ROUTLEDGE HANDBOOK OF MIGRATION AND DEVELOPMENT

The *Routledge Handbook of Migration and Development* provides an interdisciplinary, agenda-setting survey of the fields of migration and development, bringing together over 60 expert contributors from around the world to chart current and future trends in research on this topic.

The links between migration and development can be traced back to the post-war period, if not further, yet it is only in the last 20 years that the 'migration–development nexus' has risen to prominence for academics and policymakers. Starting by mapping the different theoretical approaches to migration and development, this book goes on to present cutting edge research in poverty and inequality, displacement, climate change, health, family, social policy, interventions, and the key challenges surrounding migration and development. While much of the migration literature continues to be dominated by US and British perspectives, this volume includes original contributions from most regions of the world to offer alternative non-Anglophone perspectives.

Given the increasing importance of migration in both international development and current affairs, the *Routledge Handbook of Migration and Development* will be of interest both to policymakers and to students and researchers of geography, development studies, political science, sociology, demography, and development economics.

Tanja Bastia is a Reader at the Global Development Institute, University of Manchester, UK.

Ronald Skeldon is an Emeritus Professor, University of Sussex, UK, and Honorary Professor, Maastricht University, The Netherlands.

"When I open the pages of this Handbook, I find many an entry challenging established wisdom and asking new questions in the field of migration and development. I trust that it will come to be an indispensable source of inspiration for focusing crucial debates and sharpening existing research in this vital area of scholarship."

– Thomas Faist, Professor of Sociology of Transnationalization, Migration and Development, University of Bielefeld, Germany

"This volume includes contributions from leading scholars working at the interface of migration and development. The emphasis on inequality and on migration 'corridors' in the Global South offers new insights into the complexity of these relationships and the need to situate migration within wider economic, political and social processes."

– Heaven Crawley, Director, UKRI GCRF South-South Migration, Inequality and Development Hub, Coventry University, UK

ROUTLEDGE HANDBOOK OF MIGRATION AND DEVELOPMENT

Edited by Tanja Bastia and Ronald Skeldon

LONDON AND NEW YORK

First published 2020
by Routledge
2 Park Square, Milton Park, Abingdon, Oxon OX14 4RN

and by Routledge
52 Vanderbilt Avenue, New York, NY 10017

Routledge is an imprint of the Taylor & Francis Group, an informa business

British Library Cataloguing-in-Publication Data
A catalogue record for this book is available from the British Library

Library of Congress Cataloging-in-Publication Data
Names: Bastia, Tanja, editor. | Skeldon, Ronald, editor. | Routledge (Firm)
Title: Routledge handbook of migration and development / edited by Tanja Bastia and Ronald Skeldon.
Other titles: Handbook of migration and development
Description: First Edition. | New York : Routledge, 2020. | Includes bibliographical references and index.
Identifiers: LCCN 2019031426 (print) | ISBN 9781138244450 (Hardback) | ISBN 9781315276908 (eBook)
Subjects: LCSH: Emigration and immigration. | Economic development.
Classification: LCC JV6035 .R675 2020 (print) | LCC JV6035 (ebook) | DDC 304.8–dc23
LC record available at https://lccn.loc.gov/2019031426
LC ebook record available at https://lccn.loc.gov/2019031427

ISBN: 978-1-138-24445-0 (hbk)
ISBN: 978-1-315-27690-8 (ebk)

Typeset in Bembo
by Swales & Willis, Exeter, Devon, UK

CONTENTS

Contents

FIGURES

TABLES

CONTRIBUTORS

Nermin Abadan-Unat is a Professor of Political Science at Bosporus University, Istanbul, Turkey. She taught as a Guest Professor at the Universities of Munich, City University of New York, University of Denver, and the University of California Los Angeles (UCLA). Her research interests include international migration, political parties, public opinion, women studies, and political communication. Her major publications in English are *Turkish Workers in Europe* (1976), *Women in Turkish Society* (1981), *Women in the Developing World: Evidence from Turkey* (1986), and *Turks in Europe: From Guestworker to Transnational Citizen* (2011). Her work has appeared in international journals in English, German, French, and Turkish.

W. Neil Adger is a Professor of Geography at the University of Exeter. He has researched the social dynamics and consequences of climate change, highlighting human security, well-being, and public health as dilemmas for resilient societies in the face of environmental change.

Oliver Bakewell is a Senior Lecturer at the Global Development Institute, University of Manchester. His work focuses on the intersections between migration and mobility and processes of development and change, with an empirical focus on migration within Africa. Prior to joining GDI, he spent over a decade at the University of Oxford at the International Migration Institute in the Department of International Development. He holds a PhD and MSc in Development Studies from the University of Bath and a BA in Mathematics from the University of Cambridge.

Nicholas Bascuñan-Wiley is a PhD student in Sociology and a Mellon Cluster Fellow in Middle East and North African studies at Northwestern University. His ethnographic research explores Palestinian diasporic culture and translocal connections within the global South. His most recent project focuses on the culture of food and eating as it is shaped by the long-term and long-distance connections between communities in Chile and Palestine.

Tanja Bastia is Reader at the Global Development Institute at the University of Manchester, United Kingdom. Her research focuses on transnational migration for work, particularly on the relationship between power relations, mobility, and space. She has conducted multi-sited ethnographic research with Bolivian migrants in Bolivia, Argentina, and Spain since the year 2000 and currently holds a Leverhulme Research Fellowship to develop her research into ageing and migration. Her most recent research articles have been published in *Geoforum*, *Urban Studies*, *Cities*, and *Environment and Planning A*. She has published a monograph *Gender, Migration and Social Transformation: Intersectionality in Bolivian Itinerant Migrations* (Routledge, 2019), and edited *Migration and Inequality* (2013, also published by Routledge).

Başak Bilecen is an Assistant Professor of Sociology at the University of Groningen, the Netherlands, and affiliated researcher at Bielefeld University, Germany. For the academic year of 2017–18 she has received the JFK Memorial Fellowship from German Academic Exchange Services (DAAD) and worked at the Centre for European Studies, Harvard University. Her research focuses on international migration, transnational studies, social inequalities, transnational social protection, and personal network analysis. She is the author of *International Student Mobility and Transnational Friendships* (2014). She has co-edited special issues in *Population, Space and Place, Journal of Ethnic and Migration Studies, and Social Networks*.

Paolo Boccagni is a Sociologist with an expertise in transnational migration, social welfare, care, and diversity. His current research, based on the ERC HOMInG project, is on home-related views, emotions, and practices among international migrants and their 'sedentary' or 'native' counterparts. In recent years he has also done fieldwork on social remittances, on migrants' transnational housing investments and on the everyday life experience in refugee collective facilities. His last publications include the monograph *Migration and the Search for Home* (2017) and co-edited Special Issues of the *Journal of Housing and the Built Environment* (2017) and of the *International Journal of Comparative Sociology* (2019).

Erika Busse-Cárdenas is an Assistant Professor at the Department of Sociology at Macalester College. Her scholarship examines transnational migration experiences where immigrants juggle racial, class, and gender hierarchies from both their home country and the country of reception. My current research builds on my ethnographic dissertation research and expands it to focus on ethnic identity construction among Latinos in Minnesota. Specifically, I analyse the role of the racial context of reception, ethnic dance, and women leading ethnic identity construction.

Caroline Caplan has a PhD in Human Geography. During her studies she worked on the CIDESAL project funded by the EU. She is currently a history and geography teacher in Bernay. She took part in the OECD report for global development sharing her knowledge in diaspora-development policies and projects. Her work is mainly related to the migration and development nexus, brain-drain and undocumented migrants.

Jørgen Carling is Research Professor of Migration and Transnationalism Studies at the Peace Research Institute Oslo (PRIO) and holds a PhD in Human Geography. His research interests include migration theory, migrant smuggling, migrant remittances, and the links between migration and development. Among his most influential work is the analysis of aspiration and ability in international migration, and the associated concept of involuntary immobility. He currently leads the ERC Consolidator Grant project 'Future Migration as Present Fact'.

Jean-Pierre Cassarino teaches and does research on migration matters at the College of Europe in Warsaw. He is also a Research Associate at the *Institut de Recherche sur le Maghreb Contemporain* (IRMC, Tunis). Prior to this, he was a part-time Professor at the Robert Schuman Centre (European University Institute, Florence).

Leonardo Cavalcanti da Silva is a Professor at the University of Brasilia (UnB), Institute of Social Sciences, Center for Research and Graduate Studies on the Americas (CEPPAC). Coordinator of the International Migration Observatory of Brazil (OBMigra). During the period 2008–13, he was a Professor at the Department of Sociology of the Universidad Autónoma de Barcelona (UAB). He conducted postdoctoral studies at Columbia University (Institute for Social and Economic Research and Policy – ISERP) and the University of Oxford (Centre on Migration, Policy and Society – COMPAS). Specialist in international migrations, he coordinated various research projects on transnational social fields of Latin American migrants and has various publications as *Dicionário Crítico de Migrações Internacionais* (co-edited with Botega, T., Tonhati, T. and Araujo, D. S.) and *América Latina na contemporaneidade: desafios, oportunidades e riscos* (co-edited. with Pinto, S. R). Nowadays he is developing comparative studies on Latin American migration, with an emphasis on transnational perspective on migration.

Kam Wing Chan is a Professor of Geography at the University of Washington. His research focuses on China's urbanisation, migration, spatial economy, and the *hukou* (household registration) system. He has also served as a consultant for the World Bank, Asian Development Bank, and McKinsey & Co. His recent commentaries and interviews have also appeared in the public media.

Supang Chantavanich is an Emeritus Professor in Sociology and an adviser to the Center of Excellence Asian Research Center for Migration at Chulalongkorn University in Thailand. She has worked intensively in the field of international migration since the time of the refugees from Indochina and the overseas Chinese in Southeast Asia. Her research in collaboration with many UN agencies covers labour migration, displacement due to political armed conflicts and natural disasters, and human trafficking. She was the first Chairperson of the Asia-Pacific Migration Research Network and influenced migration policies in Thailand. Dr Supang received her PhD from the University of Grenoble in France.

Michael Collyer is a Professor of Geography at the University of Sussex. His most recent books are *Migration* (Routledge, 2017) with Michael Samers and *Emigration Nations: Policies and Ideologies of Emigrant Engagement* (Palgrave, 2014). He is on the executive committee of the Department for International Development (DfID) funded Migrating out of Poverty project and on the steering committee of Sanctuary on Sea, Brighton's City of Sanctuary group.

Almudena Cortés Maisonave is an Associate Professor in Social Anthropology at Universidad Complutense de Madrid, Spain, UCM. Her field of research is international migration and its link with development from a transnational and gender perspective. Her work is published in publishing houses and journals of national and international prestige (International Migration, Edward Elgar, ERLACS, Bellaterra, among others). She is the co-director of the UCM Specialization Diploma 'Género, Migración y Derechos Humanos'.

Hannah Cross is a Senior Lecturer in International Relations at the University of Westminster. She has published extensively on migration and development, including a book titled *Migrants, Borders and Global Capitalism: West African Labour Mobility and EU Borders* (Routledge, 2013/16). Her more recent focus is on migration beyond capitalism. She is Chair of the Editorial Working Group of the *Review of African Political Economy*.

Mathias Czaika is a Professor in Migration and Integration and Head of the Department for Migration and Globalization at Danube University Krems, Austria. He is also Research

Associate at the Department for International Development and former Director of the International Migration Institute (IMI), both at the University of Oxford. He has a PhD in Political Economy from the University of Freiburg. His current research interests include (i) drivers and dynamics of international migration processes; (ii) globalisation, development, inequality, and conflict; (iii) heuristics and decision-making; (iv) policy formation and policy impact; (v) migration of high-skilled workers, asylum seekers, and refugees. Across these areas he has published in journals such as *Demography*, *Population Development Review*, *International Migration Review*, or the *Journal of Peace Research*.

Arjan de Haan is the Director of IDRC's Inclusive Economies programme. He leads a multidisciplinary team that strengthens policy research capacity in developing countries on issues of economic policy, governance, and health systems. He previously led IDRC programming on poverty reduction, employment, growth, and gender equality, including the Growth and Economic Opportunities for Women (GrOW) programme. Before joining IDRC, Arjan was Social Development Adviser at the UK's Department for International Development for 10 years, in the Policy Division and in China and India, leading work on poverty analysis and social protection. He also taught international development at the Institute of Social Studies in the Netherlands, Guelph University in Canada, and University of Sussex in the United Kingdom. Arjan holds a PhD in Social History from Erasmus University Rotterdam.

Hein de Haas is a Professor of Sociology at the University of Amsterdam. Between 2006 and 2015 he was a founding member and Director of the International Migration Institute at the University of Oxford. His research focuses on the linkages between migration and broader processes of social transformation and development in origin and destination societies. He has done extensive fieldwork in the Middle East and Africa and, particularly, in Morocco. De Haas is co-author (with Stephen Castles and Mark Miller) of *The Age of Migration*, a leading text book in the field of migration studies.

Daniela DeBono is the Marie Curie COFAS Fellow at the Robert Schuman Centre for Advanced Studies, European University Institute – Fiesole (Italy), Senior Lecturer at Malmö University, and Research Fellow at the Malmö Institute for the Studies of Migration, Welfare and Diversity, Sweden. Her core research interests lie in the migration–human rights nexus. She has conducted ethnographic field research in southern Italy, Malta and Sweden on irregular and forced migration, detention and deportation.

Natalie Dietrich Jones is Research Fellow at the Sir Arthur Lewis Institute of Social and Economic Studies (SALISES) at the University of the West Indies Mona campus. Her interests include geographies of the border, managed migration, and intra-regional migration in the Caribbean. Dr Dietrich Jones is Chair of the Migration and Development Cluster, an interdisciplinary group of researchers exploring contemporary issues concerning migration in the Caribbean and its diaspora. She is also Coordinator of the course Small States' Development: Challenges and Opportunities, which is offered in the MSc Development Studies programme at SALISES.

Mike Dottridge has worked in the human rights field for four decades. Between 1977 and 2002 he was employed by non-governmental organisations (Amnesty International and Anti-Slavery International, where he was the Director). Until 1995 his focus was on sub-Saharan Africa. Since 1995 it has been on the rights of adults and children subjected to slavery, servitude, forced labour, human trafficking, or child labour. Since 2002 he has been a freelance consultant and author, advising on programmes intended to stop economic or sexual exploitation (particularly how to monitor and evaluate them), drafting handbooks and publishing articles.

Heike Drotbohm is a Professor of Social and Cultural Anthropology at the Department of Anthropology and African Studies, Johannes Gutenberg University Mainz. Her fields of specialisation include migration, transnationalism and humanitarian aid as well as kinship, care, and generational relations. Regionally she has focused on Afro-Atlantic societies in West Africa, the Caribbean, and Brazil.

Don Flynn has been active on issues concerning the rights of migrants since the 1970s. He has worked for community law centres and national organisations and in 2006 set up the Migrants' Rights Network. He is the author of many published articles on the politics of immigration control. He continues this work as an Associate of the Migrants' Rights Network.

Nina Glick Schiller's writings explore a comparative and historical perspective on migration, transnational processes and social relations, racialisation and nation-state building, city-making. diasporic connection and long-distance nationalism, methodological nationalism, and accumulation dispossession, cosmopolitanism, and new sociabilities. Founding editor of the journal *Identities: Global Studies in Culture and Power*, and co-editor of *Anthropological Theory*, Glick Schiller's books include: *Migrants and City-Making: Dispossession, Displacement, and Urban Regeneration and Locating Migration* (with A. Caglar) *Nations Unbound*, and *Towards a Transnational Perspective on Migration* (both with L. Basch and C. Blanc), *Georges Woke up Laughing* (with G. Fouron), *and Whose Cosmopolitanism* (with A. Irving). She has conducted research in Haiti, the United States, Germany, and the United Kingdom and has worked with migrants from all regions of the globe. Glick Schiller is an Emeritus Professor of Social Anthropology (University of Manchester; University of New Hampshire), and Research Associate at the Max Planck Institute for Social Anthropology.

Alejandro Grimson holds a PhD in Anthropology from the University of Brasilia (Brazil). He has researched migratory processes, border areas, social movements, political cultures, identities and the Peronism in Argentina. He has been awarded with national and international prizes. He is full Professor of the National Council for Scientific and Technological Research, at the Institute of Higher Social Studies of the National University of San Martín (Buenos Aires, Argentina).

Olga R. Gulina holds a Diploma in Law and PhD in Law (Bashkir State University, Russia), and a PhD in Migration Studies (Potsdam University, Germany). She is Founder and Senior Researcher at RUSMPI UG-Institute on Migration Policy, Berlin, Germany.

Menara Lube Guizardi holds a MA in Latin American Studies and a PhD in Social Anthropology, both from the Autonomous University of Madrid (Spain). She is an Associate Researcher at the University of Tarapacá (Arica, Chile), and Postdoctoral Researcher at the National Council for Scientific and Technological Research of at the Institute of Higher Social Studies of the National University of San Martín (Buenos Aires, Argentina).

Karlijn Haagsman is an Assistant Professor of Globalisation and Development at Maastricht University, The Netherlands. Her research looks at transnationalism between the Global North and South, with a particular focus on transnational and migrant families, youth mobility and wellbeing. In her PhD she studied the effects of transnational parent–child separation on the wellbeing of migrant parents.

Gioconda Herrera is an Ecuadorian Sociologist and a Professor at the Facultad Latinoamericana de Ciencias Sociales (FLACSO) in Quito. Her research interests concern the effects of globalisation on social inequalities in Latin America. Her work focuses on international migrations from the Andean countries to Europe and the United States from a gender perspective. She has done research on transnational families and care, return migration and deportation. Her current research deals with the Venezuelan exodus in South America.

Alfonso Hinojosa Gordonava is a Sociologist with a MA in Social Sciences with a specialisation in Anthropology. He currently teaches and does research at the Instituto de Investigaciones Interacción Social and on the post-graduate degree course in Social Work (UMSA – La Paz). He has carried out research on migration for various organisations, both national and international. He is also a former General Director of Consular Activities for the Ministry of Foreign Relations in Bolivia.

Caroline Wanjiku Kihato is a Visiting Fellow in the Oxford Department of International Development, Oxford University, and a Visiting Associate Professor at the Graduate School of Architecture, University of Johannesburg. Her research and teaching interests are migration, gender, governance, and urbanisation in the global South. She is the author of *Migrant Women of Johannesburg: Life in an In-Between City* (Palgrave Macmillan) and co-editor of *Urban Diversity: Space, Culture and Inclusive Pluralism in Cities Worldwide* (Johns Hopkins).

Russell King is a Professor of Geography at the University of Sussex, where he was also the Founder-Director of the Sussex Centre for Migration Research, including its MA and PhD programmes in Migration Studies. He has broad interests in migration and development and has carried out empirical research on remittances and return migration in various geographical contexts, ranging from Southern Europe and the Balkans to West Africa. From 2000 to 2013 he has edited the *Journal of Ethnic and Migration Studies*.

Uma Kothari is a Professor of Migration and Postcolonial Studies in the Global Development Institute, University of Manchester. She is a Co-founder of the Manchester Migration Lab and is currently Vice-Chancellor's Fellow at the University of Melbourne. Her research interests include humanitarianism and solidarity and, migration and mobility. She is the principal investigator on an ESRC-DfID funded project and an Australian Research Council Discovery project both addressing aspects of everyday lives on small island states. Her current work includes research on the cultural geography of seafarers.

Loren B. Landau is Professor of Migration and Development at the University of Oxford, and the South African Research Chair in Human Mobility and the Politics of Difference based at the University of the Witwatersrand's African Centre for Migration and Society. His interdisciplinary scholarship explores mobility, multi-scale governance, and the transformation of socio-political community across the global South. Publications include, *The Humanitarian Hangover: Displacement, Aid, and Transformation in Western Tanzania* (Wits Press); *Forging African Communities: Mobility, Integration, and Belonging* (Palgrave); *I Want to Go Home Forever: Stories of Becoming and Belonging in South Africa's Great Metropolis* (Wits Press); *Contemporary Migration to South Africa* (World Bank); and *Exorcising the Demons Within: Xenophobia, Violence and Statecraft in Contemporary South Africa* (UN University Press/ Wits Press). He holds an MSc in Development Studies (from LSE) and a PhD in Political Science (from Berkeley).

Aija Lulle is a Lecturer in Human Geography at Loughborough University, where she teaches Migration Studies. Her core research interests are in life course approaches to migration, with particular reference to youthful and ageing migrants, and inequalities within transnational families. She is co-author of *Ageing, Gender and Labour Migration* (Palgrave, 2016) with Russell King. Regionally, her expertise is in post-socialist Europe and the post-Soviet region.

Susan F. Martin is the Donald G. Herzberg Professor Emerita in the School of Foreign Service at Georgetown University. She previously served as the Director of Georgetown's Institute for the Study of International Migration. She currently chairs the Thematic Working Group on Environmental Change and Migration for the Knowledge Partnership in Migration and Development (KNOMAD) at the World Bank. Dr Martin received her BA in History from Doauglass College and her MA and PhD in the History of American Civilization from the University of Pennsylvania. She has authored or edited a dozen books and numerous articles and book chapters.

Diana Mata-Codesal is located in Barcelona, Spain, where she has been Researcher in the Humanitites Department of the Pompeu Fabra University and Lecturer at the Open University of Catalonia. Diana's research interests include articulations and meanings of im/mobility, including the links between othering/we-nessing processes, as well as between migration and autochthony; embodied and sensorial experiences of migration and interaction; and transnational families and gender, particularly in relation to remittances and the negotiations taking place around such transfers. More recently she has started working on participatory methodologies in migration research and alliances beyond academia.

Valentina Mazzucato is a Professor of Globalisation and Development at Maastricht University, The Netherlands. She has led five international and interdisciplinary projects studying the effects of transnational migration between Africa and Europe focusing on networks, families, and youth, and on the wellbeing of those who migrate and those who remain in their country of origin. She currently leads an ERC Consolidator Grant-funded project on Mobility Trajectories of Young Lives (MO-TRAYL) focusing on the wellbeing and educational pathways of youth who move between Africa and Europe.

Marie McAuliffe is head of the Migration Policy Research Division at the International Organization for Migration in Geneva, and a fellow at the Australian National University's School of Demography. She has two decades of experience in migration research, policy, and practice. Marie has published and edited widely in academic and policy spheres on migration, including as chief editor of IOM's flagship World Migration Reports (2018 and 2020 editions). In 2014, she was awarded a Sir Roland Wilson scholarship to complete her doctoral research at ANU, which was approved in 2017. She is the 2018 recipient of the Charles Price Prize in Demography for outstanding doctoral research in migration studies.

Elaine McGregor is a PhD Fellow at Maastricht University. Her PhD research focuses on the evolution of migration as an international policy issue. She holds a MA degree in Public Policy and Human Development from the Maastricht Graduate School of Governance, Maastricht University, and the United Nations University with a specialisation in Migration Studies. Prior to her study in Maastricht, she obtained an MSc in Urban Regeneration and an MA in Public Policy at the University of Glasgow.

Deirdre McKay is a Reader of Geography at Keele University. The author of *Global Filipinos* (Indiana, 2012) and *Archipelago of Care* (Indiana, 2016), her current collaborative work explores the ways digital cultures shape migration (see curatingdevelopment.com). She has carried out fieldwork in the Philippines, and with Filipino migrants in Hong Kong, Singapore, Canada, and London, and via social media.

Mahala Miller is a PhD student in Sociology at the University of Minnesota, Twin Cities. Her research interests include family, culture, food, and inequality.

Sarah Deardorff Miller is an adjunct faculty member at Columbia University and convenes a refugee protection course for the University of London. She is a Senior Fellow at Refugees International, and has consulted for UNHCR, the World Bank, and various NGOs. She has written books and articles on the politics of forced migration and humanitarianism, and has a Doctorate in International Relations from Oxford University.

Dudu S. Ndlovu is a Postdoctoral Research Fellow at the African Centre for Migration and Society. She holds a Newton Advanced Fellowship at the Centre for African Studies University of Edinburgh where she is exploring women's mobility in Johannesburg using poetry.

Ingrid Palmary Joined the University of Johannesburg as a Professor in January 2018. Prior to that she worked at the African Centre for Migration and Society at the University of the Witwatersrand. Ingrid completed her PhD (Psychology) at Manchester Metropolitan University, UK. Before entering academia, Ingrid worked at the Centre for the Study of Violence and Reconciliation as a Senior Researcher. Her research has been in the field of gender, violence, and displacement. She has published in numerous international journals and is the co-editor of *Gender and Migration: Feminist Interventions* published by Zed Press; *Handbook of International Feminisms: Perspectives on psychology, Women, Culture and Rights* published by Springer; Heali*ng and Change in the City of Gold: Case Studies of Coping and Support in Johannesburg* published by Springer. She is also the author of *Gender, Sexuality and Migration in South Africa: Governing Morality* published by Palgrave.

Nicola Piper, a Political Sociologist, is a Professor of International Migration. She is the Founding Director of the Sydney Asia-Pacific Migration Centre at the University of Sydney, Australia. She is a British Academy Global Professor Fellow at Queen Mary University of London (2019–22). Her research interests focus on international labour migration and advocacy politics in relation to a rights-based and gender-sensitive approach to global and regional migration governance which are topics about which she has published widely.

Parvati Raghuram is a Professor in Geography and Migration at the Open University. Her two most recent ESRC funded projects are titled 'Gender, skilled migration and the IT sector: a comparative study of India and the UK' and 'Facilitating equitable access and quality education for development: South African International Distance Education'. She has also been exploring the use of 'care' as a concept in social policy, postcolonial theory, and feminist ethics. She has co-authored *Gender, Migration and Social Reproduction* (Palgrave), *The Practice of Cultural Studies* (Sage), *Gender and International Migration in Europe* (Routledge) and co-edited *South Asian Women in the Diaspora* (Berg) and *Tracing Indian Diaspora: Contexts, Memories, Representations* (Sage). She has written for policy audiences having co-authored research papers for a number of think-tanks such as IPPR, UNRISD, the Hamburg Institute of International Economics, Heinrich Böll Stiftung, IPPR, and UNRISD, and co-edited a special issue of the journal *Diversities* for UNESCO. She co-edits the journal *South Asian Diaspora* with the Centre for Study of Diaspora, Hyderabad, and the Palgrave Pivot series Mobility and Politics with Martin Geiger and William Walters both at Ottawa.

Madeleine Reeves is a Senior Lecturer in Social Anthropology at the University of Manchester. She is the author of *Border Work: Spatial Lives of the State in Rural Central Asia* (Cornell, 2014) and has co-edited several volumes dealing with questions of borders, mobility, the post-Soviet state, and the politicisation of ethno-religious difference. Since 2014 she has served as editor of the *Central Asian Survey* (Taylor & Francis).

Franziska Reiffen is a PhD candidate at Johannes Gutenberg University, Mainz. Her research interests include migration, displacement, and post-migration studies, with a regional focus on South America, especially Argentina.

Stefan Rother is a Senior Research Fellow at the Arnold Bergstraesser Institute at the University of Freiburg, Germany. His research focus is on international migration, global governance, social movements, development, regional integration, and non-/post-Western theories of international relations. He has conducted extensive fieldwork in Southeast Asia as well as participant observation at global governance fora and civil society parallel and counter-events at the UN, ILO, ASEAN, and WTO-level as well as the European Forum on Migration and World Social Forum on Migration. His latest monograph is *Democratization through Migration? Political Remittances and Participation of Philippine Return Migrants* (Lexington, 2016, with Christl Kessler).

Rachel Sabates-Wheeler has been a Research Fellow at the Institute of Development Studies since 2001, and a Founder and Director of the Centre for Social Protection since 2006. Professor Sabates-Wheeler's work has focused on poverty analysis, social protection, rural livelihoods, and migration in many countries (including over ten African countries). She has published on issues of rural institutions, graduation in the context of social protection, social protection in Africa, migration, and poverty, and has worked for numerous international agencies.

Ricardo Safra de Campos is a Lecturer in Human Geography at the University of Exeter with interdisciplinary research interests at the nexus between climate science and society, with focus on the intersection between demographic processes, human security, wellbeing, and sustainability. He has experience on research exploring migrant perspectives as sources of innovation into urban planning. He has also examined migration-sustainability relations based on the changing composition of populations driven by spatial mobility and migration, adaptation and wellbeing in low-lying areas exposed to environmental change.

Kerstin Schmidt is a Lecturer and Researcher at the Faculty for Sociology at Bielefeld University, Germany. Kerstin's PhD (Sussex University, 2012) developed a conceptual and methodological approach to the climate change–migration nexus and empirically investigated the potential impact of climate change on existing migration patterns in Mexico. Her recent research interests include the transnational perspective on migration, categorisations of migrants and refugees, and migration and international development.

Melissa Siegel is a Professor of Migration Studies and Head of Migration at the Maastricht Graduate School of Governance at Maastricht University and UNU-MERIT. Her research focuses on the causes and consequences of migration with a focus on migration and development and migration policy and programming. She regularly works with international organisations and country governments and has worked as a lead on research projects spanning the globe.

Ronald Skeldon is an Emeritus Professor at the University of Sussex and an Honorary Professor at Maastricht University. Following a PhD on Peru at the University of Toronto in 1974, he moved to the Asia-Pacific region for over 25 years, where he pursued both academic careers and positions with the United Nations before returning to the United Kingdom in 2000. He has published widely on issues of migration, including his 1997 book *Migration and Development: A Global Perspective* (Longman). He continues to teach and to act as a consultant to international organisations and lives in Nairn in northern Scotland.

Yan Tan is Associate Professor of Geography, Environment, and Population at the University of Adelaide, Australia. She has a strong research interest in the field of environment- and development-induced displacement, resettlement, and social-ecological vulnerability. Her book *Resettlement in the Three Gorges Project* (Tan, 2008) was among the first studies outside China that discuss resettlement policies, processes, and impacts on people and their communities affected by the world's largest hydro project.

Dorte Thorsen is a Research Fellow in the School of Global Studies at University of Sussex. Her research focuses on family relations, gender, and generational dynamics in Africa. She is currently researching rural youths' engagement with rural and urban economies and how their aspirations are shaped by ideas about education and migration. She also coordinates comparative research focusing on social transformations surrounding migration. She is the co-author of *Child migrants in Africa* (2011, with Iman Hashim) and the co-editor of *Hope and Uncertainty in Contemporary African Migration* (2016, with Nauja Kleist).

Ilka Vari-Lavoisier holds a PhD in Sociology from the École Normale Supérieure de Paris, a joint MA degree in Social Sciences (ENS/EHESS, Paris) and a BA in Political Science (Science Po, Aix-en-Provence). Please consult her personal website for more details. Ilka is currently a Project Manager and Postdoctoral Fellow for the ERC project HOMInG led by Paolo Boccagni, at the University of Trento. She is also an Affiliate Researcher at the IRD (DIAL), and a Fellow at the IC Migrations in Paris. Since 2018, Ilka is based at COMPAS, in the University of Oxford.

María del Carmen Villarreal Villamar is a Postdoctorate Fellow (PDJ-CNPq) in Political Science at Universidade Federal do Estado do Rio de Janeiro (UNIRIO), and a Professor for the MA degree in Political Management and Governance at the Santiago de Guayaquil Catholic University (UCSG). She holds a PhD in Political Science from the Universidad Complutense de Madrid. She is also member of the International Relations and Global South research group (GRISUL)/UNIRIO and NIEM/UFRJ. Her lines of research are international migration, development, and international cooperation, comparative politics, human rights, and regional integration. Some of her more recent works are 'Pacha defending the land. Extractivism, conflicts and alternatives in Latin America and the Caribbean' (co-edited with Echart, 2018) and *Regionalismos e Migracões Internacionais na América do Sul. Contexto e perspectivas futuras sobre as experiências na CAN, no Mercosul e na Unasul* (Espaço Aberto, 2018).

Julie Vullnetari is a Lecturer in Human Geography at the University of Southampton. Previously, she studied and worked at the University of Sussex, researching migration and development, including the links between internal and international migration, the gendering of remittances, and the impact of migration on older people left behind. Beyond these areas, her research interests include everyday life in socialist societies, feminist geopolitics, and critical border studies.

Cathy Wilcock is a Postdoctoral Researcher at the International Institute of Social Studies, Erasmus University Rotterdam. She takes a socio-anthropological approach to the nexus of political participation and migration and is particularly interested in the formation and sustainment of global communities. So far, her work has focused on Sudanese political development and the Sudanese diaspora in Europe.

L. Alan Winters is a Professor of Economics at the University of Sussex. From 2008 to 2011 he was Chief Economist at the British government's Department for International Development, and from 2004 to 2007 he was Director of the Development Research Group of the World Bank. He has also recently completed terms as Chairman of the Board of the Global Development Network, Membership of the Council of the UK's Economic and Social Research Council and Chair of its Research Committee, and Chief Executive Officer of the Migrating Out of Poverty Research Programme Consortium.

Xiaxia Yang is a Doctoral Candidate in Geography at the University of Washington. Her research examines China's migration policies and the wellbeing of children of migrants.

Roger Zetter is an Emeritus Professor of Refugee Studies in the University of Oxford where he retired as Director of the Refugee Studies Centre in 2011. From 1988–2001 he was founding editor of the *Journal of Refugee Studies*. With almost 40 years research, publication, teaching, and consultancy experience in forced migration, refugee, and humanitarian affairs, his work focuses on institutional and policy dimensions of the refugee and humanitarian 'regime', including all stages of the 'refugee cycle'. The main themes of his work include refugee labelling; the economic and social costs and impacts of refugees; refugees and the political economy of development; environmental stress, climate change, and population displacement. Research and consultancy funders include UK ESRC, Joseph Rowntree Foundation, MacArthur Foundation, Brookings-Bern Project, MPI, ICRC, IFRC, UNHCR, UNDP, UNFPA, UNHabitat, IOM, ILO, EC, World Bank, Governments of Denmark, Finland, Norway, NZ, Switzerland, and the UK.

ACKNOWLEDGEMENTS

Many individuals and institutions contributed to this volume and our major debt is to all our contributors who responded so positively to our persistent questioning for clarification and badgering over deadlines. A few threw up their hands in horror but for those of you who persisted, we hope that both the wait and the final result have justified the effort. We also owe a huge debt of gratitude to the editorial staff at Routledge for both their understanding and support from Khanam Virjee, who first suggested the idea of this handbook, Helena Hurd, who commissioned this volume, to Matthew Shobbrook and the production team, who, particularly the copy editor Martin Pettitt, constantly had to shift their horizons as realities on the ground so dictated. Tanja is grateful to Juan, for always being at her side, and Ronald, as always, owes a huge debt of gratitude to Grania, his partner of many years, who has had to reinterpret what a definition of retirement really means.

INTRODUCTION

Tanja Bastia and Ronald Skeldon

Of numbers and terminologies

Migration means a change in the location of where people live. This simple statement, however, obscures a number of technical issues, the most important of which are the size of the spatial units used to define the boundaries over which a person must move and the time that a person needs to remain at a destination in order to be defined as a migrant. The United Nations defines an international migrant as someone who has moved across an international boundary for 12 months or more in coming to its estimate of a stock of international migration of 257.7 million in 2017 (United Nations 2019a). However, a move across an international boundary provides only a very general idea of the distance travelled: it could be many thousands of kilometres across an ocean or simply a short move across a land border between contiguous countries. The International Organization for Migration (IOM) adopts a more inclusive definition as those who have changed their habitual place of residence by moving across a border, regardless of length of stay (IOM 2018). Both definitions make the distinction between those moving across administrative boundaries within a country (internal migration) and those moving across international borders (international migration). Neither of these definitions, however, includes any reason for the move, whether 'forced' or 'voluntary', or any measure of the legality of the move. The estimates are simply numbers of all those who have moved from one spatial unit, however defined, to another.

Thus, migration means change: a change in the distribution of populations within and between states. 'Development' also implies change. However, the relationship between migration and development is both complex and not always obvious. Migration is both the result and the cause of what can be broadly called development. Expanding industries or commercial operations requires labour, which must often be brought into the areas. Migrants who move into previously sparsely populated areas can extend the areas under cultivation, as well as generating markets for new products. The migrants themselves require those most basic elements of development, health, and education services in order to have fulfilling lives. The migrants, too, bring new ideas and ways of doing things that impact upon the populations of destination areas, as well as upon those of the places they have left and to which they may at some point return. Hence, migration is an integral part of development and, as one of the editors of this volume has previously written, it is 'almost impossible to envisage development without migration' (Skeldon 1997, 205) just as it is almost impossible to envisage migration without some kind of development. However, the relationship between migration and development is not as linear as often imagined by policymakers, as well as some researchers. While development is often proposed as the means to decrease migration flows from a specific area, the evidence indicates that increased levels of development actually make migration more widely desirable and available, at least initially (Chapter 1 in this Handbook).

The measure given above for the number of international migrants of 257.7 million for 2017 represented just over 3 per cent of the global population, a proportion that had not changed greatly over the previous quarter-century. The impression might be given that the impact of such a small section of the global population on development might not be consequential, but four additional points have to be taken into consideration before any potential impact of migration on development can be assessed.

The first point is that the majority of people who move do so within the boundaries of their own country as internal migrants (Chapter 4 in this Handbook). Around 2010, when the number of international migrants was around 222 million, the United Nations Development Programme estimated that the number of internal migrants was 740 million, over three times the number of international migrants (UNDP 2009). This estimate for the number of global internal migrants does need to be used with particular care because it is based on the largest administrative units for any country, inter-state in India and inter-province in China, for example. If smaller spatial divisions such as districts were used as the migration-defining unit, the number of internal migrants would be significantly larger. In some countries, internal migration is estimated to be eight or nine times larger than international migration (UNDP 2009).

The second point is that as research and the chapters of this book clearly show, the migrants are linked to their communities of origin in complex networks of family and friendship ties based on social and economic forms of exchange and reciprocity that greatly extend the size of the population impacted by migration, irrespective of their own migration status. That is, many who remain in their communities of origin come to depend on material, financial, and information flows sent back by migrants in the form of financial and social remittances (Chapters 10 and 11 in this Handbook).

The third point is that the figures for international and internal migration cited above provide a snapshot at a single point of time of the number of those who are away from their habitual place of residence. Research, as well as chapters in this volume, also clearly show that return migration is an integral part of all systems of migration. Return may no longer be a neglected part of the study of migration (King 1978), but it remains one of the most difficult to study and measure. The incidence of return varies over time and is related to changing patterns of development in origin and destination areas. Data are currently unavailable to provide global estimates of return. Suffice it to say that the number of people recorded as migrants in the current stock estimates is much smaller than the number who have actually migrated during their lifetimes. There are indeed numbers of people who have never migrated, whether by choice or because they became 'trapped' for one reason or another, and the study of their experiences are as equally valid as those who have moved (see discussion in Chapter 1 on voluntary and involuntary immobility), but trying to put a number on those who have migrated as opposed to those who have never moved seems an impossible task.

This third qualification is reinforced by the fourth, final, and perhaps most important point in this discussion of the numbers, which is that many types of movement are just not captured through the principal data-gathering instruments: population censuses and large-scale surveys. Into this category fall those who have moved over distances too short to cross an administrative boundary or too short in duration to be recorded by any official source. The majority of the authors of chapters in this volume not only review a substantial literature on the specific topics in their research fields that, among other objectives, seek to assess these 'hidden' migrations but have themselves designed and/or coordinated surveys to capture such movements.

All these population movements can be incorporated under the term 'mobility', in which the change in habitual place of residence, 'migration', is a sub-set. Mobility emerged in studies of internal migration in the developing world from the late 1960s (Bedford 1973; Skeldon 1977; Chapman 1978; Goldstein 1978; Hugo 1982) and, in the twenty-first century, is increasingly recognised as a more comprehensive way to approach the complex interrelationships between migration and development (Sheller and Urry 2006). That is, approaches to migration and development need to incorporate these return, repeat, circular, and other forms of temporary movements, including tourism, into any full and robust assessment of the topic. In the policy field, too, the growing awareness of the importance of these other types of movement was reflected in the shift in the EU's Global Approach to Migration (GAM) of 2005 becoming the Global Approach to Migration and Mobility (GAMM) by 2011.

Thus, countries experience much greater movement than the internationally recognised definitions cited might suggest, even though these still represent the 'gold standard' for comparative work. The view that sedentary populations should be the norm and that migration is somehow aberrant behaviour may appeal to governments, policymakers, and many analysts alike, although the reality may be the converse (Chapters 1 and 6 in this Handbook). All people move, although some move more often and over longer distances than others, and these experiences must impact upon their world views and attitudes of the local and the global.

The association of population with territory remains a controversial topic but is associated with the changing nature of the state and political development. Within the boundaries of specific countries, the idea of citizenship has become highly contested with the British then Prime Minister, Mrs Teresa May, during the Brexit debates, referring to the British people who wished to remain in the EU as 'citizens of nowhere'. A more objective analysis of attitudes in the United Kingdom at around the same time classified the population into two main groups that transcended more traditional divisions: cosmopolitan 'Anywheres', representing 20–5 per cent of the population, and a more rooted group of 'Somewheres', who identified strongly with specific locations within the country and represented about half of the population (Goodhart 2017). The relative mobility of these two groups was an expression not just of the personal characteristics of their members, but also of the development of the areas in which they lived. 'Anywheres' would be more typically found in metropolitan London and the Southeast of England, while 'Somewheres' came from the depths of rural and small-town England, as well as post-industrial northern regions. The political decisions of Anywheres and Somewheres, irrespective of the outcome, will have profound implications for the future direction of development of the United Kingdom.

Thus, migration, in terms of change in the habitual place of residence, represents a minority of movers, need not follow an ever-increasing trajectory. The empirical evidence from across the developed world suggests recent declines in internal migration (Champion et al. 2018). However, these are accompanied by increases in other forms of mobility in a way anticipated by Zelinsky (1971) in his model of the mobility transition that hypothesised shifting forms of migration over time that could be associated with development, then called 'modernisation'. However, relatively few societies or economies have reached this stage of development and internal migration in many parts of the world, and particularly in sub-Saharan Africa, is still expected to increase markedly. The evidence on international migration is perhaps more ambivalent, although sufficient to question whether the world is becoming more migratory and with indications that a slowing is occurring in some areas (Abel and Sander 2014; Czaika and de Haas 2014).

The migration and development 'nexus'

Hence, almost since their inception, studies of migration have been concerned with development in the broadest sense. Specific combinations of migration types are associated with particular levels of development: migrations in, from, and to a Fordist-type economy are distinct from the migrations in digital economies dominated by advanced electronic communication, or in agricultural societies, for example. Thus, the patterns of the migration differ by levels of development but so, too, do the impacts of those movements, with further variations by location within the local system, but also by distributions of class and ethnicity across that system. That is, development was the essential, often implicit, context in which migration operated and no binary distinction between them existed.

These earlier approaches were reviewed and elaborated in a global interpretation of migration and development (Skeldon 1997), although earlier examples with the two terms 'migration' and 'development' in the title can be found in Thomas (1972) and Safa and Du Toit (1975). The explicit migration *and* development debates date only from around the turn of the last century and can be associated more with the emergence of 'developmentalism' and the idea that governments, influenced by various agents in the private and non-governmental sectors, could chart the course of development through policy intervention. Migration had come of age in the policy domain: initially seen as a 'problem', it later came to be understood as a process that could be 'managed' to bring about certain development objectives. Migration thus came to be seen as a 'tool' that could be used to promote development through three principal pillars: remittances; skilled migration; and diaspora, which are all considered in this volume (Chapters 10–3), although from a more critical stance than when they were originally conceived as policy areas. The jury is still out on whether this more applied approach represents but a 'passing phase' in migration studies or whether we will see a reversion to the earlier more implicit contextual perspective (Skeldon 2008).

The most influential article reviewing the relevant literature and heralding the potential for migration to contribute to development was Nyberg-Sørensen et al. (2002). Here, the complex and interlinkages between migration and development were rendered through the word 'nexus' which conveys the idea of 'a set of complex interdependencies' and two-way causality that may have contradictory effects (Carling 2017; Faist 2008). From that time, both the policy and the more academic literature, to which this volume acts as a Handbook, have expanded exponentially. We have even seen the number of migration-related nexuses increase to 36 by 2017 (Carling 2017).

International organisations, particularly IOM and the World Bank, have played leading roles in promoting research that will inform the design of policy to maximise the benefits of international migration and minimise the risks. Some of this international concern to promote migration to foster development has deep roots. For example, the IOM implemented programmes to promote Migration *for* Development (emphasis added) from 1964 (Lavenex and Kunz 2008, 446–7), but it was really during the global development programmes launched from 2000 that migration *and* development came of age. Migration was not directly part of the Millennium Development Goals (MDGs) 2000–15, even though population movements would be involved if a number of the goals were to be realised. However, international migration was an explicit part of the Global Development Agenda of the Sustainable Development Goals (SDGs), 2015–30, in a number of guises in a trajectory examined by McGregor in this Handbook (Chapter 26).

What we mean by 'development' has also changed during this period. One tension that has existed within development debates for a long time is whether we are referring to development with a large 'D' or small 'd'. Large 'D' Development has been understood as a purposive intervention that emerged after 1945 within the context of the Cold War and struggles for decolonisation. Small 'd' development, on the other hand, refers to development as a broader process of social change linked to the spatially and economically unequal consequences of capitalism (Hart 2010; also Cowen and Shenton 1996).

Lower-income countries or those deemed 'underdeveloped' have traditionally been seen as the obvious recipients of development interventions. However, critical stances towards the framing of lower-income countries as always being 'lacking' and in need of development assistance, has helped shift the focus towards development being of global relevance (Robinson 2006). This can be seen in the framing of Development Goals. While the Millennium Development Goals applied to lower- and middle-income developing countries, the Sustainable Development Goals include measures to promote sustainable development across the globe, including in higher-income countries. In fact, some have argued that we have now transitioned from international development to global development, in which the 'where' of development is no longer so obviously located in a poorer (Global) South as had previously been the case (Horner and Hulme 2019).

For migration and development debates, a key question, then, refers to who actually benefits from migration. The direction of the ways in which migration and the developmental benefits flow within the most recent round of migration and development debates which began at the turn of the century has traditionally been seen as going in the opposite direction: migration from lower-income to higher-income countries, and benefits being accrued in lower-income countries. However, stances that are more critical have for a while shown that many developmental benefits follow the same direction as migration itself. In the case of domestic workers, for example, the services they provide allow greater female labour-market participation rates in countries that have already achieved higher levels of development. Migration in this case further supports the economic development of those countries, as well as the maintenance of high levels of living standards by the families that employ migrant domestic workers (Silvey 2009). One could therefore argue that the higher-income countries where migrants migrate to experience the greatest, or at least a large proportion, of the developmental benefits related to a specific movement of people.

However, such linear arguments about migration bringing about development in specific places and at specific times can therefore be quite limiting in scope. A more useful way forward could be to think of migration linking the places it moves from, to, and through, into broader developmental systems, in which relative benefits flow in multiple directions or, as Raghuram has argued, 'we could then more fruitfully see different places as co-constituted' (2009, 113).

A further transition we have witnessed since the 'invention' of development is related to what constitutes development and how this can be measured. More traditionally, development was related to material improvements, more clearly related to income and GDP per capita. While useful as a comparative indicator that is relatively simple to measure, criticism mounted in relation to all the aspects of a person's life that income-based measurements obscured. Social inequalities related to power differentials within households and societies more broadly were not taken into account. They need to recognise the social as well as the economic dimensions of development was reflected in the introduction of the Human Development Index by the United Nations Development Programme in its annual Human Development Report from 1990. The report has emerged as one of the leading global assessments of the direction of development with its index based on life expectancy and adult literacy, as well as the more common GDP per capita. Over time, other indices were introduced such as the Gender-related Development Index, the Gender Empowerment Measure and the Human Poverty Index that were themselves later replaced by measures that better reflected emerging concerns about the impacts of inequalities on development with the Inequality-adjusted Development Index and the Gender Inequality Index adopted. To deal with a traditional reluctance to tackle inequalities themselves, many expressed a preference for focusing on absolute poverty measures. Others have argued for a focus on multi-dimensional poverty and on the causes of poverty (Hulme and Shepherd 2003; Green and Hulme 2005). Over time, the focus shifted to individual (and sometimes collective) capabilities and an understanding of development as 'freedom' (Sen 1999) and more relational understandings of wellbeing (White 2017).

Welcome though it is to see migration gain a high profile in both policy and academic circles at the international level, the principal weakness lies in the focus on the 258 million stock figure of international migration in 2017 identified at the outset of this introductory chapter. The question can surely be legitimately raised how any consideration of migration and development can be made while excluding the majority of people who move, the internal migrants and other short-term and short-distance migrants. Many of the chapters in this volume go some way towards addressing this matter and international organisations and some governments are beginning to address the issue. With more than half of the world's population now living in urban areas, the role of cities as arenas for the study of key development issues such as poverty, inequalities and the linkages between metropolitan and state competencies are coming to the fore (Chapter 14). So, too, are their roles as nodes in domestic and international migration and mobility systems, which does bring short-term movers such as tourists into consideration in any discussion of migration and development (Skeldon 2018).

Tourists are not migrants, but they represent one of the largest and fastest-growing mobility flows in the world at some 1.3 billion arrivals in 2017 (UNWTO 2018). As an industry that generates 1 in 11 jobs worldwide and an income equivalent to 7 per cent of world exports, it would seem to play a major role in issues around mobility and migration. The tourist channel provides a legal entry for those few who, through accident or design, overstay their visas and become irregular entrants to the labour force. However, the hospitality industry itself relies heavily on migrant labour. In the United Kingdom, for example, one-fifth to one-quarter of that labour force is estimated to be migrant (People First 2017; also Lucas and Mansfield 2010). In parts of the world, however, the number of tourists has placed so much pressure on services and housing costs in the areas visited that local populations feel obliged to move out, as appears to be happening in Amsterdam and Venice, for example. Hence, tourists impact upon migration in more ways than just their own mobility, with significant implications for development.

As has been argued elsewhere, the ways in which we think about 'development' and the underlying stereotypes, often implicit, about the supposed beneficiaries of 'development' has led to some forms of migration being privileged in debates about migration and development, while others have been rendered invisible (Raghuram 2009). For example, the migration of development aid workers is seldom taken into account. The migration of professionals and investors living in the Global South and remitting to the Global North is generally analysed as a 'transnational flow of capital', not as 'development'. The migration of sex workers is always framed around discourses of victimhood, rarely around avenues for potential development and empowerment (Raghuram 2009; also Agustín 2007). The migration and development debate therefore needs to be considerably broadened in terms of the types of population movements included.

Migration and development: a child of their time

All books are children of their time, and this one is no exception. However, and as will be made clear in the final section of this introduction, no three-line whip was imposed on contributors to argue for any particular point of view. Quite spontaneously, a bi-polar way of conceptualising migration flows between and within countries in a Global South and a Global North, or simply South and North, emerged in a large number of the chapters. This view certainly reflects approaches to thinking in development studies in general and in migration and development in particular, as well as in how the basic international migration flows are summarised in both the academic and policy literature. Useful in generalising overall power relationships among regions and in drawing out differences in complex migration flows from one part of the world to another, the division has virtually become institutionalised today across the social sciences. A more nuanced and critical assessment is provided by Parvati Raghuram (Chapter 3), but four points are perhaps worth emphasising in this introductory chapter.

First, the boundary between the North and South is constantly shifting with new entrants to the former as they develop. Nevertheless, categories tend to crystallise long after realities have moved on. The terms 'Global North' and 'Global South' tend to be associated with the 'developed world' and the 'developing world' respectively. Putting to one side the fact that all countries are developing in one way or another, and taking the current United Nations (2019b) definitions for these categories, we find that Hong Kong and Singapore are included amongst 'developing countries', as are Israel, Malaysia, and Taiwan Province of China. Certainly, when countries and regions are divided up by their relative wealth into high, upper-middle, lower-middle and low-income countries, a more rational distribution is created, but just how these four categories are linked to a North and a South is unclear. The use of these latter two terms perhaps conveys a general impression, but unless they are related to a specific reality their utility is limited and largely symbolic.

The second point, and following on from the first, is the implication that the North and South are characterised by some degree of homogeneity. At best, this is highly deceptive. In terms of migration and a Global North, a world of difference exists between those countries of settlement, such as Australia, Canada, New Zealand, and the United States, and one could possibly include Argentina, Brazil, and Chile, and countries in Europe and East Asia. The former have been, and still are, created by migration, where migration is part of nation-building or state-building, whereas in the latter, mass migration is more recent in their modern history and most immigrants are reluctantly accepted as citizens, if at all. Hence, migration and development vary across the Global North. Again, differences within the Global South are so marked as to make its application problematic; from highly urban Latin America to more rural Africa; but within Africa itself among North, South, East, and

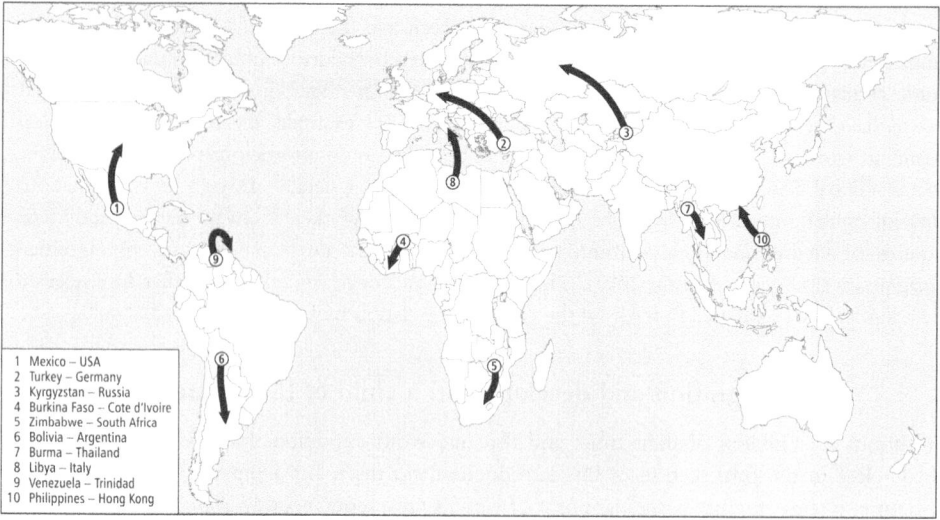

Figure 0.1 Migration corridors covered in Part VI

West Africa; and Asia is so heterogeneous as to make the term virtually meaningless as a descriptor.

The third point is that the emergence of metropolitan regions that act as key nodes in the global and regional migration and development systems are re-arranging space into transnational and sub-national units that are more meaningful than any simple binary between North and South. It is only once data become available that can be aggregated to show transnational linkages for sub-national units that more accurate assessments of migration and development will be possible, although the idea of migration corridors, as elaborated in Part VI of the Handbook, goes some way towards achieving this goal.

Finally, the distinction between the North and South is sometimes used to describe the strength of migration policies, with movements across borders in the Global South often characterised as more porous. However, the more relevant distinction here relates to income, the state's capacity to enforce its own migration policies and whether controlling or policing migration is a national priority. Poorer countries generally have fewer resources to invest in the enforcement and policing of their borders. In higher-income countries, migration often features as one of the top pressing items in election campaigns and by definition, these countries have a stronger infrastructure as well as greater budgets available for controlling the entry of foreign nationals into their territories. Over the past two decades, we have seen a steady reinforcement of migration policies in the US, Europe and Australia, sometimes implementing draconian measures to deter migration. Argentina, on the other hand, despite being one of the regional migration poles, continues to provide an exception to the global trend through its human-rights-based migration policy, albeit one that is currently under threat.

Beyond poverty and inequality

A key tension within development debates continues to be whether to focus research and policy initiatives on poverty or inequality. Many reasons exist why a focus on inequality might be preferable to the more traditional one on poverty. Poverty, however defined, will gear our attention to a specific segment of the population, those who are defined as poor; while inequality gives us the opportunity to also take into account those who have historically benefitted from specific forms of economic development and ask questions about the relationship between these two groups and unequal outcomes. Poverty can be defined as being multi-dimensional, but in its more used form, is usually reduced to income poverty. Inequality, on the other hand, while also often defined on the basis of income, includes greater scope for also taking into account social inequalities (Chapter 8). Finally, the global trends in poverty and inequality are in direct opposition. While poverty has been experiencing a downward trend globally, income inequality has steadily been rising (World Bank 2018a, 2018b).

As already indicated in the previous section, how development is defined, and what is included under this very broad term has implications for how researchers frame their questions around migration and development. However, it is encouraging to see that contributors to this volume have gone beyond a narrow definition of development and are pushing the barriers of how we (re-)define development itself. While some chapters deal with topics that have classically been seen as belonging to migration and development debates, such as remittances, diasporas, education, and skilled migration; others address specific challenges related to development, such as forced migration, climate change and disasters, as well as how development itself can be a cause of displacement (Chapter 34). Still others, look at development in terms of unfree labour, care, the reorganisation of families, new meanings of home, and the impact of the processes of ageing. Within this context, what we mean by development is both challenged and enriched by the variety of different understandings that contributors to this volume propose.

In terms of levels of analysis, then, migration also brings about the opportunity to integrate better meso-levels of analysis within development-related research. Much of development research tends to deal with either the macro- or the micro-level, that is, either with countries (states or territories) or individuals. Critical perspectives, such as those coming from feminist critiques, have been better able to integrate meso-level analyses, such as households and communities. The chapters in this Handbook are a good illustration of the cross-fertilisation of the two fields of study: migration and development. When combined, the meso-level of analysis comes more to the fore, particularly given the prominence of network analyses and the legacy of household-level analyses in migration studies, such as the New Economics of Labour Migration. Therefore, besides chapters on global governance and approaches (Chapter 25 and 26) and national-level analyses of policy (Chapter 27), the Handbook also includes chapters dealing with civil society (Chapter 28), transnational family formations (Chapters 16 and 17), and transnational forms of care (Chapter 21).

Finally, it is interesting to note that both migration and development studies have embraced gendered analysis, even if they are still to provide a thorough integration of race and ethnicity. Gender analyses in development have been available since the late 1970s, at the same time as feminist critiques of migration studies started to emerge (Chapter 9). However, development studies as a field and migration and development as a sub-field, still have a long way to go in paying sufficient attention to the historical relationship of domination and discrimination that are related to race and ethnicity. Within development studies, an agenda for thinking about race was proposed over a decade ago (Kothari 2006) but this has yet to find its way into mainstream approaches to development. Advances in the better understanding of alternative approaches to development that take into account indigenous knowledge and practices have also been made (Andolina et al. 2009). However again, this is yet to become a mainstream question within development studies. Questions related to race and/or ethnicity are seldom asked within the context of migration and development debates although Chapter 8 in this Handbook goes some way towards showing how migration and development can integrate broader questions related to social inequalities, as do many of the chapters in Part VI on 'corridors'. It is in the specific case studies where both development studies, as well as migration and development more specifically, benefit from a closer engagement with the rich literature that exists on migration, race, ethnicity, and nationalism, within the broader field of migration studies.

Integration or fragmentation

It is axiomatic that the study of migration (and mobility) crosses disciplinary boundaries. Migration is one of the basic demographic variables and the population of any area a function of only three variables: births (fertility), deaths (mortality), and the net balance of movements in and out of the area (migration). However, as migration, unlike fertility and mortality, is not a single unique life event, demographers, among others, have not been entirely comfortable with a subject whose measurement depends upon variable definitions of space and time to the extent that migration was called the 'step-child of demography' by Dudley Kirk in his presidential address to the Population Association of America in 1960 (Caldwell 1996, 308). Since then, that step-child has become richly endowed to the extent that virtually every discipline has an interest: economists, sociologists, anthropologists, political scientists, as well as the two integrating disciplines of history and geography, have all participated in the migration and development debate. A need to 'talk across disciplines' has certainly emerged (Brettell and Hollifield 2015), although the danger still exists that migration studies, born out of the burgeoning research of the last decades of the previous century, disappear into a series of disciplinary silos. This danger is reflected in the number of handbooks dealing with various dimensions of migration that have emerged in recent years and continue to emerge from three main publishing houses: Routledge, Elgar, and Palgrave Macmillan. Recent specific topics have included environmental displacement, crime, governance, and language, with region-specific volumes on particularly topical or heavily-researched areas. All are to provide both a guide through a significant literature and assessments of prevailing interpretations. Such is the volume of research today on migration that no single person can hope to dominate, or even be aware of, all the work going on across the field, or even within sub-fields within migration studies. Integration can only go so far and fragmentation is inevitable, although these handbooks can act as a kind of Baedeker guide to familiarise researchers and policymakers with the work going on right across the field and are resources to be mined.

This particular *Handbook on Migration and Development* does not adopt a disciplinary approach but incorporates the work of scholars from many disciplines, and as practised in several academic traditions, who all consider different pieces of the migration and development puzzle, but using different lenses. It seeks as broad a perspective as possible across age, gender, region of origin and practice, and educational background and training. It seeks a diverse range of perspectives within the overall objective to provide a comprehensive picture of migration and development but without according pre-eminence to any single interpretation. We are fortunate to have two chapters in this volume written by economists but for a comprehensive assessment of the work of economists in the field of migration and development, see the volume edited by Bob Lucas (2014), *International Handbook on Migration and Economic Development*, as a solid guide through the economic literature. Almost precursors to the present volume, although of longer interpretive essays, are the two collections edited by Cortina and Ochoa-Reza (2013) and van Naerssen et al. (2008). These three aforementioned collective volumes, however, primarily consider the role of international migration in development rather than the full range of mobilities that the majority of the chapters in this volume attempt to cover.

Virtually all of the contributors to this volume would consider themselves to be social scientists of one persuasion or another. If a lacuna exists, it would be the work of a group of scholars who would perhaps feel uncomfortable under a rubric of social science: the historians, whose approaches, methods and data sources are very different from those applied by the authors included in this volume. Nevertheless, historians, like geographers, have come to consider migration in the context of development in its broadest sense. Their work, covering the long term, can provide insight into more recent population flows. It seems invidious to single out just a few references from a vast literature but approaches include wide sweeps of the significance of migration over the first millennium of the Christian era for the development of Europe (Heather 2009), a study of global migration for the second millennium (Hoerder 2002), and comparative perspectives of migration across Eurasia for the second half of the second millennium (Lucassen and Lucassen 2014). Particular themes have been the great transatlantic migrations (Thomas 1972; Baines 1985; Nugent 1992), the southward migrations of the Chinese peoples (Wang 1991; McKeown 2014), and empire (Harper and Constantine 2010). Across many of the studies, the importance of diaspora, of temporary movements and of return loom large, with remittances also a consideration, reminiscent of the concerns of recent scholarship on migration and development in more modern times. The literature on Scottish migration provides a particularly insightful example of the way historians have approached these particular themes in migration and development through the work of scholars such as Harper (2003, 2005, 2018) and Devine (1992, 2011).

It would be naïve to expect that a 'migration studies' will emerge as a significant interdisciplinary alternative to more traditional disciplines, all of which will continue to claim migration and development as integral parts of their own mandate. Hence, we can expect a fragmentation of the field by discipline to continue. Nevertheless, perhaps in the way that 'development studies' has emerged as an interdisciplinary subject, in the United Kingdom at least, and albeit one still usually dominated by economists, migration studies will exist as an interdisciplinary space that will allow cross-fertilisation, and not least with development studies. In a subject in which networks are seen to be central to its understanding, surely migration and development can provide a network among the various disciplinary silos. It is in this spirit that the editors, one trained and practising in schools of development studies, and the other in a more traditional discipline, have striven to assemble as many different perspectives as realistically possible within the confines of a single volume. It is from this point of view that the current *Handbook on Migration and Development* is presented to readers.

References

Abel, G. J. and Sander, N. (2014) "Quantifying global international migration flows" *Science* 243(6178), 1520–1522.

Agustín, L. M. (2007) *Sex at the margins: migration, labour markets and the rescue industry*. Zed, London.

Andolina, R., Laurie, N., and Radcliffe, S. A. (2009) *Indigenous development in the Andes: culture, power, and transnationalism*. Duke University Press, Durham.

Baines, D. (1985) *Migration in a mature economy: emigration and internal migration in England and Wales 1961–1900*. Cambridge University Press, Cambridge.

Bedford, R. D. (1973) "A transition to circular mobility: population movement in the New Hebrides 1800-1970", in Brookfield, H. C. ed. *The Pacific in transition: geographical perspectives on adaptation and change*, Arnold, London, 187–227.

Brettell, C. B. and Hollifield, J. F. (2015) *Migration theory: talking across disciplines*. Routledge, New York, third edition.

Caldwell, J. C. (1996) "Demography and social science" *Population Studies* 50, 305–333.

Carling, J. (2017) "Thirty-six migration nexuses and counting" at: https://jorgencarling.org/2017/07/31/thirty-six-migration-nexuses-and-counting/

Champion, T., Cooke, T., and Shuttleworth, I. eds. (2018) *Internal migration in the developed world: are we becoming less mobile?* Routledge, London.

Chapman, M. (1978) "On the cross-cultural study of circulation" *International Migration Review* 12, 559–569.

Cortina, J. and Ochoa-Reza, E. eds. (2013) *New perspectives on international migration and development*. Columbia University Press, New York.

Cowen, M. P. and Shenton, R. W. (1996) *Doctrines of development*. Routledge, London.

Czaika, M. and de Haas, H. (2014) "The globalization of migration: has the world become more migratory?" *International Migration Review* 48, 283–323.

Devine, T. ed. (1992) *Scottish emigration and Scottish society*. John Donald, Edinburgh.

Devine, T. (2011) *To the ends of the earth: Scotland's global diaspora*. Allen Lane, London.

Faist T. (2008) "Migrants as transnational development agents: an inquiry into the newest round of the migration-development nexus" *Population, Space and Place* 14, 21–42.

Goldstein, S. (1978) "Circulation in the context of total mobility in Southeast Asia" *Papers of the East-West Population Institute* 53.

Goodhart, D. (2017) *The road to somewhere: the populist revolt and the future of politics*. Hurst, London.

Green, M. and Hulme, D. (2005) "From correlates and characteristics to causes: thinking about poverty from a chronic poverty perspective" *World Development* 33(6), 867–879. doi:https://doi.org/10.1016/j.worlddev.2004.09.013

Harper, M. (2003) *Adventurers and exiles: the great Scottish exodus*. Profile Books, London.

Harper, M. ed. (2005) *Emigrant homecomings: the return movement of emigrants 1600-2000*. Manchester University Press, Manchester.

Harper, M. (2018) *Testimonies of transition: voices from the Scottish diaspora*. Luath Press, Edinburgh.

Harper, M. and Constantine, S. (2010) *Migration and empire*. Oxford University Press, Oxford.

Hart, G. (2010) "D/developments after the meltdown" *Antipode* 41, 117–141. doi:10.1111/j.1467-8330.2009.00719.x

Heather, P. (2009) *Empires and barbarians: migration, development and the birth of Europe*. Macmillan, London.

Hoerder, D. (2002) *Cultures in contact: world migrations in the second millennium*. Duke University Press, Durham.

Horner, R. and Hulme, D. (2019) "From international to global development: new geographies of 21st century development" *Development and Change* 50(2), 347–378. doi:10.1111/dech.12379

Hugo, G. (1982) "Circular migration in Indonesia" *Population and Development Review* 8, 59–83.

Hulme, D. and Shepherd, A. (2003) "Conceptualizing chronic poverty" *World Development* 31(3), 403–423. doi:https://doi.org/10.1016/S0305-750X(02)00222-X

IOM. (2018) Who is a migrant? at: www.iom.int/who-is-a-migrant

King, R. (1978) "Return migration: a neglected aspect of population geography" *Area* 10, 175–182.

Kothari, U. (2006) "An agenda for thinking about 'race' in development" *Progress in Development Studies* 6(1), 9–23. doi:10.1191/1464993406ps124oa

Lavenex, S. and Kunz, R. (2008) "The migration and development nexus in EU external relations" *Journal of European Integration* 30, 439–457.

Lucas, R. and Mansfield, S. (2010) "The use of migrant labour in the hospitality sector: current and future implications", in Ruhs, M. and Anderson, B. eds. *Who needs migrant workers? Labour shortages, immigration and public policy*, Oxford University Press, Oxford, 159–186.

Lucas, R. E. B. ed. (2014) *International handbook on migration and economic development*. Elgar, Cheltenham.

Lucassen, J. and Lucassen, L. eds. (2014) *Globalising migration history: the Eurasian experience (16th–21st centuries)*. Brill, Leiden.

McKeown, A. (2014) "A different transition: human mobility in China 1600-1900", in Lucassen, J. and Lucassen, L. eds. *Globalising migration history: the Eurasian experience (16th-21st centuries)*, Leiden, Brill, 279–306.

Nugent, W. (1992) *Crossings: the great transatlantic migrations, 1870–1914*. Indiana University Press, Bloomington.

Nyberg-Sørensen, N., Hear, N. V. and Engberg-Pedersen, P. (2002) "The migration-development nexus evidence and policy options" *International Migration* 40: 49–73.

People First. (2017) "Migrant workers in the hospitality and tourism sector and the potential impact of labour restrictions" at: www.people1st.co.uk/getattachment/Research-Insight/Latest-insights/Migra tion labour-restrictions/Migrant-workers-in-the-hospitality-and-tourism-sector-and-the-potential-impact-of-labour-restrictions.pdf/?lang=en-GB

Raghuram, P. (2009) "Which migration, what development? Unsettling the edifice of migration and development" *Population, Space and Place* 15(2), 103–117. doi:10.1002/psp.536

Robinson, J. (2006) *Ordinary cities: between modernity and development*. Routledge, London; New York.

Safa, H. I. and Du Toit, B. eds. (1975) *Migration and development: implications for ethnic identity and political conflict*. Mouton, Paris.

Sen, A. (1999) *Development as freedom*. Oxford University Press, Oxford.

Sheller, M. and Urry, J. (2006) "The new mobilities paradigm" *Environment and Planning A: Economy and Space* 38(2), 207–226. doi:10.1068/a37268

Silvey, R. (2009) "Development and geography: anxious times, anemic geographies, and migration" *Progress in Human Geography* 33(4), 507–515. doi:10.1177/0309132508096351

Skeldon, R. (1977) "The evolution of migration patterns during urbanization in Peru" *Geographical Review* 67, 394–411.

Skeldon, R. (1997) *Migration and development: a global interpretation*. Longman, London.

Skeldon, R. (2008) "International migration as a tool in development policy: a passing phase?" *Population and Development Review* 34, 1–18.

Skeldon, R. (2018) "International migration, internal migration, mobility and urbanization: towards more integrated approaches", *IOM Migration Research Series No 53* at: http://publications.iom.int/books/mrs-no-53-international-migration-internal-migration-mobility

Thomas, B. (1972) *Migration and urban development*. Methuen, London.

UNDP. (2009) *Human development report 2009. Overcoming barriers: human mobility and development*. United Nations Development Programme, Palgrave Macmillan, New York.

United Nations. (2019a) *International migration stock: the 2017 revision* at: www.un.org/en/development/desa/population/migration/data/estimates2/estimates17.asp

United Nations. (2019b) *World economic situation and prospects*, New York at: www.un.org/development/desa/dpad/wp-content/uploads/sites/45/WESP2019_BOOK-web.pdf

UNWTO. (2018) *Tourism highlights 2018 edition* at: www.e-unwto.org/doi/pdf/10.18111/9789284419876

van Naerssen, T., Spaan, E. and Zoomers, A. eds. (2008) *Global migration and development*. Routledge, New York.

Wang, G. (1991) *China and the overseas Chinese*. Times Academic Press, Singapore.

White, S. C. (2017) "Relational wellbeing: re-centring the politics of happiness, policy and the self" *Policy & Politics* 45(2), 121–136. doi:10.1332/030557317X14866576265970

World Bank. (2018a) *World inequality report*. World Bank, Washington.

World Bank. (2018b) *Poverty and shared prosperity 2018: piecing together the poverty puzzle*. World Bank, Washington.

Zelinsky, W. (1971) "The hypothesis of the mobility transition" *Geographical Review* 61, 219–249.

PART I

Conceptual perspectives and approaches

Many approaches to migration and development are overtly theoretical, but apparently descriptive approaches, and most policy prescriptions also tend to have underlying conceptual assumptions and underpinnings. In order to help readers through the conceptual maze of ideas swirling around the extensive literature and debates on migration and development, Chapters 1 through 3 provide critical guides. The economic and non-economic 'drivers' of migration are placed in as broad a development context as possible and the tensions between national and transnational approaches are highlighted. Perhaps the basic tension, however, revolves around whether development causes or is caused by migration, and clearly both apply. As seen in the Introduction to this Handbook, the way in which the terms 'migration' and 'development' are defined is critical: what kinds of migration are included and how development is being applied, whether as a large or a small 'd'. In a changing context of development, with countries changing development categories at least partially the result of, or at least facilitated by migration, the migration itself can, in turn, be changed: development and migration are inextricably interlinked.

Moving on from these more conceptual/theoretical discussions, the chapters in the second half of Part I introduce three areas of both conceptual and methodological concern: the linkages between internal and international migration; the whole meaning of 'borders'; and the issue of irregular or undocumented migration. Internal migration, so often omitted from the debates on migration and development, has only recently become of interest, despite the clearly established relationships among migration, urbanisation, and development. Whether internal movements give rise to international migration or whether international migration can substitute for internal movements remain intriguing research and policy questions. Yet international migration is more than just the spatial extension of internal migration: the crossing of a national boundary is important and adds complexity. However, the creation of borders themselves leads to more than just a line in the sand but to extensive zones of engagement that are profoundly influenced by modern technologies and surveillance. Nevertheless, political developments through the creation of areas of free movement can lead to the virtual obsolescence of physical borders as a means of migration management. In so doing, any distinction between legal and illegal migration is eliminated among those with the right to move within the area of movement. Given the significance of irregular or undocumented migration within much of the so-called developing world, questions can be raised about the best strategies towards its regulation, management, or even elimination. The section concludes with an examination of the concept of unfree labour in the context of the development of a specific country, Mauritius, where labour demand simultaneously creates migration but enforces immobility. The essays in this part of the Handbook deal with such contentious and critical ideas and lay the basis for the more specific and focused chapters that follow.

1

PARADOXES OF MIGRATION AND DEVELOPMENT

Hein de Haas

Introduction

Migration is an intrinsic part of broader processes of development and social change. Yet political discourse, media, and also many researchers continue to represent migration, implicitly or explicitly, as the antithesis of development. This is evident in many policy proposals to use aid, trade, and remittances as fast-track means to accelerate development in origin countries in order to remove the need to migrate. This is grounded in the tenacious idea that poverty, violence, and other forms of human misery are the main cause of migration. Development is thus presented as a 'solution' to perceived migration problems. However, this ignores mounting evidence pointing to the fact that development initially tends to *increase* internal and international migration.

Studies of historical and contemporary migration have found overwhelming evidence that processes of state formation, infrastructure development, demographic transitions, increasing education, and transformations from agrarian toward industrial societies typically coincide with accelerating migration, particularly in early phases of development. This typically coincides with accelerating rural-to-urban migration, part of which tends to spill over into increasing international migration. Migration requires significant social, cultural, and economic resources in the form of connections, knowledge ('human capital'), and money. Extreme impoverishment, illiteracy, and inadequate infrastructure often deprive people of the resources required for migrating. Populations which are most vulnerable to violence, oppression, economic shocks, as well as environmental stress often belong to the *involuntarily immobile*, those who are unable to move in order to save their lives or build new, and possibly better, lives elsewhere (see also Carling 2002).

Development typically leads to increasing levels of migration because it simultaneously endows people with (1) the capabilities and (2) the aspirations to move (de Haas 2007, 2009). Increasing education, access to modern media, and exposure to the relative wealth of migrants typically coincide with changing ideas of the 'good life' away from agrarian or pastoral lifestyles, as well as increasing material aspirations. Increasing levels of education also tend to increase mobility levels because people are more likely to have to move in order to obtain degrees, or just finish secondary school, as well as to find jobs that match their qualifications in labour markets that grow in structural complexity. While farmworkers or construction workers are likely to find employment in close geographical proximity, the geographical extent of labour markets typically increases with specialisation levels. Such

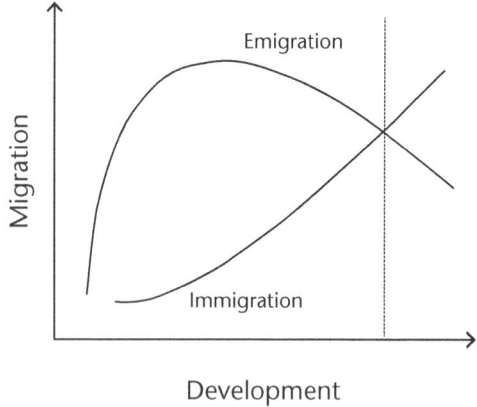

Figure 1.1   The non-linear relation between development and migration
Source: de Haas (2010b)

factors help to explain the paradox that economic and human development in low-income societies typically accelerates emigration. Only when countries achieve high-income states, and when rural-to-urban transitions have been largely completed, do emigration levels tend to go down. This typically yields a non-linear, inverted-U-shaped relation between development and emigration levels (see Figure 1.1).

Development as a migration driver

The popular idea that much 'South–North' migration is essentially driven by poverty, warfare, and environmental degradation (in recent years, climate change has frequently been added to the mix of alleged causes of South–North migration) or that such migrants would constitute a growing mass of destitute victims desperate to leave, ignores growing evidence that most long-distance migration neither occurs from the poorest countries nor from the poorest segments of the population in those countries. In fact, middle-income countries tend to be the most migratory and international migrants predominantly come from relatively better-off sections of origin populations (Czaika and de Haas 2012).

It should therefore not come as a surprise that countries such as Mexico, Morocco, Turkey, and the Philippines figure prominently among origin countries of international labour migrants. In Africa, for instance, extra-continental migration (mainly towards Europe, but also the to the Gulf and the Americas) is dominated by middle-income countries in North Africa and South Africa, while migration from most low-income sub-Saharan countries is lower on average and predominantly intra-regional. Citizens of sub-Saharan countries who are migrating to Europe or North America tend to be from among the relatively well-off and educated groups, as the relatively poor struggle to qualify for visas and generally do not have the means to assume the risks and costs involved in migrating.

According to migration transition theory (de Haas 2010b; Skeldon 1997; Zelinsky 1971), demographic shifts, economic development, and state formation initially increase internal (rural-to-urban) and international emigration. Only when countries achieve higher development levels does emigration tend to decrease alongside increasing immigration, leading to their transformation from net emigration to net immigration countries. The most comprehensive quantitative historical analysis of migration transitions is the study by Hatton and Williamson (1998) on large-scale European migration to North America between 1850 and 1913. Their analysis showed that European migration to the Americas was initially dominated by citizens of the most developed, fast-industrialising nations in northwestern Europe as they went through fast rural–urban and demographic transitions. When the emigration potential of these countries decreased, economic, demographic, and infrastructural transitions in more peripheral European countries in southern and eastern Europe started to gain ground. Their analysis revealed that emigration increased while wage rates in origin and destination countries actually *converged*. They explain this paradox by arguing that the hypothetical migration-decreasing effects of declining wage gaps were outweighed by the mass arrival of cohorts of young workers in the labour market, increasing incomes (which enabled people to migrate) and a structural shift of the labour out of agriculture. Furthermore, expanding networks partially gave migration its own momentum by reducing risks and costs of migration (Hatton and Williamson 1998, see also Massey 2000).

In recent years, the validity of migration transition theory for contemporary global migration has been assessed using new data sources. In 2010, drawing on new data from the University of Sussex/World Bank Global Bilateral Migration Database (GBMD), I provided a first global assessment of the relation between various origin and destination country migration determinants and levels of immigration and emigration (de Haas 2010a). As shown in Figure 1.2, the relation between levels of development immigration is robustly positive and largely linear, indicating that societies are likely to attract increasing numbers of immigrants as they become more prosperous. While this finding is largely intuitive, the paradox (and the inconvenient truth for policymakers and bureaucrats arguing that development can somehow be a medicine against migration), lies in the non-linear relation between development and general levels of emigration. This finding was also confirmed in multivariate regression analyses that tested the effect of other relevant variables (de Haas 2010a).

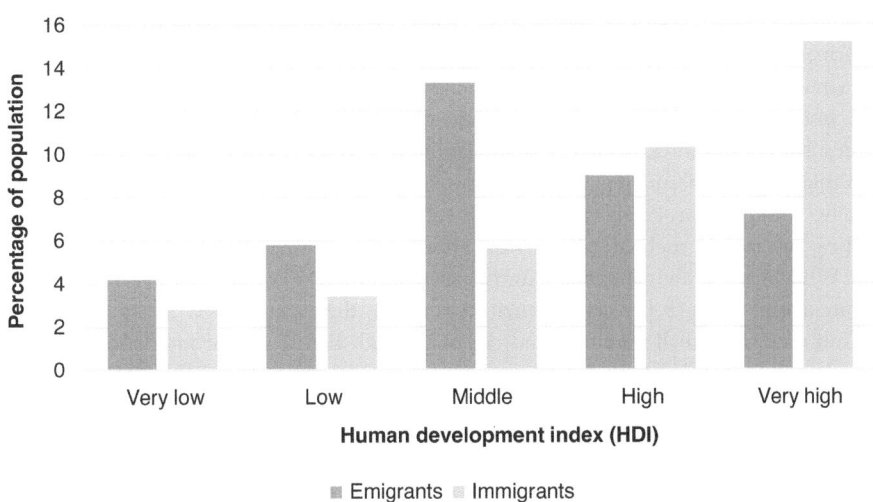

Figure 1.2 Association between levels of development and levels of immigration and emigration
Source: de Haas (2010b)

The analysis provided clear evidence of migration transition theory, finding an inverted-U-shaped association between development and emigration. Higher levels of economic and human development, whether measured by GDP per capita or the Human Development Index (HDI), are initially associated with higher levels of emigration. These findings using 2000 census data were confirmed by more recent studies that estimated the relationship between income per capita and relative emigrant levels of the 1960, 1970, 1980, and 1990 census rounds (Clemens 2014; de Haas and Fransen 2018). Only when countries shift into upper-middle-income and higher income categories, does further development lead to a decrease in emigration levels.

Of course, this data only provides national averages, and, depending upon the specific context, we find considerable variation across countries, even though some regularities can be detected. For instance, large and populous countries tend to have lower emigration levels (relative to their population) mainly because more migration is contained within their borders. The approximately ten million China-born people living abroad may appear like a high number, but they represent only about 0.7 per cent of the total Chinese population. Likewise, the 16.6 million India-born international migrants only represent 1.2 per cent of the total Indian population (de Haas et al. 2019a). By contrast, small states without large urban centres such as Lesotho or Cape Verde have high emigration rates as it is less likely that aspiring youth will find work and lifestyle opportunities that match their aspirations within their own countries.

Some countries have much lower emigration rates than one would have expected based on migration transition theory. For instance, during its economic and demographic transition of the past decades, Thailand seems to have experienced lower emigration levels compared to other countries with similar development levels, and did not experience as significant a migration transition as for instance South Korea or Malaysia. The reasons for this are not entirely clear, but are likely to be related to cultural factors and the fact that Thailand has never been colonised and hence has no extensive historical links with a metropole. Small countries with long histories of colonisation and transnational connectivity, often have extraordinary high emigration rates, such as the Caribbean nations of Guyana and Suriname, where about half of the population currently lives abroad (Vezzoli 2015). Such extremely high emigration levels are generally also linked to the introduction of immigration restrictions by former colonising nations (such as Britain and the Netherlands) and other destination countries, which created significant levels of 'now or never' migration and pushed migrants into permanent settlement by discouraging return.

Finally, immigration levels in industrialised, high-income countries vary significantly, depending on factors such as labour market structure, immigration policies, and cultural factors. While in most high-income countries such as the US, France, and the UK, immigrants constitute about 10 to 15 per cent of their population, these percentages are much higher in Arab Gulf states and small countries and city states with high levels of international connectiveness, reaching levels of 88.4 per cent in the United Arab Emirates, 75.5 per cent in Kuwait, 46 per cent in Singapore, 37 per cent in Singapore, and 29.6 per cent in Switzerland. In contrast, the 2.3 million officially registered immigrants in Japan represented only 1.8 of the total population, while the 1.2 million migrants in South Korea represented just 2.3 per cent of the Korean population (calculations based on data from UNDESA 2017).

These observations show the importance of understanding particular regional contexts and the dangers of a blind application of transition models. On the other hand, the overall pattern is clear:

- Low-income countries with low levels of global integration have low levels of internal migration as well as international emigration.
- Rural–urban and demographic transitions accompanying the transformation from agrarian to industrialised societies tend to boost migration of all kinds.
- When countries transition to higher income societies, they tend to become net immigration countries, but emigration and overall levels of mobility remain higher than in low-income societies.

Although governments can influence the actual levels and patterns of migration to a certain extent, it would be an illusion to think they can change the overall meta-trends, let alone reverse them. This insight applies to both international and internal migration. This explains why various attempts to stem the 'rural exodus' through keeping people 'down on the farm' (Rhoda 1983) have typically failed. Sometimes, such policies even produced the opposite results. For instance, the construction of rural roads, the expansion of the electricity grid into rural areas, and the establishment of schools, can actually *accelerate* out-migration through making travel and communication easier and cheaper and through the exposure of rural populations to new ideas and lifestyles, which potentially also increase their aspirations to migrate.

Practical implications

Because of the significant costs and risks involved in migration, the poorest of the poor tend to remain either stuck in involuntary immobility or, if they manage to move out, are likely to move over relatively short distances and under unfavourable conditions, such as is the case with Central American migrants trying to cross Mexico by foot (Olayo-Méndez 2018). The evidence presented here also exposes the unrealistic nature of the oft-mentioned spectre of mass long-distance migration supposedly in response to environmental degradation, whether or not affected by climate change (Christian Aid 2007; Myers and Kent 1995). In my contributions to the Migration and Global Environmental Change project conducted by the UK Government Office for Science (Foresight 2011), I argued that extreme deprivation is likely to deprive the most vulnerable and deprived groups of the means to migrate as a strategy to secure their livelihoods. If climate change would, for instance, increase the incidence of droughts in particular areas of sub-Saharan Africa, the populations most severely affected, mainly small-scale peasants and pastoralists, would be unlikely to appear on the borders of wealthy countries in Europe. They most likely will remain trapped in immobility, or forced to move or settle down in nearby agrarian areas or small towns (de Haas et al. 2019a). Even moving to larger cities requires significant resources, knowledge, and connections. This is substantiated by evidence from various sub-Saharan African countries that long-distance migration from rural areas is often *lower* in years of drought and scarcity (Henry et al. 2004; Jónsson 2010; Lewin et al. 2012).

Paradoxically, hikes in long-distance rural out-migration often occur when harvests are abundant and people have the resources to move. The relatively better-off, middle-income groups, or even small-scale entrepreneurs or peasants in possession of some land or livestock, can sell assets in order to raise the funds to migrate and are generally in a better position to move over longer distances to access jobs and other opportunities in destination areas. Likewise, those in possession of higher education degrees are more likely to find jobs in destination areas and to obtain visas and other migration permits should they aspire to migrate abroad. This partly explains why long-distance emigration from low-income countries tends to be such a selective affair. For instance, it is no coincidence that sub-Saharan Africans are amongst the highest skilled immigrant groups in the United States (Capps et al. 2012). The greater the distance, and the more stringent immigration rules are, the more selective migration tends to be.

The important lesson for policymakers is that any form of development in the poorest countries is likely to lead to accelerating emigration for the coming decades. This is the exact opposite of what 'development instead of migration' policies aim to achieve.

For instance, if we apply migration transition theory to sub-Saharan African countries – which are the target of much international aid and 'development instead of migration' programmes – it seems safe to assume that migration from sub-Saharan Africa will increase *as a consequence of* development. Higher levels of education, income, and connectivity are likely to fuel emigration to increasingly distant lands. Rather than curbing migration, development in sub-Saharan Africa will enable and inspire more people to move. In fact, high levels of poverty, illiteracy, and weak infrastructure have often prevented previous generations of Africans from migrating over longer distances. It is also no coincidence that extra-continental emigration levels have generally been highest from African countries such as Morocco, Tunisia, Egypt as well as South Africa, Senegal, Nigeria, and Ghana which are characterised by *relatively* higher levels of economic development and global integration through economic ties and infrastructure. In the future, emigration from sub-Saharan Africa is likely to increase *as a result of African development*. While many Asian countries began to massively participate in global migration from the 1960s, largely reflecting fast rates of economic development and demographic transitions in those countries, it is likely that Africans will form an increasingly large share of the future global migrant population.

The rationality of migration

The occurrence of development-driven emigration hikes shows the inability of push–pull models to explain real-world migration patterns. In fact, such models are misleading, as they predict that development in low-income societies (such as in sub-Saharan Africa) and lower geographical income gaps will decrease emigration. From a conceptual point of view, push–pull models are also misguided because of the assumption that people are 'pushed out' of origin areas. This ignores that migration requires considerable 'agency'. In concrete terms, this means that in order for migration to happen, people need to possess the willpower (or aspirations), as well as the considerable resources (or capabilities) that are required to move, particularly if this movement involves crossing borders and considerable costs involved in travel such as the procurement of immigration papers, or the payment of smugglers to cross borders.

In other words, most people have good reasons to move. Migration is generally a deliberate and largely rational attempt to gain access to better opportunities rather than a 'desperate flight from misery'. Although migrants, as people in general, have various biases, in discourses on 'South–North' migration a tendency exists to underplay or deny migrants' rationality. This tendency filters through in policy and media narratives according to which prospective migrants should be informed about the dangers of the journey and the arduous conditions in destination countries (see Pécoud 2010). However, such narratives ignore that even undocumented migrants can allow families in origin countries to significantly improve their income and livelihood security.

The emphasis of much of the current research and discourse of migration on the subjectivity of migration comes at the risks of underplaying or denying the rational dimension of migration decision making. Certainly, some migrants are misinformed about opportunities and may have an over-optimistic picture about life abroad, and each year a considerable number of migrants are deceived, extorted, or physically abused by government officials and employers. Each year, thousands of migrants are injured or die while trying to cross borders. Such risks explain why migrants are often willing to pay recruiters, smugglers, and other 'fixers' to seek some form of protection and to facilitate safer passage or the procurement of visas and other paperwork. The 'migration industry' exists by virtue of migrant controls. Certainly, smugglers and recruiters may also revert to dishonest and dangerous practices, but they are essentially service providers consciously paid for by migrants in the reasonable expectation that this will help their passage.

Given the evidence from countless surveys and field studies on the considerable long-term benefits of both internal and international migrants for the income, education, and welfare of migrants and their families (Clemens et al. 2008; McKenzie et al. 2010; UNDP 2009), it would be foolish to deny migrants a certain degree of rationality in their mobility decisions. Migration is often a carefully planned investment made by entire families for a better future. This is a crucial insight for policy makers and governments who still believe that people can be discouraged from migrating by running campaigns to highlight the dangers of migrating. Such campaigns seem to be based on the implicit idea that migrants do not know what they are doing, and that it would be in their own best interest to stay. Although perhaps largely unwittingly, such assumptions seem to buy into rather paternalistic and colonial worldviews according to which the non-Western 'other' is seen as less rational and therefore needs to be informed and enlightened. The fact that the rationality of Western internal or international migrants is rarely ever questioned further exposes this bias.

Thus, although migration usually involves risks, for most people the investment pays off, and recent evidence shows that people are willing to take considerable risks to access better opportunities abroad (see Mbaye 2014), and to live through many years of hardship either to save enough money to return or to secure residency and settle permanently with their families. As argued by the 'new economics of labor migration' (Stark 1991), migration is often a family investment because it allows families to reduce risk, increase income, and improve long-term wellbeing (Taylor 1999). Migration needs to be conceptualised as a resource in its own right, an important means for upward socioeconomic mobility for relatively disadvantaged groups.

This logic explains why migrants often show so much perseverance in reaching their long-term goals of securing better livelihoods for their families. This, too, is why migrants often try to migrate again even in the cases where they are deported, and show incredible tenacity and endurance to withstand situations of long-term hardship, sacrifice, and loneliness. Returning empty-handed is therefore an unbearable idea for many migrants, and a return home can therefore be a sign of successful rather than of failed migration. Only when migrants have obtained the money, experience, or education which motivated their movements, can they return, or, alternatively, decide to settle permanently at the destination.

The aspirations and capabilities model

To explain why development is so often associated with more, rather than less, migration we must move beyond sterile views of migrants as predictable 'respondents' to geographical opportunity gaps and other external stimuli. In order to achieve a richer understanding of migration behaviour, it can be useful to conceptualise migration as a function of people's capabilities and aspirations to move (de Haas 2014). Processes of human and economic development typically expand people's access to material resources, social networks, and knowledge. At the same time, improvements in infrastructure and transportation, which usually accompany development, make travel less costly and risky. However, as societies become wealthier, beyond a certain tipping point, overall emigration aspirations are likely to decrease because more people can imagine a future within their own country, while at the same time, immigration is likely to increase.

Development therefore increases people's capabilities to migrate over greater distances, but it does not automatically lead to migration. Migration aspirations depend on people's more general life aspirations, as well as perceptions of life 'here' and 'there'. Both are subjective and likely to change under the influence of broader processes of structural change. These include improved access to information, images, and lifestyles conveyed through education and media, which tend to broaden people's mental horizons, change perceptions of the 'good life', and increase material aspirations. Development processes initially tend to increase both people's capabilities and aspirations to move, and explain why development often boosts migration. Once sizeable migrant communities have settled in destination areas, social networks tend to reduce the costs and risks of migrating, with settled migrants frequently functioning as 'bridgeheads' (Böcker 1994). This can further accelerate migration in established migration corridors, even if wage and other opportunity gaps actually decrease because of development in origin areas (Hatton and Williamson 1998).

Although it is often assumed that technological progress increases migration, easier transportation and communication may enable people to commute or work from home, while outsourcing and trade may also partly reduce the need to migrate (see also Zelinsky 1971). In fact, from a long-term historical perspective, technology has facilitated humankind to settle. Ever since the agricultural ('Neolithic') revolution began some 12,000 years ago, technology has enabled people to shift from hunting and gathering to more sedentary lifestyles. In modern times, technological progress has certainly boosted non-migratory mobility, such

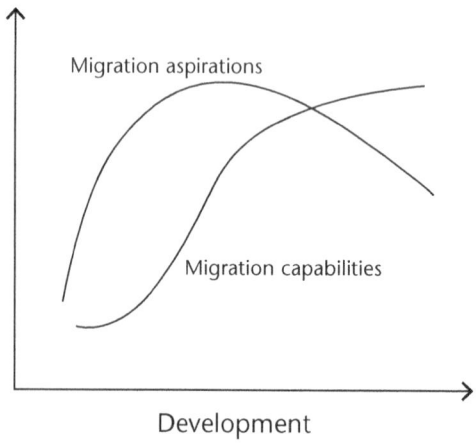

Figure 1.3 Hypothetical effects of development on migration capabilities and aspirations
Source: de Haas (2010b)

as commuting, tourism, and business travel, but its impact on (residential) migration is rather ambiguous. This may be one explanation for the fact that, over recent decades, the number of international migrants as a share of the world population has remained remarkably stable at levels of around 3 per cent. While development tends to boost migration from low-income countries, overall levels of international migration are actually rather low.

Redefining human mobility

So far, I have argued that:

- Migration is an *intrinsic* part of broader development processes.
- Development in low-income countries generally increases overall levels of migration.
- For most people involved, migration is a vital resource rather than a desperate response to destitution.
- The most deprived people are more likely to find themselves trapped in involuntary immobility and exposed to the greatest dangers in case of economic crisis, violence of environmental calamity.

At the micro-level, for most people, migration represents opportunity and the hope of a better future. At the macro-level, the profound economic, demographic, and social trans-formations that accompany processes of development and modernisation will inevitably lead to increased migration, particularly from rural-to-urban areas both within and across inter-national borders. Migration *is* development, as Skeldon (1997) already argued, instead of the antithesis of development.

This insight shows the need to reconceptualise migration and human mobility. Redefining migration as a resource, as an investment in a better future, and as an important avenue for pro-gress for non-elite groups in societies around the world, also requires rethinking the underlying concept of human mobility. Human mobility is usually seen in terms of people moving, but it can only be a freedom- and life-enhancing resource or 'capability' if people can make the actual choice to move. So, people only enjoy real mobility freedoms if they have the option to stay, if they are not forced to move. In earlier papers, I therefore proposed to define human mobility as people's capability (freedom) to choose where to live, with residential human movement (migration) as the associated outcome (de Haas 2009, 2014). Human mobility therefore also includes the freedom to stay.

The resulting view on migration does not presume either moving or staying as the norm, but acknowledges that they are the two sides of the same freedom-of-mobility coin (de Haas 2014). This allows us to move beyond the rather futile debate over whether migration or sedentary behaviour is the norm. Both are 'normal' in sedentary societies, as staying and moving occur in different phases of people's lives, and because the livelihoods of those stay-ing and moving are intimately connected. Although only 3 per cent of the world population is an international migrant, many more people (family members, communities, and entire societies) are deeply affected by migration.

From this perspective, people can still enjoy mobility capabilities without ever using them, because it adds to their sense of freedom, in the same way as people do not necessarily have to use actively certain freedoms, for instance, political rights or social benefits, in order to enjoy them: the reassuring knowledge of their existence as an 'option' or fallback position is sufficient. Awareness of the possibility of migrating can therefore function as a form of insurance, an option that is always available. This may be one of the reasons why 'open borders' regimes (such as in the EU) are often associated with much lower-than-expected (permanent) emigration levels (de Haas et al. 2019b), because people who can move around freely would otherwise have felt deprived of mobility options are no longer obsessed with moving out at the first opportunity, as is more typical for the 'involuntarily' immobile who feel blocked from opportunities to explore foreign lands.

The above argument is intrinsically related to capabilities and aspirations in two different ways. First, people need access to social (other people), economic (material), and cultural or 'human' (ideas, knowledge, and skills) resources to exert migratory agency. Under highly constrained conditions, people often lack the resources to leave, which partly explains why the poorest people are generally underrepresented in long-distance international migration. Second, if people have no real choice to stay, because of war, persecution, or environmental hazards, for example, or are pressured by their families to work abroad, they are deprived of an essential part of their human mobility freedoms, that is, the option or 'capability' to stay. On the other hand, if people feel deprived of their mobility freedoms, the concomitant feeling of being 'trapped' may further fuel their migration aspirations and can lead to an obsession with 'getting out.'

Migration and development: a reciprocal, but asymmetric relationship

Last, but not least, migration also has an impact on development processes in destination and origin societies. Overall, migration researchers have paid much more attention to the implications of migration for destination countries than to the consequences (and causes) of migration from an origin country perspective. This is part of a more general 'receiving country bias' of the research literature. Fortunately, however, since 2000, increasing attention has been paid to the impacts of migration on origin countries. This was partly prompted by a fast increase in remittances sent by migrants to their origin countries. As Figure 1.4 shows, remittance flows have far outstripped Official Development Assistance (ODA) and have approached the value of Foreign Direct Investment (FDI).

While migration tends to stimulate overall growth and innovation in destination countries (Boubtane et al. 2013; Ortega and Peri 2013; UNDP 2009), a much more contested question is whether migration encourages development of the countries of origin or, conversely, hinders such development. Over the past few decades, this issue has sparked heated debate in policy and research, opposing 'migration optimists', who argue that migration brings growth and prosperity to origin countries, to 'migration pessimists', who argue that migration undermines development through draining origin countries of their scarce human and financial resources. While the pessimists predict a 'brain drain', the optimists predict a 'brain gain'. This division reflects the more general division between historical–structural (neo-Marxist) and functionalist (neoclassical) theories that view migration as an exploitation and optimisation mechanism, respectively (de Haas 2010a). The debate about migration and development has swung back and forth, from optimism in the post-1945 period, to pessimism since the 1970s, to renewed optimism since the 2000s (de Haas 2012). This debate reflects a broader opposition between development paradigms and economic philosophies, but also ideologies.

The reality, as so often, lies in the middle because the specific impact of migration is dependent on more general development conditions. In evaluating the impacts of development, it is particularly crucial to distinguish between levels of analysis. While the evidence suggests

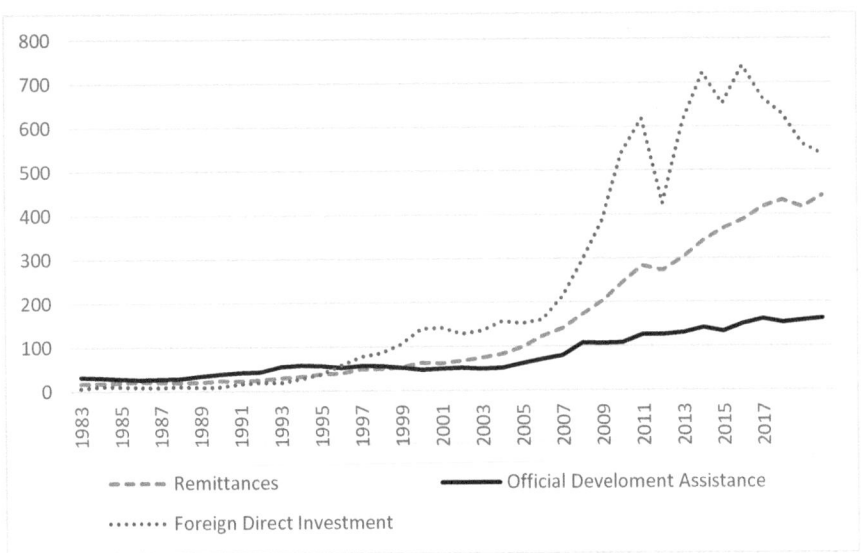

Figure 1.4 Remittances, Official Development Aid, and Foreign Direct Investment to lower- and middle-income countries

Source: World Development Indicators database, accessed 26 January 2019

Table 1.1 Opposing views on migration and development

Migration optimists		Migration pessimists
Functionalist	↔	Historical-structuralist
Brain gain	↔	Brain drain
Neoclassical	↔	Neo-Marxist
Modernisation	↔	Dependency
Net North-South transfer	↔	Net South-North transfer
More equality	↔	More inequality
Remittance investment	↔	Remittance consumption
Development	↔	Disintegration
Less migration	↔	More migration

Source: Adapted from de Haas (2010a)

there is much room for optimism when we look at the considerable potential of migration in improving the welfare and wellbeing of migrants and their communities involved (de Haas 2010a), much more scepticism is warranted with regards to expectations that migration can somehow magically 'trigger' national-level development or solve structural development problems such as corruption, lack of trust in governments, and macro-economic instability. It is therefore not surprising that studies have generally failed to identify a clear causal link between migration and origin country development trends at the macro-level, such as economic growth and investment (see Clemens and McKenzie 2018).

Notwithstanding the considerable benefits for individuals, households, and communities, a large body of empirical evidence has shown that migration and remittances can neither be blamed for lack of development ('brain drain') nor be expected to boost sustainable development ('brain gain') in generally unattractive investment environments (de Haas 2010a). Despite the benefits for families and communities at the micro- and meso-level, migration and remittances alone cannot remove structural development obstacles at the macro-level, such as corruption, nepotism, and failing institutions. Migration is unlikely to *remove* such obstacles or to *reverse* structural trends at the macro-level. Migration is therefore no panacea for development (see also Papademetriou and Martin 1991; Taylor 1999).

If states fail to implement reform, migration is unlikely to fuel national development, and can actually sustain situations of dependency, underdevelopment, and authoritarianism. Such a vicious cycle can be identified in countries such as the Philippines, Morocco, and Egypt, which have experienced large-scale emigration for decades without clear macro-level benefits, while preserving the political status quo. In these cases, migrants are also more likely to settle permanently and to reunify their families, if destination countries so permit. However, if development in origin countries takes a positive turn, and governments implement real reform, migrants often reinforce these positive trends through investing and returning, because they are often the first to recognise such improved opportunities. Such a virtuous cycle has been identified in various countries, including South Korea, China, and India (DeWind et al. 2012; Saxenian 2004).

Both migration optimists and pessimists tend to ascribe too much transformational potential to migration. This does not only apply to debates on the impacts of migration for origin societies, but for to debates on the destination country impacts of migration, which also tend to be rather polarised, pitting those arguing that migration undermines welfare, wages, and the security of destination countries against proponents of migration, who argue that migration is a solution to structural problems such as economic stagnation and population ageing. Despite these opposing views, what both migration opponents and proponents 'camps' have in common is an overestimation of the transformative potential of migration. For instance, empirical evidence suggests that the impacts of migration on wages of native workers vary depending on the context and groups under scrutiny. This has generated heated discussions in the research literature. However, what has often been ignored is that the common denominator of virtually all studies is that the actual magnitude of such wage effects, whether positive or negative, is actually very small (Dustmann et al. 2016; Ottaviano and Peri 2012; UNDP 2009).

Thus, the relation between development and migration is reciprocal but strongly asymmetrical. The conceptualisation of migration as an intrinsic part of broader development processes implies that migration is a subprocess of larger development processes (see Figure 1.5). While processes of social transformation drive migration, migration is generally less likely to fundamentally alter the deeper political and economic structures of origin and destination societies (Portes 2010). Although the short-term and local impacts of migration can initially *appear* to be significant, in the longer term most migrant groups largely adapt to the culture and economic systems of destination countries within a few generations, and the impacts of migrants and minorities on mainstream institutions and power structures remain rather negligible. The main exception on this rule are cases in which migrants come in the shape of colonisers who subjugate native populations through military force and occupation.

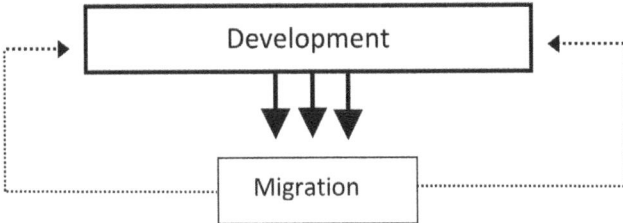

Figure 1.5 The reciprocal, but asymmetric relationship between development and migration

Conclusion

This chapter has argued that migration is an integral – and therefore inevitable – part of broader processes of economic development and social transformation that characterise societies going through 'modernisation' processes. Although specific patterns and levels of migration vary across societies, the combination of profound economic, cultural, techno-logical, political, and demographic changes typically generate major increases in overall levels of internal and international mobility. Emigration levels tend to be highest in middle-income societies where profound social transformation and rural-urban transitions simultaneously increase people's aspirations and capabilities to migrate. Low-income soci-eties generally have lower emigration levels because poverty tends to constrain people's movement. Economic development typically increases people's ability to use migration as a (family) resource to increase their long-term wellbeing, while education and cultural change typically increase people's desire to migrate as a way to pursue 'modern' lifestyles. The paradox of development-driven emigration hikes shows the inability of conventional push–pull models to explain migration, and exemplifies the need to reconceptualise migra-tion as an intrinsic part of development rather than a 'problem to be solved'. Migration is shaped by development in origin and destination societies and contributes to further change in its own right. However, the embeddedness of migration in broader develop-ment processes also means that its potential to affect structural change is fundamentally limited. This shows the logical fallacy of narratives that cast development as a 'solution' for perceived migration problems, or that cast migration and remittances as a panacea to solve fundamental development problems.

References

Böcker, A. (1994). Chain migration over legally closed borders: Settled migrants as bridgeheads and gatekeepers. *Netherlands' Journal of Social Sciences* **30**, 87–106.

Boubtane, E., Coulibaly, D., and Rault, C. (2013). Immigration, growth, and unemployment: Panel VAR evidence from OECD countries. *Labour* **27**, 399–420.

Capps, R., McCabe, K., and Fix, M. (2012). *Diverse Streams: African Migration to the United States.* Migration Policy Institute, Washington, DC.

Carling, J. (2002). Migration in the age of involuntary immobility: Theoretical reflections and Cape Ver-dean experiences. *Journal of Ethnic and Migration Studies* **28**, 5–42.

Christian Aid. (2007). *Human Tide: The Real Migration Crisis.* Christian Aid, London.

Clemens, M. A. (2014). *Does Development Reduce Migration?* Center for Global Development, Washington, DC.

Clemens, M. A., and McKenzie, D. (2018). Why don't remittances appear to affect growth? *The Economic Journal* **128**, 179–209.

Clemens, M. A., Montenegro, C. E., and Pritchett, L. (2008). *The Place Premium: Wage Differences for Identical Workers Across the US Border*. World Bank, Washington, DC.

Czaika, M., and de Haas, H. (2012). The role of internal and international relative deprivation in global migration. *Oxford Development Studies* **40**, 423–442.

de Haas, H. (2007). Turning the tide? Why development will not stop migration. *Development and Change* **38**, 819–841.

de Haas, H. (2009). *Mobility and Human Development*. UNDP, New York.

de Haas, H. (2010a). Migration and development: A theoretical perspective. *International Migration Review* **44**, 227–264.

de Haas, H. (2010b). Migration transitions: A theoretical and empirical inquiry into the developmental drivers of international migration. Working Paper No 24, International Migration Institute, University of Oxford, Oxford.

de Haas, H. (2012). The migration and development pendulum: A critical view on research and policy. *International Migration* **50**, 8–25.

de Haas, H. (2014). Migration theory: Quo vadis? International Migration Institute, University of Oxford, IMI/DEMIG working paper no 100. Oxford.

de Haas, H., and Fransen, S. (2018). Social transformation and migration: An empirical inquiry. International Migration Institute, University of Amsterdam, IMI working paper 141. Amsterdam.

de Haas, H., Castles, S., and Miller, M. J. (2019a). *The Age of Migration: International Population Movements in the Modern World*, 6th edition. MacMillan Press Ltd, Houndmills, Basingstoke, Hampshire and London.

de Haas, H., Vezzoli, S., and Villares-Varela, M. (2019b). Opening the floodgates? European migration under restrictive and liberal border regimes 1950–2010. International Migration Institute, University of Amsterdam, Amsterdam.

DeWind, J., Kim, E. M., Skeldon, R., and Yoon, I. J. (2012). Korean development and migration. *Journal of Ethnic and Migration Studies* **38**, 371–388.

Dustmann, C., Schönberg, U., and Stuhler, J. (2016). The impact of immigration: Why do studies reach such different results? *Journal of Economic Perspectives* **30**, 31–56.

Foresight. (2011). *Foresight: Migration and Global Environmental Change*. UK Government Office for Science, London.

Hatton, T. J., and Williamson, J. G. (1998). *The Age of Mass Migration: Causes and Economic Effects*. Oxford University Press, Oxford and New York.

Henry, S., Schoumaker, B., and Beauchemin, C. (2004). The impact of rainfall on the first out-migration: A multi-level event-history analysis in Burkina Faso. *Population and Environment* **25**, 423–460.

Jónsson, G. (2010). The environmental factor in migration dynamics: A review of African case studies.

Lewin, P. A., Fisher, M., and Weber, B. (2012). Do rainfall conditions push or pull rural migrants: Evidence from Malawi. *Agricultural Economics* **43**, 191–204.

Massey, D. S. (2000). Book review – The age of mass migration: Causes and economic impact by Timothy J. Hatton and Jeffrey G. Williamson. *The Journal of Modern History* **72**, 496–497.

Mbaye, L. M. (2014). "Barcelona or die": Understanding illegal migration from Senegal. *IZA Journal of Migration* **3**, 21.

McKenzie, D., Stillman, S., and Gibson, J. (2010). How important is selection? Experimental vs. non-experimental measures of the income gains from migration. *Journal of the European Economic Association* **8**, 913–945.

Myers, N., and Kent, J. (1995). *Environmental Exodus: An Emergent Crisis in the Global Arena*. Climate Institute, Washington, DC.

Olayo-Méndez, J. A. (2018). Migration, poverty, and violence in Mexico: The role of Casas de Migrantes. DPhil Thesis. University of Oxford, Oxford.

Ortega, F., and Peri, G. (2013). The effect of income and immigration policies on international migration. *Migration Studies* **1**, 47–74.

Ottaviano, G. I. P., and Peri, G. (2012). Rethinking the effect of immigration on wages. *Journal of the European Economic Association* **10**, 152–197.

Papademetriou, D. G., and Martin, P. L. eds. (1991). *The Unsettled Relationship. Labor Migration and Economic Development*. Greenwood Press, New York.

Pécoud, A. (2010). Informing migrants to manage migration? An analysis of IOM's information campaigns. In *The Politics of International Migration Management* (M. Geiger and A. Pécoud, eds.), pp. 184–201. Palgrave Macmillan UK, London.

Portes, A. (2010). Migration and social change: Some conceptual reflections. *Journal of Ethnic and Migration Studies* **36**, 1537–1563.

Rhoda, R. (1983). Rural development and urban migration: Can we keep them down on the farm? *International Migration Review* **17**, 34–64.

Saxenian, A. (2004). The silicon valley connection: Transnational networks and regional development in Taiwan, China and India. In *India in the Global Software Industry: Innovation, Firm Strategies and Development* (A. P. D'Costa and E. Sridharan, eds.), pp. 164–192. Palgrave Macmillan UK, London.

Skeldon, R. (1997). *Migration and Development: A Global Perspective*. Addison Wesley Longman, Harlow, Essex.

Stark, O. (1991). *The Migration of Labor*. Blackwell, Cambridge & Oxford.

Taylor, J. E. (1999). The new economics of labour migration and the role of remittances in the migration process. *International Migration* **37**, 63–88.

UNDESA. (2017). *2017 Revision of World Population Prospects*. United Nations Population Division, New York.

UNDP. (2009). Overcoming barriers: Human mobility and development. Human Development Report 2009, UNDP, New York City.

Vezzoli, S. (2015). Borders, independence and post-colonial ties: The role of the state in Caribbean migration.

Zelinsky, Z. (1971). The Hypothesis of the mobility transition. *Geographical Review* **61**, 219–249.

2

MIGRATION AND DEVELOPMENT

Theorising changing conditions and ongoing silences

Nina Glick Schiller

To formulate an approach to migration and development that speaks to the growing impediments to migrants' international movement and settlement, scholars and policymakers need both knowledge of previous arguments about the topic and an assessment of the changing conditions. This assessment must address the past and contemporary stance of nation-states and international organisations towards migration and people of migrant background. In assessing the political climate, it is important to ask when and why migration becomes a hot topic of political debate and migrants become contested problematic figures. Therefore, in this chapter I revisit migration and development debates, not as a review of the vast migration literature but to establish a way of assessing what is missing from contemporary discussions.

Methodological nationalism has marked many debates about migration, whether or not the discussants have been for or against migration. Methodological nationalism is an intellectual orientation that assumes that nation-states can be equated with the boundaries of society and that each state is an independent political actor, and therefore can serve as the primary unit in historical, economic, political and cultural analysis (Beck 2002; Smith 1983; Wimmer and Glick Schiller 2002). From this perspective, a state's development is primarily a product of a country's distinctive national history and political, economic, and cultural strengths and weaknesses. When translated into an argument about the causes of migration such as classic push-pull theory, migration is approached in terms of the independent development trajectories of individual states. Underdevelopment in the country of origin impels individuals to leave home, and the country of destination attracts migrants because of its separate national trajectory that produces economic opportunity, freedom, security, and safety. Modifications of push-pull explanations of migration dynamics primarily have taken the form of specifying intervening variables such as distance and cost of travel (Lee 1966).

However, by the end of the twentieth century, migration theorists, propelled by several decades of debates about dependency theory, world systems, and an emerging literature on globalisation began to explore the interconnections between migration and development in ways that connected countries of departure and settlement. Those researchers concerned with development began to speak of the migration and development 'nexus' (Nyberg–Sørensen et al. 2002). Although rarely defined, the term nexus was widely deployed to refer to 'a set of complex interdependencies between two processes or phenomena, such as migration and development' (Carling 2017). Over time, the term nexus came to signal both an acknowledgement that there were relationships between processes and policies that led to economic growth and migration dynamics and that there were transnational connections between migrants' countries and locations of settlement and their homelands.

'Nexologists' sought to examine whether and how development policies and humanitarian aid on the part of developed countries and agencies they supported contributed to various kinds of migration and resulted in the amelioration of poverty. Within these inquiries, some research specifically asked whether migration and development reduced or increased inequality in sending countries (Bastia 2013). Their findings suggested that rather than specific policies, structural variables were at work and for this reason an 'increasing body of empirical research … appeared … indicating that the development impacts of migration are fundamentally heterogeneous' (de Haas 2010, 240). Many of the relationships explored by the nexologists emerged from the transnational framework for the study of migration developed in the 1990s.

The transnational framework for the study of migration

Developing as part of the efforts to theorise globalisation, the initial transnational framework was an attempt to overcome the methodological nationalism of the migration and development discussions (Glick Schiller 1999a, 1999b; Glick Schiller et al. 1992; Kearney and Nagengast 1989; Rouse 1991). Building on the strengths and critiques of dependency and world-systems theory (Cardoso and Faletto 1979; Frank 1967; Hopkins and Wallerstein 1982; Portes and Walton 1981; Sassen 1988), the initial transnational framework spoke to the specific structures of inequality that were becoming prominent in the 1970s to 1990s. This analytic framework also was strongly influenced by the explorations in the 1980s of capital restructuring and the growth of flexible forms of accumulation (Harvey 1989), structural adjustment (Deere et al. 1990), the global assembly line (Nash and Fernández Kelly 1983), the Latin American debt crisis (1988), as well as by the critique of bounded units of analysis (Wolf 1982). Consequently, the initial transnational framework highlighted the historical conjuncture within which these transformations and transmigrants' agency were mutually constituted.

Nations Unbound: Transnational Projects, Postcolonial Dilemmas, and Deterritorialized Nation-States (Basch et al. 1994) was the first book in migration studies to offer a fully developed argument for a transnational framework for the study of migration. It argued that scholars not only must recognise transnational migration as 'inextricably linked to the changing conditions' of global capitalism and its processes of accumulation but also must connect these transformations to the political, economic, religious, cultural, and social practices and understandings within which migrants established transnational lives (Basch et al. 1994, 22). At the same time, first generation transnational migration scholars stressed that migrants' transnational strategies and identities reflected and contributed to these conjunctural conditions. It was within, and as constituters of these processes, that increasing numbers of people in the 1980s hedged their bets by becoming transmigrants and living their lives across the borders of two or more states. While many sought to settle and become permanent residents or citizens of their new land, at the same time, faced with discrimination, racialisation, and economic insecurity, many also maintained ties to their families, places, and countries of origin. These simultaneous ties, which meant that many immigrants were in fact transmigrants, took multiple forms including the sending of economic remittances, establishing businesses, building local organisations, and engaging in political, cultural, and social activities oriented toward homeland localities and nation-state building projects.

Basch et al. (1994) made it clear that nation-states remained significant through their power to regulate borders, construct categories of citizenship and illegality and foster national narratives of belonging. Nation-states continued to contribute to structures and cultures of inequality as their institutions constructed and legitimated racialisation, unequal gender and sexual empowerment, and stigmatisation and discrimination based on ancestry and religion. In other words, in order to explore the dynamics that link migration and development, analysts had to investigate the way that social relations, emotions, and identities of individuals of a migrant background were connected to various networks of power that linked households, neighbourhoods, localities, regions, nation-states, supra-national regions, and the globe. This form of transnational analysis can usefully be summarised as 'multi-scalar' (Çağlar and Glick Schiller 2018; Glick Schiller 2018).

Multi-scalar networks link individuals to institutions of differential power: businesses, banks, corporations, the media, and political and legal authorities, situated in diverse geographic locations. The often globe-spanning political, economic and cultural actions of all these players are part of the specificity of local life. Migration is not a separate story but is part of the larger processes that includes all people, migrants and non-migrants, living in a locality and connected to each other and to multiple places and institutions through diverse networks of differential power. There is no macro-, meso-, and micro-level and no push and pull. Therefore, there is no dichotomy between the local and the global or between structural and agentive analysis. Once multi-scalar processes are understood, scholars, policymakers and all the rest of us can shift our focus from differentiating natives from strangers to creating a politics that speaks to the interconnections among differentially empowered actors (Bastia and Bressán 2018; Çağlar and Glick Schiller 2018; Glick Schiller 2015; Lorey 2011; Phillips 2009; Sassen 2014).

Vision failure among the nexologists

Unfortunately, as the globalisation literature began to merge with post-modernist thinking, structural and historical analyses faded from prominence and many of those concerned with human mobility spoke primarily about global flows of capital, people, ideas, and commodities (Urry 2007). The migration–development 'mantra' (Kapur 2003) that gained prominence by 2000 paid insufficient attention to the past historical and current dialectics among global trade, capital accumulation, and multiple displacements of people from land, employment, social benefits, and rights. Moreover, rather than exploring the histories and ongoing unequal financial and corporate interconnections that have enriched colonial centres by impoverishing colonies and postcolonial states, many researchers began to promote migrant agency as the mechanism that maintained migration flows and interconnections.

For instance, in a comprehensive review of migration theories, Douglas Massey and his colleagues noted that after pioneering migrants develop transnational networks connected to their sending locality, the movement becomes one of cumulative causation in which 'each act of migration itself creates the social structure needed to sustain it'. (Massey et al. 1993, 449). Confining themselves to this insight, as subsequent researchers and policymakers explored the transnational connections that activated migration and development and examined migrant agency, many, although certainly not all, ignored the concomitant 'global perspective' of the initial transnational framework.

Unfortunately, as I have observed elsewhere (Glick Schiller 2009), by examining the differential national trajectories of development failures and successes, even the most insightful of scholars tended to reinvigorate methodological nationalist research methodologies in which each country was seen as an independent variable. Assessing differential development, international development agencies focused their attention on migrant-sending countries within which transmigrants served as agents of change. Meanwhile, financial institutions began to recognise the significance of remittances. For example, Page and Plaza (2006, 261), World Bank researchers, noted that:

> The growth of remittances has outpaced that of private capital flows and official development assistance during the last ten years. In 2004, remittance receipts were about 5% of developing countries' imports and 8% of domestic investment and were larger than official aid flows ... to developing countries. In many countries, remittances are larger than the earnings from their most important export.

They concluded that:

> Both sending and receiving countries are beginning to realise that the volume of resources currently being channelled through immigrant communities will continue to grow, and that public policies must be jointly developed to increase the development impact of both migratory movements and the remittances they generate.

In the wake of the 2008 mortgage and financial crisis in the United States and the United Kingdom and the subsequent globe-spanning economic downturn, the World Bank's migration and development experts remained optimistic about the contributions of migrants and migrant remittances to future development. In 2009, a World Bank 'Development Brief' stated that:

> in all the regions, remittance flows are likely to face three downside risks: a jobless economic recovery, tighter immigration controls, and unpredictable exchange rate movements. Despite these risks, remittances are expected to remain more resilient than private capital flows and will become even more important as a source of external financing in many developing countries. Policy responses should involve efforts to facilitate migration and remittances, to make these flows cheaper, safer and more productive for both the sending and the receiving countries.
>
> *(Ratha et al. 2009)*

In line with this mindset, after 2000, migration and development advocates popularised the concept of 'co-development' in which migrant-receiving states or localities worked with 'transnational communities' to facilitate homeland development. This strategy placed 'the migrant at the centre of attention identifying him or her as the development agent par excellence' (Faist and Fauser 2011, 7). Transmigrants were portrayed as heroic agents of development transforming their homelands through hometown organisations, remittances, diasporic communities and networks, and transnational nation-state building politics. In transnational migration studies, researchers stressed migrant agency, explored household livelihood networks (Olwig 2007) and tended to deride discussions of structure as 'top-down views, which define the properties of lower-order systems' or to confine structural factors to a different level of analysis, situating them as 'macro-structural processes and institutions' (Faist and Fauser 2011, 10, 12)

In the face of this celebration of migrant agency and remittance economies as pathways to development, some migration theorists renewed their caveats about migration and development, raising several fundamental issues (Bastia 2013; de Haas 2010; Glick Schiller 2012). First, they questioned the underlying assumption that there was a unity or at least a commonality of interests among disparate actors: migrant-receiving states; powerful financial institutions; charitable institutions; the political leadership of migrant-sending counties; migrant households; migrant associations and; individual transmigrants. Second, they demonstrated the ways that interconnected multi-scalar inequalities and interconnections, which contributed to differential migration and national, regional, and local development outcomes, were ignored in development policies (Phillips 2009).

A robust critique developed of the notion that transmigrants were uniformly development agents. Critics delineated the factors that shaped variations in migration and development outcomes, including the differential wealth and infrastructure of various sending countries or regions; their different opportunity structures; variations in migrants' class and educational backgrounds and; the differential reception accorded migrants by various migrant-receiving countries (Bastia 2013; de Haas 2010; Delgado Wise and Márquez Covarrubias 2009; Glick Schiller and Faist 2009; Skeldon 2008). Various researchers noted that migrants' remittances, international agencies' investments in development, and Euro-American development programmes intersected with receiving countries' different political-economic trajectories, including whether they are poor, middle income, or unstable, to produce different outcomes. Moreover, these critics were aware, as Darwin Munroe (1993) noted years ago, that researchers committed to development assistance often fail to fully come to terms with the degree to which the policies are organised to benefit the funders to the detriment of the recipients.

However, despite multiple authors' acknowledgement that migration and development 'is part of the ongoing structural transformation of politics, economics and culture world-wide' Faist and Fauser (2011, 23), even the critics of the migration and development mantra generally neglected the *temporality* of migration regimes. Even those migration and development scholars who did skillful work on the transnational dynamics of structures of inequality were slow to acknowledge that the conditions that had propelled and facilitated the transnational migration of the 1970s–1990s were dramatically changing. They have not reflectively theorised how their own critique and growing pessimism about development outcomes reflected and contributed to the changing conditions and new barriers to human mobility and settlement (Gamlen 2014).

In the 1970s, when the literature on the 'new migration' commenced, borders to Western Europe and North America were fairly porous. The fact that many migrants were undocumented or had temporary status kept migrant wages low but migrant labour was widely used and its utility publically acknowledged (Long 2000). Legalisation was often possible over time through various labour schemes or intermarriage. In documenting transnational migrant networks and remittance economies, scholars and policymakers assumed a continuity in legal and undocumented migration flows, asylum-seeking claims, the level of local conflicts, climatic conditions, the funding and policies of various humanitarian organisations, and the simultaneous presence and yet porosity of borders. As can be seen in the statement of the World Bank development specialists quoted above, after 2000 significant international migration and remittances were projected to continue into the future without fundamental alterations, despite various barriers and economic crises. Researchers felt comfortable generalising across time, without regard to the fundamental political-economic restructuring of the factors that affect the pace and possibility of international migration and settlement.

As Hein de Haas (2010, 228) observed in a review of the scholarship on the migration–development nexus, 'the scholarly debate on migration has tended to separate the developmental causes (determinants) and effects (impacts) of migration artificially from more general processes of social (including economic) change'. Even when analysts drew attention to dramatic alterations in migration policies and depictions of migrants, these changes were attributed to the 'self-interested actions of politicians, pundits, and bureaucrats who benefit from the social construction and political manufacture of immigration crises when none really exist' (Massey 2015, 279). Massey, in highlighting political anti-immigrant rhetoric specified that this 'transformation' has not occurred 'because of shifts in the social and economic variables'. (Massey 2015, 279). Yet, it has become increasingly clear that by dismissing rather than incorporating transformative structural forces into their analyses of migrant agency, scholars were failing to speak to the contemporary conjectural moment of massive dispossession and displacement. Transformative change is only now emerging as the research agenda of migration scholars (Çağlar and Glick Schiller 2018; Castles 2018; Feldman-Bianco 2017; Glick Schiller 2018).

The changing conjuncture and the dispossessed

The terms dispossession and displacement are increasingly used in the migration literature. However, with some thoughtful exceptions (Feldman-Bianco 2015a, 2018a, 2018b, 2018c; Phillips 2009; Ramsay, forthcoming; Torres 2015) displacement is either not defined (Drotbohm and Winters 2018; Lems 2016) or defined as a timeless state of 'subjective experience and existential life-making' (Bjarnesen and Vigh 2016, 12). Moreover, dispossession and displacement are rarely addressed together. Yet, if clearly defined in relationship to each other, these terms help make clear why this is an age of reaction and brutal repression. They can also provide the foundation of a politics of migration and development that adequately challenges contemporary migration regimes by setting aside the categories of 'migrant' and 'non-migrant' and challenging the processes of capital accumulation by dispossession. To define dispossession, we need to understand that the dynamics of capital accumulation rest within social relations. Most analyses have focused on the Marxian emphasis on the accumulation of capital by means of workers' exploitation, a process built on 'the differences between the wages paid to the worker and the value of the goods they produced' (Collins 2016, 106), However, Karl Marx (1887) [1867]), as well as Rosa Luxemburg (1951 [1913]) also spoke of 'primitive accumulation'. In the past, these processes took the form of colonial conquest, enslavement, and enclosure of the commons. Today, amassing wealth by 'accumulation by dispossession.' (Harvey 2004) has become significant in both old and new forms.

Accumulation by dispossession is a short-hand for those processes outside the point of production through which those who control force and the legal system extract or expropriate past or future labour in the form of property, rents, resources, debt, taxation, fees, and fines. These multiple forms of accumulation lead to displacement because people lose their land, housing, job security, public services, and benefits, which are appropriated by the more powerful. Displacement can therefore be defined as an outcome of accumulation by dispossession; displacement therefore includes both the processes of physical movement and downward social mobility, both of which lead to disruptions of previous relations to people and places. When the appropriation of home, property, and social position is accompanied by war and gang violence or rampant insecurity or precarity, people seek refuge within or across borders. Meanwhile, dispossession through neo-liberal privatisation of social housing, education, and healthcare and the destruction of public benefits have made even increasing numbers who stay in place socially and economically marginal: a new precariat. Those designated migrants and many of those categorised as 'native-born' confront systems of denigration that prove to be central to the extraction of capital (Cağlar and Glick Schiller 2018).

By defining dispossession and displacement in this way, we can think beyond the dichotomies of difference that haunt migration and development studies. Instead, we can identify the powerful corporate and governmental actors that benefit from anti-migrant politics, even while large numbers of 'natives' find their future is increasingly precarious and bleak. In this framework, migrant-non-migrant differences are no longer central concepts. Instead our analysis can identify the vast and growing inequalities of wealth and power that go hand in hand with the racialisation, gender differentiation, religious approbation, and criminalisation of those who are dispossessed and displaced.

The reinvigoration of processes of accumulation of capital by dispossession can be usefully understood as the emergence of a new historical conjuncture (Feldman-Bianco 2015a, 2015b). The term 'historical conjuncture' is a succinct way of speaking of changing conditions around the world as a result of the transformation of the intersections of multi-scalar, institutional, corporate, political and personal networks in which we are all embedded as co-participants, whether we are migrants or non-migrants, although with very different degrees and kinds of power (Cağlar and Glick Schiller 2018; Glick Schiller 2018; Hall 1987).

In this emerging conjuncture, increasing surveillance of borders, denials of long-standing legal rights of settlement and asylum, and mass deportations are threatening the remittance flows that global financial institutions and development agencies have so recently celebrated as stable, self-sustaining, and essential for development. At the same time, the destabilisation of states by war, debt, and related economic and political crisis makes migration more imperative. In other words, times have been changing and with them our theorisation, policies, and politics of migration and development must change too.

We are all living in a world in which the old structures do not hold. If we set aside past theories of migration and development and address the processes of dispossession and displacement that have been set in motion and legitimated by powerful actors, we can begin to explain the resurgence of nationalist politics. To understand dispossession is to discard the terminology of separate independent 'developed', 'underdeveloped', or 'developing' nation-states. Instead by analysing accumulation by dispossession, scholars, policymakers, and people everywhere can see how these processes are a source of amassing untold wealth. They can also see how these processes are used by political leaders to legitimate categories of difference by racialisation, gender, citizenship, and national origins and at the same time to criminalise the poor and dispossessed 'natives'.

Meanwhile, the dispossessed within national populations search for answers. As they intensify dispossession, politicians linked to powerful financial interests offer a vision of national security devoid of the public benefits and services that a past generation had seen as their national rights. Instead national politicians are now defining citizen's security in terms of the successful exclusion of other dispossessed people, who are defined as undesirable aliens.

However, if these processes make both the potential for more repressive, fascist type governmentality more possible, they also provide opportunities to challenge inequalities and unjust social structures and institutions. By theorising dispossession and displacement, migration and development scholars can create an analysis and politics that link migrants and the growing number of 'natives' who increasingly find themselves displaced. A powerful public critique of accumulation by dispossession can actuate policies and political movements that restructure the world in more just directions. Evidence of the sociabilities out of which such political movements are emerging is widespread but understudied. It is to be found in the local urban daily interactions in which migrants and non-migrants form social relations around common concerns and aspirations for a better life (Bastia and Bressán 2018; Çağlar and Glick Schiller 2018; Glick Schiller and Çağlar 2016; New American Economy 2019; Taran et al. 2016)

The social movements that oppose dispossession and precarity faced by migrants and non-migrants alike make it clear that a politics that works for social and redistributive economic justice is possible (Lorey 2011). Employment, education, social benefits, housing, and healthcare for all can be funded by the wealth produced from resources, crops, labour, and creativity developed from varying locations all around the world. But this can only happen if we abandon 'development aid' and adopt policies of redistribution rather than dispossessive accumulation. In a more just world, the resources deployed and extracted to build dehumanising border walls, surveillance and detentions industries, and legal and conceptual barriers to movement and settlement could be used to sustain human life and the planet. In summary, a theoretical savvy, policy-ready approach to migration and development must speak to and prepare us to confront the forces that stand against all forms of human development. Given climate change including the rapid warming of the oceans (IPCC 2018; Pierre-Louis 2019), the current powers that be enriched by accumulation by dispossession threaten not only continuing development but even the very existence of life on earth.

References

Basch, L., Glick Schiller, N. and Szanton-Blanc, C. (1994) *Nations Unbound: Transnational Projects, Postcolonial Predicaments, and Deterritorialized Nation-States.* Gordon and Breach Routledge, New York.

Bastia, T. (2013) "Migration and inequality: an introduction", in Bastia, T ed., *Migration and Inequality.* Routledge, London, 3–23.

Bastia, T. and Bressán, J. M. (2018) "Between a guest and an okupa: migration and the making of insurgent citizenship in Buenos Aires' informal settlements". *Environment and Planning A: Economy and Space,* 50(1): 31–50.

Beck, U. (2002) "The cosmopolitan society and its enemies". *Theory, Culture and Society,* 19(1–2): 17–44.

Bjarnesen, J. and Vigh, H. (2016) "The dialectics of displacement and emplacement". *Conflict and Society: Advances in Research,* 2: 9–15.

Çağlar, A. and Glick Schiller, N. (2018) *Migrants and City-making: Dispossession, Displacement, and Urban Regeneration.* Duke, Durham, NC.

Cardoso, F.H. and Faletto, E. (1979) *Dependency and Underdevelopment in Latin America.* University of California, Berkeley, CA.

Carling, J. (2017) "Thirty-six migration nexuses, and counting", at: https://jorgencarling.org/2017/07/31/thirty-six-migration-nexuses-and-counting/

Castles, S. (2018) "Social transformation and human mobility: reflections on the past, present and future of migration". *Journal of Intercultural Studies,* 39(2): 238–251.

Collins, J. (2016) "Expanding the labor theory of value". *Dialectical Anthropology,* 40(2): 103–123.

de Haas, H. (2010) "Migration and development: a theoretical perspective". *International Migration Review,* 44(1): 227–264.

Deere, C., Antrobus, P., Bolles, L., Melendez, E., Phillips, P., Rivera, M. and Safa, H. (1990) *In the Shadows of the Sun.* Westview, Boulder, CO.

Delgado Wise, R. and Márquez Covarrubias, H. (2009) "Understanding the relationship between migration and development: toward a new theoretical approach". *Social Analysis,* 53(3): 85–105.

Drotbohm, H. and Winters, N. (2018) "Transnational lives en route: African trajectories of displacement and emplacement across Central America." *Working Papers of the Department of Anthropology and African Studies of the Johannes Gutenberg University Mainz*, 175.

Faist, T. and Fauser, M. (2011) "The migration-development nexus: toward a transnational perspective", in Faist, T., Fauser, M. and Kivisto, P. eds., *The Migration-development Nexus: A Transnational Perspective*. Palgrave-Macmillan, New York, 1–26.

Feldman-Bianco, B. (2015a) "Deslocamentos, Desigualdades e Violência de Estado, in dossiê *Deslocamentos Sociais* (B. Feldman-Bianco ed.)". *Ciência e Cultura*, Revista de Divulgação Científica da SBPC, 67(2): 20–24.

Feldman-Bianco, B. (2015b) "Desarrollos de la perspectiva transnacional: migración, ciudad y economía política". *Alteridades*, 25(50): 13–26.

Feldman-Bianco, B. (2017) "Deslocamentos", in Cavalcanti, L., Botega, T., Tonhati E, T. and Araújo, D. eds., *Dicionário Crítico de migrações internacionais*, org. Editora da Universidade de Brasília, Brasilia, 208–2012.

Feldman-Bianco, B. (2018a) "Anthropology and ethnography: the transnational perspective on migration and beyond". *Etnográfica*, 22(1): 195–215.

Feldman-Bianco, B. (2018b) "Migrações e Deslocamentos: políticas nacionais, políticas globais e movimentos sociais", in de Souza Lima, A. C., Beltrão, J. F., Lobo, A., Castillo, S., Lacerda, P. e Ozório, P. eds., *A Antropologia e a esfera pública no Brasil: Perspectivas e Prospectivas sobre a Associação Brasileira de Antropologia no seu 60º aniversario*. ABA Publicações e E-papers, 2018, 547–551.

Feldman-Bianco, B. (2018c) "O Brasil frente ao regime global das migrações: Direitos Humanos, securitização e violências". *Travessias: Revista do Migrante*, 31(83): 11–36.

Frank, A. (1967) *Capitalism and Underdevelopment in Latin America*. NYU Press, New York.

Gamlen, A. (2014) "The new migration-and- development pessimism". *Progress in Human Geography*, 38(4): 581–597.

Glick Schiller, N. (1999a) "Transmigrants and nation-states: something old and something new in U.S. immigrant experience", in Hirschman, C., DeWind, J. and Kasinitz, P. eds., *Handbook of International Migration: The American Experience*. Russell Sage, New York, 94–119.

Glick Schiller, N. (1999b) "Who are these guys? a transnational perspective on national identities", in Goldin, L. ed., *Identities on the Move: Transnational Processes in North America and the Caribbean Basin*. University of Texas Press, Houston, TX, 15–44.

Glick Schiller, N. (2009) "A global perspective on migration and development". *Social Analysis*, 53(3): 14–37.

Glick Schiller, N. (2012) "Unraveling the migration and development web: research and policy implications". *International Migration*, 50(3): 92–97.

Glick Schiller, N. (2015) "Explanatory frameworks in transnational migration studies: the missing multi-scalar global perspective". *Ethnic and Racial Studies*, 8: 2275–2282.

Glick Schiller, N. (2018) "Theorizing the temporality of transnational migration: a multiscalar conjunctural perspective". *Nordic Journal of Migration Research*, 8(4): 201–212.

Glick Schiller, N., Basch, L. and Blanc-Szanton, C. eds. (1992) *Towards a Transnational Perspective on Migration: Race, Class, Ethnicity and Nationalism Reconsidered*. New York Academy of Sciences, New York.

Glick Schiller, N and Cağlar, A. (2016) "Displacement, emplacement and migrant newcomers: rethinking urban sociabilities within multiscalar power?". *Identities: Global Studies in Culture and Power*, 23(1): 17–34.

Glick Schiller, N. and Faist, T. (2009) "Introduction: migration, development, and social transformation". *Social Analysis*, 53(3): 1–13.

Hall, S. (1987) "Gramsci and us" *Marxism Today*, June16–21.

Harvey, D. (1989) *The Condition of Postmodernity: An Enquiry into the Origins of Cultural Change*. Routledge, Malden, MA.

Harvey, D. (2004) "The "new" imperialism: accumulation through dispossession". *Socialist Register*, 40: 63–87.

Hopkins, T. and Wallerstein, I. (1982) *World-systems Analysis: Theory and Methodology*. Sage, London.

IPCC. (2018) "Global warming of 1.5°C", Intergovernmental Panel on Climate Change, Switzerland, at: www.ipcc.ch/site/assets/uploads/sites/2/2018/07/SR15_SPM_High_Res.pdf

Kapur, D. (2003) "Remittances: the new development mantra?" Paper prepared for the G-24 Technical Group Meeting, September. 15–16 United Nations, New York and Geneva, at: https://wcfia.har vard.edu/files/wcfia/files/795_kapur.pdf

Kearney, M. and Nagengast, C. (1989) "Anthropological perspectives on transnational communities in rural California". Working Paper 3, Working Group on Farm Labor and Rural Poverty California Institute for Rural Studies, Davis, CA.

Lee, E.S. (1966) "A theory of migration". *Demography*, 3(1): 47–57.

Lems, A. (2016) "Placing displacement: place-making in a world of movement". *Ethnos*, 81(2): 315–337.

Long, N. (2000) "Exploring local/global transformations: a view from anthropology", in Alberto, A. and Long, N. eds., *Anthropology, Development and Modernities*. Routledge, London, 183–200.

Lorey, I. (2011) "Governmental precarization'". Centar za socijalna istraživanja Alternativna kulturna organizacija – AKO, at: www.csi-platforma.org/sites/csi-platforma.org/files/tekstovi/lorey-isabell-governmental%20precarization.pdf

Luxemburg, R. (1951 [1913]) *The Accumulation of Capital*. Yale University Press, New Haven, CT.

Marx, K. ((1887) [1867]) *Capital: A Critique of Political Economy: Volume* I. First English edition (trans. S Moore & E Aveling), ed. Engels, F., Progress Publishers, Moscow, at: www.marxists.org/archive/marx/works/download/pdf/Capital-Volume-I.pdf

Massey, D. (2015) "A missing element in migration theories". *Migration Letter*, 12(3): 279–299.

Massey, D., Arango, J., Hugo, G., Kouaouci, A., Pellegrino, A. and Taylor, J. (1993) "Theories of inter-national migration: a review and appraisal". *Population and Development Review*, 19(3): 431–466.

Munroe, D. (1993) "Reviewed Work(s): in the shadows of the sun: Caribbean development alternatives and U.S. policy". *New West Indian Guide*, 67(1 2): 129–132.

Nash, J. and Fernández Kelly, P. eds. (1983) *Women, Men, and the International Division of Labor*. State University of New York Press, Albany, NY.

New American Economy. (2019) "Stories", at: www.newamericaneconomy.org/stories/. Accessed Jan 11, 2019.

Nyberg–Sørensen, N., van der Hear, N. and Engberg–Pedersen, P. (2002) "The migration–development nexus: evidence and policy options". *International Migration*, 40(5): 3–47.

Olwig, K. (2007) *Caribbean Journeys: An Ethnography of Migration and Home in Three Family Networks*. Duke, Durham, NC.

Page, J. and Plaza, S. (2006) "Migration remittances and development: a review of global evidence". World Bank, Washington, DC, at: http://documents.worldbank.org/curated/en/479211468203649221/Migration-remittances-and-development-a-review-of-global-evidence

Phillips, N. (2009) "Migration as development strategy? The new political economy of dispossession and inequality in the Americas". *Review of International Political Economy*, 16(2): 231–259.

Pierre-Louis, K. (2019) "Ocean warming is accelerating faster than thought, new research finds". *New York Times*, 10 January, at: www.nytimes.com/2019/01/10/climate/ocean-warming-climate-change.html

Portes, A. and Walton, J. (1981) *Labor, Class, and the International System*. Academic Press, New York.

Ramsay, G. (forthcoming) "Time and the other in crisis: how anthropology makes its displaced object". *Anthropological Theory*.

Ratha, D., Mohapatra, S. and Silwal, A. (2009) "Migration and remittance trends 2009". *Development Brief* 11, Migration and Remittances Team Development Prospects Group, November 3, 2009, World Bank, Washington, DC, at: http://siteresources.worldbank.org/INTTHAILANDINTHAI/Resources/MigrationAndDevelopmentBrief11.pdf

Roddick, J. (1988) *The Dance of the Millions: Latin America and the Debt Crisis*. Latin America Bureau, London.

Rouse, R. (1991) "Mexican migration and the social space of postmodernism". *Diaspora: A Journal of Transnational Studies*, 1(1): 8–23.

Sassen, S. (1988) *The Mobility of Labor and Capital: A Study in International Investment and Labor Flow*. Cambridge University Press, Cambridge, MA.

Sassen, S. (2014) *Expulsions: Brutality and Complexity in the Global Economy*. Harvard University Press, Cambridge, MA.

Skeldon, R. (2008) "Migration and development". United Nations, The Hague, at: www.un.org/esa/population/meetings/EGM_Ittmig_Asia/P04_Skeldon.pdf

Smith, A. (1983) "Nationalism and social theory". *British Journal of Sociology*, 34: 19–38.

Taran, P., Neves de Lima, G. and Kadysheva, O. (2016) *Cities Welcoming Refugees and Migrants.* UNESCO, Paris.

Torres, A. (2015) "Migration and development: equalisation and inequalities in Ecuador's southern Sierra". *Anthropological Forum*, 25(4): 350–369.

Urry, J. (2007) *Mobilities.* Polity Press, Cambridge, UK.

Wimmer, A. and Glick Schiller, N. (2002) "Methodological nationalism and beyond: nation–state building, migration and the social sciences". *Global Networks*, 2(4): 301–334.

Wolf, E. (1982) *Europe and the People without History.* University of California Press, Berkeley, CA.

3

MIGRATION AND DEVELOPMENT

Theoretical legacies and analytical agendas in the age of rising powers

Parvati Raghuram

Introduction

Economic growth in the Global South has begun to dominate world imagination (World Bank 2011). With different nomenclatures – BRICs (Brazil, Russia, India, China), Rising Powers, emerging countries, E7 – these countries seem to occupy newspaper headlines and book stands (Sidaway 2012). China and, to some extent, India, have been at the centre of the rhetoric of Rising Power but the range of countries that are supposedly rising is much larger and is also dynamic. It includes the BRICs as well as countries like Colombia, Indonesia, Vietnam, Egypt, Turkey, and South Africa (CIVETS). This has led to what Pieterse (2011) calls a global rebalancing.

The growth of the so-called Rising Powers has had an impact on migration – some new patterns have emerged while others have intensified (Dumont, Spielvogel, Widmaier 2010). Return migration to the global South has been noted, particularly among skilled professionals who are taking advantage of the opportunities that their home countries now provide (Jain 2012). New patterns of migration from North to South have also emerged, such as, for instance, from Portugal to Angola (Åkesson 2016). Second, there has been an intensification of old South–South migration alongside new corridors of mobility (Bodomo 2009; IOM 2017; Park and Chen 2009).

The topic of migration and development has become a key area of research and policy as attempts have been made to slow South–North migration through in-situ development packages (Council of Europe 2003; de Haas 2007). Moreover, remittances now play an increasingly acknowledged part in development (Alonso 2011; World Bank 2008). However, the place of Rising Powers in theories of migration and development is yet to be analysed. This chapter fills that gap. It outlines some of the options and challenges that these Rising Powers offer for theorising migration and development.

The Rising Powers are sometimes theorised as if they are replacing or joining the countries that are developed, at other times as mid-points within the binary thinking that has haunted both the migration and development literature. They offer versions of the middle

(Fangjun 2009). However, this chapter argues that they are better conceived as disrupting these binaries (Raghuram et al., 2014). It suggests that the empirical variations within the global South as well as the different types of transformations that those countries are going through makes a multipolar world a more useful way of conceptualising the Rising Powers. The chapter ends by offering some empirical and analytical questions that the Rising Powers raises for future research on migration and development.

Dominant binaries in migration and development thinking

Binary thinking has dominated both migration and development literature and hence, the migration–development nexus literature, too. Migration theory binaries include, for instance, sending–receiving, origin–destination or some other forms of a 'here–there' analysis (IOM 2017; UN DESA 2013). Similarly, development theories also have their own binaries: modern–traditional, First World–Third World, Global North–South or core–periphery (see Table 3.1) although development practice, through, for instance, the Sustainable Development Goals has taken a more variegated, or global approach, to development. The effects of this are not yet evident in either theorisations or policy around migration and development.

As a result, approaches to migration and development, too, have a set of binaries which are widely used in tracking and analysing migration within its own analytic lens, terminology, direction of travel, location of migrants, direction of developmental efforts and location of development (see Table 3.2: de Haas 2010; Düvell et al. 2012). There are two different versions of place which are at play in this analysis of binaries. The first, often underpinned by modernisation theories, holds places as distinctive and different. The second involves theorising connections between places through Marxist influenced theories such as

Table 3.1 Dominant binaries in development thinking

Dominant binaries	Theoretical bases	Major proponents
Developing–developed	Modernisation theories	WW Rostow (1960)
Third World–First World	Non-alignment	Alfred Sauvy (1952)
Under-developed–developed	Dependency theory	Gunder Frank (1967)
Periphery–Core	World-Systems theory	Immanuel Wallerstein (1979)
Global South–North	Pluralist	Brandt Commission (1980)
Minority world–Majority world	Demographic	Shahid-ul-Alam (1990)

Table 3.2 Geographies of dominant policy concerns in migration and development debates

Characteristics of the debate	Locational analysis
Terminology	South/North
Direction of travel	South–North
Location of migrants	North
Direction of developmental efforts	North–South
Location of development	South

dependency, or phenomenology influenced theories of transnationalism. This section explores these different forms of binary thinking.

The first version of migration and development thinking is influenced by modernisation theories and by its underpinning neoclassical economic theories of migration. Here, opportunities in one country and the openings it offers are compared with those in another and the differences between the two are said to trigger migration (Grossmann and Stadelmann 2013). In these push–pull theories migration is conceptualised as linking distinctive places which are marked by difference – higher/lower wages, better/worse economic opportunities, a safer/dangerous environment, and so on. Migrants respond to these differences between places through calculation and movement (Van Hear et al. 2018). The vectors of difference between 'here' and 'there' become the causative factors for migration (see Raghuram 2013). One of the most highly political and policy-relevant versions of this difference is in the case of brain drain migration or migration of the highly skilled, especially those in the social reproduction sectors. For example, health worker migration from sub-Saharan Africa is undoubtedly shaped by wage differentials and variations in working conditions between sending and receiving countries (WHO 2010). Policies to stem such mobility and to bridge the gap between the two places often involve increasing the wages or improving working conditions in sending contexts (for a critique see Raghuram 2009).

A second version of binary thinking emphasises connections, not only difference. There are at least two connective arguments in migration and development theory. The first focuses on the economic causes and consequences of migration and the inequalities that underpin this. They differ from neoclassical theories in digging deep into the reasons why some places are more desirable and by linking this to how inequalities are produced between places. The approach is summarised by Stephen Castles (2009) as a combination of the virtuous circle and vicious circle. A virtuous circle is one where migrants who leave poor countries enhance development in areas they leave behind by drawing down fewer resources, reducing competition and by remitting. They then spur development in the countries they leave behind. Theorisations of the virtuous cycle draw on the optimism of modernisation theory.

In contrast, and drawing on Marxist thinking, a more vicious circle is envisaged in what Castles (2009) calls historical-institutional approaches to migration and development. Here, the migration leads to or is part of a wider set of negative relationships. Countries at the core of the world economy draw in highly skilled labour, for instance, from peripheral countries who lose this labour (Sassen 2002). Migrants withdraw resources through their movement and teach social behaviour, such as consumption patterns, which results in dependence on imported goods which in turn lead to greater dependence on the core countries.

A second way of theorising place connections is through the lens of transnationalism. This framework focuses on connections, seeing them as enactments of the attachments that migrants form to multiple places (Basch et al. 1994). Research adopting a transnational perspective emphasises the agency of migrants who maintain these relations across space and offers us a way of thinking about migration at scales other than that of the nation-state, a concept further emphasised through the term 'translocalism' (Greiner and Sakdapolrak 2013).

How do the Rising Powers fit into these binary theories of migration and development? Depending on how the Rising Powers are conceptualised, the answer will differ. If they are seen to replace or join existing powers (see, for instance, Ramo 2004) then the binary still stands. This is best exemplified by Samir Amin (2007) who argues that the Rising Powers do not imply change. If growth is sustained then the Rising Powers have only added to or replaced other centres of capitalist accumulation. The benefits of the same processes of accumulation by dispossession will simply be transferred to the Rising Powers. Development and migration will look the same. It is only that development is now located elsewhere and migration is oriented in a new direction. We may ask will the Rising Powers become additional destinations or alternative destinations?

Beyond the binary in migration and development thinking – versions of the middle

However, the Rising Powers may also be understood as following in the footsteps of existing powers (Fangjun 2009). Whether their 'rising' is seen as economic, as political, as the ability to influence foreign policy, they could, arguably, be seen to occupy a space in-between (Table 3.3).

As a result, at least three intermediate positions can also be envisaged in migration and development as outlined below.

First, in response to an often-posed question on whether migration leads to development or development leads to migration, theorists have identified that some degree of development is necessary for migration – it is not the poorest from any country, or indeed those from the poorest countries who migrate (Castles 2009). In Rostowian terms, then, it is the pre-take-off and the take-off countries that show the greatest migration and this was conceptualised as the migration hump: a certain degree of development was necessary for migration to take place (Martin and Taylor 1996). This necessarily focuses on the middle stages of development, positing the middle in economic terms.

Theories of a migration hump can easily be moulded into analyses of Rising Powers. For instance, the significant increase in Chinese and Indian migrants, particularly students and the entrepreneurial classes, may be seen as a direct result of economic growth. Much of the analysis of migration in the context of the Rising Powers has implicitly adopted this framework, focusing primarily on the greater numbers of people migrating out of these countries both on short-term visits (Leung 2012) and for longer stays (Xiang 2003). It is worth noting that the relationship between emigration policy and growth policies need a separate analysis, at least in the case of China, so that increase in emigration cannot simply be read as a result of growth alone. Nor is it recent. These migrations draw upon the connections and possibilities offered by earlier migrant flows and the transnational Indian and Chinese communities, for instance, that have settled in many parts of the world.

Some of this research has adopted the nuances of modernisation as a process of increasing human and cultural capital, focusing specifically on the mobility of students and highly skilled professionals (Zhang 2003; and for their deskilling see Li and Li 2008). The aspirations of the

Table 3.3 Beyond development binaries

Dominant binaries	Predominant analytic	Middle positions
Developing–developed	Economic	pre-take-off, take-off
First World–Second World	Political	Third World
Superpowers–weak power	Foreign policy	Middle power
Core–periphery	Economic	Semi-periphery

Table 3.4 Versions of the middle – migration and development

Analytics	Key concepts	Important writers
Economic	Migration hump	Martin and Taylor (1996)
Geographical	Transit zones	Schapendonk (2012)
Marxist	Border zones	Sandro Mezzadra (2010)

citizens of the Rising Powers also lead educational institutions to relocate to these countries in order to facilitate the social and class mobility that being part of the Rising Powers enables (Feng 2013). Hence, it is not only people who are becoming mobile but also, for instance, educational institutions which give existing powers, an opportunity to benefit from the Rising Powers (Ahmad and Buchanan 2016).

Second, the geographical middle in the migration trajectory, too, has become the object of attention (Table 3.4). The in-between places along the migration route, the transit zones, offer ideal places for controlling mobility (Stock 2012). In an age of anxiety over migration these places have catapulted into prominence in the imagination of those working in migration and development. Transit zones are identified as areas through which migrants move usually along a South–North axis, whether from Africa to Europe or Central America to the US. The countries in-between are those that border the destination sites (Düvell et al. 2012; IOM 2017). They have become places of investment because potentially they are sites where 'unwanted' migration can be stalled in return for development aid. They are thus both borders of control of migration and increasingly significant sites for mobilising policies on migration and development. They have also been incorporated into theories of development through the increasing significance of the mobility paradigm in social sciences. For instance, Schapendonk (2012) shows with great sensitivity the range of trajectories and experiences in the European borderlands, the transit zones, while İçduygu and Yükseker (2012) highlight the ways in which these zones are being securitised.

Some of these discussions have used the language of transition but increasingly there are also voices critiquing this terminology (Collyer and de Haas 2011). For instance, Düvell et al. (2012) argue that the term transit is dependent on and can reinforce the idea of departure and arrival, which are the central categories for a lot of migration research. For them, the term problematically denotes simultaneously a place, a destination, and a viewpoint. Currently, evidence of the extent to which Rising Powers become transit zones (as well as source and destination) is not adequate for theoretical analysis. Interesting questions may also be asked about how neighbouring countries may become transit zones on the way to the Rising Powers (or indeed destinations in their own right), but there is no research on this, thus far. There is, however, some evidence of China becoming an alternative destination to Europe and the US, a less desirable but more achievable destination for migrants from Nigeria (Haugen 2012).

A third more analytical intervention, drawing on Marxist thinking, is offered by Sandro Mezzadra and Brett Neilson (2013). They argue, writing in the context of Europe, that European borders exist not to seal off Europe from migrants from Africa but rather to selectively include and exclude migrants. He develops this into a third way of thinking about the middle. He argues that the processes of inclusion and exclusion produce the category of irregular migrants on whom the flexibility of capital in Europe and everywhere else is dependent. These transit zones are thus, simultaneously zones of inclusion and exclusion.

They are neither core nor periphery, but both sending and receiving, because it is through their position as a zone of transition that they enter global political relations. They lead to the reshuffling of the coordinates of Europe (Cobarrubias et al. 2011).

Conceptually, Mezzadra and Neilson (2013) develop this argument by positing border as method. Theirs is an important intervention for development studies because it suggests that instead of the key categories of North–South, developed–developing, First World–Third World, what we see today is both an increase in borders between nations but also an implosion of nations with new forms of connections between places irrespective of their location. They call this the multiplication of labour because labour for them is shaped by a number of power hierarchies. Although they multiply the boundaries between accumulation and dispossession, the two remain dialectically linked and in a binary relationship. The implications of a diversifying South are still viewed primarily through theories of capitalism. Nevertheless, this analysis of bordering which looks at circulation and the control of populations as an inherent part of exclusion/inclusion is in some ways the most sophisticated analysis as it recognises the multiplicity of boundaries between North and South, as enacted through everyday bordering practices. It offers the possibility of both opening up and moving beyond the North–South divide, the analytical framework to which we turn next.

Beyond the middle – pluralist positions

Empirically there are as many differences between these Rising Power countries as there are similarities. For instance, Russia has never been seen as part of the Global South as it was a colonising power which became the core of the Second World and then a part, albeit contested, of the First World post-1991. Instead, it was already part of a set of debates around the 'end of history' and the rise of a new unipolar world order. The impact of South Africa on global development has been much less marked than that of some of the other countries included as part of the Rising Powers though it remains a significant regional hegemon. The paths to development adopted have also varied as much as the bases of power. However, together the Rising Powers have altered the nature and rhetoric of discussions around global power. Although economic growth, which is often cited as the common basis for this grouping, has not been continuous or constant, the Rising Powers can be seen to foster a new global imagination (Arrighi 2007; Ramo 2004).

Empirical reconsiderations of the binaries of migration and development thinking and attempts to conceptualise multipolarity have taken many forms (Table 3.5). They have highlighted the diversity of migration trajectories, the diversity of development (Raghuram 2009), and therefore the varieties of relationships between migration and development. They draw on the notion that the Rising Powers offer the possibility of revising the terms of power itself and how it is done (Arrighi and Zhang 2011; Wade 2011).

Table 3.5 Beyond the binary

Analytical basis	Outcomes
Empirical	Diversity of migration patterns (Ratha and Shaw 2007)
Empirical and conceptual	Migration and development tiers (Skeldon 1997)
Empirical and conceptual	Transformation theories (Castles 2009)

One way of multiplying the analysis of migration and development has been to show the empirical difference and dynamism in migration patterns globally. While emigrants from low-income countries are more likely to migrate to neighbouring countries, those from middle-income countries are more likely to move to high-income ones (Lucas 2008). Also, regional wage differentials have led some middle-income countries to become both origin and destination countries, such as Mexico and Turkey, while others have become 'migration poles'. The major middle-income migration poles are Argentina and Venezuela in South America, Jordan in the Middle East, Malaysia and Thailand in Asia, the Russian Federation, South Africa in Africa and parts of Eastern Europe. These migration poles constitute a diverse group of countries with very varied histories and types of migration – in-migration, out-migration and transit-migration. Besides, there is a mix of different kinds of migratory systems in such countries. For instance, South Africa has seen some migration from Europe, regional systems of migration with neighbouring countries and internal rural–urban migrations. Moreover, these forms of migration have all coexisted through the twentieth century and been adapted and modified in this century (Kofman and Raghuram 2012). Clearly, both international and intra-national differences exist in the empirical specificities of migration and development and middle-income countries skew these variations further.

These variations arguably, challenge the efficacy of the term South–South migration and its analytical hubris. For instance, the terminology suggests a commonality across the South, which is empirically unsustainable (Bakewell 2009). Migrants from Bangladesh to India do not have the same experiences as those from Zimbabwe to South Africa. Moreover, factors such as proximity may be more important in producing similarities between countries than the geopolitical construction of a unified South.

Perhaps one of the most developed systems of analysing the complexity of migration and development, both empirically and conceptually, was that offered by Ronald Skeldon (1997). He differentiates between regions on the basis of a range of criteria – economy, politics, and migration patterns, among others. His classification is unique in that it takes up differences within countries and incorporates insights from his long-standing work on internal migration into wider debates on international migration. Like much more regionally sensitive and micro-scale analysis, his schematisation recognises the differences within countries, but he projects this into his global schema – old core, new core, core extensions, and potential cores, labour frontier, and resource niche. The complexity of his classification based on the range of criteria included places Skeldon's analysis not in a binary frame but in a pluralist framework

Finally, another pluralist tradition is that which draws on transformation itself as the basis for conceptualising plurality. For instance, Stephen Castles (2010) links the migration–development trajectory to a variety of other transitions – demographic, rural–urban, political, and economic transitions as well as shifts in the meaning of gender.

However, while he, along with others, usefully unsettles the coherence of the South in migration thinking and the dominance of the North–South axis in migration–development analyses, the challenge of theorising through and with the Rising Powers is yet to be taken up, which is the objective of the final section of this chapter.

Theoretical and empirical agenda for future research

We have looked at forms of analysis in migration and development theory where the dominance of binary thinking has been complemented by attempts to unsettle the binary (Düvell et al. 2012). These endeavours have involved both thinking through the middle where the trajectory of the binary remains largely unreconstructed, and by research and thinking that emphasises the multiplicity of flows of development as well as migration. The first places the middle alongside the other ends of the binary as part of a teleology offering, in some instances, a place and modality for development. The second purportedly moves away from a binary, although the extent to which it does so is often debatable. Nevertheless, both these approaches have offered rich, if different ways, of theorising, which complement or unsettle the binaries of both migration and development thinking.

Most of the migration and development literature looks at mobility, not as a way of allowing nations to reach out and influence, but simply as border crossing across sovereign national boundaries. Yet, in a globalising world, mobility is a central modality through which economic and political power is exercised. Both capital growth and political influence are acquired through the movement of people, and these mobilities are necessary for the countries to extend their reach. Migration and development are not cause and effect but a necessary relationship. Migration is a way of governing societies, not just an object of governance by society (Bærenholdt 2013). It is a journey, not a beginning or an endpoint, and therefore suggests the need to focus on the practices of mobility and migration as inherent to, and part of, development. This also enables us to move past the South–North binary in both migration and development.

Moreover, there exist a range of other conceptualisations from which migration and development theories can draw on in analysing the Rising Powers. I point to three rich forms of theorisation. In the first, the logic of development as a particular form of modernisation is itself questioned in this multipolar world (Table 3.6). Postcolonial theorists like Dilip Gaonkar (2001) argue that these multipolarities suggest the importance of alternative modernities where countries will forge their own path to development or to state formation (Chatterjee 1997). For instance, Kang (2007) argues, using the case of China, that instead of seeking to understand Asia's future in Europe's past (as in modernisation), it is Asia's own past that explains the story of Asia's rise. He uses history and *culture* as the basis for identifying these alternatives.

A second body of work developed by Walter Mignolo (2011) argues that these alternatives were made possible by a combination of de-westernisation and 'de-coloniality'. De-westernisation consists of the politics of the economics of rising countries. These politics may be, but are not necessarily, new as they may follow a capitalist path (albeit a different form of capitalism). Much more important for him, however, is another change that is also emerging, that of decoloniality. Decoloniality is an epistemic shift which brings far-reaching change to both the content and the nature of conversations (2011) of knowledge. It involves unsettling the coloniality of knowledge systems, which have been dominated thus far by Eurocentric processes and thought and which put European definitions of development

Table 3.6 Beyond the middle positions

Theoretical analytic	Terminology
Power (economic/political)	Multipolar world
Cultural	Alternative modernities
Cultural epistemological	Border thinking
Class, gender, race	Transnational precariat

centre stage. Instead, it requires a *cultural epistemological* shift and the importance of pluriversality for a multipolar world.

A demand to rethink the division into territorially defined North and South worlds, not through the lens of area studies, as it can sometimes appear in development studies, but through vectors of power has also been put forward by black theorists, feminists, and postcolonial theorists. They argue that the optic of *gender, race, and class* complicates the three-fold division by suggesting new kinds of alliances and different types of disagreements. Nancy Fraser (2010) calls the third world that emerges from this kind of analysis the 'transnational precariat'. The precariat exists simultaneously in different parts of the world but is caught up in the intersectional power relationships that increasingly stretch transnationally. These three theorisations offer alternative starting points for conceptualising migration and development and an opening for further research.

I want to end by asking some questions for future research. What role does the movement of people play in the flow of goods, ideas, policies, and money? When is migration a necessary party of investments abroad and what are the different kinds of mobility that these require? Thus, what role does the mobility of people play in the Rise to Power? This question may be asked historically of 'older powers' as well as of those which are currently seen to be emerging. Asking these questions effectively decentres the migrant as the object of study; instead power, its modalities, and the part played by mobility in Rising Powers, too, become part of the focus. It also unsettles terms such as integration. For instance, we rarely ask: how do Northern migrants integrate into the Global South? What infrastructures of integration are offered in Southern countries? What do the answers to these questions tell us about our implicit framing of questions around migration? Asking these questions points to the racial imaginaries that are implicitly contained in words like assimilation and the place attachments that are often used in the terminology, theory, and practice of integration policies (and see Bakewell and Jónsson 2011 for discussion of some of these issues within the context of African cities).

In sum, a long history of migration and development thinking exists into which the empirical phenomenon of economic growth and a global rebalancing interjects. There are a range of analytical legacies through which we can analyse migration at a global scale within the context of contemporary dynamics of the global economy. Migration and development may be seen as a binary relationship, albeit one with in-between steps. Others conceive migration and development along multipolar lines. This history of thought needs revisiting in order to better theorise migration and development in the context of rapidly changing realities. This chapter represents one small step towards this goal.

Acknowledgements

I would like to acknowledge Utrecht University, where these ideas were first presented as part of an inaugural lecture. Particular thanks to the IDS group there for their friendship.

References

Ahmad S and Buchanan F (2016) "Choices of destination for transnational higher education: 'pull' factors in an Asia Pacific market" *Educational Studies 42*, 163–180.

Åkesson L (2016) "Moving beyond the colonial? New Portuguese migrants in Angola" *Cahiers d'Études Africains 56*, 267–285.

Alonso J (2011) "International migration and development: a review in light of the crisis" CDP Background Paper No. 11(E). United Nations, Geneva.

Amin S (2007) "Interviewed by Amady Aly Dieng" *Development and Change 38*, 1149–1159.

Arrighi G (2007) *Adam Smith in Beijing: Lineages of the Twenty-First Century*. London: Verso.

Arrighi G and Zhang L (2011) Beyond the Washington consensus? A new bandung? In: Shefner A and Fernandez-Kelly P (eds.) *Globalization and Beyond: New Examinations of Global Power and its Alternatives*. Philadelphia: University of Pennsylvania Press, 25–57.

Bærenholdt J (2013) "Governmobility: the politics of mobility" *Mobilities 8*, 20–34.

Bakewell O (2009) *South-South Migration and Human Development: Reflections on African Experiences*. Human Development Research Papers, United Nations Development Programme, New York. Available at: http://hdr.undp.org/en/reports/global/hdr2009/papers/HDRP_2009_07.pdf. Accessed 14 October 2014.

Bakewell O and Jónsson G (2011) "Migration, mobility and the African city", IMI Working Paper 50, Oxford.

Basch L, Glick-Schiller N and Szanton-Blanc C (1994) *Nations Unbound: Transnational Projects, Postcolonial Predicaments and Deterritorialized Nation*. New York: Gordon and Breach.

Bodomo A (2009) "The African presence in contemporary China" *China Monitor 36*, 4–9.

Brandt Commission (1980) *North-South – A Programme for Survival*. Pan Books.

Castles S (2009) "Development and migration—migration and development what comes first? Global perspective and African experiences" *Theoria 56*, 121–131.

Castles S (2010) "Understanding global migration: a global transformation perspective" *Journal of Ethnic and Migration Studies 36*, 1565–1586.

Chatterjee P (1997) Modernity in two languages. In: Chatterjee P (ed.) *A Possible India: Essays in Political Criticism*. Delhi: Oxford University Press, 185–205.

Cobarrubias S, Cortes M and Pickles J (2011) "An interview with Sandro Mezzadra" *Environment & Planning D: Society & Space 29*, 584–598.

Collyer M and de Haas H (2011) "Developing dynamic categorisations of transit migration" *Population, Space and Place 18*, 468–481.

Council of Europe. (2003) *Draft Council Conclusions on Migration and Development*. 8927/03. Brussels: Council of the European Union.

de Haas H (2007) "Turning the tide? Why development will not stop migration" *Development and Change 38*, 819–840.

de Haas H (2010) "Migration and development: a theoretical perspective" *International Migration Review 44*, 227–264.

Dumont J, Spielvogel G and Widmaier S (2010) *International Migrants in Developed, Emerging and Developing Countries: An Extended Profile*. OECD Social, Employment and Migration Working Papers No.11. Available at: www.oecd.org/els/workingpapers

Düvell F, Collyer M and de Haas H (2012) "Critical approaches to transit migration" *Population, Space and Place 18*, 407–414.

Fangjun C (2009) "Modernization theory and China's road to modernization" *Chinese Studies in History 43*, 7–16.

Feng Y (2013) "University of Nottingham Ningbo China and Xi'an Jiaotong-Liverpool University: globalization of higher education in China" *Higher Education 65*, 471–485.

Fraser N (2010) "Injustice at intersecting scales: on 'social exclusion' and the 'global poor'" *European Journal of Social Theory 13*, 363–371.

Gaonkar D (2001) *Alternative Modernities*. North Carolina: Duke University Press.

Greiner C and Sakdapolrak P (2013) "Translocality: concepts, applications and emerging research perspectives" *Geography Compass 7*, 373–384.

Grossmann V and Stadelmann D (2013) "Wage effects of high-skilled migration: international evidence" *The World Bank Economic Review 27*, 297–319.

Gunder F (1967) *Capitalism and Underdevelopment in Latin America*. New York: Monthly Review Press.

Haugen H (2012) "Nigerians in China: a second state of immobility" *International Migration 50*, 65–80.

İçduygu A and Yükseker D (2012) "Rethinking transit migration in Turkey: reality and re-presentation in the creation of a migratory phenomenon" *Population, Space and Place 18*, 441–456.

IOM (2017) *Migration in the World*. Available at: www.iom.sk/en/about-migration/migration-in-the-world. Accessed 29 November 2017.

Jain S (2012) "For love and money: second-generation Indian-Americans 'return' to India" *Ethnic and Racial Studies 36*, 896–914.

Kang D (2007) *China Rising: Peace, Power and Order in East Asia*. New York: Columbia University Press.

Kofman E and Raghuram P (2012) "Women, migration, and care: explorations of diversity and dynamism in the global South" *Social Politics 19*, 408–432.

Leung M (2012) "'Read ten thousand books, walk ten thousand miles': geographical mobility and capital accumulation among Chinese scholars" *Transactions of the Institute of British Geographers 38*, 311–324.

Li P and Li E (2008) "University-educated immigrants from China to Canada: rising number and discounted value" *Canadian Ethnic Studies 40*, 1–16.

Lucas R (2008) *International Labor Migration in a Globalizing Economy*. Carnegie Papers, No. 92, Carnegie Endowment for International Peace, Washington, DC.

Martin P and Taylor J (1996) The anatomy of a migration hump. In: Taylor J (ed.) *Development Strategy, Employment, and Migration: Insights from Models*. Paris: OECD Development Centre, 43–62.

Mezzadra S and Neilson B (2013) "Border as method, or, the multiplication of labor" *Transversal* 06-08. Available at: http://eipcp.net/transversal/0608/m.... Accessed 10 May 2012.

Mignolo W (2011) "Geopolitics of sensing and knowing: on (de)coloniality, border thinking and epistemic disobedience" *Postcolonial Studies 14*, 273–283.

Park Y and Chen A (2009) "Recent Chinese migrants in small towns of post-apartheid South Africa" *REMI 25*, 25–44.

Pieterse J (2011) "Global rebalancing, crisis and the East-South turn" *Development and Change 42*, 22–48.

Raghuram P (2009) "Which migration, what development? Unsettling the edifice of migration and development" *Population, Space and Place 15*, 103–117.

Raghuram P (2013) "Theorising the spaces of student migration" *Population, Space and Place 19*(2), 138–154.

Raghuram P, Noxolo P and Madge C (2014) "Rising Asia and postcolonial geography" *Singapore Journal of Tropical Geography 35*(1), 119–135.

Ramo J (2004) *The Beijing Consensus: Notes on the New Physics of Chinese Power*. London: Foreign Policy Centre.

Ratha D and Shaw W (2007) *South-South Migration and Remittances*. Working Paper No. 102, World Bank, Washington DC.

Sassen S (2002) "Women's burden: Counter-geographies of globalization and the feminization of survival" *Nordic Journal of International Law 71*(2), 255–274.

Sauvy A (1952) "Trois mondes, une planète" *L'Observateur 118*.

Schapendonk J (2012) "Turbulent trajectories: African migrants on their way to the European Union" *Societies 2*, 27–41.

Sidaway J (2012) "Geographies of development: new maps, new visions" *The Professional Geographer 64*(1), 49–62.

Skeldon R (1997) *Migration and Development: A Global Interpretation*. London: Longman.

Stock I (2012) "Gender and the dynamics of mobility: reflections on African migrant mothers and 'transit migration' in Morocco" *Ethnic and Racial Studies 35*, 1577–1595.

UN DESA (2013) Cross-National Comparisons of Internal Migration: An Update on Global Patterns and Trends Technical Paper no. 2013/1. Available at: www.un.org/en/development/desa/population/pub lications/pdf/technical/TP2013-1.pdf. Accessed 29 November 2017.

Van Hear N, Bakewell O and Long K (2018) "Push-pull plus: reconsidering the drivers of migration" *Journal of Ethnic and Migration Studies 44*, 927–944.

Wade R (2011) "Emerging world order? From multipolarity to multilateralism in the G20, The World Bank and the IMF" *Politics and Society 39*, 347–378.

Wallerstein I (1979) *The Capitalist World-Economy*. Cambridge: Cambridge University Press.

World Bank (2008) *Migration and Remittances Factbook*. Washington, DC.

World Bank (2011) *Global Development Horizons*. Washington, DC.

World Health Organisation (2010) International Migration of Health Workers: Improving International Co-operation to Address the Global Health Workforce Crisis. Available at: www.who.int/hrh/resources/oecd-who_policy_brief_en.pdf. Accessed 20 November 2017.

Xiang B (2003) "Chinese emigration: a sending country perspective" *International Migration 41*, 21–48.

Zhang G (2003) "Migration of highly skilled Chinese to Europe: trends and perspective" *International Migration 41*, 73–97.

4

THE INTERFACE BETWEEN INTERNAL AND INTERNATIONAL MIGRATION

Julie Vullnetari

Introduction

Scholarship on migration has traditionally been fragmented between the study of internal and international migration, with the focus swinging back and forth like a pendulum (Skeldon 2006). In recent decades the field has been dominated by attention to international migration. Yet there are a number of reasons why it is imperative to engage more robustly with internal migration. First, numerically: those moving internally within a country far outnumber international migrants. By 2017, there were nearly 260 million international migrants globally according to the UN definition of having lived abroad for a year or longer, representing 3.5 per cent of the world's population (World Bank 2018). By contrast, even by 2009, there were already four times as many internal migrants: some 740 million people moved within their own respective countries, a share of 12 per cent of the global population in that year (UNDP 2009, 21). This number will have undoubtedly increased since. Within China alone internal migrant numbers stood at nearly 274 million by 2014.[1]

Second, is internal migration's link to development as this migration type is one of the most important opportunities for large numbers of poorer people in the developing countries of the Global South to improve their wellbeing. This is a dual factor of both the numerical spread of such migration, as well as by being more accessible to the poor than international movements (Deshingkar and Grimm 2005). Moreover, the development impacts of internal migration go beyond individual families. Lampert's (2014) study of Nigerian Home Town Associations (HTAs) revealed that it was the internal diaspora which was more effective and therefore, played a more important role in local development, than those based abroad.

Third, internal migration will often intertwine with international migration in complex ways, both forming part of livelihood strategies for millions of the poor in the Global South. Thus, internal and international migration may act as alternatives to each other, but often co-exist, contemporaneously or sequentially, within the same family, neighbourhood, local community, and country. As such, focusing on either of the two migration types singularly is likely to provide only a partial understanding of the lived realities of migrants (for an empirical justification of this view, see Aguayo-Téllez and Martínez-Navarro 2013). Hence the argument of this chapter is that our approach should be one that considers both migration types as linked conceptually as they are empirically (see Pryor's 1980 seminal work, and more recently, Hickey and Yeoh 2016; King and Skeldon 2010; Skeldon 2006; Vullnetari 2012; Xiao 2016). The need for such an approach is arguably more pressing than ever in light of increasing complexity and speed of global interconnections, accompanied by an equal complexity of barriers to mobility for the poor, and continued and anticipated large-scale displacements due to conflicts and environmental stressors. In making the case for such an integrated approach, the literature reviewed in this chapter both reflects these dynamic complexities and presents examples of how such research could be conceptualised and operationalised.

The remainder of this chapter is structured as follows. I first outline key similarities between internal and international migration, grouped under (i) drivers, and (ii) networks. This is followed by a discussion of key differences where my focus is on: (i) the structural impacts of immigration regimes, and (ii) migrant selectivity. Next, I outline some configurations of how the two migration types intertwine. The final section concludes. The review uses examples from Albania, where fieldwork took place between 2005 and 2006 (Vullnetari 2012) but also draws on studies and examples from around the world.

Similarities

Drivers

Key scholars of migration and development have long argued that internal and international migration share common drivers. Adepoju (1998, 389) made the case that in Africa both internal and international migration derive 'from the same set of fundamental causes'. Similarly, in Mexico, Cohen and Rios (2016) confirm that common drivers and motivations for migration were at the centre of decision making for both internal and international migrants. Nevertheless, whilst these structural drivers may be similar for both migration strands, they do not impact everyone in the same way. Moreover, individual characteristics and other cognitive factors such as desire, aspiration, and not least ability to migrate, can differ.

Networks

de Haas (2010) argues that migrant networks play a key role in supporting and perpetuating migration. This function is commonly found in studies of both internal and international migration, as examples from Mexico demonstrate (Lindstrom and Lauster 2001). In their study of migration in the Philippines, De Jong et al. (1983, 481) also found that kinship and friendship networks were the most salient factor in both internal and international migration streams. Not only have networks been important for both types of migrants separately, but they may be linked, as some internal networks may extend abroad; similarly, networks of international migrants may extend internally upon return. Moreover, these networks are important beyond their simple function of facilitating migration: they serve as key channels through which financial and social remittances are transferred, thus directly linked to how migration and development may interact.

Differences

Immigration regimes and borders

Arguably the most important difference between internal and international migration is whether a migrant's entry and stay are regulated and controlled through visas and permits. Zolberg (1989, 405) has argued that international migration is a 'distinctive social process' because of the control that states exercise over their own borders. As global interconnections have increased, including through cultural and technological diffusion, whilst options for the poor to migrate from less-developed countries to the richer Global North have narrowed, it seems migrants are undertaking increasingly dangerous journeys to escape conditions of underdevelopment or simply to improve life chances for themselves and their families. International migration, closely intertwined with these political country borders, thus becomes a very distinct movement from internal migration, especially in the resulting consequences for migrants and their families. These include financial, psychological, emotional, and physical costs, especially when migrants pay the ultimate price by losing their lives on dangerous journeys crossing these borders (Kovras and Robins 2016). Indeed, as Squire argues (2016) for the US and Europe (EU), migrant deaths and border violence have become key features of contemporary international migratory politics. If recent political developments are anything to go by, such immigration and border controls will likely increase and become more punitive for the poor, in turn raising the cost of international migration. For example, Cohen and Rios (2016) show how the tightening in recent years of border controls and punishments for Mexicans migrating to the US increased both the risks and the cost of such migration, resulting in some migrants giving up this endeavour altogether. Many re-routed their journeys to destinations within Mexico instead.

Beyond the crossing of international borders, the legal right of stay and work form the basis on which citizenship rights (voting, social housing, education, and healthcare) are subsequently accessed in the destination country. For irregular migrants, psychological costs can continue beyond the trauma experienced during the migration journey, as they try to evade arrest once they have arrived in the host country. Random, unannounced dawn raids by immigration enforcement agents at these migrants' residences or workplaces in countries such as the UK can often result in lasting mental health issues (Griffiths 2014).

Although internal migrants do not face violence and death whilst crossing administrative borders within a country as international migrants often do, the violence accompanying slum clearances and forced evictions within big cities such as Dhaka, Bangalore, Colombo, or Phnom Penh has been well documented (see Springer 2016 for Phnom Penh; Collyer et al. 2017 for Colombo). Internal rural–urban migrants, who make up a significant share of slums and other informal population settlements in cities of the developing world, are confronted with hostility from their own governments and local authorities of urban areas, who see them as a 'problem' that result in congested and unsustainable cities (Tacoli et al. 2014). For instance, a UN (2013, 107) survey of 185 countries in 2013 found that 80 per cent of governments had policies in place that aimed to reduce rural–urban migration. This share was highest (88 per cent) for least developed countries.

Arguably the most prominent (and researched) policy on limiting rural–urban migration is the *hukou* system in China, the closest we have today to an international regime for internal migration. Introduced in China in 1958, the *hukou* is a household registration system that assigns households an 'agricultural' or 'non-agricultural' status in rural and urban areas respectively. It plays a crucial role in distributing key social welfare services and benefits such as healthcare, education, social housing, and pensions. These benefits favour urban *hukou* holders, but rural–urban migrants are unable to access them as the *hukou* status is inherited by birth and an agricultural *hukou* is not readily transferable upon migration to urban areas, at least not for the poor. Despite the key role that these rural–urban migrants have played in China's spectacular economic growth since the late 1990s, the system continues to present serious challenges for them. The label 'floating population' describing these migrants reflects this sense of perpetual temporariness, resulting from the insecure migration status and the consequent limited access to social welfare (Chan 2012; Zhang 2014).[2]

In other countries, more informal ways of exclusion from accessing citizenship rights are widespread, as Abbas (2016) notes in her study of internal migrants in Mumbai and Kolkata in India where many internal migrations resemble international movements because migrants are moving between regions that are ethnically and linguistically very different from each other, albeit within the same political state boundaries. Thus, many newcomers form ethno-linguistic minorities upon arrival, leading to marginalisation and exclusion from full citizenship rights. The study underscores how, in many less-developed countries, citizenship regimes are shaped more deeply by internal than international migration.

Migrant selectivity

Internal and international migration are produced differently through segmented access but also migrant selectivity. Internal migration is more accessible to the poor, whilst international migration is often the realm of the better-off sections of society. Financial ability does not act alone in shaping selectivity, but intersects with identity markers such as gender, age, and formal education, to produce differentiated impacts not only on places and communities but more importantly on migrants themselves (see also Bastia 2011). For instance, in my research in Albania, the highly skilled migrated internally to the country's capital Tirana. Their skills would have been wasted in Greece, the key international destination for Albanians throughout the 1990s, where almost all Albanian migrants worked in manual jobs such as agriculture, construction, or domestic and care services. Those who moved to Tirana were able to find professional jobs in banking, teaching, or medicine, or started their own small businesses.

Aguayo-Téllez and Martínez-Navarro (2013) found similar patterns in Mexico. In their analysis of microdata from both Mexico and the 2000 US population census and considering both migration types in a single model, they found strong migrant selectivity. Education combined with age were noted in particular, whereby those moving internally within Mexico were often younger and better educated than international migrants to the US; migrants to the US were often older males, whereas women participated more as internal movers within Mexico. In both cases, the combination of human and social capital can provide the environment for educated and well-connected individuals to gain more from migrating internally, especially to cities. In contrast, unless using specific skilled migration schemes, such as those attracting skilled migrants in the US, Canada, or Australia, most labour migrants encounter difficulties finding jobs commensurate with their level of education abroad, both due to limited transferability of most degrees and to limited linguistic ability. Nevertheless, internal migration to cities may be followed by a move internationally at a later time, as the internal destination opens up opportunities for accumulation of financial, social, and cultural capital.

The Albanian case also showed that internal movements were particularly characterised by young, single women who were attracted to the capital for the opportunities it provided to both pursue tertiary education, and escape social control from the oppressive conservatism of their rural and small urban communities of origin. Thus, as Hondagneu-Sotelo (1994) argued in the case of Mexican migrant women to the US, migration in this context provided more gains for women than to men precisely for these reasons. Within the Albanian patriarchal society context, migration abroad of single young women for work, and outside the family unit, was viewed as morally suspect. On the other hand, education was and continues to be highly regarded for its potential for upward social mobility. Thus, beyond its intrinsic value, education for these women was also a means to 'legitimately' engage in affordable migration, as well as a door to opportunities for future onward migration abroad (see also Boehm 2012 for similar findings on Mexican migration to the US).

Moreover, international migration can be framed by society as highly dangerous and unsuitable for women. Cohen and Rios (2016) writing about historical and contemporary Mexican internal migration, found that Mexican–US border crossings were constructed in deeply gendered terms by rural Oaxacans, as posing higher risks for women than for men. Women migrated mostly internally, motivated by a combination of pursuing post-secondary education and escape from social control, including domestic violence (see also Hondagneu-Sotelo 1994). Linking this to financial ability, those who emigrated to study were not the poorest but came from households that had a certain level of financial resources. In another study of Oaxacan communities, Sandoval-Cervantes (2017) showed how it is not unusual that the same household will have migrant sons in the USA and migrant daughters in Mexico City.

The gendering that shapes selectivity of internal and international migration is not influenced simply by the patriarchal structures in (rural) areas of origin, but also by similarly patriarchal capitalist restructuring of global labour markets. For instance, in many countries of the Global South, the penetration of predatory global capital in search of cheaper labour to enable extraction of higher profit margins has shaped national economies and participation in the global markets along sharply gendered and racial lines (Silvey 2006). Garment manufacturing is a typical example of this, where the vast majority of the labour force is made up of women, who have often migrated from rural areas. Capitals such as Dhaka and Phnom Penh, key manufacturing sites for high street chains and other shops in the Global North, thus become spaces where young single migrant women negotiate a precarious existence with new-found freedom, empowerment, but also new constraints (Parsons and Lawreniuk 2016; Zhang 2014).

Intertwining internal and international migration

As the previous section has shown, whilst some differences between the two migration types are very sharp, most others blur and overlap, pointing particularly to some of the ways in which the two intertwine and connect. Parrenas' work (2000) on Filipina domestic migrant workers and the literature on 'Global Care Chains' that followed have been exemplary for engaging with both internal and international migration (see Chapter 21 in this Handbook). In this body of work, women's lives across the globe are linked together in a series of connecting 'chains', as reproductive and emotional labour are transferred amongst internal, international, and non-migrant women from rural areas of origin, to urban areas internally within a developing country, to a (often) city abroad (Hochschild 2001). Unpacking this intertwining in other contexts reveals a range of configurations at the individual, local, and national levels separately and combined. Together, they produce differentiated trajectories and outcomes for women (and children, and men) involved in these care chains, that reflect deeply unequal power geometries across gender, ethnic, racial, wealth, and geographical lines (see also Huang 2016 for an example in the Chinese context).

At the individual level, the same migrant may undertake both migrations, obviously at different times. King and Skeldon (2010, 1622) produce a typology of sequencing composed of a range of migration pathways. These include variations of a step-wise migration from the village to the nearest city to the capital and then abroad, where again movement internally within this destination country may follow, but alternatives include onward migration to a third country, or indeed return to the country of origin. This step-wise migration features particularly in the literature on Mexican migration internally and across the border to the USA (see the review in Lozano-Ascencio et al. 1999; also del Rey Poveda 2007; and for similar patterns of migrations in Indonesia, Lyons and Ford 2007). However, Skeldon (2006) has argued that step migration is only a temporary phase, most likely in the initial stages of migration from one particular origin. Once direct linkages between origin and destination (whether internally or abroad) have been established, direct migration can take place without the intermediate 'step'. The combination of many origins with different phases of development of migration patterns give an impression that step-wise migration is more important than in reality (Skeldon 2006). Nevertheless, there are also direct linkages between origin and destination that develop without any initial intermediate 'step'. This is usually outmigration from border communities to the neighbouring country and again migration from Albania to Greece and from Mexico to the US, are prime examples of this pattern. Other examples include migration through schemes such as the US visa 'lottery', Canada's skilled workers' programme or through marriage. When return takes place, this may be to the same village of origin or to another place in the country, often a city such as the capital. It is these return migrants from abroad who have contributed in large part to the rural–urban migration within developing countries such as Albania and Morocco (King et al. 2003; de Haas 2006). Savings of international migrants are used upon return to fund the construction of new and modern homes in these urban areas, in turn attracting migrant labour from other parts of the country who find employment in the construction sector, domestic and care work.

At the family level, internal and international migration can be undertaken by different members of the same family, at the same time or indeed, at different times. This configuration was prominent amongst many migrants I interviewed in my research in Albania. For instance, often the household livelihood strategy included aspirations for higher education for young family members, usually women. International migration provided the financial capital to achieve this, whilst internal relocation gave access to the site where universities were located. Usually, this was in the country's capital Tirana, where education facilities were numerous and of a higher quality than elsewhere in the country. The intertwining of the two migration types is reflected here in how different members of the same family took different migration pathways to contribute to this goal.[3] The internal migrant benefiting from the education was often a young female member of the family, whereas the remittances to enable such a move were sent by a male member of the family, usually a young brother, or sometimes the father, who had migrated clandestinely to neighbouring Greece or Italy. Direct international non-family migration for young single women through regular channels was not accessible due to the difficulty of obtaining entry visas, or affordable due to the high cost. As mentioned earlier, clandestine international journeys, usually the only ways for most Albanians to emigrate abroad at the time, were fraught with danger and enormous risks, thus considered unsuitable for women.[4] Under this configuration, in both Albania and other countries, the 'residual' parts of the international migrant's family may fully relocate internally once remittances have been sent from abroad to enable this move.

Similarly, in their study of internal and international migration in Nepal, Bohra and Massey (2009) found that international remittances financed both the cost of internal (rural–urban) migration of the recipient family and the education of young family members in the urban area on arrival.

At the meso level, both migration types can, and often do, co-exist within a local community such as a neighbourhood, village or city. The implications for such combinations can be negative for some areas, for instance, large-scale depopulation, which in turn affects the sustainability of social services and overall community life. Many remote and mountainous areas in Albania for instance, have suffered this fate, leaving behind those who either cannot (the very poor) or do not wish to (usually older people) move to fend for themselves in dire circumstances. Yet in other regions, precisely this combination ensures that village life thrives as internal migrants continue to travel back regularly to the village of origin where they maintain crops and other produce, whilst international migrants pump remittances into the local economy. These are often rural areas near main axes of transport and communication, such as my study villages in Albania located near the key motorway that links Albania to Greece, or near large cities (Vullnetari 2012). In other cases, the strategic favourable geographic position near a capital city acts as a magnet for internal rural migrants who cannot afford to settle in the city, who in turn have migrant family members abroad. In Albania again, in the late 1980s, Kamza, a small town at the edge of the capital Tirana, had merely 6000 registered residents. The 2011 census revealed that its population had shot to over 100,000 over two decades by attracting internal migrants, due primarily to its proximity to the capital, in combination with other factors such as availability of state-owned land that could be 'claimed' by in-coming poor rural migrants (Vullnetari 2012).

Finally, at a national level, the combination of internal and international migration can have regional repercussions through 'replacement migration', and more general implications for planning, urban and rural development (Skeldon 2006). For instance, in Albania migrants from the poorer northern regions, or remote mountainous villages, have migrated internally not only to the coastal parts of the country which has attracted the vast majority of those moving within the country, but also to the south where the villages have been emptied by emigration to Greece (King et al. 2003). There, these internal migrants support both the local economy and those older people who still remain in the villages, whilst, over time, they become permanent members of these communities.

Conclusions

At a time of heightened global connections, fragmented migratory journeys, increasing complexity of immigration bureaucracies to be navigated, as well as rising anti-immigrant sentiments in the Global North, migrant livelihood strategies and migrant trajectories that are composed of both internal and international migration are likely to increase. In tandem with this, increasing rural–urban migration and a rising urban population as the countries of the Global South develop economically, present new challenges for sustainable development (Tacoli et al. 2014). Understanding the ways in which such migratory trajectories and journeys entwine and interact with development processes thus becomes crucial in being able to address these challenges. It is indeed the case that key differences exist between internal and international migration, especially in crossing an international border and in migrant selectivity. However, this is only part of the story. Both migration types share common features such as drivers and networks and interact in complex and dynamic ways. This chapter has sought to unpack this complexity at various spatial scales and over time and in so doing, highlighting the need for an integrated approach to migration, from the points of view of both the research and policymaking. Whilst more remains to be done, the discussion here is a small but important step in this direction.

Notes

1 Figure quoted by Dr Nana Zhang, Lecturer in Sociology at Southampton University, at the lecture 'Rural–urban migration in China' for the 'Migration and Development' module, Geography and Environment, University of Southampton, February 2017, citing National Bureau of Statistics China 2015 www.stats.gov.cn/tjsj/zxfb/201504/t20150429_797821.html. It must be noted, however, that the figures on both internal and international migration are likely to be underestimates of the total population engaging in these respective migrations. For instance, the UNDP (2009) used large units to define internal migration for their 2009 Human Development report – provinces in China and states in India. Similarly, the 12-month criterion that the UN uses to define international migration overlooks the more voluminous, but shorter term seasonal movements that take place throughout the world (with thanks to Prof. Skeldon for his feedback on this.)
2 Whilst such examples are rare in our contemporary post-socialist/post-Cold War world, historical examples in other former communist states (Albania being an extreme such case), or the pass system in Apartheid South Africa can be instructive, not least of the importance of temporality in understanding migration processes.
3 To be clear, this was often not the *sole purpose* of migration.
4 Internal student migration increased rapidly in post-communist countries such as Albania, as the secondary and tertiary education infrastructure expanded exponentially through the emergence of a significant private sector. But internal student migration has been noted in other contexts as well (e.g. de Haas 2006 in Morocco).

References

Abbas R. (2016) "Internal migration and citizenship in India" *Journal of Ethnic and Migration Studies*, 42, 150–168.

Adepoju A. (1998) "Linkages between internal and international migration: the African situation" *International Social Science Journal*, 50, 387–395.

Aguayo-Téllez E. and Martínez-Navarro J. (2013) "Internal and international migration in Mexico: 1995–2000" *Applied Economics*, 45, 1647–1661.

Bastia T. (2011) "Migration as protest? Negotiating gender, class, and ethnicity in urban Bolivia" *Environment and Planning A*, 43, 1514–1529.

Boehm D. (2012) *Intimate migrations: gender, family, and illegality among transnational Mexicans.* New York University Press, New York.

Bohra P. and Massey D.S. (2009) "Processes of internal and international migration from Chitwan, Nepal" *International Migration Review*, 43, 621–651.

Chan K.W. (2012) "Migration and development in China: trends, geography and current issues" *Migration and Development*, 1, 187–205.

Cohen J. and Rios B. (2016) "Internal migration in Oaxaca: its role and value to rural movers" *International Journal of Sociology*, 46, 223–235.

Collyer M., Amirthalingam K. and Jayatilaka D. (2017) "The right to adequate housing following forced evictions in post-conflict Colombo, Sri Lanka" in Brickell, K., Fernández Arrigoitia, M. and Vasudevan, A. (eds.) *Geographies of Forced Eviction.* Palgrave Macmillan, London 47–69.

de Haas H. (2006) "Migration, remittances and regional development in Southern Morocco" *Geoforum*, 37, 565–580.

de Haas H. (2010) "The internal dynamics of migration processes: a theoretical inquiry" *Journal of Ethnic and Migration Studies*, 36, 1587–1617.

De Jong G.F., Abad R.G., Arnold F., Carino B.V., Fawcett J.T. and Gardner R.W. (1983) "International and internal migration decision making: a value-expectancy based analytical framework of intentions to move from a rural Philippine province" *International Migration Review*, 17, 470–484.

del Rey Poveda A. (2007) "Determinants and consequences of internal and international migration: the case of rural populations in the south of Veracruz, Mexico" *Demographic Research*, 16, 287–314.

Deshingkar P. and Grimm S. (2005) *Internal migration and development: a global perspective.* IOM, Geneva.

Griffiths M. (2014) "Out of time: the temporal uncertainties of refused asylum seekers and immigration detainees" *Journal of Ethnic and Migration Studies*, 40, 1999–2009.

Hickey M. and Yeoh B. (2016) "Crossing borders and traversing boundaries: closing the 'gap' between internal and international migration in Asia" *Population, Space and Place*, 22, 642–650.

Hochschild A.R. (2001) "Global care chains and emotional surplus value" in Hutton, W. and Giddens, A. (eds.) *On the edge: living with global capitalism*. Vintage Books, London, 130–146.

Hondagneu-Sotelo P. (1994) *Gendered transitions: Mexican experiences of immigration*. University of California Press, Berkeley, CA.

Huang S-M. (2016) "Can travelling mothers ever arrive? Articulating internal and international migration within a transnational care perspective" *Population, Space and Place*, 22, 705–717.

King R., Mai N. and Dalipaj M. (2003) *Exploding the migration myths: analysis and recommendations for the European Union, the UK and Albania*. The Fabian Society and Oxfam, London.

King R. and Skeldon R. (2010) "'Mind the gap!' Integrating approaches to internal and international migration" *Journal of Ethnic and Migration Studies*, 36, 1619–1646.

Kovras I. and Robins S. (2016) "Death as the border: managing missing migrants and unidentified bodies at the EU's Mediterranean frontier" *Political Geography*, 55, 40–49.

Lampert B. (2014) "Collective transnational power and its limits: London-based Nigerian organisations, development at 'home' and the importance of local agency and the 'internal Diaspora'" *Journal of Ethnic and Migration Studies*, 40, 829–846.

Lindstrom D. and Lauster N. (2001) "Local economic opportunity and the competing risks of internal and U.S. migration in Zacatecas, Mexico" *International Migration Review*, 35, 1232–1256.

Lozano-Ascencio F., Roberts B. and Bean F. (1999) "The interconnections of internal and international migration: the case of the United States and Mexico" in Pries L (ed.) *Migration and transnational social spaces*. Ashgate, Aldershot, 138–161.

Lyons L. and Ford M. (2007) "Where internal and international migration intersect: mobility and the formation of multi-ethnic communities in the Riau Islands Transit Zone" *IJMS: International Journal of Multicultural Societies*, 9, 236–263.

Parsons L. and Lawreniuk S. (2016) "Love in the time of Nokia: cultural change as compromise in a Cambodian migrant enclave" *Population, Space and Place*, 23. doi: 10.1002/psp.2015.

Sandoval-Cervantes I. (2017) "Navigating the city: internal migration of Oaxacan indigenous women" *Journal of Ethnic and Migration Studies*, 43, 849–865.

Silvey R. (2006) "Geographies of gender and migration: spatializing social difference" *International Migration Review*, 40, 64–81.

Skeldon R. (2006) "Interlinkages between internal and international migration and development in the Asian region" *Population, Space and Place*, 12, 15–30.

Springer S. (2016) "Homelessness in Cambodia: the terror of gentrification" in Brickell K. and Springer S. (eds.) *The handbook of contemporary Cambodia*. Routledge, London, 234–244.

Squire V. (2016) "Governing migration through death in Europe and the US: identification, burial and the crisis of modern humanism" *European Journal of International Relations*, 23, 513–532.

Tacoli C., McGranahan G. and Saerthwaite D. (2014) "Urbanization, rural-urban migration and urban poverty", Background paper to the IOM World Migration Report 2015: Migrants and Cities. New Partnerships to Manage Mobility, International Institute for Environment and Development, London.

UN. (2013) *World population policies report 2013*. UN-DESA (Department of Economic and Social Affairs), New York.

UNDP. (2009) *Overcoming barriers: human mobility and development. Human development report 2009*. United Nations Development Programme, New York.

Vullnetari J. (2012) *Albania on the move: links between internal and international migration*. Amsterdam University Press, Amsterdam.

World Bank. (2018) Migration and development brief 29. Migration and remittances: recent developments and outlook, April 2018, World Bank, Washington, DC.

Xiang B. (2016) "Beyond methodological nationalism and epistemological behaviouralism: drawing illustrations from migrations within and from China" *Population, Space and Place*, 22, 669–680.

Zhang N. (2014) "Performing identities: women in rural–urban migration in contemporary China" *Geoforum*, 54, 17–27.

Zolberg A. (1989) "The next waves: migration theory for a changing world" *International Migration Review*, 23, 403–430.

5

BORDER WORK

Frames, barriers, and disingenuous development

Michael Collyer

In August 2016, Jean-Claude Juncker, President of the European Commission was quoted as referring to national borders as 'the worst invention ever made by politicians' (*The Independent* 22 August 2016). This is a surprising statement from such a senior politician, not only for the view that borders are bad, but that they are the product of legislation, they are constructed by politicians rather than simply facts of life. Nationalist sentiment almost inevitably considers national borders as real, unquestionable, almost naturally occurring features on which the sovereignty of the state depends. It is therefore less surprising that Juncker faced so much criticism for challenging such a widely accepted view. Yet his concise statement fits well with much critical academic analysis which sees borders as accidents of history that require careful and continual work to maintain. Recent developments in border control, particularly in wealthier parts of the world such as the European Union or North America, provide a clear illustration of the significance, impact and expense that this 'border work' now involves (Vukov and Sheller 2013). Although the recognition and defence of borders is a universal human endeavour that can be traced back for millennia, contemporary border work has changed dramatically even in the last 20 years. Particularly in wealthier states, border control now describes a complex industry that accounts for a growing share of public expenditure (Andersson 2014). Such an industry could not fail to impact the relationship between migration and development in increasingly significant ways. This chapter considers the nature of this impact. In my view, the weight of critical analysis can be summarised in Juncker's terms: national borders are generally bad for development. Yet borders are bound up with what we understand both development and migration to be. The final answer is inevitably more complex and depends on the nature of the interaction between border work and development work.

This chapter focuses on national borders, though the discussion is also relevant for some sub-national borders where there are enforced administrative controls on internal migration. The chapter considers three areas in which borders impact migration and development, examined in the following three sections: frames, barriers, and 'disingenuous development'. First, like frames, borders are definitional. They frame territory, but they also define key processes, including both migration and development. The first section considers what and where borders are. Second, as barriers, the evidence is reasonably clear that increasing border controls reduces global wealth and have a particular impact on those from poorer countries. The third and final section turns to the very recent use of development and humanitarian aid to support or justify border control measures. I argue that this is not rooted in a genuine desire to support progress in poor countries but to prevent most people leaving those countries. Although the prevention of migration is increasingly legitimised as development or humanitarian aid, there appears to be no real basis to this; it is 'disingenuous development'. Arguments that border control should be a development priority or that people should be stopped from moving for their own good would have seemed shocking only a few decades ago, but these have have become normalised to the extent that under certain circumstances they may be legitimately classified as Official Development Assistance (ODA). This is bad for both migration and development.

Framing the action: borders of territory and population

In their simplest form, borders are territorial, separating and defining different spaces (Graziano 2018). In many cases, borders may have no physical form, only apparent in the normative practice which produces them. At the micro-scale, borders systematise the organisation of space within the home and may be enforced by rigid cultural or gender norms. In workplaces, borders reinforce security, separate customers and employees, or reinforce hierarchies of management and workers. Beyond households or companies, borders differentiate owners of private property or delimit administrative control of city or regional authorities. It is *national* borders that are most relevant for this chapter, defining the nation-state as the basic territorial unit of international relations from which broader international or even global political organisation may arise.

In many cases a territorial definition of borders is no longer sufficient. Strategies of control focusing on *population* rather than *territory* help explain the movement of borders outwards, beyond the territory and inwards, onto the territory itself . Foucault dated the origin of the concept of population to the mid-eighteenth century (Foucault 2007), emerging from new techniques of individualised data collection. In most situations, the population of concern to a government has been located on the territory controlled by that government. ODA provides one of the most widespread examples of *extra*-territorial governance of population. Extra-territorial engagement for purposes of migration control is even more recent. Although visas have existed in some form since the early twentieth century it is only since the 1980s that they have become a real restriction on movement, Zolberg referred to this as 'remote control' (2003). Since then successive policy developments have reinforced remote controls as wealthy states have externalised migration controls far beyond the state's territory (Bialasiewicz 2012).

The concern with population rather than territory also explains the internalisation of borders. Many border control operations occur on the territory of the controlling state. Access to a wide range of services, including right to work, healthcare or welfare benefits, is conditional on the production of proof of legal right to those services. The national border follows individuals onto the territory and continues to highlight and enforce divisions after arrival (Davies et al. 2017). As a result, national borders are no longer the 'outer bark' of the nation-state (Graziano 2018, 4). They extend outwards beyond the territory and inwards to differentiate populations present on the territory. From the perspective of population, rather than territory, a border can best be considered as anything which defines difference. In the case of a national border, this involves differences in national belonging of populations.

The shift from a territorial understanding of the border to one based on population makes analysis of the location of the border particularly challenging. A territorial border frames the territory. Yet for many travellers, the border may be entirely invisible, facilitate by a high-tech infrastructure of control, including databases of biometric information on a growing array of individuals (Amoore 2006). Population-focused strategies of control allow for the complete inclusion of some border crossers, eliminating delay to the extent that they are barely even aware of the border while simultaneously excluding others (Sparke 2006). This is the sense of the 'smart border', a system designed to facilitate the inclusion of those who belong but which also depends on the radical exclusion of those who are not judged to belong. For those who are excluded, wealthier countries go to ever greater lengths through the application of the internal border to ensure that they never feel that they have arrived; in such surveillance states, it has been argued that 'the border is everywhere' (Lyon 2006).

The most recent trend in bordering practices suggests a return to visible, territorial borders. This has become especially clear through the narratives of 'crisis' from 2015 onwards, when the construction of border walls accelerated (Jones et al. 2017). Analysis by the Economist suggested that by 2016 there were more border walls in Europe than there had been during the Cold War. Such developments appear to contradict the account of national borders moving away from territorial borders that have become established in much geopolitical writing on borders over the last few decades (Carling and Hernández-Carretero 2011; Jones et al. 2017; Lavenex and Schimmelfennig 2009). Yet these new physical borders require a slightly different explanation. New fences and walls from 2015 onwards are not (and arguably were never expected to be) an absolute barrier to unauthorised movement. Physical infrastructure at the border may re-route people or make it more expensive or time-consuming to cross the border but, with few exceptions, walls have limited impact on the numbers of unauthorised arrivals in the territory on the other side (Jones 2012). Increasing the visibility of borders reassures public opinion in that territory and may serve as a deterrent to undocumented migrants considering that particular route, but it has certainly not replaced the extra-territorial border or the internal border.

Borders are now both territorial and population-focused. Depending on who is crossing they may be perceived as everything from totally invisible to 'everywhere'. This spectrum of experience of the national border is deliberate. The fast track border crosser is able to enjoy a virtually frictionless experience at the border not purely due to financial power but because the system also has the ability to identify and detain individuals without authorisation to travel at an early stage in the process. The multiplication of the forms borders may take, effectively multiplies the number of borders, particularly for those without authorisation to cross. This matters for the impact of borders on migration and development, as the next section considers.

Borders as barriers

Borders are foundational to our understanding of both migration and development. They have both conceptual and practical effects on the relationship between migration and development. In conceptual terms, development has always been imagined and crucially measured as change in particular, territorially bounded locations, typically nation-states. Development is a desirable change within a territorially bounded place. Without borders the territory would be undefined and development could simply not be measured. Development in one location would become a component of global progress. Migration on the other hand is categorised as either internal or international, depending on the nature of the borders that are crossed. International migrants are obviously those who cross an international border, and they are therefore closest to the concerns of this chapter, but internal migrants are also relevant, not simply because they are closely connected to international migrants but because they also have to have crossed a border of some kind. For any migrant to be defined as such, their journey has to be both spatially and temporally significant; they have to have travelled a significant distance for a significant period of time. The time dimension is usually fairly straight forward. Space is rather more difficult as significance cannot be measured simply in terms of distance but only in terms of borders. Even internal migration is only recorded if individuals cross from one region into another. Like development, migration therefore depends on borders for its existence. Without borders both migration and development would be invisible, at least in statistical terms.

Beyond this commonality, migration and development depend on a different conceptualisation of the border. The definition of development remains anchored in a territorial understanding of borders. Movement of people across the territorial borders that define those locations challenges that understanding. Where people are located certainly matters, but migration also requires detailed knowledge of flows, connections and networks. These connections are not shared by everyone in the same location; in fact, they differ from one individual to another. Migration therefore requires a more challenging population-focused interpretation of borders. The territorial understanding of borders required by development and the increasingly population-focused conceptualisation of migration sets up an obvious tension.

This tension between migration and development has existed for some time and involves viewing migration as external, or at least separate from development. The interpretation of migration and development as fundamentally two different, separate things is central to the description of 'migration and development' which is common to the vast majority of theoretical and policy analysis of this topic. Yet, as Skeldon emphasised more than 20 years ago, 'migration is development' (Skeldon 1997; Sutherland 2013). Migration is not external to development or any more separate than work, education, investment, or any of the other major results of migration. This conceptual separation of migration and development is possible only because migration is seen as external, as something which is defined by border-crossing rather than border containing. A more fluid understanding of connections across borders for both migration and development would support a more integrated conceptualisation of the two processes.

The conceptual implications of borders are foundational, but borders also have clear practical effects. Where borders appear to be invisible, as in the situations mentioned in the previous section, these effects are limited, although even here the impact may be felt at certain times or by certain people so this certainly doesn't mean that they are irrelevant. In the more common cases of regular, systematic border controls, the effects are more pronounced. Where the borders are those of wealthy, welfare states, they now comprise a substantial architecture of deterrence that has been gradually constructed over the last few decades. Citizens of these countries typically face minimal barriers to movement and are often entirely unaware of how difficult international travel may be for those without privileged citizenships. The new 'smart' borders are defined by their ability to make travel for some smooth and frictionless while simultaneously making authorised travel for others almost impossible. Those for whom travel has been made more difficult are typically citizens of poorer countries. Indeed, a quantitative analysis of influences on visa controls conducted by Neumayer just over a decade ago found that poverty was one of the clearest influences on the introduction of visa restrictions. Neumayer's analysis predicted that a passport holder from a very poor country would face visa restrictions in 88 per cent of all other countries, whereas a passport holder from a very rich country would only face visa restrictions in 34 per cent of other countries (2006, 80). Neumayer concludes that 'for passport holders from poor, authoritarian countries with a history of violent political conflict travel is and remains severely restricted' (2006, 81).

This means that citizens of countries which should be a priorities for international development donors face the greatest barriers to international travel. It is not poverty alone that prevents the poorest from leaving, but borders, or more particularly the control of those borders. Other chapters in this Handbook provide detailed evidence for the fact that (under certain circumstances) international movement can dramatically increase individual opportunities, diversify risks for households, support larger collective projects, and provide valuable foreign exchange at a national level. The fact that borders prevent this movement supports the fairly straightforward conclusion: borders are bad for development. This must be carefully nuanced since these kinds of successes are far from the universal experience. Nevertheless, even a decade ago, the negative impact of borders on development was recognised at the highest level. The United Nations Development Programme (UNDP) 2009 Human Development Report (HDR), entitled 'Overcoming Barriers: Human Mobility and Development' was particularly clear on this issue. Although obviously many potential barriers to migration exist, the report was particularly concerned with the border, in all its forms; the introduction recognised that 'those wishing to migrate have increasingly come up against government-imposed barriers to movement' (UNDP 2009, 2) and went on to argue that 'large gains to human development can be achieved by lowering the barriers to movement and improving the treatment of movers' (UNDP 2009, 3).

These views were representative of a broader analysis of these issues. The final report of the Development Research Centre on Migration Globalisation and Poverty, funded by the UK's Department for International Development (DFID) was also published in 2009, after 6 years of research and came to a very similar central conclusion: 'For migration to have its full developmental impact, the most beneficial policy change would be to reduce barriers to migration, at all levels and particularly for the poorest' (Migration DRC 2009). The explanation for the positive impact of mobility is the vast and growing inequalities that exist at a global level. The annual HDR also includes comparative data on the Human Development Index (HDI) and shows how a state's position in global HDI ranking may shift enormously across a single border. In the most recent HDR (UNDP 2017), the USA is ranked 10th compared to Mexico's position at 77th; Singapore is 5th compared to Malaysia at 59 and Malaysia's neighbour, Indonesia, at 113. Yet it is unsurprisingly in the Mediterranean that the most significant cross border differentials are found. At 26th, Italy is 71 places above Tunisia and 77 above Libya; Spain is ranked 27th, 98 places above neighbouring Morocco at 123rd, which is itself 34 places above Mauritania, its neighbour to the south.

The vast inequality between states, even states which share borders, is one of the clearest pieces of evidence that reducing border controls is good for development. Yet, simply being present in a country where services are much better than a migrant's home is obviously not enough to enjoy access to those services. Border controls that explicitly seek to prevent that access are increasingly common. With the shift from territorial controls to population, those controls continue even once the migrant has arrived. The movement of border controls away from the territorial border ensures that it is extremely difficult to reach the territory, even of neighbouring states and once a state's territory has been reached it is difficult to access the excellent public services which produce high HDI scores. The ease with which the benefits of a new location may be reached and enjoyed once there depends on an individual migrants' circumstances and attributes. These include gender, ethnicity, education, financial and social capitals, linguistic ability, and previous migration experience amongst many others, but legal status has become one of the clearest routes to successful migration. Both during and after the journey one of the clearest predictors of successful migration is a migrants' ability to cross the proliferation of borders involved. The gulf between authorised, documented migration and undocumented migration is greater than it has ever been.

It is still possible for undocumented migration to lead to some of these positive outcomes, particularly if migrants are able to regularise their situation somehow once they have arrived. This hope, and the perceived impossibility of life at home for many migrants explains why undocumented migration continues. Still, undocumented migration is becoming more and more difficult and increasingly selective; those who attempt it are in the vast majority young, able men (Crawley and Duvell 2017). In the case of migration to Europe, until the early 1970s, it is thought that the large majority of migrants did not have legal status on arrival but were able to acquire it fairly quickly and secure employment (Castles et al. 2013). At that time documented and undocumented migrants were indistinguishable in terms of their means of transport and the work they did on arrival. This has now changed dramatically. Those who are denied legal access to other countries are unable to take standard means of transport and must resort to dangerous overland routes, often labelled transit migration (Collyer and de Haas 2012). Once they arrive, the development of the internal border means that undocumented migrants do not do the same jobs, live in the same places, or have the same access to services as documented migrants. Their lives are now completely separate, and they are systematically shut out from the very real benefits of living in countries with much higher HDI scores. As Neumayer (2006) has demonstrated this is much more likely to affect those with citizenship of poorer countries.

Both the HDR 2009 and the final report of the Migration RPC of the same year emphasise the significance of choice of migration destination as a way of maximising the development impact of migration (Migration DRC 2009). Freedom of mobility is always constrained but, as both reports highlight state-imposed barriers in the form of border control have become the most significant constraints on that freedom. As border controls in wealthy countries have become more rigid, it has become extremely difficult to enter through authorised channels, such as airports or seaports. The rise in arrivals in the European Union since 2015 that was somewhat inaccurately dubbed a 'migration crisis' involved the use of more spontaneous routes which are much more difficult to regulate. One response to such arrivals is the construction of new fortifications at the territorial border, though, as discussed in the previous section, this must be understood more in terms of reassurance of citizens and deterrence of potential migrants than any kind of effective barrier. A second response has been to reinforce the border control capacity of neighbouring states in order to prevent departures and in some cases to prevent arrivals in those states. In some cases border control is now defined as a legitimate development priority and financial support to poorer countries to reinforce border controls is widely defined as ODA. This latest development in the relationship between borders, migration and development is the focus of the final section of this chapter.

'Disingenuous development' and the humanitarian border

As the first and second sections argued, it is conceptually difficult to separate borders from migration and development since borders are central to basic definitions of both migration and development. Yet the overlap between borders and migration and development goes well beyond the conceptual. It has always had a clear practical basis too and this has become more obvious over the last few decades. The assumption that migration results from under-development has a long history going back to the colonial period. This led to the expectation that development could be encouraged as a way of reducing migration. There is now a very robust body of evidence undermining this idea; indeed, it is clear that far from preventing migration, development actually encourages it, at least for poorer countries (Clemens 2014). Nevertheless, the idea that development can be used to stop migration is a particularly seductive one for policymakers and has persisted in a range of national and supra-national policy settings.

The use of development policy as a tool of migration control is implicit in most donor states, often in discussions to address 'root causes' of migration, and is becoming increasingly explicit. Soon after she was appointed the UK's Secretary of State of International Development, Priti Patel wrote an article in the *Daily Mail*, a tabloid newspaper known for its anti-immigrant views, in which she argued 'I want to use our aid budget to directly address the great global challenges that affect the UK – like creating jobs in poorer countries so as to reduce the pressure for mass migration to Europe' (Patel 2016). In this context, development policy merges with the border since they share the same objectives of preventing certain forms of migration.

This use of development policy to tackle the reasons that are thought to encourage migrants to leave is now well established; López-Sala (2015) calls this the 'preventative dissuasion' of migration. More recently, development work has spread into activities more immediately associated with border control. These involve more violent forms of what López-Sala (2015) calls 'coercive' and 'repressive' dissuasion of migration that are not immediately associated with development or humanitarian action (Collyer 2019). There are two powerful legitimating forces behind this move: first, the Sustainable Development Goals (SDGs), specifically target 10.7, and second the growing tendency to push at the definitional limits of what counts as Official Development Assistance. The SDGs were officially adopted in September 2015. They include 169 targets and although several targets mention migration, target 10.7 is the only one exclusively devoted to migration (see Chapter 26 in this Handbook). Target 10.7 reads: 'facilitate orderly, safe and responsible migration and mobility of people, including through implementation of planned and well-managed migration policies' (SDG 10.7). The 'migration policies' referred to in this target clearly involve, even require, border control. For the first time ever, this target makes border control an internationally agreed objective of development. This is very different from funding employment generation projects, for example, with the idea that they may provide alternatives to emigration and so reduce international migration of the unemployed. Using development finance to fund border control operations challenges ideas of what development involves.

This fits in with the second trend, that of pushing the limits of what may be defined as ODA. The details of what the OECD considers as ODA have always been flexible and politically motivated but it is increasingly common for donors to include activities which do not obviously fit the OECD's general definition of ODA as 'government aid designed to promote the economic development and welfare of developing countries'. For example, since 2015, there has been considerable political pressure to meet the needs of individuals seeking protection in Europe using ODA. In 2016, 38 per cent of Austria's entire ODA budget was spent supporting refugees in Austria. For Italy, Germany, and Greece these 'in-donor refugee costs' accounted for over 20 per cent of total ODA (Parker 2017). No systematic accounting exists for the share of ODA spent on migration-related activities beyond the donor countries, although the signs are that this is also increasing. A large-scale review conducted by the European Centre for Development Policy Management found that since 2015 the geography of ODA spending within the EU had skewed towards those displacement crises that were likely to affect Europe (Knoll and Sherriff 2017).

The inclusion of migration control in the SDGs and the shifting understandings of ODA provide powerful legitiamation to the notion that more border control contributes to development. This is having an impact across donor countries. This 'disingenuous' development labels and finances border control as development when it is clear that it is conducted exclusively in the frequently unacknowledged interests of the funder. In the EU, the most recent policy framework for supporting migration and development is the Valletta Action Plan (VAP) of 2015. The first theme of the VAP is entitled 'Development benefits of migration and addressing the root causes of irregular migration and forced displacement' (JVAP 2017). The most recent update lists a range of projects under this theme in states in the European 'neighbourhood', funded by the EU or Member States which involve securitised approaches to migration and border control. Many of these states, such as Morocco or Egypt,[1] do not face major issues of immigration so these are unlikely to be significant domestic priorities. There are similar issues in North America, most recently concerning Mexico's *Programa Frontera Sur* (PFS). This was initiated in 2014 and funded by the USA as an explicitly development focused programme, concentrating on supporting social development on either side of the Mexico–Guatemala border. Two years into the programme the main results were an increase in deportations while the more obviously developmental elements of the project had yet to materialise (Vega 2017).

The practice of financing border control initiatives with ODA is likely to increase and is extremely difficult to monitor without a clearer approach for collecting ODA data (Knoll and Sherriff 2017). Yet it is not only ODA which is being used in this way. A similar trend is apparent in humanitarian action. This is even more difficult to investigate. Although much humanitarian action is funded through ODA budgets, there is no separate statistical accounting system in place for humanitarianism and it may simply provide a legitimising label for a range of practices which do not appear to share humanitarian principles. The 'humanitarian border' (Walters 2011) refers to a series of developments through which 'the language of humanitarianism has been co-opted and de-naturalised to respond to the immediate necessities of migrants in distress but neglecting the causes of crossings and the consequences of pre-emption, thereby disfiguring the substance of human rights' (Moreno-Lax 2018, 120). It is not a generalised global development but occurs along 'frontiers of poverty' where tremendous inequality exists on either side of a single border. The argument is that humanitarian action has become necessary because border crossing in these parts of the world is frequently a matter of life and death.

Critical analysis of the humanitarian government of borders draws attention to two trends: the use of humanitarian principles to camouflage control and the criminalisation of solidarity. In terms of camouflage, action at 'humanitarian borders' carried out by states and their representatives is essentially unchanged from previous securitised practices; any change is discursive, highlighting humanitarian motivations and framing controls as in the best interests of those whose migration they interrupt or prevent (Pallister-Wilkins 2017). Recent analysis by Violeta Moreno-Lax identifies two elements of this trend. First, 'rescue through interdiction' is the practice of describing the effective prevention of migration through repressive border control as a human rights success since the counterfactual of increased migration would have involved more migrants risking their lives. The result is that '[m] igrant safety and border security are thereby seemingly conciliated' (Moreno-Lax 2018,

121). Second, 'rescue without protection' involves the rescue of individuals in danger, but then treating their subsequent protection needs inadequately and returning them without proper procedures. The continued inadequacy of state responses to undocumented migration has left open a significant gap for non-state action and a range of NGOs and activist groups support undocumented border-crossers (Cuttitta 2018), particularly in the Mediterranean and the deserts of the US South West. Such humanitarian support from non-state agents is now widely criminalised and humanitarian workers risk being treated in the same way as those who seek to gain profit from such border crossing (Sigona 2017).

Conclusion: building bigger barriers damages development

National borders are not likely to disappear anytime soon. Indeed, as this chapter has argued, neither migration nor development would exist in the same way without them. Borders frame migration and development and allow both processes to be measured and studied. Still, a border is not necessarily a barrier; free movement within the EU or the ECOWAS region is ample illustration of that. Yet, the direction of change is for barriers to movement to become more common. Borders are becoming more rigid, better defended and harder to avoid. This has involved the spreading of borders away from their traditional locations on territorial edges; border control has moved outwards, beyond the territory and inwards so that it takes place across state territory . This process is reinforced by new technologies that have allowed population rather than territory to become a significant focus of border work, shutting undocumented migrants off from significant public services in wealthy welfare states Most recently, attention has returned to the border line itself where significant new architecture has been constructed around the world in order to reinforce control at substantial expense.

These changes have been most pronounced at the world's 'frontiers of poverty' where international borders mark massive levels of inequality, but they are not restricted solely to wealthy states. A decade ago there was already widespread agreement that increasing barriers to migration is bad for development (UNDP 2009), yet since then barriers, often in the form of physical infrastructure at borders themselves, as we have seen, have only increased. The final connection between borders and migration and development highlighted in this chapter is the use of development and humanitarian funding to reinforce border controls. This undermines the development impact of migration and increases the risks faced by migrants.

Note

1 Most notable is a cooperation agreement signed between Germany and Egypt in July 2016 which 'solidifies cooperation in preventing all types of crimes, including terrorism and corruption, as well reinforcing airport security and stemming illegal immigration. The agreement includes also the exchange of information, technical training and expertise between Egypt and Germany' (JJVAP 2017, 10).

References

Amoore, L. (2006) "Biometric borders: Governing mobilities in the war on terror" *Political Geography*, *25*(3), 336–351.

Andersson, R. (2014) *Illegality Inc. Clandestine Migration and the Business of Bordering Europe*. University of California Press, Berkeley.

Bialasiewicz, L. (2012) "Off-shoring and out-sourcing the borders of Europe: Libya and EU border work in the Mediterranean" *Geopolitics*, *17*(4), 843–866.

Carling, J., and Hernández-Carretero, M. (2011) "Protecting Europe and protecting migrants? Strategies for managing unauthorised migration from Africa" *The British Journal of Politics and International Relations, 13*(1), 42–58.

Castles, S., De Haas, H., and Miller, M.J. (2013) *The Age of Migration: International Population Movements in the Modern World.* Palgrave Macmillan, Basingstoke.

Clemens, M.A. (2014) "Does development reduce migration?" in Lucas, R.E. (ed.) *International Handbook on Migration and Economic development*, Edward Elgar, London, 152–185.

Collyer, M. (2019) "From Preventive to Repressive: the changing use of development and humanitarianism to control migration" in Mitchell, K., Jones, R., and Fluri, J. (eds.) *Handbook on Critical Geographies of Migration*, Edward Elgar, London, 170–181.

Collyer, M., and de Haas, H. (2012) "Developing dynamic categorisations of transit migration" *Population, Space and Place, 18*(4), 468–481.

Crawley, H., and Duvell, F. (2017) *Unravelling Europe's 'Migration Crisis': Journeys over Land and Sea.* Policy Press, Bristol.

Cuttitta, P. (2018) "Repoliticization through search and rescue? Humanitarian NGOs and migration management in the Central Mediterranean" *Geopolitics, 23*(3), 1–29.

Davies, T., Isakjee, A., and Dhesi, S. (2017) "Violent inaction: The necropolitical experience of refugees in Europe" *Antipode, 49*(5), 1263–1284.

Foucault, M. (2007) *Security, Territory, Population. Lectures at the College de France 1977–1978.* Palgrave, Basingstoke.

Graziano, M. (2018) *What is a Border?* Stanford University Press, Stanford.

Joint Valletta Action Plan (JVAP). (2017) "Mapping of responses to Joint Valletta Action Plan" Table 2. Policies and Legislation.

Jones, R., Johnson, C., Brown, W., Popescu, G., Pallister-Wilkins, P., Mountz, A., and Gilbert, E. (2017) "Interventions on the state of sovereignty at the border" *Political Geography, 59*, 1–10.

Jones, R. (2012) *Border Walls: Security and the War on Terror in the United States, India, and Israel.* Zed Books Ltd.

Knoll, A., and Sherriff, A. (2017) *Making Waves: Implications of the Irregular Migration and Refugee Situation on Official Development Assistance Spending and Practices in Europe.* European Centre for Development Policy Management, Maastricht. http://ecdpm.org/wp-content/uploads/ECDPM-EBA-Making-Waves-Migration-Refugee-ODA-Europe-2017.pdf (accessed 21.3.2018).

Lavenex, S., and Schimmelfennig, F. (2009) "EU rules beyond EU borders: Theorizing external governance in European politics" *Journal of European Public Policy, 16*(6), 791–812.

López-Sala, A. (2015) "Exploring dissuasion as a (geo)political instrument in irregular migration control at the Southern Spanish maritime border" *Geopolitics, 20*(3), 513–534.

Lyon, D. (2006) "The border is everywhere: ID cards, surveillance and the other" in Zuriek, E., and Salter, M. (eds.) *Global Surveillance and Policing: Borders, Security, Identity.* Willan Publishing, Cullompton, 66–82.

Migration DRC. (2009) Making Migration Work for Development, available at http://www.sussex.ac.uk/Units/SCMR/drc/publications/misc/Making_Migration_Work_for_Development.pdf (accessed 5.10.2009).

Moreno-Lax, V. (2018) "The EU humanitarian border and the securitization of human rights: The 'rescue-through-interdiction/rescue-without-protection' paradigm" *JCMS: Journal of Common Market Studies, 56*(1), 119–140.

Neumayer, E. (2006) "Unequal access to foreign spaces: How states use visa restrictions to regulate mobility in a globalized world" *Transactions of the Institute of British Geographers, 31*(1), 72–84.

Pallister-Wilkins, P. (2017) "Humanitarian rescue/sovereign capture and the policing of possible responses to violent borders" *Global Policy, 8*(S1), 19–24.

Parker, B. (2017) "Aid credibility at stake as donors haggle over reporting rules" IRIN July 21st 2017, available at www.irinnews.org/investigations/2017/07/21/aid-credibility-stake-donors-haggle-over-reporting-rules (accessed 21.3.2018).

Patel, P. (2016) "My fury at our wasted foreign aid" *Daily Mail* September 13th 2016, available at www.dailymail.co.uk/news/article-3788162/My-fury-wasted-foreign-aid-International-development-secretary-Priti-Patel-pledges-major-overhaul-12billion-budget.html#ixzz4oXqeqZbc (accessed 21.3.2018).

Sigona, N. (2017) "NGOs under attack for saving too many lives in the Mediterranean" The Conversation, March 29th, available at http://theconversation.com/ngos-under-attack-for-saving-too-many-lives-in-the-mediterranean-75086 (accessed 21.3.2018).

Skeldon, R. (1997) *Migration and Development: A Global Perspective*. Routledge, London.

Sparke, M.B. (2006) "A neoliberal nexus: Economy, security and the biopolitics of citizenship on the border" *Political geography*, *25*(2), 151–180.

Sutherland, P. (2013) "Migration is development: How migration matters to the post-2015 debate" *Migration and Development*, *2*(2), 151–156.

UNDP. (2009) *Human Development Report 2009. Overcoming Barriers: Human Mobility and Development UNDP-HDRO Human Development Reports*. UNDP, New York.

United Nations Development Programme (UNDP). (2009) *Human Development Report 2009. Overcoming Barriers: Human Mobility and Development*. UNDP, New York.

United Nations Development Programme (UNDP). (2017) *Human Development Report 2016: Human Development for Everyone*. UNDP, New York.

Vega, L.A.A. (2017) *Policy Adrift: Mexico's Southern Border Programme*. James A. Baker III Institute for Public Policy, Rice University, Houston, TX.

Vukov, T., and Sheller, M. (2013) "Border work: Surveillant assemblages, virtual fences, and tactical counter-media" *Social Semiotics*, *23*(2), 225–241.

Walters, W. (2011) "Foucault and frontiers: Notes on the birth of the humanitarian border" in Bröckling, U., Krasmann, S., and Lemke, T. (eds.) *Governmentality: Current Issues and Future Challenges*, Routledge, London, 138–164.

Zolberg, A.R. (2003) "The Archaeology of 'Remote Control'" in Fahrmeier, A. Oliver Faron, O., and Weil, P. (eds.) *Migration Control in the North Atlantic World: The Evolution of State Practices in Europe and the United States from the French Revolution to the Inter-War Period*, Berghahn Books, New York, 195–221.

6

UNDOCUMENTED MIGRATION AND DEVELOPMENT

Oliver Bakewell

Introduction

This chapter focuses on migration that is undertaken without the identity papers and permissions required by states to allow migrants to move between jurisdictions and settle in new places. It is one of the forms of irregular movement that are at the centre of contemporary concern for many states, which feel they are losing control of their borders or likely to be overwhelmed by the influx of people moving to settle on their territory. The growing literature on irregular and undocumented migration examines its scale, its impacts, and the policies adopted in response to it. While this chapter points to some of this literature, it sets out to challenge its underlying premise that casts undocumented migration as a problem which demands a solution. Instead, it suggests that in some of the poorest regions of the world, where daily life is largely undocumented for much of the population, attempts to document all international migration may introduce costs with little benefit. In short, development may be better served by leaving people to continue to move freely regardless of the paperwork. This argument is illustrated through two African case studies.

Defining undocumented migration

The term 'undocumented migration' has emerged in the last 20 years as one alternative to 'illegal migration' and its association with the idea of the 'illegal migrant'. As many academics and campaigners have noted, it is both inaccurate and dangerous to describe someone as an 'illegal migrant' as it suggests that their very person lies outside the law – it is the individual that is cast as illegal rather than their actions – and renders them vulnerable to multiple abuses (De Genova 2002; Gambino 2015; NOII 2003; Squire 2011, 4). Instead, those who move and settle across administrative boundaries without following the process laid out by the authorities are often described by a number of alternative terms. The most common are 'undocumented' and 'irregular' but some prefer 'unauthorised', 'clandestine', or 'non-status' migration. This shift in terminology has been widely adopted, including by many state actors, although there continues to be much debate about how far such terms can capture the huge array of different ways in which people move and the legal statuses that they acquire as they do so (Bloch and McKay 2016; van der Leun and Ilies 2012; Vogel and Jandl 2009).

These debates about nomenclature exacerbate the challenge of assessing the scale of these movements. There is consensus neither on the definition of irregular migration (or any of its variants) nor on the best methodology for counting how many people are involved. As a result, there is a huge variation in estimates put forward for the numbers of irregular migrants, even in the wealthiest countries where there are well-developed mechanisms for surveillance and identifying those staying illegally. For example, in the early 2000s, the European Commission suggested estimates for the numbers of irregular migrants ranged between 4.5 and 8 million (Vogel and Jandl 2009). In South Africa, the Home Affairs Minister in 2009 stated clearly she did not know how many irregular migrants were staying in the country: estimates ranged from 3 to 6 million (Mail and Guardian, 2009 cited in Mthembu-Salter et al. 2014). The International Organization for Migration (IOM) has created a website to collate migration data, which includes a section on irregular migration. When it comes to the rest of Africa (outside South Africa) and most of Asia, there are no serious attempts to provide estimates of the numbers involved. It is perhaps telling that its comments on irregular migration in Africa highlight the scale of intra-African migration, suggesting that from IOM's perspective most cross-border movement in the continent is irregular.[1]

In much of the literature, the terms irregular and undocumented migration are used interchangeably and refer both to people's movement and their ongoing legal status in the destination. In this chapter, I want to focus on the manner in which people cross borders and with this in mind I make a distinction between undocumented and irregular migration. When it comes to international borders, being undocumented refers to lacking the 'right' papers – usually a passport or identity card, often with an associated visa; this means any crossing of the border will be irregular. However, crossing the border with the full documentation that allows entry to a country, but then breaking the terms of that entry, may also make the migration irregular. In what follows, I refer to the former case, where one lacks documentation, as undocumented migration and consider it as is a subset of irregular migration; some irregular migration (such as overstaying visas) is fully documented.

This approach reflects this chapter's concern with the relationship between undocumented migration and development. Many studies have examined the situation of undocumented or irregular migrants moving to wealthy regions of the world (for example, see Andersson 2016; Bloch and Chimienti 2011). These studies show that, despite the headlines about illegal border crossings and desperate journeys across desert and sea, the majority of those who stay without any legal authorisation are those whose journey is undertaken wholly legitimately (Jandl 2009, 57). Their irregularity arises as a result of their overstaying visas, breaking conditions of entry (such as working when they are admitted as students), or other actions that contravene immigration regulations.

When it comes to discussions of irregularity in developing countries, there is much more interest in the way people cross borders without papers and find ways to settle despite their lack of documentation (Pascucci 2016). In the context of some of the poorest countries, where even citizens may lack basic documents such as birth certificates or identity cards and few would ever secure a passport, irregular migration is much more likely to arise because migrants do not have papers when they move. In practice, as I will show in what follows, in some contexts it is almost impossible to migrate in full accordance with the law; this begs the question of whether this undocumented migration is necessarily a significant problem that demands a response.

The problem of undocumented migration

Whatever definition or method of measurement is adopted, there is almost universal agreement across academic literature, policymakers, and popular discourse that undocumented migration is a problematic form of movement that is associated with a range of harms. From the perspective of individual states, the untrammelled movement of people brings concerns about security, access to resources, and socio-economic and political equilibrium among populations. Communities affected by migration may share these concerns. From a more migrant-centred perspective – evident in the work of many civil society organisations and human rights advocates – the lack of documentation opens up space for rights violations as migrants are immediately placed outside the law and vulnerable to multiple abuses.

These different perspectives give rise to contrasting responses. States and many international organisations tend to focus on reducing the volume of undocumented migration by better control of the flow of people and reducing the demand for migration. This is seen very clearly in the current EU initiatives to tackle the 'root causes' of irregular migration (Carling and Talleraas 2016). Such policy approaches, while framed in terms of improving the conditions in which people migrate, readily elide into policies of migration control and reducing the numbers of people moving, which may more accurately reflect the underlying politics guiding the interests of states.

In contrast, human rights activists and those with a more permissive approach to migration are more likely to focus on improving people's access to fully documented movement: reducing the costs of passports and other documents; opening up the legal channels for migration with more visas and less restrictive entry requirements (Appleby and Kerwin 2018). In broad terms, their interest is in increasing the availability of documented migration rather than reducing demand for migration. Or it may be to ensure that the framework of human rights is extended to cover undocumented migrants regardless of their immigration status (Bloch 2010).

Another side to the debate focuses on documentation as a way to understand and analyse migration, rather than as a means of control. For all stakeholders, whether states, human rights activists, civil society, or businesses, if there is no documentation of migration, there will be no data. Having some idea of who is moving where and why is important to track changes in societies, to identify emerging trends and to plan. This is recognised with the Sustainable Development Goals, where capacity building for data collection and analysis is identified as a target for Goal 17: strengthen the means of implementation and revitalise the global partnership for sustainable development.[2] This call for better data is one which is routinely echoed by international organisations, including IOM, the United Nations Population Division, and the World Bank.[3]

Another take on documentation is to see it as a process of documenting people's lives and journeys, not to make them legible to state bureaucracies so much as to acknowledge their existence and understand their experiences; in particular, the suffering, violence, and death they face in crossing borders. This approach is seen in the work of the Undocumented Migration Project that studies movement across the border between Mexico and the United States.[4]

Linking undocumented migration and development

Whichever approach is taken, a consensus exists that undocumented migration is a problem which needs to be addressed. In this chapter, I want to offer a different perspective focusing on undocumented migration in some of the poorest parts of the world, making particular reference to two African cases studies. In the first, I focus on movements between north-western Zambia and eastern Angola, where I have followed people's changing relationship with the border for the last 20 years. The second is drawn from recent work in the Horn of Africa examining cross-border movements and livelihoods (EUTF-REF 2016b). These are very different settings but they share some characteristics as remote areas, far from the state capitals, with high levels of poverty and very limited livelihood opportunities. I suggest that in such contexts, the rationale for seeking to reduce undocumented migration is open to question. Development, in the sense of enhancing the quality of life of poor people, may be better served by leaving them to move, with or without the right papers.

In order to understand how far undocumented migration may be seen as a problem, I suggest four useful areas of enquiry that may shape our analysis. First, we should ask about the wider role and meaning of documentation for people's lives; to what extent does it matter to people? Next, we can examine how documents are actually used in border crossing. Another important consideration is how significant migration is for the lives and livelihoods of poor people. Finally, we need to consider the implications of trying to regulate movement, both in terms of the costs of enforcing regulation and the impacts on the local socio-economic conditions as the flow of people is constrained.

What is the role of documentation?

While the documentation of life is now widely accepted as a norm across the wealthier regions of the world, in many poorer countries, the reach of formal papers issued and recognised by states is still limited. Many millions of people live without any papers – whether birth certificates, identity cards, marriage certificates or any of the routine paperwork that accompanies the passage of life for others. As noted above, this lack of documentation can represent a huge problem for people, leaving them vulnerable to exclusion from services, exploitation and the denial of rights with no legal redress. However, if in practice, services are minimal and the exploitation and abuse of rights are institutionalised regardless of one's documented status, there may be little to be gained in holding the right papers. Indeed, if the process of trying to secure them raises one's visibility to state actors, this may create new problems.

In short, how formal documentation is perceived and used will vary with the social, political, historical, and cultural context and individuals' experiences. We should not assume that because identity cards are seen as very important in the highly industrialised states or capital cities that they necessarily have the same value in all settings. It is important to distinguish between their instrumental and their affective value. Where the right to hold papers has been the outcome of great struggles or is imbued with deep historical or emotional significance, what documents say about you is likely to matter. However, if it is simply seen as a question of satisfying a bureaucratic process, their significance may lie simply in what they can do for you, which, in the context of much of the developing world, seems very little.

For example, in north-western Zambia on the border with Angola, many Angolans came into Zambia in the 1980s as refugees fleeing the civil war in their country. They settled in villages alongside Zambian families, many of whom had moved from Angola in previous generations (see Figure 6.1). In this borderland, many people did not have any identity papers and in day to day life they had little need of them. While the law stated that the children of refugees remain refugees, in practice, children growing up in these borderland villages, whatever their origin, were recognised by the local senior chief as his people and issued with

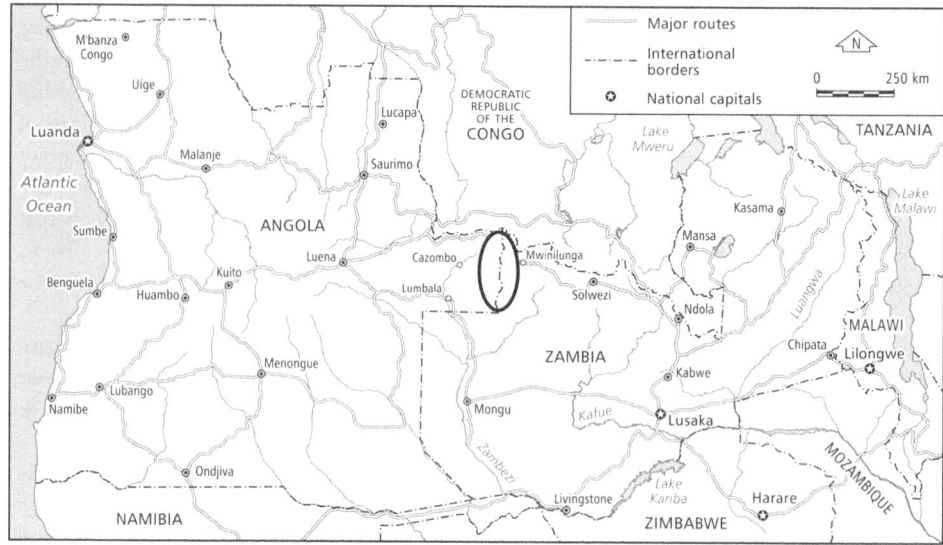

Figure 6.1   Map: north-western Zambia and Angola. Map by Cartographic Unit, University of Manchester

Zambian national identity papers as they reached adulthood. In this context, people's attitudes towards nationality and documentation varied enormously. For some, having documentary proof of citizenship was associated with their identity; it had some intrinsic value. For others, formal papers were primarily of instrumental value rather than reflecting their identity in any profound sense (Bakewell 2007).

Documentation therefore has different meanings for different people. This opens up a much wider debate about documentation, citizenship, and identity, which lies beyond the scope of this chapter. Insisting on documented migration in contexts where there are these much larger questions about the role of papers in governing the interaction of people and the state is putting the cart before the horse. It only starts to make sense when this broader issue of identification has been addressed. This is not primarily a migration problem and focusing on undocumented migration as the main challenges is perhaps missing the point.

How is documentation used in border crossing?

A second area of concern is how documentation is actually used in crossing borders. This varies enormously around the world. In much of Europe, the Schengen Area is hailed for its removal of all border controls enabling freedom of movement across 26 European states. Of course, the Schengen Area is underpinned by detailed international conventions, strong mechanisms for surveillance within states – including control of entry into labour markets – and ever-increasing restrictions on the area's external borders. In as far as these are effective, it only facilitates undocumented migration within Europe. By contrast, the lack of border formalities across many of the borders in Africa is widely seen in a much more negative light.

In many cases, there is simply no border infrastructure. For those moving between north-western Zambia and Angola, there are many tracks referred to locally as 'private roads' that move across the international border far from any formal crossing point. Those who cross by these ways come to agreements with local authorities about their presences in the country. During the time of the civil war, this meant negotiating with the rebel movement controlling the territory rather than the internationally recognised government in Luanda. The border was acknowledged and a set of local conventions about how to cross were established involving village headmen and chiefs as interlocutors for the state. This was not documented migration and did not comply with the law in books, but it could be seen as regular and in many senses regulated (Bakewell 2015).

Similarly, for thousands of labour migrants seeking to move from Ethiopia into Sudan, local conventions have emerged that facilitate border crossing in the absence of the correct papers. Like many other border areas (Walther 2014), there are weekly cross-border markets where buyers and sellers from both sides can move back and forth relatively freely – these have been allowed by both the Ethiopian and Sudanese governments since 2002. On these days, Ethiopians can easily go into Sudan by simply depositing their identity papers at the border crossing with the expectation that they will pick them up again on their return later in the day. However, many do not return but move deeper into Sudan in search of agricultural work. When they return to Ethiopia at the end of the agricultural season, most present themselves to the authorities who let them pass once they have verified their identity. Hence, their irregular outward migration is often coupled with a semi-regular (or at least regulated) return. While it is a well-established system that facilitates people's movement and enables them to pursue their livelihood, it pays little respect to the formal requirements of documented migration (EUTF-REF 2016a).

What is the value of movement for people's lives and livelihoods?

Considerable evidence exists to show that those with more capital in terms of income, higher levels of education, and stronger networks are more likely to migrate (Massey et al. 1998). It takes resources to bear both the actual cost of relocation and the risk entailed in the venture. Nonetheless, even in the poorest parts of the world, migration can play a critical role in many people's livelihood strategies. This is seen most clearly in the practice of pastoralism, which is prevalent across many parts of the Horn of Africa. In these arid and semi-arid zones, people have to move with their animals in search of water and pasture through the year. Often the livestock grazing areas used by pastoralists transect the international border; they have to be able to cross back and forth to sustain their herds. . Their livestock markets also operate across borders. For the most part, these movements associated with pastoralism remain undocumented as herders move across remote unmarked borders.

Labour migration to neighbouring countries is another an important way of securing an income for some very poor populations, such as the Ethiopians looking for seasonal work on the commercial farms of eastern Sudan (mentioned in the previous section). The wages from this seasonal labour migration plays a critical role in people's livelihoods helping them to diversify the risk of pastoralism and rain-fed agriculture (EUTF-REF 2016b). Such systems often operate largely informally with varying levels of documentation. For example, hundreds of thousands of Cambodians work in Thailand in a range of industries, including agriculture, textiles, construction, and services. The local economies of some communities in Cambodia are dependent on their remittances: Bylander (2017) found that three-quarters of households interviewed in one commune in Cambodia reported that remittances sent from Thailand were the largest component of their income. Most of this migration is undocumented although there have been various attempts to register workers and provide them with time-limited work permits, even when they do not have the papers (such as a Cambodian passport) required for securing full legal status.

A different dynamic is at play for migration across the Zambia–Angola border. Here, three important factors have shaped movement: the conflict in Angola from 1961–2002, which forced many people to flee into Zambia; the relative abundance of natural resources in Angola, which has drawn people back into the country; and the opportunities for trade. These intersect with the very long-standing social and (local) political links derived from the shared ethnicity, chieftainships divided by colonial borders, and kinship. This ability to live flexibly across the border, often with a foot in both sides, has been widely used by local people to strengthen their livelihoods in the changing circumstances regardless of any requirements for documentation (Bakewell 2015, 2007).

Weighing up the cost of documentation and disruption of mobility

These examples show that undocumented migration can play an important role in the lives of poor people. I make no claim that it is the undocumented nature of the migration that makes it valuable. At the same time, it is not obvious that the lack of documentation necessarily represents a problem that requires a solution. From the perspective of poor people, the absence of statutory recognition and the flexibility of informality may enable them better to find a place in the interstices between different regimes. This allows them to get on with their lives without putting precious resources into jumping through any bureaucratic hoops.

However, remaining undocumented can leave migrants exposed to sudden reversals should states seek to enforce immigration law. This was seen vividly in Thailand in 2014, when the military coup brought a crackdown on immigration, which triggered the mass exodus of hundreds of thousands of undocumented (or partially documented) Cambodian migrant workers. This mass movement was seen as a crisis both for Cambodia that had to deal with the return of thousands of people and the loss of remittances, and also for Thailand that lost a huge labour force almost overnight. It rapidly gave rise to some resolution that aimed to make documentation cheaper (a 4-dollar passport) and enable people to move through regular channels. However, in practice, little has changed and undocumented migration remains the norm. Relatively few of the new, low-price documents have been issued and people find it easier and cheaper to go without, using the pathways they have established over many years (Bylander 2017). In short, such a 'migration disruption' (as Bylander put it) came at a cost to both the country and the people. It is important to ask if it generated a commensurate benefit and for whom.

On the Angola–Zambia border, the end of the war in Angola in 2002 resulted in the extension of state control and the establishment of new border posts and a border force to police it. This has also created some disruption of the cross-border mobility of local people. However, unlike Cambodians in Thailand, whose lack of documents leaves them very exposed to exploitation, the undocumented Angolans in the border villages are now so well-established that have become indistinguishable from Zambians. Their route to settlement has been irregular (in terms of law) but any attempt to regularise it is likely to yield few results. Those who have become 'Zambian' would see little benefit in volunteering for a bureaucratic procedure orchestrated by the state to confirm it, when it is already accepted by the local traditional authorities in the form of the senior chief and many have national identity cards to prove it (Bakewell 2015).

In such contexts, securing documentation may be largely irrelevant for the daily lives of many people whose interaction with the state is limited. In many parts of the developing world, where the borders are extensive, poorly demarcated, and with very few formal border posts, following the letter of the law on crossing is effectively impossible for local people. Either the costs involved in securing papers is prohibitive or there are no effective administrative systems in place to provide them. Even if one has the right papers, documenting one's border crossing requires some form of border infrastructure where these documents can be checked and the movement recorded. Taking a route that passes by the nearest formal crossing point may create a huge overhead in terms of travel time and costs. In the face of weak systems and poor implementation of border management, attempts to stem irregular migration may simply put up barriers to movement and open up room for corruption as people cut their way through the system with cash.

Regular undocumented migrations

In offering these examples, I am not suggesting that they provide a model for international migration. It is true that moving between countries without documentation often leaves migrants and wider society exposed to multiple threats; in particular, the risk of exploitation, abuse of right, violence, and death. It can also represent a major threat to the security of states. My contention is that the extent to which these are significant concerns for different actors depends on the setting. In particular, if we are concerned about the relationship between undocumented migration and development, it is important to ask about the implications of any attempts to regularise or enforce documented migration for the lives of those likely to be most affected.

This calls into question the idea that ensuring all migration is documented is necessarily a worthwhile aim in itself. One of the main problems with the term 'undocumented migration' is that it inflates the significance of documentation. It is redolent with the interests of states. However, it is legitimate to ask if states need to know about everyone who is crossing their borders. Is undocumented movement necessarily a major concern, in and of itself? Focusing on documentation tends to make the *movement* into the problem and distract attention from other fundamental changes that might make a much more substantial difference to the lives of poor people.

As I have shown with the above examples, national authorities or local officials and migrants may reach some form of accommodation that makes it possible to turn a blind eye to the lack of documentation while enabling migration to continue. For some, the process of documentation such as the one that I outline for Angolans moving to Zambia is an illustration of the dangers of 'illegal migration' in the developing world. It enables people to acquire 'documentary citizenship' by fraudulent means, allowing anyone to blend in as citizens without any proper checks. This opens up a gateway for malefactors to infiltrate the state, gain fully legal documentation of citizenship with which they can then cross the world (Sadiq 2009). Without denying that these dangers may be prominent in some parts of the world – illustrated by Sadiq's case studies that include Afghans moving into Pakistan – they seem to have little relevance to others.

These arguments resonate strongly in the Horn of Africa, where irregular migration, smuggling, and trafficking generate huge concern. Across the region, migration is widely associated with insecurity, criminality, and the gross exploitation of people on the move. These are certainly major challenges. However, attempts to regulate migration more intensely are having mixed results, with many suggesting that one of its major impacts is to expand the migration industry, one branch of which is dedicated to providing documentation, monitoring its use, and punishing infractions (Andersson 2016; Dini 2018; Gammeltoft-Hansen and Sørensen 2013; Schapendonk 2018).

For those who call into question the right of states to control migration across international borders, whether advocating for open borders or no borders, the arguments of this chapter will be largely irrelevant (Anderson et al. 2009; Bauder 2015). If borders are open, the bureaucracy underpinning border control, including documentation becomes redundant; undocumented migration becomes meaningless. To some extent, we may see some echoes of this openness in the remote African borderlands that I have discussed in this chapter. However, given the political and economic weight of the migration industry that is clamouring for state oversight of people's migration in the poorest regions of the world, there is huge pressure to close down the space for undocumented movement. I am not making an argument from an open border perspective, but there is common ground as I call into question states' efforts to stop undocumented migration.

I have argued that in some of the poorest parts of the world, migration plays a critical role in securing people's lives and livelihoods. I have shown that while this may be not be documented, it may be both regular – in the sense of routine and unexceptional – and regulated by institutional mechanisms other than the state. Inhibiting this regular undocumented migration may act against development by disrupting valuable economic exchanges, reducing people's opportunities and increasing their costs. The assumption that documentation and regularity (in the sense of regulated and endorsed by states) of migration is a good in itself and is an intrinsic part of development (as suggested by its inclusion in the Sustainable Development Goals 10.7) needs to be held up to scrutiny. The case needs to be argued depending on the context. In many parts of the developing world, perhaps (regular) undocumented migration has equal, if not greater, scope to contribute to positive social development.

Notes

1 https://migrationdataportal.org/themes/irregular-migration
2 https://sustainabledevelopment.un.org/sdg17
3 https://migrationdataportal.org/themes/sustainable-development-goals-sdgs#the-need-for-better-migration-data
4 http://undocumentedmigrationproject.com/

References

Anderson, B., Sharma, N. and Wright, C. (2009) 'Editorial: Why no borders?', *Refuge: Canada's Periodical on Refugees*, 26(2), pp. 5–18.

Andersson, R. (2016) 'Europe's failed 'fight' against irregular migration: Ethnographic notes on a counterproductive industry', *Journal of Ethnic and Migration Studies*, 42(7), pp. 1055–1075.

Appleby, J. K. and Kerwin, D. (eds.) (2018) *2018 International Migration Policy Report: Perspectives on the Content and Implementation of the Global Compact for Safe, Orderly, and Regular Migration.* New York: Scalabrini Migration Study Centers.

Bakewell, O. (2007) *The Meaning and Use of Identity Papers: Handheld and Heartfelt Nationality in the Borderlands of North-West Zambia*, Oxford: International Migration Institute. Available at: www.imi-n.org/publications/wp-05-07.

Bakewell, O. (2015) 'Moving from war to peace in the Zambia-Angola Borderlands', in Vigneswaran, D. and Quirk, J. (eds.) *Mobility Makes States.* Philadelphia: University of Pennsylvania Press, pp. 194–217.

Bauder, H. (2015) 'Perspectives of open borders and no border', *Geography Compass*, 9(7), pp. 395–405.

Bloch, A. (2010) 'The right to rights?: Undocumented migrants from Zimbabwe living in South Africa', *Sociology*, 44(2), pp. 233–250.

Bloch, A. and Chimienti, M. (2011) 'Irregular migration in a globalizing world', *Ethnic and Racial Studies*, 34(8), pp. 1271–1285.

Bloch, A. and McKay, S. (2016) *Living on the Margins: Undocumented Migrants in a Global City*. Bristol: Policy Press.

Bylander, M. (2017) 'Migration disruption: Crisis and continuity in the Cambodian mass returns', *International Migration Review*, Advance online access.

Carling, J. and Talleraas, C. (2016) *Root Causes and Drivers of Migration: Implications for Humanitarian Efforts and Development Cooperation*. Oslo: Peace Research Institute Oslo. Available at: www.prio.org/Publications/Publication/?x=9229.

De Genova, N. P. (2002) 'Migrant "ILLEGALITY" and deportability in everyday life', *Annual Review of Anthropology*, 31(1), pp. 419–447.

Dini, S. (2018) 'Migration management, capacity building and the sovereignty of an African State: international organization for migration in Djibouti', *Journal of Ethnic and Migration Studies*, 44(10), pp. 1691–1705.

EUTF-REF. (2016a) *Cross-Border Analysis and Mapping – Cluster 3: Western Ethiopia-East Sudan*. London: Research and Evidence Facility of EU Trust Fund for Africa in Horn of Africa, School of Oriental and African Studies.

EUTF-REF. (2016b) *Cross-Border Analysis and Mapping: Final Report*. London: Research and Evidence Facility of EU Trust Fund for Africa in Horn of Africa, School of Oriental and African Studies.

Gambino, L. (2015) *'No Human Being is Illegal': Linguists Argue Against Mislabeling of Immigrants. The Guardian*. London: The Guardian. Available at: www.theguardian.com/us-news/2015/dec/06/illegal-immigrant-label-offensive-wrong-activists-say. (Accessed: 26/ 11/20182018).

Gammeltoft-Hansen, T. and Sørensen, N. N. (2013) 'Introduction', in Gammeltoft-Hansen, T. and Sørensen, N.N. (eds.) *The Migration Industry and the Commercialization of Iinternational Migration*. London: Routledge, pp. 1–23.

Jandl, M. (2009) 'Methods for estimating stocks and flows of irregular migrants', in Kraler, A. and Vogel, D. (eds.) *Report on Methodological Issues*. Clandestino Undocumented Migration: Counting the Uncountable. Data and Trends Across Europe, pp. 19–57. Available at: http://irregular-migration.net/typo3_upload/groups/31/4.Background_Information/4.1.Methodology/Methodological_Issues_Clandestino_Report__Nov09_2.pdf.

Massey, D. S., Arango, J., Hugo, G., Kouaouci, A., Pellegrino, A. and Taylor, J. E. (1998) *Worlds in Motion: Understanding International Migration at the End of the Millennium. International Studies in Demography*. Oxford: Clarendon Press.

Mthembu-Salter, G., Amit, R., Gould, C. and Landau, L. B. (2014) *Counting the Cost of Securitising South Africa's Immigration Regime*. Sussex: Migration out of Poverty, University of Sussex. Available at: http://migratingoutofpoverty.dfid.gov.uk/documents/wp20-mthembu-salter-et-al-2014-counting-the-cost.pdf.

NOII. (2003) *No One is Illegal Manifesto: No One is Illegal*. Available at: www.noii.org.uk/no-one-is-illegal-manifesto/. (Accessed: 26/11/20182018).

Pascucci, E. (2016) 'Transnational disruptions: Materialities and temporalities of transnational citizenship among Somali refugees in Cairo', *Global Networks*, 16(3), pp. 326–343.

Sadiq, K. (2009) *Paper Citizens: How Illegal Immigrants Acquire Citizenship in Developing Countries*. New York: Oxford University Press.

Schapendonk, J. (2018) 'Navigating the migration industry: Migrants moving through an African-European web of facilitation/control', *Journal of Ethnic and Migration Studies*, 4(4), pp. 663–679.

Squire, V. (2011) 'The contested politics of mobility: Politicizing mobility, mobilizing politics', in Squire, V. (ed.) *The Contested Politics of Mobility: Borderzones and Irregularity*, Vol. 87. London & New York: Routledge, pp. 1–26.

van der Leun, J. and Ilies, M. (2012) 'Undocumented migration: An explanatory framework', in Martiniello, M. and Rath, J. (eds.) *An Introduction to International Migration Studies: European Perspectives*. Amsterdam: Amsterdam University Press, pp. 305–326.

Vogel, D. and Jandl, M. (2009) 'Introduction to the methodological problem', in Kraler, A. and Vogel, D. (eds.) *Report on Methodological Issues*. Clandestino Undocumented Migration: Counting the Uncountable. Data and Trends Across Europe, pp. 5–11. Available at: http://irregular-migration.net/typo3_upload/groups/31/4.Background_Information/4.1.Methodology/Methodological_Issues_Clandestino_Report__Nov09_2.pdf.

Walther, O. (2014) 'Border markets: An introduction', *Articulo – Journal of Urban Research*, 10. Available at: http://articulo.revues.org/2532.

7

GEOGRAPHIES AND HISTORIES OF UNFREEDOM[1]

Uma Kothari

Introduction

This chapter contributes to debates on the continuities and divergences of different forms of labour migration over time and the degrees of unfreedom they manifest. It suggests that levels of (un)freedom can usefully be understood by analysing the various forms of control exercised over the movement of labour. More specifically, the chapter explores controls over labour mobility that simultaneously compel migration and enforce spatial confinement. It is argued here that the coerced or manipulated nature of the transnational movements of indentured and contract migrant labour combined with their subsequent immobility on plantations and in factory compounds shapes the degree of their unfreedom. Being compelled to move from one place to another, and then spatially confined in the place of work reflects an exercise of the power of labour that delimits a specific geography of unfreedom. Power is thus used to mobilise labour across space (Allen 2003) and exercised in place (De Certeau 1984), and as such unfreedom can be understood as a particular assemblage of spatial practices that simultaneously compel and confine movement. And, it is the particular configuration of these apparently oppositional spatial practices that shapes the form and extent of unfreedom. The chapter extends the historical trajectory of much previous work on unfreedom by exploring the connections between the colonial regime of indentured labour and the contemporary recruitment of contract labour migrants. The chapter draws on a case study of Mauritius that has always been constituted by movements of people from elsewhere, and in particular those of slaves and indentured labour, and thus provides a particularly instructive example of changing labour migrations over time and as a place thoroughly shaped by the mobility and confinement of labour. Specifically, the article examines issues of mobility and confinement that characterised the Indian indenture labour system on sugar plantations, and the more recent recruitment of Chinese labour migrant to the garment sector within the Export Processing Zone in Mauritius.

Understanding unfreedom

The extent to which different labour regimes, particularly those that followed the abolition of slavery, represent forms of servitude and unfreedom have been the subject of considerable debate (see Brass and van der Linden 1997). Scholars have traced either a unilinear transition from slavery to freedom as a natural process of human progression, or marked out a continuum where the dividing line between the free and unfree labour is blurred (Mishra 2009). Some have argued that continuities and divergences over time reflect a movement from unfree to progressively freer forms of labour often associated with the development of (post)industrial capitalism (see, for example, Lucassen 1997). However, while for Banaji (2003), for example, there is a relativity of freedom under capitalism, others posit that there is no automatic link between changes in capitalist production systems and a concomitant decline in unfreedoms (Brass 1999). For Brass, there is 'no necessarily unilinear transition from unfree to free production relations in the course of capitalist development' (Brass 1988, 188). Indeed, unfree labour remains an essential part of modern capitalism, although the particularities of the form of unfreedom may vary at different moments in time. Thus, labour remains unfree, yet 'there is a need to relate forced labour to differences within capitalist development' (Lerche 2007, 425) and changes in the wider socio-economic structure. Miles (1987; see also Cohen 1987) develops these ideas by exploring the specific historical context for different types of unfree labour, such as indenture and contract migrant labour.

These understandings of continuities, and divergences, from slavery to indentured labour have dominated much of the discourse on the relative freedom and unfreedom of labour. Most notably, Hugh Tinker argued that the indentured labour system was 'slavery by another name' (1974, 27) and that indenture merely replaced slavery after its abolition to fill the labour shortage (Harris 2010). That the expansion of the capitalist world economy in the nineteenth century necessitated huge demand for labour that could not be fulfilled by the locally available labour force in the regions of expansion is well documented. Similarly, the fact that this was made worse following the abolition of slavery is now widely accepted. Miles (1987) developed this notion of a labour gap by exploring the relationship between labour shortages, unfree labour, and capitalism suggesting that 'the concept of unfree labour refers to relations of production where labour power distributed, exploited and retained by politic-legal mechanisms and/or by physical compulsion' (Miles 1987, 175).

Mishra (2009), however, challenges these forms of representation. He argues that because the indentured labour system began 'over the debris of slavery', a perception of slavery as 'the closed model of reference for all forms of labour servitude' problematically underpins these debates. That is, that 'classic' slavery is invoked and used as a benchmark with which to compare other forms of labour and evaluate their relative freedom/unfreedom. As Allen writes:

> studies of the British colonial plantation world have tended to draw a sharp dividing line between the pre- and post-emancipation eras, emphasising either the character and dynamics of local slave regimes and the debates over the viability of 'free' versus chattel labour before 1834 or the nature and dynamics of the indentured experience after 1834.
>
> *(Allen 2008, 52)*

Northrup also warns that the 'progressive redefining of unfree and unfair labour practices makes it necessary to exercise extreme caution in categorising the labour systems of earlier historical eras' (2003, 129). Mishra instead shifts the debate from these 'institutional definitions to the decisive role of circumstantial necessities and perspectives culminating in multiple forms of labour servitude' (Mishra 2009, 229). Based on research on Indian indentured labour in Mauritius, he concludes that while the indenture labour regime was a form of servitude it was 'not essentially a new system of slavery' (Mishra 2009, 229). On a continuum from free to unfree, others, while not denying that indentured regimes reflect forms of servitude, claims that indentured labour have 'more in common with the experiences of "free" migrants of the same era than with the victims of the slave trade' (Northrup 1995, x) since 'Western imperial hegemony added new constraints, but with the end of slavery it also offered new opportunities' (Northrup 2003, 130).

Foundational to these differing perceptions of changing labour regimes over time is how concepts of freedom and unfreedom are defined and how the 'characteristics of working relations which makes a labourer free or unfree' (Mishra 2009, 234) are conceived. To trace the multiple meanings of 'freedom' and 'unfreedom' of labour, much useful discussion has focused on economic coercions such as debt-bondage, systems of recruitment and levels of exploitation (see Breman 2007). Others have invoked dichotomies of forced/voluntary and coercion/choice to explore levels of freedom/unfreedom, particularly in the context of labour mobility and migration. For example, Emmer (1986) suggests that due to the less compulsive and more voluntary processes of recruitment, indenture was a free labour system. This freedom of choice, combined with the economic freedom attained through wage payments and freedom from coercion through protective legislative regulations are for some the key ways in which indenture is distinct from, and free when compared with, slavery. Additionally, for some, the limited period of indenture represents another important difference from enslavement (Engerman 1983, 645).

Distinctions between coerced and voluntary movements that are subsequently mapped onto notions of unfree and free labour can homogenise highly complex and diverse processes. For Lerche (2007) dichotomies of free/unfree, forced/voluntary and coercion/choice are largely unhelpful as they conceal the 'fluidity of the actually occurring levels of unfreedom'. Furthermore, 'forms of labor often fall ambiguously in between in complex ways confounding and challenging these distinctions' (Khan 1996, 92; see also Lerche 2011). For example, when migration is interpreted as a largely voluntary activity, a means of escaping poverty in search of a better life, this supposed exercise of 'choice' conceals aspects of manipulation and compulsion. It is debatable whether moving as a consequence of extreme poverty can be seen as 'voluntary' when unequal social and economic relations may compel people to move. Thus, movement may be definitionally 'voluntary', and there may be a greater element of choice to enter into a contract of indenture, but in reality, the decision to move is made within a context where the individual or group is faced with no alternative since staying *in situ* is not a realistic option (Kothari 2003). Thus, indenture can be perceived as an escape from harsh social and economic circumstances and, as Northrup suggests:

> at times, the constraints of war, famine, epidemic, and social disadvantage were severe enough to drive people to leave their homes for work elsewhere or even into slavery or other forms of social bondage ... at its best, it offered them a chance for a better life.
>
> *(Northrup 2003, 130)*

Whether forms of bondage and servitude are preferable to living in extreme poverty raises important moral and philosophical questions that are, however, beyond the scope of this chapter. While studies have focused on the extent to which the labourer can choose where, how, and under what conditions they are able to migrate to work, it is also necessary to examine restrictions imposed on their further movement by employers. Importantly, as is shown below, 'choosing' to move, is not necessarily evidence of the free and equal nature of the labour relations into which migrants subsequently enter. Thus, the migration may be voluntary but the labour forced (Khan 1996).

This chapter attempts to move beyond some of these awkward dichotomies by examining how simultaneous processes of mobility and confinement characterise forms of unfreedom and the extent to which they are reproduced over time. Additionally, it extends the historical trajectory of much previous research by comparing past and contemporary labour regimes. The ways in which unfreedom can be understood through an analysis of how power is exercised to both compulsorily move and restrict the movement of labour and, the importance of considering historical and present-day forms of labour recruitment are discussed in more detail below.

Geographies and histories of unfreedom

While a substantial body of work on mobility and migration exists, together with an emerging literature on geographies of imprisonment, the relationship between the two remains neglected despite the fact that detention often necessitates prior movement to centres of confinement – as the transportation of slaves harrowingly testifies. As indicated, this article moves beyond dichotomies of free/unfree, voluntary/coerced, and choice/involution that bedevil much research on labour regimes, by considering how movements across transnational space coupled with immobility can illuminate the particularities of forms of unfreedom and identify distinctions and continuities of unfree labour over time. Thus, there are not only a variety of ways but also a variety of spaces in which people can be unfree. For example, those who are understood to have 'voluntarily chosen' to migrate to work on colonial plantations, in garment factories or as domestic servants have their mobility subsequently constrained, confined, and coerced in multiple ways. Similarly, asylum seekers and refugees are compelled to move, but following their movement may be restrained in detention centres.

The recruitment and conditions of work for indentured and contracted labour involve spatial processes that necessitate both *fixity* through confinement and *flows* through population movement (Martin and Mitchelson 2009). Indeed, these regimes are premised on the prior movement and subsequent detention of labour. Unfree migrant labour is sustained, then, through a 'dialectic of fixity and flow – a dynamic that produces confinement through mobility, and mobility through confinement'. This 'assemblage of spatial practices', 'constituted through social, political, cultural, and economic relationships', produces and sustains spatialities of control and power through various disciplinary tools and legal categorisations (Martin and Mitchelson 2009, 470–1). Under the indenture system, movement and confinement were intimately connected colonial practices. Imperial networks and colonial innovations in transportation, with maritime technology making possible an unprecedented movement of people, were combined with restrictions on mobilities that ensured the continuing supply of labour. Today, labour may be free to move for employment, but their subsequent movement beyond the factory or place of work is often severely constrained. So, for example, states may encourage the transnational movement of domestic workers, but they subsequently lose their freedom of mobility through passport confiscation and employer restrictions of where and how often they can leave their place of work. Migratory routes of labourers thus reveal geographies of confinement in which the 'detached geographies' caused by dislocation and social rupture of indentured and contract workers from their homelands (Sinha 2000), and from outside the plantation or factory, impacts upon their levels of freedom and access to rights and information (Hyndman and Mountz 2008). Furthermore, as O'Neill (2011, 37) writes, 'blocks on the exit of the worker are increasingly bound up with the very mobility of labour which removes it from legal and social protections against domination'.

Much previous research has focused primarily on continuities and divergences between slavery and indenture to understand the extent to which indentured labour represented 'a new system of slavery' (Tinker 1974). By extending this historical trajectory to explore the kinds of unfreedoms evident in the use and structure of Indian indentured labour and the extent to which they are being recast in the recruitment and experiences of contract migrant workers in the present, this article moves beyond this 'common historiographical framework' (Anderson 2009, 94). Research on the compulsory movement of people in the Indian Ocean region has tended to focus on slavery (see Campbell 2004; Jayasuriya and Pankhurst 2003) and indentured labour (see Tinker 1974; Torabully and Carter 2002). Until recently, with few exceptions, there has been limited scholarship that discusses how these historical forms of unfreedom have continued into the present, and in particular the extent to which contemporary labour migrations within new global divisions of labour represent forms of unfreedom akin to those of indenture and, by implication, slavery. Maurer, for example, demonstrates:

> many points of comparison between past and present forms of labour migration and that one finds elements of bondage in both of them, the red line therefore very thin indeed between indentured labour of the colonial period and present-day globalisation migrant workers recruitment and employment practices.
>
> *(Maurer 2010, 866)*

Despite differences, particularly in terms of the temporality of their unfreedom and their historical and political contexts, there are similar elements of exploitation and compulsion between labour regimes that took place in the context of global capitalist investment in the nineteenth century and contemporary accelerated globalisation (Maurer 2010). Parallels between indentured labour and contemporary contract workers include deception in recruitment and debt-bondage. Additionally, there are similarities in terms of state collusion with employers, migrants' ignorance about destinations and nature of work, duration of servitude and lack of agency.

This chapter examines geographies of unfreedom by highlighting how mobility and confinement work simultaneously to control labour. While there is a rise in mobility-based discourses (Sheller and Urry 2006) and an emerging literature on geographies of detention, the relationship between the two remains neglected. Although movement and confinement imply spatial contradictions, confinement is 'fundamentally reliant on *spatial tactics*, or the use of space to control people, objects, and their movement' (Martin and Mitchelson 2009, 459, italics added). By extending the historical trajectory of studies on unfree labour to the present day, the chapter also contributes to histories of unfreedom, identifying the historical legacy of contemporary labour regimes. These comparisons over time and across space are evident in studies of migration and diasporas (see Yeoh 2003) and those of transnational encounters in colonial and postcolonial contexts (Stoler 2001, 2006). How mobility, movement, displacement, and confinement change over time are key to understanding different forms of labour and their unfreedom, since spatial control is a fundamental means of exercising power. A study of those who move to become immobile further challenges dichotomous and generalised understandings whereby unfreedom connotes restrictions on movement, while freedom implies the ability to move. The free/unfree dichotomy mapped onto a mobility/immobility dualism is thus challenged and complicated by the experiences of indentured labour and contract workers. The case study of Mauritius provides a particularly instructive example of changing labour migrations over time and as a place thoroughly shaped by the mobility and confinement of labour.

Migrant labour in Mauritius

Prior to independence in 1968, the Indian Ocean island of Mauritius was primarily a monocrop economy that depended almost exclusively on sugar exports to Europe, the production of which had begun in the early 1700s. The development of the Mauritian economy and its reliance on sugar production has, however, not been unproblematic. By the late 1950s, for example, rising population growth coupled with the stagnating of the sugar sector produced an unemployment rate of 20 per cent and increasing levels of poverty. In 1960, the development of a manufacturing sector was initiated to break the cycle of poverty and social unrest perpetuated by the over-reliance on sugar exports. Following independence, the island was established as an Export Processing Zone (EPZ), which drove an impressive economic transition. In 1988, the EPZ outstripped the sugar sector, and by 2000 the EPZ, dominated by clothing manufacturing, employed 13 per cent of the population and provided 25 per cent of gross domestic product (GDP) (Gibbon 2000, 3). Together, the recovery of the sugar industry, the establishment of a garment manufacturing sector and the rise in luxury tourism has led to high growth rates, and by the 1990s Mauritius was well established as a middle-income country (Kothari and Wilkinson 2010).

Having no indigenous population, Mauritius has always been constituted by flows of people and inhabited by a diverse population including, for example, colonial administrators, sugar plantation owners, African slaves, Indian indentured labourers, and Chinese traders and workers (Edensor and Kothari 2006). As such, it relied for much of its history on successive waves of labour migration. Two key pillars of the Mauritian economy depended heavily on the movement of labour: indentured labourers who came to work on the sugar plantations established in the early eighteenth century; and Chinese migrant labourers who began to arrive in Mauritius in the 1980s to work in the expanding garment sector.

Sugar production since the early eighteenth century relied initially on slaves from Madagascar and elsewhere, and, following the abolition of slavery, on Indian indentured labour. Mauritius was among the first colonies to recruit indentured labourers and unlike other colonies 'the search for additional sources of labour for sugar plantations had begun well before the abolition of slavery' (Allen 2008, 154) as the 'pre-existent slave labour supply had already proved to be inadequate to meet the massive demand for labourers required by the labour-intensive sugar plantation' (Mishra 2009, 231). Additionally, by 1810, the colonial government had already begun to make use of Indian convict labour (Allen 2008).

Abolition of slavery in the British Empire in 1834 and the ensuing shortages of labour were felt more keenly in colonies like Mauritius, where the expansion of sugar plantations had already begun. With their economic fortunes adversely affected by the end of slavery and a depressed sugar industry market, sugar planters put severe pressure on the British government. Subsequently, more than 451,000 Indian indentured labourers were brought to Mauritius from 1834 until government-sanctioned immigration ended in 1910. Those who left India were, at least initially, poor peasants in search of a better life away from the famines that periodically plagued the country. They were first brought in on 5-year contracts, during which time they were not entitled to change employer nor place of work. Employers bore the costs of recruitment, labourers' passage from India and paid a fixed wage. Once their contracts were over, they were entitled to return to India, with their crossing again paid by the employer. However, the majority remained in Mauritius, and it is of 'historical and political relevance that they and their descendants by the end of the nineteenth century already constituted two-thirds of the island's population' (Allen 1999, 17).

In the mid-1980s, less than 80 years after the end of the indentured labour system, the problem of labour scarcity in Mauritius, a newly industrialised country supplying garments for European markets, was again addressed by the importation of contract workers from low-wage economies (Lincoln 2009). This contemporary contractual labour migration to Mauritius was, as Lincoln writes, 'fore-shadowed by the indentured labour system' (2009, 138). Although acknowledging differences, Lincoln draws parallels between the nineteenth century and current contractual labour migrations, highlighting the sourcing of labour over-seas to compensate for the withdrawal of workers in low-wage sectors (2009, 139). The context for this in the 1980s was the expansion and success of the clothing sector that led to full employment, and subsequently some firms, particularly those from Hong Kong, began to import Chinese migrant workers (Kothari and Nababsing 1996).

In 1970, the government of Mauritius established the EPZ to attract foreign investors. This was a successful strategy, and employment in EPZ enterprises increased from 644 in 1971 to 10,267 in 1975, of which 82 per cent were women primarily involved in the textile and garment factories. Mauritius enjoyed unprecedented high growth rates, and the EPZ sector contributed 13.5 per cent to the GDP in 1988 and employment increased to 90,000. However, from the mid-1980s, in the face of acute labour shortage, the government agreed to employers recruiting foreign workers. Many large and medium companies in the EPZ sector started importing labour and the Mauritian economy subsequently became heavily dependent on migrant labour, particularly within the textile sector. Although the import-ation of foreign workers was initiated as a short-term strategy, by 2000 there were over 30,000 migrant workers in Mauritius, of which more than 80 per cent were made up of those from India, Bangladesh, and China (IHRB 2011, 2).

During the country's period of full employment in the 1990s, the majority of foreign workers in the textile and clothing factories came from China, given that a large number of manufacturing units were Hong Kong-owned and had established networks in China. Most were offered 3-year contracts with free or subsidised accommodation and paid 100 dollars a month, plus 40 dollars food allowance, although many were able to earn more through overtime. While the primary reason given for the importation of labour was a scarcity of local labour, employers also perceived local labour as unprepared to accept the poor conditions of work in the EPZ and to perform overtime, and were frustrated by their apparently high levels of absenteeism and low productivity. Employers, therefore, have a distinct preference for imported labour, and because of their greater labour flexibility and higher productivity levels could maintain competitiveness on the world market (Kothari and Nababsing 1996).

The Mauritian economy has always relied on migrant workers, be they indentured labour from India under colonialism or Chinese garment workers in the contemporary period. How-ever, these forms of labour migration took place in different political and economic contexts that enabled and produced particular kinds of labour regimes. The political-economic impera-tives of colonialism and the plantation economy shaped the very nature of colonial labour regimes characterised here by the indentured labour system. Within the context of a modern nation-state, however, economic concerns were largely shaped by the need to develop a strong and stable post-independence economic environment and to address rising poverty and social unrest. Despite these differences that have implications for the analysis of labour regimes, tem-poral comparisons highlight points of congruence and similarities in systems of labour recruit-ment and control over time. As seen above, Mauritius has been thoroughly constituted as a migrant space, one with significant global and historical economic, social, cultural and political linkages (Crush and McDonald 2002, 14). Furthermore, colonial and postcolonial networks have shaped the constitution of the labour force such that the migrations of Indians and Chinese 'reflect much larger patterns of earlier local and external migrations' (Northrup 1995, 60).

Conclusion

As indicated above, it is neither necessary nor feasible to identify a clear-cut distinction between 'free' and 'unfree'. Attempts to do so have always problematically used slavery as a benchmark to measure all levels of unfreedom and invoked unhelpful dichotomies. Instead, spatial geographies of (im)mobility that characterise indenture and contemporary migrant labour can contribute to understandings of what constitutes unfree labour. Specifically, the extent to which mobility, in terms of the movements of labour, and confinement, with respect to constraints on the mobility of workers, shape a spatiality of power and produces geographies of unfreedom. When labour is coerced/manipulated into migrating and is subsequently constrained within the confines of the workplace, be it the plantation or the factory compound, labourers' unfreedoms are produced and sustained through particular configurations of mobility and confinement in and through different geographical spaces. Thus, the extent to which labour is free or unfree can, in part, be understood through an analysis of the extent to which they can choose whether, how, when and where to move. Furthermore, exploring forms of mobility and confinement can contribute to understanding continuities and divergences of different labour regimes over time, recognising that there is 'only a thin red line dividing indentured labour in the past from certain forms of contract labour migration today' (Maurer 2010, 877).

Note

1 This is a shorter version of a previously published article Kothari, U. (2013) "Geographies and histories of unfreedom: indentured labourers and contract workers in Mauritius" *Journal of Development Studies*, 49(8), 1042–57.

References

Allen J. (2003) *Lost geographies of power*. Blackwell, Oxford.

Allen R. B. (1999) *Slaves, freedmen, and indentured laborers in colonial Mauritius*. Cambridge University Press, Cambridge.

Allen R. B. (2008) "Capital, illegal slaves, indentured labourers and the creation of a sugar plantation economy in Mauritius, 1810–60" *The Journal of Imperial and Commonwealth History*, 362, 151–170.

Anderson C. (2009) "Convicts and coolies: Rethinking indentured labour in the nineteenth century" *Slavery and Abolition*, 301, 93–109.

Banaji J. (2003) "The fictions of free labour: Contract, coercion, and so-called unfree labour" *Historical Materialism*, 113, 69–95.

Brass T. (1988) "Slavery now: Unfree labour and modern capitalism" *Slavery and Abolition*, 9, 102–117.

Brass T. (1999) *Towards a comparative political economy of unfree labour: Case studies and debates*. Frank Cass, London.

Brass T. and Van Der Linden M. eds. (1997) *Free and unfree labour: The debate continues*. Peter Lang, New York.

Breman J. (2007) *Labour bondage in West India. From past to present*. Oxford University Press, New Delhi.

Campbell G. (2004) *The structure of slavery in Indian Ocean Africa and Asia*. Frank Cass, London.

Cohen R. (1987) *The new helots: Migrants in the international division of labour*. Gower, Aldershot.

Crush J. and McDonald D. A. eds. (2002) *Transnationalism and new African immigration to South Africa*. Canadian Association of African Studies, Toronto.

De Certeau M. (1984) *The practice of everyday life*. University of California Press, Berkeley.

Edensor T. and Kothari U. (2006) "Extending networks and mediating brands: Stallholder strategies in a Mauritian market" *Transactions of the Institute of British Geographers*, 313, 323–336.

Emmer C. (1986) "The meek Hindu: The recruitment of Indian indentured labourers for services overseas, 1870–1916" In Emmer C ed., *Colonialism and migration: Indentured labour before and after and slavery*. Martinus Nijhoff, Dordrecht, 187–207.

Engerman S. L. (1983) "Contract labour, sugar and technology in the nineteenth" *Journal of Economic History*, 433, 635–660.

Gibbon P. (2000) *Back to basics through delocalisation: The Mauritian garment industry at the end of the twentieth century*, CDR Working Paper 007, Centre for Development Research, Copenhagen.

Harris K. L. (2010) "Sugar and gold: Indentured Indian and Chinese labour in South Africa" *Journal of Social Science*, 251, 147–158.

Hyndman J. and Mountz A. (2008) "Another brick in the wall? Neo-refoulement and the externalisation of asylum in Australia and Europe" *Government & Opposition*, 432, 249–269.

Institute for Human Rights and Business IHRB. (2011) *Migrant labour in the apparel sector in Mauritius: Responsible recruitment, responsible employment Mauritius*, Business and Migration Roundtables for Collective Action–Meeting Report, Institute for Human Rights and Business, Port Louis.

Jayasuriya S. de S. and Pankhurst R. (2003) *The African diaspora in the Indian Ocean*. Africa World Press, New Jersey.

Khan A. (1996) "Untold stories of unfree labor: Asians in the Americas" *New West Indian Guide/Nieuwe West-Indische Gids*, 70, 91–99. Retrieved from www.kitlv-journals.nl.

Kothari U. (2003) "Staying put and staying poor?" *Journal of International Development*, 15, 645–657.

Kothari U. and Nababsing V. (1996) *Gender, adjustment and export processing zones in Mauritius, Bangladesh and Sri Lanka*. EOI, Mauritius.

Kothari U. and Wilkinson R. (2010) "Colonial imaginaries: Exiles, bases, beaches" *Third World Quarterly*, 318, 1395–1412.

Lerche J. (2007) "A global alliance against forced labour? Unfree labour, neo-liberal globalization and the International Labour Organization" *Journal of Agrarian Change*, 74, 425–452.

Lerche J. (2011) "The unfree labour category and unfree labour estimates: A continuum within low-end labour relations?" *Manchester Papers in Political Economy* 10/11.

Lincoln D. (2009) "Labour migration in the global division of labour: Migrant workers in Mauritius" *International Migration*, 474, 129–156.

Lucassen J. (1997) "Free and unfree labour before the twentieth century: A brief overview" In Brass T. and van der Linden M. eds., *Free and unfree labour the debate continues*. Peter Lang, Bern, 45–56.

Martin L. and Mitchelson M. L. (2009) "Geographies of detention and imprisonment: Interrogating spatial practices of confinement, discipline, law, and state power" *Geography Compass*, 31, 459–477.

Maurer J.-L. (2010) "The thin red line between indentured and bonded labour: Javanese workers in New Caledonia in the early 20th century" *Asian Journal of Social Science*, 38, 866–879.

Miles R. (1987) *Capitalism and unfree labour*. Routledge, London.

Mishra A. (2009) "Indian indentured labourers in Mauritius: Reassessing the 'new system of slavery' vs free labour debate" *Studies in History*, 252, 229–251.

Northrup D. (1995) *Indentured labor in the age of imperialism, 1834–1922*. University Press Cambridge, Cambridge.

Northrup D. (2003) "Free and unfree labor migration, 1600–1900: An introduction" *Journal of World History*, 142, 125–130.

O'Neill J. (2011) "Varieties of unfreedom" Manchester Papers in Political Economy 4/11.

Sheller M. and Urry J. (2006) "The new mobilities paradigm" *Environment and Planning A*, 382, 207–226.

Sinha M. (2000) "Mapping the imperial social formation: a modest proposal for feminist history" *Signs*, 25, 1077–1082.

Stoler A. (2001) "Tense and tender ties: The politics of comparison in North American history and postcolonial studies" *The Journal of American History*, 88, 829–865.

Stoler A. (2006) "On degrees of imperial sovereignty" *Public Culture*, 18, 125–146.

Tinker H. (1974) *A new system of slavery: The export of Indian labour overseas, 1830–1920*. Oxford University Press, Oxford.

Torabully K. with Carter M. (2002) *Coolitude: An anthology of the Indian labour diaspora*. Anthem, London.

Yeoh B. (2003) "Postcolonial geographies of place and migration" In Anderson K., Domosh M., Pile S. and Thrift N. eds., *Handbook of cultural geography*. Sage, London, 370–380.

PART II

Economic and social dimensions

Poverty and inequalities

The chapters in this second part of the Handbook, whilst not abandoning concepts, shift the attention clearly to the meso-level to focus on topics that have been central to the migration and development debate: inequality, gender, remittances (monetary and social), skilled migration, diasporas, and poverty. The migration and development debate is clearly about 'more than remittances', even if these have tended to dominate certain approaches to both research and policy: other dimensions are equally, if not more, important. Remittances can indeed help to relieve poverty but they can also increase dependence and reinforce existing inequalities. International migrants represent a minority from any population and tend to come from specific origins, which in turn, concentrate the benefits from that migration. Yet, it may be that ideas that are communicated back from destinations to origins in the form of social remittances have the greater development impact. On the other hand, the absence of some of the most energetic and skilled members from any community is so often seen to be detrimental to development, although the available evidence suggests that no such simple conclusion can be made, counterintuitive though this might at first appear. One of the reasons is that so much migration is circular, with the return of migrants to their origins, even for short periods of time with new ideas and skills, can make an impact. The importance of these transnational links in the form of a diaspora extends the process of development from the local to the global as migrants can participate in the economies and broader lives of their communities of origin from afar.

Migration is intrinsically linked to inequality as primarily a response to inequalities between places of origin and destinations. Migration in turn can also exacerbate, or ameliorate, existing levels of inequality. These include both economic levels of inequality as well as different forms of social inequalities, such as gender, race, and ethnicity.

Some of the chapters in this section deal with more 'classical' questions within migration and development debates, related to whether migration alleviates poverty. Others, on the other hand, deal with a newer, yet now well-established literature related to various forms of inequality, which ask questions about how social inequalities related to age, gender, and ethnicity are reproduced through the migration process. This part ends with two chapters. The first examines the whole process of informalisation that has proved to be so important in the creation of employment and in the provision of services across poorer parts of the world, particularly in urban areas. The specific case examines the role of informal govern-ance in urban development in sub-Saharan Africa. The second and final chapter in this part of the Handbook returns to the critical issues of migration, poverty, and inequality to re-emphasise the importance of internal migration in the migration and development debate.

8

MIGRATION AND INEQUALITY

An interdisciplinary overview

Ingrid Palmary

Introduction

Inequality is a complex concept that has been used in multiple ways in the study of migration. Much early work has focused on poverty, measured as income (such as 1 dollar per day as in the case of work by Adams and Page 2005). However, researchers have recognised that inequality, both across and within country contexts, might well be a more important influence on migration patterns or, at the very least, may have a different relationship to migration than poverty. As a result, most of the more recent research (and most of the literature reviewed in this chapter) measures the relationship between migration and both inequality and poverty. Migration studies has equally focused on various forms of social inequality such as the exclusion of migrant groups from basic service provision such as health, education, or safety, or prejudicial treatment by state institutions on the basis of migration status. In this chapter, I will consider both income and social inequality in order to outline three key points of intersection between inequality and migration. First, I will briefly review the literature that maps the relationship between poverty, inequality, and migration with an emphasis on how poverty and inequality shape who is able to migrate and how migration, and the remittances that are sent back to the place of origin, impact on levels of poverty and inequality in the sending community. Second, I will consider the limits of a focus on income and how understanding social inequalities alongside financial ones can improve our understanding of migration patterns and their meanings. Drawing this out further, I will, finally, illustrate the ways in which migration practices and policies themselves create forms of inequality that otherwise might not exist.

Inequality as a driver of migration

An important theme in migration studies has been to understand whether migration increases or decreases poverty in sending areas. The work of Adams and Page (2005) offers a useful overview of evidence from 71 sending countries. They conclude that across the studies they reviewed international migration results in a 3.5 per cent decrease in poverty in sending countries. Whilst their conclusions primarily relate to the impact of migration on poverty, there are many studies that concur that migration decreases both poverty and inequality (see Jones 1998). For example, Skeldon (1997) notes that, overall, migration reduced inequality for sending communities even though, in his research, the reduction in inequality was more significant for families with international migrants than those with internal migrants. However, these findings are far from consistent. Black et al. (2005) correctly points out the difficulty in assessing the impact that migration has on inequality even at a localised level and how contradictory many of the studies are in this field. Offering an overview of case studies across Eastern Europe, Central America, West Africa, and South Asia, their research shows markedly varied impacts of migration on poverty and inequality in these different contexts (Black et al. 2005). For example, reviewing a study on Mexican migration, they found that remittances from internal migration reduced income inequality whilst international migration to the United States exacerbated income inequality. In contrast, they offer another example from work on international migrants in South Asia showing that remittances into a sending area pushed up land prices, effectively making land too expensive to buy for those without a migrant worker in the family in a predominantly farming community. In this way, migration increased inequality between households with and without migrant workers. Thus, whilst this literature on migration, poverty, and inequality is extensive, one of its most defining characteristics is its contradictory findings. These have led more than one author to conclude that we simply do not know at any aggregate level whether migration increases or decreases poverty and inequality. Of course there are many possible explanations for these complex and contradictory findings. Drawing out the discussion by Bastia (2013) and Fraser (2007) we could suggest that this variation in findings is a consequence of the absence of any clear and consistent conceptualisation of inequality across these many studies. However, it would also appear that that inequality is related to a number of other factors outside of migration status, a point reiterated by De Haan in his review of the literature prior to 1999 when claims that:

> There are diverging opinions about the effects of migration on agriculture, on poverty alleviation and inequality, but the literature also suggests it is not migration *per se*, but the forms of migration and the conditions under which it takes place that determine the outcome.
>
> *(1999, 30)*

The lesson therefore is that one cannot understand the financial impact of migration outside of its social context. One such contextual factor that seems likely to influence the impact that migration has on poverty and inequality is historical migration patterns to and from a specific area. Several authors point out that, where migration from one sending context to one destination context has been ongoing for many years, the costs of migration, both in financial terms and in terms of the information required for successful migration, reduce, making it possible for families with fewer resources to also benefit from migration (see Carrington et al. 1996, for example). This may mean that whether or not migration is successful as a livelihood strategy depends on well-established networks and routes with the impacts for early migrants being less positive than those for later migrants (see also Palloni et al. 2001).

Similarly, Kothari (2003) has shown how migration is a livelihood strategy only for those with greater access to resources be they economic, social, or cultural (see Moore 2001; Skeldon 1997 for additional examples). Indeed, Kothari (2003) identifies no less than six different 'capitals' that may ultimately influence whether a person migrates or not. This literature represents something of a step forward from early migration research that focused on individual, often financially oriented, motivations for migration in that it considers the complex range of conditions that shape migration decision-making (see for example King 1995 for an analysis of push and pull factors). As Kothari (2003) notes, many studies have also omitted to consider why people remain in contexts where migration is frequent, and, I would add, implicitly normalise staying put and imagine migration as something that happens only with significant and usually negative pressure (a topic I return to in the examples below). Like many in migration studies, she calls for greater attention to the economic political and social conditions that shape decision-making and in particular, to understand the ways that individual agency intersects with structural constraints rather than seeing these constraints as deterministic.

Another contextual factor that shapes whether migration is successful in reducing poverty and inequality is likely to be the accuracy of migrants' perceptions about the destination country. In other words, leaving aside the question of its empirical reality, the *perception* that migration creates economic opportunity has been sufficient, in many instances, to drive migration. The work of Lipton (1980), for example, has shown how perceptions of inequality within sending communities can be a driver of increased migration where people believe migrant households are better off than non-migrant households. This complex relationship between perceptions and migration is well captured in the work on Kihato (2013), who notes the pressure on migrants to portray their migration as a financial due to social pressures in sending communities. She notes how her participants in Johannesburg often take photographs that imply a lavish lifestyle to send back home and refer to an economically unsuccessful migration to Johannesburg as a 'social death'. These perceptions about opportunities elsewhere, based on information from social networks, are likely to shape migration decisions as much if not more than objective facts about the impact of migration on poverty and inequality.

In addition, there has been a growing body of literature that considers how the impact that migration might have is shaped by factors such as the policy environment and structural inequalities such as race, gender, or ethnicity. By way of example, the fairly extensive work on gender and migration has focused on assessing the relative benefits of migration for men and women (see, for example, Chant 1992; Shauman 2010). Whilst this literature is fairly well established, several authors have attempted to understand how gender roles shape migration decisions as well as how migration, in turn, can impact gender role expectations. For example, Kothari (2003) notes that gendered role expectations can mean women do not migrate even where it might be an economic possibility for them due to their gendered position in the family (see also Curran and Saguy 2001). However, Smits et al. (2003) have also shown how migration can result in changed social norms thus freeing women from the gender constraints they may have faced in their place of origin. This may improve women's employment conditions depending on the policy and legal environment or at least allow them to transcend some of the gender norms that constrain their employment choices in their place of origin (for a useful selection of case studies see Amrith and Sahraoui 2018). Indeed, the feminisation of labour that is typically performed by migrants has been a theme in recent research (see Dodson 2018). As with studies on poverty, studies on how gender inequality shapes migration are also somewhat contradictory in their findings, suggesting there is no simple advantage or disadvantage for women who migrate. Rather a complex set of social conditions shaped by gender impact on the success of their mobility.

Inequality and migration are also shaped by the political context that shifts according to how migration is conceptualised in the political, social, and cultural domains (see also Thielemann 2003). Attending adequately to these domains requires that we understand how the local everyday experiences of exclusion and identity construction shape, and are themselves shaped by, broader social and political changes. Bastia (2013) notes that this is an approach that requires us to 'understand underdevelopment as a fundamentally historical process and a problem of the unequal distribution of power in the global political arena' (2013, 6). In other words, whilst the literature above indicates the need for greater understanding of local-level migration decision-making, there is also a need to recognise the political nature of migration in ways that connect local decision-making to global inequalities. In addition, the impact of migration is constrained by a range of global institutions and policies as well as local practices and norms that require an in-depth understanding of their differential impacts on different groups of people. This suggests that migrants cannot be assumed to be rational decision-makers outside of social pressures, hierarchies and emotions. This requires researchers to focus on the intersection of different factors that shape migrant decision-making as well as very localised studies that attend to how these local conditions are impacted by national ones. Indeed, the issue of the level of analysis that is most appropriate is key and the examples that follow suggest that these levels of analysis should be treated as intersectional with the global, national and local influencing one another. In the next section of this chapter, I will move on to consider some of the local level conditions in order to provide illustrations of how inequality is produced at local level through national-level practices of migration control and identity construction.

Producing vulnerable children: law and everyday life on South African borderlands

The first example comes from ethnographic work with children on rural South African borders. In this research, Mahati and Palmary (2017) analysed how Basotho children who cross borders, and their motivations for doing so, bear little resemblance to the policies that are designed to protect unaccompanied migrant children. Within the Children's Act (No. 38 of 2005), which is the primary piece of legislation guiding child protection in South Africa, a number of assumptions are implicit concerning the nature of children and why they might migrate. The first assumption is in fact that children do not typically move. Even in the Immigration Act (No. 13 of 2002) and Refugees Act (No. 130 of 1998) children are conspicuous in their absence, appearing only as dependents of their adult guardians. The absence of children in migration policy reflects the assumption that under 'normal' conditions children are domestically rooted and sedentary. The second key assumption is that children's migration is permanent. If they leave home, then they are doing so under conditions that mean they will not go back. The third is that children's migration stems from a breakdown in family relationships. In other words, a child will only migrate on their own when she can no longer be part of their family.

Because these assumptions do not reflect social realities, the solutions presented in the Children's Act are those that have little value for the migrant children who are frequently crossing borders on a daily or weekly basis and have families that they return to regularly. The border between Lesotho and South Africa is the Caledon river which is often dry and runs through flat easy to navigate terrain. There are strong family ties on both sides of the border and fairly minimal border control. People therefore live their lives on both sides of the border. Nevertheless, the significant income disparities between South Africa and

Lesotho provide an incentive to move across the border for everyday activities such as shopping or even making a phone call (which is much cheaper from South Africa than from Lesotho). In this way, children who are simply attending a school or carrying out other daily activities such as shopping are produced as 'unaccompanied migrants' by the practices and politics of border control. In terms of the Children's Act, they become children 'in need of care', and they require state intervention through accommodation in a place of safety or family reunification. In reality, this intervention would ironically separate them from the families that they continue to be part of in spite of their frequent border crossings. Although they often face violence, much of this violence is created by the presence of the border rather than the risks of migration. There are no legal avenues for them to cross the border routinely as they currently do. In this instance, the consequence is that the border is managed by a range of informal rules negotiated between border officials and children that bear little resemblance to formal policy. In this example, it is precisely the practices of border control that make children's movement remarkable and create barriers to their access to education and other basic needs. Their vulnerability to social inequality in particular is produced by the presence of a border.

Gendered work and the regulation of migration

A second example comes from a collaborative study of migration policymaking in South Africa, Bangladesh and Singapore.[1] The case study from Singapore (Koh et al. 2017), detailed the process of passing the 'day off policy' for migrant workers who engage in domestic labour. Until 2013, it was not mandatory for employers to give migrant domestic workers a day off each week. There were also other provisions that pregnancy would result in their contract being revoked and that their right to remain in Singapore is only for as long as they have an employment contract. In instances such as these, domestic workers' migrant status creates inequality within the host state. Similarly, in Bangladesh, as in many contexts, migrant domestic workers who move from rural to urban areas usually to work in the households of wealthier family members were excluded from the Labour Act of 2006 which, for the first time, offered protections for domestic workers (for details see Ashraf 2016). In each of these cases structural inequalities based on the gendered nature of work and the migrants' place of origin shape what becomes possible for them and their ability to migrate in ways that improve their livelihoods. Inequality is embedded in most migration policy based on a combination of assumed economic costs and benefits, even though these are often poorly assessed, and populist sentiment (see Geddes and Scholten 2016). For example, the South African Immigration Act (No. 13 of 2002), as with most in the world, actively distinguishes between and discriminates against low skilled migration in a context where this is the majority of migrants. In Singapore, highly regulated systems for the migration of low skilled domestic workers are based on meeting the needs of a population with high levels of formal employment and little time for low skilled work. Whilst the details of these case studies are beyond the scope of this chapter, there are three conclusions that have relevance for this chapter. First, policymaking in each of these three country contexts was shaped by global influences. In particular, powerful states such as the US, through the 'Trafficking in Persons' report produced by the Department of State, influenced each of the three countries to create migration law and shaped the form it took and the debates that emerged during the policy process. Similarly, international NGOs often acted as a catalyst for the creation of global lobbying for what had previously been a concern only of nationally based NGOs in each country. Finally, research evidence did relatively little to shape the policy and the debates were rather emotive, moral and drew of popular mythology surrounding migration.

Implications for the study of inequality

A number of implications are evident in these examples. First, what is clear is that migration policy does not reflect the realities of migration. Whilst it is often taken for granted that migrants are vulnerable (as is the case in the South African Children's Act which is considered exemplary for its child protection focus), what these examples show is that it is not migration that creates their vulnerability but rather the practices of migration policymaking and border control. The form that the policy frameworks take in each of these examples renders the migrants that they purport to protect more vulnerable to exclusion and prejudice. Indeed, migration control is, in both instances, the reason for their social inequality with citizens. Whilst their poverty might well have motivated them to migrate, inequality is sustained through the migration framework that they operate in. This reinforces the emphasis in the literature described above on attending to the political context of migration when trying to understand its impact.

The second key lesson is that whilst the policy might apply to all migrants, the impact it has is likely to be different depending on their social position and the inequalities associated with it – such as whether someone is an adult or a child. Thus, the second implication of these examples is that the ability of any one country to address inequality is shaped by global influences. In order to understand whether migration increases or decreases inequality in a sending community one needs to attend to how identity (such as citizenship, gender, etc.) and related entitlements are created and the differential role expectations that come with each. In other words, it is not simply a matter of establishing whether inequality is to be studied at the macro, meso, or micro-level but rather understanding how each of these levels intersects to produce different access to resources. Migration interventions are taking place in a context where powerful nation-states frequently shape and impact on the policies of less powerful ones in ways that may or may not improve the lives of migrants themselves. At the very least there is considerable risk that these policies ride roughshod over local migration conditions and patterns.

Shifting the analysis in this way inevitably shifts the kinds of interventions that are possible. As the example of migrant children shows, very often our responses fail to deal with the actual practices of family decision-making and patterns of movement. A stark example of this comes from the trafficking legislation was implemented in South Africa. Throughout the campaigns for the development of counter-trafficking legislation, extensive misinformation, poor-quality research, and inaccurate information about migrants, particularly female migrants, was used. In reality, the legislation that South Africa developed bore little resemblance to local needs. In particular, it failed to account for the circular nature of migration and the very extensive smuggling that occurs on South African borders but nevertheless falls short of the definition of trafficking. The global debates and expectations about trafficking – what it is and who was likely to be a victim – constrained the local policy process rendering it impossible to develop meaningful interventions. Instead, the advocacy drew on and perpetuated some of the worst racial and gender stereotypes to explain the presence of trafficking. In particular, the debates on trafficking eclipsed the impact that border control has (as was evident in the example of Basotho children who migrate) and instead set border control up as the solution to protect vulnerable women. This is exactly the same logic at work in the ways that the Children's Act imagined that border control plays a central role in protecting migrant children rather than being the source of their vulnerability. An analysis of the ways in which class and gender shape trafficking that attended to the structural global inequalities and how they are reproduced at a local level would have resulted in very different kinds of intervention. At the very least the demand for more heavily protected borders would not have been such a taken for granted response (Palmary 2016).

Expanding on this discussion, debates about migration at the international and national level clearly impact on the local level. Certainly, the examples given above show that research is often not at the heart of what drives migration policy and interventions posing particular challenges to creating migration policy that could decrease inequality. In particular the examples given and the literature reviewed suggests that we should not assume rationality either on the part of migrants or on the part of policymakers. Perhaps the greatest challenge to unpacking the connections between migration and inequality are the popular assumptions about, and preoccupations with, migration. Contemporary movement across borders has almost inevitably been associated with a sense of crisis and the nation under threat. This makes for a dangerous political populism that legitimates inequality rather than breaking it down. Thus, policies that could protect, such as allowing free temporary movement for school going children as in the example above, lack popular support.

Conclusions

This chapter has provided a brief overview of the literature that connects migration with inequality and poverty. What is most evident from this review is how contradictory some of the research findings are, leading to little clear agreement about whether migration indeed reduces poverty or inequality. What seems to be emerging from the literature is a recognition of whether migration increases or decreases inequality and poverty is shaped by a number of contextual and political factors. These include local-level factors such as social capital or gender norms as well as global debates that constrain local migration decision-making such as practices of border control. As a result the relationship between economic measures of inequality and social ones has been too often ignored in research.

I have suggested there are two useful ways to take these debates forward. First, a greater attention to how social inequality is connected to and in some instances creates income inequality. Second, connect micro-, macro-, and meso-level studies in order to understand, first, how migration policymaking, as just one kind of intervention, might sustain or even create inequality, and, second, its differential impact on different kinds of migrants. In this way, the examples I have used have shown how social position such as age or poverty might result in a policy having a different impact on the success of migration. Using examples of policymaking that are ostensibly about reducing the vulnerability of migrants, we see that these policies in fact fail to attend to the local forms that migration takes and the global influences on the nature of the policy. Thus, the calls within migration studies for local-level understanding are important but without adequate attention to how the local and the global are mutually-constituting local studies risk failing to capture the political and institutional constraints on individual migrants. Whilst this line of analysis offers productive ways of taking research and understanding of migration further, the political and popular resistance to migration framed as a security and moral threat makes such a focus all the more difficult.

Note

1 This study was funded by DFID under the Migrating out of Poverty research consortium. For details on the individual papers see http://migratingoutofpoverty.dfid.gov.uk/

References

Adams, R.H. and Page, J., 2005. Do international migration and remittances reduce poverty in developing countries? *World Development*, 33(10), pp. 1645–1669.

Amrith, M. and Sahraoui, N. (eds.) (2018). *Gender, Work and Migration*. London: Routledge.

Ashraf, A.A., 2016. Public policy formulation: a case study of domestic workers in Bangladesh.

Bastia, T. (ed.). (2013). *Migration and Inequality* (Vol. 100). London: Routledge.

Black, R., Natali, C. and Skinner, J., 2005. *Migration and Inequality* (pp. 1–26). Washington, DC: World Bank.

Carrington, W.J., Detragiache, E. and Vishwanath, T., 1996. Migration with endogenous moving costs. *The American Economic Review*, 86(4), pp. 909–930.

Chant, S., 1992. Conclusion: towards a framework for the analysis of gender-selective migration.

Curran, S.R. and Saguy, A.C., 2001. Migration and cultural change: a role for gender and social networks? *Journal of International Women's Studies*, 2(3), pp. 54–77.

Dodson, B., 2018. Gender, mobility and precarity: The experiences of migrant African women in Cape Town, South Africa. In M. Amrith and N. Sahraoui (eds.), *Gender, Work and Migration Agency in Gendered Labour Settings* (99–117). London: Routledge.

Fraser, N., 2007. Reframing justice in a globalizing world. In N. Fraser and P Bourdieu (eds.), *(Mis)recognition, Social Inequality and Social Justice*. New York: Routledge.

Geddes, A. and Scholten, P., 2016. *The Politics of Migration and Immigration in Europe*. London: Sage.

Jones, R.C., 1998. Remittances and inequality: a question of migration stage and geographic scale. *Economic Geography*, 74(1), pp. 8–25.

Kihato, C., 2013. *Migrant Women of Johannesburg: Everyday Life in an in-Between City*. New York: Palgrave Macmillan.

Koh, C.Y., Goh, C., Wee, K. and Yeoh, B.S., 2017. Drivers of migration policy reform: the day off policy for migrant domestic workers in Singapore. *Global Social Policy*, 17(2), pp. 188–205.

Kothari, U., 2003. Introduction: migration, staying put and livelihoods. *Journal of International Development*, 15(5), p. 607.

Lipton, M., 1980. Migration from rural areas of poor countries: the impact on rural productivity and income distribution. *World Development*, 8(1), pp. 1–24.

Mahati, S.T. and Palmary, I., 2017. Independent migrant children, humanitarian work and statecraft. Different childhoods: non/Normative development and transgressive trajectories.

Moore, K., 2001. Frameworks for Understanding the inter-generational transmission of poverty and well-being in developing countries.

Palloni, A., Massey, D.S., Ceballos, M., Espinosa, K. and Spittel, M., 2001. Social capital and international migration: a test using information on family networks. *American Journal of Sociology*, 106(5), pp. 1262–1298.

Palmary, I., 2016. Governing morality: Placing gender and sexuality in migration. In *Gender, Sexuality and Migration in South Africa* (pp. 1–18). London: Springer International Publishing.

Shauman, K.A., 2010. Gender asymmetry in family migration: occupational inequality or interspousal comparative advantage? *Journal of Marriage and Family*, 72(2), pp. 375–392.

Skeldon, R., 1997. Rural-to-urban migration and its implications for poverty alleviation. *Asia-Pacific Population Journal*, 12(1), pp. 3–16.

Smits, J., Mulder, C.H. and Hooimeijer, P., 2003. Changing gender roles, shifting power balance and long-distance migration of couples. *Urban Studies*, 40(3), pp. 603–613.

Thielemann, E.R., 2003. Between interests and norms: explaining burden-sharing in the European Union. *Journal of Refugee Studies*, 16(3), pp. 253–273.

9

GENDER, MIGRATION, AND DEVELOPMENT

Tanja Bastia and Karlijn Haagsman

Introduction

Policymakers and scholars today recognise the important role that women play in international migration and that migration is a gendered process. However, this has not always been the case. Much of migration scholarship was gender-blind for most of the twentieth century, despite the fact that women have migrated throughout human history (Donato and Gabaccia 2016). In fact, since the 1960s women have made up almost half of all international migrants. Since the 1980s, women started to migrate independently as labour migrants in ever greater numbers. Today, in some countries of immigration, particularly in the Global North, the rate of female migration is increasing more steeply than male migration (Fleury 2016; Zlotnik 2003). In other cases, it is the emigration figures, which demonstrate a greater outflow of women than men, as in the case of Indonesia, Sri Lanka, or the Philippines. The overall assessment clearly depends on which migration stream we look at. Men dominate in some migration streams, while women are more numerous in others. This is a result of gender norms, gendered labour markets at origin and destination, ageing populations, the migration of carers, and domestic workers globally, most of whom are women (Parreñas 2000; Piper 2008b).

Migration is a gendered process, as both women and men migrants are involved in the migration process as gendered beings. Women's social roles as women and men's as men have repercussions for who migrates, when, for how long, what that experience is like, what type of jobs they get, and how they relate to remittances, or to their families. However, most scholarship on gender and migration has focused on women. This is a logical consequence of the fact that they had been ignored for such a long time. But men are also affected by gendered norms. For example, men might feel compelled to migrate in order to fulfil their role as economic provider. They might feel that they have 'failed' in their role, if they are unable to send remittances, in a similar way that social norms compel young women migrants to send large proportions of their money to their parents in order to fulfil their role of 'dutiful daughters' (Sobieszczyk 2015). Attention to gender relations, and women's and men's social roles helps us better understand the formation of gendered migration streams, migration policies, the temporality of migration, and the consequences that migration has for places of origin and destination.

By the time the current phase of renewed interest in the link between migration and development came along, at the turn of the century, women migrants and gender as an integral part of the migration process were well on the scene (Piper 2009a). However, most of the policy and research interest within migration–development debates focus on a relatively narrow range of topics. Much of the work continues to be centred on product-ive investment. Women are taken into account but only in as far as they are considered 'good remitters', or at least, better than men, a bias that continues in mainstream policy cir-cles to date (Bastia and Piper 2019; Vullnetari and King 2011). When women are taken into account, they are often stripped of their agency. For example, feminist scholars who study mothers who migrated independently, tend to focus on the negative effects of globalisation forcing these women to leave their families 'behind', leading to high social costs (Hochschild 2000; Hondagneu-Sotelo and Avila 1997; Parreñas 2000). However, because these scholars focus on structural factors within an unjust political economy, they often obscure the fact that migrant women exercised agency in their migration decision and that sometimes migra-tion also leads to the empowerment of these women (Fréguin-Gresh et al. 2015; Hondag-neu-Sotelo 1994).

Moreover, migration involves productive and reproductive aspects of people's lives. Care concerns are always associated with any type of migration, whether this is in relation to the children, or parents that migrants 'leave behind' in their countries of origin or the type of jobs that migrants undertake. However, preoccupations with children 'left behind' have emerged as a concern only once policymakers became aware of the scale of women's migra-tion, especially mothers. Migrant men also used to leave children behind, but this never fea-tured as a particular concern, because it was assumed that the primary carer, the mother, remained in the countries of origin to care for their children. A gendered assessment of these changes, as well as adequate attention to reproductive lives continues to be missing, given that development in general and migration–development debates in particular, con-tinue to highlight economic, productive aspects of people's lives.

In this chapter, we begin by providing a brief review of the gender and migration litera-ture to provide the backdrop to the discussions of gender in debates about migration and development, for those who may not be familiar with this literature. The section that fol-lows focuses more directly on gender in the 'migration–development nexus' debates. We then move to briefly outline how gender may be understood in development as a process of immanent social change, before making the case for also including destination countries in debates about 'migration and development'. Most of what we discuss deals with labour migration or migration for work, as it would be impossible in a chapter of this size to also include forced migration, refugees, and internal displacement. We also do not deal in any detail with other more specific topics within debates around migration and development, such as skilled migration, migration for education or the role of diasporas, given that other chapters in this Handbook focus specifically on these topics.

Approaches to gender and migration

Despite Ravenstein's early recognition that women were more important in local migration flows than men in the United Kingdom, women hardly featured in migration studies until feminist critiques from the early 1970s. Until then, most scholars assumed that men were the primary economic migrants. Women were largely seen as 'associational migrants' or 'trailing wives'. Given the greater value placed on labour or economic migration, women's migration was deemed unimportant, despite the fact that they often end up working in places of destination. Most observers, therefore, considered men to be the primary migrants and took men as the 'norm' in migration studies.

This started changing during the 1970s as the result of emergent feminist critiques of social sciences in general and migration studies more specifically. These early critiques highlighted that: (i) women formed a large percentage of international migration flows; (ii) in some regions, women in fact dominated cross-border migration flows; (iii) many women migrated independently of the men in their families; and (iv) many of these female migrants, including some of those who had migrated as spouses, held active economic roles at their destinations (Hondagneu-Sotelo 1994; Morokvasic 1984; Phizacklea 1983). What followed were two decades of detailed scrutiny of 'the migrant woman'.

Greater recognition of women as migrants in their own right at the conceptual level went hand-in-hand with the so-called 'feminisation of migration'. While female migrants have migrated predominantly through family formation and reunification until the 1980s, women have increasingly migrated independently (United Nations 2006). One of the reasons for this change has been the global division of labour which demanded cheap female labour in the form of domestic and care work from the Global South in the North (Hochschild 2000; Hondagneu-Sotelo and Avila 1997; Parreñas 2000). This trend of increased independent female migration is commonly referred to as the feminisation of migration. While some refer to the term 'feminisation of migration' as a numerical increase in the percentage of women migrating, the term also refers to a qualitative change in women increasingly migrating independently. This phenomenon triggered a wave of interest by feminist scholars wanting to study how women's independent migration affected gender relations and their families back home (Piper 2008a).

Scholars studying developing countries led the way in recognising the importance of looking at gender relations, as opposed to focusing just on migrant women. Sarah Radcliffe (1986), for example, published an early work looking at gender and migration in the Peruvian peasant economy (Radcliffe 1986). She then expanded on this, with a collaboration with Sylvia Chant, who published an important collection on gender and migration in developing countries (Chant 1992). They argued that, while it was important to recognise the role played by migrant women, a focus on gender relations would allow a more precise analysis of how power relations between men and women shape migration flows. Many of these early studies focused on internal migration. Their intention was more on taking into account gender relations to understand migration flows better, as opposed to how gender relations change as a result of migration. By the turn of the century, gender was recognised as an intrinsic part of the process of migration (Willis and Yeoh 2000).

As the scholarship on gender and migration expanded, so did the conceptual tools used to carry out these analyses. Intersectionality had been around in feminist theory since the 1980s but started being used in an explicit manner in studies of migration only in the last 10 years (Bastia 2014; Lutz et al. 2011). Intersectionality argues that a focus on gender alone is insufficient and that it is necessary to take into account other axes of differentiation – such as race or class – in order to fully understand the disadvantage that migrants might be experiencing. Intersectionality challenges the prominence of gender as the most significant source of discrimination and alerts analysts to pay attention to other bases on which migrants, particularly women migrants, might be discriminated against. Politically, though, although it can be used with any group of people, given its roots in feminist thinking, it remains attentive on the disadvantages experienced by women. The inclusion of a generational perspective as well as greater attention to social class currently remain a challenge in this literature (Fresnoza-Flot and Shinozaki 2017).

Gender in migration–development nexus

What is included under the migration–development nexus largely depends on how we define 'development'. 'Development' can be defined as a purposeful action to improve the well-being of a segment of the population, usually the poorest. However, it can also be used to describe an immanent process of social and economic change (Hart 2010). Within the former, we need to take into account the actions that governments or non-governmental actors, such as civil society organisations, take to promote social or economic changes. 'Development', in this sense, is often seen as being located in 'poorer countries' or in the Global South (Hart 2010). In terms of the migration–development nexus, therefore, the interest here would be whether specific policies that target migration for bringing about development take into account the different experiences of women and men. For example, the SDGs now represent an improvement in relation to the MDGs given that they include migrants and migration in relation to pursuing development goals (Hennebry, Hari, and Piper 2018; Piper 2017) (see also Chapter 26 in this Handbook). As with the MDGs, the SDGs also include a specific goal and various targets related to gender. However, to what extent the migration-related goals are gender-sensitive, is still debatable. Positive aspects include a recognition of women as migrants, highlighting areas of concern such as trafficking, and a recognition of the importance of care and domestic work. However, although women migrants are now included in the SDGs, they still feature primarily as victims; of trafficking, for example. Additional areas of concern include: the focus on the 'management of migration' and temporary migration with the objective of promoting 'regular' migration practices but neglecting actual employment practices, a lack of an explicit focus on the well-being of migrants, the victimisation of female migrants, or a lack of recognition of the complex change brought about by migration in places of origin.

As the current phase of renewed interest in the relationship between migration and development erupted at the turn of the century, there was already a significant amount of information available on the ways in which gender relations influenced migration flows; and how these in turn promoted changes in gender relations. However, as Piper (2009a) has noted, interest in migration and development largely focused on economic aspects of the migration experience, for example, how the emigration (of both men and women) alleviates unemployment pressures in home labour markets while at the same time the money they send home as remittances provides important contributions to national incomes (Piper 2009b) (see also Chapter 10 in this Handbook). Social aspects have been largely side-lined. This has started changing, slightly and slowly, with the recognition in the SDGs of the importance of domestic work and care work (SDG 5.4, although this SDG focuses on unpaid care and domestic work and is not related to migration).

As financial remittances overcame foreign direct investment in terms of annual flows and proved to be resilient during financial downturns, policymakers turned to migrants to alleviate the balance of payment deficits. At this time, interest in women migrants flourished as a number of micro-level studies showed that women are better remitters than men (King, Castaldo, and Vullnetari 2011; Kunz 2008; Nyberg-Sørensen 2007). Women were supposedly more generous with the amount they sent, sending a larger proportion of their total income, and were more regular remitters. However, as others have shown, these assumptions are infused with stereotypes. They also do not hold in some contexts. Vullnetari and King (2011), for example, have shown that in the case of Albania, the responsibility to remit falls on sons and that sending remittances is a 'male thing'. In their study, they found that remittances were usually sent by men to men but that many variations existed. They also questioned the presumptive distinction between women as being more altruistic and men as more self-interested and argued that both motivations can co-exist (Vullnetari and King 2011). Other studies found that women and men often remit for different purposes (McKay 2007).

Even with the widespread circulation of the stereotype of 'women are better remitters', policymakers continue to have an ambivalent relationship towards the migration of women. While benefitting the nation's coffers and therefore something that governments would wish to promote, the migration of women is often seen in negative terms. Some women migrant workers find jobs in unregulated sectors of the labour market, such as domestic work, care work, or the provision of services such as sex work, leading to the occasional ban imposed by some governments on the emigration of women, mainly in Asia (for example, Bangladesh, Sri Lanka, Nepal, Indonesia, and the Philippines). Many women also find work in well-paid, skilled occupations, but relatively less attention is paid to these women in the literature or at the policy-level. When speaking of 'migrant women' in relation to development, the image is generally one of low-income women migrating from poor households for low-paid, usually exploitative types of work. It is no surprise, then, that migrant women continued to be portrayed as being victims of migration processes and that policymakers often see women's migration as more detrimental for the families 'left behind' (see Chapter 16 in this Handbook).

Women are often mentioned as needing protection given the dangers of becoming victims of trafficking. One of the two mentions of human trafficking in the SDGs is under Goal 5 on gender equality and empowerment of all women and girls (the other being where it should be, under Goal 8 on inclusive economic growth and decent work). Trafficking has been associated with the 'white slave' trade and the prostitution of women and girls (Doezema 2010; Kempadoo, Sanghera, and Pattanaik 2005). The association between trafficking, sex work, and the vulnerability of women is also present in the Trafficking Protocol of 2000 (see Chapter 37 in this Handbook). Most research and implementation on human trafficking fails to recognise that trafficking takes place in sectors other than sex work; for example, in domestic work, or construction and agriculture, where men migrants may predominate. The sex work sector itself is highly heterogeneous, with both high-end, very well-paid workers to women working in very exploitative working conditions in brothels (Skeldon 2000). The result is that the Trafficking Protocol is often used to limit women's mobility and instil fear around the migration of women, instead of being used to target serious labour exploitation and provide migrants with alternatives (Bastia 2005).

While it is undeniable that migrants, both men and women, experience exploitation, some of which is severe, and these clearly need to be condemned and fought, using some of these tools to try to limit people's mobility goes against what we have learned thus far. If people's mobility is curtailed, they will continue to migrate, but through more vulnerable and risky channels. How we present the findings of research on gender, migration, and development and what we do with the results requires a careful balancing act. Women do enter jobs in occupations that are exploitative, poorly paid, and unregulated, but they also organise and achieve considerable success. The new ILO Convention on Decent Work for Domestic Workers from 2011 is one such example (Bastia and Piper 2019).

Development as a process of immanent social change

Macro-level approaches in development studies, such as modernisation theory, dependency theory, and world systems theories have all included some analysis of migration, whether related to the search for modernity by internal migrants to cities; the relative benefits of movements of labour and goods in dependency theories; or the counter-movement of labour (in relation to goods) in world systems theories. However, because of the scale at which these analyses took place, little recognition was given to who migrates or to the migrants' experiences. While the implications of these analyses were also gendered, this has seldom been recognised.

A recognition of gender relations was more common in studies carried out at the micro- or meso- level. However, even here, it was common for some approaches to disregard intra-household inequalities. The New Economics of Labour Migration (NELM), for example, which became popular during the 1980s, takes into account the household as a unit of analysis, but fails to take into account gender (and generational) inequalities within the household. It does not ask who sends and who receives remittances, or why women (or men) migrate. Only some applications of the model, such as the one by Radcliffe (1986) mentioned above, begin to unpack intra-household inequalities and provide useful informa- tion in relation to migration (in her case, internal). However, over time, these micro- and meso-level studies, including the New Economics of Labour Migration literature, started taking into account gender relations more systematically. Micro-level studies, particularly those carried out from a transnational perspective, are most likely to also include a gender perspective (see, for example, Gamburd 2000; George 2005). Families separate as a result of migration and here is where most studies on gender, migration, and development have focused, taking development as an immanent process of social change.

Non-migrants, such as family-members of migrants who remain in the country of origin, are a key concern in this literature (see Chapter 16 in this Handbook). Migration often leads to spousal or partner separation, especially at the beginning of the migration trajectory. The effects of this separation are highly gendered. Stayer spouses often have to take over house- hold tasks performed by their migrant partners before migration, significantly increasing their workload, which can lead to lower overall well-being (Pribilsky 2004; Roy and Nangia 2005; Wu and Ye 2016). Moreover, those who remain in the country of origin often have to engage in wage-earning labour while their migrant partner settles into new jobs or experience low economic status because of their partner's migration (de Haas and van Rooij 2010; Pribilsky 2004; Wu and Ye 2016). Migrants are not always able to send remittances, so partners of low-skilled and undocumented migrants in particular, can experi- ence financial hardship. The wives of circular migrants in China, for example, had lower economic status because their husbands were economically unsuccessful (Yabiku, Agadja- nian, and Sevoyan 2010).

At the same time, migration can be empowering for spouses of migrants. Pribilsky (2004) points to an awareness of gender roles that resulted from migrant men having to take up domestic duties in host societies, which led to more appreciation and respect for the domes- tic labour their wives performed back home. In addition, away from the watchful eye of their husbands, some wives experience more freedom. If accepted by society, this can be liberating, leading to more physical and social mobility. Furthermore, by taking up paid work in the absence of their husbands, making household decisions and managing remit- tances, wives perform tasks previously associated with men and as a result gain more power and authority in and outside the household (Hugo 2000; Pribilsky 2004; Yabiku, Agadja- nian, and Sevoyan 2010).

However, migration of a partner does not always lead to more equal gender roles or empowerment for the stayers. Several studies showed that migration reinforced gender roles or that changes are not lasting with couples taking up traditional roles once reunified (Aghajanian, Alihoseini, and Thompson 2014; de Haas and van Rooij 2010; Gamburd 2000; Menjívar and Agadjanian 2007). Conversely, couples adopting changed gender roles, but in a way not acceptable to their home society, can lead to the stayer being more controlled by the extended family and increased social stigma against them (Aghajanian et al. 2014; de Haas and van Rooij 2010; Pribilsky 2004). A study by de Haas and van Rooij (2010) in Morocco found that a clash arose between the wants and needs of the migrants' wives and elder male family members of the husband. This interference was even greater if the wives did not receive remittances directly but through these relatives. Thus, migration can also lead to a sense of disempowerment and can exacerbate existing gender hierarchies (Gallo 2006; Hegland 2010). Several studies found that stayer men also struggled with their masculinity and self-esteem when their migrant wives become the main breadwinner, leading to marital tension (Gallo 2006; Gamburd 2000; Waters 2010).

Another reason for strained relations and lower mental well-being of partners are the extramarital relations and risky sexual behaviour migrants engage in when in the host country. Pribilsky (2004) found that away from the watchful eye of their wives and because of loneliness, some Ecuadorian men engaged in extramarital relations in the US, something their wives were well aware of. Losing their husbands to other women could mean not only a reduction or cessation of remittances, but also being stigmatised by extended family members and neighbours, as the blame would be placed on the wives. Similar findings have emerged from Armenia, Guatemala, and Mexico (Boehm 2012; Menjívar and Agadjanian 2007).

Finally, the migration of a partner can lead to union dissolution, as a result of (dis) empowerment, extramarital relations, and worsened well-being (Boyle, Kulu, and Cooke 2008; Frank and Wildsmith 2005; Hill 2004). A greater chance of marital tension and divorce emerges when women migrate and the husband stays behind, especially when partners have different gender expectations (Boyle, Kulu, and Cooke 2008; Caarls and Mazzucato 2015; Pribilsky 2004).

Calling for a 'development' perspective at destination

Most 'development' concerns are located in so-called 'developing countries', although with the SDGs the focus is now shifting more towards the global level. As others have argued, there is a geography to development. Lower-income countries are generally approached from a developmentalist perspective, as always lacking something and therefore needing development (Hart 2004). Thus far, we have focused on the gendered effects of migration in countries of origin, given that 'development' concers are traditionally thought of as being located, in the countries where most migrants originate from. However, needless to say, migrants themselves should also be considered not just as agents of development but the subjects of development itself. The migration and development debates, therefore, should place greater attention on what happens to migrants (both men and women) at destination, especially in relation to the protection of their rights.

Critical perspectives to migration and development have already identified the fact that, while most of the interest in development is in lower-income countries, higher-income countries benefit tremendously from the migration of workers. As Silvey (2009) argued: "Migration as a process includes transnational gendered and racialized labor value transfers between low and high-income countries and is integral to the production of hierarchies of privilege and power across scales" (2009, 508) "and that the transnational migration of labor supports the economic development of labor receiving nations while costing low income economies" (2009, 512).

Therefore, while the so-called 'migration–development nexus' has largely focused on the benefits that countries of origin draw from migration, a critical perspective would call on us to expand the analysis to also include the many benefits that already better-off countries draw from the movement of people (Silvey 2009).

A full analysis of this process is beyond the scope of this chapter. However, given our interest in gender relations and women migrants, we would like to also highlight the need to take into account the position of women migrants in countries of destination. Migration policies, gender, and labour regimes often interact to produce significant challenges for protecting the rights of women migrants. Those already disadvantaged by education, income, ethnic, or racial position are most likely to find employment only in precarious jobs in the informal sector. Sometimes, even those who have been brought up with the benefits of income security and education, experience a process of deskilling, given that they cannot find jobs in the sectors in which they have been trained.

Organising for women migrant workers is challenging, given they often work long hours and for little pay, leaving little time and resources for collective bargaining initiatives with other women. However, some examples do exist and these provide fundamental support services to women migrant workers and for lobbying governments for fairer migration policies. One example is Kalayaan, a small organisation in London which supports migrant domestic workers in both practical ways as well as in policy and advocacy work.[1]

Conclusion

We have come a long way. From women migrants being basically invisible in the middle of the twentieth century, we now have a burgeoning literature and a wealth of information on different types of mobilities in which women engage, and the consequences that these have for places of origin and destination. The fact that migration is a gendered process is now firmly established in academic research but also in policy circles. Although there is still some way to go in terms of acknowledging the full complexity of what is involved, an enormous amount of progress has been achieved, not least in highlighting the areas where women face the greatest vulnerabilities. In this chapter, we have mostly focused on women. This is a reflection of the literature but also of the fact that women have historically been overlooked. However, as we have mentioned, migration also leads to gendered changes for men. Gender is multifaceted and there is still a lot that we need to explore in terms of how migration affects men, from a gendered perspective, not as the assumed gender-neutral actors of migration decisions.

The danger, as we have outlined, is that we may sway the other way and start to equate migration only with threats and risks, portraying women migrants as victims of broader processes, in which they only end up losing or being cast as 'victims'. Migration is built on different types of social and economic inequalities. It is therefore expected that migration will not necessarily have equalising effects. However, we would be doing women migrants a disservice if we only saw them as victims. Women migrants are generally active participants in their own migration decisions. As we have shown, they also often draw significant benefits from their own migrations and those of others.

We have discussed many examples of 'development as an immanent process of change' and described the ways in which families and societies in places of origin change as a result of migration. However, we have also cast a note of caution on just focusing on places of origin, when talking about development. Migration is by definition a movement between different places and 'developmental' benefits are far from being confined to the places of origin. Places of destination, those that were already better-off, often benefit tremendously from migration, whether in the form of provision of services, extra taxes paid on income, or the setting up of migrant businesses. These benefits, because they occur in so-called 'developed' countries, are often overlooked as development outcomes.

Women migrants themselves need to be framed as both development agents and recipients, particularly when in their roles as migrant workers, they require additional support to be able to defend their rights. This is where we feel the gender, migration, and development debates are currently at their weakest, given the continued framing of development as being located in lower-income countries.

Note

1 See www.kalayaan.org.uk/about-us/

References

Aghajanian, A., Alihoseini, J., & Thompson, V. (2014). Husband's circular migration and the status of women left behind in Lamerd District, Iran. *Asian Population Studies*, *10*(1), 40–59.

Bastia, T. (2005). Child trafficking or teenage migration? Bolivian migrants in Argentina. *International Migration*, *43*(4), 58–89.

Bastia, T. (2014). Intersectionality, migration and development. *Progress in Development Studies*, *14*(3), 237–248.

Bastia, T., & Piper, N. (2019). Women migrants in the global economy: A global overview (and regional perspectives). *Gender & Development*, *27*(1), 15–30.

Boehm, D. A. (2012). *Intimate migrations: Gender, family, and illegality among transnational Mexicans.* New York: New York University Press.

Boyle, P. J., Kulu, H., Cooke, T., Gayle, V., & Mulder, C. (2008). Moving and union dissolution. *Demography*, *45*(1), 209–222.

Caarls, K., & Mazzucato, V. (2015). Does international migration lead to divorce? Ghanaian couples in Ghana and abroad. *Population*, *70*(1), 135–161.

Chant, S. H. (1992). *Gender and migration in developing countries.* London: Belhaven.

de Haas, H., & van Rooij, A. (2010). Migration as emancipation? The impact of internal and international migration on the position of women left behind in Rural Morocco. *Oxford Development Studies*, *38*(1), 43–62.

Doezema, J. (2010). *Sex slaves and discourse masters: The construction of trafficking.* London: Zed.

Donato, K. M., & Gabaccia, D. R. (2016). *Gender and international migration: From the slavery era to the global age.* New York: Russell Sage Foundation.

Fleury, A. (2016). *Understanding women and migration: A literature review.* KNOMAD Working Paper 8. Washington, DC: The World Bank/Global Knowledge Partnership on Migration and Development (KNOMAD).

Frank, R., & Wildsmith, E. (2005). The grass widows of Mexico: Migration and union dissolution in a binational context. *Social Forces*, *83*(3), 919–947.

Fréguin-Gresh, S., Cortes, G., Trousselle, A., Sourisseau, J.-M., & Guetat-Bernard, H. (2015). Multi-sited family systems: Proposal for an analytical and methodological framework to explore the links between migration and rural development in the South. [Le système familial multilocalisé. Proposition analytique et méthodologique pour interroger les liens entre migrations et développement rural au Sud]. *Mondes en développement*, *172*(4), 13–32.

Fresnoza-Flot, A., & Shinozaki, K. (2017). Transnational perspectives on intersecting experiences: Gender, social class and generation among Southeast Asian migrants and their families. *Journal of Ethnic and Migration Studies*, *43*(6), 867–884.

Gallo, E. (2006). Italy is not a good place for men: Narratives of places, marriage and masculinity among Malayali migrants. *Global Networks, 6*(4), 357–372.

Gamburd, M. R. (2000). *The kitchen spoon's handle. Transnationalism and Sri Lanka's migrant housemaids.* Ithaca, NY: Cornell University Press.

George, S. M. (2005). *When women come first: Gender and class in transnational migration.* Berkeley, CA and London: University of California Press.

Hart, G. (2004). Geography and development: Critical ethnographies. *Progress in Human Geography, 28*(1), 91–100.

Hart, G. (2010). D/developments after the meltdown. *Antipode, 41*, 117–141.

Hegland, M. E. (2010). Tajik male labour migration and women left behind. *Anthropology of the Middle East, 5*(2), 16, 16–35.

Hennebry, J., Hari, H.C. & Piper, N. (2018). Not without them: Realising the sustainable development goals for women migrant workers. *Journal of Ethnic and Migration Studies,* 1–17.

Hill, L. E. (2004). Connections between U.S. female migration and family formation and dissolution. *Migraciones Internacionales, 2*(3), 60–82.

Hochschild, A. R. (2000). Global care chains and emotional surplus value. In A. Giddens & W. Hutton (eds.), *On the edge: Living with global capitalism* (pp. 130–146). London: Jonathan Cape.

Hondagneu-Sotelo, P. (1994). *Gendered transitions: Mexican experiences of immigration.* Berkeley, CA and London: University of California Press.

Hondagneu-Sotelo, P., & Avila, E. (1997). "I'm here, but I'm there": The meanings of Latina transnational motherhood. *Gender and Society, 11*(5), 548–571.

Hugo, G. (2000). Migration and women's empowerment. In H. Presser & G. Sen (eds.), *Women's empowerment and demographic processes: Moving beyond Cairo* (pp. 287–317). New York: Oxford University Press.

Kempadoo, K., Sanghera, J., & Pattanaik, B. (2005). *Trafficking and prostitution reconsidered: New perspectives on migration, sex work, and human rights* (1st ed.). Boulder, CO and London: Paradigm Publishers.

King, R., Castaldo, A., & Vullnetari, J. (2011). Gendered relations and filial duties along the Greek-Albanian Remittance Corridor. *Economic Geography, 87*(4), 393–419.

Kunz, R. (2008). 'Remittances are beautiful'? Gender implications of the new global remittances trend. *Third World Quarterly, 29*(7), 1389–1409.

Lutz, H., Herrera Vivar, M. T., & Supik, L. (2011). *Framing intersectionality: Debates on a multi-faceted concept in gender studies.* Farnham: Ashgate.

McKay, D. (2007). 'Sending dollars shows feeling' – Emotions and economies in Filipino migration. *Mobilities, 2*(2), 175–194.

Menjívar, C., & Agadjanian, V. (2007). Men's migration and women's lives: Views from rural Armenia and Guatemal. *Social Science Quarterly, 88*(5), 1243–1262.

Morokvasic, M. (1984). Birds of passage are also women … *International Migration Review, 18*(4), 886–907.

Nyberg-Sørensen, N. (2007). *Migrant remittances, development and gender.* Copenhagen: Dansk Institut for Internationale Studier.

Parreñas, R. S. (2000). Migrant Filipina domestic workers and the international division of reproductive labor. *Gender & Society, 14*(4), 560–580.

Phizacklea, A. (1983). *One way ticket: Migration and female labour.* London: Routledge & Kegan Paul.

Piper, N. (2008a). Feminisation of migration and the social dimensions of development: The Asian case. *Third World Quarterly, 29*(7), 1287–1303.

Piper, N. (2008b). *New perspectives on gender and migration: Livelihood, rights and entitlements.* London: Routledge.

Piper, N. (2009a). The complex interconnections of the migration–development nexus: A social perspective. *Population, Space and Place, 15*(2), 93–101.

Piper, N. (2009b). *Migration and social development: Organizational and political dimensions.* Social Policy and Development Programme Paper Number 39, UNRISD, Geneva.

Piper, N. (2017). Migration and the SDGs. *Global Social Policy, 17*(2), 231–238.

Pribilsky, J. (2004). 'Aprendemos a convivir': Conjugal relations, co-parenting, and family life among Ecuadorian transnational migrants in New York City and the Ecuadorian Andes. *Global Networks-A Journal of Transnational Affairs, 4*(3), 313–334.

Radcliffe, S. A. (1986). Gender relations, peasant livelihood strategies and migration: A case study from Cuzco, Peru. *Bulletin of Latin American Research, 5*(2), 29–47.

Roy, A., & Nangia, P. (2005). *Impact of male out-migration on health status of left behind wives – A study of Bihar, India.* Paper presented at the International Union for the Scientific Study of Population. Available https://iussp2005.princeton.edu/papers/51906

Silvey, R. (2009). Development and geography: Anxious times, anemic geographies, and migration. *Progress in Human Geography, 33*(4), 507–515.

Skeldon, R. (2000). Trafficking: A perspective from Asia. *International Migration, 38*(3), 7–30.

Sobieszczyk, T. (2015). "Good" sons and "Dutiful" daughters: A structural symbolic interactionist analysis of the migration and remittance behaviour of Northern Thai International Migrants. In L. A. Hoang & B. S. A. Yeoh (eds.), *Transnational labour migration, remittances and the changing family in Asia* (pp. 82–110). London: Palgrave Macmillan UK.

United Nations. (2006). *2004 world survey on the role of women in development.* New York: DESA.

Vullnetari, J., & King, R. (2011). *Remittances, gender and development: Albania's society and economy in transition.* London: Tauris Academic Studies.

Waters, J. L. (2010). Becoming a father, missing a wife: Chinese transnational families and the male experience of lone parenting in Canada. *Population, Space and Place, 16*(1), 63–74.

Willis, K., & Yeoh, B. S. A. (2000). *Gender and migration.* Cheltenham: Edward Elgar.

Wu, H., & Ye, J. (2016). Hollow lives: Women left behind in rural China. *Journal of Agrarian Change, 16*(1), 50–69.

Yabiku, S. T., Agadjanian, V., & Sevoyan, A. (2010). Husbands' labour migration and wives' autonomy, Mozambique 2000–2006. *Population Studies, 64*(3), 293–306.

Zlotnik, H. (2003). The global dimensions of female migration. Retrieved from www.migrationinformation.org/feature/display.cfm?ID=109

10

REMITTANCES

Eight analytical perspectives

Jørgen Carling

Introduction

The billions of dollars that migrants send to their countries of origin every year might be the most obvious and direct link between migration and development. Remittances represent a major shift of wealth from rich to poor countries, nearly three times as large as official development assistance.

Countless papers have been written with introductions akin to this one, heralding the global value of remittances. In fact, remittances have come to be seen as an over-researched and increasingly lacklustre aspect of the migration and development agenda. Yet, there is much more to be said, explored, and challenged. Remittances not only remain overwhelmingly important to migration–development connections; they are also specific and concrete. Therefore, remittances serve as a unifying focal point for thematic, disciplinary, and methodological perspectives that differ and complement each other.

This chapter takes such a diversity-driven approach and addresses the many roles that remittances play in the migration–development nexus. The sections that follow provide eight complementary perspectives on the significance of remittances in research and policy on migration and development.

Remittances as a pivot in the migration–development nexus

The literature on migration and development took a new turn with the term 'migration–development nexus' (Sørensen et al. 2002). And the underlying ideas have implications for how we should understand remittances. No explicit definition was offered when the migration–development nexus was introduced, but I would define it as *the totality of mechanisms through which migration and development dynamics affect each other*. In other words, the nexus does not give primacy to either migration or development, but emphasises the multiple two-way relationships.

Seeing remittances as a pivot in the migration–development nexus means regarding them not only as a conduit for development impacts once migration occurs, but also as potential influences on migration dynamics. The *prospect of remitting* can be a powerful driver of migration aspirations. Working abroad can be seen as the best way of providing for one's children or elderly parents, for instance, or for financing investments such as constructing a house or establishing a business in the community of origin. *Receiving remittances* could potentially affect migration aspirations in contradictory ways. On the one hand, the money illustrates the potential benefits of migration and the prospect of becoming someone who gives, rather than someone who receives. On the other hand, remittances can make it possible, and desirable, to stay. Remittances can even be a form of compensation for not migrating, as when emigrants remit to a sibling who stays to care for their elderly parents (Carling 2014). Remittances can also *finance migration*, be it by covering the cost of travel, agency fees, permits, or smuggling.

The interaction of remittances and migration decision-making was central to the so-called new economics of labour migration (NELM) that emerged in the 1980s and 1990s (Taylor 1999). This approach took the household as the primary unit of analysis and demonstrated that migration and remittances serve to reduce risk. Many of the insights from NELM remain valid, but the approach incorporated a somewhat naïve notion of 'household decisions'. Thinking about migration and remittances at the household level should raise questions about gendered and generational power dynamics. It is not given that the prospective remitter simply makes a selfless decision to leave and provide for those who stay. Yet, it might not be as simple as a powerful patriarch deploying family members to work elsewhere. These micro-level power dynamics of migration and remittances have been examined in more recent research (Dannecker 2005; Vullnetari and King 2011). What shuttled remittances to prominence on the international development agenda, however, was observations of financial flows at the macro level.

Remittances as development finance

At some point around the turn of the millennium, interest in remittances among policy-makers, practitioners, and academics surged. Part of the explanation was an eye-opening statistic: the comparison of migrant remittances to official development assistance (ODA). Why did this comparison have such a dramatic impact?

Pedagogically, such comparisons are useful because big numbers are hard to fathom. A - 100 billion dollars is clearly a lot of money, but how important is that amount in the big scheme of things? The comparison with official development assistance provides a heuristically useful anchor for the significance of remittances.

Empirically, the comparison captured a striking trend, illustrated in Figure 10.1. During the 1990s, the value of ODA remained roughly constant while the value of recorded remittances increased steadily and surpassed ODA in 1996. Since the turn of the Millennium, ODA too has risen, but remittance amounts have skyrocketed, reaching 200 per cent of ODA in 2006 and quickly approaching 300 per cent. A key question, which we will return to, is whether these numbers can be trusted.

Thematically, the comparison with ODA represented a particular framing of remittances *as development finance*. Seen in this way remittances were not simply transfers between family members, but rather a form of crowdfunding for national development. The World Bank, the Inter-American Development Bank (IDB), and the International Fund for Agricultural Development (IFAD), for instance, increasingly saw remittances as part of their agenda.

Politically, the idea of remittances as development finance had broad appeal. Since these were private funds with a strong grassroots foundation, they were viewed favourably by sceptics of big government as well as by sceptics of big business. The implication of seeing remittances as development finance was not that the state should retreat, but rather that it

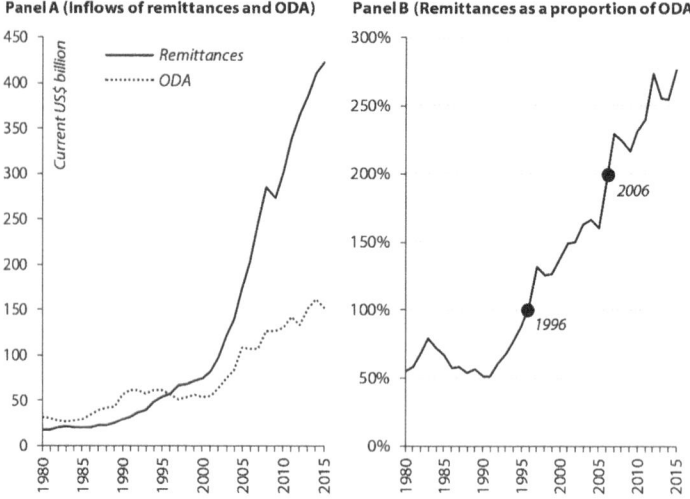

Figure 10.1 Remittances and official development assistance (ODA) to low and middle-income countries 1980–2015

Data source: World Development Indicators. Remittances are 'personal remittances'; figures for official development assistance include transfers classified as aid

should facilitate and leverage remittances-led development. A prominent example was Mexico's *tres-por-uno* programme, under which remittance-funded development projects received triply matched funding from the government.

The 'remittance euphoria' was not without its critics, though. As one report poignantly warned, 'remittances do not automatically generate development and there is a real danger that they may be seen as a substitute for policies that do' (Mitchell 2006, 3). Moreover, is it fair that low-income migrants in the Global North should have to shoulder the cost of reducing global inequality? Or that government funds boost the development of villages that receive remittances while the neighbouring village gets neither?

Such questions stimulated critical research, which proliferated alongside mainstream studies on the determinants and impacts of remittances (de Haas 2005; Kapur 2004; Kunz 2011). In fact, since the 1980s, the number of academic publications on remittances has risen three times as fast as the value of the transfers.

Remittances as a research topic

The number of journal articles about remittances increased ten-fold from the late 1990s to 2012 (Figure 10.2, Panel A).[1] Since the number of journal articles in general has risen, it is also worth asking whether a larger *proportion* of migration-related articles now address remittances. Indeed, the proportion has risen from less than 1 per cent in the early 1980s to about 5 per cent in the early 2010s (Panel B).

Yet, the graphs in Figure 10.1 suggest a rise *and fall* of interest in remittances. What happened in the early 2010s that turned the trend? Part of the explanation, I believe, is remittance fatigue. There had simply been such a wealth of studies on remittances that many scholars felt it was time to move on. This sentiment was exemplified by a special issue of the journal *World Development* in 2014, that opened with an introduction entitled 'Migration

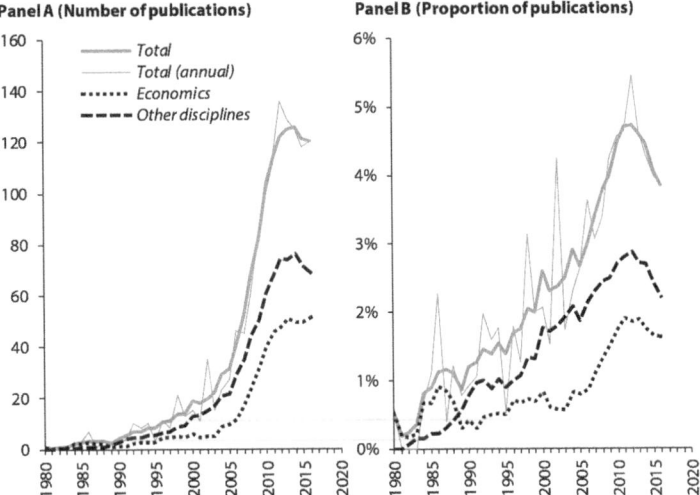

Figure 10.2 Articles on remittances in international peer-reviewed journals 1980–2016, 5-year sliding averages

Data source: Web of Science. See endnote 1 for details

and development research is moving far beyond remittances' (Clemens et al. 2014). Perhaps the peak also reflects a broader turnaround in sentiments about migration and development, with pessimistic views gaining greater influence (Gamlen 2014).

Alongside the variation in the volume of research on remittances, changes in composition have been observed. The discipline of economics dominated the study of remittances until the late 1980s, as Figure 10.2, Panel B, shows, but the expansion of research over the subsequent two decades took place in other disciplines. When sociologists, anthropologists and other social scientists increasingly became interested in remittances, it was intertwined with the rise of transnational perspectives on migration.

Remittances as a transnational practice

The concept of transnationalism provided a new and different frame for the study of remittances. Transnationalism was initially defined as 'the processes by which immigrants forge and sustain multi-stranded social relations that link together their societies of origin and settlement' (Basch et al. 1994, 7). Remittance-sending was an obvious part of these processes, which were often referred to as transnational practices. In the research literature, remittances have thus led a dual existence: partly as a form of development finance alongside foreign direct investment and development assistance, and partly as a transnational practice alongside activities such as return visits and cross-border communication (Figure 10.3).

The notion of transnational practices offers different answers to the question 'what do remittances do?' Remittances transfer wealth, but they also forge and sustain relationships. Remittance-sending, like return visits and social media communication, are practices that a large proportion of migrants engage in, at least occasionally. They thus represent one end of a spectrum, with the other end being the more intensive and institutionalised transnational practices of a small minority, such as transnational entrepreneurs and political activists.

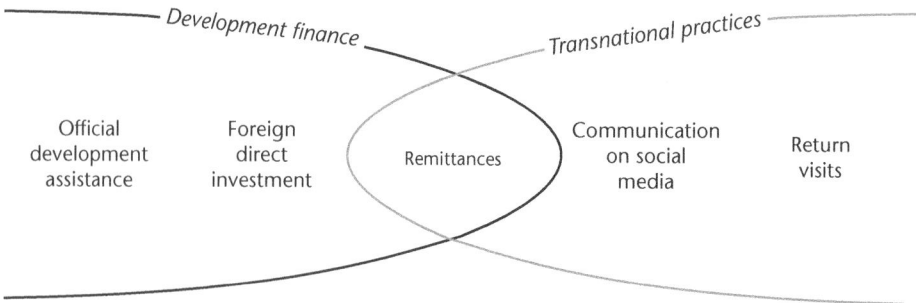

Figure 10.3 Two contexts of remittances in the research literature

Remittances as scripted transactions

Much of the research on transnationalism has drawn on ethnographic methods, which focus on building relationships with informants and examining processes and experiences that were unknown before fieldwork began. Since the 1990s, many such studies have broached remittances, even if remittances have rarely been the focus of analysis. More recently, however, researchers in anthropology, geography, and sociology have also used ethnographic methods to explore the specific social dynamics of remittance-sending (Åkesson 2011; Paerregaard 2015; Page and Mercer 2012; Thai 2014).

The ethnographic literature has yielded new insights on remittances, but they have been fragmented and faint amidst other lines of research. In Carling (2014), I sought to consolidate findings from a large body of ethnographic studies in a coherent theoretical framework with three key elements. First, *remittances are the core of composite transactions*. In other words, the money that is transferred by migrants is merely the most visible and quantifiable element in a multi-faceted exchange. For instance, remittance transactions can confirm the migrant's continued social membership, challenge hierarchical relations between the transactors, or alter the social status of both the sender and the recipient. They can induce feelings of gratification or humiliation and generate social debt. Remittance transactions thus always have other intended or unintended effects than the transfer of purchasing power.

Second, *remittance transactions reflect and encompass two-sided agency*. In other words, remittance recipients are not passively receiving, but actively participating in the transaction. They can make *requests* for remittances, for instance, which is a central but often overlooked part of remittance dynamics. Such requests reflect choices about when to ask, whom to ask, and how to ask. In addition, recipients exercise agency through all the ways in which remittances are reciprocated.

Third, *remittance transactions reflect a combination of pre-existing and migration-induced aspects of relationships*. On the one hand, remittances can reflect pre-existing social obligations between individuals, such as an adult child's responsibility to support elderly parents. In this case, transfers would have taken place regardless of migration; they simply become transnational and perhaps change in size. On the other hand, remittances can reflect new asymmetries between people that arise as a result of migration (Carling 2008b). In some cases, the same disparities in wealth, opportunities, or security that motivated migration in the first place translate into a privileged situation for migrants relative to those who stay behind. These inequalities can produce obligations or expectations of remittances.

These three premises are valuable entry points for understanding remittance transactions, but enormous variation occurs in how the actual transactions play out. Remittance transactions typically relate to specific *scripts*, or structures of expectations for specific types of situations, which facilitate social interaction (Carling 2014). For instance, remittances are in some cases conceived as 'help' that the sender extends to the recipient. In other cases, this interpretation would be entirely inappropriate. The difference is not simply about the sender's motivations; when remittances are understood as 'help', it concerns perceptions of needs and worthiness, defines the relationship between the sender and recipient, elicits particular feelings surrounding the transaction, carries implications for appropriate uses of the money, and embodies expectations for behaviour, such as the expression of gratitude. I identify 12 such scripts, including allowance, investment, repayment, and sacrifice.

Remittances as a methodological challenge

Ethnographic studies are not so dependent on systematically quantifying the volume or frequency of remittances. But such quantification is obviously central to other methodologies, as well as for development planning and policy development. Quantitative data on remittances come primarily from two sources: balance of payments statistics and sample surveys. Both encompass significant challenges.

The spectacular rise in remittances, illustrated in Figure 10.1, reflects officially recorded flows and leave out unregistered remittances such as hand-carried cash and *hawala* transfers.[2] Such transfers remain significant in many countries but have become less important over time. Official figures therefore provide a more accurate picture today than they did in the past. But this shift suggests that the officially recorded *increase* over time is an overstatement. Over the past couple of decades, regular transfers, too, are increasingly likely to be recorded as remittances in official statistics, partly because intensified efforts to combat money laundering and terrorist financing have tightened reporting requirements. Against this background, Clemens and McKenzie (in press) recently asked how much of the rise in remittances might be attributed to changes in measurement. Based on a diversity of evidence for the 1990–2010 period they surprisingly conclude that as much as 80 per cent of the rise in remittances probably results from changes in measurement. If this is the case, comparisons between countries, too, should be interpreted with caution.

Part of the reason why remittances may be overstated or understated in official records is that they can be difficult to distinguish from other transfers, or that such distinctions are not made consistently. Remittances are generally understood as money transferred by migrants to their families in the country of origin, but the diversity of actual transfers quickly raise questions about how 'remittances' should be understood.[3] In fact, money that we think of as remittances might be transferred from senders who are *not migrants* (but descendants of migrants, or collective institutions such as hometown associations) to recipients who are *not relatives* (but friends, or charitable organisations, for instance), to communities that are *not in the country of origin* (but, for instance, in the near diaspora such as Somali communities in Kenya or Afghan communities in Pakistan). A sizeable share of 'remittances' are *not even transfers* from one person to another, but rather money that remains the migrant's but is sent to the country of origin, for instance for the purpose of constructing a house.

All these considerations complicate the official accounting of remittances, and they also present challenges to researchers, analysts, and others who relate to 'remittances' as a concept. The familiar model from the economics literature, based on a dyadic relationship between households of origin and migrants who remit a share of their income, might account for a shrinking proportion of global remittance-like transfers. This is especially the case in contexts where family reunification is possible and migrants and their descendants have diverse forms of financial engagement with their country of origin.

Survey research has the advantage of not being bound by existing systems for accounting and reporting. It can therefore more flexibly capture the transfers of interest. But how are questions about remittances to be asked in a survey? Despite the multitude of survey data on remittances, little methodological reflection on this challenge has been made. In Brown et al. (2014) two overarching dilemmas were identified that must be tackled on a case-by-case basis: the complexity dilemma and the diversity dilemma.

Remittance-related transfers can be dauntingly complex. How much of that complexity should a questionnaire aim to capture? Within a given budget for the survey, every additional question has an impact on the sample size and must be justified. But shortcuts based on misleading assumptions can reduce the value of the data. For example, most surveys in communities of origin would only ask about *receiving* remittances, but there are situations in which money is rather sent *to* the migrant *from* the family at home – for instance in the case of international student migration, or when irregular migrants are trapped in transit or struggle to survive after arrival. In order to decide whether the survey questions should also address so-called reverse remittances, researchers must be knowledgeable about the context at hand and balance different priorities.

The second overarching dilemma results from variability across contexts. One key issue that is known to vary is the relationship between individuals and households (cf. Brown et al. 2014; Erdal 2012). Are remittances in practice sent to and from households or individuals within them? How is information about remittance transfers to or from the household shared between household members? And how should this affect the selection of respondents and the phrasing of questions? The best questionnaire in a given context will reflect the specifics of that setting and the remittance transactions within it. Yet, when the questions are heavily adapted to local conditions, the results can be difficult to compare with findings from surveys elsewhere.

Remittances as a driver of development

Survey data has been essential for understanding the impacts of remittances on development. A widespread, but misguided, approach is to ask recipients how remittance income is spent, and to assess the development-enhancing potential of the spending pattern. This is flawed because income is fungible; there might not be any direct link between specific income sources and specific expenditures. Moreover, the impact of remittances can only be measured by comparing with an imaginary counterfactual situation. In cases where individual migrants are working elsewhere and remitting money to their household of origin, the counterfactual situation is one in which they are living in the household, contributing from a local salary, and consuming household resources. Estimating what this situation would have been like is challenging, but doable with the right type of data (Adams 2011; Brown and Jimenez 2008; Jimenez-Soto and Brown 2012).

The most extensive review to date concluded that international remittances consistently reduce poverty in the developing world (Adams 2011). Remittances are usually also found to improve child health and reduce infant mortality. At the same time, however, they tend to reduce the labour supply because people who receive remittances choose to work less. The effects on inequality are less conclusive, and may even be divergent at national versus local levels (Jones 1998; Skeldon 2008).

The specific impact of remittances will vary across contexts and over time. But a conceptual issue always lingers in the background: where do we set the threshold for saying that remittances drive development? We could simply focus on typical development indicators, such as levels of poverty and income, and estimate the effect of remittance inflows. But if progress in those areas remains directly funded by remittances, the development gains would be dependent on continued migration and remittance-sending. If this is the case, one might argue, remittances are just a temporary band-aid. An alternative view, therefore, is that remittance-driven 'development' only occurs if there is progress that would survive the elimination of remittance inflows. This conceptual issue translates into a strategic question: can remittance-led growth be a development strategy?

A decade before remittances attained prominence on the global development agenda their strategic potential was already hotly debated in the Pacific, where remittances and aid appeared to be the cornerstones of the *de facto* development strategy of many small island states. Economist Geoffrey Bertram (1986) suggested that this is a perfectly 'sustainable' development strategy as long as the transfers can be maintained over time. However, much of the international development community in the region saw it as invalid and unsustainable, fostering dependency and undermining productive investment. In a review of the debate, Poirine (1998) argued that that the negative views fail to recognise that aid and remittances are not just handouts, but also represent exchanges with the rest of the world. These exchanges might represent pragmatic ways of making the most of a small and remote country's few comparative advantages.

Also, at the micro-level of household spending, one might ask what it takes for remittances to generate development. One scenario, which has fuelled pessimistic views on remittances in the past, is that the increased purchasing power is spent on imported luxury goods that have no meaningful impact on local or national development. The experience of Yemen in the 1980s, for instance, corroborated this fear (Carling 1996). Also, the direct investment of remittances in productive assets often fell short of expectations (cf. de Haas 2010).

Yet, remittances might be driving development in more subtle ways. They have often been found to increase expenditure on health and education, for instance. Even the construction of lavish houses, which has often been dismissed as unproductive vanity projects, may deliver indirect development benefits. The construction process provides employment for local workers and thereby diffuses remittance income across socio-economic strata, and the houses, once finished, may anchor transnational ties that persist across generations.

Another subtle but widely appreciated effect of remittances is as a driver of financial inclusion. In low-income countries, remittances often induce recipients' first interactions with financial institutions and may pave the way towards use of financial services such as credit, savings, and insurance. In this way, remittances support social transformations that are essential to the development process and likely to survive a decline in remittance income.

Remittances as unforeseen burdens

Research and policy on remittances have traditionally focused on the receiving end, where development impacts may materialise. Remittance senders have primarily figured in the part of the literature that examines determinants of remittances (Carling 2008a). These studies aiming to model variations in remittance flows across time and across groups, which are important to understand also from a development perspective.

More recently, and partly under the influence of the transnational turn, researchers have explored the broader roles of remittances within migrants' lives. Some of this work has examined the experiences of migrants who clearly did not migrate in order to remit but eventually found remittance-sending to be a big part of life as a migrant. In a seminal publication based on research among Sudanese refugees, Akuei (2005) described remittances as 'unforeseen burdens'. Within 2 years of settling in the in the US, one of Akuei's informants

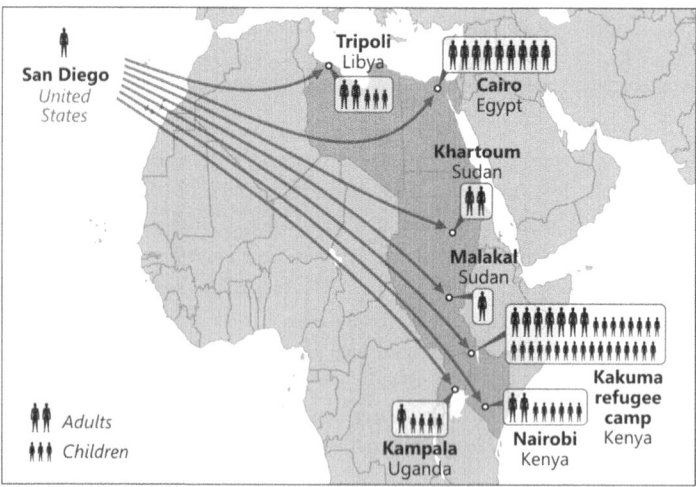

Figure 10.4 A Sudanese refugee's responsibility for supporting extended family members through remittances

Data source: Akuei (2005)

became directly responsible for supporting 24 adult relatives and 38 children across north-eastern Africa (Figure 10.4).

Three factors combine to produce powerful remittance obligations, also for low-income migrants who struggle to make ends meet (Carling 2014; Carling et al. 2012; Hernández-Carretero 2015; Lindley 2010). First, the contrasts in well-being among transnational family members can be stark. Beyond a general situation of poverty, relatives in poor or conflict-affected countries may face urgent crises that result in remittance requests that are impossible to resist. Second, many migrants come from societies with powerful norms of kinship-based redistribution. The expectation of sharing one's (relative) wealth does not cease with migration. Third, increasing possibilities for long-distance communication allow migrants' relatives in the Global South to request remittances.

Conclusion: refining or imploding the concept of remittances?

Research on remittances has swelled in volume and scope. New perspectives, methodologies, and thematic foci have been introduced and revived remittance research at a time when it appeared to be falling out of fashion. Perhaps we will see a smaller volume of research in years to come, but even greater theoretical inventiveness.

However, another development has swept into the field with potentially disruptive consequences: the rise of 'social remittances' as a label for the migration-driven forms of cultural diffusion (Levitt 1998). Levitt's seminal article employed 'remittances' in a metaphorical fashion to describe the non-economic impacts of migration. It was highly successful in this regard and gave rise to new research on changing norms, values and behaviours in the context of migrant transnationalism. But it also spawned a mushrooming of alternative 'remittances' that essentially implode the concept's meaning.

If migrants' monetary transfers become known as 'financial remittances' alongside social remittances, political remittances, professional remittances, artistic remittances, emotional remittances, and so on, the meaning of 'remittances' inadvertently changes. In a rare attempt to pin down this new and abstract meaning of remittances, Page and Mercer (2012, 4) state that they use it 'as a basket category that includes far more than just sending money'. Their usage includes 'those contacts such as conversations on the phone that convey ideas, information, and values, those journeys that move skills and knowledge around the world and the plethora of activities by which national and international connections are maintained'. I am not convinced that remittances in the conventional sense are a good metaphor for all such interactions, and I believe it would be a loss if 'remittances' were bereaved of its meaning as one distinct form of transnational practice among many others.

Remittances in the traditional sense of money transfers are interesting not least because the financial transaction is simply the crux of multi-faceted exchanges, experiences, and social consequences that reach far beyond the economic realm. Their significance is aptly summarised in the old marketing slogan of the world's leading remittance company, Western Union: 'sending so much more than money'.

Notes

1 The analysis covers migration-related articles within anthropology, area studies, demography, economics, ethnic studies, geography, history, international relations, law, planning development, political science, sociology, or urban studies. The disciplinary limitation minimises the number of instances where words derived from 'migrate' or 'remit' are used in irrelevant ways (e.g. 'relapsing–remitting multiple sclerosis', or 'tumor cell migration'). 'Migration-related' is defined by having any of the word stems migrat*, migrant*, emigra*, immigra*, or refuge* in the title, abstract, or keywords. Articles 'about remittances' are those with the word stem remit* in the title, abstract, or keywords.
2 Hawala refers to a diversity of more or less informal value transfer systems that operate alongside regular banks and money transfer operators.
3 There are detailed instructions for compiling balance of payments statistics, which clarify some distinctions. However, the question of what to include in 'remittances' is of broader relevance.

References

Adams, R.H. (2011) 'Evaluating the economic impact of international remittances on developing countries using household surveys: A literature review.' *Journal of Development Studies*, 47(6): 809–828.

Åkesson, L. (2011) 'Remittances and relationships: Exchange in cape verdean transnational families.' *Ethnos*, 76(3): 326–347.

Akuei, S.R. (2005) *Remittances as unforeseen burdens: The livelihoods and social obligations of Sudanese refugees.* Global Migration Perspectives, 18. Geneva: Global Commission on International Migration.

Basch, L., Glick Schiller, N. and Szanton Blanc, C. (1994) *Nations unbound: Transnational projects, postcolonial predicaments and deterritorialized nation-states.* Amsterdam: Gordon and Breach Publishers.

Bertram, I.G. (1986) "Sustainable development' in Pacific micro-economies.' *World Development*, 14(7): 809–822.

Brown, R.P.C., Carling, J., Fransen, S. and Siegel, M. (2014) 'Measuring remittances through surveys: Methodological and conceptual issues for survey designers and data analysts.' *Demographic Research*, 31: 1243–1274.

Brown, R.P.C. and Jimenez, E. (2008) 'Estimating the net effects of migration and remitances on poverty and inequality: Comparison of Fiji and Tonga.' In Kumar, N. and Ramani, V.V. (eds.) *Migration and Remittances in Developing Countries.* Hyderabad: Icfai University Press, 86–119.

Carling, J. (1996) *International labour migration: Consequences for countries of origin.* Occasional Paper #21, Human Geography. Oslo: Department of Sociology and Human Geography, University of Oslo.

Carling, J. (2008a) 'The determinants of migrant remittances.' *Oxford Review of Economic Policy*, 24(3): 582–599.

Carling, J. (2008b) 'The human dynamics of migrant transnationalism.' *Ethnic and Racial Studies*, 31(8): 1452–1477.

Carling, J. (2014) 'Scripting remittances: Making sense of money transfers in transnational relationships.' *International Migration Review*, 48: S218-S262.

Carling, J., Erdal, M.B. and Horst, C. (2012) 'How does conflict in migrants' country of origin affect remittance-sending? Financial priorities and transnational obligations among Somalis and Pakistanis in Norway.' *International Migration Review*, 46(2): 283–309.

Clemens, M.A. and McKenzie, D. (in press) 'Why don't remittances appear to affect growth?' *Economic Journal*, 128: F179–F209. doi:10.1111/ecoj.12463.

Clemens, M.A., Özden, Ç. and Rapoport, H. (2014) 'Migration and development research is moving far beyond remittances.' *World Development*, 64: 121–124.

Dannecker, P. (2005) 'Transnational migration and the transformation of gender relations: The case of Bangladeshi labour migrants.' *Current Sociology*, 53(4): 655–674.

de Haas, H. (2005) 'International migration, remittances and development: Myths and facts.' *Third World Quarterly*, 26(8): 1269–1284.

de Haas, H. (2010) 'Migration and development: A theoretical perspective.' *International Migration Review*, 44(1): 227–264.

Erdal, M.B. (2012) 'Who is the money for? Remittances within and beyond the household in Pakistan.' *Asian and Pacific Migration Journal*, 21(4): 437–457.

Gamlen, A. (2014) 'The new migration-and-development pessimism.' *Progress in Human Geography*, 38(4): 581–597.

Hernández-Carretero, M. (2015) 'Renegotiating obligations through migration: Senegalese transnationalism and the quest for the right distance.' *Journal of Ethnic and Migration Studies*, 41(12): 2021–2040.

Jimenez-Soto, E.V. and Brown, R.P.C. (2012) 'Assessing the poverty impacts of migrants' remittances using propensity score matching: The case of Tonga.' *Economic Record*, 88(282): 425–439.

Jones, R.C. (1998) 'Remittances and inequality: A question of migration stage and geographical scale.' *Economic Geography*, 74(1): 8–25.

Kapur, D. (2004) *Remittances: The new development mantra?* G–24 Discussion Paper, 29. New York: United Nations.

Kunz, R. (2011) *The political economy of global remittances. Gender, governmentality and neoliberalism.* Abingdon: Routledge.

Levitt, P. (1998) 'Social remittances: Migration driven local-level forms of cultural diffusion.' *International Migration Review*, 32(4): 926–948.

Lindley, A. (2010) *The early morning phone call: Somali refugees' remittances.* New York: Berghahn Books.

Mitchell, S. (2006) *Migration and the remittance euphoria: Development or dependency?* London: New Economics Foundation.

Paerregaard, K. (2015) *Return to sender. The moral economy of Peru's migrant remittances.* Oakland, CA: University of California Press.

Page, B. and Mercer, C. (2012) 'Why do people do stuff? Reconceptualizing remittance behaviour in diaspora-development research and policy.' *Progress in Development Studies*, 12(1): 1–18.

Poirine, B. (1998) 'Should we hate or love MIRAB?' *Contemporary Pacific*, 10(1): 65–105.

Skeldon, R. (2008) 'International migration as a tool in development policy: A passing phase?' *Population and Development Review*, 34(1): 1–18.

Sørensen, N.N., Van Hear, N. and Engberg-Pedersen, P. (2002) 'The migration-development nexus evidence and policy options state-of-the-art overview.' *International Migration*, 40(5): 3–47.

Taylor, J.E. (1999) 'The new economics of labour migration and the role of remittances in the migration process.' *International Migration*, 37(1): 63–86.

Thai, H.C. (2014) *Insufficient funds. The culture of money in low-wage transnational families.* Stanford: Stanford University Press.

Vullnetari, J. and King, R. (2011) *Remittances, gender and development: Albania's society and economy in transition.* London: IB Tauris.

11

SOCIAL REMITTANCES

Ilka Vari-Lavoisier

Introduction

Human mobility reshapes contemporary societies – but 'what kinds of change does migration set in motion? How does such change come about?' (Van Hear 2010). Calling attention to the societal implications of international migration (Levitt 1998, 2001), the concept of social remittances emphasised that, along with material resources (money and goods), migrants participate in the circulation of immaterial resources (knowledge and know-how, ideas and practices) between their home and host societies. In other words, the initial definition of social remittances points towards the ways of speaking, ways of doing, and ways of thinking that circulate along migratory paths.

The concept of social remittances, by providing migration scholars with a terminology and a space in which to discuss the non-economic consequences of transnational mobility, flagged a new area of inquiry. Since the early 2000s, a stimulating body of work has explored the impact of migrants' intangible resources on tangible outcomes – such as fertility rates, election results, or art forms – in the social, political, and cultural realms. Subsequent questions and critics pushed towards more nuanced views on social remittances and led to refine the epistemological, theoretical, and methodological approaches to social transfers, within and beyond the field of migration studies.

As we reflect today on of the relevance of thinking in terms of social remittances, let us consider the incidence of this concept on the scholarship over the two last decades. What is, indeed, the role of a concept? This is my contention that, despite limitations, the term 'social remittances' generated original empirical studies and stimulated a productive conversation. As such, if we consider concepts as 'exploratory tools' (Olivier de Sardan 2014) that primarily aim to 'stimulate the sociological imagination' (Siméant 2015), then the debates spurred by this concept speak for themselves.

Genesis and refinements of a concept

Of disciplines: from economics to development studies

The scholarship on migrants' remittances reflects broader evolutions in the social sciences. Until the 1990s, the overarching position of economics in the analysis of migration translated, into an abundant literature focusing on the economic stakes raised by mobility. Economic development (or its lack, thereof) appeared to spur migration; while, in turn, migration-induced economic transfers proved to impact significantly the economic life of sending countries (Clemens, Özden, and Rapoport 2015; Gubert 2007). A sustained scholarly interest in migrants' financial transfers (see Chapter 10 in this Handbook; Carling 2014; Garip, Eskici, and Snyder 2014 for recent literature reviews) revealed that economic remittances are irreducible to their monetary value, and should be analysed as *composite* transactions with material, emotional, and relational elements (Zelizer 2014).

To be sure, 'economics is not the whole story' (Levitt and Lamba-Nieves 2011, 2). The concept of social remittances called attention to the migration-driven circulation of norms and behaviours (Levitt 1998, 2001), at a time where the 'superiority of economists' began to be called into questions by cognate disciplines (Fourcade, Ollion, and Algan 2015). Consequently, the 2000s witnessed the booming of a whole new field of research, discussing the powerful impact of mobility on various social, political, and cultural outcomes. This body of evidence established that, albeit non-quantifiable, non-monetary flows critically influence the socio-political environment of sending, and receiving countries (De Haas 2007; Kapur 2014; Lacroix 2014; Lafleur 2013; Piper 2009; Portes 2008; Sasse 2013).

The impact of social transfers remains, however, unclear. Nuancing the enthusiasm of early publications, the 2010s were also marked by a series of critics, that stressed notably the need to conceptualise more firmly: both the positive and negative consequences of social remittances, the failures and resistances faced by social remitters, at the micro- or macro-level, or the need to think harder about the difficulty to operationalise a concept encompassing such a large array of phenomena (Boccagni and Decimo 2013; Grabowska et al. 2017). A new generation of scholarship, attuned to the limits and drawbacks of social transfers, emerged in the mid-2010s (Boccagni, Lafleur, and Levitt 2016; Levitt and Rajaram 2013a; Lacroix, Levitt, and Vari-Lavoisier 2016). This line of research, particularly prolific today, illustrates the inherently interdisciplinary nature of migration studies, by bringing into the conversation qualitative and quantitative studies, conducted by scholars from various fields, ranging from political science to geography, development studies, or anthropology.

Of methods: from the micro to the macro

A set of pioneer studies, that contributed to launching social remittances as a core concept, used qualitative methods to investigate the impact of mobility on intra-familial relations and households' structures (Gardner 1995; Hondagneu-Sotelo and Avila 1997). Scholars noted the powerful implications of migration for gender roles and intra-household power dynamics in various contexts (Hondagneu-Sotelo 2013; Lopez-Ekra et al. 2011; Mizanur Rahman 2013; Marchetti and Venturini 2014; Vianello 2013; Yngvesson 2017). Indeed, mobility seems to provide avenues to challenge pervasive inequalities, by offering room for emancipation, or by allowing for the acquisition of useful knowledge and know-how (see Grabowska and Garapich 2016).

This fast-growing body of evidence confirmed the relevance of studying how social remittances affect both positive and negative social change, to produce policy-relevant evidence, aiming notably to support positive migration–development links (Nyberg-Sørensen 2005; Nyberg-Sørensen, Van Hear, and Engberg-Pedersen 2002). Along those lines, a series of recent studies focus on social remittances in the health domain, as a strategic field site in which to analyse the tangible implications of intangible flows. These contributions also implement innovative collaborative qualitative methods to capture the implications of mobility at the meso- and macro-level (Holdaway et al. 2015; Lafleur and Lizin 2015, 2016; Levitt and Rajaram 2013b). By doing so, this line of inquiry sheds new light on the implications of cross-border circulation for global health today (Boccagni 2017; Dobbs and Levitt 2017; Levitt et al. 2017).

Quantitatively-minded scholars entered this discussion in the early 2010s. The seminal work of Philippes Fargues, on fertility norms showed that birth rates declined faster in regions with high emigration rates to the OECD countries (Fargues 2010, 2011). He attributed those drops in fertility rates to changing norms and values, among migrants – and paved the way for a series of statistical studies to the socio-political implications of international migration. Expanding upon this line of thought, his last piece explores the interrelations between population changes and political upheaval in the Arab world (Fargues 2017). By doing so, he contributes to the currently lively debate examining how we should think of, and go about, the relations between social remittances and political remittances.

Of conceptual distinctions between social, political, and economic remittances

The term 'political remittances' emerged at the turn of the 2010s (Kapur 2014; Nyblade and O'Mahony 2014; Pérez-Armendáriz and Crow 2010; Rother 2009; Tabar 2014; Vélez-Torres and Agergaard 2014), in an effort to parse out the different forms of transfers that migrants channel back home. Indeed, the fortune of the concept of 'social remittances' triggered questions regarding the contours of the term. As it was becoming ubiquitous in the migration literature, the term of 'social remittances' was increasingly resembling a 'moving target', mostly defined negatively (as the non-economic implications of migration; *cf.* Boccagni and Decimo 2013). Critics led migration thinkers to further refine their thinking and further research how social and political transfers interrelate, in light of new data. This debate brought into conversation qualitatively- and quantitively-minded scholars interested in the socio-political implications of mobility. Even though terminologies differ, there is considerable overlap between studies focusing on 'political remittances', political diffusion, 'democratic diffusion', 'transfers of norms', that ultimately seeks to document the different facets of one core phenomenon: the impact of migration on ideas and behaviours.

The relation between migration and political outcomes is at the core of a series of publications, using large quantitative dataset to provide new insights on the temporal sequence of events leading migration to bring about political change. For instance, Li and McHale compiled an extensive database to analyse the links between high-skilled migration in 1990 and the quality of institutions in sending areas in 2000. They found that migration had a negative impact on economic institutions, but a positive impact on political institutions[1] (Li and Mchale 2006). Convincing evidence further suggests that foreign-educated individuals play a key role in promoting 'democratic practices' back home (Artuc et al. 2015; Docquier et al. 2011; Mercier 2016; Spilimbergo 2009). Being understood that the characteristics of the destination countries mediate migrants' influence on the sending states (Beine and Sekkat 2013; Gift and Krcmaric 2015; Mahmoud et al. 2014).

Several studies attempted to quantify the impact of migration by focusing on political behaviours and electoral outcomes (Ahmadov and Sasse 2016; Dedieu et al. 2014; Jaulin 2016; Jaulin and Nilsson 2015; Nyblade and O'Mahony 2014). For instance, Catia Batista and Pedro Vicente (2011) conducted a voting experiment to assess the impact of international emigration on the political institution of Cape Verde and showed a positive impact of returnees from OECD countries on the demand for democracy. In this vein, Lisa

Chauvet and Marion Mercier studied the links between migration, electoral participation, and political competition in Mali. Using a panel dataset combing the Malian censuses, with electoral results covering a decade, the authors found a positive impact of migrants coming back from non-African countries on indicators of electoral competitiveness (Chauvet and Mercier 2014). Accordingly, a study comparing Malian migrants living in France and in Cote d'Ivoire provided evidence that the institutional context of the host country matters for the adoption of political norms (Chauvet, Gubert, and Mesplé-Somps 2016). As a whole, this body of literature underlines that migrants coming back from OECD countries tend to be more influential that migrants coming back from developing countries, although, these findings beg the question whether differences in migrants' political influence result from individual unobserved characteristics or from migrants increased social and economic resources. In other words, this line of inquiry raises questions about the extent of the inter-relations between political, social, and economic remittances.

From social to economic remittances

A core challenge of the migration studies literature is the necessity to disentangle better how social remittances relate to other forms of transnational flows. A critical need exists to conceptualise better the interrelations between economic transfers and social remittances, a question that has largely understudied thus far. This line of research has been mostly investigated by political scientists to date. For instance, Merino (2005) was among the first to argue that the receipt of remittances undermines clientelistic practices, by stimulating an increased political competition in areas receiving the most economic transfers. In the same vein, Thomas Pfutze (2012, 2014) argues that international migration promotes the 'quality of democracy' in the sending country. He puts forth a simple mechanism: economic remittances contribute to increases in households' income that 'make clientelism unambiguously more costly and, therefore, reduce turnout for the party engaging in clientelistic arrangements' (Pfutze 2014, 306). Along the same lines, a few scholars discuss the impact of economic transfers on political outcomes (Meseguer and Aparicio 2012; Meseguer, Lavezzolo, and Aparicio 2016), but tend to adopt an instrumental approach to political behaviour.

Seeking to offer a sociological perspective on transnational politics, another line of research stresses the importance of transnational power asymmetries. Elaborating further on the interrelations between material dynamics and intangible transfers of ideas and practices, some stress that unequal transnational exchanges, such as migrants' economic transfers, 'contribute to and reinforce honor, prestige, and authority' of one actor on the other (Eckstein 2010, 1651). The fact that migrants' resources loom large in the economy of sending countries contributes to migrants' social influence and political voice. The prestige associated with migrating, the economic resources, and the social capital that migrants acquire, in their countries of destination, participate in their enhanced ability to be listened to. This is all the more true in emigration countries, where common discourses depict emigrants as a symbol of success or 'gold mines'; the latter being preferred by women and mothers as potential husbands (Riccio 2005, 107) and admired by the young as role models (Fall, Carretero, and Sarr 2010). Poised with increased economic resources and prestige, migrants who maintain lively transnational ties are also likely to be more influential, because they can leverage their resources to foster their influence (Vari-Lavoisier 2015). In this respect, further studying social transfers might not only advance migration studies but could more broadly contribute to re-conceptualise how economic exchanges, political power, and social change interrelate today. To advance this research agenda, there is a need to re-embed the social remittances literature in the broader progress of migration studies and, beyond, within the broader theories of social change (Van Hear 2010).

What's next? Challenges ahead of us

Towards an epistemological framework for migration studies

The next section reviews some of the epistemological, theoretical, and empirical challenges ahead for migration scholars – and reflects on the potential contribution of the social remittance's literature to the broader objective of theorising how economic, social, and political remittances mutually shape each other in a world on the move.

A closer look at the existing literature reveals congruent findings from the macro-level, on political outcomes (Chauvet, Gubert, and Mesplé-Somps 2016; Fargues 2017), to the micro-level, on reproductive behaviours (Fargues 2011; Mesplé-Somps 2016), on the one hand; and from the political to the economic realm (Lacroix, Levitt, and Vari-Lavoisier 2016). In other words, recent studies discuss the relations between social and political remittances, while another line of research documents the links between social and economic transfers. However, an overarching synthesis is still lacking.

An overview of the literature, however, suggests that migration-driven learning effects spill over from one domain to another. The critical issue to resolve is how to develop methodologies for rigorously analysing these interrelations. A few avenues have already been sketched, to try explore specific instances where 'social remittances' scale out, to affect other domains, or 'scale-up', from the micro- to the macro-level, for instance, to affect national changes (Boccagni, Lafleur, and Levitt 2016, 460; Levitt and Lamba-Nieves 2011, 16–7). Some offer an encompassing approach, considering that '*many social remittances are political*' (Boccagni, Lafleur, and Levitt 2016), while others talk about 'social remittances', per domain, to study the *interactions* between the effects of migration on gender, health, or elections. More efforts are needed to refine the analytical tools suitable to understand how transnational economic, social, and political dynamics interrelate.

Of channels: how social change cross borders

Since its inception, the concept of social remittances has raised questions about the specificity (or lack thereof) of migrants' role in our interconnected world: to what extent migrants ontologically differ (or not) from other transnational actors (such as diplomats, Europeans politicians, or UN officials, to name a few)? And to what extent they play a particular role in linking local and global political contexts? This raises the question of the *channels* through which social remittances circulate. Indeed, social remittances are meant to circulate through exchanges of letters, videos, cassettes, e-mails, blog posts, and telephone calls. Perhaps more importantly, individual social remittances occur through interpersonal exchanges between individual family members and friends, while collective social remittances are exchanged between individuals in their roles as organisational actors. In this respect, we still a need to better understand the extent to what social remittances circulation 'reinforces and is reinforced by, other forms of global cultural circulation' (Boccagni, Lafleur, and Levitt 2016).

Indeed, at both ends of the process, there is also a need to better understand how global ideas are adapted locally (Levitt and Merry 2009). The concept of vernacularisation precisely aims to nail down the operation of translation and adaptation that migrants take in charge, as their ideas cross borders. The term vernacularisation, by describing *'the process of appropri-ation and local adoption of globally generated ideas and strategies'*, indeed calls attention to the work and characteristics of *'vernacularisers'* as well as to the *'channels and technologies of transmis-sion, and the local geographies of history and culture within which circulation'* of ideas and practices take place (Levitt and Merry 2009, 441).

Empirical challenges ahead: of directionality, intentionality, and methodology

This line of research is prone to reflect on the extent to which migrants convey *unwittingly* or *deliberately* new ideas and practices (Lacroix, Levitt, and Vari-Lavoisier 2016). This question can be traced back to the 1970s, and the notion of middlemen, coined to describe how migrants can, accidentally or voluntarily, transfer ideas between their host and home communities (Spengler 1970). The extent to which migrants intentionally transfer ideas and practices matters, to reflect on the appropriateness of thinking in terms of *remittances.*. In the case of economic remittances, migrants decide how much, when, and largely to whom they send money (Gubert 2000) The intentionality of the transfer is less clear in the case of ideas and practices, that can also be conveyed by virtue of acting (and being imitated). Is then the term 'social remittances' another instance of intellectual colonisation, by economics? Or is it a useful way to think of migrants deliberate and active efforts to promote changes in their countries of birth?

How fast and pervasive are migration-induced social changes? There is a growing aware-ness of the need to better account for the temporal dynamics implicated in the circulation of norms and behaviours. Studies of contemporary migration might advance our understanding of the temporal dimensions of transnational circulation (Levitt and Rajaram 2013a; Massey 2010). However, as historians enter this conversation, they bring methods and concepts that could critically advance our understanding of mobility (Nowicka and Šerbedžija 2016) – and more is yet to come (Krawatzek and Muller-Funk 2019).

In this regard, a tangible merit of the concept of social remittances is certainly to favour comparisons of cases studies across time and space. Today, at the empirical level, much more comparative research is needed, especially to compare more rigorously migrants coming back from different countries. To date, contributions contrast the influence of migrants coming back from OECD countries, versus migrants coming back from non-OECD countries (see, for instance, Chauvet, Gubert, and Mesplé-Somps 2016; Fargues 2011; Mesplé-Somps 2016), without controlling rigorously for the fact that migrants located in OECD countries are also more likely to benefit from more economic and social capital, that might enhance their political influence. In other words, due to the lack of longitudinal data, most studies cannot fully adjust to the role of selection effects.

Finally, there is a recurring lack of research accounting for the impact of social remit-tances on *destination countries* (see Grabowska et al. 2016 for an exception). Along those lines, migration studies need to develop *multi-directional* approaches to social transfers. Indeed, the intuition that social remittances are not unidirectional but *'circulate, continu-ously and iteratively'* (Levitt and Lamba-Nieves 2011, 19) calls for further empirical evi-dence, to explore the existence, consistence, and implications of *'reverse social remittances'* (Mazzucato 2009). Capturing the simultaneous and ubiquitous manifestations of trans-national phenomenon raises methodological challenges that are neither new to migration scholars, nor yet resolved (Beauchemin and González-Ferrier 2011; Boccagni 2016; Durand and Massey 2006; Faist 2012; Gubert et al. 2016; Massey 1987; Mazzucato 2008; Willekens et al. 2016).

Conclusion

The concept of social remittances opened a new subfield, illustrating the interdisciplinary nature of migration studies. To be sure, the broad array of phenomena it sought to encompass can, and should, be questioned. It triggered a welcome shift in research focus from the economic to the socio-political implications of human mobility. However, placing the social at the centre of research agendas, should not lead to the isolation of social transfers from the economic, political, social, and emotional environments in which they occur. Critics and debates triggered by the term of social remittances helped refine the methodological and conceptual approach to transnational social change and arguably advanced our understanding of the implications of human mobility. In this respect, the notion of 'social remittances' stimulated the collective sociological imagination.

Today, scholars interested in the socio-political implications of migration have an exciting research programme ahead to re-embed the analysis of social transfers in the social science literature. To this end, migration scholars could enter in conversation with specialists interested in cognate questions, through the lens of the circulation of public policies (Olivier de Sardan and Piccoli 2017), policy learning, and global knowledge circulation or, more broadly, on diffusion processes (Wimmer 2013). In sum, migration scholars must be responsible for this impressive and exciting task to understand human mobility in our interconnected world. By doing so, they will have to engage with critical issues that still pervade contemporary social sciences, which, in turn, will search critically advance the conceptualisation of social change.

Note

1 Their indicators reflect the six following categories: 'Voice and Accountability (VA), Political Stability (PS), Government Effectiveness (GE), Regulatory Quality (RQ), Rule of Law (RL), and Control of Corruption (CC) covering about 200 countries and territories for 5 years: 1996, 1998, 2000, 2002, and 2004' (Li and McHale 2006, 10).

References

Ahmadov, Anar K., and Gwendolyn Sasse. 2016 Empowering to Engage with the Homeland: Do Migration Experience and Environment Foster Political Remittances? *Comparative Migration Studies* 4: 12.

Artuc, Erhan, Frédéric Docquier, Çaglar Özden, and Christopher Parsons. 2015 A Global Assessment of Human Capital Mobility: The Role of Non-OECD Destinations. *World Development* 65 (C) Migration and Development: 6–26.

Batista, Catia, and Pedro C. Vicente. 2011 Do Migrants Improve Governance at Home? Evidence from a Voting Experiment. CEPR Discussion Paper, 8202. C.E.P.R. Discussion Papers. https://ideas.repec.org/p/cpr/ceprdp/8202.html, accessed January 2, 2015.

Beauchemin, Cris, and Amparo González-Ferrier. 2011 Sampling International Migrants with Origin-Based Snowballing Method: New Evidence on Biases and Limitations. *Demographic Research* 25: 103–134.

Beine, Michel, and Khalid Sekkat. 2013 Skilled Migration and the Transfer of Institutional Norms. *IZA Journal of Migration* 2(1): 9.

Boccagni, Paolo. 2016 From the Multi-Sited to the in-between: Ethnography as a Way of Delving into Migrants' Transnational Relationships. *International Journal of Social Research Methodology* 19(1): 1–16.

Boccagni, Paolo. 2017 Addressing Transnational Needs through Migration? An Inquiry into the Reach and Consequences of Migrants' Social Protection across Borders. *Global Social Policy* 17(2): 168–187.

Boccagni, Paolo, and Francesca Decimo. 2013 Mapping Social Remittances. *Migration Letters* 10(1): 1–10.

Boccagni, Paolo, Jean-Michel Lafleur, and Peggy Levitt. 2016 Transnational Politics as Cultural Circulation: Toward a Conceptual Understanding of Migrant Political Participation on the Move. *Mobilities* 11(3): 444–463.

Carling, Jørgen. 2014 Scripting Remittances: Making Sense of Money Transfers in Transnational Relationships. *International Migration Review* 48: S218–S262.

Chauvet, Lisa, Flore Gubert, and Sandrine Mesplé-Somps. 2016 Do Migrants Adopt New Political Attitudes from Abroad? Evidence Using a Multi-Sited Exit-Poll Survey during the 2013 Malian Elections. *Comparative Migration Studies* 4(1): 19.

Chauvet, Lisa, and Marion Mercier. 2014 Do Return Migrants Transfer Political Norms to Their Origin Country? Evidence from Mali. Economics Papers from University Paris Dauphine, 123456789/ 12585. Paris Dauphine University. http://ideas.repec.org/p/dau/papers/123456789-12585.html, accessed September 27, 2014.

Clemens, Michael A., Çağlar Özden, and Hillel Rapoport. 2015 Reprint of: Migration and Development Research Is Moving Far beyond Remittances. *World Development* 65: 1–5. Migration and Development.

De Haas, Hein. 2007 Remittances, Migration and Social Development: A Conceptual Review of Literature Publications. UNRISD. www.unrisd.org/80256B3C005BCCF9/search/8B7D005E37FF C77EC12573A600439846, accessed December 28, 2017.

Dedieu, Jean-Philippe, Lisa Chauvet, Flore Gubert, Sandrine Mesplé-Somps, and Étienne Smith. 2014 The "Battles" of Paris and New York. *Revue française de science politique* 63(5): 53–80.

Dobbs, Erica, and Peggy Levitt. 2017 The Missing Link? The Role of Sub-National Governance in Transnational Social Protections. *Oxford Development Studies* 45(1): 47–63.

Docquier, Frederic, Elisabetta Lodigiani, Hillel Rapoport, and Maurice Schiff. 2011 Emigration and Democracy. Policy Research Working Paper Series, 5557. The World Bank. https://ideas.repec.org/ p/wbk/wbrwps/5557.html, accessed January 12, 2015.

Durand, Jorge, and Douglas S. Massey. 2006 *Crossing the Border: Research from the Mexican Migration Project*. New York: Russell Sage Foundation.

Eckstein, Susan. 2010 Immigration, Remittances, and Transnational Social Capital Formation: A Cuban Case Study. *Ethnic and Racial Studies* 33(9): 1648–1667.

Faist, Thomas. 2012 Toward a Transnational Methodology: Methods to Address Methodological Nationalism, Essentialism, and Positionality. *Revue Européenne Des Migrations Internationales* 28(1): 51–70.

Fall, Papa Demba, Maria Hernandez Carretero, and Mame Yassine Sarr. 2010 Eumagine (Imagining Europe from the Outside). Senegal Country and Research Areas Report. Université Cheikh Anta Diop de Dakar (UCAD) Peace Research Institute Oslo (PRIO).

Fargues, Philippe. 2010/1 (Janvier) Migration et identité : le paradoxe des influences réciproques , *Esprit*, p. 6–16. DOI : 10.3917/espri.1001.0006. URL: https://www.cairn.info/revue-esprit-2010-1-page-6.htm

Fargues, Philippe. 2011 International Migration and the Demographic Transition: A Two-Way Interaction. *International Migration Review* 45(3): 588–614.

Fargues, Philippe. 2017 Mass Migration and Uprisings in Arab Countries: An Analytical Framework. In *Combining Economic and Political Development. The Experience of MENA*, pp. 170–183. Brill. www.jstor. org/stable/10.1163/j.ctt1w8h356.16, accessed December 20, 2017.

Fourcade, Marion, Etienne Ollion, and Yann Algan. 2015 The Superiority of Economists. *Journal of Economic Perspectives* 29(1): 89–114.

Gardner, Katy. 1995 *Global migrants, local lives : travel and transformation in rural Bangladesh*. Clarendon Press ; New York, NY: Oxford University Press, Oxford [England].

Garip, Filiz, Burak Eskici, and Ben Snyder. 2014 Network Effects in Migrant Remittances: Evidence from Household, Sibling and Village Ties in Nang Rong, Thailand.

Gift, Thomas, and Daniel Krcmaric. 2015 Who Democratizes? Western-Educated Leaders and Regime Transitions. *Journal of Conflict Resolution* 61. 10.1177/0022002715590878.

Grabowska, Izabela, and Michal P. Garapich. 2016 Social Remittances and Intra-EU Mobility: Non-Financial Transfers between U.K. and Poland. *Journal of Ethnic and Migration Studies* 42(13): 2146–2162.

Grabowska, Izabela, Michał P. Garapich, Ewa Jaźwińska, and Agnieszka Radziwinowiczówna. 2016 *Migrants as Agents of Change: Social Remittances in an Enlarged European Union*. Palgrave Macmillan UK: Migration, Diasporas and Citizenship. https://books.google.co.uk/books?id=6z54DQAAQBAJ.

Grabowska, Izabela, Michał P. Garapich, Ewa Jaźwińska, and Agnieszka Radziwinowiczówna. 2017 Introduction: Social Remittances and "Hand-Made" Change by Migrants. In *Migrants as Agents of Change. Migration, Diasporas and Citizenship*, pp. 1–10. London: Palgrave Macmillan. https://link. springer.com/chapter/10.1057/978-1-137-59066-4_1, accessed December 28, 2017.

Gubert, Flore. 2000 Migration et gestion collective des risques. L'exemple de la région de Kayes (Mali). Thèse de doctorat ès Sciences Economiques, Université d'Auvergne, Clermont Ferrrand I.

Gubert, Flore. 2007 Migrations et Transferts de Fonds. Impact Sur Les Pays d'origine. Commentaires. *Revue d'économie Du Développement* 21(2): 183–188.

Gubert, Flore, Inssa, Sane, Sandrine Mesplé-Somps, and Ilka Vari-Lavoisier 2016 Paris – Dakar – Boukanao : retour sur une aventure collective transnationale. Ethnographiques.org(Numéro 32). www.eth nographiques.org/2016/Gubert,Mesple-Somps,Inssa-Sane,Vari-Lavoisier, accessed July 11, 2016.

Holdaway, Jennifer, Peggy Levitt, Jing Fang, and Narasimhan Rajaram. 2015 Mobility and Health Sector Development in China and India. *Social Science & Medicine* 130(Supplement C): 268–276.

Hondagneu-Sotelo, Pierette, and Ernestine Avila. 1997 "I'M HERE, BUT I'M THERE": The Meanings of Latina Transnational Motherhood. *Gender & Society* 11(5): 548–571.

Hondagneu-Sotelo, Pierrette. 2013 New Directions in Gender and Immigration Research. In Steven J. Gold and Stephanie Nawyn, editors, *The Routledge International Handbook of Migration Studies*, pp. 180–188, London and New York: Routledge.

Jaulin, Thibaut. 2016 Geographies of External Voting: The Tunisian Elections Abroad since the 2011 Uprising. *Comparative Migration Studies* 4: 14.

Jaulin, Thibaut, and Björn Nilsson. 2015 Voter ici et là-bas : les Tunisiens à l'étranger depuis 2011. *Revue européenne des migrations internationales* 31(3): 41–71.

Kapur, Devesh. 2014 Political Effects of International Migration. *Annual Review of Political Science* 17(1): 479–502.

Krawatzek, Félix, and Lea Müller-Funk 2019. Two Centuries of Flows between 'Here' and 'There': Political Remittances and Their Transformative Potential. *Journal of Ethnic and Migration Studies*: 1–22.

Lacroix, Thomas. 2014 Conceptualizing Transnational Engagements: A Structure and Agency Perspective on (Hometown) Transnationalism. *International Migration Review* 48(3): 643–679.

Lacroix, Thomas, Peggy Levitt, and Ilka Vari-Lavoisier. 2016 Social Remittances and the Changing Transnational Political Landscape. *Journal of Comparative Migration Studies*. 4(1): 16.

Lafleur, Jean-Michel. 2013 Beyond Dutch Borders: Transnational Politics among Colonial Migrants, Guest Workers and the Second Generation. *Contemporary Sociology: A Journal of Reviews* 42(5): 750–751.

Lafleur, Jean-Michel, and Olivier Lizin. 2015 Transnational Health Insurance Schemes: A New Avenue for Congolese Immigrants in Belgium to Care for Their Relatives' Health from Abroad? http://orbi. ulg.ac.be/handle/2268/172046, accessed October 30, 2017.

Lafleur, Jean-Michel, and Olivier Lizin. 2016 Transnational Health Insurances as Social Remittances: The Case of Congolese Immigrants in Belgium. In *Migration and Social Remittances in a Global Europe. Europe in a Global Context*, pp. 211–233. London: Palgrave Macmillan. https://link.springer.com/ chapter/10.1057/978-1-137-60126-1_10, accessed October 30, 2017.

Levitt, Peggy. 1998 Social Remittances: Migration Driven Local-Level Forms of Cultural Diffusion. *International Migration Review* 32(4): 926–948.

Levitt, Peggy. 2001 *The Transnational Villagers*. Berkeley: University of California Press.

Levitt, Peggy, and Deepak Lamba-Nieves. 2011 Social Remittances Revisited. *Journal of Ethnic and Migration Studies* 37(1): 1–22.

Levitt, Peggy, and Sally Merry. 2009 Vernacularization on the Ground: Local Uses of Global Women's Rights in Peru, China, India and the United States. *Global Networks* 9(4): 441–461.

Levitt, Peggy, and Narasimhan Rajaram. 2013a The Migration–Development Nexus and Organizational Time. *International Migration Review* 47(3): 483–507.

Levitt, Peggy, and Narasimhan Rajaram. 2013b Moving toward Reform? Mobility, Health, and Development in the Context of Neoliberalism. *Migration Studies* 1(3): 338–362.

Levitt, Peggy, Jocelyn Viterna, Armin Mueller, and Charlotte Lloyd. 2017 Transnational Social Protection: Setting the Agenda. *Oxford Development Studies* 45(1): 2–19.

Li, Xiaoyang, and John McHale. 2006 Does Brain Drain Lead to Institutional Gain? A Cross Country Empirical Investigation.

Lopez-Ekra, Sylvia, Christine Aghazarm, Henriette Kötter, and Blandine Mollard. 2011 The Impact of Remittances on Gender Roles and Opportunities for Children in Recipient Families: Research from the International Organization for Migration. *Gender & Development* 19(1): 69–80.

Mahmoud, Toman Omar, Hillel Rapoport, Andreas Steinmayr, and Christoph Trebesch. 2014 *The Effect of Labor Migration on the Diffusion of Democracy: Evidence from a Former Soviet Republic*. IZA Discussion Paper, 7980. Institute for the Study of Labor (IZA). https://ideas.repec.org/p/iza/izadps/dp7980. html, accessed August 27, 2015.

Marchetti, Sabrina, and Alessandra Venturini. 2014 Mothers and Grandmothers on the Move: Labour Mobility and the Household Strategies of Moldovan and Ukrainian Migrant Women in Italy. *International Migration* 52(5): 111–126.

Massey, Douglas S. 1987 Understanding Mexican Migration to the United States. *American Journal of Sociology* 92(6): 1372–1403.

Massey, Douglas S. 2010 *Brokered Boundaries: Creating Immigrant Identity in Anti-Immigrant Times.* New York: Russell Sage Foundation.

Mazzucato, Valentina. 2008 Simultaneity and Networks in Transnational Migration: Lessons Learned from a Simultaneous Matched Sample Methodology, International Organization for Migration (IOM). In Josh DeWind and Jennifer Holdaway Eds, *Migration and Development within and across Borders: Research and Policy Perspectives on Internal and International Migration*, pp. 69–100. Geneva: International Organization for Migration.

Mazzucato, Valentina. 2009 Informal Insurance Arrangements in Ghanaian Migrants' Transnational Networks: The Role of Reverse Remittances and Geographic Proximity. *World Development* 37(6): 1105–1115.

Mercier, Marion. 2016 The Return of the Prodigy Son: Do Return Migrants Make Better Leaders? *Journal of Development Economics* 122: 76–91.

Merino, Jose. 2005 Transition to Democracy under a Clientelistic Autocracy: The Making of Independent Citizens in Mexico. http://citation.allacademic.com/meta/p_mla_apa_research_citation/0/4/1/8/8/p41887_index.html, accessed August 9, 2015.

Meseguer, Covadonga, and Francisco Javier Aparicio. 2012 Migration and Distributive Politics: The Political Economy of Mexico's 3 × 1 Program. *Latin American Politics and Society* 54(4): 147–178.

Meseguer, Covadonga, Sebastián Lavezzolo, and Javier Aparicio. 2016 Financial Remittances, Trans-Border Conversations, and the State. *Comparative Migration Studies* 4: 13.

Mesplé-Somps, Sandrine. 2016 Migration and Female Genital Mutilation. IZA World of Labor. https://wol.iza.org/articles/migration-and-female-genital-mutilation/long, accessed December 28, 2017.

Mizanur Rahman, Md. 2013 Gendering Migrant Remittances: Evidence from Bangladesh and the United Arab Emirates. *International Migration* 51: e159–e178.

Nowicka, Magdalena, and Vojin Šerbedžija. 2016 *Migration and Social Remittances in a Global Europe.* London: Palgrave Macmillan UK.

Nyberg-Sørensen, Ninna. 2005 Migrant Remittances, Development and Gender. *Danish Institute for International Studies (DIIS)*. Www.Diis.Dk/Graphics/Publications/Briefs2005/Nns_migrant_remittances.Pdf, accessed November 25, 2009.

Nyberg-Sørensen, Ninna, Nicholas Van Hear, and Poul Engberg-Pedersen. 2002 The Migration–Development Nexus Evidence and Policy Options State-of-the-Art Overview. *International Migration* 40(5): 3–47.

Nyblade, Benjamin, and Angela O'Mahony. 2014 Migrants' Remittances and Home Country Elections: Cross-National and Subnational Evidence. *Studies in Comparative International Development* 49(1): 44–66.

Olivier de Sardan, Jean-Pierre. 2014 Abandoning the Neo-Patrimonialist Paradigm · For a Pluralist Approach to the Bureaucratie Mode of Governance in Africa.

Olivier de Sardan, Jean-Pierre, and Emmanuelle Piccoli. 2017 *Cash Transfers: The Revenge of Contexts, An Anthropological Approach.* New York: Berghahn Books. https://dial.uclouvain.be/pr/boreal/object/boreal:177419, accessed October 27, 2017.

Pérez-Armendáriz, Clarisa, and David Crow. 2010 Do Migrants Remit Democracy? International Migration, Political Beliefs, and Behavior in Mexico. *Comparative Political Studies* 43(1): 119–148.

Pfutze, Tobias. 2012 Does Migration Promote Democratization? Evidence from the Mexican Transition. *Journal of Comparative Economics* 40(2): 159–175.

Pfutze, Tobias. 2014 Clientelism Versus Social Learning: The Electoral Effects of International Migration. *International Studies Quarterly* 58(2): 295–307.

Piper, Nicola. 2009 The Complex Interconnections of the Migration–development Nexus: A Social Perspective. *Population, Space and Place* 15(2): 93–101.

Portes, Alejandro. 2008 Migration and Social Change: Some Conceptual Reflections. *Journal of Ethnic and Migration Studies* 36(10): 1537–1563.

Riccio, Bruno. 2005 Talkin' about Migration - Some Ethnographic Notes on the Ambivalent Representation of Migrants in Contemporary Senegal. Stichproben. Wiener Zeitschrift Für Kritische Afrikastudien Nr.8/2005, 5. Jg. http://stichproben.univie.ac.at/fileadmin/user_upload/p_stichproben/Artikel/Nummer08/07_Riccio.pdf.

Rother, Stefan. 2009 Changed in Migration? Philippine Return Migrants and (Un)Democratic Remittances. *European Journal of East Asian Studies* 8(2): 245–274.

Sasse, Gwendolyn. 2013 Linkages and the Promotion of Democracy: The EU's Eastern Neighbourhood. *Democratization* 20(4): 553–591.

Siméant, Johanna. 2015 Three Bodies of Moral Economy: The Diffusion of a Concept. *Journal of Global Ethics* 11(2): 163–175.

Spengler, Joseph J. 1970. Notes on the International Transmission of Economic Ideas. History of Political Economy 2(1): 133–151.

Spilimbergo, Antonio 2009 Foreign Students and Democracy. *American Economic Review* 99(1): 528–543.

Tabar, Paul. 2014 "Political Remittances": The Case of Lebanese Expatriates Voting in National Elections. *Journal of Intercultural Studies* 35(4): 442–460.

Vari-Lavoisier, Ilka. 2015. Social Remittances as Mimetic Diffusion Processes: From Homophily to Imitation in Transnational Networks. The Transnational Studies Initiative Working Paper, Harvard University. https://seminars.wcfia.harvard.edu/files/tsi/files/4-varilavoisier_2015_tsiworkingpaper.pdf, accessed August 11, 2017.

Van Hear, Nicholas. 2010 Theories of Migration and Social Change. *Journal of Ethnic and Migration Studies* 36(10): 1531–1536.

Vélez-Torres, Irene, and Jytte Agergaard. 2014 Political Remittances, Connectivity, and the Trans-Local Politics of Place: An Alternative Approach to the Dominant Narratives on "Displacement" in Colombia. *Geoforum* 53: 116–125.

Vianello, Francesca Alice. 2013 Ukrainian Migrant Women's Social Remittances: Contents and Effects on Families Left Behind. *Migration Letters* 10(1): 91–100.

Willekens, Frans, Douglas Massey, James Raymer, and Cris Beauchemin. 2016 International Migration under the Microscope. *Science* 352(6288): 897–899.

Wimmer, Andreas. 2013 *Waves of War: Nationalism, State Formation, and Ethnic Exclusion in the Modern World*. Cambridge Studies in Comparative Politics. Cambridge, England; New York: Cambridge University Press.

Yngvesson, Andreas. 2017 The Social Impact of Remittances on Gender Roles in Kosovo; a Catalyst for Women Empowerment?

Zelizer, Viviana A. Rotman. 2014 Remittance Circuits. Working Paper Presented at the Workshop on "Following the Intangible Flows: Transnational Approaches to Immaterial Remittances". Princeton University, September 19, 2014.

12

SKILLED MIGRATION

Ronald Skeldon

Skilled migration has been one of the principal academic and policy concerns in both research and debate on migration and development. Developed countries view the skilled as necessary for their continued competitiveness in a globalised world. Virtually all developed counties wish to attract and retain skilled migrants, while at the same time restricting the inflow of the less-skilled. Given this global diffusion of skilled migration policies, a so-called global competition for the best and brightest has emerged (Czaika 2018, 2; OECD 2008). However, important regional dimensions are also significant with, for example, the number of skilled migrants from Western countries in Japan having decreased over recent years, but the number of skilled migrants from other Asian countries having increased (Wakisaka 2018). Cultural practices, as well as propinquity, are factors in the equation.

Less-developed countries, on the other hand, view the emigration of their skilled to the more developed world with concern, fearing that their loss will prejudice their own development. Issues of brain drain, brain gain, and brain circulation have been important parts of the research and debate but the real impact on both origins and destinations has proved to be more complex and nuanced than these simple categories might suggest. This entry will review the main dimensions of the debate, a debate that can be traced back into the 1960s. (See Adams (1968), for example, but more recent overall reviews and assessments include those by Czaika (2018), Solimano (2008), Part II of Özden and Schiff (2006), Cornelius, Espenshade, and Salehyan (2001), Clemens (2013) and Skeldon (2009).)

Of definitions and categories

Central to the debate is a definition of the skilled, who can be defined in a number of ways, with those ways differing from country to country. Data availability is thus crucial and, at the global level, the most readily accessible information across countries relates to the highest level of education completed. In the seminal work of Docquier and Marfouk (2006), for example, the population 25 years of age and over with a tertiary-level qualification, disaggregated by migrant status, was deemed to be skilled. While providing an invaluable assessment of the movement of human capital around the world, it provided but a partial picture of the migration of the skilled. To include those currently in higher education as a measure of the creation of skills adds a further dimension by extending the age range to include younger people: the future skilled.

In the context of a total global international migration stock of 221.7 million in 2010, some 28 million highly-skilled, defined as those 25 years of age with at least 1 year of tertiary education, were recorded in the OECD countries, a 130 per cent increase over the number recorded in 1990 (Kerr et al. 2016, 85). The same source showed that the number of less-skilled migrants increased by only 40 per cent over the same period. The United States was by far the dominant destination for the highly-skilled, with over 12 million in 2010–11, followed by Canada and the United Kingdom with between 3 and 4 million each (Czaika and Parsons 2018, 21–2). India was the main supplier of the skilled with 2.2 million, followed by the Philippines and China, both supplying 1.5 million, the United Kingdom with 1.3 million and Germany with 1.2 million (World Bank 2016). Definitions may vary between countries but the overall trend seems robust.

For the majority of the most developed OECD countries, however, much more detailed data are generally available. Both stocks and flows of migrants can be disaggregated by profession with the top three categories of the ISCO (International Standard Classification of Occupations) assumed to be 'highly-skilled'. See Czaika and Parsons (2018, 23) for a review. These incorporate the following:

- Managers, senior officials, and legislators
- Professionals, such as doctors, engineers
- Technicians and associate technicians

Although not all in the first and third of these categories should be assumed to have a university education, these categories are generally occupations associated with a tertiary-level education. Many will have entered large organisations straight from school and worked their way up through the system on the basis of competence and/or influence. As not all who go to university emerge with a skill as such, further disaggregation can be achieved through focussing only on those who had followed courses in technical and scientific subjects, producing Human Resources in Science and Technology (HRST, see OECD 2002).

The focus on these high-level occupations and tertiary-level qualifications does exclude some who are clearly skilled, such as leading sportsmen and women, as well as many artists and musicians. Provision is often made for their inclusion, but questions might also be raised about whether all in the high-level occupations are really 'skilled': many certainly are, but not all. All, however, will tend to be highly paid. Many who have business or entrepreneurial acumen and left school early or lower-paid workers without tertiary-level qualifications who possess technical skills in plumbing or carpentry are excluded using such approaches. Hence, the basic comparative data available, that is, the numbers with tertiary education, tend to exclude many who are skilled but probably also include some who are not so skilled. Nevertheless, a basic positive association between advanced levels of education, professional occupations, and levels of remuneration generally holds.

The emergence of a distinction between the 'highly-skilled', sometimes also called 'talent', to refer to those at the higher end of the spectrum, as opposed to the just 'skilled' tries to deal with this relative difference. Certainly, in country-specific, as opposed to regional and global comparative, approaches to the skilled, provision is made for a broad spectrum of skills. For example, the United Kingdom's Tier 2 visa for skilled workers includes occupations such as nurses, chefs, and dancers that are not generally seen to involve high-level skills. Like the Canadian points-based system, these are identified by, and shift with, observable labour-market shortages. However, matching real labour-market needs with supply through immigration policies is extremely complex and plagued with difficulty (see the essays in Ruhs and

Anderson 2010), not the least of which is due to labour-market needs moving faster than any immigration policy response. Sponsorship by employers, in the case of the United Kingdom, is one example that does attempt to link demand with supply. The evidence of high earnings that has to be produced prior to application limits the migrants to those at high levels or to an origin in a relatively high-cost economy. Investors and entrepreneurs tend fall into other visa categories, Tier 1 in the case of the UK.

The focus on the skilled or the highly-skilled and talented ignores the very real linkages that exist between these migrants and the less-skilled, an issue that throws into question the validity of identifying the skilled as the cornerstone of any immigration policy. The skilled require battalions of less-skilled to service their economy and lifestyles. Quite apart from the construction workers required to build the office complexes, many of whom will be skilled in one trade or another in their own right, it is the service workers who are central to the skilled system: office and window cleaners, delivery drivers, dishwashers, and serving staff in the up-market restaurants in and around the business districts and so on. They must either come from the local population or be imported. Given the rising expectations and education of local populations, it seems unlikely that they will be willing to supply the large number of basic service workers required. Hence, a policy that focuses simply on the highly-skilled seems short-sighted and a more balanced approach is needed.

The developmental impact of the highly-skilled: developed urban societies of destination

It is axiomatic that the destinations of skilled migrants benefit from that migration. The concentration of people with brains and abilities brings economies of scale and the exchange of knowledge stimulates enterprise. These developments are most clearly seen in the process of urbanisation. No highly developed country remains primarily rural and cities have always provided the seat for religious and secular elites and for that quintessential skilled migrant: the trader. The wealth created through these 'trading diasporas' (Cohen 1997; Curtin 1984) was used to extend the power of the city, projected so often in great architecture but also in the creation of industry that required and attracted more skilled migrants and the establishment of schools and universities to create the skilled, particularly the political and administrative elites. Cities have been for centuries, but particularly since the onset of rapid urbanisation from the early eighteenth century, the nodes for the accumulation and interchange of skilled people and the centres around which states were created.

Today, the largest cities in destination countries remain the principal destinations for international migration, both skilled and less-skilled. As emphasised earlier, government policy across the developed world favours the skilled and here the issue of retention arises. The skilled are not only in demand globally, but they see migration as part of their career development. Skills are enhanced through experience in different contexts and the skilled are characterised by high mobility and much onward and return migration. The expatriate population in Hong Kong includes a significant number of the skilled and their migration experience is instructive. Between 2001 and 2011, only half of the 440,000 expatriates in the city in 2001 'survived' to be recorded in 2011 and some 310,000 new expatriates arrived (Skeldon 2014). Hence, a significant turnover in that population in Hong Kong existed but whether such a pattern exists in other global cities must await further research. Nevertheless, it would be naïve for governments wishing to attract the skilled through manpower planning in order to fill specific vacancies in the labour force to assume that all will stay on. Those trained to global standards will tend to migrate globally, a theme to which we shall return in this chapter.

Governments that bias their immigration policy towards the highly-skilled may find that they attract more skilled than they have available and appropriate jobs for them. Accounts of PhD holders driving taxis in Canada are legendary and it is easy to exaggerate the real situation. Nevertheless, among the more than 50,000 taxi drivers in Canada as a whole in 2006, half were immigrants of whom fully one fifth had a first degree or higher, including some 200 with PhDs, compared with just under 5 per cent of Canadian-born drivers with university degrees, of whom 55 had PhDs (Li 2012). Over 80 per cent of the taxi drivers in Toronto and Vancouver were immigrants, with the vast majority established migrants rather than new arrivals, suggesting that taxi driving is not a temporary job on the way to something better.

This situation of highly-skilled migrants in less qualified occupations has given rise to the idea of a 'brain waste' amongst skilled migrants in the developed world. However, three points need to be taken into consideration. First is the complex issue of accreditation: whether the training received by an immigrant, particularly in professions such as medicine, architecture, or engineering, meets the criteria of the destination country. Certainly, professional associations may have vested interests in limiting the numbers admitted into their ranks, but standards are important and it may take time to establish equivalency. Immigrants established in their fields back home may not have the time, finance, or inclination to return to education to complete bridging courses in order to gain local qualifications. Second, from the point of view of the destination country, skilled migrants irrespective of what they do, make 'good' immigrants: they are more likely to pick up the local language quickly, to adjust to a different society and culture and to have high aspirations for their children, who may be able to achieve what they themselves have been unable to achieve. Third, is the more general issue of overqualification of tertiary-trained workers in labour forces in general in the developed world: across OECD countries, an average of 14 per cent of those with university education are in occupations that do not require such a high level of education, a percentage that rises to 28 per cent in the United Kingdom and 29 per cent in Japan. See OECD (2018, 77) and *The Telegraph Education* of 19 September 2018 for introductions to this issue. While such data might raise questions about the direct relevance of a university education to many, a more charitable interpretation might see an educated population as both a public good and a basic human right and feel that we need to move away from narrow associations between education and type of occupation. Basic questions remain about 'who pays?' but this takes the discussion far beyond the theme of this entry. Nevertheless, central to a migration and development debate remains the question who makes the 'best' immigrants for host societies: whether 'best' for future state-building or 'best' for filling places in the labour market, or even whether this is a false dichotomy entirely. When selecting these skilled immigrants, developed economies rarely take into consideration the impact that the selection has on the countries of origin and it is to that issue that our attention now turns.

The developmental impact of the highly-skilled: developing countries of origin

In the migration and development debate, most attention has focused on the impact of the exodus of the highly-skilled on countries of origin: that the loss of the skilled has been prejudicial to the development prospects of countries across the developing world. This viewpoint has been at the root of the so-called 'brain drain' and developed countries are seen to be 'poaching' the best and brightest, perhaps most particularly from the health sectors of the developing world. Thus, the developed world, by taking the skilled whose education and training were paid in whole or part by poorer countries, is part of a global system of unequal relations. This interpretation is but part of dependency theory, in which the developed world/Global North stymies the development of the developing world/ Global South through the exploitation of its human capital. However, the evidence from recent decades has not been supportive of this simple binary interpretation and more nuanced views have emerged.

The starting point must be the underlying pattern of the absolute size of global flows of the highly-skilled. These are dominated by movement originating within the countries of the developed world itself, plus a relatively small number of middle-income developing countries such as the Philippines, India, Mexico, and China. Size, location, and historical ties are important explanatory factors, plus the fact that in order to be significant sources of skilled migrants, the institutions to produce them must be well established in those countries. This means that certain countries in Europe that are now seen as countries of net-immigration, such as the United Kingdom and Germany, are amongst the largest suppliers of skilled migrants. Around the year 2000, the United Kingdom, for example, had a larger stock of skilled migrants overseas than any other country at 1.14 million (Docquier and Marfouk 2006, 175) and in 2013, it had a larger stock of emigrants as a percentage of total population than a country normally seen as a 'classic' country of emigration, the Philippines: 8 per cent for the United Kingdom against 6.2 per cent for the Philippines (World Bank 2016). The composition and pattern of the flows are very different from the two countries but the United Kingdom remains a major country of emigration; its out movements are mainly to other OECD countries and some 37.8 per cent of the UK stock in those countries consist of the tertiary educated (World Bank 2016, 259). The term 'brain drain' was first coined with reference to the movement of large numbers of scientists and engineers from the United Kingdom, mainly to the United States, Canada, and Australia from the late 1950s, but evidence of a strong negative impact of this movement on the economy remains elusive (Hatton and Price 2005, 164). The key point remains, however, that the skilled migration system is not simply from the developing to the developed world but, at the global level, is largely an interchange of brains within the developed world.

One can argue that any impact of the skilled on countries of origin is not simply a matter of numbers: a small number of skilled workers leaving a poor country could have a major impact on weak economies. The global data shows that the vast majority of countries where the highest proportion of skilled were to be found outside, were small and primarily island countries (Docquier and Marfouk 2006). Some 89 per cent of skilled Guyanans were to be found outside Guyana, for example. The figures for Grenada, Jamaica, St Vincent, and the Grenadines and Haiti were all in excess of 80 per cent and many countries had over half of their skilled overseas. Such figures for small countries are suggestive of a serious loss of skilled personnel and perhaps evidence of a brain drain.

The impact of emigration of skilled people is going to have different consequences depending upon the size and robustness of the economy of origin. However, a number of factors need to be brought into the discussion before any conclusion of either a negative or a positive impact can be drawn. The first relates to the types of data available. The data presented above refer only to the number of skilled by country of birth and country of present residence, which follow the current international definitions of international migration. The data tell us nothing about where the migrants received their education and training. While the majority may have received their basic primary, and even secondary, schooling in their countries of origin, an assumption that certainly may not universally apply, the critical tertiary education for them to be classified as 'skilled' is more likely to have been gained abroad. Conversely, if data is only available on the place of training, the loss to countries where the leading universities or training schools are located will be exaggerated. Rarely is information on birthplace (or citizenship), place of training and place of practice available.

As mentioned above, many poorer and smaller economies do not have the institutions to provide advanced education within their boundaries and those wishing to pursue tertiary training will first have to migrate as students to a more developed country or to a regional centre. For example, the University of the West Indies serves all 18 English-speaking Caribbean countries from its largest campus at Mona in Jamaica, and other campuses in Trinidad and Tobago and Barbados. For the island economies of the Pacific, the University of the South Pacific in Suva, Fiji, performs a similar function, although more recent campuses have been established across that vast region, with the largest in Samoa and Vanuatu.

Like the flows of the skilled in general, it is the developed countries of North America, Australasia, and Europe that dominate the destinations of the global inflows of students. From less than a million international students around the world in 1975, through 2.1 million in 2001, the total had risen to over 5 million students in 2018, about half originating in China and India (IIE 2018). Large numbers do go back to participate in the development of their home economies as long as opportunities exist. This has been the case with China where the incidence of return in 2017 represented about 90 per cent of the number leaving, compared with only 10 per cent in 2000 (Zhou 2018). Increasing rates of return were also observed during the much earlier development of Taiwan from the 1960s and Korea from the 1970s (Skeldon 1992) and yet the pronounced 'loss' of these bright young people was not negative, as shown by the subsequent rapid development of these economies (Adams 1968). Rather, these flows are an integral part of the development of origin countries and their future volume and direction will be a function of the subsequent economic transformation and evolution of their education systems.

These flows are about securing credentials that have weight in the country of origin and are recognised internationally, hence widening access to labour markets. However, part of the 'brain drain' argument is that the exodus of the skilled also represents a loss to countries of origin in terms of the costs of training, which for tertiary education are high in terms of investment per capita. Certainly, the cost to a country like Ghana, where over one third of Ghana-trained doctors leave (Bhargava, Docquier, and Moullan 2011), might be seen to fit this scenario but a look at the sources of funding of foreign students in the United States in 2017–18 showed that the primary source of funding was family or personal: some 82 per cent for undergraduates and 60 per cent for graduate students. Foreign government sources accounted for 7.7 per cent of undergraduate education of foreign students and 3.8 per cent for graduate students (IIE 2018). Thus, the new wealthy of China and India in particular are the main sources of student funds for overseas education in which remittances must play a not insignificant part.

Whether a country would have developed faster had the youth and the skilled stayed at home is the counterfactual, which raises a number of different issues, the most important of which is if migrants could have been either gainfully employed or absorbed into appropriate further education in their economies of origin. Those economies might lack the facilities to provide adequate tertiary education or are already experiencing high unemployment. That is, does the migration of the skilled or educated youth act as a safety valve to reduce the number of talented people who might become un- or underemployed and who ultimately might cause problems for origin governments? Such hypothetical questions are difficult to answer but attempting to prevent the migration of clever people seems counterproductive.

They will always find ways to migrate irregularly, which is never in the best interests of the country of origin or destination, or the migrants themselves.

An extension of this argument is the question of the most appropriate training needed by developing countries of origin. Clearly, a country like Ghana should have a first-rate medical school to train medical personnel to the highest standards, but policies to educate students to global standards will mean that many will choose to migrate globally. A question exists whether such highly-trained doctors are the best suited to work in isolated rural areas where facilities will be limited and where the key health-development challenges will be in the area of public health to reduce infant, child, and maternal mortality. The deployment of doctors trained to the highest international standards to isolated parts of rural developing countries may not be the best use of a scarce resource and would not be the most appropriate personnel to deal with the basic challenges facing these areas (Clemens 2007). Many will be unwilling to go to isolated areas in the first place and rates of drop out are likely to be high for those who do go. In order to produce and retain a cadre of medical personnel that will meet the main demands of the least developed parts of poor countries, policies to recruit in those areas and train to basic levels of medical care may be a more viable strategy than relying on highly-trained personnel. Specialist skills will be required but these may be better supplied through volunteer doctors, see below, or the use of modern communication between those with paramedical skills in the rural sector and specialists in base hospitals.

Any crisis facing health in some of the poorest countries in the world seems unlikely to be caused by the emigration of the skilled. More trained health professionals in some African countries are to be found outside the public health sector but within their country than there are medical personnel from those countries practising outside the country. (Clemens 2007, 37). For example, in South Africa, at a time when 32,000 vacancies for nurses existed, some 35,000 nurses were inactive or unemployed in the country itself (OECD 2004). Trying to slow or stop the emigration of skilled medical personnel from developing countries might help to reduce child mortality and increase the uptake of vaccinations but not to the extent of having a significant impact on overall trends (Bhargava, Docquier, and Moullan 2011). Even for small island economies alone, it has proved difficult to attribute any specifically negative impact on the health service to the loss of skills through migration (Connell 2009, 150). Other factors such as levels of pay, promotion prospects and working conditions within the service that have given rise to strikes and low morale are likely to be more important. Nevertheless, the international community has taken on commitments to introduce codes of practice that will, if not prohibit, at least encourage responsible recruitment of skilled migrants from developing countries. The 2010 WHO voluntary code to promote ethical recruitment of medical personnel or the United Kingdom's commitment to prohibit direct recruitment into the National Health Service from all developing countries except India and the Philippines, which have government-to-government agreements on this issue, are examples of this intent.

In contradistinction to the dominant brain discourse, some have argued that the exodus of skilled migrants can be beneficial to countries of origin (Mountford 1997; Stark 2004). Once the idea that leaving a country to obtain employment in a specific profession becomes diffused within the society, more and more young people will enrol in the types of courses or training that will then allow them to follow in the footsteps of earlier skilled migrants. However, because the skilled are required to pass through the filter of the immigration policies of destination countries, not all will be selected and at the end of any specific period, a country is likely to be left with more people in these skill categories than it started with at the beginning of the period. Assessments of this 'new brain drain' literature, however, suggest that the empirical evidence to support the case is weak (Schiff 2006; Lucas 2005). Nevertheless, as suggested above, the evidence to support the argument that the exodus of the skilled stymies development is equally weak. Other factors are more important and the movement of the skilled has to be conceptualised within a broader matrix of change in which the movement is more a consequence than a driver of that development.

This does not deny that the migration of the skilled is important as a provider of critical services at particular times and in particular places. Often excluded from the discussion of brain drain is the importation of skills to the developing world on a temporary or longer-term basis. These can come from two, not necessarily separate, sources. The first are foreign civil society organisations, medical missionaries or organisations such as Doctors Without Borders, or directly through foreign government programmes. In the health field, perhaps the most famous programme involves many thousand Cuban doctors providing services in some of the most isolated parts of Latin America and sub-Saharan Africa. Estimates vary, but perhaps 37,000 doctors and nurses are working in 77 countries, bringing not only basic medical care to poor people but also some 8 billion dollars a year to Cuba itself in revenue (Wharton 2015). Such flows are subject to the vagaries of political change with the expulsion of up to 8500 doctors from Brazil following the accession of Jair Bolsonaro as president in January 2019. This mass expulsion will have a profound impact on millions of poor Brazilians in some 1500 remote municipalities where Cuban doctors provide the only source of medical care (Alves 2018). Thus, brain drains can indeed occur with potentially devasting effects in scenarios of forced migration, emphasising the need to bring such flows into the discussion of migration and development.

The second source of outside expertise, and one which has been a recurrent theme in the global migration and development debate, is the diaspora. Countries of origin may seek the skilled living in destination countries in the 'Global North' on a temporary or longer-term basis to provide training in universities or medical schools or the financial investment required for particular development projects. Circular migration of skilled long-term residents, immigrants to the developed world, back to their home countries may be one viable pathway through which to promote development (see Chapter 13 in this Handbook on diasporas). This form of migration is a key part of the international knowledge transfers that are central to the whole idea of development.

While the skilled in the health sector relate to the provision of services that impact on key developmental variables associated with mortality, the movement of the skilled from other sectors can be as important and no more so than in education, where several parallels with health exist. Teacher shortages and the difficulty of retaining teachers in rural areas are serious policy concerns, together with the perceived loss of skilled personnel, perhaps particularly from small and mainly island countries. In 2004, a Protocol for the recruitment of teachers, with clear parallels to the code of conduct for medical personnel, was adopted by Ministers from Commonwealth Countries (Commonwealth 2004). Equally clearly, those with other skills in IT, agronomy, engineering, and so on are also important to the whole process of development. Nevertheless, any attempt to associate the movements in or out of any country with developmental variables is likely to be fraught with difficulty. Not everyone in any particular skill category is equal, which introduces the importance of that nebulous issue of quality into the discussion. A very few driven skilled individuals may make all the difference in implementing health, education or other development programmes in ways that are difficult to measure even if the results are clear to all.

Conclusion

In common with so many aspects of the migration and development debate, the role of skilled migrants is ambivalent and ranges from the definition of who a skilled migrant actually is through to the implications of the impact of the skilled on origins and destinations. The emphasis on skilled immigration in the policies of countries in the developed world and attempts to limit the numbers of skilled emigrants from the developing world introduces tensions and contradictions into the global system that divert attention away from both the real drivers of the movements and the interlinkages with other types of migration and their broader development contexts. Unless skilled migration is placed into a wider matrix of change, the limited policy responses are likely to prove both illusory and counterproductive. This short entry has attempted to introduce the reader to the main interpretations relevant to the topic and to sketch what we know, as well as the lacunae in our existing knowledge.

References

Adams, W. ed (1968) *The brain drain*, Macmillan, New York.

Alves, L. (2018) "Cuban doctors' withdrawal from Brazil could impact health" *The Lancet*, 392(10161): 2255.

Bhargava, A, F. Docquier and Y. Moullan (2011) "Modeling the effects of physician emigration on human development" *Economics and Human Biology*, 9(2): 172–183.

Clemens, M. A. (2007) "Do visas kill? health effects of African health professional emigration" Center for Global Development, Working Paper No 114 Washington.

Clemens, M. A. (2013) "What do we know about skilled migration and development?" Migration Policy Institute, Policy Brief, No 3 Washington.

Cohen, R. (1997) *Global diasporas: an introduction* UCL Press, London.

Commonwealth. (2004) *Commonwealth teacher recruitment protocol* Commonwealth Secretariat at: www.teachers.org.uk/files/ProtocolA6-5143.pdf

Connell, J. (2009) *The global health chain: from the Pacific to the world* Routledge, New York.

Cornelius, W. A., T. J. Espenshade and I. Salehyan eds (2001) *The international migration of the highly skilled: demand, supply and development consequences in sending and receiving countries center for comparative immigration studies*, University of California, La Jolla, San Diego.

Curtin, P. D. (1984) *Cross-cultural trade in world history* Cambridge University Press, Cambridge.

Czaika, M. ed (2018) *High skilled migration: drivers and policies*, Oxford University Press, Oxford.

Czaika, M. and C. R. Parsons (2018) "High skilled migrants in times of global economic crisis" in M. Czaika ed, *High skilled migration: drivers and policies* Oxford University Press, Oxford 20–47.

Docquier, F. and A. Marfouk (2006) "International migration by educational attainment, 1990–2000" in Ç. Özden and M. Schiff eds, *International migration, remittances and the brain drain* The World Bank, Washington 151–199.

Hatton, T. J. and S. W. Price (2005) "Migration, migrants and policy in the United Kingdom" in K. F. Zimmermann ed, *European migration: what do we know?* Oxford University Press, Oxford 113–172.

IIE. (2018) *Open doors 2018* International Institute for Education, New York at: www.iie.org/Research-and-Insights/Open-Doors/Data/International-Students

Kerr, S. P., W. Kerr, Ç. Özden and C. Parsons. (2016) "Global talent flows" *Journal of Economic Perspectives*, 30(4): 83–106.

Li X. (2012) *Who drives a taxi in Canada?* Citizenship and Immigration Canada, Ottawa at: www.canada.ca/content/dam/ircc/migration/ircc/english/pdf/research-stats/taxi.pdf

Lucas, R. E. B. (2005) *International migration and economic development* Elgar, Cheltenham.

Mountford, A. (1997) "Can a brain drain be good for growth in the source economy?" *Journal of Development Economics*, 52(2): 287–303.

OECD. (2002) *International mobility of the highly skilled* Organisation for Economic Co-operation and Development, Paris.

OECD. (2004) "The international mobility of health professionals: an evaluation and analysis based on the case of South Africa" in *Trends in international migration: SOPEMI 2003* Organisation for Economic Co-operation and Development, Paris 116–151.

OECD. (2008) *The global competition for talent: mobility of the highly skilled* Organisation for Economic Co-operation and Development, Paris.

OECD (2018) *Education at a glance 2018* Organisation for Economic Co-operation and Development, Paris at: www.oecd-ilibrary.org/docserver/eag-2018-en.pdf?expires=1547051052&id=id&accname=guest&checksum=BE65C2FDCDA321498D908E83D595A9A9

Özden, Ç. and M. Schiff. eds (2006) *International migration, remittances and the brain drain*, The World Bank, Washington.

Ruhs, M. and B. Anderson. eds (2010) *Who needs migrant workers? Labour shortages, immigration and public policy* Oxford University Press, Oxford.

Schiff, M. (2006) "Brain gain: claims about its size and impact on welfare and growth are greatly exaggerated" in Ç. Özden and M. Schiff eds, *International migration, remittances and the brain drain* The World Bank, Washington 201–225.

Skeldon, R. (1992) "International migration in and from the East and Southeast Asian region: a review essay" *Asian and Pacific Migration Journal*, 1(1): 19–63.

Skeldon, R. (2009) "Of skilled migration, brain drains and policy responses" *International Migration*, 47(4): 3–29.

Skeldon, R. (2014) *Hong Kong's future population and manpower needs to 2030* Bauhinia Foundation Research Centre, Hong Kong at: www.bauhinia.org/assets/document/doc173eng.pdf

Solimano, A. (2008) *The international mobility of talent: types, causes, and development impact* Oxford University Press, Oxford.

Stark, O. (2004) "Rethinking the brain drain" *World Development*, 32(1): 15–22.

Wakisaka D. (2018) Labyrinth of highly skilled migration in Japan: society, labour and policy. Unpublished PhD thesis School for Policy Studies, University of Bristol.

Wharton. (2015) *How Cuba's health sector aims to gain a greater foothold* University of Pennsylvania, Knowledge@Wharton, at: http://knowledge.wharton.upenn.edu/article/how-cubas-health-care-sector-aims-to-gain-a-greater-foothold/

World Bank. (2016) *Migration and remittances factbook 2016* The World Bank, Washington, 3rd edition at: https://openknowledge.worldbank.org/bitstream/handle/10986/23743/9781464803192.pdf?sequence=3&isAllowed=

Zhou, Y. (2018) *Chinese students increasingly return after studying abroad* Quartz Education. at: https://qz.com/1342525/chinese-students-increasingly-return-home-after-studying-abroad/

13

DIASPORAS AND DEVELOPMENT IN THE GLOBAL AGE

Cathy Wilcock

Introduction

Diasporas have participated in the development of their homelands for as long as it has been possible to send financial, social, and political remittances (see Chapters 10 and 11 in this Handbook). Currently, through their lobbying and advocacy work, their partnerships with Northern NGOs, and through their role in the development strategies of their homeland states, diasporic contributions to development go way 'beyond remittances' (Newland and Patrick 2004). Now considered as part of 'the fourth pillar' of development cooperation (Guribye and Tharmalingam 2017, 172), diasporas are a different kind of social actor to traditional development players: they have different interests, motives, historical relationships, and identifications with the development of their places of origin when compared to states, NGOs, philanthropists, and community-based organisations. As such, in the context of the development in their homelands, diasporas have been described as both 'heroes of development' (Castles 2008, 279), and 'radically unaccountable' globalisers (Conversi 2012, 1360). This chapter demonstrates how diasporas contribute to homeland development in ways that go beyond remittances. It discusses the challenges and opportunities brought about by their rise as the new 'agents of development' (Sinatti and Horst 2015; Turner and Kleist 2013; Faist 2008).

Diasporas and homelands

Diaspora is 'an old concept whose uses and meaning have recently undergone dramatic change' (Faist 2010, 12). Etymologically originating from the Greek verb 'to scatter', even the term itself has become estranged from its primary semantic kernel. To begin with, 'diaspora' described the specific historical experience of Jewish dispersal and was rooted in a primordial conceptualisation of identity which posits the existence of innate blood-ties (Safran 2005). Over time, as primordial conceptions of identity have given way to constructivist approaches based on the societal creation of identities, diaspora has come to denote all kinds of migratory populations who constitute 'imagined communities' (Anderson 1983) Whereas forced dispersal formed an integral part of its original meaning, the nature of dispersal has now become far less descriptively relevant for diaspora (Bruneau 2010, 35).

Labour or economic migrants, for example, along with exiles or refugees, are now said to comprise diasporic communities (Cohen 2008). In addition, the original desire to return to the homeland has since given way to a less specific desire to conserve 'continuous linkages' (Faist 2008) and to 'maintain connections, psychological or material' to their place of origin (Brinkerhoff 2011, 116). In primordial definitions, diaspora was conceived as an identity of deliberate boundary-keeping in the place of residence and implied a reluctance to assimilate politically, culturally, and socially (Brubaker 2005, 6–7; Safran 2005, 37). Now, however, it suffices to exist as a 'distinct community' in residence states (Kim 2014, 38). In these contemporary constructivist approaches to diaspora, the term denotes both a 'category of practice' (Brubaker 2005, 12) and a 'type of consciousness' (Clifford 1994, 312), in which connections with a shared homeland are 'mobilised' by migrants themselves (Sökefeld 2006).

What and where is the homeland? The homeland is the *sine qua non* of diaspora (Cohen 2009, 117), yet outside of ethnonational primordialism, it is not self-evident to what 'homeland' refers. Since the turn away from primordialism and blood-bonds, diasporic connections with a homeland are neither 'eternal' nor 'pre-given social formations' (Cohen and Story 2015, xxii); they do not necessarily arise from migratory experiences and are not automatically made towards ethnonational origins. In this sense, the homeland has been 'liquefied' (Cohen 2009). Reflecting this, contemporary diasporas have mobilised towards several forms of 'homeland' including *inter alia* continental homelands; see, for example, Creese (2011) on African diasporas in Vancouver; national homelands, see Bloch (2008) on Zimbabwean diasporas in the UK; and regional homelands, as shown by Budabin (2014) in relation to the global Darfuri diaspora. In addition, homelands among some diasporic groups are 'non-locative' and can instead refer to religious and cultural heritages; see, for example, Fábos (2012) on Muslim Arab diasporas; or specific shared experiences of historical trauma as shown by Axel (2004).

How coherent are diasporas? According to Adamson and Demetriou (2007, 497) diasporas mobilise around 'a sense of internal cohesion'. Despite this, it should be noted that diasporas are neither fixed nor homogeneous entities: their membership often consists of a committed organisational core – often members of the homeland elite – which is supplemented by peripheral 'passive or silent' members (Shain and Barth 2003, 425) who are 'mobilised and demobilised' to come in and out of the collectivity over time (Redclift 2017). Furthermore, like other forms of collective organisations, diasporas often have internal tensions to the point where they 'do not act in unity and may have as much in common with people outside the group as inside' (Sinatti and Horst 2015, 136). For a discussion of diaspora fragmentation see Beyene (2015) on the Ethiopian diaspora in the Netherlands.

To summarise, diaspora is a term which has roots in primordial identity theory, but which has been reimagined as a socially constructed collective identity or 'imagined community' (Anderson 1983). It refers to communities of migrants with some degree of internal cohesion who are mobilised to come together to maintain connections with their real or imagined homeland(s).

Diasporas and lobbying

It is well known that diasporas contribute to the development of their homelands through financial remittances. They contribute on average 15–20 per cent of GDP in developing states (Woo 2008) and by far outstrip Overseas Development Assistance (Raghuram 2009, 104). As well as these financial transfers, social and political remittances – representing the 'ideas, behaviours and social capital that flow from receiving-country to sending-country-communities' (Levitt 1998, 927) during 'multiple exchanges of cultural features, social thoughts, and political ideas' (Sheffer 2013, 17) – are also instrumental in homeland development processes. These multiple forms of remittance represent 'direct transfers' (Hägel and Peretz 2005, 473) which are supplemented by far less studied 'indirect transfers' (Newland 2010, 4). One key aspect of indirect transfer which contributes to homeland development is diaspora lobbying. It comprises attempts to exert influence on the development of the homeland through the foreign policy of residence states and the activities of publics in places of residence.

Lobbying refers to 'influencing the government and its leaders in an attempt to sway policymakers and legislators to address specific issues' (Perazzi 2011, 40). According to Laguerre (2006, 99), diaspora lobbying can be segmented into 'cold and hot' forms. Cold lobbying involves contacting elected officials in the residence state in an effort to influence policy-making pertinent to the home state. South African diaspora activists during apartheid lobbied the governments in their residence states for trade boycotts which would pressurise the regime in South Africa (Okpewho, Davies, and Mazrui 2001). This government lobbying was combined with boycotting campaigns directed at the corporate and business sectors, sports federations, and international news outlets. A combination of such efforts was instrumental in isolating South Africa from global economies and networks, which significantly limited the National Party's ability to withstand resistance within its borders.

Supplementing these cold campaigns are forms of 'hot lobbying' which range from mass demonstrations, public protests, to sit-ins and hunger strikes. This form of diaspora lobbying has the aim of shaping not only policy-making but also public opinion in residence states (Laguerre 2006, 99). The Senegalese diaspora in Europe in the 1960s campaigned for Senegalese independence from France, and mobilised again in the 1980s to protest against government corruption and police brutality in Senegal (Pojmann 2008, 18). Their tactics involved subversive activism, including occupying the Senegalese embassy in Paris in order to gain support from the French public (Pojmann 2008, 18).

Diaspora lobbying, while being applauded for its role in bringing down oppressive regimes and supporting important social and political change in homelands, is nevertheless controversial for a number of reasons. In particular, diaspora lobbies have been scrutinised for their claims of representation. Residence states and public audiences are often unaware of the complexities of identification and representation involved in diasporic campaigning. As Sinatti and Horst (2015, 147) have noted, it is often assumed that diasporas will want to develop their nation-state of origin over and above their regions or communities of origin (see Aguinas and Newland (2013, 15) for an example of a development handbook stating that diasporas are defined by their connections with their origin *country*). While this may be the case for many, it is problematic to make this assumption since diasporic stances can be made towards a multitude of real or imagined homelands. In some cases, diaspora groups have claimed to represent the interests of entire nation-states, regions, or ethnic groups when in reality they belong to smaller identity groups or political movements which have particular interests in campaigning for specific kinds of change. See for example the multiple Tamil diasporic groups across the world, and who campaign as 'Tamils' but who cannot realistically claim to represent a single and unified Tamil stance (Amarasingam and Poologaindran 2016). This is also complicated somewhat by the class dimensions of diaspora activism. Especially among the non-elite migrants, it is common to find 'hometown associations' which build links to a small town or village, rather than an entire nation or region (Lamba-Nieves 2017).

Furthermore, while often serving as the 'mouthpiece' for campaigns for change ongoing in their homelands (Georgiou 2003, 62), in many cases, diaspora lobbying is also used by diaspora groups as part of attempts to protect their own status and interests in their residence states. As Abusharaf (2010) has argued, Darfuri diaspora lobbyists in the USA have mobilised for the intervention of the International Criminal Court in Sudan. Their mobilisation serves as a way to express their belonging to American culture and society. This, argues Abusharaf (2010), has profoundly affected their campaign messages in ways which have alienated them from some of the Darfuri campaigners in Sudan itself. As such, it is important to understand the extent to which diaspora lobbying is representative of homeland actors, and if so, who in particular.

Another challenge to the representativeness of diaspora lobbying arises from their necessary positioning within political and discursive opportunity structures (Koopmans 2004; Orjuela 2017). Diaspora lobbying, much like other forms of political expression, takes place within parameters of acceptable discourses and behaviours (Kreisi 2004, 72). Because of the need to fit in with these or else be ignored or marginalised, diaspora lobbyists must become adept at 'translating' their political campaign messages into ones which their audience can not only understand but also find 'palatable' (Demir 2015, 71). In many cases, this tactical necessity has involved the 'boomeranging' (Keck and Sikkink 1998) of essentially local concerns onto globally legitimate campaigns such as human rights or transitional justice (Orjuela 2017). While in some cases diasporas lobbies have been praised for placing homeland concerns on the global stage. In other cases, this diaspora lobbying strategy has resulted in the misrepresentation of local development concerns (Lyons and Mandaville 2012). Consequently, some forms of diaspora lobbying have been said to represent a form of 'globalisation from below' and contribute to the erasure of locally-driven change in favour of global agendas (Mohan and Zack-Williams 2002).

Diasporas and the development industry

While diasporas have played roles in homeland development for as long as there have been diasporas, the incorporation of diasporas into the development industry, is a much more recent phenomenon. An alleged 'diaspora turn' in development practice (Boyle and Ho 2017, 592) has brought about the incorporation of diasporas into the programming of development corporations. The incorporation of diasporas into development must be seen in the light of two key anxieties which arose in the late 1990s and early 2000s. First, damning critiques of top-down NGO interventions which designated development as 'neo-colonial' made it imperative for development organisations to incorporate local actors and knowledges into their planning and management (Narayan et al. 2000). It was in this context that Northern NGOs and states began recognising diasporas with globally Southern origins as 'development actors' whose agency could be 'harnessed' in order to facilitate the 'localisation' of their development interventions (Ghai 2013; Plaza and Ratha 2011; Gaynor et al. 2007, 10).

Second, the early 2000s saw a rise in apprehensions around the impact of diaspora remittances. Remittances, since they do not go evenly distributed to the poorest on a needs-based basis but rather on the basis of connections and affiliation, have been viewed by development actors as ultimately biased, unregulated, and unaccountable (Sinatti and Horst 2015). This was compounded by concerns that diasporas could be, either knowingly or unknowingly, facilitating conflict and underdevelopment in their homelands through their remittance practices. Collier and Hoeffler's (2004) study on risk factors for civil war concluded that states with large diasporas were far more likely to have failed peace agreements and to re-enter civil war. It was suggested that 'presumably this effect works through the financial contributions of diasporas to rebel organisations' (Collier 2000, 2355). These dual concerns resulted in the desire among development practitioners to divert and harness remittances but also to control, regulate, and securitise diasporas as development actors.

This enthusiasm for diaspora engagement in development programming was institutionalised in several forums, the most significant being the Global Forum of Migration and Development which, since its inception in 2007, has been moving towards establishing a good governance agenda around diaspora-NGO partnerships (Omelaniuk 2016, 19). Many large development NGOs have launched diaspora engagement programmes or partnerships, which attempt to support and incorporate diasporic actors into formalised development interventions. Examples of this in the UK context include the British Council's Common Purpose programme; Comic Relief's Common Ground Initiative; The Royal Society of Art's UpRising Project. These combine with global networks such as the UNDP's Joint Migration and Development Initiative (JIMDI) and USAID's International Diaspora Engagement Alliance (IdEA).

While these partnerships primarily seek to subsume remittances into aid, the roles of diaspora in NGO partnerships go way beyond remittances. Diasporas, being neither purely domestic nor purely international, are deployed in partnerships as effective brokers between development aid-givers and local populations (Al-Ali and Koser 2003; Cohen and Story 2015, xxii). Due to their domestic and international connections, they are well placed to engage in 'transnational brokerage' since they can connect groups or networks that are otherwise isolated from each other (Adamson 2013, 72). During the peace process, members of the Afghan diaspora were instrumental in creating a 'third level' of mediation between international and domestic actors (Baser and Swain 2008, 12). The Somaliland diaspora has significantly contributed to the establishment of forums such as the Somaliland Peace Committee which brings disparate local and international agencies together in the project of nation-building (Bradbury 2008, 174–9).

In addition to this, diasporas have also performed roles as consultors or watchdogs during development partnerships. In 2010, members of Haitian diaspora groups in the United States were celebrated for their important role in assisting American aid workers following the earthquake. They were able to supply aid workers with vital practical information as well as translating emergency response messages which were used to create an online map of casualties (Munro 2010). Furthermore, it was the diaspora communities during the Somali peace talks in Nairobi in 2002, which were able to pressurise external actors to properly monitor the peace processes (Zunzer 2004, 33). The pressure from the diaspora effectively acts as 'soft power' (Fullilove 2008) in both advising and holding foreign states and INGOs to account.

While the integration of diaspora into the development industry has been met with enthusiasm sufficient to signal a 'diaspora turn' in development studies, challenges and critiques also exist. Among those critical of any form of Northern-led development intervention in the South, diaspora-NGO partnerships represent the co-optation of what would otherwise be diaspora-led development into another top-down framework. As Boyle and Ho (2017, 592) argue, diaspora-NGO partnerships can be seen as 'Western attempts to degrade and instrumentalise diaspora-homeland relationships' which removes the prospect for 'bottom-up' forms of development. As noted by critical scholars, the development interventions before and after diaspora partnerships through consultation, mediation, brokering are strikingly similar. This suggests that NGOs 'approach, valorise, and incorporate only a subset of overseas migrant communities' (Boyle and Kitchin 2014, 31; Ho 2011) whom they determine as already compliant with their development planning. In this sense, diaspora partnerships have been critiqued as 'a new breed of *mission civilisatrice*' (Boyle and Ho 2017, 591).

In addition to the issues of representation, which have already been discussed in relation to diaspora lobbying, serious concerns around the legitimacy of diasporas in development planning and management have also been raised. While extolled by NGOs as those who can localise development interventions, in the eyes of many homelanders, diasporas are often viewed as outsiders who lack legitimacy. Homelanders often argue that diaspora are out of touch or that they gave up their rights to comment and to be influential on the path their homeland will take. For example, in Bréant's (2013, 110) reading of the relations between Togo communities and their diasporas, it is the diasporas which are constructed as 'whitened and Europeanised'. Therefore, diasporas may struggle from the same kinds of legitimacy issues that external development actors face when intervening in developing contexts. While it must be noted that many diaspora communities have positive and highly legitimate relationships with their home communities, it is perhaps fair to say that NGO's enthusiasm for diaspora as a talisman for the local is a drastic oversimplification.

Diasporas in national development planning

The third key way in which diasporas engage in their homelands beyond remittances is through the outreach of their sending states. Whereas in the late twentieth century, sending states often disparaged diasporas as 'unpatriotic' (Mohan 2008, 464) 'disloyal quitters, deserters or sojourners' (Boyle and Ho 2017, 578), in the twenty-first century, there has been a turn towards diaspora engagement (Gamlen 2008; Kuznetsov 2006). In 2014, over half of all UN member states had emigrant focused institutions compared with less than 20 per cent in 2000 and less than 10 per cent in 1980 (Gamlen 2014, 182). There has also been a new trend in the establishment of ministerial departments dedicated to diaspora affairs (Sahai 2013). An increasing number of states have been introducing 'diaspora strategies' which are the formal and explicit policy initiatives 'aimed at fortifying and developing relationships with expatriate communities' (Boyle and Kitchin 2014, 18). These are accompanied by the incorporation of diasporas into national development planning where states seek to 'activate the diaspora's latent potential to promote homeland development' (Minto-Coy 2016, 129, 121). See for example the Jamaican national development plan which states its aim to 'expand the involvement of the Jamaican diaspora in national development' (PIOJ 2009, xxviii) citing them as a 'major resource' who can play a 'strategic role' (see also GoJ 2013).

Three key ways exist in which homeland states involve diaspora in their development strategies and planning. First, as 'brain gain' via utilising 'diaspora knowledge networks' during planning, architectural projects, and emergency response (Trotz 2008). Diasporas have also been instrumental in founding knowledge institutions such as universities in their homelands; for example, the Tamil diaspora in Norway has established a faculty of medicine in Eastern University in partnership with the University of Tromso (Cheran 2003, 14). Brain gain also works via the encouragement of temporary return migration in which skilled diaspora members would be recruited for specific assignments (Sinatti and Horst 2015, 145).

Second, the diaspora is utilised by home states as 'a transnational political lobby' (Resende-Santos 2016, 86) to promote the interests and particular images of homelands on the world stage. This 'diaspora diplomacy' can be seen as part of diaspora lobbying discussed earlier but where the impetus comes directly from the homeland state elites, rather from the diaspora themselves and the diaspora (or specific sections within it) are used by the homeland state for their own diplomatic ends. For example, the Turkish state attempted to engage Turks abroad to upscale its political agenda during its bid to gain EU entry (Østergaard-Nielsen 2003) while New Zealand 'ultimately sees diaspora engagement as a device to help it climb its way back up OECD country rankings' (Gamlen 2006, 35).

Third, states are increasingly recognising their diasporas as a market for products and services, as well as investment opportunities. Especially in small island states such as the Caribbean, diaspora engagement is a means through which developing states can 'creatively and proactively insert themselves into the global economy' (Minto-Coy 2016, 122). Suriname has introduced a diaspora investment programme, IntENT, where business support and mentorship are provided for potential investors. In addition, the raising of funds through taxation or mandatory payments is another avenue for harnessing the diaspora for homeland development, as is the case for the USA, Switzerland, Libya, Eritrea, and the Philippines (Gamlen 2006, 43). Diaspora communities also comprise another huge market for the tourism industry. While the migrant 'sojourn' in the homeland was a common practice among diplomatic elites, as travel has become more accessible and affordable in general, the market for middle-class diaspora tourists has grown widely (Ley and Kobayashi 2005). This has been picked up by both state and private travel companies looking to capitalise on 'heritage tourism' or 'nostalgia trade' (Newland and Taylor 2010)

Diaspora engagement strategies have been critiqued as a 'uni-directional endeavour' whereby diaspora communities are expected to give to the country of origin (Minto-Coy 2016, 135) in return for very little. However, by 2008, 111 states had implemented policies on absentee voting (Délano 2014, 93) and numerous states offer diaspora the rights to form political parties and run for political office. See for example the 'Justice and Welfare Party' in Somaliland which is widely known as 'the diaspora party' (Stremlau 2013, 242) and the Croatian parliament which reserves 12 seats for diaspora members (Kasapović 2012). In addition, extending social service provision is one of the most nascent forms of diaspora engagement. These efforts can be analysed as the externalisation and deterritorialisation of regimes of citizenship and social contracts.

Diaspora engagement strategies have had variable success. Success seems to depend largely upon the nature of the relationship between the state and those who have migrated. In Cape Verde, diaspora engagement is very strong but 'Cape Verde does not need to activate a dormant diaspora or convince an unwilling and suspicious one' (Resende-Santos 2016, 84). On the other hand, in cases such as Eritrea where out-migration is linked with the avoidance of compulsory and indefinite national service, and where diasporic groups campaign regularly against governance failures, the state has problems claiming taxes from its diaspora, and mobilising them for development. As put by Minto-Coy (2016: 121) 'trust' is 'one of the key challenges to activating the full potential of the diaspora'. Partnerships are only possible only where there is mutual trust, 'where the diaspora was well understood, and where the objectives of diaspora engagement were clearly articulated' (Omelaniuk 2016, 23). The success of diaspora engagement, or even its possibility, relies heavily on the relationship between the sending state and those who have left.

Conclusions

Diaspora contributions to development go way beyond the sending of financial, social, and political remittances. Diasporic communities have profoundly influenced development processes in homelands indirectly through their lobbying and advocacy work. In addition, they have contributed to development in homelands through their participation in 'diaspora partnerships' with NGOs during the diaspora engagement strategies of their states of residence. Through these distinct but related spheres of activity, diasporas have played roles such as influencers, brokers, consultants, watchdogs, knowledge networks, distant citizens, investors, and markets. The challenges can be summarised as their inherent lack of impartiality, their claims of representation and legitimacy, and the complexities of maintaining a relationship with a place from which they have migrated away. Whether characterised as distant national heroes, meddlers, or uniquely-placed partners, the development trajectories of their homelands cannot be fully understood without the incorporation of the roles of its numerous and varied diasporic communities. It is clear that in an age of ever-burgeoning globalisation, these roles will continue to grow way beyond remittances.

References

Abusharaf, R. M. (2010) "Debating Darfur in the world", *The Annals of the American Academy of Political and Social Science*, 632(1), 67–85. doi:10.1177/0002716210378631.

Adamson, F. (2013) "Mechanisms of diaspora mobilization and the transnationalization of civil war", in Checkel, J. T. ed., *Transnational dynamics of civil war*. Cambridge: Cambridge University Press, pp. 63–88.

Adamson, F. and Demetriou, M. (2007) "Remapping the boundaries of 'state' and 'national identity': incorporating diasporas into IR theorizing", *European Journal of International Relations*, 13(4), 489–526. doi:10.1177/1354066107083145.

Aguinas, D. and Newland, K. (2013) "Developing a road map for engaging diasporas in development: a handbook for policymakers and practitioners in home and host countries", *IOM*. Available at: www.tandfonline.com/doi/abs/10.1080/1369183X.2013.799909 (Accessed: 31 October 2018).

Al-Ali, N. and Koser, K. (2003). *New approaches to migration? Transnational communities and the transformation of home*. London: Routledge.

Amarasingam, A. and Poologaindran, A. (2016) "Diaspora, development, and intra-community politics: Sri Lankan Tamils in Canada and post-war debates", in Chikand, A., Crush, J. and Walton-Roberts, M. eds., *Diasporas, development and governance*. Springer, Cham. Global Migration Issues, pp. 49–63. doi:10.1007/978-3-319-22165-6_4.

Anderson, B. R. O. (1983) *Imagined communities: reflections on the origin and spread of nationalism*. London: Verso.

Axel, B. K. (2004) "The context of diaspora", *Cultural Anthropology*, 19(1), 26–60. doi:10.1525/can.2004.19.1.26.

Baser, B. and Swain, A. (2008) "Diasporas as peacemakers: third party mediation in homeland conflicts", *International Journal on World Peace*, 25(3), 7–28.

Beyene, H. G. (2015) "Are African diasporas development partners, peace-makers or spoilers? The case of Ethiopia, Kenya and Nigeria", *Diaspora Studies*, 8(2), 145–161. doi:10.1080/09739572.2015.1029714.

Bloch, A. (2008) "Zimbabweans in Britain: transnational activities and capabilities", *Journal of Ethnic and Migration Studies*, 34(2), 287–305. doi:10.1080/13691830701823822.

Boyle, M. and Ho, E. L.-E. (2017) "Sovereign power, biopower, and the reach of the West in an age of diaspora-centred development", *Antipode*, 49(3), 577–596. doi:10.1111/anti.12281.

Boyle, M. and Kitchin, R. (2014) "Diaspora-centred development: current practice, critical commentaries, and research priorities", in Sahoo, S. and Pattanaik, B. K. eds., *Global diasporas and development*. India: Springer, pp. 17–37. doi: 10.1007/978-81-322-1047-4_2.

Bradbury, M. (2008). *Becoming Somaliland*. MI: Progressio.

Bréant, H. (2013) "What if diasporas didn't think about development? A critical approach of the international discourse on migration and development", *African and Black Diaspora: An International Journal*, 6(2), 99–112. doi:10.1080/17528631.2013.793132.

Brinkerhoff, J. M. (2011) "Diasporas and conflict societies: conflict entrepreneurs, competing interests or contributors to stability and development?", *Conflict, Security & Development*, 11(2), 115–143. doi:10.1080/14678802.2011.572453.

Brubaker, R. (2005) "The 'diaspora' diaspora", *Ethnic and Racial Studies*, 28(1), 1–19.

Bruneau, M. (2010) "Diaspora, transnational spaces and communities", in Bauböck, R. and Faist, T. eds., *Diaspora and transnationalism: concepts, theories, methods*. Amsterdam: Amsterdam University Press, pp. 35–50.

Budabin, A. C. (2014) "Diasporas as development partners for peace? The alliance between the Darfuri diaspora and the Save Darfur Coalition", *Third World Quarterly*, 35(1), 163–180. doi:10.1080/01436597.2014.868996.

Castles, S. (2008) "Comparing the experience of five major emigration countries", in Castles, S. and Delgado Wise, R. eds., *Migration and development: perspectives from the South*. Geneva: IOM International Organization for Migration, pp. 258–285.

Cheran, R. (2003) "Diaspora circulation and transnationalism as agents for change in the post conflict zones of Sri Lanka", *Berghof Foundation for Conflict Studies (September 2003)*. Available at: www.sangam. org/articles/view2/523. pdf.

Clifford, J. (1994) "Diasporas", *Cultural Anthropology*, 9(3), 302–338.

Cohen, R. (2008). *Global diasporas: an introduction*. London: Routledge.

Cohen, R. (2009) "Solid, ductile and liquid: changing notions of homeland and home in diaspora studies", in Rafael, E. B. and Sternberg, Y. eds., *Transnationalism: diasporas and the advent of a new (Dis) order*. Leiden: BRILL, pp. 117–135.

Cohen, R. and Story, J (2015) "Introduction", in Cohen, R. and Story, J. eds., *The Impact of Diasporas: Foreword*. Oxford: Oxford Diasporas Programme, pp. 5–7.

Collier, P. and others (2000) *Economic causes of civil conflict and their implications for policy*. Washington, DC: World Bank. Available at: http://users.ox.ac.uk/~econpco/research/pdfs/EconomicCausesofCivil Conflict-ImplicationsforPolicy.pdf (Accessed: 18 January 2015).

Collier, P. and Hoeffler, A. (2004) "Greed and grievance in civil war", *Oxford Economic Papers*, 56(4), 563–595. doi:10.1093/oep/gpf064.

Conversi, D. (2012) "Irresponsible radicalisation: diasporas, globalisation and long-distance nationalism in the digital age", *Journal of Ethnic and Migration Studies*, 38(9), 1357–1379. doi:10.1080/1369183X.2012.698204.

Creese, G. L. (2011). *The new African diaspora in Vancouver: migration, exclusion, and belonging*. Toronto: University of Toronto Press.

Délano, A. (2014) "The diffusion of diaspora engagement policies: a Latin American agenda", *Political Geography*, 41, 90–100. doi:10.1016/j.polgeo.2013.11.007.

Demir, I. (2015) "Battlespace diaspora: how the Kurds of Turkey revive, construct and translate the Kurdish struggle in London", in Christou, D. A. and Mavroudi, D. E. eds., *Dismantling diasporas: rethinking the geographies of diasporic identity, connection and development*. Surrey: Ashgate Publishing, Ltd., pp. 71–94.

Fábos, A. (2012) "Resisting blackness, embracing rightness: how Muslim Arab Sudanese women negotiate their identity in the diaspora", *Ethnic and Racial Studies*, 35(2), 218–237. doi:10.1080/01419870.2011.592594.

Faist, T. (2008) "Migrants as transnational development agents: an inquiry into the newest round of the migration–development nexus", *Population, Space and Place*, 14(1), 21–42. doi:10.1002/psp.471.

Faist, T. (2010) "Diaspora and transnationalism: what kind of dance partners?", in Bauböck, R. and Faist, T. eds., *Diaspora and transnationalism: concepts, theories and methods*. Amsterdam: Amsterdam University Press, pp. 9–34.

Fullilove, M. (2008) World wide webs: diasporas and the international system. Lowy Institute for International Policy Australia. Available at: http://kms1.isn.ethz.ch/serviceengine/Files/ISN/87136/ipubli cationdocument_singledocument/f7e71647-feda-433e-8507-9265180ad285/en/2008-02-18.pdf (Accessed: 26 February 2015).

Gamlen, A. (2006) "Diaspora engagement policies", *Compas Working Paper*, 31.

Gamlen, A. (2008) "The emigration state and the modern geopolitical imagination", *Political Geography*, 27(8), 840–856. doi:10.1016/j.polgeo.2008.10.004.

Gamlen, A. (2014) "Diaspora institutions and diaspora governance", *International Migration Review*, 48, S180–S217. doi:10.1111/imre.12136.

Gaynor, C., Watson, S., et al. (2007). *Evaluating DFID's policy on tackling social exclusion: baseline, framework and indicators*. London: Department for International Development.

Georgiou, M. (2003) "Mapping diasporic media across the EU: addressing cultural exclusion". Available at: http://eprints.lse.ac.uk/26420/(Accessed: 3 August 2017).

Ghai, D. (2013) "Diaspora for development in Africa", *Development in Practice*, 23(2), 315–316. doi:10.1080/09614524.2013.772125.

Guribye, E. and Tharmalingam, S. (2017) "Tamil Diaspora-driven development aid: towards an understanding of context, networks and historical changes", *Forum for Development Studies*, 44(2), 171–188. doi:10.1080/08039410.2016.1273849.

Hägel, P. and Peretz, P. (2005) "States and transnational actors: who's influencing whom? A case study in Jewish diaspora politics during the Cold War", *European Journal of International Relations*, 11(4), 467–493. doi:10.1177/1354066105057893.

Ho, E. L.-E. (2011) "'Claiming' the diaspora: elite mobility, sending state strategies and the spatialities of citizenship"", *Progress in Human Geography*, 35(6), 757–772. doi:10.1177/0309132511401463.

Kasapović, M. (2012) "Voting rights, electoral systems, and political representation of diaspora in Croatia", *East European Politics & Societies*, 26(4), 777–791. doi:10.1177/0888325412450537.

Keck, M. E. and Sikkink, K. (1998). *Activists beyond borders: advocacy networks in international politics*. Ithaca, NY: Cornell University Press.

Kim, H. (2014). *Making diaspora in a global city: South Asian youth cultures in London*. London: Routledge.

Koopmans, R. (2004) "Migrant mobilisation and political opportunities: variation among German cities and a comparison with the United Kingdom and the Netherlands", *Journal of Ethnic and Migration Studies*, 30(3), 449–470. doi:10.1080/13691830410001682034.

Kreisi, H. (2004) "Political context and opportunity", in Snow, D., Soule, S., and Kreisi, H. eds., *Blackwell companion to social movements*. London: Blackwell Publishing, pp. 67–91.

Kuznetsov, Y. (2006) *Diaspora networks and the international migration of skills: how countries can draw on their talent abroad*. Washington, DC: The World Bank. doi:10.1596/978-0-8213-6647-9.

Laguerre, M. (2006). *Diaspora, politics, and globalization*. New York: Springer.

Lamba-Nieves, D. (2017) "Hometown associations and the micropolitics of transnational community development", *Journal of Ethnic and Migration Studies*, 0(0), 1–19. doi:10.1080/1369183X.2017.1366850.

Levitt, P. (1998) "Social remittances: migration driven local-level forms of cultural diffusion", *The International Migration Review*, 32(4), 926–948. doi:10.2307/2547666.

Ley, D. and Kobayashi, A. (2005) "Back to Hong Kong: return migration or transnational sojourn?", *Global Networks*, 5(2), 111–127. doi:10.1111/j.1471-0374.2005.00110.x.

Lyons, T. and Mandaville, P. (eds). (2012). *Politics from afar: transnational diasporas and networks*. London: Hurst Publishers.

Minto-Coy, I. D. (2016) "Diaspora engagement for development in the Caribbean", in Chikanda, A., Crush, J., and Walton-Roberts, M. eds., *Diasporas, development and governance*. Cham: Springer International Publishing (Global Migration Issues), pp. 121–139. doi: 10.1007/978-3-319-22165-6_8.

Mohan, G. (2008) "Making neoliberal states of development: the Ghanaian diaspora and the politics of homelands", *Environment and Planning D: Society and Space*, 26(3), 464–479. doi:10.1068/dcos3.

Mohan, G. and Zack-Williams, A. B. (2002) "Globalisation from below: conceptualising the role of the African diasporas in Africa's development", *Review of African Political Economy*, 29(92), 211–236. doi:10.1080/03056240208704610.

Munro, R. (2010) "Crowd-sourced translation for emergency response in Haiti: the global collaboration of local knowledge" 4.

Narayan, D., et al. (2000) *Crying out for change*. Oxford: Oxford University Press.

Newland, K. (2010) "Voice after exit: diaspora advocacy", *Migration Policy Institute*. Available at: www.migration4development.org/sites/m4d.emakina-eu.net/files/diasporas-advocacy.pdf (Accessed: 15 July 2016).

Newland, K. and Patrick, E. (2004) "Beyond remittances: the role of diaspora in poverty reduction in their countries of origin, a scoping study by the Migration Policy Institute for the Department of International Development", *Migration Policy Institute*. Available at: www.migrationpolicy.org/sites/default/files/publications/Beyond_Remittances_0704.pdf (Accessed: 11 August 2018).

Newland, K. and Taylor, C. (2010). *Heritage tourism and nostalgia trade: a diaspora niche in the development landscape*. London: Migration Policy Institute, USAID.

Okpewho, I., Davies, C. B. and Mazrui, A. A. (2001). *The African diaspora: African origins and new world identities*. Bloomington, IN: Indiana University Press.

Omelaniuk, I. (2016) "The global forum on migration and development and diaspora engagement", in Chikanda, A., Crush, J., and Walton-Roberts, M. eds., *Diasporas, development and governance*. Cham: Springer International Publishing (Global Migration Issues), pp. 19–32. doi: 10.1007/978-3-319-22165-6_2.

Orjuela, C. (2017) "Mobilising diasporas for justice. Opportunity structures and the presencing of a violent past", *Journal of Ethnic and Migration Studies*, 0(0), 1–17. doi:10.1080/1369183X.2017.1354163.

Østergaard-Nielsen, E. (2003). *Transnational politics: the case of Turks and Kurds in Germany*. London: Routledge.

Perazzi, M. (2011) "Civic engagement of transnational communities", in Feron, E. and Orrnert, A. eds., *Transnational communities and conflicts, The INFOCON housebook*. Brussels: Internationalist Foundation, pp. 36–52. Available at www.infocon-project.org

Plaza, S. and Ratha, D. (2011) *Harnessing diaspora resources for Africa*. Washington, DC: World Bank 1–54. Available at: http://siteresources.worldbank.org/EXTDECPROSPECTS/Resources/476882-1157133580628/DfD_FullReport.pdf#page=27 (Accessed: 21 March 2018).

Pojmann, W. (2008). *Migration and activism in Europe since 1945*. Basingstoke: Palgrave Macmillan.

Raghuram, P. (2009) "Which migration, what development? Unsettling the edifice of migration and development", *Population, Space and Place*, 15(2), 103–117. doi:10.1002/psp.536.

Redclift, V. (2017) "The demobilization of diaspora: history, memory and 'latent identity'", *Global Networks*, 17(4), 500–517. doi:10.1111/glob.12150.

Resende-Santos, J. (2016) "Cape Verde: rethinking diaspora in development policy", *International Migration*, 54(2), 82–97. doi:10.1111/imig.12212.

Safran, W. (2005) "The Jewish diaspora in a comparative and theoretical perspective", *Israel Studies*, 10 (1), 36–60.

Sahai, P. S. (2013) "India's engagement with Diaspora: government communication, platforms and structures", *Diaspora Studies*, 6(1), 50–60. doi:10.1080/09739572.2013.843292.

Shain, Y. and Barth, A. (2003) "Diasporas and international relations theory", *International Organization*, 57, 03. doi:10.1017/S0020818303573015.

Sheffer, G. (2013) "Integration impacts on Diaspora–homeland relations", *Diaspora Studies*, 6(1), 13–30. doi:10.1080/09739572.2013.843289.

Sinatti, G. and Horst, C. (2015) "Migrants as agents of development: diaspora engagement discourse and practice in Europe", *Ethnicities*, 15(1), 134–152. doi:10.1177/1468796814530120.

Sökefeld, M. (2006) "Mobilizing in transnational space: a social movement approach to the formation of diaspora", *Global Networks*, 6(3), 265–284.

Stremlau, N. (2013) "Hostages of peace: the politics of radio liberalization in Somaliland", *Journal of Eastern African Studies*, 7(2), 239–257. doi:10.1080/17531055.2013.776274.

Trotz, M. A. (2008) "Diaspora communities and sustainable urban development: Lessons from floods in Guyana", in *Third international conference on sustainability engineering and science*. New Zealand: Auckland, pp. 1–21. Available at: www.thesustainabilitysociety.org.nz/conference/2008/presentations/Trotz.pdf (Accessed: 11 August 2015).

Turner, S. and Kleist, N. (2013) "Introduction: agents of change? Staging and governing diasporas and the African state", *African Studies*, 72(2), 192–206. doi:10.1080/00020184.2013.812882.

Woo, G. (2008) "Diaspora support for earthquake microinsurance in China", in *The 14th world conference on earthquake engineering*. Beijing: Available at: www.iitk.ac.in/nicee/wcee/article/14_S01-01-008. PDF (Accessed: 24 February 2016).

Zunzer, W. (2004) "Diaspora communities and civil conflict transformation". Available at: http://edoc.vifapol.de/opus/volltexte/2011/2543/pdf/boc26e.pdf (Accessed: 11 August 2018).

14

THE INFORMALISATION OF MIGRATION GOVERNANCE ACROSS AFRICA'S URBAN ARCHIPELAGOS

Loren B. Landau and Caroline Wanjiku Kihato

Human mobility and development are increasingly urban and informalised. The intersection of movements of people and trade are repositioning cities and people's positions within circuits of commerce, information and meaning. Municipalities of all sizes are destinations and stations in people's search for profit, passage, or protection. In this role, they are also sites of intersecting networks of regulation operating at multiple geographic and temporal scales. As Glick-Schiller and Çağlar (2009) note, people's varied forms of movements within, into, and through cities demands transversal analysis: a perspective that horizontally and vertically spans otherwise delimited policy fields. Doing so connects local events and outcomes with activities and interventions occurring on other scales. Given the spatiality of human mobility, it also connects the specificities of a locale – a city, neighbourhood, or even a street corner – in archipelagos of rural and urban sites that may be spatially distant but are temporally and materially entangled.

Such mobility gives cause to question what it means when we think of urban inclusivity or the right to the city. For Lefebvre, the right to the city was the right to reframe labour's relationship to capital, through everyday modes of resistance (Lefebvre 1996). Harvey (2003) argues all urban residents should have rights to use and distribute surplus value in the city. Others embed the right to the city in local struggles around access to housing, land, water, and decent work. Glick-Schiller and Çağlar (2009) focus their arguments on varied modes of urban incorporation revealing an implicit normative bias regarding a goal presumably shared by migrants and scholars. Like many scholars, they associate rights to the city with, *inter alia*, the ability to make decisions around the planning, budgeting, and design of urban spaces. The right to the city infuses calls for urban citizenship, and immigrants' rights to urban space. This logic has also critically informed tenets of UN Habitat's new urban agenda (2016, see http://habitat3.org/the-new-urban-agenda/) and the Sustainable Development Goals (particularly number 11).

The question animating this chapter is what the practicality of urban inclusion mean and how it might be achieved in an era of mass mobility, decentralisation, and precarious work. In doing so, it asks a series of questions about the nature of work, regulation, and ethics. It follows Glick-Schiller and Çağlar (2009) in calling for *rescaling* approaches to the study of migration and development in city spaces. But going beyond their realisation that migrants help shape cities, we explore how mobility reshapes the of spatial foundations of development. Doing so, pushes us to broaden what is considered 'migration' and 'urban' policy. Given the micro and translocal (often transnational or diasporic) processes informing migrants' experiences, connections creating archipelagos of linked geographic spaces, policy approaches and analysis need to be both more and less geographically targeted so as to capture specific migrant spaces and their connections beyond urban boundaries. In recognising the myriad formal and informal mechanisms regulating access to and use of these spaces, it points to forms of regulation rarely reflected in 'state law' (cf. Merry 1986). Lastly, and perhaps most fundamentally, it suggests that the informalisation of work, politics, and regulation means revisiting what we mean by the right to the city. It questions the normative basis of inclusion and the ancillary questions this raises for the objectives and efficacy of participation, representation, and incorporation.

Informalisation and the urban archipelago

Interrogating the relationship between mobility and development draws attention to the nature of cities in the global south and the questions they raise for the understanding of inclusion, informalisation, and policymaking. In this regard, African urbanism and mobility conform poorly to patterns of industrially driven, Western urbanism that form the basis of social and much urban theory (Simmel 1964; Tilly and Blockmans 1994; Weber 1958). From a formal development perspective, the results often appear Malthusian. Undoubtedly, urban growth is far outpacing cities' ability to offer employment, services, or other support. Given economic forecasts for the coming decades and even further population pressures, the results will be heightening informality and precarity across many African spaces. Although extreme, African cities speak to the future of global mobility and urbanism across the global south and beyond (Comaroff and Comaroff 2011).

Yet amidst the informalisation of work and institutions, mobility, ambition, and social interactions are forging new institutions. Whatever the economic consequences, the dispersion of families, communities, and life courses transform and contribute to novel, emerging socio-economic and political orders. Some of these look familiar from other increasingly diverse urban centres: ethnic groups hunkering down and forming enclaves or creating neighbourhood and hometown associations. Others take the forms of localised disconnection, where individuals actively resist local incorporation while building relationships, platonic and intimate, material and imagined, that are fleeting or far-flung. These 'new possibilities for social life' reinforce the necessity to see individuals, cities, villages, and camps across multiple geographic and temporal scales (Robinson 2013, 660).

What is emerging in this era of decentralisation, dispersion, and informalisation is more than the simple translocalism and transformation fostered by oscillating movement: of people coming to the city while investing in rural villages for purposes of economic advancement and social respectability (Bank 2011; Cohen 1969; Geschiere 2009; Portes 2007; Potts 2011). Such oscillations continue, but current African migrations and mobility reflect structural, institutional, social formations far less stable or geographically discreet. The continent's remarkable urbanisation produces continued mobility, with people regularly shifting locations and connections due to uncertainties of housing and employment or forging or fragmenting relationships that enable and bind (Landau and Freemantle 2016; Simone 2009). Even those who remain close to their birthplace or entrapped in refugee camps are becoming 'inscribed' in forms of translocal consciousness (Auyero 2000, 111). Such inscriptions offer a global imagination filled with possibilities both real and chimerical that produce longings and frustrations. This is an awareness of processes and possibilities elsewhere and the barriers to accessing them. Geographic movements are shaped by these varied imaginations, visions of home, diasporas, and other 'multiple elsewheres' (Mbembe and Nuttall 2004; also Soja 1996).

Even the most seemingly materially untouched sites are rapidly becoming parts of continental and global archipelagos: islands of space and time interconnected through material exchange, social recognition, moral disciplines, and future imaginations. This leaves few people across Africa self-contained, free of dependence on money, information, or status from other spaces and times (Dzingirai et al. 2014; also Potts 2011). Those excluded from the benefits of material circulation nonetheless are affected by the mobility of resources, ideas, and values. They may become economically marginalised as neighbours accumulate wealth and opportunities or be shamed by their translocal exclusion and parochialism.

To cope with the uncertainty of work and social life, people's real and imagined mobility gives rise to varied forms of intersecting systems of moral authority centred on individuals who are nodes in networks spanning space and time. Vivet et al. (2013, 78) describes a local authority figure, Alhaji Abdullahi Salihu Olowo,

> whose title is Oba Yoruba Kano. To maintain traditional loyalties in his home town, Ilesha, where he has never lived, Olowo holds chieftaincy titles but accepted the Hausa Muslim turban as a symbol of authority to rule over the Yorubas in Kano.

Those under his leadership remain villagers of a certain kind with urban futures: urbanites who must simultaneously maintain status in multiple sites – some urban, some rural – where they may have never been or only occasionally visit (Vivet et al. 2013, 80–1). Elsewhere, people attend churches, go to community meetings, or help repatriate corpses to maintain their status in villages they otherwise visit only now and again (also Dzingirai et al. 2014; Geschiere 2009). Disconnection from distant relatives and projects not only separates them from ancestral sites, but can also alienate them from those embedded in such translocal systems of economic and social generation. Offending people at 'home' can close urban opportunities just as easily as shame shared in an urban area blocks the possibility of eventual 'return'. In spaces where people straddle multiple, distinct yet connected, social worlds, status and stigma travel, shaping what is possible and what is required (Kankonde 2010).

Pentecostalism, one of Africa's most muscular social forces, is perhaps the greatest driver of archipelagic belonging and the informalisation of social regulation (Comaroff 2014; Landau and Freemantle 2010). It is a diverse movement, but almost all churches draw liturgically, materially, and for their reputation on strong connections to institutions in Nigeria, Ghana, Congo, and the United States. For many of church founders, themselves often rural or international migrants, the pulpit is a gateway to a global social universe that exists beyond the state or spatially bound community (Garbin 2018). Their preaching is often extraterritorial, overtly denying the legitimacy of state laws while speaking of the dangers of local connections. Both the state and the sullied are enemies of salvation.

As they pray, parishioners draw on variegated liturgical language to make demands on cities while positioning them in an ephemeral, superior, and unrooted condition in which they can escape localised social and political obligations and formal regulation. This is a kind of particularistic, parochial cosmopolitanism that is not necessarily grounded in normative ideas of 'openness' or intended to promote universal values of any form. Rather, they co-opt the language and imagery of the global cosmopolitan elite, planes, cars, mansions, endless travel, to position themselves as global players through discourses melding the individual with distinct and indistinct spaces in this world and the next (Cazarin 2018; also Pogge 1992; Roudometof 2005). Their churches in Nairobi, Lagos, or Johannesburg connect those cities with others in Alabama, London, or the Parisian *banlieues* (Garbin 2012). Such an approach often leaves them – as intended – 'betwixt and between without being liminal … participating in many worlds without becoming part of them' (see Simmel 1964; Vertovec 2006). Underlying these messages is the possibility of living in multiple spaces: the space you are in and in the global space. The church also compresses multiple temporalities: the ancient battles of good and evil that led to Jesus' death; a death that allows Jesus to provide his followers with success in the here and now as a down payment for eternal grace.

Whether liturgical or popular, informed by current affairs or historical and cultural bequests, archipelagic imaginations include trajectories and markers of progress often closely associated with geographic mobility: a move to the city, a move across borders, a journey to Europe or America. Yet due to economic circumstances, most notably the precarious and informal nature of employment and income generation (DeBoeck 2012), people experience what Ramakrishnan terms 'spatiotemporal disruption … where their futures within the city remain stalled and fixed in uncertainty, ultimately influencing notions of belonging and urban governance' (Ramakrishnan 2013, 755). Fostered by the unpredictability of regulation and employment, people may move with expectations of improved financial or physical security, but feel unable to reach their goal. Without such achievements, they cannot return 'home', but nor can they move forward. Others simply wait for the state or others to provide (see Oldfield and Greyling 2015; also Jeffrey 2010). Katz (2004) characterises Sudanese youths as being 'marooned by modernity' (Appadurai 2002; Bayart 2007; Mains 2007). People can remain stuck in time: experiencing endless, empty capacious, and continuous days peppered with temporal panic for having not reached their geographic or material aims and with little in the way of formal institutions or employment to guide them.

Implications for informalisation

The intersection of mobility, cities, and informality are redefining the scale and nature of sociality and politics. What will become of these (dis)connected islands of space-time? Undoubtedly, given vast contingencies, the future for people and the spaces they create will require time to 'work themselves out' (Rast 2012, 6). Translocal or oscillating lives, diasporic imaginaries, and deterritorialised politics may become the new normal. The future is contingent and stochastic (Dalberto et al. 2013), but the rapid growth of cities, which coincides with decentralisation and a demographic bounty, means that this period of 'openness and contingency' may be put under strain and eventually solidify into new orders. While variations will continue, mobilities among these sites are likely to stabilise, creating isomorphism that concentrates connection and entrenches archipelagos. Within the planetary urbanism described by Schmid (2014) and others, micro-level socialities and individual and familial projects will make real, and reshape, global forms of extraction, exclusion, and expectation.

What determines the future will depend heavily on varied forms and scales of localised governance regimes. However, the sheer speed at which cities have grown and continue to churn means that policies and those implementing them consistently, confront, subvert, and evade institutions, often bending them to meet personal or political needs. This is of course not unique to African cities. Take Brodkin's (2013, 32) street-level organisations (SLOs) – formal and informal – that 'mediate politics by structuring the possibilities for advancing claims on the state, asserting rights, and pursuing redress,' serving as 'sites within which individuals indirectly negotiate socio-political status'. They may also exclude arbitrarily or according to logic not outlined in policy priorities or standard operating procedures. SLOs' significant effects make them critical to understanding if and how law and policy influences practice. This background disparity intersects with municipalities which are relatively free to determine their commitments to engage with, protect, or effectively prosecute vulnerable populations. Below this are a range of informal (if often deeply institutionalised) governance regimes determining access to space and opportunities (Holston and Appadurai 1996; Landau and Amit 2014; Misago 2016).

The consequence is that in many instances 'state law', particularly regarding the regulation of mobility, poorly predicts developmental outcomes. In surveys across four African cities, legal status, and documentation, factors intended to guarantee basic security and entry in housing and labour markets, unreliably predicted someone's substantive experience and, when controlling for other variables, have limited effects on welfare or security (Landau and Duponchel 2011). Indeed, the primary determinants of substantive protection, whether someone is doing well in terms of income, housing, and physical security, correspond less with anything labelled as 'migration' (including direct assistance and legal status) than individual choices, skills, and social relations. Indeed, the most significant factor in explaining 'success' (that is accessing food, jobs, housing, and physical security) was social networks, a finding in line with Simone's argument that people are the new infrastructure (Simone 2004). Although they are clearly important in exchanging information on housing and work, advising people on evading the police (or escaping from custody), and providing moderate (usually once-off) material assistance, additional work is needed on the role that these networks play. They are invaluable, but not evenly accessible and may prove to be a negative form of social capital, particularly for women (Landau et al. 2017).

Rescaling regulation[1]

Given the mobile lives people are forging amidst precarity and informality, there is a need to rethink the scale of interventions intended to counter poverty or promote development. As noted early, this demands analysts simultaneously drill down to neighbourhood or municipal regulatory spaces while incorporating the translocal and transnational processes shaping migrants' lives and trajectories. Doing so also provides insights into people and processes shaping the lives of all urban residents while revealing the political battles and interactions within sub-sections of a settlement. It is these that most directly inform conflict, helping to define who is the insider and who can be excluded from working, business formation, residence, or other resources necessary to make a successful urban life. In this case it is not an immigration issue at stake, but rather how conflicts over access to political resources are managed which create incentives to exclude. In one neighbourhood in Nairobi, for example, subtle forms of exclusion were developed around access to newly installed 'Iko toilets'. Introduced by the municipality to improve sanitation, they were intended to be free to locals, while others needed to pay a fee. For one neighbourhood, the local 'chiefs' (administrators) determined that keeping residents 'foreign' was an important way to ensure a revenue stream (see Paller 2015). The consequence was the continued exclusion of people, not just from toilets, but from full participation in local politics (see Chalfin 2017).

Respatialisation also means recognising that the overlapping memberships through which people claim protection extend beyond neighbourhoods, cities, and national boundaries. For many, urban sites are 'places of flows' (Castells 1996) or 'nowherevilles'

(Bauman 2000) where rooting and local representation – legal and otherwise – offer little appeal. Moreover, the burdens and bindings that come from engaging in formal legal regimes are to be avoided (Kankonde 2010). Given the insecurity of land tenure, the possibility of violence, and ongoing economic deprivation, urban residents are well aware that workable durable solutions mean actively maintaining feet in multiple sites without firmly rooting themselves in any (Landau and Freemantle 2016). This helps generate a kind of permanent temporariness in which people actively resist incorporation into space-bound social and regulatory regimes by maintaining lives that span multiple sites, countries, and world regions (Kihato 2013). Inasmuch as a formal policy is premised on place-bound interventions, the perspective often misses the policies shaping people's lives and calculations. These may be policies forged at supra-national levels (particularly regarding immigration) (Mainwaring and Walton-Roberts 2018). They may also be distinctly not urban in their subjects and focus. Policies about rural land ownership or affecting the possibility of accessing agricultural inputs may determine the kind of resources residents hope to extract from the city for investments elsewhere (Dzingirai et al. 2014). As urban areas expand over the rural, these policy spheres become increasingly enmeshed at one scale (Roy 2016) while ever more long-haul movements geographically distance them.

Self-alienation and usufruct rights

Lastly, within the informalisation and precarity that characterises many migrant lives, a need emerges to reconsider the meaning of inclusion and public participation. As decentralisation proceeds across the continent, participatory planning. often referencing Puerto Alegre's participatory planning pioneers, has become normalised as a means of realising democratic transformation and local accountability. One of its primary goals is an effort to channel the interests of 'marginalised groups' into planning initiatives. Along with formalisations of land and property rights, such incorporation is also intended to heighten security and public order (De Soto 2002)

In the kind of environment described above, emphasising participatory planning and policy-making runs into a number of critical problems. Most importantly, by privileging the voice of current 'bona fide' residents, it may exclude transient populations. Moreover, it discounts the future by emphasising the needs of current residents over future planning. Since by its definition, participatory planning only includes people already *in situ*, and residents rarely ask municipalities to dedicate resources to future, potential residents, which means migrant interests are excluded. Depending on the demographic pace of change and the frequency of engagement, a significant portion of residents may have been excluded from planning simply because they were not yet there when the consultations took place.[2] The desire of long-term residents to ensure their needs are first met may also lead them to actively exclude newcomers from participating. Analysis of South African participation planning processes found no overt prohibition on such participation, although such prohibitions were anecdotally reported. Yet despite opportunities for inclusion, almost all of the officials and community members interviewed indicated an almost total absence of foreigners and recent migrants in such fora (Landau et al., 2013).

Part of the absence of migrants from public deliberations may be rooted in officials' preferences to reach out to the people they understand as 'proper citizens' who occupy 'proper living environments'(Watson 2003, 396). Such preferences generate entitlements and exclusions, sometimes explicit and sometimes implicitly couched under the rubric of assisting 'registered ratepayers'. Nonetheless, the priorities were clear. But this presumes little migrant agency.

Perhaps more fundamental is the presumptions often made about mobile populations' interest in participation and incorporation. Rather than seeking ways into space-bound social or legal communities as Glick-Schiller and Çağlar (2009) implicitly presume, the forms of solidarity and recognition people seek are increasingly fluid, syncretic, and translocal. Even churches, often seen as instruments of local integration, community formation, or stable transnational mobilisation (Cadge and Ecklund 2007), are now sites for 'tactical cosmopolitanism' and other means of gaining recognition (Garbin 2012; Glick-Schiller et al. 2006; Landau and Freemantle 2016). Within them and similar bodies, people find ways to maintain the levels of social engagement and recognition necessary to negotiate everyday life, but without the kind of place-based fixity which often underlies long-term investments in place. Whereas De Soto (2002) fears these kind of exclusions can breed anti-state or revolutionary movements, this requires a population angered at their exclusion from space, society, or political influence. Instead, the forms of solidarity forged through these bodies are often inherently transient, translocal, post-territorial, and, in the case of millenarian religious configurations, potentially post-terrestrial (Kankonde 2016).

Durable forms of place-based solidarity remain a strong normative guide for urban planners and policymakers. City government decisions around upgrading slums, investing in housing, expanding urban services assume a *quid pro quo* relationship with residents. If cities invest in spaces, households will expand their businesses, participate in political processes, build their communities, and generate wealth. Yet this social contract is often absent in cities – or parts of them – with rapid turnover in populations, as well as limited regulatory capacity and frail formal institutions. Within the highly precarious cities of the south, there is little sense or expectation of staying put. Rather, migrants imagine the city as a temporary stop that enables the accumulation of wealth for a future 'back home', or on the way third countries or more prosperous neighbourhoods nearby. In an informal era in which finding economic security increasingly means spreading family and individual risk across multiple spaces, fluidity may allow opportunities to meet social and economic demands within existing and emerging translocal relationships and diasporas. In some instances, urban residents' success (or even survival) depends on radically limiting investments in the city. Indeed, what first appears as social marginalisation and alienation from family, kin, and community represents tactical agency: a quest for access to the city, but without the responsibility that this entails. Such conditions demand we rethink the ethical and practical basis of political representation, membership, and inclusion. For many residents, inclusion is not about ownership and belonging, but about usufruct rights – the ability to live in and extract from the city without being bound by it.

Conclusions

What this brief excursion suggests is that there is value in socialising, spatialising, and nuancing understandings of laws' practical and political function. Indeed, intervening in particular policy spheres with the intention of reaching specific places or peoples can be like pulling a lever in a Goldbergian creation. It may have little impact or potentially deleterious consequences for those it is intended to assist. In the kinds of environments alluded to above, granting legal or principled rights to the city may have value for some (normative if not practical), but with only limited enforcement capacity and a minimal reliance on state-provided services, schools, clinics, jobs, it is safe to say that formal rights often do little.

Even in South Africa, arguably Africa's 'strongest' state, these processes are negotiated on the ground through a panoply of rationalities and calculations, sometimes involving laws and state actors but not always in predictable ways (Hansen and Stepputat 2010).

Apart from what this means for policy analysis, it raises at least three questions about what rights to the city might mean for people in Africa's urban areas. First, it asks us to rethink the geographic scales of justice. Harvey and Lefebvre's reading of the city is rooted in Marxist understandings of labour and capital, and the belief that rights to the city belong to those who labour in it. But what if cities were built on the back of workers elsewhere? The growth of cities in Africa is not largely based on urban industry but on surpluses generated elsewhere through agriculture, oil, and mining. The labour that makes cities possible is not necessarily based there. Moreover, cities rarely carry the welfare burden of sick and ageing labour, that burden disproportionately falls on rural areas. The question then is can we envision a right to the city that moves beyond its geographic boundary to incorporate the places outside of it that have made it possible? For an African city to be just, it cannot only be for those who live in the city, but for all those who need to come to it from elsewhere. It must be open for all those who built and continue to build its wealth. Where the institutions exist, this may mean new means of allocating budgets across space to redistribute urban wealth generation. It almost certainly means shifting planning modalities and mindsets in ways that welcome – or are at least neutral – to newcomers. For various reasons, this is often not the case (Landau et al. 2013).

Second, we need to shift the metrics of urban development, the way we measure success, and recognise how people use urban spaces. For a city to be accessible, for justice to be accessible, we need to understand how people keep a foothold in the city and what kinds of spaces make it possible for them to realise their aspirations. Many urban dwellers live in informal settlements or slums framed as failed spaces in development discourses. The 'failure of capital to equitably distribute surplus value, the failure of the state to regulate such distribution and invest resources in habitats where the poor live'. This is not to say that slums and informal settlements are perfect: they are not. But it is to recognise, as Huchzermeyer (2011) and others do, that these spaces work for the poor because of their low entry costs and enable people to access the opportunities they seek to fulfil their objectives which may often be elsewhere. Pushing for justice along a metric of success that focuses on consumerism, 'quality of life', the provision of urban amenities, and land titles, can inadvertently make the city inaccessible to the poor.

Third, we need to rethink the ethics and practices of urban participation and representation. As noted in the paragraphs above, participatory planning has become an almost universal mechanism for realising democratic local government. This works from a normative position that inclusion is what everyone desires. It also overlooks how, despite its inclusive and just ethos, participation can create incentives for excluding the interests of migrants coming to the city. Those participating in planning processes rarely ask municipalities to dedicate resources to future residents when they themselves face acute immediate needs. That new arrivals are often unpopular outsiders facing formal and informal obstacles to public planning mechanisms, only heightens the probability of their exclusion. Such conditions demand we rethink the ethical and practical basis of political representation, membership, and inclusion. For many residents, inclusion is not about ownership and belonging but about usufruct rights – the ability to live in and extract from the city without being bound by it.

In an era of informalised work and regulation, a focus on law and formal migration policy – even at multiple scales – is inadequate to explain developmental outcomes. Instead, we must understand the migration experience simultaneously across multiple geographic and temporal scales. At the very least, it requires a more substantive understanding of the multiple trajectories under which urban residents are living their lives and the spatial and temporal horizons that inform them.

Notes

1 This section draws heavily from Kihato and Landau (2017).
2 For the large South African cities, internal migrants (people born in another province) make up approximately 30 per cent of the population. In Gauteng Province – home to Pretoria and Johannesburg – more than half the population is born elsewhere beyond the Province's borders.

References

Appadurai, A. (2002) "Deep Democracy: Urban Governmentality and the Horizon of Politics," *Public Culture 14(1)*, 21–47.

Auyero, J. (2000) "The Hyper-Shantytown: Neo-Liberal Violence(s) in the Argentine Slum," *Ethnography 1(1)*, 93–116.

Bank, L.J. (2011) *Home Spaces, Street Styles: Contesting Power and Identity in a South African City*, Pluto Press, London.

Bauman, Z. (2000) *Globalization: The Human Consequences*, Columbia University Press, New York.

Bayart, J.F. (2007) *Global Subjects: A Political Critique of Globalization*, Polity Press, Cambridge.

Brodkin, E. (2013) "Street-level Organisations and the Welfare State," in Brodkin, E. and Marston, G. eds., *Work & the Welfare State: Street-level Organisations and Workfare Politics*, Georgetown University Press, Washington, DC, 3–16.

Cadge, W. and Ecklund, E.H. (2007) "Immigration and Religion," *Annual Review of Sociology 33*, 359–379.

Castells, M. (1996) "The Space of Flows," in Susser, I. ed., *The Castells Reader on Cities and Social Theory*, Blackwell, Oxford, 314–365.

Cazarin, R. (2018) "Pentecostalism and a Global Community of Sentiment: The Cases of Nigerian and Congolese Pastors in Diaspora," in Bakewell, O. and Landau, L.B. eds., *Forging African Communities: Mobilities, Integration, and Belonging*, Palgrave, London, 255–275.

Chalfin, B. (2017) "'Wastelandia': Infrastructure and the Commonwealth of Waste in Urban Ghana," *Ethnos 82(4)*, 648–671.

Cohen, R. (1969) *Custom and Politics in Urban Africa: A Study of Hausa Migrants in Yoruba Towns*, University of California Press, Berkeley.

Comaroff, J. (2014) "Pentacostalism, 'Post-Secularism, and the Politics of Affect," in Lindhardt, M. ed., *Pentecostalism in Africa: Presence and Impact of Pneumatic Christianity in Postcolonial Societies*, Brill, Leiden, 220–247.

Comaroff, J. and Comaroff, J. (2011) *Theory from the South: Or, How Euro-America is Evolving toward Africa*, Routledge, London.

Dalberto, S.A., Charton, H. and Goerg, O. (2013) "Urban Planning, Housing and the Making of 'Responsible Citizens' in the Late Colonial Period: Dakar, Nairobi and Conakry," in Bekker, S. and Fouchard, L. eds., *Governing Cities in Africa*, HSRC Press, Cape Town, 43–64.

De Soto, H. (2002) *The Other Path*, Basic Books, New York.

DeBoeck, F. (2012) "Spectral Kinshasa: Building the City through an Architecture of Words," in Edensor, T. and Jayne, M. eds., *Urban Theory Beyond the West: A World of Cities*, Routledge, London, 311–328.

Dzingirai, V., Mutopo, P. and Landau, L.B. (2014) *Confirmations, Coffins and Corn: Kinship, Social Networks and Remittances from South Africa to Zimbabwe*, Migrating out of Poverty Research Programme Consortium, Working Paper 18, University of Sussex.

Garbin, D. (2018) "Sacred Remittances: Money, Migration and the Moral Economy of Development in a Transnational African Church," *Journal of Ethnic and Migration Studies* 10.1080/1369183X.2018.1433528.

Garbin, G. (2012) "Marching for God in the Global City: Public Space, Religion and Diasporic Identities in a Transnational African Church," *Culture and Religion 13(4)*, 425–447.

Geschiere, P. (2009) *The Perils of Belonging: Autochthony, Citizenship, and Exclusion in Africa and Europe*, University of Chicago Press, Chicago.

Glick-Schiller, N. and Çağlar, A. (2009) "Towards a Comparative Theory of Locality in Migration Studies: Migrant Incorporation and City Scale," *Journal of Ethnic and Migration Studies 35(2)*, 177–202.

Glick-Schiller, N., Çağlar, A. and Guldbrandsen, T.C. (2006) "Beyond the Ethnic Lens: Locality, Globality, and Born-again Incorporation," *American Ethnologist 33(4)*, 612–633.

Hansen, T.B. and Stepputat, F. eds. (2010) *States of Imagination: Ethnographic Explorations of the Postcolonial State*, Duke University Press, Durham.

Harvey, D. (2003) "The Right to the City," *International Journal of Urban and Regional Research 27(4)*, 939–941.

Holston, J. and Appadurai, A. (1996) "Cities and Citizenship," *Public Culture 8*, 199–200.

Huchzermeyer, M. (2011) *Cities with 'Slums': From Informal Settlement Eradication to a Right to the City in Africa*, University of Cape Town Press, Cape Town.

Jeffrey, C. (2010) "Timepass: Youth, Class, and Time among Unemployed Men in India," *American Ethnologist 37(3)*, 465–481.

Kankonde, P. (2010) "Transnational Family Ties, Remittance Motives, and Social Death among Congolese Migrants: A Socio-Anthropological Analysis," *Journal of Comparative Family Studies 41(2)*, 225–244.

Kankonde, P. (2016) "Taking Roots in the Name of God?: Super Diversity and Migrant Pentecostal Churches' Legitimation and Social Integration in Post-Apartheid South Africa," Doctoral Dissertation, University of Göttingen.

Katz, C. (2004) *Growing Up Global: Economic Restructuring and Children's Everyday Lives*, University of Minnesota Press, Minneapolis.

Kihato, C.W. (2013) *Migrant Women of Johannesburg: Everyday Life in an In-Between City*, Palgrave, London.

Kihato, C.W. and Landau, L.B. (2017) "Migration, Membership, and Multi-Level Governance: Incentivising Inclusion in an Era of Urban Mobility," *International Development Planning Review 39(4)*, 371–374.

Landau, L.B. and Amit, R. (2014) "Wither Policy? Southern African Perspectives on Understanding Law, 'Refugee' Policy and Protection," *Journal of Refugee Studies 27(4)*, 534–552.

Landau, L.B., Bule, K., Malik, A.A. Kihato, C.W., Irvin-Erickson, Y., Edwards, B. and Mohr, E. (2017) *Displacement and Disconnection? Exploring the Role of Social Networks in the Livelihoods of Refugees in Gaziantep, Nairobi, and Peshawar*, Urban Institute, Washington, DC.

Landau, L.B. and Duponchel, M. (2011) "Laws, Policies, or Social Position? Capabilities and the Determinants of Effective Protection in Four African Cities," *Journal of Refugee Studies 24(1)*, 1–22.

Landau, L.B. and Freemantle, I. (2010) "Tactical Cosmopolitanism and Idioms of Belonging: Insertion and Self-Exclusion in Johannesburg," *Journal of Ethnic and Migration Studies 36(3)*, 375–390.

Landau, L.B. and Freemantle, I. (2016) "Beggaring Belonging in Africa's No-Man's Lands: Diversity, Usufruct and the Ethics of Accommodation," *Journal for Ethnic and Migration Studies 42(6)*, 933–951.

Landau, L.B. and Segatti, A. with Misago, J.P. (2013) "Planning and Participation in Cities that Move: Identifying Obstacles to Municipal Mobility Management," *Public Administration and Development 33(2)*, 113–124.

Lefebvre, H. (1996). *Writings on Cities*, Translated and Edited by Eleonore Kofman and Elizabeth Lebas. Wiley-Blackwell, Hoboken.

Mains, D. (2007) "Neoliberal Times: Progress, Boredom, and Shame among Young Men in Urban Ethiopia," *American Ethnologist 34(4)*, 659–673.

Mainwaring, C. and Walton-Roberts, M. (2018) "Governing Migration from the Margins," *Social & Legal Studies 27(2)*, 131–141.

Mbembe, A. and Nuttall, S. (2004) "Writing the World from an African Metropolis," *Public Culture 16(3)*, 347–372.

Merry, S. (1986) "Everyday Understandings of the Law in Working-class America," *American Ethnologist 13(2)*, 253–270.

Misago, J.P. (2016) "Migration, Governance and Violent Exclusion: Exploring the Politics of Xenophobic Violence in Post-Apartheid South Africa," Doctor of Philosophy, University of the Witwatersrand.

Oldfield, S. and Greyling, S. (2015) "Waiting for the State: A Politics of Housing in South Africa," *Environment and Planning A 47(5)*, 1100–1112.

Paller, J. (2015) "Informal Networks and Access to Power to Obtain Housing in Urban Slums in Ghana," *Africa Today 62(1)*, 31–55.

Pogge, T.W. (1992) "Cosmopolitanism and Sovereignty," *Ethics 103(1)*, 48–75.

Portes, A. (2007) "Migration, Development, and Segmented Assimilation: A Conceptual Review of the Evidence," *Annals, AAPSS 610*, 73–97.

Potts, D. (2011) *Circular Migration in Zimbabwe and Contemporary Sub-Saharan Africa*, University of Cape Town Press, Cape Town.

Ramakrishnan, K. (2013) "Disrupted Futures: Unpacking Metaphors of Marginalization in Eviction and Resettlement Narratives," *Antipode 46(3)*, 754–772.

Rast, J. (2012) "Why History (Still) Matters: Time and Temporality in Urban Political Analysis," *Urban Affairs Review 48(1)*, 3–36.

Robinson, J. (2013) "The Urban Now: Theorising Cities beyond the New," *European Journal of Cultural Studies 16(6)*, 659–677.

Roudometof, V. (2005) "Transnationalism, Cosmopolitanism and Glocalization," *Current Sociology 53(1)*, 113–135.

Roy, A. (2016) "What is Urban about Critical Urban Theory?" *Geography 37(6)*, 810–823.

Schmid, C. (2014) "Patterns and Pathways of Global Urbanization: Towards Comparative Analysis," in Brenner, N. ed., *Implosions/Explosions: Towards a Study of Planetary Urbanization*, Jovis, Berlin, 203–217.

Simmel, G. (1964) *The Sociology of George Simmel*, translated by Wolff, K., The Free Press, New York.

Simone, A. (2004) "People as Infrastructure: Intersecting Fragments in Johannesburg," *Public Culture 16(3)*, 407–429.

Simone, A. (2009) *City Life from Jakarta to Dakar: Movements at the Crossroads*, Routledge, New York.

Soja, E. (1996) *Thirdspace: Journeys to Los Angeles and Other Real-and-Imagined Places*, Blackwell, Oxford.

Tilly, C. and Blockmans, W. eds. (1994) *Cities and the Rise of States in Europe, A.D. 1000 to 1800*, Routledge, London.

Vertovec, S. (2006) "Fostering Cosmopolitanisms: A Conceptual Survey and a Media Experiment in Berlin," in Lenz, G., Ulfers, F. and Dallmann, A. eds., *Toward a New Metropolitanism: Reconstituting Public Culture, Urban Citizenship, and the Multicultural Imaginary in New York and Berlin*, Universitätsverlag, Heidelberg, 3–10.

Vivet, J., Bregand, D., Olaniyi, R. and Spire, A. (2013) "Changing Minority Identities in Urban Africa: Cotonou, Kano, Lomé and Maputo," in Bekker, S. and Fourchard, L. eds., *Governing Cities in Africa: Politics and Policies*, HSRC Press, Cape Town, 67–84.

Watson, V. (2003) "Conflicting Rationalities: Implications for Planning Theory and Ethics," *Planning Theory & Practice 4(4)*, 395–407.

Weber, M. (1958) *The City*, Trans. Martindale, D. and Neuwirth, G., Free Press, New York.

15

LABOUR MIGRATION, POVERTY, AND INEQUALITY

A gap in the development debate

Arjan de Haan

While much academic and policy attention focuses on international migration, the largest numbers of migrants remain in the Global South, and within national borders. Moreover, while rural–urban migration, such as has happened on a massive scale in China, attracts the most attention, large numbers of migrants in the Global South remain within rural areas. Typically, this is even more the case for poorer migrants.

Focusing on the latter, and comparing different types of migration, this chapter discusses links between migration for work, and poverty and inequality. It looks at who the labour migrants typically are, how many they are, what socioeconomic status they belong to, what causes people to migrate, and what the impact of such migration is on people's and home communities' well-being, and the inequality within these communities. These apparently simple questions do not have simple or straightforward answers, for different reasons – including ambivalence about the desirability of migration, which informed the writing of this chapter and I discuss first.

Migrants: essential yet not welcome

The different views on migration, and how they relate to poverty have different causes. Data shortage is one of them. National statistics tend to under-record and underestimate the complexity of migration. For India, for example, Shanthi (2006, 5) provides insights into reasons for under-recording of female migration in surveys, which can be related to the prevalent cultural inappropriateness to emphasise the economic role of the women, particularly vis-à-vis a male interviewer, and the emphasis on primary and full-time work. Many migration studies do not have representative samples (Litchfield 2018), thus limiting macro-level analysis. Very few studies have information on migrants in both areas of origin and destination (de Brauw et al. 2018). Analysis like Munshi and Rosenzweig (2009) emphasise 'low mobility' in India, ignoring the qualitative evidence of mobility, particularly of more vulnerable groups.

Strong disciplinary differences in conceptualising migration have also hampered clear understanding. On the one hand, approaches to migration typically by economists see migrants as rational economic agents. On the other hand, alternative and critical political-economy approaches emphasise the exploitation and powerlessness of migrants. These theoretical backgrounds tend to provide different answers to questions regarding links between migration and poverty.

The differences are not only academic. They are often deeply political and ideological. Indeed, data collection and analysis can be directly informed by these political and ideological differences. While there is generally a preference for, or at least acceptance of, people moving when there is a demand for labour, there are at least equally strong voices, often strengthened in times of crises, for reducing the number of migrants.

Countries with centrally managed economies have tended to restrict migration, and this perspective often continues to filter through after reforms. China demonstrates such ambivalence. Migrants on the one hand have been regarded as drivers of economic transformation. On the other hand, the *hukou* (household registration) system continued to exclude migrants from many public services in urban areas. This has been gradually reformed, since the early 2000s becoming more permissive to migrants without *hukou* status, and since the mid-2010s entitlements to social services are in principle no longer linked to *hukou* status. In Ethiopia, similarly, its government has historically tried to control and prevent migration, and this perspective continues to inform development strategies, such as Poverty Reduction Strategies (Atnafu et al. 2014).

Policies to limit rural–urban migration are not restricted to former centrally planned economies. According to the UNDESA World Population Policies Database (2010–15), countries that have higher rates of urbanisation, which typically are lower-income countries, were more likely to have policies to reduce rural-to-urban migration. The data suggests that in the majority of countries these restrictive policies were adopted in the last 5 years (UNDESA 2016, 5 and 10–9).

Moreover, there is a common focus on reducing migration in development and anti-poverty programmes. This was articulated, for example, within India's employment guarantee scheme (NREGA), the world's largest public works scheme. Reminiscent of the Maharashtra employment scheme, NREGA's objectives include significantly reducing labour migration through the provision of locally available work in rural areas (Datta 2019, 39–40; Solinski 2012). The ambivalent and differentiated treatment of migrants in India in the official discourse is described in detail by Deshingkar (2017).

How many people move for work?

Movement of people is much more common than is usually assumed and has existed for much longer than often acknowledged in both academic and policy circles (see Czaika and de Haas 2014, for an overview). Moreover, scholarship on international migration literature tends to underplay the fact that most migration remains within the Global South, and within national borders. Therefore, much migration – and many of the most vulnerable migrants – may remain unrecorded.

Using a 'conservative' definition, UNDP's 2009 *Human Development Report* estimated there were almost a billion migrants globally; as far as I am aware this is the only existing global estimate including internal and international migration. These included four times as many internal migrants, 740 million, as international migrants (214 million, some 3 per cent of the world's population). Twice as many migrants moved across borders within the Global South compared to international migrants moving South–North. No longitudinal data is available, as far I am aware, but it seems reasonable to assume that internal migration in much of the Global South continues to increase, and cross-border migration within the Global South continues to be a larger share of total share of population mobility than

South–North migration (including because growth rates in OECD economies have been below those in many emerging economies).

In Africa, data from the new Global Migration Database shows migration within Africa increased from 6.2 million in 1960 to 10.5 million, while migration to the rest of the world increased from 1.8 million to 8.7 million in the same period (this refers to cross-border migration, migration within countries is not described): 'the bulk of African migration is contained within the continent and, more specifically, occurs between neighbouring countries'. While economic growth poles and improved communication increases the likelihood of migration, other factors may deter larger movements of people, such as strengthened borders after decolonisation, and xenophobia in a number of places (Flahaux and de Haas 2016).

While publications like the *World Migration Report 2018* focus on international migration – despite the title – internal migration in Africa is far more significant than international migration (Awumbila 2017). It plays a major role for the majority of households in, for example, Ghana, Mali, Nigeria and Tanzania. Research on regional migration, like that by Konan and Kuakou (2012) in West Africa, is relatively scarce.

Estimates of numbers of international migrants remain uncertain, given the importance of undocumented migrants in particular. Estimates of internal migrants can be equally uncertain.

Definitions of migrants are part of the reason for this, and can vary, for example, regarding length of time away from home, and causes of migration (for example, refugee, labour migrant, student migration, and family/marriage migration). Statistical systems can be part of the problem too, particularly in countries with a tradition of control over population movements.

Estimates of numbers of migrants in China remained unclear for a long period of time since economic reforms started in 1978. This was to a large extent the result of or related to the lack of legal status of rural *hukou* holders when they migrate to other areas. But it was also partly because the data collection system is divided between rural and urban survey divisions, thus complicating estimates of the people who move between these regions. Currently, the official statistics provide a reliable estimate of the large-scale internal migration that has taken place in China. In 2015, there were 278 million rural migrant workers, over one-third of the labour force. The majority (159 million) worked in other provinces (China Labour Bulletin 2010). Among younger migrants in China, women migrate as much as men do (Chiang et al. 2015).

But in countries with more 'liberal' policies vis-à-vis population movements, too, estimates of migrants can be problematic. For example, in India, which has well developed statistical measures, data on numbers of migrants leave much room for interpretation (de Haan 2011; Srivastava and Sutradhar 2016). According to the National Sample Survey, 26 per cent of the rural population was classified as migrant in 2007–08, and 35 per cent of the urban population. The majority of these (over 80 per cent) were women, and the largest group of migrants is that of 'migration for marriage'. If this category is excluded about 10 per cent of the total population is classified as migrant; the share of women migrating for work is low (in line with women's labour force participation rates), and has actually declined according to official statistics (Rao 2014).

The 2007–08 survey in India recorded a mere 1.7 per cent of the rural population and under 1 per cent of the urban population as short-term migrants, defined as persons who had moved for employment between one and six months in the previous year. There are clear indications that these figures underestimate significant parts of population movements, particularly that of poorest workers who move for unskilled and seasonal jobs, as described from fieldwork for example by Jan Breman (1985, 1996) and Ben Rogaly and colleagues (2002), and in the review of India's booming construction sector by Srivastava and Sutradhar (2016). This under-recording is relevant for what we know about the links between migration and poverty, as discussed later.

Migration for labour is not only very common; it also takes many forms, of which a rural–urban transition is only one. A common form is the move of one member of the household who retains links with her or his origins, migrating for varying and often unknown periods of time. Return, and urban–rural migration, can happen as a result of declining job opportunities, as described in my own historical research of migration to Calcutta (de Haan 1997), and for the West African context during the period of structural adjustment (Beauchemin et al. 2004). Migrants' backgrounds and motives are very diverse, as we discuss next.

Who migrates?

The question who migrates does not have a simple answer either. Different regions and countries have varying levels of migration. UNDP (2009) estimates suggest that international migrants are twice as likely to come from countries with high standards of living as from those with lower living standards. In Africa, data from the Global Migration Database suggests

> a rather clear relation between levels of socio-economic development and the volume and geographical orientation of African emigration. More marginal, poorer or landlocked countries tend to have lower absolute and relative levels of extra-continental migration, and their migration is primarily directed towards other African countries.
>
> *(Flahaux and de Haas 2016)*

As mentioned, this database does not include reference to internal migrants, but does suggest that poorer sections of populations have less opportunity to migrate.

In South Asia, Punjab, Mirpur, Sylhet, and Sri Lanka were major (and early) areas of international outmigration. Research has shown that these were only partly related to levels of poverty in those regions, and also to a significant extent due to historical links and the role of social networks forming patterns of chain migration, for example, linked to soldiers having travelled with colonial armies. In the case of India, only in the last decades has, for example, the state of Uttar Pradesh overtaken richer Indian states as a major sending area of international migrants. This was despite high levels of deprivation, which have long been associated with outmigration (and as important areas of recruitment of indentured labourers), but mostly to other parts of India. Again, poorer migrants have fewer migration opportunities – even though this might involve long-distance migration, such as nineteenth-century migration from Northern India to agricultural occupations in what is now Bangladesh, or migration from poor parts of Orissa to industrial work in western India.

In different contexts, different socioeconomic groups migrate, prompted by different opportunities, and differentiated access – which is unlikely to be captured in simple push–pull and economic models of migration. For example, in Mahabubnagar village in Andhra Pradesh in India, each Reddi (powerful caste) household had a migrant in urban areas, whereas migration to rural areas was much more common among the Madiga (Dalit) and landless marginal farmer households (Korra 2010).

Gender is a critical determinant of this, and gender analysis 'is an essential tool for unpicking the migration process' (Wright 1995; also Sinclair 1998). There are no meaningful generalisations about whether men or women migrate. Young men tend to be over-represented among migrants in many places, constituting particular gendered and household impacts. But women have always been mobile. According to estimates, they constitute half of the total global migrant workforce. They move for 'traditional' female occupations (and the 'care economy') as well as newer ones (Gaetano and Yeoh 2010). Female migrants tend to be particularly vulnerable and suffer from labour market discrimination and violence, often ending up in the 'informal sector' (Mehra and Gammage 1999). A great deal of path dependency and gender stereotyping exists. Whether men or women migrate may also determine the kind of impact migration has on families left behind (see, for example, Heymann et al. 2009).

While people move for better opportunities, and from relatively poor to better-off areas, patterns of migration are also determined by chain migration (de Haas 2008; Del Carmen and Sousa 2018; Massey et al. 1994). People move to places where relatives or friends have moved to before them, as these connections are critical to finding jobs, and in poor economic conditions 'outsiders' may be considered unwelcome. In certain jobs, for both international and national migrants, it is common to find a large concentration of workers from one particular area. Bangladeshi migrants to the United Kingdom have tended to come from Sylhet. Punjab and Kerala have been the main areas of out migration in India, despite the fact that these are not the poorest parts of those countries, nor were the migrants the poorest among the population in those areas. Outmigration from Kerala, both internationally and nationally, was likely promoted by its historically high levels of human development.

Similar dynamics operate at a country level, thus leading to, for example, a high concentration of workers from Orissa in industrial work in Surat, despite the distance. Social networks, often linked to specific occupations for generations, have played an important role, as descriptions of tea sellers in Mumbai illustrate (Subramaniam 2018). In an historical narrative of Bihar, Arvind Das (1986) highlighted that the sons of landowners were amongst the first to migrate, and they were followed by the less well-off. In the 1980s, Oberai et al. (1989) showed that in Bihar, the poor and landless were (slightly) more likely to migrate.

The poorest people – in terms of income, or health, or those lacking sufficient labour-power within the household – may not be able to migrate, and if they do, they migrate to work in the most exploitative jobs. Globally, with technological change, migration has tended to become more selective; there are fewer opportunities for unskilled workers, and anti-immigrant sentiments in Europe have led to declining international migration, particularly of the less-skilled. In low-income countries, such selectivity also seems to affect internal migration. For example, relatively low rates of urbanisation in Asia has been attributed to increasing difficulties and the high costs to migrants of settling in urban areas (Kundu 2009), and anti-migrant sentiments can equally affect migrants within large and socially and ethnically diverse countries.

Different reasons for migration can present a macro–micro paradox. Data from Indian national surveys showed that migrants were *on average* better-off than non-migrants, in terms of levels of income and education. This does not concur with micro-studies that highlight the severe deprivation of migrants; for example, movements of workers who often remain within rural areas (Rogaly et al. 2002), migrations in western India (Mosse et al. 2002), migrants from Orissa's most deprived districts who work in brick kilns in Andra Pradesh

(CREATE 2008, 11), and the large number of migrants in construction (Srivastava and Sutradhar 2016).

This paradox can likely be explained with the fact that migrants constitute very diverse groups. As Deshingkar (2017) notes for India, different strata receive different treatments in public debate and policy. Inspired by research among international migrants in the UK that highlighted diversity of migration, we used NSS to assess diversity of internal migrants in India. We found that income inequality among migrants was larger than the inequality in the population as a whole (de Haan and Dubey 2006; as mentioned, poor migrants in particular are likely under-recorded in the survey).

Moreover, reasons for migrating are diverse, as Litchfield (2018) describes for Ghana, Ethiopia, and Zimbabwe. Much migration is driven by the hope of better opportunities, broadening horizons, or simply a rite of passage for young men and women. But migration often arises from desperation, lack of work, or indebtedness. Seasonal migration, both rural–rural and rural–urban, is for many households a regular household strategy, where income from migrants' work is (intended) to complement the livelihood in the village. Also, as statistical data tends to record only one reason for migration, it underestimates the complexity of migration. This can be particularly pertinent for female migrants, who often – particularly in South Asian context – have marriage as the main purpose, but this can involve labour market participation as well (and of course has critical reproductive functions). Since reasons and patterns of migration are diverse, the impacts of migration are very diverse too, as described next.

Consequences of migration

Assessing the impact of migration remains a relatively uncharted field of study. Comparatively, more research exists on the impact on 'host' societies, which of course is heavily politically charged; the impact on sending communities has not received much attention, neither in the literature on international nor internal migration. Moreover, research on impacts is complicated by technical questions regarding the selectivity of migrants and distinguishing cause and effect. Study of the counter-factual, as done by Adams for Guatemala (2006), is critical but an exception. Particularly if migration is a recurring phenomenon, and part of households' livelihoods strategies, distinguishing causes and impact of migration is nearly impossible.

As patterns, causes, and motives of migration are diverse, it follows almost logically that the impacts of migration cannot easily be summarised. For example, migration can help to alleviate local unemployment (Ghosh 1992), but it can also contribute to a shortage of workers, as it did for example in China (Croll and Ping 1997) and labour-scarce West Africa (David 1995). As migrants tend to be young, populations in sending areas of course tend to become relatively older. Those varied impacts have received relatively little attention; most emphasis has been on the impact of remittances.

International remittances have received most interest over the last two decades because they now far outstrip official ODA flows. The interest has been accompanied by significant efforts to reduce costs of remitting money, and optimism regarding possible beneficial development effects, including remittances as a source of foreign earnings (Kapur 2004). This largely overtook concerns about brain drain (which for example influential UK Minister Clare Short emphasised in the late 1990s) despite evidence that international migration has become increasingly selective (Docquier and Rapoport 2004). Similar research on transfers within countries, to my knowledge, hardly exists, with Adams (2006) study of Guatemala that analyses both international and international migration and remittances an important exception.

The impacts of remittances are often clearly visible in the areas of migrants' origin. Opportunities for migration have in some areas become an integral part of the local economy, including in the provision of education: Jamaica and Kerala train more nurses than the local economy can absorb (Connell 2007; Zachariah and Rajan 2012). There is also evidence that migrants contribute to the building of schools or other community activities (Russell et al. 1990), and that it can contribute to modernising agriculture (Lakshmansamy 1990) or diversification (Zhunusova and Herrmann 2018). Remittances by themselves appear not to lead to the economic transformation of sending communities. The conditions for, and potentials of, returns to investment in areas of origin may be as important as the mere fact of remittances itself.

At a household level, migration usually improves incomes and well-being. For example, de Brauw et al. (2018) finds large increases in consumption and income measures for migrants in Ethiopia; these increases are much larger than in other studies, which may be linked to relatively low development levels in the villages, and traditional barriers to migration (as earlier research in the IDS livelihoods programme highlighted; de Haan et al. 2000).

The impacts on well-being and poverty can be modest, and many studies find that the overwhelming share of income from migration is used for what tends to be labelled (partly misleadingly) consumptive purposes, for daily necessities, household goods, housing (Adams 2006), marriage expenses, and so on. In the case of farming families, migration and remittances are often seen as a way to maintain their mode of agricultural production, against the risk of losing their land: remittances can play a key part as insurance against risks of seasonality and annual harvest failure. As summarised by Srivastava and Sasikumar (2003), in India, most remittances function as a 'safety valve' (see also Dinkelman et al. 2018). My research of the long-standing migration links between Bihar, one of India's poorest states, and cities like Kolkata led me to conclude that migration contributed to maintaining economic structures in sending areas, as migrants expressed it the earnings in Kolkata allowed them to maintain their primarily agricultural livelihoods.

Remittances can also increase inequalities in areas of origin. As inequality within areas of origin may be a cause of people moving out (as Lipton et al. showed in the 1970s), migration in turn may also increase that inequality. Better-off people, such as sons of landowners, move for more rewarding opportunities. At the bottom of the income hierarchy the benefits from migration are likely to be lowest. In cases of bonded labour, migration may actually reinforce those very conditions of bondage, as described by David Mosse and colleagues (2002) for western India. If better-off people migrate for relatively beneficial opportunities, the disparities between them and those with fewer opportunities have the potential to become larger.

Migration dynamics are not necessarily static. Deshingkar et al. (2008) showed that over time conditions of circular migration in Madhya Pradesh improved: it led to more accumulation for the poor, and increased wages and decreased dependence on contractors. Migration reduced borrowing for consumption, improved debt repayment capacity, and enhanced the migrants' confidence. Migration also brought greater returns to those with skills or strong social networks. The study showed increased migration by higher castes (and women) as opportunities became more rewarding (see also Rogaly and Coppard 2003, for Puruliya). In the US, research indicated that inequalities among Asian immigrants has been increasing, and this is in part because well- educated immigrants recruit their educated relatives (Hassab and Carlsen 2018).

It is important to take account of costs when considering the benefits of migration. Data on remittances often neglect the investment migrants and their families have to make before moving, and indeed the investment societies or countries have made in educating young people who move after obtaining their education. The health of migrants is adversely affected by poor living and working conditions, increased exposure to infectious diseases, lack of access to health care, and emotional stress. Middlemen who provide access to migration opportunities also restrict that access, and often make migrants even more vulnerable. Further, many migrant labourers have no option but to take children along. In India, children aged under 14 may constitute one-third of all migrants, thus potentially contributing to increased child labour, gaps in education, and potentially transmitting poverty across generations (CREATE 2008, 5). Conversely, the conditions of children left behind with families also can transmit disadvantages inter-generationally.

Can policies alter these dynamics?

This essay has emphasised that there are no easy empirical conclusions regarding links between migration on the one hand, and poverty and inequality on the other. The broader relationship between migration and development is still, I believe, to a great extent 'unsettled' as Papademetriou and Martin argued in 1991. Migration is both a consequence and a cause of well-being and disparities. Patterns of migration are complex and caused by a range of factors. The impacts depend on conditions for investment as much as the amount of remittances. Which groups benefit from migration, and impacts on inequality and poverty, are questions that have even less clear answers.

Migration is a common part of livelihoods in many areas, and should be seen as an integral part of development. While the literature on migration has grown tremendously in the last 20 years, migration is still often regarded as exceptional or new, and this 'sedentary bias' may well reduce the ability to understand the complexity, and formulate effective policies. Migration studies continue to focus on international migration, this paying less attention to the largest groups of migrants, and typically those that are less well-off.

Policymakers, pushed by popular opinion or mobilising anti-immigrant sentiments, tend see migration as undesirable. They often deny its existence. Both sets of beliefs and attitudes can make migrants more vulnerable, particularly poorer migrants, as they have fewer opportunities to shelter themselves against negative repercussions.

Policy can and needs to play a role in enhancing the well-being of migrants, making migration less risky, *simultaneously* enhancing their contribution to broader society. Guaranteeing access to health care, schools for their children, safety net provisions, and legal assistance – can all contribute to win-wins. Policies can support the process of migration itself, trying to limit exploitation by middlemen, providing information, opportunities for training, etc. And policies can – and examples of this exist – make it more rewarding for migrants to invest back home.

Role of international community

Migration is now included in the SDG framework, reflecting the international community's growing attention. Migrants are referred to in a number of the goals and targets (IOM, undated), and specifically in target 10.7: to 'facilitate orderly, safe, and responsible migration and mobility of people, including through implementation of planned and well-managed migration policies'.

The Global Compact for Migration is trying to strengthen a development perspective in international migration policy, with a non-binding agreement on support to migrants and migration processes reached in December 2018.

These debates focus on international migration; the absence of attention to internal migration in the SDG framework seems to reflect a continued ambivalence around the movement of people. There may be much to gain to extend the current focus on international migration to better understanding and supporting national migration. Economic transformation, investment in infrastructure and education, and technological change – as well as, for example, commercialisation of land – will all likely lead to the greater potential mobility of people across the developing world. Much is known already about the potential costs of such mobility, costs that are likely to be larger in the absence of supportive policies.

References

Adams, R. (2006) Remittances, Poverty and Investment in Guatemala. In Ç. Ozden and M. Schiff (eds.), *International Migration, Remittances and Brain Drain.* Washington, DC: World Bank, pp. 53–80.

Atnafu, A. et al. (2014) Poverty, Youth and Rural-Urban Migration in Ethiopia. http://migratingoutof poverty.dfid.gov.uk/files/file.php?name=wp-17—atnafu-oucho-zeitlyn-2014-poverty-youth-and-rural-urban-migration-in-ethiopia.pdf&site=354.

Awumbila, M. (2017) Drivers of Migration and Urbanization: Key Trends and Issues. United Nations Expert Group Meeting on Sustainable Cities, Human Mobility and International Migration, UN New York, 7–8 September.

Beauchemin, C., Henry, S., and Schoumaker, B. (2004) Rural-urban Migration in West Africa: Toward a reversal? Migration Trends and Economic Conjuncture in Burkina Faso and Côte d'Ivoire. Paper presented at Population Association of America (PAA) annual meeting, April 1–3, 2004, Boston, MA.

Breman, J. (1985) *Of Peasants, Migrants and Paupers: Rural Labour Circulation and Capitalist Production in West India.* Oxford: Oxford University Press.

Breman, J. C. (1996) *Footloose Labour. Working in India's Informal Economy.* Cambridge: Cambridge University Press.

Chiang, Y.-L., Hannum, E., and Kao, G. (2015) It's Not Just about the Money: Gender and Youth Migration from Rural China. *Chinese Sociological Review* 47(2), 177–201. doi:10.1080/21620555.2014.990328.

China Labour Bulletin (2010) Migrant Workers and Their Children. www.clb.org.hk/content/migrant-workers-and-their-children (accessed 22 July 2018).

Connell, J. (2007) Local Skills and Global Markets? The Migration of Health Workers from Carribean and Pacific Island States. *Social and Economic Studies* 56, 67–95.

CREATE (2008) *Distress Seasonal Migration and Its Impact on Children's Education.* Create Pathways to Access Research Monograph No. 28, Centre for International Education, Sussex School of Education, University of Sussex. www.create-rpc.org/pdf_documents/PTA28.pdf (accessed 7 February 2012).

Croll, E. J. and Ping, H. (1997) Migration for and against Agriculture in Eight Chinese Villages. *The China Quarterly* 149, 128–146.

Czaika, M. and de Haas, H. (2014) The Globalization of Migration: Has the World Become More Migratory? *International Migration Review* 48(2), 283–323. doi:10.1111/imre.12095.

Das, A. (1986) *The 'Longue Duree': Continuity and Change in Changel. Historiography Ofan Indian Village from the 18th towards the 21st Century.* Rotterdam: CASP 14.

Datta, A. (2019) *Continuity and Change: Migration and Development in India. The Case of Bihar.* PhD Thesis. International Institute for Social Studies, Erasmus University Rotterdam, Rotterdam.

David, R. (1995) *Changing Places: Women, Resource Management and Migration in the Sahel.* London: SOS Sahel.

de Brauw, A., Mueller, V., and Woldehanna, T. (2018) Does Internal Migration Improve Overall Well-Being in Ethiopia? *Journal of African Economies* 27(3), 347–365, doi:10.1093/jae/ejx026.

de Haan, A. (1997) Unsettled Settlers. Migrant Workers and Industrial Capitalism in Calcutta. *Modern Asian Studies* 31(4), 919–949.

de Haan, A. (2011) *Inclusive Growth? Labour Migration and Poverty in India.* ISS Working Paper 513. Institute of Social Studies, The Hague.

de Haan, A., Brock, K., Carswell, G., Coulibaly, N., Seba, H., and Ali Toufique, K. (2000) *Migration and Livelihoods: Case Studies in Bangladesh, Ethiopia and Mali*. IDS Research Report 46. Institute of Development Studies, Sussex.

de Haan, A. and Dubey, A. (2006) Are Migrants Worse off or Better Off? Asking the Right Questions. *Margin – Journal of Applied Economic Research* 38(3), 9–26.

de Haas, H. (2008) *The Internal Dynamics of Migration Processes*. Paper presented at IMSCOE Conference on Theories of Migration and Social Change, St. Anne's College, University of Oxford, July 1–3 2008, www.heindehaas.com/Publications/de%20Haas%202008%20The%20internal%20dynamics%20of%20migration%20processes.pdf (accessed 16 December 2011).

Del Carmen, G. and Sousa, L. D. (2018) *Human Capital Outflows: Selection into Migration from the Northern Triangle*. World Bank Policy Research Working paper 8334. World Bank, Washington, DC.

Deshingkar, P. (2017) Towards Contextualised, Disaggregated and Intersectional Understandings of Migration in India. *Asian Population Studies* 13(2), 119–123. doi:10.1080/17441730.2016.1189655.

Deshingkar, P., Sharma, P., Kumar, S., Akter, S., and Farrington, J. (2008) Circular Migration in Madhya Pradesh: Changing Patterns and Social Protection Needs. *The European Journal of Development Research* 20(4), 612–628.

Dinkelman, T., Kumchulesi, G., and Mariotti, M. (2018) *Labor Migration, Capital Accumulation, and the Structure of Rural Labor Markets*. GLM|LIC Working Paper No. 22. IZI – Institute of Labor Economics, Bonn. https://glm-lic.iza.org/publications/wp/wp22.

Docquier, F. and Rapoport, H. (2004) *Skilled Migration: the Perspective of Developing Countries*. mimeo. Washington, DC: World Bank. http://documents.worldbank.org/curated/en/856971468761964198/129529322_20041117165105/additional/WPS3382.pdf.

Flahaux, M.-L. and de Haas, H. (2016) African Migration: Trends, Patterns, Drivers. *Comparative Migration Studies* 4(1). https://comparativemigrationstudies.springeropen.com/track/pdf/10.1186/s40878-015-0015-6?site=comparativemigrationstudies.springeropen.com.

Gaetano, A. M. and Yeoh, B. S. A. (2010) Introduction to the Special Issue on Women and Migration in Globalizing Asia: Gendered Experiences, Agency, and Activism. *International Migration* 48(6), 1–12.

Ghosh, B. (1992) Migration–development Linkages: Some Specific Issues and Practical Policy Measures. *International Migration* 30(3/4), 423–452.

Hassab, A. and Carlsen, A. (2018) 'Some Are Crazy Rich', but Asians' Inequality Is Widest in the U.S. *New York Times*, August 19. www.nytimes.com/interactive/2018/08/17/us/asian-income-inequality.html.

Heymann, J., Flores-Macias, F., Hayes, J. A., Kennedy, M., Lahaie, C., and Earle, A. (2009) The Impact of Migration on the Well-being of Transnational Families: New Data from Sending Communities in Mexico. *Community, Work & Family* 12(1), 91–103. doi:10.1080/13668800802155704.

IOM (International Organization for Migration) (undated) 2030 Agenda for Sustainable Development. https://unofficeny.iom.int/2030-agenda-sustainable-development

Kapur, D. (2004) *Remittances: the New Development Mantra?* G24 Discussion Papers 29. UNCTAD, Geneva.

Konan, S. Y. and Kuakou, A. K. (2012) Migration Et Marché Du Travail Sous-Régional: Analyse De Cas De a Côte d'Ivoire Et Du Gana. *Journal of West African Integration* 1(1), 44–81.

Korra, V. (2010) *Nature and Characteristics of Seasonal Labour Migration: A Case Study in Mahabubnagar District of Andhra Pradesh*. CDS Working Paper 433. Centre for Development Studies Thiruvananthapuram.

Kundu, A. (2009) Exclusionary Urbanisation in Asia: A Macro Overview. *Economic and Political Weekly* XLIV(48), 48–58.

Lakshmansamy, T. (1990) Family Survival Strategy and Migration: An Analysis of Returns to Migration. *The Indian Journal of Social Work* 51(3), 473–485.

Litchfield, J. (2018) http://migratingoutofpoverty.dfid.gov.uk/files/file.php?name=wp53-litchfield-2018-drivers-of-intra-regional-and-inter-regional-migration-in-africa.pdf&site=354 (accessed 16 July 2018).

Massey, D. et al. (1994) An Evaluation of International Migration Theory. *Population and Development Review* 20(4), 699–751.

Mehra, R. and Gammage, S. (1999) Trends, Countertrends, and Gaps in Women's Employment. *World Development* 27(3), 533–550.

Mosse, D., Gupta, S., Mehta, M., Shah, V., Rees, J. F., and KRIBP Project Team. (2002) Brokered Livelihoods: Debt, Labour Migration and Development in Tribal Western India. *Journal of Development Studies, Taylor & Francis Journals* 38(5), 59–88.

Munshi, K. and Rosenzweig, M. (2009) Why Is Mobility in India so Low? Social Insurance, Inequality, and Growth. www.stanford.edu/group/SITE/SITE_2009/segment_2/2009_s2_papers/rosenzwieg. pdf (accessed December 2010).

Oberai, A. S., Prasad, P. H., and Sardana, M. G. (1989) *Determinants and Consequences of Internal Migration in India. Studies in Bihar, Kerala and Uttar Pradesh*. Delhi: Oxford University Press.

Rao, S. (2014) Women and the Urban Economy in India: Insights from the Data on Migration. www. insightsonindia.com/2014/10/29/urbanization-in-india-facts-and-issues/ (accessed 6 October 2019).

Rogaly, B. and Coppard, D. (2003) They Used to Go to Eat, Now They Go to Earn: the Changing Meanings of Seasonal Migration from Puruliya District in West Bengal. *Journal of Agrarian Change* 3(3), 395.

Rogaly, B., Coppard, D., Rafique, A., Rana, K., Sengupta, A., and Biswas, J. (2002) Seasonal Migration and Welfare/Illfare in Eastern India: A Social Analysis. *The Journal of Development Studies* 38, 89–114. doi:10.1080/00220380412331322521.

Russell, S. S., Jacobsen, K., and Stanley, W. D. (1990) International Migration and Development in Sub-Saharan Africa. *World Bank Discussion Papers 101 and 102 (2 Issues)*, Africa Technical Department Series. World Bank, Washington, DC.

Shanthi, K. (2006) *Female Labour Migration in India: Insights from NSSO Data*. Working Paper 4/2006. Madras School of Economics, Chennai.

Sinclair, M. R. (1998) Community, Identity and Gender in Migrant Societies of Southern Africa: Emerging Epistemological Challenges. *International Affairs* 74(2), 339–353.

Solinski, T. (2012) NREGA and Labour Migration in India: Is Village Life What the 'Rural' Poor Want? *The South Asianist* 1(1), 17–30.

Srivastava, R. and Sasikumar, S. K. (2003) An Overview of Migration in India, Its Impacts and Key Issues. Impacts of Internal and International Migration on Indian Development. Paper for Regional Conference on Migration, Development and Pro-Poor Policy Choices in Asia, www.eldis.org/go/home&id=17521&type=Document (accessed 4 December 2017).

Srivastava, R. and Sutradhar, R. (2016) Migrating Out of Poverty? A Study of Migrant Construction Sector Workers in India. www.ihdindia.org/1.pdf

Subramaniam, R. R. (2018) Chai Migrants: For Decades, This Region in Rajasthan Has Been Providing Mumbai Its Tea Sellers, Cityscapes. https://scroll.in/magazine/887831/chai-migrants-for-decades-this-region-in-rajasthan-has-been-providing-mumbai-its-tea-sellers.

UNDESA (United Nations, Department of Economic and Social Affairs) (2016) Policies on Spatial Distribution and Migration. *Data Booklet*, www.un.org/en/development/desa/population/publications/pdf/policy/Data%20Booklet%20Urbanization%20Policies.pdf (accessed 15 July 2018).

UNDP (United Nations Development Programme) (2009) *Human Development Report 2009. Overcoming Barriers. Human Mobility and Development*. Basingstoke, UK: Palgrave Macmillan.

Wright, C. (1995) Gender Awareness in Migration Theory: Synthesizing Actor and Structure in Southern Africa. *Development and Change* 26(4), 771–791.

Zachariah, K. C. and Rajan, S. I. (2012) Inflexion in Kerala's Gulf Connection. Report on Kerala Migration Survey 2011, www.cds.edu/wp-content/uploads/2012/11/WP450.pdf

Zhunusova, E. and Herrmann, R. (2018) Development Impacts of International Migration on "Sending Communities". The Case of Rural Kyrgyzstan. *European Journal of Development Research* 30(5), 871–891. doi:10.1057/s41287-018-0136-5.

PART III

Families and social policy

The chapters in this part bring the discussion on migration and development down to the micro-level with a clear focus on the family and on specific dimensions that impact on individuals and families: those who remain at home, the impact of movement on the family itself, the migration of children, the ageing of populations, care, health, education, housing, and social protection. These issues, like so many in the migration and development debate, are so often misinterpreted or oversimplified. The idea that the impact that the migration of one or both parents, but particularly the mother, leaving children in the origin area, is necessarily detrimental to the development of the child needs to be examined with greater care. Negative consequences may not be the outcome. Likewise, the independent migration of children need not necessarily lead to exploitation and increased vulnerability, although that can occur. The ageing of human populations impacts on migration in many ways, most directly through reducing the number of people in age groups most likely to migrate, but also in the migration of older people themselves: to retire or to follow their children to look after their grandchildren, for example. The care of the elderly, too, creates challenges for governments insomuch as local populations appear unwilling to undertake such demanding but poorly paid and insecure employment, placing the onus increasingly on immigrants.

Health and education, two of the most basic development variables, affect migration in multiple ways. The health of immigrant populations may show distinct patterns relative to host populations, partially due to poor knowledge about how to access services locally. Mobile populations may contribute to the diffusion of certain diseases, although fears among host populations are likely to be more perceived than real as it is generally the younger and healthier who move. There is also the issue of sourcing health workers and their migration from poorer to richer countries, which is mainly covered in Part II. Migrants tend to be selected by education, with the more educated moving. However, those with higher levels of education may find that their credentials are not recognised in destination societies and tensions emerge between how to upgrade these levels and the need to ensure that all professional qualifications meet local standards in host populations. Migrants increasingly move as students to obtain qualifications in destination countries in a system that has become increasingly stratified and hierarchical.

The impact of migration on the landscape is examined through one of the most visible measures of development: the construction of houses in areas of origin and what this means for concepts of home. The final chapter in this part returns to a key policy area: the social protection of migrants abroad and on their return home. The challenge is to ensure that migrants can access all social benefits due to them in destinations and that these are portable should they return or move on. All the chapters in this part deal with very specific policy areas in the current migration and development debate.

16

THE WELL-BEING OF STAY BEHIND FAMILY MEMBERS IN MIGRANT HOUSEHOLDS

Karlijn Haagsman and Valentina Mazzucato

Introduction

Until the turn of the century, most work on migration focused on migrants and the effects migration has on the host society. But for every migrant that leaves his or her origin country, there are also family members and loved ones that he/she 'leaves behind'. This geographic separation has well-being consequences on both sides and involves complex transnational caring arrangements when it concerns dependent children or elderly (Toyota et al. 2007). Bryceson and Vuorela (2002) highlighted the existence of these so-called transnational families in 2002 and started a sub-field of transnational migration scholarship that turned to studying how families continue to function over great distances.

The effects of migration on origin countries was researched before the sub-field of transnational family scholarship evolved. Starting with the Manchester school in 1947, anthropologists studied how migration to the Copper Belt in southern Africa affected communities of origin (Epstein 1992; Mayer 1962; Schapera 1947). Yet, most of this literature, and the subsequent field of migration and development studies focused on the realm of development, mostly at the macro-level and on economic gains. It looked at households as an entire unit not distinguishing the effects on individual members (Mazzucato 2015). In short, until the turn of the century there was little scholarly attention on the experiences of individual members 'left behind' by migrants. Only around 3.4 per cent of the world's population is classified as an international migrant at any one time (UNDESA 2017), but those affected by migration, or those 'left behind', are considerably more numerous. The relative lack of studies that address the experience of the 'left behind' is noteworthy, particularly because studying the 'left behind' can give important insights into the lives of migrants as well (Mazzucato 2011).

Starting in the 2000s, the literature on transnational families brought the 'left behind' into scholarly view. Transnational families are those in which one or more members of a family live in another country or region for extended periods of time. When members migrate, they remain connected to their home communities and family members and engage in family practices and maintain relationships despite geographical separation (Bryceson and Vuorela 2002; Glick Schiller et al. 1992). This was a break from most literature in family studies which focused on families living together or separated through divorce, crisis, or death (Mazzucato and Schans 2011; Suarez-Orozco et al. 2002). Despite the emphasis of transnational family studies on the importance of considering the whole family, even those who are separated by great distances, most of the early work still focused on the migrants in these families and how they coped with the separation. Since the 2010s, however, this literature has started to focus on the effects of migration on the 'left behind'. This chapter will provide an overview of this recent literature.

The term 'left behind' is quite broad. Most studies focus on nuclear family members, but others include extended family and friends, while others even go as far as to include the communities migrants leave behind (Nguyen et al. 2006). The term 'left behind' is also ambiguous because it has a negative condition: that of abandonment or neglect and implicitly depicts the 'left behind' as passive victims who are forced to stay in the country of origin and do not have any say (Archambault 2010; Nguyen et al. 2006). As we will see in this chapter, this is far from true. Therefore, increasingly, researchers are moving away from the term and use, for example, 'stayers', to refer to the 'left behind'. We will use the term stayers but when the literature itself uses the term 'left behind' we employ it in our review yet denote it in quotation marks to remind the reader that this is a term with implicit meanings with which we do not necessarily agree.

This review focuses on the two groups that are most often considered in the literature: children and elderly parents. Although spouses and partners are also an important group of stayers, we do not discuss them here as they are discussed in Chapter 9 on gender and migration. When discussing each group, we review both qualitative anthropological and sociological in-depth studies focusing on a small number of cases, as well as quantitative sociological, demographic, and psychological literature based on large samples. We structure the review around the main topic that these studies investigate: the effect on stayers' well-being, broadly defined and including mental and physical health, education, social behaviour, household labour, and economic security, and look into important mediating and explanatory factors.

Children

Several million children are estimated to stay at origin while one or both of their parents migrate overseas. Although exact numbers are unknown, estimates illustrate the extent of this phenomenon for some developing countries. It has been estimated that up to 1 million Sri Lankan children have a migrant mother abroad (Save the Children 2006); 9 million Filipino minors (27 per cent of all Filipino children) have at least one parent working abroad (Kakammpi in Parreñas 2005); and 21 per cent of Dominican children and one in six children under 18 in El Salvador, Mexico, Puerto Rico, and Nicaragua live apart from a migrant parent (Dewaard et al. 2018). This has not gone unnoticed by NGOs and governments who are afraid that parent–child separation can lead to adverse outcomes for children, especially if they are separated from their mothers. Moreover, next to transnational family scholars, family sociologists and child psychologists have shown increasing concern and have investigated the well-being of these children. Most studies refer to children as being under the age of 18.

Most studies find that parental migration has negative impacts on children's overall well-being. Several anthropological studies found that transnational parent–child separation can lead to conflict and resentment (Coe 2008; Dreby 2007; Schmalzbauer 2004), depressive symptoms, loneliness, and feelings of abandonment (Dreby 2010; Levitt 2001; Parreñas 2005; Pribilsky 2001), and behavioural problems (Moran-Taylor 2008; Schmalzbauer 2004; Smith

2006), which can also affect the migrant parents' well-being. For example, an anthropological study on Mexican children reports that some felt abandoned and developed strategies to 'punish' their parents for leaving them behind such as refusing to speak to them on the phone or refusing to accept their parent's parental authority (Dreby 2007). Furthermore, some studies indicated that educational aspirations and performance of stayer children could also be affected (Dreby 2010; Moran-Taylor 2008).

More recently, child psychology and family sociology studies have looked into the effects of parental migration on children's well-being using survey data. Generally, these quantitative studies have corroborated the findings in the qualitative literature that separation can affect the child negatively. They find that parental migration can affect children's emotional health (Jordan and Graham 2012; Mazzucato et al. 2015; Wen and Lin 2012), physical health, and health behaviour (Salah 2008; Wen and Lin 2012), and social behaviour (Fan et al. 2010). Likewise, parental migration can affect school behaviour, educational outcomes, and aspirations negatively (Battistella and Conaco 1998; Mckenzie and Rapoport 2007; Robles and Oropesa 2011; Wen and Lin 2012). However, conversely through remittances children can be sent to better schools which can lead to the better educational performance of these children (Kandel and Kao 2001; Lu 2012).

Although much of the literature concludes that the overall well-being of 'left behind' children might be negatively affected by parental migration, some studies find no effect or even a positive effect of migration on children's emotional well-being (Asis 2006; Cebotari et al. 2017; Wen and Lin 2012), physical health and nutrition (Asis 2006; Carling and Tønnessen 2013; Cebotari et al. 2017), and education (Antman 2012; Cebotari and Mazzucato 2016; Kandel and Kao 2001). More importantly, recent literature points to the importance of specific characteristics of the transnational child-raising arrangement and points to factors that mediate this relation and/or explain it. As such these studies nuance the findings of the poor well-being of stayer children and show the importance of taking micro- and meso-level characteristics into account. In general, three conditions are found to be of importance: 1) communication; 2) the environment; and 3) the structure of the transnational child-raising arrangement.

First, communication between parent and child is very important for the well-being of both (Dreby 2010; Madianou and Miller 2011; Parreñas 2005; Zentgraf and Chinchilla 2012), as irregular or little contact can be seen by the child as disinterest or abandonment (Suarez-Orozco et al. 2002; Zentgraf and Chinchilla 2012). And, as remittances are 'the currency of contact across borders' (Dreby and Adkins 2010, 680), not being able to send these because of low socio-economic well-being or undocumented status can affect relationships between migrant parents, caregivers, and children (Dreby 2006; Haagsman 2015; Pribilsky 2004), and hence affect the well-being of the 'left behind' child.

Second, the physical and social environment in which the child grows up plays a major role. Quantitative studies find that socio-economic status, care arrangements, child's psychological traits, parent's and caregiver's education, and teacher involvement are important mediators in the relation between child well-being and parental migration (Fan et al. 2010; Wen and Lin 2012). Potential negative effects on children's well-being can be exacerbated when children are left in inadequate care, get little parental guidance, and have gained more responsibilities in the household because of the absence of one or both parents (Vanore 2015).

Last, but not least, how the transnational child-raising arrangement is set up is of great significance: who takes care of the child and who has migrated? Although results are not conclusive (Graham and Jordan 2011; He et al. 2012; Mazzucato et al. 2015; Vanore et al.

2015), most of these studies concur that children are worse off when mothers migrate (Dreby 2010; Gao et al. 2010; Jia and Tian 2010; Liu et al. 2009; Parreñas 2005; Wen and Lin 2012). Different reasons are given. Some authors argue that it is because of the special bond children have with their mothers (Parreñas 2008) and/or because of gender norms in place that create different expectations from mothers and fathers. While fathers are expected to provide mostly financial care, mothers are expected to provide emotional care, which is more difficult to provide across borders (Dreby 2006, 2007; Hondagneu-Sotelo and Avila 1997; Parreñas 2005). Therefore, children can feel more abandoned when their mothers migrate. Others argue that these differences arise because mother-away and father-away families are differently structured and face different structural constraints making migrant mothers more vulnerable (Caarls et al. 2018; Hondagneu-Sotelo and Avila 1997; Parreñas 2001). For instance, Mazzucato et al. (2015) found that migrant mothers, possibly through their structural constraints, 'leave' their children in less stable care arrangements than migrant fathers, which leads to the next important factor in the transnational child-raising arrangement: the caregiver of the child.

Caregivers are essential in helping children cope with the separation and alleviating emotional hardships and are important mediators in the relation between migrant parent and child (Hoang and Yeoh 2012; Schmalzbauer 2008; Suarez-Orozco et al. 2002), making the relationship between migrant parent and caregiver essential. If the relationship between caregiver and parent is strained because they are divorced or separated this harmfully affects the migrant parent–child relationship (Dreby 2006; Haagsman and Mazzucato 2014; Nobles 2011). Additionally, the specific characteristics of the caregiver are also important for the well-being of the child, such as the caregiver's mental health (Jordan and Graham 2012), human capital (Fan et al. 2010; Vanore et al. 2015), gender, and position in the family. For example, children might reproach their parents if they perceive the care provided as bad (Poeze and Mazzucato 2013), which can happen especially if the caregiver is not one of the parents. Moreover, children in the care of their grandparents do less well than children whose caregiver is one of the parents (Jia and Tian 2010) Although uncommon, non-relatives can be caregivers (Dankyi 2015), although Fan et al. (2010) find that children in such care are more prone to emotional and behavioural problems.

Elderly

Migration can also affect elderly stayers. This is an important category as the elderly compose a vulnerable group in the Global South, of which a relatively large share is living in poverty. Emigration can lead to more elderly persons living alone (Du et al. 2004; Kanaiaupuni 2000), challenging the traditional role of the family in elderly care (Guo et al. 2009). As with children, ageing parents often need care which requires physical presence and close geographic proximity (King and Vullnetari 2006). Indeed, it has even been found that care of elderly or sick parents is often a reason for return migration (King et al. 1983). And, as with children, good relationships, and caregiving practices can be established across borders. Despite not living geographically close, migrant children are often actively involved in the caring process and often try to provide for their elderly parents through regular visits, remittances, gifts, and calls to their parents and their caretakers (Baldock 2000; Zechner 2008; Zimmer and Knodel 2013).

Adult children who migrate overseas or to urban areas often provide an important source of income for elderly parents (Guo et al. 2009; Knodel et al. 2010; Knodel and Saengtienchai 2007). Most studies find that the economic well-being of the elderly substantially increases with migration (Du et al. 2004; Guo et al. 2009; Knodel and Saengtienchai 2007), although in exceptional cases, such as in rural Albania, it was found to lead to more economic insecurity (King and Vullnetari 2006). Yet, migrant children have difficulties providing other support that the elderly may need such as food, help with household chores, and assistance in the businesses of their elderly parents (Du et al. 2004; Knodel et al. 2010). Moreover, daily care for the elderly, especially if they are ill or disabled, requires regular physical presence which migrants cannot provide. Therefore, the elderly who are in need of physical care can be especially vulnerable when their children migrate (Guo et al. 2009).

Mental and physical health effects can also arise. Various studies have found that the stay-behind elderly experience a greater risk of psychosocial and emotional distress, loneliness, and depression (Adhikari et al. 2011; De Soto et al. 2002; King and Vullnetari 2006). In addition, the physical health of the stay-behind elderly can also be affected. Antman (2010) found that in Mexico, elderly persons who had a child abroad were more likely to suffer from a heart attack or stroke. Through the migration of their children, elderly people lose their social support, as migrant children cannot assist their elderly parents directly in times of crisis, such as illness or moments of weak mental health. Studies report even worse effects for elderly in rural areas where the remote and often rough location makes them already more prone to isolation and out-migration is often high (King et al. 2003; King and Vullnetari 2006). However, again results are inconclusive with some studies finding no effects or even positive effects on health (Adhikari et al. 2011; Guo et al. 2009; Kuhn et al. 2011). For example, Abas et al. (2009) found no relation between children's out-migration and levels of depression amongst elderly parents in rural Thailand. Even more so, when taking parental characteristics, social support, health, and wealth into account, the elderly with migrant children were less often depressed than their counterparts who had non-migrant children.

On the other hand, while migrant children cannot provide direct care, it does not mean they are not involved in their parent's health care. The elderly with migrant children can make better use of health services (Adhikari et al. 2011) because their migrant children may have better access to information, set up specific savings schemes that allow parents to receive financing for their health needs and can send remittances when parents are in need of treatment (Knodel et al. 2010; Mazzucato 2008). Moreover, if elderly parents are really ill, migrant children often decide to visit and provide the care they need or return if their situation allows it (King et al. 1983; Knodel et al. 2010). Again, communication is key to the well-being of stayer parents. But how often and how long children call is also dependent on the economic and legal status of the migrant child and, if children cannot visit, they sometimes ask other migrants to visit and bring remittances and gifts (King and Vullnetari 2006).

While remittances can improve elderly people's material and emotional well-being (Guo et al. 2009; Silverstein et al. 2006), they are also an unstable source of income. King and Vullnetari (2006) found that remittances tend to slow down, first, when migrant children have their own children and, second, the longer migrant children are away. Mazzucato (2008) found that elderly people in Ghana actively seek to care for their migrant children's children, as a way to gain access to material care, such as household chores, and to ensure a steady flow of remittances, knowing that their adult child will be more likely to send remittances for their own child.

How care for elderly parents is organised depends on how far the migrant is located from the elderly parent, the resources, such as remittances and housing, the migrant has available for caregiving, cultural filial norms, and resulting feelings of obligation, and the (care) provisions of the origin country (Baldassar 2007; Zechner 2008). In addition, the well-being of parents also depends on whether, besides the migrant child, they have other non-migrant children who can provide daily care, which is often the case (Knodel et al. 2010).

The elderly are not only care receivers, they can also be essential care providers in the post-migration household, which can increase their workload (Gassmann et al. 2013). For example, they can be asked to take care of property or administrative issues while their migrant child is away (Mazzucato 2008). Moreover, elderly are sometimes asked by their migrant children to take care of their grandchildren while they are abroad. This could be for a short period until the migrant is settled and reunifies with his/her child abroad, but this could also be for an extended period of time. Chang et al. (2011) found that elderly people in Chinese migrant households dedicated significantly more time to domestic work and subsistence labour than elderly people in non-migrant households. For some of the elderly, the childcare burden is difficult to manage because of limited resources, their old age, their worries over the child's well-being, and their heightened responsibility, which can lead to decreased well-being (Dankyi et al. 2017; Salah 2008; Yarris 2014).

Conclusion

This chapter has shown that migration impacts people in origin countries in ways other than the economic even if the latter has been the main focus of studies on the impact of migration on origin countries. Yet family members who remain in the country of origin can be impacted in various other domains that relate to their general well-being, including health, psychological well-being, education, aspirations, social behaviour, and household labour. The various studies reviewed here, showed that the effect of migration on overall well-being is not clear cut. As gender and family norms are different across the world and conditions of migration vary, so do the effects of migration on stayers. Therefore, it is indispensable to take contextual factors into account in the study of stayers. This includes norms, structural factors such as the socio-economic status of the family and who migrates.

Moreover, although cross-country analyses have been scarce, they have shown that the macro-level, too, is of importance for the well-being of stayers. For example, the few cross-country comparisons that exist find that the destination country of migrants matters for the well-being of stayers (Graham et al. 2015; Mazzucato et al. 2015). Migration policies in countries of destination are important because transnational separations can be the result of strict policies that make it difficult for families to reunify. This in turn affects the well-being of both migrants and stayers (Coe 2014; Dreby 2010; King and Vullnetari 2006). Other kinds of policies matter as well, such as those affecting which sectors of the economy migrants can work in and whether they are able to gain stable employment (Dito et al. 2017). Finally, the conditions at home also matter, such as whether a country is recovering from civil strife (Mazzucato et al. 2015).

Importantly, this chapter has shown that migration does not necessarily impact stayers negatively, and at times can even have positive effects. Some NGOs, policymakers, and academics, stress negative effects. Yet while negative effects exist, they do not depict the full story and only portraying the negative side can stigmatise stayers and migrants. It is important for research to further investigate the circumstances under which migration leads to negative consequences for stayers. It is through answering this question that research can guide policymakers to address the well-being of stayers.

References

Abas, M. A., Punpuing, S., Jirapramukpitak, T., Guest, P., Tangchonlatip, K., Leese, M., and Prince, M. (2009) "Rural–urban migration and depression in ageing family members left behind", *British Journal of Psychiatry*, *195*, 54–60.

Adhikari, R., Jampaklay, A., and Chamratrithirong, A. (2011) "Impact of children's migration on health and health care-seeking behavior of elderly left behind", *BMC Public Health*, *11*, 143.

Antman, F. M. (2010) "Adult child migration and the health of elderly parents left behind in Mexico", *The American Economic Review*, *100*, 205–208.

Antman, F. M. (2012) "Gender, educational attainment, and the impact of parental migration on children left behind", *Journal of Population Economics*, *25*, 1187–1214.

Archambault, C. S. (2010) "Women left behind? Migration, spousal separation, and the autonomy of rural women in Ugweno, Tanzania", *Signs*, *35*, 919–942.

Asis, M. M. B. (2006) "Living with migration", *Asian Population Studies*, *2*, 45–67.

Baldassar, L. (2007) "Transnational families and aged care: The mobility of care and the migrancy of ageing", *Journal of Ethnic and Migration Studies*, *33*, 275–297.

Baldock, C. (2000) "Migrants and their parents: Caregiving from a distance", *Journal of Family Issues*, *21*, 205–224.

Battistella, G. and Conaco, M. C. G. (1998) "The impact of labour migration on the children left behind: A study of elementary school children in the Philippines", *Sojourn: Journal of Social Issues in Southeast Asia*, *13*, 220–241.

Bryceson, D. and Vuorela, U. (2002) *The transnational family*, New European frontiers and global networks, Berg, Oxford & New York.

Caarls, K., Haagsman, K., Kraus, E. K., and Mazzucato, V. (2018) "African transnational families: Cross-country and gendered comparisons", *Population, Space and Place*, *24*, e2162.

Carling, J. and Tønnessen, M. (2013) "Fathers' whereabouts and children's welfare in Malawi", *Development Southern Africa*, *30*, 724–742.

Cebotari, V. and Mazzucato, V. (2016) "Educational performance of children of migrant parents in Ghana, Nigeria and Angola", *Journal of Ethnic and Migration Studies*, *42*, 834–856.

Cebotari, V., Mazzucato, V., and Siegel, M. (2017) "Child development and migrant transnationalism: The health of children who stay behind in Ghana and Nigeria", *The Journal of Development Studies*, *53*, 444–459.

Chang, H., Dong, X.-Y., and Macphail, F. (2011) "Labor migration and time use patterns of the left-behind children and elderly in rural China", *World Development*, *39*, 2199–2210.

Coe, C. (2008) "The structuring of feeling in Ghanaian transnational families", *City & Society*, *20*, 222–250.

Coe, C. (2014) *The scattered family: Parenting, African migrants, and global inequality*, University of Chicago Press, Chicago, IL.

Dankyi, E. (2015) *Transnational Child Raising Arrangements: An Ethnographic study of Transnational Caregivers in Ghana*, PhD dissertation, University of Ghana.

Dankyi, E., Mazzucato, V., and Manuh, T. (2017) "Reciprocity in global social protection: Providing care for migrants' children", *Oxford Development Studies*, *45*, 80–95.

De Soto, H., Gordon, P., Gedeshi, I., and Sinoimeri, Z. (2002) Poverty in Albania. A qualitative assesment. *World Bank Technical Paper 520*, World Bank, Washington, DC.

Dewaard, J., Nobles, J., and Donato, K. M. (2018) "Migration and parental absence: A comparative assessment of transnational families in Latin America", *Population, Space and Place*, *24*, e2166.

Dito, B., Mazzucato, V., and Schans, D. (2017) "The effects of transnational parenting on the subjective health and well-being of Ghanaian migrants in The Netherlands", *Population, Space and Place*, *23*, e2006.

Dreby, J. (2006) "Honor and virtue - Mexican parenting in the transnational context", *Gender & Society*, *20*, 32–59.

Dreby, J. (2007) "Children and power in Mexican transnational families", *Journal of Marriage and Family*, *69*, 1050–1064.

Dreby, J. (2010) *Divided by borders. Mexican migrants and their children*, University of California Press, Berkeley, CA.

Dreby, J. and Adkins, T. (2010) "Inequalities in transnational families", *Sociology Compass*, *4*, 673–689.

Du, P., Ding, Z., Li, Q., and Gui, J. (2004) "The impact of out labor migration on the elderly stayers in rural areas", *Population Research*, *28*, 44–52.

Epstein, A. L. (1992) *Scenes from African urban life: Collected copperbelt papers*, Edinburgh University Press, Edinburgh.

Fan, F., Su, L., Gill, M. K., and Birmaher, B. (2010) "Emotional and behavioral problems of Chinese left-behind children: A preliminary study", *Social Psychiatry & Psychiatric Epidemiology*, *45*, 655–664.

Gao, Y., Li, L. P., Kim, J. H., Congdon, N., Lau, J., and Griffiths, S. (2010) "The impact of parental migration on health status and health behaviours among left behind adolescent school children in China", *BMC Public Health*, *10*, 56.

Gassmann, F., Siegel, M., Vanore, M., and Waidler, J. (2013) The impact of migration on children left behind in Moldova. *UNU-MERIT Working Papers*, Maastricht.

Glick Schiller, N., Basch, L., and Blanc-Szanton, C. (1992) "Transnationalism – A new analytic framework for understanding migration", *Annals of the New York Academy of Sciences*, *645*, 1–24.

Graham, E. and Jordan, L. P. (2011) "Migrant parents and the psychological well-being of left-behind children in Southeast Asia", *Journal of Marriage and Family*, *73*, 763–787.

Graham, E., Jordan, L. P., and Yeoh, B. S. A. (2015) "Parental migration and the mental health of those who stay behind to care for children in South-East Asia", *Social Science & Medicine*, *132*, 225–235.

Guo, M., Aranda, M. P., and Silverstein, M. (2009) "The impact of out-migration on the inter-generational support and psychological wellbeing of older adults in rural China", *Ageing & Society*, *29*, 1085–1104.

Haagsman, K. (2015) *Parenting across Borders: Effects of Transnational Parenting on the Lives of Angolan and Nigerian Migrant Parents in the Netherlands*. PhD dissertation, Maastricht University, Maastricht.

Haagsman, K. and Mazzucato, V. (2014) "The quality of parent–child relationships in transnational families: Angolan and Nigerian migrant parents in The Netherlands", *Journal of Ethnic and Migration Studies*, *40*, 1677–1696.

He, B., Fan, J., Liu, N., Li, H., Wang, Y., Williams, J., and Wong, K. (2012) "Depression risk of 'left-behind children' in rural China", *Psychiatry Research*, *200*, 306–312.

Hoang, L. A. and Yeoh, B. S. A. (2012) "Sustaining families across transnational spaces: Vietnamese migrant parents and their left-behind children", *Asian Studies Review*, *36*, 307–325.

Hondagneu-Sotelo, P. and Avila, E. (1997) "'I'm here, but I'm there': The meanings of Latina transnational motherhood", *Gender & Society*, *11*, 548–571.

Jia, Z. and Tian, W. (2010) "Loneliness of left-behind children: A cross-sectional survey in a sample of rural China", *Child: Care, Health and Development*, *36*, 812–817.

Jordan, L. P. and Graham, E. (2012) "Resilience and well-being among children of migrant parents in South-East Asia", *Child Development*, *83*, 1672–1688.

Kanaiaupuni, S. M. (2000) *Leaving parents behind: Migration and elderly living arrangements in Mexico*, Center for Demography and Ecology, University of Wisconsin, Madison, WI.

Kandel, W. and Kao, G. (2001) "The impact of temporary labor migration on Mexican children's educational aspirations and performance", *International Migration Review*, *35*, 1205–1231.

King, R., Mai, N., and Dalipaj, M. (2003) *Exploding the migration myths: Analysis and recommendations for the European Union, the UK and Albania*, The Fabian Society and Oxfam, London.

King, R., Strachan, A., and Mortimer, J. (1983). Return migration: A review of the literature. *Discussion Papers in Geography 19*, Oxford Polytechnic, Oxford.

King, R. and Vullnetari, J. (2006) "Orphan pensioners and migrating grandparents: The impact of mass migration on older people in rural Albania", *Ageing & Society*, 26(5), 783–816.

Knodel, J., Kespichayawattana, J., Saengtienchai, C., and Wiwatwanich, S. (2010) "How left behind are rural parents of migrant children? Evidence from Thailand", *Ageing & Society*, *30*, 811–841.

Knodel, J. and Saengtienchai, C. (2007) "Rural parents with urban children: Social and economic implications of migration for the rural elderly in Thailand", *Population, Space and Place*, *13*, 193–210.

Kuhn, R., Everett, B., and Silvey, R. (2011) "The effects of children's migration on elderly kin's health: A counterfactual approach", *Demography*, *48*, 183–209.

Levitt, P. (2001) *The transnational villagers*, University of California Press, Berkeley, CA.

Liu, Z., Li, X., and Ge, X. (2009) "Left too early: The effects of age at separation from parents on Chinese rural children's symptoms of anxiety and depression", *American Journal of Public Health*, *99*, 2049–2054.

Lu, Y. (2012) "Education of children left behind in rural China", *Journal of Marriage and Family*, *74*, 328–341.

Madianou, M. and Miller, D. (2011) "Mobile phone parenting: Reconfiguring relationships between Filipina migrant mothers and their left-behind children", *New Media & Society*, *13*, 457–470.

Mayer, P. (1962) "Migrancy and the study of Africans in Towns1", *American Anthropologist*, *64*, 576–592.

Mazzucato, V. (2008) "Transnational reciprocity: Ghanaian migrants and the care of their parents back home", In E. Alber, S. V. D. Geest, W. Geissler, and S. Whyte, eds, *Generations in Africa: Connections and conflicts*, LIT Verlag, Münster, 91–109.

Mazzucato, V. (2011) "Reverse remittances in the migration–development nexus: Two-way flows between Ghana and the Netherlands", *Population, Space and Place*, *17*, 454–468.

Mazzucato, V. (2015) "Transnational families and the well-being of children and caregivers who stay in origin countries", *Social Science & Medicine*, *132*, 208–214.

Mazzucato, V., Cebotari, V., Veale, A., White, A., Grassi, M., and Vivet, J. (2015) "International parental migration and the psychological well-being of children in Ghana, Nigeria, and Angola", *Social Science & Medicine*, *132*, 215–224.

Mazzucato, V. and Schans, D. (2011) "Transnational families and the well-being of children: Conceptual and methodological challenges", *Journal of Marriage and Family*, *73*, 704–712.

Mckenzie, D. and Rapoport, H. (2007) "Migration and education inequality in rural Mexico", *Integration and Trade Journal*, *24*, 135–158.

Moran-Taylor, M. J. (2008) "When mothers and fathers migrate North: Caretakers, children, and child rearing in Guatemala", *Latin American Perspectives*, *35*, 79–95.

Nguyen, L., Yeoh, B. S. A., and Toyota, M. (2006) "Migration and the well-being of the left behind in Asia", *Asian Population Studies*, *2*, 37–44.

Nobles, J. (2011) "Parenting from abroad: Migration, nonresident father involvement, and children's education in Mexico", *Journal of Marriage and Family*, *73*, 729–746.

Parreñas, R. S. (2001) *Servants of globalization and domestic work*, Stanford University Press, Stanford, CA.

Parreñas, R. S. (2005) "Long distance intimacy: Class, gender and intergenerational relations between mothers and children in Filipino transnational families", *Global Networks-a Journal of Transnational Affairs*, *5*, 317–336.

Parreñas, R. S. (2008) "Transnational fathering: Gendered conflicts, distant disciplining and emotional gaps", *Journal of Ethnic and Migration Studies*, *34*, 1057–1072.

Poeze, M. and Mazzucato, V. (2013) "African transnational families: Child fostering of Ghanaian youths when mothers and fathers migrate to the global North", In L. Baldassar, and L. Merla, eds, *Transnational families, migration and kin-work: From care chains to care circulation*, Routledge Transnationalism Series, New York, 149–169.

Pribilsky, J. (2001) "Nervios and 'modern childhood': Migration and shifting contexts of child life in the Ecuadorian Andes", *Childhood*, *8*, 251–273.

Pribilsky, J. (2004) "'Aprendemos a convivir': Conjugal relations, co-parenting, and family life among Ecuadorian transnational migrants in New York City and the Ecuadorian Andes", *Global Networks-a Journal of Transnational Affairs*, *4*, 313–334.

Robles, V. F. and Oropesa, R. S. (2011) "International migration and the education of children: Evidence from Lima, Peru", *Population Research and Policy Review*, *30*, 591–618.

Salah, M. A. (2008) *The impacts of migration on children in Moldova*, UNICEF, New York.

Save the Children (2006) *Left behind, left out. The impact on children and families of mothers migrating for work abroad*, Save the Children in Sri Lanka, Colombo.

Schapera, I. (1947) *Migrant labour and tribal life: A study of conditions in the Bechuanaland protectorate*, Oxford University Press, London.

Schmalzbauer, L. (2004) "Searching for wages and mothering from Afar: The case of Honduran transnational families", *Journal of Marriage and Family*, *66*, 1317–1331.

Schmalzbauer, L. (2008) "Family divided: The class formation of Honduran transnational families", *Global Networks*, *8*, 329–346.

Silverstein, M., Cong, Z., and Li, S. (2006) "Intergenerational transfers and living arrangements of older people in rural China: Consequences for psychological well-being", *The Journals of Gerontology: Series B*, *61*, S256–S266.

Smith, R. C. (2006) *Mexican New York: Transnational lives of new immigrants*, University of California Press, Berkeley, CA.

Suarez-Orozco, C., Todorova, I. L. G., and Louie, J. (2002) "Making up for lost time: The experience of separation and reunification among immigrant families", *Family Process*, *41*, 625–643.

Toyota, M., Yeoh, B. S. A., and Nguyen, L. (2007) "Bringing the 'left behind' back into view in Asia: A framework for understanding the 'migration–left behind nexus'", *Population, Space and Place*, *13*, 157–161.

Undesa (2017) *International migration report 2017*, UNDESA (United Nations Department of Economic and Social Affairs), New York.

Vanore, M. (2015) *Family-Member Migration and the Psychosocial Health Outcomes of Children in Moldova and Georgia*. PhD dissertation, Maastricht University, Maastricht.

Vanore, M., Mazzucato, V., and Siegel, M. (2015) "Left behind' but not left alone: Parental migration and the psychosocial health of children in Moldova", *Social Science & Medicine*, *132*, 252–260.

Wen, M. and Lin, D. (2012) "Child development in rural China: Children left behind by their migrant parents and children of nonmigrant families", *Child Development*, 83, 120–136.

Yarris, K. E. (2014) "Pensando mucho" ("thinking too much"): Embodied distress among grandmothers in Nicaraguan transnational families", *Culture, Medicine, and Psychiatry*, *38*, 473–498.

Zechner, M. (2008) "Care of older persons in transnational settings", *Journal of Aging Studies*, *22*, 32–44.

Zentgraf, K. M. and Chinchilla, N. S. (2012) "Transnational family separation: A framework for analysis", *Journal of Ethnic and Migration Studies*, *38*, 345–366.

Zimmer, Z. and Knodel, J. (2013) "Older-age parents in rural Cambodia and migration of adult children", *Asian Population Studies*, *9*, 156–174.

17

FAMILIES AND MIGRATION IN THE TWENTY-FIRST CENTURY

Mahala Miller, Nicholas Bascuñan-Wiley, and Erika Busse-Cárdenas

Introduction

How does migration shape family practices? In turn, how do family practices influence migration experiences? At this particular historical moment, analysing the role of family in migration is of great importance. Over the past decades, cyber technology has created the potential for heightened transnational engagement. Additionally, many receiving nation-states have increasingly emphasised security and nativism, visible in growing anti-immigrant sentiment and conservative legislative policy reform (Abdi 2015; Terrio 2015).

Concurrently, advances in the social sciences have provided for greater consideration of the complexities of family life, through the inclusion of men in discussions of gender relations and an emphasis on the importance of children as autonomous actors. Scholarly work has also shown how sexuality and citizenship status shape both families and the migration experience (Acosta 2013; Adamson et al. 2011; Carrillo 2017; Dreby 2007; Hoang and Yeoh 2011; Montes 2013).

Thus, at present, an amalgamation of forces has increased the possibility of studying family interaction across borders. This includes greater hostility and vulnerability for migrants in many host societies, which has potentially limited return migration and increased the focus on migration experiences, as well as a scholarly consideration of new actors. Despite these developments, the migration and development literature demonstrates an ongoing reluctance to fully address the noneconomic causes and effects of migration. The nature of the current climate for migrant families, as well as a long-standing silence in the migration and development literature on the role of family, calls for attention to scholarly work that centralises family practices within migration. In this review, we draw on diverse research on gender, intergenerational relations, immigration law and policy, race, and sexuality, to show the significance of family in the migration literature and, in consequence, development scholarship. In doing so, we focus primarily, but not exclusively, on migration to the United States.

This chapter emphasises family practice as the social activities and routines that individuals engage in to create and define their families, rather than strict family structure (Morgan 1996). This perspective allows us to view a wide variety of personal relationships through the lens of family and emphasises the emotional and practical work individuals engage in to support the family commitments that are important to them (Spencer and Pahl 2006). Although this theoretical position considers a diversity of family forms, we acknowledge the significance of ideological definitions of the family, embedded in state policy, which shape both the social recognition and legal status of individuals and families (Menjívar et al. 2016). Furthermore, defining family as a set of dynamic practices rather than a discrete structure provides for a nuanced understanding of the ways in which gender, race, class, and sexuality influence individual and family abilities to pursue and fulfil their commitments (Crow 2002; Jamieson 1999; Menjívar et al. 2016; Smart and Neale 1999). Finally, focusing on family practices suggests two focuses of analysis: both the subject, in their understandings and enactment of their familial roles, and the functioning of family relationships and networks (Parreñas 2001).

We focus specifically on the past two decades of literature on family and migration. In doing so, we aim to examine advancements in the field that have occurred since two important developments in the 1990s. The first was the feminist critique of the consequences of migration for women, following growth in female-led migration (Hondagneu-Sotelo 1994; Parreñas 2001). The second was the rise of the transnationalist perspective that challenged assimilation as an end-goal, in response to increases in migration from resource-poor countries to resource-rich countries in accordance with globalisation (Portes et al. 1999). Drawing on the literature across a range of disciplines, this review focuses on the nexus between migration and family in the context of development. First, we provide an overview of the theoretical intersection between the literature on family and on migration and consider how incorporation of family scholarship could address some of the central concerns and limitations of development scholarship. Then, we demonstrate how advancements in the literature have demonstrated both the challenges and possibilities of migration for maintaining and creating family practices. We pay particular attention to how inequalities such as gender, position in the life course, and race and citizenship status, shape migrants' abilities to fulfil their family obligations and seek familial support.

Development, migration, and family

Defining the family and situating it within contemporary social, economic, and political contexts has been a long-standing theoretical and empirical goal. Early sociological and anthropological thinking on families emphasised the biological basis of family ties with a focus on the imperative to produce and raise children, viewing monogamy as evolving naturally to accomplish these needs (Chambers 2012). Of course, this perspective ignores the significance of polygamous relationships, both historically and contemporarily, which is particularly influential for migrant families whose movement can place them spontaneously into conflict with receiving nations' marital norms and laws (Abdi 2015; Charsley and Liversage 2013).

Later scholars emphasised the influence of social and economic changes on family structure, suggesting that the nuclear family developed functionally to meet the needs of society in response to industrialisation (Goode 1963; Parsons 1956). Beginning in the 1970s, theorists focused their attention on how social change brought on family instability, giving rise to the 'individualisation' thesis which suggests that modernity's increased emphasis on individual agency and autonomy has shifted traditional and patriarchal structures, towards constructs such as democratised 'pure relationships' between kin or 'post-familial' families of elective affinity (Burgess 1973; Giddens 1992). However, some scholars have criticised the individualisation thesis for not adequately capturing the diversity of families' lived experiences and over-emphasising individual agency without a nuanced consideration of the influence of systems of oppression, such as race, class, and gender, on families (Meadow and Stacey 2006; Williams 2008).

Within a rapidly developing technological, political, and social environment, the dynamics of global migration and human movement are constantly changing. Thus, it is essential to consider the ways and directions that families today move within a context of global capitalism and globalisation (Sheller 2014). Immigrant families face both new pressures, legislative changes to immigration policy that determine the legality and norms surrounding family, and the long-standing need to seek and maintain employment in order to provide material resources for themselves and other family members (Menjívar et al. 2016). Migration is often the result of family decisions, and families that migrate together must navigate through both local networks and global systems. Much of the existing canonical migration theory has excluded these analyses of family, focusing instead on individual interpretations of why people move, how they choose a destination, and their process of incorporating into a new society. Yet, some new approaches have started to incorporate family as both a motivation for migration, as well as a unit of analysis. As a next step, migration theories must centralise the importance of both emotional and economic familial obligations and support for migrants. The burden and benefit of family endure despite physical separation, challenging normative ideals of the nuclear family.

Many theorists have tried to interpret the motivations, methods, and implications of migration in sending and receiving nations. Early theories focused heavily on the movement of the individual, such as functionalist and historical-structural theories that speculated about which actors and what motivations were relevant in the inception and process of international movement (Castles 2003; Massey et al. 1999). While functionalists argued that individuals are autonomous and are pushed and pulled from their origin by a variety of social forces (Passaris 1989), historical-structuralists conceptualised migration as a result of a larger capitalist system that subjects individuals to social pressures leading to increased social stratification (Cohen 1987; Sassen 1990).

Both functionalists and historical-structural theories emphasised the role that society plays in the lives of migrants, but ignored the agency of individuals, families, and communities to determine the path of their own migration. Other migration theories did include these groups in their analyses, but failed to incorporate the nuances of race, gender, and sexuality that are essential to immigrant family dynamics. Household approaches, for example, focus on the cooperative connections between family members and how they share risk, diversify income sources, and draw on social resources in times of need (Massey et al. 1993). Similarly, migration network theory examines the connections and relationships present in the migratory process by highlighting social ties and social capital (Massey et al. 1993). In these two approaches, the family is central to the migratory process as a source of the social capital, economic resources, and knowledge necessary for successful migration. Yet, these theories lack the contributions that recent transnational and feminist scholars have raised about intra-household inequalities, sexuality, and citizenship, and racial and citizenship-based hierarchies.

More recent approaches to family migration have incorporated analyses of power to show the multiplicity of family structure. MacDonald and MacDonald (1964) set the stage for family migration studies with their discussion of 'chain migration' which posits that opportunities to migrate stem primarily from 'social relationships with previous migrants' (1964, 82). Scholarship that followed took this theory as a base and built in a number of directions. For instance, transnational and diaspora theories centred membership in international diasporic communities and transnational families as a hub for cultural and economic relations, thereby complicating both approaches to migration and definitions of family (Parreñas 2001, 2005). These more recent works shift scholarly understanding of migration through their focus on the connections between individuals, communities, and families. In this way, diasporic and transnational literature understands both migration decisions, and migrant's agency, as influenced by familial obligations and support.

The development literature, in contrast to migration and family social science scholarship, is motivated by a self-conscious mandate to better individual living conditions. From this perspective, the development literature focuses on migration's power to create remittances as a socioeconomic mobilising resource (Delgado-Wise 2014). In this sense, development scholarship understands migration as a temporary phenomenon that will end as living standards improve and the poor are led out of poverty, in part through remittances (Bastia 2013).

Additionally, much of the development literature has focused on economic migration from the global south to the global north (see de Haas 2005). The development literature fails to reflect the effect of migration on the lived experiences of families as a result of this narrow focus on the individual economic effects of migration and a single flow of movement. New scholarship regarding migration and family practices addresses these limitations while considering some of the central concerns of development scholarship, including the flow of remittances between host and receiving nations and family members.

In the context of ongoing migration, focusing on the family provides the opportunity to understand the consequences of migration for daily life (Chamberlain and Leydesdorff 2004). Expanding analysis from the stories of individuals to include the perspectives of families illuminates the social implications of movement and mobility. Focusing on family practices in migration demonstrates an understanding of family as both a set of obligations and demands, and a resource of support and care. With this perspective, this chapter centres the intersection of family and migration studies to demonstrate how family intimately interacts with the process of migration, both challenging and empowering migrants as they encounter structural constraints. At this historical moment, considering the connections between migration, development, and family scholarship is of particular importance as advances in communication technology and the growing threat of anti-immigrant and nativist attitudes, as well as conservative migration policy reform, have increased the salience of familial responsibilities for the lives and well-being of migrants (Abdi 2015; Baldassar 2007; Peng and Wong 2013; Terrio 2015).

Family and migration: two decades of research

Centralising the family as a unit of analysis, and considering the reality of transnational families divided by geographical distance, allows for attention to be paid to the noneconomic effects of migration on individuals, such as the impact on their emotional lives and relationships (Mai and King 2009; Mazzucato and Schans 2011). Family, in the context of a family practices approach, is particularly useful in this sense because of its duality. Family both places individual responsibilities and duties on migrants, in their enactment of familial roles, and can provide care and support to migrants through relationships and networks (Parreñas 2001). The geographical proximity of migrants to their family, the complex identities of migrants, and the context of sending and receiving communities, shapes both the familial expectations of migrants and their ability to perform care. In turn, state-level policy and community-level ideologies interact closely with the emotional power of the family as a socially-constructed ideal reflective of the collective identities of nations and communities. New scholarship has focused on the emotional, interpersonal, and economic difficulties associated with maintaining family relationships and forms in migration and demonstrates the potential for migration to enable the creation of new family forms. An emphasis on the influence of inequalities in identity and legal context on the abilities of migrants to seek or maintain familial support and care undergirds the consideration of this chapter to both the difficulties and possibilities of migration for family practices.

Over the past 20 years, transnational families have become an increasingly important consideration for many migration scholars (Castles et al. 2013; Dreby 2010; Massey et al. 1999). Transnational family life provides the potential for social mobility for all members and stands in opposition to family reunification as an end-goal, reflecting an understanding of living-apart-together as a long-term strategy rather than a temporary phenomenon (Mazzucato and Schans 2011). However, it is also necessary to consider the associations of complex emotional strain on interpersonal relationships within families, particularly when living apart. For instance, a great deal of research on the feminisation of migration has highlighted the requirement for women to express and experience deep suffering when apart from their children, in demonstration of the resilience of the women-as-carer model and in accordance with the significant difficulty of experiencing downward mobility into domestic work (Ho 2006; Hoang 2016; Parreñas 2005).

Complementing this long-standing research trend is new work that demonstrates the emotional costs for men, who have often been left out of the conversation regarding transnational parenting (Mazzucato and Schans 2011). Men must undergo both the complex navigation of masculinity while performing care work locally while mothers live abroad, and experience emotional distance from their children when migrating themselves (Vásquez del Águila 2013; Dreby 2010). Strict expectations for the emotional inexpressiveness of men make these negotiations all the more difficult (Montes 2013). In addition to increased scholarly attention to men, there is greater engagement with children as autonomous actors with individualised experiences. This literature illuminates how children experience a lack of intimacy and affection when parents migrate and use emotional expressiveness to demonstrate the costs of migration to their parents (Dreby 2007; Haagsman et al. 2015). However, the inclusion of men and children as actors engaged in interpersonal and emotional familial relationships also demonstrates that migration and transnational family life provide the potential for relational growth and increased intimacy. The increased engagement of men with emotion, following either their own migration or the migration of a family member, and the leveraging of emotion by children to shape the migration decisions of their parents provide the potential for this increased relational affinity (Dreby 2007; Montes 2013).

Distance strains financial, as well as personal, relationships. Family members use remittances to demonstrate care and connection across distance (Aranda 2003; Dreby 2007). However, remittances and transnational economic exchanges are also a source of interpersonal tension. Migrants and family members use remittance negotiations to communicate ambivalence or commitment to their families (Hoang 2016; Peng and Wong 2013). Additionally, migrants with families in both sending and receiving nations must navigate competing economic needs that translate to both emotional and tangible difficulty in providing family support (Abdi 2015; Espiritu 2009). Often, migrants must navigate conflicting definitions of the family in sending remittances. For instance, remitting first-generation migrants may work to address the expectations of family in the host nation that conflict with the definitions of the family in the receiving nation, embodied in the experiences of any children born or raised in the new context (Espiritu 2009; Singh et al. 2010). In this sense, the quotidian difficulties of managing familial relationships is intimately connected to the broad focus of migration and development literature: the potential for migration to expand community financial resources.

The difficulties associated with navigating the emotional realities of family-at-a-distance emphasise the importance of considering who is able to maintain or access physical proximity to the family. Individuals both migrate with their family to maintain an emotional support system, and make temporary and permanent return trips to their sending communities for the provision of care (Aranda 2003; Gilbertson 2009; Montes 2013). In turn, the legal regimes of receiving nations, and the legal status of migrants, shapes the ability to migrate with or visit their families. Both liberal migration regimes, with an ostensibly open migration policy, provisions of citizenship, and the right to family reunification, and conservative migration regimes, emphasising the ethnic basis of citizenship with limited pathways to citizenship for foreign migrants, make it difficult to establish familial residency (Adamson et al. 2011). However, conservative regimes may allow for greater temporary legal migration that enables intermittent re-connection with families of origin (Choo 2013). Liberal migration regimes, in contrast, provide long-term potential for documented familial migration while paradoxically necessitating extended separation from family in the sending country to establish legal residency (Parreñas 2005). Additionally, in liberal migration regimes, such as the United States, an increased emphasis on security has both narrowed the definition of families for whom family reunification is a legal possibility and increased the real and perceived danger of border crossings and the potential for deportation dividing mixed-status families (Gonzales 2016). This has increased the privilege of mobility, and access to extended family care, for documented individuals and the vulnerability and isolation for those without legal status (Aranda 2003; Gilbertson 2009). Separation from extended care networks is particularly difficult for women, given their ongoing responsibility for child-rearing and familial care work (Baldassar 2007; Deeb-Sossa and Bickham Mendez 2008).

While geographical separation from family of origin can strain the emotional lives of migrants, it can also enable the creation of new family forms and support networks. Geographical separation from family of origin can decrease the demands of migrants to comply with the norms of family creation in their sending countries and networks (Gorman-Murray 2009). Migration often provides the opportunity for transwomen, gay men, and lesbian women to create new relationships in line with their sexual and gender identities and enter into 'chosen families' of friends and lovers (Carrillo 2017; Manalasan 2006; Parreñas 2011; Vásquez del Águila 2013). However, when migration to more permissive societies is not possible, gay and lesbian individuals may migrate internally to create distance from their families of origin while maintaining close connections to this original family unit (Wimark 2016). Furthermore, migration allows for sexual exploration and sexual identity transformation not only for non-heterosexual or transgender migrants but, also, for individuals in heterosexual relationships (Hirsch 2004; Luibhéid 2013). This demonstrates the importance of complicating the scholarship on migrants with children, particularly women, with further attention to the sexual agency of migrants of all genders living within diverse families (Mai and King 2009; Manalasan 2006).

In addition to chosen family networks that support gay, lesbian, and transgender migrants, co-ethnic support networks assist many migrants and their children in navigating host societies (D'Alisera 2009; Schmalzbauer 2009; Yoo and Kim 2014; Zhou 2009). However, new family forms and networks are, in turn, shaped by inequality, in particular, the racial and legal hierarchies of receiving contexts which both stratify migrant positions within support communities and weaken the efficacy of peer networks in the face of racial and political domination (Acosta 2008; Kibria 2009). Additionally, migrant access to co-ethnic networks that allows them to leverage community resources and strengthen the ethnic identity of migrant children, and their ability to engage in return migration in order to bolster children's racial and ethnic identities, is unequally influenced by cultural and social capital (Shah 2007; Zontini 2010). Intimate family and community relationships can allow migrants to create and engage with their racial and ethnic identities, which are often significant following migration in the face of racist social and political contexts in host societies (Foner 2018; Reynolds 2006).

In addition to family, this path towards relational family and community formation clarifies the close connection between the emotional power of the family and the political and social reception of migrants in host communities. In conservative migration regimes where alternative pathways to citizenship are barred, migrant women who marry local men at once create new family units while attaining legal status. The combination of this pragmatic and intimate action draws attention and criticism to migrant wives in manners that deny their agency. Both government and NGO discourse and political actions suggest that these migrant women are either sexually and economically exploited victims in need of state protection from their means of material advancement or shrewd and calculating economic actors, undeserving of the legal and communal benefits of citizenship (Choo 2013; Lan 2003; Parreñas 2001). As this example illustrates, while some communities embrace migrants, in many contexts both national policy and local interaction draw on the emotional and ideological power of the 'ideal' family to sanction the control of migrants' mobility and access to resources. In these instances, both law and policy-in-action require migrants to embody specific family structures and practices (Abdi 2015; Terrio 2015). For instance, the state intervening to provide protection for the children of West Indian migrants in response to the physical disciplining of their parents, thereby delineating the state-sanctioned boundaries between legitimate and illegitimate family relations (Waters and Sykes 2009). As with the difficulties and possibilities of transnational families, the mobilisation of the emotional power of the family to control migrants is closely connected to other systems of oppression and domination including gender, race, and position in the life course.

The scholarly move to embrace transnationalism has been celebratory, viewing the transition in analysis as better able to capture the empowerment and agency of migrants (Baldassar 2007). However, the continued emphasis on economic effects in the migration and development literature has not considered the repercussions of maintaining and establishing community-at-a-distance for people's everyday lives. Engaging with the family as a unit of analysis captures both the emotional difficulties associated with living apart and the possibilities for community and family creation associated with migration (Acosta 2008; Montes 2013; Parreñas 2005, 2001). Moreover, it demonstrates that the emotional and social challenges for families in migration are intimately connected to the flow of money and resources transnationally, reinforcing the notion that one cannot truly understand even the economic effects of migration without considering the social context (Abrego 2009; Carrasco 2010; Peter 2010). This social context demonstrates, in turn, the significance of inequality for migration and underscores the importance of considering individuals' social location and identities (Faist 2016). Doing so requires acknowledging the diverse identities, legal statuses, and compositions that shape migrant family practices.

References

Abdi, C. (2015) *Elusive Jannah: The Somali Diaspora and a Borderless Muslim Identity*, University of Minnesota Press, Minneapolis.

Abrego, L. (2009) "Economic Well-being in Salvadoran Transnational Families: How Gender Affects Remittance Practices," *Journal of Marriage and Family 71*, 4, 1070–1085.

Acosta, K.L. (2008) "Lesbianas in the Borderlands: Shifting Identities and Imagined Communities," *Gender & Society 22*, 5, 639–659.

Acosta, K.L. (2013) *Amigas y Amantes: Sexually Nonconforming Latinas Negotiate Family*, Rutgers University Press, New Brunswick.

Adamson, F., T. Triadafilopoulos, and A. Zolberg (2011) "The Limits of the Liberal State: Migration, Identity and Belonging in Europe," *Journal of Ethnic and Migration Studies 37*, 6, 843–859.

Aranda, E.M. (2003) "Global Care Work and Gendered Constraints: The Case of Puerto Rican Transmigrants," *Gender & Society 17*, 4, 609–626.

Baldassar, L. (2007) "Transnational Families and Aged Care: The Mobility of Care and the Migrancy of Ageing," *Journal of Ethnic and Migration Studies 33*, 2, 275–297.

Bastia, T. (2013) "Migration-Development Nexus," *Geography Compass 7*, 7, 464–477.

Burgess, E. (1973) *On Community, Family and Delinquency: Selected Writings*, University of Chicago Press, Chicago.

Carrasco, L.N. (2010) "Transnational Family Life among Peruvian Migrants in Chile: Multiple Commitments and the Role of Social Remittances," *Journal of Comparative Family Studies 41*, 2, 187–204.

Carrillo, H. (2017) *Pathways of Desire. The Sexual Migration of Mexican Gay Men*, University of Chicago Press, Chicago.

Castles, S. (2003) "Towards a Sociology of Forced Migration and Social Transformation," *Sociology 37*, 1, 13–34.

Castles, S., H. De Haas, and M.J. Miller (2013) *The Age of Migration: International Population Movements in the Modern World*, Palgrave Macmillan, Basingstoke.

Chamberlain, M. and S. Leydesdorff (2004) "Transnational Families: Memories and Narratives," *Global Networks 4*, 3, 227–241.

Chambers, D. (2012) *A Sociology of Family Life: Change and Diversity in Intimate Relations*, Polity Press, Cambridge.

Charsley, K. and A. Liversage (2013) "Transforming Polygamy: Migration, Transnationalism and Multiple Marriages among Muslim Minorities," *Global Networks 13*, 1, 60–78.

Choo, H.Y. (2013) "The Cost of Rights: Migrant Women, Feminist Advocacy, and Gendered Morality in South Korea," *Gender & Society 27*, 4, 445–468.

Cohen, R. (1987) *The New Helots: Migrants in the International Division of Labour*, Gower, Aldershot.

Crow, G. (2002) "Families, Moralities, Rationalities and Social Change," in A. Carling, S. Duncan, and R. Edwards (eds.) *Analysing Families*, Routledge, London, 285–297.

D'Alisera, J. (2009) "Images of a Wounded Homeland: Sierra Leonean Children and the New Heart of Darkness," in N Foner (ed.) *Across Generations: Immigrant Families in America*, New York University Press, New York, 114–134.

de Haas, H. (2005) "International Migration, Remittances and Development: Myths and Facts," *Third World Quarterly 26*, 8, 1269–1284.

Deeb-Sossa, N. and J. Bickham Mendez (2008) "Enforcing Borders in the Nuevo South: Gender and Migration in Williamsburg, Virginia, and the Research Triangle, North Carolina," *Gender & Society 22*, 5, 613–638.

Delgado-Wise, R. (2014) "A Critical Overview of Migration and Development: The Latin American Challenge," *Annual Review of Sociology 40*, 643–663.

Dreby, J. (2007) "Children and Power in Mexican Transnational Families," *Journal of Marriage and Family 69*, 4, 1050–1064.

Dreby, J. (2010) *Divided by Borders: Mexican Migrants and Their Children*, University of California Press, Berkeley.

Espiritu, Y.L. (2009) "Emotions, Sex, and Money: The Lives of Filipino Children of Immigrants," in N. Foner (ed.) *Across Generations: Immigrant Families in America*, New York University Press, New York, 47–71.

Faist, T. (2016) "Cross-Border Migration and Social Inequalities," *Annual Review of Sociology 42*, 1, 323–346.

Foner, N. (2018) "Race in an Era of Mass Migration: Black Migrants in Europe and the United States," *Ethnic and Racial Studies 41*, 6, 1113–1130.

Giddens, A. (1992) *The Transformation of Intimacy: Sexuality, Love and Eroticism in Modern Societies*, Polity Press, Cambridge.

Gilbertson, G. (2009) "Caregiving across Generations: Aging, State Assistance, and Multigenerational Ties among Immigrants from the Dominican Republic," in N. Foner (ed.) *Across Generations: Immigrant Families in America*, New York University Press, New York, 135–159.

Gonzales, R. (2016) *Lives in Limbo: Undocumented and Coming of Age in America*, University of California Press, Oakland.

Goode, W.J. (1963) *World Revolution and Family Patterns*, The Free Press, New York.

Gorman-Murray, A. (2009) "Intimate Mobilities: Emotional Embodiment and Queer Migration," *Social & Cultural Geography 10, 4*, 441–460.

Haagsman, K., V. Mazzucato, and B.B. Dito (2015) "Transnational Families and the Subjective Well-Being of Migrant Parents: Angolan and Nigerian Parents in the Netherlands," *Ethnic and Racial Studies 38, 15*, 652–671.

Hirsch, J. (2004) *A Courtship after Marriage: Sexuality and Love in Mexican Transnational Families*, University of California Press, Berkeley.

Hoang, L. (2016) "Moral Dilemmas of Transnational Migration: Vietnamese Women in Taiwan," *Gender & Society 38, 3*, 404–434.

Ho, C. (2006) "Migration as Feminisation? Chinese Women's Experiences of Work and Family in Australia," *Journal of Ethnic and Migration Studies 32, 3*, 497–514.

Hoang, L.A. and B.S.A. Yeoh (2011) "Breadwinning Wives and 'Left-Behind' Husbands: Men and Masculinities in the Vietnamese Transnational Family," *Gender & Society 25, 6*, 717–739.

Hondagneu-Sotelo, P. (1994) *Gendered Transitions: Mexican Experiences of Immigration*, University of California Press, Berkeley.

Jamieson, L. (1999) "Intimacy Transformed: A Critical Look at the Pure Relationship," *Sociology 33*, 477–494.

Kibria, N. (2009) "Marry into a Good Family: Transnational Reproduction and Intergenerational Relations in Bangladeshi American Families," in N. Foner (ed.) *Across Generations: Immigrant Families in America*, New York University Press, New York, 98–113.

Luibhéid, E. (2013) *Pregnant on Arrival: Making the Illegal Immigrant*, University of Minnesota Press, Minneapolis.

MacDonald, J.S. and L.D. MacDonald (1964) "Chain Migration Ethnic Neighborhood Formation and Social Networks," *The Milbank Memorial Fund Quarterly 42, 1*, 82–97.

Mai, N. and R. King (2009) "Love, Sexuality, and Migration: Mapping the Issue(s)," *Mobilities 4, 3*, 295–307.

Manalasan, M.F. (2006) "Queer Intersections: Sexuality and Gender in Migration Studies," *The International Migration Review 40, 1*, 224–249.

Massey, D.S., J. Arango, G. Hugo, A. Kouaouci, and A. Pellegrino (1999) *Worlds in Motion: Understanding International Migration at the End of the Millennium: Understanding International Migration at the End of the Millennium*, Clarendon Press, Oxford.

Massey, D.S., J. Arango, G. Hugo, A. Kouaouci, A. Pellegrino, and J.E. Taylor (1993) "Theories of International Migration: A Review and Appraisal," *Population and Development Review 19, 3*, 431–466.

Mazzucato, V. and D. Schans (2011) "Transnational Families and the Well-being of Children: Conceptual and Methodological Challenges," *Journal of Marriage and Family 73, 4*, 704–712.

Meadow, T. and J. Stacey (2006) "Families," *Contexts 5, 4*, 55–57.

Menjívar, C., L.J. Abrego, and L. Schmalzbauer (2016) *Immigrant Families*, Polity Press, Cambridge.

Montes, V. (2013) "The Role of Emotions in the Construction of Masculinity: Guatemalan Migrant Men, Transnational Migration, and Family Relations," *Gender & Society 27, 4*, 469–490.

Morgan, D. (1996) *Family Connections: An Introduction to Family Studies*, Polity Press, Cambridge.

Parreñas, R.S. (2001) *Servants of Globalization: Migration and Domestic Work*, Stanford University Press, Stanford.

Parreñas, R.S. (2005) *Children of Global Migration: Transnational Families and Gendered Woes*, Stanford University Press, Stanford.

Parreñas, R.S. (2011) *Illicit Flirtations: Labor, Migration, and Sex Trafficking in Tokyo*, Stanford University Press, Stanford.

Parsons, T. (1956) "The Normal American Family," in B. Adams and T. Weirath (eds.) *Readings on the Sociology of the Family*, Markham, Chicago, 53–66.

Passaris, C. (1989) "Immigration and the Evolution of Economic Theory," *International Migration 27, 4*, 525–542.

Peng, Y. and O.M.H. Wong (2013) "Diversified Transnational Mothering via Telecommunication," *Gender & Society 27, 4*, 491–513.

Peter, K.B. (2010) "Transnational Family Ties, Remittance Motives, and Social Death among Congolese Migrants: A Socio-anthropological Analysis," *Journal of Comparative Family Studies 41, 2*, 225–243.

Portes, A., L.E. Guarnizo, and P. Landolt (1999) "The Study of Transnationalism: Pitfalls and Promise of an Emergent Research Field," *Ethnic and Racial Studies 22*, 2, 217–237.

Reynolds, T. (2006) "Carribean Families: Social Capital and Young People's Diasporic Identities," *Ethnic and Racial Studies 29*, 6, 1087–1103.

Sassen, S. (1990) *The Mobility of Labor and Capital: A Study in International Investment and Labor Flow*, Cambridge University Press, Cambridge.

Schmalzbauer, L. (2009) "Gender on a New Frontier: Mexican Migration in the Rural Mountain West," *Gender & Society 23*, 6, 747–767.

Shah, B. (2007) "Being Young, Female and Loatian: Ethnicity as Social Capital at the Intersection of Gender, Generation, "Race" and Age," *Ethnic and Racial Studies 30*, 1, 28–50.

Sheller, M. (2014) "The New Mobilities Paradigm for a Live Sociology," *Current Sociology 62*, 6, 789–811.

Singh, S., A. Cabraal, and S. Robertson (2010) "Remittances as a Currency of Care: A Focus on 'Twice Migrants' among the Indian Diaspora in Australia," *Journal of Comparative Family Studies 41*, 2, 245–263.

Smart, C. and B. Neale (1999) *Family Fragments?* Polity Press, Cambridge.

Spencer, L. and R. Pahl (2006) *Rethinking Friendship: Hidden Solidarities Today*, Princeton University Press, Princeton.

Terrio, S.J. (2015) *Whose Child Am I?: Unaccompanied, Undocumented Children in U.S. Immigration Custody*, University of California Press, Berkeley.

Vásquez del Águila, E (2013) *Being a Man in a Transnational World: The Masculinity and Sexuality of Migration*, Routledge, Abingdon.

Waters, M.C. and J.E. Sykes (2009) "Spare the Rod, Ruin the Child? First-and Second-Generation West Indian Child-rearing Practices," in N. Foner (ed.) *Across Generations: Immigrant Families in America*, New York University Press, New York, 72–97.

Williams, F. (2008) "What is Fatherhood? Searching for the Reflexive Father," *Sociology 42*, 487–502.

Wimark, T. (2016) "The Impact of Family Ties on the Mobility Decisions of Gay Men and Lesbians," *Geography Compass 23*, 5, 659–676.

Yoo, G.J. and B.W. Kim (2014) *Caring Across Generations: The Linked Lives of Korean American Families*, New York University Press, New York.

Zhou, M. (2009) "Conflict, Coping, and Reconciliation: Intergenerational Relations in Chinese Immigrant Families," in N. Foner (ed.) *Across Generations: Immigrant Families in America*, New York University Press, New York, 21–46.

Zontini, E. (2010) "Enabling and Constraining Aspects of Social Capital in Migrant Families: Ethnicity, Gender, and Generation," *Ethnic and Racial Studies 33*, 5, 816–831.

18

INDEPENDENT CHILD MIGRATION

Mobilities and life course transitions

Dorte Thorsen

Introduction

Children in migration used to be portrayed either as 'children of migrants' or as 'left-behind'. Both depictions tally with an increasingly globalised notion of childhood as a time of dependence, education and play with few responsibilities. However, since the early 2000s, children in the Global South have been recognised as migrants in their own right. This has sparked concern in policy and advocacy circles that children of poor families are pawns in their parents' survival or risk aversion strategies or are victims of parents' obliviousness to the exploitation endured by child migrants (Fitzgibbon 2003; ILO 2001). Children are not seen as having any influence on their whereabouts. This perspective is problematic because children are treated as a homogenous group without acknowledging gender and age differences and without understanding the importance of seeing children's lives in context (Hashim and Thorsen 2011).

The globalised model of childhood as a carefree phase of life 'fails to recognise the actual experiences of millions of people under the age of 18 throughout the world' (Willis 2011, 156). Such experiences include amongst others paid and unpaid work, incorporation into the economic spheres of a household, and ruptures to lifepaths due to unforeseeable contingencies. What work children do and the ways they contribute to the well-being of their families are highly contingent on their age, gender and class (Bourdillon et al. 2010; Whitehead and Hashim 2005). The globalised model also fails to recognise that ideas about parents and parenthood are embedded in cultural and social notions of family and home. It conceptualises parents narrowly as birth parents or as adults legally designated as parents. However, in West Africa, where we will be directing our attention in this chapter, parenthood is a more elastic concept. More people are involved in raising a child and thus contributing to its care, education, and well-being (Alber 2004; Hashim 2005; Thorsen 2007b; Whitehead and Hashim 2005). Children's part in establishing and maintaining affective relationships – or in shunning detrimental ones – is rarely considered, except in a few academic studies as, for example, in Peru (Leinaweaver 2008), Cameroon (Notermans 2008), Indonesia (Schrauwers 1999), and Burkina Faso (Thorsen 2009a).

This chapter focuses on children in the later phase of childhood – also categorised as adolescents or youth – as this is the point in life when the majority of young migrants start their migratory path. Drawing on a corpus of child/youth-centred research, the chapter challenges the vulnerability rhetoric and victimisation of children on the move that often has defined global advocacy and child protection work. My aim is to demonstrate the ways that migration contributes to girls' and boys' life course transitions and eventually leads to social adulthood. A better understanding of how intersecting mobilities shape adolescents' lives should facilitate their incorporation into a broader range of development initiatives, which consider their interests as workers, providers, and, not least, dynamic actors with ideas and goals of their own.

The emergence of independent child migration as 'a problem'

Children's relocation to other households and localities is not a new phenomenon. Citing archival records, Alber (2019) describes the frustration among colonial administrators posted in northern Benin at their difficulty to keep track of the population of both children and adults who relocated frequently and not necessarily to the same location. For children in this region, growing up with members of the extended family was seen to be part of childhood well into the twentieth century. Nonetheless, mobility practices involving children went unnoticed among scholars until the 1970s when anthropologists and demographers began to focus on practices of fosterage (Goody 1982; Isiugo-Abanihe 1985; Jonckers 1997). Hashim and Thorsen (2011, 14–6) note that these early studies were situated within either a structural-functionalist (Anglophone) or a structuralist (Francophone) paradigm to explain children's relocation in terms of kin-based solidarity and the redistribution of resources to increase survival, strengthen social ties, and retain power. In these perspectives, children's relocation was not perceived as particularly troublesome: children were seen as a resource on a par with other resources in a context where, as Whitehead has pointed out (1994), social and material resources interlocked in implicit contracts of entitlements and obligations.

That children's relocation in the Global South came to be seen as 'a problem' is linked with two global policy processes. One was the increasing focus on children's rights in the late 1980s, which resulted in the UN Convention on the Rights of the Child (CRC). In broad brush strokes, the CRC formulated a set of universal rights pertaining to education, health care, and protection from violence, neglect, and exploitation. The CRC also set out the obligation of states to provide these rights, and to ensure children's participation in decision-making in matters concerning themselves. While the CRC and the momentum it gained with NGOs and policymakers has contributed significantly to the emergence of children as a social category in development practice (Boyden 2001, 176), it also contributed to universalising a very specific conceptualisation of childhood. This conceptualisation gives primacy to Western middle-class practices while seeing children who are not in education, who work and/or who live outside the parental home as anomalies in need of protection (Ennew 1995; cf. Ansell 2005, 230; Boyden 1997).

The other policy process that impacted significantly on southern childhoods was the expansion of neoliberal development ideologies through structural adjustment programmes to resolve indebtedness and stagnating economic growth in many southern countries. Cuts in public spending had a direct impact on children as education and health provision declined and became more costly due to increased 'user payment'. Moreover, privatisation of public services combined with mistrust in governments' capacity to ensure the provision of children's rights led to donor money being channelled to NGOs, and often international NGOs, rather than to state institutions (Ansell 2005, 44–50; Katz 2004). These organisations have played a significant role in defining which issues were prioritised.

NGO-led child protection since the late 1990s and early 2000s has focused on tackling what was seen as unequivocal impediments to schooling and child protection: work and relocation to work (Andvig et al. 2001; Bourdillon 2006; Nieuwenhuys 2007). Programmes under the auspice of ILO, UNICEF, bilateral donors, and large NGOs were premised on the perception that many child labour migrants were victims of trafficking and exploitation (Dottridge 2004). It was assumed that children living away from their birth parents were particularly vulnerable to exploitation without considering the age – chronological or social – of the children in question and without considering local notions of childhood. National policy environments were often ambiguous. Despite the fact that the globalisation of the notion of childhood prompted governments in the Global South to adopt legislation to curb child labour and to increase education levels, enforcement was generally low. So, although the ILO Conventions No. 138 concerning the minimum age for admission to employment and No. 182 concerning the worst forms of child labour were written into national legislation, they had limited effect (Abebe and Bessell 2011; ILO 2007b).

Early programmes financed by ILO sought to limit the supply of child workers as part of anti-trafficking initiatives, amongst others, by establishing local vigilance committees mandated to prevent children from being trafficked (Dottridge and Feneyrol 2007; Human Rights Watch 2007; ILO 2007a). In practice, these committees often tried to prevent all young people from travelling, including those above the minimum age of admission to employment and without knowing what work they were going to do and for whom. Importantly, they failed to take into account children's own views on how their lives should unfold. They also ignored the question of life course transitions and social age; that is, the fact that some children shoulder, or take on, full or partial responsibilities associated with adulthood because of their family situation (Hashim and Thorsen 2011). Rural populations did not always welcome anti-trafficking measures, and many of the adolescents who were intercepted and repatriated from cities and neighbouring countries set off again a few days after returning home (Castle and Diarra 2003; Dottridge 2008; Imorou 2008).

The fervent attention to children's work and migration in policy and practitioner circles sparked renewed interest among scholars. In trying to debunk some of the misconceptions surrounding children's work and independent child migration, researchers working with child-centred approaches began to unpick changes in children's mobilities. Despite statistical information on children being scarce (Deleigne and Pilon 2011; Whitehead and Hashim 2005), a few studies used population censuses or comprehensive, longitudinal surveys to map out population movements (Hertrich and Lesclingand 2007; Jacquemin 2012). Highlighting gender differences, Hertrich and Lesclingand (2007, 9–11) showed that in southeastern Mali, rural boys' labour migration rose steadily in the 1940s and 1950s whereas girls' labour migration only picked up in the early 1970s. This difference was closely linked with what work was considered to be gender appropriate: boys migrated primarily to do farm work or herding, whereas girls left to go to urban areas to become domestic workers when a labour market for this type of labour developed.

Broader social and economic transformations in Africa thus affected children and youth. The growth of labour markets, especially in urban areas, and increasing interest in education have resulted in a diversification of children's mobilities since the 1990s. Although the early explanatory model of children's relocation as fosterage based on kin-based solidarity is sometimes replicated in analyses of larger statistical data sets modelling the effects of fostering practices (Akresh 2004; Kielland 2009), qualitative studies emphasise that a more nuanced understanding of kinship relations and gender dynamics is needed (Hashim 2006; Notermans 2008; Thorsen 2009b).

Child migrants' embeddedness in complex family constellations

Migration has been a substantial source of livelihood in much of Africa for several generations, and the migratory systems of West Africa are well documented (Amin 1974; Beauchemin and Bocquier 2004; Cordell et al. 1996). Most families are thus trans-local in that they have members in several locations, whose membership of the family or household might be invoked at different times. The notions of family and household are indisputably fuzzy and often overlapping. Both are used to describe the intimate nucleus of a father, mother, and children; the slightly bigger nucleus of a polygynous father with several wives and their children; larger compounds containing several subunits organised around production or reproduction; the extended family and sometimes even larger groups founded on ethnicity, origin, or religion which are dispersed over shorter or longer distances. It is thus imperative to distinguish between the different levels at which family relations are articulated (Murray 1980, 141), and to be aware that kinship provides a flexible language for forging social ties both inside and across descent groups (O'Laughlin 1995, 71). The specific cultural and social context must be taken into account to understand children's place in these relations.

In West Africa, the economic spheres of women and men are separate. In addition to the household head's productive unit, women and junior members of the household have their individual farming or income-generating activities in which they participate when they are not obliged to work for the household head (Whitehead 1996). Children learn both practical tasks and the structuring of the economic spheres through participating in work and being encouraged to develop their own activities when they reach adolescence (Thorsen 2005). Not just in West Africa but more globally, the work that children and adolescents do depends on gender, age, ethnicity, class, whether they are enrolled in school or not, access to land and local markets, and on socio-cultural notions of age- and gender appropriate work (Abebe 2007; Bonnet et al. 2006; Hashim 2004; Katz 2004; Reynolds 1991; Thorsen 2007a). Adolescents' engagement in independent economic activities contributes to their transition to youth and young adulthood. It is also a driver to migrate, either because they are encouraged to seek more opportunities, are pushed to do so by parents who arrange work or accommodation for them, or they themselves are keen to try out activities in a different location (Thorsen 2014).

The advocacy surrounding anti-trafficking discourses has focused substantially on girls who were trafficked. In contrast, migrant girls who do not fall into the victim category have attracted little interest among development and child rights actors (Temin et al. 2013). The involvement of intermediaries in adolescent boys' labour migration also tends to be overlooked. In fact, academic studies have found little evidence of traffickers who facilitate children's internal or regional labour migration with the intention of exploiting them (Howard 2017). Instead, they have identified different types of intermediaries whose involvement in children's and adolescents' labour migration is explained as transmutations of long-standing practices of fosterage.

In Abidjan, the economic capital and largest city of Côte d'Ivoire, transformations in the placement of rural girls in domestic work has been charted by Jacquemin (2012). In the early 2000s, adolescent girls were not just recruited to work in a relative's household, they were also recruited to be put to work in other households. The arrangements varied in form; at one end of the spectrum they resembled the more traditional articulations of family relations, the employer was framed as an aunt and the remuneration as upkeep and a large gift at the end of the stay-cum-employment. At the other end of the spectrum, the arrangement was more like salaried employment; only the relative would collect the salary to save up on behalf of the adolescent, to send to the rural parents or to keep. Some of these placement practices gave rise to discontent if the remuneration or gift offered at the end of a contract was perceived as substandard. Increasingly, rural parents preferred their direct siblings to facilitate employment for adolescents rather than distant or loosely associated relatives (Jacquemin 2009).

Even though we use the terms 'fosterage' and 'placement' in this chapter, it is important to note that these terms carry the risk of feeding perceptions of adolescent migrants as younger children, victims, and as particularly vulnerable to negative effects of social change. Recent research with Togolese adolescents in Ghana and Côte d'Ivoire reveals that boys and girls often responded to job offers relayed to them or their families in Togo by an intermediary. Alternatively, they came to a well-established intermediary with the prospect of being placed in employment (Howard et al. 2018). The morality surrounding relationships between adolescents, parents, and intermediaries is complicated by the fact that family relations are articulated at different levels. An intermediary can be a relative or a more distant social relation, and – what is often forgotten because it is assumed that fosterage is arranged by adults – the intermediary can be an adult but just as well an adolescent who already has migration experience (Djobokou 2008; Jacquemin 2002; Thorsen 2009a).

Another issue that is important for understanding adolescents' place in complex family constellations is the widespread presence of a dense network of relatives, in which several members may have an affinity with an adolescent due to their social or structural position in the family, due to affective sentiments or just due to ordinary decency. Adolescents are not without agency in making and consolidating kinship relations. Through calling on the support of different relatives when the time is right, they are able to influence their lifepaths, albeit with a range of constraints that may differ across gender, ethnicity, religion, and class (Hashim and Thorsen 2011; Notermans 2008; Thorsen 2016).

Negotiations of relative status and social position

Migration is generally perceived as a rite of passage for both boys and girls in West Africa because they are exposed to different situations and social settings. In local parlance, this is articulated as 'opening one's eyes' (Castle and Diarra 2003). Paid employment is also regarded as a path to upward social mobility because of the skills gained and the ability to cultivate one's appearance, accumulate symbols of wealth, and contribute to the family economy (Abdul-Korah 2007; Thorsen 2010, 2014). But, as intimated above, adolescents do not always succeed in having paid employment when they come to the city. The elastic use of kinship terms to forge social ties by adults and adolescents alike blurs the distinction between unpaid family labour and paid employment. Contractual arrangements are oral and rarely settled in every detail, presenting ample ground for divergence but also highlighting that employment relationships are deeply social.

In Ouagadougou, the capital of Burkina Faso, arrangements of working for an urban relative often created tensions. Adolescent boys who were new to employment expected to work as if they were at home with the freedom to take frequent breaks, whereas urban relatives tried to impart a more structured labour market logic on them. When it came to remuneration, however, adolescents saw themselves as employees and expected a wage. Employers, on the other hand, used kinship logics of implicitly framing the wage as a gift that was offered at the end of the stay, or as deferring the remuneration to help teach adolescents to save up. Regardless of their intentions, this practice afforded employers-cum-relatives immediate control over the young migrant's means and opened the possibility of withdrawing or reducing the premeditated remuneration (Thorsen 2009b).

Not all adolescents accepted being framed as a junior family member if that required them to do unpaid work. Some left quickly to find other employment to avoid being exploited by relatives or to seek greater autonomy in the city (Thorsen 2009b). Adolescents were negotiating their status as workers and with that their ability to generate an income. But they were also negotiating their social position as migrants by gradually asserting their know-how of how to navigate the urban setting. Their ability to create space for acting upon their choices hinged on the constitution of the labour market. In Ouagadougou, they could find lowly paid work in food stalls and small restaurants, as itinerant traders and casual labourers by going from door to door, or they could provide services such as shoe-shining, transporting goods, act as parking guards, and so on, In Abidjan, Burkinabè migrants did not have the same possibilities. Newcomers were inhibited by lacking language skills in French or Jola but, more importantly, the informal labour market was characterised by distrust. They were required to have someone to vouch for them to get a job.

Rural Ivorian girls also changed job frequently according to Jacquemin's (2012) study; sometimes because relatives competed over their labour and sometimes because they were able to assert their dissatisfaction with an employer to the relative who had mediated the work. Here age and gender appropriate behaviour plays a role. Girls and young boys were under much more surveillance by their relatives because they were perceived to be in need of protection, whereas adolescent boys were left to fend for themselves as part of learning to cope with problems. Adolescent girls gradually won more opportunity to shape their lifepath, as they learned the full range of domestic tasks and therefore commanded jobs with more responsibility and higher salaries. Skilfully, these girls with little opportunity to speak up against their senior relatives, used the trans-local household to seek support from those parents who had authority and were likely to back their wishes of asserting their social maturity by taking salaried employment on their own account (Thorsen and Jacquemin 2015).

Adolescents are not given much space to navigate their own path but nevertheless seek to negotiate their social position through proving to others that they have the resilience of youth to endure hardship and the capacity to earn an income, or through resisting being treated like children. To do so, they draw on the common discourses about youth and migrants in their communities. These categories are not set in stone; for example, the qualities ascribed to the category of youth depends on whether the youth is female or male. Moreover, the delineation of social categories is not singular but hinges on divergent interpretations both of what it takes to be a youth and of an individual's performance (Durham 2000). Adolescents' social positioning changes in the course of their migratory path, as they gradually add new elements to their interpretation and embodiment of what it takes to be a youth in that social context (Thorsen 2006, 2014).

Conclusion: transitions and transformations in independent child migration

The study of independent child migration has seen a number of transitions and transformations since the mid-2000s when the research field emerged in response to anti-trafficking advocacy and development interventions concerning child protection. Using a child-centred approach to explore the motivations and experiences of migrants who had set off on migration before the age of 18, a number of qualitative studies in the Global South demonstrated that some anti-trafficking measures inadvertently reduced the opportunities for children of poor families and made their pathways more precarious (Whitehead and Hashim 2005).

This chapter exposes some of the misconceptions that underpin the term 'independent child migration'. First, the vast majority of adolescents, who migrate on their own accord, are not independent. They move within a dense network of migrants who interfere with their lives in numerous ways, to varying degrees, and for better or for worse. Although migration may bestow them with some autonomy, adolescents are rarely given space to behave in ways that are not condoned by their community. Second, the variety in social positions and identities unsettles age-based categorisation and highlights that the portrayal of these young migrants as children is misleading. This issue is not solved by using the 'adolescent' label, which still homogenises a very diverse group but at least infers that the discussion does not address young children. Finally, adolescents' migration is intertwined with different forms of mobilities. Their assertion of specific identities is a testimony of transitions, informed by imagined futures and possibilities (Whyte 2006), and whether linked with material accumulation *in situ* or continued migration to other destinations, is part of rural children and youth's social becoming (Bastia 2005; Boyden 2013; Buchbinder 2013; Huijsmans 2017; Punch 2015; Thorsen 2013). These reflections have prompted a shift to speak about 'children on the move' among some scholars and international NGOs. However, the concept of 'independent child migrants' and its close ally 'unaccompanied minors' still hold sway over many scholars and practitioners, taking no notice of evidence based on small deeply qualitative studies.

Another important transition in the field of child migration and development is the decline in anti-trafficking rhetoric, especially when the focus is on internal and regional mobilities. In light of ongoing social changes stemming from an increased focus on schooling and other types of education, and the ensuing transformations in the aspirations of adolescents and their parents, there is an urgent need for in-depth studies of how migration, gender, class, and ethnicity intersect with aspirations and with practices surrounding access and completion. It could be argued that the focus on education is firmly grounded in the globalised notion of childhood. However, if going beyond a focus on enrolment and retention rates, an exploration of the choices made in relation to education and the experience of constraints, offers valuable insights into the politics of inequality and the potential for empowerment and social justice.

References

Abdul-Korah, G. B. (2007) "'Where is not home?' Dagaaba migrants in the Brong Ahafo region, 1980 to the present", *African Affairs*, 106, 71–94.

Abebe, T. (2007) "Changing livelihoods, changing childhoods: Patterns of children's work in rural southern Ethiopia", *Children's Geographies*, 5, 77–93.

Abebe, T. and Bessell, S. (2011) "Dominant Discourses, Debates and Silences on Child Labour in Africa and Asia", *Third World Quarterly*, 32, 765–786.

Akresh, R. (2004) "Risk, network quality, and family structure: Child fostering decisions in Burkina Faso", Bureau for Research in Economic Analysis of Development.

Alber, E. (2004) "Grandparents as foster-parents: Transformations in foster relations between grandparents and grandchildren in northern Benin", *Africa*, 74, 28–46.

Alber, E. (2019) "Politics of kinship: Child fostering in Dahomey/Benin", *Cahiers d'Études africaines*, 234, 359–379.

Amin, S. (1974) *Modern migrations in Western Africa*, Oxford University Press, London.

Andvig, J. C., Canagarajah, S. and Kielland, A. (2001) *Issues in child labor in Africa*, The World Bank, Washington, DC.

Ansell, N. (2005) *Children, youth and development*, Routledge, London.

Bastia, T. (2005) "Child trafficking or teenage migration? Bolivian migrants in Argentina", *International Migration*, 43, 58–89.

Beauchemin, C. and Bocquier, P. (2004) "Migration and urbanisation in Francophone West Africa: An overview of the recent empirical evidence", *Urban Studies*, 41, 2245–2272.

Bonnet, M., Hanson, K., Lange, M.-F., Paillet, G., Nieuwenhuys, O. and Schlemmer, B. eds. (2006) *Enfants travailleurs, repenser l'enfance*, Editions Page deux, Paris.

Bourdillon, M., Levinson, D., Myers, W. and White, B. (2010) *Rights and wrongs of children's work*, Rutgers University Press, New Brunswick, New Jersey and London.

Bourdillon, M. C. F. (2006) "Children and work: A review of current literature and debates", *Development and Change*, 37, 1201–1226.

Boyden, J. (1997) "Childhood and the policy makers: A comparative perspective on the globalization of childhood", in James, A. and Prout, A. eds. *Constructing and reconstructing childhood: Contemporary issues in the sociological study of childhood*. Falmer Press, London, 190–229.

Boyden, J. (2001) "Some reflections on scientific conceptualisations of childhood and youth", in Tremayne, S ed. *Managing reproductive life. Cross-cultural themes in sexuality and fertility*. Berghahn Books, New York and Oxford, 175–193.

Boyden, J. (2013) "'We're not going to suffer like this in the mud': Educational aspirations, social mobility and independent child migration among populations living in poverty", *Compare: A Journal of Comparative and International Education*, 43, 580–600.

Buchbinder, L. (2013) "After trafficking: Togolese girls' orientations to life in a West African city", *Cultural Dynamics*, 25, 141–164.

Castle, S. and Diarra, A. (2003) *The international migration of young Malians: Tradition, necessity or rite of passage?* London School of Hygiene and Tropical Medicine, London.

Cordell, D. D., Gregory, J. W. and Piché, V. (1996) *Hoe and wage. A social history of a circular migration system in West Africa*, Westview, Colorado, Boulder.

Deleigne, M.-C. and Pilon, M. (2011) "Migrations dans l'enfance et scolarisation en Afrique subsaharienne: Apports et limites des approches quantitatives", *Journal des africanistes*, 81, 87–117.

Djobokou, K. P. (2008) *Étude sur le flux Akébou – Accra des jeunes filles domestiques*, Terre des Hommes Foundation, Lausanne and Lomé.

Dottridge, M. (2004) Kids as commodities? Child trafficking and what to do about it, Terre des Hommes, Lausanne.

Dottridge, M. (2008) *Kids abroad: Ignore them, abuse them or protect them? Lessons on how to protect children on the move from being exploited*, Terre des Hommes, Laussane.

Dottridge, M. and Feneyrol, O. (2007) *Action to strengthen indigenous child protection mechanisms in West Africa to prevent migrant children from being subjected to abuse*, Terre des Hommes Foundation, Lausanne. https://www.terredeshommes.org/a-handbook-on-planning-projects-to-prevent-child-trafficking/

Durham, D. (2000) "Youth and the social imagination in Africa: Introduction to parts 1 and 2", *Anthropological Quarterly*, 73, 113–120.

Ennew, J. (1995) "Outside childhood: Street children's rights", in Franklin, B. ed. *The handbook of children's rights: Comparative policy and practice*. Routledge, London, 201–215.

Fitzgibbon, K. (2003) "Modern-day slavery? The scope of trafficking in persons in Africa", *African Security Review*, 12, 81–89.

Goody, E. N. (1982) *Parenthood and social reproduction. Fostering and occupational roles in West Africa*, Cambridge University Press, Cambridge.

Hashim, I. M. (2004) "Working with working children: Child labour and the barriers to education in rural Northeastern Ghana", Unpublished DPhil Thesis, University of Sussex.

Hashim, I. M. (2005) "Exploring the linkages between children's independent migration and education: Evidence from Ghana", Development Research Centre on Migration, Globalisation and Poverty, University of Sussex, Brighton.

Hashim, I. M. (2006) "The positives and negatives of children's independent migration: Assessing the evidence and the debates", Development Research Centre on Migration, Globalisation and Poverty, University of Sussex, Brighton.

Hashim, I. M. and Thorsen, D. (2011) *Child migrants in Africa*, Zed Books, London.

Hertrich, V. and Lesclingand, M. (2007) *Transition to adulthood and gender: Changes in rural Mali*, INED, Paris.

Howard, N. (2017) *Child trafficking, youth labour mobility and the politics of protection*, Palgrave Macmillan, London, New York and Shanghai.

Howard, N., Jacquemin, M. and Thorsen, D. (2018) *Baseline research report. Project for the protection of child migrants along the Abidjan-Lagos Corridor*, Terre des Hommes, Cotonou.

Huijsmans, R. (2017) "'Generationing' development: An introduction", in Huijsmans, R ed. *Generationing development. A relational approach to children, youth and development*. Palgrave Macmillan, London, 1–31.

Humanrightswatch. (2007) *Bottom of the ladder. Exploitation and abuse of girl domestic workers in Guinea*, Human Rights Watch, New York.

ILO. (2001) *Combating trafficking in children for labour exploitation in West and Central Africa: Synthesis report*, International Labour Office, Geneva.

ILO. (2007a) *Combating the trafficking of children for labour exploitation in West and Central Africa*, International Programme on the Elimination of Child Labour (IPEC), Geneva.

ILO. (2007b) "Rooting out child labour from cocoa farms. Paper No. 4: Child labour monitoring – A partnership of communities and government", International Programme on the Elimination of Child Labour (IPEC), Geneva.

Imorou, A.-B. (2008) *Le coton et la mobilité: les implications d'une culture de rente sur les trajectoires sociales des jeunes et enfants au Nord-Bénin (Cotton and mobility: implications of cash-cropping on children and youth's social trajectories in northern Benin)*, Plan-Waro/Terre des Hommes/Lasdel-Bénin, Dakar.

Isiugo-Abanihe, U. C. (1985) "Child fosterage in West Africa", *Population and Development Review*, 11, 53–73.

Jacquemin, M. (2012) *'Petites bonnes' d'Abidjan. Sociologie des filles en service domestique*, L'Harmattan, Paris.

Jacquemin, M. Y. (2002) "Travail domestique et travail des enfants, le cas d'Abidjan (Côte d'Ivoire)", *Revue Tiers Monde*, XLIII, 307–326.

Jacquemin, M. Y. (2009) "De jeunes travailleuses migrantes si (in)visibles: les "petites domestiques" d'Afrique de l'Ouest. Perspectives comparatives à partir de l'exemple des fillettes et jeunes filles au travail à Abidjan", Centre d'Etudes africaines, Paris.

Jonckers, D. (1997) "Les enfants confiés", in Pilon, M., Locoh, T., Vignikin, E. and Vimard, P. eds. *Ménages et familles en Afrique. Approches des dynamiques contemporaines*. CEPED, Paris, 193–208.

Katz, C. (2004) *Growing up global: Economic restructuring and children's everyday lives*, University of Minnesota Press, Minneapolis.

Kielland, A. (2009) "Child mobility as household risk management", *Forum for Development Studies*, 36, 257–273.

Leinaweaver, J. B. (2008) *The circulation of children. Kinship, adoption and morality in Andean Peru*, Duke University Press, Durham and London.

Murray, C. (1980) "Migrant labour and changing family structure in the rural periphery of southern Africa", *Journal of Southern African Studies*, 6, 139–156.

Nieuwenhuys, O. (2007) "Embedding the global womb: Global child labour and the new policy agenda", *Children's Geographies*, 5, 149–163.

Notermans, C. (2008) "The emotional world of kinship: Children's experiences of fosterage in East Cameroon", *Childhood*, 15, 355–377.

O'laughlin, B. (1995) "Myth of the African family in the world of development", in Bryceson, D. F. ed. *Women wielding the hoe*. Berg Publishers, Oxford, 63–91.

Punch, S. (2015) "Youth transitions and migration: Negotiated and constrained interdependencies within and across generations", *Journal of Youth Studies*, 18, 266–276.

Reynolds, P. (1991) *Dance civet cat: Child labour in the Zambezi Valley*, Zed Books, London.

Schrauwers, A. (1999) "Negotiating parentage: The political economy of "kinship" in central Sulawesi, Indonesia", *American Ethnologist*, 26, 310–323.

Temin, M., Montgomery, M. R., Engebretsen, S. and Barker, K. M. (2013) "Girls on the move: Adolescent girls & migration in the developing world", A GIRLS COUNT report on adolescent girls Population Council, New York.

Thorsen, D. (2005) "Sons, husbands, mothers and brothers. Finding room for manoeuvre in rural Burkina Faso", Unpublished DPhil Thesis, University of Sussex.

Thorsen, D. (2006) "Child migrants in transit. Strategies to become adult in rural Burkina Faso", in Christiansen, C., Utas, M. and Vigh, H. E. eds. *Navigating youth, generating adulthood: Social becoming in an African context*. Nordic Africa Institute, Uppsala, 88–114.

Thorsen, D. (2007a) "'If only I get enough money for a bicycle!' A study of childhoods, migration and adolescent aspirations against a backdrop of exploitation and trafficking in Burkina Faso", Development Research Centre on Migration, Globalisation & Poverty, University of Sussex, Brighton.

Thorsen, D. (2007b) "Junior-senior linkages. Youngsters' perceptions of migration in rural Burkina Faso", in Hahn, H. P. and Klute, G eds. *Cultures of migration. African perspectives*. Lit Verlag, Berlin, 175–199.

Thorsen, D. (2009a) "From shackles to links in the chain. Theorising adolescent boys' relocation in Burkina Faso", *Forum for Development Studies*, 36, 81–107.

Thorsen, D. (2009b) "L'échec de la famille traditionnelle ou l'étirement des relations familiales? L'exode des jeunes Burkinabé des zones rurales vers Ouagadougou et Abidjan", *Hommes et migrations*, 1279, 66–78.

Thorsen, D. (2010) "The place of migration in girls' imagination", *Journal of Comparative Family Studies*, XXXXI, 256–280.

Thorsen, D. (2013) "Weaving in and out of employment and self-employment: Young rural migrants in the informal economy of Ouagadougou", *International Development Planning Review*, 35, 203–218.

Thorsen, D. (2014) "Jeans, bicycles and mobile phones. Adolescent migrants' material consumption in Burkina Faso", in Veale, A. and Donà, G eds. *Child and youth migration. Mobility-in-migration in an era of globalization*. Palgrave Macmillan, Basingstoke, 67–90.

Thorsen, D. (2016) "La migration des enfants bissa: diversité des comportements, pluralité des représentations", in Zongo, M. and Bredeloup, S. eds. *Repenser les mobilités burkinabé*. L'Harmattan, Paris, 95–120.

Thorsen, D. and Jacquemin, M. (2015) "Temporalités, savoir-faire et modes d'action des enfants travailleurs migrants au sein de la parenté élargie en Afrique de l'Ouest", *Canadian Journal of African Studies/ La Revue canadienne des études africaines*, 49, 285–299.

Whitehead, A. (1994) "Wives and mothers: Female farmers in Africa", in Adepoju, A. and Oppong, C. eds. *Gender, work and population in sub-Saharan Africa*. ILO, London, 35–53.

Whitehead, A. (1996) "Poverty in North East Ghana. A report to ESCOR", Economic and Social Committee on Research, Department for International Development (DfID), London.

Whitehead, A. and Hashim, I. M. (2005) *Children and migration: Background paper for DfID Migration Team*, Department for International Development (DfID), London.

Whyte, M. A. (2006) "Afterword", in Christiansen, C., Utas, M. and Vigh, H. E. eds. *Navigating youth, generating adulthood: Social becoming in an African context*. Nordic Africa Institute, Uppsala, 255–265.

Willis, K. (2011) *Theories and practices of development*, Routledge, London and New York.

19

AGEING, MIGRATION, AND DEVELOPMENT

Russell King and Aija Lulle

Introduction

Wary of further inflating what Carling (2017) has called the 'nexification' of the migration literature, this chapter brings into conversation with each other the established conceptual frame of the 'migration–development nexus' (Faist et al. 2011; Van Hear and Sørensen 2003), and the newly-coined 'ageing–migration nexus' (King et al. 2017; Lulle and King 2016, 5). We therefore construct 'ageing–migration–development' as a triple nexus which examines the various ways that ageing migrants (and non-migrants) interact with the process of 'development' through the medium of migration. The key focus of the chapter, *ageing*, is routinely left out of the general debate on migration and development, which tacitly assumes that migrants, as potential agents of development, either in their home countries or in the places they move to, are young and economically active.[1] Where older people are brought into this debate, they are usually cast in a negative or problematic light – for instance as 'left behind' in shrinking residual populations in peripheral regions, as responsible for the 'crisis' in pensions and healthcare provision affecting ageing societies, or as retirement migrants putting pressure on health services in attractive destination regions (Lucas 2005, 295–6; Skeldon 1997, 87–8). Yet, when introducing older migrants into the migration–development debate, we must be careful not to over-compensate their previous omission by an over-celebratory or exaggeratedly positive role. We pay heed, therefore, to the fragilities and vulnerabilities that they are also prone to.

Defining ageing in the context of migration and development

At the risk of tautology, we define ageing as a biological process of becoming older. More disputable are the age thresholds for becoming an 'older person' or 'senior citizen', with the privileges and penalties that such critical junctures bring – for instance pensions and free healthcare vs old-age discrimination and loss of the right to work. A fundamental point to stress is the variable ways in which 'older-age' is culturally constructed across different societies which are also reflected in different policy stances towards older people, including ageing migrants. Ageing is geographically emplaced (Andrews and Phillips 2005) and the significance of this is enhanced in a context of migration between societies at different levels of development, through for example citizenship empowerment, income returns, rights to work, pensions, and welfare, and the emic perspective of how older migrants 'feel' in different geographical settings (McHugh 2003). A major gap in research concerns lower-income countries where studies on ageing migrants, except as returnees, are seriously lacking.

Different 'models' of ageing also compete for attention, and these orthodoxies, too, can be projected into the context of migration and development. On the one hand, there is the traditional, dominant trope of vulnerability and of the need to somehow cope with old age in migratory contexts: ageing migrants are seen as marginalised and excluded from policy and practices, except as a welfare need (King et al. 2017). This is contrasted with the notion of 'healthy', 'active' ageing (Bytheway 2000) – a celebratory view of independent self-reliance and valorisation of experience which can have positive development impacts, in ways which will be discussed later. Yet this neoliberal, individualistic construction of a 'good' and active older age also has its downside. The danger is that it overlooks the real developmental questions relating to care needs, community engagement, and exclusionary infrastructures and bureaucracies, and the fact that, in many countries, successful ageing is less about individual independence and more about dignity, respect, family support, and physical relaxation (Gardner 2002).

Ageing, then, is not suddenly being an older person at a fixed age threshold (60, 65, etc.). Rather, it is a multi-faceted process of gradually 'becoming': seeing oneself, and being seen by others, as older than before (Worth 2009). We envision ageing as a long-term process which typically starts with a mid-life consciousness of impending older-age. The onset of ageing may thus start in one's 40s and last for another 40 years or more – half the life cycle (Lulle and King 2016, 2–3). The longer-term perspective on ageing enables us to draw a broad contrast between the 'young-old' – still active, independent, and energetic – and the 'old-old' – more dependent, frail, and vulnerable. Whilst recognising this division as heuristically useful, especially in a developmental context, it is not absolute and, pushed too far, reflects age determinism and ignores the variety of individual experience.

After this wide-ranging discussion on the nature of ageing, we look more briefly at definitions of migration, development, and the migration–development nexus. There exists a litany of definitions of migration which are also scoped by other contributions to this Handbook. For our purposes here, migration is a straightforward notion. It is the movement of a person or people from one country or place to another, with the intention of residing there for a significant period of time, such as at least six months or a year (Hammar and Tamas 1997, 16). Development is a much more 'chaotic' concept expressed at multiple scales – global, national, local, and individual. It has been subject to an evolution of meanings, starting with mainly economic variables but progressively encompassing more social, humanitarian, and quality-of-life elements, including choice and control over one's life. Like both ageing and migration, development is a dynamic term that implies change, growth, advancement (Skeldon 1997, 1); 'a comprehensive concept that expresses positive change in society' (Sinatti and Horst 2015, 139). Increasingly, development connotes an egalitarian principle: 'change for the many, not for the few'.[2]

Carling's (2017) recent definition of the migration–development nexus as 'the totality of mechanisms through which migration and development dynamics affect each other' implies that causality goes in both directions and plays out in multiple ways. Likewise, with ageing and migration, there are multiple connections, and they feed through to influence, and are shaped by, development in a variety of interactions which are the main components of the rest of this chapter. Much work lays ahead to understand how these interactions co-produce and build on each other, shaping migration flows, producing development outcomes, and affecting ageing migrants themselves – in their countries/regions of origin, in the countries/ regions where they reside, and in the transnational/translocal spaces which constitute their lifeworlds.

Older people and their varying positionality within structures of uneven development

Both ageing and migration, as well as ageing migrants, are closely linked to the phenomenon of uneven spatial development, at a variety of scales from the local to the global. Forty years ago, Seers (1979) mapped out the pessimistic, neo-Marxist scenario of migration–development inter-dependencies for Europe, and more recently Delgado Wise and Márquez Covarrubias (2011) have re-articulated these ideas in the Mexico–US context. Migration from 'peripheral' countries to the global and regional 'core' economies reflects and perpetuates two-way but asymmetrical relations of dependency. Core economies need cheap and flexible migrant labour to keep costs down, remain competitive, and to do the jobs that native workers shun. Peripheral countries become structurally reliant on core countries as the market for their chief export, labour, thereby creating and reinforcing their own form of dependent development, reliant chiefly on remit-tances. In the past, such labour migrations were governed by specific schemes such as the Mexi-can *bracero* programme or the West German *Gastarbeiter* (guestworker) model of temporary labour recruitment, both with past echoes of slavery and indenture (Cohen 1987; Potts 1990). Nowadays, 'Western' neoliberal ideals of 'free movement' (as in Europe) are tempered by ambiguous policies of migration control designed to appease electorates who have been per-suaded by right-wing (and some left-wing) ideologies that migration is a 'problem' that needs to be 'solved', if necessary by creating a 'fortress' around Europe or by trumpeting the need for a 'great, big beautiful wall' along the US–Mexico border.

Underdevelopment due to historical oppression, wars, colonial and neo-colonial exploitation on the one hand, and to neoliberal policies of individual responsibility, state roll-back, austerity, and structural adjustment on the other, have created migration paths with specific age and gender characteristics. The typical 1960s guestworker was a young man, poor but fit and healthy, ready for work in the factory or construction site; as soon as he became older or sick, the labour rotation system sent him back to his home country.[3] This masculinist model, bril-liantly but one-sidedly analysed in two classic texts of the era (Berger and Mohr 1975; Piore 1979), tended to overlook the fundamental role of women as labour migrants in the early post-war decades of Europe's reconstruction and growth. Women, too, were recruited, as factory workers, cleaners, and health services staff in Britain and the other North-west European econ-omies – as recorded by McDowell (2005, 2013). In more recent decades, as ageing has become a major demographic challenge of Western societies, the need for female migrant workers to plug the care gap, especially for older and frail people, has become an increasingly important component of the global labour market (Hondagneu-Sotelo 2001; Parreñas 2001). In short, migrant women from poor countries, many of whom are ageing themselves, are called upon to look after the elderly of the rich West. Thereby they contribute to the development of the higher-income countries, often to the detriment of their own care duties and preferences back home (Silvey 2009).

In our recent critical review of studies on ageing and migration (King et al. 2017; Lulle and King 2016, 5–9), we have developed a typology which we now extend within a more explicit developmental context. The typology comprises four main scenarios: i) intergenerational care in a context of uneven global development, ii) international retirement migration, iii) ageing eco-nomic migrants, and iv) ageing return migrants. We consider each in turn.

Development, migration and the challenge of intergenerational care

Toyota et al. (2007) have pointed out that the category of older people 'left behind' by their migrating children has itself been largely left behind by the literature on migration and its impacts.[4] Termed by King and Vullnetari (2006) 'orphan pensioners', these semi-abandoned older people have recently become the focus of increased scholarly attention in places as far apart as Albania (King and Vullnetari 2006), Bolivia (Bastia 2009), and China (Congzhi and Jingzhong 2014). The ageing parents of migrants face both material and emotional vulnerability, coping as best they can on meagre pensions (perhaps boosted by remittances from their children) but above all beset by loneliness in a setting where population is declining along with other aspects of the rural economy and social life. These realities of peripheral underdevelopment need policies to foster community building and infrastructure for all older people living in places that are profoundly shaped by the mass outflow of younger people.

However, research is also emerging to show that more active caring and even economic roles of erstwhile 'abandoned' older people are recognised (Bastia 2009; King and Vullnetari 2009). These studies emphasise the care-giving work done by older parents, and especially grandparents (looking after grandchildren so that both parents can migrate for work), as well as the more economic role played by these older non-migrants as the managers and investors of remittances. Managing households, making investments, administering remittances, and supervising formal as well as informal business practices on behalf of children who live and work abroad requires considerable and diverse skills, including knowledge of financial planning, communication technologies, building techniques, and continuing embeddedness in local networks.

Yet, migrants' parents are not always condemned to 'stay put'. Depending on visa regulations, they may engage in 'follow-the-children' migration, either for temporary stays conditioned by visitor or tourist visa time-limits, or longer-term. Such mobilities can have many purposes or functions: to both give and receive family care; to work, perhaps on a casual or part-time basis; and to access a better healthcare system. All these circumstances – both in their positive and negative elements – are exemplified in recent research on the migration experiences of the Albanian 'zero-generation' parents of the first-generation migrants (King et al. 2014). Along similar lines, Tiaynen-Qadir (2016) has studied the phenomenon of 'transnational babushka' – Russian grandmothers and even great-grandmothers who travel to Finland to help with childcare. They also help to educate the younger generations, taking them to private lessons, teaching them Russian and engaging them in Russian diaspora life. For the Russian older women themselves, they are able to enrich their own self-development, pursuing lives that are less constrained by gender and age stereotypes, forming new intimate relationships and developing small business activities, thanks to their mobile positioning across borders.

International retirement migration

International retirement migration (IRM) is one of the most readily recognised intersections between ageing and migration and has been thoroughly studied in recent years, although research gaps remain. The overviews of IRM provided by Casado-Díaz et al. (2004) and King (2012) summarise all but the very latest literature and draw the typical contours of the phenomenon. Less, however, has been written on the developmental and care implications of IRM. IRM evokes an image of wealthy North Europeans who seek a peaceful life and good amenities in a warmer and sunnier climate, where they can also avail themselves of cheaper living costs – housing, heating, food and drink, and health-care services – where their pensions and dividends from investments will stretch further than in their home countries. The portability of pensions is crucial to IRM, and also gives an insight into its spatial distribution. For the British case, data from the Department of Work and Pensions show that two groups of countries stand out as key destinations where the DWP pays pensions: anglophone countries such as Australia, New Zealand, the USA, and Canada, where many retirement migrants have either moved independently or, more likely, followed their already-settled children; and European 'sun-belt' countries where IRM has been most intensively studied (Spain, Italy, Portugal, Cyprus, and Malta). Taking the Spanish case, data from the Office for National Statistics for 2016 reveal that 40 per cent of British citizens resident in Spain are over 65, up from 32 per cent in 2011.[5]

Outside of Europe, IRM is also well-established in North America (from Canada and the northern and central US states to destinations in Florida and California, and latterly also Mexico), and in South-East Asia, notably to Thailand (Gustafson 2001; Truly 2002). As well as the geographical variations in these latitude-spanning retirement migrations, there are different temporal regimes, ranging from permanent, year-round relocation, to seasonal 'snowbirds' escaping the northern winters.

The developmental aspects of IRM are less commonly addressed. Apart from those who deliberately seek an isolated, 'off-grid' environment, retirement migrants are in need of physical infrastructures such as good-quality housing (sometimes restored older properties in rural areas), fast transport links, and decent healthcare services. Along many stretches of the Spanish Mediterranean coast, and in the larger Canary Islands, the scale of IRM (combined with tourism) has shaped the entire character of the built environment, economy and 'culture' of the resorts and their associated *urbanizaciones* – purpose-built estates. Whilst retirement migrants bring many benefits to the local economy, stimulating the demand for housing, goods and services, there are downsides too. These include squeezing local people out of the coastal housing market, environmental pressures, and a kind of neo-colonial reshaping of the 'culture', with many foreign retirees failing to integrate or learn the local language (O'Reilly 2000).

The final set of issues concerns satisfying the health and care needs of this elderly migrant population. Whilst most retirees move when they are 'young-old', inevitably they sooner or later transition to the frailer 'old-old' and generate pressures in multiple dimensions – on themselves in terms of how to cope with failing health and reduced mobility, on local doctors and hospitals, and on their families to arrange transnational care. These transitions, including the final transition to death, need further research, both in terms of care services and from a psycho-social well-being perspective (Hardill et al. 2005; Oliver 2008). The end-game may be a painful return to the country of origin.

Ageing economic migrants

For this category of people within the ageing–migration–development nexus, we consider both those who migrated for economic reasons as young men and women and who subsequently remained in their migration destination through the rest of their working lives and beyond, and those who embarked on the migration trail as mature-age economic migrants, for instance in their 40s, 50s, and 60s.

We call the first subgroup 'ageing-in-place' migrants. They stay abroad as migrant workers for a variety of reasons – economic (there is no future for them back home), family (their children and grandchildren are abroad), socio-cultural (they feel more 'integrated' abroad than they now would in their home countries), and health/welfare (access to better medical facilities, pension payments, and other welfare services). From a development point of view, provided they remain in work, they make a net contribution to the economy of their country of settlement. However, as soon as they reach pensionable age, and if they start to make costly demands on the health service, their net annual fiscal contribution becomes negative.[6] They suffer what Dowd and Bengtson (1978) called the 'double jeopardy' of being both an older person and a migrant, which leads potentially to an interlinked range of vulnerabilities – weak physical and mental health, low income, poor housing, and (self-) exclusion from care and welfare services (Fokkema and Naderi 2013). Some of these problems may be compensated by the strength of family and ethnic-community support mechanisms. Writing respectively on the Cypriot and Bengali migrant communities in London, Cylwik (2002) and Gardner (2002) have demonstrated how a strong ethos of family solidarity inculcated inter-generationally leads to older migrants being cared for as far as possible within the family sphere. For these ageing-in-place migrants, a 'good' old age is not so much about being active, independent and self-reliant, but being surrounded by caring and respectful family members.

For other economic migrants growing older in their destination countries, a relaxed old age is beyond their reach. They may need to continue working in order to keep sending remittances to support their families in the country of origin. Two examples illustrate this economic entrapment. Hunter (2011) has studied the lives of older North African men who continue to live in migrant-worker hostels in France, even beyond retirement age. They remain there in order to maximise their pension rights and avail of better health services, and also because, in some cases, they have been estranged from their families for so long that they fear the challenges of return and reintegration. The second example is of Filipina care-workers in Los Angeles, who need to keep working because they have no pension rights and are responsible both for supporting themselves, and family members in the Philippines. Most are carers for single elderly or frail men and women, who in some cases are actually younger than themselves. The result is that 'the unretirable elderly care for the retired elderly' (Nazareno et al. 2014).

Finally, there are older economic migrants who depart their home country at a mature age. Our own research on Latvian women in the UK is arguably the most detailed study of this genre (Lulle and King 2016). Condemned to the prospect of a poverty-stricken old age in Latvia due to pension and welfare cuts in the neoliberal post-Soviet era, these older women, many of whom are divorced, separated, or widowed, have been coming to Britain since the 1990s, but especially since Latvia's entry to the EU in 2004, in order to find work to support themselves, and their children and grandchildren back home. Most have found employment as agricultural workers, cleaners, nannies, and carers. Given the devaluation of Latvian pensions to a pittance, they become 'target earners' in a dual sense – to build up surplus income to support family members and invest in real estate back home, and to accumulate sufficient years in order to qualify for a more valuable UK pension. However, we found that these women's migratory trajectories did not solely lead to a better economic future; they also achieved enhanced personal and emotional well-being through their experiences of independence, self-development, and more active social and romantic lives.

The developmental potential of ageing return migrants

In his well-known typology of return migration and development, Cerase (1974) posits different stages, based on research on migrants returning from the United States to Southern Italy in the early post-war decades. The 'return of conservatism' occurs when the migrant returns after just a few years: the developmental impact is rather weak because the migrant has not changed much and still thinks and behaves according to the norms and values of the home society, which were still somewhat 'traditional' in Southern Italy at this time. For those who return after a longer period away – typically 10 years or more – there is the potential of the 'return of innovation'. By this time, it is hypothesised that migrants will have internalised new values and behaviours from the host society, regarding for instance business practices, politics, and social principles, and be ready to transfer these innovative stimuli to the home country setting. This developmental potential is rarely realised, at least in Cerase's study, for two main reasons. First, few migrants return at this stage in their migratory careers (typically in their 30s or early 40s) because they see their futures as much brighter, also for their children, in the United States. Second, for those who do return fired with energy and enthusiasm, their ambitions are thwarted by the enduring power of the entrenched local elites and clientelistic social networks. The final element in Cerase's life-stage model of return is the 'return of retirement', which the author assumes to have minimal developmental impact as these older migrants merely wish to live out their final years in a quiet and relaxed manner.

At a distance of more than 40 years, Cerase's model, with its simplistic linear logic, seems dated and ageist. Being a sociological model, it ignores the economic impact of retired migrants who return to their countries of origin. Like the IRM category described earlier, they 'import' their pensions and savings, and make investments in the local economy, as well as generating consumer demand for goods and services. Even as a social model, it is deficient as it overlooks the impact of retirees' accumulated experience and of their own changed attitudes – what Levitt (1998) has proposed as 'social remittances'. Nevertheless, we must be careful not to brush aside the more problematic aspects of the 'return of retirement'. Long-absent migrants tend to hold idealistic images of their homeland, often frozen in the past, and envision it as an idyllic place to which to retire. They fail to appreciate that nothing is static: both the homeland and they themselves have changed, and the return may bring disillusionment. As an example, a study by Barrett and Mosca (2013) of Irish older returnees found that their imaginations of a peaceful life in the Irish countryside were negated by significant readjustment challenges and experiences of social isolation.

Very different from this picture of retired Irish migrants from urban Britain struggling to re-adapt to life in rural Ireland is Sun's research on high-skill older Taiwanese migrants returning to their homeland from the USA. Whilst some return-migrated in order to access affordable, yet good-quality healthcare, which can be prohibitively expensive in the US (Sun 2014), many were motivated by altruistic economics – they wanted to 'give something back' to their motherland. Despite being officially retired from their professional jobs in the US, they in fact do not retire, but start a new later-life career in Taiwan. Working especially in science, technology, and medicine, they take, or are offered, posts in universities, research institutes, hospitals, and private companies. They bring specialist knowledge, social and cultural capital, new ideas, and practices acquired during their professional working lives in the US, and aspire to apply these 'professional remittances' (Sun 2016) to help the development of Taiwan. However, this was not always a smooth process, and Sun's research participants also articulate a narrative of frustration at some of the barriers to their 'modernising' aspirations, which brought out the disjuncture between them as 'Americanised Taiwanese' and their co-ethnics in Taiwan.

Conclusion

In challenging the dominant 'vulnerability trope' associated with ageing migrants, this chapter has explored the connections between ageing migrants and a more positive range of development scenarios, both for the places they migrate from, to, and then return to, and in terms of older migrants' own active agency and self-development. Against the 'double jeopardy' of being both an ageing person and a migrant, we have sought to stress the values of knowledge, experience, respect, and intergenerational solidarity. The fact that migrants are moving towards and beyond the end of a 'normal' working life, does not mean that they cannot be economically active, innovative, and resourceful. The Latvian and Taiwanese cases reviewed above are good illustrations of this important principle (Lulle and King 2016; Sun 2016). At the same time, we should be careful not to righteously impose neoliberal Western models of active, independent ageing on migrants who originate from cultures where 'good' ageing is associated with a different set of values and customs.

We must also be careful to avoid viewing all ageing migrants through a simplistic bifocal lens of origin and destination. Many ageing migrants – ageing-in-place labour migrants, late-life economic migrants, international retirement migrants, returned emigrants, and even non-migrant family members – wish to engage in regular transnational mobility which keeps them in touch with both 'here' and 'there', and perhaps other 'theres' too. The ability to lead a transnationally mobile lifestyle is a privilege not open to all older people: good health, financial resources, and the legal ability to be mobile across borders are some of the conditioning factors. But, where and for as long as it can be sustained, a transnational mode of living in older age, with frequent contact with scattered family members, is often found to be desirable for those embedded in migrant families, and a crucial component of their well-being.

Finally, we return to the issue of care, a central theme in any discussion of older migrants' well-being – not only the ability and right to receive care from the family or from state welfare services, but also the ability to give care to children and grandchildren. Pension rights and their transferability across borders are another element in older migrants' economic, and hence psycho-social well-being, but only for those employed in the formal economy where pension rights are recognised. Above all, we stress that, just as there are many types of migration, and many facets to development, so there are 'many ageings' (King 2016) which take place biologically, socially, culturally, and economically. These multiple diversities within the ageing–migration–development nexus pose ongoing challenges for both scholarly research and policy.

Notes

1 A scanning of the standard texts on migration and development (Castles and Delgado Wise 2008; Faist et al. 2011; Hammar et al. 1997; Lucas 2005; Skeldon 1997; Van Hear and Sørensen 2003) and of the 150 or so articles thus far published in the journal *Migration and Development* fails to uncover any reference to older migrants as positive actors in the development process.
2 Echoing a phrase from the Labour Party manifesto for the UK general election of June 2017, which helped to turn round the Party's fortunes.
3 This was the *Gastarbeiter* theory: in practice it worked out somewhat differently, as many guestworkers stayed and 'aged in place' in Germany and other European labour-recruitment countries (Castles et al. 1984).
4 Indeed, most of the literature on the phenomenon of family members left behind by migration focuses on the young children of the migrants.
5 See ONS (2017) Living abroad: migration between Britain and Spain. Available at: www.ons.gov. uk/peoplepopulationsandcommunity/populationandmigration/internationalmigration/articles/livin gabroad/migrationbetweenbritainandspain#how-many-british-citizens-are-there-in-spain (accessed 30 August 2017).
6 This focus on pensions should be qualified. In lower-income countries, most people, including especially migrants, work in the informal sector and are not covered by pension schemes (see Barrientos 2009).

References

Andrews, G. J. and Phillips, D. eds. (2005) *Ageing and place: Perspectives, policy, practice*. Routledge, London.

Barrett, A. and Mosca, I. (2013) "Social isolation, loneliness and return migration: evidence from older Irish adults", *Journal of Ethnic and Migration Studies* 39(10): 1659–1677.

Barrientos, A. (2009) "Social pensions in low-income countries", in Holzmann, R., Robalino, D. A., and Takayama, N. eds., *Closing the coverage gap: The role of social pensions and other retirement income transfers*. World Bank, Washington, DC, 73–83.

Bastia, T. (2009) "Women's migration and the crisis of care: grandmothers caring for grandchildren in urban Bolivia", *Gender and Development* 17(3): 389–401.

Berger, J. and Mohr, J. (1975) *A seventh man*. Penguin, Harmondsworth.

Bytheway, B. (2000) "Youthfulness and agelessness: a comment", *Ageing and Society* 20(6): 781–789.

Carling, J. (2017) "Thirty-six migration nexuses, and counting" Blog post at https://jorgencarling.org/2017/07/31/thirty-six-migration-nexus-and-counting/

Casado-Díaz, M. A., Kaiser, C., and Warnes, A. M. (2004) "Northern European retired residents in nine Southern European areas: characteristics, motivations and adjustments", *Ageing and Society* 24(3): 353–381.

Castles, S., Booth, H., and Wallace, T. (1984) *Here for good: Western Europe's new ethnic minorities*. Pluto Press, London.

Castles, S. and Delgado Wise, R. eds. (2008) *Migration and development: Perspectives from the South*. International Organization for Migration, Geneva.

Cerase, F. P. (1974) "Migration and social change: expectations and reality. A study of return migration from the United States to Italy", *International Migration Review* 8(2): 245–262.

Cohen, R. (1987) *The new helots: Migrants in the international division of labour*. Avebury, Aldershot.

Congzhi, H. and Jingzhong, Y. (2014) "Lonely sunsets: impacts of rural-urban migration on the left-behind elderly in rural China", *Population, Space and Place* 20(4): 352–369.

Cylwik, H. (2002) "Expectations of inter-generational reciprocity among older Greek Cypriot migrants in London", *Ageing and Society* 22(5): 599–613.

Delgado Wise, R. and Márquez Covarrubias, H. (2011) "The dialectic between development and forced migration: toward a political economy framework", in Faist, T., Fauser, M., and Kivisto, P. eds., *The migration-development nexus: A transnational perspective*. Palgrave Macmillan, Basingstoke, 57–82.

Dowd, J. J. and Bengtson, V. L. (1978) "Aging in minority populations and examination of the double jeopardy hypothesis", *Journal of Gerontology* 33(3): 427–436.

Faist, T., Fauser, M., and Kivisto, P. eds. (2011) *The migration-development nexus: A transnational perspective*. Palgrave Macmillan, Basingstoke.

Fokkema, T. and Naderi, R. (2013) "Differences in late-life loneliness: a comparison between Turkish and native-born older adults in Germany", *European Journal of Ageing* 10(4): 289–300.

Gardner, K. (2002) *Age, narrative and migration: The life-course and life histories of Bengali elders in London*. Berg, Oxford.

Gustafson, P. (2001) "Retirement migration and transnational lifestyles", *Ageing and Society* 21(4): 371–394.

Hammar, T., Brochmann, G., Tamas, K., and Faist, T. eds. (1997) *International migration, immobility and development: Multidisciplinary perspectives*. Berg, Oxford.

Hammar, T. and Tamas, K. (1997) "Why do people go or stay?", in Hammar, T., Brochmann, G., Tamas, K., and Faist, T. eds., *International migration, immobility and development: Multidisciplinary perspectives*. Berg, Oxford, 1–19.

Hardill, I., Spradbery, J., Arnold-Boakes, J., and Marrugat, M. L. (2005) "Severe health and social care issues amongst British migrants who retire to Spain", *Ageing and Society* 25(5): 769–783.

Hondagneu-Sotelo, P. (2001) *Doméstica: Immigrant workers cleaning and caring in the shadow of affluence*. University of California Press, Berkeley.

Hunter, A. (2011) "Theory and practice of return migration at retirement: the case of migrant worker hostel residents in France", *Population, Space and Place* 17(2): 179–192.

King, R. (2012) "Sunset migration", in Martiniello, M. and Rath, J. eds., *An introduction to international migration studies: European perspectives*. Amsterdam University Press, Amsterdam, 281–304.

King, R. (2016) "Many ageings, multiple migrations, and ambiguous homes", in Walsh, K. and Näre, L. eds., *Transnational migration and home in old age*. Routledge, London, 239–252.

King, R., Cela, E., Fokkema, T., and Vullnetari, J. (2014) "The migration and well-being of the zero generation: transgenerational care, grandparenting, and loneliness amongst Albanian older people", *Population, Space and Place* 20(8): 728–738.

King, R., Lulle, A., Sampaio, D., and Vullnetari, J. (2017) "Unpacking the ageing-migration nexus and challenging the vulnerability trope", *Journal of Ethnic and Migration Studies* 43(2): 182–198.

King, R. and Vullnetari, J. (2006) "Orphan pensioners and migrating grandparents: the impact of mass migration on older people in rural Albania", *Ageing and Society* 26(5): 783–816.

King, R. and Vullnetari, J. (2009) "The intersection of gender and generation in Albanian migration, remittances and transnational care", *Geografiska Annaler B* 91(1): 17–38.

Levitt, P. (1998) "Social remittances: migration driven local-level forms of cultural diffusion". *The International Migration Review* 32(4): 926–948.

Lucas, R. E. B. (2005) *International migration and economic development: Lessons from low-income countries.* Edward Elgar, Cheltenham.

Lulle, A. and King, R. (2016) *Ageing, gender, and labour migration.* Palgrave Macmillan, New York.

McDowell, L. (2005) *Hard labour: The forgotten voices of Latvian women 'volunteer' workers.* UCL Press, London.

McDowell, L. (2013) *Working lives: Gender, migration and employment in Britain 1945–2007.* Wiley-Blackwell, London.

McHugh, K. (2003) "The three faces of ageism: society, image and place", *Ageing and Society* 23(2): 165–185.

Nazareno, J. P., Parreñas, R. S., and Yung-Kang, F. (2014) *Can I ever retire? The plight of migrant Filipino caregivers in Los Angeles.* UCLA Institute for Research on Labor and Employment, Los Angeles.

O'Reilly, K. (2000) *The British on the Costa Del Sol.* Routledge, London.

Oliver, C. (2008) *Retirement migration: Paradoxes of ageing.* Routledge, London.

Parreñas, R. S. (2001) *Servants of globalization: Women, migration, and domestic work.* Stanford University Press, Stanford.

Piore, M. J. (1979) *Birds of passage: Migrant labor in industrial societies.* Cambridge University Press, New York.

Potts, L. (1990) *The world labour market: A history of migration.* Zed Books, London.

Seers, D. (1979) "The periphery of Europe", in Seers, D., Schaffer, B., and Kiljunen, M.-L. eds., *Underdeveloped Europe: Studies in core-periphery relations.* Harvester Press, Hassocks, 3–34.

Silvey, R. (2009) "Development and geography: anxious times, anemic geographies, and migration", *Progress in Human Geography* 33(4): 507–515.

Sinatti, G. and Horst, C. (2015) "Migrants as agents of development: diaspora engagement discourse and practice in Europe", *Ethnicities* 15(1): 134–152.

Skeldon, R. (1997) *Migration and development: A global perspective.* Longman, London.

Sun, K. C.-Y. (2014) "Transnational healthcare seeking: how ageing Taiwanese return migrants think about homeland public benefits", *Global Networks* 14(4): 533–550.

Sun, K. C.-Y. (2016) "Professional remittances: how ageing migrants seek to contribute to the homeland", *Journal of Ethnic and Migration Studies* 42(14): 2413–2429.

Tiaynen-Qadir, T. (2016) "Transnational babushka: grandmothering and family making between Russian Karelia and Finland", in Horn, V. and Schweppe, C. eds., *Transnational aging: Current insights and future challenges.* Routledge, New York, 85–105.

Toyota, M., Yeoh, B. S. A., and Nguyen, L. (2007) "Bringing the 'left behind' back into view in Asia: a framework for understanding the 'migration-left behind nexus'", *Population, Space and Place* 13(3): 157–161.

Truly, D. (2002) "International retirement migration and tourism along the Lake Chapala Riviera: developing a matrix of retirement migration behaviour", *Tourism Geographies* 4(3): 261–281.

Van Hear, N. and Sørensen, N. N. eds. (2003) *The migration-development nexus.* International Organization for Migration, Geneva.

Worth, N. (2009) "Understanding youth transition as 'becoming': identity, time and futurity", *Geoforum* 40(6): 1050–1060.

20

MIGRATION AND HEALTH

Melissa Siegel

Introduction

The purpose of this chapter is to familiarise the reader with some of the most common linkages between migration and health. The term 'health' is used to convey not only the health outcomes of the person who migrates or those who stay behind but also access to healthcare. Additionally, food habits and nutrition are also coupled under the concept of health. Migration in this chapter mainly refers to international migration and used to convey the movement of a person from one county to another for the purpose of residence for a period of time. The reason for this migration could be both forced and voluntary and could even be for health reasons such as access to health services or specific types of treatment in a different country.

This chapter covers various linkages between migration and health but mostly focuses on the effects of migration and remittances on health and nutrition and is broken down into: (1) the effects of migration health outcomes and access to healthcare of migrants in the country of destination; (2) the health of those who stay behind in the country of origin; (3) migration and the spread of communicable diseases; and (4) the health of migrants during travel/in transit, which is linked to sections 1 and 3. The impact of the migration of health workers on development is covered in Chapter 12 in this Handbook.

Health of the migrants in the country of destination

The health of immigrants in the country of destination is one of the most studied areas of health and migration and refers to both healthcare access and health outcomes of immigrant populations, which are often compared to native populations. Bollini et al. (2009) reviewed 64 studies on pregnancy outcome and international migration, revealing that immigrant women are at a disadvantage compared to native women in relation to birth weight, preterm delivery, and other key birth variables. Access to healthcare includes three key areas: physical accessibility, financial affordability, and acceptability (Evans, Hsu, and, Boerma 2013). Access to healthcare can play into the health outcomes that we see in different populations and refers to the health that is observed along a range of different indicators such as heart disease, high blood pressure, obesity, the absence or presence of infectious diseases, and so on. This section begins with a discussion of immigrant health outcomes and then moves on to access to healthcare by immigrants.

Health outcomes

When studying the effects of migration on health outcomes in countries of destination, scholars look at both communicable and non-communicable diseases. A communicable disease (CD) is an infectious disease transmissible from person to person by direct contact with an affected individual or the individual's discharges, or by indirect means of a vector such as a mosquito (Babaie et al. 2015). Transmission may occur in a variety of ways, including direct physical contact with an infected person, consuming contaminated foods or beverages, contact with contaminated body fluids, contact with contaminated inanimate objects, airborne (inhalation), or being bitten by an infected insect or tick (Parrish 2010). Examples of communicable diseases are tuberculosis, HIV/AIDS, influenza and Ebola. A non-communicable disease (NCD) is a disease that is not transmissible directly from one person to another. According to the WHO, these diseases are often chronic in nature, tending to be of a long duration and include Parkinson's disease, autoimmune diseases, strokes, most heart diseases, most cancers, diabetes, chronic kidney disease, Alzheimer's disease, and cataracts, among others.

While we do see a higher prevalence of communicable diseases among some immigrant groups, which is discussed more in the section on the transmission of disease) much of the more recent literature has focused on NCDs, particularly in developed country contexts. NDCs have gained in importance given the diet and lifestyle changes that have been observed by many immigrants to Western countries. Changes in dietary patterns in the context of the destination country occur mainly due to the new food environment and socio-economic status, although changes in physical activity level and new work and living environments can also play a role.

Particular health outcomes associated with migration include a higher prevalence of non-communicable diseases triggered by changes in dietary patterns, including obesity, type 2 diabetes, cardiovascular disease, and some types of cancer (Saleh, Amanatidis, and Samman 2002; Kirchengast and Schober 2006). Common changes in dietary patterns usually include the use of foods high in calories, saturated fat, and simple sugars including fast food, processed soda, and to a lesser extent, artificial juices as well as a decrease in dietary fibre, fruits, and vegetables. Studies with Asian populations in Europe and North America find that the main changes in dietary patterns of migrants relate to increased energy and fat intake, a reduction in carbohydrates, and a switch from whole grains to more refined sources of carbohydrates, resulting in a low intake of fibre. Additionally, an increase in the intake of meat and dairy foods and a reduced vegetable intake was found among some groups (Rosenmöller et al. 2011; Holmboe-Ottesen and Wandel 2012).

Negative changes in food habits are not only seen in moves from developing to developed countries but a study conducted with Finnish migrants in Sweden showed that even when migration occurs between highly developed countries, migrants report a change in dietary pattern which is not always beneficial. Migration from Finland to Sweden was associated with differences in the food pattern that reflect population differences in eating habits between the two countries including a reduced consumption of typical Finnish foods like dark bread and berries (Hammar et al. 2009).

Mental health and well-being factors such as stress Delavari et al. (2013) and depression may also impact dietary and lifestyle changes that lead to poorer physical health outcomes.

Immigrants may be more prone to stress and depression because of their legal status, socio-economic situation and separation from loved ones.

Migrants are also seen to be working in jobs that have more health risks, including construction and agriculture. Immigrants may be exposed to dangerous chemicals, risk of accidents, or are more affected by the weather as many jobs are undertaken are outdoors: immigrants are known to be more highly represented in what are called 3D jobs, dirty, dangerous, and demeaning, which does not only affect their physical but also their mental health.

While many studies and policy interventions in destination countries focus on integration as being important for immigrants to be able to live decent lives, in the areas of nutrition and dietary behaviour, it seems that the less integrated or acculturated, the better. Acculturation is the cultural modification of an individual or group usually to the prevailing or dominant culture. In this case, acculturation into the food culture of the Western diet of highly processed foods and low fibre can be harmful to immigrants' health. Migration from low- and middle-income countries to developed countries has been associated with negative changes to dietary patterns, partially explained by acculturation. An increased time of stay in the host country leads to increasing similarities between migrants and natives regarding lifestyle, social norms, health practices, and nutritional practices, and consequently health outcomes (Antecol and Bedard 2006).

The 'Healthy Migrant Effect'

When looking at health outcomes of immigrants in destination countries, a phenomenon referred to as the 'Healthy Migrant Effect' has been observed. According to the Encyclopaedia of Public Health 2008 (Razum 2008, 110):

> The 'Healthy Migrant Effect' describes an empirically observed mortality advantage of migrants from certain countries of origin, relative to the majority population in the host countries, usually in the industrialized world. Occasionally, it relates to a relatively lower morbidity of immigrants as well. The Healthy Migrant Effect also serves as an ad hoc explanation when migrants are found to have a better health status in spite of being socioeconomically disadvantaged

On many measures, first-generation migrants are often healthier than natives in the country of destination, but this effect seems to diminish as migrants increase their duration of stay in the destination country. However, and this advantage is usually not present in the second generation who were born and usually grow up in the country of destination. Migrants who stay in the host country for extended periods of time are subject to several environmental/ socio-economic and behavioural aspects that may impact their health outcomes. Environmental and socio-economics aspects include poverty, housing conditions, and access to care. Behavioural factors include changes to diet and increased use of tobacco, alcohol, and drugs, as well as less physical activity.

The reason we often see that migrants are healthier than natives has to do with several factors, which may be overstated. The first reason is that there is a selection effect of who migrates. First, it is generally the working-age population that migrates, which is also the healthiest group in any population. Additionally, it is generally the most capable people who migrate meaning that is also the healthiest who are able to work. People do not migrate if they have health conditions if they can help it. Immigrants are also often used to more regular physical activity and have jobs that are physically demanding as well as bringing better food habits from their countries of origin.

Mental health

Although most studies centre on the damaging effects that migration can have on mental health, it can also lead to improved mental well-being when in the country of destination. The improvement or deterioration of the mental health situation of a migrant is highly dependent on both the pre- and post-migration contexts, as well as their context in transit. Generally, migrants who find themselves in more vulnerable situations as a refugee or an irregular migrant, for example, post-migration is likely to present poorer mental health outcomes (Weishaar 2008; Ziol-Guest and Kalil 2012). Undocumented women have shown higher rates of unintended pregnancies and delayed prenatal care, less use of preventative measures, and higher exposure to violence during pregnancy (Wolff et al. 2008). A migrant's state of mental health is also associated with the length of stay in a country and their adaptation abilities (Weishaar 2008). Some of the factors that may increase stress include language and cultural barriers, work-related stress, and social stress (Weishaar 2008).

While there is a concern particularly for vulnerable migrant groups with regard to negative mental health outcomes, research also points to neutral or even positive impacts of migration on mental health. For example, Stevens and Vollebergh (2008) in a review of 20 studies published since the 1990s, did not find any increased risk of mental health problems among migrant children. This study also underlined the importance of varied social and cultural values attributed to the informants of children's mental well-being. Using the New Zealand-Tonga migration lottery as a natural experiment, where it's possible to compare successful and unsuccessful applicants, Stillman, McKenzie, and Gibson (2009) found that migration may have had an important positive impact on the overall welfare of individuals, including mental health. These positive mental health changes may have been a consequence of the large income gains experienced by Tongans in New Zealand and were observed particularly among women and by those with prior poor mental health.

Healthcare access

Health outcomes of migrants in the destination country are affected by the migrants' capacity not only to access healthcare, but also to their behaviour in relation to seeking both preventative and curative care. Their access to healthcare depends greatly on the country they have migrated to and the public or private healthcare provisions offered to the migrant populations, as well as their own legal and socio-economic status. Rights and entitlements are of particular concern for healthcare access. These vary greatly around the world and across different segments of the healthcare system with many legal and financial barriers to access (Medecines du Monde 2015). In a study of healthcare access in the European Union, O'Donnell (2018) found that the lack of the right to receive primary and secondary care was a significant barrier for many asylum seekers and refugees and an even greater barrier for undocumented migrants. Barriers for migrants in general included financial and administrative barriers, different health profiles and awareness of chronic disease risk amongst migrants, migrants' awareness of the organisation of health systems, and entitlements in host countries and language and communication (Medecines du Monde 2016; O'Donnell 2018).

In developing countries, physical accessibility is a particularly pressing problem for refugees. A common problem is a lack of capacity or overcrowded and overstretched resources, particularly following an increase in refugee flows. For example, Syrian refugees in Jordan not residing in camps reported facing long waiting times, long distances to clinics, and unavailability of medicines for chronic diseases (Ay, Arcos González, and Castro Delgado 2016; UNHCR 2017). Physical accessibility is often even more of a problem in refugee camps, which are often located in remote areas (Adler et al. 2008).

Some studies found an over-use of emergency rooms and under-utilisation of preventative care among immigrants. This is usually found among populations that have a more difficult time accessing preventative and early care due to lack of entitlements or difficulty understanding and navigating healthcare systems. For instance, a study conducted in Norway with Polish, German, Iraqi, and Somalian immigrants concluded that immigrants used emergency services less than native Norwegians, but large variations among immigrant groups existed. Labour immigrants from Germany and Poland used emergency services considerably less, while asylum seekers from Somalia and Iraq used these services more than native Norwegians (Sandvik, Hunskaar, and, Diaz 2012). Another study in Spain found that while migrants displayed better lifestyle-related parameters, in that they consumed less alcohol and smoked less than the native population, they also had higher percentages of hospitalisation compared with the Spanish population. However, the study concluded that there was no evidence of excessive and inappropriate use of other health care resources (Carrasco-Garrido et al. 2009).

Besides the other barriers already mentioned, discrimination and xenophobic attitudes from health professionals and providers further discourage migrants from use of health services (European Centre for Disease Prevention and Control 2009; HUMA 2011; Médecins du Monde 2012). Differing ideas about how best to respond to health issues across cultures is another barrier to migrants seeking treatment as they sometimes opt-out of formal healthcare and seek informal treatment (Thomas 2013). At the same time, approaches to dealing with diverse populations from different immigrant backgrounds are lacking in many health systems, such as the provision of free or inexpensive language services and community-based cultural support staff, culturally informed care delivery, and culturally tailored health promotion, disease prevention, and treatment (WHO 2010; Suess et al. 2014).

Health of those who stay behind in the country of origin

Migration not only affects the health of those who travel and live in a new place, but it also affects those who stay behind through changes in monetary resources, additional knowledge that is transferred, as well as the absence of a household member. The linkages that are sustained through migrant transnational networks allow migrants and their friends and families in the countries of origin to transfer not only money but also knowledge, norms, and values, which are referred to as social remittances (Levitt 1998; also Chapter 11 in this Handbook). Financial remittances provide those who stay behind with additional purchasing power to enter the formal healthcare system, which is often not available otherwise (Lindstrom and Muñoz-Franco 2006; Valero-Gil 2009; Amuedo-Dorantes and Pozo 2011). The additional resources allow households to buy better food, preventative care, and to have access to health services when health shocks happen. Knowledge transfers increase information and may induce behavioural changes in those who stay behind regarding health, nutrition, and hygiene (Kanaiaupuni and Donato 1999; Beine, Docquier, and Schiff 2013). These effects can be both positive and negative. For instance, while many studies have shown better health outcomes for maternal and child health, another study found that higher community-level migration intensity is associated with the individual risk of being overweight and obese (Riosmena et al. 2012).

Several studies on those who stay behind focus on maternal and child health. Most of the studies on nutrition have focused on how migration and remittances can be beneficial or detrimental to child health and development, using measures such as nutritional status, height for age, and weight for age (Antón 2010). Remittances in particular have been a focus of many of these studies. Frank (2005) and Frank and Hummer (2002) found that remittances and migration may have had positive long-term effects on child health outcomes including infant mortality rates and low birth weight since migrant households have more disposable income to spend on healthcare services and/or health insurance.

Another area that has received considerable attention is around sexual and reproductive health and specifically fertility. Social remittances have been found to have an impact on fertility levels of origin countries because of the transfer of norms from migrants in low fertility destinations to their origin countries as well as knowledge and usage of contraception (Beine, Docquier, and Schiff 2013; Roosen and Siegel 2018).

The elderly who stay behind are increasingly being studied because it is generally the working-age population that migrates, leaving care responsibilities to others, including the elderly, but who are also often dependent on this care for their own well-being. (Adhikari, Jampaklay, and Chamratrithirong 2011; Vanore et al. 2018). More and more studies are also focusing on children who stay behind with or without a parent. While some studies show negative effects on children who stay behind when their parents migrate (Graham and Jordan 2011), others do not (Cebotari, Siegel, and Mazzucato 2018; Gassmann et al. 2018).

The migration of individuals from households can not only have health effects on the household members who stay behind but it can also have effects on other households in the community without migrants. (Kanaiaupuni and Donato 1999). For instance, better access to healthcare among migrant households reduces the emergence and transmission of preventable diseases within the community at large (Lindstrom and Muñoz-Franco 2006). Remittances have been reported to be specifically used to increase health care expenditures, leading to greater access to private clinics and medicine in case of sickness, as well as improved health knowledge which can have spillover effects to the entire community. Additional, Frank and Hummer (2002) emphasise how migration can raise expectations of health services coupled with additional resources with the new demand leading to a supply of better healthcare.

Migration and the spread of communicable diseases

With increased globalisation and mobility, individuals are increasingly connected, which increases the challenges associated with the management and control of public health, particularly regarding infectious diseases (Gushulak and MacPherson 2004). Although much of the literature has focused on HIV/AIDS (Deane, Parkhurst, and Johnston 2010), the spread of other infectious diseases such as hepatitis, tuberculosis, malaria, and dengue has been associated with migration (Rees et al. 2010). Circular migration may present simultaneous risks to both the origin and destination communities.

When addressing malaria risks associated with migration, it is important to take into consideration the specific conditions in which they occur, and socio-economic and environmental factors that increase the risk of migrant populations to malaria (Martens and Hall 2000; Prothero 2001; Jitthai 2013). Also, migrants who return home to visit friends and relatives must make sure they are vaccinated and are aware of other necessary pre-travel health arrangements (LaRocque et al. 2013) Tuberculosis (TB) is a disease of poverty, and is often associated with highly vulnerable migrant groups (Welshman and Bashford 2006) with factors that increase risk including poor housing and overcrowded conditions (Carballo and Nerukar 2001). Migrants can then bring TB back with them on returns to their family in the country of origin and is particularly a concern with seasonal or circular migrants who regularly travel back and forth between their country of origin and the country of destination. A study in Kazakhstan concluded that the high incidence of TB among seasonal Uzbek workers was caused by a series of barriers, including limited access to healthcare, vulnerable and exploitative work conditions, and continued exposure to the disease (Huffman et al. 2012). The seasonal character of this migration led to treatment interruption, which can also lead to drug-resistant forms of TB.

HIV/AIDS is one of the more studied areas of disease transmission through migration. Migrants travelling to their country of origin may be a bridge population for HIV transmission upon return (Kramer et al. 2008). Both male and female migrants may be at risk of contracting HIV and transmitting it to their partners in the country of origin. High risk groups include migrant miners, truck drivers, (trafficked) sex workers, and soldiers. This has to do with the nature of the work and the conditions in which theses migrants live. Studies indicate that migrant female sex workers are generally more at risk of contracting HIV and other sexually transmitted diseases than non-migrant female sex workers, particularly when working conditions are poor and with undocumented legal status (Skeldon 2006; Wong, Yim, and Lynn 2011; Platt et al. 2013). Many countries have taken a hard stance on immigrants with HIV/AIDS. UNDP and other international organisations such as the Human Rights Watch have highlighted the deportation of HIV-positive migrants by host countries (Carballo and Nerukar 2001; Human Rights Watch 2009). Countries in Asia and the Middle East have particularly strict policies in this regard.

Migrants can be more susceptible to spreading infectious diseases in certain contexts because of poor access to information. Excessive recruitment fees and poor wages may lead migrant into debt traps and consequently into sexual exploitation. Abusive and exploitative working conditions lead men and women into cycles of poverty and vulnerability. Although there is a general concern about migration and the transmission of infectious disease, little evidence to support this claim exists. Research suggests that, on average, migrant health problems are similar to those of the general population (The Lancet 2016). According to the WHO (n.d.), no systematic association between migration and infectious disease exists. Infectious disease is much more associated with poverty, than with migration and much of the importation of infectious disease is more associated with tourist movements and specialist groups such as the military.

Health of migrants during travel/in transit

Numerous studies have looked at health hazards in transit. The longer it takes for migrants to move from their origin to their destination country and the more precarious their legal situation, the greater risk of negative health issues they have (Kasl and Berkman 1983). Many of the studies focus on health issues associated with migrant smuggling and migrant trafficking (Gushulak and MacPherson 2000). Long, precarious journeys can have a number of negative effects, both physical and psychological, one of the most obvious of which is the interruption of care because of a lack of available medication and treatment while in transit. Additional factors affecting health include a lack of food, water, shelter and psychological stress, which can lead to the worsening of health conditions during the migratory journey for individuals already affected by NCDs (Scholz 2016) or the contraction of new ailments. These issues are exacerbated in humanitarian emergency settings (Hayman et al. 2015).

Conclusion

The purpose of this chapter has been to give the reader an overview of the migration and health research landscape. In this regard, this chapter has covered key areas in migration and health, namely: the effects of migration in the country of destination; the effect of migration on those who stay behind; the transfer of disease across borders; and the health situation of migrants in transit.

This chapter showed that there are both positive and negative effects of migration and these affects are transmitted through multiple mechanisms including financial remittances, social remittances, the absence of a family member, and selection effects. Factors such as length of stay of the migrant in the destination country, access to healthcare, specific vulnerabilities of migrants, and cultural differences all effect health outcomes. A particular challenge is that most research on health and migration only captures a snapshot in time, which does not allow for the detailed examination of the long-term impacts of various diseases and their drivers on human populations.

References

Adhikari, R., Jampaklay, A. and Chamratrithirong, A. (2011) 'Impact of children's migration on health and health care-seeking behavior of elderly left behind', *BMC Public Health*, 11, p. 143. doi: 10.1186/1471-2458-11-143.

Adler, D. *et al.* (2008) 'Introduction of a portable ultrasound unit into the health services of the Lugufu refugee camp, Kigoma District, Tanzania', *International Journal of Emergency Medicine*, 1(4), pp. 261–266. doi: 10.1007/s12245-008-0074-7.

Amuedo-Dorantes, C. and Pozo, S. (2011) 'New evidence on the role of remittances on healthcare expenditures by Mexican households', *Review of Economics of the Household*, 9(1), pp. 69–98.

Antecol, H. and Bedard, K. (2006) 'Unhealthy assimilation: Why do immigrants converge to American health status levels?', *Demography*, 43(2), pp. 337–360. doi: 10.1353/dem.2006.0011.

Antón, J.-I. (2010) 'The impact of remittances on nutritional status of children in Ecuador1', *International Migration Review*, 44(2), pp. 269–299. doi: 10.1111/j.1747-7379.2010.00806.x.

Ay, M., Arcos González, P. and Castro Delgado, R. (2016) 'The perceived barriers of access to health care among a group of non-camp Syrian refugees in Jordan', *International Journal of Health Services: Planning, Administration, Evaluation*, 46(3), pp. 566–589. doi: 10.1177/0020731416636831.

Babaie, J. *et al.* (2015) 'Performance assessment of communicable disease surveillance in disasters: A systematic review', *PLoS Currents*, 7. doi: 10.1371/currents.dis.c72864d9c7ee99ff8fbe9ea707fe4465.

Beine, M., Docquier, F. and Schiff, M. (2013) 'International migration, transfer of norms and home country fertility: International migration, transfer of norms', *Canadian Journal of Economics/Revue canadienne d'économique*, 46(4), pp. 1406–1430. doi: 10.1111/caje.12062.

Bollini, P. *et al.* (2009) 'Pregnancy outcome of migrant women and integration policy: A systematic review of the international literature', *Social Science & Medicine*, 68(3), pp. 452–461. doi: 10.1016/j.socscimed.2008.10.018.

Carballo, M. and Nerukar, A. (2001) 'Migration, refugees, and health risks', *Emerging Infectious Diseases*, 7(3 Suppl), pp. 556–560.

Carrasco-Garrido, P. *et al.* (2009) 'Patterns of medication use in the immigrant population resident in Spain: Associated factors', *Pharmacoepidemiology and Drug Safety*, 18(8), pp. 743–750. doi: 10.1002/pds.1776.

Cebotari, V., Siegel, M. and Mazzucato, V. (2018) 'Migration and child health in Moldova and Georgia', *Comparative Migration Studies*, 6(1), p. 3. doi: 10.1186/s40878-017-0068-9.

Deane, K. D., Parkhurst, J. O. and Johnston, D. (2010) 'Linking migration, mobility and HIV', *Tropical Medicine & International Health*, 15(12), pp. 1458–1463. doi: 10.1111/j.1365-3156.2010.02647.x.

Delavari, M. *et al.* (2013) 'Experiences of migration and the determinants of obesity among recent Iranian immigrants in Victoria, Australia', *Ethnicity & Health*, 18(1), pp. 66–82. doi: 10.1080/13557858.2012.698255.

European Centre for Disease Prevention and Control (2009) *Migrant health series: Access to HIV prevention, treatment and care for migrant populations in EU/EEA countries.* Available at: http://ecdc.europa.eu/en/publications-data/migrant-health-series-access-hiv-prevention-treatment-and-care-migrant (Accessed: 6 March 2019).

Evans, D. B., Hsu, J. and Boerma, T. (2013) 'Universal health coverage and universal access', *Bulletin of the World Health Organization*, 91(8), pp. 546–546A. doi: 10.2471/BLT.13.125450.

Frank, R. (2005) 'International migration and infant health in Mexico', *Journal of Immigrant Health*, 7(1), pp. 11–22. doi: 10.1007/s10903-005-1386-9.

Frank, R. and Hummer, R. A. (2002) 'The other side of the paradox: The risk of low birth weight among infants of migrant and nonmigrant households within Mexico', *International Migration Review*, 36(3), pp. 746–765. doi: 10.1111/j.1747-7379.2002.tb00103.x.

Gassmann, F. *et al.* (2018) 'Unpacking the relationship between parental migration and child well-being: Evidence from Moldova and Georgia', *Child Indicators Research*, 11(2), pp. 423–440. doi: 10.1007/s12187-017-9461-z.

Graham, E. and Jordan, L. P. (2011) 'Migrant parents and the psychological well-being of left-behind children in Southeast Asia', *Journal of Marriage and the Family*, 73(4), pp. 763–787. doi: 10.1111/j.1741-3737.2011.00844.x.

Gushulak, B. D. and MacPherson, D. W. (2000) 'Health issues associated with the smuggling and trafficking of migrants', *Journal of Immigrant Health*, 2(2), pp. 67–78. doi: 10.1023/A:1009581817682.

Gushulak, B. D. and MacPherson, D. W. (2004) 'Globalization of infectious diseases: The impact of migration', *Clinical Infectious Diseases: An Official Publication of the Infectious Diseases Society of America*, 38(12), pp. 1742–1748. doi: 10.1086/421268.

Hammar, N. *et al.* (2009) 'Migration and differences in dietary habits—A cross sectional study of Finnish twins in Sweden', *European Journal of Clinical Nutrition*, 63(3), pp. 312–322. doi: 10.1038/sj.ejcn.1602931.

Hayman, K. G. *et al.* (2015) 'Burden of cardiovascular morbidity and mortality following humanitarian emergencies: A systematic literature review', *Prehospital and Disaster Medicine*, 30(1), pp. 80–88. doi: 10.1017/S1049023X14001356.

Holmboe-Ottesen, G. and Wandel, M. (2012) 'Changes in dietary habits after migration and consequences for health: A focus on South Asians in Europe', *Food & Nutrition Research*, 56. doi: 10.3402/fnr.v56i0.18891.

Huffman, S. A. *et al.* (2012) 'Exploitation, vulnerability to tuberculosis and access to treatment among Uzbek labor migrants in Kazakhstan', *Social Science & Medicine (1982)*, 74(6), pp. 864–872. doi: 10.1016/j.socscimed.2011.07.019.

HUMA (2011) *Access to healthcare and living conditions of asylum seekers and undocumented migrants in Cyprus, Malta, Poland and Romania.* Available at: https://interwencjaprawna.pl/docs/wpdt2011_1_en.pdf (Accessed: 6 March 2019).

Human Rights Watch (2009) 'Discrimination, denial, and deportation | human rights abuses affecting migrants living with HIV', *Human Rights Watch*. Available at: www.hrw.org/report/2009/06/18/discrimination-denial-and-deportation/human-rights-abuses-affecting-migrants (Accessed: 6 March 2019).

Jitthai, N. (2013) 'Migration and malaria', *The Southeast Asian Journal of Tropical Medicine and Public Health*, 44(Suppl 1), pp. 166–200; discussion 306-307.

Kanaiaupuni, S. M. and Donato, K. M. (1999) 'Migradollars and mortality: The effects of migration on infant survival in Mexico', *Demography*, 36(3), pp. 339–353. doi: 10.2307/2648057.

Kasl, S. V. and Berkman, L. (1983) 'Health consequences of the experience of migration', *Annual Review of Public Health*, 4(1), pp. 69–90. doi: 10.1146/annurev.pu.04.050183.000441.

Kirchengast, S. and Schober, E. (2006) 'To be an immigrant: A risk factor for developing overweight and obesity during childhood and adolescence?', *Journal of Biosocial Science*, 38(5), pp. 695–705. doi: 10.1017/S0021932005027094.

Kramer, M. A. *et al.* (2008) 'Migrants travelling to their country of origin: A bridge population for HIV transmission?', *Sexually Transmitted Infections*, 84(7), pp. 554–555. doi: 10.1136/sti.2008.032094.

The Lancet (2016) 'Migration and health', *The Lancet Infectious Diseases*, 16(8), p. 867. doi: 10.1016/S1473-3099(16)30218-3.

LaRocque, R. C. *et al.* (2013) 'Pre-travel health care of immigrants returning home to visit friends and relatives', *The American Journal of Tropical Medicine and Hygiene*, 88(2), pp. 376–380. doi: 10.4269/ajtmh.2012.12-0460.

Levitt, P. (1998) 'Social remittances: Migration driven local-level forms of cultural diffusion', *International Migration Review*, 32(4), pp. 926–948. doi: 10.2307/2547666.

Lindstrom, D. P. and Muñoz-Franco, E. (2006) 'Migration and maternal health services utilization in rural Guatemala', *Social Science & Medicine*, 63(3), pp. 706–721. doi: 10.1016/j.socscimed.2006.02.007.

Martens, P. and Hall, L. (2000) 'Malaria on the move: Human population movement and malaria transmission', *Emerging Infectious Diseases*, 6(2), pp. 103–109. doi: 10.3201/eid0602.000202.

Medecines du Monde (2015) *Legal report on access to healthcare in 12 countries*. Available at: https://mdmeuroblog.files.wordpress.com/2014/05/mdm-legal-report-on-access-to-healthcare-in-12-countries-3rd-june-20151.pdf (Accessed: 6 March 2019).

Medecines du Monde (2016) 'International report 2016: Access to healthcare for people facing multiple vulnerabilities in health in 31 cities in 12 countries', Available at: https://mdmeuroblog.files.wordpress.com/2016/11/observatory-report2016_en-mdm-international.pdf.

Médecins du Monde (2012) *Access to health care for vulnerable groups in the European Union in 2012*. Available at: www.europarl.europa.eu/document/activities/cont/201302/20130208ATT60776/20130208ATT60776EN.pdf (Accessed: 6 March 2019).

O'Donnell, C. A. (2018) 'Health care access for migrants in Europe', *Oxford Research Encyclopedia of Global Public Health*. doi: 10.1093/acrefore/9780190632366.013.6.

Parrish, R. G. (2010) 'Measuring population health outcomes', *Preventing Chronic Disease*, 7(4). Available at: www.cdc.gov/pcd/issues/2010/jul/10_0005.htm#Definitions (Accessed: 6 March 2019).

Platt, L. *et al.* (2013) 'Factors mediating HIV risk among female sex workers in Europe: A systematic review and ecological analysis', *BMJ Open*, 3(7), p. e002836. doi: 10.1136/bmjopen-2013-002836.

Prothero, R. M. (2001) 'Migration and malaria risk', *Health, Risk & Society*, 3(1), pp. 19–38. doi: 10.1080/713670171.

Razum, O. (2008) 'Migrant mortality, healthy migrant effect migrant mortality, healthy migrant effect', in Kirch, W. (ed.) *Encyclopaedia of public health*. Dordrecht: Springer Netherlands, pp. 932–935. doi: 10.1007/978-1-4020-5614-7_2188.

Rees, D. *et al.* (2010) 'Oscillating migration and the epidemics of silicosis, tuberculosis, and HIV infection in South African gold miners', *American Journal of Industrial Medicine*, 53(4), pp. 398–404. doi: 10.1002/ajim.20716.

Riosmena, F. *et al.* (2012) 'U.S. Migration, Translocality, and the Acceleration of the Nutrition Transition in Mexico', *Annals of the Association of American Geographers. Association of American Geographers*, 102(5), pp. 1209–1218. doi: 10.1080/00045608.2012.659629.

Roosen, I. and Siegel, M. (2018) 'Migration and its influence on the knowledge and usage of birth control methods among Afghan women who stay behind', *Public Health*, 158(Special issue on Migration: A global public health issue), pp. 183–197. doi: 10.1016/j.puhe.2018.03.014.

Rosenmöller, D. L. *et al.* (2011) 'Determinants of changes in dietary patterns among Chinese immigrants: A cross-sectional analysis', *The International Journal of Behavioral Nutrition and Physical Activity*, 8, p. 42. doi: 10.1186/1479-5868-8-42.

Saleh, A., Amanatidis, S. and Samman, S. (2002) 'The effect of migration on dietary intake, type 2 diabetes and obesity: The Ghanaian health and nutrition analysis in Sydney, Australia (Ghanaisa)', *Ecology of Food and Nutrition*, 41(3), pp. 255–270. doi: 10.1080/03670244.2002.9991686.

Sandvik, H., Hunskaar, S. and Diaz, E. (2012) 'Immigrants' use of emergency primary health care in Norway: A registry-based observational study', *BMC Health Services Research*, 12, p. 308. doi: 10.1186/1472-6963-12-308.

Scholz, N. (2016) 'The public health dimension of the European migrant crisis', *EPRS | European Parliamentary Research Service Brief*, January 2016, p. 8.

Skeldon, R. (2006) 'The global challenge of HIV/AIDS', in R. Black and H. White (eds.) *Targeting development: Critical perspectives on the millennium development goals*. London: Routledge, pp. 256–272.

Stevens, G. W. J. M. and Vollebergh, W. A. M. (2008) 'Mental health in migrant children', *Journal of Child Psychology and Psychiatry*, 49(3), pp. 276–294. doi: 10.1111/j.1469-7610.2007.01848.x.

Stillman, S., McKenzie, D. and Gibson, J. (2009) 'Migration and mental health: Evidence from a natural experiment', *Journal of Health Economics*, 28(3), pp. 677–687.

Suess, A. *et al.* (2014) 'The right of access to health care for undocumented migrants: A revision of comparative analysis in the European context', *European Journal of Public Health*, 24(5), pp. 712–720. doi: 10.1093/eurpub/cku036.

Thomas, F. (2013) 'Multiple medicaments: Looking beyond structural inequalities in migrant healthcare', in Felicity Thomas and Jasmine Gideon (eds.), *Migration, health and inequality*. London: Zed Books.

UNHCR (2017) *Health access and utilization survey among Syrian refugees in Lebanon*. Available at: https://data2.unhcr.org/en/documents/download/61329 (Accessed: 6 March 2019).

Valero-Gil, J. N. (2009) 'Remittances and the household's expenditures on health', *Journal of Business Strategies*, 26(1), p. 119.

Vanore, M. *et al.* (2018) 'Adult child migration and elderly multidimensional well-being: Comparative analysis between Moldova and Georgia', *Research on Aging*, 40(7), pp. 599–622. doi: 10.1177/0164027517723077.

Weishaar, H. B. (2008) 'Consequences of international migration: A qualitative study on stress among Polish migrant workers in Scotland', *Public Health*, 122(11), pp. 1250–1256. doi: 10.1016/j.puhe.2008.03.016.

Welshman, J. and Bashford, A. (2006) 'Tuberculosis, migration, and medical examination: Lessons from history', *Journal of Epidemiology and Community Health*, 60(4), pp. 282–284. doi: 10.1136/jech.2005.038604.

WHO (2010) 'Migrant-sensitive health systems'. Available at: www.who.int/hac/events/2_migrant_sensitive_health_services_22Feb2010.pdf.

Wolff, H. *et al.* (2008) 'Undocumented migrants lack access to pregnancy care and prevention', *BMC Public Health*, 8(1), p. 93. doi: 10.1186/1471-2458-8-93.

Wong, W. C. W., Yim, Y. L. and Lynn, H. (2011) 'Sexually transmitted infections among female sex workers in Hong Kong: The role of migration status', *Journal of Travel Medicine*, 18(1), pp. 1–7. doi: 10.1111/j.1708-8305.2010.00453.x.

Ziol-Guest, K. M. and Kalil, A. (2012) 'Health and medical care among the children of immigrants', *Child Development*, 83(5), pp. 1494–1500. doi: 10.1111/j.1467-8624.2012.01795.x.

21

CARE, SOCIAL REPRODUCTION, AND MIGRATION

Gioconda Herrera

While the concept of care has been part of feminist sociology and economics since the 1980s, its relationship with migration and development studies is more recent and is connected to discussions of gender and globalisation. One may trace at least two different sources for this relationship. One of them is the concept of 'global care chains', which has dominated discussions on the relationship between care, migration, and development since its inception almost 20 years ago (Ehrenreich and Hochschild 2002). Around the same time, several studies on migrant domestic work led to conceptual debates on the transnational character of social reproduction in contemporary capitalism (Parreñas 2001). Parreñas (2001) uses the term 'international division of reproductive work' to refer to the increasing relevance of migrant women in the lives of middle-class households in countries of the Global North, taking care of reproductive duties that states and families were reluctant to assume. She also coined the term 'international transfer of care' to make sense of the organisation of reproductive work in the hands of migrant women at different scales and in different countries. Similar to the global care chains, the issue at stake was to highlight that together with the transnational flows of commodities and finances, reproductive work was circulating globally. Looking at globalisation through the lens of social reproduction is a way to address gendered social inequalities beyond the nation-state (Bakker and Gill 2003, Bakker and Silvey 2008). For Verschur (2013), the concept of care has been essential for understanding 'the relational character of reproductive activities and the impossibility of separating material and non-material labour' (2013, 156).

However, social reproduction goes beyond care and involves many other aspects that need to be taken into account when analysing contemporary global migrations. For Kofman (2014), it is important to differentiate care from social reproduction. The latter is a complex array of activities that involves many sites and institutions: the state, the market, the community, and the household. An approach through social reproduction allows a more comprehensive interpretation of women's migration and labour transfers, whereas care usually involves a narrower focus on women, household, and domestic work (Kofman 2014).

This chapter traces the debates surrounding care, social reproduction, and migration by looking at how the concept of global care chains has evolved, particularly in Latin America. When initially coined, the concept of global care chains was very useful in linking the experience of women's migration with social inequality at the global level. However, limitations became evident over time, particularly when looking at more recent Latin American migrations to Europe and migration flows within the region. I argue that this experience contributes to the literature on care and social reproduction and migration in two ways: it problematises the idea of 'care deficit' by looking more carefully at gender and family arrangements in the countries of departure of migration, and it opens new paths of inquiry surrounding the relationship between women's migrant work and colonial legacies around unpaid and paid domestic labour. The chapter is organised as follows: first, I present some of the debates on the concept of care and its relationship with social reproduction in the migration literature. Then, I discuss some of the research done in Latin America on global care chains, social reproduction, and migration and the emergence of new concepts such as the circulation of care, transnational care regimes, the right to care, and transnational social protection as they apply to the study of both North–South as well as South–South migrations.

Care work, global care chains, and social reproduction

While the term care started to become popular in feminist economy and sociology in the 1990s, Marxist feminism worked on the link between social reproduction and production, and to make domestic labour visible in the process of capitalist accumulation for the last 50 years (Beneria 1979, Eldholm, Harris, and Young 1977). These discussions initially centred around two aspects that are crucial for understanding what would later be labelled care: the sexual division of labour and the definition of work itself. On the one hand, the origin of women's subordination was often explained by the existence of a gendered organisation of human activity that places women in the private realm in charge of reproductive duties whereas men were in the public sphere of production. On the other hand, emphasis was placed on the need to recognise both paid and unpaid labour as part of a new definition of work (Beneria 2007).

The term care, however, also brought into the debate an aspect that was not necessarily taken into account in definitions of social reproduction or unpaid work: the emotional and bonding aspect of care. Going beyond the obvious materiality it involves, care-work also has emotional and relational dimensions. It is this connotation that has given rise to a series of conceptual developments on different forms of care work as activities that deserve not only economic but fundamentally social recognition (Aguirre et al. 2014; Carrasco, Borderías, and Torns 2001).

Ehrenreich and Hochschild's book *Global Women* (2002) was a first recognition that care spanned across national borders. The book brought together research that examined areas of women's migrant work related to the care of older adults, children, the sick, and sex work. Each case combines physical and emotional work. As for the 'chain' aspect of the concept, it was coined by Hochschild (2000) and refers to 'a series of personal links between people across the globe based on the paid or unpaid work of caring' (2000, 131). She describes a global care chain as one in which the oldest sister of a low-income family cares for her siblings while her mother works as a nanny caring for other children whose mother, in turn, migrated and cares for the children of a different family in a wealthy country (2000, 131).

The basic idea behind the concept is that as one moves further down the chain, the value of work gradually decreases and, little by little, it becomes unpaid. These transfers of care take place on the basis of transnational relationships built upon axes of power relating to class, gender, and ethnicity; as a result, some people enjoy privileged care while others experience a care deficit (Ehrenreich and Hochschild 2002; Pérez Orozco 2011). The chain concept renders visible the links that make up the unequal processes of care transfer between families in destination countries, migrant families, and families in origin countries (Parreñas 2001). Thus, the concept of global care chains allows us to sketch a new geography of inequality, parallel to the geography of global supply chains and the circulation of financial capital. By showing the configuration of chains of care in experiences of migration, this concept reveals the hierarchical nature of caring relationships at the global level and how these hierarchies were transformed (or not) across borders.

In addition to linking inequality in care arrangements on a global scale, this concept led to a reconceptualisation of paid and unpaid work by including the emotional dimension of care in the analysis. Indeed, Hochschild (2000) speaks of emotional surplus value and analyses care work as a set of material and emotional tasks. Beyond the stratification and historical persistence of the material and symbolic inequality of domestic work, the notion of care introduces this emotional dimension into the universe of persistent inequalities. In short, the concept of global care chains sought to illustrate the double character of migrant care work: globally unequal and made of simultaneously material and emotional work.

Some scholars are cautious in the use of the terms 'care' and 'social reproduction'. They point out some important distinctions between the two concepts that may help to better grasp the articulation of paid and unpaid labour with global inequalities. For Christine Verschur, social reproduction is a more encompassing concept that enables a better appreciation of the articulation of labour reproduction within capitalism. According to Verschur, the debate should not focus on the nature of work (paid, unpaid, emotional, or moral) but on the articulation of different social relations where activities are undertaken (2013, 155). Analyses through the lens of care usually overlook some activities, such as subsistence agriculture or non-nurturing activities that are part of the reproduction of the labour force. In addition, they tend to focus on the care of dependents, such as children, the elderly, and the sick, and do not pay attention to the entire workforce. They also neglect the role played by communities and neighbourhoods in social reproduction (Verschur 2013).

Kofman (2014) shares some of these criticisms and argues that the concept of global care chains falls short in explaining many non-face-to-face activities that are part of households' activities of social reproduction. For her, a variety of care activities have been commodified and outsourced, while many external agents and institutions interact with households. In that sense, the concept of social reproduction is better suited to understand the complexity of the transfer of labour as well as the increasing social and gender inequalities of global migrations (Kofman 2014; Verschur 2013).

Yeates (2005, 2009) also raises criticisms of the concept of global care chains. She argues that it is necessary to make the care work performed by men more visible, especially in relation to caring for the sick or older adults. It is also important to address more specialised and institutional care work, such as nursing, family doctors, and domiciliary care providers. She points to the necessity to open up research towards other care configurations and actors beyond domestic work (nannies and maids), and to take into consideration activities such as care for the elderly or for the sick. Such lines of inquiry were pursued by other work that examined the global care chains of the elderly (Escrivá 2004; Genta 2017; Martínez Buján 2010; Skornia 2014). Yates also suggests that any analysis should take into account different family and household configurations. While many studies centred on nuclear families and married women leaving children behind and taking care of other children, Yeates argues that single women migrant, who are working as caretakers of the elderly and may be in charge of their elder parents at home in their countries should also be included. Thus, Yeates (2005) calls attention to the multi-dimensional nature of 'care' services and the need to encompass other institutional activities, and not only care within families, in the analysis of global care chains. In that sense, she joins many of the criticisms raised by Kofman (2014).

Global care chains, development and the right to care in Latin America

The concept of global care chains was an important tool for understanding the new feminisation of Andean migrations to Europe that took place in the late 1990s, as well as the more traditional Asian migrations to the Middle East and Europe. In fact, the need to address the care gaps in Southern European societies became attractive for Andean women who, when migrating to care for minors and older adults in these countries, often left their dependent relatives in the care of other women in their communities of origin.

According to Amaia Pérez Orozco (2011), the concept of global care chains became a strategic site for the study of gender dynamics within the current processes of globalisation and 'a strategic positioning, from which to debate the interrelation between migration and development' (Pérez Orozco 2011, 4). Starting in 2008, the use of the concept led to a series of studies on different migration circuits in Latin America that analysed the construction of these chains and their specificities in the regional context. Several of these studies were part of the United Nations Women project 'Latin American women in global care chains' the purpose of which was to understand the configuration of global chains in South–South and South–North migration circuits. In addition to Spain as the main destination for Latin American women, the research included many other destination countries within Latin America such as Chile, Argentina, and Costa Rica, underlying the need to take into account the specificities of intraregional migrations of women domestic workers. For instance, the work of Arriagada and Todaro (2011) on Peruvian migrant women in Chile shows that paid care work was historically done by internal rural migrants and that it was connected with social asymmetries grounded in historical and social inequalities. Care work was only recently replaced by Peruvian migrant women and the transnational organisation of care work in the countries of origin differs from other countries of destination due to proximity; frequent visits of migrant women to their communities contribute to maintaining a more fluid relationship with children left behind.

Other researchers look at different countries of origin such as Ecuador, Bolivia, and Paraguay whose migrant women participate both in South–South and South–North migrations, adding more complexity and highlighting the need to look at cultural and historical specificities in the analysis (Soto, González, and Dobrée 2012; Herrera 2013; Salazar, Jimenez, and Wanderley 2011).

One of the contributions of this research was to integrate the role of the state and social policies into the analysis of the transnational organisation of care. These studies highlighted the need to connect the concept of care chains to the institutional organisation of care at local, national, and regional levels, both where migration originates and at its destination. The need to look at migrant care arrangements in relation to existing government actions and policies (or the absence thereof) was emphasised. The work of Pérez Orozco and Lopez Gil (2011) in Spain, of Carcedo, Chavez, and Larraitz (2011) in Costa Rica, of Sanchís and Rodriguez (2011) on Paraguayan migrants in Argentina, and of Arriagada and Todaro (2012) on Peruvians in Chile all analysed these chains in relation to a deficient institutional organisation of care in the receiving countries and to the role of migrants in the their provision.

In these works, prevailing views on the concept of care chains, which place these relationships mainly as inequalities between women and families in the South and North, are surpassed. Hence, the concept of care chains comes to be understood as connected to institutional care delivery systems, and Molano, Robert and García promoted the notion of an 'unfair global regime of care', the features of which are:

> the lack of social responsibility for care so that responsibility for their provision falls upon the household; the lack of participation and responsibility for care on the part of men; and strong inequalities and stratification in access to care, by which some social groups access decent care while others access precarious or vulnerable care.
>
> *(2012, 15)*

Thus, they pointed towards a specific agenda that linked care, migration, and development. From these studies emerged policy proposals around the right to care as part of both the construction of citizenship and of development (Pérez Orozco 2011). The right to care includes, first, receiving care in different moments of the life cycle no matter where the person lives; second, caregivers should have the right to decide whom to take care of; and third the care sector should enjoy correct labour conditions. In sum, Pérez Orozco (2011) calls for a global regime of 'fair care'.

Care deficit and care arrangements in transnational migration

This literature also suggests that the analysis of the dynamics of care in the cities and communities where migration originated added nuance to one of the implications of the concept of care chains: the notion of lack or deficit of care as the chain reaches the communities where the families of migrants are left. In contrast, these studies showed that communities of origin deployed various forms of care that, although they took place in environments of inequality and vulnerability, did not necessarily imply an absence of care (Herrera 2013). Work was carried out on the social and institutional arrangements surrounding care in places of origin of migration, showing that an endless array of practices exists that involve not only mothers and daughters but many members of the nuclear and extended family, in different places and moments of the transnational relationship. The studies of Anderson (2012) on the trajectories of Peruvian migrants in Chile and Spain and their families arrangements, as well as the works of Herrera and Carrillo (2009) and Herrera (2013) on Ecuador; Soto, Gonzalez, and Dobrée (2012) on Paraguay; and Salazar, Jimenez, and Wanderley (2011) on Bolivia, showed that what was perceived as a care deficit from the perspective of the receiving countries translated into myriad care arrangements and disarrangements in the families of migrant women.

In other words, these works challenge the concept of care deficit and show that although the migration of women, and particularly of mothers, did alter the lives of children and partners in their communities and neighbourhoods, there were many forms in which material and emotional care was provided by other people: grandparents, elder daughters, and even neighbours. Moreover, the experience of both internal migration and family separation during childhood was part of the lives of many international migrants (Anderson 2012; Herrera 2013). Thus, mother and father separation from their children was not immediately connected with a care deficit but as a strategy of social reproduction rather common among these families.

Likewise, the work of Skornia and Cifuentes (2016) in Peru details the dynamic configurations of transnational care for Peruvian migrants in Italy, as well as the perspective of actors in the communities of origin. These authors support their analysis with the notion of entangled inequalities in which asymmetries based on different power axes such as gender, generation, race, or ethnicity are combined with distinct, but interdependent, geographic scales: local, national, and global. Their goal was to demonstrate that the intergenerational and gender asymmetries that affect familial and care relationships locally are intensified in a context where care becomes transnational. In addition, the authors show that these asymmetries are also related to aspects such as citizenship, or the absence of citizenship, and the right to care. These views went beyond the idea of care deficit or care drain and made the interpretations of care practices from migration societies of origin more complex.

The multi-sited and multi-scale quality of these works also showed that notions of care also travelled and changed, leading to tensions and negotiations over representations of care among family members and also creating possibilities for transformation. This approach, when applied to various parts of Latin America, meant emphasising the importance of the social and cultural context for the understanding of care practices, taking the concept of global care chains beyond networks and flows of people, emotions, and goods, and adding other actors to the analysis: those who migrate and those who do not, as well as other scales that are useful to evaluate the influence of national institutions and global markets on care practices.

Acosta's comparative study (2015) on migrant care work in Spain and Chile offers an analysis of the representations of care upheld by employers, in addition to analysing the social organisation of care, which highlight the connections among the state, the market, and families in the provision of care, from an institutional point of view. The author finds that despite the cultural, social, and economic differences between Chile and Spain, in both cases, a historical substratum of servitude and devaluation of migrant work still persists in the representations of employers, an attitude derived from discriminatory notions relating to gender and race. From Acosta's study, we can derive a further dimension to the debate on the right to care. In addition to examining structural connections and global inequality through the concept of global care chains and addressing the role of the state and the rights of care workers, it is also necessary to take into account the historical and cultural representation of care in any analysis.

In summary, the focus on social arrangements of care in countries of departure lends a greater complexity to the analysis of the effects of female migration on families and communities, and interrogates the interpretative potential of the concepts of care deficit and care drain. Besides, historical and cultural considerations of the meaning of care are taken into account when analysing care transfer through migration in the Latin American cases. Some of these criticisms were highlighted by Yeates (2005, 2009) and Kofman and Raghuram (2012) when referring to other regions of the world. Yeates (2005) insists on the importance of historical analyses that may give a deeper perspective on contemporary and global analysis of care chains by looking at the origins of cultures of servitude. Kofman and Raghuram (2012) seek to unsettle some of the assumptions underlying the analysis of care in South–North migrations by looking at examples of South–South migrations 'tied into global circuits of care in distinctive ways and with different care provisioning and histories of gendered migrations' (2012, 1). The Latin American cases illustrate these historical specificities through the analysis of continuities between internal and international migrations and the persistence of colonial notions of servitude through which care is understood.

Research questions remain with regard to how certain cultural representations of care are being transformed with migration. For example, male caregivers and the transformation of masculinities with migration is an important topic as yet understudied that is explored in the work of Gallo and Scrinzi (2015). Their analysis focuses on the practices and strategies of migrant men employed as domestic/care workers in Italy, and it highlights how migrant men negotiate the transformations and conflicts that their 'feminised' jobs entail. Datta et al. (2010) also looked at how migrant men and women in London's low-paid economy may be constructing a new ethic of care, thus transforming the cultural representation of care. In order to understand the character of these transformations the historical and cultural dimensions of care need to be taken into account.

Circulation of care

Balsaddar and Merla (2014) proposed the concept of a 'circulation of care' to describe the forms of asymmetric reciprocity surrounding care that take place in transnational kinship networks. While the literature on global care chains makes visible a unidirectional transfer of care between women in asymmetric pairs (dyads), according to the authors, the notion of circulation would allow us to consider the complete network of social relationships within which care circulates. In this sense, care is conceived as a process rather than as an occasional event or a discrete linkage; as such, it needs to be addressed longitudinally throughout the life cycle. To the spatial dimension of care chains, the authors add temporality as an important factor that contributes to circulation. This proposal may be useful to examine the experience of migrants' return, particularly of women, who often decide to come back to take care of elderly parents (Herrera and Pérez 2017). Through the circulation of care, one can understand how economic crises in destination countries may articulate with the absence of care policies for the elderly in countries of origin and, thus, push for the return of migrant women.

Furthermore, Balsaddar and Merla (2014) consider that, as a concept, the circulation of care allows us to think of transnational families as social structures in which mobility and absence are part of family life instead of exceptions to the rule. Thus, exchanges of care become central activities in the process of 'making family' at a distance (Bryceson and Vuorela 2002). The exchange of care becomes especially important in the absence of other ways of expressing feelings of family belonging or solidarity. Thus, for the authors, the circulation of care is a privileged methodological entry point to study transnational families and is useful for the study of migrant return.

Finally, Balsaddar and Merla (2014) include the interaction between social and institutional actors, in addition to the individual practices of subjects or families, in their notion of the circulation of care. We are facing de-territorialised conceptions of care that are nonetheless highly determined by territoriality: migrants negotiate expectations and regulations surrounding care and family in at least two countries. Because of this, multiple local and national contexts produce different conditions for the circulation of care.

Transnational care regimes

Along similar lines, Skornia's work on Peruvian migrants who care for older adults in Italy (2014) speaks of 'transnational care regimes'. The author highlights the importance of looking at the way that family, state, market, and networks beyond the national territory interact. For Skornia, using the term 'regime' captures the institutional, social, and spatial arrangements that organise the provision of care. This overcomes a vision of welfare organisation and care that centres on national states in order to focus on how class, gender, race, ethnicity, and nationality produce inequalities in access to care both within national states and across borders.

Thus, different segmented care regimes coexist and stratify care within the national territory. In these hierarchical care regimes, migration introduces nationality as an increasingly prominent dimension of inequality, one that links up with social categorisations based on class and race to generate exclusion or the negotiation of the conditions of subordination (Skornia 2014).

Concluding remarks: Care, citizenship, and mobility

All of the above has led to reflections on citizenship and rights that go beyond the framework of the national state and examine how they may be connected with the transnational dimension of care and families. Thus, notions of citizenship that were once criticised by feminists for their false universalism, assuming the national state as the locus of social inequality that administers social justice are beginning to be rethought with reference to globalisation, migration and its feminisation (Benhabib and Resnik 2009; Herrera 2013).

That is, transnational care challenges our conceptions of citizenship. Concepts such as the transnational care regime, unfair care regimes, and/or the right to care have allowed us to understand better how these processes are linked with the behaviour of states and the social organisation of care. Moreover, thinking about transnational care also propels us to take the discussion of rights and social protection beyond national borders. The fact that more people on the planet must solve their care needs and those of their families in a transnational manner poses a series of analytical challenges to thinking about public policies in a way that links the local, the national, and the global. Levitt et al.'s (2017) proposal for a transnational social protection agenda that takes into account the way in which people in mobility and their families construct their care arrangements is an important step in this direction. Their proposal not only considers the relationships of care that exist at the micro family level but also takes into account the ecology of formal and informal institutional resources with which people interact to meet their needs for protection. Thus, Levitt et al. (2017) propose to analyse how people and their families can make use of transnational state protection and how states, private institutions, or social networks protect (or fail to protect) people in mobility. Overall, the relationship between care and migration has been a fruitful way to expand our interpretation of global migration and social inequalities and global care chains have been a central concept in this reflection. However, both theoretical debate on care, social reproduction, and care regimes, as well as empirical studies on the care arrangements and the transfer of care, have interrogated this concept in a constructive manner, enabling a more complex understanding of global social inequalities and their relationship with renewed notions of citizenship.

References

Acosta Gonzalez E. (2015) *Cuidados en crisis: Mujeres migrantes hacia España y Chile*. Bilbao: Universidad de Deusto.

Aguirre R., Batthyány K., Genta N. and Perrota V. (2014) "Los cuidados en la agenda de investigación y en las políticas públicas en Uruguay", *Quito: Íconos*, 50: 43–60.

Anderson J. (2012) "La migración femenina peruana en las cadenas globales de cuidados en Chile y España: transferencia de cuidados y desigualdades de género" Documento de trabajo. PUCP-ONU -Mujeres. Lima, p. 144.

Arriagada I. and Todaro R. (2011) *Cadenas globales de cuidados: el papel de las migrantes peruanas en la provisión de cuidados en Chile*. Santiago de Chile: ONU- Mujeres.

Bakker I. and Gill S. (2003) *Power, Production, and Social Reproduction. Human Insecurity in the Global Political Economy*. New York: Palgrave Macmillan.

Bakker I. and Silvey R. (2008) *Beyond States and Markets. The Challenges of Social Reproduction*. London and New York: Routledge, p. 224.

Balsaddar L. and Merla L. (2014) "Introduction: Transnational family caregiving through the lens of circulation", in Balsaddar L. and Merla L. (eds.) *Transnational Families, Migration and the Circulation of Care. Understanding Mobility and Absence in Family Life*, pp. 3–24. New York: Routledge.

Beneria L. (1979) "Reproduction, production and the sexual division of labor", *Cambridge Journal of Economics*, 3: 203–225.

Beneria L. (2007) *Paid/Unpaid Work and the Globalization of Reproduction*. GEM-IWG Working Paper 01-1.

Benhabib S. and Resnik J. (eds.). (2009) *Migrations and Mobilities. Citizenship, Borders, and Gender.* New York: New York University Press.

Bryceson D. and Vuorela U. (2002) "Transnational families in the twenty-first century". In D. Bryceson and U. Vuorela (eds.) *The Transnational Family: New European Frontiers and Global Networks.* Oxford: Berg.

Carcedo A., Chavez M.J. and Larraitz L. (2011) *Cadenas globales de cuidados: el papel de las migrantes nicaragüenses en la provisión de cuidados en costa rica.* San José: ONU-Mujeres.

Carrasco C., Borderías C. and Torns T. (2001) "Introducción. El trabajo de cuidados: antecedentes históricos y debates actuales", in Carrasco C., Borderías C. and Torns T. (eds.) *El trabajo de cuidados: historia, teorías y política*, pp. 13–95. Madrid: Catarata.

Datta K., McIlwaine C., Evans Y., Herbert J., May J. and Will J. (2010) "A migrant ethic of care? Negotiating care and caring among migrant workers in London low paid economy", *Feminist Review*, 94: 93–116.

Ehrenreich B. and Hochschild A.R. (2002) *Global Woman: Nannies, Maids and Sex Workers in the New Economy.* New York: Henry Holt and Company, llc.

Eldholm F., Harris O. and Young K. (1977) "Conceptualising women", *Critique of Anthropology*, 3(9/10): 101–130.

Escrivá A. (2004) *Securing the Care and Welfare of Dependants Transnationally: Peruvians and Spaniards in Spain.* Working Paper Number WP404. Oxford: Oxford Institute of Ageing.

Gallo E. and Scrinzi F. (2015) "Outsourcing elderly care to migrant workers: The impact of gender and class on the experience of male employers", *Sociology*, 50(2), April 2015.

Genta N. (2017) "Amor de abuela': redistribución intergeneracional del cuidado en el contexto de la migración ecuatoriana a España", in Oso L. and Torres A. (eds.) *Migración ecuatoriana, género y desarrollo.* Quito: FLACSO.

Herrera G. (2013) *Lejos de tus pupilas. Familias transnacionales, cuidados y desigualdad social en ecuador.* Quito: Onu-Muejres, FLACSO.

Herrera G. and Carrillo M.C. (2009) "Transformaciones familiares en la experiencia migratoria ecuatoriana. Una mirada desde los contextos de salida", *Mélanges de la Casa Velasquez*, 39(1): 97–114.

Herrera G. and Pérez L. (2017) "Times of Crisis, Time to return?", in Youkana E. (ed.) *Borders Trangression. Mobilities and Mobilizations*, pp. 99–116. Bonn: Bonn University Press.

Hochschild A.R. (2000) "Global Care Chains and Emotional Surplus Value", in Hutton W. and Giddens A. (eds.) *On the Edge: Living with Global Capitalism*, pp. 130–146. London: Jonathan Cape.

Kofman E. (2014) "Gendered migrations, social reproduction and the household in Europe", *Dialetic Anthropology*, 38: 79–94.

Kofman E. and Raghuram P. (2012) "Women, migration, and care: Explorations of diversity and dynamism in the Global South", *Social Politics*, 19(3): 408–432.

Levitt P., Viterna J., Mueller A. and Loyed C. (2017) "Transnational social protection: Setting the Agenda", *Oxford Development Studies*, 45: 2–19.

Martínez Buján R. (2010) *Bienestar y cuidados: el oficio del cariño. Mujeres inmigrantes y mayores nativos.* Madrid: CSIC.

Molano A., Robert E. and García M. (2012) *Cadenas globales de cuidados. Síntesis de resultados de nueve estudios en América Latina y España.* Santo Domingo: ONU-Mujeres.

Parreñas R.S. (2001) *Servants of Globalization: Women, Migration and Domestic Work.* Stanford: Stanford University Press.

Pérez Orozco A. (2011) *Cadenas globales de cuidados. Qué derechos para un régimen global de cuidado justo?* Santo Domingo: INSTRAW.

Pérez Orozco A. and Lopez Gil S. (2011) *Desigualdades a flor de piel. Cadenas globales de cuidado. Concreciones a nivel del hogar y articulaciones políticas.* Santo Domingo: ONU-Mujeres.

Salazar C., Jimenez E. and Wanderley F. (2011) *Migración, cuidado y sostenibilidad de la vida.* La Paz: Onu Mujeres.

Sanchís N. and Rodriguez C. (2011) *Cadenas globales de cuidado. El papel de las migrantes paraguayas en la provisión de cuidados en Argentina.* Buenos Aires: ONU –Mujeres.

Skornia A. (2014) *Entangled Inequalities in Transnational Care: Practices across the Borders of Peru and Italy.* Bielefeld: Transcript verlag.

Skornia A. and Cifuentes J. (2016) "Cuidados transnacionales y desigualdades entrelazadas en la experiencia migratoria peruana: una mirada desde los hogares de origen", *Desacatos*, 52(Sept.- Dec): 32–49.

Soto C., González M., and Dobrée P., (2012) *La migración femenina paraguaya en las cadenas globales de cuidados en Argentina: transferencia de cuidados y desigualdades de género*. Asunción: ONU Mujeres.

Verschur C. (2013) "Theoretical debates on social reproduction and care: The articulation between the domestic and the global economy.", in Oso L. and Ribas Matos N. (eds.) *International Handbook of Gender, Migration and Transnationalism*, pp. 145–160. Cheltenham and Camberley (UK) and Northampton (US): Edward Elgar Publishing.

Yeates N. (2005) "Global care chains: A critical introduction", in *Global Migration Perspectives*, pp. 1–19. Geneva: Global Commission on International Migration, no. 44. September.

Yeates N. (2009) *Globalizing Care Economies and Migrant Workers: Explorations in Global Care Chains*. New York: Palgrave MacMillan.

22

EDUCATION AND MIGRATION

Başak Bilecen

Introduction[1]

Market-driven neoliberal policies and practices have implications for all institutions, including education and training, that are key in preparing the labour force for economic competition, which helps to direct the development path of a country. The shifts in types and sites of production such as an increase in technological innovation and the increased share of the service sector comes with requirements for the labour force to possess matching skills. The education systems of a society essentially prepare the population for such transformations. In other words, 'the quality of a nation's education and training system is seen to hold the key to future economic prosperity' (Brown and Lauder 1996, 1). This has implications for social structure both within and across nation-states. Education as a proxy for social position is one of the most important determinants of how other goods are being distributed not only at the nation-state level but also at the individual, family, and community levels.

Given the interconnectivity of production systems, circulation of goods, capital, and labour became the norm, at least in the Global North. An emphasis on skills and knowledge over other areas of economic production came to the fore, highlighting the importance of education while facilitating greater internal and international mobility of persons. In the neoliberal era, the struggle for the 'best and brightest' became an expression of economic advantage and competition. The link between education and mobility/migration operates at manifold levels which this chapter examines while pinpointing the developmental effects of this link in three subsections: student and academic mobility, the education of first-generation labour migrants, and the implications of second-generation status for education in countries of destination. The concept of development is contested and has many definitions (see also Faist 2008 and the Introduction in this Handbook). In this chapter, and following Sen (1997), development is understood to be progress towards the betterment of persons and their well-being through the improvement of state infrastructures, political governance, and social protection systems, as well as balanced economic growth in harmony with resources, environment, and human rights. However, inequalities are the major obstacles to achieving such progress and improvement in well-being and hence the development of societies.

Categories of migrations and migrants are rather fluid indicating that one's mobility might start with the motivation to work in another country and it might change over the course of the years and this person can start to study in the same or in a third country or vice versa indicating that migration is not a unidirectional phenomenon but open-ended (Skeldon 1997). While recognising this proviso, this chapter uses the terms such as international students or labour migrants to indicate a single type of mobility either for study or work for the sake of simplicity. First, this chapter investigates the mobilities of students, academics, and the highly skilled as one expression of the role of higher education in development. Second, the chapter examines the selectivity effects of education for first-generation international labour migrants and engages in discussions on formal and informal recognition of their educational credentials. Third, the chapter explores the education and social mobility of second-generation migrants as a result of their parents' international migration. In so doing, it draws upon literature often not explicitly considered in the migration and development debate. By examining these three different aspects of education and international migration/mobility, the reproduction of social (dis)advantage emerges as a significant theme.

Education, stratification, and knowledge

Education systems, in general, and higher education, in particular, are institutions that structure societies. Following Bourdieu (1984), universities can be seen as places (re)producing human and cultural capital but at the same time have been under pressure to restructure in order to survive in the organisation of the 'knowledge economy' (Scott 1997). Through the second half of the twentieth century, the numbers of higher education institutions increased rapidly across the globe as did enrolments from a variety of class backgrounds to produce skilled labour forces across the developed world (Meyer et al. 1992). This situation increased the hopes for a decrease in the inequality of educational opportunity through which intergenerational social mobility would be possible within a given nation-state. At the very least, across most countries in the Global North, a more diverse student population from the working, middle, and upper-middle classes emerged.

Nevertheless, the socio-economic position of the parents of students enrolling in higher education institutions is still important, indicating the reproduction of classes and the favouritism of the already privileged. This is particularly the case when one considers the privatisation of higher education institutions mainly in the Anglophone-world where financial means are needed to cover at least the tuition fees and parental networks facilitate access. As more and more people from different backgrounds entered universities and started to gain skills and certificates, one strategy adopted by privileged classes has been to maintain the scarcity value of educational credentials. In order to do so, graduate parents, as alumni and stakeholders, support their higher education institutions through donations, as well as often being formally active members in selecting the next generation of students. It is not so much a degree that is important but more from which institution it was awarded. Access to elite institutions is critical and if no equivalent opportunities are available locally, families look to their children's participation in international education programmes. This trend can be observed both in the Global North, itself, as well as in the Global South, where the emergence of the transnational capitalist class (Sklair 2001) has seen the new wealthy send their children either to elite universities in their own countries or overseas. This trend matched the aims of universities in the Global North that under the neoliberal regime became much more autonomous while relying on revenues generated through international education programmes offered, such as tuition fees. For the supply side, international study through experiences, knowledge, and educational credentials serve as symbolic capital to their holders (Findlay 2011; Waters 2009). For instance, Xiang and Shen (2009) argued that higher education has expanded massively in China, which led to a devaluation of national degrees and the middle class began to favour international education for their children justifying their often recently acquired economic capital through its conversion into cultural capital. In addition, the highly ranked universities in China maintained or improved their standards to the extent that many of the new middle-income groups could not access these institutions and chose instead to place their children overseas, often not in the top universities but in second- or third-tier institutions. According to Skeldon (2009), this is not a new phenomenon: already in Hong Kong of the 1970s, migration for education to the UK had started to grow rapidly because the local universities could only offer a limited number of places and the rising demand essentially 'pushed' new middle-income families to look overseas.

Family background has a direct effect on a student's opportunities to attend higher education and become part of international student mobility programmes (Bilecen and Van Mol 2017; Bourdieu 1996; Findlay et al. 2012). According to Bourdieu (1984, 1993, 1996), those who already have an advantageous socio-economic family background will continue to hold these positions in their later life as they have the necessary economic, social, cultural, and symbolic capitals to enter to the field of higher education to keep their status in society. In addition, institutions and nation-states are engaged in branding their degrees as status symbols. This is not to suggest that all international students belong to upper classes in their societies of origin. Through expansion of education to include a larger body of students and scholarship programmes, those in less advantaged positions today have more opportunities to participate in such programmes. For instance, student mobility within the EU is regulated under the Bologna Framework Erasmus programme. It aims to standardise national educational systems across the EU so that the educational credentials earned in one member-state are recognised in the other one. It has been designed to increase the mobility of youth, aiming to foster European identity (King and Ruiz-Gelices 2003). Of course, the first step for such mobility is to be 'successful' enough to enrol at a university.

International student mobility is usually considered as a type of mobility that is temporary and entailing a triple win for countries of origin, education, and the students themselves. The very definition of an international student is a person whose sole purpose of being in another country is to study for a defined period of education, set according to their a student visa. However, students might have multiple reasons to be internally or internationally mobile and studying might have coincided with another incident at this life stage. Due to increased unemployment, young persons might go back to study to enhance their skills so that they can find jobs or simply to do 'something enriching'.

Previous research has shown that international students transfer the knowledge and thus foster economic development and social transformation in a variety of places, not only during their studies but also after graduation: in their countries of origin but also through their transnational networks elsewhere across the globe. For instance, Bilecen and Faist (2015) argued that international doctoral students act as transnational brokers of knowledge across multiple nation-state borders. The authors highlight the importance of communication and transportation technologies in such cross-border knowledge dissemination which do not necessarily require international students to be physically present. Moreover, Saxenian (2008) shows that US-educated engineers from China and India play an economic developmental role by transferring their knowledge back to their countries of origin through their entrepreneurial activities. This is possible for both international students and alumni not only because of ease in communication and transportation technologies, but also because of their insider understandings on how things operate in origin contexts. Thus, Chinese and Indian graduates can 'locate foreign partners quickly and manage complex business relationships and teamwork across cultural and linguistic barriers' where it is 'particularly challenging in high-tech industries in which products, markets, and technologies are continually redefined' (Saxenian 2008, 122). Therefore, international students often represent a wanted category of mobile populations because of the skills, knowledge, social values, and financial contributions they bring with them (as the universities in the countries of education need the tuition fees) and generate during and after their studies.

Another category of mobile persons at the nexus of education and development are the educators themselves. Through academic exchanges across borders, academics cooperate with one another, learn from each other, and thus have developmental effects in the regions in which they work. Through international collaborations and visits, they exchange and produce new ideas, products, and patents. Geographical propinquity is not considered as the main requirement: through increased speed of the transmission of information and technologies of transportation, they can transfer knowledge across regions and nation-state borders. For instance, according to the study conducted by Edler and colleagues (2011) based on evidence collected from 950 German academics in science and engineering faculties, the international mobility of scientists improves their productivity, their scientific and human capital, as well as their propensity to circulate knowledge. A similar study conducted by Jöns (2009) investigating circular movements of academics, found that short academic stays intensified international collaboration and knowledge circulation through networks.

Previously, migration of highly skilled workforce such as academics or business people as 'brain drain' from the Global South to Global North usually characterised as loss of skills, knowledge, or decrease in economic productivity and growth. According to this understanding, international mobility of the highly skilled was conceptualised as a 'brain gain' for countries of destination usually located in the Global North with already advantaged economic positions at the expense of making origin countries in the Global South lose their human capital and become dependent, thereby deepening the existing global inequalities (Lowell and Findlay 2001). Today, mobility of the highly skilled workforce is not necessarily perceived as such a loss anymore, but rather is acknowledged to be beneficial for the home regions as well destinations (De Haas 2012). The main argument is that through mobility, the highly skilled increase their social capital and diversify their formal and informal ties resulting in knowledge circulation, investments, innovations, and patent applications. Nevertheless, the exodus of medical personnel from the poorest regions in the world may still pose a challenging issue (Martin et al. 2006; see also Chapter 12 in this Handbook).

According to Altbach and Knight (2007, 291), the direction of student and faculty flows is usually from Global South to Global North favouring 'well-developed education systems and institutions, thereby compounding existing inequalities'. Therefore, mobility for academic purposes needs to take into account specific case-studies but also the macroeconomic and structural factors and their wider implications. Moreover, more research on South–South mobilities and their implications is needed to counterbalance the dominant narrative of the South–North movement of students, academic faculty and skilled migrants.

Education and labour migration

Another important strand of research has been on labour migrants whose mobility is not primarily motivated for education as such but intricately tied to their levels of education, skills, and experience. Educational qualifications of individuals not only influence their labour market opportunities but also their propensity to migrate. Previous research indicates that the least educated and the poorest tend not to have the means to migrate, given that migration, initially at least, requires capital, education, and skills, which are usually only available to those who are relatively better off. The higher the education, the higher the propensity to migrate (Todaro 1976), although those with tertiary education, as a minority of most populations, are certainly not necessarily the most mobile in that population.

Clearly, it is not only higher education systems that are being expanded around the world, but perhaps more importantly, primary, secondary, and vocational levels of education are being promoted to produce necessary labour force for production and consumption. In fact, indicators of enrolment and retention at these more basic levels of education are seen to be among the most fundamental measures of development. Concomitantly, given the ageing populations and lower fertility rates in the Global North, the demand for unskilled and skilled labour force has also increased, driving much international migration of labour force from disadvantaged to advantaged areas (Skeldon 1997).

While education levels are important to determine internal or international migratory patterns of individuals, it is only one criterion among many. Decisions to migrate are either constrained or enabled within opportunity structures of the nation-states that regulate exits and entries through border controls and policies (Faist 2000). Examples of state policies regulating labour migration include guest-worker agreements in the European countries starting as early as the 1950s. Despite their drawbacks, recent recruitment of nurses from the Philippines through bilateral agreements of nation-states constitutes an example of a more equitable North–South agreement trying to create win-win situations, even if Northern countries are usually the main architects of such agreements (Adepoju et al. 2010). Another contemporary state policy targeting the migration of highly skilled persons is the Blue Card Directive introduced in the EU in 2009 based on Lisbon Strategy. Given relatively low levels of intra-EU mobility of highly skilled persons, together with the ageing demographics of member states, the Blue Card scheme aims to attract skilled third-country nationals to maintain economic competitiveness. While aiming at a unified and simplified procedure of admission, its criteria has been criticised on the grounds of different salary thresholds required from member states, as well as different definitions of skill, qualification levels, and the recognition of foreign degrees (Zimmermann 2009).

As the numbers of labour migrants with educational credentials obtained elsewhere has increased, the issue of transferability of degrees has come to importance, particularly in professional fields. The expectations of international migrants with high levels of education are high but these will be conditional upon the recognition of their qualifications. However, not all foreign educational credentials are recognised on crossing an international border, which often results in deskilling and downward mobility of labour migrants. For example, studying ethnic re-settlers from the former Soviet Union and Eastern Europe to Germany, Bauder (2005) concluded that even though they quickly received citizenship, their educational degrees and certificates were formally accredited only once they arrived in Germany, and often at a lower level. The reasons for this often included the shorter length of education and training in their areas of origin. Moreover, Kofman and Raghuram (2006) argued that it is usually women whose skills were not being formally recognised, and thus led to more marginal positions.

While formal recognition of educational credentials is important in order for labour migrants to find employment that would ideally yield matching earnings and comparable social positions in host countries, research has indicated that informal recognition of degrees by peers is equally significant. Weiss (2016) observed that even though educational credentials were fully recognised formally, as in the case of physicians in the EU member states, degrees and experiences gained abroad also needed to be recognised by their peers in the workplace pointing to the symbolic dimension of educational credentials. Similarly, according to the study of Alexis and colleagues (2007), which was conducted with nurses from Asia, Africa, and the Caribbean who earned their qualifications overseas but worked in south England, found the processes of devaluation of foreign nurses and lack of trust from their peers at their workplace. Therefore, both formal and informal recognition of educational credentials in international labour migration serve as mechanisms of production and reproduction of social (dis)advantage mainly in the countries of immigration.

Labour migrants tend to send financial remittances back 'home' given that most of them are bound by expectations to do so. However, quite apart from financial remittances, 'social remittances' (Levitt 1999) are transmitted to countries of origin, which have developmental effects through the exchange of ideas, knowledge, material goods, and investments in businesses, healthcare, and education (see also Chapter 11 in this Handbook). Nevertheless, a question remains whether financial remittances do increase the education of left-behind family members (see Chapter 10 in this Handbook). While the educational aspirations and investments might increase in the countries or regions of origin, international migration might also increase the opportunity costs and lower the expected return on education. In addition, absence of either one or both parents from the household might also discourage younger generations from obtaining a higher educational degree (McKenzie and Rapoport 2011).

Education might also have a bearing on the migrants' ability/likelihood to send remittances/on their remittance behaviour. Theoretically, the more educated the international migrant, the higher the income and the more they can send back to their families in the countries of origin. However, more educated international migrants from higher socio-economic backgrounds are often accompanied by their families and thus have a lower propensity to send financial remittances back 'home' (Bollard et al. 2011).

Education and second-generation

Both education and training levels of first-generation labour migrants, as well as their formal and informal recognition, have an impact on their children's access to education systems and their educational attainment and ultimately their social position. While early research argued that second-generation would experience a 'downward assimilation' (Portes and Zhou 1993), paradoxically children of immigrants in the United States have been shown to outperform local populations and are labelled as 'overachievers' to the extent that the gap in educational attainment between migrant and non-migrant populations widened (with consequences for social position, social inequalities, and thus, development) (Heath et al. 2008; Lee and Zhou 2015).

However, in Europe, unlike in the US, second-generation migrant groups still do not outperform their non-migrant counterparts in terms of their educational achievements. In studying Western Europe, Turkish and Moroccan first- and second-generation migrants have been widely investigated because they represent the largest and often marginalised groups. When compared to the non-migrants, second-generation migrants in Europe have fundamentally lower educational achievements with higher dropout rates and lower access to higher education than the native-born. (For an extensive and refined review, see Heath et al. 2008.) This academic gap is usually explained by lower socio-economic status of their first-generation immigrant parents, limited language proficiency, educational resources as well as the education infrastructure of the European countries of immigration (Crul and Vermeulen 2003; Pasztor 2014; Song 2011). For instance, investigating Turkish second-generation migrants' educational achievements in Austria, Pasztor (2014) found that seemingly free and open structures of higher education is highly selective and equipped with structural barriers particularly for the second-generation. In addition, Song (2011) found evidence that Turkish second-generation migrants in Austria, Germany, and Switzerland were at a disadvantage in regards to resources at home and at school, which explains their educational achievement gap.

Although, in general, studies pinpoint a significant educational achievement gap in Europe for second-generation migrants, some successes can be found. Focusing on those successful second-generation migrants who achieved upward social mobility in Crul (2000, 2015) argued that social background, the help of siblings and peers, and aspirations together with structural conditions in the education systems and the transition to the labour markets were important factors in explaining their success.

Education of second-generation migrants will continue to be crucial for an understanding of both the achievements and barriers facing immigrant populations over the long-run together with relevant implications for social policy and institutional opportunities. The study of education and the second-generation also has implications for how researchers and policymakers think about migrant incorporation and development in both contexts of immigration and emigration. We know that second-generation migrants have transnational ties and practices (Levitt and Waters 2006). For example, Jain (2013) has argued that transnational ties and cultural affinity, together with the perception of better job opportunities, may have encouraged second-generation Indian-Americans to 'return' to India. This line of research could be expanded in the future to take into account the aspirations and meanings of education, its successes and failures, within the context of families in immigrant communities.

Conclusion

This chapter has outlined three potential relationships between education and international migration: the migration of students and academic personnel; the education of first-generation migrants; and the implications of second-generation status for education in countries of destination. Because education is such a crucial determinant of social position, the aim was to generate further discussion on the reproduction of social (dis)advantage. This chapter argued that social positions, and the ways in which they are evaluated by a variety of actors, are crucial in access to, and distribution of, resources that are crucial to the reproduction of social (dis)advantage. Moreover, values to education and jobs, and thus social positions that were once assigned within national frameworks, are now achieved transnationally, involving multiple actors of individuals, families, communities, employers, institutions, and nation-states. In such an understanding, this chapter gave examples involving cross-border practices tied to education, but also provided a transnational perspective through which social inequalities in different geographies could be discussed.

It is crucial to understand the (e)valuation processes of social positions in the context of education and international migration/mobility within and across different nation-state borders. It is mainly because they are being used to draw social boundaries of who gets what kind of jobs and where that have fundamental implications for migrants' and their families' life chances in both contexts of emigration and immigration. To this end, this chapter gave the example of the recognition of educational credentials: while transferability of degrees is rather a smooth process for some groups such as international students and academics due to standards set by international institutions, for other groups it is rather difficult. Even if the degrees are recognised in the course of international migration, other factors such as other qualifications, experiences, and where the diploma is obtained are also considered in the formal evaluations of the employers. Nevertheless, formal recognition of degrees is not always enough because informally they might not be recognised, for example, by co-workers. This situation has a variety of implications and one of them is traced in the next generations of migrants whose success and social position largely dependent on the previous generation.

Note

1 I would like to thank the editors Tanja Bastia and Ronald Skeldon as well as Thomas Faist and Peggy Levitt for their invaluable comments on the earlier drafts of this chapter.

References

Adepoju A., Van Noorloos F. and Zoomers A. (2010) "Europe's migration agreements with migrant-sending countries in the Global South: a critical review" *International Migration*, 48, 42–75.

Alexis O., Vydelingum V. and Robbins I. (2007) "Engaging with a new reality: experiences of overseas minority ethnic nurses in the NHS" *Journal of Clinical Nursing*, 16, 2221–2228.

Altbach P. and Knight J. (2007) "The internationalization of higher education: motivations and realities" *Journal of Studies in International Education*, 11, 290–305.

Bauder H. (2005) "Institutional capital and labour devaluation: the non-recognition of foreign credentials in Germany" *Journal of Economics*, 2, 75–93.

Bilecen B. and Faist T. (2015) "International doctoral students as knowledge brokers: reciprocity, trust and solidarity in transnational networks" *Global Networks*, 15, 217–235.

Bilecen B. and Van Mol C. (2017) "Introduction: international academic mobility and inequalities" *Journal of Ethnic and Migration Studies*, 43, 1241–1255.

Bollard A., McKenzie D., Morten M. and Rapoport H. (2011) "Remittances and the brain drain revisited: the microdata show that more educated migrants remit more" *World Bank Economic Review*, 25, 132–156.

Bourdieu P. (1984) *Distinction: A Social Critique of the Judgement of Taste*, Cambridge MA: Harvard University Press.

Bourdieu P. (1993) *The Field of Cultural Production*, Cambridge: Polity Press.

Bourdieu P. (1996) *The State Nobility: Elite Schools in the Field of Power*, Cambridge: Polity Press.

Brown P. and Lauder H. (1996) "Education, globalization and economic development" *Journal of Education Policy*, 11, 1–25.

Crul M. (2000) "Breaking the circle of disadvantage. social mobility of second-generation Moroccans and Turks in the Netherlands" in Vermeulen H. and Perlmann J. eds., *Immigrants, Schooling and Social Mobility*, London: Palgrave Macmillan, 225–244.

Crul M. (2015) "Is education the pathway to success? a comparison of second-generation Turkish professionals in Sweden, France, Germany and The Netherlands" *European Journal of Education*, 50, 325–339.

Crul M. and Vermeulen H. (2003) "The Second Generation in Europe" *International Migration Review*, 37, 965–986.

De Haas H. (2012) "The migration and development pendulum: a critical view on research and policy" *International Migration*, 50, 8–25.

Edler J., Fier H. and Grimpe C. (2011) "International scientist mobility and the locus of knowledge and technology transfer" *Research Policy*, 40, 791–805.

Faist T. (2000) *The Volume and Dynamics of International Migration and Transnational Social Spaces*, Oxford: Oxford University Press.

Faist T. (2008) "Migrants as transnational development agents: an inquiry into the newest round of the migration–development nexus" *Population, Space and Place*, 14, 21–42.

Findlay A. (2011) "An assessment of supply and demand-side theorizations of international student mobility" *International Migration*, 49, 2, 162–190.

Findlay A., King R., Smith F.M., Geddes A. and Skeldon R. (2012) "World class? an investigation of globalisation, difference and international student mobility" *Transactions of the Institute of British Geographers*, 37, 118–131.

Heath A.F., Rothon C. and Kilpi E. (2008) "The second generation in Western Europe: education, unemployment, and occupational attainment" *Annual Review of Sociology*, 34, 211–235.

Jain S. (2013) "For love and money: second-generation Indian-Americans 'return' to India" *Ethnic and Racial Studies*, 36, 896–914.

Jöns H. (2009) "'Brain circulation' and transnational knowledge networks: studying long-term effects of academic mobility to Germany, 1954–2000" *Global Networks*, 9, 315–338.

King R. and Ruiz-Gelices E. (2003) "International student migration and the European Year Abroad: effects on European identity and subsequent migration behavior" *International Journal of Population Geography*, 9, 229–252.

Kofman E. and Raghuram P. (2006) "Gender and global labour migrations: incorporating skilled workers" *Antipode*, 38, 282–303.

Lee J. and Zhou M. (2015) *The Asian American Achievement Paradox*, New York: Russell Sage Foundation.

Levitt P. (1999) "Social remittances: a local-level, migration-driven form of cultural diffusion" *International Migration Review*, 32, 926–949.

Levitt P. and Waters M.C. (eds.) (2006) *The Changing Face of Home: The Transnational Lives of the Second-Generation*, New York: Russell Sage Foundation.

Lowell L. and Findlay A. (2001) *Migration of Highly Skilled Persons from Developing Countries: Impact and Policy Responses*, Geneva: ILO.

Martin P., Abella M. and Kuptsch C. (2006) *Managing Labor Migration in the Twenty First Century*, New Haven: Yale University Press.

McKenzie D. and Rapoport H. (2011) "Can migration reduce educational attainment Evidence from Mexico" *Journal of Population Economics*, 24, 1331–1358.

Meyer J., Ramirez F.O. and Soysal Y. (1992) "World expansion of mass education, 1870–1980" *Sociology of Education*, 65, 128–149.

Pasztor A. (2014) "Divergent pathways: the road to higher education for second-generation Turks in Austria" *Race and Ethnicity in Education*, 19, 880–900.

Portes A. and Zhou M. (1993) "The new second generation: segmented assimilation and its variants" *Annals of the American Academy of Political and Social Science*, 530, 74–96.

Saxenian A. (2008) "The international mobility of entrepreneurs and regional upgrading in India and China", in Solimano A. ed., *The International Mobility of Talent: Types, Causes, and Development Impact*, Oxford: Oxford University Press, 117–144.

Scott P. (1997) "The changing role of the university in the production of new knowledge" *Tertiary Education and Management*, 3, 5–14.

Sen A. (1997) *Resources, Values, and Development*, Cambridge MA: Harvard University Press.

Skeldon R. (1997) *Migration and Development. A Global Perspective*, London: Longman.

Skeldon R. (2009) "Of skilled migration, brain drain and policy responses" *International Migration*, 47, 3–29.

Sklair L. (2001) *The Transnational Capitalist Class*, Oxford: Blackwell Publishers.

Song S. (2011) "Second-generation Turkish youth in Europe: explaining the academic disadvantage in Austria, Germany, and Switzerland" *Economics of Education Review*, 30, 938–949.

Todaro M. (1976) *Internal Migration in Developing Countries: A Review of Theory, Evidence, Methodology, and Research Priorities*, Geneva: ILO.

Waters J.L. (2009) "Transnational geographies of academic distinction: the role of social capital in the recognition and evaluation of 'overseas' credentials" *Globalisation, Societies and Education*, 7, 113–129.

Weiss A. (2016) "Understanding physicians' professional knowledge and practice in research on skilled migration" *Ethnicity & Health*, 21, 397–409.

Xiang B. and Shen W. (2009) "International student migration and social stratification in China" *International Journal of Educational Development*, 29, 5, 513–522.

Zimmermann K. (2009) *Labor Mobility and the Integration of European Labor Markets*. Berlin: German Institute for Economic Research, Discussion Paper 862. http://hdl.handle.net/10419/27385.

23

SO MANY HOUSES, AS MANY HOMES?

Transnational housing, migration, and development

Paolo Boccagni[1]

Introduction

Migrants' cross-border housing strategies and practices, and their ways of locating and establishing 'home' across countries, are not the most obvious of topics in the context of migration and development. On the one hand, the building or refurbishment of migrants' houses in the countries of origin has been ethnographically highlighted all across migration systems (e.g. Bivand 2012; López 2015; Smith and Mazzucato 2009). Housing is often mentioned among the main targets for remittance expenditure (Adams et al. 2012; Cohen 2011). On the other hand, migrant real estate investments, as transnational processes at the intersection between their life prospects in different countries, are little studied in their developmental impact. This is unfortunate and even surprising, since remittance-funded houses are a unique way of embodying migrant transnational engagement, with all of its ambiguities. They are also critical to a better understanding of development, both in a descriptive sense (what comes after migration) and in a policy-oriented one (how far social and economic conditions and life opportunities in sending communities are affected by migration).

In terms of the society of origin, remittance houses are a hallmark of migrant claims for visibility, membership and recognition, even while living elsewhere. In terms of the individual migrant, the houses are a visible symbol of their expectations to translate migration into better life opportunities for their families at present, and into a potential safe haven for themselves in the future. At both levels, these houses embody the persistent identification with the country of origin, or parts of it, as *home*: a centre for their life projects and aspirations, regardless whether they will return for good or not. As such, remittance houses are indeed a fundamental aspect of the migration–development interaction and require more systematic and comparative research. While house-building is a matter of household micro and private choices, it has much to say on the broader socio-economic impact of migration. It also illuminates the evolving gap between migrants' dreams and their actual achievements, and between migrants themselves and their homelands, over time.

This chapter provides a conceptual overview of the homebound housing investments of international labour migrants, by considering four aspects:

- the meanings and functions that remittance houses embody in the communities of origin and in migrants' own biographies, which I term 'unpacking the remittance house';
- the ways in which remittances for housing are transnationally allocated and managed or 'from the product to the process';
- the role of institutional actors and of the broader structure of opportunities in shaping migrant transnational building initiatives;
- the mixed significance of these buildings and of the social and economic processes associated with them for the migration–development nexus.

Some final remarks are dedicated to the potential transition from *house-building* to *home-making*, as an indicator of the developmental prospects of the remittance landscape in migrants' countries of origin.

Unpacking the remittance house

A rich literature is available, from a large number of case studies, on the new or improved houses that migrants build in their countries of origin, through their remittances (Boccagni 2017; López 2015). A remarkable continuity exists across migration systems in the prevalence, visibility, and 'atypicality' of these houses, particularly in rural contexts. Most ethnographies of migrants' home communities contain at least some mention to remittance houses and to what makes them distinctive, in several respects (e.g. Aguilar 2009; Bivand 2012; Freeman 2013; Mata-Codesal 2014; Smith and Mazzucato 2009; Van der Horst 2010):

- as ways of embodying and displaying the dreams and aspirations associated with migration;
- as powerful symbols of migrants' simultaneous claim for belonging to the community of origin, and distinction from it;
- as arenas for the reproduction of migrant family life and investments across generations;
- as tangible manifestations of the friction between what/who comes from abroad and what was already there, all the more so when they are left unfinished or unoccupied.

Nonetheless, a comparative and theory-driven approach to the study of remittance houses is yet to be developed, particularly with reference to their architectural patterns, societal functions, and interactions with the larger built and social environment. In fact, an abundance of ethnographic details is available on what these houses look like to the eyes of migrants and their counterparts (including researchers) (Boccagni 2014; Freeman 2013; Grigolini 2005). However, less research has been done on two fundamental aspects: first, what comes *before*, so that the weight and significance of housing among other ways of spending remittances can be appreciated in terms of the interpersonal and institutional mediations required for these houses to be built; second, what comes *after*, or the ways in which these houses are experienced and used, as a more or less effective investment of migrants' savings and a part, for better or worse, of the developmental impact of migration.

Clearly, remittance houses are a research object in themselves, as artefacts and lived spaces, as much as, or even more than, any domestic setting (López 2015; Miller 2001).

A number of questions on domesticity, everyday life, and material culture can be addressed by investigating them, even when they are 'houses in process' or 'not-yet-houses' (Melly 2010). The same holds for migrants' own biographies. These houses are a powerful elicitor of narratives about the migrants themselves and their attitudes to 'home' (Leinaweaver 2009; Sandoval-Cervantes 2017).

That said, less consideration has been given to a systematic reflection on the social and economic processes that precede and follow the material construction of the houses. Such a reflection ideally brings together the bottom-up initiatives of migrants and the transnational structures of opportunity in which they operate. Expanding along these lines is critical to an understanding of the consequences of migrant housing investment in home societies. The influence of remittances-for-housing on local development also has to be considered in the light of public policies, the housing market, and the housing needs and resources of the local populations. The 'place' of house-building in the broader economy of migrant remittances will first be discussed.

From the product to the process: remittances and transnational housing practices

Achieving homeownership is a life-goal for many people (Atkinson and Jacobs 2016) and international labour migrants are no exception. Migration is also a strategy instrumental to such an aim. The construction of new or better houses in home communities is often a core expectation that is at the root of labour migration itself. This tends to be the case, regardless of the outcome. That is, whether the houses are eventually built and inhabited and regardless, too, of their actual location which, as several ethnographies suggest (Melly 2010; Perraudin 2017), is not always in the local community of origin. That community may be perceived as inadequate, possibly for security reasons because violence is endemic, but perhaps more importantly because *internal* mobility towards better locations and opportunities, typically from rural to urban areas, is part of the expected *social* mobility that migration should facilitate. Thus, and as increasingly demonstrated, important links between international and internal migrations exist at many levels (King and Skeldon 2010).

Housing-related expenses, in terms of rent, mortgage or investment, have been shown to be common among remittance recipient households (Maimbo and Ratha 2005; Mezger and Beauchemin 2015). Certainly, the bulk of remittances is generally intended, apart from repaying debts, to finance everyday consumption and welfare, including health and education. Yet, a share is also allocated for less short-term concerns such as housing – and at certain times and places, that share can be even higher (Zachariah et al. 2001). Relevant estimates are highly variable between and even within emigration countries (Saenz 2007) and the argument in the next sections must be somewhat exploratory. It attempts to take stock of the available evidence to open up new research prospects, rather than providing conclusive statements.

Much has already been written on the determinants of migrant remittances and of their uses (Adams et al. 2012; Cohen 2011; De Haas 2007). However, accounting for migrants' investments in housing, rather than for other purposes, deserves more discussion. This will be framed around the idea that the construction of a house is primarily a way of articulating an apparently universal need for belonging, recognition, and respect. More instrumentally, it can be seen as a means to obtain a higher expected return, relative to other potential investments, assuming these alternatives do exist. Where migrants have a high expectation of return in a literal sense, new houses are instrumental to 'secure their membership rights' in the communities of origin (Osili 2004, 826).

Several factors can lead migrants to invest in transnational housing. Status maintenance in terms of displaying migrants' presence-in-absence in a community and preparation for future homecoming are as significant as other drivers, such as the aspiration to homeownership. Equally important and central to the emotional, moral, and material value of these buildings is the influence of kinship. This revolves around family-related obligations to provide housing for family members, including ageing parents and other dependents (see Grigolini 2005 on Mexico, and Kuuire et al. 2016 on Ghana, for example). A new or better house is a marker of achieved adulthood and autonomy for younger cohorts of migrants. It is also an ideal setting for transnational family life, as long as close kin live apart from each other. Migrants can host, or perhaps rent to, family members remaining in the community. In the most 'successful' cases, they rent some flats or buildings, while keeping others for themselves or their kin. Investing remittances in housing, then, is also a way of taking care of left-behind family members, a strategy that reflects a strong pattern of reciprocity. Stayers are expected to take care of the homes of movers, in often gendered ways (Melly 2010; Sandoval-Cervantes 2017). In doing so, they provide a form of reverse remittance, with all of the frailties associated with the negotiation of mutual commitments and obligations over a large distance (Boccagni 2015).

However, migrant transnational housing also has an economic rationality of its own, one that should not be obscured by the bizarre and ostentatious structures of some remittance houses. Neither should we be distracted by the public discourse about them, which is often negative. Remittance houses are fundamentally an investment, both socially (Smith and Mazzucato 2009) and economically (Mezger and Beauchemin 2015). They are a lever for reproducing meaningful relationships over time, while providing a tangible way of investing remittances in contexts where no viable alternatives exist. Whatever their symbolic meanings and implications, these houses have a very pragmatic side. They are expected to be a relatively safe 'deposit' for migrant savings; an insurance mechanism against a background of poor public welfare and unstable credit markets.

Houses, and housing tenure, are also a powerful indicator of social inclusion or exclusion in each locality involved in the migration process. It follows that housing investments over migrants' life trajectories can be appreciated as an entry point into the debate on the interface between integration and transnationalism (Carling and Hoelscher 2013). There is nothing academic in this: the dilemmas of where to allocate the scarce resources available are part and parcel of migrants' everyday lives (Kuuire et al. 2016). Indeed, the interaction between their housing choices and practices in different countries is a key area for more empirical and comparative research. A number of case studies suggest that relatively few migrants can afford both a mortgage 'here' and a new house 'there', within already difficult housing careers. Many more people tend to engage in one of these projects at a time, at best, while leaving the other behind. The temporality of this process is then a critical indicator of migrants' balancing act between integration and transnational engagement. As long as they are able to save money at all, they may well privilege investment in remittance houses during their earlier migration experience, with less of an interest in, and remarkable adaptation to, poor dwelling conditions abroad (Van der Horst 2010). At some point, though, migrants may find this investment to be at odds with their own everyday needs, and with their chances for homeownership in the place where they live most of the time. For housing, no less than for other ways of spending remittances, the potential of transnational resources, and engagement should not go unnoticed. At the same time, it should not be over-estimated or over-stretched, considering migrants' typically disadvantaged life conditions and the expectations to which they are subject from their left-behind counterparts (Boccagni 2015).

Bringing institutional actors in: policies, markets and the migration industry

After considering the family-based moral economies of transnational housing, and the special place of remittance houses in the migrant life course, we move on to examine more institutional factors. Investing in houses, particularly across international borders, is not just a matter of spontaneous bottom-up initiatives. The broader structure of opportunities, including the influence of several transnational and local institutions, also needs consideration. First, governments in sending countries have a role to play. Emigration countries tend to have a strategic interest in cultivating the allegiance and the investments of their citizens abroad. Although research on diaspora policies has received attention at a global scale (Collyer 2013), its relevance to transnational housing has been primarily explored in Latin America. This is what can be inferred from the very few studies of remittance-for-housing programmes, as co-designed initiatives involving national and local authorities, often with the support of international organisations and local partners such as credit unions and housing associations, besides migrants themselves (see, for instance, on Colombia, Zapata 2018; on Mexico, López 2015; on Guatemala and Salvador, Klaufus 2010). As long as diaspora policies channel migrants' remittances into the formal banking system, through dedicated financial products and saving or borrowing schemes, the housing sector is a significant outlet for their investments (Saenz 2007). Indeed, remittance-driven house-building is just an instance of foreign investment being attracted into massive urban construction, and of governmental attempts to reshape housing policies along neoliberal lines (Melly 2010; Zapata 2018). Yet, throughout the literature on migration and development, scant attention has been given to remittance-for-housing programmes. Limited empirical research exists, and little data are available, on the actual take-up and impact of government-led schemes to promote 'diasporic housing'.

However, the relevance of public institutions for migrant transnational housing is not limited to dedicated flagship programmes, which may serve primarily symbolic purposes. It has also to do more fundamentally with the expected aims of housing policy: to design and implement social housing, set and enforce the rules for the housing market and the construction sector, facilitate access to housing credit, and ultimately fix a balance between building anew and recovering the pre-existent housing stock (see Bredenoord et al. [2014] for an overview across the Global South). The characteristics of formal and informal housing markets, and the role, orientations, and impact of public policies in managing them, are the really critical variables for transnational housing.

Whether in housing or in other domains, migrants are an elusive target for public policy in emigration countries. This is not only for their mixed relations with political institutions, or for income levels that make them an unlikely target for basic welfare schemes, but also for their room to manoeuvre within the housing market. Whenever they have enough savings, migrants or returnees may invest in housing anyway, regardless of dedicated public measures and even with little interest in them. As several studies have shown (Page and Sunjo 2018; Zachariah et al. 2001), their housing needs and initiatives generally lie in the grey area of middle-class buildings, more than in that of social housing for low-income households.

For the same reason, migrants are often an ideal target for private construction companies and real estate developers in their countries of origin (Klaufus 2010). This calls for more empirical analysis of the interaction between transnational building projects and local housing dynamics and conflicts. The weight of remittance housing on the local demand for craftsmen, bricklayers, and less specialised labour is also an obvious topic for further research (López 2015; Page and Sunjo 2018). Less obvious, but equally remarkable, is that migration-driven building may enlarge and transnationalise the field of housing players, well beyond the dyad of migrants (or their left-behind counterparts) vs construction companies.

The construction or refurbishment of a house from afar is a complex endeavour and one exposed to moral and financial hazards, as is so often the case with cross-border social practices in general (Grigolini 2005; Osili 2004). Against this background, institutional and transnational actors such as remittance and banking agencies may do more than channel a share of migrant money: they can play an active role as managers of migrant investments, including for housing purposes. Transnational construction companies may also act for family members left behind in cases of major misconduct. For example, the labour migrant who, after remitting for years for a new house, returns only to find that there is no house or that someone else has occupied it. Against the failures of informal networks, the mediation of formal agencies, whereby contract replaces personal trust, is an option. This is all the more the case if migrants have little control in their countries of origin, or little chance to return there, due to their undocumented status. It may then happen that, for instance, Mexican migrants in the United States purchase building materials in Los Angeles and Chicago (to be delivered in subsidy shops in Mexico), or engage with architecture or design studios in the US, rather than relying on kin, friends, or other contact persons in their own communities of origin (Hernández León 2012; López 2015). Aside from all other considerations, this can be expected to reduce the multiplier effect of migrant housing expenditure, as long as key steps of the building process, such as designing and providing technical equipment, are no longer located in their sending countries.

No matter the plans transnational migrants might have for housing in their places of origin, the influence of the opportunity structure in the countries of settlement, legally, socially, and economically, is also a major issue. There is little point in exploring migrant contribution to development in the countries of origin without assessing their evolving position 'abroad', including their dwelling conditions and tenure. Hence an assessment of their income and assets and the potential ways of spending them needs to be made. This holds true at any moment of their migration trajectories and, most notably, whenever they make upward or downward moves in their residential, housing, and labour market careers and have to rearrange their transnational commitments accordingly, in light of the resources available to them. It is then an empirical question of how distinct, potentially conflictive housing needs and aspirations 'here' and 'there' interact with each other over time, parallel to migrants' individual and family life course.

Migrant house-building and development: a conceptual revisit

Returning to the broader debate on migration and development, the available research suggests that the place of transnational housing is variable, context-dependent, and ultimately mixed. It cannot be reduced to the dichotomy between 'productive' and 'unproductive ways' of spending migrants' capital (Melly 2010; Smith and Mazzucato 2009). Rather, it calls for a systemic understanding of the political and economic conditions of emigration countries, rather than for a focus on the housing issue alone.

From an analytical point of view, the developmental significance of remittance houses invites a threefold transition in approaching the migration–development nexus: first, from the *individual* level of remittance recipient households, to the *collective* level of the surrounding communities, with a focus on the often limited transferability of private wealth into the public domain; second, from the *infrastructural* dimension of the remittance landscape, the developmental relevance of which is clear from the revitalisation of the local economy, to the actual utilisation of the house as a *lived space*; third, from the *present* to the *future*, or from a static view of the built environment, to the projects that the building of remittance houses enables over time.

In a symbolic sense, the construction of remittance houses tells us much about development in the very places in which they are built. If migration is inherently a future-oriented project, these houses, occupied or not, well-finished, incomplete, or dilapidated, are a unique mirror of migrants' 'attempt to "spatialise" their hopes for the future' (Sandoval-Cervantes 2017, 210). They are a powerful image, first, of how 'successful' migration was for the households involved and, second, of how 'homebound' or not the migrants tend to be over time (Boccagni 2014). Migration-related advances and migrants' interest in keeping connected with their homelands are made critically visible by these houses. At least from the point of view of the communities of origin, remittance-based buildings embody and display the promise of material improvement associated with migration, as much as they epitomise the 'failure' of migration-driven social mobility whenever they are half-finished or in disrepair.

If migration-driven development is based on gaining greater investment capacities (than before, and relative to non-migrants) (Mezger and Beauchemin 2015), well-finished remittance houses indicate that such a capacity has been gained. Thus, remittance houses can be appreciated as 'the first stage of a broader investment relationship between migrants and their countries of origin' (Osili 2004, 844). Whether this leads to further investments with income-generating potential is however a different question. Among other things, their transformation into properties with a significant investment value as financial assets, rather than dwellings (Guyer 2015), is unlikely to take place where the broader economic and political context is not stable.

As most ethnographic research shows, remittance houses are not generally occupied by migrants themselves, unless on an intermittent basis or after retirement. It is exactly the *absence* of the owners that enables the *presence* of these new and distinctive buildings (López 2015). As long as this is the case, remittance houses can be appreciated as a visible embodiment of *dependence* on migration, rather than of new forms of endogenous development stemming out of it.

At an individual or a household level, remittance houses are there to show that a symbolic and material investment in the homeland has been made: migrants 'voted with their bricks' in favour of it, just as they 'voted with their feet' against it when they moved away. Through their housing initiatives, migrants pave the way for the investment, accumulation, and intergenerational transmission of the wealth they made abroad. They also enable left-behind kin to enjoy better dwelling conditions, or gain extra-income by becoming landlords, besides creating the pre-conditions for their own return. Lastly, they exert at least some spill-over effect on the local economy and labour market. Furthermore, migrants' transnational housing can reach beyond the reconstruction of their own private dwellings. It can also result in new or better *public* buildings and infrastructures such as schools, hospitals, leisure facilities, and so on. This is a highly celebrated, context-dependent and relatively infrequent development, as the literature on collective remittances has shown (e.g. Goldring 2004; López 2015).

Once these premises have been made, however, the construction of new and better houses as a result of migration has no straightforward correlation with broader trends in social and economic development in regions of origin. Indeed, the cumulation of private wealth (via housing) does not necessarily make for better housing or living conditions in the public realm, out of the circles of remittance recipients.

Remittance houses, therefore, are only one aspect of the broader housing question, just as migration is one aspect of social change in home communities. At either level, international migration is a highly visible influence, and a catalyst for all sorts of social representations. Its causal powers, nonetheless, should not be over-emphasised. Remittance houses are typically a middle-class option; or, at most, an embodiment of social mobility for migrants with a working-class (and/or rural) background. They can hardly be a solution for deep-rooted questions of housing affordability – no more than remittances can be a solution for urban or rural poverty on a large scale (rather than only for recipient households). This is not a marginal point, in light of all that has been written on remittances as 'panacea for development'. More recently, this celebratory approach has been increasingly criticised, for it disregards the need for more effective and better resourced public policies. By the same token, migrant houses should not be blamed for failing to address an issue, the lack of affordable housing, which is simply out of their remit, as a private investment. Generally speaking, one can hardly deny that migrant transnational housing tends to enhance 'spatial social segregation, visibly increasing inequality, and new scales of intergenerational transfers of wealth and privilege' (Page and Sunjo 2018, 6). In all of these respects, though, the diffusion of remittance houses is a mirror of the limitations and weaknesses of public governance – not the cause of it.

Overall, a disjuncture can be traced between the mainly positive economic effects of transnational housing at a micro level, and more mixed consequences on larger scales. There is a remarkable 'disconnection between the improved livelihoods that households acquire through migration, particularly through their ability to materialise their dream of homeownership, and the macro-level political, social, and economic policies needed to transform the structural conditions of migrant-sending localities' (Zapata 2018, 2). Even when the migrant 'dream house' comes true, its prevalent location in areas with poor public facilities and infrastructures is emblematic in this sense.

To conclude: from house-building to home-making

If the meanings and implications of remittance houses for the migration–development nexus are context-dependent, more empirical research on them is needed. Yet, within the burgeoning field of remittance studies, the comparative study of migrant housing and of its consequences over time is still rare. Against this background, the way ahead for research on transnational housing and development would also benefit from a distinctive optic, which borrows from 'home studies' (Blunt and Dowling 2007; Boccagni 2017). In order to better understand the development significance of remittance houses, one could empirically investigate their potential transition from houses to homes – or, from objects of house-building to venues and channels of home-making. The real question is if and how these houses are viewed and felt like homes at all by those inhabiting them. Whenever they are indeed experienced as home-like spaces, and taken care of as such, they do create a background for migrants to be fruitfully connected to their homelands, even while living elsewhere most of the time. They are also a privileged setting for the materialisation and diffusion of social remittances: the processes whereby particular home-related values, styles, and architectural patterns, encountered in migrants' countries of destination, are reproduced and brought back – in more or less hybridised and stereotyped ways – into the housing arrangements of their countries of origin (López 2015; Melly 2010).

Migrants' remittance houses, to conclude, are *not* a source of development in themselves, unless in the sense discussed above. They are, however, an implicit precondition for it: the background and the starting point for all forms of social and economic development associated with migration. Wherever they are left unoccupied, not taken care of, or dilapidated – wherever they do not turn into *homes* – a clear warning is there of the dubious prospects for local development, at least as a consequence of international migration.

Note

1 This project has received funding from the European Research Council (ERC) under the European Union's Horizon 2020 research and innovation programme (grant agreement No. 678456).

References

Adams R., et al. (2012) *Migrant remittances and development: Research perspectives*, New York: SSRC Web Anthology, 2nd Edition.

Aguilar F. (2009) "Labour migration and ties of relatedness: diasporic houses and investments in memory in a rural Philippine village", *Thesis Eleven*, 98(1): 88–114.

Atkinson R., Jacobs K. (2016) *House, home and society*, London: Palgrave.

Bivand M. (2012) "A place to stay in Pakistan: why migrants build houses in their countries of origin", *Population, Space and Place*, 18(5): 629–641.

Blunt A., Dowling R. (2007) *Home*, London: Routledge.

Boccagni P. (2014) "What's in a migrant house? Changing domestic spaces, the negotiation of belonging and home-making in Ecuadorian migration", *Housing, Theory and Society*, 31(3): 277–293.

Boccagni P. (2015) "Burden, blessing or both? On the mixed role of transnational ties in migrant informal social support", *International Sociology*, 30(3): 250–268.

Boccagni P. (2017) *Migration and the search for home*, New York: Palgrave.

Bredenoord J., Van Lindert P., Smets P. eds. (2014) *Affordable housing in the global urban south*, London: Routledge.

Carling J., Hoelscher K. (2013) "The capacity and desire to remit: comparing local and transnational influences", *Journal of Ethnic and Migration Studies*, 39(6): 939–958.

Cohen J. (2011) "Migration, remittances and household strategies", *Annual Review of Anthropology*, 40: 103–114.

Collyer M. ed. (2013) *Emigration nations: Policies and ideologies of emigrant engagement*, Basingstoke: Palgrave.

De Haas H. (2007) "Remittances, migration and social development", UNRISD paper no. 34/2007.

Freeman L. (2013) "Separation, connection and the ambiguous nature of émigré houses in rural highland Madagascar", *Home Cultures*, 10(2): 93–110.

Goldring L. (2004) "Family and collective remittances to Mexico", *Development and Change*, 35(4): 799–840.

Grigolini S. (2005) "When houses provide more than shelter: Analyzing the use of remittances within their sociocultural context", in Trager L. (ed.), *Migration and economy*, pp. 193–224, Oxford: Altamira Press.

Guyer J. (2015) "Housing as 'capital'", *HAU*, 5(1): 495–500.

Hernández León R. (2012) "La industria de la migración en el sistema migratorio México-Estados Unidos", *TRACE*, 61: 41–61.

King R., Skeldon R. (2010) "'Mind the gap': integrating approaches to internal and international migration", *Journal of Ethnic and Migration Studies*, 36(10): 1619–1646.

Klaufus C. (2010) "Watching the city grow: remittances and sprawl in intermediate Central American cities", *Environment and Urbanization*, 22(1): 125–137.

Kuuirc V., et al. (2016) "Obligations and expectations: perceived relationship between transnational housing investment and housing consumption decisions among Ghanaian immigrants in Canada", *Housing, Theory and Society*, 33(4): 445–468.

Leinaweaver J. (2009) "Raising the roof in the transnational Andes: building houses, forging kinship", *Journal of the Royal Anthropological Institute*, 15: 777–796.

López S. (2015) *The remittance landscape: Spaces of migration in rural Mexico and urban USA*, Chicago: University of Chicago Press.

Maimbo S., Ratha D. (2005) *Remittances: Development impact and future prospects*, Washington, DC: The World Bank.

Mata-Codesal D. (2014) "From 'mud houses' to 'wasted houses': remittances and housing in rural highland Ecuador", *REMHU*, 22(42): 263–280.

Melly C. (2010) "Inside-out houses: urban belonging and imagined futures in Dakar, Senegal", *Comparative Studies in Society and History*, 52(10): 37–65.

Mezger C. K., Beauchemin C. (2015) "The role of international migration experience for investment at home: direct, indirect and equalising effects in Senegal", *Population, Space and Place*, 21: 535–552.

Miller D. ed. (2001) *Home possessions: Material culture behind closed doors*, London: Bloomsbury.

Osili U.O. (2004) "Migrants and housing investments", *Economic Development and Cultural Change*, 52(4): 821–849.

Page B., Sunjo E. (2018) "Africa's middle class: building houses and constructing identities in the small town of Buea, Cameroon", *Urban Geography*, 39(1): 75–103.

Perraudin A. (2017) Home ownership as an investment in the country of origin, paper given at the HOMInG kick-off meeting *Researching home and migration*, University of Trento, June.

Saenz M. (2007) *Framing the debate: Use of family remittances for housing finance*, Atlanta: Habitat for Humanity International, Working paper.

Sandoval-Cervantes I. (2017) "Uncertain futures: the unfinished houses of undocumented migrants in Oaxaca, Mexico", *American Anthropologist*, 119(2): 209–222.

Smith L., Mazzucato V. (2009) "Constructing homes, building relationships", *Tijdschrift Voor Economische En Sociale Geografie*, 100(5): 662–673.

Van der Horst H. (2010) "Dwellings in transnational lives: a biographical perspective on 'Turkish–Dutch' houses in Turkey", *Journal of Ethnic and Migration Studies*, 36(7): 1175–1192.

Zachariah K., et al. (2001) "Impact of migration on Kerala's economy and society", *International Migration*, 39(1): 63–87.

Zapata G. (2018) "Transnational migration, remittances and the financialization of housing in Colombia", *Housing Studies*, 33(3): 343–360.

24

SOCIAL PROTECTION, DEVELOPMENT, AND MIGRATION

Challenges and prospects

Rachel Sabates-Wheeler

Introduction

Globally 244 million people are currently estimated to be living in a country other than that of their birth.[1] This group of people includes wealthier migrants, able to access high levels of livelihood security and protection in their place of destination, as well as those moving away from situations of extreme poverty and insecurity, who are often unprotected upon their arrival, and may lack documents to establish resident or work status in the country they currently live in. All of these mobile groups of people experience vulnerabilities at different points of their journeys and all have the need for social protection and access to social services – whether this is provided through official means or through less formal relation-based networks. The topic of welfare provision for migrants is not new and covers a range of issues from social cohesion, integration, access to basic services, health, and education (Bommes and Geddes 2000; Castles and Davidson 2000; Castles and Miller 2003; Schierup et al. 2006). However, it is only in recent years that social protection, a sub-area of the broader welfare agenda, has started to struggle with how to cater for migrants and forcibly displaced groups (Sabates-Wheeler 2009; Sabates-Wheeler and Feldman 2011). Social protection is often framed as an instrument-based agenda for dealing with vulnerability. So, for instance, safety nets for the poorest in the form of cash transfers and consumption support; and social insurance mechanisms for the less poor, yet vulnerable, in the form of pensions, unemployment, and maternity benefits. Social protection does not extend to the whole range of policies and initiatives offered under the traditional social welfare sectors of health and education.

In line with the emergence of the human rights-based approach and the resilience development paradigm some 10 years ago, we might have anticipated the opening of an economic and political space for discussing, catering for, and providing social provision for vulnerable mobile groups. Recently quite the opposite sentiment has prevailed: the space for thinking about migrants' rights is being squeezed as nationalism, the rise of far-right politics, and populist concerns about 'floods' of migrants dominate political discussion, particularly in the west. These sentiments stand in contrast with the 'leave no one behind' agenda dominating the sustainable development goals (SDGs). It is precisely this tension, in the context of increasing migrant numbers and uncertain welfare provision, that necessitates action on the part of social scientists, development professionals, policymakers, and civil society groups to think through, lobby for, and demonstrate sustainable social protection solutions for migrants and forcibly displaced populations.

The term 'migrants' is being used here in its broadest possible sense, to include all types of mobile groups: labour migrants, forcibly displaced persons, refugees, and IDPs. The author recognises the distinctions between these groups (as reviewed in Long and Sabates-Wheeler 2017). However, the purpose of this paper is to highlight the commonalities in social protection needs that these groups experience. Where differences exist, the paper will be specific about the group being discussed.

This chapter will reflect on the last 10–15 years of research and attention given to the linkages between social protection and migration. The timeframe is chosen to coincide with the rise in the interest on social protection, particularly in the Global South. Of course, the provision of welfare for migrants has been a topic of research for a much longer time and overlaps in some ways with this work. However, the marked rise of social protection to the status of what is now arguably dubbed as a 'new development paradigm' (Elkins et al. 2015) justifies more focused attention. I will describe some of the challenges that 'migration' introduces into the relationship between development and social protection. I do this in order to promote a more progressive framing of social provision, one that encourages us to pay attention to the design and delivery of social protection such that migrants and displaced populations are able to live and pursue livelihoods with dignity and in line with their universal human rights.

The rise of social protection

The rise of social protection as a policy response to vulnerability and chronic poverty has been remarkable (see Barrientos and Hulme 2008; Devereux and Sabates-Wheeler 2004; Gentilini and Omamo 2011; Surender and Walker 2013). Following the financial and food crises of the 1980s, international development agencies have taken centre stage on the global social protection agenda, particularly in Africa and Asia. While many governments in the Global South were initially sceptical about the cost implications of taking on social protection at such a scale, in recent years many of the same governments have been formulating, instituting, and investing in social protection policies, strategies, and systems. Most of these policies contain national-level mandates for coverage and provision. A review of the policy arena shows that social protection is increasingly being seen as an important government mandate, justified on the basis of productive inclusion, poverty reduction, and livelihoods strengthening. As pointed out by Sabates-Wheeler and Devereux (2018), the impetus for this change in 'global' attitude and attention comes from four main directions:

1) increased political attention to the importance of equity in promoting stability;
2) improvements in technology that enables more accurate and efficient identification and targeting of the most vulnerable people;
3) increased number and duration of disasters and crises;
4) greater momentum behind coherence, integration and government ownership agendas.

(2018, 10)

A number of approaches for justifying the provision of social protection exist. Risk-based framings focus on the ability of different social protection instruments to manage or prevent negative outcomes from shocks and hazards (Holzmann et al. 2003). Rights-based models emphasise social security and protection as legally enshrined human rights that every person should have (UNICEF 2012), while justice-based approaches stress the ethical view that all people should have access to social protection, but especially the most poor and vulnerable. Regardless of the framing, there is agreement that social protection should comprise two core functions of 'protection' and 'prevention'. 'Protection' usually refers to safety nets and social assistance, while 'prevention' describes social insurance mechanisms such as contributory social security schemes for employed workers. The 'promotive' function is commonly included within social protection policies and programmes, as this emphasises the ability of social protection to support the building of sustainable and resilient livelihoods. For instance, cash transfers can be used to promote education and health uptake, which can have long-term positive development impacts. There is less agreement on the 'transformative' function. Social protection policies and programmes can be 'transformative' if they address the structural determinants of poverty and insecurity (see Devereux and Sabates-Wheeler 2004 for a full description of these functions).

As a policy response to vulnerability, the provision of social protection has obvious relevance to the lives and livelihoods of migrants and forcibly displaced people. Clearly, these groups face many of the same risks and hazards as anyone else in the population. However, they also face migrant-specific risks, such as those related to their registration, citizenship status, and language barriers. Other migrant-specific vulnerabilities relate to the spatial dislocation associated with mobility and transit. Spatial dislocation, and the remoteness of transit migrations in particular, make it very difficult for the government to provide formal social protection schemes. Furthermore, some risks are intensified for migrants due to the fact that migrants may be disproportionally located in ghettos, camps, or in sectors where work practices and living arrangements are unsafe. For instance, migrants tend to be over-represented in informal sectors, and therefore any vulnerability affecting this sector will disproportionately affect migrants. Migrant-specific disadvantage applies by virtue of having migrated. Migrant-intensified disadvantage occurs when a negative outcome is intensified for a migrant (see Sabates-Wheeler and Waite 2003, for a full discussion of these vulnerabilities).

Social protection, development, and migration

As economies develop and grow the nature of social protection provision changes. For the sake of illustration, take a simplistic version of societal and economic transformation; it is clear that in pre-industrial societies the extended family/clan provided basic survival strategies and safety nets for members that were unable to provide for themselves. This holds true when we look back at the history of highly developed countries, but it is also true of regions and countries that still, today, share characteristics similar to those of pre-industrial societies. For instance, in the pastoralist areas of Ethiopia and northern Kenya we see that, even with the provision of basic social assistance from the government and the development community, clan-based sharing and provision constitute the norm of protection (Sabates-Wheeler et al. 2013). But, as the basis of economy and society shift, the family changes towards a less extended, more nuclear unit, and the state in its various forms takes on greater responsibility for social provision. This also coincides with a structural transition from agricultural to urban-based living where the cash economy becomes increasingly relevant as a means of exchange and service provision (see Rostow 1959; Timmer 2009). Forms of social assistance and social insurance are required to fill the space left in the absence of familial support or as relation-based provision becomes overburdened as population increases and employability, especially of the rural poor, lags behind employment possibilities provided by an emerging non-rural sector. This absence of support is particularly obvious in situations of conflict and fragility, especially where family and community support structures are weakened. Whether 'official' provision is state-led or international/humanitarian-led will depend on the capacity and willingness of those states to respond in such situations.

In advanced stages of development, the formal, private sector emerges as both a complementary and alternative provider of services and basic needs provision, with markets emerging for health, old-age insurance, and education. Furthermore, occupation-linked benefits expand as the formal sector grows. These social protection instruments are largely related to the growth of the formal labour market and other private markets. Dorward et al. (2006) develop a framework to show how social protection interventions evolve as the agricultural sector becomes more commercialised and economic growth takes off. Other empirically-informed literature reviews the differences between social policy instruments in highly industrialised countries and in developing countries (Walker 2013).

Generally speaking, then, there is an empirically observed relationship between economic development and the evolution, emergence, and type of social protection provision – with a move from predominantly extended family and clan-based provision, to the state and NGO sector and then in later stages to the market as a significant provider. In other words, development brings the state and market into the picture: and as the state extends its influence, the protection regime changes. Development itself, and the associated increasing concentration of people in urban areas, is likely to be a causal factor in the demand for formal, official social protection. Furthermore, it may be easier for the state and market to provide that protection to concentrated, rather than geographically scattered populations.[2]

The challenges that migration brings to social protection provision in a differing-stages-of-development scenario

Complicating this linear national economic transformation story, is the fact that each country is at a different stage in this process. Social protection contexts are very different. Winder Rossi et al (2016) specify five categories of social protection system maturity based on state capacity, and flexibility to respond. The categories range from a case in which the provision of social protection is completely absent (e.g. Somalia), to a situation in which the social protection system is flexible and able to respond in an appropriate and efficient manner after a shock (e.g. Kenya). The social protection strategies and interventions vary widely according the specific contexts at local level.

Now, what happens when we introduce human mobility and migration into the development story described above? There are some obvious (and some less obvious) conclusions to be drawn about social protection provision and access. Below we identify challenges to providing social protection for mobile populations within a dynamic development perspective.

i. *Differential levels of maturity of social protection systems across countries*

Migrants move between countries and hence between distinctively regulated labour markets and social security systems, which creates specific provision challenges and vulnerabilities.

a. Portability problems: portability of social security rights is important to migrants to avoid financial losses, but also to social security institutions out of concerns of actuarial fairness.

Portability ensures the ability to preserve, maintain, and transfer vested social security rights or rights in the process of being vested, independent of nationality and country of residence (Cruz 2004; Holzman et al. 2005). The research and policy in this area has focused predominantly on regular labour migration and higher-income labour migrants who were tied to formal labour markets and, therefore, had accrued various types of insurance payments, whether for health or old age. They, and their 'sending' countries, had a vested interest in ensuring these savings were accessible regardless of their country of residence or nationality. One concern is how better to facilitate movement of labour both across international orders as well as internally within national states. The World Bank, and others (particularly legal scholars), led a substantial amount of work in the early 2000s detailing the legal and economic contexts and conditions by which the social security and pensions payments can become portable across different countries or groups of countries, such as the EU, CARICOM, and MERCOSUR.

Other researchers, interested in the plight of labour migrants from poor regions of the Global South, focused their attention on replicating this 'portability' research by conducting case studies of poorer regions and countries (Avato et al. 2010; Olivier and Kalula 2004). Overall, provision of formal social protection for South–South migrants is not well developed. Hence, while a regional bloc, such as the EU, might have very successful regional agreements the replicability of these agreements to less developed countries/ regions, such as ECOWAS, stumbles on a number of grounds. First, success requires a fair degree of homogeneity between countries' social systems. Second, these systems need to be well developed so that it is easier to connect and coordinate financial transfers and insurance products. Third, the capacity to administer agreements, including record-keeping, tracking contributions and actuarial operations, must be well developed (Sabates-Wheeler and Feldman 2011).

Given these requirements and the technical and administrative barriers to setting up portable systems of payments, together with the fact that only around 23 per cent of labour migrants (mainly North–North) are actually in occupations that enable them to accrue such payments (Avato et al. 2010), the actual numbers of lower-income migrants that benefit from such arrangements is likely to be minimal. Clearly, for scholars and policymakers interested in the plight of low-income labour migrants as well as forcibly displaced populations, a focus on portability of accrued benefits is unsatisfying and misplaced.

b. Access barriers: even when social protection is available for migrants, access to it can be extremely challenging for mobile populations as they move across administrative boundaries. This includes access to health care benefits, long-term social security benefits like old-age and disability benefits, and short-term benefits like social assistance, maternity and unemployment benefits, family and housing allowances, as well as public housing and education. Migrants often do not fully benefit from these provisions, either because access is only granted sometime after arrival, if at all, or because family members are spread across various countries. In addition, it is clear that the rights of different migrants and displaced groups will be governed by a range of national and international laws and conventions, which can be incredibly difficult to navigate. These are not discussed in detail here but see Long and Sabates-Wheeler (2017) for a review of legal frameworks relevant for social protection and related to different migrant statuses.

Other access constraints hinge on the socio-cultural determinants of vulnerability for migrants, reflected in differences in the norms, values, and customs which constitute local constructions of the 'migrant'. These constructions are often interwoven with culturally held notions of race, gender, and illegality, which can constrain the nature of migrants' participation in labour markets (obviously depending on different categories of migrants and demographic characteristics). That is, social constraints may militate against migrants taking up certain occupations. This is likely to hamper migrants' search for employment, especially in situations of recession and unemployment. Outside of the labour market, perceptions of the 'other' promote barriers to social integration and promote the ghetto-isation of refugees and other displaced groups. These socio-cultural constraints can lead migrants to be relatively excluded from access to public goods, such as health and educa-tion, and from civic engagement.

ii. *Mobility between equally deficient social protection systems*

The most disadvantaged migrants are those moving within low-income regions. In these regions, formal social security provisions are less developed, and migration is often character-ised by high numbers of undocumented migrants. Furthermore, most migrants (as well as local people) work in the informal sector and live in informal settlements; hence, they have limited eligibility to access social protection schemes linked to formal employment, even where these exist. It is no surprise that southern countries have little to offer with respect to portability of benefits. Most benefits are tax-financed social assistance benefits and social security often relies primarily on provident funds, if there are any. The weak development of social security provisions in low-income countries and the lack of administrative capacity are likely to be the reasons why poorer countries are not in a position to engage in bilateral or multilateral negotiations regarding the social security for their emigrants. Since the large majority of emigrants from low-income countries go to other low- or lower-middle-income countries, the concern is not so much how developing countries can coordinate with high-income countries in order to enhance the social security of their emigrants, but how low-income countries can coordinate among themselves to enhance the social protection of South–South migrants.

The plight of refugees and forcibly displaced people is of particular relevance here. Refu-gees, for instance, frequently move from places with shattered or non-existent social protec-tion systems to locations with only slightly better provision (for instance, refugees moving from Burundi to Tanzania, where national social protection systems are nascent but access for refugees is heavily restricted). Displaced populations or poorer labour migrants might move from weak social protection contexts to destinations where systems have the ability to accommodate shocks and stresses (such as, migrants from Malawi to South Africa), but they may lack formal documentation, limiting their access (see Sabates-Wheeler 2011, for an example of this). Moreover, some states will simply refuse to recognise welfare responsibil-ities for certain categories of migrants (see Section iii below).

It is precisely because of this lack of provision, that extra-governmental organisations, development agencies and NGOs have developed a range of social protection provisions to ease the livelihood transition and adaptation of migrants, refugees, and other forcibly dis-placed people. One important future focus of social protection for migrants and those in need of international protection, both in places of origin and destination, is to investigate ways in which the international community might support and strengthen the development of national social protection systems and reduce dependency upon funding-contingent short-term programming that in practice becomes a long-term substitute for effective state-based social protection.

In fact, social protection programmes are increasingly being designed, and re-designed, with contingency funds and plans to be able to scale up in the event of seasonal or recurrent crises (Slater and Bhuvanendra 2013). Shock-responsive social protection means that programmes and systems are designed to be able to respond to what is traditionally understood as an 'emergency' by the humanitarian community: a covariate shock that affects a large number of people at once, such as a natural disaster (OPM 2015). Much of the institutional architecture required for a shock-responsive system is identical to that established for an existing social protection system. For instance, in the event of a sudden drought, in order to address an increased caseload of food-insecure people, trigger events, pre-registration of potential beneficiaries, delivery systems, beneficiary identification systems, etc., must all be in place so that response is timely and efficient. This is a relatively new area of work within the social protection arena, yet there have been some successful cases (in Kenya and Ethiopia) of contingency planning and the ability of the system to scale up and out in the context of an emergency.

An often-overlooked aspect of the provision of social protection for refugees and/or poor migrants is the complex relationship between migrants and host communities. In situations of substantial influxes of refugees, such as in the Kosovar–Albanian crisis of 1999, it is possible that the refugee population, on average, has more financial liquidity at their disposal than the host population. That is, the local host population may be very poor. Cash or food transfers and social support targeted only to the refugee population can further exacerbate this economic difference, causing social and economic tension between the two groups. This can lead to local price hikes and a two-tier market for host and refugee populations, as well as conflict and unrest. Governments and communities can try to minimise these tensions through various social cohesion initiatives, and also through extending provision of social protection to the host community in addition to the refugee community. Recent work by Hagen-Zanker et al. (2017) on the impacts of a cash transfer for Syrian refugees in Jordan shows that the Jordanian government has a policy that requires equitable provision of support to both refugees and host populations. This is not a policy that relates to the government's responsibility, but to extra-state provision that ensures that any provision incorporates Jordanian citizens as beneficiaries. This is one way of helping to resolve local tensions.

iii.   *Ambiguous rights in relation to a state*

Migrants often live and gain a living outside the parameters of the state. At times they strategically choose how to interact with state provisioning and negotiate other regimes of provision that may be transnational, cross-border, charity-based, or non-formal. However, more often, migrants and displaced populations are purposely excluded from welfare systems and social protection initiatives, due to both political and cultural motives. Neither welfare regime analysis nor social protection frameworks attend to the plight of migrants and their relation to welfare. This is largely because these framings do not incorporate institutional, social, and political barriers to welfare provision, which are characteristics of migrant-specific vulnerability.

Socio-political determinants of vulnerability refer to the institutional constraints facing migrants and typically reflect the lack of political commitment from the destination government/society to the migrant. This type of vulnerability is especially pronounced for illegal migrants and forcibly displaced populations, who by definition are excluded from participation in political life, from access to legal institutions, and also from social and economic benefits. The exclusionary processes resulting from this determinant of vulnerability often causes the migrant to become further marginalised over time and prone to exploitation and discrimination, leading to a spiral into poverty. Furthermore, governments may actively discourage legalisation of certain categories of migrants and forcibly displaced peoples so that the economy is able to benefit from access to cheap (exploited) labour.

National social protection systems are predicated on citizen–state contracts, whereby citizens can, theoretically, appeal to legally enshrined rights to a minimum level of welfare provision and social protection. When citizens move beyond state boundaries, these rights come into question (as explained in relation to portability arrangements). These boundaries may be international boundaries, such that a right to free health care in the UK does not translate to free health care in Bangladesh; but they can also be internal, administrative boundaries. MacAuslan (2011) describes the plight of Indian migrants' access to the Public Distribution System (PDS). He describes the substantial challenges facing internal migrants in terms of their access to the PDS in the event that the move across state boundaries. A similar story told by Pong (2014) from her extensive fieldwork in four suburban districts of Bejing, illustrates the politically imposed constraints to rural–urban migrants when attempting to access education for their children. The *hukou* system of residence implies that the educational rights of rural populations are not easily transferable to urban areas. This case shows very vividly the way in which governments are able to use residency and boundaries to designate rights and responsibilities. The response has been the setting up of private schools by migrants in destination areas. However, the state, even if it accepts these schools, still retains control over the access to the nationally recognised examinations that must be taken in the place of *hukou* registration. In summary, the national political appetite for provision of social protection to non-citizens is a huge challenge to supporting the inclusion of migrants into national distribution systems.

iv.   *Limited social protection design and distribution options for mobile populations*

While domestic migration that is stimulated through national structural transformation might concentrate populations and help to facilitate social protection provision among poorer people, certain types of migration mean that people become more scattered and dislocated from social protection provision. This is particularly the case in situations of conflict or protracted crisis, where people may be on the move, or geographically remote or dislocated. It is also the case for internally mobile population groups, such as pastoralists. It is much more difficult to organise social protection among dispersed populations, especially if they are dispersed across administrative and national boundaries.

Mobility raises specific challenges for social protection design and delivery, ones that are not adequately dealt with in mainstream social protection provision. For instance, how is it possible to target and register people on the move? Which organisation or country will be responsible for registering them and updating the registry? An interesting example of these challenges can be seen in the roll out of Ethiopia's Productive Safety Net Programme (PSNP) to the lowland pastoralist areas of Ethiopia. Pastoralist households are characterised by the mobility of the household head and some adult males, with the herd, over large tracts of land and over long periods of time. Setting up the PSNP in the lowland areas required that all vulnerable households were registered and that the designated household representative (typically the male head of household) be available to come to a 'local' collection point on a bi-monthly basis to pick up the food transfer. Difficulties in registering households emerge due the absence of the head of household (given that they are out with the herds), the movement of the household and also use to the high levels of insecurity and conflict in a number of the districts. Furthermore, if households prioritise receipt of the food transfer, the requirement for household heads to be present at a specific collection point means that usual mobility and herd pasturing patterns would be severely disrupted. On the other hand, some mobile groups might deliberately choose to opt out of the programme as their livelihoods are not conducive to sedentarisation (see Scott 2009). Moreover, survey evaluation that requires interviews with households is very complicated and costly due in large part to the process of locating the migrant. This relatively straightforward case illustrates the large challenges that human mobility/migration has for the design of social protection. This is an example of a voluntary internally mobile group. These problems are exacerbated for internationally mobile and forcibly displaced.

Another challenge of delivering social transfers to migrants and forcibly displaced peoples is the lack of coordination and harmonisation between different delivering agencies. Cash transfers frequently use some form of software or digital transfer system to distribute cash. They often also use a combination of software systems, phones, and vouchers or cash. However, these cash transfer systems are mainly bespoke, disconnected, and non-interoperable. This is exacerbated when people cross international borders, particularly in the event of humanitarian and protracted crises. So, it is possible that an IDP family might receive several entitlements in response to the same crisis, each through different modalities (cash, voucher) and cash transfer systems (mobile phones, biometric cards) and from different agencies. Hagen-Zanker et al. (2017) show this to be the case in a number of protracted crises where harmonisation and common platforms are slow to emerge. There is increasing research on the value for money and performance of different models of cash delivery (at humanitarian response/sector level); however, less is known about the recipient's experience and the nature and modalities of access. How does the aggregated package optimise the family's choices and financial inclusion? Innovations in cash transfer systems for populations on the move need to be developed that are efficient, user-friendly, and open-source, which integrate well with existing systems and ultimately respond to people's needs and aspirations within what is possible in a particular context.

Conclusions

The discussion in this chapter shows clearly that migrants and forcibly displaced populations face substantial hurdles in both the provision of, and access to, social protection. This is especially true for the poorest and most vulnerable and, by definition, those most in need of protection. In large part, this is down to the lack of resources of developing nations. In many cases, governments are unable to provide for their own citizens, let alone non-citizens, and so the perceived 'exclusion' of migrants is not always deliberate. In other cases, the lack of access is politically motivated.

How does migration impact on the development-social protection relationship? What is clear is that highly skilled migrants moving between regions with mature social protection systems are likely to be able to access social protection and social services on equivalence to their national counterparts and ones that are fairly homogenous across countries. Some migrants move from contexts of weak social protections systems to mature systems, but access remains restricted due to lack of vested rights. However, these groups of migrants represent just a small proportion of the world's migrant stock. The vast majority of migrants and mobile populations move from less developed regions to other less developed regions with shattered or poorly developed social protection provision. Governments are unlikely to be able to develop policies and programmes for migrants when the national population itself has restricted access to such policies. However, it does raise the obvious point, that unless social protection exists for native populations, migrants are unlikely to be considered in national policy formulation. In all cases, there exists a role for extra-governmental actors to set up distribution mechanisms and systems, prioritising the most vulnerable. At the same time, migrants will need to be proactive agents in the creation of their own social protection.

The bigger solution, however, relates to development more broadly: balanced growth, and equitable opportunities for growth, across regions and countries. Recent focus on a 'universal development' approach (Longhurst 2017)

> is particularly relevant against the backdrop of shared and interconnected challenges such as climate change, resource degradation, migration and trafficking, shared technology, and growing inequality, and when the rise of populism and nationalism is undermining attempts to address many of these challenges in both North and South.
>
> *(2017, 2)*

With regard to migration there has been no time as pressing as the current to think innovatively about universal workable solutions for people on the move. The SDGs take us some way towards this, but there is much space for innovations in social protection implementation and delivery for people on the move, for non-citizen populations, for refugees and the forcibly displaced. There is also appetite for ensuring that human rights are available and accessible to all and that migrants are treated in a socially just way within any new development paradigm.

As currently construed, social protection is largely an offer of a technocratic solution to persistent poverty and vulnerability resulting from various development strategies. The offer is bounded by the geography of nation-states and is therefore usually only available to citizens and legal residents in a specific country or region. Progressive framings and implementation of social protection policy are limited, yet this is precisely what is needed if migrants and displaced peoples' needs are going to be addressed. Justice-based innovations in social protection for migrants will include complementary interventions that promote social integration, the removal of information bottlenecks, sensitivity to language and culture in the design of social protection instruments, and advances in digital payment delivery and targeting.

Notes

1 UN Department of Economic and Social Affairs (DESA), *International Migration Report 2015: Highlights*. ST/ESA/SER.A/375, 2016, p.1.
2 Despite this general pattern of transformation, regional differences obviously persist, with some highly industrialised countries, such as the USA and Japan going much more strongly down the market social protection route, while Nordic countries have substantial, universal state benefits for their populations.

References

Avato, J., J. Koettl and R. Sabates-Wheeler (2010) Social Security Regimes, Global Estimates and Good Practices: The Status of Social Protection for International Migrants. *World Development*, 38(4).

Barrientos, A. and D. Hulme (2008) Social protection for the poor and poorest: An introduction, in *Social protection for the poor and poorest*. London: Palgrave Macmillan, 3–24.

Barrientos, A. and D. Hulme (Eds.). (2016) *Social Protection for the Poor and Poorest: Concepts, Policies and Politics*. Basingstoke, UK: Palgrave Macmillan.

Bommes, M. and A. Geddes (Eds.). (2000) *Immigration and Welfare: Challenging the Borders of the Welfare State*. London: Routledge.

Castles, S. and A. Davidson (2000) *Citizenship and Migration: Globalisation and the Politics of Belonging*. London: Macmillan.

Castles S. and M. Miller (2003) *The Age of Migration*. Basingstoke: Palgrave.

Cruz, A. T. (2004) *Portability of Benefit Rights in Response to External and Internal Labour Mobility: The Philippine Experience* (Conference paper, ISSA 13th Regional Conference for Asia and the Pacific, Kuwait, 8-10 March). Geneva: International Social Security Association.

Devereux, S. and R. Sabates-Wheeler (2004) *Transformative Social Protection, IDS Working Paper No. 232*. IDS: Brighton..

Dorward, A, R. Sabates-Wheeler, I. Macauslan, C. Penrose-Buckley, J. Kydd and E. Chirwa (2006), Promoting Agriculture for Social Protection or Social Protection for Agriculture: Strategic Policy and Research Issues. Discussion Paper for the Future Agricultures Consortium. www.future-agricultures.org.

Elkins, M., S. Feeny and D. Prentice (2015) Do Poverty Reduction Strategy Papers Reduce Poverty and Improve Well-being? Discussion Paper No. 15/02, University of Nottingham. Accessed on 26/01/2018 www.nottingham.ac.uk/economics/documents/discussion-papers/sdp15-02.pdf

Gentilini, U. and S. W. Omamo (2011) Social Protection 2.0: Exploring Issues, Evidence and Debates in a Globalizing World. *Food policy*, 36(3), 329–340.

Hagen-Zanker, J., M. Ulrichs, R. Holmes and Z. Nimeh (2017) *Cash Transfers for Refugees: The Economic and Social Effects of a Programme in JORDAN*. Research reports and studies, London: ODI.

Holzman, R., J. Koettl and T. Chernetsky (2005) *Portability Regimes of Pension and Health Care Benefits for International Migrants: An Analysis of Issues and Good Practices*. Geneva, Switzerland: Global Commission on International Migration.

Holzmann, R and S. Jorgensen (2000). Social Risk Management: A New Conceptual Framework for Social Protection and Beyond. Social Protection Discussion Paper 0006, Human Development Network, World Bank, Washington, DC.

Holzmann, R., L. Sherburn-Benz and E. Tesliuc (2003) *Social Risk Management: The World Bank's Approach to Social Protection in a Globalizing World*. Washington, DC: World Bank.

Lerner, D. (1958) The Passing of Traditional Society. London: The Free Press, Glencoe, Ill and MacMillan.

Long, K. and R. Sabates-Wheeler (2017) *Migration, Forced Displacement and Social Protection. (GSDRC Rapid Literature Review)*. Birmingham, UK: University of Birmingham.

Longhurst, R. (2017) *Universal Development, Has it Come of Age?* Vol 48, Number 1A, October 2017, Brighton, UK: IDS Bulletin.

MacAuslan (2011) Crossing Internal Boundaries: Political and Physical Access to the Public Distribution System in India, in R. Sabates-Wheeler and R. Feldman, eds. *Migration and Social Protection: Claiming Social Rights Beyond Borders*. London: Palgrave Macmillan, 183–209.

Massey, D; Durand, J; Capoferro, C (2005) The New Geography of Mexican Immigration, in Rubén Hernández León and Victor Zúniga, eds. *New Destinations of Mexican Migration in the United States: Community* Formation, *Local* Responses *and* Inter-Group Relations. New York: Russell Sage Foundation, 1–20.

Massey, D. S. (1987) Do Undocumented Migrants Earn Lower Wages than Legal Immigrants? New Evidence from Mexico. *International Migration Review*, 21(2), 236–274.

Massey, D. S. (2005) *Backfire at the Border: Why Enforcement Without Legalization Cannot Stop Illegal Immigration*. Washington, DC: Cato Institute.

Olivier, M. (2008) *Regional Overview of Social Protection for Non-Citizens in the Southern African Development* Community *(SADC)*. Background Paper for joint IDS/World Bank research project.

Olivier, M. P. and E. Kalula (Eds.). (2004) *Social Protection in SADC: Developing an Integrated and Inclusive Framework*. Cape Town, South Africa: Centre for International and Comparative Labour and Social Security Law (CICLASS), RAU [and] Institute of Development and Labour Law, UCT.

Oxford Policy Management (2015) *Shock-Responsive Social Protection Systems, Working Paper 1: Conceptualizing Shock-Responsive Social Protection*. Oxford: Oxford Policy Management Limited.

Pong, M. (2014) *Educating the Children of Migrant Workers in Beijing: Migration, Education, and Policy in Urban China*. Abingdon, Oxon, UK: Routledge.

Portes, A. (1976) Determinants of the Brain Drain. *International Migration Review*, 10, 489–508.

Rostow, W. W. (1959) The Stages of Economic Growth. *The Economic History Review*, 12(1), 1–16.

Sabates-Wheeler, R. (2009), *The Impact of Irregular Status on Human Development Outcomes for Migrants*. Published in: Human Development Research Paper (HDRP) Series, Vol. 26, No. 2009.

Sabates-Wheeler, R. (2011) Coping and investment strategies of migrants in the South: Malawian migrants in South Africa, in *Migration and Social Protection*. London: Palgrave Macmillan, 232–261.

Sabates-Wheeler, R. and S. Devereux (2018). Social Protection and the World Food Programme, Occasional Paper WFP 25. www.wfp.org/content/occasional-paper-25-social-protection.

Sabates-Wheeler, R. and R. Feldman (2011) *Migration and Social Protection: Claiming Social Rights Beyond Borders*. London: Palgrave Macmillan.

Sabates-Wheeler, R., J. Lind and J. Hoddinott (2013) Implementing Social Protection in Pastoralist Areas: How Local Distribution Structures Moderate PSNP Outcomes in Ethiopia. *World Development*, 50, 1–12.

Sabates-Wheeler, R and M. Waite (2003) Migration and Social Protection. Working Paper Series of the Migration DRC, Sussex University, Sussex.

Schierup C. U., P. Hansen and S. Castles (2006) *Migration, Citizenship, and the European Welfare State*. Oxford: Oxford University Press.

Scott, J.C. (2009) The Art of Not Being Governed: An Anarchist History of Upland Southeast Asia. New Haven, CT: Yale University Press. *Comparative Political Studies*, *43*(11), 1527-1531.

Slater, R. and Bhuvanendra, D. (2013). Scaling up Existing Social Safety Nets to Provide Humanitarian Response. www.cashlearning.org/downloads/calpfffannex3web.pdf.

Surender, R. and R. Walker (Eds.). (2013) *Social Policy in a Developing World*. Earthscan: Edward Elgar Publishing.

Timmer, C.P. (2009) A World Without Agriculture. Washington, DC: AEI Press.

UNICEF (2012) *Social Protection Strategic Framework: Integrated Social Protection Systems: Enhancing equity for children*. New York: UNICEF.

Walker, R. (2013). Conclusion: Towards the Analysis of Social Policy in a Developing World, Ch. 13, in R. Surender and R. Walker, eds. *Social Policy in a Developing World*. Earthscan.

Winder Rossi N., F. Spano, R. Sabates-Wheeler and S. Kohnstamm (2016). FAO Position Paper - Social Protection and Resilience Building: Supporting Livelihoods in Protracted Crises, Fragile and Humanitarian Contexts. Food and Agriculture Organization of the United Nations and Institute for Development Studies. www.fao.org/3/a-i7606e.pdf.

PART IV

Policies, rights, and interventions

The chapters in Part IV return the discussion on migration and development back to the macro-level by addressing two critical global issues: the role of rights in the treatment of migrants and the role of both national policy and the global architecture to manage migration and development better. The rights of migrants have been a highly contested area simply because rights are granted normally to citizens and residents of nation-states, which should include all those within a specific state irrespective of migrant status. To accord specific rights to anyone simply because they are a migrant appears to single out a particular group for special attention. Yet, the evidence shows that some migrants are indeed more vulnerable to abuse and exploitation. The International Labour Organisation of the United Nations has been in the forefront of developing standards for labour migrants and attempts have been made through international organisations to extend common rights to migrants more generally, although with mixed success.

The application of rights-based approaches and the evolution of the global architecture to implement these and other migration and development policies are examined in this part of the Handbook, together with an assessment of current national-based migration policies. The greater attention being paid to migration and to migrants, in the key, internationally-agreed architecture for development, the Sustainable Development Goals, is to be welcomed but, at the same time, concerns regarding which types of migration and which groups of migrants are privileged and taken into account, and which are overlooked and silenced are emerging. The increasing role of civil society organisations in the context of this national and inter-governmental environment is also examined, a role complicated by the variety of competing agendas among the many participating groups. The final two chapters in this part illustrate the challenges involved in implementing rights-based policies in the context of one developed economy, the United Kingdom, with a final chapter providing a view on academic research in the design of policy from an experienced practitioner at both national and multilateral levels.

25

RIGHTS-BASED APPROACHES TO MIGRATION AND DEVELOPMENT

Nicola Piper

Introduction

Rights have come to be treated as an integral dimension of development (Piron and Watkins 2004; UNDP 2000). Rights discourses have made substantial contributions in terms of emphasising the importance of agency by placing the individual, ordinary person at the centre of development, in relation to the broader developmental process as well as specific development projects. In doing so, greater attention, if not priority, is given to 'bottom-up' change derived from a more complex and comprehensive understanding of social transformation. This shift in focus strikes a balance to the macro-structural emphasis of conventional concerns with development which have tended to treat the costs of development for individuals as collateral damage and, thus, as unavoidable in the name of (and on the road to) 'big change' (Grugel and Piper 2009).

This has not always been the case. In fact, the 'rise of rights' was separated from development for a long time, and rights have entered development debates only fairly recently (Nyamu-Musembi and Cornwall 2004; Veneklasen et al. 2004). A key explanatory factor for this separation is that 'rights' had long, primarily if not exclusively, been viewed as profoundly normative and legalistic, preoccupied with global standard-setting and the building of liberal states. In contrast, 'development' tended to concern itself with macro-level change, approached primarily from an economistic angle. With mainstream economic discourse being intrinsically opposed to the promotion of economic, social, and cultural rights, human rights were regarded as 'competing rather than complementary' (Branco 2009). As a result, human rights were at best a means by which to engage in window-dressing in the development process, if they were viewed as relevant at all. Rights, on the other hand, were initially attached to debates about governance and globalisation, but not to development as such. The meeting point between rights and development was until recently far from obvious (Grugel and Piper 2009).

The rights of *migrants* are part and parcel of the rising importance of the rights discourse in general, and in relation to development in particular. This is so because the key drivers of people movement across borders include structural inequality within and between countries, lacking economic opportunities, and discrimination. The most extreme rights' violations – forced labour and human trafficking – have also been related to under-development (Skeldon 2000). Yet, international migrants, as non-citizens, are a particular group whose rights are still among the most contentious, and endeavours aimed at the advancement and realisation of their rights are being met with great resistance around the world (Basok 2009; Berg 2015). Innovative thinking about migrant rights and an integrated rights-based approach at the intersection of migration and development has begun to emanate from rising political activism by migrants located in the Global South (Piper 2015).

When the understanding and analysis of migration is approached from an intersecting human rights and development angle, it involves addressing the drivers and consequences of migration from a rights perspective, and thus the situation in countries of origin and destination. Consequently, such a discussion has to engage with global justice perspectives, scholarship on regulation/governance, and the proliferation of globalisation studies, as argued here. Those fields of inquiry all have one central contribution in common: the decentring of the state as the pertinent unit of social scientific analysis, by bringing the role of non-state or transnational actors to the fore (private sector, civil society, and international organisations) and the complex range of institutional actors involved at various levels of policymaking or policy engagement: local, national, regional, and global. An intricate institutional analysis paves the way for future thinking about a rights-based approach to migration.

The birth of the rights-based approach

The shift in thinking about human rights as a central feature of the development process has first and foremost been triggered by the belief that state-led approaches to development have failed in the delivery of individual well-being and empowerment – and the resultant realisation that a need exists to place the individual at the centre of the development process (Sen 1999). Rights have thereby come to be seen as a useful conduit, since rights theory serves to define individual injustice and to frame advocacy efforts as urgent and justified claims in the short term: and in order to tackle the multiple forms of exclusion experienced by 'the marginalised many' (the poor, women, children, and migrants) in relation to certain issues or policy fields in the long term (e.g. food, water, housing, social protection, and decent work). In this sense, a focus on rights has emerged as *the* moral or intellectual framework for challenging injustices leading to deprivation and disempowerment as they have occurred at the global, national and local level. Apart from its philosophical appeal, the effectiveness of the rights discourse in the political process has also been acknowledged by scholars of social movements as has been the use of 'rights language' in framing and moving issues up on political agendas. This has been demonstrated in relation to various, but not all, 'issue-areas'. As 'absentee citizens' or 'noncitizens', migrants have been particularly marginalised.

This 'seismic shift in the global system' is further attributed by Grugel and Piper (2009, 81) to the post-communist liberal triumphalism since 1989 in which rights entered global politics more forcefully. As a result, human rights began to be talked about more seriously as having the potential to transform global politics. This shift is also related to the rise of international rights movements in 1990s as reflected in a series of UN world conferences and the adoption of 'rights-based approaches' (Nyamu-Musembi and Cornwall 2004; Veneklasen et al. 2004). Although 'rights talk' in development may be new amongst international (donor and UN) agencies, struggles for the realisation of economic, social, and cultural rights have long featured in resistance and liberation movements in developing countries, as part of nationalist and anti-colonial movements for instance. In such context, rights were understood as something that needed to be fought for and won on the basis of the exclusion of the majority of the population. Rights in the broader sense of awareness of injustice thus sprang from popular opposition to colonial rule (Rajagopal 2002) and anti-dictatorship movements across Latin America and Asia (Eckstein 2013; Uhlin 1997). This indicates the importance of a social movement perspective and an understanding of rights as the product of social struggle (Stammers 2009).

Then came 'development', leading to a shift from rights to development, thereby hastening the depoliticisation of poverty (Marks 2004). The innocuous language of development, couched in technicalities and indicators, tended to deflect from the issue of power inequality on a global scale. The common practice of treating 'development' and 'human rights' as separate domains, however, began to change with the entry of newly independent southern countries into the UN in the 1960s and 1970s. Their key demand was for a new international economic order, which would transform notions of aid as charity to becoming a matter of social justice, power and entitlement. Such thinking emanated from a host of developing country-led initiatives, one of whose outcomes was the *Declaration on the Right to Development* in 1986 (Marks 2004). Despite its non-binding nature, this declaration is seen as constituting a key milestone since

> rather than confine itself to a conventional understanding of rights as being about state-citizen relations, it places an emphasis on the global dimension, pointing to inequalities between North and South. In doing so, it stresses the collective obligation of all states.
>
> *(Nyamu-Musembi and Cornwall 2004, 20)*

The aim of this declaration was, thus, to create a just and equitable international environment for the realisation of the Right to Development as a collective duty of all states by eliminating barriers such as unfair trade rules and debt burden.

Evidently, this led to the re-politicisation of under-development and poverty which was, however, soon countered over the course of the later 1980s and 1990s by certain countries questioning the types of rights that were seen as development concerns. Unsurprisingly much resistance to economic and social rights came from the West (especially the USA) since this resistance had its roots in the ideological clash during the Cold War. At that time, the human rights movement tended to remain aloof to issues of economic and social justice.

The end of the Cold War made possible a more comprehensive view of rights encompassing all rights (including economic, social, and cultural rights), as explicitly emphasised at the 1993 Vienna World Conference on Human Rights whose final declaration referred to the integrated nature of all rights. Since then, collaboration between mainstream human rights NGOs and development-oriented NGOs has increased. Amnesty International, for example, started to adopt the language of a rights-based approach to development as of 2001–2. In the world of practitioners, a range of both governmental and non-governmental actors has also been affected by this shift in thinking and, over time, a consensus has begun to emerge on the important link between human rights and development. This is reflected in the new programming ethos of a number of international NGOs (O'Neill 2003). A clear link between the concepts of 'human development' and 'human rights' has also been established by UNDP and its human development reports.

One of the reasons for the 'rise in rights-based approaches' (RBA), at least as far as rhetorics are concerned, has been suggested to be of political nature, and thus attributed to the perceived need to distance the discourse of rights from the 'Right to Development'. As convincingly speculated by Veneklasen et al. (2004), one of the reasons for rendering the language of a rights-based approach tolerable to institutions that had been cautious before is the severing of the mid-1990s dialect of the rights language from any reference to global inequality that is the central focus of the 1986 declaration. While insisting that they now see the people in recipient countries as rights-bearers, donor countries do indeed not see themselves as bearing any defined duties that contribute to the concrete realisation of these rights. Perhaps it is this lack of clarity on corresponding duties that makes the contemporary language of rights in development less threatening to the governments of rich countries. This heavily summarised historical account of the rights-based approach, thus, indicates the complexities involved in the politics and efforts to realise a rights-based approach to development. Future study and analysis into the intricate details and nuances would benefit from an interdisciplinary, multi-methods approach.

The rights-based approach: a multi-actor, multi-institutional perspective

A human rights-based approach is premised on the belief that people experiencing disempowerment as the result of poverty or other forms of disadvantage should understand their experiences of want, fear, and exclusion in terms of human rights abuses and violations. A rights-based approach thus differs from the traditional approach to development in that it focuses on discrimination and disempowerment, which in turn requires 'development work' to be viewed as a struggle for justice. The rights-based approach highlights the human rights entitlements of people, or rights holders, and the corresponding responsibilities of governments and other actors as duty bearers in the endeavour 'to respect, protect, and fulfil' human rights. Rights in their link to development have, thus, come to be conceptualised beyond the law and remit of courts, and instead as an expression of political agency. In this context, rights are understood in two major ways: first, as participation in a political process involving advocacy and mobilisation; second, as a means through which projects are implemented.

From their review of the plurality of rights-based approaches and their different implications for development practice, Nyamu-Musembi and Cornwall (2004) discerned a generalisable divide between narrow legal interpretations and broader rights frameworks. The rights-based approach to development as understood by the United Nations is more typical of a legal interpretation of the concept, emphasising the importance of compliance with the international legal human rights framework. By contrast, many development NGOs have moved beyond narrow legal interpretations to articulate a more expansive approach to a rights-based understanding of development, often on the basis of integrating empowerment, solidarity, and campaigning/advocacy programmes. The idea behind this approach is to enable affected communities' collective analysis of the 'problem' and the development of collective 'action' with the view to instigating change organically, or from 'within', rather than externally imposed.

Rights are thus rooted in the context of power as well as in the analysis of exclusion. The way forward is to ensure the agency and inclusion of affected groups into development projects by enabling rights holders to self-organise and mobilise and to articulate their agenda and demand the kind of change they wish to see. By emphasising the issue of power and decision making, rights-based approaches move beyond technical solutions to consider the political and social dynamics that underpin deprivation and exclusion. As an overall result, attention is shifted from macro-development or global achievements to a finer-grained analysis that includes questions of inequality and (re-)distribution.

Amartya Sen's path-breaking study of *Development as Freedom* (1999) fundamentally changed how development was perceived by arguing that the object of development should not solely be macro-economic outcomes, but centre upon, and emanate from, the enrichment of people's capabilities. Martha Nussbaum contributed to the globalising of the capabilities approach, which proposed that development should be re-evaluated in terms of the expansion of people's capabilities, by linking it to global economic and political powers in an increasingly interdependent and interconnected world (2004). She explains her preference for capabilities over rights in the following way: 'only because a right exists on paper does not mean that people really have this right. They only have it if there are effective measures to make people truly capable of political exercise' (2004, 240). Yet, she concedes that the language of rights has its valid use because 'the rights language reminds us that people have justified and urgent claims to certain types of urgent treatment' (1999, 241) and because the rights language is 'rhetorically more direct' (1999, 242).

The 'responsibility approach' to human rights as put forward by Andrew Kuper (2005) also builds on the discrepancy between 'rights on paper' and 'rights in practice'. To move beyond this impasse, Kuper argues for a shift from a 'recipient-centric' articulation of rights to an 'agent-centric' approach, which focuses on the capacities and obligations to deliver on rights. Both approaches de-emphasise the sole role of the state as the only agent, by attributing the role, and power of effecting change, to a variety of non-governmental actors ranging from NGOs to corporations. This resonated with social movement scholarship, especially the work on transnational advocacy networks, which highlights the importance of collective action 'from below'. 'Collective action may seem superfluous to capability but for the less privileged attaining development as freedom requires collective action' (Evans 2002, 56). Of fundamental importance, therefore, is collective capability as the first step towards securing other kinds of freedoms.

The fact that state-based multilateralism seems inadequate if not even obsolete in a world 'morphing into a multilevel complex of institutions, networks, coalitions, and informal arrangements' (Kuper 2005, xi) is also reflected in scholarship on regulation and governance. Notions of 'multi-sourced', 'nodal', and 'networked' governance are all indicative of regulatory theory having moved beyond narrow confines of a rules-based vision tied to the state and the legal sphere (Drahos 2017). The advantage of reconceptualising the advancement and enforcement of rights from a multi-actor or multi-institutional perspective is to ensure that powerless groups, such as migrants, are not robbed by state managerialism of the promise of rights, thereby turning them into pawns of economic and political management (Piper 2017). The push emanating from civil society actors is captured by the notion of 'bottom-up' governance or 'governance from below' as an integral aspect of a rights-based approach to governance (Grugel and Piper 2007).

On a similar wave, the notion of 'Everyday International Political Economy' has been proposed by Dobson and Seabrooke (2007) to shift attention from hegemony to legitimacy by paying attention to the political activism by the 'weak'. These shifts to more sociological frameworks have introduced more nuanced analyses to the predominant accounts of macro-level institutions' preoccupation with order as per elites' interest by highlighting the complexity of interactive relationships at multiple institutional levels.

The adoption of new global rights codes (such as the International Convention on the Rights of All Migrant Workers and their Families) or the reaffirmation of existing ones (such as the International Labour Organisation's Forced Labour Convention) have opened up, or were partly created by, political opportunity structures for collective advocacy. Such codes have begun to be taken more seriously by states and international policymakers with the result that more support appears to be forthcoming for the creation of global forms of regulation in which demands can be made and expressed across a range of domains including development and migration.

Rights-based approach to migration and development

The relationship between migration, development, and human rights has become subject to rising interest over the last decade which coincided with, or is in fact a reflection of, the emerging attention paid to shifts in the realm of global politics. This is evident from gradually expanding scholarship on global governance in general, and scholarly contributions on global governance of migration in particular (Betts 2011; Grugel and Piper 2007; Koser 2010) and the work by primarily sociologists on world society which has allowed the discussion of migrant rights to move beyond the traditional frame of (national) citizenship (Basok and Piper 2013).

Conventionally, the discussion of rights was set within the parameters of two extant overlapping rights-related frameworks, citizenship and human rights. Rights were conferred via citizenship, understood as a legal and social status that defined responsibilities, prescribed collective identity, and bestowed political membership through the exercise of democratic rights (Benhabib 2007). People's increasing mobility across international borders, however, has propelled scholars and activists to question this concept of national citizenship (Benhabib 2007; Sassen 2002; Urry 2000). Since the adoption of the Universal Declaration on Human Rights in 1948, national and regional institutions have by way of ratification in fact committed to implement such rights. At the same time, the idea of bestowing rights to non-citizens, especially when they entered in an unauthorised manner, is still considered 'counter-hegemonic' in reality (Basok 2009). Thus, despite existing on paper, migrant rights are still met with great obstacles in terms of their actual fulfilment.

In addition to the controversies surrounding the rights of *migrants*, another debate concerns the question of whether the rights of migrant *workers* should be regarded as separate from the rights of other, so-called 'vulnerable' migrants (children, refugees, and victims of trafficking). The more specific discussion over how best to secure *labour* rights in the globally networked economy of the twenty-first century has also begun to centre upon two related debates: (1) on how best to define the human rights and responsibilities of non-state actors, and (2) on how labour rights apply to migratory or non-citizen workers, including undocumented migrants as the most vulnerable of all.

The dominant experience at the centre of current articulations of migrant rights claims by the fledgling global migrant rights movement, the Global Coalition on Migration, is that of a (oftentimes female) worker who hails from the Global South labouring at the bottom ranks of the global economy (Piper 2015). Given the significance of so-called South–South migration, regional advocacy networks such as the *Migrant Forum in Asia*, are addressing the situation of the many migrants who labour under temporary contract conditions or in an unauthorised manner by targeting countries of origin, destination, regional, and global institutions. Such migrants find themselves in a highly vulnerable situation on several accounts: first, by the severe limitation of their mobility and residential rights; second, the extent and nature of the type of exploitation and discrimination they are exposed to in the receiving countries; and lastly, temporary migrants may not only receive limited or no support from their sending countries, but also face extortion (for instance by recruitment agencies) throughout the migration process. Furthermore, the restrictive approach to their migration and work permits in temporal and spatial terms by national, regional, and global regulatory bodies has implications for the practice of their political rights. It is in this specific context that migrant rights communities have begun to evoke the Declaration of the Right to Development and begun to develop an integrated rights-based approach to migration and development (Piper 2016; Piper and Rother 2014).

Since, globally, the fewest workers work in formal sector jobs, another issue in the labour rights debate concerns how to tackle informal work and (migrant and non-migrant) worker precarity. Growing recognition of workplace precarity (Standing 2016) alongside the specifics of migrant precarity (Lewis et al. 2015; Piper et al. 2017) has led the International Labour Organisation (ILO) to develop a rights-based approach to labour migration based on the 'decent work' concept. The new ILO Convention 189 from 2011 on 'Decent Work for Domestic Workers' is one concrete result of the 'decent work' agenda launched by the ILO in 1999. As concerns *migrant* precarity, the ILO marked further significant success in 2015 by managing to have decent work incorporated as a key objective in targeting world poverty by the Sustainable Development Goals (SDG). SDG Goal 8 explicitly calls for 'decent work' at the heart of all processes of economic growth and for the protection of the labour rights of all workers, 'including migrant workers', while SDG 10.7 calls for not only 'well managed migration policies' but also for efforts to 'facilitate orderly, safe, regular, and responsible migration and mobility'. Achieving this goal will require a more contextually specific understanding of how decent work is situated within the 'push' and 'pull' factors shaping labour migration patterns and, thus, necessitate the development of reliable indicators for measuring improvements in these areas (Piper 2016; Piper et al. 2017).

In summary, migrant rights are still a highly contested notion in regard to the rights to free movement, the right to work and rights at work (Estevez Lopez 2010) which are not widely recognised, let alone translated into practice. The definition of 'rights-based approach' to development and migration as being primarily about the capability of civil society actors falls on fertile ground. The promotion and protection of migrant rights through participation by migrant rights organisations constitutes a central pillar of rights-based migration governance. The 'new rights' agenda emanating from the global migrant rights movement has placed migration squarely in the context of debates about global justice and the combined responsibilities of multiple agents in multiple sites (Piper 2015). Such a 'new rights agenda' reflects the growing centrality of rights in debates about global development (Grugel and Piper 2009). Applied to migrants' rights, it is a decolonised understanding of global justice based on the general principles of the Right to Development and the right to mobility that has been proposed as a way forward (Estevez Lopez 2010).

Concluding remarks

The one element that rights-based approaches have in common with other relevant fields of study – globalisation, regulation/governance, social movements – is process. Development and migration are processes, not events, nor are they final products that are realised at a specific point in time. For both, per capita income (including monetary remittances) may not be the most appropriate manner of measuring well-being of those affected. As Arjun Sengupta who served as the UN's Independent Expert on the Right to Development (1999–2004), the UN's Independent Expert on Human Rights and Extreme Poverty (2004–2008) has reminded us, a rights-based approach goes in fact further in identifying the notion of well-being with the realisation of fundamental freedoms, so both development and migration become processes of improvement of well-being. When those freedoms are identified with rights which are claimed by people, development and migration are a realisation of human rights. The aspect of 'rights-based' thereby refers to consistency with human rights standards and corresponding obligations of policies, carried out in a rights-based manner which relates to conditions of participation, equity, non-discrimination, accountability and transparency (Sengupta 2004).

Regulation and governance scholarship has similarly pointed to the importance of process when highlighting the fragmentation and multiplication of institutional actors. Resonating with social movement scholarship and constructivist strands within International Relations, a rights-based approach is evidenced in the political struggle for a more inclusive and 'just' global governance of migration. This is an activity that has shown some positive effects on global democracy by diversifying recognition and increasing representation amidst interstate concerns.

The rights-based approach articulates an alternative vision, expressed in a new migrant rights agenda, to the elitist, top-down project of global migration governance. This new rights agenda which centres upon a comprehensive rights-based approach to migration is promoted by the global migrant rights network to democratise migration with the aim of turning migration into a more emancipatory and less oppressive (or forced) phenomenon. To what extent it will be successful in combining rights-producing politics and rights-assuming advocacy is yet to be seen.

References

Basok T. (2009) "Counter-Hegemonic Human Rights Discourses and Migrant Rights Activism in the US and Canada", *International Journal of Comparative Sociology* 50(2), 179–201.

Basok T. and Piper N. (2013) "Justice for Migrants: Mobilizing a Rights-Based Understanding of Migration", in Ilcan S. ed., *Mobilities, Knowledge and Social Justice*, Montreal, McGill-Queen's University Press, pp. 255–276.

Benhabib S. (2007) "Twilight of Sovereignty or the Emergence of Cosmopolitan Norms? Rethinking Citizenship in Volatile Times", *Citizenship Studies* 11, 19–36.

Berg L. (2015) *Migrant Rights at Work: Law's Precariousness at the Intersection of Immigration and Labour*, London, Routledge.

Betts A. ed. (2011) *Global Migration Governance*, Oxford, University of Oxford Press.

Boehning R. (2009) "Getting a Handle on the Migration Rights-Development Nexus", *International Migration Review* 4, 1–19.

Branco M.C. (2009) *Economic versus Human Rights*, London, Routledge.

Castles S. (2011) "Bringing Human Rights into the Migration and Development Debate", *Global Policy* 2(3), 248–258.

Dobson J. and Seabrooke J. eds. (2007) *Everyday International Political Economy*, Cambridge, Cambridge University Press.

Drahos P. ed. (2017) *Regulatory Theory – Foundations and Applications*, Canberra, ANU University Press.

Eckstein S. (2013) "The Latin Amerian Social Movement Repertoire: How It Has Changed, When and Why", *Moving the Social* 50, 81–102.

Estevez Lopez A. (2010) "Taking the Human Rights of Migrants Seriously: Towards a Decolonized Global Justice", *The International Journal of Human Rights* 14, 658–677.

Evans P. (2002) "Collective Capabilities, Culture, and Amartya Sen's *Development as Freedom*", *Studies in Comparative International Development* 37(2), 54–60.

Grugel J.B. and Piper N. (2007) *Critical Perspectives on Global Governance: Rights and Regulation in Governing Regimes*, London, Routledge.

Grugel J.B. and Piper N. (2009) "Do Rights Promote Development?", *Global Social Policy* 9(1), 79–98.

Jönsson C. and Tallberg J. eds. (2010) *Transnational Actors in Global Governance: Patterns, Explanations, and Implications*, Houndmills and Basingstoke, Palgrave Macmillan.

Koser K. (2010) "Introduction: International Migration and Global Governance", *Global Governance* 16, 301–315.

Kuper A. ed. (2005) *Global Responsibilities – Who Must Deliver on Human Rights?* London, Routledge.

Lewis H., Dwyer P., Hodkinson S. and Waite L. (2015) "Hyper-Precarious Lives: Migrants, Work and Forced Labour in the Global North", *Progress in Human Geography* 1–21.

Marks S. (2004) "The Human Right to Development: Between Rhetoric and Reality", *Harvard Human Rights Journal* 17, 137–168.

Nussbaum M. (1999) "Women and Equality: The Capabilities Approach", *International Labour Review* 138, 227–245.

Nussbaum M. (2004) "Beyond the Social Contract: Capabilities and Global Justice", *Oxford Development Studies* 32, 3–18.

Nyamu-Musembi C. and Cornwall A. (2004) "What Is the "Rights-based Approach" All About? Perspectives from International Development Agencies", *IDS Working Paper 234* Brighton, IDS.

O'Neill W.G. (2003) *An Introduction to the Concept of Rights-Based Approach to Development: A Paper for Inter Action*, Washington, DC, InterAction.

Piper N. (2015) "Democratising Migration from the Bottom Up: The Rise of the Global Migrant Rights Movement", *Globalizations* 12(5), 788–802.

Piper N. (2008) "The 'Migration-Development Nexus' Revisited from a Rights Perspective", *Journal of Human Rights* 7, 1–18.

Piper N. (2016) "Migration and the SDGs", *Global Social Policy* 17(2), 231–238.

Piper N. (2017) "Global Governance of Labour Migration: From "Management" of Migration to an Integrated Rights-Based Approach", in Drahos P. ed., *Regulatory Theory – Foundations and Applications*, Canberra, ANU University Press, pp. 377–394.

Piper N., Rosewarne S. and Withers M. (2017) "Migrant Precarity: 'Networks of Labour' for a Rights-Based Governance of Migration", *Development and Change* 48(5), 1089–1110.

Piper N. and Rother S. (2014) "More than Remittances – Resisting the Global Governance of Migration", *Journal fuer Entwicklungspolitik/Austrian Journal for Development Studies* 30(1), 30–45.

Piron L. and Watkins F. (2004) *DFID Human Rights Review. A Review of How DFID Has Integrated Human Rights into Its Work*, London, ODI.

Rajagopal B. (2002) "International Law and Social Movements: Challenges to Theorizing Resistance", *Columbia Journal of Transnational Law* 41, 397–432.

Sassen S. (2002) "Global City and Survival Circuits", in Ehrenreich B. and Hochschild A.R. eds., *Global Woman: Nannies, Maids and Sex Workers in the New Economy*, New York, A Metropolitan/Owl Books, pp. 254–274.

Scholte J.A. (2011) *Building Global Democracy? Civil Society and Accountable Global Governance*, Cambridge, Cambridge University Press.

Sen A. (1999) *Development as Freedom*, Oxford, Oxford University Press.

Sengupta A. (2004) "The Right to Development: An Interview with Dr Arjun Sengupta", *Essex Human Rights Review* 1(1), 93–97. http://projects.essex.ac.uk/ehrr/V1N1/Interview1.pdf

Skeldon R. (2000) "Trafficking: A Perspective from Asia", *International Migration* 38(3), 7–30.

Stammers N. (2009) *Human Rights and Social Movements*, London, Pluto Press.

Standing G. (2016) *The Precariat: The New Dangerous Class*, London, Bloomsbury Press.

Uhlin A. (1997) *Indonesia and the "Third Wave of Democratization": The Indonesian Pro-Democracy Movement in a Changing World*, Richmond, Curzon.

UNDP. (2000) *Human Development Report: Human Rights and Human Development*, New York, UNDP.

Urry J. (2000) "Global Flows and Global Citizenship", in Isin E. ed., *Democracy, Citizenship and the Global City*, London, Routledge, pp. 62–78.

Veneklasen L., Miller V., Clark C. and Reilly M. (2004) "Rights-Based Approaches and Beyond: Challenges of Linking Rights and Participation", *IDS Working Paper 235*, Brighton, IDS.

26

MIGRATION, THE MDGS, AND SDGS

Context and complexity[1]

Elaine McGregor

Introduction: human development in the twenty-first century

The MDGs and the SDGs have – for better or worse – provided guiding principles for human development in the twenty-first century. Migration was not a MDG and, at the time, there were few who argued that it should have been, with the notable caveat that 'it is virtually impossible to envisage progress towards achieving the existing MDGs without some kind of migration' (Skeldon 2008, 2). However, in the run-up to the adoption of the SDGs, there was an observable push by many actors operating in the area of migration to see it included in the Post-2015 Development Agenda. Its subsequent inclusion has been celebrated by many international actors, but what does this actually imply? How is migration to be included, and what does this tell us about the relationship between migration and development? Situating the inclusion of migration in the SDGs into the broader context of the formulation and acceptance of global goals on development, this chapter offers a brief commentary on the evolution of migration as an international policy issue.

The millennium development goals

Described as 'the world's biggest promise' the MDGs were a set of eight goals, 18 targets, and 48 indicators with the broad aim of reducing poverty around the world (Hulme 2009). While it is speculated that the MDGs were written on a napkin (McArthur 2014), the goals were ultimately the product of two ongoing processes that gained momentum after the end of the Cold War (Hulme 2009). One of these took place within the context of the United Nations and the other amongst donor States, driven primarily by OECD's Development Assistance Committee (DAC).

Within the United Nations, the 1990s witnessed a renewed focus on global summitry in which the concept of poverty reduction, having waned in the context of structural adjustment policies of the World Bank and the International Monetary Fund (IMF) in the 1970s and 1980s, was accepted as the cornerstone of development (Fukuda-Parr and Hulme 2011). The number of global conferences, recommendations, and declarations skyrocketed (Hulme 2009).

However, for many aid agencies, the 1990s saw shrinkage in budgets with an overall decline in Overseas Development Assistance (ODA) owing to a growing concern about the effectiveness of aid from both ends of the political spectrum (Carbone 2013). Facing organisational downsizing, the high level meeting of the DAC in 1995 focused on reframing development cooperation as an investment. It was in this context that the *Groupe de Réflexion* was formed and, although it had no clear end goal at inception, sought to reinvigorate discussions surrounding aid. One of the concrete outputs of the group was a set of goals – the International Development Goals (IDGs) which were a culmination of a review and synthesis of the declarations agreed upon at the many UN summits of the early 1990s.

This led to some concern within the UN that the DAC were 'taking control of a UN agenda' (Hulme 2009, 19) and, by comparing the IDGs with the UNDP Human Development Report of 1997, a few noteworthy differences can be observed. First, while the UN approach cited moral reasons for its recommendations, the DAC narrative focused more on the economic benefits of development for donors. Second, while the UN sought the overall eradication of poverty, DAC opted for a more modest approach to poverty reduction. Third, the DAC goals were pitched at the global level, while the UN viewed such a goal-setting exercise as being a national endeavour, with countries setting their own targets and implementation plans. Finally, the DAC placed more emphasis on economic growth as a poverty reduction strategy where the UN acknowledge its importance but drew much more attention to human development and human rights (Hulme 2009).

Towards the end of the 1990s, preparations began for the Millennium Assembly of the United Nations. Kofi Annan appointed John Ruggie to prepare a document based on previous UN conference and summit declarations that would be acceptable to UN members. This document became 'We the Peoples'. In June 2000, another key document was released, '2000: A Better World for All: Progress towards the International Development Goals' which was published by, in alphabetical order, IMF, OECD, UN, and the World Bank. The document provided legitimacy to the IDGs although there was still some concern that donor countries were over influencing the agenda (Hulme 2009).

After negotiations, which primarily took place behind closed doors, the Millennium Declaration was unanimously accepted on the 8 September 2000. However, the MDGs themselves had still to be finalised and a road-map developed. As this process began, UN officials consulted with the DAC where work had continued on the IDGs. To avoid what would ultimately add complexity, efforts to reconcile the IDGs with the MDGs took place at a World Bank convened meeting in 2001. This was a largely technical exercise, and from the resulting goals it can be said that the IDGs are strongly mirrored in the MDGs, with the notable exception of reproductive rights as an issue with political opposition among UN Member States (Bernstein 2005).

International migration as a major development issue

Long held at arms-length from the United Nations by States defending migration as the 'last bastion of state sovereignty' (Dauvergne 2004, 588), migration, and particularly migrant rights, were, like reproductive rights, a topic of contention between Member States. Although like reproductive rights, migration was not destined to be included as an explicit MDG, an often forgotten fact is that migrants did receive an explicit mention in the Millennium Declaration alongside other goals in areas 'too difficult to measure unambiguously or too sensitive to handle politically' (Browne and Weiss 2014, 6). This mention took the form of a commitment:

to take measures to ensure respect for and protection of the human rights of migrants, migrant workers and their families, to eliminate the increasing acts of racism and xenophobia in many societies and to promote greater harmony and tolerance in all societies.

(UN General Assembly 2000)

Despite the fact that a focus on the human rights of migrants has been overshadowed by migration management and migration and development discourses (Piper 2017), it is interesting nevertheless to take note of this commitment since it is reflective of the position of migration as an international policy issue at the time.

Prior to IOM joining the UN in September 2016, no UN agency, with the exception of the normative mandates of ILO (rights of migrant workers) and UNHCR (displaced populations), had a specific mandate to work on migration. Ultimately this meant that international migration – a phenomenon that by definition involves at least two countries – did not share the same degree of international cooperation as other cross-border issues such as trade or transnational crime, and instead commenters bemoaned the lack of global migration governance (Betts 2011). This was the context of the famed 2002 'Doyle Report'[2] which assessed the feasibility of creating a global organisation for migration, be it through the designation of an existing organisation as 'lead agency', merging existing organisations, or creating a new one. The report concluded that not enough consensus on migration existed at the international level and thus the best interim solution would be to enhance inter-agency coordination and to pay more attention to the 'management' of international migration. On 9 December 2003, Kofi Annan, at the behest of Member States, launched the first-ever global panel addressing international migration. The Global Commission on International Migration (GCIM) had 19 members from across the world. The GCIM led to the formalisation and enlargement of the Geneva Migration Group (later the Global Migration Group) from six members in 2003 (IOM, ILO, UNHCR, OHCHR, UNODC, UNCTAD) to a membership of 22 before it was superseded by the United Nations Network on Migration in 2019.

However, it was at this point that there was a slight narrative shift in the way migration was discussed at the international level. While concerns regarding the management of migration prevailed, the GCIM report also drew attention to the relationship between migration and development. This was potentially a reflection of the realisation that remittances far exceeded ODA in the early years of the millennium (de Haas 2010). The appointment of the late Sir Peter Sutherland by Kofi Annan to be his Special Representative on Migration and Development for the first High Level Dialogue (HLD) on International Migration and Development in New York in 2006 marked an important moment in further solidifying migration as a development issue. As former and youngest Attorney General of Ireland, Director of the General Agreement on Tariffs and Trade (GATT) and the World Trade Organization (WTO) and Chairman of BP plc and Goldman Sachs International, Peter Sutherland came with international authority and a strong message:

Migration can be an enormous force for good: one of the great drivers of economic growth, individual liberty and personal prosperity. As such, I am delighted to undertake this assignment for Kofi Annan. The goal is to maximise the benefits of migration and minimise potentially negative impacts.

(United Nations 2006)

Peter Sutherland was instrumental in steering the first HLD which led to the creation of the Global Forum on Migration and Development (GFMD), which has been held annually since 2007 with the exception of 2013 when the second HLD took place. This has kept the momentum going on discussions of international migration and development at the global level. UNDP's 2009 Human Development Report is symbolic of the acceptance of migration as a development issue. These developments gave international migration a high global profile and, arguably, provided the context for the acceptance of migration into the Sustainable Development Goals.

However, the inclusion of migration in the SDGs is not the end of the story for migration as a global policy issue. Propelled into the spotlight by governments, primarily in Europe, facing increased numbers of migrants, including refugees, migration has not witnessed such sustained global attention in recent history. In October 2016, in addition to IOM joining the UN as a 'related agency', 193 States unanimously agreed upon the New York Declaration as the closing of High Level Summit for Refugees and Migrants, committing themselves to negotiate two global compacts by 2018, one on migration and the other on refugees. This commenced 2 years of consultations and negotiation which have now concluded. While development may have been the vehicle upon which migration entered the UN, migration management continues to be a dominant feature of UN deliberations on migration (Piper 2017).

The Sustainable Development Goals

Where the MDGs were in part a product of serendipitous events such as the formation of the *Groupe de Réflexion* in a carpark (see Hulme (2009) for a comprehensive account of this), the development of the SDGs was far more intentional, perhaps owing to the fact that the task of gaining acceptance of global goals as a general principle had already been achieved by the MDGs. Discussions officially started at the United Nations Conference on Sustainable Development in Rio de Janeiro in 2012 which also led to the formation of the High Level Political Forum on Sustainable Development. In the 3 years to follow numerous consultations and meetings were organised allowing space for different interest groups to lobby for their specific issues they would like to see included in the Post-2015 Development Agenda. Perhaps the success of the MDGs in structuring development financing lent further impetus to those excluded from the initial goals to make a (stronger) case the second time around. As Steven Sinding succinctly stated of reproductive health, 'if you are not an MDG, you're not on the agenda' (cited in Hulme 2009, 25). The sheer expansion of the eight goals, 18 targets and 48 indicators of the MDGs to the 17 goals, 169 targets and 230 indicators of the SDGs provides support for this statement.

In 2014, and the first half of 2015 in particular, civil society organisations around the world actively advocated for the inclusion of migration in the Post-2015 Development Agenda, with 312 organisations signing the 'Stockholm Agenda on Migration and Migration Related Goals and Targets' at the GFMD Civil Society Days in 2014. In the Stockholm Agenda, civil society organisations called for the moral necessity of addressing the rights of migrants and the root causes of migration. The Stockholm Agenda also called for a significant decrease in the cost of sending remittances, for reducing the risks and guaranteeing the safety of migrants on the move, and for increasing the mobility of skills, wages, and social security (GFMD Civil Society 2014).

Within the UN, the existence of an informal working group organised around Peter Sutherland and his team, and composed of representatives of different international organisations galvanised efforts to create consistent messaging around the relevance of migration to any discussions of development at the global policy level. This process was not particularly well documented. However, the outward communication of the international organisations with an interest in seeing migration included in the Post-2015 Development Agenda are more readily available.

Between 2012 and 2015, an outpouring of publications and countless meetings were organised by members of the Global Migration Group (and others) with the aim to see migration included in the Post-2015 Development Agenda. IOM was particularly prolific in lobbying for migration's inclusion in the SDGs, producing numerous publications that solely focused on migration and the Post-2015 Development Agenda (see McGregor 2017 for a full list). IOM perhaps had more incentive to see migration included since migration is the sole business of the organisation. ILO also made a concerted effort to see labour rights for migrants particularly with respect to recruitment costs and the rights of domestic workers, included in the SDGs. In the case of UNHCR, references primarily related to a call to promote ties between humanitarian and development actors in the context of promoting durable solutions for refugees. For other GMG members, migration represented a topic at the periphery of their daily business and thus, while still discursively connecting migration as an issue of relevance to the SDGs, were more likely to do so in the context of their broader remit (McGregor 2017).

In McGregor (2017), I analysed a sample of these publications (n=166), identifying five key arguments made by international organisations for including migration in the SDGs:

1. Under the right conditions, migration can be an enabler of development and thus can support the implementation of the SDGs. This is the most prominent narrative which is not entirely surprising given that the concept of 'development enablers' was a key principle guiding the formulation of the Post-2015 Development Agenda (UNTT, 2012).
2. Migration can be a threat to development and if not addressed, may undermine other development goals.
3. Migrants are a vulnerable population group at risk of exclusion from development opportunities.
4. Development can drive migration from both a 'development failure' (negative) and 'development enabled migration' (positive) perspective.
5. Displacement can disrupt development and thus should also be a focus for development actors, particularly in the context of promoting durable solutions for displaced populations.

This diversity in narratives on migration highlight the complexity of migration as an international policy issue and, as will be demonstrated in the next section, are manifested in the ways in which migration is reflected in the SDGs, both directly and indirectly.

Migration in the Sustainable Development Goals

The result of these efforts was a place for migration in the Sustainable Development Goals including an entire paragraph in the preamble devoted solely to migration:

> We recognize the positive contribution of migrants for inclusive growth and sustainable development. We also recognize that international migration is a multidimensional reality of major relevance for the development of countries of origin, transit and destination, which requires coherent and comprehensive responses. We will cooperate internationally

to ensure safe, orderly and regular migration involving full respect for human rights and the humane treatment of migrants regardless of migration status, of refugees and of displaced persons. Such cooperation should also strengthen the resilience of communities hosting refugees, particularly in developing countries. We underline the right of migrants to return to their country of citizenship, and recall that States must ensure that their returning nationals are duly received.

(UN General Assembly 2015, 8)

Migration is explicitly mentioned under the goals on reducing inequality (Goal 10 Targets 7 and c), promoting decent work and economic growth (Goal 8 Target 8) and the context of data disaggregation in Goal 17 (Target 18) (see Table 26.1). Further references to mobility-related phenomena include human trafficking, mentioned in the context of Goal 5 on achieving gender equality (Target 2), in Goal 8 on decent work and economic growth (Target 7), and Goal 16 on promoting peaceful and inclusive societies (Target 2). Mobility in the context of higher education is captured in Goal 4 (Target 4b).

Migrants are also represented by the pledge to 'leave no one behind'.

People who are vulnerable must be empowered. Those whose needs are reflected in the Agenda include all children, youth, persons with disabilities (of whom more than 80 per cent live in poverty), people living with HIV/AIDS, older persons, indigenous peoples, *refugees and internally displaced persons and migrants*.

(UN General Assembly 2015, 7, own emphasis)

With this in mind, migration relevant goals and targets could be increased to include all goals and targets where inclusive language is used. In total, seven Goals (3, 4, 5, 6, 7, 8, and 16) and 27 Targets (see Appendix 26.1 for a full list) stipulate that the specific goals or target is 'for all', thus inclusive of migrant populations.

Even before adding these goals and targets to the arsenal of migration-related SDGs, the dominant narrative evident in the way migration is covered in the SDGs is that of migrants as a distinct social group at risk of being excluded from development, as opposed to migration being conceptualised as an enabler of development, which was the most prominent narrative prior to their adoption. However, this latter narrative is captured in SDG 10 (reducing

Table 26.1 Explicit migration references in the Sustainable Development Goals

---

8.8 Protect labour rights and promote safe and secure working environments for all workers, including **migrant** *workers, in particular women* **migrants**, *and those in precarious employment*

10.7 Facilitate orderly, safe, regular and responsible **migration** *and mobility of people, including through the implementation of planned and well-managed* **migration** *policies*

10.c By 2030, reduce to less than 3 per cent the transaction costs of **migrant remittances** *and eliminate remittance corridors with costs higher than 5 per cent*

17.18 By 2020, enhance capacity-building support to developing countries, including for least developed countries and small island developing States, to increase significantly the availability of high-quality, timely and reliable data disaggregated by income, gender, age, race, ethnicity, **migratory status,** *disability, geographic location and other characteristics relevant in national contexts*

---

inequalities). The proposed indicators for measuring Target 10.7 include a measure of recruitment cost, for which ILO is responsible, and an indicator on the number of countries who have implemented 'orderly, safe, regular, and responsible' migration policies, however this may be defined. Target 10.c focuses on reducing the cost of migrant remittances. Remittances have been a dominant part of the migration and development discourse and it is unsurprising that they continue to hold their weight as a central aspect of the migration and development debate in the SDGs.

While there appears to be a general sense of achievement with regards to the inclusion of migration in the SDGs, not everyone appears satisfied with its coverage, and this discontentment comes with different justifications. For example, some commenters argue that the coverage is reductionist:

> While it is significant that the advocacy of migration and development groups succeeded in having migration included in the 2030 Agenda, challenges exist in that migration is reduced within certain goals and targets thus overlooking the broader relation between migration and development and the particular role of migrant women workers in contributing to development in countries of origin and destination.
>
> *(Maulik and Petrozziello 2016, 263)*

However, as was also true of the MDGs (McGregor et al. 2014; Skeldon 2008), it is possible to connect almost all goals to migration in one way or another. To illustrate, several publications outlining the connections between migration and the SDGs were released in 2017 (Table 26.2). In the first of these examples, the Global Migration Policy Associates (GMPA) identify 43 targets and 3 Goal statements that cover 15 of the 17 SDGs that 'apply directly to migrants, refugees, returnees, potential migrants, and migration-compelling situations'. In IOM's (2017b) 'Migration in the 2030 Agenda', a total of 41 targets across all 17 goals are highlighted. The 'Guidelines on Mainstreaming Migration into Local Development Planning', published by the Joint Migration and Development Initiative (JMDI 2017) makes reference to 59 relevant targets across 12 SDGs. Finally, in a collection of policy briefs, the Overseas Development Initiative (ODI 2017) make specific reference to 63 indicators covering 13 of the 17 SDGs.

One might expect to find much overlap between these mappings, and it is therefore of note that just 14 of the 100 targets identified in these reports, appear in all four

Table 26.2 Mapping migration in the Sustainable Development Goals

Author	Title	Year	Goals	Targets
Global Migration Policy Associates (GMPA)	The Sustainable Development Goals and Migrants/Migration *Version 3.2*	2017	15	43
International Organization for Migration (IOM)	Migration in the 2030 Agenda	2017	17	41
Joint Migration and Development Initiative (JMDI)	Guidelines on Mainstreaming Migration into Local Development Planning	2017	12	59
Overseas Development Institute (ODI)	Migration and the 2030 Agenda for Sustainable Development	2017	13	63

documents (see Appendix 26.1 for the full text of these 14 indicators). Excluding those indicators that have already been identified for their explicit references to migration (Targets 8.7; 8.8; 10.7; 10.c; and 17.18), the remaining nine indicators draw connections between migration in the context of climate-change (Targets 1.5, 13.1, and 13b); migration and the labour market including education provision that matches labour market needs (Targets 4.4), job creation (Target 8.3) and recognising domestic work, which is often carried out by migrant workers (Target 5.4); and access to services including health, education, and justice (Targets 3.8, 4.a, 16.3).

The limited overlap of common indicators points to different ways of conceptualising the connections between migration and development, which can, in part, be explained by looking at the methodology behind each mapping. GMPA (2017) – currently a work in progress – offers a systematic listing of the SDGs and provides the rationale and justification for their relevance to migration based on several premises including: that migrants are rights-holders; that migrants are actors in development that can often be more vulnerable to exclusion; and that development is a multifaceted concept.

In the remaining publications (IOM 2017b; JMDI 2017; and ODI 2017), the exercise of mapping migration in the SDGs is approached by looking at the intersections between migration and specific thematic issues, an increasingly common approach in the area of migration studies (Carling 2017). For IOM, these thematic issues are diaspora engagement, environment, and climate change, health, gender equality, labour mobility, cities, displacement, and children. ODI (2017) look at poverty, gender equality, cities, education, health, social protection, climate change, and citizenship. In JMDI (2017), the mapping is approached from the perspective of policy coherence at the local level and focuses on considering mobility in the context of a range of different policy areas including education, health, employment, infrastructure, agriculture, and food security, environment, and climate change, investment, and social cohesion/xenophobia. Depending on the thematic area selected, it is conceivable that 'almost all of the SDGs are relevant to migration, and can only be fully achieved if migrants are taken into account during implementation' (IOM 2017b, 10).

Concluding remarks

The MDGs and SDGs are essentially the products of the concerted efforts of different constellations of interest groups to put forth their particular vision of development, at a particular point in time. While the MDGs were created in a far more top-down fashion, the development of the SDGs was a far more bottom-up process. While the MDGs were criticised for being solely focused on the developing world, the SDGs broaden this scope to conceive of a set of goals with universal applicability. However, the SDGs are far from representing a 'compact among nations' and their complexity and all-encompassing nature represents more a compact among international organisations than anything else.[3] Where the MDGs were applauded for their simplicity, the SDGs are anything but simple. The sheer number of issues covered makes it possible to create many connections, explicit or otherwise between migration and the SDGs.

Framing migration as a development issue has been a vehicle for bringing migration into the UN. By focusing on economic development and the positive societal contributions that migration can make through monetary and social transfers, a series of events unfolded that have culminated in the acceptance of migration as a global policy issue. The inclusion of migration in the SDGs reflects this acceptance. However, the ongoing fragmentation and lack of clarity among migration actors continues to be seen in the way in which migration is conceptualised in the context of the SDGs and we are far from reaching consensus on how migration should be treated at the level of international policymaking. Perhaps the most important, if not new, observation, that can be made is that migration is intrinsically part of development and, by reducing migration to a single narrative that supports a particular organisational focus, is reductionist and fails to capture the essence of the migration and development 'nexus': that migration *is* – has, and most probably always will be – development (Skeldon 1997).

Notes

1 I am grateful to Tanja Bastia, Ronald Skeldon and Michaella Vanore for comments on an earlier draft of this chapter. Any errors remain my own.
2 Report to the Secretary-General on Migration by the Migration Working Group chaired by Michael W. Doyle on 20 December 2002.
3 Credit is owed to Ronald Skeldon for this observation.

References

Bernstein, S. (2005). "The changing discourse on population and development: Toward a new political demography". *Studies in Family Planning*, *36*(2), 127–132.
Betts, A. (ed.). (2011). *Global Migration Governance*. Oxford University Press, Oxford, United Kingdom.
Browne, S. and Weiss, T. G. (2014). "The UN we want for the world we want", in Browne, S. and Weiss, T. G. (eds.), *Post-2015 UN Development: Making Change Happen?* Routledge, London and New York, pp. 1–14.
Carbone, M. (2013). *Policy Coherence and EU Development Policy*. Routledge, Oxon, United Kingdom and New York, United States of America.
Carling, J. (2017). "Thirty-six migration nexuses, and counting". (https://jorgencarling.org/2017/07/31/thirty-six-migration-nexuses-and-counting/) Accessed 8 January 2018.
Dauvergne, C. (2004). "Sovereignty, migration and the rule of law in global times". *The Modern Law Review*, *67*(4), 588–615.
de Haas, H. (2010). "Migration and development: A theoretical perspective". *International Migration Review*, *44*(1), 227–264.
Fukuda-Parr, S. and Hulme, D. (2011). "International norm dynamics and the "end of poverty": Understanding the millennium development goals". *Global Governance: A Review of Multilateralism and International Organizations*, *17*(1), 17–36.
Global Forum on Migration and Development (GFMD) Civil Society. (2014). "Civil society "Stockholm Agenda" on migrant and migration-related goals and targets in the post-2015 global and national development agendas". (http://gfmdcivilsociety.org/wp-content/uploads/2014/06/Civil-Society-Migration-Stockholm-Agenda-June-2014.pdf) Accessed 8 January 2018.
Global Migration Policy Associates (GMPA). (2017). "The sustainable development goals and migrants/migration: Regarding the UN 2030 sustainable development agenda: Relevant SDGs and targets, rationales for inclusion, implementation actions, and realization measurement indicators, Version 3.2. Contribution to the fifteenth coordination meeting on international migration: global migration policy associates (GMPA)". (www.un.org/en/development/desa/population/migration/events/coordination/15/documents/papers/20_GMPA.pdf) Accessed 16 November 2017.
Hulme, D. (2009). *The Millennium Development Goals (MDGs): A Short History of the World's Biggest Promise*. Brooks World Poverty Institute (BWPI), Manchester, United Kingdom. Working Paper 100.
International Organization for Migration (IOM). (2017a). "Migration in the 2030 agenda". (https://publications.iom.int/system/files/pdf/migration_in_the_2030_agenda.pdf) Accessed 30 October 2017.
International Organization for Migration. (2017b). *Follow-Up and Review of Migration in the Sustainable Development Goals*. International Dialogue on Migration No. 26. International Organization for Migration, Geneva, Switzerland. (www.deslibris.ca/ID/10089612) Accessed 30 October 2017.
Joint Migration and Development Initiative (JMDI) (2017). "Guidelines on mainstreaming migration into local development planning". (http://migration4development.org/sites/default/files/guidelines_on_mainstreaming_migration.pdf) Accessed 20 November 2017.

McArthur, J. W. (2014). "The origins of the millennium development goals". *SAIS Review of International Affairs*, *34*(2), 5–24.

McGregor, E. (2017). "Intergovernmental organizations, migration and the sustainable development goals". Conference paper presented at the migrating out of poverty conference, London.

McGregor, E., Siegel, M., Ragab, N., and Juzwiak, T. (2014). *A New Global Partnership for Development: Factoring in the Contribution of Migration. IOM Migration Research Series, 50.* International Organization for Migration, Geneva, Switzerland.

Overseas Development Initiative (ODI). (2017). "Migration and the 2030 agenda for sustainable development". (www.odi.org/projects/2849-migration-and-2030-agenda-sustainable-development) Accessed 20 November 2017.

Piper, N. (2017). "Migration and the SDGs". *Global Social Policy*, *17*(2), 231–238.

Skeldon, R. (1997). *Migration and Development: A Global Perspective.* Addison Wesley Longman Limited, Essex.

Skeldon, R. (2008). "Migration policies and the millennium development goals". paper commissioned for the progressive governance conference, London, Policy Network, March, 2008, (www.policy-network.net/uploadedFiles/Publications/Publications/Ronald_Skeldon.pdf) Accessed 23 November 2017.

UN System Task Team on the Post-2015 UN Development Agenda (UNTT). (2012). "Realizing the future we want for all". (www.un.org/en/development/desa/policy/untaskteam_undf/presentatio n_untt_report.pdf) Accessed 15 October 2017.

UN Women. (2016). *Gender on the Move: Working on the Migration-Development Nexus from a Gender Perspective*, 2nd ed. UN Women Training Centre, Santa Domingo, Dominican Republic. (www.migration4 development.org/sites/default/files/genderonthemove_low2b_pdf.pdf) Accessed 26 October 2017.

United Nations (2006) "Secretary general appoints peter sutherland as special representative for migration". *SG/A/976-BIO/3735*, (www.un.org/press/en/2006/sga976.doc.htm) Accessed 8 January 2018.

United Nations General Assembly. (2000) "United Nations millennium declaration". 18 September 2000, A/RES/55/2, (www.un.org/millennium/declaration/ares552e.pdf) Accessed 16 March 2018.

United Nations General Assembly. (2015) "Transforming our world: The 2030 agenda for sustainable development". 21 October 2015, A/RES/70/1, (www.refworld.org/docid/57b6e3e44.html) Accessed 23 October 2017.

Appendix 26.1

Migration and the SDGs

SDG Target	Relevance to Migration
1.1 By 2030, eradicate extreme poverty for all people everywhere, currently measured as people living on less than $1.25 a day.	Inclusive Language
1.2 By 2030, reduce at least by half the proportion of men, women and children of all ages living in poverty in all its dimensions according to national definitions.	Inclusive Language
1.3 Implement nationally appropriate social protection systems and measures for all, including floors, and by 2030 achieve substantial coverage of the poor and the vulnerable.	Inclusive Language
1.4 By 2030, ensure that all men and women, in particular the poor and the vulnerable, have equal rights to economic resources, as well as access to basic services, ownership and control over land and other forms of property, inheritance, natural resources, appropriate new technology and financial services, including microfinance.	Inclusive Language
1.5 By 2030, build the resilience of the poor and those in vulnerable situations and reduce their exposure and vulnerability to climate-related extreme events and other economic, social and environmental shocks and disasters.	Appears in **all four** SDG review publications (IOM, ODI, JMDI and GMPA)
2.1 By 2030, end hunger and ensure access by all people, in particular the poor and people in vulnerable situations, including infants, to safe, nutritious and sufficient food all year round.	Inclusive Language
3.8 Achieve universal health coverage, including financial risk protection, access to quality essential health-care services and access to safe, effective, quality and affordable essential medicines and vaccines for all.	Inclusive Language, Appears in **all four** SDG review publications (IOM, ODI, JMDI and GMPA)
3.b Support the research and development of vaccines and medicines for the communicable and non-communicable diseases that primarily affect developing countries, provide access to affordable essential medicines and vaccines, in accordance with the Doha Declaration on the TRIPS Agreement and Public Health, which affirms the right of developing countries to use to the full the provisions in the Agreement on Trade-Related Aspects of Intellectual Property Rights regarding flexibilities to protect public health, and, in particular, provide access to medicines for all.	Inclusive Language
4.1 By 2030, ensure that all girls and boys complete free, equitable and quality primary and secondary education leading to relevant and effective learning outcomes.	Inclusive Language

(Continued)

(Cont).

SDG Target	Relevance to Migration
4.2 By 2030, ensure that all girls and boys have access to quality early childhood development, care and pre-primary education so that they are ready for primary education.	Inclusive Language
4.3 By 2030, ensure equal access for all women and men to affordable and quality technical, vocational and tertiary education, including university.	Inclusive Language
4.4 By 2030, substantially increase the number of youth and adults who have relevant skills, including technical and vocational skills, for employment, decent jobs and entrepreneurship.	Appears in **all four** SDG review publications (IOM, ODI, JMDI and GMPA)
4.6 By 2030, ensure that all youth and a substantial proportion of adults, both men and women, achieve literacy and numeracy.	Inclusive Language
4.7 By 2030, ensure that all learners acquire the knowledge and skills needed to promote sustainable development, including, among others, through education for sustainable development and sustainable lifestyles, human rights, gender equality, promotion of a culture of peace and non-violence, global citizenship and appreciation of cultural diversity and of culture's contribution to sustainable development.	Inclusive Language
4.a Build and upgrade education facilities that are child, disability and gender sensitive and provide safe, non-violent, inclusive and effective learning environments for all.	Inclusive Language, Appears in **all four** SDG review publications (IOM, ODI, JMDI and GMPA)
5.1 End all forms of discrimination against all women and girls everywhere	Inclusive Language
5.2 Eliminate all forms of violence against all women and girls in the public and private spheres, including trafficking and sexual and other types of exploitation.	Inclusive Language
5.4 Recognise and value unpaid care and domestic work through the provision of public services, infrastructure and social protection policies and the promotion of shared responsibility within the household and the family as nationally appropriate.	Appears in **all four** SDG review publications (IOM, ODI, JMDI and GMPA)
5.c Adopt and strengthen sound policies and enforceable legislation for the promotion of gender equality and the empowerment of all women and girls at all levels.	Inclusive Language
6.1 By 2030, achieve universal and equitable access to safe and affordable drinking water for all.	Inclusive Language
6.2 By 2030, achieve access to adequate and equitable sanitation and hygiene for all and end open defecation, paying special attention to the needs of women and girls and those in vulnerable situations.	Inclusive Language
8.10 Strengthen the capacity of domestic financial institutions to encourage and expand access to banking, insurance and financial services for all.	Inclusive Language
8.3 Promote development-oriented policies that support productive activities, decent job creation, entrepreneurship,	Appears in **all four** SDG review publications (IOM, ODI, JMDI, and GMPA)

(*Continued*)

(Cont).

SDG Target	Relevance to Migration
creativity and innovation, and encourage the formalisation and growth of micro-, small- and medium-sized enterprises, including through access to financial services.	
8.5 By 2030, achieve full and productive employment and decent work for all women and men, including for young people and persons with disabilities, and equal pay for work of equal value.	Inclusive Language
8.7 Take immediate and effective measures to eradicate forced labour, end modern slavery and human trafficking and secure the prohibition and elimination of the worst forms of child labour, including recruitment and use of child soldiers, and by 2025 end child labour in all its forms.	Appears in **all four** SDG review publications (IOM, ODI, JMDI, and GMPA)
8.8 Protect labour rights and promote safe and secure working environments for all workers, including migrant workers, in particular women migrants, and those in precarious employment.	*Explicit Reference*, Inclusive Language, Appears in **all four** SDG review publications (IOM, ODI, JMDI, and GMPA)
9.1 Develop quality, reliable, sustainable and resilient infrastructure, including regional and trans-border infrastructure, to support economic development and human well-being, with a focus on affordable and equitable access for all.	Inclusive Language
10.2 By 2030, empower and promote the social, economic and political inclusion of all, irrespective of age, sex, disability, race, ethnicity, origin, religion or economic or other status.	Inclusive Language
10.7 Facilitate orderly, safe, regular and responsible migration and mobility of people, including through the implementation of planned and well-managed migration policies.	*Explicit Reference*, Appears in **all four** SDG review publications (IOM, ODI, JMDI and GMPA)
10.c By 2030, reduce to less than 3 per cent the transaction costs of migrant remittances and eliminate remittance corridors with costs higher than 5 per cent.	*Explicit Reference*, Appears in **all four** SDG review publications (IOM, ODI, JMDI, and GMPA)
11.1 By 2030, ensure access for all to adequate, safe and affordable housing and basic services and upgrade slums.	Inclusive Language
11.2 By 2030, provide access to safe, affordable, accessible and sustainable transport systems for all, improving road safety, notably by expanding public transport, with special attention to the needs of those in vulnerable situations, women, children, persons with disabilities and older persons.	Inclusive Language
13.1 Strengthen resilience and adaptive capacity to climate-related hazards and natural disasters in all countries.	Appears in **all four** SDG review publications (IOM, ODI, JMDI, and GMPA)
13.b Promote mechanisms for raising capacity for effective climate change-related planning and management in least developed countries and small island developing States, including focusing on women, youth and local and marginalised communities.	Appears in **all four** SDG review publications (IOM, ODI, JMDI, and GMPA)
16.3 Promote the rule of law at the national and international levels and ensure equal access to justice for all.	Inclusive Language Appears in **all four** SDG review publications (IOM, ODI, JMDI. and GMPA)

(*Continued*)

(Cont).

SDG Target	Relevance to Migration
16.9 By 2030, provide legal identity for all, including birth registration.	Inclusive Language
17.18 By 2020, enhance capacity-building support to developing countries, including for least developed countries and small island developing States, to increase significantly the availability of high-quality, timely and reliable data disaggregated by income, gender, age, race, ethnicity, migratory status, disability, geographic location and other characteristics relevant in national contexts.	*Explicit Reference*, Appears in **all four** SDG review publications (IOM, ODI, JMDI, and GMPA)

27

NATIONAL MIGRATION POLICY

Nature, patterns, and effects

Mathias Czaika

Introduction

The ongoing European migration crisis fundamentally challenges the way immigration has been managed over the past few decades. Existing immigration regimes largely originate from periods where nation-states could deal with human mobility solely at and within their borders. Reactive migration policy 'on-territory' was sufficient as long as the scale of mostly unwanted, low-skilled immigrants were not too large and the demand for wanted high-skilled workers was not too high. Until recently, aversion against unwanted and the desire for wanted migration were mostly at levels where policy-makers did not face the need to re-think the fundamental principles and mechanisms of their national immigration systems.

In Europe, national migration policies towards non-European migrants have changed only gradually over the past decades, and often only at the margin. Aside from some paradigmatic shifts in intra-regional migration and mobility regimes, first and foremost, of course, the free mobility and free movement of worker regimes within the European Union and the Schengen area, international cross-border migration follows largely the same rules and practices for decades: nation-states wait and see what type of and how many human beings arrive on their territory, and if considered necessary, states usually respond unilaterally and in mostly uncoordinated ways by making admission and stay regulations slightly more or less restrictive, putting more or less effort in the apprehension of irregularly entering or residing migrants, or trying to attract and select much needed labour migrants for employment in shortage occupations.

Understanding the making and unmaking of immigration policy has been the objective of some academic debate (e.g. Castles 2004). Immigration policy changes, which are usually the outcome of political processes and interactions among stakeholders in bureaucratic, legislative, judicial, and public arenas, aim to encourage, discourage, or otherwise regulate the flow of immigrants (Massey 1999, 307). Or, put differently, explicit migration policies are established in order to affect (migratory) behaviour of a target population, which includes actual and potential migrants, in an intended direction (Czaika and de Haas 2013). The underlying objectives, patterns, scope, and effects of immigration policies may change over time and certainly do across states (Rosenblum and Cornelius 2012).

Besides *explicit* migration policies, that is, policies that target potential migrants aiming to influence their migration decisions in a certain direction, other public policies may affect international migration processes more indirectly and implicitly by changing the socio-economic context within which migration takes place. These more *implicit* migration policies, including industrial policies, education and labour market policies, taxation and welfare policies, etc., are certainly migration-relevant and have the potential to shape migration, but to what extent is still very much under-researched and therefore beyond the scope of this chapter.

This chapter therefore aims to take stock of the current state of (explicit) national migration policies and their role in influencing international migration and integration processes. I will address the nature and making of migration policies by elaborating on the evolution of existing migration regimes and reviewing conceptual and empirical insights and evidence on the effects of migration policies including their unintended consequences. I conclude with some suggestions for further research in this area.

Migration policy transition

Migration policy regimes evolve over longer time periods and change only very rarely suddenly and substantially. Migration policies reflect and adapt their designs and characteristics to major trends and patterns of emigration and immigration. Most countries have at least some migration in both directions – people simultaneously moving in and out – which in a broader sense defines any country as both a country of emigration *and* immigration. Obviously, this definition is not very helpful when we want to classify a country's migration regime. Therefore, only countries with significant and long-term *net* immigration should be called *countries of immigration*. Likewise, *a country of emigration* is characterised by a significant and persistent net outflow of its native population. Most immigration countries have developed immigration regimes that use an array of regulatory and administrative measures to monitor, regulate, and control immigration processes. Emigration of native population, on the other hand, remains in most countries largely unregulated.[1]

Globally, the majority of countries are net emigration countries, and over recent decades, the number of countries and territories with net immigration has been continuously decreasing (Czaika and de Haas 2014). This phenomenon can be explained by migration transition theory (Zelinsky 1971), which predicts a non-linear, hump-shaped pattern and relationship between economic development and its effect on (net) migration. Emigration from a country dominates immigration into this country at early stages of its development process. However, when countries continue to develop into economically-thriving middle-income countries, emigration and immigration patterns and dynamics change and adapt to the new, rapidly emerging economic, social, and political structures (De Haas 2010; Skeldon 2012). In most countries, following a sustainable economic growth and development path, emigration tends to decrease while immigration is continuously increasing as a result of expanding domestic opportunities.

Less developed, low-income countries which often suffer under severe economic and political fragility and vulnerability, are often characterised by significant absolute and relative emigration and only very little, if any, immigration. As a consequence, net emigration is significant. That is, the number of people leaving those countries due to economic or political reasons is usually larger than the number of people moving in the opposite direction. In these contexts, migration flows remain largely unregulated as these countries usually lack the necessary capacity to control and manage the movement of people in an orderly manner. Emerging middle-income economies have usually established growth-enhancing institutions and some reliable governance structures, which turn these countries into increasingly attractive places for low- and high-skilled workers from abroad. In these more developed countries, inflows and outflows tend to shift gradually towards more balanced net migration with ongoing outmigration increasingly being compensated by both growing return movements of nationals living abroad and immigration of foreign workers.

In contrast to most low- and middle-income countries, the majority of high-income (OECD and non-OECD) countries have grown into major destinations for an increasingly diverse range of immigrant groups (Vertovec 2007). As a consequence, these net immigration countries have developed sophisticated immigration systems employing an array of policy instruments to manage the admission, selection, and integration of various immigrant groups, including students, high- and less-skilled workers, family migrants, intra-company transferees, investors and entrepreneurs, and refugees and asylum seekers.

International migration is an inherent part of multiple socio-economic, political, and demographic transitions (Castles 2010), which, in the long run, transforms some countries from net emigration into net immigration countries (Figure 27.1). This transition of migration processes from net emigration to net immigration is usually associated with a concomitant migration *policy* transition. This policy transition is reflected by the evolution of sophisticated and complex immigration systems which establish a multitude of immigration categories for temporary, circular, and permanent, economic and non-economic, forced and voluntary migrants. Despite some variation in the timing and sequencing of immigration policy changes and innovations across this group of high-income destinations, most countries in this group have been moving towards immigration systems which follow two major objectives: first, controlling, and if necessary restricting unwanted, mostly low-skilled and irregular migrant workers and other non-economic migrants; second, facilitating migration and mobility of high-skilled migrants and knowledge workers recruited for sectors such as health or ICT in which many countries perceive growing shortages. Over the last one or two decades, several emerging, middle-income economies like Brazil, China, Malaysia, or Turkey have gradually been developing immigration policies which resemble in some aspects those of Western liberal states, although many emerging economies still face slightly different needs and policy priorities compared to Western immigration countries with a longer tradition of immigration (Cerna and Czaika 2018).

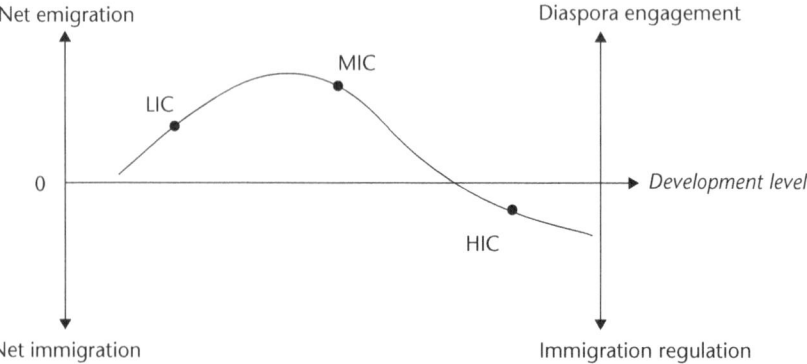

Figure 27.1 Migration transition and changing policy priorities ('migration policy transition')
Note: LIC=Low-income countries; MIC=Middle-income countries; HIC=High-income countries

Figure 27.1 illustrates this non-linear relationship between level of development, net migration, and migration policy priorities. High-income countries are situated at one end of this transition process, characterised by significant net immigration flows, sophisticated immigration policy regimes, and a growing diversity of the immigrant population. Low-income countries are mostly characterised by a significant net outflow of their, in particular, young and skilled population. These countries sit at the other end of this development–migration–policy continuum and focus mostly on policies which target their diaspora either by providing protection services for their vulnerable, mostly low-skilled migrant workers abroad or by actively engaging with their potent, often high-skilled diaspora to generate remittances or facilitate return.

Emerging, mostly middle-income, countries are often active in both policy dimensions as they often experience major inflows and outflows at the same time. In fact, emerging economies do not only continue to lose skilled emigrants from their growing middle class, but also start attracting low and high-skilled workers from abroad. Policy priorities are not only protecting workers abroad (Martin et al. 2004) or engaging with the diaspora (Gamlen 2008), but these countries also start experimenting with policies that aim to attract sought-after talent (Cerna and Czaika 2018) or controlling unwanted (irregular) immigration (e.g. Shah 2009; Düvell 2012).

Immigration policy evolution

Over the past half-century, immigration policies in most net immigration countries have become more sophisticated, and overall, less restrictive than the period between World War I and II (Meyers 2000; De Haas et al. 2016). In particular in the late nineteenth and early twentieth century, due to the fading preoccupation on exit policies ('exit revolution'), as well as the introduction of modern passport systems reflecting the growing focus on immigration policies, established a major policy transition (Torpey 2000, Zolberg 2007).

Since then, the evolution of migration policies has been neither linear nor uniform across countries and policy areas. Figure 27.2 reveals that over the past 70 years, policy changes in major (mostly Western) destination countries have been heavily concentrated on border control and more recently on exit and return measures, while admission regulations and post-entry integration policies have become overall less restrictive over the past few decades. However, policies have become more fine-grained and targeted on specific migrant groups which are reflected in the creation of multiple entry channels for low and high-skilled workers, permanent and temporary migrants, family members, students, entrepreneurs, and asylum seekers. Obviously, for each of these migrant categories, entry and post-entry regulations have not changed uniformly for the different legal categories but have become stricter for some migrant groups while turning more liberal for other groups. These trends and patterns reflect the extent to which governments have liberalised regular entry channels and stay perspectives for 'wanted' migrants, while border control and enforcement policies, as well as return and deportation measures, have become more restrictive in an apparent attempt to prevent the entry and (irregular) stay of 'unwanted' migrants.

Policies seeking to attract and select 'wanted' migrant workers are proliferating rapidly across the globe. In 2015, almost half of all UN member states and two-thirds of all 35 OECD member states aimed to increase the numbers of high-skilled immigrants (Czaika and Parsons 2017). Thus, high-income countries are at the forefront of this policy trend by which states have established policy instruments aimed at selecting highly qualified immigrants to fill domestic labour shortages and address structural undersupply of qualified labour

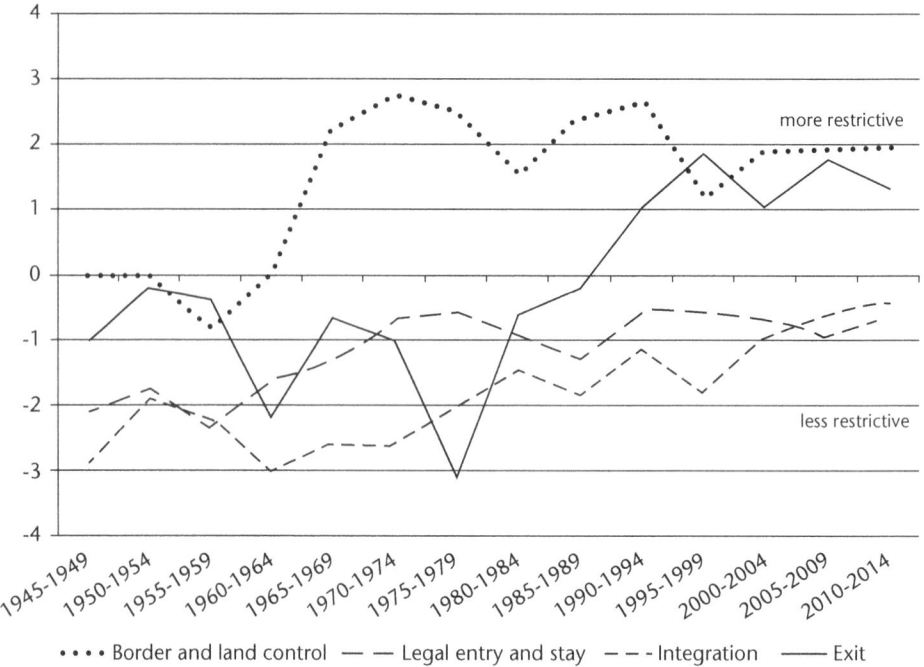

Figure 27.2 Immigration regime evolution in 22 Western liberal states, 1945–2014
Source: De Haas et al. (2016)

in specific sectors such as health services, ICT, or engineering (Bhagwati and Hanson 2009; Chaloff and Lemaitre 2009). Whether these policies are conducive and effective in addressing structural and temporal occupational shortages is highly contested, not least since the identification and quantification of labour and skill shortages in the first place is rather problematic (Ruhs and Anderson 2010).

Czaika and Parsons (2017) identify enhanced policymaking activity in this policy areas since the early 2000s by which primarily OECD countries increasingly employ instruments such as quotas, occupational shortage lists, job contingency requirements, labour market tests, points-based systems, (student) job-seeker visas, employer portability rights, immediate family reunion rights, spousal work rights, permanency rights, financial incentive schemes, labour market protection regulations, and more for facilitating and filtering immigration of labour.[2]

Figure 27.3 indicates the percentage of 19 OECD countries that have implemented any of these instruments since 2000. Three out of four countries implement job offer systems, while around half have implemented some 'demand-driven' policy instruments such as occupational shortage lists or labour market tests. Ten out of nineteen countries also use quotas. Points-based systems are only implemented in six countries. The selection tool that became very popular over the past two decades is the post-study job seeker visa. In 2000, none of the 19 countries implemented such schemes, while 15 years later, more than half of the countries have introduced such measures that aim to retain foreign-born graduates (Czaika and Parsons 2018).

Beyond skill-selection policy instruments, Figure 27.3 also illustrates that immigration packages that regulate post-entry rights of migrant workers have gained wide importance. These policies typically regulate pathways to permanent residency, which includes immediate

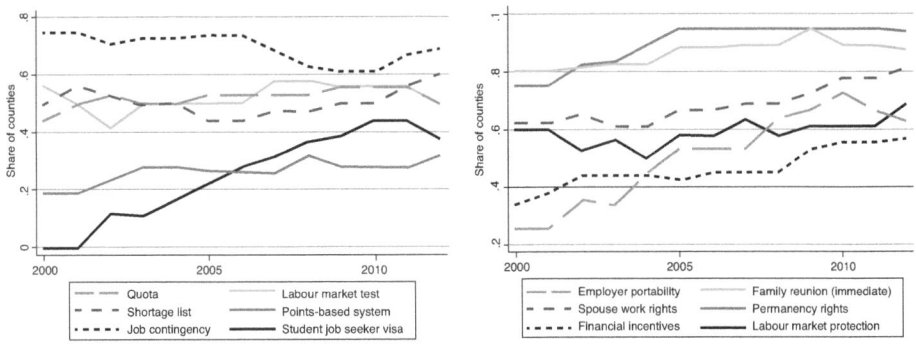

Figure 27.3 Labour migration policies OECD countries since 2000: entry (*left*) and post-entry (*right*)
Source: Czaika and Parsons (2018)

settlement rights for high-skilled work permit grantees which often provide similar rights to the family members of skilled migrants. Four out of five countries provide immediate family reunification rights, and in addition, some work rights for accompanying spouses, either immediately or after a fixed period of time. Countries increasingly use financial incentives schemes including tax cuts and allowances, to attract and retain high-skilled migrants.

In addition to non-discriminatory unilateral policy measures, many countries have signed bi- and multilateral agreements which shall regulate, for instance, social security provision, double taxation, and tax evasion or the recognition of foreign-earned diplomas and credentials. These arrangements shall facilitate and increase mobility and circularity of wanted foreign workers, which are mostly skilled or high-skilled. Diploma recognition agreements in particular have gained eminent attention over the last decade.

Despite an overall tendency towards more liberal admission and integration policies in favour of wanted labour migrants, modern states have simultaneously developed a desire to monitor and control population movements more systematically. Besides the multiple immigration policy instruments available to regulate entry and stay of migration unilaterally, travel visas in combination with carrier sanctions are a central instrument of mobility control intensively used by modern states (Salter 2006; Finotelli and Sciortino 2013). Although visa policies primarily regulate the entry of travellers and other temporary visitors such as business people, in practice they also function as instruments of migration control. Modern visa systems are often used to reduce the 'risk' of entry of potential asylum seekers and unauthorised migrants overstaying their temporary visa (Schoorl et al. 2000; Neumayer 2006). Travel visa restrictions are therefore a key instrument in the migration policy toolbox. Many immigration states use visa restrictions as an extraterritorial 'upstream' instrument to prevent unwanted migrants from approaching and accessing the national territory (Mau et al. 2012). The nature of travel visas allow nation-states to discriminate between nationalities and to impose restrictions on only those nationalities which are considered 'high risk' of overstaying visas and/or claiming asylum (Neumayer 2006; Czaika and de Haas 2017).

Figure 27.4 shows that not only net immigration countries in Western liberal states use visa restrictions as a 'legitimate means of movement' (cf. Torpey 1998). Over the past four decades, Africa, for instance, has become a continent with relatively high levels of inbound visa restrictiveness, particularly in West Africa, East Africa, and Central Africa. Countries in

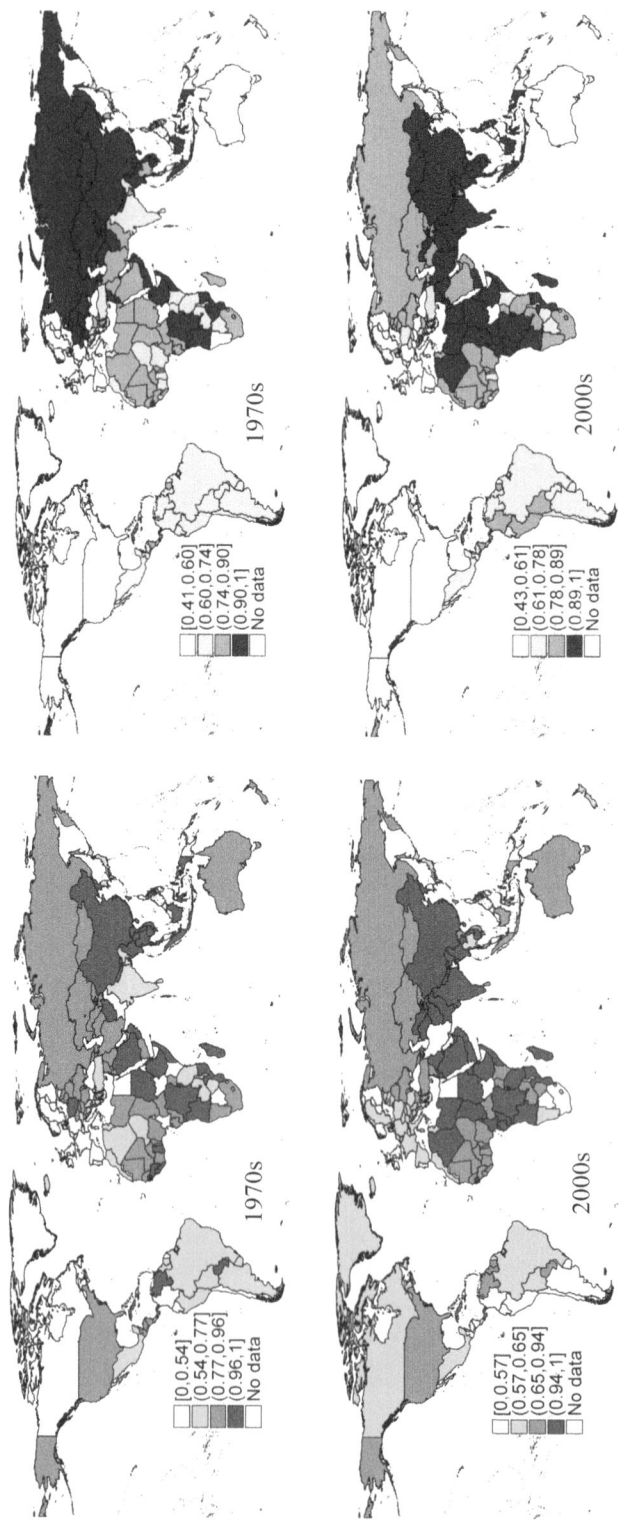

Figure 27.4 Inbound (*left*) and outbound (*right*) visa restrictiveness, 1970s versus 2000s

Source: Czaika et al. (2018)

the Middle East and parts of Asia also employ increasingly restrictive visa regimes (Czaika et al. 2018). Over the past four decades, visa restrictions across Europe show a mixed pattern, with a clear East–West divide before 1989 but some convergence at moderate levels since then (see a discussion of the 'policy convergence hypothesis' by Hollifield et al. 2014).

From the perspective of prospective migrants or travellers, the outbound visa restrictiveness yields a more clear-cut pattern compared to those of inbound visa restrictiveness (Figure 27.3, right). From this perspective, Western citizens, but also Latin Americans, are among those enjoying the greatest visa-free travel opportunities, measured by the degree to which citizens of each country require visas to enter other countries. While citizens of the former Soviet Union and communist Eastern European countries faced high levels of outbound visa restrictiveness before 1989, these restrictions have receded remarkably since then. Outbound visa restrictiveness has become comparatively high for mobile people in Africa and the Middle East, as well as for most South, East, and South-East Asian countries, despite a few exceptions such as Japan, South Korea, and Malaysia (Czaika et al. 2018).

Visa policy regimes reflect not only the general openness or closed-ness of countries towards the mobile people but also the strength of political, social, cultural, and economic ties between states and societies. Czaika et al. (2018) propose visa reciprocity, or the degree to which state A can impose a visa requirement on citizens from state B without state A having to fear a retaliating measure by state B for their own citizens, as an indicator of international power asymmetries. According to this study, visa reciprocity has slightly increased over the past decades with more bilateral corridors being simultaneously either visa-restricted or visa-free for citizens of both sides. This decline in bilateral power asymmetries has been significantly influenced by economic and political regionalisation processes which lead to an incremental intra-regional opening and extra-regional closure of mobility regimes.

Migration policy effects

Migration policy scholarship has not yet conclusively answered the question whether restrictive immigration and border control policies are an effective way to curb unwanted immigration (Brochmann and Hammar 1999; Bhagwati 2003; Massey and Pren 2012; Czaika and de Haas 2013). The assessment of the effects and effectiveness of immigration policies is a highly contested issue as empirically it shows only mixed results. While in some historical cases some immigration policies have largely been effective, other anecdotal and contemporary evidence shows that states often fail to control and restrict immigration, at least when evaluated with regard to the explicit or implicit policy objectives (Hollifield et al. 2014).

Migration scholars are particularly sceptical about the capacity of (liberal democratic) nation-states to control migration given that migration itself is mostly driven by structural factors such as labour market imbalances, inequalities in wealth and opportunities and violent conflicts and persecution in origin countries, which all lie largely beyond the reach of national policymaking, at least in the short run. In contrast to a dominant scepticism, some scholars have highlighted that, by and large, immigration policies are effective (Brochmann and Hammar 1999; Geddes 2003; Bonjour 2011).

Whether migration policies are effective or not, or whether they simply generate some partial effects is an important distinction. The notion of 'effectiveness' requires a quantitative or qualitative yardstick or benchmark against which migration outcomes can be evaluated. Migration policy effects, however, only require that some change in migration outcomes can be (causally) linked to some preceding policy changes. These effects might be intended or not, at least their assessment is largely value-free.

If not only used symbolically to signal an appearance of control (Massey 1999), migration policies are usually established in order to affect the behaviour of a target population in an intended direction (Czaika and de Haas 2013). Migration policy effects can be evaluated by changes in the volume, the spatial orientation, the legal and illegal channels, the migrant characteristics, the timing, and the direction of migration flows. Several authors (e.g. Borjas 1999; De Haas 2011; Czaika and de Haas 2013; Bjerre 2017) have identified and conceptualised various migration policy effects. Assuming that a policy change (i.e. an introduction or removal of a migration restriction) is properly implemented, the following types of immigration policy effects, or mechanisms through which a policy intervention may lead to a certain migration outcome, can be distinguished. Admission effects are hereby the result of new entry opportunities and they usually increase the absolute inflow of migrants. Deterrence effects are the result of policy changes towards more restrictiveness and work in the opposite direction; removal of entry opportunities should reduce absolute numbers of entries, as a consequence of a reduced number of attempts or a higher number of failed attempts. Czaika and de Haas (2017), for instance, estimate that a visa requirement reduces bilateral migration flows by more than 30 per cent. Other authors identify similar deterrence effects of entire immigration systems (see Mayda 2010) or specific immigration policy areas such as border policies, admission, or integration (De Haas et al. 2019).

Deflection effects are the result of a (partial) reorientation of migrants to other destinations (spatial deflection) or other entry channels (categorical deflection). While spatial deflection usually reduces absolute inflows of migrants into the migration policy-restricting destination, categorical deflection may leave absolute inflows of migrants unaffected but rather affects the composition of gross inflows. For instance, Czaika and Hobolth (2016) find evidence for a 'deflection into irregularity' as a consequence of restrictive asylum policies. This implies that although restrictive changes in government regulations and practices may deter some potential asylum seekers, a more comprehensive assessment suggests that this conclusion is at least incomplete since some of the 'deterred' regular migrants are re-directed towards other, usually irregular entry channels.

Furthermore, migration policy effects are usually highly asymmetrical. That is, a policy change in a more liberal direction does not necessarily create the same reverse effects of a policy change in the opposite direction towards greater restrictiveness. For instance, Czaika and de Haas (2016) found that policy changes towards greater restrictiveness (such as a visa introduction) usually generate very delayed effects with only gradually declining immigration flows whereas policy changes towards more liberal regulations such as the lifting of a visa requirement have an almost immediate effect on respective immigration levels. The high responsiveness of migration movements upon policy liberalisation can indicate so-called intertemporal substitution effects (De Haas 2011), whereby people partake in 'now or never' or 'beat the ban' migration, for instance because prospective migrants may fear re-introduction of migration restrictions. It is often against the best interests and objectives of policy-makers when immigration restrictions not only deter migrants and reduce the respective gross inflow of migrants, but also affect the return flows to an extent that *net migration* may not necessarily be negative. Czaika and de Haas (2016) show that visa restrictions significantly decrease immigration *and* emigration, or the deterrence effect is partly counterbalanced by a settlement effect of those who would otherwise return and potentially re-enter in the future. This combined inflow and reverse flow effect of immigration policy restrictions results usually in diminished circularity.

Conclusion

National migration policies have become increasingly complex and multifaceted in their objectives, design, functions, and effects. The boundaries of migration policy and 'non-migration' policy are relatively blurred as many public policies that are usually not classified as migration policies – because they do not target (potential) migrants – nevertheless influence migration processes, and the effects of such policies may in certain cases be even larger than those of immigration policies targeting migrants. For instance, labour market and higher education policies are likely to affect immigration, although this is not the prime aim of such policies. This implies that the lines between migration and other migration-relevant public policies are often blurred.

To understand the specific role and effects of migration policy, we must first better understand the way structural conditions within and between destination and origin countries affect migration patterns and dynamics. Structural factors such as economic and political (in-) stability, (changing) labour market structures, social stratifications, income inequality, poverty, welfare provisions, and social security systems are important drivers of international migration processes. Development as a multidimensional driver of migration involves much more than economic growth and progress. Development as freedom (Sen 2001) to choose and realise the kind of lives people have reason to value, either in situ or elsewhere, simultaneously constrains and facilitates migration processes and mediates the effects of migration policies. As a consequence, the volume, composition, timing, or geographic direction of international migration flows are only partially affected by migration policies and work mostly in interaction with those other migration drivers. Understanding these configurations of policy and non-policy drivers of migration, and testing the scope of these 'driver complexes' (Van Hear et al. 2017), remains a task for further research in this area.

Notes

1 However, some countries still employ much targeted exit restrictions and barriers for instance of single females or males conscribed for military service.
2 One of the editors of this volume noticed that the development of all these migration policy instruments seems to have occurred without much attention given to the policies that are designed to attract the industries that will require these people in the first place. That is, migration policy instruments are rarely designed and implemented within the context of industrial and regional development policy.

References

Bhagwati, J. and Hanson, G. (2009) *Skilled Immigration Today: Prospects, Problems, and Policies*. Oxford: Oxford University Press.

Bhagwati, J. (2003) 'Borders beyond control'. *Foreign Affairs*, 82, 98–104.

Bjerre, L. (2017) 'Immigration policy effects – a conceptual framework'. IMI working paper No. 139, University of Oxford.

Bonjour, S. (2011) 'The power and morals of policy makers: Reassessing the control gap debate'. *International Migration Review*, 45(1): 89–112.

Borjas, G. J. (1999) 'Immigration and welfare magnets'. *Journal of labor economics*, 17(4): 607–637.

Brochmann, G. and Hammar, T. (Eds.). (1999) *Mechanisms of Immigration Control*. Oxford/New York: Berg.

Castles, S. (2004) 'The factors that make and unmake migration policies'. *International Migration Review*, 38(3): 852–884.

Castles, S. (2010) 'Understanding global migration: A social transformation perspective'. *Journal of ethnic and migration studies*, 36(10): 1565–1586.

Cerna, L. and Czaika, M. (2018) Rising Stars in the Global Race for Skill? A Comparative Analysis of Brazil, India and Malaysia, forthcoming as IMI-n working paper.

Chaloff, J. and Lemaitre, G.. 2009. "Managing Highly-Skilled Labour Migration: A Comparative Analysis of Migration Policies and Challenges in OECD Countries." DELSA/ELSA/WD/SEM(2009)5, OECD Publishing, Paris.

Czaika, M. and de Haas, H. (2017) 'The effect of visas on migration processes'. *International Migration Review*, 51(4): 893–926.

Czaika, M., de Haas, H. and Villares-Varela, M. (2018). The global evolution of travel visa regimes: an analysis of the DEMIG VISA database. *Population and Development Review*, 44(3): 589–622.

Czaika, M. and de Haas, H. (2014) 'The globalization of migration: Has the world become more migratory?' *International Migration Review*, 48(2): 283–323.

Czaika, M. and de Haas, H. (2013) 'The effectiveness of immigration policies'. *Population and Development Review*, 39(3): 487–508.

Czaika, M., & Hobolth, M. (2016). Do restrictive asylum and visa policies increase irregular migration into Europe?. *European Union Politics*, 17(3), 345–365.

Czaika, M. and Parsons, C. R. (2017) 'The gravity of high-skilled migration policies'. *Demography*, 54(2): 603–630.

Czaika, M. and Parsons, C. (2018). "High-skilled Migration in Times of Global Economic Crisis." In Mathias Czaika (Ed.)*High-Skilled Migration: Drivers and Policies*. Oxford: Oxford University Press, 20-47.

De Haas, H. (2011). 'The determinants of international migration'. IMI working paper No 32. Oxford: International Migration Institute, University of Oxford

De Haas, H. (2010) "Migration transitions: A theoretical and empirical inquiry into the developmental drivers of international migration." IMI working paper. Oxford: Working Paper, International Migration Institute, University of Oxford

De Haas, H., Czaika, M., Flahaux, M., Mahendra, E., Natter, K., Vezzoli, S. and Villares-Varela, M. (2019), 'International migration: Trends, determinants, and policy effects.' *Population and Development Review*, 45(4): 885–922. doi: 10.1111/padr.12291.

De Haas, H., Natter, K. and Vezzoli, S. (2016) "Growing restrictiveness or changing selection? The nature and evolution of migration policies." *International Migration Review*.

Düvell, F. (2012) 'Transit migration: a blurred and politicised concept'. *Population, Space and Place*, 18(4): 415–427.

Finotelli, C. and Sciortino, G. (2013) 'Through the gates of the fortress: European visa policies and the limits of immigration control'. *Perspectives on European Politics and Society*, 14(1): 80–101.

Gamlen, A. (2008) 'The emigration state and the modern geopolitical imagination'. *Political Geography*, 27(8): 840–856.

Geddes, A. (2003) *The Politics of Migration and Immigration in Europe*. London: Sage.

Hollifield, J., Martin, P. L. and Orrenius, P. (Eds.). (2014) *Controlling immigration: A global perspective*. Redwood City: Stanford University Press.

Martin, P., Abella, M. and Midgley, E. (2004) 'Best practices to manage migration: The Philippines'. *International Migration Review*, 38(4): 1544–1559.

Massey, D. and Pren, K. (2012) 'Unintended consequences of US immigration policy: Explaining the post-1965 surge from Latin America'. *Population and Development Review*, 38(1): 1–29.

Massey, D. S. (1999) 'International migration at the dawn of the twenty-first century: The role of the state'. *Population and Development Review*, 25(2): 303–322.

Mau, S., Brabandt, H., Laube, L. and Roos, C. (2012) "Visa Policies and the Regulation of Territorial Access." In Mau, S., Brabandt, H., Laube, L. and Roos, C.*Liberal States and the Freedom of Movement*. London: Palgrave Macmillan, 54–87.

Mayda, A. M. (2010) 'International migration: A panel data analysis of the determinants of bilateral flows'. *Journal of Population Economics*, 23(4): 1249–1274.

Meyers, Eytan. 'Theories of international immigration policy—A comparative analysis'. *International migration review* 34(4) (2000): 1245–1282.

Neumayer, E. (2006) 'Unequal access to foreign spaces: How states use visa restrictions to regulate mobility in a globalized world'. *Transactions of the Institute of British Geographers*, 31(1): 72–84.

Rosenblum, M. R. and Cornelius, W. A. (2012) "Dimensions of Immigration Policy (Chapter 11)." In Rosenblum, M. R. and Tichenor D. J. (Eds.) *The Oxford Handbook of the Politics of International Migration*. Oxford University Press, 245-273.

Ruhs, M. and Anderson, B. (Eds.). (2010) *Who needs Migrant Workers?: Labour Shortages, Immigration, and Public Policy*. Oxford: Oxford University Press.

Salter, M. B. (2006) 'The global visa regime and the political technologies of the international self: Borders, bodies, biopolitics'. *Alternatives: Global, Local, Political*, 31(2): 167–189.

Schoorl, J., Heering, L., Esveldt, I., Groenewold, G., van der Erf, R., Bosch, A., de Valk, H. and de Bruijn, B. (2000) *Push and Pull Factors of International Migration: A Comparative Report*. Luxembourg: Eurostat, European Communities.

Sen, A. K. (2001) *Development as freedom*. Oxford: Oxford University Press.

Shah, N. M. (2009). The management of irregular migration and its consequence for development: Gulf cooperation council (No. 431863). International Labour Organization.

Skeldon, R. (2012) 'Migration transitions revisited: Their continued relevance for the development of migration theory'. *Population, Space and place*, 18(2): 154–166.

Torpey, J. (1998) 'Coming and going: On the state monopolization of the legitimate "means of movement"'. *Sociological Theory*, 16(3): 239–259.

Torpey, J. (2000) *The Invention of the Passport: Surveillance, Citizenship and the State*. Cambridge: Cambridge University Press.

Van Hear, N., Bakewell, O. and Long, K. (2017) 'Push-pull plus: Reconsidering the drivers of migration'. *Journal of Ethnic and Migration Studies*. doi.org/10.1080/1369183X.2017.1384135.

Vertovec, S. (2007) 'Super-diversity and its implications'. *Ethnic and racial studies*, 30(6): 1024–1054.

Zelinsky, Z. (1971) 'The Hypothesis of the Mobility Transition'. *Geographical Review*, 61(2): 219–249.

Zolberg, Aristide R. 2007. "The Exit revolution." In Green N. L. and Weil F. (Ed.), *Citizenship and Those Who Leave: The Politics of Emigration and Expatriation*. Urbana and Chicago: University of Illinois Press, 33–60.

28

GLOBAL CIVIL SOCIETY, MIGRATION, AND DEVELOPMENT

Stefan Rother

Introduction

Over the past two decades, development has entered global migration debates, and the perceived 'migration and development nexus' has received increasing attention up to the point where it has become a 'mantra' (Kapur 2003). For migrant civil society, this development turned out to be a double-edged sword. On the one hand, it brought with it a positive framing of an issue that previously had been mostly discussed as a matter of security or social cohesion. Painting migrants as 'agents of development' highlighted the positive contributions they could make and ascribed to them a certain agency, in contrast to still dominant paradigms, where migrants are foremost seen as objects of policies that need to be 'managed'. On the other hand, the debate was, at least initially, characterised by a very limited view on migration's contribution to development – locating it mostly in the country of origin and focusing on financial contributions through remittances. Furthermore, this discourse was replicated and enforced in so many large-scale policy reports and conferences, that it became, as Antoine Pécoud observed, a part of international migration narratives. This could lead to the depoliticisation of migration by taking the global socioeconomic and political context in which migration takes place for granted (and thus leaving it unchallenged) and through a 'technocratic reliance on expertise and empirical evidence to avoid political controversies' (Pécoud 2015, 95).

This tension between seeing the debate as beneficial *per se*, but being critical about the way it was conducted, led to probably the most significant outcome: it served as a catalyst for migrant organising on a global level be it in support of, in critical engagement with, or in fierce opposition against, the migration and development paradigm. Networks of migrant organisations have joined forces and created umbrella organisations, global networks of networks, and central events such as the United Nations High-Level Dialogue on Migration and Development (UN-HLD) or the Global Forum on Migration and Development (GFMD) have provided structures for political opportunity for these various forms of engagement. Parallel processes to these 'official' events as well as independent gatherings have been set up, and today we can witness a very lively migrant civil society, which has contributed to the *re-politicisation* of global migration discourses. However, no one single migrant civil society exists: rather, as with any usage of 'civil society', the term refers to a heterogeneous group of actors, which operates on various levels and with a multitude of, often conflicting, agendas.

This chapter therefore starts with a discussion of the meaning and scope of civil society and maps out which forms civil society engagement can take with regards to the issue of migration and development. The next section looks at how development is viewed, framed and advocated among a variety of actors within global migrant civil society. The conclusion discusses the question of the role of civil society.

Global civil society

Some concepts are in danger of falling victim to their own success: similar to other popular terms such as 'globalisation', the term 'civil society' has been used so frequently and in so many contexts that as a result its meaning has become rather blurred.[1] It has become a buzzword, usually conveying the notion that civil society is a positive force or at the very least well-intentioned, and that including its representatives in the political process is a desirable goal in itself. But what about actors such as anti-immigrant groups, the alt-right movement or the 'Identitarian movement' ('*Identitäre Bewegung*')? In their own perceptions, these groups might see themselves as fighting for the good of the community even when in the eyes of others the view is strongly contested. If these groups become militant, they could be categorised as 'uncivil society' (Beittinger-Lee 2009). The ambiguity regarding right-wing groups remains and, it is not sufficient to simply subsume all non-state actors under the umbrella term 'civil society'.

A narrower definition has been proposed by Larry Diamond, who defines civil society as encompassing 'the realm of organized social life that is open, voluntary, self-generating, at least partially self-supporting, autonomous from the state, [and] that is bound by a legal order or a set of shared collective rules' (Diamond 1999, 221). This definition still needs further specification, since it could be argued that it also includes business organisations, which are more commonly seen as forming a separate category, the private sector. The widely used definition proposed by the World Bank therefore highlights the non-profit dimension of civil society and defines the term as referring to the

> wide array of non-governmental and not-for-profit organizations that have a presence in public life, expressing the interests and values of their members or others, based on ethical, cultural, political, scientific, religious or philanthropic considerations. Civil Society Organizations (CSOs) therefore refer to a wide of array of organizations: community groups, non-governmental organizations (NGOs), labor unions, indigenous groups, charitable organizations, faith-based organizations, professional associations, and foundations.
>
> *(World Bank 2013)*

Churches, and other forms of organised religion, are also usually defined as being distinct from civil society. If they form issue-specific organisations, however, then they can be considered faith-based groups within civil society. Other distinct groups include think tanks and expert groups, which are referred to as epistemic communities (Haas 1992), and trade unions, wherein the concept of social movement unionism has emerged as a bridge to civil society (Scipes 1992).

After having clarified what CSOs are, we should look at what they actually do and what roles they can play. The stakes are high, because, as Francis Fukuyama writes, civil society 'has been almost universally seen as a necessary condition for modern liberal democracy (in Ernest Gellner's phrase, "no civil society, no democracy")' (Fukuyama 2001, 11). For him, the role of civil society is to balance the power of the state by protecting individuals from the state. Writing on how the Sustainable Development Goals can be realised for women migrant workers, Hennebry et al. (2018) see civil society as not only responding to the states they are based in but as taking an active role of their own. 'We understand CSOs as non-state actors that build new structures and rules to solve problems, change outcomes and transform international life' (Hennebry et al. 2018, 13). These actors can operate beyond the confines of the nation-states expanding or building alliances to form transnational activist networks (TANs) (Keck and Sikkink 1998). Their outreach can go up to the regional and global level. These organisations can form part of (but are not identical with) what has been termed global civil society, 'a vast, interconnected, and multi-layered social space that comprises many hundreds of thousands of self-directing or nongovernmental institutions and ways of life' (Keane 2001, 23).

At such levels of engagement beyond the nation-state, there might be no established mechanisms for deliberation and civil society might have to fight even to establish such spaces. The strategies employed to this end usually take place in the public sphere. Creating or enlarging such a sphere might be part of civil society advocacy. Civil society can see itself predominantly as an observer of the political process, serving therein in a watchdog capacity, or become a political actor in its own right with the aim of promoting its agenda. To achieve this goal, CSOs can fall back on an established toolkit, including strategies such as *agenda setting*, *deliberations*, *blaming*, *shaming*, and *naming*. The strategies employed are often related to the political opportunity structures available for civil society (Meyer 2004). When the political environment is open, civil society might deliberate directly with other relevant actors, usually the state, international organisations, or the private sector. Although the resources at hand are usually not distributed in their favour, civil society might hope for the triumph of the power of persuasion, specifically by providing the better argument for their own particular case and by identifying like-minded actors to serve as supporters (Deitelhoff 2009). If the environments for deliberations have become institutionalised, civil society can serve as a transmission belt by articulating the interests of their constituency from the bottom up while, simultaneously, informing them about negotiations, policies, and the like from the top down (Nanz and Steffek 2007). As one downside to such arrangements, however, civil society organisations might face accusations of having been co-opted by governments and having made too many concessions to the latter in order to be able to participate in these processes.

This is just one of several criticisms directed towards CSOs. Even when one takes controversial groups and 'uncivil society' (Stewart 1997) out of the picture, one should avoid the pitfalls of glorifying civil society. Issues of transparency, accountability, and the underlying motivation of their work arise, for example. In particular, international aid and development charities have increasingly faced criticisms for lack of transparency and, in some cases, misspending. While we consider CSOs to be non-profit, they usually still have to generate some income to pay for salaries, uphold the organisational structure, and so on. Although some of them might operate through member fees, smaller CSOs and particularly organisations situated in the Global South rely to a large degree on third-party funding. This might have an influence on their agenda, for instance, if they have to shift their thematic focus in order to be able even to apply for certain programmes. If part of their funding stems from government funds, the legitimacy of civil society might be called into question. If they are mostly funded, or even formed, through government channels then they might constitute (or be perceived as constituting) 'fake' civil society, in the form of GONGOs (government-organised NGOs). These might be established by governments in order to reach, in some cases incorporate, sectors of society that they could not reach through direct means or that might be set up to compete with, or sometimes delegitimise, existing independent NGOs.

Even if there is no external intervention, the internal dimension deserves closer scrutiny. How democratic is their organisational form and their election of leadership, for example, is there a transparent structure based on open elections or do they have a professionalised, *de facto* permanent leadership and insufficient control mechanism? This leads to probably the most controversial question of all. What is the legitimacy of CSOs? Critics usually highlight the lack of a clear mandate, and, particularly in the case of NGOs, the description of civil society as a middle-class phenomenon susceptible to the influences of dominant 'Western' organisations, funding, and ways of thinking. While this criticism is often valid and important to take on board, one has to keep in mind that the latter argument is often used by authoritarian regimes in order to discredit human rights NGOs as nothing more than 'Western agents'. A holistic approach to CSOs should therefore acknowledge that these organisations are market participants, competing for resources and influence. This observation does not rule out their potential to contribute to democratic participation – particularly in regions with only limited performance of formal democratic institutions, or by representing transnational groups such as migrants.

Civil society, migration, and development

We have seen that the term civil society covers a variety of organisational forms, levels of operation, and advocacy. A similarly broad spectrum can be found when looking at CSOs in the field of migration and development. A significant number of organisations exist in both migration and development that do not necessarily make a link between these two fields. The number of CSOs in the field of development significantly rose in the 1990s when the 'good governance' discourse gained prominence in the international development agenda. Increasingly, donors such as the World Bank built conditionalities into their aid programmes and the existence and involvement of civil society was one of these prerequisites (Lewis and Kanji 2009, 128–9). This led to some 'civil-society building' (Lewis and Kanji 2009, 130) or at least support from above, often carrying a clear liberal, market society agenda. While these endeavours can be situated in the field of democratic development, the spectrum also includes service-oriented CSOs on the ground. While they may not be as explicitly political as, say, human rights organisations, implicitly they still are. In fact, civil society is always political, no matter the form or content of their work. A similar variety can be found in the fields of migrant civil society organisations. These can be composed of 'concerned citizens' advocating for the rights of migrants or focusing on specific service provisions such as legal aid, or language training. Migrant self-organisations can provide such services for their members but they can also follow an explicitly political agenda, if the political opportunity structures allow it. In some countries, such as Singapore, the formation of organisations and political engagement is not allowed.

The most obvious actors where development and migrant civil society connect, are probably Hometown Associations (HTAs). A rich literature on these grassroots processes exists with much work done on Latino migration (La Garza and Lowell 2002), in particular, the role of Mexican migration to the US (Oroczo and Lapointe 2004). These HTAs might have started out as providing a network for newcomers in the destination country as well as upholding social and cultural links to the place of origin. Over time and with growing income, however, some of these organisations started to look into the contribution they could make to the development of their hometowns. Ayse Caglar, who has worked on Turkish HTAs in Germany, sees similarities between HTAs in various parts of the world: 'their main defining characteristics are their informal and voluntary structure and their sporadic relationship with their hometowns' (Caglar 2006, 2).

Besides conventional development projects, HTAs might also be involved in the democratic development of their home countries (Rother 2016). Itzigsohn and Villacrés (2008) have shown how Dominican and Salvadoran HTAs in the US fought for dual citizenship and external voting rights. They also point out the problematic aspects of private actors such as HTAs being involved in development projects. While the Washington-based Fundación Unidos por Intipuca was regarded as one of El Salvador's best-organised and successful HTAs having implemented many development projects, they also had some shortcomings. Most decisions on which projects to choose were made in Washington by a small group of wealthier migrants who selected projects that overwhelmingly benefited the urban centre of Intipuca, neglecting the poorer outlying districts (Itzigsohn and Villacrés 2008, 678–9). This uneven distribution was illustrated by the investment of half a million US dollars in the building of a soccer stadium, while other districts of the municipality were still lacking basic necessities such as electricity or drinkable water.

Such observations call into question the implicit 'migrants know best' assumption underlying many of the discourses on migration and development. That is because the migrants in question may have been away for many years from their home communities and may not be aware of the real development needs in their home communities but rather are motivated by the social, ethnic, religious, or political ties that bind them to the place of origin. As Sinatti and Horst (2015) point out, 'diaspora engagement' often takes the form of philanthropy or charity, which is clearly something different from development.

While HTAs often develop on the ground, increasing support for diaspora organisations has grown in development agencies. For example, the German Deutsche Gesellschaft für Internationale Zusammenarbeit (GIZ) runs a global programme *Migration for Development*, which is currently active in 24 countries. Since 2011 'over 100 diaspora organizations have received support and sustainably improved the lives of people in partner countries through their projects'. (GIZ 2018) A government-related agency in Germany thus supports the transnational engagement of migrant civil society in the specific issue of migration and development such as voluntary short-term assignments for diaspora experts. Further components focus on private sector engagement, such as migrants starting businesses, and skill transfer through return migration. This transnational component is thus a decisive factor in civil society involvement in development programmes: the example of the Fundación discussed above has shown the need for these programmes to be rooted in the reality on the ground back home.

These HTAs are by no means a new phenomenon. An influential article by Kenneth Little from 1957 discusses the role of voluntary associations in West African Urbanisation (Little 1957). Revisiting this article from a time and region with loosely defined and shifting national boundaries also puts into question strict definitions of what we consider transnational. Even within clearly defined nation-states, we can find HTAs as a result of rural–urban migration (Skeldon 1980). But this domestic/internal dimension seems to be mostly neglected in the current policy and research debate on HTAs. The main focus is on their role as transnational advocacy networks with a particular emphasis on economic and political development. HTAs are not static actors but change over time, a process which is especially affected by their relation to government(s):

> It can be argued that HTAs work less autonomously after they have accepted the support of the government. Also, that the HTAs are hindering the decision-making process of the community back home because the needs being met are those of migrants.
>
> *(Muñoz and Collazo 2014, 138)*

While HTAs tend to be composed of migrants who have left their countries of origin for extended periods of time, if not for good, in many regions of the world such as contemporary South and Southeast Asia, migration is often temporary in nature. This labour migration is contract-based which limits the time spent in the country of destination and offers no opportunities for permanent residency. For example, even if a migrant domestic worker spends 20 years in Hong Kong, she will remain 'permanent temporary' migrant workers (Rother 2017, 961). The migrants in this scenario might still form associations based on their place of origin, which in the case of the Philippines often happens along regional lines, such as island groups. These might consist of cultural or support groups in the place of destination but can also take on a clearer transnational component. The Migrants Coordinating Group in Western Visayas (MCG-WV) is such a CSO, which also has its own Facebook group that serves as an 'online information sharing, mutual-help, referral and support group for Western Visayan migrants (overseas Filipinos, OFWs, seafarers), their families, communities and groups based in Western Visayas or overseas'. (MCG-WV 2018).

Besides the online dimension, the activities of this CSO are multi-local: they can include a 'Preparedness Seminar on Migration, Development & Reintegration', held in Singapore in March 2018 with a focus on savings, assets, and livelihood, a nation-wide campaign in the Philippines in April 2018 that asked the government to adopt a 'National Provident Savings Program for Filipino Migrants and Families' (NPSP) or a general assembly in May the same year in Iloilo City (Visayas, Philippines), that adopted several training modules and discussed how to build links and redress channels and reintegration pathways between Filipino migrant groups abroad and the migrants' hometowns in the Philippines.

This snapshot of the agenda shows that migrant CSOs can play an important role in all parts of the migration process: providing preparatory information before departure; organising the migrants while being abroad as well as their families back home; and providing training and education throughout in order to help with reintegration. Financial literacy seems to be of particular importance. In the case of Hong Kong, on the one hand, this is offered by Enrich, a classic charity run by supportive citizens with the mission to 'empower migrant domestic workers in Hong Kong, regardless of nationality or background, to transform their lives through financial education and personal development programmes' (Enrich 2018). On the other hand, migrant self-organisations such as The Asian Migrants Credit Union (AMCU) (AMCU 2018) exist as a savings and credit cooperative of and for migrants. While what it offers may seem far away from the large-scale infrastructure projects of the Fundación – one of their information sessions was taking place 'outside Starbucks Coffee shop, in the Atrium' of a University building, for example – being able to save money is a central prerequisite for migrants to have any development impact, either through remittances or when they return home.

One long-established CSO that links savings abroad and investment back home is Unlad Kabayan that was founded in 1996 in the Philippines. It started out with mobilising migrant savings in destinations such as Hong Kong and Japan, but now the Migrant Savings for Alternative Investment (MSAI) has 'evolved from a reintegration strategy for migrant workers to an alternative economic model' (Unlad Kabayan 2018). Since then, the mission of the CSO has been to 'promote social entrepreneurship and social enterprises by mobilizing migrant workers, the marginalized in the community and their resources to build a sustainable local economy' through a series of programmes that include savings, microcredits, and skills training up to enterprise development. Unlad Kabayan is also involved in disaster relief, such as after Typhoon Yolanda that hit the Philippines in November 2013.

Most of the examples given above focused on very specific measures on the ground, such as service provision, training, and establishing financial programmes. However, during their work, CSOs also encounter regional and global policy frameworks, programmes, or conventions as well as more fundamental questions relating to migration and development. Because dealing with these issues on their various levels would often stretch or go beyond the capacities of single CSOs, many of them have formed networks of networks that allow for multi-level advocacy.

Global migrant civil society

It took a long time for migration to enter the arena of global politics, and the aspect of development played a crucial part in this process. For a long time, states considered migration policy and the related entry and exit rules as the prerogative of their sovereignty. While the International Convention on the Protection of the Rights of All Migrant Workers and Members of Their Families was signed back in 1990, its further fate did not counter this opposition to binding multilateralism but rather underlined it: it took 13 years for the convention to gather the 20 ratifications necessary to enter into force and even at the time of writing there is no established major country of destination among the 51 states who have ratified the convention.

Global deliberations on migration thus emerged in a different context: the 1994 UN International Conference on Population and Development (ICPD), in Cairo, Egypt, somewhat unexpectedly, because the initial 'conference's focus was not on migration but rather on population growth, sustainable development, and gender issues' (Thouez 2018, 5). Still, for the first time, states signed a text that not only outlined their perspectives on international migration but also recognised that migration could assist countries in forwarding their development agenda.

It took 12 more years for the UN General Assembly to convene a High-Level Dialogue on Migration and Development (UN-HLD). Because no consensus could be reached on how to address the issue within the UN System, an informal, non-binding, and state-led process was initiated outside of it: the Global Forum on Migration and Development (GFMD). It has met annually since the first gathering in Belgium in 2007 (except 2013, when it was replaced by a second UN-HLD to review progress) and might have contributed to socialising states into more cooperative behaviour on the issue, amongst each other, but also towards migrant civil society (Rother 2019).

What kind of role does civil society play in these global processes? Once it was granted an, albeit small, place on the table from the first GFMD,[2] a dedicated space was given to CSOs to interact amongst themselves: the Civil Society Days (CSDs). These have evolved over the years into two full days of deliberations followed by a 'common space' with governments on a third day before government representatives confer among themselves for the final two days.

The strategy of a cluster of migrant-rights CSOs towards the GFMD was two-fold. First, to take part in the discussions in the official fora and to try influence what is talked about and how it is talked about, or as one activist put it: 'to mainstream our agenda' (Ellene Sana, see Piper and Rother 2012, 1743). Second, to organise an independent space for broader and inclusive discussions on migration and development, and try to let its outcomes also feed into the official discussions. This forum was termed People's Global Action on Migration, Development and Human Rights (PGA) and is usually held before or in parallel to the GFMD. The global CSO behind these activities is the Global Coalition on Migration (GCM), which brings together several regional networks such as the Migrant Forum in Asia (MFA), which in turn counts some of the Asian CSOs introduced in the previous section among its members. Hence, a link from the global to the local exists and activists such as the Migrants Coordinating Group in Western Visayas founder Rex Verona are active at all levels. The Global Coalition on Migration has also been involved in the negotiations for the Global Compact on Safe, Orderly and Regular Migration and, since it was agreed in Marrakesh and New York at the end of 2018, the main advocacy of the coalition has been to press for a rights-based implementation.

While these CSOs follow an 'inside-outside strategy', others have decided upon a more fundamental opposition (Rother 2009). The International Migrants' Alliance (IMA), founded as 'the first-ever global alliance of organizations of grassroots migrants, refugees and displaced peoples' in Hong Kong in 2008, sees the GFMD as a forum of 'modern day slavery' through the commodification of labour migrants. It holds its own counter-event, the International Assembly of Migrants and Refugees (IAMR) with the goal to 'expose' the agenda behind the GFMD. It has a more open attitude towards Global Compact negotiations but considers them not far-reaching enough.

Since the GFMD (and even the Global Compact) is non-legally binding, many of the advancements are discursive in nature. The expectation exists that these processes and documents might lead to policy recommendations and ultimately specific policies on the ground. Starting with the Global Coalition and its related fora, it can be said that that it has significantly contributed to widening the scope of the agenda. While the first GFMD meetings were characterised by a fairly narrow focus on 'migration management' and the economic dimension, in particular remittances, other issues such as gender, undocumented migration, climate change, and rights-based approaches (see Chapter 25 in this Handbook) were off the agenda but all now form part of the discussion, including in the 'zero draft' of the Global Compact (Rother 2018a). This has been achieved through alliances with like-minded states, such as Mexico, and, to a lesser degree, cooperation with think tanks and scholar-activists who provide a bridge between the various sectors since they are usually employed and paid by the state but might consider themselves as part of civil society. The demands and recommendations of these CSOs were manifested in several documents, one of them being the 'Civil Society "Stockholm Agenda" on migrant and migration-related goals and targets in the post-2015 global and national development agendas' (GFMD Civil Society 2014). It stressed that migrants have to be seen as both actors and subjects of human and economic development and that policies such as the Sustainable Development Goals (SDGs, see Chapter 26 in this Handbook) would have to connect migrants and migration with a human and economic development that is decent, sustainable, and transformative. Among the goals raised are a decrease in remittance transfer costs as well as a reduction of risks to migrants on the move, in particular: recruitment costs; lack of fair, regular and orderly channels of migration; criminalization of migrants; and risks to women and to children in contexts of human trafficking, transit and crisis; portability of social security, pension and skills, including recognition of qualifications.

(*GFMD Civil Society, 2014*)

There is scepticism towards the very much 'en vogue' circular migration programmes (Skeldon 2012) since they might be highly restrictive and require migrants to give up fundamental rights and freedoms for the opportunity to work in another country (Global Coalition on Migration 2017).

The goals of the cluster around the IMA are not all that different, but the CSOs do not believe that the GFMD is a place to achieve them; they also put even more emphasis on the root causes of migration, which they connect to imperialism and which has

a strategic interest in keeping social or geographical divisions by genderising, racialising or territorialising the humanity. Migration politics aims to keep the system of borders and territories whilst in the same time exploits the wage and reproduction cost differential between countries.

(*International Migrants Alliance (IMA) 2008, 4*)

While these two CSO clusters have separate and often competing agendas, occasional interaction occurs in independent spaces for migrant advocacy such as the World Social Forum on Migration (WSFM): 'make migration a choice, not a necessity' is a slogan regularly used by almost all of the CSOs involved.

Concluding remarks

This chapter has shown that migrant civil society is as diverse in its organisational forms, levels of engagement and social and political agenda as civil society as a whole. CSOs such as the HTAs can be directly involved in development measures, but the outcome of these projects is varied. One necessary condition that has been identified is the transnational dimension, where knowledge 'back home' can help to identify measures adequate for local circumstances. While HTAs often work independently, more network-based projects have been presented that ideally include all stages of the migration process from pre-departure training, to measures such as financial literacy training or the establishment of credit unions for the migrants abroad as well as their families back home to reintegration programme and social entrepreneurship after return.

Several open questions remain. Regarding HTAs, it has become clear that these are not a new phenomenon, that they have a longer history in particular with regards to internal migration and that their structure and advocacy may change over time. A major factor influencing this change has been the relation of HTAs to government, or more precisely, governments, both of the countries of origin and countries of destination, but also third countries, regional institutions, or state-led international organisations which might support 'diaspora engagement'. This leads to the wider question of the internal democratic structure and the legitimacy of civil society organisations and to the even harder question of which actors constitute civil society and which do not, and on which criteria the boundaries are drawn. Does 'the diaspora' really 'know what's best' for the homeland? When cooperation with governments exists, such as in the case of the Mexican *Tres Por Uno* programme, questions of the legitimacy of private money influencing the distribution of public resources arise. Examples such as those from the Philippines have shown, that a close involvement and equal participation of the home communities are crucial for successful and sustainable programmes.

While the activities discussed in this chapter may not seem explicitly political, implicitly they certainly are since they touch upon issues such as emigration and immigration policies, root causes of migration such as lack of development, as well as the rights and support of migrant workers. In order to voice their advocacy on multiple levels, migrant CSOs have formed networks of networks that participate in deliberations up to the global level such as the GFMD. Here, they have shown marked success in influencing the discourse at the global arena towards a more far-reaching notion of development and a rights-based approach. The challenge for both states and CSOs alike remains to link these discourses to the policies on the ground and move towards their implementation.

Notes

1 Parts of this section draw from Rother (2015).
2 Unlike the first HLD, where only a very small number of accredited CSOs were allowed to observe the discussion.

References

AMCU. 2018. "Asian migrants credit union." www.amcu-hk.org/home.

Beittinger-Lee, Verena. 2009. *(Un)civil society and political change in Indonesia: A contested arena. Routledge studies on civil society in Asia.* London, New York: Routledge.

Caglar, Ayse. 2006. "Hometown associations, the rescaling of state spatiality and migrant grassroots transnationalism." *Global Networks* 6 (1): 1–22.

Deitelhoff, Nicole. 2009. "The discursive process of legalization: Charting Islands of persuasion in the ICC case." [[en]]. *International Organization* 63 (1): 33.

Diamond, Larry. 1999. *Developing democracy: Toward consolidation* [eng]. Baltimore: Johns Hopkins University Press.

Enrich. 2018. "About Enrich HK." www.enrichhk.org/about-enrich-financial-education-migrant-domestic-worker-ngo/.

Fukuyama, Francis. 2001. "Social capital, civil society and development." *Third World Quarterly* 22 (1): 7–20.

GFMD Civil Society. 2014. Stockholm Agenda. http://gfmdcivilsociety.org/wp-content/uploads/2014/06/Civil-Society-Migration-Stockholm-Agenda-June-2014.pdf (Accessed February 5, 2019).

GIZ. 2018. "Programme "migration for development"." www.giz.de/en/worldwide/62318.html.

Global Coalition on Migration. 2017. "What is the global compact on migration?" http://gcmigration.org/2017/04/what-is-the-global-compact-on-migration/.

Haas, Peter M. 1992. "Introduction: Epistemic communities and international policy coordination." [[en]]. *International Organization* 46 (1): 1–35.

Hennebry, Jenna, Hari Kc, and Nicola Piper. 2018. "Not without them: Realising the Sustainable Development Goals for women migrant workers." *Journal of Ethnic and Migration Studies* 19: 1–17.

International Migrants Alliance (IMA), ed. 2008. Founding assembly documents. June 15-16. Hong Kong: SAR.

Itzigsohn, José, and Daniela Villacrés. 2008. "Migrant political transnationalism and the practice of democracy: Dominican external voting rights and Salvadoran home town associations." [[en]]. *Ethnic and Racial Studies* 31 (4): 664–686.

Kapur, Devesh. 2003. *Remittances: The new development mantra?* Washington, DC: The World Bank. G-24 Discussion Paper Series, 29.

Keane, John. 2001. "Global civil society?" In *Global civil society 2001*, eds. Helmut K. Anheier, Marlies Glasius and Mary Kaldor.. Oxford: Oxford University Press, 23–47.

Keck, Margaret E., and Kathryn Sikkink. 1998. *Activists beyond borders: Advocacy networks in international politics* [en]. Ithaca, NY: Cornell University Press.

La Garza, Rodolfo O. de, and Briant L. Lowell, eds. 2002. *Sending money home: Hispanic remittances and community development.* Lanham, MD: Rowman & Littlefield.

Lewis, David, and Nazneen Kanji. 2009. *Non-governmental organizations and development* [eng]. *Routledge perspectives on development.* Milton Park, Abingdon, Oxon, New York: Routledge.

Little, Kenneth. 1957. "The role of voluntary associations in West African urbanization." *American Anthropologist* 59 (4): 579–596.

MCG-WV. 2018. "Migrants coordinating group in Western Visayas, Inc." Facebook Group. www.facebook.com/groups/mcgwv2015/about/.

Meyer, David S. 2004. "Protest and political opportunities." [[en]]. *Annual Review of Sociology* 30 (1): 125–145.

Muñoz, José A., and José L. Collazo. 2014. "Looking out for Paisanos: Latino hometown associations as transnational advocacy networks." *Migration and Development* 3 (1): 130–141.

Nanz, Patrizia, and Jens Steffek. 2007. "Zivilgesellschaftliche Partizipation und die Demokratisierung internationalen Regierens." [de]. *Anarchie der kommunikativen Freiheit: Jürgen Habermas und die Theorie der internationalen Politik* [de], eds.. Peter Niesen and Benjamin Herborth. Frankfurt am Main: Suhrkampp. 87–110.

Oroczo, Manuel, and Michelle Lapointe. 2004. "Mexican hometown associations and development opportunities." *Journal of International Affairs* 57 (2): 31–51.

Pécoud, Antoine. 2015. *Depoliticising migration: Global governance and international migration narratives.* Basingstoke: Palgrave Pivot.

Piper, Nicola, and Stefan Rother. 2012. "Let's argue about migration: Advancing a right(s) discourse via communicative opportunities." *Third World Quarterly* 33 (9): 1735–1750.

Rother, Stefan. 2009. "Inside-Outside" or "Outsiders by choice"? Civil society strategies towards the 2nd Global Forum on Migration and Development (GFMD) in Manila." [en]. *ASIEN – The German Journal on Contemporary Asia* (111): 95–107. www.asienkunde.de/content/zeitschrift_asien/archiv/pdf/111_rother.pdf.

Rother, Stefan. 2015. "Civil society and democracy in South and Southeast Asia — An introduction." *ASIEN – The German Journal on Contemporary Asia* 136: 5–13.

Rother, Stefan., ed. 2016. *Migration und Demokratie.* Wiesbaden: Springer VS.

Rother, Stefan. 2017. "Indonesian migrant domestic workers in transnational political spaces: Agency, gender roles and social class formation." *Journal of Ethnic and Migration Studies* 43 (6): 956–973.

Rother, Stefan. 2018a. "Nur ein erster Schritt: Der globale Pakt für Migration." *Vereinte Nationen* 66 (2): 78.

Rother, Stefan. 2019. "The Global Forum on Migration and Development (GFMD) as a venue of state socialization: A stepping stone for multi-level migration governance?" *Journal of Ethnic and Migration Studies* 45 (8): 1258–1274.

Scipes, Kim. 1992. "Understanding the new labor movements in the "third world": The emergence of social movement unionism." [en]. *Critical Sociology* 19 (2): 81–101.

Sinatti, Giulia, and Cindy Horst. 2015. "Migrants as agents of development: Diaspora engagement discourse and practice in Europe." *Ethnicities* 15 (1): 134–152.

Skeldon, Ronald. 1980. "Regional associations among urban migrants in Papua New Guinea." *Oceania* 50 (4): 248–272.

Skeldon, Ronald. 2012. "Going round in circles: Circular migration, poverty alleviation and marginality." *International Migration* 50 (3): 43–60.

Stewart, Sheelagh. 1997. "Happy ever after in the marketplace: Non-government organisations and uncivil society." *Review of African Political Economy* 24 (71): 11–34.

Thouez, Colleen. 2018. "Strengthening migration governance: The UN as 'wingman'." *Journal of Ethnic and Migration Studies* 16 (3): 1–16.

Unlad Kabayan. 2018. "Our history." www.unladkabayan.org/history.html.

World Bank. 2013. "Defining civil society." http://web.worldbank.org/WBSITE/EXTERNAL/TOPICS/CSO/0,contentMDK:20101499~menuPK:244752~pagePK:220503~piPK:220476~theSitePK:228717,00.html (January 7, 2019).

29

WHEN LIBERAL DEMOCRACY PULLS APART

Challenges for protecting migrants' rights in the UK

Don Flynn

A dilemma exists for advocates of greater rights for migrants in the shape of the decline of what we have become used to calling liberal democracy for most of the last 70-odd years. Over this period, liberal democracy was the favoured way of governing states that relied on relatively open, or 'free' markets to drive economic growth. Its precedence across North America, Western Europe, and Japan rested on the hegemonic position of the United States in the post-World War II order. Its fundamental principles were those of representative democracy which itself was restrained by the rule of law. This rule of law protected, first and foremost, the rights of property, with other liberties following on as a natural consequence of the rights invested in ownership of goods and assets.

The political scientist James F. Hollifield, borrowing from James Ruggie, described the system that came into being under this settlement as 'embedded liberalism' (Hollifield 1992, 26) and argued that it had implications for the way in which migration came to be managed across these decades.

> Such simple constitutional protections as equality before the law and due process are important constraints on the power of liberal states. Rights are doubly important for aliens, who as noncitizens, are among the most vulnerable individuals in liberal societies.
>
> *(Ibid., 27)*

Hollifield argued that embedded liberalism had a ratchet effect which ensured that rights, once gained, became a more-or-less permanent feature of social life. Both the wider society which conceded rights and those who are beneficiaries will adapt to the new regime that had been established and social and political life will move on to deal with new issues and challenges. Liberal democracy in short was presumed to have fixed the direction of change firmly towards constant, gradual progress; an ideology which was comfortably adapted to the political parties of the centre-right and centre-left during the middle decades of the twentieth century.

Liberalism and democracy have been political currents pulling in opposite directions throughout most of history, but during post-World War II period conditions allowed them to be yoked together by a settlement that combined a high rate of return on capital investment with economic redistribution through the structures of welfare states (Esping-Andersen 1990). Versions of the welfare state became the provider of an array of public services on principles that approximated to rights-based universalism across virtually all liberal democratic states during this period. However, the entire system came under severe pressure during the latter decades of the twentieth century as planned capitalism gave way to neoliberalism.

The transition from planned corporate capitalism to free-market neoliberalism was marked by a vast increase in the mobility of capital between sectors of the economy and across national borders (Epstein 2000, Part II). As early as the 1970s the social scientist Claus Offe argued that the increasingly footloose character of capital was opening up contradictions within the structure of the welfare state (Offe 1984). More recently Wolfgang Streeck has argued that this has been critical in undermining of the rights of the majority of wage-dependent citizens in liberal democratic countries (Streeck 2016, Chapter 2). An implicit contract existed between parliamentary states and capitalist firms during this period, with public authorities taking on responsibility for providing an educated, healthy, disciplined labour force which private sector enterprises would utilise to make profits in sufficient volume as to support the taxation necessary for the schools, healthcare and family welfare services.

These arrangements presumed limited opportunities for the mobility of capital, with firms retaining an organic connection with the states in which they had been incubated. This degree of dependency eroded when transnational companies discovered that new opportunities for foreign direct investment, subcontracting, outsourcing, and joint venture partnerships gave them access to workforces that were coming into existence in jurisdictions with lower costs of social reproduction. In a work which explores outflow of capital investment to developing regions under the conditions of neoliberal globalisation, the economist John Smith argues that the capacity to draw on the labour resources of regions in Asia and Latin America is the defining feature of a new age of capitalist imperialism. He goes so far as to state that 'outsourcing and migration have become two aspects of the same wage-differential-driven transformation of the global production' (Smith 2016, 44). He cites Jeffrey Henderson and Robin Cohen to make this point:

> While some fractions of metropolitan capital have taken flight to low-wage areas, partly in response to the class struggle of metropolitan workers, less mobile sections of Western capital have enormously increased their reliance on imported migrant labour to cheapen the labour process and lower the costs of the reproduction of labour in the advanced countries.
>
> *(Smith 2016, 44)*

However, the entry of ever-larger segments of the populations of less developed countries should not be mistaken for a progressive form of development which will eventually eliminate poverty and inequality. Smith cites a UNTAD study, which found that despite the higher skill and technology intensity of exports from developing countries this still did not 'signify a rapid and sustained technological upgrading in the exports of developing countries'. This was because, 'The involvement of developing countries is usually limited to the labour-intensive stages in the production process' (Smith 2016, 42). Moreover, the size of the wage-earning workforce in less developed countries had expanded from 60 million people in 1950 to over 500 million in 2010 according to statistics compiled by the International Labour Organisation and cited in an earlier article by Smith (2015). At the same time the workforce in developed countries had remained broadly similar to its mid-twentieth century figure of around 120 million. In short, the metropolitan worker, once benefiting from the effect of regulating factors such as trade unions, health and safety regulation, and job security, was now outnumbered in the global labour market by a factor of 4.5 to 1 by wage earners who had none of these protections. In a world in which the mobility of capital had been increased by neoliberal globalisation the greater access to these low-wage, precarious workers in far-off countries presented a greater challenge to the working conditions attained by workers in the developed world than was represented by migration alone.

Just as the mobility of capital precipitated the crisis of the welfare state model as it existed in the developed capitalist nations so the social rights associated with citizenship, were also eroded. This happened, firstly, through the de-regulation of labour markets and the reduced power of trade unions to represent workers, and then by way of the under-funding of public services which promoted the well-being of the population. In a succession of steps, liberal democracy gave up on its role as a promotor of social rights, instead directing citizens concerned about their standards of life to commit themselves more whole-heartedly to what the market had to offer for their welfare (Streeck 2016, 90).

If, as Hollifield has argued, liberal democracy and the rights regimes it fostered have been proportionately greater in importance to vulnerable groups like immigrants then the trend towards relying on markets as the means of securing welfare would prove especially challenging given their over-representation in particularly precarious forms of employment (Waite et al. 2015). At the same time, as capital sought out more opportunities to access cheap labour across the globe, the quality of a larger proportion of jobs left in domestic labour markets was downgraded as employment contracts became less secure and the scope for worker representation through trade unions was reduced. The jobs being brought into existence were those which vulnerable migrants were recruited to fill.

Employers resort to the recruitment of workers from migration sources when there is insufficient supply to be found in domestic labour markets. Examples of active migrant recruitment programmes are found in the heyday years of liberal democracy and the welfare state in the form of the guestworker schemes being used in many continental European countries (Castles and Kosack 1973). In other instances, the recruitment of citizens of colonial dependencies served this purpose (Castles, De Haas, and Miller 2014, 108–10). However, the commitment to some degree of the state regulation of labour markets and the provision of welfare services to legal residents at this time provided an environment that proved favourable to the success of migrant and ethnic minority struggle for inclusion and more equal outcomes. We should have no doubt that the energy and drive for progress in this direction came from migrants and sympathetic groups in the majority communities and was not just a matter of the unfolding of the intrinsic generosity of liberal society. But the chance of making progress will be optimised when external conditions are favourable, and the gradual increase in equality of treatment for migrants owed something to the character of a reasonably coherent liberal democratic social order.

This contrasts with the types of migration management schemes which have become typical of neoliberalism. The numerical volume of migration has increased during this latter period, and with it the policy emphasis on maintaining the effectiveness of markets as the drivers of economic growth and social well-being of the population. This brought in tow an ideological commitment to the instrumentality of migrants as *workers* (or in some cases, such as higher education, the fee-paying users of services). This has severely undermined the rights element, such as it existed, associated with the movement of *people*. Even in areas like the humanitarian right to protection for individuals who are the victims of persecution, the sense of a safety net being in place to support the most needy has been put in disarray by governments, which have brought the neoliberal mindset to bear on the issue (Kushner and Knox 2001, Part 5).

The plight of migrants in the United Kingdom

Why are, as Hollifield puts it, non-citizens among the most vulnerable people in liberal societies? There is nothing intrinsic in their personal characteristics which render prone to this situation, and indeed a proportion manage to escape this fate. As individuals, they are often comparatively well-educated and exhibit qualities of resilience and enterprise which are not always present in non-mobile populations (Neuwirth 2011; Goldin, Cameron, and Balarajan 2012). Individuals who establish themselves in more prestigious occupations are generally accorded higher social standing and this acts as a counterbalance to the deficit in rights which is a consequence of their non-citizen status. The risk of harm is borne in the main by the large group of migrants who seek employment in work that is regarded as being less-skilled. Sectors like agriculture and food processing, construction, hospitality, social care, and basic process work in manufacturing concentrate on migrant workers because the employment offered is poorly remunerated and insecure. According to an article published in *The Guardian* on 29 July 2017, statistics from the government's Office for National Statistics identify 18 employment sectors where migrants make up over 20 per cent of the workforce. The common ascription of this work as '3D' jobs – dirty–dangerous–demeaning (Ethical Trade Initiative n.d.) – has made it unappealing to the majority of native citizens who are strongly inclined to seek alternative occupations in less arduous positions.

The proportion of less desirable, 3D jobs in Britain increased after the economic crises of the 1970s which had led to a marked move in the direction of de-industrialisation. The manufacturing sector had up until that point employed around one-third of the workforce, much of which was in relatively well-paid jobs which enjoyed the security of trade union protection. As discussed above, the outsourcing of these jobs to lower-wage regions abroad during the 1980s and after led to this being replaced with an employment structure in which 80 per cent of jobs where in the service sector (Kitson and Mitchie 2014; Clarke 2017).

Many service sector jobs, in areas like finance, law, and management services, were well-paid and on relatively secure conditions of employment. But a large proportion of the businesses that emerged when the UK economy returned to growth in the late 1980s operated on the basis of precarious business plans which are dependent on access to credit to finance day-to-day cash flow. Changes to the financial system brought more lenders to the market. The traditional high street bank system also reformed itself in the competitive pressure to find borrowers, considerably lowering the terms of the conditions in which credit was extended to small businesses (Kay 2016). These relaxed conditions brought about an expansion of the small business sector (Blackburn 2002). The absence of detailed evidence about the ways in which migrant labour is used in this expanding sector makes it difficult to judge whether the experience of employment by small and medium-size enterprises (SMEs) are any more exploitative than in larger companies. Surveys of employer attitudes to migrant staff tend not to differentiate between the size of the firm but findings by studies on the issue point towards a consensus which was expressed by Blauw as:

> when confronted with labour shortages and confronted by high ambitions concerning cost reductions or maximum utilisation of labour an orientation towards a foreign labour market becomes in sight.
>
> *(Dench et al. 2006, 16)*

No doubt, this attitude also existed among large companies operating in migrant-dense sectors such as food production, construction, and hospitality, but given the even greater financial pressure on small businesses, it is probable that the struggle to contain wages and other costs associated with the hire of workers was even greater among SMEs. Writings on the emergence of a new workforce with the characteristics of a 'precariat' have discussed the ways in which employers in general find ways to eliminate the cost of unproductive hours of wage labour through casual and part-time contracts as well as the use of 'just-in-time' workers who are contracted through second-tier agencies or digital information technologies of the 'Uber' type (Standing 2016). The use of extended supply chains, in which end-user firms subcontract operations out to companies which assume responsibility for the production of basic goods, transport, and warehouse logistics and back office management services, has also played a role in generating new layers of risk-laden businesses. Through these chains, large firms are able to transfer the hazards coming from hold-ups in the supply of goods and components and fluctuations in demand during low seasons from companies to their workers in the form of staff lay-offs (Gebel and Giesecke 2008).

In her studies of the food production industry in Britain, the journalist Felicity Lawrence has explained how the migrant worker has come to be the epitome of the type of operative needed in industries which manage risk through extended supply chains. The penalties incurred by the failure to supply goods on time or at the quality required are subcontracted downwards, from the supermarket chain to the packhouses, farms, and transport companies, and from these to the gangmasters and employment agencies that specialise in providing labour at short notice, until the risk finally falls on the most vulnerable sectors of the workforce – typically migrant workers – who lack sufficient bargaining power to avoid fines and wage deductions which employers use to recoup losses from failure to meet contractual terms (Lawrence 2004).

The paradox for migrants in countries with free-market economies is that, while their labour is unquestionably needed, dependency on employment opportunities in sectors where precarity is intrinsic means that opportunities for gaining the rights that put them at the same level as citizens will be chronically limited. This contrasts with the offers made to migrants working as highly skilled professionals in fields such as business management, law, medicine, financial services, and higher education. For this group migration management grants rights and privileges in the form of secure residence status, family reunification opportunities, and the prospect of long-term settlement and citizenship if it is desired. However, this divergence serves to emphasise the fact that the rights of migrants in market-based liberal democracies are aligned to the perception of the utility of the individual as a member of the country's workforce. What is offered to skilled migrants as compensation for the insecurities of being non-citizens brings into sharper focus the losses in social and economic status that have to be endured by those labouring in less prestigious occupations.

The hope that 'embedded liberalism' would work overtime to diminish the gap that exists between the newcomer and the native is fading in mature, post-industrial societies as conditions in labour markets become more precarious and insecure. In truth, liberalism as an ideology was in any event deeply ambiguous about the degree of obligation that society owed to non-citizens. Prominent thinkers in the tradition of the stature of John Rawls and Michael Walzer argued that this could be kept to a minimum because migrants had views on social justice which were formed in countries which operated according to different value systems. If a sense of injustice took root in the country to which the individual had migrated then a remedy was at hand in the form of returning to the place of origin (Grey 2015). Another strand of liberal thought saw migrants contributing to the dissolution of the community values needed to sustain generosity towards people considered deserving because they had not contributed to the long-term building of social trust which was the necessary condition for mutual aid (Freeman 1986). The flaccidness of liberalism's ideological support for the rights of migrants suggests that whatever might have been on offer during the heyday of the liberal democratic settlement was always at risk of being withdrawn whenever the political mood changed.

Beyond the crisis of the liberal order

Yet, although as per Hollifield, a view of 'embedded liberalism' as providing firm ground for further advances in the rights of migrants could be sustained right up to the 1990s, it has subsequently been displaced by new political ideologies which openly sneer at notions of universal human and social rights. Social security now has a conditionality clause in its social contract: the ideal of a cradle-to-grave covenant committing the state to support the welfare of the population against all the hazards of existence has been ditched by acquiescence to the logic of neoliberalism.

Yet the forms of democracy seem to be surviving the passing of liberalism, with multi-party contestation of elections now standard across a larger proportion of the world. What is different is the fact that the successful politicians under these new systems are less inclined to advocate for legal protection for workers in the labour markets or enhancements to the social wage through improved public services. Risks to the well-being of citizens, once seen as arising from structural defects inherent in free-market capitalism, are now routinely attributed to the work-shy, chronically maladjusted families of the lower working classes, 'welfare mothers', feral adolescents, and selfish, cynical migrants out to grab things to which they have no entitlement (Jones 2012).

In the context of political discussion in Britain over the past 20 years, arguments in support of the rights of migrants have come up against their representation in the public discourse as a mistake which owes its origin to the arrogance of a liberal elite which is indifferent to the interests and aspirations of 'ordinary' people (West 2013). Politicians responded by rolling out legislation that aimed to squeeze the rights available to immigrants to an irreducible minimum. The courts themselves became increasingly closed to aggrieved migrants looking for a right of appeal against deprivation of residence rights and the threat of deportation (Webber 2012).

Politics in Britain, as is the case in much of the rest of the ostensibly democratic world, is now decidedly populist rather than liberal. Its world view is dominated by a sense of deep crisis extending across the whole of society, which can no longer be resolved by the timid policy tinkering that was the hallmark of the old system. The radical potential of democracy can only be regained in response to the following urgent questions; 'what went wrong; who is to blame; and what is to be done to reverse the situation'? (Betz and Johnson 2004, 323).

With immigration figuring so prominently in the populist case for what was supposedly going wrong, the simplest answer to what needed to be done was 'stop it'. But it is in reaching such hasty conclusions that a chronic instability is introduced into the populist outlook which holds out the prospect that complex questions might have to be looked at again, with the possibility of arriving at very different outcomes. There are reasons to believe that this revision of opinions might have been set in train as a direct consequence of the achievement of the populist insurgency in influencing the outcome of the 2016 referendum on Britain's membership of the European Union in favour of the vote for Brexit. Public misgivings about immigration played an important role in securing victory for the leave position (Ford and Goodwin 2014). Yet the view that the presence of migrants poses a critical problem for the country has given way in more recent times to apprehension about what will happen when the revitalisation of border controls made possible by Brexit will cause the flow of fresh cohorts of workers is reduced.[1] Problems for the recruitment of staff are predicted in the politically sensitive area of health and social care in particularly, bringing up doubts about the consequences of tightly-controlled immigration which hard-line Brexiteers have struggled to deal with.

In the midst of the political turbulence which the debate about Britain's membership has provoked it is not out the question that opportunities will present themselves to bring a positive, rights-based approach to immigration into the public conversation. The grounds for optimism here lie with the fact that the previous decades of contention about the direc-tion policy has been taking have ushered into existence an array of migrant support groups which have roots within local communities across the country (MCOP 2006). Initially responding to policies promoted by the New Labour government between 1997–2010 which were seen as being hostile to asylum-seeking refugees, by the middle of the following decade these groups were increasingly working to support economic migrants, including citizens of the EU accession countries from 2004 onwards.

The British situation has not yet produced a unified response to immigration from pro-gressive quarters, in the sense of there being a single organisation which confidently repre-sents a consensus on what needs to be done. Engagement with these issues has come from a wide spectrum of interests and concerns which range from faith communities concerned with the ethics of the treatment of strangers, mutual aid groups working to provide practical help to the people threatened with hardship or expulsion as a consequence of immigration policies, through to radicals aligned to leftist and libertarian outlooks which are committed to challenging the authority of the state and the capitalist system.

The heterogeneity of what can be described as a loosely associated migrant rights movement does not need to be regarded as a weakness, at least not at this point in time. The radical journalist Paul Mason has written persuasively of the virtue of working as a flexible, adaptive network of projects which have claimed for themselves licence to tackle an agreed social problem in separative but overlapping ways (Mason 2015). In the context of working on migration issues this opens up the prospect of a swarm of human and civil rights activism, each working on different aspects of public thinking and moods, bringing the ethical thinking of religious communities, the legal defence of civil liberties, trade union confrontation with exploitation, and the willingness to confront authority through tactics of disobedience into alignment with one another. Work of this type reaches out to professionals involved in the provision of public services – health service workers, social security administrators, local government officials, educationalists, social workers, and others – who occupy spaces where eruptions of obvious injustice have an impact on the value they put on their own sense of worth. If this has the effect of gen-erating and sustaining resistance to overtly anti-immigrant social policies, then the popu-list agenda might well be held in check and the areas of social life created where the human rights of migrants continue to be sustained in defiance of whatever is intended state authorities.

In recent times the example of the response to the government's attempts to create a regulatory 'hostile environment' for migrants, and the effect this had on long-settled migrants of the 'Windrush Generation' has given us a sense of what battles for the rights of migrants might look like in the future.[2] In this work, the experiences of scores of support organisations came together to provide an account of the predicament of now elderly British Caribbean people whose right to be in the country after decades of work and paying tax was being challenged by the authorities. It spoke in terms of moral outrage that Britain had become such a country as a consequence of its government pursuit of an agenda which marginalised immigrant communities and rendered them less secure. Ironically, in reaching a crescendo of its criticism during the months of revelations about what was happening to immigration policy, the discourse followed the logic of angry questioning closer to the logics of populism than traditional liberal democracy. What went wrong; who is to blame; and what is to be done to reverse the situation? This time the angry upholders of the rights of migrants had the better answers.

Notes

1 See 'The British jobs Brexit makes hard to fill' by Julia Kollewe, *The Guardian*, Sat 25 March 2017. Available at: www.theguardian.com/business/2017/mar/25/brexit-eu-nationals-exodus-jobs-recruitment.
2 See 'The week that took Windrush from low-profile investigation to national scandal' by Amelia Gentleman, *The Guardian*, 20 April 2018. Available at: www.theguardian.com/uk-news/2018/apr/20/the-week-that-took-windrush-from-low-profile-investigation-to-national-scandal.

References

Betz, H.G. and Johnson, C. (2004) Against the current—stemming the tide: the nostalgic ideology of the contemporary radical populist right, *Journal of Political Ideologies*, 9:3, 311–327. doi: 10.1080/1356931042000263546

Blackburn, R. (2002) *Small businesses in the UK: From hard times to great expectations* Paper Presented to the 22nd Japanese Annual Small Business Society (JASBS) National Annual Conference Senshu University Kawasaki City Japan, Small Business Research Centre Kingston University.

Castles, S., De Haas, H. and Miller, M.J. (2014) *The Age of Migration: International Population Movements in the Modern World* (5th Edition), Palgrave Macmillan, Basingstoke and New York.

Castles, S. and Kosack, G. (1973) *Immigrant Workers and Class Structure in Western Europe*, Institute of Race Relations, London.

Clarke, S. (2017) *Migration and the Past, Present and Future of the British Labour Market*, Resolution Foundation website. Available at: https://www.resolutionfoundation.org/comment/migration-and-the-past-present-and-future-of-the-british-labour-market/

Dench, S., Hurstfield, J., Hill, D' and Akroyd, K. (2006) *Employers' Use of Migrant Labour: Main report Home Office Online report 04/06*.

Epstein, G. (2000) *Threat Effects and the Impact of Capital Mobility on Wages and Public Finances: Developing a research agenda*, Working paper series 7, University of Massachusetts Amherst, PERI.

Esping-Andersen, G. (1990) *Three Worlds of Welfare Capitalism*, Princeton University Press, Princeton, NJ.

Ethical Trading Initiative. (n.d.) *Migrant Workers – "We are the people at the lowest level of society'*. Available at: www.ethicaltrade.org/issues/migrant-workers

Ford, R. and Goodwin, M. (2014) *Revolt on the Right – Explaining Support for the Radical Right in Britain*, Routledge, London.

Freeman, G. (1986) Migration and the political economy of the welfare state, *The Annals of the American Academy of Political and Social Science*, 485, 51–63.

Gebel, M. and Giesecke, J. (2008) *Labour Market Flexibility and Inequality the Changing Risk Patterns of Temporary Employment in Germany*, Working Papers 112, Mannheim Centre for European Social Research (MZES), Mannheim.

Goldin, I., Cameron, G. and Balarajan, M. (2012) *Exceptional People: How Migration Shaped Our World and Will Define Our Future*, Princeton University Press, Princetown, NJ and Woodstock, Oxfordshire.

Grey, C. (2015) *Justice and Authority in Immigration Law*, Hart Publishing, Oxford and Portland Oregon.

Hollifield, J.F. (1992) *Immigrants, Markets, and States: The Political Economy of Postwar Europe*, Harvard University Press, Cambridge, MA and London.

Jones, O. (2012) *Chavs: The Demonization of the Working Class*, Verso, London and New York.

Kay, J. (2016) *Other People's Money: Masters of the Universe or Servants of the People?* Profile Books, London.

Kitson, M. and Mitchie, J. (2014) *The Deindustrial Revolution: The rise and fall of UK manufacturing, 1870–2010*, Centre for Business Research, University of Cambridge Working Paper No. 459.

Kushner, T. and Knox, K. (2012) *Refugees in Age of Genocide*, Frank Cass, London and Portland.

Lawrence, F. (2004) *Not on the Label*, Penguin, Harmondsworth.

Mason, P. (2015) *Postcapitalism: A Guide to Our Future*, Allen Lane, Harmondsworth, Middlesex.

MCOP. (2006) *Migrant Voices, Migrant Rights: Can migrant community organisations change the immigration debate in Britain today?* Barrow Cadbury Trust, London. Available at: www.qmul.ac.uk/geog/media/geography/docs/research/migrantvoices.pdf

Neuwirth, R. (2011) *Stealth of Nations: The Global Rise of the Informal Economy*, Knopf Doubleday Publishing Group, New York.

Offe, C. (1984) *Contradictions of the Welfare State*, MIT Press, Cambridge, MA.

Smith, J. (2015) *Imperialism in the Twenty-First Century*, Monthly review Volume 67, Number 3, New York. Available at: https://monthlyreview.org/2015/07/01/imperialism-in-the-twenty-first-century/

Smith, J. (2016) *Imperialism in the Twenty-First Century: Globalization, Super-Exploitation, and Capitalism's Final Crisis*, Monthly Review Press, New York.

Standing, G. (2016) *The Precariat: The New Dangerous Class*, Bloomsbury, London.

Streeck, W. (2016) *How Will Capitalism End?* Verso, London and New York.

Waite, L., Craig, G., Lewis, H. and Skrivankova, K. (editors) (2015), *Vulnerability, Exploitation and Migrants: Insecure Work in a Globalised Economy*, Palgrave Macmillan, Basingstoke.

Webber, F. (2012) *Borderline Justice: The Fight for Refugee and Migrant Rights*, Pluto Press, London.

West, E. (2013) *The Diversity Illusion: What We Got Wrong About Immigration and How to Set It Right*, Gibson Square, London.

30

RESEARCH AND POLICY IN MIGRATION AND DEVELOPMENT

Some personal reflections

L. Alan Winters

Research and policy in migration: some personal reflections

This chapter is an embarrassingly personal account of what I think I have learned over four decades about the intersection between policy and research. Although the majority of my research has been devoted to international trade policy, a fair proportion has been expended on migration, and that is the context of the current chapter.

Migration is possibly the most difficult of all areas in which to bring evidence to bear on policy. First, it is multifaceted, so there is no readily accepted intellectual framework within which to pitch policy research on migration. Oftentimes it has been explained to me that, as an economist, my focus is too narrow; I accept that, but not to the extent of agreeing that economics has next to nothing to offer. Economic incentives and the supposed economic outcomes are major drivers of migration and of the responses to it. Nonetheless, much research, and any serious attempt to summarise research findings for the sake of policy-makers must be multi-disciplinary.

Second, migration touches the most sensitive of social issues – the boundary between 'us' and 'them'; what is the group for which we intuitively feel some affinity – and hence for whom we are prepared to bear some inconvenience – and who lies outside it. This is not necessarily only a matter of race or nationality. Even immigration within national boundaries and racial groups arouses unease and potential animosities if people in one location feel crowded or threatened economically by inflows from another, or indeed, on occasion, if they feel their communities are undermined by emigration to more prosperous regions. Policy-makers cannot entirely ignore such issues.

The third, related, source of sensitivity is political. 'Them' and 'us' provides a potent political message – and so can become magnified beyond the social concerns just alluded to. Moreover, in the liberal democracies and indeed in most other countries, it is difficult to discuss migration without racial or nativist rhetoric setting in. Thus, it is difficult to debate options for migration calmly and before a crisis sets in: politicians want to avoid the issue for as long as they can and constituents find it difficult to raise it without incurring suspicions of unworthy motives.

These difficulties do not make it impossible to use research for policy-making in the field of migration, but they certainly make it challenging.

Research and policy: a personal account

Virtually all my research has been empirical and/or policy-related. Much has been in academia, including within the network the Centre for Economic Policy Research, and in the World Bank, where I held posts of Economist, Head of International Trade, and Director of Research in the 1980s, 1990s, and 2000s, respectively. I have also been a consumer of research as Chief Economist in the British government's Department for International Development (DFID). These experiences have led me to reflect deeply on the interface between policy and research; indeed, I felt that I spent half my time as Director of Research explaining to the rest of the World Bank why they had a Research Department.[1]

My first effort to pursue research in migration was in the 1990s in the World Bank, where I concluded that considering international trade without also considering international migration gave you only half a loaf. I approved a little work and employed one consultant but soon my director explained that if I persisted with such controversial subjects my career (I think he meant *his* career) would progress no further!

After I moved to the University of Sussex in 1999, Roman Grynberg of the Commonwealth Secretariat approached me to see if I would explore the practical implementation of the clauses in the 1994 General Agreement on Trade in Services (GATS) on the temporary movement of natural persons and quantify their potential benefits for developing countries. The GATS distinguishes four modes of delivery for services, of which the movement of natural persons is 'Mode 4'. It has generated far less trade liberalisation since 1995 than the other modes – (1) cross-border trade, (2) movement of consumers, and (3) commercial presence (movement of supplying firms, i.e. foreign investment).

Roman's request led to a flurry of work, co-produced with Roman, Terrie Walmsley, and Zhen Kun Wang, which attracted significant policy attention in capitals and organisations like UNCTAD, IOM, and OECD. The work was quite novel, but I suspect that the main reason for its popularity was that it offered a big number on the potential gains. We estimated that increasing the international mobility of people from developing to developed countries by 3 per cent of the latter's workforces, offered economic gains half as large again as abolishing every barrier to international trade in the world! You must take such numbers with a large pinch of salt, but the idea is very simple: as far as we can tell, when a worker moves from a low-productivity location to a high-productivity one, his or her output and income increase very substantially, even without any extra training or education. At the same time as the Mode 4 research, I also worked on the 'brain drain' – especially that of medical and software professionals.

One handicap facing the work on Mode 4 was the absence of a bilateral dataset on levels of international migration, and so, with the support of DFID, Terrie Walmsley, Ron Skeldon, Chris Parsons, and I set off to construct one. It reports, for about 220 countries, the 'countries of origin' (variously defined) of their populations in their census years. The database started life in Sussex, migrated to the World Bank, and from there became a co-production between the World Bank and the UN Population Department, and it is now a standard resource – the Global Bilateral Migration Database (https://esa.un.org/unmigra tion/). It also underpins the more frequent, but less complete, UN Trends in International Migration Stock: Migrants by Destination and Origin, which is updated on a regular basis, UN (2015).

Meanwhile, Francois Bourguignon and Ian Goldin had rekindled World Bank interest in migration, and in 2004 Francois invited me back to the Bank as Director of Research with establishing a migration research programme as part of the deal. This started as a collaboration with Maurice Schiff, who then introduced Caglar Ozden and David McKenzie to the team, all of whom continue to produce high-class research in the area. For a couple of years, I feared that the Bank's Board would suggest that migration was too hot to handle, but gradually interest took hold with work springing up in several locations in the Bank, including in the Economic Policy and the Economic Prospects Groups, see, for example, World Bank (2006) and the Bank's periodic Migration and Remittances Briefs. I note in passing, partly to illustrate the delights of managing research in institutions, the pressure to produce outputs quickly meant (mean) that these latter references do not use the migration data referred to in the previous paragraph, but their own approximations to them!

At the same time as in the World Bank, economists around the world took up the migration with vigour, and strong migration research programmes emerged from both the international trade and the labour economics sides of the profession. From an extremely small base 15 years ago, migration is now a firmly established part of the economics profession, matching the longer-standing interest in the subject from other disciplines. While some institutions may choose not to invest in it, the set of issues that scholars have identified can no longer be entirely ignored by the policy-making community.

A particular success at the Bank arose from the informal connections between Research and Operations – in particular, the East Asia and Pacific Regional staff. In the mid-2000s the New Zealand authorities were edging towards a seasonal migration programme for the Pacific to provide labour for their vinicultural and horticultural industries. Recognising the sensitivities and technical challenges of such schemes, they approached the World Bank's Sydney office for advice. Manjula Luthria from that office worked closely with them and also asked me for any advice/evidence I could offer based on my work on Mode 4. I was pleased to be asked for advice but I was even more pleased to hear about a probable change in migration policy in advance of its implementation. We persuaded the New Zealand government that, as well as conducting an evaluation of the effects of any new policy in New Zealand (as they had planned), they should also allow the Bank to undertake a formal impact evaluation in the Pacific. We were able to do pre-policy base-line surveys of households in Tonga and Vanuatu followed by three post-policy surveys. This was the first formal evaluation of a migration policy and it established beyond reasonable doubt that for the households which supplied workers for New Zealand, incomes increased by around 30 per cent – an almost unprecedented boon for a specific development policy. The hard work that went into the design and evaluation of the policy, led the ILO to declare that the Recognised Seasonal Employers (RES) scheme was a best-practice model for other countries to follow.

After returning to Sussex from the Bank, I became Chief Economist at the UK Department for International Development, 2008–11. My tenure was largely taken up with the international financial crisis, although I was involved in some migration work. However, the subject was extremely sensitive, and, especially after the formation of a new government in May 2010, DFID largely ceased to work on it. Its principal engagement with migration was, indeed, to fund a large research centre at the University of Sussex. I was precluded from any contact with it, for conflict of interest reasons, but in September 2013, 2 years after leaving DFID, I became CEO of the Migrating out of Poverty Research Partnership Consortium (MOOP) when the incumbent left Sussex. The Consortium is concerned with migration within and between developing countries and is staffed mainly by academics in non-economic social sciences, and so it proved highly educational for me.

It is greatly to the credit of DID staff, especially those in the Research Department, that the contribution of migration to development gradually returned to the policy narrative. This is partly as a result of MOOP's work, but also that of many other academics and organisations. By 2018, Migration and Modern-Day Slavery warranted a whole Department to themselves.

Bringing research into policy

Having divided my career between the thinking end of policy and the policy end of thinking, I have reflected a good deal on the symbiosis between them. This section collates some of the lessons I think I have learned.

What is 'policy research'?

Research in development and in the social sciences is mostly about acquiring a general understanding of economic and social processes. Even where it comprises a carefully defined experiment on a specific policy instrument (for example, a randomised control trial) that experiment has to be located in a general understanding and its results only take on major significance when they are part of that understanding rather than just a simple correlation of the nature of 'we did X and A happened'. That said, instrumental results are very attractive in terms of both their intellectual clarity and the concreteness of their results; and they can consequently be politically persuasive. However, such an approach is only rarely applicable to the broader issues development policy. Partly this is because of the nature of the question but partly also because, on sensitive issues like migration, political authorities are suspicious of such forensic examination. For example, in the mid-2000s, development economists had a strong focus on impact evaluations (excessively so in my view), and prior to the initiation of the evaluation of New Zealand's RES described above I had spent a year looking for a migration policy we could subject to that treatment. Among the reasons I failed to persuade policy-makers to go along with one were their unwillingness to discuss a sensitive policy with outsiders prior to its formal announcement and their recognition that the existence of a technical evaluation could make it difficult to retreat from a policy which had become too hot politically.

Policy is normally made with less than complete information and what there is has to be tailored to the policy-makers' exact question, often over a very short period. This suggests to me two needs. First, it requires skilled intermediaries – possibly in a multi-layered hierarchy – to transmit the results from the researcher to the policy discussion and well-conceived research questions in the opposite direction. At one end of the chain, the skill of accessible writing and presentation is invaluable – and it almost always resides elsewhere than the skill of doing research. Researchers should accept help, subject only to keeping a veto over meaning. At the other end one needs a trusted and skilled first point of contact for the policy-maker as he or she contemplates seeking (or even producing) evidence; someone who can say broadly what is known, what is knowable, what is essentially unknowable (at least in advance) and translate policy requests into research questions. For several years DFID had a set of Senior Research Fellows – academics working part-time in the Department – who worked with policy staff on the early stages of policy and analysis tasks. I always felt they greatly strengthened the foundations on which such work proceeded.

The intermediary is also an essential part of research quality control. Plenty of research is second rate and it needs to be weeded out. But also, perish the thought, researchers can be a bit lazy and if they think their 'policy client' cannot tell the difference, they will not always exert themselves to produce their best work.[2]

Policy-relevant research does have to be technically correct. This entails using the most appropriate methods, not necessarily the most sophisticated or newest methods, a trade-off that poses real challenges in marrying policy and academia. Academia values originality and cleverness more highly than worthy rectitude or replication, and so quickly tires of the work that most policy-making requires. Indeed, the search for originality can be a negative force in policy work. First, it can divert the research away from the (often simple) key practical questions and second policy ought to be made on the basis of a broad understanding backed by a body of evidence not on the latest wizard idea from a fevered academic imagination. On the other hand, policy often requires original solutions and so research qua research is still important.

The correct aim for policy research is to be 'policy relevant' – that is, to focus substantively on issues of practical importance. But this does not necessarily mean analysing a specific policy lever or proposal, and nor does it necessarily have to be empirical research. However, given that policy requires policy levers and is about the real world, it should support and eventually help to lead to these features.

Taking policy seriously

One often hears requests for academic authors to make their work 'policy relevant', and it often seems that tacking a couple of policy conclusions onto the end of an article is held to be an adequate response. This is a travesty: the paragraphs are frequently tangential to the analysis that precedes them and often amount to no more than a parade of conventional wisdom or prejudice. Actually, policy is serious, sometimes, deadly serious.

Any policy statement is a statement about causality – you are asserting that if you change a policy in a particular way, something specific will happen. Economists take causality very seriously, and have developed tools that attempt (often inadequately) to deal with it, but I am afraid I do not detect the same care throughout social science. It is also a particular challenge in migration research, because migrants are special people (typically more adventurous and risk-loving than average) who decide consciously to migrate because they think it will offer better life-chances than not migrating. In technical terms the sample of actual migrants is subject to a selectivity bias. Hence, if you observe that migrants earn more than those who stay at home, you do not know without further analysis whether that is because migration generates higher incomes or because migrants are the sort of people who would be successful anyway. Among the most elegant pieces of analysis that side-steps this problem is Gibson and McKenzie (2014) who study permanent migration from Tonga and Samoa to New Zealand. The right to such migration is allocated by ballot. Hence, to simplify a little, you can observe the differences due to being a migrant-type by comparing people who entered the ballot with those who did not, while, by comparing the people who won the ballot with those who did not, you can isolate the effects of migration.

There is still an immense amount of highly valuable work to be done describing and understanding migration processes, but one should not look to it to offer direct policy statements. Under the best of circumstances, such work contributes to the policy process, but too often it describes a problem and concludes that 'therefore something must be done', usually implicitly or explicitly by the government. This is the second complexity in using research to recommend policy. Even if the diagnosis is perfectly correct, someone still needs to identify an appropriate instrument and how to apply it. This is often not an area of strength for the researchers, and that is acceptable, but, given that this is the case, the researchers should not claim – nor be encouraged to claim – that they have solved the problem. Researchers are often aware of their lack of experience in practical policy application, but are nonetheless encouraged by sponsors and journalists – and increasingly by their institutions' Public Relations operations – to over-claim.

The third – related – complication is that one needs to balance solving a problem with the cost of doing so and the possible unintended consequences (collateral damage) that doing so entails. An awful example of the latter came to public attention in the UK in May 2018, under the name of the 'Windrush Generation'. It emerged that in an attempt to clamp down on 'illegal' migration in Britain – an objective that to some people is perfectly reasonable – the UK authorities had withheld critical services from, and even expelled, some very long-term residents because they could not document their right to remain to the standards being applied in 2018. When they entered Britain, no such paperwork was required and no-one had ever suggested that they should accumulate it over time. This is a case of focussing exclusively on the 'technical' solution to the 'illegality' problem without thinking through its unacceptable spill over effects on another. The alternative explanation for this outcome is too chilling to contemplate

Again, the issue is not that policy researchers should think through every possible pathology of a policy before suggesting it, but that they and the demanders of policy research should recognise what research can and cannot reasonably do and accept that actually defining and implementing policy solutions requires further, and usually differently-skilled, work than doing the initial diagnostic research.

Engaging with policy-makers

One of the lessons I have learned is to listen very carefully to policy-makers. This is partly so that you have a ready audience for your research results (and perhaps some material support for your research), but this advice also reflects a more substantive goal. Researchers can be rather supercilious about policy-makers' lack of rigour, but this is not generally because policymakers are stupid, but because they have a different job from the researchers. Hence one should always ask oneself, 'Why are they asking this question?' 'What don't they understand that I do?' 'What do they understand that I don't?' Often the answer is that policy-makers bring context to a question of the sort that researchers – at least in economics – tend to place on one side in order to make a question manageable. They bring exactly the sort of 'balance' that should have been applied in the 'Windrush' scandal.

Let me be completely clear, however, that the plea for balance is not a critique of making simplifying assumptions. Our job as scientists is to make a complex world sufficiently simple that we can understand it and answer important questions clearly and rigorously. Every discipline makes assumptions – for example, in how to set up a problem and what to ignore from the mass of observational data; the important thing is never to forget that one has made assumptions and then periodically to ask whether they were the right ones.

Listening to policy-makers does not mean having to adopt their view of a problem: having an impact does not mean being on the winning side of every (any?) policy debate. I think it means accepting that sometimes, while the research points in one direction, the policy-maker decides, for good or bad reasons, to go in a different one. In these circumstances, the researcher's duty to his or her profession is not to compromise the research by calling bad economics (or sociology) good economics (sociology), but to say 'this is what the research says and I recognise that you have decided differently'. In the end researchers are playing a long game and to compromise on analysis rather than just on outcome will eventually turn out to be costly.

Several colleagues have observed to me that over the last two decades policy-making has regressed in this regard in the UK. Whereas the Labour government of 1997–2010 advocated 'evidence-based policy' and lived up to that to at least some extent, this seemed to give way to the 'policy-based evidence' of the Coalition (2010–15) and to an ideological and more or less 'evidence-free' approach to policy in the (Brexit-obsessed) Conservative government of 2017 onwards.

Politicians, and therefore the civil servants who work for them, have to make compromises to achieve anything. One technique to resolve policy conflicts is to try to find 'win-win' narratives that offer political cover for their preferred policies or find strategies that clothe the policy in terms to which no-one can object. These narratives and strategies often depend upon myths and as such pose serious dilemmas for the researchers. Migration research furnishes two classic cases. Developed country politicians have long justified foreign aid or trade concessions with the argument that only by helping developing countries to grow can they stop the latter's citizens from migrating to the rich countries. No evidence in favour of this view exists except, possibly, in the very long run (Parsons and Winters 2016), and yet both aid and trade concession are generally held to be policies that we would wish to promote. The second example is the current tendency among politicians to equate migration with modern-day slavery. This permits governments to talk about migration in a way that was not possible previously and yet is clearly not true: most migrants are not slaves and, most likely, most slaves are not migrants.

It does not seem helpful always to declare loudly that the politicians are mistaken or mendacious but equally one cannot let the assertions pass unchallenged. The best policy that I have managed to devise is to stick to our analytical conclusions in any debate but not necessarily to make debunking the myth the headline of every encounter. It may be that policy-makers have just learned not to discuss the matter with me anymore, but I think that the 'aid cuts migration' myth is in recession.

Having an impact

Contradicting policy-makers arises at another point in the researcher–policy interaction. Emmanuel Tumusiime-Mutebile was the Permanent Secretary of the Ugandan Finance Ministry and then Governor of the Central Bank, and was widely credited as the architect of Uganda's resurrection from being the worst of states into a star economic performer under President Museveni. He frequently said that his principal task was 'just to say no' to the President. Nearly every senior economist in government has the same experience, and I believe it is true also for other senior social scientists. Moderating bad policy ideas at an early stage is another critical contribution of senior, in-house, intermediaries between policy and research.

Even from the outside, and at less august levels, researchers can contribute to heading off bad policy. Research affects policy at least as much indirectly as directly, by influencing the way in which people think, the questions they ask, their view of the trade-offs, and even what constitutes evidence. Thus, the accumulation of evidence and its broad dissemination can gradually block off the space for bad policy because a general understanding of the actual situation emerges. Parallel to the injunction not to bless bad policy as good analysis, persistently explaining the logic of a policy dilemma can, at least on some occasions, eventually prevail. The road that British policy-makers have travelled over the last 5 years, from denial to an understanding that migration plays an important role in development is substantially due, I believe, to the persistence of the message from researchers.

Related to this is my belief that generally the best route to having an impact in the long run is to work with mid-level civil servants rather than with the ministers of the day.[3] Of course, on occasion ministerial enthusiasm is enough to get a policy adopted but this is typically more the case in times of crises and narrowly defined issues than of the broad contours of development. Usually, when dealing with a problem becomes unavoidable, a mid-level official is asked to prepare an issues paper. If that paper contains only sensible suggestions, it is relatively rare in my experience for higher officials to replace them wholesale. Hence, if, through our teaching or through relatively technical and interesting discussions of policy questions, researchers can persuade the middle-level civil service, we contribute substantially towards avoiding the worst policy errors. Moreover, I have come more recently to believe that the most useful interactions between researchers and officials are open-form private discussions in which officials feel enough confidence to test their, and their ministers', ideas with experts and listen to the answers without feeling the need to defend government positions. There is rarely an identifiable impact from any one such meeting, but by creating trust it increases the civil servants' openness to analysis and confidence in implementing its results.

It is also important in these meetings that researchers be prepared to call upon their knowledge of the field in general, rather than merely promote just the thing they are working on at present. Indeed, policy should not be made on the strength of single pieces of work – and certainly not those that are very recent – for the process of testing and fully understanding research results is a long one. Policy advice should rely on a body of work developed over a number of years. This was brought home to me in an excrutiating interview I had during an evaluation of World Bank research conducted when I was Director of Research. The chair of the Evaluation Committee – now a Nobel laureate – started one meeting by saying 'we want to talk about impact – the cases where you had impact but should not have had'.

A significant danger for in-house researchers, and also for others charged with having 'impact', is that sometimes results can be brought into play prematurely. Not only researchers, but also funders and commissioners of research, must not let their urges to justify their work (funding decisions) and to have an impact, get ahead of the necessary part of research played by peer review and challenge. Certainly, some problems are so urgent that society needs answers quickly and so the risks of premature application are justified, but in my experience there are cases where the urgency is a purely personal or institutional one and deserves to be resisted. A proud moment for me when I was Director of Research in the World Bank was when, despite considerable pressure, one of my Research Managers refused to report some preliminary research results to the Bank's President (the disgraced Paul Wolfowitz) because he was not yet sure of their reliability.

Making policy is like making sausage[4]

It would be easy to think from the above that policy proceeds in a simple linear fashion from research and analysis to implementation, but this is not the case. As I noted above, policy-makers face a wide range of pressures and objectives – e.g. efficiency, equity, history, identity, and politics – whose relative weight can vary, often rapidly, over time. (It is not that policy-makers are irrational, they just have a different job from that of the researcher.)

One consequence of this is that timing is important, and that is more commonly a matter of luck than of judgement. Most policy is initiated much more quickly than research can be organised and executed and so the critical first formulations (around which political positions tend to crystallise) rely on the existing stock of knowledge. This has several implications.

- Policy advisers should be an important reservoir of previous research – again the role for the local expert;
- Researchers should not be shy of returning to and promoting old results when they suddenly attain relevance;
- A research culture in which current 'relevance' is the only or even the main criterion is likely to be quite deficient;
- As a researcher, you can do all the right things to achieve impact and still have no effect, if there is no 'market' for the question to which you have an answer. It is almost always necessary to find a champion inside the policy-making process if your results are to be directly influential.

Many examples exist and I will give only two. First, the key to preventing the spread of Ebola in West Africa in 2014–15, which was clearly a huge potential global health crisis, was anthropological research on burial practices in West Africa over the previous decade. No-one would have predicted in, say, 2004 that this would have had a practical impact. Melissa Leach, the director of the work, also notes another key input to impact on development – the existence of local researchers in developing countries able to position the research in the local context, see Leach (2016). This is also a guiding principle of The Global Development Network with which I have had a long association (www.gdn.int/). It is devoted to building local research capacity as the key to better policy-making and thus better lives in developing countries

Second, in the Migrating out of Poverty Research Partnership Consortium, we had a small programme with three projects exploring the process whereby migration policy was actually formed: granting a day a week off to domestic workers in Singapore and Bangladesh and preventing human trafficking in South Africa. Each project describes a decade-long process specific to its own country, but in fact the cases turned out to have a number of similarities (see Palmary and de Gruchy 2016).

Perhaps because the policies concerned poor, vulnerable workers, almost exclusively women, the arguments were all moral, moralistic, and highly gendered. Legal human rights arguments supported reform positions whereas opponents focused on the infeasibility or high cost of protecting or granting rights to migrants. Behind each discourse, was concern about the 'burden' that unskilled poor migrants placed on receiving societies.

International actors and norms played significant roles in each case. So, in addition to politicians, did coalitions of NGOs and particular civil servants who championed the cause of reform. In each case, the policies took almost a decade to develop, starting with the elaboration of the case for reform followed by a hiatus until a catalyst, for example, international pressure, emerged.

Turning to the role of research Palmary and de Gruchy (2016) state that 'research was used by coalitions and policy-makers in ad hoc and problematic ways'. And that:

Notably, lawmakers were remarkably passive in their consumption of research. They did not seek out researchers nor did they search for research themselves. Rather, they relied on people coming to them with research findings. In spite of this, in all three cases they lamented the absence of research on the topic. Thus, if one thing is clear it is that advocacy is an important influencer of policy development even if the advocacy is not evidence-based. In addition, the quality of research did not influence whether the research had impact or not. In fact, many members of civil society and civil servants appeared relatively illiterate in terms of their abilities to discern between methodologically sound research and problematic research.

(2016, 22)

Conclusion

The previous paragraph sounds rather depressing for those of us who believe that policy should be made by rational argument from a factual base. Rather, however, I would prefer to interpret it as a dose of realism for those who believe that all that is necessary to get good policy is putting a few million into universities and urging (incentivising?) them to 'have impact'. The integration of research into policy will always be partial, and to researchers' minds, inadequate, but we can improve immensely on the position of having none at all. But it takes time. The sort of environment we need to aim for requires:

- a strong, argumentative, research community which can debate ideas freely and openly, and which debates policy analyses in a rigorous and objective way, independent of the palatability of the results. This, in turn, requires rewarding scholars for research and debate, not for 'winning' the policy argument;
- recognising that the process of understanding policy problems and being trusted enough to contribute to the answers requires a long-term commitment by people who understand research; and that there is a major role in this for insiders who span the research-policy space, often as a result of splitting their time between the academy and government;
- persuading academics that policy-making is not merely a parking lot for failed researchers, but that it is fundamental to a sound society and that policy-making is different from research;
- allowing researchers space to identify at least some of the issues they will work on, while requiring them to show that the resulting research contributes towards finding solutions to important social and economic problems; and
- cultivating in policy-makers an appetite for analytical results, partly by affording them research experiences as part of their education, and partly by engaging with them in mature way; on the policy-makers' part this requires a greater willingness to spend time with research and to make resources available to cover this time.

Notes

1 The two biggest influences on the way in which I think about policy and research are Michael Finger, who led the International Economics Research Division in the World Bank in the 1980s and Richard Portes, founding Director of the Centre for Economic Policy Research.
2 Being sufficiently grumpy to complain about poor work was, I believe, one of my larger contributions in both DFID and the Migrating out of Poverty Consortium.
3 This was essentially the philosophy of the Centre for Economic Policy Research (CEPR).
4 Otto von Bismarck is (mis-)reported as saying 'Laws, like sausages, cease to inspire respect in proportion as we know how they are made'. In fact, according to WikiQuote, it should be attributed to John Godfrey Saxe 'University Chronicle', University of Michigan (27 March 1869). It's still true, though.

Acknowledgements

I am grateful to Tanja Bastia and Ron Skeldon for comments on an earlier draft and to the myriad of people who helped me sort out some of these ideas over many years.

References

Gibson, John, and David McKenzie. "The development impact of a best practice seasonal worker policy." *Review of Economics and Statistics* 96.2 (2014): 229–243.

Leach, Melissa (2016) 'Ebola anthropology: From real-time social science to building future local capacity', https://blog.esrc.ac.uk/2016/10/27/ebola-anthropology-from-real-time-social-science-to-building-future-local-capacity/#more-1484.

Palmary, Ingrid and Thea de Gruchy (2016) 'How unpopular policies are made: Policy making for migrant women in South Africa, Bangladesh and Singapore', Migrating Out of Poverty Working Paper 45, University of Sussex, October 2016.

Parsons, Christopher R. and L. Alan Winters (2016) 'International Migration, Trade and Aid: A Survey', *Chapter 4 of International Handbook on Migration and Development*, eds. Robert E.B. Lucas, Cheltenham, Edward Elgar, 2014, pp.65–112.

United Nations (2015) 'Trends in international migrant stock: Migrants by destination and origin'. *United Nations database*, New York, Population Division, Department of Economic and Social Affairs, POP/DB/MIG/Stock/Rev.2015, available at: www.un.org/en/development/desa/population/migration/data/estimates2/estimates17.shtml.

World Bank (2006) *Global Economic Prospects 2006: Economic Implications of Remittances and Migration*, Washington DC, World Bank.

PART V

Key challenges for migration and development

In this fifth part of the Handbook, the chapters deal with critical current and future issues in the migration and development debate. The role of return migration and return policies in development in a context where development policy can be predicated upon acceptance by origin countries of the return of their citizens is examined. A critical perspective is provided to propose a more balanced interpretation of 'voluntary' and 'forced' return. Forced migration and refugees are often not an integral part of the migration and development debate and yet a clear relationship exists between the distribution of forced migrants and low levels of development. How best to consider the role of people who are forced to move as a consequence of development? While conflict forces people to flee, development itself can force people off their land. The construction of dams and the expansion of cities or the extraction of minerals displace large numbers of people who will often have little opportunity to return.

Perhaps the biggest questions revolve around migration and environmental change, and particularly the impact of climate change. Many myths and unknowns beset this debate and the two chapters, critically assess the conceptualisation of and the impact on migration of both man-made and naturally induced disasters, to the extent that these can be clearly separated. Part V ends with yet another two critical policy issues, with chapters on trafficking and smuggling, raising questions about the abuse and protection of migrants, not all of which are intuitively obvious.

Essentially, the underlying question of the chapters in Part V asks whether development, and the migrations that are associated with it, are sustainable over the longer term. They remind us that development, as we understand it in its broadest sense of improving the well-being of human populations, may not be guaranteed. Similarly, the migrations associated with that development can bring misery as much as improvement into the human condition.

31

ARE CURRENT 'RETURN POLICIES' RETURN POLICIES?

A reflection and critique

Jean-Pierre Cassarino

The title of this chapter may be puzzling when considering the plethora of official statements, reports, and communiqués that have been produced, over the last two decades, to address 'the sustainability of return' in migrants' countries of origin. To be sure, this question raises a host of challenges having concrete relevance in contemporary policy-making and research methods which will be tackled in this contribution.

Talking about return today differs markedly from talking about return a few decades ago. Today, the understanding is all too often associated with the end of the migration cycle. Its meaning even incorporates deportation or removal. This meaning has become so hegemonic in policy discourse that a reference to *return* implies a form of pressure or coercion exerted by the state and its law-enforcement agencies.

The first part of this article analyses the factors and policy developments that have been conducive to a different coinage of return, its global diffusion and banal acceptance. It also examines the implications stemming from this definitional shift whereby return is equated with removal in official rhetoric. Critically examining these powerful policy developments constitutes a daunting challenge. To do so, we need to adopt a grounded method which empirically examines what current 'return policies' really address and prioritise. This chapter concludes by arguing that comparing without equating return with removal is possible and necessary through the lens of migration cycles. It is also useful to highlight the security-oriented biases that drive current policy priorities as well as their own limits when addressing the link between return, re-integration, and development.

Recalling the individuality of return migrants

More than 40 years ago, in his oft-cited 1974 essay on the sociology of return migration, Frank Bovenkerk dedicated a section entitled '"Return" that is not return'. He called for a basic distinction between repatriation and return (Bovenkerk 1974, 19). The former takes place as a result of external forces or coercion exerted by 'political authorities' as he put it, whereas the latter occurs as a result of migrants' subjective motivations, ill-grounded or not. Return migration is broadly defined in his essay as the act of returning to a migrant's country of departure before emigration. In other words, return is part and parcel of a migratory cycle that includes three stages: departure, immigration, and return. A few years later, George Gmelch suggests that return is the 'movement of emigrants back to their homelands to resettle' (1980, 136) and that return motives may be favourable (for example, job achievement, sufficient savings earned whilst abroad, loyalty, desire to reunite) or unfavourable (for example, economic recession in the host country, discrimination abroad, family pressure) or a combination of the two. As rightly stressed in his comprehensive review, motives for return are always diverse and never mono-causal. They tend to overlap so much that eliciting *the* factor which influenced the decision to return might be risky, if not biased. Empirical works with return migrants show that they tend to mention a plurality of factors which, in their opinion, were conducive to their return. Face-to-face interviews are essential for identifying which factors are primarily significant in migrants' decision to return, and to understanding how agency intersects with social, economic, and structural factors and under which circumstances both in countries of destination and in countries of origin (King 1986; Cassarino 2004).

Over the last five decades, a rich and abundant academic literature has addressed return migrants' motivations, re-adaptation processes, resources, and patterns of reintegration back to their countries. Nermin Abadan-Unat (1976), Roger Böhning (1975), Frank Bovenkerk (1974), Francesco Cerase (1971), George Gmelch (1980), Russell King (1986), Daniel Kubat (1984), Elizabeth Thomas-Hope (1999), and Frieda Wilder-Okladek (1969), to name but a few scholars, have produced important and seminal works on return migration *and* returnees. Beyond their inherent diversity, major research interests across various disciplines revolve around how return migrants affected and were affected by the social economic cultural and political context in both their countries of origin and their former countries of destination. Today, their works and heuristic devices continue to be instrumental when analysing the ways in which the duration of the migration experience, context, and structure interplay and, at the same time, shape the agency of return migrants and their patterns of reintegration. That is, the individuality of return migrants, defined as *persons* having individual motivations, aspirations, and resources – just like any other human being – was a major research topic.

The shifts

Today, laying emphasis on the individuality of return migrants may be viewed as an eccentric endeavour when one considers the powerful paradigms that have been conducive to the predominant state-centred approach to migration matters in international policy talks, including return migration. In a recent study, Blitz et al. rightly noted that 'the notion of return has shifted from being a voluntary decision made by individuals to a policy option which is exercised by governments' (2005, 196) on individual migrants. This shift is perceptible in migration talks and official rhetoric as applied to return migration. It results from other 'shifts' that need to be addressed together with key policy and economic events.

The first of these shifts refers to the need to ensure the temporariness of labour migration which, since the 1973 oil crisis onwards, has gained momentum in migration talks (Castles 2006a, 2006b). Temporary migration schemes have been implemented for various decades. In practice, however, the return and rotation of foreign workers, on which temporary migration schemes were premised, did not occur systematically (Dustmann 1996, 221). With reference to the German guest worker programmes, Philip Martin explains that such programmes lasted longer than expected because 'employers often encouraged migrants to stay longer, saving them the cost of recruiting and training a replacement' (Martin 2006, 14). At the same time, two additional effects contributed to the time extension of such schemes. In

Martin's opinion, the first one relates to 'dependence', namely the fact that migrants and their families could come to depend on foreign jobs through family reunification. The second effect pertains to 'distortion' which, to quote Martin, refers to 'the fact that employers make investment decisions on the assumption that migrants will continue to be available' (Martin 2006, 2), leading to an adjustment of domestic labour markets to the presence of foreign workers. Both the dependence and distortion effects prevented the rotation of foreign labour and the expected return of foreign workers to their home countries. Other unintended consequences also included the capacity of foreign workers to organise themselves through trade unions and to voice their claims for equal treatment through strikes. Martin's remark is important to understand that a combination of economic and non-economic factors combined together, making the temporary stay of foreign workers less temporary, if not permanent. Also, a mix of economic performance and a complex socialisation process within the firm contributed to the prolonged stay of migrant workers.

The second of the shifts pertains to the gradual prioritisation (and acceptance) of job flexibility over protection from uncertainty in Western labour markets (Holgate 2011; Standing 2011; Schierup et al. 2015). To date, this shift has contributed to making the current emphasis placed by some economic and political elites on workers' employability more acceptable and thinkable. Actually, this reference reflects the 'adjustment of labour supply to the requirements of the market, deregulation and rising labour market flexibility' (Burroni and Keune 2011, 76). In European destination countries, this shift also entailed a process of labour market deregulation which concomitantly has gone hand in hand with the reinforced regulation of migration by the state administration. One emblematic illustration of the reinforced regulation of international migration lies in the adoption of restrictive immigration laws aimed at channelling given human resources to specific sectors of industry, on a temporary basis. Moreover, in various EU member states, the right to stay became subordinated to migrant workers having a job contract. Moreover, family reunification was made more difficult following the introduction of restrictive criteria. Later on, these restrictions were accompanied by the implementation of state-led 'return aid' programmes aimed at inducing migrants to leave. In France, such programmes were initially questioned and subsequently suspended, but during the late 1980s, they were re-introduced by the French government. Their reintroduction was not only a response to the resilient economic downturn in France and to the growing politicisation of such domestic concerns as the 'integration of immigrants', citizenship, and national identity. These programmes also constituted and still constitute today the most explicit form of state interventionism, above all in a context marked by growing labour market deregulation, subcontracting, weakened social dialogue, industrial delocalisation, the retrenchment of the welfare state, and state divestiture (Delgado Wise 2015).

The third shift results from the combination of the former two. In order to ensure the temporariness of labour migration, while making the drive for temporariness a mainstay of current labour market policies (Cassarino 2013), removal mechanisms had to be designed with a view to deterring labour migrants from overstaying their job contract. Concomitantly, flows of asylum-seekers from Iraq, the Balkans, Pakistan, Afghanistan, and African countries became a major crossover issue in the numerous governmental and intergovernmental talks on migration and asylum that have proliferated since the early 1990s. These informal intergovernmental meetings are not only aimed at sharing knowledge and experiences among government officials on migration management and asylum matters. Through their repetition, they have instilled guiding principles which in turn have been erected as normative values and principles shaping how international migration should best be administered, regulated, and understood.

For example, the dichotomy opposing 'voluntary' with 'enforced' return results from a political construct that is emblematic of these recent policy developments. Its acceptance by policymakers and stakeholders from all countries of migration has been extraordinary when one realises that it is shaped by a receiving-country bias. Moreover, it hardly reflects the composite nature of return flows and returnees' realities in the broadest sense. Finally, despite the seemingly impeccable reference to voluntariness, the line between 'voluntary' and enforced return has turned out to be too blurry (Bivand Erdal and Oeppen 2018), given the security-driven purposes this political construct has served (Chimni 1995; Blitz et al. 2005; Webber 2011; Kleist and Vammen 2012, 56–63; Kalir 2017). This was precisely what the Parliamentary Assembly of the Council of Europe (PACE) denounced when it decided in June 2010 to adopt Resolution 1742 calling on the member states of the Council of Europe to ensure that:

> Assisted voluntary return programmes are indeed voluntary, that [migrants'] consent is not obtained under pressure or blackmail and that [they] have access to independent and impartial actors in the return process to make free and informed decisions, [...] [and that] assisted voluntary return should never put in jeopardy the right of an asylum seeker to claim asylum and protection.[1]

In the European Union (EU), this vision of return has been presented as an integral part of the instruments aimed at dealing with unauthorised migration and at protecting the integrity of immigration and asylum systems in most destination countries (European Commission 2005, 2). Since the early 2000s, 'return' policies of the EU and its Member States have been predominantly, if not exclusively, viewed as instruments for combating irregular migration. In the parlance of the EU, return merely refers to the act of removing irregular migrants and rejected asylum-seekers from the European territory. Moreover, it does not take into account migrants' post-return conditions, let alone their human and financial potential as participants in development.

Over the last two decades, this security-driven vision of 'return' has invested official discourses and means of action with an extraordinary sense of rationality, so much so that mixing return with expulsion or re-admission has become commonly accepted. As mentioned before, this terminological usage results from a political construct that finds its roots in the growing politicisation of international migration movements in Western countries, the ensuing adoption of selective laws regarding the conditions of entry and (temporary) residence of labour migrants, asylum-seekers and refugees, the reinforcement of border controls, and the protracted crisis of European political integration. This is not the place to delve into these complex causes. Suffice to say that these policy developments have gradually contributed to altering the meaning of return while equating it with removal or deportation.

The epitome of this altered meaning lies probably in the Green Paper on a 'Community Return Policy on Illegal Residents' that the European Commission presented in April 2002 (European Commission 2002). The Green Paper was not only aimed at opening consultations with EU stakeholders on so-called return matters. It also contributed to a skilful reframing of such consultations in its preliminary remarks. For example, in the text of the Green Paper, the European Commission acknowledged the existence of various categories of returnees. It made a distinction between those who decide autonomously to go back to their countries of origin and those who are forced to. The European Commission, however, opted to focus on the latter, namely on the forced and assisted return of foreigners living irregularly in the European Union. The Commission also mentioned in the 2002 Green Paper that the autonomous return of migrants should deserve further attention, owing to its potential impact on countries of origin, and that it should be 'subject to further reflection on the part of the Commission, at a later stage' (2002, 7). To date, this reflection has not taken place.

It could be argued that the gradual acceptance and diffusion of this altered meaning among governmental and intergovernmental agencies date back to the early 2000s. Concomitantly, acceptance and diffusion have been contingent on sending to oblivion past research and theoretical findings able to explain return migrants' patterns of re-integration as well as their unequal contribution to local development. Instead of tilling a vast and rich academic corpus on return migrants' motivations and patterns of reintegration, dating back to the 1960s onwards, the land was, as it were, cleared before the co-opted expertise was mobilised to grow 'policy-relevant' research outputs on so-called 'voluntary and enforced return', 'the nexus between reintegration of voluntary return', and last but not least the 'sustainability of return'. A form of land clearance was a prerequisite to uprooting large segments of academic research on return migrants with a view to paradigmatically equating return with the removal or deportation of irregular migrants and rejected asylum-seekers.

Moreover, the drive for operability and 'effectiveness' has shaped the rationale for these programmes. Financial schemes have been created to ensure migrants' 'sustainable return' at all costs, regardless of whether the economic and political conditions back in the country of origin are suitable.[2]

Comparing without equating

Perhaps never before has the need to make a clear-cut distinction between return and deportation been so relevant both politically and analytically. This distinction is essential when realising that implications for migrants are extremely diverse.

Return, viewed as a stage in the migration cycle (Cassarino 2004; Sinatti 2014), markedly differs from removal. Removal or expulsion represents the interruption of a migration cycle, which has severe consequences for a migrant's likelihood and opportunities to reintegrate. As argued before, confounding removal and return stands in stark contrast with what scholars across disciplines have observed and documented since the 1960s. Perhaps, the only common denominator between migrants who return back home and those who are removed (be they rejected asylum-seekers or irregular migrants subjected to a removal order) is that they all have a migration cycle. The basic and substantial difference between both groups lies in their types of migration cycle as explained below. It is through the lens of migration cycles that the conditions of removed migrants and return migrants can be compared and analysed without, however, equating the former with the latter.

Three types of migration cycle

A migration cycle may be complete, incomplete, or interrupted.

A migration cycle is complete when migrants consider that it is time to return owing to factors and conditions in both countries of destination and of origin that are subjectively viewed as being favourable or positive to their life plans. They feel they gathered sufficient tangible and intangible resources to carry out their projects in their home countries. They may have developed valuable contacts, as well as acquired skills and knowledge that can add significantly to their initiatives. These migrants not only opted to return, but they also had the opportunity to evaluate the costs and benefits of return while considering the changes that occurred in their countries of origin at institutional, economic, social, and political levels. Some of them may maintain their residential status in their host country; others may have acquired citizenship abroad, with a view to securing their cross-border mobility.

Conversely, a migration cycle is incomplete when unexpected factors and conditions prompted migrants to return, whereas they intended to stay abroad for longer. Their length of stay abroad was too short to allow tangible and intangible resources to be mobilised. They decided indeed to return, but their option was taken owing to unfavourable or adverse factors – examples being unexpected family problems, ostracism, or even lack of real opportunities for social and professional advancement in host countries. Migrants having an incomplete migration cycle consider that the costs of remaining are higher than returning home, even if few resources were mobilised before their return. Hence, resource mobilisation in receiving countries remains extremely limited, and the returnee will tend to rely on resources available at the level of the family or the community back home in order to reintegrate.

Finally, a migration cycle is interrupted when disruptive events compel migrants to leave the territory of the host country. They intended to stay abroad for longer. However, unlike migrants having an incomplete migration cycle, they never had the possibility of weighing the costs and benefits of their return, for factors external to their own volition prompted them to leave. For some, this may result from their asylum application being rejected or from a removal order by the law-enforcement authorities in their destination country. Undoubtedly, these constitute the most violent and upsetting factors prompting a person to leave a destination country. There are, however, additional factors that abruptly interrupt a migration cycle and invariably jeopardise the reintegration process of migrants back home. Women migrants' families may exert pressures strong enough to demand their return back home in order to arrange their marriage while disregarding whether or not such pressures will compromise their migratory projects and aspirations abroad. Scant attention has been paid to these profoundly gendered implications where the family and traditions turn out to disrupt a personal migratory and emancipatory project. In a similar vein, war and insecurity in the host country also constitute factors which may disrupt a migration cycle, leading to the compelled repatriation of migrants. Finally, the unexpected non-renewal of a job contract inevitably disrupts a migration cycle if one considers that labour migrants will have no choice but to shorten their stay abroad and to leave their destination countries against their will, lest they become irregular.

It is clear that the three abovementioned types of migration cycles make up a rough plot of the plurality of conditions faced by migrants once they decide or are prompted to come back. However, the significance of this heuristic device lies precisely in emphasising that, beyond the heterogeneity of migrants' experiences and profiles, the degree of completeness of their migration cycles constitutes a key explanatory element of their various patterns of reintegration. It is only by focusing on the degree of completeness of migration cycles that migrants' patterns of reintegration can be compared without equating removed or deported migrants with return migrants.

These considerations have concrete and significant implications for policy-making when, for example, it comes to defining measures aimed at offsetting the incompleteness and interruption of the migration cycle. Particularly in the current context marked by the resilience of adverse economic conditions in Western destination countries that negatively impact on migrants' likelihood to complete their migration cycle and on their option (if any) to return. Such a decision also springs from a personal evaluation of these circumstances which cannot be dismissed. Moreover, over the last two decades or so, the temporariness of labour migration has gained tremendous momentum in current bilateral and multilateral talks on migration matters. The drive for temporariness (Cassarino 2013) which is enshrined in current labour migrant schemes and circular migration programmes (Castles 2006a, 2006b; Anderson 2010; Holgate 2011) invariably raises a host of critical issues when understanding whether the temporary duration of the experience of migration will foster the completeness of foreign workers' migration cycles and their ensuing reintegration in their countries of origin, be it permanent or temporary. Public authorities will be faced, at a certain point, with the need to ensure that the abovementioned drive for temporariness will not jeopardise the social and occupational reintegration of their nationals returning back home.

Likewise, these considerations are of paramount importance to realise that the abrupt interruption of migration cycles might well have severe consequences for the reintegration of migrants and their livelihood (Blitz et al. 2005; Cassarino 2008; Schuster and Majidi 2013; Kalir 2017), regardless of the disruptive factors that contributed to their interruption. Field surveys carried out in various countries of origin with migrants have already demonstrated the analytical and empirical relevance of the three types of migration cycles described above (Cassarino 2008). Opportunities to find a job, to transfer one's own skills and social rights, to stay mobile, to start a family, to realise one's own life plans are all contingent on adequate conditions in the former country of destination and in the country of origin. Such conditions have a bearing on the completeness, incompleteness, or interruption of migration cycles. In sum, empirical work invariably requires a 'grounded distance' from the pervasive dichotomic construct opposing 'voluntary' with 'enforced' return in current EU policy debates.

Conclusion

Today, the growing politicisation of international migration and mobility in the West as well as the reinforced drive for the temporariness of labour migration have called for a paradigmatic shift as applied to return. This shift is symptomatic of the strengthened centrality of the state in the reinforced regulation of labour migration and asylum. Incidentally, this process of reinforced regulation has gone hand in hand with the perceptible deregulation of labour market policies including the withdrawal of the state from the direct administration of the economy through the privatisation of state-owned assets, the crisis of the welfare state and unrestrained industrial delocalisation, to mention but a few (Standing 2011; Delgado Wise 2015). It could even be argued that the abovementioned shift has coincided with the need of various Western governments to bolster their own credentials in the 'fight against illegal migration' at a time when market reforms had already exposed large segments of their own constituencies to growing labour uncertainties (Schierup et al. 2015). It is against this backdrop that the understanding of 'return' has changed while being equated, in official rhetoric, with expulsion or removal.

The reflection proposed in this chapter is not aimed at denouncing the banal usage of euphemisms and double-talk which, by all accounts, characterise policy discourse. Rather, it is aimed at explaining that using 'return' as a laconic umbrella term to refer to deportation, expulsion, removal, and pushbacks invariably deflects policy attention from the real causes of the problem and from the need to respect migrants' safety and human rights. Equating return with removal or deportation hence constitutes a subtle denial of migrants' human conditions in the broadest sense. More problematically, the uncritical acceptance of this figure of speech reflects an alignment with a powerful narrative that has surreptitiously dispossessed migrants from their own agency.

These developments raise a host of ethical challenges for policy-making and academia alike. From a political perspective, they have been detrimental to the exploration of the link between return, reintegration, and development, for current 'return' policies have been predominantly guided by the need to ensure the removal of irregular migrants while disregarding their conditions back home, let alone migrants' willingness to leave. Another policy implication lies in the oft-reported reluctance of many countries of origin to adopt and implement mechanisms aimed at sustaining the reintegration of their own nationals. Faced with the securitisation of migration policy priorities in the West, including the issue of 'return' (or re-admission), cooperation with third countries has been more than erratic owing to the domestic social political and economic costs that such a cooperation would incur.

Strong paradigms as applied to 'return' have consolidated over the last two decades or so. Scholars currently working on return migration issues are well aware that scientific production and outcomes that critically question such paradigms and policy priorities (be they explicit or not) may be viewed as a threat to the established consensus. Such outcomes may even trigger self-defence, for never before has research on return been so politically sensitive. Nonetheless, the all-pervasiveness of the abovementioned consensus does not justify any form of intellectual alignment ('we cannot do otherwise'). Nor does it justify the uncritical acceptance of the pervasive dichotomy 'voluntary vs. enforced return', let alone the spurious argument that re-admission or removal *is* a form of return, as some intergovernmental actors, UN agencies, and their experts would have it.

The reference to the completeness of return migrants' migration cycles can be viewed as an attempt to overcome the epistemological hurdles that policy discourses on 'return' have created over the last two decades or so. It draws on a vast academic corpus not to resurrect it but to show that the state-of-the-art has already produced devices that continue to be analytically relevant to research on return migration. Both removal and return can be compared through the lens of migration cycles without, however, equating re-admission or removal with return. Comparison is important here to show that the interruption of a migration cycle severely jeopardises access to opportunities back home. Readmission, expulsion, removal, and pushbacks epitomise the abrupt interruption of a migration cycle.

More generally, realising that a migration cycle's degree of completeness or incompleteness strongly shapes migrants' ability to reintegrate in their countries of origin is a prerequisite to establishing a credible link between return migration and development. Empirical data confirm that the more complete the migration cycle, the more prepared for return migrants are. In this light, the issue at stake is to foster the legal, economic, and institutional *conditions* for ensuring the completeness of returnees' migration cycles, not to ensure at all costs that migrants leave the territory of their host countries.

Defining concrete policy measures aimed at ensuring the completeness of returnees' migration cycles will, at a certain point, be a key challenge that migration and development stakeholders will have to address in both countries of origin and of destination. Admittedly, this challenge is all the more daunting when considering the consensus on which the current security-driven approach to 'return' rests in bilateral and multilateral migration talks. Hence, addressing the completeness of migration cycles implies questioning such a consensus by rethinking the policy priorities that have been considered to date.

It is time to recognise that the following categories cannot be mixed together under a uniform heading of 'return': migrants expelled or removed from abroad and migrants who return to their countries of origin. This basic difference can no longer be ignored, analytically or in practical terms. As long as no distinction is made, the policy debates on the link between return, reintegration, and development will remain biased. As long as no distinction is made, current 'return' policies are not return policies.

Notes

1 See points 10.1 and 10.4 of Resolution 1742 (Council of Europe 2010).
2 For a critique, see Cassarino (2004), Turner and Kleist (2013), Kleist (2015), and Vathi and King (2017).

References

Abadan-Unat N. ed. (1976) *Turkish workers in Europe 1960–1975: A socio-economic reappraisal.* Brill, Leiden.

Anderson B. (2010) "Migration, immigration controls and the fashioning of precarious workers" *Work, Employment & Society* 24(2): 300–317.

Bivand Erdal M. and Oeppen C. (2018) "Forced to leave? The discursive and analytical significance of describing migration as forced and voluntary" *Journal of Ethnic and Migration Studies* 44(6): 981–998.

Blitz B., Sales R. and Marzano L. (2005) "Non-voluntary return? The politics of return to Afghanistan" *Political Studies* 53(1): 182–200.

Böhning R. W. (1975) *Return migrants' contribution to the development process. The issue involved.* International Labour Office, Geneva.

Bovenkerk F. (1974) *The sociology of return migration.* Martinus Nijhoff, The Hague.

Burroni L. and Keune M. (2011) "Flexicurity: A conceptual critique" *European Journal of Industrial Relations* 17(1): 75–91.

Cassarino J.-P. (2004) "Theorising return migration: The conceptual approach to return migrants revisited" *International Journal on Multicultural Societies* 6(2): 253–279.

Cassarino J.-P. ed. (2008) *Return migrants to the Maghreb countries: Reintegration and development challenges* RSCAS, European University Institute.

Cassarino J.-P. (2013) "The drive for securitised temporariness" in Triandafyllidou A. ed., *Circular migration between Europe and its neighbourhood: Choice or necessity?* Oxford University Press, Oxford, 22–41.

Cassarino J.-P. (2016) "Return migration and development: The significance of migration cycles" in Triandafyllidou A. ed., *Routledge handbook of immigration and refugee studies.* Routledge, New York, 216–222.

Castles S. (2006a) "Back to the future? Can Europe meet its labour needs through temporary migration?" *IMI Working Paper*, International Migration Institute, University of Oxford.

Castles S. (2006b) "Guestworkers in Europe: A resurrection?" *International Migration Review* 40(4): 741–766.

Cerase F. P. (1971) *L'emigrazione di ritorno: Innovazione o reazione? L'esperienza dell'emigrazione di ritorno dagli Stati Uniti d'America.* Istituto di statistica e ricerca sociale "C. GINI", Roma.

Chimni B. S. (1995) "The meaning of words and the role of UNHCR in voluntary repatriation" *International Journal of Refugee Law* 5(3): 442–460.

Council of Europe. (2010) "Voluntary return programmes: An effective, humane and cost-effective mechanism for returning irregular migrants" *PACE, Resolution* 1742(2010): 18.

Delgado Wise R. (2015) "Migration and labour under neoliberal globalization: Key issues and challenges" in Schierup C.-U., Munck R., Likić-Brborić B. and Neergaard A. eds., *Migration, precarity, and global governance: Challenges and opportunities for labour.* Oxford University Press, Oxford, 25–45.

Dustmann C. (1996) "Return migration: The European experience" *Economic Policy* 11(22): 215–250.

European Commission. (2002) *Green paper on a community return policy on illegal residents.* Brussels, COM (2002) 175 final.

European Commission. (2005) *Proposal for a directive of the European parliament and the council on common standards and procedures in member states for returning illegally staying third-country nationals.* COM (2005) 391 final, Brussels.

Gmelch G. (1980) "Return migration" *Annual Review of Anthropology* 9(1): 135–159.

Holgate J. (2011) "Temporary migrant workers and labor organization" *WorkingUSA: The Journal of Labor and Society* 14(2): 191–199.

Kalir B. (2017) "Between 'voluntary' return programs and soft deportation: Sending vulnerable migrants in Spain back 'home'" in Vathi Z. and King R. eds., *Return migration and psychosocial wellbeing: Discourses, policy-making and outcomes for migrants and their families*. Routledge, New York, 56–71.

King R. ed. (1986) *Return migration and regional economic problems*. Croom Helm, London.

Kleist, N. and I. Vammen. (2012). "Diaspora groups and development in fragile situations: Lessons learnt". *DIIS Report 2012:09*. Danish Institute for International Studies, Copenhagen, 84.

Kleist N. (2015) "Pushing development: A case study of highly skilled male return migration to Ghana" in Åkesson L. and Eriksson Baaz M. eds., *Africa's return migrants: The new developers?* Zed Books, London, 64–86.

Kubat D. ed. (1984) *The politics of return. International return migration in Europe (proceedings of the first European conference on international return migration, Rome, 11-14 November 1981)*. Center for Migration Studies, New York.

Martin Ph. (2006) *Managing labor migration: Temporary worker programmes for the 21st century*. United Nations Secretariat, Turin.

Schierup C.-U., Munck R., Likić-Brborić B. and Neergaard A. eds. (2015) *Migration, precarity, and global governance: Challenges and opportunities for labour*. Oxford University Press, Oxford.

Schuster L. and Majidi N. (2013) "What happens post-deportation? The experience of deported Afghans" *Migration Studies* 1(2): 221–240.

Sinatti G. (2014) "Return migration as a win-win-win scenario? Visions of return among Senegalese migrants, the state of origin and receiving countries" *Ethnic and Racial Studies* 38(2): 275–291.

Standing G. (2011) *The precariat: The new dangerous class*. Bloomsbury Academic, London.

Thomas-Hope E. (1999) "Return migration to Jamaica and its development potential" *International Migration* 37(1): 183–207.

Turner S. and Kleist N. (2013) "Introduction: Agents of change? Staging and governing diasporas and the African state" *African Studies* 72(2): 192–206.

Vathi Z. and King R. eds. (2017) *Return migration and psychosocial wellbeing: Discourses, policy-making and outcomes for migrants and their families*. Routledge, New York.

Webber F. (2011) "How voluntary are voluntary returns?" *Race and Class* 52(4): 98–107.

Wilder-Okladek F. (1969) *The return movement of jews to Austria after the Second World War: With special consideration of the return from Israel*. Martinus Nijhoff, The Hague.

32

FROM HUMANITARIANISM TO DEVELOPMENT

Reconfiguring the international refugee response regime

Roger Zetter

Introduction and context

After a brief contextual overview of the global refugee situation, this chapter explores the emergence and the characteristics of development-led approaches to refugee crises, popularly termed the humanitarian–development nexus. This is a recent and significant reformulation of international responses to large-scale protracted forced displacement.

In an era of unprecedented population mobility, the global total of refugees and forcibly displaced people is the highest recorded in contemporary times and is increasing. According to the UNHCR (UNHCR 2019), the total reached 70.8 million people in 2017. Of this total, 20.4 million were officially recorded as refugees under the terms of the 1951 Geneva Convention Relating to the Status of Refugees while 3.5 million were asylum seekers awaiting determination of their claim for refugee status. Some 41.3 million were internally displaced, while 5.5 million were Palestinian refugees. These of course are official figures: millions more people are forcibly displaced in their own countries or across international borders but are not recorded in national or international data, or do not fit the defining characteristics of the 1951 Geneva Convention – a well-founded fear of persecution. In 2018, the forcibly displaced population increased by 5.2 million people over 2016 total; and almost 78 per cent of UNHCR documented refugees, some 15.9 million, have been displaced for more than 5 years and the mean duration of exile is about 10 years (UNHCR 2019). Significantly, refugees overwhelmingly originate from and are located in the developing regions of the world, which host some 85 per cent of the total. Indeed, more than two-thirds of the world's refugees originate from just five countries, which, Syria excepted, are low-income countries – Afghanistan, Myanmar, South Sudan, and Somalia.

Forced displacement of refugees and others is the result of a complex interplay of socio-economic and political circumstances and existential threats that are manifest in different configurations (Zetter 2018). Armed conflict, other situations of violence, and severe human rights violations are the most obvious and familiar drivers of people seeking to 'escape from violence' (Zolberg et al. 1993). This is predominantly the result of civil wars and internal conflict in countries such as Syria, Somalia, Afghanistan, and Rohingya from Myanmar (Keen 2007; Lindley 2014: Martin et al. 2014), rather than interstate conflict which was more typical in the past, for example in World War II. While it is too simplistic to assert that refugees are the result of 'failed development', it is the case that socio-economic vulnerability and the lack of sustainable livelihoods emanating from food insecurity and drought, environmental degradation, and climate change (McAdam 2010; Zetter 2011) as well as governance fragility (Zetter 2012, 2014; Betts 2013) constitute significant drivers of forced displacement. The key point is that often these factors occur in combination – hence the need to recognise the multi-causality that underpins the displacement of the majority of refugees: Somalia is a good example, where there have been repeated displacements over several decades due to overlapping episodes of conflict, drought, food insecurity, and governance fragility.

The humanitarian–development nexus and its origins

Recognising the continuing need for humanitarian assistance, a reconfiguration of international responses to refugee crises has taken place in recent years. This emphasises sustainable, development-led strategies that address the scale and protracted nature of forced displacement described above, underpinned by the fact that displacement is overwhelmingly concentrated in countries of the Global South already struggling to achieve their own development aspirations without the added 'burden' of refugees.

This approach is summarised in the phrase the humanitarian–development nexus (HDN). Although this nexus is by no means a fully formed or uniform paradigm (Sande Le 2017), a working definition offered here is that it is a multi-agency and multi-sectoral approach to refugee crises that seeks complementarity between humanitarian and development programming, funding, time scales, and priorities. It aims to achieve coherence between short-term emergency assistance and sustainable, resilience-building development for refugees and their host communities. To this end, the HDN tackles two enduring challenges in refugee crises. The first is to mediate the impacts of protracted forced displacement on receiving countries and communities. The second is to transition to longer-term sustainable livelihoods for the refugees themselves and their hosts.

For very many decades, the displacement of refugees has pre-eminently been framed as a humanitarian challenge. But the aim of promoting development responses to refugee crises has also been an on-going, although inconsistent, objective of international donors, in part frustrated by the escalating costs of the dominant humanitarian model. But the objective also recognised that protracted conditions of refugee displacement require sustainable livelihood solutions for displaced people and hosts where none of the three orthodox, durable 'solutions' (repatriation, resettlement, or local integration) could be realised.

Several attempts in the last three decades to promote and co-ordinate developmental responses that complement humanitarian assistance have been initiated but have failed to gain traction. Major constraints have been: the nature of the international institutional architecture to manage and co-ordinate the interplay between humanitarian and development actors; and the difficulty of resolving the contrasting precepts of humanitarian and development interventions, which are discussed in more detail below.

In the 1990s, linking relief to rehabilitation and development (LRRD), the mantra of the humanitarian actors (Ross et al. 1994; Mosel and Levine 2014), offered some recognition that displacement conditions also create significant development challenges and opportunities (Zetter 2014; World Bank 2017). The UNHCR took up this challenge of promoting developmental responses, but this sat somewhat uneasily alongside its primary mandate as the refugee protection agency, and its well-established humanitarian/emergency role (Crisp 2001).

The reform of the UN humanitarian system in 2005 created an 'early recovery' cluster (one of 13 sectoral clusters). Led, significantly, by a development agency, the UNDP, rather than UNHCR, the cluster was designed to bridge humanitarian assistance to longer-term recovery and development, the dynamic for which the UNDP as expected to provide. But this failed to gain the traction that was anticipated, partly due to the unfamiliarity of the concept, partly the lack of buy-in by donors, and partly due to the lack of effective policy and programme instruments.

The Transitional Solutions Initiative (TSI) in 2010 marked a further stage in international momentum for a stronger development response to protracted situations of forced displacement (UNHCR 2010). The TSI, a collaboration between the World Bank, UNHCR, and UNDP, established a wider grouping of development and humanitarian actors to overcome the limitations of a single lead-agency model of the early recovery cluster. However, this approach encountered similar constraints to earlier initiatives: these were how to design and implement a coherent and comprehensive framework to deliver developmentally oriented responses that involved many stakeholders and governments, as well as the need to establish effective funding mechanisms.

Global developments: the humanitarian–development nexus

The conjuncture of two factors over the last decade has imparted a renewed impetus to link humanitarian assistance to development-led responses. These factors have accelerated the international approach to strategy and policymaking, and underpin the reconfiguring of global responses governing protracted refugee crises.

On the one hand, there have been renewed attempts for global level institutional reform to build governmental commitment and institutional capacity and capability, collectively termed the 'New Way of Working' (OCHA 2017). The process has been demarcated by the 2015 'Grand Bargain' by the world's leading humanitarian donors; the World Humanitarian Summit 2016 where the stakeholders (donors, NGOs, crisis-affected States) promoted a key priority of strengthening the humanitarian–development nexus; the 2016 UN High-Level Meeting on Addressing Large Movements of Refugees and Migrants and the 2016 New York Declaration which noted that 'to meet the challenges posed by large movements of refugees close co-ordination will be required among a range of humanitarian and *development* actors' (emphasis added). The 2016 processes led to the UNHCR-led 2018 Global Compact on Refugees (GCR); and the Comprehensive Refugee Response Framework (CRRF) which are discussed in more detail below. These initiatives are transforming the structure, funding mechanisms, and instruments that are embodied in the humanitarian–development nexus.

The GCR actively promotes development-led approaches to situations of refugee displacement involving bilateral, multilateral, and private stakeholders. Streamlined funding processes for responsibility-sharing, elaborated in the GCR but not yet operationalised, potentially commit international donors to long-term, predictable, development-led assistance for countries impacted by protracted refugee displacement.

On the other hand, more prosaically but with greater practical force, the resurgent interest has been precipitated by the regional and global impacts of the large-scale refugee displacement of Syrian refugees in the Middle East, and the operational and political challenges this has presented. The response to the Syrian refugee crisis reflects both international concern at the scale and socio-economic impact on middle-income countries in the region; but also, their proximity to Europe, and thus a 'securitisation' agenda motivated by the backdrop of the so-called refugee crisis in Europe in 2015.

In many ways, the response to the Syrian refugee crisis has become the testing ground for the humanitarian–development nexus. Yet, it transcends this immediate setting and the political interests it has provoked, by crystallising innovative policies and programmes which are firmly development-led. This framework has been further rolled out, inter alia, by international responses to regional displacement in the Horn of Africa, by a small scale archetype of the development-led approach in Rwanda, and by a more indigenously crafted model which has been developed in Uganda (Clements et al. 2016).

Some indication of the traction of the new paradigm is reflected by the fact that in 2018 it was possible for a UN meta-evaluation to sample almost 100 evaluations from nine countries and a further 26 global, thematic, strategic evaluations, and reviews in order to assess how humanitarian and development project evaluations considered the topic of the nexus (UNEG-HEIG 2018).

Reconciling the humanitarian and development interface

The humanitarian system and its normative and international legal framework of protection, embodied in the 1951 Geneva Convention on Refugees, are vital but insufficient conditions to provide comprehensive responses to the complex and prevalent situations of protracted forced displacement. Nevertheless, bridging humanitarian to longer-term development objectives introduces not only institutional challenges, discussed above, but also different principles and mandates that have to be reconciled.

Humanitarian assistance is unconditionally 'needs-based', predicated on the principles of humanity, neutrality, impartiality, and independence. Even where displacement is protracted, humanitarian principles still obtain, although the often-political nature of displacement crises poses enormous challenges to these principles as the case of Syria and in the recent past Iraq, illustrate. A second precept is that humanitarian assistance is provided according to short-term and flexible funding, programming, and reporting priorities, often on no more than an annual basis, to tackle the 'emergency', life-saving conditions which usually characterise the early stages of refugee crises.

By contrast, development is a medium to long-term project for, inter alia, improving social and economic conditions, and is essentially a political project. Whereas humanitarian assistance is explicitly targeted to countries and projects on the basis of needs and vulnerability – the 'humanitarian imperative' – development assistance, particularly under OECD-DAC guidance, tends to be focused on a limited set of countries, over a longer time scale and mediated by political interests and objectives of both donor and recipient counties. However, donor countries have preferred partner countries for development that may not include refugee impacted countries; and the lack of flexibility of development instruments can make it difficult to use them in volatile contexts. Development actors may need to work in partnership with governments that may be scarcely functioning, weak, or even party to the conflict that creates refugees; or they may have criteria that prevent them undertaking development programmes in refugee-hosting countries, notably middle-income countries such as Lebanon, Jordan, and Turkey which are amongst those currently most impacted.

Accordingly, these humanitarian and development precepts play out rather differently; funding and programming have to align with these different circumstances and reconciling these different precepts, in other words achieving policy coherence, lies at the heart of establishing the humanitarian–development nexus – a challenge faced by all donors and other stakeholders.

However, it is possible to argue that the distinction between humanitarian needs and development interventions can be somewhat artificial – for example, child protection, education, and healthcare, indeed all the basic services and infrastructure that refugees need require both modes of action and they may overlap. This means that development strategies and programmes should be built in from the beginning of a crisis, aligned simultaneously with humanitarian assistance and ensuring complementarity between the two modes. Alignment and co-ordination can take different forms. For example this could involve; the sequencing of funding instruments and programming, with humanitarian interventions targeted to meeting short-term needs while development actors mobilise longer-term measures; or the layering and complementarity of the two elements by the provision of different kinds of assistance or assistance to overlapping or different groups (for example refugees and hosts) in the same or different parts of the affected country (Scott et al. 2016).

The main parameters of development-led approaches

Development modalities

Development plays a key role in mitigating the macro- and micro-economic impacts of refugees on host countries, and in supporting the resilience and self-reliance of refugees and affected communities. For these reasons, a diverse range of actors and new modes of development engagement now constitute part of the reconfiguration of development-led modalities in the refugee regime (Zetter 2014).

At the macro-economic level, new funding mechanisms have been instituted to tackle the fiscal stress and the developmental shocks that large-scale refugee influxes produce for host countries. In this regard, the World Bank has substantially scaled-up its involvement in refugee impacted countries to stabilise the national and regional economies, and protect their development investment and gains of recent decades (World Bank 2016, 2017, 2019). For example, it has provided concessionary funding for countries such as Jordan, heavily impacted by Syrian refugees. Facilitated through the IDA-18 refugee sub-window of the World Bank, such funding would normally be made available only to the world's poorest countries: middle-income countries are not normally eligible for IDA. Similarly, the European Investment Bank (EIB) has also scaled-up its involvement with concessionary funding to Ethiopia linked to that country's development-led strategies for refugees.

Alongside new modalities of bilateral and multilateral funding, the HDN opens opportunities for other development actors such as private and corporate sector funding for development operations (Zetter 2014; Boyer and DuPont 2016; World Commission 2019a, 2019b). Traditionally sub-contractors to the main humanitarian agencies, the private sector is now promoted from the micro-economic to national levels as a mainstream development actor that can bring investment, funding, and entrepreneurship to the nexus (Binder and Witte 2007; Drummond and Crawford 2014; Zetter 2014; Zyck and Armstrong 2014; Carbonnier and Lightfoot 2016). Private humanitarian assistance accounted for 24 per cent (6.5 billion dollars) of the global total of 27.3 billion dollars in 2017 (Development Initiatives 2018). The risky investment environments and the search for commercially viable undertakings act as impediments to significant uptake by the private sector; but a proposal for a merchant bank to underwrite these risks is symptomatic of the structural changes in a refugee regime that for decades has been perceived as the domain of public and welfare policy interventions (World Commission 2019a).

At the micro-economic level, cash transfer programming is now the universal standard for the distribution of assistance to refugees by humanitarian actors (UNHCR 2016). But this is also an essential instrument of development-led responses because injecting cash into aid delivery renders refugees as market actors, directly incorporating them into economic development processes as consumers and potentially as suppliers, for example, through micro-enterprise activity (ODI 2015).

Employment generation for refugees and local host communities is the leading policy sector of development-led strategies with the aim of promoting sustainable livelihoods (Jacobsen and Fratzke 2016). To this end, impacted countries are increasingly pressurised by donors (e.g. DFID, EIB), and multilateral actors (UNHCR, UNDP, ILO), to open up their labour markets to refugees and relax their usually stringent limitations on refugees' rights to work under Articles 17–19 of the 1951 Geneva Convention on Refugees as the quid pro quo of additional development assistance (Zetter and Ruaudel 2016). At the same time, there is a drive for donor and private sector funded employment generation policies to include nationals and diversify local labour markets. In this way development-led approaches seek to protect nationals from the negative economic impacts of refugees; for example, the depression of wage levels by the entry of refugees.

The challenges of strategic planning and programme co-ordination in a multi-stakeholder setting exert a critical demand for policy coherence at every level of the humanitarian–development nexus – donor precepts, strategic planning, project design, needs assessment, local programming and multi-stakeholder co-ordination, and funding and reporting protocols. In this context, new operational instruments have been created to underpin development-led responses, notably the Comprehensive Refugee Response Framework, contained in Annex I of the New York Declaration. The CRRF provides for improved strategic planning and co-ordination of responses in situations of protracted refugee displacement.

Refugees and hosts – agency and support

Creating income-generating projects for refugees has, for many years, been an enduring but largely unsuccessful and 'token' activity of humanitarian actors. Refugee camps have been unpropitious locations: limited markets, low-level unsustainable investment, weak project design, and a limited range of projects and sectors which usually set refugees in competition with each other.

Rather than living in camps, now the majority of refugees, almost 70 per cent, are self-settled (UNHCR 2018, 60), mostly in urban areas, where more diverse economic opportunities and wider access to markets complement the development modalities described above. The scaling-up of development-led approaches offers a much greater potential for capitalising on the resources and skills of refugees, as well as their economic demand and supply functions which can add to the productive capacity of impacted countries.

This approach is underpinned by the concept of the resilience-building of refugees (and, where relevant, their host communities), a familiar strategy in disaster risk reduction policies, but less recognised until recently in the refugee context (Betts and Collier 2017, 156–81; Easton-Calabria and Omata 2018). Promoting self-reliance and resilience, by designating forcibly displaced people as development actors, appeals to the wider aspirations of humanitarian agencies keen to foster the image of refugees as agentive contributors rather than passive recipients of assistance and thus very much aligned with the 2030 Sustainable Development Goals. At the same time, if successful, it will relieve donors of long-term funding commitments.

The humanitarian–development nexus: experience so far

This nexus reconfiguration still remains experimental and pragmatic; it does not, as yet, constitute a coherent model or a set of norms in the way that the humanitarian assistance paradigm has come to be structured through many decades of experience. In any case, a standardised approach cannot be applied in different contexts of displacement (Sande Le 2017; UNEG-HEIG 2018). Yet uptake is wide (see, e.g. Danida 2017; OCHA 2017; Save the Children 2018; UNDP-UNHCR 2018; UNEG-HEIG 2018; UNICEF 2019; World Bank 2019), and the development-led paradigm is now being rolled out both in a reshaped global response architecture underpinned by the 2018 GCR (UNHCR 2018a), and at an operational level of international responses through the CRRF, adopted in 15 countries including for example Chad, Ethiopia, Kenya, Somalia, and Uganda.

The CRRF sits alongside other operational innovations such as the Syrian Regional Refugee and Resilience Plan (colloquially known as the 3RP) (UNDP-UNHCR 2018, latest iteration); and the Jordan and Ethiopian Compacts, agreed with various international donors and the EC, with the aim of stimulating job creation for refugees and host populations by concessionary trading agreements and investment incentives.

In the UNHCR's Middle East-North Africa region, the UNHCR-UNDP co-ordinated Syrian 3RP has been promoted as an archetype of a more sustainable longer-term humanitarian–development nexus response. This coordinates country-driven resilience plans and funding processes across the region impacted by Syrian refugees. In Jordan, a national Compact between international donors and the government aims to promote investment and development incentives to provide 200,000 new jobs for refugees and nationals in order to promote livelihoods, principally in designated Special Enterprise Zones (SEZs), and supported by concessionary trading agreements with the EU. The right to work for refugees, as we have seen, is a key instrument for achieving sustainable livelihoods for them, but is usually denied or heavily circumscribed in many low-income countries. However, it is being promoted in Jordan by the World Bank, the ILO as well as UNHCR and UNDP (Zetter and Ruaudel 2016). Turning theory into practice has not been without numerous problems, for example: the extent to which the Syrian Regional Refugee and Resilience Plan is a regional strategy rather than an assembly of non-compatible country plans; very substantial underfunding; the sheer scale of the programme; the uneasy relationship between the twin institutional protagonists, the UNHCR and the UNDP. For these reasons it is often described as a pilot even after 5 years in existence. It is certainly evolving. Perhaps the main achievement has been to mainstream resilience as the core objective.

Albeit rather pragmatically conceived, together these instruments, modalities, and precepts constitute what, on the face of it, is an international strategy for a public welfare model response to contemporary refugee crises; but it is a paradigm which has the seeds of a privatised refugee assistance model firmly embedded in it.

Humanitarian–peace–development nexus

While the humanitarian–development nexus has been rolled out in host countries impacted by refugees and forced displacement, as the Secretary General's Report for the 2016 World Humanitarian Summit noted, conflict remains 'the biggest obstacle to human development'. For these reasons, there is growing international interest in promoting peace and security as an essential missing link in the nexus between humanitarian action and sustainable development in those countries that are actually caught up in conflict itself – the so-called 'triple nexus' of the humanitarian–peace–development nexus (Uvin 2002; Barnett 2011; Chandler 2014). Although this ordering of the processes is used internationally, the obvious logic is to consider peace as an essential transitional stage between humanitarian and development interventions in countries impacted by conflict, hence the humanitarian–peace–development nexus (HPDN). In Iraq in recent years, potentially in Somalia and Afghanistan, and ultimately in Syria sometime in the future, the triple nexus constitutes a critical platform whereby civilian crisis management, peace-building, security, rule of law, and governance processes, link humanitarian assistance (during and in the immediate aftermath of conflict) to longer-term reconstruction and development. Peace-building is a significant niche traditionally filled by Nordic donors and Switzerland, but usually enacted as a distinct activity by these actors. However, the HPDN, by setting peace-building in the wider context of their role as humanitarian and development actors, may offer a potentially valuable way of averting the conditions that precipitate forced displacement, and certainly in facilitating refugee return and undertaking the essential international challenge of reconstructing war-torn countries.

References

Barnett M. (2011) *Empire of Humanity: A History of Humanitarianism*. Ithaca: Cornell University Press.

Betts A. (2013) *Survival Migration: Failed Governance and the Crisis of Displacement*. Ithaca: Cornell University Press.

Betts A. and Collier P. (2017) *Refuge: Rethinking Refugee Policy in a Changing World*. New York: OUP.

Binder A., and Witte J. (2007) *Business Engagement in Humanitarian Relief: Key Trends and Policy Implications*. London: HPG.

Boyer G. and DuPont Y. (2016) "The Contribution of the Private Sector to Solutions for Displacement" *Forced Migration Review 52, 36–38*. Oxford Refugee Studies Centre.

Carbonnier G. and Lightfoot P. (2016) "Business in Humanitarian Crises for Better or for Worse?" in Sezgin Z. and Dijkzeul D. eds. *The New Humanitarians in International Practice: Emerging actors and Contested Principles*. Abingdon: Routledge Humanitarian Studies, 169–191.

Chandler D. (2014) "Humanitarianism, Development and the Liberal Peace" in Acuto M. ed. *Negotiating Relief: The Politics of Humanitarian Space*. London: Hurst, 231–246.

Clements K., Shoffner T. and Zamore L. (2016) "Uganda's approach to Refugee Self-Reliance" *Oxford Refugee Studies Centre Forced Migration Review 52, 49–51*.

Crisp J. (2001) *Mind the gap! UNHCR, humanitarian assistance and the development process*. New Issues in Refugee Research Working Paper 43 Geneva UNHCR.

Danida. (2017) *The World 2030 - Denmark's Strategy for Development Cooperation and Humanitarian Action*. Copenhagen The Ministry of Foreign Affairs of Denmark. http://amg.um.dk/en/policies-and-strategies/stategy-for-danish-development-cooperation/

Development Initiatives. (2018) *The Global Humanitarian Assistance Report 2018*. Bristol Development Initiatives.

Drummond J. and Crawford N. (2014) *Humanitarian Crises, Emergency Preparedness and Response: The Role of Business and the Private Sector Kenya Case Study*. London: ODI.

Easton-Calabria E. and Omata N. (2018) "Panacea for the Refugee Crisis? Rethinking the Promotion of 'Self-reliance' for Refugees" *Third World Quarterly 39(8), 1458–1474*.

Jacobsen K. and Fratzke S. (2016) *Building Livelihood Opportunities for Refugee Populations: Lessons from Past Practice*. Washington, DC: Migration Policy Institute.

Keen D. (2007) *Complex Emergencies*. London: Polity.

Lindley A. (2014) *Crisis Migration: Critical Perspectives*. London: Routledge.

Martin S., Weerasinghe S. and Taylor A. eds. (2014) *Humanitarian Crises and Migration: Causes, Consequences and Responses*. London: Routledge.

McAdam J. ed. (2010) *Climate Change and Displacement: Multidisciplinary Perspectives*. Oxford and Portland: Oregon Hart Publishing.

Mosel I. and Levine S. (2014) *Remaking the Case for Linking Rehabilitation and Development. How LRRD Can Become a Practically Useful Concept for Assistance in Complex Places*. London: ODI.

OCHA. (2017) *New Way of Working*. New York Policy Development and Studies Branch (PDSB). https://www.unocha.org/sites/unocha/files/NWOW%20Booklet%20low%20res.002_0.pdf.

ODI. (2015) *Doing Cash Differently: How Cash Transfers Can Transform Humanitarian Aid*. London: ODI.

Ross J., Maxwell S. and Buchanan-Smith M. (1994) *Linking Relief and Recovery*. London: Overseas Development Institute. www.ids.ac.uk/files/dmfile/DP344.pdf

Sande Le J. (2017) "From Humanitarian Action to Development Aid in Northern Uganda and the Formation of a Humanitarian Development Nexus" *Development in Practice* 27(2), 196–207.

Save the Children. (2018) *Addressing the Humanitarian-Development Nexus in the Horn of Africa New York Save the Children*. https://resourcecentre.savethechildren.net/library/addressing-humanitarian-develop ment-nexus-horn-africa

Scott L., Garloch A. and Shepherd A. (2016) *Resilience and Sustainable Poverty Escapes: Implications for programming*. USAID Leveraging Economic Opportunities and Chronic Poverty Advisory Network. www.marketlinks.org/sites/marketlinks.org/files/resource/files/LEO_Brief_Sustainable_Poverty_Es capes_Implications_-_508_compliant.pdf

UNDP-UNHCR. (2018) *3RP Regional Refugee & Resilience Plan 2018–19 in Response to the Syria Crisis*. New York and Geneva: UNDP-UNHCR. https://reliefweb.int/report/lebanon/3rp-regional-refu gee-resilience-plan-2018–2019-response-syria-crisis-regional

UNEG-HEIG (United Nations Evaluation Group (UNEG) Humanitarian Evaluation Interest Group (HEIG)) (2018) *The Humanitarian-Development Nexus – What do Evaluations have to Say? Mapping and Synthesis of Evaluations*. Working paper.

UNHCR. (2010) *Concept Note Transitional Solutions Initiative UNDP and UNHCR in collaboration with the Washington DC World Bank Geneva UNHCR*. www.unhcr.org/uk/partners/partners/4e27e2f06/con cept-note-transitional-solutions-initiative-tsi-undp-unhcr-collaboration.html

UNHCR. (2016) *Strategy for the Institutionalisation of Cash-Based Interventions 2016–2020*. Geneva: UNHCR. www.unhcr.org/uk/584131cd7

UNHCR. (2019) *Global Trends: Forced Displacement in 2018*. Geneva: UNHCR. https://www.unhcr. org/5d08d7ee7.pdf.

UNHCR. (2018a) *The Global Compact on Refugees*. Final Draft 26 June 2018. www.unhcr.org/events/ conferences/5b3295167/official-version-final-draft-global-compact-refugees.html

UNICEF. (2019) *UNICEF Study on Linking Development and Humanitarian Programming (Final Report)*. Update on UNICEF Humanitarian Action with a Focus on Linking Humanitarian and Development Programming UNICEF/2019/EB/3 New York UNICEF. www.unicef.org/spanish/about/exec board/files/2019-EB3-Humanitarian_action-EN-2018.12.21.pdf

Uvin P. (2002) "The Development/Peacebuilding Nexus: A Typology and History of Changing Paradigms" *Journal of Peacebuilding & Development* 11, 5–24.

World Bank. (2016) *Global Concessional Financing Facility*. Washington, DC: World Bank. http://pub docs.worldbank.org/en/222001475547774765/FlyerGlobalCFF.pdf

World Bank. (2017) *Forcibly Displaced: Toward a Development Approach Supporting Refugees, the Internally Displaced, and Their Hosts*. Washington, DC: World Bank. https://openknowledge.worldbank.org/bit stream/handle/10986/25016/9781464809385.pdf?sequence=11&isAllowed=y

World Bank. (2019) *World Bank Group Support in Situations Involving Conflict-Induced Displacement*. Washington, DC: World Bank.

World Commission. (2019a) *Report of the World Commission on Forced Displacement*. New York: Chumir Foundation. https://chumirethicsfoundation.org/programs/forced-displacement/reports/world-com mission-on-forced-displacement

World Commission. (2019b) *A Merchant Bank: A Proposal from the World Commission New York Chumir Foundation*. https://chumirethicsfoundation.org/programs/forced-displacement/reports/world-com mission-on-forced-displacement

Zetter R. (2011) *Protecting Environmentally Displaced People: Developing the Capacity Legal and Normative Frameworks*. Report commissioned by UNHCR and Governments of Switzerland and Norway Oxford Refugee Studies Centre. www.rsc.ox.ac.uk/files/publications/other/rr-protecting-environ mentally-displaced-people-2011.pdf

Zetter R. ed. (2012) *IFRC World Disasters Report 2012 Focus on Forced Migration and Displacement*. Geneva: IFRC. www.ifrc.org/en/publications-and-reports/world-disasters-report/world-disasters- report-2012—focus-on-forced-migration-and-displacement/

Zetter R. (2014) *Reframing Displacement Crises as Development Opportunities*. Development Solutions Initiative Copenhagen Danish Ministry of Foreign Affairs. https://www.rsc.ox.ac.uk/files/files-1/pn-reframing-displacement-crises-2014.pdf

Zetter R. (2015) *Protection in Crisis: Forced Migration and Protection in a Global Era*. Policy Paper for Transatlantic Council on Migration. Washington, DC: Migration Policy Institute http://migrationpolicy.org/research/protection-crisis-forced-migration-and-protection-global-era

Zetter R. (2018) "Conceptualising Forced Displacement: Praxis, Scholarship and Empirics" in Dona G. and Bloch A. eds. *Forced Migration: Current Issues and Debates*. London: Routledge, 19–43. www.rsc.ox.ac.uk/files/files-1/pn-reframing-displacement-crises-2014.pdf

Zetter R and Ruaudel H. (2016) *Refugees' Right to Work and Access to Labor Markets – An Assessment* World Bank KNOMAD Study. www.knomad.org/publication/refugees-right-work-and-access-labor-markets

Zolberg A. Suhrke A. and Aguayo S. (1993) *Escape from Violence: Conflict and the Refugee Crisis in the Developing World*. Oxford: Oxford University Press.

Zyck S. and Armstrong J. (2014) *Humanitarian Crises, Emergency Preparedness and Response: The Role of Business and the Private Sector - Jordan Case Study*. London: ODI.

33

CONFLICT-INDUCED DISPLACEMENT AND DEVELOPMENT

Sarah Deardorff Miller

Introduction

People fleeing conflict, including refugees, internally displaced persons, and other groups of migrants, have been a central part of many of the world's most complex crises and political debates. The United Nations High Commissioner for Refugees now reports that there are some 68.5 million forcibly displaced persons in the world, the highest recorded number in recent years (UNHCR 2019). News headlines suggest hand wringing and chaos as the world lurches from one crisis to another, and the UN and humanitarian actors seem stretched more than ever to meet increasing need, desperately trying to convince weary donors that more funds are needed. Even amidst the recent New York Declaration, Global Compacts, and Comprehensive Refugee Response Framework (CRRF), ongoing conflicts in places like Syria, Yemen, the Democratic Republic of the Congo, South Sudan, and Venezuela continue to produce displaced persons at alarming rates, causing many states to close their doors to those seeking refuge. Amidst this complexity, there remains confusion over how different groups of displaced persons vary – differences that are very important for legal and normative reasons.

Forced migration scholars continue to rethink these labels or categories of migrants, wondering about the usefulness of such groupings, and rethinking the concepts, policies and ideas underpinning the international system responding to displacement (Betts 2015; Castles and Miller 2003; Harrell-Bond 1986; Zetter 1991, 2007). Conflict-induced displacement is one of these broad categories focused on the root causes of flight, and that provides a lens under which displacement can be distinguished from other reasons of flight, including development-, climate-, or natural-disaster-induced displacement.

However, the concept of conflict-induced displacement is more than just a label. It is a foundation for methods and theories that frame the way scholars, policymakers, practitioners and the global humanitarian and development community at large think about and respond to displaced persons in the short and long-term. As Muggah (2003) writes, '... there is no more obvious case of the importance of clear definitions than in debates on forced migration'.

Understanding conflict-induced displacement: definitions, conceptions, causes

Conflict-induced displacement is not a commonly used phrase in the general refugee/forced migration-focused literature. Certainly, some scholars mention it, but for the most part, it is used in development- or IDP-related research. It covers a broader range of reasons why people might flee, and is often used to differentiate from other types of forced migration, such as development-induced or natural disaster-induced displacement.

Conflict-induced displacement is a broad category that can describe any situation in which people leave their homes to escape political violence (Lischer 2007). It can thus describe refugees, asylum seekers, or internally displaced people who have fled conflict – be it civil war, genocide, a failed state, or politicide (Lischer 2007). Other types of conflicts that produce refugees include interstate wars, anti-colonial wars, ethnic conflicts, non-ethnic conflicts, and flights from authoritarian and revolutionary regimes (Weiner 1996). These groups are differentiated from other groups of forced migrants, including those fleeing natural disasters, persecution, or development projects like a dam or road (Muggah 2000, 133).

This type of displacement thus involves some level of force, is involuntary, and involves some type of deterritorialisation (Hyndman 2000). It is commonly described as taking place within the confines of a state (e.g. internally displaced person) or across an internationally recognised border (e.g. refugee) (Muggah 2003, 3). Some, like Holtzman and Nezam (2004), use the term conflict-displaced population to refer to both IDPs and refugees, but think of this group in terms of socioeconomic conditions, poverty and vulnerabilities. They write that conflict-induced displacement often conjures images of temporary displacement during fighting, where people can quickly return home once fighting is finished. Of course, the reality of most conflict – and the fact that the average duration of a protracted refugee situation is now a staggering 26 years (UNHCR 2016) – proves otherwise (Holtzman and Nezam 2004).

One way of thinking about categories of migrants, then, would be according to the level of choice with each group – for example, refugees fleeing persecution are deemed to be running for their lives, meaning they have little choice; others migrating for, say, educational opportunities, have a greater level of choice. Someone that fits the broad category of economic migrant might theoretically fit somewhere in the middle. Approaches like this, however, oversimplify and do a disservice to the displaced and those seeking to understand their flight. A broad definition of conflict-induced displacement, rather, echoes an understanding of some type of coercion where choices are restricted, and where the affected populations are facing more risks than opportunities by staying in their 'place' of residence, which distinguishes it from 'voluntary' or 'economic' migration (Muggah 2003, 3).

Another helpful approach to understanding conflict-induced displacement vis-à-vis other groups of migrants is to think of it as a broader category encompassing sub-categories. Betts and Loescher, for example, offer a helpful discussion of how different groups of forced migrants, including conflict-induced displaced, are connected, many of whom are described as refugees, whether they fit the formal Convention definition or not. They write,

> Conceptually what connects these categories of people is that the assumed relationship between state and citizen is likely to have broken down....The most salient characteristic which connects different categories of the vernacular 'refugee' is not geographical movement *per se* but rather the inability or unwillingness of the country of origin to ensure a citizen's protection.
>
> *(Betts and Loescher 2011, 6)*

Theoretical lenses and applications

In contrast to refugee or forced migration studies that tend to be studied through relief or humanitarian studies lenses, the term 'conflict-induced displacement' tends to be used in reference to internal displacement, or to differentiate the cause of displacement from other causes like development or disaster-induced displacement (Muggah 2003). Topically those who have employed the term have tended to focus on development-related issues like poverty reduction. The World Bank, for example, is increasingly involved in situations of refugees and IDPs in light of the New York Declaration and Global Compacts. It is now developing a more nuanced understanding of forced migration as it is further involved in the space, but in the past has tended to use broader categories like conflict-induced displacement in its approaches (Holtzman and Nezam 2004).

Conflict-induced displacement can be studied by the type of conflict; the 'location and timing' of displacement; the determinants of individual and family decision-making processes; how people interpret their own situations; and larger political and historical contexts and processes (Lischer 2007). Conflict-induced displacement has also been studied from a range of theoretical approaches, including international relations, which tends to focus on the relationship between forced migrants and security; critical theoretical approaches; macro-level analysis on patterns of power and resource allocation; and approaches that look at how displacement is used as a tool in conflict, domestic factors, reasons people remain versus flee, and literature on civil wars (2009, 320). These theoretical approaches thus focus on both root causes and proximate causes (2009, 320).

Scholars like Lischer also highlight the practical implications of how conflict-induced displacement is viewed:

> focusing myopically on either causes or solutions narrows the usefulness of a research agenda, since, in order to identify meaningful solutions it is first necessary to learn about the causes of the crisis. Indeed, understanding the characteristics of conflict can help predict, and hopefully prevent, displacement as policymakers note warning signs. For example, wars in Iraq and Syria created large outflows of refugees and IDPs which could have been predicted, and even prevented, had more attention been paid to the causes of conflict induced displacement. This effort requires political attention and resources to ensure the validity of research and the application of findings, rather than merely adopting an apolitical lens and promoting a palliative humanitarian response.
>
> *(Lischer 2007, 325)*

Likewise many scholars, particularly those who focus on international development, urge humanitarian and development researchers to realise how the root causes – often related to development issues – 'can lay the foundations for conflict-induced displacement, as has been the case … in Sri Lanka, Ethiopia, and Latin America' (Cernea 2006, 26). Cernea argues that while the types of or reasons for displacement might vary widely, the 'impoverishing consequences on people's lives are largely similar' (2006, 26). This view varies somewhat from protection-focused humanitarian actors like UNHCR, who see the needs of the displaced as having some overlap with other groups, but deserving of specialised protection.

Comparing and contrasting disaster- and development-induced displacement

Conflict- and natural disaster-induced displacement often evoke similar human experiences. Ferris (2008) writes that whether displaced by flooding or fighting, the displaced often

> lose family members, endure family separation, lose their possessions, and experience trauma and depression. They have similar protection and assistance needs. They lose important documents which limits their access to public services. They lose property and it may take years (if ever) before they receive compensation for their loss.

In both conflict- and natural disaster-induced displacement, vulnerable groups suffer more, including women, children, the elderly, and the disabled. They may experience discrimination in the provision of assistance – 'In many camps where persons displaced by conflict live, food is – at least initially – more likely to go to healthy and strong men than to children or the disabled' (Ferris 2008). Some can be displaced by both natural disasters and conflict, and may also be susceptible to gender-based violence or recruitment by armed forces. In addition to unequal access to assistance or discrimination in aid provision, they may face enforced relocation; sexual and gender-based violence; loss of documentation; recruitment of children into fighting forces; unsafe or involuntary return or resettlement; and issues of property restitution. For both conflict- and natural disaster-induced displaced, the majority remain inside the borders of their country as IDPs, and for both groups, poverty makes things worse. There may also be great initial responses to high-profile crises, but less as the situation becomes protracted. The weakest part for both is in prevention or mitigation (Ferris 2008).

Conflict-induced displacement and natural disaster-induced displacement also highlight the disparity in how poorer and wealthy countries are affected, as well as the relationship between poverty and conflict. According to Ferris (2008), natural disasters in poorer countries have higher casualties than disasters of similar magnitude in wealthier countries. She goes on to emphasise the relationship between poverty and conflict: 'An analysis of state weakness in the developing world found a strong relationship between poverty and failed states which are more likely to have conflict-induced displacement'.

Coercion and the use of or threat of violence are common features of conflict- and development-induced displacement (Muggah 2003, 10). They also have common patterns of vulnerability and risk (Muggah 2003, 14). For this reason, Muggah argues that processes and solutions relating to both types of displacement should not be seen as mutually exclusive. He writes, 'In practical terms, both development-induced displacement and conflict-induced displacement can be characterised as having three phases', including a period of relief assistance and transportation to settlements where houses are built beforehand or, as if often the case, by relocated populations themselves; a physical settlement on the land; and a working/livelihood phase where they are expected to resume their livelihoods as assistance decreases (2003, 13–4).

Those fleeing conflict have a greater likelihood of crossing a border (possibly becoming a refugee), unlike those fleeing natural disaster, who are more likely to remain in the country (Ferris 2008), though it is not clear whether they are more or less likely to return than other groups of migrants. Those fleeing natural disaster, for example, may be unable to return if the damage is so extensive rendering it impossible (Ferris 2008). Though it is worth noting that in 'cases where people have crossed national borders because of natural disasters, such as those fleeing Ethiopian famine in 1984–85, the humanitarian community has responded as if they were indeed refugees' (Ferris 2008). Some argue that national authorities are more likely to accept international assistance for people displaced by natural disasters than conflict, but this is not necessarily the case. Likewise, in some cases, multinational forces are more likely to be used in conflict situations, and yet at the same time, military assistance is more generally accepted in natural disasters than in conflict.

Conflict-induced situations may also be more spontaneous or unpredictable than other types of displacement – a violation of international humanitarian and human rights law (Muggah 2003). It is often seen as a challenge to those hosting – an unplanned hardship that requires international assistance, is meant to be temporary, and demonstrates where something has gone wrong. By way of contrast, development-induced displacement is planned, and while it may be a violation of rights as well, is often viewed as for the overall advantage of the nation. The displaced in these cases may be compensated according to legal agreements: 'It is perceived by many donors and policymakers to be a process leading to *permanent* relocation' (Muggah 2003, 11).

Responses

While the normative and institutional aspects of the global refugee regime, for example, are quite explicit and involved in that there is a Refugee Convention and key actors such as UNHCR who seek to uphold these norms and institutions vis-à-vis refugee situations, those fleeing conflict more broadly – who may or may not meet the definition of a refugee – do not necessarily enjoy a global response framework amongst international actors that covers legal, social, and physical protections. There can be a range of actors who take the lead in responding, and plans can vary with respect to the traditional durable solutions to displacement (return, local integration, and resettlement). With respect to resettling those who have been displaced, Muggah writes that both conflict-induced and development-induced displacement can represent explicit violations of human rights, and both can lead to impoverishment if planned resettlement programmes or solutions are not considered. Conflict-induced displacement, however, tends to be more immediate than development-induced displacement. He also writes that involuntary resettlement during conflict tends to be transitory while development-induced displacement is more permanent, and notes that conflict-induced displacement 'does not capture the electorate's imagination in the same way as [development-induced displacement]' (Muggah 2000, 158).

For most persons displaced by conflict, however, resettlement is the rare exception, and the other traditional durable solutions of return and local integration are also elusive. This is certainly the case with refugees, where less than 1 per cent are resettled, with the majority remaining without a solution (UNHCR 2018a). Refugees are rather at the mercy of the host country, who may or may not enable UNHCR and other actors to respond to their protection and assistance needs. IDPs have even fewer guaranteed responses in place – fewer actors devoted to their needs and less predictable international standards and institutions working for their protection. The Guiding Principles on Internal Displacement were established in 1998 and provide a comprehensive list of standards and protections available to IDPs. The Kampala Convention, the IASC Framework on Durable Solutions for Internally Displaced Persons, and other regional or national instruments and agreements have also been devised to respond to internal displacement. Likewise, the cluster approach, which emerged during the 2005 Humanitarian Reform Process, was meant to improve coordination, transparency, predictability, and accountability in responding to IDP situations. It divided the response into sectors and assigned sector leads to ensure that that sector was provided for (e.g. health, WASH, food security, shelter).

For those who are not IDPs or refugees, but are still displaced by conflict (perhaps they have crossed a border but do not meet the 1951 Convention definition), there are not standardised response mechanisms in place. Certainly, the full gamut of human rights treaties applies to these individuals, but there are no groups, institutions or treaties fully devoted to this broad group's protection and assistance. Rather, it is governments that maintain the first responsibility for any displaced persons on their territory. Governments from Afghanistan to Somalia, Yemen, Syria, South Sudan, and the DRC tend to prefer the return of those they are hosting, however, and are often lacking the capacity or willingness to fully respond to the needs of the displaced. Nevertheless, there are cases where a state has attempted to respond more fully to protection and assistance needs, such as in the case of Colombia developing judicial protection and truth-and-reconciliation processes (Rivadeneira 2009; Sandvik and Lemaitre 2015).

In reality, then, responses are context-specific, and may involve a large number of international actors helping in the response to displaced persons. Responses may also vary based on how long the displacement lasts (i.e. it may become a care and maintenance situation in a protracted case), if it is cyclical (i.e. the displaced are moving back and forth across a border or returning home to the unsafe area to check on property or family, and then fleeing back into exile), if it is urban versus rural or a camp or non-camp situation.

Criticism from scholars of the category/calls for merging

Among the most important and critical of concerns among refugee scholars is the worry that labelling, categorising, and grouping displaced persons is dehumanising and over-simplifies, and also exploits displaced persons' already vulnerable positions, reinforcing latent and overt power dynamics (Zetter 1991). Horst and Grabska (2015, 3) write, 'In academia as well as in policy and practice, refugees are increasingly understood as a subcategory of migrants, as if physical mobility is the most defining aspect of the refugee experience'. They instead argue that the uncertainty associated with conflict, flight, and exile is central to their experiences and thus that conflict-induced displacement should therefore be viewed in these terms and this broader context. Thus, the exercise of this chapter and other scholarship like it must remain mindful of the pitfalls of categorising, labelling, and grouping, even as it is a natural way of carrying out research and inquiry.

Another key criticism of focusing on conflict-induced displacement has been that it is too isolated from other causes of displacement, and does not recognise the interconnected-ness between causes of forced displacement. Rather, it separates areas of study – theoretic-ally, methodologically, and practically – where scholars of each track are not learning from one another (Lischer 2014; Muggah 2003). This is problematic because the reality of displacement is that it includes a number of interlinked reasons why people flee that might be rooted in conflict, political tensions, and economic reasons. Looking only through one lens thus means missing important parts of the full picture. Resource scarcity, for example, can lead to political violence as different groups struggle to control the government, and thereby control diverse resources. Acknowledging the interaction among various root causes can help explain the crisis. For example, Newland notes that 'a number of the ethnic conflicts that have erupted into violence and generated refugees in the developing world can be char-acterised as resource wars, in which battle lines reflect ethnic or tribal affiliations' (Newland 1993, 90).

Likewise, the dichotomy between research focused on development-induced displacement and conflict-induced displacement is still largely separate and lacks communication between the two (Cernea 2006, 25).[1] He finds this 'unjustified dichotomy' to lead to weak scholarship, and praises scholars like Cohen, who managed to bridge this divide with regards to internal displacement (Muggah 2003, 12). When scholars and policymakers remain narrowly focused on their area of expertise, they may miss important factors that could help solve the crisis – since displacement crises have so many interwoven causes, a holistic approach is necessary for creating rigorous, generalisable explanations for forced migration (Lischer 2014, 327). Conflict-induced displacement thus needs to be more integrated with other studies on crisis-induced displacement, 'rather than a continual reinvention of typologies, datasets, and conceptualizations' (Lischer 2014, 327).

This divided thinking is clearly evidenced in the sluggish, if not impotent, response of the 'early recovery' cluster to bring development actors into crises in the earlier stages – arguably a clear recognition of the diverse underlying causes of displacement. In an article evaluating humanitarian reform for IDPs, Ferris asserts that 'the single biggest failing of the cluster system is the Early Recovery cluster' (Brookings 2014, 9). In case studies of Colombia, the DRC and Somalia, she found almost no significant early recovery cluster activity for IDPs – a surprise given the 'obvious opportunities for early recovery programs' (Brookings 2014, 9). Indeed, Holtzman and Nezam (2004) recognise that, particularly as a displacement situation becomes protracted, 'the venue for actions concerning displaced groups has changed to the sphere of national development planners and development agencies, including the World Bank and the United Nations Development Programme (UNDP)' (Holtzman and Nezam 2004, 9–10). They continue, 'In this new sphere, the identification of a group as refugees or IDPs does not, in and of itself, denote a justifiable focus of attention', but rather the level of impoverishment compared to others in society, and the extent to which they are excluded from channels of assistance and empowerment. In this view, 'it is necessary to demonstrate that displaced populations, when compared with other groups in an affected society, have a specific pattern of vulnerability' (Holtzman and Nezam 2004, 10). This perspective might surprise some refugee/IDP advocates, who insist that specific protections must be upheld over the short- and long-term for the displaced in particular. Nevertheless, it speaks to the need for greater side-by-side work between those who look at conflict-induced displacement and those who look at development-induced displacement, as well as outlets for development actors to be more involved early on in recognising and responding to root causes. There is current momentum around this type of work, not least with new initiatives by the World Bank to work with displaced persons.

This problem does not arise from a lack of awareness. Indeed, calls for closer work between relief and development; causes of displacement and broader root causes; and other false dichotomies are in full supply and have been for decades (Crisp 2001; Kaiser 2005; Van Hear and Sorenson 2003). Muggah argues that

> one of the reasons why development-induced displacement and conflict-induced displacement are treated as distinct regimes is because development and conflict are frequently conceived as two separate and non-continguous phenomena – the former a linear trajectory of growth and expansion of human capacities and potential and the latter an exogenous 'disruption' in the system (Luckham et al. 2001; Duffield 2001).
>
> *(2003, 12)*

He argues that literature shows causal interconnection instead: 'Just as it is now widely accepted that conflict contributes to underdevelopment, it is also acknowledged that unevenly distributed development and underdevelopment … are positively correlated with the outbreak of conflict' (2003, 12). He further asserts that 'there is a tendency to compartmentalise internal displacement and involuntary resettlement into simplistic mono-causal categories, such as "development" and "war"', and that this subsequently misses complex interrelationships (Muggah 2003, 12).

There is other literature that calls for merging understandings of disaster-induced/environmental displacement with conflict-induced displacement (Bohnet, Cottier, and Hug 2014) but these tend to emphasise their distinct security and policy implications, and do not go as far as literature relating to conflict- and development-induced displacement. For these reasons, the recent New York Declaration, upcoming Global Compacts, and CRRF all call on greater bridges between development and humanitarian actors.

Conclusions: why conflict-induced displacement still offers an important lens

In spite of these criticisms, however, the lens of conflict-induced displacement still offers important methodological, theoretical, and practical leverage for thinking through root causes of displacement. For one, it is natural and useful in scholarship to categorise, label and organise information for analysis. Lischer writes of separating reasons for conflict-induced displacement: 'The benefit of disaggregation is that it "allows the researcher to examine how conflict affects displacement and also how aspects of the displacement crisis may in turn affect the conflict"'. (Lischer 2007, 2014).

Likewise, there is the obvious need to be more precise in describing the causes of flight. Yes, root causes are often interlinked with more immediate, life-threatening reasons for flight. This is a clear reason for emphasising greater study of the two in tandem. But this can also go too far. One need look no further than international law – the Refugee Convention in particular – to point out the importance of distinguishing reasons of flight – recognising asylum seekers apart from other groups. Likewise, the merits of thinking about root causes in the field during an emergency are clear. But reality has its limits.

This chapter has also noted that drawing on the idea of conflict-induced displacement is often done in research on internal displacement and development-induced displacement for the purpose of differentiation from other causes of flight. This literature is obviously less developed with regards to displaced persons than refugee-focused literature, for example, and benefit from the broad contours that conflict-induced displacement offers.

The criticisms are clear and valid: those who study conflict-induced displacement would better serve the displaced, practitioners, and their own academic understanding if they were to take a more integrated approach to understand the linkages between conflict-induced displacement and other causes of flight. This logic is akin to the calls for looking at root causes, as well as calls for addressing the relief-development gap that have echoed loudly for decades. In the end, however, conflict-induced displacement as a category or label has merit, and will likely remain in use for the foreseeable future.

Note

1 More than a decade ago, Cernea (2006) described the lack of communication and collaboration between proponents of refugee studies and researchers of development-induced displacement as leading to an

'unjustified dichotomy' in the social science literature. He found that the resettlement literature separated the study of refugees from the study of populations uprooted by development projects and that the 'literature on refugees co-exists side by side with a literature on development-caused involuntary resettlement' without any interplay between the two. And yet, the case for a comparative analysis of internally displaced people from war and development is even more compelling than that of refugees and development-displaced and resettled populations (Muggah 2003, 12).

References

Betts A. (2015) "The Normative Terrain of the Global Refugee Regime" *Ethics and International Affairs* 29(4), Winter 2015, 363–375.

Betts A. and Loescher G. (2011) *Refugees in International Relations*. Oxford University Press, Oxford.

Bohnet H., Cottier F. and Hug S. (2014) "Conflict versus Disaster-Induced Migration: Similar or Distinct Implications for Security?" Working paper, October 13, 2014 (www.unige.ch/ses/spo/static/simonhug/cvdim/BohnetCottierHug2014_Uppsala.pdf) Accessed 31 March 2018.

Brookings. (2014) "Ten Years after Humanitarian Reform: How are IDPs Faring? A Summary" Brookings-LSE Project on Internal Displacement (www.brookings.edu/wp-content/uploads/2016/06/Brookings-IDP-Study-Summary-Dec-2014-3.pdf) Accessed 30 March 2018.

Castles S. and Miller M. (2003) *The Age of Migration*. Guilford Press, New York.

Cernea M. (2006) "Development-Induced and Conflict-Induced IDPs: Bridging the Research Divide" Forced Migration Review, "Putting IDPs on the Map" (www.fmreview.org/sites/fmr/files/FMRdownloads/en/FMRpdfs/BrookingsSpecial/15.pdf) Accessed 31 March 2018.

Crisp J. (2001) "Mind the Gap! UNHCR, Humanitarian Assistance and the Development Process" *International Migration Review* 35(1): 168–191.

Ferris E. (2008) "Displacement, Natural Disasters, and Human Rights" Brookings Institution (www.brookings.edu/on-the-record/displacement-natural-disasters-and-human-rights/) Accessed 21 March 2018.

Harrell-Bond B. (1986) *Imposing Aid: Emergency Assistance to Refugees*. Oxford University Press, Oxford.

Holtzman S. and Nezam T. (2004) *Living in Limbo: Conflict-Induced Displacement in Europe and Central Asia*. The World Bank. (https://openknowledge.worldbank.org/bitstream/handle/10986/14943/296970PAPER0Living0in0limbo.pdf?sequence=1&isAllowed=y) Accessed 31 March 2018.

Horst C. and Grabska K. (2015) "Flight and Exile—Uncertainty in the Context of Conflict-Induced Displacement" *Social Analysis* 59(1): 1–18.

Hyndman J. (2000) *Managing Displacement:Refugees and the Politics of Humanitarianism*. University of Minnesota Press, Minneapolis.

Kaiser T. (2005) "Participating in Development? Refugee Protection, Politics and Developmental Approaches to Refugee Management in Uganda" *Third World Quarterly* 26(2): 351–367.

Lischer S. (2014) "Conflict and Crisis Induced Displacement" in Fiddian-Qasmiyeh E., Loescher G., Long K., and Sigona N. eds. *The Oxford Handbook of Refugee and Forced Migration Studies*. Oxford University Press, Oxford, 317–329.

Lischer S.K. (2007) "Causes and Consequences of Conflict-Induced Displacement" *Civil Wars* 9(2): 142–155, DOI: 10.1080/13698240701207302

Muggah R. (2000) "Through the Developmentalist's Looking Glass: Conflict-Induced Displacement and Involuntary Resettlement in Colombia" *Journal of Refugee Studies* 13 (2): 1, 133–133164.

Muggah R. (2003) "A Tale of Two Solitudes: Comparing Conflict and Development-induced Internal Displacement and Involuntary Resettlement" *International Migration* 41(5): 2–24.

Newland K. (1993) "Ethnic Conflict and Refugees" *Survival* 35(1): 81–101.

Rivadeneira R. (2009) "Judicial Protection of Internally Displaced Persons: The Colombian Experience" Brookings Institution (www.brookings.edu/research/judicial-protection-of-internally-displaced-persons-the-colombian-experience/) Accessed 31 March 2018.

Sandvik K. and Lemaitre J. (2015) "From IDPs to Victims in Colombia: Transition from Humanitarian Crisis through Law Reform?" Norwegian Centre for Humanitarian Studies (https://reliefweb.int/report/colombia/idps-victims-colombia-transition-humanitarian-crisis-through-law-reform) Accessed 31 March 2018.

UNHCR. (2016) "Global Trends: Forced Displacement in 2015" p. 20 (www.refworld.org/docid/57678f3d4.html) Accessed 31 March 2018.

UNHCR (2018a) "Resettlement" (www.unhcr.org/en-us/resettlement.html) Accessed 31 March 2018.

UNHCR. (2019) "Figures at a Glance" (www.unhcr.org/en-us/statistics/unhcrstats/5b27be547/unhcr-global-trends-2017.html) Accessed 3 March 2019.

Van Hear N. and Sorenson N. eds. (2003) *The Migration-Development Nexus*. IOM/United Nations Publications, Geneva.

Weiner M. (1996) "Bad Neighbors, Bad Neighborhoods: An Inquiry into the Causes of Refugee Flows" *International Security* 21(1): 5–42.

Zetter R. (1991) "Labelling Refugees: Forming and Transforming a Bureaucratic Identity" *Journal of Refugee Studies* 4(1): 39–62.

Zetter R. (2007) "More Labels, Fewer Refugees: Remaking the Refugee Label in an Era of Globalization" *Journal of Refugee Studies* 20 (2): 1, 172–172192.

34

DEVELOPMENT-INDUCED DISPLACEMENT AND RESETTLEMENT

An overview of issues and interventions

Yan Tan

Introduction

The Geneva-based Internal Displacement Monitoring Centre (IDMC 2017, 2) estimated that 'over the past 20 years, as many as 300 million people have been displaced around the world by development – a rate of 10 to 15 million people a year', and that '80 million people have been displaced by dam projects worldwide'. Many of those affected 'live in developing countries where economic growth and poverty alleviation are considered top policy priorities, but displacement tends to leave people impoverished and marginalised, contrary to the very goals of development' (IIDMC 2017, 2). Among diverse types of development projects, displacement produced by major infrastructure projects is significant, with economic, social, and environmental consequences for the displaced population (World Bank 2001). This chapter uses the term 'development-induced displacement and resettlement' (DIDR) and focuses on reservoir induced displacement and resettlement because the construction of dams is the most common type of development project, and displaces more people than other development projects (IDMC 2017).

This chapter employs China as a key country for discussions as it has displaced more people through public infrastructure projects than any other country in the world. Shi et al. (2012) estimated that 70 million people have been displaced by three major types of infrastructure projects (dams/reservoirs, transportation, and urban construction) over the last 60 years. China has built almost half of the world's large dams (estimated at 45,000), and these have directly caused the displacement of some 15 million people. The Three Gorges Project (TGP) on the Yangtze River was used as the main case for discussion due to its unprecedented scale and significant geopolitical and environmental effects (Heggelund 2004; Xu et al. 2013). Success in implementation of China's resettlement regulations and policies in mega hydro projects, such as the TGP and Xiaolangdi (184,000 people displaced) on the Yellow River, has provided the foundation for China's national 'resettlement with development' policy, which is likely to be best practice by global standards, endeavouring to mitigate the intrinsic risks of impoverishment from becoming a firm or partial reality.

The remainder of this chapter is structured into four sections. First, it briefly reviews the main theoretical frameworks (or models) and perspectives of DIDR, and some recent advancements in the field. It then addresses key resettlement approaches and challenges by highlighting rural versus urban resettlement strategies and social impacts. The next section outlines some issues in the existing literature, before the chapter concludes by reflecting on emerging issues in the developing world that require future studies in DIDR research and practice.

Theoretical frameworks (or models), perspectives of DIDR, and recent advancement

Two fundamental models best describe DIDR: the Stress model and the Impoverishment Risk and Reconstruction (IRR) model. The Stress model is the earliest attempt to understand how communities, households, and individuals act in response to resettlement, and reveals that the stress caused by relocation is multi-dimensional, with physiological, socio-cultural, and psycho-logical ramifications. Moreover, four-stages of relocation were identified within this model: recruitment, transition, preferential development, and handing over/incorporation (Scudder and Colson 1982). Although this model is widely acknowledged, its linear nature, as a smooth and orderly process, has been critiqued as being far removed from reality (Muggah 2000; Wilmsen and Webber 2010). Scudder (2005, 2011) has continued to develop this model and specified physiological stress as a factor in health impacts of dam-induced displacement and resettlement – communicable diseases, water-borne diseases, vector-borne diseases, and malnutrition. He high-lights the impact that resettlement has on displaced communities: the loss of a home syndrome and anxiety over the future (Scudder 2011). Though still under-researched, many scholars have applied this model and its developments to analyse resettlement impacts, especially the psycho-logical impacts of dam-induced displacement and resettlement (Hwang et al. 2007; Cao et al. 2012; Xi and Hwang 2011).

The IRR model (Cernea 1997; Cernea and Mcdowell 2000) denounces the impoverish-ment caused by development-induced displacement and breaks down the complex and multi-dimensional process of displacement into eight risks: landlessness, joblessness, home-lessness, marginalisation, increased morbidity, and mortality, food insecurity, loss of access to common property, and social disintegration. The IRR model has been widely used by resettlement practitioners and researchers as:

1. a diagnostic tool (diagnosing the recurrent pathologies of forced displacement);
2. a predictive tool (warning about the adverse effects before the displacement occurs);
3. a problem-resolution tool (directing proactive responses to risks); and
4. a research guidance tool (a conceptual framework for designing hypotheses for testing).

While the model continues to undergo modifications, it has proven to be an influential approach that scholars employ to analyse DIDR issues today and researchers have applied the model to assess the impacts of displacement caused by various projects. Assessments of the displacement impacts from reservoirs and dams (Wilmsen 2018), mining (Alexandrescu 2013), national parks, and urbanisation and urban gentrification (Patel et al. 2015) provide but some examples.

Achieving a sustainable livelihood is an ultimate objective in human displacement and resettlement. Failure to mitigate impoverishment risks may generate new poverty, as opposed to the old poverty that millions of people displaced commonly experience before relocation.

Sustainability of livelihood has three features: a sustainable improvement in livelihood measured by poverty alleviation and livelihood enhancement; ecological sustainability; and long-term resilience to future shocks and stresses (Cernea and Mcdowell 2000). In 'Sustainable Livelihood' research (Sen 1984), the key concerns include dynamic processes and livelihood systems that incorporate social institutions and vulnerability. A sustainable livelihood perspective, therefore, marks a move away from static measurements of absolute levels of poverty and well-being, towards a concern with how displaced people make a living over time and what factors significantly influence security or vulnerability. Of particular interest in this approach is the institutional process that mediates the ability to carry out sustainable livelihood strategies and achieve outcomes of development (Scoones 1998).

A recent study by Kirchherr and Charles (2016) unified scholarly understanding of dams' social impacts through systematically analysing and aggregating 27 frameworks used by scholars. The authors particularly examined five frameworks: the Relocation framework (or Stress model) (Scudder 2005; Scudder and Colson 1982), the IRR model (Cernea 1997), the Sustainable Livelihood framework (DFID 1999), the World Commission of Dams framework (WCD 2000), and the Integrative Dam Assessment model (IDAM) (Kibler et al. 2012). These five frameworks (models) provide a wide spectrum of perspectives on the social impacts of dams from which the authors developed a 'matrix framework' for studying the social impacts of dams. This framework captures three key dimensions (space, time, and value) and three key components (infrastructure, community, and livelihood) of social impacts, and emphasises their interlinked nature. The matrix framework advanced the literature by synthesising the complex and multi-dimensional issues of the social impacts of dams in a holistic manner.

Major resettlement approaches and issues

Rural resettlement versus urban resettlement

China's resettlement practice endeavours to minimise both the appropriation of cultivated land for the use of infrastructure projects and urban expansion, and the magnitude of the population displaced. Often, the majority of those displaced by infrastructure projects or urban expansion are farmers living in rural areas or peri-urban villagers. Insufficient understanding of the human carrying capacity in both the settler sending and receiving communities is a key factor impeding the process of resettlement with many rural residents displaced. This leads to irrational rural resettlement in many hydro projects, including the early stages of the Three Gorges Project resettlement in China (Chen et al. 1995). The major restrictions of land reclamation and improvement of low-yielding land were exacerbated by the scarcity of uncultivated land, the requirement of national reforestation, lack of capital investment for building water conservation engineering works, deteriorating water supply, and soil erosion arising mainly from runoff on steeply sloping land in the reservoir area (Tan 2008). Similarly, land provision to minority groups and vulnerable groups has been observed as a major problem in rural resettlement in other developing countries (IDMC 2016; OED 1998).

Urbanisation further constrains the potential supply of agricultural land and water for settling displaced rural residents. Over the past three decades, China has experienced massive rural-to-urban migration, rising from a stock of 6.6 million migrants in cities in 1982 to 221 million in 2010 (see Chapter 55 in this Handbook). Urbanisation has reached a critical point; the number of migrant workers is expected to increase from 253 million in 2014 to 291 million by 2020, of which over three-quarters are rural-to-urban migrants (NHFPCC 2015). The proportion of the population in urban areas has increased from 17.9 to 50 per cent between 1978 and 2010 and is expected to rise further to 70 per cent by 2030 (World Bank 2014). Urban expansion has encroached upon cropland, forest and river-lake bodies by converting them into urban land use since the mid-1990s (Xu et al. 2014). Competition for water resources between the industrial and agricultural sectors has also added pressure on the water supply in mega-cities, including Shanghai, jeopardising agricultural productivity levels (Finlayson et al. 2013). Notably, the average per capita cultivatable land (<0.1 ha) and renewable freshwater resources (2083 m^3 in 2013) in China is around half and one-quarter of the world's average (Liu and Diamond 2005). Thus, any reduction to the already limited land and water resources will impose tremendous pressure on the rural resettlement of displaced people in China.

Resettling people in urban and peri-urban areas may facilitate displaced people to find jobs in secondary and tertiary industry sectors, revitalise rural towns, and foster in-situ urbanisation processes in less developed regions. Research suggests that urban resettlement has imposed substantial challenges for the settlers produced by the Three Gorges Project, including difficulties in adapting to an urban lifestyle with different cultural backgrounds and languages, high unemployment, a struggle to meet non-agricultural job requirements due to low skills, and potential loss of their traditional values and belief systems (Tan 2008; Padovani 2016). However, cutting across the rapid urbanisation issues in country-specific contexts, large infrastructure projects such as dams and reservoirs, urban expansion, and other development projects are expected to generate major urban impacts that need to be monitored and analysed in future research. One of the issues is to understand how people resettled in peri-urban and urban areas gain access to basic infrastructural, social security, health, housing, and educational services that become essential for ensuring their integration into urban life and re-building livelihoods in urban settings.

Massive migration to cities certainly creates new risks related to pressures on existing infrastructure and institutions responsible for safeguarding shelter, utilities, economic activity, and livelihoods; it changes the social-ecological systems that sustain urban life. These are important issues given that urbanisation is one of the most profound demographic and social processes facing the world today and that social and environmental challenges posed by climate change are expected to have significant ramifications in the urbanisation process through impacts on urban sustainability, human security, institutional, and infrastructural integrity, and urban economic activities and livelihoods (ISSC and UNESCO 2013). There is a pressing need, in both research and policy, to develop risk management approaches that avert, minimise, plan for, and put contingency arrangements in place for human mobility and resettlement in a climate-resilient and sustainable future; this is especially urgent for environmentally vulnerable and rapidly urbanising areas of developing countries.

Social impact and social inclusion

Coupled with economic impoverishment, the social impacts of DIDR are enormous and multi-faceted. A systematic review of 217 peer-viewed articles published in the past 25 years, conducted by Kirchherr et al. (2016), showed that only a handful of studies (5--6 per cent of articles surveyed) reported largely positive social impacts of dams, compared to 44–46 per cent largely negative and 49–50 per cent balanced. Kirchherr et al. (2016, 121) stated that not a single article within their sample investigated 'the implications of irrigation, water provision or flood control for food security in the resettlement area, upstream region, downstream region or nation'. No study focused on second-generation impacts, and health and nutrition impacts remained the least studied livelihood impacts of dams. In terms of time frame, the planning and design phase was least studied, and a probable reason for this was 'lack of transparency and accessibility, as the public opposition to dams that has developed in the past 45 years' (Kirchherr et al. 2016, 120). Importantly, the planning and design phase was an integral part of Scudder's four-stage relocation framework, and ignoring impacts (especially psychological stress associated with high rates of death among the elderly) at this stage may have misled practitioners (Scudder 2012). The social impacts of dam-induced resettlement on women upstream and downstream were also understudied. Moreover, women experienced displacement and resettlement differently compared to men, but this difference was often excluded from the DIDR narrative and policy making (Asthana 2012).

A consensus emerged that the people affected by the development ought to be consulted in the whole process of resettlement, especially at the planning stages (Cernea 1990; Wilmsen and Webber 2010; Vanclay 2017). If displaced people were consulted sufficiently and had control over their futures, they could be sufficiently empowered. Wilmsen and Webber (2015) pointed to managerial approaches that appeared to entrench the DIDR processes. They argued that the participation of affected people was often tokenistic in nature and did not carry through into practice. A rare example of successful participation was the Minashtuk Project in Canada, and examples of partly successful participation, where settlers participated in planning and implementation, included the Three Gorges and Xiaolangdi dam projects in China. Here, 190,000 rural residents displaced from the Three Gorges reservoir area were resettled in 11 distant provinces, and 184,000 settlers displaced from the Xiaolangdi reservoir area participated in the selection, design, and construction of resettlement sites (World Bank 2007; Tan 2008).

Displacement and resettlement often resulted in 'a painful and traumatic experience of socio-cultural dismantling' (Bartolome et al. 2000, 6). This often led to a profound sense of loss of identity and belonging among settlers who may have become an underclass in their new socio-cultural resettlement communities. Thus, social inclusion becomes a core issue of social reconstruction and development. In a case study of resettlement of rural residents who were displaced by the Three Gorge Project and resettled in 11 far-away provinces in China, Padovani (2016) revealed that integration does not equal acculturation as the settlers held strong attachments to their hometowns and identities and that they experienced enormous difficulties in creating new networks.

Key issues in DIDR literature

Among the other issues embedded in the current DIDR literature, three deserve particular mention. *First*, an inter-disciplinary dialogue in DIDR research is still lacking, leading to incomplete analysis and policy solutions that have entrenched poverty and inequality among those affected. DIDR scholars have long called for the inter-disciplinary expansion of DIDR dialogue. However, decision-makers and scholars are often put in positions where their scope is restricted, are subject to narrow disciplinary and bureaucratic interests, and they are unwilling to cross institutional boundaries (Castles 2003). Castles (2003) argued that social scientists have largely been at fault as they have allowed their research agenda to be oriented by policy needs and funding, which has resulted in misinformed policies and short-term planning and outlook. Cernea (1990, 1995) and Scudder (1993) have repeatedly emphasised how different literatures have coexisted side by side, untouched and unexplored among the various authors, which has restricted any advancement in research, let alone comparative research among diverse disciplines.

Second, neoliberalism has been the dominant approach to DIDR research and practice. This has brought about a narrow perspective to the topic and, driven by market-based approaches, the displaced are perceived to be the inevitable 'losers' within the process of economic development and modernisation (Muggah 2003; Cernea 2007). As a common practice, governments backed by the financial agencies such as the World Bank or the International Monetary Fund, initiate the massive infrastructure spending by enforcing their power over 'eminent domain' (the compulsory acquisition of land). Eminent domain is usually undertaken legally through the process of expropriation (although differing from country to country), even against people's will (Vanclay 2017). Researchers (Oliver-Smith 2010) contend that countries are coerced into loans and subjected to policies regarding trade, investment, financial deregulation, and privatisation, despite knowing the impact these policies may have on local populations. As large, rapidly developing, and key countries, which have produced large numbers of displaced people with development projects, such as China and India, have the financial capabilities to fund their own development projects, financial institutions are prioritising their competitiveness as lenders over their social and environmental responsibilities (Wilmsen and Webber 2015). This has become a major concern within the literature and is seen as a weakening of key resettlement policies (Wilmsen and Webber 2010). Research that monitors and addresses how dynamic and complex political economy, at regional, national, and transnational scales, influences policies and implementations of DIDR will contribute to the literature in the development and migration research field.

Third, many countries do not have a complete or up-to-date set of the baseline data on the number, location, and needs of people displaced by development projects, nor on the patterns of their resettlement and movement, leading to underestimates of the scale and consequences of displacement (IDMC 2016, 2017). It is therefore important for relevant countries to regularly collect and analyse national data on DIDR and identify the most disadvantaged among them, to ensure their needs are included in resettlement or development plans. Development and migration research has found that, globally, the extent of planned, well-financed, and successful DIDR processes is tiny compared to the sheer magnitude and disastrous effects of failed resettlements (Scudder 2011). How can this vast problem be solved? Future research needs to be centred on this fundamental question.

Concluding remarks

Policymakers argue that the affected populations benefit from the 'trickle-down' effect of development, but this does not always happen in reality. Wilmsen and Webber (2015) provided evidence from the Three Gorges Project in China and the Ciarata and Saguling dams in Indonesia to show that the benefits of development are unequal and enjoyed only by a minority. The fairness and equality of development across diverse groups of the population remains questionable and the debate is dominated by western ideals of modernisation (Wilmsen and Webber 2015).

Global interest and investment in dams and hydropower projects in recent years is on the rise, despite contentious debate on the benefits and costs of building large hydropower dams. A recent study estimated that at least 3700 dams of greater than 1 MW are planned or under construction, of which 847 are large dams of greater than 100 MW (Zarfl et al. 2014). As of 2012, Chinese companies and financiers were involved in more than 300 ongoing dam projects in 70 countries, from Southeast Asia to sub-Saharan Africa, (IDMC 2017). Large-scale infrastructure projects such as hydropower, irrigation and water transfer projects, increasingly have become an integral part of climate change mitigation and adaptation projects. This is particularly the case in China (NDRC

2007) and other parts of the world (Pittock 2010; Lindström and Ruud 2017). In China, hydro projects have gained and continue to gain considerable political and institutional support. In '*China's Policy and Actions to Adapt to Climate Change*' and in the '*National Plans for Renewable Energy in the Medium- and Long-Term Future of China*', the Beijing government firmly stated that developing hydropower (and other forms of new energy) is a crucial strategy for adapting to climate change (NDRC 2007). China aims to improve the percentage of hydroelectricity and other new forms of energy in the total energy consumption from 12 per cent in 2015 to 20 per cent by 2030 (NDRC 2016). Two-thirds of hydropower resources are concentrated in the southwest region (particularly Sichuan, Yunnan, and Tibet), especially the Yangtze, Jinsha, Yalong, Dadu, Wu, Hongshui, Lancang, Yellow, and Nu rivers. Of these, Lancang and Nu are international waterways, and thus construction of dams on the upper reaches of such rivers has significant implications for the long-term sustainability of dam development and food security in downstream countries of Southeast Asia. In the process of ongoing and approved large hydropower projects such as the Baihetan, Yebatan, Lawa, Batang, and Jinsha projects on the Jinsha River in the upper section of the Yangtze, further displacement of people will occur in the next decade. The term 'actively and steadily develop' hydropower was reiterated by the Chinese government in its recent report on the '*13th Five-Year Plan of Renewable Energy Development (2015–2020)*' (NDRC 2016). To date, China's hydropower development model entails 'coordinating the ecological environment protection and resettlement and promoting economic and social development' (Li et al. 2018, 239). How 'resettlement with development', instead of resettlement with impoverishment, can be accomplished remains the central research question and policy concern for China and many other developing countries.

The livelihoods of displaced people are or should be of central concern to policymakers. Studies of migration, including the displacement of people and resettlement produced by development projects and by environmental change, need to be put into the current global context of continuing economic downturn, climate change, and other structural changes such as demographic and socio-economic transformations. Any successes and failures that can be drawn from human displacement produced by large-scale development projects are needed to help people reconstruct livelihoods as quickly as possible in their new environments and to help policymakers and practitioners plan displacement and resettlement more effectively.

Issues of impoverishment and reconstruction of livelihoods need to be studied in a coherent way to safeguard development gains and should be tackled by working towards the sustainable development goals (SDGs) set up by the United Nations in the 2030 Agenda for Sustainable Development (see Chapter 26 in this Handbook). The Agenda commits to 'leave no one behind' and explicitly includes internally displaced persons and migrants. How can it help solve the risks of impoverishment and marginalisation of millions of people displaced by development projects? DIDR and resultant poverty and inequality may undermine achievement of SDG 1 (on poverty) and SDG 10 (on inequality) if the risks of impoverishment are not sufficiently eliminated. Addressing DIDR, both in future research and policy, can facilitate progress across many goals in the 2030 Agenda. Displaced people will not escape impoverishment without significant government support and systematic changes to social, economic and environmental policies in a country.

References

Alexandrescu, F. 2013. Mediated risks: The Roşia Montană displacement and a new perspective on the IRR model. *Canadian Journal of Development Studies*, 34, 498–517.

Asthana, V. 2012. Forced displacement: A gendered analysis of the Tehri Dam project. *Economic and Political Weekly*, 47, 96–102.

Bartolome, L. J., Wet, C., Mander, H. & Nagraj, V. K. 2000. Displacement, resettlement, rehabilitation, reparation, and development. Working paper for the World Commission on Dams, WCD Thematic Review, Social Issues I.3. Cape Town, South Africa.

Cao, Y., Hwang, S. S. & Xi, J. 2012. Project-induced displacement, secondary stressors, and health. *Social Science and Medicine*, 74, 1130–1138.

Castles, S. 2003. Towards a sociology of forced migration and social transformation. *Sociology*, 37, 13–34.

Cernea, M. M. 1990. Internal refugee flows and development-induced population displacement. *Journal of Refugee Studies*, 3, 320–339.

Cernea, M. M. 1995. Social integration and population displacement: the contribution of social science. *International Social Science Journal*, 143, 91–112.

Cernea, M. M. 1997. The risks and reconstruction model for resettling displaced populations. *World Development*, 25, 1569–1587.

Cernea, M. M. 2007. Financing for development benefit-sharing mechanisms in population resettlement. *Economic and Political Weekly*, 42, 1033–1046.

Cernea, M. M. & Mcdowell, C. 2000. *Risks and Reconstruction: Experiences of Resettlers and Refugees*: Washington, DC: The World Bank.

Chen, G. J., Xu, Q. & Du, R. H. (eds.). 1995. *Studies on the Effects of the Three Gorges Project on the Eco-environment and Countermeasures*. Beijing: Chinese Science Press.

Department for International Development (DFID). 1999. *Sustainable livelihoods guidance sheets* [Online]. Available: www.eldis.org/vfile/upload/1/document/0901/section2.pdf

Finlayson, B. L., Barnett, J., Wei, T., Webber, M., LI, M., Wang, M. Y., Chen, J., Xu, H. & Chen, Z. 2013. The drivers of risk to water security in Shanghai. *Regional Environmental Change*, 13, 329–340.

Heggelund, G. 2004. *Environment and Resettlement Politics in China: The Three Gorges Project*: Hampshire (UK): Ashgate.

Hwang, S. S., Xi, J., Cao, Y., Feng, X. & Qiao, X. 2007. Anticipation of migration and psychological stress and the Three Gorges Dam project, China. *Social Science and Medicine*, 65, 1012–1024.

Internal Displacement Monitoring Centre (IDMC). 2017. *Dams and Internal Displacement: An Introduction*. Geneva, Switzerland.

International Displacement Monitoring Centre (IDMC) 2016. Pushed aside: Displacement for 'Development' in India.

ISSC & UNESCO 2013. *World Social Science Report 2013, Changing Global Environments*. Paris: OECD Publishing and UNESCO Publishing.

Kibler, K., Tullos, D., Tilt, B., Wolf, A., Magee, D., Foster-Moore, E. & Gassert, F. 2012. *Integrative Dam Assessment Model (IDAM) Documentation: Users Guide to the IDAM Methodology and a Case Study from Southwestern China*. Corvallis, Oregon: Oregon State University.

Kirchherr, J. & Charles, K. J. 2016. The social impacts of dams: A new framework for scholarly analysis. *Environmental Impact Assessment Review*, 60, 99–114.

Kirchherr, J., Pohlner, H. & Charles, K. J. 2016. Cleaning up the big muddy: A meta-synthesis of the research on the social impact of dams. *Environmental Impact Assessment Review*, 60, 115–125.

Li, X. Z., Chen, Z. J., Fan, X. C. & Cheng, Z. J. 2018. Hydropower development situation and prospects in China. *Renewable and Sustainable Energy Reviews*, 82, 232–239.

Lindström, A. & Ruud, A. 2017. Who's hydropower? From conflictual management into an era of reconciling environmental concerns; A retake of hydropower governance towards win-win solutions? *Sustainability (Switzerland)*, 9.

Liu, J. & Diamond, J. 2005. China's environment in a globalizing world. *Nature*, 435, 1179–1186.

Muggah, R. 2000. Through the developmentalist's looking glass: Conflict-induced displacement and involuntary resettlement in Colombia. *Journal of Refugee Studies*, 13, 133–164.

Muggah, R. 2003. A tale of two solitudes: Comparing conflict and development-induced internal displacement and involuntary resettlement. *International Migration*, 41, 5–32.

National Development and Reform Commission (NDRC). 2007. *National Plans for Renewable Energy in the Medium- and Long-Term Future of China* [Online]. Beijing: State Council of China. Available: www.ndrc.gov.cn/125gh.pdf [Accessed 8 April 2018].

National Development and Reform Commission (NDRC). 2016. *13th Five-Year Plan of Renewable Energy Development (2015-2020)* [Online]. Available: www.ndrc.gov.cn/zcfb/zcfbtz/201612/W020161216659579206185.pdf [Accessed 8 April 2018].

National Health and Family Planning Commission of China (NHFPCC). 2015. *2015 Report on China's Floating Population Development Report*. Beijing: China Population Publishing House.

Oliver-Smith, A. 2010. *Defying Displacement: Grassroots Resistance and the Critique of Development*: Austin: University of Texas Press.

Operation Evaluation Department (OED). 1998. *Recent Experience with Involuntary Resettlement: Overview.* Washington, DC: World Bank.

Padovani, F. (ed.). 2016. *Development-induced Displacement in India and China.* Lanham: Lexington Books.

Patel, S., Sliuzas, R. & Mathur, N. 2015. The risk of impoverishment in urban development-induced displacement and resettlement in Ahmedabad. *Environment and Urbanization*, 27, 231–256.

Pittock, J. 2010. Viewpoint - Better management of hydropower in an era of climate change. *Water Alternatives*, 3, 444–452.

Scoones, I. 1998. Sustainable Rural Livelihoods: A Framework for Analysis. Sussex, UK: IDS working paper No. 72, June 1998.

Scudder, T. 1993. Development-induced relocation and refugee studies: 37 years of change and continuity among Zambia's gwembe tonga. *Journal of Refugee Studies*, 6, 123–152.

Scudder, T. 2005. *The Future of Large Dams: Dealing with Social, Environmental, Institutional and Political Costs*: London: Routledge.

Scudder, T. 2011. Development-induced community resettlement. *In:* Vanclay, F. & Esteves, A. M. (eds.). *New Directions in Social Impact Assessment: Conceptual and Methodological Advances.* Cheltenham (UK): Edward Elgar Publishing, pp. 186–201.

Scudder, T. 2012. Resettlement outcomes of large dams. *In:* Tortajada, C., Altinbilek, D. & Biswas, A. K. (eds.). *Impacts of Large Dams: A Global Assessment.* Verlag Berlin Heidelberg, pp. 37–68.

Scudder, T. & Colson, E. 1982. From welfare to development: A conceptual framework for the analysis of dislocated people. *In:* Hansen, A. & Oliver-Smith, A. (eds.). *Involuntary Migration and Resettlement: The Problems and Responses of Dislocated People.* Boulder, Colorado: Westview Press, pp. 267–287.

Sen, A. 1984. Rights and capabilities. *In:* Sen, A. (ed.). *Resources, Values and Development.* Oxford: Basil Blackwell, pp. 307–324.

Shi, G., Zhou, J. & Yu, Q. 2012. Resettlement in China. *In:* Tortajada, C., Altinbilek, D. & Biswas, A. K. (eds.). *Impacts of Large Dams: A Global Assessment, Water Resources Development and Management.* Verlag Berlin Heidelberg: Springer, pp. 219–241.

Tan, Y. 2008. *Resettlement in the Three Gorges Project*: Hong Kong: Hong Kong University Press.

Vanclay, F. 2017. Project-induced displacement and resettlement: from impoverishment risks to an opportunity for development? *Impact Assessment and Project Appraisal*, 35, 3–21.

Wilmsen, B. 2018. Is Land-based resettlement still appropriate for rural people in China? A longitudinal study of displacement at the Three Gorges Dam. *Development and Change*, 49, 170–198.

Wilmsen, B. & Webber, M. 2010. Dams and displacement: Raising the standards and broadening the research agenda. *Water Alternatives*, 3, 142–161.

Wilmsen, B. & Webber, M. 2015. What can we learn from the practice of development-forced displacement and resettlement for organised resettlements in response to climate change? *Geoforum*, 58, 76–85.

World Bank. 2001. *Involuntary Resettlement: Operational Policy (OP) 4.12.* Washington, DC: World Bank.

World Bank 2007. *China – Xiaolangdi Resettlement Project. Project Performance Assessment Report No. 43061.* Washington, DC: World Bank.

World Bank. 2014. *Urban China: Toward Efficient, Inclusive, and Sustainable Urbanization.* Washington, DC: World Bank.

World Commission of Dams (WCD). 2000. *Dams and Development: A New Framework for Decision-making.* London: Earthscan.

Xi, J. & Hwang, S. S. 2011. Relocation stress, coping, and sense of control among resettlers resulting from China's Three Gorges Dam project. *Social Indicators Research*, 104, 507–522.

Xu, X., Tan, Y., Chen, S. & Yang, G. 2014. Changing patterns and determinants of natural capital in the Yangtze River Delta of China 2000–2010. *Science of the Total Environment*, 466-467, 326–337.

Xu, X., Tan, Y. & Yang, G. 2013. Environmental impact assessments of the Three Gorges Project in China: Issues and interventions. *Earth-Science Reviews*, 124, 115–125.

Zarfl, C., Lumsdon, A. E., Berlekamp, J., Tydecks, L. & Tockner, K. 2014. A global boom in hydropower dam construction. *Aquatic Sciences*, 77, 161–170.

35

CLIMATE-CHANGE DISRUPTIONS TO MIGRATION SYSTEMS

W. Neil Adger and Ricardo Safra de Campos

Introduction

It is inevitable that climate change will have impacts both on migration and on development processes in every region and corner of the world. No place, no economy, and no population is immune. The reasons for this ubiquitous impact are first that human-induced climate change will affect biological and physical systems and hence the spatial distribution of resources on which humans depend. Second, changes in climate affect the distribution of the substantial risks associated with weather extremes in both their spatial and social dimensions. So, these two elements, changing the spatial distribution of the productivity of resources and weather-related risks, will inevitably alter human settlement patterns in the long term. But these trends and projections on future climates raise a number of issues for migration and development: Who will be affected? How sensitive is migration to environmental resources and risks? Will these changes in migration be attributable to the underlying environmental change? And can the challenges of migration and climate change be managed through policy and collective action? The evidence used to inform the answers to these empirical questions is scattered throughout the migration, economic, demographic, historical, and physical sciences.

It is well established that climate change has affected migration flows for all of human history. This has included the opening up of new frontiers of habitability, through to places that have in effect been abandoned as climate, resources, and circumstances change (McLeman 2014). Every well-documented example of how environmental change affects settlement patterns, of course, raises the multi-faceted nature of the interaction of climate with other factors. Climate has rarely been dominant but interacts with demographic change through the twin aspects of biological productivity and weather risks in conjunction with technology, politics, and other social complexities.

Some analysis of migration–climate interactions has, inevitably, been overly deterministic, such as attributing major population declines to climate change in historical cases, through to projections of populations likely to be displaced by expected current climate change (Gemenne 2011b). The over-deterministic pronouncements of the mass movements of people, and the designation of climate refugees, diverges from demographic realities and has led to major scepticism in the social sciences of the whole idea that climate change is important for migration systems. Much of the work in this area has sought to attribute complex social change to simplified climate factors and involved projections of movement of people out of the context of established migration trends (Piguet 2013).

Yet, increasing evidence exists that climate change will indeed affect all elements of migration systems. Such evidence is based on an understanding of migration decision-making processes at individual levels and the increasing resolution of projected environmental changes (Hugo 2011; Piguet et al. 2011; McLeman 2014; Adger et al. 2015; Neumann et al. 2015). Hence this chapter sets out the principal mechanisms by which climate change may affect migration, highlights how these affect well-established migration systems, and examines the policy challenges associated with these impacts.

Mechanisms linking climate change with migration outcomes

The physical impacts of human-induced climate change in the contemporary world and the prospects for the incoming decades and centuries are, in their broad scope, well established from multiple lines of evidence and with multiple methods. First, the climate over the past century has altered globally, with some areas, notably in the high latitudes, experiencing rapid warming. Second, the biological world and many physical processes have already begun to adapt to these altered climates. The evidence is irrefutable that ecosystems have altered in line with the observed climatic changes in both the plant and animal kingdoms (Rosenzweig et al. 2008). Further, physical systems have been significantly altered, not least in the coverage and extent of ice and glaciers, and permafrost, and in altered patterns of water availability and river flows in all parts of the world (Betts et al. 2018). Third, all projections suggest that climatic changes will accelerate because of the physical processes of response to increased trapped energy in the atmosphere and oceans, and that the impacts of those climatic changes are significant to physical and biological systems globally.

The significance of changes to the climate is highlighted in great detail in the physical, ecological, and social sciences. The risks of climate change are potentially major destabilisers to ecosystems, and represent a huge challenge to public health, as well as to geo-political stability (Watts et al. 2015; Challinor et al. 2018). The scientific community focuses on the uncertainty and the possibility of significant emerging risks: reasons for concern include the probability of critical transitions in the Asian monsoon and long-term commitments to many metres of sea-level rise globally from the loss of Greenland and Antarctic (Smith et al. 2009; Bathiany et al. 2018). Integrated global analyses of the impacts of climate change emphasise the highly uneven geographic distribution of risks, often on populations with less ability to adapt, and often with irreversible consequences (Bathiany et al. 2018)

How will the impacts play out in terms of changes in productivity, habitability, and risk? Table 35.1 summarises three major elements of climate-change impacts that have variously been identified as affecting migration patterns (McLeman and Hunter 2010; Gemenne 2011a). It describes their global extent and variation as well as likely mechanisms of how they will affect migration. These elements are water availability, land inundation and habitability, and the increase in intensity or frequency of weather-related hazards. Ecological impacts on biodiversity and processes of ocean acidification brought about by increased carbon dioxide may also have profound long-term consequences. But the three issues raised in Table 35.1 in effect have the most immediate and also long-term impacts on settlement patterns and migration trends.

A primary impact of climate change is on the distribution and availability of rainfall. Every part of the world will be affected by the changing availability of water, and in low latitudes in particular with changes in evapotranspiration. Changes to water availability impact upon the

Table 35.1 Impacts associated with climate-change impacts and their implications for migration

Climate-change impacts	Geographical distribution	Potential interactions with migration and mobility
Drought and water availability	Global extent. Impacts acute in agriculture-dominated regions	Constraints on urban growth in drying areas. Impacts on long-term productivity of marginal agricultural lands leading to leading term population declines. Increased distressed populations movement within drought-prone areas. Significant economic and social impacts on pastoralist farming systems and nomadic populations in arid and semi-arid areas.
Land inundation and habitability	Impacts concentrated in coastal lowlands and small islands	Increased risks from salinisation and land productivity in the short term. Long-term decline in accretion rates in deltas and sustainability of littoral settlements. Dilemmas of coastal protection and planned relocation of coastal populations.
Increases in intensity or frequency of extreme events		
Flooding	Global extent with rainfall intensity increasing in all regions	Increased incidence of short-term displacement of populations from river flooding, and coastal flooding. Global phenomenon.
Storms	Cyclones and hurricanes in tropics and extra-tropics	Significant economic damage and evacuation and displacement from storms, interacting with longer-term economic viability, signalled through availability of insurance and disinvestment.
Heatwave and extreme temperatures	Global extent: impacts extend even in temperate regions, especially in urban areas	Less impact on mobility. Some indications of acclimatisation and adaptation to heat impacts.
Wildfire	Concentrated in semi-arid and drying regions	Economic damage and evacuation and displacement from wildfire events, interacting with longer-term economic viability, signalled through availability of insurance and disinvestment.

viability of agriculture and the productivity of ecosystems. Societies where populations have been highly mobile within economies, based for example on pastoralism, would inevitably be significantly affected through direct changes in forage quality and species composition. In particular, evidence exists for the changing nature of pastoralism practices in high latitude areas where climatic changes have been dramatic in the past three decades (Dong et al. 2011). Agricultural systems everywhere have been shown to be susceptible to changes in extremes of rainfall and water availability (Thornton et al. 2014).

What do such risks to agricultural production and the viability of economies mean for mobility and migration? Evidence suggests that long-term drought leads to greater levels of outward migration from agricultural areas, but this is limited to those parts of populations that can, in effect, afford to move. Nawrotzki et al. (2015), for example, show that hot and dry periods are correlated with increased out-migration from rural areas across Mexico throughout the most recent decades. Urban populations and non-farming parts of the rural economy are, of course, much less sensitive to droughts in terms of migration decisions. A review of evidence in Adger et al. (2014) documented many studies that showed both increased or decreased migration rates during drought periods: the common factor being the impact of drought on the availability of resources for long-distance and duration migration by choice.

Land inundation and habitability is a second major climate impact that has consequences for migration (Table 35.1). The impacts of sea-level change in coastal regions, amplified by habitat change and salinisation processes, have been analysed as routes to the large-scale displacement of populations (Neumann et al. 2015), but such displacement is not inevitable, but rather depends on adaptive responses and the protection of coastal areas (Dasgupta et al. 2015; Seto 2011). The impacts of climate change on net out-migration are not yet detectable. De Sherbinin et al. (2011) show a net migration increase to coastal regions globally over the past four decades: but much of that drift is to coastal cities and thus not necessarily away from the risks of climate change. Codjoe et al. (2019) examine recent movements in low-lying deltas from the 2000 and 2010 census periods and find that some coastal districts in highly populous deltas in India, Bangladesh, and Ghana are indeed losing population to outward migration, though they do not attribute this solely to environmental change. But the predicted impacts of coastal impacts and inundation suggest that large-scale investment would be required to maintain land in many coastal areas (Neumann et al. 2015).

The third major element of climate-change impacts that have consequences for migration, as shown in in Table 35.1, is the short-term impact of weather-related disasters. Clearly, cyclones, hurricanes, coastal surges, and even wildfires continually displace populations (Fussell, Curtis, and DeWaard 2014) . The populations affected by such events and the economic cost of these disasters is rising, partly through the changing frequency and severity of climate extremes, but also because of the rising number of populations in harms' way (Bouwer 2011). Nevertheless, the monitoring of current populations affected globally suggests more than 20 million people are affected by weather-related events each year. Such impacts disrupt livelihoods and have negative effects on mental health (Munro et al. 2017), even if most of those evacuated during such events return home quickly. Well studied events such as Hurricane Katrina in the US in 2005 show that, of those displaced, poorer populations were less likely to return to New Orleans and that such large-scale disruption has caused significant demographic shifts and population loss for some areas within the region (Groen and Polivka 2010). Hence short-term weather-related disasters, while leading mainly to short-term displacement, have impacts on permanent migration flows.

How the impacts of climate change highlighted in Table 35.1 are realised and distributed depends on migration and demographic processes and the multi-dimensional nature of individuals' migration decision-making. Even where climate change impacts are stark, as in small low-lying islands, for example, populations persist and live with environmental risks where models would predict population decline or abandonment. Mortreux and Barnett (2009) and Adams (2016), for example, highlight cultural and identity issues and place attachment as explaining persistent populations, from island settings such as Tuvalu to the depopulating highland areas of Peru. In these cases, sections of populations actively decide to remain in environmentally vulnerable places for a multitude of rational and deeply held reasons.

How individuals make migration decisions in the face of climate change risks

Large-scale economic and social structures drive migration and population movements, which include urbanisation, land-use transitions, globalisation, and postcolonial relations. Hence, intricate relationships exist between migration, development, and climate change, with the observed aggregate flows the sum of myriad individual decisions. The incentives for individual migration decisions are well established: individuals and households respond to drivers depending on their socioeconomic and cultural characteristics, demographic composition, and contexts that include environmental risks (Black et al. 2011). There is limited evidence to suggest that slow-onset impacts derived from climate change have been significant in reconfiguring the existing direction of migration flows to date. For example, internal migration is prevalent in both developed and developing countries and will continue to increase even without the projected impacts of climate change (Rigaud et al. 2018).

These issues, of the relative importance of climate change in migration decision-making, are illustrated in new evidence obtained from low-lying coastal areas across India, Ghana, and Bangladesh that have been regularly affected by a range of environmental hazard events and are also vulnerable to future climate change. The high dependency on climate-sensitive livelihoods, such as fishing and agriculture, makes the population living in coastal, river basin, and semi-arid regions particularly vulnerable to climate variability and change (Safra de Campos et al. 2020). A high degree of exposure to environmental hazards, stalled development, and poverty in those areas clearly play some part in a well-documented recent trend of net out-migration towards urban centres (Szabo et al. 2016).

When examining the overall patterns of population movement, it is tempting to suggest that existing or future environmental factors are influential in driving individual decisions on migration, more so in already vulnerable locations. A new cross-sectional survey of 5450 households across delta locations in India, Ghana, and Bangladesh showed that more than 30 per cent of these representative households reported at least one migrant. The survey collected data on the motivation to migrate by one or more household members: eliciting all relevant motivations for migration and ranking them to ascertain the principal driver. Figure 35.1 shows that only 2.8 per cent of respondents perceived the main reason behind the decision to move to have been environmental stress: the vast majority of respondents perceived economic and social benefits to have accounted for the migration of their household members.

The results in Figure 35.1 show therefore that few migrants, even in places significantly exposed to climate variability and potentially to the impacts of climate change, self-report as environmental migrants. Yet environmental risks may still have a significant role in migration decisions. The households in coastal Ghana, India, and Bangladesh also reported significant exposure to environmental risks and perceived economic insecurity associated with environmental hazards. One-third of all respondents perceived that there was an increased exposure to hazards (from a list that included cyclone, drought, erosion, flooding, salinity, and storm surge) over the previous 5 years. Over one-third of respondents (37.5 per cent) also reported the environment to be more hazardous and extreme events to be more frequent. Similarly, between 40 and 80 per cent of the respondents associated environmental factors with more insecure livelihoods. These perceptions of underlying environmental degradation and insecurity were also positively correlated with increased odds of household members migrating (Adger et al. 2019).

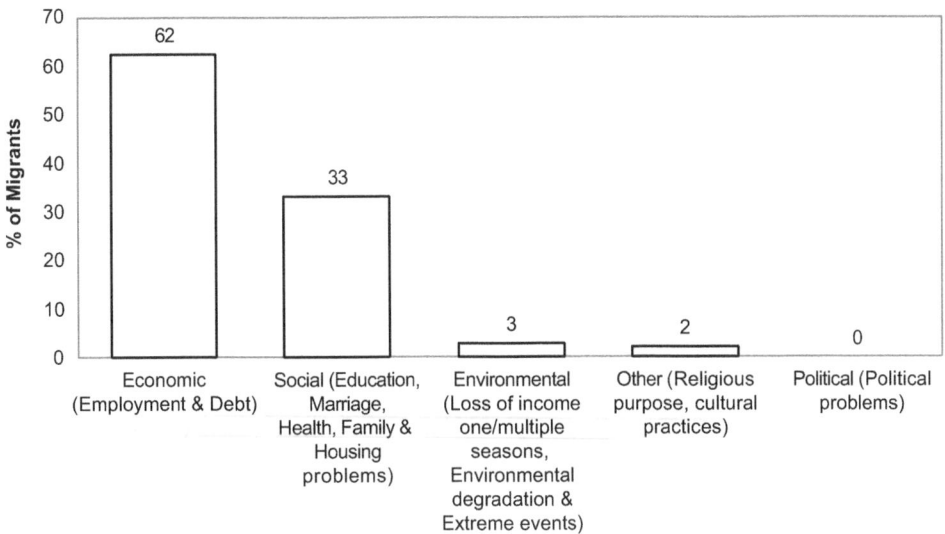

Figure 35.1 Perceived principal motivations for migration in households where at least one family member
has migrated, in low-lying coastal areas in India, Bangladesh, and Ghana, 2016 (N=1668)

Source: Adger et al. (2019)

The most important potential impact of climate change on migration systems is, in effect, the potential for climate change impacts to affect livelihoods and push vulnerable populations into poverty. Previous large-scale weather-related extremes, impacts on food prices, along with disease burdens and threats to state capacity, are identified as reasons for concern associated with poverty and health. The food price spike of 2011, which was partially driven by droughts in cereal-growing regions globally, for example, pushed 45 million people below the poverty line in African, Asian, and Latin American countries (Ivanic et al. 2012). The underlying cascading impacts linked to climate change are projected to shift patterns of population movement and impact on the size and direction of flows, especially for internal migration (Groundswell 2018 with Rigaud et al., 2018).

Migration studies have associated rural to urban migration with regional disparities and livelihood strategies (see De Haas 2010). Our own representative survey work referred to above, shows the contemporary reality of these patterns for coastal Bangladesh: surveys in villages across coastal parts of southern Bangladesh reveal that migration is primarily domestic and permanent. Irrespective of migration drivers, population movements to the two largest urban centres of Bangladesh continue to be the prevalent direction of internal flows. Dhaka represented nearly 40 per cent of the urban population of Bangladesh, and had net annual migration arrivals during the 2000–10 period of 300,000–400,000 (te Lintelo et al. 2017), while the population of Chittagong (now Chattogram) grew by 3.6 per cent per year across the 1990–2011 period, and had an aggregate population of 4 million in 2011 compared to 3.3 million in 2001 (Figure 35.2). Over the same period, new arrivals accounted for 330,000 people or 8.2 per cent of the population (Mia et al. 2015). Migration into Chittagong has consistently increased in trend terms over the period 1975–2005 and is projected to increase until 2025 (Mia et al. 2015). Dhaka and Chittagong are the destinations of almost 43 per cent of internal migration from our survey (see Figure 35.3). The purpose of these movements is dominated by opportunities in both formal and informal sectors of the economy associated with the rapid industrialisation and urban growth of the country (Siddiqui et al. 2018).

Figure 35.2 Roads in Chattogram, Bangladesh, congested with traffic, street hawkers, and pedestrians as a result of rapid urbanisation

Photo credit: Rezaul Karim

Even from rural coastal Bangladesh, there is a significant element of direct international migration, particularly to the Middle East and across Asia (see Figure 35.3). The survey shows 37 per cent of all migrants relocating to international destinations: preferred destinations are the Gulf and Arab countries as well as emerging economies in South East Asia, where migrants are most frequently employed under temporary contracts. Siddiqui et al. (2018) has documented significant changes in the make-up of such international migration, with over 100,000 female international migrant workers departing Bangladesh in 2017. Aggregate migration flows, even from rural delta regions at risk in Bangladesh, are affected therefore by economic opportunities and the policies and regulations of migration in source and destination regions.

Environmental stressors are, rather, more likely to impact migration through the disruption of livelihoods rather than directly, through natural hazards (Call et al. 2017). However, an increased frequency and exposure to environmental stressors associated with climate change, particularly sudden-onset events such as flooding, cyclones have potentially significant effects on migration decision-making processes in vulnerable areas of developed and developing countries. Moreover, there are various established migration systems across the globe and, under present conditions, it is difficult to establish the impact of climate change on the size or direction of existing migration flows. However, the occurrence of large extreme events or persistent changes in the frequency of slow-onset hazards could induce new population movements and change the size and the direction of current migration flows.

Division level flows (N=292)

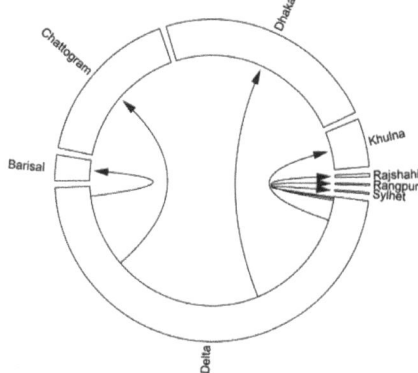

District level flows (N=292)

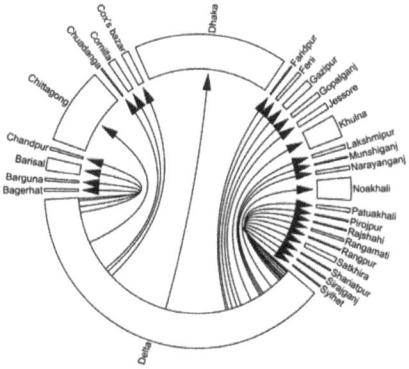

International migration (N=173)

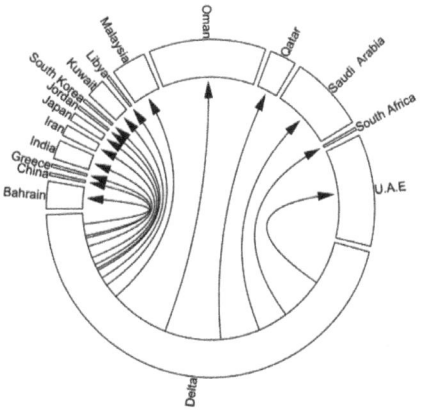

Figure 35.3 Destinations of migrants from low-lying coastal regions in the Ganges Brahmaputra delta, Bangladesh, 2016: localised, regional, and international migration flows (N=465)

Source: Safra de Campos et al. (2019)

Policy and governance dilemmas of climate migration interactions

The discussion in this chapter has summarised what is known about migration systems and the impacts and consequences of climate change. In summary, the most significant policy challenges concerning migration associated with climate change are immobility, planned relocation, and regulation and government responses to migration and displacement. These issues pertain, to a very large degree, to domestic rather than international movements. At the same time the potential linkages between the international governance of migration and the international governance of climate change are only now beginning to emerge.

Mass displacement

Climate change has the potential to disrupt migration systems and hence create significant challenges to the governance of migration. Much public discourse on climate change has, inevitably, focused on the prospect of the international mass displacement of people, often playing to negative stereotypes or highlighting security and border control concerns associated with this potential. Any realistic assessment of the potential for mass displacement shows that this is a significant reason for concern, especially for marginalised populations in places dependent on productive natural resources and in low-lying areas affected by changing sea levels.

The portrayal of the impacts of climatic change on mass displacement as having universally negative impacts on social cohesion in destination areas is wildly off the mark. Studies that have

Figure 35.4 Vulnerable communities frequently affected by flooding along the banks of the Karnaphuli River, Bangladesh

Photo credit: Rasheda

deconstructed the discourses in this area show that migrants are predominantly portrayed as victims or security threats, with less common portrayals as people making rational adaptive actions, or having some agency in their future (Ransan-Cooper et al. 2015). The security threat discourse pervades much analysis in mainstream climate-change governance (Bettini 2013).

The moral and economic concern about the impacts of climate change only portrays migration as an unintended and negative outcome of newly emerging risks, rather than part of social, economic, and demographic processes. Hence the reformulation of the migration–environment relations over the past decade has, for the first time, shown that a lack of agency in migration decision-making results in immobility as a key governance challenge (Foresight 2011). Place attachment, identity, the loss of culture, and occupational identity are therefore parameters that override apparently stark environmental and climate change risks. Analyses of why populations persist in the face of climate change risks show that environmental change is often already central to perceptions of place, and that a lack of mobility potential compounds these perceptions (Adams 2016).

Involuntary immobility and planned relocation

A second, related issue, is the involuntary nature of immobility, often referred to as populations being trapped. Call et al. (2017), for example, shows that temporary migration is often disrupted and is reduced following flood events in Bangladesh. Similar reductions in the ability of populations to migrate are demonstrated for dryland agriculture (Suckall et al. 2017). Hence migration, particularly temporary movement for livelihood security, is in danger from the impacts of climate change in resource-dependent economies. The implications of reduced mobility and migration are profound, not least with increased demand for humanitarian assistance and the need for co-operation between states on issues of the lack of mobility (Challinor et al. 2018).

Given the risks of climate change, governments will increasingly be compelled to intervene in spatial planning and deciding whether to protect or abandon settlements. Environmental disasters have always affected the calculus of displacement and return. In places subject to persistent environmental risks associated with changing hydrology and climate change, such as riverbank erosion or coastal inundation, the physical space where people live simply disappears and no meaningful alternative option for populations to decide to move or be formally relocated elsewhere exists. Settlements that are periodically affected by floods and storm surges, experience disruption to livelihoods and properties, and public services are compromised (Figure 35.4). For some of these places, the calculus for protecting or abandonment will eventually be in favour of relocation. In other words, planned relocation is often associated with a combination of both directly uninhabitable land and places becoming too risky.

Hence the practice of planned relocation, also referred to as resettlement, is now widely discussed as a necessary or potentially effective intervention for vulnerable communities (McAdam and Ferris 2015; Hino et al. 2017). Given the history of resettlement associated with development projects such as dams, where whole communities have been involuntarily relocated, planned relocation initiatives are often detrimental for those involved in the process, including the disruption of livelihoods and loss of income, socioeconomic networks, and cultural heritage (Cernea and McDowell 2000; de Sherbinin et al. 2011; see also Chapter 34 in this Handbook on development-induced migration).

Several studies have focused on the outcome for people involved in planned relocation, which is directly affected by the legitimacy and levels of agency in the process (Bronen and Chapin 2013; Sipe and Vella 2014). Yet decisions by governments on whether to intervene and undertake planned relocation interventions are often ad hoc responses ranging from the full-scale movement of communities to no intervention at all (Warner et al. 2013). With increasing environmental risks brought about by climate change, an underlying political economy emerges around how governments decide whether to support communities in need of relocation. Furthermore, cases have arisen where governments have deliberately taken no action to move vulnerable communities or yet other cases where various barriers have prevented a more direct intervention (Hino et al. 2017; McNamara et al. 2018; Mortreux et al. 2018)

Policy inaction is a result of the systematic under-reaction to external circumstances with policy processes, either through under-estimating the risks of not acting, or through inertia and the persistence with existing processes guiding decisions. Inaction can be a manifestation of risk aversion in order to avoid risks to political reputation, whereas action is often associated with accountability to civil society (Mortreux et al. 2018). Incentives and disincentives emerge that mediate government action and inaction in the context of planned relocation associated with environmental risks.

Government accountability creates a set of institutional incentives for actions that are associated with political credibility and reputational and economic gains that can solidify authority. Inaction or non-action tends to result from aversion to perceived risks such as prohibitive costs, defensive avoidance, or institutional paralysis or blinds spots (Mortreux et al. 2018). If patchy and uneven approaches to planned relocation occur, in places where a need exists for relocation initiatives because of environmental risks, this may have significant implications for the safety and well-being of vulnerable communities leading to outcomes such as displacement or distress migration.

International coordination

A third major arena of policy action is in the international coordination of migration policies and governance. Various initiatives that seek to enhance the rights of the displaced as a direct result of climate change have been set in motion, which incorporate suggestions on how to empower and protect displaced populations, including those who may cross international borders. The Nansen initiative, for example, is seeking to build principles for action and protection for those displaced across borders by weather-related disasters such as droughts and floods (Gemenne and Brücker 2015). Significant ethical arguments concerning the involuntary nature of migration induced by climate change have been made to draw attention to the harm imposed by polluters disrupting the climate through the global emissions of greenhouse gases (Williams 2008). Specific calls to recognise climate refugees under the Geneva Convention Relating to the Status of Refugees have not progressed (Biermann and Boas 2010). Such changes remain unlikely to be implemented for both political and practical reasons. First, the multi-dimensional nature of every migration decision, as discussed above, means that distinguishing and categorising a climate refugee or climate migrant is not meaningful. Second, there is significant reluctance to destabilise the Geneva Convention, not least given contemporary global refugee flows and perceived crises in the current system. Progress on the governance of migration–climate interactions, however, is progressing through the recognition of migration as a legitimate adaptation action under the Cancun Accords of the UN Framework Convention on Climate Change and in evolving discussions on protocols on Loss and Damage under the Convention.

Conclusions

The prospects for sustainable development are restricted and constrained by climate changes which will be disruptive of many environmental processes and economic activities. Progress on sustainable development which leaves no-one behind appear to be particularly at risk, because of the uneven and disproportionate impact of climate changes on vulnerable and marginalised populations globally. The global climate regime has long recognised the potential for disruption to processes of sustainable development, and indeed defines dangerous climate change in those terms in Article 2 of the Climate Change Convention in 1992 (Dessai et al. 2004). Mounting evidence shows that resource-based economies and primary sector activities such as agriculture, forestry, and fishing are vulnerable to changes, with profound consequences for rural areas and food systems everywhere.

In summary, climate change therefore has the potential to significantly and fundamentally disrupt migration flows and individual migration decisions everywhere. This is inevitable given the highly likely uneven impacts of climate change across space where people live. Migration systems can be altered in multiple ways, ranging from temporary displacement from weather-related disasters to the long-term decline of regions and settlements. For individuals, such imposed harm in effect limits their choice, agency, and mobility in ways that are not easily predictable. It may at the extreme represent an existential threat to identity and the sovereignty of places and cultures. The crucible for these interactions and dilemmas is increasingly going to be in urban settings globally, where new populations may be exposed to new risks and new dilemmas. These issues demonstrate how climate change is tied up with the political economy of development processes.

Acknowledgements

Funding is acknowledged from the Deltas, Vulnerability and Climate Change: Migration and Adaptation project (IDRC 107642) under the Collaborative Adaptation Research Initiative in Africa and Asia Programme of the UK Department for International Development and the International Development Research Centre, Canada, and from the UK Economic and Social Research Council (ES/R002371/1) for Safe and Sustainable Cities: Human Security, Migration and Well-Being and for Migration, Transformations and Sustainability projects (ES/S007687/1).

References

Adams, H. (2016) Why populations persist: Mobility, place attachment and climate change. *Population and Environment* 37, 429–448.

Adger, W.N., Arnell, N.W., Black, R., Dercon, S., Geddes, A. & Thomas, D.S. (2015) Focus on environmental risks and migration: Causes and consequences. *Environmental Research Letters* 10, 060201.

Adger, W.N., Pulhin, J. M., Barnett, J. et al. (2014) Human security. In Field, C.B., V.R. Barros, D. J. Dokken, K.J. Mach, M.D. Mastrandrea, T.E. Bilir, M. Chatterjee, K.L. Ebi, Y.O. Estrada, R. C. Genova, B. Girma, E.S. Kissel, A.N. Levy, S. MacCracken, P.R. Mastrandrea, & L.L. White eds. *Climate change 2014: Impacts, adaptation, and vulnerability. Contribution of working group ii to the fifth assessment report of the Intergovernmental Panel on Climate Change.* Cambridge University Press, Cambridge, pp. 755–791.

Adger, W.N., Safra de Campos, R., Codjoe, S.N.A., Siddiqui, T., Hazra, S., Adams, H., Mortreux, C., Das, S. & Abu, M. (2019) Perceived exposure to environmental risks and insecurity are significant in migration decisions. *One Earth*. submitted.

Bathiany, S., Dakos, V., Scheffer, M. & Lenton, T.M. (2018) Climate models predict increasing temperature variability in poor countries. *Science Advances* 4, 5809.

Bettini, G. (2013) Climate barbarians at the gate? A critique of apocalyptic narratives on climate refugees. *Geoforum* 45, 63–72.

Betts, R.A., Alfieri, L., Bradshaw, C. et al. (2018) Changes in climate extremes, fresh water availability and vulnerability to food insecurity projected at 1.5° C and 2° C global warming with a higher-resolution global climate model. *Philosophical Transactions of the Royal Society A* 376, 20160452.

Biermann, F. & Boas, I. (2010) Preparing for a warmer world: Towards a global governance system to protect climate refugees. *Global Environmental Politics* 10(1), 60–88.

Black, R., Adger, W.N., Arnell, N.W., Dercon, S., Geddes, A. & Thomas, D. (2011) The effect of environmental change on human migration. *Global Environmental Change* 21, S3-S11.

Bouwer, L.M. (2011) Have disaster losses increased due to anthropogenic climate change? *Bulletin of the American Meteorological Society* 92, 39–46.

Bronen, R. & Chapin, F.S. (2013) Adaptive governance and institutional strategies for climate-induced community relocations in Alaska. *Proceedings of the National Academy of Sciences* 110, 9320–9325.

Call, M.A., Gray, C., Yunus, M. & Emch, M. (2017) Disruption, not displacement: Environmental variability and temporary migration in Bangladesh. *Global Environmental Change* 46, 157–165.

Cernea, M.M. & McDowell, C. eds. (2000) *Risks and reconstruction: Experiences of resettlers and refugees.* World Bank, Washington, DC.

Challinor, A.J., Adger, W.N., Benton, T.G., Conway, D., Joshi, M. & Frame, D. (2018) Transmission of climate risks across sectors and borders. *Philosophical Transactions of the Royal Society A* 376, 20170301.

Codjoe, S.N.A., Abu, M., Adger, W.N., Safra de Campos, R., Hazra, S., Das, S., Atiglo, Y. & Islam, N. (2019) Do deltas remain attractive? Testing the migration to coast hypothesis. *Ambio.* submitted.

De Haas, H. (2010) Migration and development: A theoretical perspective. *International Migration Review* 44, 227–264.

Dasgupta, S., Hossain, M. M., Huq, M., & Wheeler, D. (2015). Climate change and soil salinity: The case of coastal Bangladesh. *Ambio*, 44(8), 815–826.

de Sherbinin, A., Castro, M., Gemenne, F., Cernea, M.M., Adamo, S., Fearnside, P.M.,Krieger, G., Lahmani, S., Oliver-Smith, A., Pankhurst, A. & Scudder, T. (2011) Preparing for resettlement associated with climate change. *Science* 334, 456–457.

Dessai, S., Adger, W.N., Hulme, M., Turnpenny, J., Köhler, J. & Warren, R. (2004) Defining and experiencing dangerous climate change. *Climatic Change* 64, 11–25.

Dong, S., Wen, L., Liu, S., Zhang, X., Lassoie, J.P., Yi, S., Li, X., Li, J. & Li, Y. (2011) Vulnerability of worldwide pastoralism to global changes and interdisciplinary strategies for sustainable pastoralism. *Ecology and Society* 16(2), 10.

Foresight (2011). *Migration and Global Environmental Change: Future Challenges and Opportunities. Final Project Report.* London, UK: UK Government Office for Science, 236 pp.

Fussell, E., Curtis, K.J. & DeWaard, J. (2014) Recovery migration to the City of New Orleans after Hurricane Katrina: A migration systems approach. *Population and Environment* 35, 305–322.

Gemenne, F. (2011a) Climate-induced population displacements in a 4°C+ world. *Philosophical Transactions of the Royal Society A* 369, 182–195.

Gemenne, F. (2011b) Why the numbers don't add up: A review of estimates and predictions of people displaced by environmental changes. *Global Environmental Change* 21, S41–S49.

Gemenne, F. & Brücker, P. (2015) From the guiding principles on internal displacement to the Nansen initiative: What the governance of environmental migration can learn from the governance of internal displacement. *International Journal of Refugee Law* 27(2), 245–263.

Groen, J.A. & Polivka, A.E. (2010) Going home after Hurricane Katrina: Determinants of return migration and changes in affected areas. *Demography* 47, 821–844.

Hino, M., Field, C.B. & Mach, K.J. (2017) Managed retreat as a response to natural hazard risk. *Nature Climate Change* 7, 364–370.

Hugo, G. (2011) Future demographic change and its interactions with migration and climate change. *Global Environmental Change* 21, S21-S33.

Ivanic, M., Martin, W. & Zaman, H. (2012) Estimating the short-run poverty impacts of the 2010–11 surge in food prices. *World Development* 40, 2302–2317.

McAdam, J. & Ferris, E. (2015) Planned relocations in the context of climate change: Unpacking the legal and conceptual issues. *Cambridge Journal of International Comparative Law* 4, 137.

McLeman, R.A. (2014) *Climate and human migration: Past experiences, future challenges.* Cambridge University Press, New York, NY.

McLeman, R.A. & Hunter, L.M. (2010) Migration in the context of vulnerability and adaptation to climate change: Insights from analogues. *Wiley Interdisciplinary Reviews: Climate Change* 1, 450–461.

McNamara, K.E., Bronen, R., Fernando, N. & Klepp, S. (2018) The complex decision-making of climate-induced relocation: Adaptation and loss and damage. *Climate Policy* 18(1), 111–117.

Mia, M.A., Nasrin, S., Zhang, M. & Rasiah, R. (2015) Chittagong, Bangladesh. *Cities* 48, 31–41.

Mortreux, C., & Barnett, J. (2009). Climate change, migration and adaptation in Funafuti, Tuvalu. *Global Environmental Change*, 19(1), 105–112.

Mortreux, C., de Campos, R.S., Adger, W.N., Ghosh, T., Das, S., Adams, H. & Hazra, S. (2018) Political economy of planned relocation: A model of action and inaction in government responses. *Global Environmental Change* 50, 123–132.

Munro, A., Kovats, R. S., Rubin, G. J., Waite, T. D., Bone, A., Armstrong, B., ... & Oliver, I. (2017). Effect of evacuation and displacement on the association between flooding and mental health outcomes: a cross-sectional analysis of UK survey data. *The Lancet Planetary Health*, 1(4), e134–e141.

Nawrotzki, R.J., Hunter, L.M., Runfola, D.M. & Riosmena, F. (2015) Climate change as a migration driver from rural and urban Mexico. *Environmental Research Letters* 10, 114023.

Neumann, B., Vafeidis, A.T., Zimmermann, J. & Nicholls, R.J. (2015) Future coastal population growth and exposure to sea-level rise and coastal flooding-a global assessment. *PloS One* 10, e0118571.

Piguet, E. (2013) From primitive migration to climate refugees: The curious fate of the natural environment in migration studies. *Annals of the Association of American Geographers* 103, 148–162.

Piguet, E., Pécoud, A. & De Guchteneire, P. eds. (2011) *Migration and climate change*. Cambridge University Press, Cambridge.

Ransan-Cooper, H., Farbotko, C., McNamara, K.E., Thornton, F. & Chevalier, E. (2015) Beings framed: The means and ends of framing environmental migrants. *Global Environmental Change* 35, 106–115.

Rigaud, K.K., De Sherbinin, A.M., Jones, B., Bergmann, J., Clement, V., Ober, K., Schewe, J., Adamo, S.B., McCusker, B., Heuser, S. & Midgley, A. (2018) *Groundswell: Preparing for internal climate migration*. World Bank, Washington, DC.

Rigaud, K. K., Jones, B., Bergmann, J., Clement, V., Ober, K., Schewe, J., ... & Midgley, A. (2018). *Groundswell: Preparing for Internal Climate Migration*. Washington, DC: World Bank.

Rosenzweig, C., Karoly, D., Vicarelli, M., Neofotis, P., Wu, Q., Casassa, G., Menzel, A., Root, T.L., Estrella, N., Seguin, B. & Tryjanowski, P. (2008) Attributing physical and biological impacts to anthropogenic climate change. *Nature* 453, 353.

de Campos, R. S., Ardey Codjoe, S. N., Adger, W. N., Mortreux, C., Hazra, S., Siddiqui, T., Das, S., Atiglo, D. Y., Alam Bhuiyan, M. R., Rocky, M. H. & Abu, M. (2019) Where people live and move in deltas. In Nicholls, R.J., Adger, W.N., Hutton, C. & Hanson, S.E. eds. *Deltas in the Anthropecene*. Palgrave, London, pp. 153–177.

Seto, K. C. (2011). Exploring the dynamics of migration to mega-delta cities in Asia and Africa: Contemporary drivers and future scenarios. *Global Environmental Change*, 21, S94–S107.

Siddiqui, T., Neelim, A., Shabab, C.R. & Hasan, M. (2018) *Impact of migration on poverty and growth in Bangladesh*. Refugee and Migratory Movements Research Unit, Dhaka.

Sipe, N. & Vella, K. (2014) Relocating a flood-affected community: Good planning or good politics? *Journal of the American Planning Association* 80, 400–412.

Smith, J.B., Schneider, S.H., Oppenheimer, M. et al. (2009) Assessing dangerous climate change through an update of the Intergovernmental Panel on Climate Change reasons for concern. *Proceedings of the National Academy of Sciences* 106, 4133–4137.

Suckall, N., Fraser, E. & Forster, P. (2017) Reduced migration under climate change: Evidence from Malawi using an aspirations and capabilities framework. *Climate and Development* 9, 298–312.

Szabo, S., Brondizio, E., Renaud, F.G. et al. (2016) Population dynamics, delta vulnerability and environmental change: Comparison of the Mekong, Ganges–Brahmaputra and Amazon delta regions. *Sustainability Science* 11, 539–554.

te Lintelo, D.J.H., Gupte, J., McGregor, J.A., Lakshman, R. & Jahan, F. (2017) Wellbeing and urban governance: Who fails, survives or thrives in informal settlements in Bangladeshi cities? *Cities* 72, 391–402.

Thornton, P.K., Ericksen, P.J., Herrero, M. & Challinor, A.J. (2014) Climate variability and vulnerability to climate change: A review. *Global Change Biology* 20, 3313–3328.

Warner, K., Afifi, T., Kälin, W., Leckie, S., Ferris, B., Martin, S.F. & Wrathall, D. (2013) *Changing climate, moving people: Framing migration, displacement and planned relocation*. UNU-EHS, Bonn.

Watts, N., Adger, W.N., Agnolucci, P. et al. (2015) Lancet commission on health and climate change: Policy responses to protect public health. *The Lancet* 386, 1861–1914.

Williams, A. (2008) Turning the tide: Recognizing climate change refugees in international law. *Law and Policy* 30, 502–529.

36

ACUTE NATURAL DISASTERS AND DISPLACEMENT

Susan F. Martin

Introduction

Acute natural disasters are a principal cause of displacement, affecting all countries in the world. According to the Internal Displacement Monitoring Centre,

> With 24.2 million new displacements in 2016, disasters triggered by sudden onset hazard events continue to bring about the highest numbers of new displacements each year. A majority of these occur in low and lower-middle income countries and as a result of large-scale weather events, and predominantly in South and East Asia.
>
> *(IDMC 2017, 10)*

These disasters are caused by natural hazards that arrive with little or no warning. The International Federation of the Red Cross groups these hazards into four categories: geophysical (earthquakes, landslides, tsunamis, and volcanic activity), hydrological (avalanches and floods), climatological (extreme temperatures, drought and wildfires), meteorological (cyclones and storms/wave surges), or biological (disease epidemics and insect/animal plagues) (IFRC 2018). This chapter does not address displacement from slow-onset natural or human-made hazards, such as drought or rising sea levels. These slowly developing processes may trigger acute events, however, such as storm surges. Acute events of this type are within the scope of the chapter.

While potentially damaging, not all of these hazards result in large-scale disasters. Generally, it is only when the scale of the hazard exceeds the coping capacity at the local level that these situations rise to a crisis level (Ferris 2007; Martin et al. 2014). A confluence of natural hazards and poor governance in addressing the causes and consequences of such events may render large numbers of people at significant risk for their lives and well-being. In many of these situations, large-scale movements of people are the direct result.

Most movements resulting from acute disasters are internal to the countries experiencing the disaster (Foresight 2011). Large-scale internal displacement in the context of Typhoon Haiyan in the Philippines (Yonetani and Yuen 2014), the triple emergency of earthquake, tsunami, and nuclear accident in Japan (Meybatyan 2014), and Hurricanes Harvey and Maria in the United States (Campbell 2017; Raphelson 2017) are illustrative. Cross-border movements may also occur as people seek safety outside of their own countries to find safety and assistance (Weiss Fagen 2013; Martin et al. 2014; Nansen Initiative 2015). Most of these movements are temporary yet some people may remain displaced for long periods and still others may never be able to return to their home communities. These longer-term displacements are often the result of recurring hazards that prevent people from rebuilding their homes and communities.

At present, significant gaps exist in the capacity of states and international organisations to address the needs of those who are displaced by disasters of this type. This chapter begins with definitions of displacement, focusing on three dimensions that affect how people affected by disasters may be categorised – where movements take place, why they occur, and what is the phase of their displacement. The needs of disaster-displaced persons are then discussed. The chapter then turns to the laws and policies that apply to disaster displacement and the gaps that remain. It then describes recent efforts to improve policy responses. It concludes with reflections on the likely success of these efforts in filling the existing gaps and meeting new challenges ahead.

Definitions and dimensions of displacement

Policymakers tend to use a classification system that places those who flee life-threatening situations, such as disasters, in specific 'boxes', with the assumption that standards, mandates, and programmes will follow the designated classification. These categories reflect a number of dimensions. First, displaced persons are characterised by where the displacement takes place. Those who cross international borders are designated 'refugees' or 'externally displaced persons'; which label applies largely depends on the cause of the movement, as discussed below. Depending on whether they have received permission to enter another country, they may also be designated 'undocumented, unauthorised, or illegal' migrants. By contrast, those who remain within their national borders are 'internally-displaced persons' (IDPs).

Second, those who flee dangerous situations are defined in accordance with the causes of their movements. The United Nations Convention Relating to the Status of Refugees (1951) gives specific recognition to people who flee because of a well-founded fear of persecution. If they cross an international boundary, they are 'refugees'. Those fleeing conflict may also be specially designated, either by convention (e.g. the Organization of African Unity 1969 Refugee Convention) or because the UN High Commissioner for Refugees, the international organisation granted responsibility for protecting and assisting refugees, designates them as persons of concern. By contrast, no binding international legal framework exists to address displacement due to other causes, regardless of how life threatening they may be. Those who cross international borders as a result of natural disasters, for example, are generally not covered by the refugee convention. The *Guiding Principles on Internal Displacement* (UN Office of the High Commissioner for Human Rights 1998), which draws on existing human rights instruments to describe the protections that should be accorded to IDPs, apply to a broad range of causes of displacement, including disasters, but unlike refugee law, they are not legally binding.

The third dimension relates to time. Persons are often defined by the phase of their displacement. During the emergency phase, those who are displaced may need special attention because of the instability of the situation (MICIC 2016; Nansen Initiative 2015). Many are and may remain for days or weeks in life-threatening conditions. Most refugees and IDPs, however, are in protracted situations, sometimes lasting for decades (UNHCR 2018). There is scant information about the numbers of disaster displaced who have been displaced for longer periods but that appears to be the case in many situations (IDMC 2015). The needs and challenges differ in many ways from the emergency phase. While no longer facing life-threatening conditions, those in protracted situations may be in camps or makeshift accommodation and most lack economic opportunities for themselves and their families. Still other challenges arise for those who find solutions to their displacement. These people may be re-designated 'returnees' if they are able to go back to their home communities or 'resettled' if they are able to integrate into new communities. These formulations have arisen in the context of conflict-induced displacement, but they often apply in other situations. Those forced to migrate because of acute disasters, for example, may remain displaced for protracted periods, finding that they are unable to return, perhaps permanently, to homes that have been destroyed and places that are no longer habitable. Some may be required to be relocated to other locations under these circumstances.

To a large extent, this approach has succeeded in raising the visibility of groups of displaced persons who heretofore had been either ignored or had fallen between the cracks in the international system. This has particularly been the case in designating IDPs as a category of concern to the international community. It also allows targeted responses to issues arising from the specific cause or phase of an emergency. Options for those driven from their homes by conflict are different in nature and scope than those applicable to persons driven from their homes by natural disasters. The same approach does not make sense in every stage of a crisis or in the context of each of the various solutions outlined here.

There are limits to the approach that has been taken to date, however. The categories of displacement are not mutually exclusive; more often they are overlapping, not only among themselves but with forms of migration that are generally seen as 'voluntary'. The victims of humanitarian emergencies may belong to more than one group, either at the same time or in close sequence. To take the 2004 tsunami as an example, many of the survivors in Sri Lanka and Indonesia were displaced by conflict as well as natural disaster. In other situations, people repatriate following a disaster, thereby earning the designation 'returnees', only to find themselves newly designated 'IDPs' because they are unable to go back to their home communities. In still other cases, migrants have mixed motives in moving to another location: they may be leaving because conflict, natural disasters, or environmental factors (or a combination of all three) have disrupted their lives, but they are attracted by the economic opportunities available in destination countries or communities.

Needs of disaster-displaced persons

All displaced populations, regardless of cause, require protection, assistance, and recovery. Protection involves legal protection of the rights of the displaced, particularly the right not to be forced to return to a situation in which their lives would be endangered (Nansen Initiative 2015). Protection also requires that those affected by natural disasters are physically safe during and after their displacement (Cohen and Bradley 2010). Natural disaster victims are highly vulnerable, particularly when they have lost their possessions and are separated from family and community; host populations grow concerned about competition for resources or the displaced themselves lash out against what they see as an untenable situation (Cohen and Bradley 2010; Martin et al. 2014; MICIC 2016). Women and children often bear the brunt of violence; rates of sexual and gender-based violence may increase in the aftermath of disasters along with human trafficking (IASC 2006, Nansen Initiative 2015; MICIC 2016).

Those who are uprooted also require food and non-food items, health care, sanitation, water, shelter, education, and restoration of their livelihood. Distribution of food, cooking utensils, clothing, sanitary materials, and other customary items that families need are among the highest priorities in displacement from natural disasters (Sphere Project 2011). During the emergency phase, assistance tends to focus on immediate needs, but as these situations become more protracted, and in the absence of functioning markets, the assistance system may take on greater and greater responsibilities to ensure that basic needs are met.

Persons with pre-existing physical and socio-economic vulnerabilities are at high risk during displacement. Difficulties accessing food, poor sanitation, and contaminated water supplies contribute to high death rates in many of these situations; at the same time, standard public health practices in displaced persons' camps can afford protection and reduce the risk of epidemics in these situations. In Haiti, for example, many people fled from the cholera epidemic that occurred following the earthquake but those who were already living in IDP camps were less likely than other populations to succumb to the disease because of the public health measures enacted (Piarroux et al. 2011). Those who are forced to move can suffer from physical disabilities resulting from the disaster itself or the flight thereafter. For example, they may be the victims of collapsed construction. Loss of limbs is not uncommon both in flight and during displacement.

Displaced women have higher mortality rates during and after natural disasters than men, due largely to their lower socio-economic status (Neumayer 2007). Complications from pregnancy exacerbate the situation when there is a lack of training of midwives and traditional birth attendants (TBA); septic abortions, unsanitary conditions during birth, septic instruments, poor lighting during deliveries, and frequency of pregnancies all lead to difficulties. The December 2004 tsunami, for example,

> caused sex-specific death on a scale that has devastated families and family life ... It also devastated many of the healthcare services that are essential to sound antenatal care and delivery, killing large numbers of midwives in Indonesia and medical personnel in other countries, and destroying vital physical infrastructures.
>
> *(Carballo 2005, 402)*

At a minimum, the displaced may face emotional problems and difficulties in adjustment resulting from loss of family and community support. Depression and post-traumatic stress disorder (PTSD) sometimes follow disasters.

Shelter is a principal need of those displaced by a natural disaster. Unlike settled populations, displaced persons arrive in camps or urban areas without ready access to housing. Decisions about shelter and camp location and layout, more generally, greatly affect the physical security of displaced persons. Where shelter is located also affects access to services and work. Female-headed households, elderly persons without family, disabled persons, and those who were already living in extreme poverty are often particularly disadvantaged in obtaining decent shelter when displaced. Often, they find themselves on the periphery of camps or in slums in urban areas. Women heads of households may find it difficult to return and rebuild their homes because of restrictive property rights (Sphere Project 2011).

Displacement also disrupts education and work. During emergencies, households are often unable to continue their regular activities, whether in farming, trades, businesses, professions, or other sectors. Children often experience abrupt closure of schools and interruptions in their education. This loss of the capacity for self-support often precipitates displacement, which further disrupts access to work, particularly if displaced persons have no access to land, employment, or markets in which they can sell their products. Survival may then lead to longer-term dependency on humanitarian assistance or, if that assistance is not available, a range of negative coping strategies, including prostitution and crime. Returning home or integrating into a new location may not mean that displaced persons regain their livelihoods. Damage to the economy, loss of infrastructure, and continuing instability and insecurity may well make it difficult for them to find the means of making a living.

A group of particular concern in natural disasters are foreign nationals living in the affected areas (MICIC 2016). Although natural disasters generally affect all persons equally, migrants may be at a heightened risk because of pre-existing vulnerabilities; they

> may disproportionately live in poor neighbourhoods with no access to transportation to flee from harm's way. They may not be able to afford to live in houses that conform to earthquake resistant and other building codes. Specific groups of migrants, such as domestic workers may be left behind as their employers flee in the face of crises.
>
> *(Martin 2016, 3)*

Evacuation during disasters can be difficult for migrant workers. A study of migrant workers from Myanmar attempting to return home during massive floods in Thailand found many were 'detained at the border by immigration authorities, charged excessive amounts by brokers, and extorted once inside Burma', according to a Thai Ministry of Finance and World Bank report (Ministry of Finance 2012, 244).

Disaster-induced displacement: legal and institutional frameworks

As natural disasters have grown in intensity and frequency and knowledge about the often-significant loss of life accompanying some disasters has also increased, concerns have mounted that many governments have little capacity and still others have little will to assist and protect those who are displaced by such events. Some disasters are of such scale that the affected population is displaced beyond the borders of the country or cannot return home because of the devastation to their communities, creating an international, not just a domestic, issue. Haiti after the 2010 earthquake is a case in point, as people fled internally, across the border into the Dominican Republic and to further destinations such as Brazil and the United States (Ferris 2014).

Most disaster displacement is internal. The Internal Displacement Monitoring Centre estimates that 'since 2008, an average of 26.4 million people per year have been displaced from their homes by disasters brought on by natural hazards' (IDMC 2015, 8). The Guiding Principles on Internal Displacement define the internally displaced as

> persons or groups of persons who have been forced or obliged to flee or to leave their homes or places of habitual residence, in particular as a result of or in order to avoid the effects of armed conflict, situations of generalized violence, violations of human rights or meant [emphasis added] *natural or human-made disasters*, and who have not crossed an internationally recognized State border.
>
> *(UN Office of the High Commissioner for Human Rights 1998)*

Although the Guiding Principles are not binding, many governments have incorporated their provisions into national law. Significantly, the African Union's Convention on Internally Displaced Persons specifically calls on States Parties to 'take measures to protect and assist persons who have been internally displaced due to natural or human-made disasters, including climate change' (African Union 2009, 8).

No legally binding conventions exist that apply specifically to persons whose displacement across borders results from natural disasters. The UN Convention on the Protection of All Migrant Workers and Members of their Families would apply if those who move enter the labour market in a host country. There are no specific provisions, however, within the Migrant Workers Convention for those moving because of disasters compared to any other reasons. Some may be covered under the 1951 UN Convention Relating to the Status of Refugees and its 1967 Protocol[1]. The Convention uses a persecution-based definition of a refugee and few persons seeking protection because of natural disasters are likely to meet the criteria unless they are unable to access aid because they fear persecution.[2]

Despite the lack of law and formal policies, governments frequently respond, albeit mostly in an ad hoc way, to those who have been displaced by natural hazards. The 2010 earthquake in Haiti provides a good example of humanitarian admissions policies that were used by governments to protect persons not already on their territory and who did not qualify as refugees. The Dominican Republic responded almost immediately, permitting an estimated 160,000 Haitians to cross onto its territory. Many of those permitted entry had been seriously injured and required medical care. Family members of patients were also allowed to enter the Dominican Republic to stay with the injured during their convalescence (Weiss Fagen 2013).

Other Haitians received humanitarian visas to enter Brazil. At first, the Haitians applied for asylum but the Brazilian government determined that they did not fit the refugee definition. Also, recognising that they were not seeking admission for purely economic reasons, Brazil offered the alternative of humanitarian visas. Initially, the determinations were made at the border. Thousands of Haitians had travelled to Ecuador, which had suspended visa requirements for Haitians in 2008, and then made their way to the Brazilian border. Subsequently, Brazil instituted processing procedures in Haiti for persons seeking humanitarian admissions. At first, these were for temporary admissions, but Brazil now has a category for permanent admissions. In September 2015, the International Organization for Migration (IOM) established the Brazil Visa Application Centre (BVAC) to facilitate applications for these visas.

Countries such as Canada and the United States sped up the entry of persons who had already applied for admission, recognising that they would remain in life-threatening situations if forced to wait for their turn in the admissions queue. In Canada, for example, 'this meant expediting and to some extent stretching the existing immigration categories through which Haitians would be eligible to come to Canada without changing existing immigration rules and regulations' (Weiss Fagen 2013, 23). These applied primarily to family reunification applications. The province of Quebec, which controls its own immigration policy, expanded its notion of family reunification to include 'formerly inadmissible categories of adult brothers and sisters, step-brothers and -sisters and adult children, along with their own families' (Ibid., 24). As a result, Quebec admitted about 9000 Haitians in 2010 alone.

Governments have also applied policies for the deferral of deportation of those displaced by natural disasters. These range from statutory measures to ad hoc ones. One of the most well-developed statutory provisions is in US legislation enacted in 1990 to provide temporary protected status to persons 'in the United States who are temporarily unable to safely return to their home country because of ongoing armed conflict, an environmental disaster, or other extraordinary and temporary conditions' (Immigration and Naturalization Act, as amended in, 1990). Environmental disaster may include 'an earthquake, flood, drought, epidemic, or other environmental disaster in the state resulting in a substantial, but temporary, disruption of living conditions in the area affected'. Importantly, TPS only applies to persons already in the United States at the time of the designation. It is not meant to be a mechanism to respond to an unfolding crisis in which people seek admission from outside of the country. It also only pertains to situations that are temporary in nature. Countries are often re-designated and 'temporary' protection is offered to their nationals over lengthy periods. For example, TPS was originally triggered in 1999 by Hurricane Mitch, which had severe impacts on Nicaragua and Honduras. Its most recent extension is until 5 January 2018.[3] Those granted TPS are left in limbo throughout these periods; they are unable to become permanent residents unless they meet the criteria of other immigration statuses (e.g. they have married a US citizen).[4]

A number of other countries provide exceptions to removal on an ad hoc basis for persons whose countries of origin have experienced significant disruption because of natural disasters. After the 2004 tsunami, for example, Switzerland, the United Kingdom, and Canada suspended deportations of those from such countries as Sri Lanka, India, Somalia, Maldives, Seychelles, Indonesia, and Thailand. A number of governments announced similar plans after the 2010 earthquake in Haiti.

The international institutional framework for responding to natural-disaster-induced displacement is equally weak. Under the cluster approach, the International Organization for Migration has lead responsibility for camp management when people are displaced by natural disasters. As in the case of conflict-induced displacement, the arrangement is new and largely untested. Moreover, unlike UNHCR, IOM does not have a mandate for or significant experience in protecting displaced populations, and as noted above, in the cluster system UNHCR's protection responsibilities are limited to those displaced by conflict. When a government is willing to offer its own protection, the absence of international protection may not be a problem, but when governments are unwilling or unable to protect their citizens, the displaced may be left without access to assistance or safety and security, as evidenced by the case of cyclone Nargis in Burma/Myanmar.

The UNHCR has been drawn, albeit in an ad hoc way, into providing assistance during several notable natural disasters, particularly in countries in which it was already working with conflict-induced displaced. For example, in the *State of the World's Refugees*, UNHCR explained its involvement in tsunami relief in Sri Lanka: 'UNHCR's presence in the country prior to the tsunami allowed for a comparatively swift and sustained humanitarian intervention – including efforts focused on the protection of internally displaced persons' (UNHCR 2006, 21). The UNHCR also assisted tsunami victims in Somalia and Aceh, Indonesia, pointing out that, 'The protection of displaced populations was especially urgent in areas of protracted conflict and internal displacement in Aceh, Somalia and Sri Lanka' (UNHCR 2006, 21).

New developments

Given the dearth of legal, policy, and institutional frameworks at the international, regional, or national level specifically focused on disaster displacement, a number of initiatives have been launched to promote guidelines that would be applicable in these situations. Sir Peter Sutherland (2016), the first Special Representative of the Secretary General on International Migration, dubbed these efforts mini-multilateralism, that is, efforts by states to develop non-binding guidance based on existing principles and effective practices. The success of the Guiding Principles on Internal Displacement in shifting perceptions and practices in countries throughout the world (including the promulgation of a regional convention in Africa) is the backdrop for these efforts. This section discusses two such initiatives that pertain to displacement in the context of natural disasters: (1) the Nansen Initiative and its successor, the Platform on Disaster Displacement; and (2) the Migrants in Countries in Crisis (MICIC) initiative. It also discusses two initiatives at the global level that culminated in recommendations related to disaster displacement: (1) The Task Force on Disaster Displacement, established under the UN Framework Convention on Climate Change (UNFCCC); and (2) the Global Compact for Safe, Orderly and Regular Migration.

The Nansen Initiative and the platform on disaster displacement

The Nansen Initiative was launched in 2011 at a Ministerial Conference commemorating the 60th anniversary of UNHCR's founding and adoption of the 1951 Refugee Convention (UNHCR 2011). The aim was to develop an agenda for improving the protection of people displaced across borders by natural disasters and the slow onset effects of climate change. The Nansen Initiative did 'not seek to develop new legal standards, but rather to build consensus among states on the elements of a protection agenda, which may include standards of treatment'.[5] There was no expectation that the process would lead to a set of Guiding Principles on Cross-Border Displacement that would be equivalent to the ones developed for internally-displaced persons. Rather, the Nansen Initiative sought to identify existing practices that complement refugee and other humanitarian protection regimes in use by countries in protecting those who are displaced by natural disasters and other forms of environmental change.

The Agenda for Protection, adopted as the outcome of the Nansen Initiative, focuses on three principal areas of action. The first is to improve the collection of data and to enhance knowledge on cross-border disaster-induced displacement. The second area of the agenda focuses on 'humanitarian protection measures for cross-border disaster-displaced persons, including mechanisms for lasting solutions' (Nansen Initiative 2015, 44). The agenda points to the need for new legal instruments and policies that would, for example, grant 'temporary entry and stay for cross-border disaster-displaced persons, such as through the issuance of humanitarian visas or other exceptional migration measures' (Nansen Initiative 2015, 26). The third set of recommendations is aimed at strengthening the management of disaster displacement risk in the country of origin so that those affected by natural disasters and the effects of climate change would not need to cross international borders. Finally, the agenda notes that legal migration provisions can prevent displacement since they allow people to move in a safe and orderly manner.

The agenda was endorsed by 109 governmental delegations during a global multi-sectoral consultation in October 2015. Those who spoke at the consultation noted the utility of the agenda and the flexibility of governments to adopt its recommendations in accord with national law. Subsequently, the German government took on the chairmanship of the process, announcing the Platform on Disaster Displacement (PDD) in May 2016 at the World Humanitarian Summit in Istanbul. The PDD has four main goals in furthering the Agenda for Protection. First, it seeks to address knowledge and data gaps (Platform on Disaster Displacement 2016a). The second aim is to promote policy and normative development to fill gaps in protection, as outlined in the protection agenda (Platform on Disaster Displacement 2016b). The third aim flows naturally from the second area for the PDD. The aim is to enhance the use of effective practices identified by the Nansen Initiative. Mainstreaming disaster-induced displacement across sectors, mandates and areas of expertise related to its multi-causality is the fourth aim of the PDD.

Migrants in countries in crisis

The origins of the MICIC Initiative are similar to Nansen, whose success influenced its development. The mass displacement of migrant workers in Libya during the 2011 conflict, followed by similar conflict-related crises in Cote d'Ivoire and Syria, in addition to the natural disasters in Japan, Thailand, and the United States that affected millions of non-nationals, generated substantial interest among governments, civil society, and the private sector.

Following regional consultations and research, MICIC developed a set of principles, guidelines, and effective practices that were presented on 15 June 2016 in the United Nations. The principles focused on core rights and responsibilities and set out the duty to save lives in conflict and disasters. The principles and resulting guidelines emphasise that States have primary responsibility but that other stakeholders, including non-nationals themselves, play an important role in ensuring protection (MICIC 2016).

MICIC emphasised integration of the needs and capabilities of migrants into existing disaster risk reduction, early warning, emergency preparedness, and emergency response systems, with particular attention to migrant-specific issues such as their ability to read and comprehend the host language. It urged states to institute awareness-raising programmes for migrants about prevention, preparedness, and emergency response procedures in host countries. Recognising that some migrants may leave post natural disaster, while others enter affected areas, MICIC also recommended measures to prevent exploitation of migrants working in post-disaster reconstruction jobs by providing prevailing wages, monitoring work conditions, providing safety equipment as needed, and enforcing laws against human smuggling, trafficking in persons, and occupational health and safety and other labour violations (MICIC 2016).

UNFCCC task force on displacement

In 2015, the parties to the UNFCCC adopted a resolution to establish a task force to 'develop recommendations for integrated approaches to avert, minimise and address displacement related to the adverse impacts of climate change' (UNFCCC 2018). The task force was to focus on both cross-border and internal movements. Its members included 13 representatives, mostly from UN agencies. Its 2018 report outlined a number of recommendations for states and the UN system. In particular, the task force called on parties to the UNFCCC to consider formulating human rights oriented national and subnational legislation, policies, and strategies, using an integrated approach, to avert, minimise, and address climate-change related displacement; enhance research, data collection, risk analysis, and sharing of information, in a way that involves communities affected and at-risk of displacement; strengthen preparedness through early warning systems, contingency planning, evacuation planning, and resilience building strategies and plans; integrate displacement into national planning processes; consider ways to assist internally-displaced persons, taking into account the Guiding Principles on Internal Displacement; and facilitate orderly, safe, regular, and responsible migration and mobility of people (Task Force 2018). This last recommendation is addressed more fully by the global compact discussed next.

Global Compact for Safe, Orderly, and Regular Migration

The 2016 High Level Meeting on Large Movements of Refugees and Migrants resulted in the NY Declaration, which in turn committed to the negotiation of a global compact that would address all sectors of migration, with the exception of refugees (which would be addressed in a separate compact).[6] The process through which the global compact on migration would be adopted began with a fact-finding stage, culminating in a global stock-taking meeting, and then a negotiation stage during which states set out commitments with regard to both substance and process moving forward. The compact itself would be non-binding but represent the consensus of states with regard to best practice. It laid out objectives, commitments, and recommended actions in 23 areas, ranging from prevention of irregular migration to (re-)integration of migrants.

The compact included a number of commitments related to migration, displacement, and relocation across borders as a result of sudden- and slow-onset natural disasters, environmental degradation, and the adverse effects of climate change. The most detailed relate to the drivers of disaster displacement. Objective 2 of the compact sets out commitments

> to create conducive political, economic, social and environmental conditions for people to lead peaceful, productive and sustainable lives in their own country … while ensuring that desperation and deteriorating environments do not compel them to seek a livelihood elsewhere through irregular migration (para 17).
> *(Global Compact 2018)*

The compact is specific in setting out a series of actions related to the environmental drivers that are deemed instrumental in helping States deliver on their commitments. For example, they could invest in programmes to ameliorate adverse drivers and structural factors that compel people to leave their home countries from either sudden-onset events (e.g. natural disasters) or slow-onset processes, such as 'desertification, land degradation, drought and sea level rise' (para 17j). The actions include 'resilience and disaster risk reduction' and 'climate change mitigation and adaptation' strategies (para 17d). The compact references the need for cooperation among neighbouring and other countries to ensure more effective 'early warning, contingency planning, stockpiling, coordination mechanisms, evacuation planning, reception and assistance arrangements, and public information' (para 17k). Recognising that large-scale displacement often results from a lack of capacity to respond quickly and effectively to acute natural hazards, the compact notes strategies to identify 'risks and threats that might trigger or affect internal and onward cross-border migration movements' (para 17e) and 'joint analysis and sharing of information to better map, understand, predict and address migration movements' (para 17f) (Global Compact 2018).

Objective 5 sets out policies that may help manage situations arising from disaster displacement. It aims to enhance the availability and flexibility of pathways for regular migration (para 20). Paragraph 20(g) recommends that States develop or build on existing national and regional practices that provide for admission and stay 'based on compassionate, humanitarian or other considerations' when migrants 'face unsurmountable obstacles to return, including due to sudden-onset natural disasters' (Global Compact 2018). Paragraph 20(h) cites humanitarian visas, private sponsorships, access to education for children, and temporary work permits as potential strategies for accomplishing the objective (Global Compact 2018).

The negotiations culminated in a summit in Marrakesh, in which the final language was approved, and then a formal vote in the General Assembly. The compact was approved by a large majority. However, some countries with high levels of immigration, such as the US, Australia, and some EU countries, either rejected it outright or abstained from voting for it.

Conclusion

This review of trends in disaster displacement identifies some areas of research and policy development that are needed to respond more effectively. In the area of research, more attention is needed for improving the evidence base on the multi-faceted ways in which disasters affect displacement and the need for better solutions. Further, additional research is needed on the impact of disaster displacement on the well-being of the displaced, communities of origin, and communities of destination. As compared to even 10 years ago, however, there has been great progress in filling the gaps in evidence and knowledge of the mobility implications of disasters. The Nansen Initiative commissioned considerable research on the topic and the Internal Displacement Monitoring Centre is now producing estimates of the numbers displaced by disasters each year. With the increasing attention of governments to these issues, there is reason for cautious optimism that this progress will continue.

At the law and policy level, there are also grounds for cautious optimism from the mini-multilateralism of the Nansen and MICIC Initiatives as well as the Task Force on Displacement and the global compact. Unlike earlier efforts that focused primarily on the adoption of binding international conventions, these initiatives are less formal, more ad hoc and less binding. The ad hoc nature of these processes allows them to address emerging issues and concerns more effectively than more formal mechanisms that are often tied to specific mandates. They also represent a more pragmatic approach given the reluctance of states to adopt and ratify new binding instruments related to movements of people.

They are also very practical in setting out an agenda for action. The Nansen Initiative has been succeeded by the Platform for Disaster Displacement. The MICIC initiative also included a follow-up mechanism for helping states implement the guidelines. A similar process, led by Georgetown University, UNHCR and other international organisations, has developed principles, guidelines, and an operational toolkit to help states plan and implement planned relocation policies and programmes when needed to avert displacement or find solutions for those already displaced by disasters. At the global level, the Task Force on Displacement has set out an agenda for parties to the UNFCCC, the global compact has outlined specific objectives and commitments as well as a review mechanism to assess implementation, and a new Network on Migration was established to help coordinate UN agency activities.

Further, these processes have been highly inclusive in terms of regional scope and participation. Members of the steering/working groups have come from all regions. Regional variations have been solicited in consultations that brought together governments, civil society, the private sector, international organisations, and the research community. The resulting recommendations have been vetted with multiple stakeholders.

This is not to say that the ad hoc, non-binding nature of the process is without problems. Protection of the disaster displaced is still highly dependent on the willingness of States to implement the guiding principles and the international community to intercede when States are unwilling or unable to fulfil their responsibilities. Enhancing protection of those displaced by natural disasters and the impacts of climate change will require sustained attention. Mechanisms described herein, and their follow-up, are promising ways to foster greater attention to the protection gaps and practical solutions to improve the lives of millions of people affected by crises. In the long term, however, they will only be as effective as the willingness of states and other stakeholders to implement the recommendations and offer protection on a non-discriminatory basis to all who are affected by disasters.

Notes

1 The protocol eliminated geographic (that refugees be from Europe) and time limits (pre-1951) on the Convention, making it a universal document.
2 In Africa, the scope of coverage might be greater because the 1969 OAU (now AU) Refugee Convention includes those who,

> owing to external aggression, occupation, foreign domination or *events seriously disturbing public order in either part or the whole of his country of origin or nationality* (emphasis added), is compelled to leave his place of habitual residence in order to seek refuge in another place outside his country of origin or nationality.

3 The Trump administration has tried to end TPS protections for several countries affected by natural disasters, including Nicaragua, Haiti, and El Salvador, but the case is still in litigation.
4 If the environmental disaster has permanent consequences, however, a designation of Temporary Protected Status is not available or it may be lifted. When a volcano erupted in Montserrat in 1997, TPS was granted to its citizens and was extended six times. In 2005, however, it was ended because 'it is likely that the eruptions will continue for decades, [and] the situation that led to Montserrat's designation can no longer be considered "temporary" as required by Congress when it enacted the TPS statute'.
5 The Nansen Initiative website, 'About us', available at www.nanseninitiative.org/secretariat/
6 The discussion of environmental drivers was less well developed in the Global Compact on Refugees than in the migration compact.

References

African Union. (2009). *Convention for the Protection and Assistance of Internally Displaced Persons in Africa (Kampala Convention)*. https://au.int/en/treaties/african-union-convention-protection-and-assistance-internally-displaced-persons-africa, last accessed 26th April 2019.

Campbell, A.F. (2017). *5 things to know about Puerto Rico 100 days after Hurricane Maria*. Vox News. www.vox.com/2017/12/23/16795342/puerto-rico-maria-christmas, last accessed 26th April 2019.

Carballo, M., M. Hernandez, K. Schneider and E. Welle. (2005) "Impact of the Tsunami on reproductive health." *Journal of the Royal Society of Medicine*, 98, 400–403.

Cohen, R. and M. Bradley. (2010) "Disasters and Displacement: Gaps in Protection." *Journal of International Humanitarian Legal Studies*, 1, 63–78.

Ferris, E. (2007) *Making Sense of Climate Change, Natural Disasters, and Displacement: A Work in Progress.* Lecture at The Calcutta Research Group Winter Course, 14 December 2007. Washington, DC: Brookings Institution.

Ferris, E. (2014) "Recurrent Acute Disasters, Crisis Migration: Haiti Has Had It All" in S. Martin, S. Weerasinghe and A. Taylor, eds. *Humanitarian Crises and Migration: Causes, Consequences and Responses.* New York: Routledge Press, 77–96.

Foresight. (2011) *Migration and Global Environmental Change: Final Project Report.* London: The Government Office for Science.

Global Compact for Safe, Orderly and Regular Migration. (2018) https://refugeesmigrants.un.org/sites/default/files/180711_final_draft_0.pdf, last accessed 26th April 2019.

Immigration and Naturalization Act, as amended in 1990. *Temporary Protected Status.* Sec. 244. 1/[8 U.S. C. 1254].

Interagency Standing Committee (IASC). (2011) *Protecting Persons Affected by Natural Disasters: IASC Operational Guidelines on Human Rights and Natural Disasters.* Washington DC: Brookings Institution.

Internal Displacement Monitoring Centre. (2015) *Estimates 2015: People Displaced by Disasters.* Geneva: IDMC, www.internal-displacement.org/publications/global-estimates-2015-people-displaced-by-disasters, last accessed 26th April 2019.

Internal Displacement Monitoring Centre. (2017) *Global Report on Internal Displacement.* Geneva: IDMC. www.internal-displacement.org/global-report/grid2017/, Last accessed on 01/ 23/2018.

International Federation of Red Cross Societies. (2018) *Types of disasters: Definition of hazard.* Web resource. www.ifrc.org/en/what-we-do/disaster-management/about-disasters/definition-of-hazard/, last accessed 26th April 2019.

Martin, S. (2016) *Conflict or Natural Disaster: Does It Matter for Migrants?* Geneva: IOM. https://micici nitiative.iom.int/resources-and-publications/conflict-or-natural-disaster-does-it-matter-migrants, last accessed 26th April 2019.

Martin, S., S. Weerasinghe and A. Taylor, eds. (2014) *Humanitarian Crises and Migration: Causes, Consequences and Responses.* New York: Routledge Press.

Meybatyan, S. (2014) Nuclear Disasters and Displacement. *Forced Migration Review* 45 www.fmreview. org/crisis.html, last accessed 26th April 2019.

MICIC (Migrants in Countries in Crisis Initiative) (2016) *Guidelines to Protect Migrants in Countries Experiencing Conflict or Natural Disaster.* Geneva: IOM.

Ministry of Finance, Royal Thai Government and The World Bank. (18 January 2012) *Thailand Flooding 2554: Rapid Assessment for Resilient Recovery and Reconstruction Planning.*

Nansen Initiative. (2015) *Agenda for the Protection of Cross-Border Displaced Persons in the Context of Disasters and Climate Change.* Vol. I, Geneva: Nansen Initiative.

Neumayer, E. (2007) "The Gendered Nature of Natural Disasters: The Impact of Catastrophic Events on the Gender Gap in Life Expectancy, 1981–2002." *Annals of the Association of American Geographers*, 97(3), 551–566.

Organization of African Unity (1969) *Convention Governing the Specific Aspects of Refugee Problems in Africa*, United Nations, Treaty Series No. 14691. www.unhcr.org/45dc1a682.html, last accessed 26th April 2019.

Piarroux, R., R. Barrais, B. Faucher, R. Haus, M. Piarroux, J. Gaudart, R. Magloire, and D. Raoult. (2011) "Understanding the Cholera Epidemic, Haiti." *Emerging Infectious Disease*, 17(7): 1161–1168.

Platform on Disaster Displacement. (2016a) *Address Knowledge and Data Gaps.* http://disasterdisplace ment.org/address-knowledge-and-data-gaps, Last accessed on 10/4/2017.

Platform on Disaster Displacement. (2016b) *Promote Policy and Normative Development in Gap Areas.* Geneva: Platform on Disaster Displacement. http://disasterdisplacement.org/promote-policy-and-nor mative-development-in-gap-areas/, Last accessed on 10/4/2017.

Raphelson, S. (2017) *In Houston, Thousands Remain Displaced As Harvey Recovery Continues.* National Public Radio. www.npr.org/2017/12/28/574166438/in-houston-thousands-remain-displaced-as-harvey-recovery-continues.

Sphere Project. (2011) *The Sphere Handbook: Humanitarian Charter and Minimum Standards in Humanitarian Response.* Geneva: Sphere Project.

Sutherland, P.D. (2016) Remarks by the Special Representative of the UN Secretary General on International Migration. Delivered at the UN DESA Coordination Meeting. 25 February 2016. https:// www.un.org/en/development/desa/population/migration/events/coordination/14/documents/pres entations/Peter_Sutherland_14CM.pdf.

UNFCCC (2018) Report of the Task Force on Displacement. https://unfccc.int/sites/default/files/ resource/2018_TFD_report_17_Sep.pdf, accessed on 8 October 2018.

UNHCR. (2006) *State of the World's Refugees: Human Displacement in the New Millennium.* Geneva: UNHCR.

UNHCR. (2011) *Ministerial Communique: Intergovernmental Event at the Ministerial Level of Member States of the United Nations on the Occasion of the 60th Anniversary of the 1951 Convention Relating to the Status of Refugees and the 50th Anniversary of the 1961 Convention on the Reduction of Statelessness.* HCR/MIN-COMMS/2011/6 (8 December 2011). www.unhcr.org/4ee210d89.pdf, last accessed on 10/4/2017.

UNHCR. (2018) *First Draft Global Compact on Refugees.* Geneva: UNHCR.

United Nations Convention Relating to the Status of Refugees. (1951) www.unhcr.org/cgi-bin/texis/ vtx/home/opendocPDFViewer.html?docid=3b66c2aa10&query=UN%20Convention%20Relating% 20to%20the%20Status%20of%20Refugees, last accessed 26th April 2019.

United Nations Office for the Coordination of Humanitarian Affairs, Guiding Principles on Internal Displacement. (1998) available at www.ohchr.org/EN/Issues/IDPersons/Pages/Standards.aspx, last accessed 26th April 2019.

Weiss Fagen, P. (2013) *Receiving Haitian Migrants in the Context of the 2010 Earthquake.* Geneva: Nansen Initiative.

Yonetani, M. and Lorell Y. (2014). The Evolving Picture of Displacement in the Wake of Typhoon Haiyan. Geneva: International Organization for Migration. www.iom.int/files/live/sites/iom/files/ Country/docs/The-Evolving-Picture-of-Displacement-in-the-Wake-of-Typhoon-Haiyan.pdf (last accessed 26th April 2019).

37

EFFECTS OF ANTI-TRAFFICKING POLICIES ON MIGRANTS

Mike Dottridge

Introduction

Migrants routinely experience abuse, both international migrants and individuals working far from home in their own country. Various international agreements have been adopted in recent decades to minimise abuse and ensure that migrants and their families are not the subject of discrimination. Those migrants who have been trafficked are by definition known to be in a particularly vulnerable situation. In theory, the United Nations (UN) addressed their vulnerability when it adopted a new international Protocol on trafficking in persons in 2000. In practice, however, much evidence exists that, rather than protecting migrants, this Protocol has caused problems for many. This chapter explains what international agreements mean by 'trafficking in persons', how various governments have chosen to interpret the term and what some of the impacts have been for migrants themselves.

What is human trafficking – definitions

In the late 1990s, the UN developed an international Convention on Transnational Organized Crime, adopted by the UN General Assembly in November 2000. It set out to facilitate cooperation between law enforcement officials in different countries in investigating, prosecuting, and punishing criminal organisations which engaged in cross-border crime or which were based in one country while committing offences in another: 'to promote cooperation to prevent and combat transnational organized crime more effectively' (UN Convention on Transnational Organized Crime, Article 1). By 'organized crime', the Convention referred to a 'structured group of three or more persons'.

However, discussions on the new Convention occurred a decade after the end of the Cold War and in the immediate aftermath of the wars in former Yugoslavia. This was when politicians in Western Europe, in particular, were concerned about an increase in irregular immigration from former communist countries in central and eastern Europe. At this time, there were also reports that large numbers of women and girls had been brought to Bosnia and Herzegovina and forced into prostitution, notably to provide sexual services for peace-keepers and other men deployed by intergovernmental organisations.

Alongside the new Convention, the UN developed three supplementary protocols. The first was the Protocol to Prevent, Suppress and Punish Trafficking in Persons, especially Women and Children (the UN Trafficking Protocol), which was adopted in November 2000 (UN General Assembly 2000) and entered into force in December 2003. This set out to provide a clear definition of human trafficking. A second Protocol developed at the same time focused on the 'smuggling' of migrants and a third, adopted later, concerned the illicit trade in firearms.

Article 3 of the Trafficking Protocol contains a complex definition of the crime of trafficking in persons. It involves three elements: (i) an action ('recruitment, transportation, transfer, harbouring, or receipt of persons'), which is undertaken with (ii) abusive means and is (iii) 'for the purpose of exploitation'. The abusive means mentioned are

> the threat or use of force or other forms of coercion, of abduction, of fraud, of deception, of the abuse of power or of a position of vulnerability or of the giving or receiving of payments or benefits to achieve the consent of a person having control over another person.

However, when committed for the purpose of exploiting a child (anyone aged under 18), the definition specifies that any of the actions mentioned constitutes trafficking in persons, even if no abusive means are used. The exploitative purposes of trafficking listed in the definition are 'the exploitation of the prostitution of others or other forms of sexual exploitation, forced labour or services, slavery or practices similar to slavery, servitude or the removal of organs'. With the exception of the term 'sexual exploitation', each of these terms had featured and been defined fully or partially in previous international conventions (Dottridge 2017a). However, rather than presenting this as a definitive list of forms of exploitation, the Trafficking Protocol indicates that these must, at a minimum, be categorised in law as purposes of trafficking, leaving individual countries the option of categorising other forms of exploitation as purposes of trafficking.

The definition of trafficking in persons was complex because it was the product of protracted negotiations between states with quite different laws and policies on prostitution (Jordan 2002). A number of countries, such as the Netherlands, had already decided to decriminalise or legalise both the acts of offering or paying for commercial sex and of making money from someone who earns it from commercial sex, such as a pimp or brothel owner. However, they were ready to categorise as crimes all cases in which children were recruited into prostitution or making pornography and also those in which adult women (or men) were forced or tricked into prostitution. They also wanted to include various forms of extreme economic exploitation, later renamed 'labour exploitation', as cases of trafficking. Representatives of other states wanted any form of recruitment into prostitution to be regarded as trafficking, whether or not the person involved concurred (Simm 2004). Hence the definition in Article 3 of the Trafficking Protocol became complicated, requiring three elements for an offence to secure international agreement on the definition.

In principle, the Trafficking Protocol has been tremendously influential. By mid-2018 it was in force in more than 170 countries,[1] each of which is required to enact a law defining and punishing the offence of trafficking in persons in terms consistent with the Protocol. However, the complexity of the definition meant that, when national laws were enacted or amended, the definition of the offence was also often complicated, making it difficult for law enforcement officials, potential victims of the crime, and members of the public to understand what constituted the crime, or to know what evidence was required to prove that the crime had been committed.

Although the Trafficking Protocol is concerned with transnational organised crime, and with cases of human trafficking that involve people being trafficked from one country to another, its definition of trafficking in persons has also been applied more widely to offences committed uniquely within one country ('domestic' or 'internal' trafficking) and by individuals, as well as by 'organised crime'.

In addition to defining an offence, the UN Trafficking Protocol also specifies general measures for ratifying states to prevent human trafficking and to protect and assist trafficked victims. Most of the protection provisions in the Protocol are not mandatory, however. As it was intended to focus on transnational crimes in which victims of the crime were moved from one country to another, this meant that governments ratifying the Protocol were not bound by specific standards to protect migrants that had been exploited by traffickers (although some states had already ratified international human rights conventions requiring them to provide protection and assistance). Even so, within a few years, some concluded from experience that prosecutions of traffickers were more likely to be successful if people who had been trafficked and who were potential witnesses at trials, were protected and assisted by the authorities.

Most of the measures required by the UN Protocol to prevent human trafficking were vague. For example, ratifying states made a commitment to 'endeavour to undertake measures such as research, information and mass media campaigns and social and economic initiatives' (Article 9.2). It also required states to implement border controls and to take action 'to discourage the demand that fosters all forms of exploitation of persons, especially women and children, that leads to trafficking' (Article 9.5). This was a novel use of the term 'demand' in the context of an international agreement to stop crime and was pushed in particular by delegates at drafting sessions who considered that 'demand' for commercial sex was a major causal factor responsible for human trafficking (Ezeilo 2013).

Implementation of the UN Trafficking Protocol

The first decade following the adoption of the UN Trafficking Protocol saw the publication of commentaries and guidelines by international organisations and others about what constituted human trafficking and what responses were appropriate (e.g. UNODC 2008). Most endeavoured to challenge the assumption by law enforcement officials in many countries that 'trafficking' was uniquely about recruitment into prostitution. Both international organisations and some non-governmental organisations (NGOs) began issuing their own analyses of particular patterns of trafficking, some about patterns involving just two countries and some at a regional level. It was apparent early on that some of these were influenced by the specific interests of the organisations involved and that they, in turn, were influenced by what particular governments did or did not consider to constitute human trafficking. Thus, although the definition of human trafficking in the UN Protocol was intended to bring about consensus on the meaning of the term, in practice it was interpreted to mean what a particular government or organisation wanted it to mean.

The Trafficking Protocol was drafted and adopted at the same time as other initiatives at an international level to halt exploitation. These included two optional protocols to the UN Convention on the Rights of the Child adopted in 2000 (one concerning the sale of children and the other on the involvement of children in armed conflicts and their recruitment into military units) and the International Labour Organization's Convention No. 182 on the worst forms of child labour (1999). However, each of these was developed under the auspices of a different part of the UN, with the result that the first decade after the adoption of the UN Trafficking Protocol was marked by competition between them, rather than cooperation within the UN system. In some cases, the competition was for funding to implement anti-trafficking programmes, which increased markedly during the decade. In others, it concerned the agencies' mandates and the strategies they considered appropriate to stop trafficking.

This jockeying for position by international organisations took various forms. In 1999 the attention of the International Labour Office (ILO) was on a related but different issue, the worst forms of child labour. It was consequently not represented by a senior official during discussions about the proposed Trafficking Protocol and had minimal influence on its provisions as a result. It was not until 2001 that the ILO issued the first of a series of what it called 'global reports' on forced labour and set up a unit dedicated to responding to it. The ILO's reorientation to the new definition of human trafficking (instead of referring uniquely to 'forced labour') took a decade, culminating in the adoption of the Protocol of 2014 to the ILO's Convention No. 29 on Forced Labour (1930). In its preamble, this recognised that

> the context and forms of forced or compulsory labour have changed and trafficking in persons for the purposes of forced or compulsory labour, which may involve sexual exploitation, is the subject of growing international concern and requires urgent action for its effective elimination
>
> *(ILO 2014)*

In the meantime, in 2010 the UN adopted a UN Global Plan of Action to Combat Trafficking in Persons, confirming that the UN Office on Drugs and Crime (UNODC) was the lead international agency on the topic of human trafficking. By this time, the international organisation playing the most substantial role in assisting people who had been trafficked and supporting what was called the 'assisted voluntary return' of people identified as trafficking victims in a country other than their own was the International Organization for Migration (IOM).

Although the definition of what constitutes trafficking in persons in the UN Trafficking Protocol might appear long and definitive, in practice governments have emphasised or omitted particular aspects according to their priorities. As the understanding of the term trafficking in persons that law enforcement agencies in many countries had before the Protocol was adopted focused on recruitment into prostitution and exploiting the prostitution of others, their focus once the Protocol was adopted tended to be on the sex industry. For example, when Vietnam adopted its first National Action Plan on Combating Trafficking in Women and Children (for the period 2004 to 2010), it focused uniquely on sexual exploitation and made no reference to forced labour (David et al. 2011, 13). Indeed, the Vietnamese authorities were concerned mainly with what happened to Vietnamese women and girls when they left Vietnam, particularly when they worked in brothels in Cambodia and China, but also when they married men in China and other countries in East Asia. Only some women were forced into marriage as a result of deception or abduction (and could be considered victims of trafficking), but the authorities had difficulty in distinguishing between marriage migration in general and trafficking for the purpose of forcing women or girls into marriage (Bélanger 2010). In 2011, Vietnam adopted an anti-trafficking law that was more closely aligned to the definition in the Trafficking Protocol.

a. *The role of the United States*

Action by the United States of America had a strong influence on anti-trafficking laws and policies implemented around the world. Shortly before the UN adopted the Trafficking Protocol, in October 2000, the US adopted the *Trafficking Victims Protection Act* of 2000 (TVPA), defining and stipulating penalties for trafficking-related offences in the US. Its definitions of offences were not identical to those in the UN Protocol and the law distinguished what it called 'severe forms of trafficking' from others. The TVPA contained provisions intended to encourage action against trafficking by other governments. It listed ten factors to be considered as 'indicia of serious and sustained efforts to eliminate severe forms of trafficking in persons' which were to be assessed once a year in a Trafficking in Persons report published by the US Department of State. Eighteen of these reports had been published by July 2018. They categorise countries into four tiers, according to their perceived performance, with those in the lowest tier threatened with the loss of certain forms of assistance from the US.

Within months of the adoption of the TVPA, President George W. Bush became President. His administration chose to emphasise the importance of measures by other governments to stop trafficking for the purpose of sexual exploitation, with the added complication that this was often conflated in the US with any form of recruitment into sex work, whether or not abusive means were involved. Since 2000, sex workers in general and migrant sex workers in particular have complained that they have suffered considerable prejudice as a result of law enforcement actions taken in the name of stopping human trafficking. The protests have been noisiest in the US itself, both against the effects of US anti-trafficking laws and of US measures taken to discourage prostitution elsewhere in the world. Presenting findings in the US in 2009, the Sex Workers Project reported that US law enforcement officials routinely presumed 'that all immigrant sex workers have been trafficked, and that sex workers who have not been trafficked must be punished' (Ditmore 2009, 12). The author argued that such presumptions were wrong and noted that they had 'led to the disproportionate allocation of anti-trafficking resources to local vice raids targeting prostitution venues' (Ditmore 2009, 12).

b. *Impact of criminal justice measures (investigations and prosecutions)*

Statistics about prosecutions for trafficking offences have been published on a biennial basis by the UNODC since 2012. These are based on statistical information provided to the UNODC by governments, so reflect national interpretations of what constitutes human trafficking and only reveal what numbers of traffickers have been prosecuted or victims of trafficking have been identified by government officials, rather than presenting more objective estimates of the scale of the phenomenon. Nevertheless, the data about the origins of both convicted traffickers and their victims is revealing.

Evidence exists that prosecutions for trafficking have targeted migrants who facilitate irregular migration and who help people from the same country or ethnic background following their arrival in a new country. The UNODC global report in 2016 observed that 'Traffickers and their victims often come from the same place, speak the same language, or have the same ethnic background. Such commonalities help traffickers generate trust to carry out the trafficking crime' (UNODC 2016, 7). Evidently, migrants routinely depend on the advice and assistance of people from the same country or community, and these services vary from benign (and free or cheap) to exploitative and extremely costly. The question raised by the UNODC findings is whether the individuals convicted of trafficking people with similar social origins have indeed recruited and exploited them in the ways listed in the UN Trafficking Protocol. In some countries it appears that law enforcement authorities have interpreted methods for informally (and sometimes illegally) assisting new migrants to be trafficking offences, when the supposed victims regarded the methods used as an acceptable way (indeed, the only option open to them) to enter a country and earn a living (see Chapter 38 in this Handbook). Assessing this objectively is difficult, as most information about prosecutions comes from official sources, supplemented by the observations of independent legal experts who have watched proceedings, usually to assess the quality of the legal process or its fairness for victims of crime, rather than for the defendants (ASTRA 2018). No anti-trafficking initiatives are reported to have examined the informal credit markets open to migrants, although there have been recent initiatives to prevent migrant workers having to pay fees to recruitment agencies (ILO 2016). These, too, seem to ignore the positive services that migrants obtain from the brokers they pay, which are sometimes more effective than the protection from abuse that law enforcement agencies are supposed to provide, but often fail to deliver.

Although some offences against migrants and nationals have been prosecuted under new anti-trafficking laws, many countries have avoided identifying migrant workers in their territory as 'trafficked', preferring to see it as a crime committed against their own nationals when they seek a living abroad (Nikolić-Ristanović and Ćopić 2011, 280). In the case of workers who accept contracts to work abroad, many are relatively powerless to protest if their contract is changed once they arrive in a new country where they are unfamiliar with the rules or culture. This is notoriously the case if their visa or work permit is tied to their job or employer, as in the case of the *kafala* system in force in many countries in the Middle East, where migrant construction or domestic workers, for example, are 'sponsored' by a specific employer and are not entitled to remain in the country if they run away from an abusive employer. In the case of those who enter a country as irregular or undocumented and find work which the authorities categorise as 'illegal', there is even less they can do to prevent themselves from being exploited, as they fear arrest and deportation if they contact the police or other officials to complain about abuse. This means that there are many forms of exploitation (some mentioned explicitly in the UN Trafficking Protocol and others not) which migrants put up with in silence.

c. Debt bondage and migration: how migrants dependent on informal sources of credit are labelled as 'trafficked'

Several forms of exploitation mentioned in the UN Trafficking Protocol as purposes of trafficking, such as 'forced labour' and 'practices similar to slavery', relate to a UN Convention of 1956 (the UN Supplementary Convention on the Abolition of Slavery, the Slave Trade, and Institutions and Practices Similar to Slavery) which categorises debt bondage or bonded labour as an 'institution or practice similar to slavery'. Those responsible for drafting this Convention were not thinking about the costs of migration, but rather about patterns of debt bondage in agrarian South Asia (Miers 2003, 325). The Convention defines debt bondage as

> the status or condition arising from a pledge by a debtor of his personal services or those of a person under his control as security for a debt, if the value of those services as reasonably assessed is not applied towards the liquidation of the debt or the length and nature of those services are not respectively limited and defined
>
> *(Article 1(a) of the Supplementary Convention)*

Publications about human trafficking have routinely reported that migrants are told upon their arrival that they owe tens of thousands of dollars and must stay in a particular job until the debt is repaid. For example, a research paper prepared for the UN High Commissioner for Refugees (UNHCR) noted that

Sex trafficking victims come mainly from West Africa, especially from Nigeria with roughly 90 per cent of these women from the Delta and Edo states ... One characteristic of African sex networks is the debt system. These debts are typically quite high, taking between one to four years to repay ....

(García 2013, 6)

A report by the European Asylum Support Office similarly estimated that debts owed by Nigerians amounted to 35,000 to 50,000 Euros and would take 2 to 5 years to repay (EASO 2015, 25). There are indeed many situations in which migrants are duped by those recruiting them about the amounts they will have to repay, or about the nature of the work they will be given, meaning that their recruitment does indeed entail deception, one of the abusive means used by traffickers. However, the informal methods used to finance regular and irregular migration have led to some migrants being considered to be in debt bondage, and therefore to be 'trafficked' or 'modern slaves', inappropriately. Many migrants cannot obtain credit from formal institutions, such as banks. They can either raise a loan in advance from relatives, friends, or informal money lenders in their home community, or seek credit from individuals who will facilitate their journey and help find them an income-earning opportunity at their destination. In both cases, the interest charged on credit is routinely exorbitant (such as 10 or even 20 per cent per month; see Lainez 2018), for those offering such credit are exposed to higher risks than formal credit institutions. However, it is only when credit advanced by a broker or employer obliges a migrant to stay in a job that they want to leave that it can reasonably be categorised as servitude or forced labour. As Julia O'Connell Davidson has observed, 'To think of debt is to think of obligations, and we cannot state that all involuntary debts that generate personal dependencies imply a condition of "slavery" without making almost all of us "slaves"' (O'Connell Davidson 2015, 203).

d. *Publications about human trafficking and about the impact of anti-trafficking laws*

It took several years for academic researchers (rather than legal commentators) to take an interest and to begin publishing independent findings about what constituted human trafficking and how this related to the actual experience of migrant workers (see Bastia 2005; Raigrodski 2015; Rijken 2011, for example). Most based their comments directly on their research findings; however, the analyses and comments of some were influenced by the attitudes of a particular government, notably once the US Department of State began publishing an annual 'Trafficking in Persons' report in 2001. A few researchers assumed this was a dependable source for information about trafficking, while others perceived the US reports to be a highly politicised tool used by a powerful government.

'Collateral damage'

A Global Alliance Against Traffic in Women (GAATW) publication, *Collateral Damage* (Dottridge 2007), reviewed the human rights impact of anti-trafficking laws and policies in eight countries. This was by no means the first publication reporting that anti-trafficking laws and policies were counterproductive for the very people they were supposed to benefit – migrants. *Collateral Damage* observed that: 'The evidence available suggests that especially marginalised categories of people, such as migrants, internally-displaced persons, refugees and asylum-seekers, have suffered unacceptably negative consequences' as a result of anti-trafficking laws or policies (Dottridge 2007, 2).

a. *Restrictions on freedom of movement*

As early as 2000, the UN Special Rapporteur on Violence against Women, Radhika Coomaras-wamy, criticised anti-trafficking initiatives which restricted women from emigrating or from entering a country to work. She noted that: '[S]ome legal reforms may create new opportunities for trafficking and may be counterproductive for women'. She criticised Germany for introducing special visa requirements for citizens of the Philippines and Thailand, commenting that:

> Such restrictions generally do not limit trafficking or forced labour. Rather, they increase women's reliance on extra-legal means of migration, and the costs associated with such migration. Responses that target specific nationalities also serve to stigmatize women from certain countries as potential sex workers or undocumented migrants and increase patterns of discrimination against migrant women.
>
> *(Coomaraswamy 2000, 27)*

Restrictions of this sort have been widely reported since 2000, both in industrialised and developing countries.

In developing countries, measures to prevent migrants being trafficked have been cruder and, under political pressure from wealthier countries, anti-trafficking measures have gradually merged with those taken to limit irregular emigration in general. A Nigerian author noted that 'The Nigerian government has a laissez-faire emigration policy, leaving it up to individuals to decide for themselves whether to accept employment offers abroad and under what terms' (Nwogu 2007, 152). However, once airport immigration officials were informed that women from a particular part of Nigeria (Edo State) were going to Italy and other destinations in Europe to earn money as sex workers, they began stopping some women from boarding flights leaving Nigeria, even when the women concerned could prove that they were going to be employed in a quite different job. Not surprisingly, one side effect of these measures was to fuel emigration across land borders, including northwards, across the Sahara. The numbers of irregular migrants from Nigeria and other West African countries seeking to enter Europe after crossing the Sahara increased substantially after the fall of the Gadhafi government in Libya, once again resulting in the authorities in Europe concluding that stemming emigration would be a way to prevent human trafficking as well as migrant smuggling and the terrible toll of deaths on unsafe vessels crossing the Mediterranean.

b. *Gender-based restrictions*

Already in the 1990s, governments in several countries supplying domestic workers for countries in the Middle East banned such migration following incidents in which their citizens had been abused or unfairly punished. From 2000 onwards, the risk that women would be trafficked was invoked by several governments to justify prohibiting women from travelling to certain countries to take up jobs, particularly as live-in domestic workers. The general result has been that women have continued to migrate, albeit in smaller numbers, but in less safe conditions. Such restrictions were imposed by five different governments in Asia: Bangladesh, Burma/Myanmar, India, Nepal, and the Philippines (GAATW 2010). After a Nepali domestic worker died in Kuwait in 1998, the Nepalese authorities decided that no Nepali women should work anywhere in the Gulf. This ban was lifted in 2003 to allow women to travel for certain types of employment, but not domestic work. In 2008, a similar ban for women was extended to Lebanon and Malaysia. In 2010, Nepal's ban on women working in Gulf countries was lifted, only to be re-imposed in 2012, again due to reports of the abuse of domestic workers, this time to prohibit women under 30 from working as domestic workers. In 2014, the ban was extended to prohibit Nepalis emigrating to engage in domestic work anywhere, even though this was the main type of overseas employment available to women (Shrestha and Taylor-Nicholson 2015).

c. Measures affecting child migrants adversely

In several regions, initiatives to stop children being trafficked and exploited have confused independent child migrants who are not exploited in ways condemned by the UN Trafficking Protocol, with children who are trafficked (see also Chapter 8 in this Handbook). For example, several West African countries implemented initiatives to stop children who work away from home from being exploited, either by preventing them leaving home in the first place or by intercepting them while travelling during the 1990s (Dottridge 2002). Repackaged from 2000 onwards as 'anti-child trafficking measures', the first substantial criticism of such measures came in 2003 (Castle and Diarra 2003), focusing on the prejudice caused to children in Mali. This presented evidence about the impact of village-based 'vigilance committees' that were supposed to prevent children from being trafficked. The principle of encouraging responsibility at the community level sounded good, but the reality of the vigilance committees was found to be abusive. Two years after they were set up, the study found that committee members did not distinguish between trafficked children and other children leaving their homes to earn a living. It found that young people were resorting to methods of migrating which increased risks rather than reducing them.

The Mali example was one of the first to point to the 'collateral damage' of anti-trafficking measures in cases which did not involve sex workers. It also demonstrated that it was easier to launch such measures than to reverse them, for ensuring that harmful practice is discontinued has been hard to achieve both in West Africa and elsewhere. In the Mali case, the international organisations which had supported the establishment of vigilance committees were reluctant to recognise their failings. Child protection specialists in various West African countries became more vocal in pointing out that migration to earn money was a long-established tradition in the region and that only a small proportion of the children concerned were subjected to forms of exploitation listed in the UN Trafficking Protocol. Ironically, in cases which did have the hallmarks of trafficking, law enforcement institutions in the region were often reluctant to take action, so the courts across West Africa have not yet provided a yardstick for agreeing which cases constitute child trafficking. Eventually, a coalition of international organisations and NGOs pooled their resources in an effort to stop child migrants being misdiagnosed as 'trafficked' and to identify more appropriate methods to protect them from harm (Feneyrol 2011). However, disagreement continues among child protection organisations in the region about precisely which children should be regarded as trafficking victims, with some continuing to intercept children who are away from home, while others do not consider the same children to be in need of 'rescue' or repatriation (Boiro and Einarsdóttir 2018).

d. Politicians exploiting the emotive power of the term 'trafficking'

The term 'trafficking' has been used repeatedly since 2000 by politicians in industrialised countries to justify restrictions on irregular migration (by claiming that the measures would stop human trafficking). For example, the British Home Secretary was reported in 2009 to be 'delighted' by the destruction of a camp for migrants in France, situated near the port of Calais, from where migrants attempted to enter the United Kingdom. He reportedly said that 'The measures that we have put in place are not only there to prevent illegal immigration but also to stop people trafficking' (Black 2009). Evidently, by making it more difficult for migrants to enter a country, government officials can indeed claim to be on the side of the angels – even though the migrants concerned are sometimes precipitated into worse living conditions and accrue larger debts and consequently are even more vulnerable to being exploited.

Conclusion

Efforts to stop migrants or others being subjected to the various forms of exploitation that are the purposes of trafficking in persons have certainly had an impact, but some of the effects have harmed rather than helped migrants and others who were nominally intended to benefit. To a great extent, this is because there has been an intensive focus on promoting criminal justice responses to human trafficking (to bring about the conviction of traffickers and thereby deter others), while this has not been counterbalanced by appropriate measures by governments to prevent extreme exploitation or to protect the victims. Indeed, even criminal justice responses have been rendered less effective by the complexity of the definition of trafficking adopted by the UN in 2000, as well as by ongoing difficulties in coordinating investigations by law enforcement officials in two or more countries.

The near-exclusive focus on criminal justice solutions has also inhibited effective cooperation among intergovernmental organisations. For example, the preoccupation of governments in North America and Europe with large-scale immigration, in particular from 2014 and 2015 onwards respectively, has increased their determination to stem irregular migration. While international agreements and political rhetoric continue to mention their commitment to stop trafficking in persons, by 2018 the issue was no longer receiving the same level of resources or being flagged as a political priority in the same way as in the first decade of the twenty-first century. The governments of several industrialised countries have couched statements about measures designed to stop or reduce immigration in terms of 'stopping human trafficking' and 'saving' unfortunate migrants. Indeed, it is worrying that there still seems to be a basic misunderstanding of how migration works in lower-income countries and how people in and from such countries habitually earn a living (such as children who migrate to the nearest city to find work, often across a frontier in a different country; see Dottridge 2017b). Perhaps the best way of measuring whether governments are genuinely committed to stopping human trafficking and the exploitation of migrants will be to see when they start responding positively to the calls to implement migration policies which increase the possibility of regular migration into decent jobs, including unskilled jobs, and introduce firewalls between law enforcement actions to detect cases of trafficking and illegal exploitation and those to detect and deport irregular migrant workers.

Note

1 The countries which have ratified or acceded to the UN Trafficking Protocol are listed at https://treaties.un.org/pages/ViewDetails.aspx?src=TREATY&mtdsg_no=XVIII-12-a&chapter=18&clang=_en

References

ASTRA Anti-trafficking action. (2018) *Position of Human Trafficking Victims in Court* Proceedings. *Analysis of Judicial Practice for 2017*, (www.astra.rs/en/reports-and-studies/) Accessed 31 August 2018.

Bastia T. (2005) "Child Trafficking or Teenage Migration? Bolivian Migrants in Argentina", *International Migration*, 43, 4, 58–89.

Bélanger D. (2010) "Marriages with Foreign Women in East Asia: Bride Trafficking or Voluntary Migration?", *Population & Societies*, 469, 1–4.

Black, P. (2009) "France Bulldozes Migrant 'Jungle'" (CNN, 22 September 2009), (http://edition.cnn.com/2009/WORLD/europe/09/22/calais.france.illegal.migrants.removal) Accessed 20 August 2018.

Boiro H. and Einarsdóttir J. (2018) "'A vicious circle': Repatriation of Bissau-Guinean Quranic School-boys from Senegal", *Journal of Human Trafficking*. DOI: 10.1080/23322705.2018.1521643

Castle S. and Diarra A. (2003) *The International Migration of Young Malians: Tradition, Necessity or Rite of Passage?* London: London School of Hygiene and Tropical Medicine.

Coomaraswamy R. (2000) *Report of the Special Rapporteur on Violence Against Women, Its Causes and Consequences, Ms. Radhika Coomaraswamy, on Trafficking in Women, Women's Migration and Violence Against Women*, Submitted in accordance with Commission on Human Rights Resolution 1997/44. (UN document E/CN.4/2000/68, 29 February 2000).

David F., Gallagher A., Holmes P. and Moskowitz A. (2011) *Progress Report on Criminal Justice Responses to Trafficking in Persons in the ASEAN Region*. Jakarta: Association for of Southeast Asian, Nations (ASEAN).

Ditmore, M. (2009) *The Use of Raids to Fight Trafficking in Persons*, Sex Workers Project. http://sexworkersproject.org/downloads/swp-2009-raids-and-trafficking-report.pdf.

Dottridge M. (2002) "Trafficking in children in West and Central Africa", *Gender and Development*, March 2002, 10, 1, 38–42.

Dottridge M. (2007) *Collateral Damage. The Impact of Anti-Trafficking Measures on Human Rights around the World*, Global Alliance against Traffic in Women, Bangkok.

Dottridge M. (2017a) "Trafficked and Exploited: The Urgent Needs for Coherence in International Law", in Kotiswaran P. (ed.), *Revisiting the Law and Governance of Trafficking, Forced Labor and Slavery*. Cambridge: Cambridge Studies in Law and Society, Cambridge University Press, 59–82.

Dottridge M. (2017b) *Eight Reasons Why We Shouldn't Use the Term 'Modern Slavery'*, Beyond Trafficking and Slavery. 17 October 2017.

European Asylum Support Office (EASO). (2015) Nigeria. *Sex Trafficking of Women*, EASO Country of Origin Information Report, Valleta (Malta).

Ezeilo J. N. (2013) *Report of the Special Rapporteur on Trafficking in Persons, Especially Women and Children*, Joy Ngozi Ezeilo UN Document A/HRC/2013/23/48 (18 March 2013).

Feneyrol O. (2011) *Quelle Protection pour les enfants concernés par la mobilité en Afrique de l'Ouest? Nos positions et recommandations. Rapport régional de synthèse* Projet "Mobilités" (African Movement of Working Children and Youth, International Labour Organization, International Organization for Migration, Plan International, Save the Children, Terre des Hommes International Foundation and UNICEF). Dakar.

García A. D. (2013) *Voodoo, Witchcraft and Human Trafficking in Europe New Issues in Refugee Research*, Research Paper No. 263, Policy Development and Evaluation Service. United Nations High Commissioner for Refugees (UNHCR).

Global Alliance Against Traffic in Women (GAATW). (2010) *Beyond Borders: Exploring Links Between Trafficking and Migration* GAATW Working Papers Series, Bangkok.

International Labour Organization (ILO). (2014) *Protocol of 2014 to the Forced Labour Convention, 1930.* Geneva.

International Labour Organization (ILO). (2016) *General Principles and Operational Guidelines for Fair Recruitment adopted by the Meeting of Experts on Fair Recruitment.* (Geneva, 5–7 September 2016).

Jordan A. D. (2002) "Human Rights or Wrongs? The Struggle for a Rights-based Response to Trafficking in Human Beings", *Gender and Development*, March 2002, 10, 1, 28–37.

Lainez N. (2018) "The Contested Legacies of Indigenous Debt Bondage in Southeast Asia: Indebtedness in the Vietnamese Sex Sector", *American Anthropologist*, 120, 4, 671–683.

Miers S. (2003) *Slavery in the Twentieth Century. The Evolution of a Global Problem*, Altamira Press

Nikolić-Ristanović, V. and Ćopić S. (2011) "Combating Trafficking in Human Beings for Labour Exploitation in Serbia", in Rijken, C. ed., *Combating Trafficking in Human Beings for Labour Exploitation*, Wolf Legal Publishers, Nijmegen, 223–284.

Nwogu V. I. (2007) "Nigeria", in Dottridge, M. ed., *Collateral Damage. The Impact of Anti-Trafficking Measures on Human Rights around the World*, Global Alliance against Traffic in Women, Bangkok, 142–170.

O'Connell Davidson J. (2015) *Modern Slavery. The Margins of Freedom*, Palgrave Macmillan (UK), London.

Raigrodski D. (2015) "Economic Migration Gone Wrong: Trafficking in Persons Through The Lens of Gender, Labor, and Globalization", *Indiana International & Comparative Law Review*, 25, 1, 79–114.

Rijken, C. ed (2011) *Combating Trafficking in Human Beings for Labour Exploitation*, Wolf Legal Publishers, Nijmegen.

Shrestha J. and Taylor-Nicholson E. (2015) *No Easy Exit – Migration Bans Affecting Women From Nepal*, International Labour Office, Fundamental Principles and Rights at Work (FUNDAMENTALS) and Labour Migration Branch (MIGRANT), Geneva.

Simm G. (2004) *Negotiating the United Nations Trafficking Protocol: Feminist Debates. Australian Year Book of International Law*.

United Nations General Assembly. (2000) *Protocol to Prevent, Suppress and Punish Trafficking in Persons, Especially Women and Children*, Supplementing the United Nations Convention Against Transnational Organized Crime, General Assembly resolution 55/25, 55th Session, UN Document A/45/49 (2001).

United Nations Office on Drugs and Crime (UNODC). (2008) *Toolkit to Combat Trafficking in Persons. Global Programme against Trafficking in Human Beings*, United Nations, New York.

UNODC. (2016) *Global Report on Trafficking in Persons 2016*, United Nations, New York.

38

ON THE MARGINS

Migrant smuggling in the context of development

Marie McAuliffe[1]

Introduction

The examination of migrant smuggling within a migration and development context is important for several reasons. The more important revolve around the myriad policy issues the two phenomena raise, which have grown in prominence in recent years, particularly in public and political discourses. Among these issues is the human impact of migrant smuggling on migrants, their families, and home communities, as well as on the societies of transit and destination. A smuggled migrant, for example, is at greater risk of serious abuse, exploitation, or even death during a journey, than a migrant who is travelling on a valid visa and travel document (IOM 2018; McAuliffe et al. 2017, 178–9). Migrant smuggling, therefore, is often examined with reference to human rights, migrant vulnerability, as well as to the criminality of smugglers and smuggling practices. Critical analysis of how migrant smuggling intersects with aspects of development is less common.

Notwithstanding the importance of the topic, it is essential to acknowledge that any discussion of migrant smuggling contains a potential risk of overstating the scale and prevalence of the phenomenon. From what we know, migrant smuggling globally remains marginal when compared with the migration and mobility of people who are not smuggled. For example, there were an estimated 1322 million international tourist arrivals in 2017 (UNWTO 2018) and around 258 million international migrants living outside their country of birth in the same year (UN DESA 2017).[2] In contrast, a recent study on smuggling has estimated that 2.5 million people were smuggled globally in 2016 (UNODC 2018). That a small fraction of all people moving internationally are smuggled makes intuitive sense, because of the high risks, costs, and difficulties involved in such illicit practices, but it can sometimes be overlooked or forgotten. Acknowledging the relatively small scale of smuggling globally is not to understate the human rights abuses and severe exploitation that are often associated with the phenomenon but a sense of proportionality is required when critically examining migrant smuggling, including in a development context. It is also worth noting that people who are irregular migrants generally become so after entering a country lawfully; they are not smuggled (see discussion on the difference between irregular *migrants* and irregular *migration* in IOM 2017, 20–1, 25).

The second issue requiring consideration is that we know little about migrant smuggling globally, especially when compared with other forms of migration and mobility. A key reason for this is the clandestine nature of smuggling, making it difficult to collect accurate data and other information on smuggling (Icduygu 2018; UNODC 2018). Consequently, our ability to assess trends over time is severely hampered, with often only 'one-off' estimates able to be compiled intermittently on, for example, the numbers smuggled, profits made, changes in smuggling practices, and impacts of policies.

A noticeable absence of robust data on smuggling combined with often horrifying accounts of those who are smuggled makes for compelling narratives that can loom large in the minds of readers or viewers. It is easy to understand why migrant smuggling may, at times, seem as if they are becoming the norm. What we do know, however, is that migrant smuggling largely occurs in the margins of much larger migration corridors. Most international movement globally occurs as part of regulated systems (or informal systems that do not require being smuggled) with much of it increasingly facilitated by the ongoing reduced costs of international air travel, enhanced visa programming, bilateral or regional mobility regimes as well as border management systems (IOM 2017, 150–2). A wide variability in the prevalence of smuggling by geographic location and transportation type exists, with some migration corridors being more prone to smuggling than others, because of specific events such as civil conflict, environmental degradation, or disaster (McAuliffe and Koser 2015; McAuliffe and Laczko 2016; UNODC 2018). The current toxic and unbalanced political debate on immigration in some parts of the world appears to have been fuelled by political expediency, further encouraging misinformation and disproportionate policy responses to 'curb' migration generally, not just irregular migration (Hester et al. 2018). It is more important than ever, therefore, to be mindful of presenting the challenges and risks of migrant smuggling while also acknowledging its exceptional status within broader migration systems globally.

The purpose of this chapter is to provide an overview of current conceptualisations and analyses of migrant smuggling within a migration and development context, so that it may assist readers in their own empirical or theoretical research and analysis. First, a brief discussion on definitions is provided. The chapter then examines the core components of the migration and development debate posed by Skeldon (2008) – remittances, diaspora, and brain circulation – as they relate to migrant smuggling. The chapter then concludes by reiterating the need for proportionality, both in research and analysis and in operational and policy responses, as well as for greater acknowledgement of multi-faceted perspectives of smuggling. It also briefly outlines areas most in need of further enquiry and examination.

Definitions matter

Definitions reflect specific perspectives that can be applied to a set of circumstances, group(s) of people, or events. They help make sense of the world around us and are central to analysis, legal-policy frameworks, and practical implementation of law and policy. In the migration context, IOM notes that there are specific definitions of migration-related terms that are technical in nature and relate to a range of contexts, including legal, administrative, research, and statistical (IOM 2017, 14). The definition of 'migrant', may differ depending on the context in which it is applied: such as, estimating the number of international migrants, providing services to specific population groups, or applying entry and stay conditions on visa holders for example.

The most widely accepted definition of 'migrant smuggling' at the international level is set out in the Protocol against the Smuggling of Migrants by Land, Sea and Air (the Protocol), which stems from the United Nations Convention against Transnational Organized Crime, and has been ratified by 147 member states globally (UNTC 2018). The Protocol defines migrant smuggling as a crime: 'The procurement, in order to obtain, directly or indirectly, a financial or other material benefit, of the illegal entry of a person into a State Party of which the person is not a national or a permanent resident' (Article 3). According to the Protocol, the act of smuggling is defined as criminal and the smugglers as criminals who pose a security threat, but it does not seek to criminalise migrants who are smuggled (UNODC 2018, 17). Part of the reason is that smuggled migrants may be seeking safety from danger or harm, and may in fact be asylum seekers or refugees. For some people, using a smuggler to leave a country and/or enter another can be a life-saving necessity.

In contrast to migrant smuggling, human trafficking involves coercion and is defined by the Protocol to Prevent, Suppress and Punish Trafficking in Persons as

> the recruitment, transportation, transfer, harbouring or receipt of persons, by means of the threat or use of force or other forms of coercion, of abduction, of fraud, of deception, of the abuse of power or of a position of vulnerability or of the giving or receiving of payments or benefits to achieve the consent of a person having control over another person, for the purpose of exploitation.
>
> *(Article 3(a))*

The smuggling and trafficking Protocols both stem from the Convention against Transnational Organized Crime and were finalised at the same time in 2000. Since then, there has been increasing recognition that changes in illicit migration processes have further blurred the line between smuggling and trafficking (Carlin, Gallagher, and Horwood 2015). In some situations, what may start out as a simple transaction involving a person seeking the services of a smuggler may end up with the migrant being deceived, coerced and/or exploited somewhere during the journey – a smuggled migrant may quickly and unwillingly become a trafficked person (RMMS 2015).

Within the academic sphere, additional conceptualisations of migrant smuggling exist in the context of a rich body of literature on the topic spanning several decades. Of note is Salt and Stein's seminal work on migrant smuggling as being part of the illicit migration business, with emphasis on services, supply and demand, and profit motives (Salt and Stein 1997). Alongside this, the notion of 'altruistic' smuggling that does not involve financial or material gain has been further articulated (Salt and Hogarth 2000), which may relate to forms of support within ethnic or political minorities (UNODC 2018). Smuggling for humanitarian reasons (including of refugees) regardless of payment has also gained prominence in the literature (Koser 2011; van Liempt and Doomernik 2006), and has been a notable feature of smuggling dynamics in key corridors, such as the Aegean Sea between Turkey and Greece, land routes from Greece through to Austria and Germany, and sea routes from Bangladesh to Thailand, Malaysia, and Indonesia (Angeli and Triandafyllidou 2016; Icduygu and Akcapar 2016; McAuliffe 2016).

In examining smuggling in the context of migration and development, the Protocol definition, as well as the additional conceptualisations, are all relevant. However, it could be argued that more emphasis should be placed on longer-term, systemic issues underpinning smuggling routes and flows, and less emphasis be afforded large-scale displacement and related onward movement, such as undertaken by large groups of people who have fled transnational or civil conflict. Notwithstanding the complexities and differences involved in the motivations of the smugglers and the smuggled, the unifying aspect of migrant smuggling is that it occurs outside regulated systems (so is 'irregular' in nature), involves unauthorised border crossings and is clandestine in nature. Statistical trends, impacts and outcomes are therefore extremely difficult to measure (if at all). In turn, the effects of smuggling on development are 'loose', unable to be linked directly to this illicit and clandestine practice.

Notwithstanding these realities, some proxy indicators exist that can point to how smuggling might be acting to inhibit or enable aspects of development, such as those relating to detections of irregular arrivals, estimates of smuggler profits, migrant returns (voluntary or involuntary), although most are not able to be disaggregated by migration type (whether regular or irregular, for example) or mode of entry (smuggled or not smuggled). Most data, even where it is available, are not sufficiently granular to be able to support analysis that distinguishes the specific effects of migration supported by smuggling. Only broad estimates and analyses are able to be undertaken. Nevertheless, this type of work can be useful in highlighting potential systemic issues as well as some of the underlying incentives underpinning migrant smuggling from a development perspective.

Remittances

It is widely acknowledged that remittances deliver significant positive impacts in origin countries, where they support households with basics such as food, shelter, health, and education as well as fund further/expanded education opportunities, income-generating activities, and investments. In 2016, official remittances amounted to 573 billion dollars globally, most of which (73.6 per cent) was received by recipients in developing countries (World Bank 2018). In addition, the value of remittances is estimated to be as high as double the official figure globally if informal money transfers were also to be included (UNDP 2017), with informal transactions estimated to be worth between 20 to 55 per cent of total remittances in developing countries (UNDP 2016). This does raise the issue of potential 'incentivisation' of international migration, including irregular migration and smuggling, with migration being perceived as a quick fix to economic ills or faltering national development in some origin countries. Recent analysis, for example, has found that origin and transit countries of significance when it comes to irregular migration and smuggled migrants, are less likely to sign and ratify the Smuggling Protocol, which is in part related to levels of development (Schloenhardt and Macdonald 2017).

Remittances now dwarf Official Development Assistance (ODA) globally, accounting for three times that of ODA annually (World Bank 2017). However, we also know that most remittance flows are directed to households in specific locations. In many origin countries, inbound remittance flows mirror outbound emigration patterns that have developed over many years, such that high proportions of remittances being transferred back home may end up being concentrated in only specific, limited geographic areas of a country (Aredo 2005; Skeldon 2008). This typically means that some of the poorest areas in origin countries are not able to benefit from remittances. In contrast, the distribution of ODA can be better managed, enabling the poorest communities to receive access to poverty alleviating measures, which is not dependent on whether emigration has occurred from that locality.

But what does this mean for irregular migration and smuggling? First, it is likely that similar emigration–remittance patterns exist, with informal remittances reflecting irregular migration corridors. Notwithstanding the difficulties in attempting to analyse such patterns, some studies have successfully been able to employ a range of techniques to assess these features. Zewdu's (2018) recent study of irregular migration and informal remittances in Ethiopia, for example, found that:

> Another feature born out of irregular migration is informal remittance transfer from migrants to communities of origin...patterns of migration and remittance channels are interrelated. In Hadiya and Kembata-Tembaro region, where migrants predominantly depart to South Africa as irregular migrants, remittances are sent through informal channels.

This of course makes intuitive sense, as those who enter and stay irregularly are likely to find it more difficult to use formal remittance channels and may only have access to informal transfer networks. Migrant smugglers themselves can also be involved in the smuggling of money along specific corridors (FATF 2011; Zewdu 2018). Irregularity and precariousness, therefore, continue to feature in migrants' lives beyond the more immediate migration-related aspects (such as unauthorised entry), and relate to more limited options to remit. Irregularity in destination also often translates into lower wages with greater risk of exploitation, higher relative living costs, and reduced choice, which can in turn translate into a lower capacity to remit (Baldwin-Edwards 2008; Kanko and Teller 2014; Shah 2009). In addition, studies have found that the greater precariousness associated with working as an irregular migrant in informal settings results in workers ensuring they have enough money to deal with uncertainties, which again negatively affects their ability to remit (Schluter and Wahba 2009). The implications of this have been articulated by Schluter and Wabha (2009, 24):

> These results are relevant to migration policy as they quantify the substantial losses to the migrant arising from the lack of legal status; turning this around, these illegality effects quantify the substantial gains that would arise from amnesty-style policies or the losses to the migrant from more restrictive migration policies.

The impacts on the receiving communities also need to be considered. In communities where remittances feature, the high status that can come with additional income from family members working abroad can create significant social pressures. In corridors where irregular migration and smuggling feature, the pressures for others to undertake such journeys can be immense (Grabska et al. 2016; Mbaye 2017; Zewdu 2018), sometimes resulting in riskier migration and (ultimately) higher numbers of missing or deceased migrants, as captured in IOM's work on fatal journeys (see, for Brian and Laczko 2014, 2016) and missing migrants (IOM 2018). Remittances may also play a role in financing irregular migration of family members, such as was found in recent studies on irregular migration in Africa (Kanko and Teller 2014; Majidi and Oucho 2016; Zewdu 2018).

The additional income can also evolve into dependency, which can have extremely negative effects when destination country economies contract and migrants find themselves without work or resorting to lower-skilled, lower-paid work including as irregular migrants in the informal economy, as has been seen in recent years in Russia with significant impact on the more remittance-dependent countries such as Kyrgyzstan and Tajikistan (IOM 2016). There are also sometimes direct economic benefits that come with being a transit country for smuggling, notwithstanding the significant downsides that may eventuate, including those related to insecurity and risks to efforts to improve regulatory capacities (see the text box below).

What incentives does Niger have for cracking down on migrant smuggling? Not many

Agadez, a small city deep in Niger's northern desert, has become the hub for trans-Saharan migration. A reported 3000 people a week, from all over West Africa and the Horn, have been congregating there waiting for a place on the convoy that leaves every Monday night, heading north into Libya. In the last four years, the sea crossing between Libya and Italy has been one of the principal gateways for the massive surge in migration into Europe.

Closing down the smuggling trade would have a devastating effect on the economy in Agadez. Few of these nationalities stand a chance of successfully negotiating their way through the EU's asylum policy and being legally admitted ... The administrative burden of processing their claims and then the significant costs of financing their return makes it therefore a high priority of European states to stem this flow closer to source. For this they need the cooperation of the littoral states in North Africa. Mauritania maintains a longstanding partnership with the Spaniards to prevent the reopening of the route to the Canary Islands, for example. Gaddafi's Libya used to play the same role for the Italians – in 2011, right before his fall, the dictator was negotiating a $4 billion incentive package to control illicit emigration – but since the revolution, the bifurcated and highly contested Libyan state is in no position to control its own coastlines and offer the same guarantees. The EU is thus appealing to inland states – namely Niger – to prevent the flow of migrants closer to source.

There are a number of deep-seated economic reasons that will make Niger reluctant to take a serious stance against migrant smuggling. Firstly, remittances from migrants working overseas are an important source of revenue in the country ... Agadez has been a trade and smuggling hub in the Sahara for centuries, and there are basically no alternative livelihoods for the nomadic groups such as the Tebu and Toureg that reside there ... The economies of the Sahel are closely tied to the petroleum rich countries of the Maghreb: Algeria and Libya. Not only do a large proportion of West Africans go north to seek employment in these countries, but cross border smuggling in basic goods subsidised in the north, are a mainstay for many communities in the Sahel ... The economies of key cities along the route have developed in support of these transit trades, and with the migration surge, business is booming. The entire community revolves around providing facilities for migrants and smugglers: accommodation, food, equipment and security. To close down the smuggling trade in Agadez would bring the economy crashing down, and as the government has basically no capacity to provide alternative livelihoods, this would risk raising tensions in the region.

Abridged excerpt of Tuesday Reitano's post of 13 January 2016, originally published in the Africa Migration blog series by the London School of Economics and Political Science.

Diaspora

Discussion of diaspora in the context of migrant smuggling and irregular migration is difficult in a number of key ways, and care needs to be taken when discussing their potential linkages. First, is the ongoing debate about what the term 'diaspora' means and who it includes (and excludes) (Castles et al. 2014; Faist 2010; see also Chapter 13 in this Handbook), making it difficult to examine with precision as the definitions have implications for examination of migration processes, such as smuggling. Second, much of the literature on diaspora and migration tends to focus on the much sought after high-skilled migrants, for which smuggling is typically much less of a necessity. This is the case for origin country policy and practice as it relates to diaspora engagement, which has sought to attract various types of investment from diaspora (Dickerson and Ozden 2018; Weinar 2010; see also Chapter 13 in this Handbook). Third, is the need to acknowledge the tensions that emerge when considering diaspora in the context of migrant smuggling, especially given the increased recognition of the central role of social networking in smuggling processes. Recent research, for example, has found that members of diaspora may act as facilitators, funders or even migrant smugglers (Demir, Sever, and Kahya 2017; van Liempt 2018).

Skeldon notes that when contemplating the role of diaspora in development, individuals can only have limited effect at the household or community level, and that diasporas 'need to work within some effective structures if they are to have an impact on their countries of origin' (2008, 6). Countries with the capability to establish and support both clear policies and effective structures for diaspora engagement, such as Argentina, China, and Malaysia (Dickerson and Ozden 2018), are able to reap the benefits. However, countries without this capacity, including those that may be suffering conflict or a post-conflict phase, have reduced ability to secure diaspora investment such that it remains marginal for the poorest and most fragile countries (Skeldon 2008).

Irregular migration, illicit activities such as smuggling, and illegal work abroad all act to minimise the ability of those members of a diaspora to engage in such 'effective structures', which are formalised and likely segmented, with a greater focus on skilled migrants and those from higher socio-economic strata. As we saw with remittances, when irregular migration and smuggling are considered, we can see the ways in which they can act to limit potential benefits and contributions of migrants to development. Full engagement with government programmes seeking to facilitate diaspora investments and contributions would typically be beyond those in irregular situations in destination countries, lest they are detained or deported. In this sense, and with irregular migrants being more likely to be effectively 'locked out' of formal inclusive structures that encourage diaspora investment, the relevance of diaspora falls more to political engagement and/or informal engagement outside of regulated systems (e.g. informal remittances).

Brain circulation, mobility, and the 'management' of irregularity

The third component of the migration and development debate, brain circulation, or brain drain, again tends to focus on those with high-skill levels. This is understandable and it is important to also acknowledge the global competition for skilled migrants and their relative mobility globally compared with those with low or no skills (Skeldon 2018b). Doctors, scientists, IT professionals, and others with high skills are much less likely to need to engage in irregular migration and be smuggled into a country. (One significant exception relates to those high-skilled migrants who have been displaced due to conflict and/or persecution.) The linkages between brain circulation and smuggling is somewhat remote. That said, it is critical that we also acknowledge that the main sources of skilled migrants are in highly developed countries along with a small number of middle-income developing countries (Docquier and Marfouk 2006). In this context, 'brain' circulation is not necessarily the most useful construct to consider migrant smuggling. Rather, international labour mobility encompassing both 'brain' and 'brawn' provides a more appropriate framework to examine smuggling and irregular migration in a development context, as demonstrated by Figure 38.1, which clearly shows

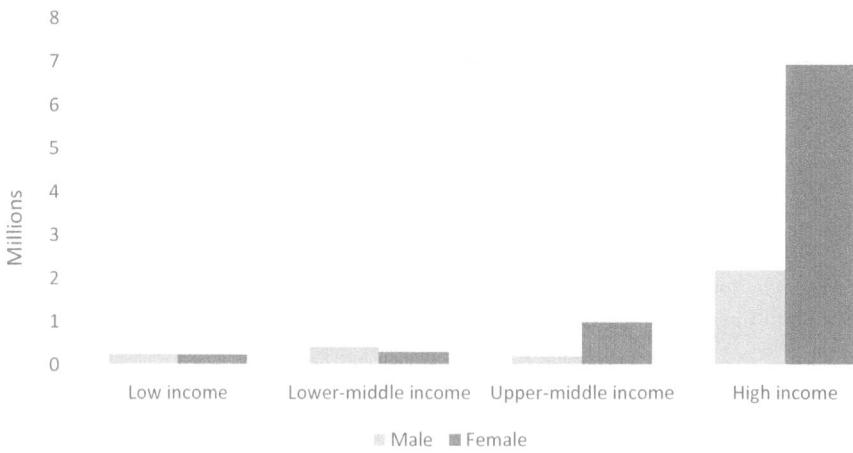

Figure 38.1 Migration domestic workers by country income level and sex as of 2013 (millions)
Source: IOM 2017, based on data from ILO 2015

the relevance of unskilled migrant workers in the domestic sector – a sector we know is often characterised by irregular migration, informal employment, exploitation, and heightened vulnerability, most especially for women and girls (Triandafyllidou 2013; Van Hooren 2012). Unlike people migrating through skilled migration pathways, unskilled migrant workers are more likely to need to resort to irregular migration pathways to access labour markets in higher-income countries (Triandafyllidou et al. 2019).

Taking a step back and considering the relative mobility of the people who are most often smuggled is useful. There is a strong correlation, as shown in Table 38.1, between levels of development, state fragility and passport 'strength'. Citizens of countries with low human development and high fragility, such as Afghanistan, have weaker passports, and much more limited mobility, compared with citizens from countries with high human development and low fragility. They are also much less likely to be part of the global pool of high-skilled talent pursued by many countries. Often therefore, one of the few feasible options available for Afghans and others from low human development countries seeking to migrate internationally is through irregular migration pathways involving smuggling.

Currently, no clear answers exist on whether and how this 'lottery of birth' may be overcome globally so that large groups of people have expanded choices that include options beyond irregular migration and smuggling. The Global Compact on Migration has the potential to support iterative advances toward achieving safe, orderly, and regular migration for all but overcoming the structural and systemic barriers will be considerable. Work at the regional and national levels continue to address these issues, including through Regional Consultative Processes and via bilateral mobility agreements between origin and destination countries (Dacanay 2018; Shah 2009). The need to examine impacts on the evermore pressing gender dimensions of irregular migration and smuggling is also a key consideration in the Compact's implementation (Hennebry 2018). In the meantime, a considerable body of research and analysis confirms that irregularity acts to undermine circulation and mobility (Gallagher 2015; Shah 2009), making irregular migrants' decisions about return migration as well as onward movement risky, expensive, and challenging. The advances in biometric technology in recent years also means that much more is at stake for those who may want to return home temporarily but who risk being unable to (re-)migrate internationally to key destination countries in the future.

Table 38.1 Human development, passport, and fragility rankings, selected countries

Country (in HDI rank order)	Human Development Index 2016	Passport Index 2018	Fragile States Index 2018
	Rank	Rank	Rank
Very High Human Development			
Norway	1	5	177
Germany	4	3	167
United States	10	5	154
Sweden	14	4	170
UK	16	5	159
France	21	3	160
Italy	26	4	143
High Human Development			
Mauritius	64	31	151
Turkey	71	51	58
Sri Lanka	73	99	50
Mexico	77	22	94
Thailand	87	68	77
Tunisia	97	75	92
Medium Human Development			
Egypt	111	92	36
Indonesia	113	72	91
Morocco	123	80	83
India	131	81	72
Ghana	139	78	108
Pakistan	147	104	20
Low Human Development			
Syria	149	105	4
Haiti	163	89	12
Sudan	165	102	7
Yemen	168	103	3
Afghanistan	169	106	9
Eritrea	179	102	19
A number 1 ranking means:	Very high human development	Most mobile passport citizenship	Most fragile country
The lowest ranking means:	Low human development	Least mobile passport citizenship	Least fragile country

Sources: Based on IOM 2017 with data sources from UNDP, Human Development Index 2016; Henley & Partners, Passport Index 2018; Fund for Peace, Fragile States Index 2018.

The 'winners' in all this, some argue, are the receiving countries, who are able to benefit from a steady supply of workers in the informal economy and so keep wage costs down (Shah 2009). This is not uniform, however, and certain sectors in many economies (such as the agricultural, fishery, and care sectors) rely more heavily on irregular migrant workers. Employers in these sectors continue to operate as 'bad actors' by exploiting irregular migrant workers, who are more likely to accept lower pay and working conditions (Papademetriou 2014). Segmentation of the labour market can occur over time, which acts to entrench practices whereby migrant workers undertake the so-called three dimensional jobs – dirty, dangerous, demanding jobs – with local workers increasingly unwilling to do such work (Shah 2009). It is perhaps specific industry sectors, some of which are controlled by multi-nationals with business practices transcending national boundaries, that are increasingly 'winning' through the exploitation of migrants (Ndiaye 2012; Yazd 2014). Multi-faceted responses to combat migrant smuggling and reduce migrant vulnerability and exploitation will only get so far if transnational business practices in high-risk sectors are not comprehensively examined and addressed. The increased focus in recent decades on global supply chains has had some success in uncovering and addressing labour exploitation, including of migrant workers. However, global competition, industry self-regulation and consumer awareness pose ongoing challenges to improving labour practices in transnational supply chains (LeBaron et al. 2017; Parker 2015).

Conclusions

In this chapter, the main interlinkages between smuggling and development have been examined with particular reference to the core components of the migration and development debate: remittances, diaspora, and brain circulation. Importantly, the examination has been situated within a broader migration context that acknowledges smuggling as occurring on the margins of much larger systems regulating migration and mobility globally. This is important, because of the need to bring proportionality to the discussion of smuggling and development, notwithstanding the critical need to highlight issues of human rights abuses and migrant exploitation often associated with smuggling.

One of the more difficult aspects of analysing migrant smuggling, whether it be in relation to human rights, criminality, or development, is that data supporting longitudinal analysis is not available. This makes it extraordinarily difficult to assess trends in smuggling over any period, let alone how they might intersect with other trend data, including on remittances, ODA, human development, and international migrant stock. The picture is unavoidably an incomplete one. Nevertheless, a case is to be made for further examination of the potential impacts of irregular migration and smuggling in terms of costs and benefits over the longer term. What may be perceived as securing access to overseas labour markets and enabling remittances back home – a short-term gain – needs to be assessed against the human costs and losses as well as the potential for continued systematic erosion of regulatory systems, structures and processes that are interlinked to development progress while at the same time helping to ensure more equitable development within and between countries. In addition, our current knowledge of the systemic problems that exist within those industry sectors more likely to engage irregular migrant workers, warrants further examination. The focus on national regulatory environments needs to continue to be supplemented with the scrutiny of transnational systems and practices supporting 'bad actors' and unethical supply chains, creating further incentives for short-term gains at the expense of sustainable development.

Notes

1 The opinions, comments, and analyses expressed in this chapter are those of the author and do not necessarily represent the views of any of the organisations with which the author is affiliated.
2 Migration and mobility are referred to including because of the linkages between the two (see discussion in Skeldon 2018a). The link between regular entry and subsequent overstaying as an irregular migrant, while only a small proportion of all entries, is also relevant to the discussion in this chapter.

References

Angeli, D. and A. Triandafyllidou. (2016). 'Europe', in McAuliffe, M. and F. Laczko (eds.), *Migrant smuggling data and research: A global review of the emerging evidence base*. IOM, Geneva, pp. 105–136.

Aredo, D. (2005). *Migrant remittances, shocks and poverty in urban Ethiopia: An analysis of micro-level panel data.* Addis Ababa University, Addis Ababa.

Baldwin-Edwards, M. (2008). Towards a theory of illegal migration: Historical and structural components. *Third World Quarterly* 29(7): 1449–1459.

Brian, T. and F. Laczko (eds.) (2014) *Fatal journeys: Tracking lives lost during migration.* International Organization for Migration (IOM), Geneva. Available from https://publications.iom.int/system/files/pdf/fataljourneys_countingtheuncounted.pdf

Brian, T. and F. Laczko (eds.). (2016). *Fatal journeys volume 2: Identification and tracing of dead and missing migrants.* IOM, Geneva.

Carling, J. (2016). 'West and Central Africa', in McAuliffe, M. and F. Laczko (eds.), *Migrant smuggling data and research: A global review of the emerging evidence base.* IOM, Geneva, pp. 24–53.

Carling, J., A. Gallagher, and C. Horwood. (2015). *Beyond definitions: Global migration and the smuggling–trafficking nexus* November 2015 Regional Mixed Migration Secretariat, Nairobi.

Castles, S., H. de Haas, and M. Miller. (2014). *The age of migration.* Palgrave Macmillan, London.

Dacanay, B. M. (2018) China's deal to hire 300,000 Filipinos finalised, *The Gulf News,* 14 April 2018.

Dickerson, S. and C. Ozden. (2018). 'Diaspora engagement and return migration policies', in Triandafyllidou, A. (ed.), *Handbook on migration and globalisation.* Edward Elgar Publishing, Cheltenham, UK, pp. 140–154.

Docquier, F. and A. Marfouk. (2006). 'International migration by educational attainment, 1990-2000', in Ozden, C. and M. Schiff (eds.), *International migration, remittances and the brain drain.* World Bank, Washington, DC, pp. 151–200.

Faist, T. (2010). 'Diaspora and transnationalism: What kind of dance partners?', in *Diaspora and transnationalism: Concepts, theories and methods* Baubock R. and T. Faist (eds.), Amsterdam University Press, Amsterdam, pp. 9–34.

Financial Action Task Force (FATF). (2011). *Money laundering risks arising from trafficking in human beings and smuggling of migrants.* FATF Secretariat, Paris.

Frontex. (2018). *FRAN quarterly report, Q4, 2017,* Available at: https://frontex.europa.eu/assets/Publications/Risk_Analysis/Risk_Analysis/FRAN_Q4_2017.pdf

Fund for Peace (FFP). (2018). *Fragile states index 2018.* Available from http://fundforpeace.org/fsi/.

Gallagher, A. T. (2015). Exploitation in migration: Unacceptable but inevitable. *Journal of International Affairs* 68(2): 55–74.

Grabska, K., N. Del Franco and M. de Regt. (2016). *Comparative research report: Time to look at girls: adolescent girls' migration in the South,* Global Migration Centre, Graduate Institute of International and Development Studies, Geneva.

Haider, H. (2015). *Radicalisation of diaspora communities.* GSDRC, University of Birmingham, UK. Available at http://gsdrc.org/docs/open/hdq1187.pdf

Henley & Partners. (2018). The Henley & Partners Passport Index 2018. Available from www.henleypassportindex.com/passport-index

Hennebry, J. (2018). The global compact for migration: From gender-rhetoric to gender-responsive? *Global Social Policy* 18(3): 332–338.

Hester T., M. E. Mendoza, D. Moloney, and M. Ngai. (2018). 'Now the Trump administration is trying to punish legal immigrants for being poor', in *The Washington Post,* 9 August 2018.

Icdugyu, A. (2018). 'Middle East', in Triandafyllidou, A. and M. McAuliffe (eds.), *Migrant smuggling data and research: A global review of the emerging evidence base, volume 2.* IOM, Geneva, pp. 19–44.

Icdugyu, A. and S.K. Akcapar. (2016). 'Turkey', in McAuliffe, M. and F. Laczko (eds.), *Migrant smuggling data and research: A global review of the emerging evidence base.* IOM, Geneva, pp. 137–160.

IOM. (2017). *World migration report 2018.* IOM, Geneva. Available from https://publications.iom.int/books/world-migration-report-2018

IOM. (2016). *Migrant vulnerabilities and integration needs in Central Asia: Root causes, social and economic impact of return migration.* IOM, Astana. Available from www.iom.kz/images/inform/FinalFullReport18SBNlogocom.pdf.

IOM. (2018). Missing Migrants project. Available from http://missingmigrants.iom.int/

Kanko, T. and T. Teller. (2014). *Irregular migration in Sub-Saharan Africa: Causes and consequences of young adult migration from Southern Ethiopia to South Africa.* Princeton conference paper. Available at http://paa2014.princeton.edu/papers/140147.

Koser, K. (2011). 'The smuggling of refugees', in Kyle, D. and R. Koslowksi (eds.), *Global human smuggling: Comparative perspectives.* The John Hopkins University Press, Baltimore, pp. 256–272.

LeBaron, G., J. Lister and P. Dauvergne. (2017). Governing global supply chain sustainability through the ethical audit regime. *Globalizations* 14(6): 958–975.

Majidi, N. and L. Oucho. (2016). 'East Africa', in McAuliffe, M. and F. Laczko (eds.), *Migrant smuggling data and research: A global review of the emerging evidence base*. IOM, Geneva, pp. 55–84.

Mbaye, L. (2017). 'Supporting communities under migration pressure: The role of opportunities, information and resilience to shocks', in McAuliffe, M. and Klein Solomon, M. (eds.), *Migration research leaders syndicate: Ideas to inform international cooperation on safe, orderly and regular migration*. IOM, Geneva, pp. 91–96.

McAuliffe, M. and K. Koser (2015) Unintended consequences: How migrant smugglers are exploiting the international protection system. *Advance*, Australian National University, Winter 2015, pp. 30–33.

McAuliffe, M. and F. Laczko (eds.) (2016). *Migrant Smuggling Data and Research: A Global Review of the Emerging Evidence Base*. IOM, Geneva. Available from https://publications.iom.int/system/files/smuggling_report.pdf.

McAuliffe, M. (2016). *Resolving policy conundrums: Enhancing cooperation on protection in Southeast Asia*, Migration Policy Institute, Washington, DC.

McAuliffe, M., A. Kitimbo, A. M. Goossens and A. K. M. Ullah. (2017). 'Understanding migration journeys from migrants' perspectives', in *World migration report 2018*, IOM: Geneva.

McAuliffe, M. and V. Mence. (2017). 'Irregular maritime migration as a global phenomenon', in McAuliffe, M. and K. Koser (eds.), *A long way to go: Irregular migration patterns, processes, drivers and decision making*. ANU Press, Canberra, pp. 11–47.

Ndiaye, N. (2012). 'Labour migration, human trafficking and multinational corporations within the ECOWAS region: Challenges and opportunities', in Quayson, A. and A. Arhin (eds.) 2012 *Labour migration, human trafficking and multinational corporations*. Routledge, Oxon, pp. 90–106.

Newland, K. and E. Patrick. (2004). *Beyond remittances: The role of diaspora in poverty reduction in their countries of origin*, Migration Policy Institute, Washington, DC.

Papademetriou, D. (2014). *Curbing the influence of "Bad Actors" in international migration*. Council statement, Transatlantic Council on Migration. Available from www.migrationpolicy.org/research/curbing-influence-bad-actorsinternational-migration

Parker, L. (2015). *Broken? The ethical dilemma of the modern supply chain*, UTS Business School News, 4 August 2015, at www.uts.edu.au/about/uts-business-school/news/broken-ethical-dilemma-modern-supply-chain

Regional Mixed Migration Secretariat (RMMS). (2015). *Regional mixed migration summary for October 2015*. http://regionalmms.org/fileadmin/content/monthly%20summaries/RMMS_Monthly_Summary_October_2015.pdf

Retaino, T. (2016). What incentives does Niger have for cracking down on migrant smuggling? Not many, LSE Centre for Africa, 13 January 2016, at: http://blogs.lse.ac.uk/africaatlse/2016/01/13/what-incentives-does-niger-have-for-cracking-down-on-migrant-smuggling-not-many/

Salt, J. and J. Hogarth. (2000). 'Migrant trafficking and human smuggling in Europe: A review of the evidence', in Laczko, F. and D. Thompson (eds.), *Migrant trafficking and human smuggling in Europe: A review of the evidence with case studies from Hungary, Poland and Ukraine*. IOM, Geneva, pp. 11–164.

Salt, J. and J. Stein. (1997). Migration as a business: The case of trafficking. *International Migration* 35(4): 467–494.

Schloenhardt, A. and H. Macdonald. (2017). Barriers to ratification of the United Nations protocol against the smuggling of migrants. *Asian Journal of International Law* 7(1): 13–38.

Schluter, C., and J. Wahba. (2009). *Illegal migration, wages, and remittances: Semi-parametric estimation of illegality effects*. IZA Discussion Paper no. 4527. IZA, Bonn.

Shah, N. (2009). *The management of irregular migration and its consequence for development: Gulf Cooperation Council*, Working Paper No 19, Asian Regional Programme on Governance of Labour Migration, ILO Regional Office for Asia and the Pacific ILO, Bangkok.

Skeldon, R. (2008). *Migration and development*, Paper for the United Nations expert group meeting on international migration and development in Asia and the pacific, 20–21 September 2008, United Nations Department of Economic and Social Affairs, Bangkok.

Skeldon, R. (2018a). *International migration, internal migration, mobility and urbanization: Towards more integrated approaches*. Migration Research Series Paper No 53 International Organization for Migration, Geneva.

Skeldon, R. (2018b). 'High-skilled migration and the limits of migration policies', in Czaika, M. (ed.), *High-skilled migration: Drivers and policies*. Oxford University Press, Oxford, pp. 48–64.

Triandafyllidou, A. (2013). Irregular migrant domestic workers in Europe. Who cares? *Research in Migration and Ethnic Relations Series* Ashgate Publishing Ltd, pp. 1–16.

Triandafyllidou, A. L. Bartolini, and C. Guidi. (2019). *Exploring the links between enhancing regular pathways and discouraging irregular migration: A discussion paper to inform future policy deliberations*, IOM, Geneva.

United Nations Department of Economic and Social Affairs (UN DESA) (2017) *Trends in International Migrant Stock: The 2017 Revision*. United Nations database, POP/DB/MIG/Stock/Rev.2017. Available from http://www.un.org/en/development/desa/population/migration/data/estimates2/esti mates17.shtml

United Nations Development Programme (UNDP). (2016). *2016 human development report*. Available at http://hdr.undp.org/en/2016-report

United Nations Development Programme (UNDP). (2017). *Remittances (diaspora financing)*, Available at www.undp.org/content/sdfinance/en/home/solutions/remittances.html

United Nations Treaty Collection (UNTC). Status of the protocol against the smuggling of migrants by land, sea and air, supplementing the United Nations convention against transnational organized crime, available at https://treaties.un.org/, accessed 31 October 2018.

United Nations World Tourism Organization (UNWTO). (2018). *2017 international tourism results: The highest in seven years*. Press release, UNWTO, Madrid.

UNODC. (2018). *Global study on smuggling of migrants*. United Nations publication, Vienna. Sales No. E.18.IV.9.

Van Hooren, F. (2012). Varieties of migrant care work: Comparing patterns of migrant labour in social care. *Journal of European Social Policy* 22(2): 133–147.

van Liempt, I. (2018). 'Human smuggling: A global migration industry', in Triandafyllidou, A. (ed.), *Handbook on migration and globalisation*. Edward Elgar Publishing, Cheltenham UK, pp. 140–154.

van Liempt, I. and J. Doomernik. (2006). Migrant's agency in the smuggling process: The perspectives of smuggled migrants in the Netherlands. *International Migration* 44(4): 165–190.

Weinar, A. (2010). 'Instrumentalising diasporas for development: International and European policy discourses', in Bauböck, R. and T. Faist (eds.), Amsterdam University Press, Amsterdam.

World Bank. (2017). Migration and remittances: Recent developments and outlook special topic: Global compact on migration, migration and development brief 27, at: http://pubdocs.worldbank.org/en/ 992371492706371662/MigrationandDevelopmentBrief27.pdf

World Bank (2018) Migration and remittances: Recent developments and outlook brief 29, at: www. knomad.org/publication/migration-and-development-brief-29

Yazd, A. (2014) Multinational corporations play key role in Qatar labor abuses, *Aljazeera*, 14 May 2014, at http://america.aljazeera.com/opinions/2014/5/qatar-labor-abusesworldcupmultinationalcorpora tions.html

Zewdu, G.A. (2018). Irregular migration, informal remittances: Evidence from Ethiopian villages. *GeoJournal* 83: 1019–1034.

PART VI

Migration corridors
Large and small

Migration is highly concentrated. Just under one-fifth of the total number of international migrations as defined using the United Nations database, go to a single destination, the United States, and over one-quarter of that flow comes from a single origin, Mexico. Hence, although migrants come from and can be found in every country, the majority of global migrants move to relatively few destinations, and from relatively few origins. That is, they are concentrated into a relatively small number of origin-destination flows that we can call 'migration corridors'. About 14 per cent of all international migration is accounted for by the ten leading origin-destination corridors, the most important of which include, after Mexico to the United States, flows from the Ukraine and Kazakhstan to the Russian Federation, from Bangladesh to India, and from China to the United States (World Bank 2017). In this section, we provide examples of some of the major migration corridors in the Americas, Europe, Southeast Asia, and sub-Saharan Africa. However, to provide a sense of perspective, and to show how small flows impact development, we include one example of a relatively unknown corridor in the Caribbean.

The corridors discussed here are defined by national origin and destination simply because the data at the global level are most readily available for states. However, where disaggregated data are available, they show that the cities in destination countries have higher proportions of migrants than the national populations as a whole. In the United Kingdom, for example, almost 40 per cent of the population of London is foreign-born compared with about 14 per cent for the population as a whole. Certainly, small numbers of migrants can have a profound impact on rural populations but the migration to states as a whole does tend to be heavily urban-weighted. Migrants are also often over-represented in specific regions of origin and destinations. Some chapters in this section in fact talk of 'corridors within corridors'.

Urban areas also play an important role in the origins of migrants, although data on urban origins are difficult to obtain. It is in the cities, and the urban sector of origin countries in general, where greater numbers have the physical and human capital available to move, for example. Again rural-origin migrants are not missing from international flows, but they may have first moved to urban centres in their own countries before proceeding overseas. This sub-national dimension of origins and destinations of corridors seems a particularly fertile area for future research into the role of international migration and development.

39

THE PHILIPPINES–
HONG KONG MIGRATION
CORRIDOR

Deirdre McKay

The movement of workers between the Philippines and Hong Kong has been a stable feature of Filipino labour migration since the 1970s. Most migrants in this corridor are domestic workers. Of the world's estimated 53 million domestic workers, 83 per cent female, and 41 per cent of them work in the Asia-Pacific (ILO 2013). Hong Kong is a unique destination in that the city recognises domestic work as 'work' and requires migrants and employers to sign a contract.

In Hong Kong, the contract specifies that the migrant must live in the employer's home and sets their minimum monthly wage (currently 4520 Hong Kong dollars). Employers of Foreign Domestic Workers in Hong Kong must provide a food allowance of 1075 dollars, or free food and free accommodation. Employers are required to set agreed working hours and days off, observe holidays, offer coverage for medical expenses, and pay for the migrant's return home at the end of the contract (Government of Hong Kong 2019). Domestic workers can complete multiple contracts, but are not permitted to apply for a Hong Kong residency card. Domestic worker migrants can thus reside in Hong Kong for decades but cannot settle in the city: they are denizens but not legal permanent residents, let alone citizens.

The number of Filipino migrants in Hong Kong has grown from 158,000 in 1997 to 201,000 in 2013, with the vast majority being women on temporary domestic work contracts (POEA 2013). Many Filipino migrants have some tertiary education but were underemployed in the Philippines, unable to find work commensurate to their qualifications (Scalabrini 2013, 123–30). Though the work Hong Kong offers is low-status, it comes with relatively transparent salary and contract provisions, public freedoms, social life, and close communications with the Philippines.

While the numbers of migrants going to Hong Kong from the Philippines have been overtaken by those leaving for other destinations for construction, medical, or care work, Hong Kong has remained a top destination for Filipino domestic workers. At the same time, the labour market in Hong Kong has shifted to incorporate more migrants of other nationalities, especially Indonesians. Following the historical trajectory described by Constable (2007), Filipinos replaced Chinese *amahs* (maids) because they were considered more tractable; now Filipinos are considered more demanding and less tractable than Indonesians. Filipinos are also considered more capable of taking on complex, additional tasks that extend their role beyond domestic work in a city short of labour.

Exploitation

Migrants experience exploitation in all live-in domestic worker migration schemes. Hong Kong is no exception. Long hours, emotional labour, lack of privacy, loss of personal life, intrusion on personal space and activities are concomitant with living in a workspace that is also the employer's home and the migrant's place of residence (Constable 2007). Workers regularly report non-payment of wages – salary deductions for spurious reasons, lack of a day off, insufficient food, and employers 'holding' the migrant's passport. These circumstances were once frequent, but are now less common, largely due to activist campaigns and the presence of several Filipino and international NGOs which assist migrants in distress (Constable 2009).

Migrants and would-be migrants from the Philippines compare experiences in destination countries and choose according to both conditions and their means. It is more expensive, in terms of visa fees and agency fees, to find a placement in a 'good' country. In the hierarchy of Filipino domestic worker migration destinations, Hong Kong is reputed to be less awful than Singapore, Taiwan, and Israel, the Gulf or Jordan and Greece (McKay 2012). The city offers relatively more freedoms and better salaries for Filipinos (Constable 2007). While salaries and working conditions for domestic workers may be better in France or the UK, access to that work now usually means following an irregular strategy (McKay 2016). Canada is usually better than Hong Kong or Europe, with a route to permanent resident status, but there are a surprising number of 'bad employers' in Canada who force migrants to work 'shared' between households or outsource them to other work, as they do in Hong Kong (McKay 2012). Exploitation of domestic worker visa-holders in other labour sectors is not uncommon around the world. In Hong Kong, some employers have forced their domestic workers to work in retail outlets of factories on the weekends, for example. But exploitation is not always the outcome; domestic workers operate in a complex environment with many hidden (and irregular) opportunities for earning or changing work and workplaces.

Figure 39.1 'High Rise' – one of the art pieces made by our Hong Kong group for Curating Development
Photo credit: Deirdre McKay

438

Filipino migrants who remain in Hong Kong long-term thus tend to be comparatively entrepreneurial. The city experiences labour scarcity at the lower end of the job market, so cash-in-hand and part-time work that tops up a maid's salary is common. Filipinos call this 'aerobics' – taking multiple part-time jobs. This means breaking the formal conditions of their contract to work, part-time, for additional employers doing cleaning, pet care, babysitting, or other work. Hong Kong's domestic worker contract can even conceal work in accounting or managing home renovations (McKay 2012). Doing 'aerobics' can raise migrants' salaries well above the government-stipulated minimum rate (Gibson, Law, and McKay 2001). Some migrants also find work in the service sector, including the night time entertainment economy of Wanchai.

While many Filipino migrants initially understand the city as a gateway to their eventual on-migration to third countries, Hong Kong's informal sector opportunities entice them to stay. The city thus has a significant population of long-term Filipino migrant workers and a social infrastructure that supports them.

Public life and development

Hong Kong offers informal spaces where migrants can meet to socialise and share information. 'Central' is the business district of Hong Kong Island, a centre of high-rise office buildings with luxury goods outlets in their bottom-floor malls. Each Sunday, streets and parks of the Central district fill with Filipino migrants. This Filipino gathering extends into the open spaces under several of the city's major office buildings. Here, migrants are tolerated, rather than invited per se. Protests require official permissions from the Hong Kong government, but spontaneous socialising is accepted, with the clean-up costs for this day of migrant sociality borne by the city. Filipino domestic workers are generally tolerated but not welcomed into Hong Kong's public spaces during the working week. On Sunday afternoons, however, they are allowed to take over the heart of the city.

Beginning mid-morning, small groups put down picnic blankets around Central's Star Ferry terminal, on Statue Square, under the headquarters of the Hong Kong and Shanghai Bank, and in the Chater Gardens park. As the day goes on, more women emerge from churches and public transit to join in. They sit and exchange news, gossip, food, and money late into the evening. NGOs representing migrant groups, Philippine municipal mayors looking for the overseas workers' vote, consular officials, and researchers all visit workers here. These people would usually be inaccessible, attending to their work in private homes, doing the shopping, or shepherding charges to and from school but, on Sunday, they are free. Mobile Chinese vendors arrive to sell food and drink and Filipinos offer each other services: manicures, pedicures, haircuts, phone-credit top-ups and the like. Filipinos in Hong Kong are at their most anonymous and most comfortable in this crowd.

For Filipinos, the word '*Central*' describes *both* the city district and their Sunday gathering itself (McKay 2012). Their social space is laid out by province, municipality, and then village. For example, migrants from Benguet Province congregate under the HSBC building near the escalators. Ask at their picnic blankets and they can point you not only to groups from each of the province's municipalities but also the gathering spots for migrants from neighbouring provinces, Ifugao and La Union. During the gathering, migrants compare notes on their remittance plans and investment strategies back home. Businesses in Central not only offer these migrants remittance services and banking in the Philippines, but they also advertise house-and-land packages, agricultural equipment, furniture, and cars on instalment. These services are discussed and marketed, person-to-person, in the gathering.

Beneficiaries of NGO training schemes or church-sponsored skills-building activities also report back on their experiences. At the same time, people in the gathering share photographs and make phone calls, send texts, or chat online with kin and friends back in the Philippines, drawing the two nations into a single, translocal social space.

Central as the translocal social corridor connecting Hong Kong to the Philippines is where the individual, intimate, and collective work of 'doing development' through migration happens. Families send in their requests for loans and allowances to migrant workers, report on schoolwork and house-building or agricultural projects. By sending back Hong Kong dollars in response, migrants express their complex feelings of obligation, alienation, love, and homesickness engendered by long separations (McKay 2007). At the same time, migrants compare notes, and complain to each other. *Central* not only lets migrants offer support and advice to each other in face-to-face sociality, it enables them to assess the successes and failures of transnational relationships, whether that's parenting, marriage, or ties mediated through their broader family obligations.

Central's Sunday gathering also facilitates political organising and access to migrants for advocacy groups. These groups are powerful advocates for, and opinion leaders among, migrants in Hong Kong and in the Philippines (Constable 2009; Hsia 2009; Law 2003). Migrants are able to vote in Philippine national elections and shape politics back home through their financial and social remittances. Migrant engagement with activism in Hong Kong goes on to shape their politics on return to the Philippines and that of their families (Rother and Kessler 2016). In this respect, Filipino *Central* is also a training ground for development and activism.

Obstacles to remittance-led development

Central offers a spatial and temporal site to target initiatives designed to facilitate remittance-led development. Filipino civil society groups focussed on development have long operated branch offices in Hong Kong and sent staff over to work with migrants to shape their investment and business strategies (Gibson et al. 2001). Other service-oriented groups offer migrants in-depth training on financial management.

Women's migration is often debt-financed, relying on loans or mortgages to pay placement fees, and remittances are used to pay off these Philippine-based debts. Most migrants need to work for up to a full year to pay off their recruitment debt, all the while fielding requests for additional funds from their family. When faced with emergencies or what seemed to be urgent investment opportunities, migrants often negotiate unsecured loans from Hong Kong finance companies against their salaries (McKay 2012). Having borrowed the maximum amount and failing to service their loans, they turn to their employers for advances or borrow additional funds from other migrants who have savings in the bank. Hong Kong thus has an extensive secondary market for credit and agencies often harass migrants' employers and friends for repayment. Loan-sharking among migrants themselves is also prevalent. Extortionate interest rates and transfer fees in the Hong Kong–Philippines corridor eat into the money available for migrants to invest at home.

Locating sites of productive investment and managing projects from a distance is a huge challenge for migrants despite new communication technologies (McKay 2012, 2016). In a recent project with migrant clients of Enrich, an NGO specialising in training migrants in financial literacy, our research team found Filipino migrants considered their biggest obstacle to successful development investments to be their family's lack of financial acumen (see curatingdevelopment.com and Figure 39.1, p. 436).

Our project worked with 24 of Enrich's clients. With an average age of 45 years old, they were each remitting approximately £300 per month. Before engaging with Enrich, most of their money had been going to school fees and home improvements, as well as status-building gifts for family members and food for celebrations. While it was vital for migrants to share their success with those they loved, it was also evident that their lack of a savings buffer or productive assets forced them to turn to finance agencies when faced with an emergency. Moreover, they were putting very little aside, if anything, for investments that would generate ongoing income on their return to the Philippines. Attending Enrich's financial training workshops changed the ways they understood both their own salaries but also their family obligations. Enrich's programme enabled them to give themselves permission to save and to invest in themselves and for themselves.

The alternative to strategic investment is returning as a 'one-day millionaire'. Without an investment strategy and a portfolio of activities, many Filipino domestic worker migrants in Hong Kong take successive contracts, working in the city for 15–25 years. They return home hoping that the beneficiaries of their gifts, school fees, and house renovations will to support them in their old age. Migrants in the Enrich group knew this was not a secure strategy. However, they needed courage and strong arguments to deprive their families of the short-term pleasures of consumer goods and celebratory meals. Once they had given themselves permission to save and invest, they made not only individual investments but identified collective and community-based projects such as community water tanks to irrigate agricultural land and supply domestic water. Collective planning and management were more easily undertaken by women who met each other in *Central* each week.

Interest rate and transaction costs combined with low wages and little opportunity for wage rises dampen remittance-led development. Those factors aside, the largest obstacle for migrants seeking to invest is the dearth of viable project ideas. Returning migrants, often college-educated and former professionals, encounter government training offers that don't match their experience or the scope of their earnings and ambitions. Research participants with whom I have remained in contact report that investment and business advice for returnees is sorely lacking. Having given up a career in teaching or similar to become a domestic worker in Hong Kong and remitting £50,000 or more back to the Philippines, the re-integration training they access on their return doesn't meet their ambitions.

Government re-integration programmes tend to offer returnees skills such as baking cookies, sewing, repairing shoes and umbrellas, and managing a small piggery. These activities are typically already familiar to returnees and only suitable as 'sidelines' that generate a small bit of extra income. Little training is available in the skills they need to take advantage of emerging digital business opportunities or on what would be required to launch a larger-scale enterprise. The development need, then, is to consider domestic workers as incipient owners of small-to-medium enterprises. Migrants need appropriate training on finances and management, and the Hong Kong corridor is an ideal incubator to pilot and test accessible, well-targeted schemes and measure their development effects.

Conclusion

Hong Kong offers Filipinos opportunities and that is why they remain. Even with the challenges outlined here, many choose to stay (Asis, 2013). The city offers migrants comparatively secure and dignified working conditions, which, when combined with its proximity to the Philippines, can make further risk-taking seem unwise. Should something go wrong, migrants perceive they'll be able to rely on fellow Filipinos for support and easily return home. This imagined ease of work and travel is compared to Singapore, Malaysia, Taiwan, and the Arabian Gulf, which offer much lower wages and greater isolation. The comparative ease of return between contracts and for vacations during contracts enable migrants in Hong Kong to exert greater influence and control over the ways in which their remittances are invested in the Philippines. Being able to direct and monitor investments is crucial to migrant wellbeing, as is the sense of camaraderie in the Filipino social life of the city. Moreover, in a city where labour is scarce, lucky long-timers have been able to transition their work, if not their domestic worker visa, into new and more remunerative roles in the informal economy. Thus, Hong Kong is a place where a canny migrant can find opportunity and establish networks of support that, despite the nature of the work and the attached social status of 'maid', make their sojourns worthwhile.

Acknowledgement

Data on Enrich's work comes from Curating Development (AHRC P007678/1), a collaborative project led by Prof Mark Johnson (Anthropology, Goldsmiths) with Dr Gabriela Nicolescu, Nathalie Dagmang, and Lenlen Mesina (Enrich) alongside community participants in Hong Kong.

References

Asis, M. (2013) "Here Today and Tomorrow: Transnational Domestic Workers" Asia Research Institute, Singapore at: www.youtube.com/watch?v=4Q1Pkqsstgo
Constable, N. (2007) *Maid to Order in Hong Kong*. Ithaca: Cornell University Press.
Constable, N. (2009) "Migrant Workers and the Many States of Protest in Hong Kong", *Critical Asian Studies*, 41(1): 143–164.
Gibson, K., Law, L. and McKay, D. (2001) "Beyond Heroes and Victims: Filipina Contract Migrants, Economic Activism, and Class transformations", *International Feminist Journal of Politics*, 3(3): 365–386.
Government of Hong Kong. (2019) Recruitment: Hiring Foreign Domestic Helpers. Available at: www.gov.hk/en/residents/employment/recruitment/foreigndomestichelper.htm
Hsia, H.-C. (2009) "The Making of a Transnational Grassroots Migrant Movement in Hong Kong: A Case Study of Hong Kong's Asian Migrants' Coordinating Body", *Critical Asian Studies*, 41(1): 113–141.
International Labour Organisation. (2013) Domestic Workers Across the World. Geneva: ILO. Available at: www.ilo.org/public/libdoc/ilo/2013/113B09_2_engl.pdf
Kessler, C. and Rother, S. (2016). *Democratisation Through Migration*. London: Lexington Books.
Law, L. (2003) "Transnational Cyberpublics: New Political Spaces for Labour Migrants in Asia", *Ethnic and Racial Studies*, 26(2): 234–252.
McKay, D. (2007) "Sending Dollars Shows Feeling: Emotions and Economies in Filipino Migration", *Mobilities*, 2(2): 175–194.
McKay, D. (2012) *Global Filipinos*. Bloomington: Indiana University Press.
McKay, D. (2016) *Archipelago of Care*. Bloomington: Indiana University Press.
Philippines Overseas Employment Agency (POEA) (2013). Stock Estimates. https://cfo.gov.ph/down loads/statistics/stock-estimates.html (Last accessed 30/01/2019).
Scalabrini Migration Centre 2013 Country Migration Report: The Philippines 2013. Prepared for the International Organisation for Migration. Available at: www.iom.int/files/live/sites/iom/files/Country/docs/CMReport-Philipines-2013.pdf. See pp. 123–130.

40

THAILAND–MYANMAR INTERNATIONAL MIGRATION CORRIDOR

From battlefield to marketplace

Supang Chantavanich

Thailand and Myanmar, formerly known as Siam and Burma, share more than 2000 km of borders. The corridor is demarcated by the Tenasserim Range, which separates the two countries. Three major corridor immigration crossings are located in the north, central, and south of the borders. From 2013–15, two new border crossings were open on the corridor.

North: Mae Sai (Chiengrai Province) – Thachilek Eastern Shan State
North: Mae Sot (Tak Province) – Mywaddy (Karen State)
Central: Phu Nam Ron (Kanchanaburi Province) – Thee Khee (Karen State)
South: Ranong Province – Kaw Thaung (Tanintharyi Region)
South: Dan Singkorn (Prachuab Province) – Mudong (Tanintharyi Region)

From the sixteenth to the nineteenth century, Siamese and Burmese relations were mainly through warfare (Chutintaranond and Than Tun 1995, 33). The Burmese Army captured the Siamese capital of Ayuthaya twice in 1569 and 1767. After Burma became a British colony in 1824, the relationship between the two states was frozen until Burma's Independence in 1948. Later, from the end of the twentieth and beginning of the twenty-first centuries, the two states resumed their diplomatic relations and trade flourished at an accelerated phase, changing this corridor from battlefield to marketplace.

Thai and Burmese people are not the only main actors here. Ethnic minorities especially the Mon, Karen, Karenni, and Shan who live along the corridor have been actively involved in the relationship. These ethnic minorities were indigenous to the area before colonisation. During wartime, they were drafted to participate in the army by both powers (Slezak, Singer, and Ramadurai 2015, 59). They also played the role of buffer zone, which separated Thailand and Myanmar from direct contact. When the wars between the two states were over, some of them became traders, loggers, weapons, drugs smugglers, and resistant groups fighting against Myanmar. Doubtlessly, the corridor has always been lively and porous. After the period of fighting, the situation changed and the borders became more pervious. According to the ADB, the East–West Economic Corridor (EWEC) is located on this Myanmar–Thailand corridor. Flows of people, trades, and investment are on the rise.

Figure 40.1 Thailand–Myanmar migration corridor

Source: Asian Research Center for Migration 2019, adapted from Samak Kosem ed. (2016) Border Twists and Burma Trajectories: Perceptions Reforms, and Adaptations, p. iii

Transformation of the corridor 1990–2018

Movements of people along the corridor have been known for centuries. Ethnic minorities commuted across the mountain during the colonial period. Small towns and markets could be found everywhere, as described by an ethnologist:

> Mong Tai [alias] is located on the old trade route between Northern Thailand and Shan State of Myanmar. It is a market town where traders from various places of origin bring their goods to exchange with local people … Ethnic Karen women brought forest products and sold them to northern Tai women who sold them to others while

ethnic Hmong carried cabbages from the mountain in their van and brought them to Mong Tai market for sale. It seems that everybody is a trader in Mong Tai.

(Niti Pawakhapan 2015, 93–7)

The narrative of Mong Tai illustrates how a small market town historically emerged in the corridor. Various groups of mobile people crossed borders for economic motivation. However, the Thai–Myanmar corridor is not without conflict. After Independence in 1948, Myanmar has been challenged by ethnic minorities who possess their own armed groups and continuously fight against the military government. The latter fought back violently. Ethnic political refugees crossed the borders to Thailand as asylum seekers. More than 100,000 persons were displaced and accepted in nine shelters along the corridor in Thailand (Chantavanich and Kmonpetch 2017). They are mainly Karen, Karenni, Shan, and other minorities. The Thai government and UNHCR cooperate to offer humanitarian assistance. During 2008–16, 80,000 asylum seekers were resettled. However, currently there are still 120,000 displaced persons including new arrivals. Repatriation has been discussed, but limited progress can be observed as the Peace Process between the government and the ethnic groups in Myanmar has been delayed creating a protracted refugee situation (Chantavanich and Kmonpetch 2017). The existence of refugee

Figure 40.2 Myeik port in Myanmar, and end of the migration corridor

shelters in the corridor reflects another aspect of displacement flows. The borders have been transformed from battlefield to marketplace at the state level, yet local realities show a different scenario of armed conflict in some parts of the corridor.

Another feature of the corridor transformation is cross-border labour migration. Since the 1990s, a significant number of job seekers from Myanmar have crossed the borders to work in Thailand. Sea fishery was the first sector to employ them. In 1992, Thailand started its policy to employ migrant workers from Myanmar in coastal provinces. Later, more workers were employed in other sectors. In 2018, the total number of registered migrant workers from Myanmar, Cambodia, and Laos was 1.8 million persons. Of this number, 75 per cent are from Myanmar (IOM 2018; MOL 2018). A Memorandum of Understanding was signed to address the irregular flows of migrants and to arrange a more formal recruitment system. However, due to long porous borders, measures to manage a totally documented labour migration is a challenge despite the Thai government's policy to regularise all migrant workers from the three source countries. Migrants bring along their families and some use the services of unscrupulous transborder human smuggling networks to cross the corridor. In the south, Muslim Rohingya migrants take the boat journey from western Myanmar. Some disembark on Thai shores due to unfavourable weather conditions. Current research finds that the mixed flows comprise of asylum seekers, victims of human trafficking, and economic migrants (Kaewkuekoonkit and Chantavanich 2018). The corridors have witnessed migration flows of asylum seekers, migrant workers as well as victims of human trafficking during the last 20 years.

The increasing number of people who cross the borders has led to the establishment of new border crossing points in border towns. Usually, the main natural passes in the Tenessarim Range serve as major border crossings with towns located at each crossing. Most of the official immigration checkpoints are equipped with the necessary infrastructure including roads, warehouse, immigration, customs, and quarantine.

On the Thai side, Mae Sai, Mae Sot, and Ranong are the three biggest border towns where trade flourishes at an exceptional speed. Similarly, Thachilek, Myawaddy, and Khawthaung have economically developed quickly with trade, tourism, and human mobility. Since the transformation of the turning policy from battlefield to marketplace, trades in the corridor have increased steadily (Department of Foreign Trade, Thailand 2017).

Figure 40.3 Thailand–Myanmar border

Impacts of migration on development

International migration has yielded impacts on both sides at the micro and macro levels (De Haas 2010 p.227)

Economic

Labour mobility has had a significant impact on remittance flows. The World Bank indicated that 1.7 billion dollars had been sent from Thailand to Myanmar in 2015, accounting for 2.78 per cent of Myanmar's GDP (World Bank 2017). Another study indicated that sending remittance through brokers was less costly than through the banks (IOM-ILO 2017). A tracer study of remittance flows from Thailand to Myanmar in 2007 found that remittances were used mainly for daily household consumption, thus significantly supporting the families left behind with food consumption, shelter, clothing, the education and healthcare (Khine 2007).

The rise of trade and investment is another consequence of migration in the corridor. While more people moved from Myanmar to Thailand, the direction of trade and investment is in the reverse direction. Export value from Thailand to Myanmar increased from 2.1 billion dollars in 2012 to 3.3 billion in 2016 (Department of Foreign Trade, Thailand 2017). The investment has created local employment and brought economic growth to both countries.

Political

The diplomatic relationship between the two countries has much developed after the extension of the corridor. However, illegal border crossing is a major concern in the corridor and is associated with the trafficking of drugs and weapons, as well as human beings. The northern part of the corridor called the 'Golden Triangle' has been known as the location of drug production and exportation. Contraband arms were also found due to past internal political conflicts in Myanmar (Boutry and Ivanoff 2009, 49–68; Phongpaichit, Piriyarangsan, and Treerat 1998, 86–97). As for human trafficking, some migrant workers were brought to Thailand and ended up in forced labour in the fisheries industry (Chantavanich, Laodamrongchai, and Stringer 2016, 1–7). More recently, male and female Rohingya migrants were trafficked to the south of Thailand. The two governments have signed several memoranda of understanding to tackle the challenges arising from the illegality and cross-border crimes indicating that cooperation is underway.

Border demarcation is a security challenge between the two countries although a Joint Border Committee (JBC) has been set up, the process is slow. There exist some border points that the JBC cannot agree upon.

Socio-cultural

The majority of Myanmar migrants who come to Thailand are young people and those who have been living in Thailand for more than a decade have reconstructed their identities. Interethnic marriage and inter-marriage with Thais (formally and informally) have led them to take on a new identity as Thai people. To the extent that some see Thailand as their homeland (Boutry and Ivanoff 2009, 124–5; Makchareon 2011, 119). The newly adopted identity leads to the consumption of Thai cultural commodities such as media, language, and food. Nevertheless, diaspora communities of Burmese and other ethnic groups can be found along the corridor in Thailand interacting with their co-ethnics in Myanmar.

In 2005, the Thai government addressed the issue of statelessness. Children of some ethnic minorities, who live along the borders and were formerly stateless, received a permanent resident card issued by the Thai government. The spouses of Thai citizens both men and women are granted Thai citizenship. Obviously, the impacts of migration on economic, political, and socio-cultural development on the corridor are both positive and negative. Yet the positive consequences are more evident.

Future of the corridor

The corridor in context

The Thailand–Myanmar corridor is the western part of the East–West Economic Corridor, initiated in the 1990s by the Asian Development Bank, and is an ASEAN regional land link between the Pacific and Indian Oceans (Figure 40.4) . The eastern part of the corridor was finished in 2000 but the progress of the western corridor was slow. However, recently, the road links from Mae Sot to Pa-an and Kanchanaburi to Dawei have been constructed and repaired, making the EWEC almost complete. The Thailand–Myanmar corridor is but one part of the broader EWEC designed ultimately to bring development to Myanmar, Thailand, and the region.

Direction of the flows

Cross-border migrations between 1990 and 2017 have changed in unpredictable ways. In the 1990s, the direction of the flows was one way: from Myanmar to Thailand. When Thailand expanded its labour market, migrants from Myanmar came from States and Divisions, which are located both near and far from the borders. The corridor of migration expanded to cover the central and western part of Myanmar. In Thailand, labour migration extended from border provinces to inner towns. The new millennium witnessed economic and political developments in the corridor (Callahan 2002). In Myanmar, trade and investment from Thailand and the ASEAN flourished in Yangon. On the Thailand side, the new restrictive labour migration policy effected massive temporary return flows to Myanmar in 2016 (see Schiller 2009, 14–37). The pattern of mobility became unpredictable, depending on push and pull factors from both sides. Migration flows have become *multi-directional* with a high level of diversification. According to Truong (2015, 7–27), the transformation of borders and migration flows is a twin process which is significant for the development on both sides of the corridor. Later in 2017–18, mobility became stabilised on both sides with tourists, traders, and investors crossing the borders to Myanmar compensating for movements in the other direction. The new trend of translocality is emerging in the corridor.

Conclusion

The arrival of China has brought profound change to Southeast Asia and to the Thailand–Myanmar corridor. The upper part of the corridor is traversed by an unknown but large number of Chinese traders and visitors from the southern provinces but also from as far away as Beijing. The traders invest mostly in informal business like the export of Chinese commodities and agro-industry. A significant number of Chinese tourists came to the mainland ASEAN especially Thailand and Myanmar. It is estimated that more than 9 million Chinese are travelling in the ASEAN (Santasombat 2015). They have

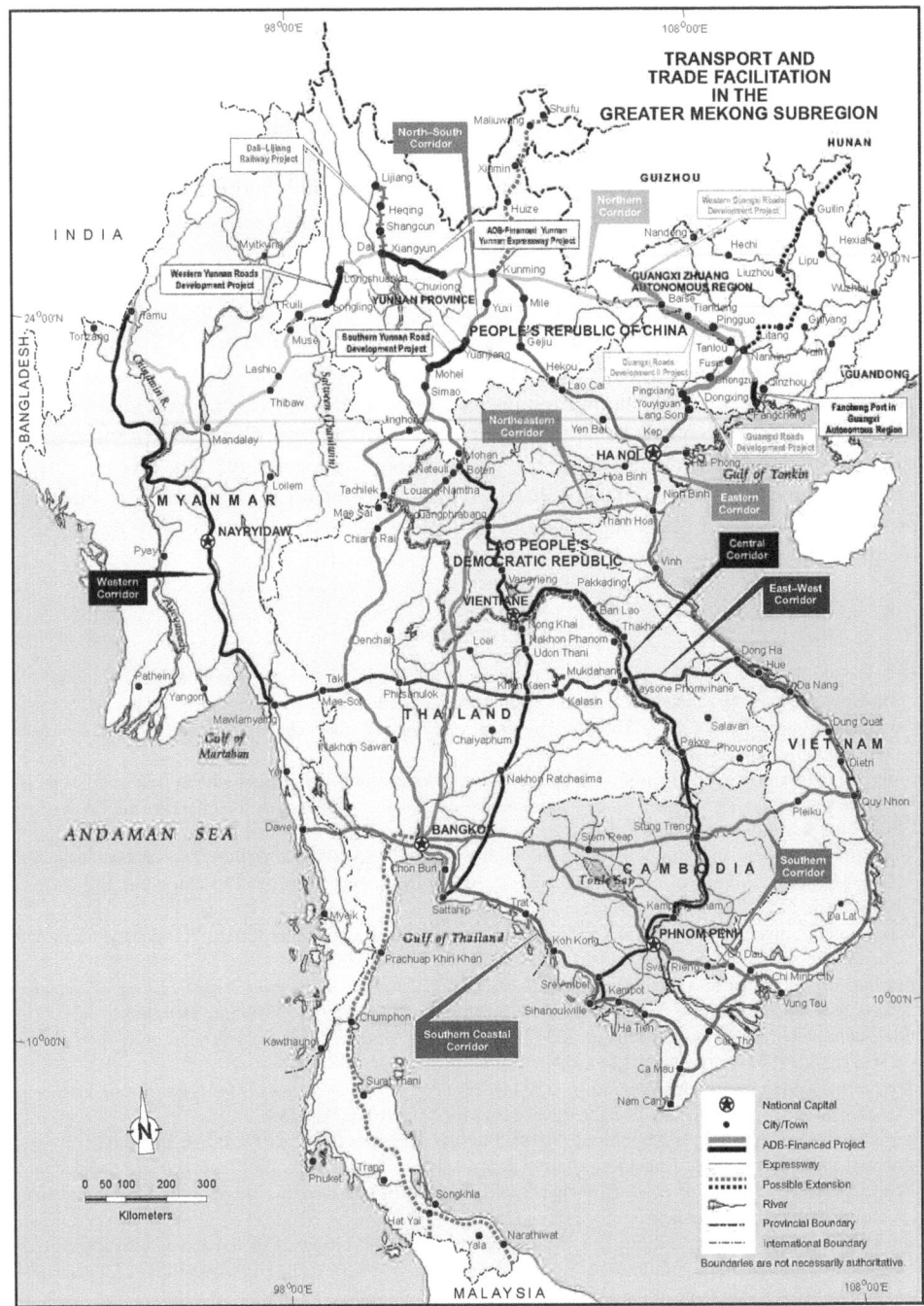

Figure 40.4 East–West Economic Corridor

Source: Asian Development Bank (2014) *Economic Corridor Development for Inclusive Asian Regional Integration: Modeling Approach to Economic Corridors*, p. 65

made impacts on the consumption of food, energy, the physical and cultural environment as well as on transport and tourism services. Tourism also created linkages to many sectors of production and contributed to the national GDP in Myanmar and Thailand (ADB 2017). The migration flows of Chinese tourists, businessmen, and students reflect China's rising influence, which will certainly change this corridor. In 2017, 9.8 million Chinese tourists visited Thailand (Thailand Ministry of Tourism and Sports Tourism Statistics 2017). More than 200,000 Chinese visited Myanmar in the same year (Myanmar Ministry of Hotel and Tourism 2017).

The future of the corridor will be predominantly economic. Regional migration policy including the Asian Development Bank Tourism Roadmap for Cambodia, Laos, Myanmar, Thailand, and Vietnam (CLMTV) and the ASEAN Master Plan of Action 2025 on Tourism Connectivity on the East–West Economic Corridor will enhance the development of infrastructure and services to facilitate more human and commodity flows on Thailand–Myanmar International Migration Corridor and make it a real marketplace. Cross-border integration depends on national immigration policy and economic cooperation. Unexpected forces from environmental changes and uncertain security concerns on the corridor may bring in new migration patterns like temporary and multiple relocation and translocality due to the diversification of livelihoods.

References

Asian Development Bank (2014) *Economic Corridor Development for Inclusive Asian Regional Integration: Modeling Approach to Economic Corridors*. Asian Development Bank, Manila.

Asian Development Bank (2017) *Tourism Assessment Strategy and Roadmap for CLMV 2016-2018*. Asian Development Bank, Manila.

Boutry, Maxim and Jacques Ivanoff (2009) *La Monnaie des frontieres: Migrations birmanes dans le sud de la Thailande, structure des reseaux et internationalisation des frontieres*. Institut de Recherche sur l'Asie-du-Sud-Est Contemporaine, Bangkok.

Chantavanich, Supang and Aungkhana Kmonpetch eds. (2017) *Refugee and Return: Displacement along the Thai–Myanmar Border*. Vol. 28. Springer Briefs in Environment, Security, Development and Peace, New York, NY, Springer, Printforce, the Netherlands.

Chantavanich, Supang, with Samarn Laodamrongchai and Christina Stringer (2016) "Under the Shadow: Forced Labour among Sea Fishers in Thailand" *Marine Policy*, 68, 1–7.

Chutintaranond, Sunait and Than Tun (1995) *On Both Sides of the Tenasserim Range: History of Siamese-Burmese Relations*. Institute of Asian Studies Chulalongkorn University, Thailand, Bangkok.

Department of Foreign Trade, Thailand. (2017) "Statistics of Border Trades". (www.dft.go.th/bts/trade-statistics/cid/153/-4) Accessed 12 October 2017.

International Organization for Migration. (2014) *Thailand Migration Report: Highlights Social, Economic Challenges of Migration*. International Organization for Migration, Bangkok.

International Organization for Migration. (2018) *Thailand Migration Report 2018*. IOM, Bangkok.

International Organization for Migration – International Labour Organization. (2017) *Risks and Rewards: Outcomes of labour migration in South-East Asia*. International Organization for Migration and International Labour Organization, Bangkok.

Kaewkuekoonkit, Angkana and Supang Chantavanich (2018) "Rohingyas in Thailand: Existing Social Protection in Dynamic Circumstance", *Asian Review*, 33, 5–24. Institute of Asian Studies, Chulalongkorn University, Bangkok.

Khine, Nwet Kay (2007) Migration as a Development Strategy: A Case Study of Remittance Flows from Thailand to Mawlamyine, Mon State, Myanmar. MA Thesis in International Development Studies Programme, Chulalongkorn University, Thailand.

Makchareon, Pairin (2011) "Myanmar Migrant Worker's Adaptation for Settlement in Mae Sot, Thailand" *Asia Parithat*, 32, 111–136. Institute of Asian Studies, Chulalongkorn University, Bangkok.

Ministry of Hotel and Tourism, Myanmar. (2017) "Myanmar Tourism Plan", (http://tourism.gov.mm/wp-content/uploads/2018/06/Myanmar-Tourism-Statictics-2017.pdf) Accessed October 12, 2018.

Ministry of Tourism and Sports Thailand. (2017) Tourism Statistics 2017. Accessed from http://www.thaiwebsites.com/tourists-nationalities-Thailand.asp (22 October 2019).

Pawakhapan, Niti (2015) *Narrative of Mong Tai: Dynamism of a Thai–Myanmar Border Town*. Center for ASEAN Studies, Chiengmai University, Chiengmai.

Phongpaichit, Pasuk with Sungsidh Piriyarangsan and Nualnoi Treerat (1998) *Guns, Girls, Gambling, Ganja: Thailand's Illegal Economy and Public Policy*. Silkworm Books, Chiengmai.

Santasombat, Yos ed. (2015) *Impact of China's Rise on the Mekong Region*. Palgrave Macmillan, New York.

Schiller, Nina Glick (2009) "A Global Perspective on Migration and Development" *Social Analysis*, 53 (3), 14–37.

Slezak, Amanda Crews with Thalia Singer and Rupa Ramadurai (2015) "Stateless and Fleeing Persecution: The Situation of the Rohingya in Thailand" *Children's Legal Rights Journal*, 35, 44–78.

Truong, Thanh-Dam (2015) "Migration, security and development: Reflections on integrating migration into border studies" *Asian Review*, 28(1), 7–27.

World Bank (2017) "Bilateral Remittance Estimates (Thailand–Myanmar)" (www.worldbank.org/en/topic/migrationremittancesdiasporaissues/brief/migration-remittances-data) Accessed 22 September 2017.

41

THE KYRGYZSTAN–RUSSIA MIGRATION CORRIDOR

Madeleine Reeves

Kyrgyzstan, with a population of 6.2 million, is today ranked among the most remittance-dependent states in the world. Annual remittance transfers of 2.7 billion dollars equated to 35.1 per cent of the country's GDP in 2018, making Kyrgyzstan second only to Tonga in its degree of remittance dependence (World Bank 2018). The scale and the intensity of Kyrgyzstan's transformation into a 'remittance state' over the course of the previous 15 years has had profound structural impacts on the country's economy and society at every level, from the dynamics of the urban housing market and the transformation of the agricultural economy to the micro-politics of multi-generation households in contexts of protracted family absence (Isabaeva 2011; Reeves 2012; Sagynbekova 2016; Schoch, Steimann and Thieme 2010). Meanwhile, the transformation of the Russian Federation, the primary destination for migrant workers from Kyrgyzstan, into a state with one of the highest global rates of in-migration, has had significant impacts on the country's social, economic, and political life. In 2017 Russia had a non-citizen population of 11.2 million. With over a million migrants from the Commonwealth of Independent States in Moscow alone, migration has become a particularly intense topic of public debate in the Russian capital, figuring as the dominant election issue in the 2013 Moscow mayoral race (Blakkisrud and Kolstø 2018; Reeves 2013).

Post-Soviet remittance corridors, while relatively new and comparatively under-researched, have become integral to the architecture of the labour markets in both receiving and sending countries and have come to have a significant impact on development priorities and agendas, nationally and internationally. Visa-free access to Russia, along with well-developed transport links by rail, air, and chartered bus, and the linguistic and cultural familiarity born of a shared Soviet heritage, have created the conditions for relatively easy integration for Kyrgyzstani migrant workers into a largely unregulated labour market. Changes in visa regulations in Turkey and the ongoing impact of sanctions on the Russian economy, which have led to a significant devaluation of the Russian rouble against the Kyrgyz som, have made Turkey an increasingly popular destination for Kyrgyzstani migrant workers since 2014. Nonetheless, Russia, where a declining domestic population has created the conditions for seasonal workers to find employment and accommodation relatively easily through informal networks of friends and acquaintances, remains by far the primary destination hosting 640,000 of Kyrgyzstan's 800,000 migrant workers in 2018 according to Kyrgyzstan's State Migration Service (Interfaks 2018).

The transformations brought about by this emergent migrant economy have been profound. As well as coming to serve as a social safety net against the most acute shocks of post-Soviet economic implosion, recent empirical studies in Central Asia have drawn attention to the ways that migration is incorporated into the fabric of family life, including changing patterns of marriage and long-distance intimacy (Aitieva 2015; Ismailbekova 2014), new patterns of divorce and polygamy (Thibault 2018), the changing cost of bride-price (Reeves 2012), and emergent patterns of urban investment brought about by the remittance economy (Nasritdinov 2015). This chapter focuses on the Kyrgyzstan–Russia migration corridor and its social impacts, drawing upon the author's ongoing, multi-sited ethnographic research among migrant workers from Batken region of Kyrgyzstan and their encounter with life *shaarda* ('in town').

The development of a post-Soviet migration 'corridor'

The end of the Soviet Union and of its centralised, planned economy had far-reaching consequences for the newly-independent, mountainous republic of Kyrgyzstan. In the early 1990s, the country became a poster-child for experiments in 'shock therapy', with the liberalisation of the currency, the privatisation of land, and the auctioning of formerly collectively-owned livestock, equipment, and farm-buildings. The 1990s witnessed a precipitous decline in living standards, with many rural families resorting to eating their livestock and migrating to the peri-urban informal settlements that rapidly developed around the country's largest cities, Bishkek and Osh (Falkingham 2005; Pétric 2012).

Policymakers and government officials at this time were primarily concerned with two sets of migratory dynamics that were distinct from the patterns of seasonal or long-term labour migration that were later to emerge: the first was the internal migration of ethnic Kyrgyz families from rural areas to the peri-urban informal settlements of the larger cities; the second was the large-scale out-migration of Kyrgyzstan's Russian-speaking population, in which ethnic Russians, Ukrainians, Germans, and others returned to their so-called 'historical homeland', often benefitting from preferential resettlement policies aimed at 'compatriots' (*sootechestvenniki*). Between 1989 and 1999, 688,000 people left Kyrgyzstan permanently, around one in six of the population (Schmidt and Sagynbekova 2008, 116). This migration has typically been characterised as 'political' rather than 'economic', though motivations were often complex, combining fears of ongoing economic decline in Central Asia with a generalised sense that life as a visible minority in Kyrgyzstan in a context of resurgent ethno-nationalism constrained the life-chances of one's children (Pilkington 1998). It is notable at this time that Russia did not have a migration policy as such: the Russian state viewed ethnic Russians and Russian-speakers as 'returnees' rather than as migrants who might continue to maintain material and affective ties with the country they had recently left.

Labour migration among ethnic Kyrgyz was rarely discussed in public discourse in the 1990s, and in the Russian media, the *gastarbaiter* ('guest worker', a term incorporated into the Russian language from the German in the post-Soviet period) was typically used to denote Russians who had migrated west, rather than Central Asians or other visible minorities who had travelled to Russia from other states of the former Soviet Union. Russia in the 1990s was also in a state of precipitous economic decline. Infrastructure and construction projects were limited and families, even in highly urbanised areas, came to rely increasingly on garden plots and rural relatives to keep them supplied in fresh fruit and vegetables (Ries 2009). This was hardly an attractive environment for seasonal labourers.

In this first post-Soviet decade, international migration from Kyrgyzstan was dominated by ad hoc market trade, typically by those established entrepreneurs who had developed trade relations in the late Soviet period, importing single lorry-loads of fresh or dried fruits from a cluster of villages or a single district to be sold at a farmers' market (*kolkhoz bazaar*) on the edges of urban settlements. Many of these early trade connections developed from informal links developed through shared military service or the privileges enjoyed by long-distance drivers for state farms. Such journeys were primarily undertaken by men who had been socialised during the Soviet period, who spoke fluent Russian and felt quite at home in the Russian metropolis. Often those trading had a primary employment elsewhere and would make a single annual journey to sell produce such as apricots, cherries, or pomegranates in the cooler climes of Russia during a short summer season.

It was in the early 2000s that migration came to shift from the adventurous seasonal activity of a few 'pioneer' young men to a year-round activity and a source of regular livelihood. The particular pattern and dynamic of migration varied by region, and rates of out-migration, though high everywhere, still vary considerably by region. Migration became widespread first in those southern districts of the country, such as Batken and Osh, where land plots tend to be smaller and supplies of irrigation water more constrained. Districts where livelihoods were more embedded in a pastoral, rather than an agricultural economy, were (and remain) less dependent upon seasonal migration since livestock can serve as a store of wealth that can more easily be converted to cash than agricultural products with seasonal cycles of production and sale. In regions of Kyrgyzstan immediately bordering Tajikistan, patterns of out-migration have also been influenced by dynamics across the border. The civil war that devastated Tajikistan between 1992 and 1997 pushed many Tajik men to migrate as a form of economic necessity, and migration remains critical to economic well-being in large parts of the country two decades after the end of the civil war. In the early 2000s, these men returned with cash and contacts, often travelling through Kyrgyzstan by road, and sharing their stories of success.

In the Batken region, for instance, which immediately borders Tajikistan's Soghd region, my informants often spoke of following where Tajiks had started, though ultimately developing rather different economic niches within the Russian labour market. They also spoke of migration becoming a 'fashion' (*moda*) in the mid-2000s: no longer an exceptional or 'pioneer' activity, migration was now the primary destination for male school-leavers and a season or more 'in town', increasingly became a necessity to be able to defray the demanding costs of marriage and to prove oneself capable of providing for one's family. In 2005 a survey that I conducted in a cluster of land-poor villages in the Batken region revealed that around 40 per cent of households relied directly or indirectly upon remittance transfers for their livelihoods; by 2010, a repeat survey in the same cluster of villages revealed that it was more than double this figure, with 85 per cent of surveyed families indicating migration and its associated intermediary businesses serving as a significant or primary source of domestic incomes. While this data is locally specific, the general trend towards the normalisation of migration as a livelihood strategy in land-poor regions of southern Kyrgyzstan is substantiated by national-level data on out-migration. Migration rates increased throughout the 2000s, in line with Russia's growing economy. Although the 2009–10 financial crisis and the impositions of sanctions on Russia in 2014 led to dips in the rate of migration, migration rates to Russia have since recovered, boosted by Kyrgyzstan's accession to the Eurasian Customs Union in 2015 (Turdukulov 2018).

The corridor that developed was facilitated by the development of air connections between Kyrgyzstan and Russia alongside the previous rail and road connections. It was magnified by economic differentials between the two states, such that by the mid-2000s the monthly salary as an entry-level construction worker (*raznorabochii*) on an informal construction site would earn 4–5 times as much as a state salaried worker employed by the local education authority or the provincial government. The mid-2000s 'snowball effect' was facilitated by the drastic oil-fuelled growth in the Russian economy beginning in the year 2000, which prompted a construction boom in Moscow and other cities, and created a ready demand for small, informal construction brigades who would update or remodel Soviet-era apartments or turn former one-story dachas into large out-of-town villas for an emergent middle class.

The corridor also brought about its own infrastructures of communication and exchange. Beginning in 2004, the gradual appearance of a mobile phone signal in rural Kyrgyzstan and the emergence of cheap international calling cards facilitated communication and the transfer of remittances. Until the mid-2000s it was still common for remittances to be transferred by a trust and kin-based mechanism analogous to the South Asian *hawala* system known as a *perekidka* ('throwing'), in which brothers or other close relatives would negotiate the (virtual) transfer of funds to a relative in the sending village for a small fee. By the late 2000s such systems of unregulated transfer were gradually displaced by Russia-based commercial companies and by the proliferation of local banks. At the time of writing (2018), smartphone technology has transformed the process of remittance transfer once again, both in terms of the mechanisms for the transfer of funds and the ubiquity of demands upon migrant workers who were previously much harder to reach (see also Urinboyev 2017). Calls between Russia and Kyrgyzstan are relatively cheap, particularly when compared with other global remittance corridors. Given the size of the migrant population, multiple mobile phone operators deliberately target the migrant market in their advertisements and their offerings, charging calls to Kyrgyzstan at the same rate as those to other parts of the Russian Federation. As a result, the transaction costs of remittance transfers between Russia and Kyrgyzstan are some of the lowest in the world (UNDP 2013, 21).

Changing gender dynamics of migration

The initial phase of labour migration, from the early to the mid-2000s, was dominated by men. The typical pattern would be for a male household head and/or his eldest son to depart for work first, undertaking work in a construction 'brigade' (*brigada*) of other men from the man's village or district. Work was typically organised informally, without written contracts, and based on a trust-based system of informal regulation in case of non- or under-payment of wages. In such a situation, accommodation typically consisted of an informal area within the construction site, or a designated 'dormitory' (*jatakana* in Kyrgyz) for which expenses would be taken directly from the monthly wages. Such arrangements reduced costs in an exceptionally expensive housing market, by providing accommodation that was free or low-cost. As more men became established, however, so patterns of occupation and residency changed. There emerged a network of informal intermediaries (*posredniki*) who facilitated access to the Russian housing market, either by serving as an informal tenant who then sub-let mattress space (*koiko-mesto*) on an individual basis, and/or by facilitating contact with landlords who would, for a significant percentage, countenance renting their apartment as a *de facto* dormitory apartment. Such arrangements, colloquially known as 'rubber apartments' because of the number of people notionally registered as resident, exist in violation of housing codes and are thus extremely vulnerable to police or vigilante raids.

As mattress-spaces and, for the more financially able, individual rooms within shared apartments became more popular as a system of tenancy, so migration itself shifted from a predominantly seasonal pattern undertaken (almost) exclusively by men to a livelihood strategy of both men and women, including married couples who would typically leave children in the care of grandparents or other relatives. This so-called 'family migration' (*semeinaia migratsiia*) became much more widespread by the late 2000s, facilitated by a growing demand for service-sector jobs, including in catering, cleaning, and domestic service, undertaken primarily by women (Aitieva 2015). The shift towards family migration has altered patterns of seasonality, with more families coming to see migration as a long-term survival strategy, with the children of migrant workers increasingly enrolled in kindergarten and school in the Russian Federation. The relative ease of obtaining Russian citizenship has also led many migrant workers to seek to regularise their situation by buying a Russian passport, often at considerable expense. This is typically undertaken as a pragmatic response to the challenges of remaining regularised in a context of economic and administrative precarity, and it remains to be seen whether, longer term, the current orientation towards an imagined (if increasingly distant) return 'home' persists among the generation of children born and raised of migrant workers in Russia. Current migration trends suggest that while migrant destinations are likely to continue to diversify, the expectation in large parts of rural Kyrgyzstan that seasonal work abroad is the pre-condition for a socially-meaningful adult life and the possibility to construct an independent family home is unlikely to disappear any time soon.

References

Aitieva, Medina. 2015. "Reconstituting Transnational Families. An Ethnography of Family Practices Between Kyrgyzstan and Russia". PhD dissertation, University of Manchester.

Blakkisrud, Helge and Pål Kolstø. 2018. "'Restore Moscow to the Muscovites': Othering 'the Migrants; in the 2013 Moscow Mayoral Elections." In Pål Kolstø and Helge Blakkisrud, eds., *Russia Before And After Crimea: Nationalism and Identity, 2010-2017*. Edinburgh: Edinburgh University Press, 236–257.

Falkingham, Jane. 2005. "The End of the Rollercoaster? Growth, Inequality and Poverty in Central Asia and the Caucasus." *Social Policy and Administration* 39 (4): 340–360.

Interfaks. 2018. "Vlasti Kirgizii nazvali kolichestvo migrantov v Rossii." 14th September. www.interfax. ru/russia/629250

Isabaeva, Eliza. 2011. "Leaving to Enable Others to Remain: Remittances and New Moral Economies of Migration in Southern Kyrgyzstan." *Central Asian Survey* 30 (3-4): 541–554.

Ismailbekova, Aksana. 2014. "Migration and Patrilineal Descent: the Role of Women in Kyrgyzstan." *Central Asian Survey* 33 (3): 375–389.

Nasritdinov, Emil. 2015. "Building the Future: Materialisation of Kyrgyz and Tajik Migrants' Remittances in the Construction Sectors of their Home Countries." Unpublished manuscript, American University Central Asia.

Pétric, Boris. 2012. *On a mangé nos moutons: le Kirghizstan, du berger au biznessman*. Paris: Belin.

Pilkington, Hilary. 1998. *Migration, Displacement and Identity in Post-Soviet Russia*. Abingdon: Routledge.

Reeves, Madeleine. 2011. "Staying Put? Towards a Relational Politics of Mobility at a Time of Migration." *Central Asian Survey* 30 (3-4): 555–576.

Reeves, Madeleine. 2012. "Black Work, Green Money: Remittances, Ritual and Domestic Economies in Southern Kyrgyzstan." *Slavic Review* 71 (1): 108–134.

Reeves, Madeleine. 2013. "Mayoral Politics and the Migrant Economy: Talking Elections and 'Illegals' in Moscow." Cities@Manchester blog. 5th September. https://citiesmcr.wordpress.com/2013/09/05/mayoral-politics-and-the-migrant-economy-talking-elections-and-illegals-in-moscow-3/

Ries, Nancy. 2009. "Potato Ontology: Surviving Postsocialist Russia." *Cultural Anthropology* 24 (2): 181–212.

Sagynbekova, Lira. 2016. *The Impact of International Migration. Process and Contemporary Trends in Kyrgyzstan*. Basel: Springer Publishing.

Schmidt, Matthias and Lira Sagynbekova. 2008. "Migration Past and Present: Changing Patterns in Kyrgyzstan." *Central Asian Survey* 27 (2): 111–127.

Schoch, Nadia, Berndt Steimann and Susan Thieme. 2010. "Migration and Animal Husbandry: Competing or Complementary Livelihood Strategies. Evidence from Kyrgyzstan." *Natural Resources Forum* 34 (3): 211–221.

Thibault, Hélène. 2018. "Labour Migration, Sex, and Polygyny: Negotiating Patriarchy in Tajikistan." *Ethnic and Racial Studies* 41 (15): 2809–2826.

Turdukulov, Adil. 2018. "Chislo migrantov iz Kyrgyzstana rastet." *Res Publica*, 2nd February. http://respub.kg/2018/02/02/chislo-migrantov-iz-kyrgyzstana-rastet/

UNDP. 2013. *Labour Migration, Remittances, and Human Development in Central Asia*. UNDP: Regional Bureau for Europe and the Commonwealth of Independent States. www.undp.org/content/dam/rbec/docs/CAM&RHDpaperFINAL.pdf

Urinboyev, Rustamjon. 2017. "Establishing an 'Uzbek Mahalla' via Smartphones and Social Media: Everyday Transnational Lives of Uzbek Labor Migrants in Russia." In Marlène Laruelle, ed., *Constructing the Uzbek State: Narratives of Post-Soviet Years*. Lanham, MD: Lexington Books, 119–147.

World Bank. 2018. *Migration and Remittances: Recent Developments and Outlook. Migration and Development Brief 30*, December 2018. www.knomad.org/sites/default/files/2018-12/Migration%20and%20Development%20Brief%2030.pdf

42

THE TURKEY–GERMANY MIGRATION CORRIDOR

Nermin Abadan-Unat and Başak Bilecen

Introduction

In Europe, one of the largest migration corridors is between Turkey and Germany, a function of their longstanding migration history. According to the latest census data, in 2017, there were 2.77 million persons from Turkey with a migration background living in Germany (Destatis 2018). Although labour migration from Turkey to Germany is the most well-known type of mobility between the two countries, in this chapter we demonstrate that there are multiple population movements in this specific corridor. We examine six phases of migration between the two countries while concentrating on their developmental impacts. In so doing, we argue for a nuanced understanding of a migration corridor given the heterogeneity of mobility and two-way flows over the years between cities and regions leading to corridors within country corridors.

Linkages between Turkey and Germany have existed for a long time, as both countries have been allies leading to economic, political, and societal exchanges throughout recent history. Starting as early as the nineteenth century, the German empire was sending military personnel to the Ottoman empire for training purposes that also continued in the early years of the Turkish republic. During World War I, the Ottomans allied with the German empire leading to more population movements of businessmen, craftsmen, and their spouses (Pusch and Splitt 2013). Those relations had positive implications in the political and economic relations between the two republics. Against this background, we identify six phases consolidating the migration corridor between Germany and Turkey: (1) the migration of academics escaping from Nazi persecution to Turkey (1930–50); (2) the entrepreneurial small-scale migration from Turkey to Germany (1950–60); (3) guest worker recruitment starting the official labour migration (1961–73); (4) the settlement phase with family unification (1973–90); (5) the asylum seeking period (1989–2000); (6) contemporary two-way flows (2000–present).

Migration streams between Turkey and Germany

During the 1930s, the first Turkish President Mustafa Kemal Atatürk invited Jewish intellectuals including professors, teachers, and physicians who escaped from Nazi persecution to settle in Turkey. German professors contributed to the development of the higher education system in

Turkey and trained future intellectuals (Widman 1973). This migration flow was a two-step process directed initially towards Istanbul, Ankara, and Izmir. From there, some moved abroad, mainly to the US. Upon their further mobility during the 1940s, those intellectuals kept their ties and initiated partnerships with universities in Turkey. Moreover, they also led important institutions such as the German Hospital, German schools, and German-speaking churches (Radt 2006). Their mobility allowed different segments of Turkish society in large cities to familiarise themselves with German culture, and as a result they became more sympathetic towards Germany paving the way for subsequent migrations (Akgündüz 2008).

In the second phase of migration, in the 1950s, Turkish businessmen and entrepreneurs were invited to West Germany not only to improve their skills but also to strengthen foreign trade and the economy between the two countries (Abadan-Unat 2011). During this phase, migration was organised by individuals and small groups for entrepreneurial activities. This is usually an overlooked stage of migration between the two countries because of low numbers of migrants. For example, during that period, high school graduates in Turkey in technical fields were invited to Germany for training with the aim to post them as foremen in German plants operating in Turkey. Later, those who were trained in Germany opted to stay in the country rather than going back to Turkey for work (Akgündüz 2008).

The third phase, in the 1960s, was characterised by the state-organised guest worker agreement. During that decade, Turkey was facing higher unemployment rates and pursuing state-led industrialisation. Turkey aimed to send workers to gain skills and send financial remittances to contribute to the country's development goals while at the same time reducing the demographic pressure. It coincided with the era when Germany was restructuring its economy and experiencing labour shortages after World War II, particularly after the erection of the Berlin Wall in 1962. Against this background, both nation-states conceptualised this short-term agreement for their mutual economic development (Abadan-Unat 2011, 7–13; Martin 2014). Migrants were mainly male and working in specific industrial sectors and accommodated in dormitories. Migrants' financial remittances in this period played a crucial role in Turkey's economy, and thus development (İçduygu 2006). Guestworkers were from villages in central Anatolia, such as Boğazlıyan (Yozgat) or from the Black Sea region, for example, the city of Trabzon. The Black Sea shores are well known as a region where both rural and urban migrants originated.

The oil crisis of 1973 ushered in the fourth phase, the settlement of Turkish migrants in Germany. Labour recruitment from Turkey officially stopped while family reunification increased (Martin 2014). This was a time when the social rights of workers and their families became an important policy issue. As a result of intergovernmental negotiations, migrants gained access to state welfare provisions such as healthcare, unemployment, and pension rights in Germany. In addition, more young women migrated independently to improve the prospects of their households, when they and their families in Turkey learned about the demand for workers in the German labour market. They were usually not well-educated and eventually employed in jobs requiring no qualifications such as in the textile sector. Migration profoundly influenced family life both in the emigration and immigration contexts, because women became breadwinners that changed the division of labour within families. (Abadan-Unat 2011, 88–111).When families arrived in this era, they settled in cities and concentrated in certain neighbourhoods such as Kreuzberg and Neukölln in Berlin, Marxloh in Duisburg, and Keup in Cologne, changing the urban landscape of Germany. For instance, North Rhine-Westphalia is the most foreign populated federal state mainly because of the Ruhr area, where heavy industries were located, which recruited migrant labourers. Macro-level changes such as deindustrialisation together with different migration streams over time and lack of integration policies made the area ethnically segregated resulting in poor housing and schooling leading to further marginalisation (Reuschke and Weck 2013).

The fifth phase, between 1989–2000, was characterised by conflicts in the South-eastern region in Turkey from the 1980s, which dramatically increased the number of people seeking political asylum in Germany (Martin 2014, 229–31). That migration stream added another layer of heterogeneity to the existing migrant population in terms of ethnicity and region of origin from Turkey. In Europe, this period was also characterised by other refugee movements such as from Bosnia-Herzegovina. The Christian Democratic Union party was in power in Germany with the idea that their country was not a country of immigration and the main discourse revolved around immigrants having the 'right' to choose between return or full assimilation into German society. In that context, in 1983, the 'Foreigners Repatriation Incentive' law encouraged around 5 per cent of Turkish migrants to return through granting a lump sum return incentive together with pension premiums. Return migrants were usually elderly and unskilled who invested their savings in property or small family businesses. They therefore did not necessarily contribute to the industrialisation of Turkey as originally anticipated. The policy worked as a retirement strategy for the first-generation labour migrants. However, for their children, who have been brought up in Germany, the situation was different. When parents returned to Turkey, they often took their youngest children with them to be sent to schools in Turkey where they had re-adaptation issues. Over time, some of these children returned to Germany either to study or through marriage. Concurrently, migrants who stayed in Germany established small independent businesses and created further employment for fellow workers. The 'Foreigners Law' in 1992 eased the process of becoming a German citizen and particularly for younger generations with longer residence, school attendance, and who renounced their right to Turkish citizenship. The law also put emphasis on continuous employment and residency for social rights and naturalisation while favouring those with good prospects of integration (Abadan-Unat 2011, 13–25).

During this fifth phase, religious, political, and business associations were financed by Turkish migrants and the state. The Turkish–Islamic Union of the Presidency of Religious Affairs (DITIB) (1984), Islamic Community Millî Görüş (1985), and the Federation of Alevitic Communities of Europe (AABF) (1991) were the major religious associations with transnational activities (Amelina and Faist 2008). Millî Görüş had strong ties with the extreme right and Islamic political parties such as Millî Nizam, Faziler, Saadet, whereas DITIB became the mouthpiece of the Justice and Development Party (AKP) in the early 2000s, so that the transnational religious and political ties were consolidated.

In the sixth phase, from 2000 onwards, we observe a mix of movements including students and highly skilled persons pointing to an increase in more circulatory movements and a decline in the number of marriage migrations. Baykara-Krumme and Fuss (2009) explain marriage migration as taking place between migrants who had at least 5 years of residency in Germany and their new arriving spouses from Turkey. This definition excludes family reunification of already married migrant couples. This definition covers the 49 per cent of Turkish first-generation male migrants' marriage and family reunification patterns in Germany. In this last phase, the tendency to choose a spouse from Turkey declined for male migrants, while it slightly increased for females (Baykara-Krumme and Fuss 2009). Some of the marriages were arranged because for some families having a groom from Turkey in Europe was financially appealing, together with the idea of raising the next generations with an 'appropriate culture' (Abadan-Unat 2011, 108–10).

When we look at the developmental effects of the various streams of migration, we can say that not everything is economic. Social remittances, or the idea that norms, practices, identities, and social capital circulate between the two countries through the simultaneous involvement of the migrants in both contexts, play a major developmental role, too (Levitt and Lamba-Nieves 2011). For instance, women's participation in migration and paid work allowed a rethinking of authority in the household and a division of labour between migrating and non-migrating families in Turkey. The emergence of 'kaleidoscopic' type families (Kıray in Abadan-Unat 1976, 210–34) indicates that size, membership, and authority is decided by the breadwinner, in many cases the female migrant. In this process, families located in both contexts have been transformed in terms of gender relations, division of labour, and what is considered culturally and socially appropriate.

Other types of mobilities in this sixth phase of migration between Turkey and Germany include returned guest workers and their children, exchange students, skilled professionals, and German retirees (Fauser 2016). While some of the first-generation guest workers and their spouses return to Turkey for good, some of them prefer to circulate between the two countries as a lifestyle choice. For instance, Bilecen and Tezcan-Güntekin (2014) found that first-generation retired migrants tend to live in both countries simultaneously, usually maintaining ties to their own communities in Turkey where they have property and personal ties. Moreover, some of the guest workers have had previous internal migration experience in Turkey from rural to urban areas, particularly to the big cities such as Istanbul, Ankara, Izmir, and Antalya. In such cases, guest workers tend to return to those cities while also visiting their villages and communities.

According to King and Kılınç (2016), three types of 'return' by second-generation Turkish migrants exist. First, 'return' as teenagers based on parental decision. Second, 'return' through marriage, usually observed among women. Third, 'return' as a self-realisation and a quest for identity and belonging through which ambivalences in an imagined 'ethnic motherland' arise. While the first and second types were usually observed in the fifth phase, the third type of 'return' is a main aspect of the sixth phase. The now grown-up second-generation whose parents chose to stay in Germany during the fifth phase started to enrol in universities or find jobs in Turkey and wanted like to experience their 'motherland' for themselves.

The latest research on exchange students and skilled professionals shows a mixture of flows in both directions (Bilecen Süoglu 2012; Fauser 2016; Pusch and Aydın 2012). While Germany has always been an attractive study place for exchange and degree-seeking students from Turkey, recently both German and second-generation migrants also go to Turkey for educational purposes. For instance, Pusch and Aydın (2012) conducted research with highly skilled German citizens with a Turkish background, who were sent to Istanbul by the businesses they work for. In their findings, they show how they question their identities when they work in Turkey. Their return to Germany is always an option indicating another type of circular movement between the two countries.

The last type of mobility found in the sixth phase is characterised by German retirees living in Antalya and its provinces mainly in Alanya due to affordable living conditions and good weather. Their impact has been the creation of a de-facto municipal foreigner council in Alanya, but also in changing the daily landscape of the province through for example opening their shops, bakeries, and building churches.

One major and recent type of mobility consists of academics from Turkey seeking refuge in Germany, thus reversing the very early trend in this migratory corridor. In January 2016 'academics for peace' group signed a petition to draw attention to human rights violations in the South-eastern region of Turkey. Moreover, on 15 July 2016, there was a coup attempt against the state institutions. In such a political climate, academics were charged of being members of terrorist group and 8,000 were fired. The most substantial support for the Turkish academics has been by the Humbolt Foundation's Phillip Schwartz Initiative, who once had to flee Nazi Germany and convinced the Turkish government to appoint the persecuted German professors in 1930s.

Conclusion

In this chapter, we have shown different population flows that contributed to the heterogeneity of migration and consolidated the corridor between Turkey and Germany. We argued that such international flows have impacts on the two countries in economic and sociocultural terms. What is implicit in the migration corridor concept is that once migration is initiated, either individually or through state-led initiatives, later networks of people, businesses, and institutions/organisations sustain such channels and turn the migration into a corridor where both ends are transformed. Once the networks gain momentum, migration tends to become more diversified. As we have shown, sometimes the corridors can be geographically circumscribed. For example, due to the industrialisation of a region, such as the Ruhr area, migrant flows tend to be directed towards such regions. From the perspective of the sending area, however, the networks channel them into certain cities and neighbourhoods to create networks of networks, or corridors within corridors. In this chapter, we have shown, that the concept of 'the corridor' is quite restricted because it gives the impression of a homogeneous and often uni-directional flow of people. As the history of migration between Turkey and Germany throughout the twentieth and twenty-first century demonstrates, this is far from being the case.

References

Abadan-Unat, N. (1976) *Turkish Workers in Europe, 1960-1975*. Leiden: E.J.Brill.

Abadan-Unat, N. (2011) *Turks in Europe. From Guest Worker to Transnational Citizen*. Oxford: Berghahn Books.

Akgündüz, A. (2008) *Labour Migration from Turkey to Western Europe, 1960–1974. A Multidisciplinary Analysis*. Aldershot: Ashgate.

Amelina, A. and Faist, T. (2008) Turkish Migrant Associations in Germany: Between Integration Pressure and Transnational Linkages. *Revue européenne des migrations internationals* 24(2): 91–120.

Baykara-Krumme, H. and Fuss, D. (2009) Heiratsmigration nach Deutschland: Determinanten der transnationalen Partnerwahl türkeistämmiger Migranten. *Zeitschrift für Bevölkerungswissenschaft* 34(1–2): 135–164.

Bilecen, B. and Tezcan-Güntekin, H. (2014) Transnational Healthcare Practices of Retired Circular Migrants. *COMCAD Working Papers*, No. 127. COMCAD: Bielefeld.

Bilecen Süoglu, B. (2012) Trends in Student Mobility from Turkey to Germany. *Perceptions: Journal of International Affairs* 17(2): 61–84.

Destatis. (2018) Bevölkerung und Erwerbstätigkeit. Bevölkerung mit Migrationshintergrund. Ergebnisse des Mikrozensus 2017. Available at: www.destatis.de/DE/Themen/Gesellschaft-Umwelt/Bevoelker ung/Migration-Integration/Publikationen/Downloads-Migration/bevoelkerung-migrationsstatus-5125203117004.pdf?__blob=publicationFile&v=3, last accessed March 21, 2018.

Fauser, M. (2016) A View on the Reverse Map of Migration between Germany and Turkey. *Turkish Review* 6(3): 116–124.

Içduygu, A. (2006) International Migrants Remittances in Turkey (Research Reports No. 7). Florence: European University Institute, Euro-Mediterranean Consortium for Applied Research on International Migration.

King, R. and Kılınç, N. (2016) The Counter-Diasporic Migration of Turkish-Germans to Turkey: Gendered Narratives of Home and Belonging, in R. Nadler, Z. Kovács, B. Glorius and T. Lang (eds.), *Return Migration and Regional Development in Europe. New Geographies of Europe*. London: Palgrave, pp. 167–194.

Levitt, P. and Lamba-Nieves, D. (2011) Social Remittances Revisited. *Journal of Ethnic and Migration Studies* 37(1): 1–22.

Martin, P. L. (2014) Germany: Managing Migration in the Twenty-first Century, in J. F. Hollifield, P. L. Martin and P. M. Orrenius (eds.), *Controlling Immigration: A Global Perspective*. Stanford: Stanford University Press, pp. 224–250.

Pusch, B. and Aydın, Y. (2012) Migration of Highly Qualified German Citizens with Turkish Background from Germany to Turkey: Socio-Political Factors and Individual Motives. *International Journal of Business and Globalisation* 8(4): 471–490.

Pusch, B. and Splitt, J. (2013) Binding the *Almancı* to the "Homeland" – Notes from Turkey. *Perceptions* 17(3): 129–166.

Radt, B. (2006) Von der Teutonia bis zur Brücke-Zur Deutschsprachigen Infrastruktur in Istanbul. *Zeitschrift für Türkeistudien* 19(1): 152–159.

Reuschke, D. and Weck, S. (2013) Residential Segregation of Turkish Migrants in the Ruhr Area—Reasons, Patterns and Policies, in D. Reuschke, M. Salzbrunn and K. Schönhärl (eds.), *The Economies of Urban Diversity*. New York: Palgrave, pp. 191–215.

Widman, H. (1973) *Exile und Bildungshilfe: die deutschsprachige akademische Emigration in die Türkei nach 1933*. Frankfurt: P. Lang.

43

THE LIBYA–ITALY MIGRATION CORRIDOR

Daniela DeBono

Introduction

The Libya–Italy corridor is one of the main corridors used by migrants to irregularly cross the Mediterranean Sea. In 2017, it registered 119,369 sea border crossers, a drop from previous years when on average some 170,000 would be registered every year (UNHCR 2018). However, even though the deaths at sea dropped from 4578 in 2016 to 2846 in 2017, this remains the most deadly border in the world (UNHCR 2018).

The Libya–Italy corridor is part of a broader route, also encompassing Tunisia and Malta, which is equally subject to border control and migration governance and is often referred to as the Central Mediterranean Route. For many, this corridor is a small part of a longer route across Western or Eastern African countries and an equally long route ahead after the sea crossing to destination countries in northern Europe. For this reason, the Mediterranean can be considered a geo-racial border zone (Van Reekum 2016).

Human smuggling and other geopolitical interests in the area have contributed towards an intense governance game played by bordering states and also by more powerful actors such as the European Union (EU) and the United States (US). The aim of this article is to encourage an appreciation of the political and socio-economic 'factors, dynamics, and actors' (Ciabarri 2014, 258) which contribute to the production of this migratory corridor, thus challenging a superficial representation of this corridor as a fixed or straightforward reality.

The background: the making of this corridor

The manner in which the Libya–Italy route became a corridor, duly governed and organised by different actors, sheds light on the choice of style of migration governance undertaken by the EU. This point can be extended to the whole Central Mediterranean Route. In 2015, the entry point of this corridor, together with the Eastern Mediterranean Route (Turkey–Greece), both part of the EU's external border, became 'irregular entry hotspots'. Building on relations already established between the two countries, the EU machinery moved in to support the border management along this corridor leading to political and technocratic interventions, which in practice entail a shift of sovereignty towards centralised European institutions legitimated through these dominations (Kasparek 2016). The portrayal by the EU of the Mediterranean as a 'maritime void' or 'reserved' for state and EU (border) authorities (Stierl 2016, 561) has been criticised for it absolves states from their responsibility for deaths as a result of border control (Spijkerboer 2009). Indeed, the Mediterranean Sea is highly regulated, as might be expected in an area with such political, social and economic activity.

Three kinds of operations take place in and around the sea passage. First, are operations related to border control led by national coastguards and FRONTEX (the EU's border agency). Second, are Search and Rescue operations, which are handled primarily by Italian and Maltese authorities since most of this corridor runs through the Maltese Search and Rescue zone. However, these Rescue and Coordination Centres can call on any vessels for assistance, such as merchant vessels. Since 2015, non-governmental organisations are also conducting a fair share of Search and Rescue operations. Third, the presence of a wide spectrum of international military vessels of which there has been a proliferation since the revolution in Libya.

Before proceeding to discuss human smuggling/irregular migration and its governance, it is important to bear in mind five key factors. First, mobility and exchange, for trade and military purposes, between countries across the central Mediterranean have a long history (Ben-Yehoyada 2017). Libya itself from the middle of the nineteenth century to the first half of the twentieth century was gradually shaped into a 'borderscape' not only due to Italian–Libyan relations but also due to its strategic position in North Africa on the Mediterranean coast (Brambilla 2014, 225).

Second, although Italy maintained and developed new relations with Arab Governments, including Libya in the second half of the twentieth century (Del Boca 2014), this region is still largely characterised by the after-effects of independence movements in North African countries and the birth of the European Coal and Steel Community/the European Union. In particular, the Schengen Treaty, which abolished internal border controls in the EU, created the need for greater enforcement of the external EU borders to try to make these as impermeable as possible. This resulted in a highly securitised and militarised border. The Schengen agreement, however, could not work without a common visa policy governing legal entries into the EU. As a result of the centralisation of the visa regime, it became more selective, with interests led by common EU policy, ignoring previous ties between individual Member States and third countries (Finotelli and Sciortino 2013). This selective visa regime in turn produced a situation whereby people seeking asylum are forced into taking irregular routes. Those people, such as the Tunisians in Sicily, who until then had relatively easy access to temporary work across the border, had to stop the practice or cross irregularly.

Third, this corridor runs across a Global South and Global North border. The economic asymmetry, the emerging conflicts in the region and to the south, and the greater awareness of perceived opportunities in the north between the European and African sides of the corridor are key factors conditioning its existence as an irregular migration corridor. Indeed, as argued by King and DeBono (2013) irregular migration is constitutive of the Southern European migration regime.

Fourth, this corridor is located in a regional area of instability. Since 2011, Libya has been in a state of turmoil and civil strife brought about by local rival groups seeking control of the territory, and failing to enter into lasting agreements with each other. Furthermore, competing international stakeholders have tried to establish a link with those factions in Libya, creating a wider spectrum of mismatching interests. In 2017 an estimated 1.3 million people were in need of basic humanitarian assistance in Libya (UNHCR 2017).

Fifth, Libya was an immigration country, and not, as often described, a country of transit (Bredeloup and Pliez 2011). In 2002, Libya hosted 1.6–1.8 million migrants (HRW 2006), mostly labour migrants from sub-Saharan countries, from which only a few transited the country to Europe. For example, in 2004, only 10,000 migrants arrived by boat to Italy and not all of them departed from Libya. The numbers of people leaving Libya rose sharply during and after the 2011 revolution. This increase was a result of the conflict and included both Libyans and foreigners resident in Libya. In 2017, UNHCR estimated that there were 217,002 internally displaced persons, 278,559 returnees, and 43,113 refugees and asylum seekers registered with UNHCR resident in Libya (UNHCR 2017).

Human smuggling

Smuggling networks facilitate the crossing of borders without a permit (see also Chapter 38 in this Handbook). Research shows that the choice of routes is often dictated by less policing of entry points (Mountz and Kempin 2013). At the same time as enforcement measures intensify, human smuggling networks intensify their efforts, and the prices for irregular journeys increase as do the risks taken by migrants (Abdel Aziz et al. 2015).

Human smuggling networks have been active in Libya for some considerable time, but there has been a dramatic increase in the post-revolution years. This is a feature of Libya's post-war division into competing armed factions. It is an activity that goes beyond the coastline and can be found across the country, incorporating and feeding on the political economy and geopolitics of Libya's Southern, Eastern, and Western borders (Micallef 2017). Reports on the threat to the human security of migrants, including the use of torture are now widely available. What is less often considered is the human security threat to local communities, which rely on local militias for protection, and/or rely on human smuggling for their own livelihoods (Micallef 2017).

The Italian–Libyan cooperation in border and migration management acted as a precursor and supported the creation of this corridor. The roots of this cooperation, economic ties and strong diplomatic relations, can be found in the period when Italy colonised Libya between 1911 and 1947. This was a relatively short, but bloody, period of time. Nevertheless, close diplomatic relationships were established between the two countries and still persist today. Within the EU, Italy is seen as the natural ally/broker with Libya. Italy's close relationship and its colonial past with Libya came to the fore with treaties such as the Treaty of Friendship, Partnership and Cooperation between the Italian Republic and Great Socialist People's Libyan Arab Jamahiriya of 2008. Gaddafi himself actively pursued such relations to augment internal legitimacy (Trupiano 2016). It also included a section, denounced as in violation of international law (Frelick 2009), by which Libya would accept to take back irregular border crossers and would step up its border control through funding provided by Italy.

In contrast to the establishment of close ties with Libya, Italian relations with Malta, another EU Member State, suffered a series of diplomatic incidents in relation to Search and Rescue operations. This generally concerns rescues, which take place within Malta's Search and Rescue Zone, but where the closest safe port is the Italian island of Lampedusa. Italy and Malta disagree on the interpretation of the notion of a 'place of safety' which in the international law of the sea denotes the place where migrants should be disembarked (Klepp 2011). This has led to a series of unfortunate standoffs between Italy and Malta whereby rescue or disembarkation are delayed by the disputing states. One of the first widely publicised incidents of this kind took place in 2009 and concerned the Turkish cargo ship 'Pinar E' which was refused entry to Malta with 154 migrants onboard. But these incidents have been ongoing: for example, in December 2018, 49 migrants who had been saved by Sea-Watch, a small German NGO, in the Mediterranean close to Lampedusa, were first denied entry by Italy and eventually even by Malta. After 19 days at sea, with rough weather approaching and an agreement reached between Malta and other EU Member States, the migrants were finally disembarked in Malta.

Governance: control, containment, and humanitarianism?

The critical tension that characterises the governance of this migration corridor by the EU and Member States rests between the protection of human lives and border control. National and European law, in this regard, provides the obligations of states and international laws, but in practice the fulfilment of these obligations depends on the countries' political and military interests.

EU policy on this corridor employs the Italian–Libyan model of joint governance. By doing so, Italy as well as the EU, de-localise the EU's external border from South Italy beyond the Libyan coastline into its territory. Examples of such de-localisation can be found both pre-Gaddafi and after: the construction of Italy-funded detention centres on Libyan territory, the material provision of vehicles and communication equipment to facilitate Libyan patrols, deportations to and from Libya, and joint Italian–Libyan police patrolling of the Libyan coastline (Andrijasevic 2006, 123).

On land, two contrasting logics have been identified: the logic of reception and the logic of containment (Cuttitta 2016). The EU promises a dignified reception for all irregular migrants. This is in line with international human rights law and, in view of the high number of asylum applicants, in agreement with international refugee law. In recent decades, detention as a means of control and deterrence is increasingly supported by the EU both in Libya (with direct EU financing) and in Italy and other border states for the purposes of reception and repatriation. Evidence of this policy is the recent model of the 'first reception'/'hotspots' designed by the EU and implemented in Italy (and Greece), whereby the administrative detention of all irregular migrants is enforced upon arrival (DeBono 2019), in the absence, unfortunately, of adequate human rights monitoring (DeBono 2018).

Mobility along this route is not only in one direction. Indeed, forced migration in the form of deportation and involuntary returns regularly takes place. Widely publicised at the time were operations of detention and deportations from the detention centre in Lampedusa in the autumn of 2004 when, between 3 and 7 October, more than a thousand irregular migrants were expelled from Lampedusa to Libya on military aeroplanes. These collective deportations occurred in a politically charged atmosphere surrounding the proposal to set up refugee processing centres in North Africa (Andrijasevic 2006, 121). The collective deportations from Lampedusa to Libya resumed in March, April, and June 2005. In August 2005, they acquired almost a weekly regularity after the International Organisation of Migration signed an agreement with Libya aimed at deterring irregular migration from and into the country (Andrijasevic 2006, 121). Returns and deportations to Libya were suspended at the start of the revolution in Libya (although they continue to Tunisia). In 2017, amidst considerable controversy due to the unstable situation in Libya and the reports of torture of sub-Saharan migrants, the pushbacks of migrants by Italy (meeting the interests of Italy, Libya, and the EU) were resumed, albeit not on a regular basis. The criminalisation of Search and Rescue NGOs which, since 2015 have been operating on the Central Mediterranean Route, has continued unabated by both Italy and Malta.

Conclusion

In conclusion, the Italy–Libya migration corridor best known for its use as an irregular migration route into the EU, and the most deadly, should be approached as a corridor constructed and sustained by geopolitical interests over the years. This can be seen in its governance model presented as driven by humanitarianism, but characterised by the control and containment of irregular migrants, hiding the competitive tensions and interests of different national and regional powers.

References

Abdel Aziz, N., Monzini, P. and Pastore, F. (2015) *The Changing Dynamics of Cross-border Human Smuggling and Trafficking in the Mediterranean*, Istituto Affari Internazionali, Roma.

Andrijasevic, R. (2006) "Lampedusa in Focus: Migrants Caught between the Libyan Desert and the Deep Sea", *Feminist Review 82*: 120–125.

Ben-Yehoyada, N. (2017) *The Mediterranean Incarnate: Region Formation between Sicily and Tunisia since World War II*, University of Chicago Press, Chicago.

Brambilla, C. (2014). "Shifting Italy/Libya Borderscapes at the Interface of EU/Africa Borderland: A 'Genealogical' Outlook from the Colonial Era to Post-Colonial Scenarios", *ACME: An International Journal for Critical Geographies 13(2)*: 220–245.

Bredeloup, S. and Pliez, O. (2011) *The Libyan Migration Corridor*, European University Institute, Fiesole.

Ciabarri, L. (2014) "Dynamics and Representations of Migration Corridors: The Rise and Fall of the Libya-Lampedusa Route and Forms of Mobility from the Horn of Africa (2000-2009)", *ACME: An International E-Journal for Critical Geographies 13(2)*: 246–262.

Cuttitta, P. (2016) "The Way to the Italian Hotspots. The Space of the Sea between Reception and Containment", *Society and Space* (http://societyandspace.org/2016/11/15/the-way-to-the-italian-hotspots-the-space-of-the-sea-between-reception-andcontainment/) accessed 15 January 2018.

DeBono, D. (2018) "In Defiance of the Reception Logic: The Case for Including NGOs as Human Rights Monitors in the EU's Policies of First Reception of Irregular Migrants", *Peace and Conflict: Journal of Peace Psychology 24(3)*: 291–295.

DeBono, D. (2019) "Plastic Hospitality: The Empty Signifier at the EU's Mediterranean Border", *Migration Studies 7(3)*: 340–361.

Del Boca, A. (2014) *Gheddafi. Una sfida dal deserto*, Laterza, Bari.

Finotelli, C. and Sciortino, G. (2013) "Through the Gates of the Fortress: European Visa Policies and the Limits of Immigration Control", *Perspectives on European Politics and Society 14(1)*: 80–101.

Frelick, B. (2009) *Pushed Back, Pushed around: Italy's Forced Return of Boat Migrants and Asylum Seekers, Libya's Mistreatment of Migrants and Asylum Seekers*, Human Rights Watch, USA.

Human Rights Watch (HRW) (2006) "Stemming the Flow: Abuses Against Migrants, Asylum Seekers and Refugees", (https://www.hrw.org/report/2006/09/12/stemming-flow/abuses-against-migrants-asylum-seekers-and-refugees) accessed 22 October 2019.

Kasparek, B. (2016) "Routes, Corridors, and Spaces of Exception: Governing Migration and Europe" Near Futures Online "Europe at Crossroads", (http://nearfuturesonline.org/routes-corridors-and-spaces-of-exception-governing-migration-and-europe/) accessed 15 January 2018.

King, R. and DeBono, D. (2013) "Irregular Migration and the 'Southern European Model' of Migration", Journal of *Mediterranean Studies 22(1)*: 1–31.

Klepp, S. (2011) "A Double Bind: Malta and the Rescue of Unwanted Migrants at Sea, a Legal Anthropological Perspective on the Humanitarian Law of the Sea", *International Journal of Refugee Law 23(3)*: 538–557.

Micallef, M. (2017) *The Human Conveyor Belt: Trends in Human Trafficking and Smuggling in Post-revolution Libya*, Global Initiative Against Transnational Crime, Geneva.

Mountz, A. and Kempin, R. (2013) "The Spatial Logics of Migration Governance along the Southern Frontier of the European Union" in Walton-Roberts, M. and Hennebry, J. eds., *Territoriality and Migration in the E.U. Neighbourhood: Spilling over the Wall*, Springer, Dordrecht, 85–95.

Spijkerboer, T. (2009) "The Human Costs of Border Control", *European Journal of Migration and Law 9(1)*: 127–139.

Stierl, M. (2016) "A Sea of Struggle – Activist Border Interventions in the Mediterranean Sea", *Citizenship Studies 20(5)*: 561–578.

Trupiano, F. (2016) *Un Ambasciatore nella Libia di Gheddafi*, Greco e Greco, Milano.

UNHCR. (2017) Libya 23 October 2017 (www.unhcr.org/libya.html) accessed 15 January 2018.

UNHCR. (2018) "Operational Portal: Mediterranean Situation", (https://data2.unhcr.org/en/situations/mediterranean/location/5205) accessed 15 January 2018.

Van Reekum, R. (2016) "The Mediterranean: Migration Corridor, Border Spectacle, Ethical Landscape", *Mediterranean Politics 21(2)*: 336–341.

44

THE BURKINA FASO–CÔTE D'IVOIRE MIGRATION CORRIDOR

Hannah Cross

Introduction[1]

Côte d'Ivoire is the main destination for migrants from Burkina Faso and likewise, the Burkinabè are the largest migrant group in Côte d'Ivoire. Owing to the often circular and temporary nature of these migrations and to different ways of classifying who is a migrant, estimates vary from 1.5 million to 3.5 million migrants out of a Burkinabè population of over 19 million (Devillard et al. 2016; Zanou and Lougue 2009, 1). The Burkina Faso–Côte d'Ivoire migration corridor is an almost century-old exchange that originated in a policy from the French colonial administration to use the Burkinabè territory (then Upper Volta) as a labour reservoir to supply Ivoirian agriculture and major transport projects. France did not only administer people within the landlocked territory of Upper Volta, but also, as this chapter will show, adjusted its borders to keep labour power under control. Nearly 60 years on from independence, labour migration continues to be the primary focus of the corridor, and the majority of the migrant population works in the informal sector, largely in agriculture (Devillard et al. 2016; IOM 2009).

Both former colonies belong to the West African Economic and Monetary Union (WAEMU), a group of countries whose currency, the CFA franc, is pegged to the euro (previously the French franc) and that are mainly classified as 'least developed countries'. The numerous migration systems in this region have been squeezed by austerity and associated economic and political crises, especially since the CFA franc was dramatically devalued in 1994. Migration is a household survival strategy in Burkina Faso, where almost half of the country lives below the poverty line and more than 70 per cent of the population lives in rural areas, their livelihoods being based on peasant farming, animal husbandry, and artisanal mining. All regions participate but the Mossi in the central part and the north of the country are the largest ethnic group and the main one to face environmental and economic pressures to migrate (Loada 2006, 345). Côte d'Ivoire is WAEMU's largest economy and the world's largest producer of cocoa beans, for which it relies on a significant migrant labour force. Yet it has experienced persistent economic problems and is unable to recapture the growth experienced from independence up to the mid-1980s (Sylla 2016, 165–6). The rest of this chapter will firstly outline the historical development of the migration corridor; and second, will examine its impact on development both between and within the two countries. This includes analysis of the patterns of dependency that are associated with migrant labour in West Africa and the role of migrant workers in the development process.

Historical origins – from forced labour to migration dependence

In 1923, the French Colonial Minister Albert Sarrault argued that France had yet to profit from its entry to West Africa, so he would assign to each region between two and four products for export. The pattern of development would be orientated around commercial crop zones in the coastal areas, using migrant labour from the interior that would be coerced –through the use of a head tax system and various regimes of forced labour including *prestations* (6–10 days of free labour for public works) and military conscriptions (Cooper 1996, 32; Cordell and Gregory 1982, 209; Courtin et al. 2010, 14). These attempts to extract labour contrasted with the needs of the rural economy, hindering food crop production and creating famine in Upper Volta and Niger by 1931. After people began to flee the colonial regime, mainly going to the Gold Coast (now Ghana), the colonial administration dissolved Upper Volta in 1933 into Côte d'Ivoire, Soudan (now Mali) and Niger with the aim of sending the Mossi population to work on major development projects and industrial plantations where they were taken as directly exploitable labour for the expansion of cocoa and coffee production. The railway from Abidjan to Bobo-Dioulasso, launched in 1934, opened up more of the Voltaic labour force for Côte d'Ivoire (Blion and Bredeloup 1997, 711; Cordell and Gregory 1982, 213; Zanou and Lougue 2009).

Félix Houphouët-Boigny, who would be the first Ivoirian President after independence, led the abolition of forced labour in 1946 amidst major labour struggles and strikes around francophone West Africa and in a mass-movement alliance between African planters, peasants, and workers. Colonial authorities soon re-established the territory of Upper Volta to prevent the influence of 'communism' from Côte d'Ivoire, though Houphouët-Boigny in reality promoted capitalist economic relations (Amin 1971, 13–5; Cooper 1996, 188). He encouraged the recruitment of migrant labour after independence and the country experienced a 'growth miracle' by the mid-1970s that brought male, largely Mossi migrants to work on road and rail projects or in agricultural production in conditions of rapid urbanisation and commercialisation of the rural economy. Increasing numbers of migrants could start their own plantations and use family labour under exemption from taxes, in the south-west where land had not been exploited (Blion and Bredeloup 1997, 719–20; Cordell and Gregory 1982, 218). It ultimately amounted to a form of 'growth without development', also found in Ghana and Senegal, by which large tracts of land were dominated by agribusiness and multinationals that profited from low wages (Amin 1971, 10; Adepoju 1995, 91; Arthur 1991, 70; Blion and Bredeloup 1997, 712; Cross 2013, 40–1).

This growth would be reversed by the world economic upheaval that, by the early 1980s, created serious balance of payment problems and a decline in terms of trade for countries that had specialised their economies for the export of primary products. Like many other former colonies, Côte d'Ivoire plunged into indebtedness and international financial institutions gained increasing power over its deteriorating economic and financial situation (Losch 2000, 7–8). In a restructured, brutally competitive world economy, the price of cacao plunged in 1989 to less than 60 per cent of its 1984 nominal dollar price. Houphouët-Boigny appointed Alassane Ouattara as Prime Minister in 1991, a US-educated economist who would oversee a programme of neoliberal austerity (Cagnolari 2011; ODI 1990, 1). Ouattara was also a major proponent of the 1994 devaluation of the CFA franc, which despite mitigating measures from the International Monetary Fund and France, left people half as rich while the cost of imported goods, on which people were dependent, shot up.

In this economic setting, Henri Konan Bédié, President after Houphouët-Boigny's death in 1993, established the nationalist conception of 'Ivoirité' (Ivorianness), which interrupted the process of naturalisation for immigrants and deprived them of the right to vote. Burkinabè workers, even if they belonged to the million people who were born in Côte d'Ivoire, were not Ivoirian in law: both parents had to be born in the country. This legislation excluded Ouattara from standing for election, though he eventually became President in 2010 under highly contested circumstances. While the previous principle had been that the land belonged to those who develop it; as of 1998, only the state, local public authorities, and Ivorians could be owners (Courtin et al. 2010, 15–6; Devillard et al. 2016; Zongo 2003, 116).

By the 1990s, the forest was already becoming exhausted in Côte d'Ivoire, bringing diminishing returns from the land, continuous reliance on cheap labour from migrants and the expansion of trafficked child labour. Methods of labour and land exploitation became more intense in response to land pressures and low commodity prices (Odijie 2015; Woods 2003). Towards the end of 1999, locals in Tabou to the south-west of the country started a movement against 'foreign' workers who had been there for more than a decade, which led to mass flight. More provocations to leave followed the 2000 election of Laurent Gbagbo and the attempted *coup d'état* in 2002, which started a civil war. Though the war itself lasted less than a year, the country was divided by a buffer zone, 'secured' by French and UN troops, between the rebel-held north and the south controlled by Gbagbo and his loyalist forces (Galy 2008). At this time, around 500,000 Burkinabè were displaced to Burkina Faso (Loada 2006, 354). The Burkinabè government avoided the establishment of refugee camps, instead channelling *repatriés* to their villages of origin, but on return many were no longer considered to belong there, had never lived there, or they were unable to access quality land. Many settled elsewhere in the country, and high numbers appear to have re-emigrated to Côte d'Ivoire, sustaining their social links with the country, although it has become more difficult to travel. The military buffer zone was successively dismantled after a peace accord was signed in March 2007. In 2011, however, it faced further political crisis and, more recently, economic shocks of a sharp decline in cocoa prices and higher oil prices.

Migrant labour and development

This section considers the extent to which migration from Burkina Faso to Côte d'Ivoire encourages development and promotes socio-economic mobility for migrant workers and their communities. In 1975, the average length of migration was 4.5 years, and for the over-30s, 6.5 years, while the number of women migrating doubled to one-third. Individual labour migrations of unmarried men shifted and cascaded towards family migration, while the collective solidarity of diaspora and community associations expanded as Côte d'Ivoire had taken an integrationist approach towards Burkinabè (Blion and Bredeloup 1997, 714). Villages and urban quarters in Côte d'Ivoire gained Burkinabè names including Koudougou in the Bouaflé region and 'petit Ouaga' in a neighbourhood of Abidjan. Most Burkinabè worked on plantations but there were also records of their type of employment changing after 5 years towards industry, artisanal work, and the service sector, yet the change in Côte d'Ivoire's fortune a decade later reversed many of these gains. As men dominated these migration flows, salaried employment for women in Burkina Faso was relatively high, constituting one-third of civil service personnel, but women also faced restricted land rights, disproportionately higher levels of poverty and higher risks to health (Harsch 1998, 632). Women have since migrated to work in cities as well as for family reasons, and migrations for education have also advanced, with representation for Burkinabè students found in Tocsin, an association that focuses on the concerns of the diaspora.

While these indicators suggest some positive impacts on development, the overwhelming evidence shows the centrality of such a labour regime to underdevelopment and dependence. One reflection on Burkina Faso's century of labour migration finds that it is 'approved' in society only because it is a household survival strategy (Piché 2015, 14). It has had profound effects on poverty since transfers of remittances, affecting most families, have been unstable, local economic and subsistence activities are abandoned, and there is a reliance on imported products whose prices are determined by financial speculators. Although Côte d'Ivoire is the better-off country in this relationship, it is best understood as an international class relation because it benefits a small capitalist elite under the dominance of the international financial institutions. Agricultural production is submitted to world prices and societies in both countries are held back from substantive development.

Samir Amin argued that West Africa's colonial trade economy persists, challenging the mainstream conception of migration patterns as a process of accelerated industrialisation, by which short-term migration by lone males would eventually give way to a settled urban working class (Amin and Bush 2014). While some settlement patterns developed in Côte d'Ivoire, the broader linearity of migrations has been proven a myth because chronic dependence on migration, under unstable conditions, continues in Burkina Faso. This reflects continuing patterns of circulatory movement and evidence of counter-urbanising trends in Africa's regions (Piché 2015, 9; Potts 2010, 20–1). Alternative destinations are highly restricted, with some diversification of routes to Ghana, Togo, and Benin, while attempts to go further afield, towards the United States or Europe, are confronted with the closure of safe routes and North African labour and transit zones are destabilised: one indicator of the scale of the regional crisis of migration was revealed in 2012, when 1661 Burkinabè returnees had fled the Libyan civil war (Devillard et al. 2016, 92; Loada 2006, 354). Dependence on labour migration has kept West Africa in a peripheral position in the global economy and has sustained an economic geography by which the coastal countries of Côte d'Ivoire, Ghana, Nigeria, and the Gambia have higher urban populations and net immigration, and relatively higher gains in GDP and social development; while the interior countries, especially Burkina Faso and Mali, continue to have 'traditional' economic sectors with a surplus of labour, marking the interdependence rather than dualism between these countries (Amin 1995, 37; Arthur 1991, 71; Devillard et al. 2016, 25; Cross and Cliffe 2017, 3–4; Sylla 2016).

Note

1 Thank you to Bettina Engels for contributing her knowledge and insight to this chapter.

References

Adepoju A. (1995) "Migration in Africa: An overview", in Baker J. and Aida T. A. eds, *The migration experience in Africa*, Nordiska Afrikainstitutet, Uppsala, 29–40.

Amin S. (1971) "The development of capitalism in the Ivory Coast", *IDEP/REPRODUCTION/209*. United Nations African Institute for Economic Development and Planning, Dakar.

Amin S. (1995) "Migrations in contemporary Africa: A retrospective view", in Baker J. and Aida T. A. eds, *The migration experience in Africa*, Nordiska Afrikainstitutet, Uppsala, 29–40.

Amin S. and Bush R. (2014) "An interview with Samir Amin", *Review of African Political Economy* 41 (S1), S108–S114.

Arthur J. A. (1991) "International labor migration patterns in West Africa", *African Studies Review* 34 (3), 65–87.

Blion R. and Bredeloup S. (1997) "La Côte d'Ivoire dans les stratégies migratoires des Burkinabés et des Sénégalais", in Cotamin B. and Memel Foté H. eds, *La modèle ivoirien en questions. Crises, ajustements, recomposition*, Karthala-Orstrom, Paris, 707–737.

Cagnolari V. (2011) "Ivory Coast's struggle for succession", *Le Monde Diplomatique*, February.

Cooper F. (1996) *Decolonization and African society: The labor question in French and British Africa*, Cambridge University Press, Cambridge.

Cordell D. D. and Gregory J. W. (1982) "Labour reservoirs and population: French colonial strategies in Koudougou, Upper Volta, 1914–1939", *Journal of African History* 23, 205–224.

Courtin F., et al. (2010) "La crise ivoirienne et les migrants burkinabès. L'effet boomerang d'une migration international", *Afrique contemporaine* 2010/4 (236), 11–27.

Cross H. (2013) *Migrants, borders and global capitalism: West African labour mobility and EU borders*, Routledge, Abingdon.

Cross H. and Cliffe L. (2017) "A comparative political economy of regional migration and labour mobility in West and Southern Africa", *Review of African Political Economy* 44 (153), 381–398.

Devillard A., et al. (2016) *A survey on migration policies in West Africa*, Second Edition, International Centre for Migration Policy Development (ICMPD) and International Organisation for Migration (IOM), Vienna and Dakar.

Galy M. (2008) "Transition to peace in Ivory Coast", *Le Monde Diplomatique*, January.

Harsch E. (1998) "Burkina Faso in the winds of liberalisation", *Review of African Political Economy* 25 (78), 625–641.

IOM. (2009) "Migration in Côte d'Ivoire: 2009 national", International Organisation for Migration.

Loada A. (2006) "L'émigration burkinabè face à la crise de 'l'ivoirité'", *Outre-Terre* 4 (17), 343–356.

Losch B. (2000) "Coup de cacao en Côte d'Ivoire [Économie politique d'une crise structurelle]", *Critique internationale* 9, 6–14.

ODI (Overseas Development Institute). (1990) "Crisis in the franc zone", *Briefing Paper*, July.

Odijie E. M. (2015) "Diminishing returns and agricultural involution in Côte d'Ivoire's cocoa sector", *Review of African Political Economy* 43 (149), 504–517.

Piché V. (2015) "Un siècle d'histoire migratoire au Burkina Faso: quelles leçons?", Paper presented for international colloquium: Les migrations burkinabè: permanences et changements, Homage au Professor Dieudonné Ouédraogo, Institut supérieur des sciences de la population, Université de Ouagadougou, 28-30 May.

Potts D. (2010) *Circular migration in Zimbabwe and contemporary sub-Saharan Africa*, James Currey, Rochester, NY.

Sylla N. S. (2016) "Emerger avec le franc CFA ou émerger du franc CFA?", in Nubukpo K., ed, et al. *Sortir l'Afrique de la servitude monétaire: A qui profite le franc CFA?* La Dispute, Paris, 161–177.

Woods D. (2003) "The tragedy of the cocoa pod: Rent-seeking, land and ethnic conflict in Ivory Coast", *Journal of Modern African Studies* 41 (4), 641–655.

Zanou B and Lougue S. (2009) "Impact de la crise ivoirienne sur les migrations de retour au Burkina Faso". Paper presented at Congrès de l'Union internationale pour l'étude scientifique de la population (IUSSP), Marrakech, 2 October.

Zongo M. (2003) "La diaspora Burkinabè en Côte d'Ivoire: Trajectories historique, recomposition des dynamiques migratoires et rapport avec le pays d'origins", *Politique africaine* 2003/2 (90), 113–126.

45

THE ZIMBABWE–SOUTH AFRICA MIGRATION CORRIDOR

Dudu S. Ndlovu and Loren B. Landau

Migration route development

The corridor between Zimbabwe and South Africa has developed over time, linking the two countries and their peoples. It dates back to the importation of labour in South Africa during apartheid (1948–91), with changes when Zimbabwe gained its independence in 1980, South Africa's democratisation in the mid-1990s, and Zimbabwe's ongoing, almost two-decade-long economic crisis. Driving and facilitating factors include disparities of wealth within and between countries; South Africa's industrial and service economies; and the spatial proximity and ethnic affinity between Matabeleland and South Africa. Although not a border spanning solidarity, cultural affinity of the Ndebele from Zimbabwe's Matabeleland region and the Zulu of South Africa influences some of this migration. A proportion of the Zimbabweans from Matabeleland are descendants of the Ndebele who moved from South Africa to Zimbabwe in the migrations of Mfecane in the 1800s. The cultural affinity of the migrants from Matabeleland and similar language historically facilitated the integration of some Zimbabwean foreigners in South Africa. Although few Zimbabweans travel to the 'Zulu heartland' in KwaZulu Natal Province, Zulu is the lingua franca of many mining areas and of the wealthy and migrant-rich Gauteng Province. Socio-political solidarity and cultural affinity between white Rhodesians and Apartheid White South Africans similarly facilitated the migration of white Rhodesians pre- and post-Zimbabwean independence, although this movement is rarely the subject of debates (Mlambo 2010; Simon 1988).

During the apartheid era (approximately 1948–91), movements from Zimbabwe (formerly Rhodesia) were closely regulated by bi-lateral labour agreements between the two countries (Mlambo 2016). Mining companies actively recruited Zimbabwean and other African workers from the region using a number of bodies including the Witwatersrand Native Labour Association (WNLA) and The Employment Bureau of Africa (TEBA) (Crush 1999). Such strategies allowed them to meet labour needs without empowering black South Africans. The reliance on foreign labour helped keep black South Africans in the homelands and reduced the likelihood of an organised mobilisation against employers or the state (Prothero 1974).

During the apartheid era, Zimbabweans were largely able to form solidarities with their South African co-workers. They also adopted ways to fit into South Africa's culture and society, such as adopting local language and style (Sisulu, Moyo, and Tshuma 2007). The mostly male migrants sometimes married into South African families or surreptitiously acquired South African or 'homeland' citizenship. While some stayed in South Africa or its apartheid era-homelands, most were unable to do so and were forced to return home to collect their salaries or renew contracts (Mlambo 2016). The migration was typically circular with South Africa as only a base for work to amass the resources to build a life back home in Zimbabwe (Maphosa 2010).

Changes in South African labour law and a decline in mining jobs have largely eroded these formal frameworks. In 1980, when Zimbabwe gained independence, there was a ban on the

Figure 45.1 Map of Zimbabwe indicating international and provincial boundaries

Source: www.mapcruzin.com

recruitment of mineworkers from Zimbabwe but individuals could seek work. The established migration route remained a part of the culture of Southern Zimbabwe. It became a rite of passage for young men from these provinces (Maphosa 2010). This was popularly called *ukutshaya idabulaphu*, an adaptation from the English phrase to double up and referring to the clandestine border crossing by mostly young men from Matabeleland seeking employment opportunities in South Africa. Soon after independence, state-sponsored violence in the Matabeleland regions of Zimbabwe led young men to flee, intensifying the migration routes, which pre-dated Zimbabwean independence (Alexander 1998; Sisulu, Moyo, and Tshuma 2007).

Since the late 1990s, there has been a steady increase of migration from Zimbabwe to South Africa owing to Zimbabwe's economic decline and political instability (Crush and Tevera 2010). The intensification of mobility along the South Africa–Zimbabwe corridor has transformed long-standing migration patterns. Bolt (2010) speaks of a diversification of the origin of Zimbabwean workers on the farms who previously came from the areas near the border, now spread further afield. Yet movements also continue to flow through the channels carved in years past. Many Zimbabweans – estimates vary between 1 and 3 million (Wilkinson 2017) – travel to South Africa.

The formal and informal regulation of Zimbabwe–South Africa migration

Although South Africa continues to dedicate additional resources to physically controlling its borders, its efforts are stymied by widespread corruption, extended and remote distances, and intensive cross-border social networks. It is then, perhaps, not surprising that even with an escalation of police crackdowns and deportations, the South African public broadly imagines a porous borderland across which millions of Zimbabwean migrants more or less represents an invading army (Mthembu-Salter et al. 2014). South Africa's pragmatic effort to regularise Zimbabweans – including the 2010 Zimbabwean Dispensation Project (ZDP) – have helped tens of thousands to legalise their stay in the country. Although it is not a permanent guarantee of residence and has left many Zimbabweans in a state of limbo, it has nonetheless fostered further fears and resentment among South African citizens (Amit 2015). For poor South Africans who have seen few economic benefits from the country's political freedom, Zimbabweans represent the quintessential threat: educated, English speaking, and largely able to disappear within the South African body politic. Moreover, they can compete at multiple levels of the economy: the highly skilled challenge South Africans for executive and professional positions while the majority compete with an underemployed, working-class majority. Those who can be identified – those who have yet to perfect invisibility – become the focus of much unwanted attention. While the threats vary by class – the poor are the most vulnerable – patterns of social resentment and exclusion are widespread (Hassim et al. 2008; Landau 2012).

Johannesburg

At the heart of South Africa's mining and industrial production, Johannesburg has long been at the centre of migrant journeys and imaginations. Johannesburg is popularly called eGoli, referring to the gold mines but also denoting the hopes that many people who come here have of striking gold in the 'New York of Africa' (Grant and Thompson 2015). With its immediate surroundings, it accounts for close to 10 per cent of sub-Saharan Africa's gross domestic product. The highest concentration of Zimbabweans is in Johannesburg, a city whose prosperity does not translate to economic or physical security for migrants (Palmary, Hamber, and Núñez 2015).

Indeed, those in Johannesburg and elsewhere work, live, and/or stay for varied periods with varying legal status. A small percentage are professionals with permanent resident status and permanent jobs. Others have naturalised through marriage, other legal channels, or back channels. Many, if not most, live and work in South Africa with both precarious professions and papers. Historically Zimbabwean migrants were typically unmarried, unskilled young men but this has shifted to a more diverse profile that includes the highly skilled holders of university degrees; young and old; male and female; single and married (Crush and Tevera 2010). Those who migrate regardless of skill level typically maintain strong ties with Zimbabwe through remittances and regular visits (Dzingirai, Mutopo, and Landau 2014).

Perhaps more importantly, migrants no longer originate mostly from the Matabeleland regions of the country that are spatially and culturally proximate to South Africa. Zimbabweans from across the country have turned to migration for relief from the country's economic challenges (Dzingirai, Mutopo, and Landau 2014). Migrants from other parts of Zimbabwe do not share the cultural and linguistic similarities and find it more difficult to assimilate or invisibilise. Moreover, they often lack the social capital of long-established routes into the city. Needing help to survive, they have become highly visible in spaces of refuge including Johannesburg's Central Methodist Church (Kuljian 2013)

This has led to a socialisation of geographic diversification of border making: a transfer of negotiations from the borderlands to places such as Johannesburg. Cultural performances of identity and social processes including xenophobia (Landau 2012), construct boundaries between migrants and their hosts within Johannesburg, South Africa's primary city that is 500 km from any formal border. Migrants' reciprocal attitudes are not far from the negative sentiments from their hosts. They may remain embedded in their communities in Zimbabwe, but in South Africa they often remain at the edges of local communities and cultures (Landau and Freemantle 2016, 2010). Many see themselves as morally superior to locals. Some Zimbabweans conform to this cosmopolitanism and take pride in being stereotyped as more educated and hardworking than locals in response to their xenophobic reception.

Conclusion

Borders are both objective geographic sites and dynamic sites of socio-spatial differentiation (Brambilla 2016). This chapter highlights the ways the Zimbabwe–South Africa border is configured between the states and among people, the social processes in people's negotiation of the border and the processes of agency and subjectification associated with the movements. The social bordering in South Africa's cities combined with challenges in obtaining work permits leaves migrants at the margins in precarious working positions that do not always translate to making a good living. This reduces the likelihood of the transmission of significant remittances that can be used to successfully lead to development. Many, if not all Zimbabwean migrants, send remittances home although this does not necessarily translate to development. Remittances are usually to replace incomes lost due to Zimbabwe's economic decline (Dzingirai, Mutopo, and Landau 2014; Maphosa 2007). Furthermore, the wages are not significant enough for use for anything other than daily sustenance. However, while remittances may not translate to development in Zimbabwe, they contribute positively to the welfare of receiving individuals and families and at times the immediate community. The modalities of migration between Zimbabwe and South Africa are presented in this chapter framed by the socio-political context of the two countries. Through both the apartheid and post-apartheid period, the movements of ethnically white Rhodesians (later Zimbabwean) largely went unnoticed by policy makers, police, and scholars.. The movement of black Zimbabweans initially not recognised by apartheid South Africa in the post-2000 political moment is visible, pathologised, and abhorred. The link between the two countries however endures as the migration continues to maintain connections through remittances and other exchanges cultural and otherwise.

References

Alexander, J. 1998. 'Dissident Perspectives on Zimbabwe's Post-Independence War'. *Africa* 68 (2): 151–182.

Amit, R. 2015. 'The Expansion of Illegality'. In *Immigration Detention: The Migration of a Policy and Its Human Impact*, edited by A. Nethery and Silverman, S. J., 145–153. Abingdon: Routledge.

Bolt, M. 2010. 'Camaraderie and its Discontents: Class Consciousness, Ethnicity and Divergent Masculinities among Zimbabwean Migrant Farmworkers in South Africa'. *Journal of Southern African Studies* 36 (2): 377–393.

Brambilla, C. 2016. *Borderscaping: Imaginations and Practices of Border Making*. Abingdon: Routledge.

Crush, J. 1999. 'Fortress South Africa and the Deconstruction of Apartheid's Migration Regime'. *Geoforum* 30 (1): 1–11.

Crush, J. and Tevera, D. S. (Editors). 2010. *Zimbabwe's Exodus: Crisis, Migration, Survival*. Cape Town: SAMP.

Dzingirai, V., Mutopo, P., and Landau, L. B. 2014. *Confirmations, Coffins and Corn: Kinship, Social Networks and Remittances from South Africa to Zimbabwe*. Migrating out of Poverty. DFID, September. http://migratingoutofpoverty.dfid.gov.uk/files/file.php?name=wp18-dzingerai–mutopo-landau-2014-confirmations-coffins–corn-final.pdf&site=354

Grant, R. and Thompson, D. 2015. 'City on Edge: Immigrant Businesses and the Right to Urban Space in Inner-City Johannesburg'. *Urban Geography* 36 (2): 181–200.

Hassim, S., Kupe, T., Worby, E., and Skuy, A. (Editors). 2008. *Go Home or Die Here: Violence, Xenophobia and the Reinvention of Difference in South Africa*. Johannesburg: Wits University Press.

Kuljian, C. 2013. *Sanctuary: How an Inner-City Church Spilled onto a Sidewalk*. Johannesburg: Jacana Media.

Landau, L. B. 2012. *Exorcising the Demons within: Xenophobia, Violence and Statecraft in Contemporary South Africa*. Johannesburg: Wits University Press.

Landau, L. B. and Freemantle, I. 2010. 'Tactical Cosmopolitanism and Idioms of Belonging: Insertion and Self-Exclusion in Johannesburg'. *Journal of Ethnic and Migration Studies* 36 (3): 375–390.

Landau, L. B. and Freemantle, I. 2016. 'Beggaring Belonging in Africa's No-Man's Lands: Diversity, Usufruct and the Ethics of accommodationxmlambo, Alois S.'. *Journal for Ethnic and Migration Studies* 42 (6): 933–951.

Maphosa, F. 2007. 'Remittances and Development: The Impact of Migration to South Africa on Rural Livelihoods in Southern Zimbabwe'. *Development Southern Africa* 24 (1): 123–136.

Maphosa, F. 2010. 'Transnationalism and Undocumented Migration between Rural Zimbabwe and South Africa'. In *Zimbabwe's Exodus: Crisis, Migration, Survival*, edited by J. Crush and D. S. Tevera, 346–362. Cape Town: SAMP.

Meuser, M. 2018. Map of Zimbabwe. Digital image viewed 15 January 2018, https://mapcruzin.com/free-maps-zimbabwe/zimbabwe_pol_2002.pdf.

Mlambo, A. S. 2010. '2. A History of Zimbabwean Migration to 1990'. In *Zimbabwe's Exodus: Crisis, Migration, Survival*, edited by J. Crush and D. S. Tevera, 52–76. Cape Town: SAMP, African Books Collective.

Mlambo, A. S. 2016. '"Zimbabwe Is Not a South African Province": Historicising SouthAfrica's Zimbabwe Policy since the 1960s'. *Historia* 61 (1): 18–40.

Mthembu-Salter, G., Amit, R., Gould, C., and Landau, L. B. 2014. *Counting the Cost of Securitising South Africa's Immigration Regime*. Migrating out of Poverty. DFID, September. http://migratingoutofpoverty.dfid.gov.uk/files/file.php?name=wp20-mthembu-salter-et-al-2014-counting-the-cost.pdf&site=354

Palmary, I., Hamber, B., and Núñez, L. (Editors). 2015. *Healing and Change in the City of Gold*. Cham: Springer International Publishing.

Prothero, R. M. 1974. 'Foreign Migrant Labour for South Africa'. *The International Migration Review* 8 (3): 383–394. https://doi.org/10.2307/3002372.

Simon, A. 1988. 'Rhodesian Immigrants in South Africa: Government, Media and a Lesson for South Africa'. *African Affairs* 87 (346): 53–68.

Sisulu, E., Moyo, B., and Tshuma, N. 2007. 'The Zimbabwean Community in South Africa'. In *State of the Nation: South Africa*, edited by S. Buhlungu, J. Daniel and R. Southall, Cape Town: HSRC Press, 552–573.

Wilkinson, K. 2017. 'Claim that 13 Million International Migrants Live in SA Wildly Incorrect,' *AfricaCheck* (21 February 2017): https://africacheck.org/reports/claim-13-million-international-migrants-live-sa-wildly-incorrect/

46

THE MEXICO–US MIGRATION CORRIDOR

Diana Mata-Codesal and Kerstin Schmidt

Introduction

Mexico and the US have been closely linked by migration throughout history. Currently, this is the most transited migration corridor in the world (World Bank 2016). In 2015, about 11.6 million Mexicans lived in the US, which is about 27 per cent of the total foreign-born population in the country (OECD 2017). An estimated 5.6 million of them were undocumented (Passel and Cohn 2017). Yet, despite the still high importance in terms of numbers of Mexicans residing in the US, Mexicans have been overtaken by migrants from China and India in more recent immigration streams (Chishti and Hipsman 2015).

It is not only the movement of Mexicans to the US that shapes the Mexico–US migration corridor, but transit and return migration are also relevant. There is a lack of data about the number of people – mainly from Guatemala, Honduras, and El Salvador – crossing Mexico en route to the US. However, statistics on US border apprehensions indicate an increase in migration from Central America to the US after a decline in 2007 (Alba 2013). Furthermore, since 2009 Mexican returnees outnumber new arrivals from Mexico. In line with this trend, the number of US-born foreigners living in Mexico reached 750,000 in 2015, equalling about 75 per cent of the foreign-born population in Mexico (OECD 2017); many of whom are people of Mexican descent born in the US or naturalised US citizens.

In addition to the movement of people, the volume of financial transfers taking place between the two countries also contributes to making this corridor one of the most dynamic worldwide. Recent World Bank statistics estimate that in terms of volume in 2018 Mexico was the fourth most important receiving country of remittances after India, China, and the Philippines (World Bank 2018).

Although, in terms of GDP percentage, remittances are arguably more important for smaller countries, they are one of the main items in the Mexican Balance of Payments (CONAPO and Fundación BBVA Bancomer 2017). Contrary to the global trend of declining remittances, officially recorded financial transfers to Mexico have increased over the past few years, reaching a historical peak in 2017 (see Figure 46.1). In 2017, 95 per cent of these financial transfers came from the US (Cervantes and Li Ng 2018).

Thus, while experiencing some changes, the Mexico–US migration corridor remains highly relevant in terms of flows of people and financial transfers. However, as will be shown in the next section, the picture is not as clear-cut as suggested by the above-presented statistics.

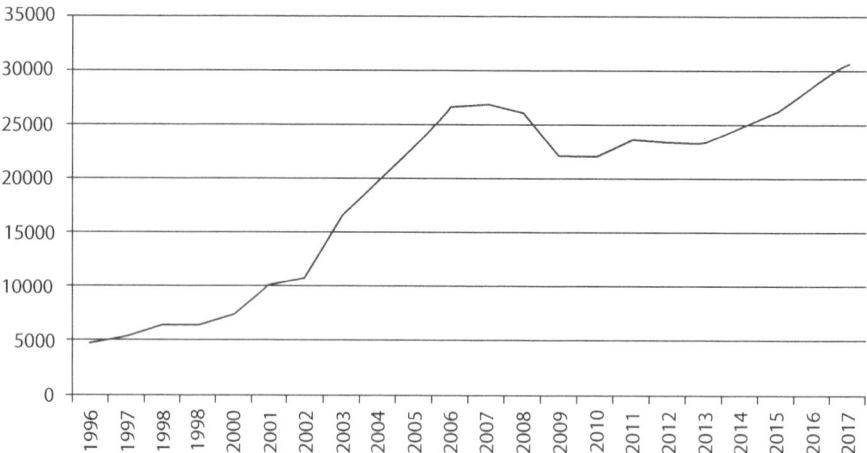

Figure 46.1 Migrant remittance inflows in Mexico (in million US dollars) 1996–2017

Source: Authors' compilation based on World Bank data, 2017

The complex empirical picture of migration in the Mexico–US context

Although the Mexico–US migration corridor has been extensively researched, the very same concept of a single migration corridor obscures more complex realities, and calls for more detailed analyses. The Mexico–US migration links are neither unidirectional, nor unrelated to other international or internal mobility patterns (Arizpe 1983; King and Skeldon 2010). Against mainstream ideas which seem to focus disproportionally on human crossings from Mexico to the US and financial returns from the US, the number and typology of crossings from the US into Mexico are also relevant including US lifestyle migration to Mexico (Lizárraga Morales et al. 2015), returned Mexicans (Hagan and Wassink 2016), or deported Mexican and other Central and South American citizens to Mexico (Slack 2015).

In addition, the idea of one overarching corridor for migrants between Mexico and the US does not do justice to the complex realities of migration trajectories between the two countries. A finer look reveals the existence of multiple and entangled corridors that link specific localities and regions on both sides of the border. The resulting labyrinthine panorama questions the linearity conveyed with the image of the corridor. As many studies on transnational communities have shown, the two countries are not linked in geographically homogeneous ways, but rather produce arrays of intensity, many times in the form of transnational fields between federal states, regions, or cities at both sides of the border – e.g. Oaxacalifornia (Kearney 2000), la Mixteca, and New York City (Rivera 2007), or some municipalities in the South of Morelos with the state of Minnesota (Bobes 2010).

Authors tend to agree on a four-item regional typology for Mexican states: the historical or traditional states of emigration in the Central-West, Northern states or states in the border region, the Central region, and the Southeast (see for instance CONAPO 2012; Riosmena and Massey 2012; Zuñiga et al. 2005).

Traditionally, the states in the Central-West of Mexico – Guanajuato, Jalisco, Michoacán, San Luis Potosí, and Zacatecas – have been the origin of most migrants to the US (the darkest region in the map in Figure 46.2). After the turn of the millennium, the links between these 'classic' Mexican migration states with the states of Texas, Illinois, and California remain strong.

Traditonal Emigration States

Border Region

Central Region

Southeast

Figure 46.2 Regions of migrants' origin in Mexico

Source: Authors' elaboration based on CONAPO 2012

In this context, transnational links are often used to compensate the lack of financial resources and/or education needed for outmigration (Chort and de la Rupelle 2016). Since the 1980s, states in the centre of the country – Guerrero, Morelos, the State of Mexico, Puebla, and Morelos – started to appear in migration statistics (CONAPO 2012). A few years later, at the turn of the millennium, the diversification intensified with an extension toward the South to incorporate states like Oaxaca or Chiapas, Mexico's most Southern state (Riosmena and Massey 2012).

As the case of Veracruz, which only started to become a state of origin of international migrants in the 1990s (Canales 2010) shows, the diversification of migrant origin regions in Mexico in some cases also increased the diversity of Mexican migrants in destination regions in the US. First-time migrants from Veracruz tended to make use of the transnational networks of friends and colleagues from other Mexican states. This situation entailed the fact that even international migrants from the same village in Veracruz went to different cities in the US because they made use of their personal networks due to a lack of transnational spaces established at the village level (Schmidt-Verkerk 2012).

In addition, Mexican migrant destination regions in the US also diversified mainly due to a restructuring and relocation of important industries in the country. Related to this development, the diversification of destination regions has also been a consequence of an economic downturn in some of the traditional destination regions (see Figure 46.3). Moreover, the regularisation of their residence status by the Immigration Reform and Control Act (IRCA) in 1993 provided many previously undocumented Mexican migrants with more freedom to move and to pursue job opportunities elsewhere in the US (Riosmena and Massey 2012). In the late 1990s, Mexican migrants began to migrate internally from the traditional destination

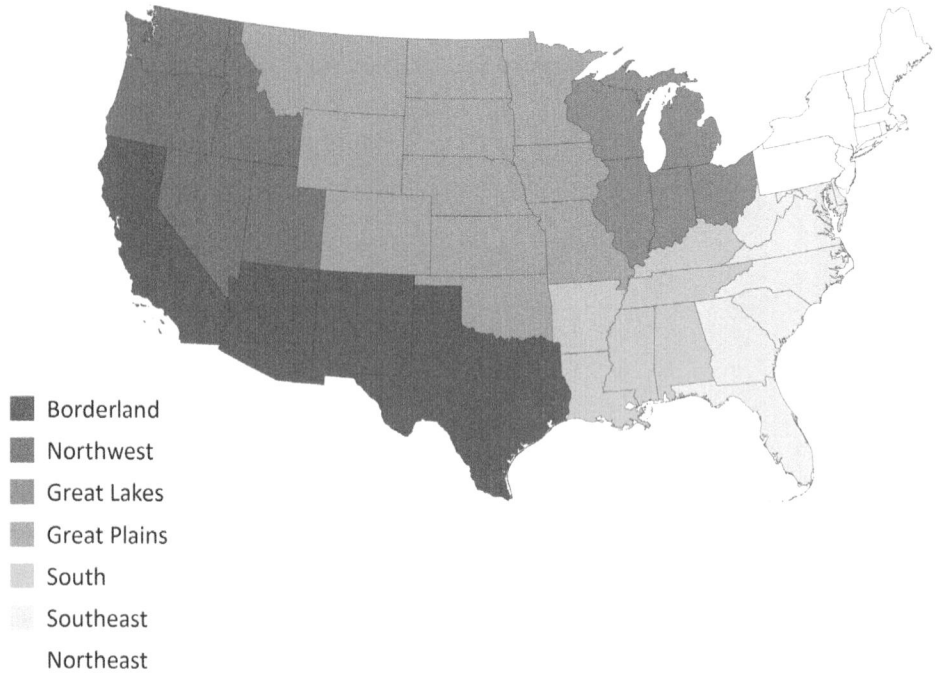

- ■ Borderland
- ■ Northwest
- ■ Great Lakes
- ■ Great Plains
- ■ South
- ■ Southeast
- Northeast

Figure 46.3 Regions of migrants' destinations in the US
Source: Authors' elaboration based on Riosmena and Massey 2012

states California, Texas, and Illinois (Zong and Batalova 2016) to other regions of the country, particularly North Carolina, Georgia, and Florida in the Southeast, Iowa, and Nebraska in the Midwest, Arizona, Colorado, and Nevada in the West, and the areas of New York, New Jersey, and Pennsylvania in the Northeast. These internal moves were then followed by direct migration flows from Mexico (Riosmena and Massey 2012).

Despite this development, nowadays, with more than 1.7 million foreign-born Mexicans in the time period of 2010 to 2014, the metropolitan area of Los Angeles continues to host the largest Mexican population in the US, followed by the metropolitan areas of Chicago, Houston, and Dallas (Zong and Batalova 2016).

The links between internal and international migration are often overlooked in the literature (King and Skeldon 2010). The Mexico–US corridor clearly points to the need to redress such lacunae, given that the linkages between internal and international migration are partially responsible for recent changes in the migration geography of the two countries. In Mexico, international emigration has been so intense from some central states that labour vacuums emerged and were filled by internal migrants from further South. These Southerners also began to migrate directly to the US through linkages developed at previous destinations within Mexico. This is, earlier migratory experience fuelled direct migration from the Southern states by-passing previous internal destinations (King and Skeldon 2010; Rivera 2007). In the US, as argued above, some authors have acknowledged the central role of internal migrations in the changing geographical distribution of Mexican migrants within the country (Riosmena and Massey 2012).

Since the continuous increase in border surveillance – which started with the Immigration Reform and Control Act in 1986 and was strengthened after 9/11 when irregular migration was conceived as a national security thread – the traditional circularity of migration from Mexico to the US has been severely reduced (Durand 2013). Apart from the option of receiving a Green Card as an immediate relative of a US citizen, which most Mexican immigrants with a legal status make use of (Zong and Batalova 2016), there are few legal channels for Mexican migrants to enter the US, except for high-skilled migrants and students (Delgado-Wise 2015; Lozano and Gandini 2010). The Trump era has so far reinforced this trend, while at the same time increasing fears of deportation and uncertainty about the future of undocumented Mexicans living in the US. It results in growing precariousness and vulnerability in migrants' lives, and therefore a growing inability to plan ahead, which have negative effects on migrants', their relatives', and communities' development options.

Mexican interpretations of migration and development in the Mexico–US migration corridor

After providing some recent figures and discussing the complex empirical reality of migration and development in the Mexico–US context, the chapter now turns to three main theoretical approaches most often applied to understand development in this corridor. The literature selection this section relies on merits clarification. Mexican migration scholars have a long tradition of solid research which we feel is sometimes not given enough recognition. Taking into consideration the format of this Handbook, we can sensibly expect its potential readership to be more acquainted with Anglo-Saxon literature, so we have tried to redress the geographical bias in references by focusing on research produced outside mainstream Anglo-Saxon areas. We have also tried to provide a gender-balanced list of publications. Although it has been possible to do it regarding the transnational approach, the other-two approaches have been traditionally male-dominated, which is reflected in the references list. The main ideas and principal representatives of the three theoretical approaches are shown in Table 46.1.

Neoclassical understandings of the migration–development nexus

Research under this approach is overly positive about the ability of migration to be conducive for development. Often understood as the perspective of the Global North and promoted by international development agencies, it focuses on the potential of remittances to enhance development in the countries of migrants' origin. Seminal works of this approach take the US–Mexico as a case in point, and emphasise the positive role of financial remittances as a stabilising force for the Mexican economy, as well as the positive impact on poverty for the receiving families. These studies often remain silent about the family costs of migration and remittances. This approach has been criticised for using a too narrow economic concept of development and portraying migrants as development agents, without giving enough consideration to the structural constraints migrants and their relatives are subjected to. These include irregular legal status, precarious labour market insertion, lack of basic infrastructures in origin areas, political and economic instability, etc. In addition, the selective nature of migration and the resulting inequalities brought about by the fact that not everyone can leave for employment or educational purposes and that not all families in origin regions receive remittances are often neglected.

Table 46.1 Overview of the main theoretical approaches

	Neoclassical developmentalist approach	Structuralist approach	Transnational approach
Stance regarding migration and development	Migration is good for development; remittances improve socio-economic conditions in regions of origin.	Migration has negative consequences for development; it feedbacks dependency of periphery regions on core regions and increases inequality.	Development is a multi-faceted reality which cannot be decontextualised; therefore, migration might lead to or reinforce social inequalities, as well as increases and decreases of life options.
Mostly carried out by	Economists Human Geographers	Sociologists Historians Critical Development Scholars Human Geographers	Anthropologists Sociologists Human Geographers
Level of analysis	Macro and micro level of analysis	Macro-level of analysis	Meso and micro level of analysis
Selected authors within each theoretical perspective	J. Edwards Taylor Richard H. Adams Germán A. Zarate-Hoyos Alejandro I. Canales	Raul Delgado-Wise Humberto Márquez-Covarrubias Rodolfo García-Zamora Arturo Escobar	Xochitl Bada Federico Besserer Michael Kearney Patricia Arias Liliana Rivera-Sánchez Douglas S. Massey Jorge Durand

Source: Authors' own elaboration

Neo-Marxist and structural critiques of the relationship between migration and development

This research paradigm, often labelled as the perspective from the Global South, has been mainly advanced by migration scholars based in Mexico (Delgado-Wise 2014). It draws on structuralist and dependency-theory related approaches to argue that underdevelopment is a result of core (US) and periphery (Mexico) relations. It also involves criticism of neo-liberal developments in Mexico and the exportation of cheap labour to the US. According to this interpretation, migration and remittances fuel dependency in Mexico, with both phenomena feeding back endlessly. The development of cultures of migration in areas with an intense and long migratory tradition is a clear consequence of this vicious circle (Cohen 2004). Due to its mainly global or macro level of analysis, this approach sometimes fails to capture the diversity of migrants' and their families' micro-level experiences of migration and development.

The transnational turn

As anticipated by the transnational fields mentioned in the first section of the chapter, the US–Mexican case has been particularly relevant for the development of the transnational paradigm given the fact that many populations – both of Mexican and US origin – inhabit dynamic transnational fields that span the national border (Besserer 2004). The antiquity of the migration(s), as well as the geographical contiguousness, are undoubtedly two factors facilitating the appearance and maintenance of transnational links. Transnational links in the Mexico–US context have been discussed with respect to different foci, including financial, social, and political remittances (Bada 2016). Research on transnational migration is dominated by discussions about remittances, yet some research has also taken into consideration the burdens of sustaining transnational lives derived from the fact that transnationality is often the migrants' response to legal and other barriers. In fact, the inability to freely cross over the US–Mexico border lies at the base of most long-distance family transnational relations developed by many Mexicans in the US. This research has shown how, contrary to some anticipated ideas about the diminishing power of states in the globalisation era, the positioning of the US State heavily defines and shapes transnational family interactions (Boehm 2012).

Conclusion

Transfers in the Mexican–US migration corridor are neither unidirectional nor linear. The features of the corridor itself are historically-deployed and context-dependent, as so are their potential development effects. The existence of the sometimes-contradictory theoretical stances presented to migration and development in the case of US–Mexico migration, impels us to carefully consider what the object and the subjects of development are, given that the very same definition of development is still under heated discussion. In fact, we can also argue that the apparently more straightforward definition of migration, is not what it seems. As some research in Mexico has shown, what is socially considered as migration is not gender-neutral given that reasons for moving place are important in the definition of who is or who is not a migrant and these are gender-specific (Mata-Codesal 2017). Assuming that both development and migration are social phenomena with effects, causes, and consequences at different levels, which can even contradict each other, researchers and practitioners interested in US–Mexico migration are necessarily compelled to integrate, or at least acknowledge, the existence of such different arenas in their theoretical as well as methodological stances.

References

Alba F. (2013) Mexico: The New Migration Narrative, Migration Policy Institute (www.migrationpolicy.org/article/mexico-new-migration-narrative) Accessed 5 March 2019.

Arizpe L. (1983) "El éxoco rural en México y su relación con la migración a Estados Unidos", *Estudios Sociológicos*, *1(1)*, 9–33.

Bada X. (2016) "Collective remittances and development in rural Mexico: a view from Chicago's Mexican Hometown Associations", *Population, Space and Place*, *22(4)*, 343–355.

Besserer F. (2004) *Topografías, Transnacionales* UAM, Mexico City & Plaza y Valdés.

Bobes C. (2010) *Los Tecuanes Danzan en la Nieve. Contactos transnacionales entre Axochiapan y Minnesota*, FLACSO Mexico, Mexico City.

Boehm D. (2012) *Intimate Migrations. Gender, Family, and Illegality among Transnational Mexicans*, New York University Press, New York and London.

Canales A. (2010) "Mexican labour migration to the United States in the age of globalization", *Journal of Ethnic and Migration Studies*, *29(4)*, 741–761.

Cervantes D. and Li Ng J.J. (2018) Mexico Migration Watch. 6 February 2018. Fundacion BBVA Bancomer, Mexico City.

Chishti M and Hipsman F. (2015) In historic shift, new migration flows from Mexico fall below those from China and India, Migration Policy Institute (www.migrationpolicy.org/article/historic-shift-new-migration-flows-mexico-fall-below-those-china-and-india) Accessed 5 March 2019.

Chort I. and de la Rupelle M. (2016) "Determinants of Mexico-US outward and return migration flows: a state-level panel data analysis", *Demography, 53(5),* 1453–1476.

Cohen J. (2004) *The Culture of Migration in Southern Mexico,* University of Texas Press, Austin.

CONAPO. (2012) *Índices de Intensidad Migratoria México-Estados Unidos 2010,* Consejo Nacional de Población, Mexico City.

CONAPO and Fundación BBVA Bancomer. (2017) *Yearbook of Migration and Remittances 2017.Consejo Nacional de Población-Fundación,* BBVA Bancomer-BBVA Research, Mexico City.

Delgado-Wise R. (2014) "A critical overview of migration and development: The Latin American challenge", *Annual Review of Sociology, 40,* 643–663.

Delgado-Wise R. (2015) "Unravelling highly skilled migration from Mexico in the context of neoliberal globalization", in Castles S, Ozkul D and Arias Cubas M eds., *Social Transformation and Migration: National and Local Experiences in South Korea, Turkey, Mexico and Australia,* Palgrave Macmillan, UK, London, 201–217.

Durand J. (2013) "Nueva fase migratoria", *Papeles de Población, 19(77),* 83–113.

Hagan J. and Wassink J. (2016) "New skills, new jobs: return migration, skill transfers, and business formation in Mexico", *Social Problems, 63(4),* 513–533.

Kearney M. (2000) "Transnational Oaxacan indigenous identity: the case of Mixtecs and Zapotecs", *Identities, 7(2),* 173–195.

King R. and Skeldon R. (2010) "Mind the gap! integrating approaches to internal and international migration", *Journal of Ethnic and Migration Studies, 36(10),* 1619–1646.

Lizárraga Morales O. Mantecón A. and Huete R. (2015) "Transnationality and social integration within lifestyle migration. A comparative study of two cases in Mexico and Spain", *Journal of Latin American Geography, 14(1),* 139–159.

Lozano F. and Gandini L. (2010) *Migrantes Calificados de América Latina y el Caribe. ¿Capacidades Desaprovechadas?* CRIM-UNAM, Cuernavaca.

Mata-Codesal D. (2017) "Gendered (Im)mobility: rooted women and waiting penelopes", *Crossings: Journal of Migration and Culture, 8(2),* 151–162.

OECD. (2017) *International Migration Outlook 2017,* OECD Publishing, Paris.

Passel J.S. and Cohn V. (2017) As Mexican Share Declined, U.S. Unauthorized Immigrant Population Fell in 2015 below Recession Level. Washington: Pew Research Center (www.pewresearch.org/fact-tank/2017/04/25/as-mexican-share-declined-u-s-unauthorized-immigrant-population-fell-in-2015-below-recession-level) Accessed 5 March 2019.

Riosmena F. and Massey D. S. (2012) "Pathways to El Norte: origins, destinations, and characteristics of Mexican migrants to the United States", *The International Migration Review, 46(1),* 3–36.

Rivera L. (2007) "La formación y dinámica del circuito migratorio Mixteca-Nueva York-Mixteca: los trayectos internos e internacionales", *Norteamérica, 2(1),* 171–203.

Schmidt-Verkerk K. (2012) *The Potential Influence of Climate Change on Migratory Behaviour - A Study of Drought, Hurricanes and Migration in Mexico.* PhD thesis Department of Geography, University of Sussex, Brighton.

Slack J. (2015) "Captive bodies: migrant kidnapping and deportation in Mexico", *Area, 48(3),* 271–277.

World Bank. (2016) *Migration and Remittances Factbook 2016,* 3rd edition. World Bank, Washington DC.

World Bank. (2018) Annual Remittances Data. (www.worldbank.org/en/topic/migrationremittances diasporaissues/brief/migration-remittances-data) Accessed 5 March 2019.

Zong J. and Batalova J. (2016) Mexican Immigrants in the United States, Migration Policy Institute (www.migrationpolicy.org/article/mexican-immigrants-united-states) Accessed 5 March 2019.

Zuñiga E., Leite P. and Acevedo L. (2005) *Migración México-Estados Unidos. Panorama Regional y Estatal,* CONAPO, Mexico City.

47

THE BOLIVIA–ARGENTINA MIGRATION CORRIDOR

Alfonso Hinojosa Gordonava[1]

Introduction

Argentina today continues to be the principal destination for Bolivian migrants, as it had been for the whole of the twentieth century. Although this migration has been a constant throughout recent history, fluctuations have occurred dependent upon a number of economic and political factors that shaped the volume at particular times. The 2012 Bolivian census included questions about international migration for the first time, which showed that almost 40 per cent of all Bolivian migrants choose Argentina as their preferred destination. Argentinean labour markets, therefore, continued to represent a significant labour niche for Bolivian labour migration.

This chapter reviews the origins as well as recent developments in migration dynamics between these two countries, in relation to their composition as well as labour market insertion, which have been and continue to be significant. Today, it is not possible to think of certain Argentinean areas of production, such as horticulture, construction, or garment manufacturing, without taking into account the contribution of Bolivian labour.

Historic context

Bolivian migration to Argentina for work has a long tradition. During the colonial period, in the eighteenth century, many of the haciendas of the north of Argentina, turned to indigenous people from the Andean highlands further north. In fact, the economic base of this region of Argentina was closely articulated with the economy of mining in Potosí, in terms of regional trade, but also given that its exports were through ports on the Pacific Ocean, and not through Buenos Aires until the beginning of the nineteenth century and the creation of independent states.

From the beginning of the Republic in the early nineteenth century, and because of the delayed process of colonisation of the region of the Chaco, which borders Argentina, significant numbers of indigenous Guaraní people were forced to abandon their territories and 'cross imaginary boundaries', moving to localities in the neighbouring country and working as 'peones' in the horticultural sector. Various missionary chronicles from this early period lead us to think that the beginnings of the Bolivian migration to Argentina responded to a scheme of forced political displacement, and that only later this transitioned into a labour type of migration.

The labour force from neighbouring countries in Argentina started gathering importance from the 1920s onwards. The phenomenon was mostly taking place in the north of the country, linked to the sugar industry, which expanded from Tucumán towards the provinces of Salta and Jujuy. This expansion and the corresponding increase in the seasonal demand for cheap labour, incentivised the migration from the South of Bolivia and the Bolivian valleys. In the Argentinean census of 1947, almost 88 per cent of Bolivian migrants were found in the provinces of Salta and Jujuy, and only 7 per cent in the Province of Buenos Aires (Grimson 1999). This situation persisted until the import substitution policies, which encouraged rural–urban migration towards the main cities, to fill in the labour demand for the nascent industry even though seasonal migration towards the northern rural areas persisted.

The rural–urban migration that went hand in hand with industrialisation led to the establishment of marginal areas in the large cities, and primarily Buenos Aires. Bolivian migrants, therefore, who were leaving precarious socio-economic conditions at home, were then finding work in occupations that were low paid and unskilled. This was the case in urban areas, in factories and construction, as well as in rural areas, given they were filling jobs left by Argentinean rural–urban migrants who were moving towards the cities to find work in factories.

During this period, Bolivian migration increased, mostly as a result of the crisis that the Bolivian economy suffered during the 1980s and the neo-liberal structural adjustment programme that followed. As part of the restructuring of the economy, a large proportion of miners were 'relocalised' (euphemism used for being made redundant), which also fed the increasing movement of people who were seeking work in Argentina. Unlike earlier migrants, who were mainly rural-indigenous farmers looking for temporary work, this was an urban population, from the mining town and main cities, with higher levels of education, who ended up in the Argentinean cities or its peripheries. During this decade, the number of Bolivian residents in the Province of Buenos Aires became equal to, or higher than, those residing in Salta and Jujuy. Thus, migration became reorganised towards the most important urban centre in search of better working and living conditions. However, a large proportion of Bolivian migrants also found work in the rural Province of Buenos Aires, working its land that they leased and eventually also owned.

The 1990s marked a period of stability and a 'migration boom' in Argentina given the convertibility plan that pegged the Argentinean peso to the US dollar but also the amnesty that allowed the legalisation of residence of around 110,000 Bolivians, mostly in Buenos Aires. This period saw the consolidation and diversification of previous migration trajectories, including urban to urban migration. These migration networks then cushioned the effects of the Argentinean crisis of 2001.

The beginning of this century was marked by crises for various countries in the region, which played an important role in the changing scenarios of Bolivian migration. The Bolivian political crisis pushed many migrants out, while the Argentinean crisis altered the pre-established material and symbolic interchanges. However, sometime after the severe Argentinean crisis, migration flows re-established themselves, but clearly with much lower levels of savings and remittances. In this sense, the process of labour flexibilisation, which resulted from the neo-liberal models imposed in the region, generated an army of unemployed who were desperate to find a job and therefore accepted conditions of extreme exploitation, cheapening the cost of labour in a direct benefit to the employers.

The consolidation of the collective

As mentioned above, most Bolivians, estimated at over 1 million people, live in the Greater Buenos Aires area (Cancillería 2011). Most of them are undocumented, despite the agreement called Patria Grande, which aimed at making regularisation more accessible and was signed by both countries in 2006. We are therefore talking of over half a million undocumented migrants, who constitute a vulnerable population in terms of their most basic rights (Abal 2014). Most Bolivians work in unskilled occupations, in construction, in garment manufacturing, informal trade, agricultural production, and domestic work (Argos 2017; Bastia 2014; Gago 2015; Vargas 2010). Many young people are students, while a minority also exercise their profession and are in Argentina as skilled migrants.

A number of studies mention that a significant part of the horticultural production in the north is carried out by Bolivian families (Benencia and Karasik 1995; Sassone 2009; Hinojosa 2001; among others). While they started working as day labourers, they then moved up the ladder, leasing land and eventually becoming property owners, linking with other co-nationals who were in charge of the horticultural trade in Buenos Aires. These studies aim to understand the complexity of this phenomenon as a transnational process, highlighting spatial occupation and structuration, as well as the nexus between rurality and international migration. They also highlight the importance of remittances in local production processes for improving quality of life and decreasing poverty. Other studies highlight the levels of illegality, labour and racial discrimination, and social and cultural exclusion, which many migrants in Argentina experience (Grimson 1999).

The history and development of garment workshops as a productive sector stems from the 1980s, a period that is usually defined as neo-liberal. Variables such as unemployment, economic convertibility, and migration stemmed directly from the economic crises and social outbreaks in the region, and reached their consolidation during the 1990s.

During this period, there have also been controversies in relation to how to frame some of the challenges that Bolivian workers experienced. Vargas (2010) admonishes that it is problematic to talk about 'slave labour', 'black economy', 'marginal and informal labour' when referring to garment workshop owners and workers. These interpretations tend to overlook the complexity, changes, and hybridisation of processes in which migrants live their daily lives. These processes, which are often carried out collectively, on the other hand, include three decades of continuous participation by Bolivian migrants in the productive spaces of the garment workshops. To use the terminology of 'slavery' to refer to a productive activity that is part of a larger social and productive system, hinders the development of appropriate tools for fighting injustice, because it simplifies a complex social, cultural, and economic reality. In terms of the Bolivian labour force, Bastia (2010) argues that 'the labour market insertion of the Bolivian migrants in Buenos Aires shows that for the women it was easier to find work immediately after their arrival' (2010, 77, original in Spanish). She also argues that, in the case of garment workshops in Buenos Aires, despite the fact that both men and women find work in this sector, in the last few years there had been a slight increase in the number of women.

The Bolivian community in Argentina is characterised by a high density of cultural associations and other organisations, which express a strong identification with socio-cultural practices through values transmitted across generations and reflected through their social networks, which are always very active (Benencia and Karasik 1995; OIM-CEMLA 2004; Santillo 2001). So, in the case of Bolivians, 'marriages and religious celebrations, baptisms and funerals, family reunions and dances are spaces more geared towards reproducing the fundamental elements of the Bolivian culture in Greater Buenos Aires' (Santillo 2001, 37). The political background of the leaders of the various organisations of Bolivian residents is important, given that most of them have previous experience of being community or trade union leaders, as well as leaders of social movements related to miners or ethnic-peasant and other grassroots organisations, during their migration trajectory.

It is important to highlight here that the social and political changes that Bolivia went through during the first decade of this century were so intense and profound – the 'gas war', nationalisation of hydrocarbons, Evo Morales' government – that they also shaped the actions of the Bolivian residents in Argentina (Hinojosa 2018).

A brief conclusion: the new characteristics of the Bolivian collective in Argentina

Even though Bolivian migration to Argentina has been taking place for a long time and includes various phases and particularities in the construction of residents abroad, the current century has seen the emergence of new organisations of young migrants. These have been linked to the emergence of the garment workshops and indicates a rupture with the traditional organisations of the Bolivian community, which have been organising folkloric events and festivities for Bolivian residents for decades. These new organisations are evidence of novel discursive practices and new forms of organising compared with the traditional forms that such organisations took in Argentina (Hinojosa 2018). The most interesting characteristics of the new forms of organising include the following.

First, they have broken free from the nationalist ghetto. That is, their areas of action and interaction have created a capacity to relate with other collectives such as trade unions, and migrant groups from other countries but also with local workers' organisations.

Second, they have distanced themselves from a victimising discourse. There has been a fundamental discursive change in that, given the victimisation of the fight against xenophobia and discrimination, they have moved on to highlight the economic contributions that migrants make. In this sense, there is a recognition of their fundamental rights but also of their role as economic actors. Therefore, an awareness of the important economic contribution they make as migrants exists. In Buenos Aires there is also a new Bolivian middle class, which is linked with productive activities, which have given some people the possibility of upward social mobility in the Bolivian community.

Third, these organisations are mostly made up of educated young people, both men and women, which is perhaps the key characteristic of the Bolivian community in Argentina today. They organise horizontally and the spaces within which they relate to other organisations are mostly made up of social media and the internet. The level of education of these younger migrants is also higher compared to previous waves of migrants. As the second and third generation of migrants gather importance, the children of migrants and the contexts within which they socialise, organise, reproduce, has allowed them to become political actors.

Fourth and finally, is the phenomenon that one can call 'migrants subject/actor'. The gender-based violence in the family context is a fundamental structural factor behind women's migration, as is the violence that women are subjected to in the garment workshops. Here we see the emergence of 'the feminine' as one of the main current powers behind the movements of migrants in Buenos Aires. They denounce the reproduction of gender-based violence and inequalities within migration spaces. All of this is crystallised in the setting up of the organisation *Ni una Migrante Menos*, 'Not one Migrant Woman Less', and their declaration (see www.marcha.org.ar/ni-una-migrante-menos-vivas-libres-y-sin-racismo-nos-queremos/).

Note

1 Docente Investigador del Instituto de Investigación, Interacción Social y Postgrado, Carrera de Trabajo Social, UMSA, La Paz-Bolivia. Translation by Tanja Bastia.

References

Abal, Antonio. 2014. El *ejercicio ciudadano de migrantes bolivianos en la Provincia de Buenos Aires*, Universidad de Buenos Aires (Tesis de Maestría en Migraciones Internacionales, mimeo).

Argos, Ayeleen. 2017. Entre *la "esclavitud" y la "cultura". Reflexiones en torno a representaciones y prácticas sobre las relaciones de trabajo y producción en talleres de costura en Buenos Aires*, Ponencia en Congreso Latinoamericano del Trabajo y Trabajadores.

Bastia, Tanja. 2010. Migración transnacional y emancipación. Relaciones de género y cambio social en las migraciones urbanas, *Decursos, Revista de Ciencias Sociales* Año xii, Número Vol. 21, pp. 67–96, Cochabamba.

Bastia, Tanja. 2014. From Mining to Garment Workshops: Bolivian Migrants in Buenos Aires, *Journal of Ethnic and Migration Studies* Vol. 33, No. 4, pp. 655–669.

Benencia, Roberto and Gabriela Karasik. 1995. *Inmigración limítrofe. Los bolivianos en Buenos Aires*, Editorial CEAL, Buenos Aires.

Cancillería. 2011. *Informe anual* (datos institucionales), La Paz.

Gago, Verónica. 2015. *La razón neoliberal. Economías barrocas y pragmática popular*, Tinta Limón, Buenos Aires.

Grimson, Alejandro. 1999. *Relatos de la diferencia y la igualdad. Los bolivianos en Buenos Aires*, Eudeba, Buenos Aires.

Hinojosa, Alfonso. (ed.). 2001. *Entre idas y venidas. Campesinos tarijeños en el norte de Argentina*, PIEB, La Paz.

Hinojosa, Alfonso. 2018. *Unos jodidos bolitas. Nuevos rostros de la bolivianeidad en Buenos Aires*. (mimeo).

OIM-CEMLA. 2004. *Relevamiento y diagnóstico de las asociaciones de la colectividad boliviana en Argentina*, Informe final. OIM-CEMLA, Buenos Aires.

Santillo, Mario. 2001. *Más allá de las fronteras culturales y religiosas: religiosidad popular de los inmigrantes bolivianos en las comunidades católicas de Buenos Aires*, Trabajo presentado en el Simposio Académico de la Comisión de Estudios de la Iglesia Latinoamericana (CEHILA) en Las Cruces, Nuevo Mexico, Estados Unidos.

Sassone, Susana. 2009. "Geografías Bolivianas en la gran ciudad. Acerca del lugar y de la identidad cultural de los migrantes", en Pedro Pírez (ed.), Buenos Aires, la larga formación del presente. OLACCHI, Quito, 176-190.

Vargas, Jorge. 2010. *Mi razón no pide piedad*. (mimeo).

48

THE VENEZUELA–TRINIDAD AND TOBAGO MIGRATION CORRIDOR

Natalie Dietrich Jones

Introduction

This chapter locates the contemporary in historical accounts of migration between (the Bolivarian Republic of) Venezuela and (the Republic of) Trinidad and Tobago, shedding light on the interplay between development and migration in these two cases. It focuses on immigration to and from Trinidad, the larger of the islands of the 'twin-island republic', as Tobago demonstrates a distinct migration profile from that of Trinidad (Anatol et al. 2013).

This chapter highlights the evolutionary dimension of this corridor, where the directionality, types, and volume of migration have ebbed and waned in response to political and economic developments taking place in each country, the wider Caribbean (that is, the insular and circum-Caribbean), as well as the global political economy. It provides useful insight into the implications of proximity, porosity of borders, synergistic (economic) development, and past migratory patterns, for contemporary migration.

Geo-historical overview: fifteenth to twentieth centuries

Trinidad and Tobago is the most southern country along the chain of Caribbean islands. It is separated from Venezuela by the Gulf of Paria by a mere 7 miles; at this distance, Trinidad is in fact closer to Venezuela than it is to Tobago, and its Caribbean neighbours.

The migratory connection between Venezuela and Trinidad precede the first settlement of the Spanish in both countries. In the earliest phases of the corridor, Amerindian populations travelled between Trinidad and Venezuela to trade, settle permanently, and transit to other destinations in the Caribbean (Toussaint 2000). Such movements continued into the seventeenth century, being augmented by commercial exchange during the period of Spanish, and later British, colonisation (Tinker Salas 2009).

In the nineteenth century newly freed slaves from the British West Indies, including Trinidad, began travelling to Venezuela for remunerated labour on cocoa plantations. They also worked in gold mining during the mid-nineteenth century (Putnam 2013; Tinker Salas 2009; Toussaint 2000). These movements took place during a high point of *intra*-regional migration in the Anglophone Caribbean, as newly emancipated slaves sought high(er) wages, as well as opportunity for settlement of arable land. They are therefore significant as

Figure 48.1 Steel Pan Man: This steel pan man greets departing passengers at the Piarco International
 Airport in Port-of-Spain Trinidad. Parang music, which some believe was brought to Trinidad by Venezuelan cocoa panyols, today incorporates the use of steel pan

Copyright: Natalie Dietrich Jones

they foreshadow later mass migration to the Hispanic Caribbean – Panama, Costa Rica, and
Cuba, during the twentieth century (cf. Putnam 2013).

In post-emancipation Trinidad, the lack of an adequate labour force impacted the agricultural sector, then dominated by cocoa and sugar. To revive the cocoa industry, the colonial
administration suggested recruitment of labour from Venezuela. Cocoa panyols from Venezuela contributed significantly to the development of the industry in Trinidad between 1860
and 1890 (Brereton 1981, 2007; Moodie-Kublalsingh 1994; Whiteman 1990).[1] Their arrival
eased a chronic labour shortage, occasioned an economic transition, as well as produced shifts
in demography by diversifying and increasing the population in Trinidad (Brereton 2007; see
Figure 48.1). The settled and seasonal migration of cocoa panyols differed from other forms of
immigration from Venezuela (see Table 48.1), which included affluent French-speaking
Venezuelans, children sent to Trinidad for a British education and political refugees who fled
revolutionary wars and repressive political regimes at various points during the nineteenth
century (Munro 2010; Reis 2009; Tinker Salas 2009).

Table 48.1 Dominant migratory patterns within the Venezuela–Trinidad corridor

Century	Venezuela to Trinidad	Trinidad to Venezuela
Pre-Columbian era	Amerindians	Amerindians
Sixteenth to eighteenth century	Itinerant traders	Itinerant traders
	Slave labour (agricultural sector)	Slave labour (agricultural sector)
	Political refugees	Escaped and manumitted slaves
Nineteenth century	Sephardic Jews	Escaped indentured workers
	Political refugees	Waged labour (agricultural, shipping
	Waged labour (agricultural sector)	and extractive sectors)
Twentieth century	Waged labour (extractive sector)	Waged labour (extractive sector)
	English language students	Female itinerant traders
Twenty-first century	English language students	Waged labour (extractive sector)
	Circular/short-term economic migrants	Smuggled and trafficked persons
	Refugees/asylum seekers	Tourists
	Smuggled and trafficked persons	

Author's elaboration Sources: Toussaint (2000); Tinker Salas (2009); Reis (2009); UNHCR (2017a)

Migration to Venezuela from Trinidad increased in the early twentieth century, when the discovery of oil led to development of the sector by multinational interests, who recruited labourers from the British and Dutch West Indies. Employment in Venezuela helped to ease the pressures of low wages and unemployment in the colonies. For Trinidadians, it enabled social mobility for afro-descended workers unable to obtain technical work in the oil fields alongside expatriates until the 1950s (Brereton 1981). Trinidad and Venezuela, both with burgeoning oil industries, served as major markets for employment. There was therefore movement between Venezuela and Trinidad, from Venezuela and Trinidad to Aruba (due to the location of an oil refinery there) and Curaçao, as well as to these three countries from the Eastern Caribbean (Marshall 1982, 1986; Tinker Salas 2009).

Although patterns were dominated by male migrants, women also obtained work as domestics in Venezuelan households, and as seamstresses, laundresses and cooks in oil companies, their travel facilitated by their connectivity to kith and kin resident in Venezuela (Tinker Salas 2009). Approximately 10,000 nationals from Curaçao, Trinidad and Barbados, travelled to work in oil fields in Venezuela between 1916 and 1929 (Marshall 1986). It should be noted that the simultaneous development of the sectors in both countries, as well as Trinidad's status an importer of labour, influenced the numbers travelling to Venezuela. In addition, lack of disaggregation of country of origin of British nationals travelling during this period also limits true assessment of the numbers (Putnam 2013). Data provided in Venezuelan censuses do, however, suggest sustained emigration from Trinidad, which until the 1940s was second only to Colombia as a source country (see Table 48.2).

Emigration to Venezuela continued despite the passage in 1936 of legislation prohibiting the employment of afro-descended workers, but eased in the 1980s when a boom in the oil sector in Trinidad decreased the emigration of the working-class population (Kiely 1996). By this time, however, Venezuela had ceased to be a primary destination. Trinidadians had, since the late 1960s, opted for North America as their destination of choice (Steele 1980). The large-scale emigration to the United Kingdom from the British West Indies was not

Table 48.2 Origin of immigrants from the Americas in Venezuela

Nationality	1926(a)	1936(a)	1941(a)	1950	1961	1971
Colombia	7798	19,421	16,979	45,969	102,314	180,144
United States of America	2480	1832	3575	10,610	13,271	11,277
Cuba	321	395	1210	3777	7953	10,415
Ecuador	10	70	135	1275	2932	5239
Chile	38	106	177	519	2051	3093
Argentina	76	103	142	618	3131	3971
Trinidad	**?**	**2821**	**?**	**3728**	**4381**	**5067**
Others	625	5401	1456	9527	16,614	20,833
Total Americas	11,348	30,149	23,674	76,023	152,647	240,039

Source: adapted and translated from Chen and Picouet (1979, 32 Cuadro1–10, Procedencia de los inmigrantes en Venezuela seg[ú]n censos nacionales)

a reality for Trinidad, with an economy buoyed by economic growth and post-independence developments. In addition, the turn to the United States, and subsequently Canada, for Trinidad came about much later than its counterparts, and was encouraged by high rates of unemployment (Andrews 1975). Despite this decline, in the late 1980s, Venezuela was an important destination for women who worked as itinerant traders. Travelling from Trinidad, as well as Grenada, St. Vincent, and Barbados, they frequented Venezuela in order to purchase manufactured goods in free-port shopping centres in Caracas and the island of Margarita (Aymer 1997).

Table 48.3 Immigration to Trinidad from Venezuela

	1990	1995	2000	2005	2010	2015
N° immigrants	1337	1213	1413	1516	1672	1732
Total immigrant/foreign born population	50,666	45,994	41,753	44,812	48,226	49,883
Migrant stock (per cent total immigrants)	2.6	2.6	3.4	3.4	3.5	3.5
Total male immigrant/foreign born population	23,528	21,303	19,288	20,647	23,152	24,326
N° male migrants	534	483	580	620	709	751
Male migrant stock (per cent Venezuelan immigrants)	40	40	41	41	42	43
Male migrant stock (per cent total male immigrants)	2	2	1	3	3	3
Total female immigrant/foreign born population	27,138	24,691	22,465	24,165	25,074	25,557
N° female migrants	803	730	833	896	963	981
Female migrant stock (per cent Venezuelan immigrants)	60	60	59	59	58	57
Female migrant stock (per cent total female immigrants)	3	3	4	4	4	4

Author's elaboration Source: United Nations Department of Economic and Social Affairs (2015)

Contemporary migratory patterns: late twentieth and early twenty-first centuries

Although migration from Trinidad to Venezuela has been on the decline (Table 48.3) migration to Trinidad from Venezuela has continued to rise (Table 48.4) since 1990. For Venezuelans, Trinidad remains an attractive location for employment, as well as educational certification (Reis 2009).

Proximity, as well as porosity of coastal borders, have over the years contributed to incidences of smuggling and trafficking. In addition, both countries serve as transit points for regional and extra-regional migrants (from Africa, Brazil, and Colombia), who travel via Venezuela to Trinidad, likely en route to other destinations in the North (Waldrop-Bonair et al. 2013). Entry into Trinidad is facilitated by regular air and sea connectivity (Ali and Shrivastava 2015), as well as a no-visa requirement for Venezuelans who intend to stay less than 90 days as outlined in the Trinidad and Tobago Immigration Division website. There is also evidence of the use of fraudulent documentation and collusion with locals who arrange travel, as well as organise employment in order to circumvent regulations regarding residence and work (Waldrop-Bonair et al. 2013).

An ongoing humanitarian crisis, following the death of former President Hugo Chavez in 2013, has further encouraged migration into Trinidad (UNHCR 2017a). The comparably low

Table 48.4 Immigration to Venezuela from Trinidad

	1990	*1995*	*2000*	*2005*	*2010*	*2015*
N° immigrants	3611	3174	2765	2746	2724	2808
Total immigrant/foreign born population	1,025,099	1,019,996	1,013,663	1,070,562	1,331,488	1,404,448
Migrant stock (per cent total immigrants)	0.3	0.3	0.2	0.2	0.2	0.1
Total male immigrant/ foreign born population	507,430	513,473	508,639	535,096	667,963	703,458
Male	1710	1504	1309	1302	1294	1314
Male migrant stock (per cent Trinidadian immigrants)	47	47	47	47	47	46
Male migrant stock (per cent total male immigrants)	0.3	0.3	0.2	0.2	0.2	0.2
Total female immigrant/foreign born population	517,669	506,523	505,024	535,466	663,525	700,990
Female	1901	1670	1456	1444	1430	1494
Female migrant stock (per cent Trinidadian immigrants)	53	53	53	53	53	54
Female migrant stock (per cent total female immigrants)	0.3	0.3	0.2	0.2	0.2	0.2

Author's elaboration Source: United Nations Department of Economic and Social Affairs (2015)

Figure 48.2 Pirogues: Fishing boats, or pirogues, docked at a boat yard in Chaguaramas. Chaguaramas, located in the northwest of Trinidad, is one of the closest Trinidadian ports to Venezuela. It is possible, to travel from this boatyard to Güiria, Venezuela, one of the more popular points of departure for Venezuelan migrants travelling by boat to Trinidad. Formal trips from this boat yard are registered by the Immigration Department, which is also located on site

Copyright: Natalie Dietrich Jones

cost of sea travel makes Trinidad, as well as other proximate Caribbean neighbours, Aruba and Curaçao, a more likely destination for migrants without the funds to travel over land to the more distant continental destinations – Colombia and Brazil (see Figure 48.2). There were noticeable jumps in arrivals in 2014 and 2015 (see Table 48.5), due to an increase in travel from Venezuela of individuals shopping for food and other essential items (Rambally 2016; Vyas and Munoz 2017). The crisis has further complicated the mixed migratory pattern, which has characterised the corridor, increasing undocumented migrants and the number of asylum seekers (UNHCR 2017b). The undocumented obtain employment primarily in the informal sectors – care work, construction, retail, and sex work – in order to remit money home to family members left behind in Venezuela (Dowlat 2018; Venezelanos de buheros 2016). Current statistics are unavailable but earlier data for 2010–12 has shown that men make up approximately two-thirds of irregular migrant flows (International Labour Organization/ILO 2017).

Recent estimates, which are contested indicate that there are 40,000 Venezuelans, with varying forms of status in Trinidad (Kowlessar 2017; La Rose 2017, 2017b; UNHCR 2017b). This figure far exceeds official statistics, which point to a migrant stock of approximately 1700 Venezuelans (United Nations Department of Social and Economic Affairs 2015). While

Table 48.5 Stopover arrivals in Trinidad by Venezuelan nationals, 1995–2016

	Venezuela	*Total*	*% Total*
1995	6293	259,784	2.4
2010	9590	387,559	2.4
2011	14,460	430,922	3.3
2012	16,415	454,683	3.6
2013	15,008	434,044	3.5
2014	21,052	412,447	5.1
2015	28,087★	439,749	6.4
2016	19,927★	408,782	4.9

Author's elaboration Sources: Trinidad and Tobago Tourism Development Company Limited (2014) ★Government of the Republic of Trinidad and Tobago Ministry of Tourism (2017)

undocumented and other irregular flows may not be reflected in these statistics, the true scope of migration is unclear. If these figures are correct, the Venezuelan immigrant population would be roughly equivalent to the total number of foreign born population in Trinidad. The figures would also be indicative of a shift in the composition of immigrant stock, which has been dominated by skilled and unskilled labour migration from Guyana, Grenada, and St. Vincent (Central Statistical Office of Trinidad and Tobago 2012; SICREMI 2015).

Conclusion

The Venezuela–Trinidad migration corridor is an exemplar of inter-Caribbean migration processes, which have been central to the economic development of the Caribbean. Past migrations between Venezuela and Trinidad have produced the musical genre of Parang in Trinidad (Munro 2010) and taken the language of Patuá to Venezuela (Ferreira 2009). These enduring cultural forms underscore the significance of this corridor. The ongoing crisis in Venezuela, which has occasioned a shift of primarily bi-directional labour flows to movement of a largely vulnerable migrant (and refugee) population from Venezuela into Trinidad, calls for renewed focus on the evolution of this corridor, which will no doubt continue to play a role in migration dynamics within the region.

Note

1 'Panyol' is a Trinidadian corruption of the word 'español', and refers to a person of mixed Spanish, Amerindian, and African heritage (Moodie-Kublalsingh 1994).

Acknowledgment

The author is grateful to Prof Jessica Byron, Director of the Institute of International Relations at the University of the West Indies (St. Augustine) who provided comments on an initial draft of this chapter.

References

Ali, Anton, and Gyan Shrivastava. 2015. "A Bridge Linking Trinidad and Venezuela: A Case Study". *The Journal of the Association of Professional Engineers of Trinidad and Tobago* 43 (2): 32–43.

Anatol, Marlon, Raymond Mark Kirton, and Nia Nanan. 2013. *Becoming an Immigration Magnet: Migrants' Profiles and the Impact of Migration on Human Development in Trinidad and Tobago*. Belgium: ACP Observatory on Migration.

Andrews, Norman. 1975. "Trinidad and Tobago". In *Population Policies in the Caribbean*, edited by Aaron Lee Segal, 73–87. Lexington, Massachusetts: Lexington Books.

Aymer, Paula L. 1997. *Uprooted Women: Migrant Domestics in the Caribbean*. Westport, CT: Praegar.

Brereton, Bridget. 1981. *A History of Modern Trinidad 1783–1962*. Kingston: Heinemann.

Brereton, Bridget. 2007. "Contesting the Past: Narratives of Trinidad and Tobago History". *New West Indian Guide/Nieuwe West-Indische Gids* 81 (3&4): 169–196.

Central Statistical Office of Trinidad and Tobago. 2012. *Trinidad and Tobago Population and Housing Census Demographic Report*. Port-of-Spain, Trinidad: Central Statistical Office of Trinidad and Tobago.

Chen, Chi-Yi, and Michel Picouet. 1979. *Dinámica de la población: Caso de Venezuela* Caracas. Universidad Catolica Andres Bello y Office de la Rescherche Scientifique et Technique Outre-Mer.

Dowlat, R. 2018. "Venezuelans Cautious Entering Cedros, Icacos." In *Trinidad and Tobago Guardian*, May 10. www.guardian.co.tt/news/2016-05-09/venezuelans-cautious-entering-cedros-icacos.

Ferreira, Jo-Anne S. 2009. "The History and Future of Patuá in Paria: Report on Initial Language Revitalization Efforts for French Creole in Venezuela". *Journal of Pidgin and Creole Languages* 24 (1): 139–157.

International Labour Organization. 2017. *Labour migration in Latin America and the Caribbean: Diagnosis, Strategy and ILO's Work in the Region*. Lima: ILO Regional Office for Latin America and the Caribbean.

Kiely, Ray. 1996. *The Politics of Labour and Development in Trinidad*. Barbados: University of the West Indies Press.

Kowlessar, Geisha. 2017. "Dillon: Decrease in Illegal in Venezuelans." *Trinidad and Tobago Guardian*, September 14. www.guardian.co.tt/news/2017-09-13/dillon-decrease-illegal-venezuelans-coming-tt

La Rose, Miranda. 2017. "40 000 Venezuelans in TT." In *Trinidad and Tobago Newsday*, September 13. http://newsday.co.tt/2017/09/13/40000-venezuelans-in-tt/.

Marshall, Dawn. 1982. "The History of Caribbean Migrations". *Caribbean Review* XI: 6–9 & 52–3.

Marshall, Dawn. 1986. "A History of West Indian Migrations: Overseas Opportunities and "Safety Valve" Policies". In *Caribbean Exodus*, edited by Barry Levine. New York: Praeger, 15–31.

Moodie-Kublalsingh, Sylvia. 1994. *The Cocoa Panyols of Trinidad: An Oral Record*. London; New York: British Academic Press.

Munro, Martin. 2010. *Different Drummers: Rhythm and Race in the Americas*. Berkeley, Los Angeles: University of California Press.

Putnam, Lara. 2013. *Radical Moves: Caribbean Migrants and the Politics of Race in the Jazz Age*. Chapel Hill: University of North Carolina Press.

Rambally, Rhonda K. 2016. "Venezuelans Flock to T&T for Supplies." *Trinidad and Tobago Guardian Online*, May 22. Trinidad: Port-of-Spain.

Reis, Michele N. 2009. "Contemporary Venezuelan Student Emigration to Trinidad". In *Freedom and constraint in Caribbean migration and diaspora*, edited by Elizabeth Thomas-Hope. Kingston: Ian Randle Publishers, 36–51.

Tinker Salas, Miguel. 2009. *The Enduring Legacy: Oil, Culture, and Society in Venezuela*. Durham, NC: Duke University Press.

SICREMI. 2015. *International Migration in the Americas: Third report of the Continuous Reporting System on International Migration in the Americas (SICREMI)*. Washington, DC: Organization of American States.

Steele, Lynette. 1980. "The Flow of Labour from the Republic of Trinidad and Tobago to the United States of America (1965-1975): An Analysis." PhD dissertation, Washington, DC: Howard University.

Toussaint, Michael F. 2000. "Afro-West Indians in Search of the Spanish Main: The Trinidad-Venezuela Referent in the Nineteenth Century." PhD dissertation, St. Augustine: The University of the West Indies.

Trinidad and Tobago Ministry of Tourism. 2017. "Arrivals to Trinidad and Tobago by Main Market 2014-2016." www.tourism.gov.tt/Resources/Statistics/Vistor-Arrivals.

Trinidad and Tobago Tourism Development Company. 2014. "Tourist Stop-over Arrivals to Trinidad and Tobago by Main Markets: 1995-2014." http://tdc.co.tt/index.php/research/visitor-stopover-statistics.

United Nations Department of Social and Economic Affairs. 2015. "Total International Migrant Stock." Accessed November 13, 2017. www.un.org/en/development/desa/population/migration/data/estimates2/estimates15.shtml.

United Nations Refugee Agency/UNHCR. 2017a. *UNHCR Situational Update Venezuela Situation*. Vol. October. Washington, DC: UNHCR.

United Nations Refugee Agency/UNHCR. 2017b. *UNHCR Situational Update Venezuela Situation: Brazil, Colombia, Trinidad and Tobago*. Vol. 19 May. Washington, DC: UNHCR.

Venezelanos de buheros. 2016. "Venezelanos de Buheros en Trinidad & Tobago." *La Patilla*, May 11. www.lapatilla.com/site/2016/05/11/venezolanos-de-buhoneros-en-trinidad-tobago/.

Vyas, Kejal, and Sara Schaefer Muñoz. 2017. "Venezuela's Shortages Spur Periolous Sea Journeys." *Wall Street Journal*, June 23. www.wsj.com/articles/venezuelas-shortages-spur-perilous-sea-journeys-1498172121.

Waldropt-Bonair, Leigh-Ann, Juliana Sherma Foster, Gerard Gray, Susan Alfonso, and Torshia Seales. 2013. *Invisible Immigrants: A Profile of Irregular Migration, Smuggling of Migrants and Trafficking in Persons in Trinidad and Tobago*. Belgium: ACP Observatory on Migration.

Whiteman, Debra. 1990. "The Immigration of Peons to Trinidad and Their Contribution to the Development of the Cocoa Industry 1811-1891." Masters dissertation, St. Augustine: The University of the West Indies.

PART VII

Translating migration and development

In common with most of the research in the social sciences in general, the literature on migration and development is heavily biased towards publications in the English language. This certainly does not mean that the research itself is concentrated on the English-speaking world, and by native English speakers, but that the publications and debate are dominated by that language. Nevertheless, literature on migration and development does exist in languages other than English. The primary purpose of the chapters in this ultimate section is to provide readers with an insight into the discourse that has existed in some of the main language groups around the world: French, German, both the Spanish of Spain and Latin American Spanish, Brazilian Portuguese, Russian, and Chinese.

The chapters also have a more subtle dimension: to tease out whether 'migration and development' are conceptualised or visualised differently by culture area as defined by language. Any such objective is complicated by the fact that so many of the researchers in the field have been trained at institutions in the English-speaking world and have absorbed the prevailing concepts in academies there. However, different underlying historical, geographical, political, and cultural realities suggest that variants distinct from the ideas prevalent in the English-speaking world are likely to emerge. The chapters in this section outline the principal patterns, concerns, and interpretations of migration and development in parts of the world distinct from those of the English-language hegemony.

One example not discussed in the chapters that follow might provide an illustration of such differences. A few years ago, one of the editors participated in discussions of possible future research on migration and development in Cuba. He suggested that it might be useful to assess the developmental impact of the large number of Cuban health workers on African countries. However, the Cuban chair of the meeting made it very clear that, as far as Cuba was concerned, such people were not migrants, even though by international definitions they clearly were: they were outside their country of origin for 12 months and more. Nevertheless, as far as Cuba was concerned, they could not be part of any migration and development debate or research project. Whom we define as 'a migrant' and what we understand as 'development' is context- and time-specific.

The chapters presented in this part provide an insight into how migration is perceived and has evolved in situations very different from those of the English-language academy. Although far from being accomplished, the aim of this section is to broaden and begin democratising migration and development debates.

49

SHIFTS IN MIGRATION AND DEVELOPMENT STUDIES

A perspective from France

Caroline Caplan[1]

Representing 3 per cent of humanity, migrants already contribute four times more to development than rich states do in the form of aid. In this sense, the role of the state loses its importance (Dumitru 2013) and more credit is given to the migration and development nexus. As economic inequalities grow, the migratory phenomenon becomes inseparable from questions related to economic development in countries of origin (Efionayi-Mäder et al. 2008).

In French literature, the work of Guilmoto Christophe and Sandron Frédéric is traditionally considered as a starting point in migration and development studies. In 2003, their work developed an origin-country perspective promoting financial remittances in order to encourage development in developing economies. By this time, international migration was understood in a South–North perspective and the literature as far as development policies were concerned, focused on how migrants could contribute actively to their home country's development. Since then, 15 years of research in the migration and development field have passed. Focusing on the French perspective, this article seeks to understand what that perspective might be and how the field has evolved in France.

In 2009, the Human Development Report concluded that mobility had the potential to optimise human development for those who migrate, for those who stay in their home countries, and for the majority of those in the destination countries. That said, the report had a great impact on French literature as it promoted a human development perspective instead of thinking solely in terms of national economic development. This allowed the human dimension to enter into the debate. This human development perspective renewed migration studies in France.

The first part of this chapter is dedicated to the scale of international migration and development focusing on recent changes in the literature. The second part of this chapter explains how the work done by the UNDP in 2009 directly contributed to a paradigmatic shift in migration studies in France.

National-level perspectives on research on migration and development

In 2003 the publication of Guilmoto and Sandron's work on migration and development opened a new field of study closely linked to global concerns on economic development.

Simultaneously with the development of the literature on migrant transnationalism, in the early 2000s, Guilmoto and Sandron made the link between transnational activities and the ability to generate economic development.

The raising awareness of the third world

In the 1970s, northern countries adopted restrictive migration policies in order to prevent South–North migration. It was widely accepted at this time that the more developed countries had become countries of net immigration; hence, they closed their borders and implemented migration policies. In the late 1970s, France established policies to control migration flows from poor countries, as it '*couldn't host the entire misery of the world*' (Michel Rocard, Prime minister, June 1989). This famous citation reflects a key period in the history of international migrations and migratory circulations in which migrants were rejected in northern economies, and borders were closing in order to reduce their number. Paradoxically, these policies had the opposite effect: closing borders led to the long-term presence of migrant populations. Until then immigrants stayed for short periods of time in France and then went back to their home countries. When immigration controls started in 1974, the consequences were the reverse of the expected and caused a mutation of migration systems (Laurens 2008): flow control was limited to family reunification and migrants tended to stay longer in the country. The mechanism was simple: visas were granted only for family reunification after 1975 and now that workers were no longer admitted, immigrants could not go back and forth between their country of origin and France. They chose to stay in France because if they returned home they would probably not be allowed to come back to France. The impact was massive in origin countries and researchers then focused their work on the impact of highly skilled migrants leaving their home countries more permanently.

The border closure at this time had a two-fold effect: on the one hand, the stabilisation of southern populations in northern countries; and on the other hand, the decrease of migrant returns to origin countries. In migration studies, this led to a strict distinction between home and host countries and to the study of transnational activities. Migration strategies changed as immigration policies tightened. In the 1990s, migrants stayed longer in their host countries. In the case of France, Mali is a widely used example to illustrate those changes: border closure favoured long-term emigration flows and family reunification in France (Daum 1994; Daum et al. 1988). Therefore, migrants circulated less than they used to.

Taking into account the risks long-term emigration represents for home-country development, the French government developed a pioneering development policy associating the migrants in development projects in southern economies. The 'co-development' policy was based on the idea that migrants, by increasing their human, economic, and social capital through their migratory experience, could participate in origin-country development. This policy was unveiled in the so-called Sami Naïr report (Naïr 1997) and aimed to transform migrants into international development actors. This co-development policy is a particular French approach, presented as a way to 'strengthen integration in France while promoting active solidarity with countries of origin, and create social conditions to help potential migrants to stay at home' (Naïr 1997, 3). However, it was commonly agreed that this 'co-development' policy consisted more in limiting migration flows than fostering financial or social exchanges towards home countries. In any case, the co-development policy took into account the new patterns of international migration in the 1990s after the reinforcement of migration controls.

The migrant as a driver for home-country development: a dogma

For decades, migration has been considered either a loss or a gain for origin and destination countries. At the dawn of the twenty-first century, the paradigm for international migration was about to change as migrants became drivers for development in the recommendations of international organisations. Hence, after 2000, migrants have been included in poverty reduction policies, even if no direct mention was made to them in the Millennium Development Goals. These policies, based on the idea diasporas would aim to contribute to their home country's development, led to the promotion of migrant associations and transnational activities.

Imported from the Anglo-Saxon world, transnationalism studies have been nourished by the founding works of Nina Glick Schiller et al. published in 1994 and followed by an abundant literature on migrant initiatives. The transnational turn taken in the 1990s led to a nuanced view of the traditional opposition between home country and host country, highlighting that the migrant could play a role in both countries at the same time. It thus became widely accepted that diasporas would lead to the promotion of development.

In France, work has focused on three geographic areas in the study of migrant initiatives: Sub-Saharan Africa, the Maghreb, and China, corresponding to the three main source areas of migration to France. This transnational turn is also characterised by a focus on 'productive remittances', which were supposed to play a greater role in development-related issues. Productive remittances have been considered to be the demonstration of a profitable migration. Collective initiatives have been created as models following the case of Mexico and its *tres por uno* experience (Lanly and Valenzuela 2004) and, in the 1990s, French literature focused on collective initiatives and their impact on home-country development. This research focused on the Sahel region (Mali, Senegal, and Mauritania), which was a major source of migrants to France (see Daum et al. 1988; Daum 1995, 1998; Quiminal 1991). Financial transfers were a key dimension in their work and responded to an interest from researchers and decision-makers worldwide for economic transfers because they are easily traceable.

It is believed that 'the combination of remittances and diasporas is a key to more rapid development' (Martin 2006, 11). France was known as a forerunner in recognising migration as a development driver in giving migrants access to financial services and by facilitating remittances through lowering their cost (Lucas 2014). France therefore pioneered the diaspora turn, which by the end of the 1990s and beginning of the 2000s scholars had identified as a major area in migration studies (Agunias 2009), which in turn, resulted in the growing interest of the migration and development nexus by international organisations. Consequently, an increasing number of governments engaged in diaspora policies. Not that the very existence of diaspora was new, rather that it became a means to foster development and reduce emigration in origin countries. As a consequence, it won the interest of host states wishing to reduce immigration. France has been a key actor in this process through its co-development policy, which is now called 'mobility and development'. This strategic change of vocabulary fitted into the mobility turn social science has taken (Faist 2013), which embraced the whole process of movement including what precedes it and extends it (Urry 2000).

By the end of the 1990s, empirical studies on transnational practices were followed by policies made to enhance technical, intellectual, and financial capacities to benefit countries of origin (Naïr 1997). The interest of origin and destination countries to foster development through migrants' initiatives led to the growth of remittances for infrastructure and productive investments (Lowell and De la Garza 2002; Ndofor-Tah 2000; Papail 2002). This participated in a renewed interest on diasporic organisations. French geographers have taken a major interest in studying the creation of transnational spaces and their role in local development (Charef 1999; Faret 2003; Lanly 2002). Their work did corroborate the fact that collective remittances had a wider impact than intra-familiar remittances.

Migration and development: a study of organisational practices and capacity building

Before the end of the 1990s. this primary focus on financial remittances, the most easily quantifiable proof of the impact of migration on development, side-lined the issue of skilled migrants. However, since neo-Marxist theories of the 1970s shed light on the brain drain, (Barré et al. 2003; Freitas et al. 2012), political attention has focused on skilled migration. Today, growing evidence has emerged that this emigration of the skilled and highly skilled no longer means an irreparable loss for the country of origin and suggests that skills, knowledge, and ideas, which can easily circulate among countries are able to contribute to scientific and technological development in countries of origin. Two ways for institutions and states to mobilise skilled migrants exist: the first is through the administration of temporary return; the second is by the creation (or mobilisation) of Diaspora Knowledge Networks (DKN). The latter aim to 'contribute to the development of their members' place of origin, through their skills input' (Meyer and Wattiaux 2006, 5)

In developing countries, DKN are urged by states to engage in science and technology development back home without thereby requiring a physical return of the migrant (Caplan 2014). However, this system is based on the use of information and communication technologies. For example, Colombia, Scotland, or South Africa are well-known examples of diaspora networks (see Crush and Williams 2005 for SANSA network (South African Network of Skills Abroad); see Meyer (2015) for Latin-America, MacRae and Wight (2006) for GlobalScot). Institutional initiatives encompass government-designed networks of ministers or state agencies but also institutions of higher education. All this generally supposes that the state (or the institution) cultivates a sense of belonging and ensures mutual respect and trust. If migrants generally trust their co-ethnics (Docquier and Lodigiani 2010), they sometimes appear suspicious of their own origin-state policies and question the legitimacy of top-down diaspora approaches. It is specifically the case for Colombians, who have been the target of several diaspora policies and lack confidence in the intentions of their government. Thus, they multiply individual initiatives competing with those of the state (Caplan 2014).

Controversial development

As Hein de Haas highlighted in 2010, the migration and development nexus is characterised by successive periods of optimism and of pessimism from which the French literature was not immune. In the 1950s and 1960s, optimism dominated as the migration process was conceived to be a redistributive force of labour power worldwide. Pessimism, however, rose in the 1970s, especially influenced by neo-Marxist dependency theory where the negative impacts of brain drain came to the fore. This decade led us to the Bhagwati tax, which is still discussed in political theory of migration, with the drain of skilled from the developing world seen as an integral part of inter-state trade and a primary responsibility of Western states that need to provide some form of compensation (Dumitru 2013).

After a celebration of mobility and circular migration in the last optimist period late in the twentieth century (Baby Collin et al. 2009; Faret and Cortes 2009), it appears that we have now entered into a new pessimist cycle in which researchers have denounced lately is the main interest on skilled migrants and the nationalist turn of the migration and development nexus. We hereby detail the four main objections made by researchers.

First, geographers have denounced the interventionist attitude of states. As Parvati Raghuram has observed, the International Monetary Fund and the World Bank shaped the language of development giving more power to states while overshadowing grassroots activities. It can be said in this sense that state diaspora policy is a verticalised control that reinforces state power over its population and legitimises governmentality (Bordes-Benayoun and Schnapper 2006; Iskander 2005; Raghuram 2009).

Second, the bias towards the skilled migrant has been subject to criticism. Skilled emigration is considered more problematic and has to be compensated somehow because it is assumed that 'skilled workers are the people most likely to build and sustain governments, schools, hospitals, and firms that promote development' (Kapur and McHale 2005), especially as they represent investments to their countries of origin. In this regard, a report from the French Development Agency introduced the notion of 'migration balance' to measure quantitatively the impact of the exit and entry of the educated on countries of origin (Melonio 2008). We identify in the literature two main objections: First that emigrants are urged to return in order to provide knowledge and services in their countries of origin without taking into consideration the ability of the migrants to do so, and without questioning whether the skilled could be productively absorbed in their countries of origin (Caplan 2014), especially because the skilled are usually underused in origin countries (Gaillard and Gaillard 1999). Moreover, these critics claim that unskilled labour emigration is, as much as skilled emigration, a loss for home countries.

Third, critics rely on the observation that migration and development have become a normative framework that do not incorporate migrant experiences. Indeed, international targets aim to increase remittances through legal and therefore controlled channels, which may be ethically problematic as migrants have sacrificed themselves to send money back home. Some authors argue against a policy that relies on migrant remittances as it removes the responsibility of developed states to contribute to the development of southern countries (Datta et al. 2007). Because migrant remittances can play a greater role than international development assistance the risk is to forget the migrants living conditions in host countries:

> Remittances ... are also about the money that is no longer available to individual migrants to secure their well-being, or indeed gain access to further education. It is through the travails and the sacrifices of Gulf migrants from Kerala, India, who share tiny accommodation with myriad others in order to send money home that our development dreams are played out.
>
> *(Raghuram 2009, 107)*

In France, this interest for the migrants' living conditions in developed countries led some researchers to conduct studies on discrimination more specifically in terms of access to health and economic resources (Berchet and Jusot 2012; Cognet 2002; Cediey and Foroni 2006; Condon and Hamel 2007). This approach facilitated a human development perspective (Dumitru 2018).

Finally, another argument made by sceptical scholars highlighted a 'sedentary bias' that is at the heart of reflexions and practices of development, which sees mobility as being symptomatic of dysfunction in origin society (Bakewell 2007; Pécoud 2014). Authors often assume that an equal society would lead to 'sedentariness' and that fostering development in southern countries would diminish the migratory pressure in northern states. This idea is generally agreed among liberal philosophers. Nonetheless, this assumption is wrong as it has been showed that development is a key driver of migrations at least until countries reach upper-middle income (Clemens 2014). This also seems to forget how migratory flows are multidirectional (Simon 2008) and that receiving and sending countries are anything but the same. Generally, these critics have fuelled in France the debate on methodological nationalism (Dumitru 2014) and enhance criticism towards migration management and the depoliticisation of migration policies (Pécoud 2009, 2017). According to Pécoud, the sedentary bias allows associating migrant vulnerability with their mobility and therefore easily promotes the solution that victims should go home to stay secure (Pécoud 2014).

Both migrants and researchers have denounced the injunction to productivity, participation in the development process and the apparent contradiction that is made between leaving one's country and feeling indebted to it (Auroi 2008; Wanner 2008). If remittances at a family scale are mainly for consumption, these expenses are 'consistent with their future' and constitute a social security the state is not able to provide (Auroi 2008). Moreover, it is now understood that economic transfers may generate or worsen social and economic inequalities and that productive investments do not necessarily generate employment (Baby-Collin et al. 2009). It is impossible to ensure that transfers are beneficial to the entire population; therefore, transfers should not be set up as a model of sustainable development for origin countries.

Migration and human development

A renewed interest in migrant's living conditions

Migration has always played an important role in sustaining families especially through savings and investments. In the 1990s, studies showed how family strategies played a great role in the production of migratory chains and transnational lives. In the case of Bolivia, for example, transnational livelihoods are well-known strategies to gain access to land and diversify household income in order to stay (Cortes 2001). Households are the main recipients of remittances, the money transfers aiming at financing education of the youngest, covering health care expenditure, financing housing renovation, and so on. Remittances also have consequences in family business systems and substantially increase their standard of living (Mercandalli 2013). But this optimism is not uncontested. In Nigeria, for example, international migration through remittances has been shown to exacerbate inequalities while internal migration has contributed to more effective income redistribution (De Haas 2010). This latter view has challenged the idea of distributive justice ordinarily granted to financial remittances in the case of international migration. Nevertheless, the international community has expressed great concern over this issue because remittances support millions of families throughout the developing world. This has explained why there is such a growing pressure on the private sector to lower transaction fees, not simply to make the transfer more affordable but also to encourage a shift away from more informal channels. In order to effect this change, the target is now set to a maximum cost of 3 per cent of the total amount of remittances transferred.

Shifts in development theory in the 1990s began to advocate for the greater empowerment of both migrant communities and migrants so that they can become more effective stakeholders in development. Yet, some authors argued that these policies hardly addressed the issue of discrimination and did not take into account the 'cost' of migration: the actual money migrants have to pay to leave their own country. Migrants need to have access to social capital (Arab 2009; Doraï 2005; Michalon 2003) and time for a long journey. There are also the actual costs of transport and other hidden costs, such as the de-skilling many migrants go through, once they arrive at their destinations and cannot validate their diplomas or find a job to match their skills (Caplan 2014; Raghuram 2009). Other studies show that the effectiveness of financial flows depends on skills and occupation position, culture, but also on gender (Ambrosetti 2008). These issues should urge states to be better informed of migrants' living conditions before involving diaspora in development policies.

Overcoming barriers: human mobility and development

The Human Development Report of 2009 *Overcoming barriers: human mobility and development* (PNUD 2009) is a major founding work for anyone interested in migration at the international level. In substance, the report argues that international migration can improve someone's health, increase household income, and open new perspectives for migrant's children. The report affirms that reducing barriers to mobility can generate huge benefits in human development. The cross-cutting nature of migration implies that it be considered through its interactions with the various traditional portfolios such as health, employment, economy, justice, and well-being. This cross-cutting nature is precisely what the Human Development Report revealed in 2009. This report was followed by the work of Roger Böhning who revealed that all forms of transfer are positively correlated with migrant's length of settlement and status (Böhning 2009). Hence policy recommendations of the Human Development Report were focused on security, rights, costs, and benefits of internal and international migration: liberalising and simplifying regular channels, ensuring basic rights for migrants, reducing transaction costs associated with movement, improving outcomes for migrants and destination communities, enabling benefits from internal mobility, making mobility an integral part of national development strategies.

The Human Development Report of UNDP in 2009 considered the impact of mobility on those who do not move. The findings are that:

> the greatest impacts are at the household level, for those who have family members who have moved, and these are largely positive for income, consumption, education and health. However, the poverty impacts are limited because those who move are mainly not the poorest. Broader community and national effects can also be observed, although these patterns are often complex, context-specific and subject to change over time.
>
> *(UNDP 2009, 92)*

The report also highlights the impact of migration on host communities and countries. In that sense the reports conclude that « *fears about migrants are generally exaggerated* » (UNDP 2009, 92).

The report also concentrates on the impact of mobility on those who move. Among other proposals, it suggests simplifying and expanding regular channels and improving outcomes for migrants and their communities in countries of destination. It suggests facilitating entry for unskilled people by expanding the number of visas; more flexibility, by preventing people from being tied to specific employers; promoting permanent residence; and facilitating circularity in order to ensure human development. This work done at the international level had a great impact on French literature, developing a specific human development approach.

The human development approach in French literature

As part of the post-2015 development agenda debate, the intergovernmental consultation on migration, asylum, and refugees recommended the making of migration policies keen to respect migrants' well-being and therefore ensure their freedom to circulate, work, and access education in worthy conditions. The consultation insisted on the freedom of individuals to move through the better management of departure, transit, and arrival, thus securing the migratory process, as well as the right to live, reside, and work in destinations. This approach was adopted to ensure the right of access to place, health services, and economy, therefore ensuring human development. The right to work and live in decent conditions and the right to healthcare are in fact key to human development which has been central at UNDP since 1990 and the first Human Development Report and its definition by Mahbub Ul-Haq. Health, education, and standard of living are the three dimensions of human development.

The failure of policies to restrict migratory flows is pushing host countries to review their policies and reconsider the whole issue of the migration–development nexus. Catherine Withol de Wenden explained this shift as a result of changes in migration path from immigration to circulation, transforming the migratory phenomenon into a mobility phenomenon. Recognising this shift should allow the elaboration of a right to migrate which is fundamental in a human development approach (Wihtol De Wenden 2017). The French literature insists on the relationship between human development and the right to migrate. Indeed, human development is in contradiction to the making of illegality (Caplan and Dumitru 2017; Dumitru and Atak 2015; McDonald 2009) as it deprives migrants of access to fundamental rights such as health or work. Defining migration as a right and not as a need, even if this need exists, is also to focus on the migratory flow, on a more just regulation of flows, on a democratisation of borders as Balibar has argued (Balibar 2002); it is to value mobility, as a source of development, democratisation, and exchange.

Yet, despite difficult access to international migration for developing country nationals, migrants contribute by their mobility to mitigate human development inequalities. A recent study led by Speranta Dumitru focused on irregular migrants in France and their role for human development (see Caplan and Dumitru 2017). The advantage of this approach is that it de-compartmentalises development dimensions usually considered separately between individuals, families, and states. In this study, development is considered in the three dimensions defined by Ul-Haq (health, education, living conditions) rather than at the different scales at which development has been traditionally considered when it comes to the migration and development nexus (host and home states and families).

Migrants already contribute to human development in their origin countries through the transfer of 466 billions of dollars in 2017 surpassing development aid since 1997. However, the production of irregularity and the casualisation of regularity deprive migrants of access to fundamental rights in their destination countries. This interest in the French literature comes from the fact that France creates 81,000 irregular migrants every year through orders to leave the country 'Obligation de Quitter le Territoire Français' (on which approximately 10 per cent leave the country see Dumitru 2018). Her work focuses more specifically on human security and shows the majority of irregular migrants feel insecure, which goes against human development (Dumitru 2018, 38).

A renewed approach to border studies

The interest in human development in migration studies has had a great impact on the study of borders in French literature. In fact, the human development approach made it clear that the status of the migrants had a great impact on remittances and therefore in home-country development. This shed light on the criminalisation of international migration and of places of confinement near airports, transit areas but also on the 'mobile border' (Amilhat-Szary 2015).

The Westphalian model of the border, which was previously dominant at the international level, has become obsolete. By becoming more complex under the effect of border externalisation policies, the border is no longer a continuous line that delimits two distinct political entities but a diffuse, pixelated space (Amilhat Szary 2015; Bigo and Guild 2005). In this context, whatever the administrative situation abroad, its mobility remains conditioned and limited by the potential threat it poses to the sovereignty of the state. Paradoxically, vulnerable migrants show a high degree of mobility within the states, in particular forced or constrained mobility. The insecurity of migratory routes must not simply be understood as the maritimisation of migration and its 'accounting' human consequences. On the contrary, it must be interpreted as a daily insecurity of the foreigner. In that sense border studies are more than ever influenced and influencing migration and development studies.

Conclusion

The French literature on migration and development has moved from its early focus on 'co-development' to its current adoption of the human development approach. It gives priority to the development of the people as a condition towards the development at the national level. This shift has introduced a renewed interest in borders and more specifically towards the border as mobile and dislocated. Indeed, migrants are playing the biggest role in terms of development contribution since they send more money than aid to developing countries. But migrants' status is key when it comes to the contribution they make to the development of their home countries and more specifically in terms of human development. Research in France has therefore advanced on these themes, exploring the different nature of borders, the making of irregularity, and how migrants play a key role in development. In this chapter, we were looking for how the migration and development nexus is considered in French literature. As we've seen, development is more and more considered at a human scale and focuses more on security, fundamental rights, and on migrants' irregularisation paths.

Note

1 Caroline Caplan is a certified Professor of History and Geography, Secondary degree, Lycée Augustin Fresnel.

References:

Agunias D. (2009) *Guiding the Invisible Hand: Making Migration Intermediaries Work for Development*, Human Development Research Paper, 2009/22.

Ambrosetti E. (2008) "Femmes, rapports de genre et dynamiques migratoires", *Population*, INED, 63(4), 767–793.

Amilhat Szary A.-L. (2015) *Qu'est-ce qu'une frontière aujourd'hui*, Presses Universitaires de France, France.

Arab C. (2009) *Les Aït Ayad. La circulation migratoire des Marocains en France, Espagne et Italie*, Presses Universitaires de Rennes, Rennes.

Auroi C. (2008) "La contribution des migrants au développement local en Amérique latine", *Annuaire Suisse de politique de développement*, 27(2), 133–153.

Baby-Collin V., Cortes G. and Faret L. (2009) *Migrants des Suds*, IRD Editions, Marseille.

Bakewell O. (2007) *Keeping Them in Their Place: The Ambivalent Relationship between Development and Migration in Africa*, IMI working papers.

Balibar E. (2002) "Démocratisation des frontières", 2002/3, Rue descartes, n°37.

Barré R., Hernandez V., Meyer J.-B. and Vinck D. (2003) *Diasporas scientifiques: Comment les pays en développement peuvent-ils tirer parti de leurs chercheurs et de leurs ingénieurs expatriés?*, IRD Editions, Marseille.

Berchet C. and Justo F. (2012) "Etat de santé et recours aux soins des immigrés: une synthèse des travaux français", *Questions d'économie de la santé*, 172, 1–8.

Bigo D. and Guild E. (2005) *Controlling Frontiers: Free Movement into and within Europe*, Ashgate, London.

Böhning R. (2009) "Getting a Handle on the Migration Rights and Development Nexus", *International Migration Review*, 43(3), 652–670.

Bordes-Benayoun C. and Schnapper D. (2006) *Diasporas et Nations*, Odile Jacob, Paris.

Caplan C. (2014) "Les réseaux transnationaux et diasporiques de la migration andine en Europe". Géographie d'un partage, Unpublished PhD Thesis, Montpellier III University.

Caplan C. and Dumitru S. (2017) "Politiques d'irrégularisation par le travail: le cas de la France", in Neuwahl N. and Barrère S. (eds), *Cohérence et incohérence de la gestion des migrations et de l'intégration*, Editions Thémis, 265–289.

Cediey E. and Foroni F. (2006) *Les discriminations à raison de l'origine dans les embauches en France. Une enquête nationale par test de discrimination selon la méthode du BIT*, BIT, Genève.

Charef M. (1999) *La circulation migratoire marocaine. Un pont entre deux rives*, Editions Sud Contact, Rabat.

Clemens M. (2014) *Does Development Reduce Migration?* IZA Discussion Paper, n°8592.

Cognet M. (2002) "La santé des immigrés à l'aune des modèles politiques d'intégration des étrangers", *Bastidiana*, 39–40, 97–130.

Condon S. and Hamel C. (2007) "Contrôle social et violences subies parmi les descendantes d'immigrés maghrébins", in Jaspard M. and Chetcuti N (eds), *Violences envers les femmes. Trois pas en avant, trois pas en arrière*, L'Harmattan, Paris, 201–222.

Cortes G. (2001) *Partir pour rester: survie et mutations de sociétés paysannes andines, Bolivie*, IRD Editions, Marseille.

Crush J. and Williams V. (2005) *International migration and development: dynamics and challenges in south and southern Africa*, Un Population division.

Datta K., Mcilwaine C., Wills J., Evans Y., Herbert J. and May J. (2007) "The New Development Finance or Exploiting Migrant Labour?" *International Development Planning Review*, 29(1), 43–68.

Daum C. (1994) "Ici et là-bas, immigration et développement", *Migrations Société*, 32, 99–110.

Daum C. (1995) *Les migrants, partenaires de la coopération inter- nationale: le cas des Maliens de France*, document de travail 107, Centre de Développement de l'OCDE.

Daum C. (1998) *Les associations maliennes en France, Migration, Développement et Citoyenneté*, Karthala, Paris.

Daum C., Diarra H., Gonin P., Philippe C., Quiminal C. and Sylla S. (1988) *La fonction émigrée dans les stratégies de développement*, Fontenay-aux-Roses-Paris, E.N.S. Fontenay-Saint-Cloud, Centre de Géographie Rurale-CNRS-ATP.

De Haas H. (2010) "Migration and Development: A Theoretical Perspective", *International Migration Review*, 44(1), 1–38.

Docquier F. and Lodigiani E. (2010) "Skilled Migration and Business Networks", *Open Economies Review*, 21(4), 565–588.

Doraï M.K. (2005) "Du Liban vers l'Europe. Réseaux migratoires et pratiques transnationales des réfugiés palestiniens", in Jaber H. and Métral F. (eds), *Mondes en mouvements, Migrants et migrations au Moyen-Orient au tournant du XXIe siècle*, Institut français du Proche Orient, Beyrouth, 95–111.

Dumitru S. (2013) "Des visas pas de l'aide! De la migration comme substitut à l'aide au développement", *Ethique Publique*, 15(2), 77–98.

Dumitru S. (2014) "Qu'est-ce que le nationalisme méthodologique? Essai de typologie", *Raisons politiques*, 54(2), 9-22.

Dumitru S. (2018) "La production de l'immigration irrégulière en France: une question d'insécurité humaine", *Migrations Société*, 1(171), 35–48.

Dumitru S. and Atak I. (2015) "Pourquoi penser l'ouverture des frontières", *Ethique publique*, 17(1), 3–6.

Efionayi-Mäder Perroulaz and Younossian Schümperli (2008) "Migration et développement: les enjeux d'une relation controversée", *Annuaire Suisse de politique de développement*, 27(12), 11–20.

Faist T. (2013) "The mobility turn: a new paradigm for the social sciences?" *Journal of Ethnic and Racial Studies*, 36(11), 1637–1646.

Faret L. (2003) *Les territoires de la mobilité. Migrations et communautés transnationales entre le Mexique et les Etats-Unis*, CNRS Editions, Paris.

Faret L.and and Cortes G. (2009) *Les circulations transnationales, Lire les turbulences migratoires contemporaines*, Armand Colin, Malakoff.

Freitas A., Levatino A. and Pécoud A. (2012) "Introduction: New perspectives on Skilled Migration", *Diversities*, 14(1), UNESCO, 1–7.

Gaillard A.-M. and Gaillard J. (1999) *Les enjeux des migrations scientifiques internationales. De la quête du savoir à la circulation des compétences*, Questions contemporaines, L'Harmattan, Paris.

Guilmoto C. and Sandron F. (2003) *Migration et développement*, Les Etudes de la documentation française, Paris.

Iskander N. (2005) *Innovating State Practices: Migration, Development, and State Learning in the Moroccan Souss*, MIT-IPC working paper series.

Kapur D. and McHale J. (2005) *Give us your best and brightest: the global hunt for talent and its impact on the developing world*, Centre for Global Development, Cambridge.

Lanly G. (2002) "Les associations de migrants internationaux dans trois communautés rurales mexicaines", *Autrepart*, 22, 109–128.

Lanly G. and Valenzuela V. (2004) *Clubes de migrantes oriundos mexicanos en los Estados Unidos. La politica transnacional de la nueva sociedad civil migrante*, Guadalajara University, Guadalajara.

Laurens S. (2008) "1974 et la fermeture des frontières, analyse critique d'une décision érigée en turning-point", *Politix*, De Boeck Supérieur, (82), 69–94.

Lowell L. and De La Garza R. (2002) *Sending money home: Hispanic Remittances and Community Development*, Rowman & Littlefield, Lanham.

Lucas V. (2014) *Les activités de l'Agence Française de Développement en matière de soutien à l'investissement productif des diasporas*, Revue Techniques financières et développement, n 114, Paris.

MacRae M. and Wight M. (2006) "A Model Diaspora Network: The Origin and Evolution of Globalscot", in Kuznetsov Y. (ed), *Diaspora Networks and the International Migration of Skills, How countries can draw on their talent abroad*, The World Bank, Washington DC.

Martin P.L. (2006) "The Trade, Migration, and Development Nexus", in Hollifield F., Orrenius M.P. and Osang T. *Migration, Trade and Development*, Texas, 11–34.

McDonald J. and Illegality M. (2009). "Nation-Building and the Politics of Regularization in Canada", *Refuge*, 26(2), 66–77.

Melonio T. (2008) *Balances migratoires. Concept, hypothèses et discussions*, AFD document de travail n°74, 45 pages.

Mercandalli S. (2013) Le rôle complexe des migrations dans les reconfigurations des systèmes d'activités des familles rurales: la circulation comme ressource? Localité de Leonzoane, Mozambique 1900-2010, Unpublished PhD thesis, Montpellier III University.

Meyer J.-B. (2015) *Diaspora, towards the new frontier*, Institut de recherche pour le développement, Online, Marseille.

Meyer J.-B. and Wattiaux J.-P. (2006) "Diaspora Knowledge Networks: Vanishing Doubts and Increasing Evidence", *International Journal on Multicultural Societies*, 8(1), 4–24.

Michalon B. (2003) "Migrations des Saxons de Transylvanie vers l'Allemagne. De l'émigration ethnique à la circulation migratoire", *Balkanologie*, VII(1), 19–42.

Naïr S. (1997) *Rapport de bilan et d'orientation sur la politique de codéveloppement liée aux flux migratoires*, Documentation Française, Paris.

Ndofor-Tah C. (2000) *Diaspora and Development: Contributions by African Organisations in the UK to Africa's Development*. www.afford-uk.org/resources/download/

Papail J. (2002) "Migrations internationales, transferts monétaires et investissements dans les milieux urbains du Centre-Ouest mexicain", *Autrepart*, 123, 89–105.

Pécoud A. (2009) "La crédibilité des politiques migratoires à l'épreuve des sans-papiers", *Migrations Sociétés*, 126, 9–18.

Pécoud A. (2014) "Etats-nations, mobilité et citoyenneté dans le discours international sur les migrations", *Raisons politiques*, 54, 67–85.

Pécoud A. (2017) "De la gestion au contrôle des migrations? Discours et pratiques de l'Organisation Internationale des Migrations", *Critiques Internationales*, 76, 81–99.

PNUD. (2009) *Overcoming Barriers: Human Mobility and Development*, PNUD, NYC, 229p.

Quiminal C. (1991) *Gens d'ici et d'ailleurs, Migrations soninké et transformations villageoises*, Christian Bourgeois, Paris.

Raghuram P. (2009) "Which Migration, What Development? Unsettling the Edifice of Migration and Development", *Population, Space and Place*, 15(2), 103–117.

Simon G. (2008) *La planète migratoire dans la mondialisation*, Armand Colin, Malakoff.

Urry J. (2000) *Sociologie des mobilités, Une nouvelle frontière pour la sociologie?* Armand Colin, Paris.

Wanner P. (2008) "L'apport des migrants au développement: une perspective économique", *Annuaire suisse de politique de développement*, 27(2), 121–131.

Wihtol De Wenden C. (2017) *Faut-il ouvrir les frontières? Nouveaux Débats*, 3d edition. Presses de Sciences Po, Paris.

50

MIGRATION, DEVELOPMENT, AND BORDER CONTROL

A review of the German literature

Heike Drotbohm and Franziska Reiffen

Introduction

By the end of the 1990s, the enthusiasm that had surrounded the migration and development nexus was criticised among German-speaking scholars from different disciplinary backgrounds. We will use the following overview to explore the positions of key authors in this debate, including mainly scholars but also some practitioners.

Many publications in the German language refer to examples from Germany, but also to examples from other German-speaking countries, such as Austria and Switzerland. Furthermore, a large part of literature summarised here points to specificities of how '*Migration und Entwicklung*' ('migration and development') is interpreted in Germany. While '*co-développement*' or 'co-development' have been discussed as political strategies in France and Great Britain, respectively, since the 1990s, the debate in Germany started later (Hilber and Baraulina 2012; Schwertl 2015a, 114). However, in 2007, migration was one of four thematic areas discussed during the Bonn conference for development policy (Nieswand 2011, 402). At that time, Germany had definitely entered the European debate on migration and development.

In the following, we will first summarise authors who trace the encounter between migration and development, especially in non-academic publications. Next, we will clarify several specificities of the German context, before examining how migrants are seen as new actors of development by different types of agencies and organisations. We will end our overview with the competing policy agendas in the context of migration management, which often result in a tightening of border control and in a securitisation of migration. By focusing on the literature in the German language, we do not intend to assign authors to nations, language groups, or territories. Rather, we follow a pragmatic selection of books and articles, most of which were published in the German language without being translated into other languages. The authors selected evidently also publish in English, French, Spanish, and several other languages. Nevertheless, we identified key authors whose positions will certainly add to the debates presented in this Handbook.

Shifting notions of development and the migration–development nexus

The meaning and implications of 'development' have changed over time, and with it the ways in which the link between migration and development was established and interpreted. Sociologist Thomas Faist and his colleagues, who were the first to combine development studies with a perspective on migration, urged migration scholars to integrate critical understandings of development into their research (Faist 2006, 2008; Faist and Fauser 2011). They discerned three phases in which development took different meanings in relation to migration. The first phase, the years of the 1950s and 1960s, corresponded to economic modernisation theory when migrants' remittances, return and the transfer of human capital were assumed to contribute positively to the development in their countries of origin. During the second phase, in the 1970s and 1980s, the term was used more critically, as it stood for a structural condition of dependency in which 'underdevelopment' in poor countries would lead to migration and, hence, the loss of skilled populations (brain drain). This would generate more emigration and underdevelopment in the so-called Global South.

Migration and development were then propagated again after the 1990s under the label of 'co-development', renewing the emphasis on remittances, by including 'social remittances', that is flows of knowledge, ideas and values, and by understanding migrants as the key actors of development. Migrants would establish social spaces through temporary and circular migration characterised by continuous economic, political, and social transactions across borders (Faist 2008, 25–6). Faist also demonstrated how interpretations and evaluations of migration's impact on development, whether it was seen as 'brain gain' or 'brain drain', shifted in accordance with the economic situation in the so-called Global North. A brain gain perspective was much favoured in the 1960s when migrants represented a greatly needed labour force. In turn, the brain drain perspective gained popularity during the economic crisis and structural changes of the 1970s and 1980s when most European countries stopped labour recruitment (Faist 2010, 68–9).

While the discursive connection of migration and development has changed, many authors agree on the unprecedented intensity and the 'new enthusiasm' (Faist 2010, 64) with which it has been discussed in the past 15 years (Faist 2010; Kraler and Noack 2014; Schwertl 2015a). Cornerstones of this latest phase include the UN Conference on Population and Development (1994), the 'discovery' of remittances by the World Bank through its report on migrant worker's remittances (2003) and the foundation of the Global Forum on Migration and Development (2007) (Kraler and Noack 2014, 37; Schwertl 2015a, 18–21; see also Chapter 26 in this Handbook). The German development agency GIZ (Deutsche Gesellschaft für Internationale Zusammenarbeit), for example, has produced more than 30 publications on migration and development since 2003, translated into several languages, including studies on different diasporas in Germany, remittances and manuals for organisational work (GIZ 2017; Schwertl 2015a, 20).

Against this background, anthropologist Maria Schwertl saw the 'excessive attention and productivity' (Schwertl 2015a, 18) around the migration–development nexus as a 'hype'. By calling the phenomenon a 'hype', Schwertl distances herself from other suggested formulations such as 'mantra' (Faist 2010, 65) or 'trend' (Kunz 2011). According to her, 'mantra' only refers to the level of discourse, and she perceives 'trend' as too lineal and teleological (Schwertl 2015a, 14). This 'hype', she states, has been produced by academic as well as non-academic statements, publications, and diagnoses regarding the link between migration and development. It is also marked by a certain *Entdeckermentalität* ('mentality of discovery'; Schwertl 2015a, 14) that accompanies the evaluation of migrants and their remittances for development purposes by banks, organisations, and development agencies. The 'hype' does not remain merely discursive, but produces and results in programmes, projects, and funding initiatives (Schwertl 2015a, 14, 2016), 'with concrete implications that stretch from the international realm to individual subjects' (Kunz 2011, 4).

Several scholars, in addition to delivering diachronic analyses of the developments mentioned above, have empirically explored how different types of actors, such as governments, international institutions, migrant organisations, individual migrants, or non-migrants, negotiate different, sometimes conflicting ideas and ideals of 'development', relating to migration in specific contexts or moments in time.

While 'development' remains both a synonym for progress and a goal set by many national and international institutions and organisations (Bierschenk 2014), it also serves as a term employed both by migrants and non-migrants. In all these cases, the term's interpretations differ (Lachenmann 2009, 90–1; Sieveking 2011, 378–9). Interestingly, Schwertl reveals that the notion of development often remains a 'blank' ('*Leerstelle*'), especially in non-academic publications on the migration–development nexus (Schwertl 2015a, 2015b). Both institutions and organisations that promote the connection between migration and development often concentrate on defining migrants, migration, and diaspora, while leaving the notion of development undefined.

These methodological reflections resonate with questions that have also been addressed by sociologist Gudrun Lachenmann. From the perspective of empirical research on globalisation, Lachenmann suggested working with a translocal, comparative perspective 'from below', which prioritises migrants as actors of globalisation (Lachenmann 2008, 2009), a perspective that considers the multiple and often contradictory notions on development and society that might meet and clash in specific local contexts (Lachenmann 2009, 98). Albert Kraler and colleagues suggest treating development as a discursively created social concept which acknowledges the transformative powers of modernisation promises (Kraler et al. 2014, 15). Until today, Faist's statement from 2008 that the term development has carried, since the 1940s, a 'vague hope of progression and betterment for those parts of the world deemed "underdeveloped"' (Faist 2008, 27), still holds true.

'Migration und Entwicklung' – a contested field in German politics

As mentioned in the introduction, the formation and timing of the debate in Germany has its specificities for historical and structural reasons. In Germany, the official self-description as an immigrant country only dates back to the beginning of the millennium. In 2000, Gerhard Schröder's government revised the citizenship and immigration law and implemented a restricted birthright citizenship law (*ius soli*). Until then, the law had exclusively followed a principle of descent (*ius sanguinis*), meaning that children born in Germany did not automatically obtain German citizenship if their parents were of another nationality. From 2000 onwards, children born in Germany obtained German citizenship at least until their legal adulthood. In 2005, the first German immigration act (*Zuwanderungsgesetz*) became effective (Hilber and Baraulina 2012, 91–2; Mannitz and Schneider 2014, 72–3).

In terms of development policies, the situation in Germany is also particular in several respects. In France, the Foreign Ministry is responsible for development policies. Hence, development policies count as an important foreign policy strategy. In Germany, a distinct ministry is responsible, the Federal Ministry for Economic Cooperation and Development (BMZ). According to Andrea Riester, the BMZ has a weak position in relation to other ministries, not least because it hardly appears in or can have any impact on domestic policy debates (Riester 2014, 209). In this respect, the situation in Germany can be compared to the one in Great Britain, where a relatively 'weak' ministry, the Department for International Development (DfID), is also responsible for migration at the multilateral level. Before the establishment of the DfID in 1997, however, its responsibility has been moved back and forth between being founded as an independent ministry and being assigned to the Foreign and Commonwealth Office (FCO). Since its establishment and until recently, DfID has faced discussions about its takeover by the FCO or its replacement by a different institution, discussions that are often linked to budgetary questions (Elgot and McVeigh 2017; Mendick et al. 2013). In Germany, despite the failed attempts of former Development Minister Dirk Niebel (2009–13) to integrate the BMZ into the Federal Foreign Office international development since 1961 has remained the responsibility of the same independent ministry. Meanwhile, the implementation of BMZ policies is handled by executing agencies separated from the ministry, namely the GIZ, which is in charge of technical cooperation, and the financial institution KfW (Kreditanstalt für Wiederaufbau) (Rauch 2015).

German development actors initially included perspectives on migration because development was increasingly linked to migration-related security debates that were considered an issue for domestic policy actors (Riester 2014, 213). According to Riester, the European Union increased the pressure to exploit the payment of official development aid (ODA) for domestic aims after the turn of the millennium. In 2002, for instance, the European Council suggested tying ODA payments to re-admission agreements (European Council 2002, para 33). Development actors rejected the Council's proposition, speaking against this intervention of domestic policy actors in matters of development policies. In Germany, especially, the BMZ would have risked losing its political significance if domestic policy actors had successfully instrumentalised development aid for their own purposes (Riester 2014, 212–13).

Migration and development remains a highly fragmented field of political action in the German context, where ministries, other state actors, and NGOs compete with each other on a federal, regional, and local level. Doris Hilber and Tatjana Baraulina (2012, 97, 108–9) underline that no central German 'agenda' for dealing with migration and development really exists. Instead, responsibilities and competences remain unclear. Such confusion might be partly explained by the focus on 'integration' that runs through the debate (Baraulina et al. 2012, 12), which brings not only actors such as the BMZ, but also, again, domestic policy actors such as the Federal Ministry of the Interior (BMI) and especially its Federal Office for Migration and Refugees (BAMF), into play.

On a federal level, the BMZ, the German development agency GIZ, the BMI, the BAMF, and the Foreign Ministry all claim to have their say in policy formulation that concerns migration and development. On a regional and municipal level, departments for migration and integration issues, so-called 'integration-commissioners' ('*Integrationsbeauftragte*'), and departments responsible for international cooperation, also share certain competences (Hilber and Baraulina 2012, 96–7). However, the migration–development nexus is not at the top of the agenda at either the regional or the municipal level (Hilber and Baraulina 2012, 101, 104).

Doris Hilber, Tatjana Baraulina, and colleagues tend to seek the 'best' way for implementing a coherent German migration and development policy strategy in their policy-oriented analyses. While this should not be understood as a key question for most of the publications summarised here, the specificities of the German context mentioned above resonate with many less policy-oriented works. Schwertl (2015a), for instance, describes the establishment of a department for international affairs in the city of Munich, where she conducted parts of her fieldwork, as an unintended effect of the 'hype' described previously.

Inspired by migration- and development-related projects and in a moment of competing responsibilities between federal and municipal level, the city created a new department for launching development-related projects and, simultaneously, polishing the city's image as 'transnational' and 'global' (Schwertl 2015a, 231–42). Finally, the responsibilities of the new department ended up competing, once again, with already established institutions and ineffectively tried to combine development with integration policies (Schwertl 2015a, 240–1).

This combination of discourses on migration and development, on the one hand, and 'integration' policies, on the other hand, can be found in several empirical studies. Migrant organisations have been addressed as actors of development (Schwertl 2015a, 2015b, 2016; Sieveking 2011). The GIZ and other institutions have launched conferences and workshops with development-related topics, mostly on a municipal level. These initiatives often addressed migrant organisations that were active in the field of cultural and social activities in Germany. According to Sieveking, 'integration' into German society seemed to be considered a prerequisite for migrants to be seen as potential development actors. According to her, both workshop organisers and migrants themselves sometimes explicitly expressed this attitude (Sieveking 2011, 391). At the same time, Schwertl (2015a, 2016) describes how workshops and conferences sometimes targeted (inter)cultural organisations that considered themselves 'neither developmental nor migrant-oriented, but rather as a hybrid set of people from different countries' (Schwertl 2016, 248). These organisations often refused to take part in or rapidly dropped out of the activities mentioned above. How individuals and collectivities have been addressed by the migration and development discourse and in which way this impacts on the subjectivities of actors involved will be discussed in the following section.

Migrants as 'new actors of development' – the discourse and its internalisation

Since Thomas Faist's re-orientation around the 'migration–development nexus' (Faist 2008), when he highlighted the significance of durable social, economic, and political connections across national borders, migrants and their diasporic settings are perceived as 'new actors' of development, who need to be courted, activated, or convinced for figuring out which types of activities would receive a higher level of acceptance in the migrants' countries of origin. Migrant institutions, such as their families and ethnic organisations, business networks, hometown organisations (HTOs), scientists and experts, cross-border religious congregations, or schools, are understood as alternatives to activities organised by governments and their development partners (such as international organisations) (Aikins 2016; Faist 2008).

In 2009, Gudrun Lachenmann considered two possible effects of the migration and development debate. On the one hand, she warned against a possible instrumentalisation of migrants. On the other hand, she believed that the debate might also lead to a true change in perspective (Lachenmann 2009, 93). Most other scholars have avoided the rhetoric of an 'either instrumentalisation or change' perspective. They rather describe the consequences of the discourse in terms of its formative effects by showing how the discourse contributes to the creation of new subjectivities and by tracing how this materialises in policy decisions.

Rahel Kunz, a political scientist at the University of Lausanne, has criticised what she calls the 'migrant bias' of this discourse. According to her, it clearly prioritises 'the voice of migrants over that of non-migrants' (Kunz 2011, 58). The expertise of other actors who also belong to these transnational networks, including those who organise migration while remaining behind or other non-migrants, is less valued or simply remains invisible in these debates (Kunz 2011, 58; Schwertl 2015a, 156–7). Certain organisations are eventually excluded from funds related to migration and development policies, because they are not sufficiently migration-related, that is, 'in deficit of migration' (Schwertl 2016, 254). Migration becomes a contested resource in the 'hype' around migration and development.

Surprisingly, the debate on migration and development produces both collectivising and individualising effects (Schwertl 2015a, 152–5). As Faist (2008) and Lachenmann (2008) noticed, actors addressed through the migration and development discourse often belong to different social strata. Against this background, the term 'diaspora' became particularly prominent both in the political realm and in academia. Boris Nieswand (2011, 404) reminds us that any reference to migrants as 'diasporas' is based on their assumed emotional connection to and identification with their country of origin. With his empirical research on Ghanaian migrants in Germany, Nieswand shows how a discourse that positively evaluates the diaspora's impact on the development of a given country of origin can contribute to the formation of a diaspora. In this manner, the discourse produces the emotional ties and identifications on which it claims to be based (Nieswand 2008, 2011). Additionally, instead of promoting individual 'human capabilities' through development, the above-mentioned individualising plus collectivising effects of the discourse demonstrate more of a bio-political understanding of human capital as national capital: The migrant body, the migrant's engagement and his/her affects are tied to his/her 'nation' (Schwertl 2015a, 155, 2015b, 8).

At the same time, Schwertl (2015a, 2015b) highlights another dominant discursive figure: The migrant-as-manager, i.e. migrants who act, or rather are expected to act, as managers or entrepreneurs in the context of development (Schwertl 2015a, 153). According to Schwertl, development agencies, like the German GIZ, consider migrants as actors with intercultural competences, which are positively valued, albeit still being in deficit. Migrants are expected to professionalise their activities in order to be eligible for funding, particularly in the realm of project management (Schwertl 2016). Therefore, the author identifies the most striking consequence of the 'hype' in its profound impact on voluntary work. She shows that the expected professionalisation of migrants' engagement towards development results in increasingly precarious working conditions. Hence, the migrant-as-manager's success or failure depends on the question of whether his or her project corresponds with the expectations of national and international organisations and institutions (Schwertl 2015a, 244–6, 2016). Consequently, migrant engagement in this exclusively economic interpretation tends to be depoliticised, an effect that is also deeply related to prominent migration management strategies, as discussed below.

Regarding female migrants, several authors have problematised their special 'discovery', first as migrants and then as potential development agents, and the ways in which the remaining gender-bias of the migration and development debate materialises in concrete policy decisions. Exploring the example of Ghanaian migrant networks in Germany, Nadine Sieveking (2011) points out how regional and communal institutions emphasise the promotion of projects that are appealing to 'strengthening the women's role'. While projects addressing women as vulnerable victims are preferred, other women's activities, such as rotating credit associations, are not considered to be development-oriented. At least in Germany, public debates on migration and development often focus on a macro-economic level, instead of considering actor-centred approaches (Sieveking 2011, 389) that would acknowledge a gender-specific embeddedness of economic activities (Lachenmann and Danneker 2001). Drawing from the examples of international documents, Rahel Kunz and Helen Schwenken (2014b) show that women are currently imagined as representing a diasporic position by means of contributing both to the improvement of living conditions in the country of origin and to processes of integration and identity building in the country of destination.

Parallel to these figures, women are also imagined as vulnerable subjects 'left behind', who must cope with their partners' absences. By examining the changing positions published in these documents over time, Kunz and Schwenken (2014a) show that women's positions are mainly framed through their assumed belonging to 'family' and much less through the gender label. According to the authors, this framing serves as a justification for implementing policy projects that aim at promoting women's engagement in 'productive' work. Kunz argues that these projects suggest implicitly that women's activities usually remain part of the 'reproductive' sphere (Kunz 2011, 112–3), which needs correction. At the same time, other 'illegitimate' subject positions, such as the one of the migrant sex worker, remain marginalised and stigmatised, even if they manage to generate a similar level of income or remittances (Kunz and Schwenken 2014b, 97).

Migration management: a new field of competing policy agendas

While the positive or even euphoric promotion of the migration–development nexus is a relatively new phenomenon, the geographers Martin Geiger and Malte Steinbrink (2012) make clear that it is based on well-known political aims. According to them, migrant-receiving states mainly aim to tackle what organisations such as the IOM call the 'root causes of migration' (IOM 2017). Migrants' contribution to development, thus, becomes an 'instrument for preventing migration' (*Instrument zur Migrationsvermeidung*, Geiger and Steinbrink 2012, 12). This apparent paradox is in line with increasingly restrictive immigration policies and the popularity of migration management approaches, both among governments and intergovernmental organisations such as the IOM (Geiger and Steinbrink 2012, 13). Migration management also characterises the EU Global Approach on Migration and Mobility (GAMM, Riester 2014, 212), which the EU itself defines as an 'overarching framework of the EU external migration and asylum policy' (European Commission 2017). The GAMM's objectives are to regulate legal and to prevent illegal migration, to foster migration and development, and to enhance refugee protection.

Several authors are inspired by new practices of 'migration management', i.e. a set of practices and discourses largely carried out and mobilised by non-state actors (Geiger and Pécoud 2010, 1–2). The anthropologist Sabine Hess (2008, 2010) conducted field research in the Vienna-based International Centre for Migration Policy Development (ICMPD), an organisation that provides consultancy in the field of migration policy and that Hess has called 'an inter-state service agency for migration management' (Hess 2008, 1). In addition to illustrating the ICMPD's leading role in the Europeanisation of migration politics (Hess 2010), Hess also describes the policy field of migration and development as serving as an instrument for expanding migration management beyond the common EU borders (Hess 2008). However, the author maintains that the same policy field could also count as 'a partial victory of the countries of the Global South inscribing some of their own interests in the European Union migration management agenda' (Hess 2008, 5).

Stefanie Kron (2014) in her analysis of the Regional Conference on Migration (RCM) meetings, traces the debate between North and Central American states in which a country's alleged degree of development depends on its capacities to manage migration. Migration management is predominantly discussed in terms of anti-trafficking initiatives in RCM meetings. When migration management is addressed in terms of trafficking, smuggling, and drug dealing, it results in policies of securitisation (Kron 2014, 61). Janicki and Böwing argue in a similar direction. Based on their fieldwork at the *Centre d'Information et de Gestion des Migrations* in Bamako, Mali, they show how projects designed for 'development' *de facto* go along both with a preventive and repressive politics of population control and a securitisation of migration. According to this interpretation, the combination of migration and development appears a 'soft' form of postcolonial population control (Janicki and Böwing 2010, 132). A comparable perspective was developed for other transit countries, such as Ukraine (Speer 2010) or Morocco (Heck 2010).

According to Stephan Dünnwald, migration management makes the 'hype' on migration and development double-edged (Dünnwald 2014, 174): The positive evaluation of migration as enhancing development is only one side of the coin. The other side displays migration as a security issue. Both interpretations remain closely connected, are promoted by the same actors, such as the IOM, and show up in the same discourses, policy initiatives, and strategies that aim at 'optimizing, directing, and combating' certain types of migration (Kron 2014, 50, original version: '*optimieren, steuern und bekämpfen*'). Especially with regard to the increasing number of asylum applications, the debate about controlled repatriation and deportation has lately increased (Rosenberger et al. 2017; Rosenberger and Trauner 2014; Scherr 2015; Steinhilper 2014).

As Schwertl puts it (2015b, 4), combining a development logic with migration policies does not result in more rights for migrants or in lower hierarchies between the Global North and Global South. Instead, it re-territorialises the 'rich' and the 'poor' through migration control (Dünnwald 2014, 175). Migration management, as it appears in the 'hype', stands for what Bernd Kasparek and Sabine Hess have called the 'neo- or rather post-liberal turn of migration policies' (Kasparek and Hess 2010, 18, original version: '*neo- bzw. postliberale Wende der Migrationspolitik*'), that is migration policies make the most profitable use of the labour force and labour-related mobility. At best, the 'hype' creates new economic possibilities for migrants (Schwertl 2015b, 4).

Concluding thoughts

Today, imaginations and ideologies of 'development' in the context of migration are negotiated among multiple actors, such as governments, international organisations, NGOs, private enterprises, migrant organisations, and other transnational actors. Our overview traces how the perception of migration in the context of the development agenda has shifted from a derogatory to a valorising one, which praised migration as improving the living conditions in the Global South. In the end, we pointed out that this euphoric attitude has been substituted again by a sceptical or even negative stance, which emerged along with new discourses on border control, migration management, and securitisation. According to our understanding, recent trends to woo certain migrants, whose subject positions make them 'ideal' entrepreneurial partners, will contribute to a new, internalised border regime which distinguishes between good, productive migrants or returnees, and those migrants claiming asylum or social assistance.

Since the so-called 'long summer of migration' (Hess et al. 2017) of 2015, migration and development have been less present in German political and academic debates than questions of displacement, asylum, and the externalisation of European borders. The short phase of open borders has deeply transformed German society and influenced policymakers. Today, social practices of receiving and supporting newcomers coexist in parallel to an often-empty discourse of '*Willkommenskultur*' ('welcome culture'), increasingly restrictive asylum policies and an upheaval of right-wing and nationalist political movements. Somehow in contradiction to the depoliticising tendencies of migration and development policies, the 'long summer of migration' highlighted the autonomy of migration as a power that has contested the European border regime (Hess and Kara-kayali 2017; Hess et al. 2017, 18). It remains to be seen in which way these recent developments will have an impact on the German and European discussion on migration and development inside and outside academia.

References

Aikins J. K. (2016) "Fallstudie: Diasporas als Akteure der Entwicklungspolitik", in Fischer K., Hauck G. and Boatcă M. eds., *Handbuch Entwicklungsforschung*, Springer, Wiesbaden, 225–230.

Baraulina T., Hilber D. and Kreienbrink A. (2012) "Migration und Entwicklung. Explorative Untersu-chung des Handlungsfelds auf Ebene des Bundes, der Länder und der Kommunen", Working Paper 49, Bundesamt für Migration und Flüchtlinge, Nuremberg.

Bierschenk T. (2014) "Entwicklungsethnologie und Ethnologie der Entwicklung. Deutschland, Europa, USA", Department of Anthropology and African Studies. Working Paper No. 150.

Dünnwald S. (2014) "Rückkehr als Risiko", in Ataç I., Fanizadeh M., Kraler A. and Manzenreiter W. eds., *Migration und Entwicklung. Neue Perspektiven*, promedia, Vienna, 173–189.

Elgot J. and McVeigh K. (2017) "UK Ethical Code to 'Stop Fat Cats Profiteering from Aid Budget'", The Guardian, 3 October 2017 (www.theguardian.com/politics/2017/oct/03/uk-ethical-code-to-stop-fat-cats-profiteering-from-aid-budget) Accessed 1 March 2018.

European Commission (2017) "Global Approach to Migration and Mobility", European Commission, Migration and Home Affairs (https://ec.europa.eu/home-affairs/what-we-do/policies/international-affairs/global-approach-to-migration_en) Accessed 15 November 2017.

European Council. (2002) "Seville European Council, Presidency Conclusions (21 and 22 June 2002)", Seville. (www.cvce.eu/en/obj/seville_european_council_presidency_conclusions_21_and_22_june_2002-en-f96751f6-9eed-4390-99a8-3174841a1b2d.html) Accessed 13 November 2017.

Faist T. (2006) "Die europäische Migrations- und Entwicklungspolitik – eine Chance für den Süden?", Center on Migration, Citizenship and Development. Working Paper No. 12.

Faist T. (2008) "Migrants as Transnational Development Agents: An Inquiry into the Newest Round of the Migration-Development Nexus", *Population, Space and Place 14*, 21–42.

Faist T. (2010) "Transnationalization and Development. Toward an Alternative Agenda", in Glick Schiller N. and Faist T. eds., *Migration, Development and Transnationalization. A Critical Stance*, Berghahn, New York, 63–99.

Faist T. and Fauser M. (2011) "The Migration-Development Nexus. Toward a Transnational Perspec-tive", in Faist T., Fauser M. and Kivisto P. eds., *The Migration-Development Nexus. A Transnational Perspective*, Palgrave Macmillan, Basingstoke, 1–28.

Geiger M. and Pécoud A. (2010) "The Politics of International Migration Management", in Geiger M. and Pécoud A. eds., *The Politics of International Migration Management*, Palgrave Macmillan, Hound-mills, Basingstoke, Hampshire, 1–20.

Geiger M. and Steinbrink M. (2012) "Migration und Entwicklung: Merging Fields in Geography", *IMIS Beiträge 42*, 7–35.

GIZ (Deutsche Gesellschaft für Internationale Zusammenarbeit). (2017) "Weitere Informationen", GIZ, Fachexpertise, Migration und Entwicklung (www.giz.de/fachexpertise/html/9702.html) Accessed 03 November 2017.

Heck G. (2010) "'Die beste Reise meines Lebens'. Migrationsmanagement und migrantische Strategien am Beispiel Marokkos", in Hess S. and Kasparek B. eds., *Grenzregime. Diskurse, Praktiken, Institutionen in Europa*, Assoziation A, Berlin, Hamburg, 43–56.

Hess S. (2008) "Migration and Development: A Governmental Twist of the EU Migration Management Policy", Paper for the workshop "Narratives of migration management and cooperation with coun-tries of origin and transit", September 18-19 2008, Sussex.

Hess S. (2010) "'We are Facilitating States!' An Ethnographic Analysis of the ICMPD", in Geiger M. and Pécoud A. eds., *The Politics of International Migration Management*, Palgrave Macmillan, Houndmills, Basingstoke, Hampshire, 96–118.

Hess S. and Karakayali S. (2017) "Fluchtlinien der Migration. Grenzen als soziale Verhältnisse", in Hess S., Kasparek B., Kron S., Rodatz M., Schwertl M. and Sontowski S. eds., *Der lange Sommer der Migration. Grenzregime III*, Assoziation A, Berlin, Hamburg, 25–37.

Hess S., Kasparek B., Kron S., Rodatz M., Schwertl M. and Sontowski S. (2017) "Der lange Sommer der Migration. Krise, Rekonstitution und ungewisse Zukunft des europäischen Grenzregimes", in Hess S., Kasparek B., Kron S., Rodatz M., Schwertl M. and Sontowski S. eds., *Der lange Sommer der Migration. Grenzregime III*, Assoziation A, Berlin, Hamburg, 6–24.

Hilber D. and Baraulina T. (2012) "Migration and Development. A New Policy Paradigm in Germany?", *IMIS Beiträge 40*, 89–112.

IOM (International Organization for Migration). (2017) "Migration and Development", IOM, Department of Migration Management (www.iom.int/migration-and-development) Accessed 03 November 2017.

Janicki J. J. and Böwing T. (2010) "Europäische Migrationskontrolle im Sahel. Das CIGEM in Mali", in Hess S. and Kasparek B. eds., *Grenzregime. Diskurse, Praktiken, Institutionen in Europa*, Assoziation A, Berlin, Hamburg, 127–144.

Kasparek B. and Hess S. (2010) ""Einleitung. Perspektiven kritischer Migrations- und Grenzregimeforschung"", in Hess S. and Kasparek B. eds., *Grenzregime. Diskurse, Praktiken, Institutionen in Europa*, Assoziation A, Berlin, Hamburg, 7–22.

Kraler A., Ataç I., Fanizadeh M. and Manzenreiter W. (2014) "Migration und Entwicklung. Eine Einleitung", in Ataç I., Fanizadeh M., Kraler A. and Manzenreiter W. eds., *Migration und Entwicklung. Neue Perspektiven*, promedia, Vienna, 7–19.

Kraler A. and Noack M. (2014) "Migration und Entwicklung. Interessen, Akteure und Arenen eines erfolgreichen Diskurses", in Ataç I., Fanizadeh M., Kraler A. and Manzenreiter W. eds., *Migration und Entwicklung. Neue Perspektiven*, promedia, Vienna, 23–47.

Kron S. (2014) "'Something had to be done in the South'. Entwicklung, *Migration Management* und Regionalisierung in den Amerikas", in Ataç I., Fanizadeh M., Kraler A. and Manzenreiter W. eds., *Migration und Entwicklung. Neue Perspektiven*, promedia, Vienna, 49–64.

Kunz R. (2011) *The Political Economy of Global Remittances. Gender, Governmentality, and Neoliberalism*, Routledge, New York.

Kunz R. and Schwenken H. (2014a) "MigrantInnen als HoffnungsträgerInnen in der Entwicklungszusammenarbeit? Geschlechterspezifische Subektivitäten im migrant-development-nexus", *PVS, Sonderheft 48 (2014)*, 283–311.

Kunz R. and Schwenken H. (2014b) "Das flexible Geschlecht. Genderskripte im Migrations- und Entwicklungsdiskurs", in Ataç I., Fanizadeh M., Kraler A. and Manzenreiter W. eds., *Migration und Entwicklung. Neue Perspektiven*, promedia, Vienna, 85–100.

Lachenmann G. (2008) "Transnationalisation, Translocal Spaces, Gender and Development – Methodological Challenges", in Anghel R. G., Gerharz E., Rescher G. and Salzbrunn M. eds., *The Making of World Society. Perspectives from Transnational Research*, transcript, Bielefeld, 51–74.

Lachenmann G. (2009) "Nachbemerkung: Transnationalismus – Migration – Entwicklung. Methodologische Herausforderungen für eine empirisch fundierte Theoriebildung", *Sociologus 59 (1)*, 89–102.

Lachenmann G. and Dannecker P. eds. (2001) *Die geschlechtsspezifische Einbettung der Ökonomie. Empirische Untersuchungen über Entwicklungs- und Transformationsprozesse*, Lit, Hamburg.

Mannitz S. and Schneider J. (2014) "Vom 'Ausländer' zum 'Migrationshintergrund': Die Modernisierung des deutschen Integrationsdiskurses und seine neuen Verwerfungen", in Nieswand B. and Drotbohm H. eds., *Kultur, Gesellschaft, Migration. Die reflexive Wende in der Migrationsforschung*, Springer, Wiesbaden, 69–96.

Mendick R., Hennessy P. and Malnick E. (2013) "Some Countries Do Not Need our Money Any More, Says Andrew Mitchell", The Telegraph, 16 June 2013 (www.telegraph.co.uk/news/politics/10122842/Some-countries-do-not-need-our-money-any-more-says-Andrew-Mitchell.html) Accessed 1 March 2018.

Nieswand B. (2008) "Ghanaian Migrants in Germany and the Social Construction of Diaspora", *African Diaspora 1*, 28–52.

Nieswand B. (2011) "Der Migrations-Entwicklungs-Nexus in Afrika. Diskurswandel und Diasporaformation", in Baraulina T., Kreienbrink A. and Riester A. eds., *Potenziale der Migration zwischen Afrika und Deutschland*, Bundesamt für Migration und Flüchtlinge und Deutsche Gesellschaft für Internationale Zusammenarbeit, Nuremberg, Eschborn, 400–425.

Rauch T. (2015) "Zur Reform der deutschen Entwicklungszusammenarbeit", *Aus Politik und Zeitgeschichte 65 (7-9)*, 36–42.

Riester A. (2014) "Verstrickt im Nationalstaat – Transnationalismus in der Entwicklungspolitik", in Nieswand B. and Drotbohm H. eds., *Kultur, Gesellschaft, Migration. Die reflexive Wende in der Migrationsforschung*, Springer, Wiesbaden, 203–223.

Rosenberger S., Schwenken H., Kirchhoff M. and Merhaut N. M. (2017) "Abschiebe-Protest-Kulturen: Abschiebungen als Konfliktfeld in Deutschland und Österreich zwischen 1993 und 2013", *Leviathan 33*, 255–281.

Rosenberger S. and Trauner F. (2014) "Abschiebepolitik: Eine sozialwissenschaftliche Annäherung", *Österreichische Zeitschrift für Politikwissenschaft (ÖZP) 2 (2014)*, 141–150.

Scherr A. (2015) "Wer soll deportiert werden? Wie die folgenreiche Unterscheidung zwischen den 'wirklichen' Flüchtlingen, den zu Duldenden und den Abzuschiebenden hergestellt wird", *Soziale Probleme 26*, 151–170.

Schwertl M. (2015a) *Faktor Migration. Projekte, Diskurse und Subjektivierungen des Hypes um Migration & Entwicklung*, Waxmann, Münster, New York.

Schwertl M. (2015b) "Wissen, (Selbst)Management, (Re)territorialisierung. Die drei Achsen des aktuellen Diskurses um Migration & Entwicklung", *Movements. Journal für kritische Migrations- und Grenzregime-forschung, 1/1* (http://movements-journal.org/issues/01.grenzregime/09.schwertl–wissen-selbstmanagement-reterritorialisierung-migration-entwicklung.html) Accessed 14 July 2017.

Schwertl M. (2016) "The Economic Diaspora: The Triple Helix of Im/mobilisation in the Hype about Migration and Development", in Gutekunst M., Hackl A., Leoncini S., Schwarz J. S. and Götz I. eds., *Bounded Mobilities. Ethnographic Perspectives on Social Hierarchies and Global Inequalities*, transcript, Bielefeld, 245–264.

Sieveking N. (2011) "Die Transformation von Geschlechterverhältnissen im Spiegel des Entwicklungs-sengagements afrikanischer Migrantinnen und Migranten in Deutschland", in Baraulina T., Kreienbrink A. and Riester A. eds., *Potenziale der Migration zwischen Afrika und Deutschland*, Bundesamt für Migration und Flüchtlinge and Deutsche Gesellschaft für Internationale Zusammenarbeit, Nuremberg, Eschborn, 378–399.

Speer M. (2010) "Die Ukraine als migrantisch genutztes Transitland", in Hess S. and Kasparek B. eds., *Grenzregime. Diskurse, Praktiken, Institutionen in Europa*, Assoziation A, Berlin, Hamburg, 57–73.

Steinhilper E. (2014) "Doing Deportation – Moral und Kontingenz in der Abschiebepraxis.17.07.2014–19.07.2014, Buchenbach", H-Soz-u-Kult 19. 09.2014 (www.hsozkult.de/conferencereport/id/tagungsberichte-5558) Accessed 28 April 2019.

51

SPANISH STUDIES ON MIGRATION AND DEVELOPMENT

Areas of prestige and knowledge production

Almudena Cortés Maisonave

Introduction

The field of research relating to migration and development in Spain has gradually consolidated since the late 1990s.[1] This is evidenced by the interest in the subject, the number and type of publications, the space given in Congresses to topics on migration and development, the calls for proposals and the research projects financed, and the specialised and non-regulated university education that has been taught on this subject since the mid-1990s.

After the impact of the economic downturn, we have been in the midst of a makeover of the Spanish migration regime, which affects the field of migration and development. This adjustment makes it relevant to consider how the knowledge on this subject had been built within Spanish studies of migration. In particular, I am interested in analysing which research topics have been chosen, which subjects have been recognised, and, to a lesser extent, which ones have been made invisible. That is to say, what has been privileged in the field of migration and development in Spain? Therefore, migration studies will be considered as a 'field' of knowledge production where competences and struggles are generated (Bourdieu 1997, 49), and studies on migration and development will be thought of as a set of approaches that define and give shape to this field composed of themes and actors. The field of migration and development is a strongly politicised field, and the Spanish case is no exception. For this reason, it is necessary to analyse the political implications of the construction of knowledge of the migration and development nexus.

To sustain this analysis, it is necessary to begin with the concept of the 'politics of place' proposed by Lila Abu-Lughod (1989, 271) who pointed out that in order to talk about the politics of the place, it was necessary to explore how a certain problem was constructed, what academic conventions were generated, the standards of relevance applied, and the political interests at stake. This leads us to think and reflect on the creation of areas of greater and lesser prestige within ethnographic areas (Appadurai 1986, 357). According to

Appadurai, certain areas have been privileged objects of attention for researchers and carry more or less prestige in anthropological theory. Therefore, in this chapter, it is argued that the nexus, migration and development, has been configured as an ethnographic area of knowledge, understood as a construction, both academic and political, and Spain as a 'place' where knowledge is produced and circulates in relation to this specific topic. To carry out the aforementioned analysis, I will draw on a variety of sources identifying Spanish academic texts and reports prepared by NGOs, and scientific papers submitted at congresses, conferences, and seminars that deal with migration and development. An introduction has been incorporated to contextualise the construction of the migration and development nexus in Spain.

The political and historical context of the studies on migration and development in Spain: the double crossing

Studies on migration and development in Spain have emerged in the context of an older European debate on the same subject. The nexus between migration and development is an area of studies resulting from certain political and historical circumstances. It is a highly politicised field (Sørensen et al. 2002), precisely because migration is a priority issue in the political agendas of European host countries. The European model of migration and development is based on the control of migratory flows, on the integration of immigrants in the labour market and in the host society, and, finally, on the extension of cooperation with sending and developing countries (Sørensen et al. 2002). In this way, policy debates have introduced cooperation with sending and developing countries, with the aim of strengthening the management and control of migration. This is possible because, from an ideological and modernising point of view, poverty continues to be viewed as the main cause of migration despite the fact that this assumption has been profoundly questioned by the data and research that have shown that the nexus between migration and development is complex, multidirectional, and specific. However, despite the empirical evidence to the contrary, this relationship between migration and development remains central in the political and social discourse in European societies on migration (Cortés 2011; Marín 2006).

In the Spanish case, the emergence of the field of study on migration and development coincided with three determining processes. In the first place, Spain, which had been a country of emigrants and refugees, became in the 2000s 'immigrant Spain' (Cachón 2002, 97). Unlike previous decades, Spain was at the forefront of international politics as a member of the EU and, together with the other countries of Southern Europe, Spain participated in the same negotiations, speeches, and migration policies, political and legal practices of border control, and the same policies of cooperation for development, including those for migration and development. Second, when Spain began to build a scientific field relating to migration and development, in the European and multilateral context, the notion that this field implied proposing a bid in which all the actors involved would win emerged. That is, sending and receiving states, migrants themselves, facilitating forms of global governance and cooperation of migration would all gain (Gamlen 2009). Third, migration ceased to be a 'technical-administrative concern', as during the 1980s and 1990s, and became a matter of state interest that affected the political agenda of Spanish political parties (Cortés 2009a; Zapata-Barrero 2002, 83). Following this logic, the Spanish government proposed co-development in the EU and introduced it to Spain within a global approach aimed at influencing the dynamics of migration flows. The ultimate aim of this policy was to avoid migration in places of origin through the co-development approach. This policy had two major components: at the border through increased control and in the place of origin of potential migrants through the creation of improved conditions so that people did not need to migrate (Declaración de Motivos de la Ley Orgánica 4/2000). This perspective was reflected in the Global Program for the Regulation and Coordination of Immigration and Immigration (Delegación del Gobierno para la Extranjería y la Inmigración 2001), 'Co-development of the countries of origin and transit of immigrants' and was divided into five initiatives:

- training of immigrants who may be agents of development upon their return to their country of origin
- aid for their reintegration in the countries of origin
- the orientation of savings towards productive investments
- the promotion of the Microcredit Grant Fund
- technical assistance directed to countries from where immigrants come.

In the 2000s, migration and development policies were used to reinforce Spanish interests. On the one hand, the scope of migration and development contributed to increasing the multilateral presence of Spain. The country presented its set of proposals on migration and development at a number of international forums, beginning with the United Nations High Level Dialogue on Migration and Development (2006). At the European level, Spain has been one of the promoters of the integration of migration and development in the EU's cooperation policies, including the framework of the financial perspectives 2007–13, the conclusions of the European Council of December 2006 and the Migration and Development Conferences held in Rabat and Tripoli.

On the other hand, these initiatives were promoted by emphasising the role of migration in shaping Spain's identity as a country of emigration in the past and a country of immigration in the present day. This national memory of migration has been showcased in development cooperation policies related to migration. The 2008 Annual International Cooperation Plan recognised this new situation and built an image of a receiving state that was sensitive to migration and contributed to forging the idea of Spain as a state committed to values that have traditionally been European, such as respect for Human Rights or tolerance. Spain opted for the definition of a model linking migration and development in the context of European policies, as an original contribution based on the premise that control policies should be complemented with prevention policies but based upon cooperation. Co-development was thus seen as different from the policy of control of migration flows, even if it helped to reinforce it.

The politics of place and the nature of studies on migration and development

The study of migration and development in Spain is a field that has been consolidated because of its connection with the transnational perspective (Escrivá and Ribas 2004). The pioneering works in the Spanish case, have contributed to framing three central themes: the linkage between migration and development and cooperation for development; studies of specific geographical areas, particularly Morocco; and the connection between migration, gender, and development. Within the first theme, studies have focused on demonstrating the application of the migration and development nexus in the field of cooperation for development (Giménez 1997; Malgesini 2001; Solé 1998). These studies are framed in an approach that critically examines the relationships among emigration, poverty, and development, and specifically its economic implications (Alonso 2004). The fundamental question was whether emigration contributed to expanding development possibilities of the countries of the South.

The applied nature of these studies is particularly apparent as they sought to meet the requirements of Spanish development cooperation, which was beginning to take an interest in the issue of migration and to request guidelines to inform its response to this new phenomenon (Atienza 2004). This set of studies gave rise to research on co-development, which will be discussed below. The critical vision of the migration and development nexus was also presented through studies that showed that the relationship between migration and development was complex and not predetermined but varied with the initial conditions of each country in terms of demographic structure, human capital, and institutional stability (Abad 2005, 2008).

In the second group, the Spanish research focused on countries with a long and complex relationship with Spain, such as the Dominican Republic or Morocco (López and Ramírez 1997). In this ground-breaking work in Spain, Moroccan migratory networks were constructed to examine their links to development. Other studies subsequently emerged focused on the relationship between migration, development, and poverty in Morocco in the form of a doctoral thesis (Marín 2006), or on the effects of emigration on development in the Moroccan case (Lacomba 2004). Finally, and in the third group, Spanish studies have analysed the relationship between migration, gender, and development in the case of Dominican women (Gregorio 2000).

Transnational practices of migrants and their relationship with development

The studies that emerged in the 2000s paid special attention to the transnational practices of migrants and their connection with development in areas of origin, whether locality, country, or region.

At first, concern revolved around the role of social and migration networks in the migration process and the ways in which these were related to the countries of origin (Aparicio and Tornos 2005; Pedone 2006). Subsequently, the studies tried to connect transnational networks with development processes, understanding them as intermediate units of analysis that allowed the channelling of social relations into development-oriented effects (Cortés et al. 2007). Fieldwork was carried out in the countries and regions with the highest migrant populations in Spain in the 2000s, such as Morocco (Lacomba 2004), sub-Saharan Africa (Carballo and Echart 2007), and Ecuador (Cortés 2011; Cortés and Sanmartin 2008). This research analysed the social and economic insertion of Asian, particular Chinese, communities in Spain (Beltrán and Sáiz 2004), transnational Asian entrepreneurship (Beltrán 2007) or the consolidation of ethnic economic niches where Chinese workers and entrepreneurs were inserted through the family businesses (Beltrán and Sáiz 2015).

Three major issues provided a focus in these studies: the relationship between remittances and development; the relationship between gender, migration, and development; and the role of migrant associations in development. First, interest in remittances and development arose early in the light of the mantra that remittances promoted development in countries of origin. The analysis showed the relevance of the specific contexts, moving away from the search for universal interpretations about the role of remittances (Abad 2005). The researchers focused on the uses of remittances by senders and receivers in the case of Moroccan migration in Spain (Criado 2009), as well as on more ethnographic analyses of the social and cultural impacts of remittances in transnational households (Cavalcanti and Parella 2006; Cortés and Ortega 2008; Rivas and Gonzálvez 2011; Sanz 2009). In this way, Spanish studies incorporated the category of social remittances and expressly linked them with human development (Lacomba and Sanz 2013). More quantitative analysis of the impacts of remittances was also undertaken as part of these studies (Grande and Del Rey 2012).

Second, research in Spain has also recognised that migration and remittances are highly gendered (Oso 2011). Thus, Spanish research into migration and development has been firmly placed into the broader economic and sociocultural contexts in which it takes place (Cortés 2013; Oso and Torres 2017), which has contributed to a more complex and complete understanding of the dynamics of the migration–development nexus.

Third, an interest in the role of migrant associations in development experienced a significant boost from the second half of the 2000s. These studies analysed how Spain, as it became a country of immigration, provided the territorial, political, economic, and sociocultural context for the emergence of transnational migrant diasporas that have promoted development-oriented activities. Through these practices, Spain is re-interpreted as a symbolic social space from which actions emerge to influence development in the areas of origin (Cortés and Sanmartin 2009). Research has focused on how migrant associations understand the migration and development nexus, what their role is, and how they participate in this discourse (Piras et al. 2012). The involvement of associations in development from a transnational and local perspective has also been examined through the mobilisation of migrant networks, both in the country of origin and destination, as well as through official interests of Spain and the states of origin in supporting these activities (Lacomba and Cloquell 2014).

Co-development in Spain

The interest in co-development pervades Spanish studies on migration and development. For this reason, the studies that initially emerged focused on the definition of co-development and on exploring the development potential of the first co-development programmes (Cortés 2004, 2005, 2009; Cortés and Torres 2009; Fernández et al. 2006; Giménez 2005; Giménez et al. 2006; Gómez Gil 2008; Malgesini 2007). More recently, works of synthesis and more critical reviews of the co-development scheme have emerged (Aboussi 2012; Lacomba and Falomir 2010).

Initial research focused on two main topics related to co-development: the political dimension and the actors. The interest in co-development as 'politics' reflects the territorial decentralisation of the Spanish state in its dealings with the countries of origin of the migrants (Aubarell et al. 2003; Pinyol and Royo 2010; Ramón Chornet 1999, 2005). The research work brought an understanding that co-development was an opportunity to broaden the capacity of those involved, together with the need to promote a model that facilitated the participation of all the actors involved in the nexus of migration and development, not just the central state. Specifically, the local dimension of the migration and development nexus was highlighted and how policies and initiatives of local governments were also closely related to the process of successful migrant incorporation into their country of residence, not just the policies relating to national integration such as citizenship (Østergaard-Nielsen 2011). As for the actors, these studies have described and analysed the various roles played by the central state, the autonomous communities and municipalities, the NGOs and immigrant associations (Sanmartin 2009). NGO representatives generated their own operational proposals based on their field of experience (Font 2009; Galán 2009;

Irazola 2009; Mauri and Gómez 2010; Peris 2009). The migrants themselves also reflected on their role in development and on their own vision of co-development (Paspuel 2009; REDCO 2008; VOMADE-VINCIT 2003). However, associations have played a paradoxical role. On the one hand, some associations have played a secondary role in comparison with the NGOs that have been the protagonists of the co-development projects. And on the other hand, other organisations have abandoned the vindication of the migratory situation to focus on projects and proposals for welfare activities (Echeverri et al. 2007; Lacomba et al. 2015). Although migrant associations initially played a leading role in development activities, research showed they have occupied a secondary place in the new cooperation schemes led by NGOs and many associations have abandoned their development interests to focus on projects and proposals for welfare activities in destination areas (Echeverri et al. 2007; Lacomba et al. 2015).

The analyses of co-development have privileged issues and geographical areas according to the political agenda. Several doctoral theses have focused on flagship projects, such as the Cañar-Murcia[2] project (Jodar 2011); the tensions between contracting at source and co-development (Morello 2015); the role of the state in the promotion of co-development in contexts of migration through the critical analysis of co-development between Ecuador and Spain (Cortés 2011); and the role of migrant associations in co-development (Cortés and Sanmartin 2018; Sanmartin 2010). The analysis of place-specific policies showed that co-development has been understood both as an opportunity for the different participating actors and as a state dimension of co-development over local contexts, to reduce migration through development cooperation, paradoxical though this might seem.

Finally, and despite the fact that a rich Spanish literature on gender and migration exists, the gender perspective has not been extensively applied to studies of co-development, with the exception of Solana (2010) and Cortés (2017). While Solana's text is a proposal on how the gender perspective should be incorporated into co-development, Cortés's text reveals how the co-development projects promoted by the Spanish cooperation have not incorporated the Gender in Development approach. Thus, co-development is still used as a way to reinforce the old hierarchies that originate gender inequality in trying to stop migration and encourage migrants to return by appealing to the 'family unit' and the role of women as mothers and carers. The study analyses the tension between the gender perspective and the programmes that link migration and development. It also highlights the tensions between the structure and agency of all the actors involved in development, not only between those who migrate and their families, but also the NGOs that implement co-development programmes and governments.

Final remarks

In this chapter, I have shown that Spanish migration and development research has been configured as an ethnographic area of knowledge, understood as a construction, both academic and political, with Spain as a 'place' where knowledge is produced and circulated. On the one hand, co-development allowed Spain to adopt its own migration management model within the EU, which was rather similar to the French model and more benign in its approach to migrants, including international development cooperation as part of its intervention. The Francophone and Spanish model have allowed the state to channel its functions in a concerted and cooperative manner through 'other actors': mainly NGOs and migrant associations, especially, giving rise to a government 'at a distance' (Morris 1998; Rose 1997). In this case, both social and geographical distance. At the policy level, the Spanish model of migration and development established a set of rules of conduct that have defined practices, assigned functions, and incorporated both sub-national and transnational, state and non-state actors. The overall objective was to reinforce border control policies, by promoting preventative actions to reduce migration through productive strategies and investment of remittances in origin. Thus, the co-development model has allowed the reinforcement of 'new legal orthodoxies' (Santos and Rodríguez 2007, 15) in and around legal migration and the legitimacy of deportations and the return of migrants from Spain. Thus, the Spanish model of migration and development has undergone a gradual process of *Europeanisation* through an adaption to European migration policies and to the EU's economic and development model.

Notes

1 For reasons of space, this chapter will only focus on the period ranging from the mid-1990s to the present.
2 The Cañar-Murcia project was directly promoted by the Spanish Agency for International Development Cooperation (AECID), in the period 2006–10 with a total funding of 6,389,310 dollars with half from the AECID and the balance from the Autonomous Community Region of Murcia and the Ecuadorian government. The general objective of the project was to enhance the effects that migrations have on improved living conditions in the populations of origin (Cañar, Ecuador) and destination (Murcia, Spain). This project achieved high visibility and became well-known both inside and outside Ecuador.

References

Abad, L.V. (2005) "Impacto de la emigración y las remesas en el desarrollo: un enfoque desde las "condiciones iniciales", *Migraciones*, 18, 105–148.

Abad, L.V. (2008) "Emigración y desarrollo. Un enfoque desde las condiciones iniciales", in García Roca, J. and Lacomba, J. (eds), *La inmigración en la sociedad española. Una radiografía multidisciplinar*, Edicions Bellaterra, Barcelona, 717–750.

Aboussi, M. (ed) (2012) *El codesarrollo a debate*, Editorial Comares, Granada.

Abu-Lughod, L. (1989) "Zones of Theory in the Anthropology of the Arab World", *Annual Review of Anthropology*, 18, 267–306.

Alonso, J.A. (ed) (2004) *Emigración, pobreza y desarrollo*, Los Libros de La Catarata, Madrid.

Aparicio, R. and Tornos, A. (2005) *Las redes sociales de los inmigrantes extranjeros en España. Un estudio sobre el terreno*, Ministerio de Trabajo y Asuntos Sociales, Madrid.

Appadurai, A. (1986) "Theory in Anthropology: Center and Periphery", *Comparative Studies in Society and History*, 29, 356–361.

Atienza, J. (2004) "La cooperación para el desarrollo en contextos de alta migración. De las ideas a la práctica: el Plan Migración, Comunicación y Desarrollo", in Alonso, J.A. (ed), *Emigración, pobreza y desarrollo*, Los Libros de La Catarata, Madrid, 185–209.

Aubarell, G., Oliván, H. and Aragall, X. (2003) "Inmigración y Codesarrollo en España", in Aubarell, G. (ed), *Perspectivas de la Inmigración en España. Una aproximación desde el territorio*, Editorial Icaria, Barcelona, 393–414.

Beltrán, J. (2007) "El transnacionalismo en el empresariado asiático de España", *Revista CIDOB d'afers internacionals*, 78, 13–32.

Beltrán, J. and Sáiz, A. (2004) "La inserción social y económica de las comunidades asiáticas en España", *Anuario Asia-Pacífico*, 1, 361–370.

Beltrán, J. and Sáiz, A. (2015) "A contracorriente. Trabajadores y empresarios chinos en España ante la crisis económica (2007-2013)", *Migraciones*, 37, 125–147.

Bourdieu, P. (1997) *Razones prácticas. Sobre la teoría de la acción*, Anagrama, Barcelona.

Cachón, L. (2002) "La formación de la "España Inmigrante": mercado y ciudadanía", *Revista de Investigaciones Sociológicas (REIS)*, 97, 95–126.

Carballo, M. and Echart, E. (2007) *Migraciones y Desarrollo. Estrategias de acción en el Sahel Occidental*, IUDC-UCM/FIAPP, Madrid.

Cavalcanti, L. and Parella, S. (2006) "Una aproximación cualitativa a las remesas de los inmigrantes peruanos y ecuatorianos en España y a su impacto en los hogares transnacionales", *Revista Española de Investigaciones Sociológicas (REIS)*, 116(1), *January 2006*, 241–257(17).

Cortés, A. and Sanmartin, A. (2018) "Asociacionismo migrante latinoamericano y codesarrollo. Ámbitos de participación política transnacional Papers", *Revista de Sociologia*, 103(4), 551–575. doi:http://dx.doi.org/10.5565/rev/papers.2506.

Cortés, A. (2004) "La emergencia del codesarrollo: una perspectiva transnacional" *4 Congreso de Inmigración a España* Girona.

Cortés, A. (2005) "La experiencia del codesarrollo entre Ecuador y España: una aproximación a un transnacionalismo desde el medio", in Herrera, G., Carrillo, M.C. and Torres, A. (eds), *La migración ecuatoriana: transnacionalismo, redes e identidades FLACSO-Ecuador y Plan Migración*, Comunicación y Desarrollo, Quito, 253–277.

Cortés, A. (2009) "Los antecedentes políticos del codesarrollo: la reinvención del vínculo entre la migración y el desarrollo en el sur de Europa", in Checa, F., Checa, J.C. and Arjona, A. (eds), *Las migraciones en el mundo, Desafíos y Esperanzas*, Icaria Antracyt, Barcelona, 55–95.

Cortés, A. (2011) *Estados, cooperación para desarrollo y migraciones: el caso del codesarrollo entre Ecuador y España* Entimema, Madrid.

Cortés, A. (2013) "Gender, Andean migration and development: analytical challenges and political debates", in Oso, L. and Ribas Mateos, N. (eds), *The international handbook on gender, migration and transnationalism*, Edward Elgar, Cheltenham, 127–145.

Cortés, A. (2017) "Mujeres ecuatorianas y proyectos de codesarrollo: modelos culturales en tensión desde el sur de Europa", in Oso, L. and Torres, A. (eds), *Migración ecuatoriana, género y desarrollo FLACSO-Ecuador*, Universidade da Coruña, Quito, 23–45.

Cortés, A., Fernández, M. and Sanmartin, A. (2007) "Redes transnacionales como espacios generadores de desarrollo", *Revista Española de Desarrollo y Cooperación*, 19(invierno), 89–105.

Cortés, A. and Ortega, C. (2008) "Si ellas no vieran por mí, no tuviera nada: remesas y estructuras financieras locales en el Austro ecuatoriano. Una mirada transnacional al dinero de los migrantes", *Migración y Desarrollo*, 11, 31–53.

Cortés, A. and Sanmartin, A. (2008) "Ecuador", in Fernández, M., Giménez, C. and Puerto, L.M. (eds), *La construcción del codesarrollo*, Los Libros de la Catarata, Madrid, 67–145.

Cortés, A. and Sanmartin, A. (2009) "Las prácticas transnacionales de los/las migrantes vinculados al desarrollo. Un estudio a partir del contexto español" *Revista del Ministerio de Trabajo e Inmigración. Migraciones Internacionales, n°80*, pp. 191–211.

Cortés, A. and Torres, A. eds. (2009) *Codesarrollo en los Andes: contextos y actores para una acción transnacional*, FLACSO – Instituto Universitario de Migraciones Etnicidad y Desarrollo (IMEDES) – Ayuntamiento de Madrid, Quito.

Criado, M.J. (2009) "Las remesas familiares a los países en desarrollo. El corredor España-Marruecos" *Revista del Ministerio de Trabajo e Inmigración. Migraciones Internacionales, n°80*, 211–237.

Echeverri, M., Ibáñez, R. and Ortí, M. (2007) *El codesarrollo desde la perspectiva de la población inmigrante. Una aproximación a las representaciones sociales y discursos sobre el desarrollo de los migrantes ecuatorianos y marroquíes en Madrid* Acsur-Las Segovias, Madrid.

Escrivá, Á. and Ribas, N. (eds) (2004) *Migración y desarrollo*, CSIC, Córdoba.

Fernández, M., Giménez, C. and Puerto, L.M. (2006) *La construcción del codesarrollo*, Los Libros de la Catarata, Madrid.

Font, J. (2009) "El codesarrollo como proceso: experiencias prácticas en Catalunya (España)", in Cortés, A. and Torres, A. (eds), *Codesarrollo en los Andes: contextos y actores para una acción transnacional*, FLACSO – Instituto Universitario de Migraciones, Etnicidad y Desarrollo (IMEDES) – Ayuntamiento de Madrid, Quito, 157–177.

Galán, E. (2009) "El codesarrollo como estrategia para el fortalecimiento de redes transnacionales", in CIDEAL (ed), *El codesarrollo y su gestión: haciendo camino al andar*, CIDEAL, Madrid, 79–95.

Gamlen, A. (2009) "El Estado de emigración y los vínculos con la diáspora", in Escrivá, A., Bermúdez, A. and Moraes, N. (eds), *Migración y participación política*, CSIC, Córdoba, 237–264.

Giménez, C. (1997) "Migración y Desarrollo. Su vinculación positiva" *Ingeniería sin fronteras. Revista de cooperación, n° 9, Madrid*.

Giménez, C. (2005) *¿Qué es el codesarrollo? Expectativas, concepciones, y escenarios de futuro* CIDEAL, Madrid.

Giménez, C., Martínez, J., Fernández, M. and Cortés, A. (2006) *El codesarrollo en España: protagonistas, discursos y experiencias*, Los Libros de la Catarata, Madrid.

Gómez Gil, C. (2008) *Potencialidades y limitaciones del codesarrollo*, Bakeaz, Bilbao.

Grande, R. and Del Rey, A. (2012) "Remesas, proyectos migratorios y relaciones familiares. El caso de los latinoamericanos y los caribeños en España", *Papeles de Población*, 18(74), 237–272.

Gregorio, C. (2000) "Mujeres inmigrantes dominicanas ¿agentes de cambio y desarrollo en sus comunidades de origen?", in Pérez Cantó, P. (ed), *Las mujeres del Caribe en el umbral del 2000*, Comunidad Autónoma de Madrid, Madrid, 147–167.

Irazola, J. (2009) "¿Co ... qué? La cooperación al codesarrollo en busca de identidad", in Cortés, A. and Torres, A. (eds), *Codesarrollo en los Andes: contextos y actores para una acción transnacional*, FLACSO – Instituto Universitario de Migraciones, Etnicidad y Desarrollo (IMEDES) – Ayuntamiento de Madrid, Quito, 51–69.

Jodar, J. (2011) "Análisis de la gestión de los proyectos de codesarrollo. Estudio de caso: el proyecto piloto de codesarrollo Cañar-Murcia", Unpublished PhD thesis, Universidad de Murcia.

Lacomba, J. (2004) *Migraciones y Desarrollo en Marruecos*, Los Libros de la Catarata, Madrid.

Lacomba, J., Boni, A., Cloquell, A. and Soledad, C. (2015) "Immigrant Associations and Co-development Policies. Among the Opportunities for Strengthening and the Risks of Cooptation in the Case of Valencia Region (Spain)", *VOLUNTAS: International Journal of Voluntary and Nonprofit Organizations*, 26(5), 1852–1873.

Lacomba, J. and Cloquell, A. (2014) "Migrants, Associations and Home Country Development: Implications for Discussions on Transnationalism", *New Diversities*, 16(2), 21–37.

Lacomba, J. and Falomir, F. (eds) (2010) *De las migraciones como problema a las migraciones como oportunidad: codesarrollo y movimientos migratorios*, Los Libros de la Catarata, Madrid.

Lacomba, J. and Sanz, J. (2013) "No es solo mandar dinero: transferencias y remesas de los migrantes más allá de su dimensión económica", *Migraciones*, 34(2013), 45–76.

López, B. and Ramírez, Á. (1997) "Emigración y desarrollo: la geografía de origen de la emigración marroquí", in Martín Rojo, L. (ed), *Hablar y dejar hablar (sobre racismo y xenofobia)*, Ediciones de la UAM, Madrid, 115–140.

Malgesini, G. (2001) "Reflexiones sobre migraciones, cooperación y codesarrollo", *Arxius de ciencies socials*, 5, 123–146.

Malgesini, G. (2007) *¿Qué es el codesarrollo y cómo participar en él?* CIDEAL, Madrid.

Marín, I. (2006) *La cooperación española para el desarrollo como "prevención" de la emigración marroquí: percepciones, discursos y realidades entre las dos orillas*, Editorial de la Universidad de Granada, Granada.

Mauri, R. and Gómez, L. (2010) "El programa Wipala: experiencias y reflexiones sobre codesarrollo", in Lacomba, J. and Falomir, F. (eds), *De las migraciones como problema a las migraciones como oportunidad: codesarrollo y movimientos migratorios*, Los Libros de la Catarata, Madrid, 435–457.

Ministerio del Interior, Delegación del Gobierno para la Extranjería y la Inmigración. (2001–2004) *Programa Global de Regulación y Coordinación de la Extranjería y la Inmigración en España*, Ministerio del Interior, Madrid.

Morello, N. (2015) Entre la oportunidad y el deseo. Contratación en origen, codesarrollo y grupos domésticos transnacionales en el mundo rural. El caso Catalunya Colombia. Unpublished PhD thesis, Universidad de Barcelona.

Morris, L. (1998) "Governing at a Distance: The Elaboration of Controls in British Immigration", *International Migration Review*, XXXII(4), invierno, 949–973.

Orgánica, L. 4/2000, de 11 de enero, sobre derechos y libertades de los extranjeros en España y su integración social, Boletín Oficial del Estado, núm. 10, 12 de enero de 2000.

Oso, L. (2011) "Género, migración y desarrollo. Entre Quito y Madrid, familias ecuatorianas y estrategias de movilidad social" *Amérique Latine Histoire et Mémoire. Les Cahiers ALHIM*, 22.

Oso, L. and Torres, A. (2017) *Migración ecuatoriana, género y desarrollo*, FLACSO-Ecuador, Universidade da Coruña, Quito.

Østergaard-Nielsen, E. (2011) "Codevelopment and Citizenship: The Nexus between Policies on Local Migrant Incorporation and Migrant Transnational Practices in Spain", *Ethnic and Racial Studies*, 34(1), 20–39.

Paspuel, V. (2009) "Visión y experiencia del codesarrollo desde las asociaciones de personas migradas", in CIDEAL (ed), *El codesarrollo y su gestión: haciendo camino al andar*, CIDEAL, Madrid, 139–155.

Pedone, C. (2006) *Tú siempre jalas a los tuyos. Estrategias migratorias y poder*, Editorial Abya-Yala, Quito.

Peris, J. (2009) "Fantasmas y potencias del codesarrollo", in Cortés, A. and Torres, A. (eds), *Codesarrollo en los Andes: contextos y actores para una acción transnacional*, FLACSO – Instituto Universitario de Migraciones, Etnicidad y Desarrollo (IMEDES) – Ayuntamiento de Madrid, Quito, 69–87.

Pinyol, G., Royo, E. (2010) "El concepto de codesarrollo en las políticas públicas: una historia inconclusa", in Centre de Cooperació per al Desenvolupament Rural et al. (eds), *Migraciones y desarrollo. El codesarrollo: del discurso a la práctica*, Anthropos, Barcelona, 83–123.

Piras, G., Cazarín, R., Rennau, A., Bianchi, G. and Blanco, C. (2012) "El asociacionismo de la población andina en Madrid y el País Vasco. Voces sobre el nexo migración y desarrollo", VII Congreso sobre Migraciones Internacionales en España, Bilbao.

Ramón Chornet, C. (1998) "Nuevas orientaciones de la política de ayuda y cooperación al desarrollo de la Unión Europea: la propuesta de codesarrollo", in *Cursos de derecho internacional de Vitoria-Gasteiz*, Universidad del País Vasco, Leioa, 45–173.

Ramón Chornet, C. (2005) "La política de codesarrollo en la Unión Europea ¿Hacia una inflexión significativa?" in CIDEAL (ed), *Codesarrollo: migraciones y desarrollo mundial*, CIDEAL, Madrid, 47–68.

REDCO. (2008) *Documento de la Red de Asociaciones de Inmigrantes y Codesarrollo*, Madrid.

Rivas, A.M. and Gonzálvez, H. (2011) "El papel de las remesas económicas y sociales en las familias transnacionales colombianas", *Migraciones internacionales*, 6(2), *Julio-Diciembre*, 75–99.

Rose, N. (1997) "El gobierno en las democracias liberales 'avanzadas': del liberalismo al neoliberalismo", *Archipiélago*, 29, 25–40.

Sanmartin, A. (2009) "Los actores del codesarrollo: el caso español", in Cortés, A. and Torres, A. (eds), *Codesarrollo en los Andes: contextos y actores para una acción transnacional*, FLACSO – Instituto Universitario de Migraciones, Etnicidad y Desarrollo (IMEDES) – Ayuntamiento de Madrid, Quito, 139–157.

Sanmartin, A. (2010) El codesarrollo en España: un análisis de la implicación de los migrantes. Unpublished PhD thesis, Instituto Universitario Ortega y Gasset-Universidad Complutense de Madrid.

Santos, B. and Rodríguez, C. (2007) "El derecho, la política y lo subalterno en la globalización contrahegemónica", in Santos, B. and Rodríguez, C. (eds), *El Derecho y la globalización desde abajo: hacia una legalidad cosmopolita*, Anthropos Editorial, Barcelona, 7–28.

Sanz, J. (2009) Entre "cumplir" y "hacer cosas". Estrategias económicas y simbolismo en el uso de las remesas de la migración ecuatoriana en España. Unpublished PhD thesis, Universitat Rovira y Virgili.

Solana, V. (2010) "Género en el codesarrollo. Una perspectiva necesaria", in Lacomba, J. and Falomir, F. (eds), *De las migraciones como problema a las migraciones como oportunidad: codesarrollo y movimientos migratorios*, La Catarata, Madrid, 369–388.

Solé, C. (1998) "Migración y cooperación: la migración como estrategia de cooperación", in Bacaria, J. (ed), *Migración y cooperación mediterráneas*, Icaria, Barcelona, 133–165.

Sørensen, N., Van Hear, N. and Engberg-Pedersen, P. (2002) "The Migration-Development Nexus: Evidence and Policy Options", Centre for Development Research, Copenhagen.

VOMADE-VINCIT. (2003) *Asociacionismo e Inmigración dominicana a España*, VOMADE-VINCIT, Madrid.

Zapata-Barrero, R. (2002) "Estructuras institucionales y redes de actores en las políticas de acomodación de los inmigrantes en España: un enfoque de cambio estructural", Granada, III Congreso Nacional de la Migración a España.

52

DEVELOPMENT AS THE AXIS OF MIGRATION POLICY

A perspective from Brazil

Leonardo Cavalcanti da Silva and María del Carmen Villarreal Villamar

Introduction

Development is a polysemic concept that contains meanings related to beliefs and values which generate multiple definitions and reflects the historical context in which it is analysed. In this regard, development carries different connotations, sometimes coinciding; other times directly opposing each other. In any of its varied meanings, development is set as an aim to be met; not only in terms of economic objectives, but also in social and cultural terms. On a historical level, the word 'development' derives from the Western notion of progress originating from Greece and it was later consolidated in Europe during the Enlightenment (Rist 2002). The current notion of development coined in the twentieth century and disseminated worldwide within the context of the Cold War was preceded by terms that include similar ideas, such as progress, civilisation, evolution, wealth, or growth. Since then, development has been seen as a word that covers approaches such as: the theory of growth, modernisation, or underdevelopment and as an object of reformulations and critiques from other perspectives, which are more sensitive to the environment, gender, ethnic-cultural differences or to the local context (Payne and Phillips 2012).

The links between migration and development have traditionally been analysed from optimistic and pessimistic perspectives (De Hass 2010; also Chapter 1 in this Handbook). Nevertheless, since the 1990s, as a consequence of the emergence of approaches such as transnationalism and new empirical evidence, the dichotomous view of the migration–development nexus was abandoned in favour of pluralist theses that accept the heterogeneity of existing relations between both variables and the contemporary presence of positive and negative effects (De Hass 2010, also Chapter 2 in this Handbook). Today, links between migration and development are a central element of global discussions concerning human mobility. In this scenario, the view concerning the migration–development nexus has become mostly optimistic and focuses on understanding how migration can affect development not only on an economic level, but also on political, social, and cultural levels (Villarreal 2017).

Brazil, as a historical host country of immigrant populations, as well as an emigration nation, has not remained unaware of this phenomenon. Throughout the country's modern history, migration policies have included ideal imaginaries and specific visions on international migrations and migrants, closely related to the current development perspective. For didactic purposes, the predominant views, outlined in the following paragraphs, are divided into four phases. In spite of the fact that the literature accepts other classifications, each phase contains various sub-phases and elements of continuity link them. The division outlined here aims solely to illustrate the key characteristics of each macro-period.

First period: 1822–88

In the territory now known as Brazil, the initiative of the Portuguese population, mainly 'white' and 'European', to occupy areas bordering with Spanish colonies began in the seventeenth century and expanded during the following periods with people mainly from the Azores. These early colonisation attempts had modest results, but laid the groundwork for future colonisation projects sponsored by the state. According to Seyferth (2008), the historical event, which marks the arrival of immigrants to the country, was the opening up of ports in 1808 and the installation of the first colony of immigrants in the city of Nova Friburgo, in the state of Rio de Janeiro in 1819, which mainly included Swiss citizens. Although the settlement was a failure in terms of numbers, due to the high mortality rate among the settlers during the trip and after arrival, as well as a high rate of return, it established a precedent for the entry of non-Catholics to the national territory, which continued from then on.

On 1 December 1822, Don Pedro I was proclaimed the Emperor of Brazil and, aiming to promote the modernization of the country., he decided to continue the policy of immigration and the creation of small settlement colonies developed by his father João VI (Iotti 2010). Despite opposition from some sectors, such as large landowners, there was a great interest among the liberal elites to promote immigration for purposes of colonisation, occupation, and defence of borders, as well as to create an economy based on small property holdings (Lesser 2015). In other words, the link between migration and development was positive and optimistic, although the terms used at the time were 'progress' and 'civilisation'.

The colonisation projects were concentrated mainly in the southern region of the country, in which the states of Rio Grande do Sul and Santa Catarina were the most important areas. On the other hand, policies to attract labour, or 'arms for agriculture', were mainly in the southeast region, especially in the state of São Paulo (Vignoli 2003). The territories intended for colonisation were, in many cases, inhabited by indigenous peoples, although the land was, in practice, regarded as 'free' and suitable for occupation. At the same time, there was a desire to 'whiten' the society and the belief in the 'civilisational ability', 'the promoters of progress', or 'superiority', which were all supposedly innate to the European immigrant. Hence, according to some authors, such as Furtado (2001) and Lesser (2015), the idea was to privilege the arrival of non-Portuguese and non-Spaniard whites, who were considered 'unacceptable'. In this scenario, the promulgation of the 1824 Constitution, recognising freedom of religion and citizenship to those born in the Brazilian territory, established the legal basis for the colonisation project financed by the Empire.

From the first legislative acts aimed at regulating the arrival of immigrants, the correlation between the migratory policy and development was clear. Decision 80, issued on 31 March 1824, for example, declared the superior advantage of the Empire to employ 'people who were white, free and industrious, both in the Arts and in agriculture'; in other words, Europeans linked to the industrial revolution and to modernity. Thus, the imagined and desirable immigrant was defined as one who could bring 'civilisation', 'progress', and 'development' to the country. As Acosta (2018, 47) points out, this attitude was not exclusive to Brazil, but was also present in policies which attracted immigrants to Argentina and Uruguay, and to countries that received smaller numbers of immigrants such as Chile, Colombia, Peru, Ecuador, and Venezuela.

In the case of Brazil, although after the abdication of Don Pedro I in 1831 and the suspension of public funding, immigration was halted. It was, however, resumed in 1848 under different modalities: public-private agreements and private projects, which meant that the immigrants were mainly assigned to work in coffee plantations and in the agricultural sector in general. In this new context of searching for a free workforce, provinces and colonisation companies became more important, as well as entities such as the Society for the Promotion of Immigration (Sociedade Promotora de Imigração), founded in 1886. During the period 1850–89, 250 colonies were created in Brazil: 197 private, 50 imperial, and 3 provincial (Iotti 2010, 8).

Despite the difficulties experienced in attracting immigrants derived from factors such as the country's poor reputation abroad and information on the difficulties immigrants had in adapting to the new territories (Prado Júnior 1994), Law 601 of 1850 on land distribution, established that foreigners could obtain naturalisation in the country after living there for two years, thereby benefiting Europeans. Moreover, the promulgation of Decree 3.784 of 1867, which regulated the colonies and offered some advantages to immigrants, as well as the approval of a series of beneficial measures, altered the panorama favouring the entry of workers, who were assigned mainly to coffee farms in the South-eastern region of the country. In this context, the number of immigrants, mainly Italians, but also Portuguese and Spaniards, increased and marked a trend that would remain in the following years.

Second period: 1888–1930

From the late nineteenth century to the early twentieth century, a transition occurred in the productive relations of Brazil, moving from a system based on slavery to one based upon a consolidation of capitalism, essentially 'development' as broadly understood. The most significant change, however, was the gradual abandonment of the production based on sugar-cane plantations in the Northeast region, which lost its centrality in favour of coffee production and the incipient industry established around the states of Minas Gerais and São Paulo (Scott and Cook-Martin 2014, 264–5).

Slavery was officially banned in Brazil in 1888, although the system had been in place for four centuries and it was estimated that the country had between 4 and 5 million slaves at the time (Fernandes 1972), even if the exact number of African slaves was unknown. Nevertheless, the volume was of such a magnitude that today Brazil is home to the largest population of African descent in the world outside the African continent.

The end of the arrival of slaves and the slow integration of former slaves into industrial production intensified the demand for foreigner labour (Fausto 1991) and, from an optimistic perspective, made the immigration process an essential factor for the development of the capitalist system in the country. Thus, the arrival of European immigrants was seen as an effective solution to address the aspirations of the governments and the ruling class. It not only supplied the labour for emerging industry and agriculture, but also, under the prevailing views of eugenics of the time, would provide the presence of a 'civilising labour' of 'smart white workers' which would improve the conditions for the development of the country as a whole (Da Matta 1987).

With the beginning of the Republic in 1889, a normative framework was decisive in the consolidation of this policy of control and selectivity from a racial point of view: Decree number 528, of 28 June 1890 in its first article pointed out the guidelines of the immigration project intimately bound to the progress of the nation. Using biological criteria, this article establishes that entry into the national territory was completely free for individuals who were: 'valid individuals', 'fit for work', and 'having no criminal records'. However, 'indigenous people from Asia' or 'black Africans', could only be admitted into the country subject to authorisation from the National Congress. In 1891, laws were also enacted that guaranteed the freedom of public worship aiming to attract even more white protestant immigrants. In the era of the 'great European migrations', these new policies, together with the socioeconomic transformations in Brazil, factors of expulsion in European societies and better and more accessible means of transport, allowed 2.6 million people to enter Brazil from 1890 to 1919 (Lesser 2015, 101).

Thus, the Brazilian immigration project was highly selective, in which European citizens were considered to be 'desirable', whereas the 'indigenous people from Asia' and the 'black Africans', as well as Afro-Americans, were considered 'undesirable'. However, the ideology of whitening and the ethnic selectivity of immigration policies contrasted openly with the myth of 'racial democracy' created by national elites or the idea that Brazil was a miscegenated population, a result of the fusion of Europeans, Africans, and indigenous people living in perfect harmony and equality (Scott and Cook-Martin 2014, 259).

The contrast between myth and reality found different forms of expression in Brazil. For example, Decree Nº. 4.247 of 6 January 1921, listed those foreigners considered undesirable, including in this category people with physical disabilities, who were mentally ill, 'subversive' or considered 'harmful' to the national security (anarchists and transgressors of legal and moral laws), prostitutes, and criminals, but apparently excluding ethnic selectivity criteria (Feldman-Bianco 2014). According to Scott and Cook-Martin (2014), the denial of racism, the strength of the myth of racial democracy over local elites, and the defence of Brazil's international image caused the ethnic selectivity to be publicly denied on a number of occasions. However, in practice, the selection was common practice and the 'undesirable' category served above all to exclude those that did not promote the 'improvement' and 'whitening' of the local population. In this respect, an emblematic example was the cancellation of concessions and the denial of entry to the Afro-American members of the *Brazilian American Colonization Syndicate* who had obtained land concessions in the state of Mato Grosso. (Scott and Cook-Martin 2014, 274).

Ultimately, European immigration was seen as an ideal part of the promotion of the national development project driven by agriculture for export, especially coffee and emerging industry. However, during this second phase, the arrival of unexpected groups that deviated from the ideal occurred (see Table 52.1). These groups included Arabs (from countries like Lebanon, Syria, Turkish, Iraq, Egypt, and Palestine) and Jews from the Middle East and Eastern Europe that worked in business and trade in states like São Paulo, Rio de Janeiro, Minas Gerais, and Rio Grande do Sul, as well as Japanese, supported by their government, that went into coffee production, especially in São Paulo and Santa Catarina, but also Mato Grosso and the North and Northeast of the country (Lesser 2015, 215).

Additionally, the preferences among 'desirable' immigrant groups changed. In fact, if in the first immigration stage, the preferred ones were the Northern Europeans (mainly Swiss and Germans), and then the Southern Europeans: Spaniards, Italians, and Portuguese, in the second stage, the selection criteria were modified because Southern Europeans were seen to comply with the three essential criteria required by the newly created Brazilian state:

Table 52.1 Immigration in Brazil by nationality (1884–1939)*

Nationality	Number of immigrants
German	170,645
Spanish	581,718
Italian	1,412,263
Japanese	185,799
Portuguese	1,204,394
Syrian and Turkish	98,962
Others	504,936
Total	4,158,717

Source: Brazilian Institute of Geography and Statistics (IBGE 2007).

* The data includes information about decadal periods (1884–93) (1924–33) and annual periods (1934–39).

they were white, Catholic, and spoke Latin languages. Thus, they were more assimilable to an imagined *Brazilianness* and national identity (Seyferth 2008).

These biological and ideological preferences became the main features of the migratory policies of this period and, as a result, immigrants from southern Europe increased exponentially. In order to consolidate this policy, until approximately 1930, the Brazilian government offered subsidies to European immigrants, either in the form of grants to help with travelling costs or by handing out small properties of land for agriculture in the south and southeast regions of the country (Bassanezi 1995; Levy 1974). However, political activism and the desires for improving life conditions led these immigrants to promote diverse political and trade union activities, as well as struggle for their rights, giving rise to concerns from Brazilian authorities. These events produced, once again, a change in the ideal of the desired immigrant for the national political and economic development project.

Third period: 1930 until the late twentieth century

During the First Republic (1889–1930), there was growing concern from various sectors in Brazil, about those immigrants considered 'undesirable' as well as those groups seen as 'not very assimilable', often referred to as 'ethnic entrenchment', particularly in the case of the Japanese and Germans, but also the Italians. In this context, in 1930, after accusations of electoral fraud, there came what in Brazilian history became known as the '1930 Revolution', which was an armed movement led by the states of Rio Grande do Sul, Minas Gerais, and Paraíba that supported the coup headed by Getúlio Vargas. The rise of Vargas to the presidency took place in a social and political climate influenced by the 1930 economic crisis, growing restrictions on immigration in countries such as the United States and Argentina, and political protagonism of anarchist and socialist groups with migrant participation. At this time, existing xenophobic and nationalist positions led to the imposition of a restrictive turn in the national migration policy (Lesser 2015). This change was reinforced by the establishment of the dictatorial regimen of the 'New State' (*Estado Novo*) (1937–45), also led by Vargas.

Within this context, policies for the assimilation of immigrants increased, even banning schools, press, or cultural activities in languages other than Portuguese. Under the influence of North American legislation (Scott and Cook-Martin 2014, 284), the Brazilian Constitution of 1934, and subsequent decrees, also established entry quotas, with severe restrictions on specific groups such as Jews, Japanese, political activists, or people with any disability (Koifman 2012). Thus, the state sought to guarantee the eugenic ideals then present in European and American scientific thinking until the first half of the twentieth century. In practice, these measures by themselves did not reduce immigration and were not always followed; the main aim was to provide the imagined *Brazilianness* through an assimilation policy for those that had already entered the country. The policy also provided advice on visa requests to favour people with acceptable 'physical and moral' qualities (Koifman 2012; Seyferth 2008).

During World War II, immigrants began to be seen as a potential military threat. In parallel, internal migration, previously favoured only in case of need, increased as a consequence of the regional development processes: the promotion of industry, and the building of infrastructure to link the north with the south of the country. Additionally, during the Vargas era, a policy was established to protect national labour, which in the context of the decreasing population flows from abroad, meant that internal migration substituted international flows (Koifman 2012). In fact, from the second half of the twentieth century, a sharp reduction in migratory flows took place and, by 1939, immigration ceased almost completely, since there were no favourable conditions for maritime traffic. After World War II, and especially from 1960, immigration resumed, but to a lesser extent and mainly as a consequence of external factors associated with the reconstruction and development in Europe.

In 1964, through a military coup, a military dictatorship came to power and governed until 1985. The dictatorial government promulgated institutional acts that abolished the Federal Constitution and allowed the suspension of political rights. Imprisonments, exile, torture, and often murder, became the fate of those who opposed the new regime (Gaspari 2002). Within this framework, Law 6.815 of 1980, also known as the 'Statute of Foreigners' (*Estatuto do Estrangeiro*), was promulgated to regulate the rights and duties of immigrants during the dictatorship and at the height of the Cold War. This law was guided by the idea of national security with foreigners considered a threat and had to be monitored and controlled. On an economic level, the national government wanted to protect the labour of the local citizens. However, it was during this period that an 'ideal' immigration, bound to the idea of development, was also conceived. In fact, Article 16 of the 'Statute of Foreigners' stated:

> immigration will primarily aim at providing skilled labour to the various sectors of the national economy, seeking to implement the National Development Policy in all its aspects and especially in relation to the increase of productivity, the assimilation of technology and obtaining resources for specific sectors.
>
> *(Brasil 1980)*

However, the political uncertainties of the return to democracy and the economic crisis of 1990 did not encourage immigration from Europe. Rather, new origins emerged with migrants coming from neighbouring countries, such as Bolivia as analysed by Silva (1997).

This period also saw the opposite phenomenon: the emigration of Brazilians. According to the Ministry of Foreign Affairs (MRE 2015), the Brazilian diaspora is made up of more than 3 million people dispersed mainly in the USA, Japan, and Europe, especially in Italy,

Portugal, the United Kingdom, and Spain. Apart from their presence in other countries such as Canada and Australia, emigration to neighbouring countries such as Paraguay, Argentina, and Bolivia has also been noticeable. In this new scenario, the Government of Fernando Henrique Cardoso, created a support programme for Brazilian citizens living abroad (1995) and approved various measures for the protection of citizens abroad, the recognition of dual-citizenship, and maintenance of their political rights (Patarra 2009; Reis 2011). Thus, discussions concerning the relation between migration and development began to consider emigrants, given the potential of their remittances and the growing importance of this group in Brazilian life.

Fourth period: beginning of the twenty-first century

From the 1980s, and the arrival of non-traditional immigrants from South America, Asia, and Africa, the profile of migration in Brazil began to change and this trend strengthened in the early 2000s. Moreover, the economic crisis that began in 2007 in the USA, and also greatly affected Europe and Japan, added to growing restrictions on immigration imposed by Northern countries, which caused shifts in the immigration in and to South America. In the Brazilian case, the economic and social development of the country and its geopolitical repositioning, the last few years have seen a radical diversification in the patterns of migration. Today, Brazil combines different scenarios: it is a country of emigration and return, but also continues to be a receiving territory of flows that are increasingly heterogeneous and mainly coming from the Southern parts of the world (Cavalcanti et al. 2015; Handerson 2015).

In addition to factors such as significant economic growth generating a wide range of jobs, improvements in political and social conditions, and greater institutional stability, the increasing number of arrivals, especially since 2007, is closely related to Brazil attaining the position as an emerging or rising power (Reis 2011; also Chapter 2 in this Handbook). The country's aim to become a *global player*, for example, generated significant results. Brazil managed to position itself as part of the BRICS group; it became a serious contender to a permanent seat on the UN Security Council; is a member of the G20; and from 2004 to 2017, conducted the United Nations Stabilization Mission in Haiti (MINUSTAH). Its representatives have been in senior positions in international organisations such as the World Trade Organization (WTO) and the Food and Agriculture Organisation of the United Nations (FAO). Brazil has hosted events of global importance, such as the Football World Cup and the Olympic Games and has also participated in different discussion forums in regions in Asia and Africa. All these factors not only positioned the country globally, converting it into a pole of attraction for international migration, but also allowed Brazilian diplomacy to adopt a protagonist role in regional and multilateral spaces in favour of migration and emigrants' rights. The country's migratory tradition and, once again, the myth about racial democracy played a predominant role (Scott and Cook-Martin 2014).

In this new scenario, the migration–development link appears again in the country's migratory policy in two ways. First, the Brazilian government resumed its selective approach towards immigrants through the idea of 'qualification' and 'investment ability' for strategic sectors of the Brazilian economy, which expanded and became increasingly international thanks to foreign investment. The desirable immigrants are, therefore, the qualified or skilled immigrants, 'useful' to the national development (Brasil 1997, 2004a, 2004b, 2008a, 2008b) and those at the level of being able to invest their own resources in productive activities (Brasil 2009). For example, in 2010 as much as 54 per cent of foreigners working in Brazil were graduates; although this situation changed in following years, showing a decreasing trend, although the ratio continued to be high and was equivalent to 30 per cent in 2016 (Cavalcanti, Oliveira, Araujo and Tonhati 2017, 83).

Second, the National Immigration Council, also encouraged the entry of 'non-qualified' but 'necessary' manpower, for sectors such as agriculture and services (Brasil 1993). For example, from 2011 to 2016, as many as 52,429 work permits were granted. From this total, 92 per cent were granted to working-age people between 20 and 49 years old, while, 83 per cent of the permits were given to people with no reported education levels (Cavalcanti et al. 2017, 39). This group can be illustrated by Haitians, who are involved in labour market activities, both formal and informal, in sectors such as construction, hotel and cleaning services, and the meat industry. At the same time, the Ministry of Foreign Affairs, in agreement with other public bodies or local governments, created various policies to favour Brazilian returnees and return from the Brazilian diaspora regarding, for example, the promotion of entrepreneurship, productive investment project remittances, or cooperation networks with their country of origin.

At the same time, and under pressure from Brazilian communities living abroad, migrant associations, activists and other groups for the defence of human rights, advocated for the need to update migration laws, particularly anachronistic features of various provisions in the 'Statute of Foreigners'. Therefore, in addition to the amnesties of 1981, 1988, 1998, and 2009, Normative Resolutions and humanitarian visas, specially designed for groups, such as Haitians (2012), Syrians (2013), and, more recently, Venezuelans (2017), have been approved. Other actions that advocated a view of the immigrant as an individual with rights demanded social integration policies for migrants and saw the realisation, in July 2014, of the First National Conference on Migration and Refugees (COMIGRAR). The social mobilisation campaign entitled 'Here I live, here I vote' lobbied for immigrants to vote in municipal elections; Reference Centres for Immigrants were created in the states with the greatest migratory inflows; and awareness campaigns in defence of the rights of immigrants emerged. No less important, were the advances and recognition of rights for South American migrants resulting from bilateral or multilateral agreements, such as the Mercosur Residency Agreement or the discussions on regional citizenship held within the Union of South American Nations (UNASUR) (Villarreal 2018).

The culmination of these activities was the creation and discussion of new legislative projects that allowed the approval of the Senate Law (PLS) 288/2013. After various changes on 24 May 2017, the then President, Michel Temer approved the new Immigration Law 13.445/2017 which, in spite of receiving 20 presidential vetoes, considered immigration as a right and was no longer a national security issue. Although lines of continuity with previous migration policies exist, in terms of migration and development, the new law overcomes unidirectional approaches and reflects a more pluralistic view of the nexus between these two variables. Thus, in Article 3, the new norm considers Brazil's migration policy as based on Brazil's economic, tourist, social, cultural, sports, scientific, and technological development; on the integration and development of border regions and promoting the link between migration and human development in the place of origin, as inalienable rights of all people (Brasil 2017).

Final considerations

The approaches adopted in the various migration policies in Brazil reflect not only the ideal views concerning development and migrants, but also the changes concerning the links between migration and development itself. Therefore, during the first and second migratory phases, optimistic, but selective, views of migration were established, mainly those based on ideological beliefs and eugenic theses. In fact, development was understood as economic growth, progress, and modernisation, although, at the same time closely related to the promotion of what the elites understood as 'enhancement' and 'civilisation' of the society. Thus, in spite of the imagined view that Brazil was a country with racial democracy, in practice, as a result of the 'whitening' ideology, the local elites promoted the selective entry of those considered 'ideal immigrants', who were seen to be white and European, since these were considered the only ones qualified to meet the objectives.

Later, the country experienced a third nationalist and restrictive period in which, under the Doctrine of National Security, foreigners were considered a threat. In this phase, the link between migration and development was inward looking, with the exception of skilled labour. This period coincided with the internalisation of the migration process and its contributions to the project for national development. That is, although development continued to be understood as economic growth and progress, the objective could only be reached through the contribution of local workers and with the exclusive participation of 'desirable immigrants', comprising specific groups of foreign labour, no longer defined by ethnic characteristics, but trained and skilled in line with the aims of national development.

At the same time, due to the increasing emigration of Brazilians, the government is taking measures to attract contributions from this group, such as remittances, but also contacts and knowledge, as a means of promoting Brazil's development. In the present stage, the selective nature of immigration policy, preferring skilled migration or people with investment capacity is maintained. Nevertheless, inward-looking perspectives of development have been abandoned in favour of a hybrid approach that accepts both disadvantages, as well as benefits in international migration. In this new scenario, the concept of the 'ideal immigrant' becomes flexible without becoming lost, while the concept of development assumes specific connotations (human, local) and expands to include contributions of both immigrants and emigrants and their impacts on the economic, social, technological, scientific, and cultural spheres.

References

Acosta D. (2018). *The national versus the foreigner in South America. 200 years of migration and citizen law.* Cambridge, Cambridge University Press.

Bassanezi M. (1995). "Imigrações internacionais no Brasil: um panorama histórico", in Patarra N. (ed.), *Emigração e imigração internacionais no Brasil contemporâneo.* São Paulo, FNUAP, pp. 1–38.

Brasil (1850). Lei N. 601 de 18 de setembro de 1850. Coleção de Leis do Império do Brasil - 1850, Página 307 Vol. 1 pt. I.

———— (1867). Decreto N. 3784 de 19 de janeiro de 1867. Coleção de Leis do Brasil - 19/1/1867, Página 31 Vol. 1 pt II.

———— (1890). Decreto N. 528 de 28 de junho de 1890. Coleção de Leis do Brasil - 1890, Página 1424 Vol. 1 fasc.VI, Brasília.

———— (1980). Lei N. 6.815 de 19 de agosto de 1980. Presidência da República, Brasília.

———— (1993). Decreto N. 840 de 22 de junho de 1993. Câmara dos Deputados, Brasília. (www2. camara.leg.br/legin/fed/decret/1993/decreto-840-22-junho-1993-449205-publicacaooriginal-1-pe. html) Accessed 1 September 2017.

———— (1997). Resolução normativa N. 1 de 29 de abril de 1997. Concessão de visto para professor ou pesquisador de alto nível e para cientistas estrangeiros. (www.icmbio.gov.br/sisbio/images/stories/ instrucoes_normativas/RN_CNImg_01_1997.pdf) Accessed 10 December 2017.

———— (2004a). Resolução Normativa N. 61 de 08 de dezembro de 2004. Disciplina a concessão de autorização de trabalho e de visto a estrangeiro sob contrato de transferência de tecnologia e/ou de prestação de serviço de assistência técnica, de acordo de cooperação ou convênio, sem vínculo empregatício ou em situação de emergência. (www.legisweb.com.br/legislacao/?id=101131) Accessed 10 December 2017.

———— (2004b). Resolução Normativa N. 62 de 08 de dezembro de 2004. Disciplina a concessão de autorização de trabalho e de visto permanente a estrangeiro, Administrador, Gerente, Diretor ou

Executivo, com poderes de gestão, de Sociedade Civil ou Comercial, Grupo ou Conglomerado econômico. (www.legisweb.com.br/legislacao/?id=101129) Accessed 10 December 2017.

_____ (2008a). Resolução normativa N. 82 de 3 de dezembro de 2008. Disciplina a concessão de visto a cientista, professor, pesquisador ou profissional estrangeiro que pretenda vir ao país para participar de conferências, seminários, congressos ou reuniões na área de pesquisa e desenvolvimento ou para a cooperação científico-tecnológica, e a estudantes de qualquer nível de graduação ou pós-graduação. (https://sistemas. mre.gov.br/kitweb/datafiles/Viena/pt-br/file/rn_20081203_82.pdf) Accessed 10 December 2017.

_____ (2008b). Resolução Normativa N. 80 de 16 de outubro de 2008. Disciplina a concessão de autorização de trabalho para a obtenção de visto temporário a estrangeiro com vínculo empregatício no Brasil. (www.usp.br/drh/novo/legislacao/dou2008/mteresnormativa802008.html) Accessed 10 December 2017.

_____ (2009). Resolução Normativa N. 84 de 2009. Disciplina a concessão de autorização para fins de obtenção de visto permanente para investidor estrangeiro -pessoa física. (www.legisweb.com.br/legis lacao/?id=111486) Accessed 10 December 2017.

_____ (2017). Presidência da República. Lei N. 13.445/2017 de 24 de maio de 2017. Brasília.

Cavalcanti L., Oliveira A. T., Araújo D., and Tonhati T. (2017). Relatório anual. A inserção dos imigrantes no mercado de trabalho brasileiro. Série Migrações, Observatório das Migrações; Ministério do Trabalho/Conselho Nacional da Imigração e Coordenação Geral da Imigração, Brasília, DF, OBMigra.

Cavalcanti L., Oliveira A. T., and Tonhati T. org. (2015). "A inserção dos imigrantes no mercado de trabalho brasileiro". *Cadernos do Observatório das Migrações Internacionais*, Ministério do Trabalho e Previdência Social/Conselho Nacional de Imigração e Coordenação Geral de Imigração. Brasília, DF, OBMigra.

Da Matta R. (1987). *Relativizando: uma introdução à antropologia social*. Rio de Janeiro, Editora Rocco.

De Hass H. (2010). "Migration and development: a theoretical perspective", *International Migration Review*, v. 44, n.1, pp. 1–38.

Fausto B. (1991). *Historiografia da Imigração para São Paulo*. São Paulo, Fapesp.

Feldman-Bianco B. (2014). "La libre circulación de las personas debería ser considerada como una utopía", *Crítica y Emancipación*, v. año VI, n.11, pp. 613–626.

Fernandes F. (1972). *O negro no mundo dos brancos*. São Paulo, Difusão Europeia do Livro.

Furtado C. (2001). *Formação Econômica do Brasil*, 30 Ed. São Paulo, Editora Nacional.

Gaspari E. (2002). *A ditadura envergonhada*. São Paulo, Companhia das Letras.

Handerson J. (2015). "Diáspora. Sentidos sociais e mobilidades haitianas", *Horizontes Antropológicos*, v. 21, n.43, pp. 51–78.

IBGE (Instituto Brasileiro de Geografia e Estatística) (2007). *Brasil, 500 anos de povoamento*. Rio de Janeiro, IBGE.

Iotti L. (2010). "A política migratória brasileira e sua legislação (1822-1914)". X Encontro Nacional de História. Santa Maria: ANPUH-RS, anais.

Koifman F. (2012). *Imigrante Ideal*. O Ministério da Justiça e a Entrada de Estrangeiros no Brasil (1941-1945). São Paulo, Civilização Brasileira.

Lesser J. (2015). *A invenção da brasilidade. Identidade nacional, etnicidade e políticas de imigração*. São Paulo, Editora UNESP.

Levy M. (1974). "O papel da migração internacional na evolução da população brasileira (1872 a 1972)", *Rev. Saúde Pública*, São Paulo, v. 8, pp. 49–90.

Ministério das Relações Exteriores (MRE) (2015). Estimativas populacionais das comunidades brasileiras no mundo. Recuperado de: www.brasileirosnomundo.itamaraty.gov.br/a-comunidade/estimativas-populacio nais-das-comunidades/Estimativas%20RCN%202015%20-%20Atualizado.pdf Accessed 11 October 2017.

Patarra N. (2009). "Governabilidade das migrações internacionais e Direitos Humanos: o Brasil como país de emigração", in Fundação Alexandre de Gusmão (FUNAG) (ed.), *I Conferência sobre as Comunidades Brasileiras no Exterior, Brasileiros no Mundo*. Brasília, Fundação Alexandre de Gusmão (FUNAG), pp. 187–211.

Payne A. and Phillips N. (2012). *Desarrollo*. Madrid, Alianza Editorial.

Prado Júnior C. (1994). *História Econômica do Brasil*, 41 Ed. São Paulo, Brasiliense.

Reis R. (2011). "A política do Brasil para as migrações internacionais", *Contexto Internacional*, v. 33, n. 1, pp. 47–69.

Rist G. (2002). *El desarrollo: historia de una creencia occidental*. Madrid, Catarata.

Scott F. David and Cook-Martin D. (2014). "Brazil. Selling the myth of racial democracy", in Scott F. D. and Cook-Martin D. (eds.), *Culling the masses. The democratic origins of racist immigration policy in the Americas.* Cambridge, MA, Harvard University Press, pp. 259–298.

Seyferth G. (2008). "Imigrantes, estrangeiros: a trajetória de uma categoria incomoda no campo político". Trabalho apresentado na Mesa Redonda Imigrantes e Emigrantes: as transformações das relações do Estado Brasileiro com a Migração. 26ª Reunião Brasileira de Antropologia, realizada entre os dias 01 e 04 de junho de 2008, Porto Seguro, Brasil.

Silva S. (1997). *Costurando sonhos. Trajetória de um grupo de imigrantes bolivianos em São Paulo*. São Paulo, Paulinas.

Vignoli F. (2003). "A imigração e a formação do mercado de trabalho", in Rego J. and Marques R. (eds.), *Formação Econômica do Brasil*. São Paulo, Saraiva, pp. 112–134.

Villarreal M. (2017). "Replanteando el debate sobre migraciones internacionales y desarrollo: nuevas direcciones y evidencias", *Revista Interdisciplinar de Mobilidade Humana (REMHU)*, v. 25, n. 51, pp. 181–198.

_____. (2018). "Regionalismos e Migrações internacionais na América do Sul. Contexto e perspectivas futuras sobre as experiências na CAN, no Mercosul e na Unasul", *Revista Espaço Aberto*, v. 8, n.2, pp. 131–148.

53

MIGRATION AND DEVELOPMENT TRANSITIONS

A perspective from Latin America

Menara Lube Guizardi and Alejandro Grimson

Categories and their fetishism

In this chapter, we trace the political, economic, and social links that migration has had with the concept of development in Latin America from the nineteenth to the twenty-first century. In order to narrate this debate, we have structured our reflections into four sections that cover the changes in the ideological make-up of the relationship between these two terms. These sections cover from 1850 to 1950 ('Fantasies of Progress'), from 1950 to 1985 (The Development Era), from 1985 to 2008 (Globalised and Transnational), and from 2016 onwards (The Adversities of Post-globalisation). In each section we will seek to characterise the socio-political contexts and the more general economic processes that frame migrations in, from, and to Latin America. However, we will focus on the semantic changes that have attributed socially contradictory, heterogeneous, and disputed meanings to the concepts of migration and development.

Certain words have a curious relationship with social contexts. To paraphrase Appadurai's reflection on commodities (1988, 14), some words take on 'a life of their own' when they acquire centrality in the symbolic frames of social meaning shared by a group or society. They become social categories: structural elements that configure the modes of action and the relation of people to the world. The concepts 'migration' and 'development' are two such words of importance in Latin America.

Some social categories have been reified: they are understood as given, immovable, and general. But this appearance of exteriority, immutability, and universalism is a historical way of relating to the categories. Naturalising this perspective constitutes, to paraphrase Marx (1996, 197), a 'fetishism of categories'. To overcome this, we would have to assume that no word – and likewise no social category – is, implicitly, a 'thing'. They are social processes and relations; their meaning is woven by historical formations.

In Latin America, few terms have had a social and political life as troubled as the concept of 'development'. The meanings and realities conceived to be 'represented' by the term varied from country to country and in different contexts within the countries (see Cardoso and Faletto 1971). Thus, the uses of development impacted on Latin American micro-relational dynamics and local spaces in a forceful and transversal manner, but always with great heterogeneity. In many places of the region, the term meant, adversely, a desired horizon and a terrible ghost presiding from the shadows over the construction of an unequal future (Quijano 2000, 73).

At the same time, the Latin American state and academic discourses on development have evolved from strongly economic representations (from the mid-twentieth century), to more critical views that situate the problem in the political, social, and cultural fields (from 1970 onwards) (Quijano 2000, 73). In addition, the word has been used as a slogan for a variety of political campaigns, whilst on other occasions it has been targeted for attack by a diverse spectrum of political forces. Therefore, although it is possible to trace permanent and common features in those meanings attributed to development in various Latin American countries, we also observe the non-stop historic transformation of the category (Rist 2008, 25), that has connected it with the macro-global processes of capitalism ever since their emergence (Wallerstein 1996, 195–207).[1]

There is then, a historical link in the complex relationship between the accepted versions – internationally hegemonic – of development, and those that have been contextualised in Latin America. This connection refers to colonisation: the understanding of development as the structural axis of a modernising process, a teleology of the expansion of political dominance from the 'great powers' first European and later from the Global North more generally (Rist 2008, 47). This criticism can be found in authors such as Wallerstein but its most forceful enunciation is found precisely amongst Latin American thinkers such as Escobar (1999) or Dussel (1994). According to the latter, the notion of 'development' should be traced from the mythology of emancipation, which permeates Latin American thinking from European colonialism to philosophical modernity. This emancipation is tacitly ethnocentric: it engenders a symbolic geography according to which Europe constitutes an epistemic centre from where a supposed moral superiority flows towards the peripheries.

For this reason, Escobar (1999) argued that we should abandon an anthropology *given to* development: that considers it as an obvious and undeniable objective. Instead, we should construct an anthropology that takes development as an object of research; taking into consideration those projects and strategies in dispute (Lins Ribeiro 2007). Our debate is aimed at these reflections in the sections that follow.

Fantasies of Progress (1950 to 1985)

At the end of the nineteenth century, the Eurocentric conceptions of progress came together in the idea of social evolution, setting out a racist correlation between the supposed 'development stages' of a society and the biological characteristics of its members (Rist 2008, 40–1). August Comte's pseudoscientific arguments of positivism are cloaked by the unquestioned legitimacy of the scientific field. But they also became a political *leitmotif*, especially in the institutionalisation of nation-states in Latin America after Independence (at the beginning of the nineteenth century).

Even though colonialism incubated many of the social categories that allowed the emergence of the development concept, before 1948 this term had not appeared as a slogan attached to capitalist geopolitics (Rist 2008, 47). What we do find alive and well from the mid-nineteenth century is a set of conceptions that make up its semantic predecessor: the conceptions of progress linked to the social physiology of positivism. For example, concepts such as 'civilisation' (predominant until World War I), 'Westernisation' and 'modernisation' constitute precedents matched with 'development' (Rist 2008, 25). Out of all these precedents, perhaps the one that has impacted most strongly on Latin America's political imaginaries is the word 'progress'. These concepts gave birth to the social perception of migration in Europe and the Americas.

Between the eighteenth and the nineteenth centuries, the Industrial Revolution in Northern Europe caused social transformations of transcendental impact (ideological, political, and economic). During the nineteenth century, European rural and urban areas underwent a complete change: the population moved suddenly to the cities (Bairoch and Goertz 1986, 288). Industrialisation was therefore linked to urbanisation and the rural exodus. The conceptions of progress were associated with the imperative to promote these three phenomena. During the second half of the nineteenth century and almost the entire twentieth, it was assumed that rural–urban migration was a synonym of progress, a view strongly criticised by those who denounced the social, economic, and political impacts of the rural exodus (Engels 1993, 106–44). But these European migration patterns were internationalised quickly, linking the continent to other places around the world. From 1824 to 1924, 52 million Europeans, who came from rural and urban areas, migrated to cities in the Americas, Australia, and New Zealand (Moch 1996, 124). Until 1964, Europe was the principal origin of the international migrant population (Sutcliffe 1998, 64).[2]

The main poles of attraction for this world migration were the United States, Argentina, Brazil, and Canada (Moch 1996). The demographic impact of the phenomenon was considerable in certain Latin American countries: between the years of 1856 and 1932 Argentina received 6.4 million migrants. 4.4 million arrived in Brazil between 1821 and 1932. Uruguay saw some 713,000 migrants arrive from 1911 to 1932; Mexico received 226,000 between 1911 and 1932, and Cuba 857,000 from 1901 to 1932 (Margulis 1977, 283).

At this stage, there were at least three central political-ideological aspects as far as the formation of the interconnection of the notions of progress and migration is concerned:

i. These transatlantic processes formed part of the invention of the very concept of 'international migration'. We are referring to a period immediately after the formation of the European nation-states (at the end of the eighteenth century). We cannot talk of international migration with today's meaning to refer to anything before the emergence of the nation-states.

ii. The idea that migration was necessary for modernisation and progress, and therefore a desired and positive phenomenon, becomes hegemonic. However, this imaginary had nuances on both sides of the Atlantic. In Europe, international migration was seen as an optimal solution to overpopulation, which, as it was understood, was threatening the accumulation of capital. And so, the exportation of the European population started the internationalisation of both the industrial reserve army of labour and industrial capital (Margulis 1977, 274)

iii. The belief in the benefits of progress was questioned in Latin America by a political imperative related to the construction of the nation-states: the control of new migrant populations to mould the countries' human contingent according to the elite's racist ideals and hegemonic progress.

Latin America's role in the Industrial Revolution was as a consumer of European industrial products: as an agricultural region and an exporter of raw materials (Ribeiro 1977, 11). This led to Latin America being labelled 'backward' in relation to the global axes of industrialisation in the North Atlantic. In Latin America, in general, the predominance of conceptions derived from social evolutionism was matched by a racist vision of European migration as a mechanism of promoting the 'evolution' of the nations. Several countries (Argentina, Brazil, Chile, Venezuela, Uruguay, and Mexico) adopted policies to encourage this migration hoping to 'whiten' their population (Margulis 1977, 289; Scott and Cook-Martín 2014, 16). This was supposed to be the quickest way to tame the three workhorses of progress: urbanisation, industrialisation, and modernisation (Cardoso and Faletto 1971, 44–5; Kearney 1986, 333; Ribeiro 1977, 475–6).

This situation would change in the first half of the twentieth century. Latin America continued to receive Europeans until the end of World War II, but in more modest proportions than at the beginning of the century. The term 'development' began to engender a transversal and international political discourse, stemming precisely from the imperialistic geopolitics that the United States deployed towards Latin America (in 1949).[3] Its conformation as a social category was still incipient, but the uses of the term began to displace the notion of progress, encompassing and substituting it. The link between progress, development, and international migration became evident in political discourses.

Between 1930 and 1950, migration policies continued to see the migrant presence as positive; only now, they supported them by putting a positive spin on the idea of mixing races. Examples of this include the melting-pot ideology in the United States, and the mestizo identity ideology in Brazil and Mexico. On the other hand, migration policies linked to the melting-pot and the notion of mixed races were also engendered from a homogenising sense, given they accepted the intrinsic cultural diverse constitution of the nation-state, but assumed that it led to a hegemonic pattern, a form of 'the social being' ideologically defined as the majority and priority. This implied a violent adaptation for the different groups making up the countries to comply with this new fiction of hegemonic diversity and so reproduce an assimilationist (and racist) sense of integration (López-Sala 2005). Indeed authors such as Glazer and Moyniham (1963) and Brubaker (2001) affirm that the melting-pot, never actually took place.

The Development Era: displace, urbanise, and modernise (1950–85)

After World War II, the start of the Cold War helped denote a difference in meanings attributed to migration and development in the framework of these regimes. In both terms, the conception that international migration and rural exodus were fundamental in the development of nations was deepened. But there was an important difference between the two blocks: internal and international migratory freedom became a distinctive feature of the capitalist world, in complete contrast to the policy of controlling the displaced in communist countries. In the latter, population movements in general, but especially those towards the industrial cities or military strategic points, were subject to state control. They were decided in the framework of the economy's general plan, to 'favour' the productive force's development and they were regulated by restrictive measures (internal and international) (Gang and Stuart 1999).

In this period, given the productive reorganisation undertaken by several countries to overcome the 1929 crisis, many Latin American states started an industrialisation process by substituting imports (Cardoso and Faletto 1971, 3–4). In parallel, a new geopolitical grammar was proposed by the rich capitalist countries dividing the planet into three spheres. The *First World*, comprised of the (self-proclaimed) 'developed' capitalist countries; the *Second World*, made up of socialist and communist countries and the *Third World*, a classification given by the capitalist countries to those others where development seemed like a chimaera (more or less distant, depending on the case). The whole of Latin America was placed in this third block. This division's semantic cut was doubly governed by the difference in political regimes and by the structuring notion that the concept development takes on in the capitalist world as a 'water divider'. Thus, the Third World becomes an ideological battlefield for the great powers, inciting a protectionist policy that would impact enormously on migration (Rist 2008, 80–1).

The concept of development, greatly influenced by the spirit President Truman gave it during Cold War geopolitics, continued to be juxtaposed to industrialisation and modernisation. But, in line with the colonialism that imbued conceptions of modernity, it was assumed that all that belonged to the Indigenous Latin Americans and those from the African diaspora was the opposite of modern (Quijano 2000). In different countries of the region, development consolidated itself as the goal of economic and political action that would give continuity to the colonialist ethos. It was not long before critical Latin American voices were raised, many of them articulated through 'Dependency Theory' – and which denounced the falsehoods reproduced by developmental 'imperatives' (Ribeiro 1977).

Development and migration continued to be semantically connected as social categories in Latin America during this period. But state political action focused on encouraging the rural exodus (Kearney 1986). In the second half of the twentieth century, Latin America had the world's greatest rural–urban migration. Between 1950 and 1990, the region changed from being predominately rural, with only 42 per cent of its population in urban areas (Da Cunha 2002, 21), to 80 per cent of its population in cities, consolidating its ranking as the second most urbanised area in today's world, below North America with 82 per cent, but above Europe with 73 per cent (UN 2015, 1–7). In Brazil, this rural–urban migration involved some 54 million people between 1950 and 1995 (Caramano and Abramovay 1999, 3). In Mexico, the rural population accounted for 68 per cent of its total inhabitants in 1920. By the end of the twentieth century, this had dropped to less than 25 per cent (Carton de Grammont 2009, 17). In Peru, the urban population grew from 35 per cent to 70 per cent, between 1950 and 2000 (Da Cunha 2002, 24). From 1940 to 1981, the population of Lima, Peru's capital, went from 645,000 people to 4.6 million (Golte and Adams 1990, 38). Argentina had an urban rate of 62 per cent in 1947, whilst by 2000 this had reached 89.9 per cent. In contradiction, the over-crowding of the population in the cities' poor sectors – shanty towns known locally as *barriadas, campamentos, favelas, or villas miserias* depending on the country, was progressively shaped as a structural problem for development in Latin American countries.

Whilst Latin America stayed focused on mobilising the rural–urban migration, new connections between development and migration emerged in the Global North at the end of the twentieth century. These would have a surprising impact on Latin Americans (especially those who migrated to the North). At the end of World War II, the concept of Universal Human Rights emerged. However, only leaving or entering your own country was considered a right; the right to enter another country was excluded (López-Sala 2005, 17). After 1947, Europe required labour for its reconstruction and so needed to import migrant workers (Sutcliffe 1998). For the first time, European countries implemented state policies to attract migration. This marked a new tendency in international migration (Arango 2005, 23).

In North America, both Canada and the United States implemented immigration policies that largely excluded non-Europeans until 1960s. But from this decade onwards, Europe and North America became poles of attraction for Latin American migration, yet the countries were caught in a contradictory scenario: they needed migrant labourers, but refused to treat them from a human rights perspective (Sutcliffe 1998, 64). In parallel extra-continental migration to Latin American countries declined dramatically, whilst there was a clear increase in international movement between the region's countries (Villa and Martínez 2001, 3). From the 1970s onwards, migratory policies in the capitalist world began to develop in an increasingly contradictory manner: controls became more restrictive, whilst at the same time there was an effort to find ways to promote 'integration' of those migrants already living in the destination countries of the North (Arango 2005, 18). Here another shift in meaning took place: it was assumed that developed countries were going through the height of a 'migratory invasion'. It was in the midst of this semantic transformation that globalisation began, and a new meaning was given to the world's movements.

Globalised and Transnational (1985–2008)

The tendency of Latin American people to flow to the Global North en masse began at the end of the 1970s with the oil crisis of 1973 stimulating significant migratory processes. However, it was the 1980s, often referred to as Latin America's 'lost decade' (CEPAL 2006, 91), that were marked by major regional economic chaos. Neoliberal reforms applied decisively in different countries aggravated and spread poverty, widened the social gaps, progressively dismantled the industrial sectors and re-established the importation of goods. All the above together proved to be a big 'push' factor in international migration from Latin America to the Global North.

It is important to draw attention to the gender dimension of the phenomenon. With working conditions becoming precarious, the figure of the 'male breadwinner' so characteristic of patriarchal patterns, was questioned. In an increasing number of homes in the poorest and middle social classes, the male figure left and women took on the productive and reproductive roles alone. However, between 1990 and 2000, international migration in the region was feminised, demographically expressed as women having faced up to the consequences of neoliberal policies (Martínez 2003).

With these precedents, Latin America entered into the third of its migratory processes. It can be said that globalisation took place from the mid-1980s until the beginning of the twenty-first century, a period during which the Cold War tensions began taking on a different shape. The fall of the Berlin Wall was perhaps a symbol that marked this process. It implied, on the one hand, a transformation of the grammar of international geopolitics. That is, the countries of the then First World led a crucial reform to the way the world's countries were divided. From the Cold War formula of 'three worlds' (First, Second, and Third), the international geopolitics advanced towards another triad – 'developed', 'underdeveloped', and 'developing' worlds – which was later substituted by the binarism 'developed' versus 'underdeveloped/developing'.

On the other hand, this phase can be considered a 'rollercoaster' in political conceptions related to migration. Firstly, the announced discourse of 'a world without walls', 'no borders' was celebrated from the capitalist powers as part of the process of the hegemony of the capitalist regime (Kymlicka 1995, 9). It was also one of the symbolic articulating axes of neoliberalism in its defence of the 'creative destruction' of the regulatory capacity of the nation-state (Harvey 2008).

The 'freedom of movement euphoria' was short-lived: it soon gave way to a process of closing borders, which was even more clearly defined by the end of the twenty-first century's first decade. The idea that we lived in a world of movement, migration, and border crossings, as seen during the transition at the end of the Cold War, was substituted by a discourse from the Global North warning about the dangers of receiving migration from the South. And so began to grow a negative perception towards the presence of Latin Americans, Africans and Asians in the developed world's backyard.

In Latin America, the effects globalisation had on the formation of migratory processes and the notions of development continued to be felt in an expansive way at least until the most recent important economic crisis affecting the Global North (from 2008 onwards). In the year 2000, immigrants accounted for 1 per cent of the Latin American population, whilst emigrants made up 4 per cent. Ten per cent of the world's migrants left from the region (Martínez 2003, 21). No less than 75 per cent of this migration (20.5 million people) ended up in the United States (2003, 27), whilst 2.8 million Latin Americans lived in other parts of the globe (concentrated especially in Spain, Canada, the United Kingdom, and Japan) (2003, 33).

> And even though geographically speaking the destinations of emigrants have ampli-fied and diversified – to not only the United States, but also Europe, Canada, Japan, Australia, and Israel – Argentina, Costa Rica, and Venezuela have continued to be traditional destinations within Latin America and the Caribbean, whilst others have become countries of origin, transit and destination all at the same time.
>
> *(Martínez 2009, 2)*

On this globalised stage, migration and development in Latin America were viewed from a transnational perspective, which was intrinsically contradictory. The supposed opportunity represented by remittances (social, economic, cultural, and symbolic) sent by migrants was deeply appreciated. But, on the other hand, the loss of human capital through this context of emigration was seen to diminish the innovative capacity of the countries of origin (Del-gado Wise and Márquez 2005, 13) even if this interpretation requires critical assessment . The emigration during this period was accompanied by a general weakening of migrant rights. At the same time, a complex situation of remittance dependency arose: for many of the region's countries they made up one of the main components of the gross national prod-uct and they surpassed 'the aid developed countries give to developing countries' (Martínez 2003, 7).

For the first few years of the twenty-first century, the increase in the prices of exported products implied a significant rise in the GNP of Latin American countries. Different states, in line with their policies, appropriated and controlled these new incomes, redistributing them (albeit to different extents) (Arnold and Jalles 2014, 8–9). This created new political configurations, which many associated with the terms 'populism' or 'swing to the left' or 'consensus of the commodities'. This period was characterised by poor populations rising to enter the middle class. However, some years later, the exchange rates began to decline again and the price of these products began to fall. These processes created a crisis situation linked specifically to the emerging popular sectors (the segments of the population that overcame the situation of poverty during the redistributive years, situating themselves in sectors of medium or low average economic stratification.), and which has become a determining factor in the new international migration in the region at present.

The adversities of post-globalisation (from 2016 onwards)

The fourth stage, which we can call 'post-globalisation', began to take shape in the previous period, but it came into full force from 2016 onwards. This implied an important step back-wards in the constitution of global semantics regarding social and human rights. The grow-ing trend in border controls (and the return of isolationist conceptions, which aims to mark the division of countries through building walls) has been accompanied by the employment of arms to control population movements towards the Global North. Migrants coming from the capitalist periphery are criminalised, with more and more deaths and persecutions.

The globalised and globalising victory of neoliberalism, with its rapid capacity to destroy or absorb alternative models, seems to push ever more crude mechanisms that reproduce inequalities. This intensifies the generalisation of forms of action that are protected by a radical realism that removes any humanising mediation of economic processes.

As a result, the concept of development took on a profoundly segregationist spirit. Huntington's idea (1997) that contact between the supposed developed countries and those developing and poor countries through the migration of populations from the latter to the former, gained strength. The migration led to an insoluble clash between 'cultural groups' (Huntington used the term 'civilisations') which are incapable of integrating. Developed countries seek to prohibit, tacitly control, or 'manage' migration, as a way to limit the 'contact' with the 'other' Backed up by segregationalist and isolationist notions according to which 'efforts to shift societies from one civilization to another are unsuccessful; and countries group themselves around the lead or core States of their civilization' (Huntington 1997, 20). Such arguments radicalise xenophobia with worrying speeches about the 'preservation of culture' in these same dominant countries. The Latin American states receiving international migration follow this tendency.

In this context, the focus on human rights, (that had had some transcendence during the 1990s) rapidly lost ground as a paradigm guiding migratory policies in Europe, North America, and Latin America. The subordinate place that Latin America now occupies in relation to decision making regarding globally implemented policies is leading to the application and reproduction of these international tendencies, which have little if anything to offer the region's countries. With almost no influence on the decisions that the destination countries of Europe and North America make, many Latin American countries end up adopting these same political trends. Indeed, the return to conservative, exclusionary, and assimilationist conceptions regarding migration comes at a time when it has not even been possible to establish the minimum rights reached by previous migratory policies in most of Latin America.

In the framework of this debate, it is fundamental to again pick up the critical efforts made by Indigenous and African descendent movements, in order to learn from their long history of struggle against political hegemony from key Latin American contexts. We need to be prepared in Latin America for this dehumanising process of migratory policies and borders. And the first thing we should do in this scenario is to recognise that this inhuman radicalisation of migrant rights is geared towards, yet again, a development logic that does not favour populations or countries from the Global South.

Notes

1 Rist (2008) argues that there is a shared global semantic on the term that places it in a general and depoliticised way, as a process of increasing economic goods, improving living conditions, and also as a synonym of any historical process (2008, 25). This semantic is articulated through four idea-forces. *Directionality*: development has a specific direction and a purpose. *Continuity*: occurs in a persistently temporarily form. *Cumulativeness*: made up of a progressive and successive growth. *Irreversibility*: it is not possible to go back (2008, 27).

2 The period is also marked by the incentive, in European nations, of migration to less populated and bordering territories as a way to ensure the territorial conformation of the nation-states, which gradually links the notions of frontier and sovereignty to State planning of migration policies (Hobsbawm 2012).

3 Rist (2008) frames the 'ideological premiere' of the term in the American President Truman's speech in 1949.

References

Appadurai, A. (1988) "Introduction. Commodities and the politics of value", in Appadurai A. ed., *The social life of things: Commodities in cultural perspective*, Cambridge University Press, Cambridge, 3–63.

Arango, J. (2005) "Dificultadesy dilemas de la política de inmigración", *Arbor 181*(713), 17–25.

Arnold, J. and Jalles, J. (2014) *Dividing the pie in Brazil: income distribution, social policies and the new middle class*, OCDE, Paris.

Bairoch, P. and Goertz, G. (1986) "Factors of urbanisation in the nineteenth century developed countries. A descriptive and econometric analysis", *Urban Studies 23*(4), 285–305.

Brubaker, R. (2001) "The return of assimilation? Changing perspectives on immigration and its sequels in France, Germany, and the United States", *Ethnic and Racial Studies 24*(4), 531–548.

Caramano, A.A. and Abramovay, R. (1999) *Éxodo Rural, envelhecimento e masculinização no Brasil: Panorama dos últimos 50 anos*, IPEA, Rio de Janeiro.

Cardoso, F.H. and Faletto, E. (1971) *Dependencia y desarrollo en América Latina: ensayo de interpretación sociológica*, Siglo XXI, México, DF.

Carton de Grammont, H. (2009) "La desagrarización del campo mexicano", *Convergencia 16*(50), 13–55.

CEPAL (2006) *Migración internacional, derechos humanos y desarrollo en América Latina y el Caribe: síntesis y conclusiones*, CEPAL, Santiago.

Da Cunha, J.M.P. (2002) *Urbanización, redistribución espacial de la población y transformaciones socioeconómicas en América Latina*, CEPAL, Santiago.

Delgado Wise, R. and Márquez, H. (2005) "Migración, políticas públicas y desarrollo: reflexiones en torno al caso de México", *Red Internacional de Migración y Desarrollo 5*(2), 7–9.

Dussel, E. (1994) *El encubrimiento del otro: hacia el origen del mito de la modernidad*, AbyaYala, La Paz.

Engels, F. (1993) *The condition of the working class in England*, Oxford University Press, Oxford.

Escobar, A. (1999) "Antropología y desarrollo", in Escobar, A. ed., *Cultura, ambiente y política en la antropología contemporánea*, INAH, Bogotá, 43–57.

Fitzgerald, D. and Cook-Martin, D. (2014) *Culling the masses: The democratic origins of racist immigration policy in the Americas*, Harvard University Press, Cambridge, MA.

Gang, I. and Stuart, R. (1999) "Mobility where mobility is illegal: Internal migration and city growth in the Soviet Union", *Journal of Population Economics 12*(1), 117–134.

Glazer, N. and Moyniham, D. (1963) *Beyond the melting pot: The Negroes, Puerto Ricans, Jews, Italians, and Irish of New York City*, MIT Press, Cambridge, MA.

Golte, J. and Adams, N. (1990) *Los caballos de Troya de los invasores. Estrategias campesinas en la conquista de la Gran Lima*, Instituto de Estudios Peruanos, Lima.

Harvey, D. (2008) "El neoliberalismo como destrucción creativa", *Revista Apuntes 27*(45), 1–24.

Hobsbawm, E.J. (2012) *Nations and nationalism since 1780: Programme, myth, reality*, Cambridge University Press, Cambridge.

Huntington, S.P. (1997) *The clash of civilizations and the remaking of world order*, Penguin, New York.

Kearney, M. (1986) "From the invisible hand to visible feet: Anthropological studies of migration and development", *Annual Review of Anthropology 15*, 331–361.

Kymlicka, W. (1995) *Multicultural citizenship. A liberal theory of minority rights*, University of Oxford Press, Oxford.

Lins Ribeiro, G. (2007) "Poder, redes e ideología en el campo del desarrollo", *Tabula Rasa 6*, 173–193.

López-Sala, A.M. (2005) *Inmigrantes y Estados: la respuesta política ante la cuestión migratoria*, Anthropos, Barcelona.

Margulis, M. (1977) "Inmigración y desarrollo capitalista. La migración europea a la Argentina", *Demografía y economía 11*(3), 273–306.

Martínez, J. (2003) *El mapa migratorio de América Latina y el Caribe, las mujeres y el género*, CEPAL, Santiago.

———— (2009) *Notas sobre las características de la fuerza laboral migrante en las Américas*, CEPAL, Santiago.

Marx, K. (1996) *O Capital. Crítica da economia política*, Editora Nova Cultural, São Paulo.

Moch, L.P. (1996) "The European perspective: Changing conditions and multiple migrations, 1790–1914", in Hoerder, D. and Moch, L.P. eds., *European migrations. Global and local perspectives*, Northeastern University Press, Boston, MA, 115–140.

Quijano, A. (2000) "El fantasma del desarrollo en América Latina", *Revista Venezolana de Economía y Ciencias Sociales 6*(2), 73–90.

Ribeiro, D. (1977) *Las Américas y la civilización. Procesos de formación y causas del desarrollo desigual de los pueblos latinoamericanos*, Extemporáneos, México, DF.

Rist, G. (2008) *The history of development: From western origins to global faith*, Zed Books, New York.

Sutcliffe, B. (1998) *Nacido en otra parte. Un ensayo sobre la migración internacional, el desarrollo y la equidad*, Hegoa, Bilbao.

United Nations [UN] (2015) *World urbanization prospects*, United Nations, New York.

Villa, M. and Martínez, J. (2001) *El mapa migratorio internacional de América Latina y el Caribe: patrones, perfiles, repercusiones e incertidumbres*, CEPAL, Santiago.

Wallerstein, I. (1996) "La re-estructuración capitalista y el sistema-mundo", *Anuario Mariateguiano 8*, 195–207.

54

MIGRATION AND THE DEVELOPMENT OF THE RUSSIAN STATE

Three centuries of migration management[1]

Olga R. Gulina

Introduction

During the last three centuries, Russia has seen a succession of turbulent changes during the epochs of Tsarist, Soviet, and post-Soviet Russia, when the management of the mobility of both local populations and newcomers perfectly reflected Churchill's words on Russia in general as 'a riddle, wrapped in a mystery, inside an enigma'. Migration management in Russia during the nineteenth and twentieth centuries was mainly subordinated to the interests of the Russian state, and very indirectly to the needs and interests of its inhabitants. A number of reforms and policies mark turning points in Russian history in which human migrations can be understood as a reflection of the disasters and changes that took place in the country. These included: Catherine II's manifesto of the late eighteenth century, the Stolypin reforms of the first half of the twentieth century, the February and October Revolutions of 1917, the civil war of 1918–22, the demographic losses of the Soviet people in World War II, the forced relocation of Germans from the Volga region, Crimean Tatars, Chechens and Ingush, the collapse of the USSR, and the mass movement of people in the post-Soviet space.

Historically, at all stages of the development of Russian statehood, the mobility of the Russian and foreign population aimed to reflect the interests of the state. The settlement or the conquest of new lands, for example, raised concern and was subject to restrictive control from state representatives. This article is thematically divided into three historical sections: regulation of population mobility in Tsarist Russia (1649–1917); migration management in the USSR (1917–91); and migration management in modern Russia (1991 to the present). These sections are designed to give the reader an understanding of the evolution of the right to freedom of movement and its legal application in Russia.

Regulation of population mobility in Tsarist Russia

Attempts to establish legislative control over the movement of the population were already made in Tsarist Russia of the seventeenth century. In 1649, Tsar Aleksei Mikhailovich fixed an obligation to have a travel permit for every person of the Grand duchy of Moscow departing abroad (Sobornoye Ulozhenie 1649, 8). By the eighteenth century, the movement of local and foreign populations were subject to detailed and comprehensive regulation particularly through the decree of Peter the Great of 30 October 1719, which laid the foundation for the Russian passport system and required:

> that none of the travellers or walkers moving from one city to another, from one village to another, not provided with a letter [of passage], would be permitted to travel or walk, and everyone would be provided with a passport or a laissez-passer issued by their superiors.

The decree, in its original intention, was aimed at preventing recruits leaving the army and navy, but very soon became the basis for limiting the mobility of serfs (peasants). Peter's further Decree of 26 June 1724 established the obligation to 'catch ... and punish [runaway peasants]'. In 1725, Catherine I made the first attempt to introduce a printed form of passport but never managed to cover the population of the whole country due to the high printing cost and the complexity of their production (Baiburin 2017, 45–54). The legal and bureaucratic framework for the certification and identification of residents of the Russian Empire was finalised in Russia only at the beginning of the World War I.

In contrast, measures were also taken to promote migration. in December 1792 Catherine II published the manifesto 'On allowing foreigners, except Jews, to leave and settle in Russia and about the free return to their homeland of Russian people who fled abroad' in order to stimulate internal and external migration in the Russian Empire. The main objective was to increase the population in the Urals, Siberia, and other sparsely populated regions of the country by attracting foreigners as well as to grant amnesty to the subjects of the Empire who left their homeland illegally or without permission.

In order to cover the largest number of Russian nationals hiding abroad and to motivate them to return to the country, the text of the manifesto was printed in Russian, German, French, English, Polish, Czech, and Arabic (Auman and Chebotareva 1993). The tensions between restricting the movement of domestic populations but facilitating the in-movement of foreigners and returnees gave rise to Catherine's dilemma (Sunderland 2014). On the one hand she had begun the promotion of the mobility of Russian and foreign populations in order to consolidate and expand the Empire. However, on the other, attempts to promote mobility would undermine the stability on which the state was predicated: the immobility of the agricultural producers. Hence their movement had to be restricted. 'Before serfdom set in, you were free to move. After serfdom was established, the Tsar was free to move you' (Sunderland 2014, 69)

Thus, the provisions of the manifesto of 1792 on the return to their homeland concerned subjects belonging to all the peoples and ethnic groups living on the territory of the Russian Empire, except for Jews. The restriction of the rights of members of the Jewish community is a special chapter in Russian history. In April 1727, for example, Catherine I had issued a decree 'On the expulsion of Jews from Russia and making sure that they will not take abroad gold and silver Russian coins', which read 'Jews, both males and females, settled in Ukraine and in other Russian towns, ... have to be all immediately sent out of Russian borders, and henceforth ... not let back in Russia'.

In 1742, Empress Elisabeth, the daughter of Catherine I, issued a decree on expelling Jews and members of their families from the territory of the entire Russian Empire, regardless of rank and type of occupation except for those who were ready to convert to the Christian faith. A Pale of Settlement was also established where Jews were allowed to live: a territory of about 1200 thousand km^2 in Lithuania, Belarus, Poland, and certain parts of today's Ukraine. Restrictions on living outside this Pale of Settlement were only lifted in the second half of the nineteenth century for Jews with higher education, doctors, craftsmen, retired military recruits, merchants of the first guild (league) whose income exceeded 50,000 roubles, as well as members of their families and their fellow believer servants (Klier 1995, 14–5).

The regulations for the procedure of obtaining a residence permit were established in 1894 and the Statute on Passports was adopted in 1903. Restrictions were imposed on the freedom of movement for certain categories of the population, such as street hawkers, gypsies, cripples, and beggars (Rogovin 1913, 36–7). The passport was issued to males at 18 years of age and to females on permission of their father or husband at the age of 21. The provisions of these documents remained almost unchanged until the October Revolution of 1917. Baiburin (2009) notes that, depending on the certifying and identifying documents, the entire population of the Russian Empire can be conditionally divided into two categories. One category of document holders consisted of people belonging to the tax-paying classes, such as petty bourgeois, artisans, and rural inhabitants. They were holders of one of the following three documents:

1. The passport booklet, which was issued for 5 years, provided that there were no arrears in the subject's fees and charges payments. The police had the right to take away passports from those subjects of the Empire who did not pay the established tax amounts on time, thereby limiting the freedom of their movement;
2. Passports issued for up to 1 year, irrespective of arrears and the consent of others;
3. Absence permits. These documents were issued free of charge for up to 1 year to victims displaced by crop failures, fire, or floods.

The second privileged group of residents of the Russian Empire were owners of perpetual passport booklets, such as noblemen, officers, merchants, and honorary citizens (Baiburin 2009). Honorary citizens of the Russian Empire were a special group of the population of the Empire. In Tsarist Russia, honorary citizenship was introduced by the manifesto of Nicholas I and was granted only to the citizens of the Empire who brought exceptional and incomparable benefits to the Russian Empire. For example, honorary citizenship of the city of Moscow was granted to Nikolay Pirogov for his work in the field of science and meritorious civilian service, and to philanthropist, collector, and entrepreneur Pavel Tretyakov for generosity and cultural dissemination. Honorary citizenship of the city of St. Petersburg was given to the geographer, ethnographer and traveller Nikolai Przhevalsky for establishing sympathy and respect (for Russia) among the Central Asian peoples. In pre-revolutionary Russia, honorary citizenship implied exemption from corporal punishment, recruitment into the army, the disciplinary procedures of the tax authorities and guaranteed a number of other privileges.

Those privileges and the honorary citizenship itself were abolished by new the Soviet leadership in 1917, although the collapse of the Soviet Union gave re-birth to the idea of the honorary citizenship for 'those who provided the outstanding services to the Russian Federation or the international community' among Russia's law makers. Today, the honorary citizenship of the Russian Federation is granted by Russia's Presidential Decree to the Russian and foreign citizens, who brought exceptional and incomparable services to the Russian Federation.

At the end of the nineteenth century and the beginning of the twentieth century, Russia was at the epicentre of external and internal migrations. The main directions for internal migration between 1897 and 1916 were Siberia and the Far East with 2.5 million new arrivals, Kazakhstan and Central Asia with 1.4 million new migrants, and the Caucasus with 0.9 million migrants (Kabuzan 2012). In terms of international migrations, more than 40 thousand crossings of the borders of the Russian Empire were registered by both Russian citizens and foreigners in 1850, which had risen to more than 4 million border crossings by 1900 and over 10 million border crossings by 1909 (Lohr 2012, Tables 1, 3–7).

Emigration was also very significant. Between 1901 and 1910 the number of emigrants from the Russian Empire to the countries of the New World reached 1.8 million, and 1.1 million between 1911 and 1915. The ethnic background of the emigrants from the Russian Empire at the end of the nineteenth century and the beginning of the twentieth century was mainly of Jewish, Polish, Finnish, German, or Lithuanian origin. Between 1871 to 1920 almost 1.5 million Jews; 0.9 million Poles; about 200,000 Finns; 150,000 Germans; and about 210,000 other subjects of the Russian Empire of Russian, Ukrainian, and Belarusian origin left Russia for the United States (Kabuzan 1998).

The October Revolution of 1917 put an end to the history of the Russian Empire and gave rise to the 70-year period of the USSR. By this time, Russia was already a country with a well-formed system of bureaucratic control over the mobility of local population and newcomers. This system of migration control was based on class division, differentiated rules of freedom of movement, and types of residence permits, depending on the gender, religion, (ethnic) origin, and occupation of the individual.

Migration management in Soviet Russia

The abdication of Emperor Nicholas II from the throne and the coming to power of the Bolsheviks in 1917 plunged the country into the whirlwind of fundamental changes that transformed the socio-economic structure of Russian society, its political regime, and its legal foundations. The task of migration management in Soviet Russia was not to ensure the mobility of the population, but the redistribution of labour resources in the interests of the state (Zayonchkovskaya 1999, 22–3; Light 2016, 21; Chudinovskikh and Denisenko 2017).

Migration management during the Soviet era consisted of three key elements: a virtual ban on emigration by Soviet citizens and severe limitation on their foreign travel, a rejection of large-scale immigration, and the subordination of internal migration to the state's imperatives (Light 2016, 21).

Such state policy yielded results very quickly. The mobility of the Russian population in the twentieth century increased markedly. In 1897 the vast majority, some 85.2 per cent of the subjects of the Russian Empire, still lived where they were born, and only one in seven had ever moved. The policy of the Soviet state, aimed at urbanisation and industrialisation, disrupted the traditional settled way of life of the population and promoted their mobility in all directions and, by 1989, some 44 per cent of the population of the USSR did not live where they had been born (Zayonchkovskaya 2000, 3–4). During the years of Soviet power, active development of the Urals, Siberia, and the Far East was underway: by 1959, 21.3 per cent of Soviet citizens lived in the towns of these regions, compared with 12.8 per cent in 1926 (Zayonchkovskaya 1999, 22–3).

The 'dark' pages of the migration history of the USSR included the expulsion of unwanted groups of the population – wealthy peasants [kulaks], church leaders, church-goers, intellectuals, the Russian nobility, the Volga Germans, Chechens, Crimean Tatars, and other ethnic groups (Polyan 2004, 201–10, 312–3), as well as the withdrawal of passports and the refusal to register certain groups of the population such as former prisoners, rural inhabitants, and collective farmers [*kolkhozniki*]. The Soviet Constitution of 1924, 1936, and 1977 did not contain any guarantees of the right to freedom of movement. Therefore, the idea and the right to free movement were poorly applied to the above groups in the population. The right to free movement within Soviet Russia generally depended on social status. The right to leave a country freely was an exceptional privilege for a small number of Soviet citizens.

In order to prevent the free movement of collective farmers in the USSR, state bodies issued passports only to residents of towns. Collective farmers, known as *kolkhozniki*, gained the right to obtain passports in the 1970s. From 1932 to 1977, they were entitled to a passport, but they were not allowed to leave the collective farm without the consent of all members of the collective farm and freely choose where to live (Decree 1934, No. 2139). According to the *Instruction on the issuance and registration of passports in cities Moscow, Leningrad, Kharkov*:

> the right to obtain passports was not granted to other groups of the population, such as: persons who are not factory workers and/or employees of state's institutions (except for pensioners and invalids); kulaks and dekulakized, even if they worked in enterprises and/or served in institutions; servants of religious institutions; persons deprived of their voting rights; persons who have served a sentence, as well as members of their families and persons who are dependent on them

In addition, in many large cities, such as Moscow and St. Petersburg, elderly parents who lived in other cities or villages could not move in with their adult children and register there, except for those who did not have other children, with whom they could live together. As Baiburin notes, the Soviet passport system for some Soviet citizens was 'a privilege, and for others – a source of information about their social inferiority' (Baiburin 2017, 188). All such measures restricting the freedom of movement of citizens of the USSR were, as a rule, regulated by administrative measures and were not subject to official publication.

External migration was also in the spotlight of the Soviet legislator. During the Soviet period, travelling abroad was not available to ordinary citizens of the country. It was both an exclusive privilege and a kind of punishment for a limited number of persons. Polyan (2005) singles out three emigration waves from the USSR:

1. The first wave of emigration – 1918–22, when some 3 million people left the country. These were military men and civilians who fled from the Soviet power that won during the October Revolution and the Civil war. During this period, the Soviet government openly pursued a policy of getting rid of 'unwanted' citizens through their internal exile or their expulsion abroad. In 1922, a decree was adopted, which stipulated that 'in order to isolate persons involved in counter-revolutionary crimes … when there is a possibility not to resort to arrest, establish expulsion abroad or exile in certain areas of the Russian Soviet Federative Socialist Republic (hereinafter RSFSR)'. The decree became the legal basis for the expulsion of more than 150 outstanding Russian politicians, public figures, scientists and artists, as well as members of their families.

A little later, a new type of punishment was established under the Criminal Code: the expulsion from the country for a term of up to 3 years or indefinitely. In this case, any arbitrary return to the RSFSR after the application of this type of punishment was subject to execution. Polyan (2005) pointed out that by 1953, 360,921 persons had been sentenced to various terms of imprisonment under the Criminal Code, 67,539 of whom were sentenced to political and administrative exile or forced settlement within the territory of the USSR; 3.70 persons had faced forced expulsion abroad.

2. The second wave of emigration – 1941–44. 8.7 million people were forcibly displaced beyond the borders of the Soviet Union during World War II and about 0.5–0.7 million of them subsequently evaded return repatriation. In this regard, it should be noted that at the end of the Second World War, the Soviet leadership defined principles and mechanisms for the repatriation of Soviet citizens from foreign countries by classifying them into different groups: former prisoners of war (privates and sergeants); former prisoners of war (officers); prisoners of war (civilians); police and 'other suspicious persons'; interned civilians; inhabitants of border regions; orphans. The destinies of those who returned to their homeland differed, but all were prohibited from settling in any of the major cities of the USSR, such as Moscow, Leningrad, or Kiev.

3. The third wave of emigration took place between 1948 and 1986/1990, when about 280,000 Jews, 105,000 Soviet people of German origin, and 52,000 Armenians left the USSR (Heitman 1987, 24). The peak of this emigration occurred at the beginning of the 1970s after the head of the Soviet government, Anatoly Kosygin, had declared in December 1966 that the Soviet leadership was ready to support 'families separated by war, who would like to meet their relatives outside the USSR or leave the USSR' (BBC 2012). This statement made in Paris by the head of the Soviet government is to be considered the beginning of legal emigration from the USSR for the purpose of family reunification abroad.

Thus, migration management of the Soviet era was a mixture of strict state control over the mobility of the population and the violations of personal rights and freedoms of certain groups of Soviet citizens.

The right to freedom of movement in the new Russia

The collapse of the Soviet Union led to the resurgence of Russia and the declaration of freedom of movement as a right of every citizen of the new Russia. Unfortunately, after almost three decades, restrictions on the right to freedom of movement in the old Soviet tradition again appears to be on the rise.

Everyone has the right to move freely in the territory of the Russian Federation. However, only lawfully resident with a permanent permit has the right to choose his place of residence. Non-citizens have the right to stay temporarily in the territory of Russia, which is initially granted through a temporary residence permit. A temporary permit can later be extended to a permanent right to reside depending upon particular situations within quotas set by the Russian Government. The right to reside (permanent residence permit) can only be obtained by a foreigner or stateless person after holding temporary residency.

In the Russian scientific literature, freedom of movement is regarded as an integral component of individual freedom (Solonchenko 2004, 20) and self-determination (Rostovshikova 2001, 8). The Constitution of the Russian Federation specifies five elements of the right to freedom of movement: (1) the right to freedom of movement; (2) the right to freely choose the place of residence; (3) the right of free choice of place of stay for foreigners; (4) the right to free exit from the country; (5) the right of unhindered return to the country for citizens of the Russian Federation (Baglai 1999, 187–95; Bezuglov and Soldatov 2001, 463–6; Tiunov 2005, 70–9; Avakyan 2006, 601–5, also Limonova 2001; Barkhatova 2010).

The Russian legislature has chosen a complex legal model for the settlement of the right to freedom of movement. Today in the Russian Federation there is no single law covering all aspects of the right to freedom of movement. So, for example, freedom of movement and free choice of place of residence, or place of stay for non-citizens are regulated by law. The right to free exit from the country and unhindered return to the Russian Federation for citizens of the Russian Federation is regulated by the law. Over the past 10 years, a discussion has taken place in Russia on the adoption of a single migration code capable of settling migration issues, staying in Russia and abroad, as well as integrating migrants in Russia. Despite numerous attempts to discuss such a legislative proposal, it has not yet been adopted (Ivakhnyuk 2017).

The Constitutional Court of the Russian Federation interprets several elements of the right to freedom of movement as an inalienable and integral part of individual self-determination. These include: (1) the right to move freely in the territory of the Russian Federation; (2) the right to legally stay and live in the territory of the Russian Federation; (3) the right to enter and exit. The above-mentioned rights meet different human needs and interests and, as a consequence, can be legally applied separately (Arutyunyan and Baglai 2006, 425) Thus, according to Russian legislation, the right to freedom of movement is in theory granted to every person regardless of their status: citizens of the Russian Federation or of other states, as well as stateless persons.

In the theory the right to freedom of movement granted to every person and may be restricted under the 1993 Constitution of Russia in case of a state of emergency and in order to ensure the security of citizens and to protect the constitutional order, in accordance with the federal constitutional law, specifying the limits and duration of their validity

For example, Article 55 of the Constitution provides for the restriction of the right to freedom of movement within Russia for Russian citizens, foreigners and stateless persons:

- in the border zones;
- in closed military towns;
- in closed administrative-territorial divisions or entities;
- in areas of ecological disaster;
- in territories and in places where, in case of danger of spread of infectious and mass non-infectious diseases and human poisoning, special conditions and regimes for the population and economic activities are established;
- in territories where an emergency or martial law is imposed.

In the Constitution, the grounds for restricting freedom of movement are thus clearly defined and not subject to broad interpretation. However, in modern Russia, a number of legal provisions and by-laws exist that legally impose restrictions on the freedom of movement of certain groups of people. For example, the Federal Law on Counteracting Terrorism provides the Federal Security Service with certain powers in the area of conducting anti-terrorist activities, such as the possibility of restricting fundamental rights, including the right to freedom of movement of Russian citizens, foreign citizens, and stateless persons, and several other restrictive measures on movement exist on the statutes.

Thus, in modern Russia, the restriction of the freedom of movement of Russian citizens is increasingly regulated by administrative measures and it is clear that, after the collapse of the Soviet Union, the new Russia has passed three different stages in its legal development of the right to freedom of movement:

1. The first stage (1991–2002) was the period of active development and adoption of a legislative framework to regulate the management of external and internal migration in the new post-Soviet Russia.
2. The second stage (2002–14) included the defining and consolidating the competence of the Federal Migration Service, expanding the system of agreements between the Russian Federation and the countries supplying migrants, detailing and diversifying migration flows, as well as conceiving state programmes and mechanisms aimed at reorienting migrants' flows from the central regions Russia to the Urals, Siberia, and the Far East. The state actively promoted and pushed forward resettlement programmes through the state programme to promote the voluntary resettlement of compatriots living abroad in the Russian Federation and the *Far Eastern hectare programme* for the provision of land allotments in sparsely populated areas of the country.
3. The third stage (from 2014 to the present) is the era of monopolisation by the Russian state of the right of its citizens to freedom of movement.

Geopolitical tensions in the post-Soviet space, resulting from the on-going Russian–Ukrainian conflict and tense relations between Russia and the West, have affected the right of freedom of movement for Russian citizens. In the autumn of 2015, a bill was submitted to the State Duma of the Russian Federation aiming at restricting the right of Russian citizens who are employees of the Ministry of Internal Affairs or state employees to travel outside of Russia. The bill also includes the prohibition of professional activities in the internal affairs bodies of the Russian Federation for Russian citizens who are hold a permanent residence permit in a foreign country.

In 2015, the Ministry of Internal Affairs of the Russian Federation issued an order that prohibits the departure of all employees of the Ministry of Internal Affairs to take vacations abroad due to the difficult international contingency. Departure outside the Russian Federation for holidays is only allowed to Abkhazia and South Ossetia, both FSU states and partially recognised republics in the Caucasus, claiming independence from Georgia as well as other CIS countries, with the exception of Ukraine. The order was not officially published, but due to the subsequent wave of mass dismissals of employees of the Ministry of Internal Affairs and their media coverage, the order became known to the general public (Vashchenko 2017).

Conclusion

The evolution of the right to freedom of movement and its legal registration in the context of three historical periods shows that the Russian legislature and law enforcement consider the needs and interests of the Russian state over interests and needs of individuals. Over decades, the conquest and the settlement of remote regions of the country; the protection of state secrets or suspicions concerning the 'loyalty' of certain peoples and representatives of ethnic groups has influenced the right to freedom of movement and the ways in which the Russian state rules mobility of its population. This common thread of state interests is due not only to the weak legal tradition of protecting individual rights and freedoms, but to the historical and geographical position of Russia and the desire of its rulers in all historical periods to keep its vast territory and its inhabitants under control.

Note

1 Translation by Ravel Kodrič.

References

Arutyunyan, G. and Baglai, M. (2006) *Constitutional Law*. Moscow: Norma Press /Арутюнян, Г., Баглай, М. (2006): Конституционноеправо, Москва: Издательство Норма.

Auman, V. and Chebotareva, V. (1993) *History of Russian Germans in Documents (1763–1992)*. Moscow: Publishing House of the International Institute for Humanitarian Programs. *Ауман, В. & Чеботарёва, В. (1993) История российских немцев в документах (1763–1992 гг.)*. Москва: Издательство Международного института гуманитарных программ.

Avakyan, S. (2006) *The Constitutional Law of Russia*, Volume. 1. Moscow: Yurist. Авакьян С. (2006): Конституционное право России. Т. 1. Москва: Юрист.

Baglai, M. (1999) *The Constitutional Law of the Russian Federation*. Moscow: Norma Press. Баглай М. (1999): Конституционное право Российской Федерации. Москва: Издательство Норма.

Baiburin, A. (2009) "Prehistory of the Soviet Passport (1917–1932)" *Neprikosnovennyy Zapas* 2(64): 140–154/Байбурин, А (2009): К предыстории советского паспорта (1917–1932). Неприкосновенный запас, 2(64): 140–154.

Baiburin, A. (2017) *Soviet Passport. History-Structure-Practice*. Saint Petersburg: *European University Publishing House*/Байбурин, А. (2017): Советский паспорт. История- структура- практики. СпБ: Издательство Европейского университета.

Barkhatova, E. (2010) *Commentary on the Constitution of the Russian Federation*. Moscow: *Prospect*/Бархатова Е. (2010): Комментарий к Конституции Российской Федерации. Москва: Проспект.

BBC (2012). Five Waves of Russian Immigration (www.bbc.com/russian/russia/2012/12/121128_russia_emigration_waves 25 May 2018)/Пять волн российской эмиграции https://www.bbc.com/russian/russia/2012/12/121128_russia_emigration_waves.

Bezuglov, A. and Soldatov, S. (2001): *The Constitutional Law of Russia*. Volume 1. Moscow/Безуглов А., Солдатов С. (2001): Конституционное право России. Т. 1. Москва.

Chudinovskikh, O. and Denisenko, M. (2017) "Russia: A Migration System with Soviet Roots". *Migration Policy Institute*. 18. May. 12 p. (https://www.migrationpolicy.org/article/russia-migration-system-soviet-roots).

Heitman, S. (1987) The Third Soviet Emigration: Jewish, German and Armenian Emigration from the USSR since World War II. Cologne: Federal Institute for Ostwiss and Boarding Studies. No. 21. 24 p./Berichte des Bundesinstituts für ostwissenschaftliche und internationale Studien. Köln: Bundesinst. für Ostwiss. und Internat. Studien. № 21. 24 S.

Ivakhnyuk, I. (2017) *Suggestions on the Russian Migration Strategy of until 2035*. Moscow: *CSR*/Ивахнюк, И. (2017): Предложения к миграционной стратегии России до 2035 года. ЦСР: Москва.

Kabuzan, V. (1998): Emigration and Re-emigration in Russia in the XVII-XX Centuries. Moscow/Кабузан, В (1998): Эмиграция и реэмиграция в России в XVIII — начале XX века. Москва.

Kabuzan, V. (2012) "Population Movement in the Russian Empire" *Otechestvennyye Zapiski* 4(19): 82–93/Кабузан, В (2012): Движение населения в Российской империи. Отечественные записки. № 4 (19): 82–93.

Klier, J.D. (1995) *Imperial Russia's Jewish Question, 1855–1881*. Cambridge: Cambridge University Press.

Light, M. (2016) *Fragile Migration Rights. Freedom of Movement in post-Soviet Russia*. London: Routledge.

Limonova, N. (2001) *The Right of Citizens to Freedom of Movement, Choice of Place of Stay and Residence*. Moscow: Knizhnyy mir/Лимонова Н. (2001): Право граждан на свободу передвижения, выбор места пребывания и жительства. Москва: Книжный мир.

Lohr, E. (2012) *Russian Citizenship. From Empire to Soviet Union*. Cambridge, MA and London: Harvard University Press.

Polyan, P. (2004) *Against Their Will: The History and Geography of Forced Migrations in the USSR*. Budapest: CEU.

Polyan, P. (2005) *Emigration: Who Left Russia in the XXth Century? Russia and Its Regions in the XX Century: Territory – Resettlement – Migration*, O. Glaser and P. Polyan (eds.) Moscow: OGI Press, pp. 493–519/Полян, П (2005): Эмиграция: кто и когда в XX веке покидал Россию. Россия и ее регионы в XX веке: территория - расселение - миграции/Под ред. О. Глезер и П. Поляна. Москва: Издательство ОГИ: 493–519.

Rogovin, L. (1913) *The Statute on Passports. Collection of Legislation*. Informal publication. Saint Petersburg: Zakonovedenie/Роговин, Л. (1913): Устав о паспортах. Собрание законодательства. Неофициальное издание. СПб.: Законоведение.

Rostovshikova, O. (2001) The Freedom of Movement, A Choice of Residence and Their Guarantees in Russia: Author's Dissertation. PhD Thesis. Volgograd/Ростовщикова О. В., Свобода передвижения и выбор места жительства и гарантии ее обеспечения и защиты в России: Авторефат диссертации. Волгоград, 2001.

Solonchenko, I. (2004) Constitutional and Legal Framework of Rights and Freedoms of Man in the Russian Federation. PhD Thesis. Rostov-on-Don./Солонченко И. (2004) Конституционно-правовая концепция содержания личных прав и свобод в Российской Федерации: Авторефат диссертации. Ростов-на-Дону.

Sunderland, W. (2014) Catherine's Dilemma: Resettlement and Power in Russia 1500s–1914, in J. Lucassen and L. Lucassen (eds.), *Globalising Migration History: the Eurasian Experience (16th-21st Centuries)*, Leiden, Brill, pp. 55–70.

Tiunov, O. (2005) *Constitutional Rights and Freedoms of Man and Citizen in the Russian Federation*. Moscow: Norma Press/Тиунов О. (2005): Конституционные права и свободы человека и гражданина в Российской Федерации. Москва: Издательство Норма.

Vashchenko, V. (2017): The Ministry of Internal Affairs Punishes Policemen for Going on Vacation Abroad. *Gazeta.Ru* (www.gazeta.ru/social/2017/09/04/10874330.shtml 25 May 2018)/Ващенко, В. (2017): Руководство МВД наказывает полицейских за выезд в отпуск за границу. Газета.РУ. https://www.gazeta.ru/social/2017/09/04/10874330.shtml.

Web-resources

Zayonchkovskaya, Zh (1999) "Internal Migration in Russia and the USSR As a Reflection of Social Modernization in the XXth Century" *Mir Rossii*. № 4: 22–34/Зайончковская, Ж (1999): Внутренняя миграция в России и в СССР в XX веке как отражение социальной модернизации. Мир России. № 4. 22–34.

Zayonchkovskaya, Zh. (2000) "Migration of the population in the USSR and Russia in the XXth Century: Evolution through Catastrophes" *Studies on Russian Economic Development* № 4: 1–15/Зайончковская, Ж (2000): Миграция населения ссср и России в XX веке: эволюция сквозь катаклизмы. Studies on Russian Economic Development, №4, pp. 1–15

55

INTERNAL MIGRATION AND DEVELOPMENT

A perspective from China[1]

Kam Wing Chan and Xiaxia Yang

Introduction

China's rise as the 'world's factory' is definitely one of the biggest stories of the twenty-first century and its dominance in manufacturing has made it a major player in the global economy. This China success story is closely intertwined with the migration story: without the epic-scale migration of peasants, which supplies almost infinite low-cost human labour to power the China economic engine. the ascent of China would be totally unthinkable. Cheap migrant labour is what makes 'China price' so unrelenting (Harney 2009) and though that era of cheap labour may be coming to an end, its story needs to be told. The three decades prior to 2010 have witnessed the world's 'Great Migration' – an estimated 200 to 250 million rural residents have moved to cities and towns within China (Chan 2012a).

Building on previous work (Chan 2012b; Liang 2007) and using the latest census and mini-census data available, this chapter analyses China's recent migration trends, spatial patterns, and their relationship with economic development. China's internal migration is special in that it is heavily controlled and regulated by the *hukou* (household registration) system (Chan 1994; Fan 2008). As will be explained below, it was through the special institutional design of the *hukou* system that China has also managed to turn this vast number of rural–urban migrants into the largest army of cheap industrial labour the world has ever seen. Moreover, China's simultaneous use of a *de jure*, *hukou*-based population registration system and a *de facto* population statistical counts have greatly complicated the task of counting migrants and measuring migration. All kinds of conceptual and technical complexities exist which have served to mislead and confuse many researchers (see Chan 2007; Liang 2007). This is briefly outlined below before analysing the trends and geographical patterns in. The section preceding the conclusion highlights the two important migration issues affecting China's development and the world. The concluding remarks place Chinese migration in a broader perspective and looks to the future.

The *hukou* system and migration

After the Communist Revolution in 1949, China opted for the traditional Stalinist growth strategy of rapid industrialisation centred on heavy industry in cities and extraction of agricultural surplus from the peasantry (Chan 1994). This strategy was predicated upon exploiting the rural labour by denying it geographic mobility and access to state welfare. From the mid-1950s, the government repeatedly introduced measures to stem rural outflows, culminating, in 1958, in the formal codification of a comprehensive registration system to control population mobility (Chan 2009; Wang 2005). The regulation decreed that all internal migration be subject to approval by the relevant local government. From that point onward, Chinese citizens lost the freedom of residence and migration within their own country. Each person was assigned a *hukou* (registration status), classified as 'rural' or 'urban', in a specific administrative unit. The *hukou* mechanism served as a central instrument of the command system designed for the big-push industrialisation, to prevent peasants from exiting the countryside. This industrialisation strategy led China to create, in effect, two very different societies: on the one hand, the urban class, whose members worked in the priority and protected industrial sector and who had access to (at least basic) social welfare and full citizenship; and on the other hand, the peasants, who were tied to the land to produce an agricultural surplus for industrialisation and who had to fend for themselves. *Hukou* conversion, referring to change from the rural to the urban category, was tightly controlled and permitted only under very limited conditions, usually when it was in accordance with state industrialisation plans. The *hukou* system was not merely a means of limiting rural–urban population and labour mobility, as it has been commonly depicted, but also a system of social control aimed at excluding the rural population from access to state-provided goods, welfare, and entitlements so that the rural population segment remains cheap and easy to be exploited.

It was under this socioeconomic context that China in the late 1970s launched its economic reform. After some experimentation, as China latched onto a labour intensive, export-oriented growth strategy in the mid-1980s, rural labour was allowed to move *en masse* to the cities to fill industry's labour demand, which later became a major state industrialisation strategy. By the mid-1990s, rural-*hukou* labour had become the backbone labour force of the export industry based on manufacturing. Today, rural-*hukou* labourers staff almost all of the low-end services in urban areas, and they are in the majority in the labour force in export centres such as Shenzhen and Dongguan since the 1990s (Liang 1999).

'Rural migrant labour' (*nongmingong*) in China has a specific meaning: it refers to industrial and service workers with rural-*hukou*. These village-origin labourers, though working in urban jobs and residing for the most part in towns and cities, are not considered legally to be 'urban' workers. Neither are they treated as 'locals': *rural migrant* is not a probational status but permanent (Wu 2011). They are not eligible for regular urban welfare benefits and social services (access to local schools, urban pension plans, public housing, and so on) and other rights that are available to people with urban-*hukou*. Instead, rural migrant workers are treated officially as part of the rural-*hukou* population, even though they may have worked and lived in an urban area for many years. In short, they are fixed, through institutional mechanisms, in a permanent social 'half-arrival' situation, belonging to the netherworld of rural or urban, and with little hope of acculturating into the permanent urban population. This also applies to their children, even to those born in the city. The legally 'temporary' status of this group's members and their *permanent* ineligibility for local 'citizenship' in the form of urban-*hukou* make them forever vulnerable, and easily exploitable and expendable (Solinger 1999; Wu 2011).

One's *hukou* classification remains unchanged no matter where he/she moves, unless that person effects a formal *hukou* conversion, which is almost impossible for ordinary rural migrants. As a result, they are consigned to low-end factory and service jobs, often in the low-skilled three-dimensional ('dangerous, dirty, and demeaning') category. The denial of local urban-*hukou* to migrant workers, combined with their plentiful supply (until recently) and lack of access to legal support, has created a large, easily exploitable, yet highly mobile, and flexible industrial workforce for China's export economy. The internal migrant labour force is similar to the cheap migrant labour in the classical Lewis (1954) model of the unlimited supply of labour. It has greatly contributed to China's emergence as the world's 'most efficient' or the least-cost producer. Figure 55.1 outlines the main components of China's dual society, with particular reference to position in the social (and economic) hierarchy (pyramid), type of *hukou* (urban or rural), and rural/urban location in two different historical periods: Mao's (pre-1979) era and the present.

The number of rural migrant workers swelled rapidly from about 20–30 million in the 1980s to close to 160 million in 2011 (see Table 55.1 below). Adding 70 million dependents, they made up a total of 230 million living in cities and towns but without local *hukou* in 2011 (NPFPC 2012). To put the number in perspective, the total number of international migrants was estimated by the United Nations (2012, Table 1) to be 214 million in 2010. The rapid expansion of China's essentially disenfranchised population, primarily in urban areas, has become its hallmark in the last quarter-century.

Based on (Chan et al. 1999), two broad categories of migrants can thus be identified:

a) Migration with 'local' residency rights (hereafter, *hukou* migration). This is usually open only to a select group (currently in big cities, the rich or the highly educated), and immediate family members of residents with local *hukou*;
b) Migration without *hukou* residency rights (non-*hukou* migration).

Officially only *hukou* migration is considered *qianyi* ('migration'). All other moves are considered *renkou liudong* (population movements or 'floating' population), implying a 'temporary' move to a destination where the person is not supposed to, and is legally not entitled to, stay permanently. China's exceptionally large numbers of people moving internally, as well as the circulatory and temporary nature of many of them, have hugely complicated the efforts to measure the movement consistently (Chan 2007, 2012b).

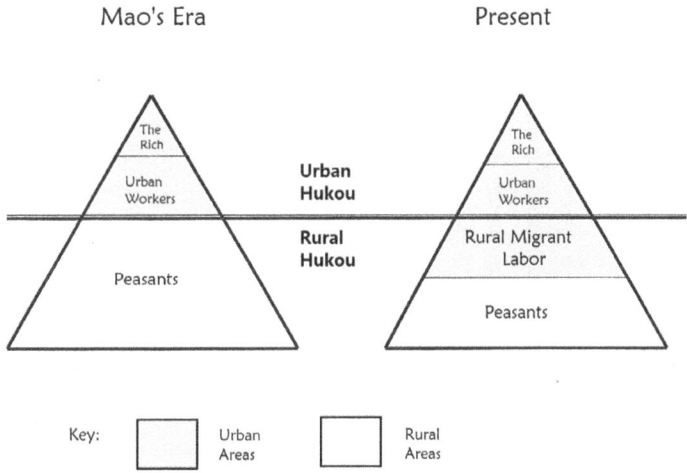

Figure 55.1 Social stratification and *hukou* type
Source: Chan (2012a)

Table 55.1 Major Aggregate Migration and Urban Population Statistics, 1982–2017 (in millions)

	Hukou Migrants (Yearly flow figures)	Non-Hukou Population (Stock Figures)						De facto Population in Urban Areas
		'Floating Population'			'Rural Migrant Labour'			
		Registered with MPS (mid-year)	NBS National Censuses/Mini-Censuses/Annual Surveys		NBS Estimates based on Sample Surveys	Rural-hukou Population in Urban Areas — Authors' Estimates		NBS Statistics
Geographic boundary (to cross)	City, town, or township	City, town, or township	Township-level unit	County or city	Township	Not applicable		Not applicable
Minimum length of stay (for those without local hukou)	No minimum	three days	six months	six months (unless otherwise specified)	Away for outside work (for six months or more)	six months		six months
Series	A	B	C	D	E	F	G (per cent)	H
1982	17.30			6.6 (1 year)		46.5	21.7	214.5
1987	19.73			15.2[a]	26.0[c]	64.0	23.1	276.7
1990	19.24			21.6 (1 year)		66.3	22.0	302.0
1995	18.46		49.7	29.1[b]	75.0	69.4	19.7	351.7
2000	19.08	44.8	144.4	121.0		136.6	29.8	459.1
2001	17.01	55.1				148.6	30.9	480.6
2002	17.22	59.8			104.7	152.8	30.4	502.1
2003	17.26	69.9			113.9	149.5	28.5	523.8
2004	19.49	78.0			118.2	151.4	27.9	542.8
2005	19.33	86.7	153.1	147	125.8	153.1	27.2	562.1
2006	20.60	95.3			132.1	162.2	27.8	582.9
2007	20.84	104.4			137.0	175.5	29.0	606.3
2008	18.92	116.6			140.4	184.3	29.5	624.0
2009	16.77	122.2			145.3	194.8	30.2	645.1
2010	17.01	131.4	261.4	221.4	153.4	210.2	31.4	669.8

2011	16.28	155.4		230	158.6	220.2	31.9	690.8
2012	17.49	167.5		236	163.4	232.1	32.6	711.8
2013		173.9		245	166.1	241.2	33.0	731.1
2014		180.1		253	168.2	258.2	34.5	749.2
2015			292.5	246	168.8	222.7	28.9	771.2
2016				245	169.3	223.1	28.1	792.8
2017				241	171.9	225.5	27.7	813.5

Notes and sources:

MPS = Ministry of Public Security; NBS = National Bureau of Statistics.

a the geographic boundary is based on city, county, or town.

b the geographic boundary is based on county-level units.

c refers to 1988

A: MPS (1988–2012); NBS and MPS (1988)

B: MPS (1997–2014)

C and D: NBS (1988, 2018), SC and NBS (1985, 1993, 2002, 2007, 2012, 2016), and NPSSO (1997).

E: 2002–08 figures are from NBS, compiled by Cai and Chan (2009, Table 1). 2009–17 figures are from NBS (2010–17b, 2018).

Earlier figures are estimates in Lu et al. (2002) and they may not be fully comparable to recent NBS figures.

F: Estimates by Chan (2012a, Table 1; 2018, 11).

G: F expressed as a percentage of H.

H: NBS (1983–2017c); NBS (2018).

Based on the above understanding and a careful differentiation of different statistics from a variety of sources and surveys in accordance with their nature (flow or stock), and temporal and geographic coverage, a matrix set up in Table 55.1 allows us to make sense of those numbers and gain an understanding of the overall volume of migration, its variety and trends over the last 35 years. Table 55.1 is organised to show the annual series of the flow of *hukou* migration and the size of non-*hukou* migrants (migration stock), based on different metrics. Detailed explanations of the various statistics are in Chan (2012b). The *hukou* migrants Series A, available till 2012, represents the total number of all types officially approved changes in *hukou* (residence) within a particular year, from townships to cities; from cities to cities; from townships to townships but most probably excluding moves *within* cities, towns and *within* townships.

The non-*hukou* population Series B–G refers to the people staying in an administrative unit (usually city, town, street, or township) other than their place of *hukou* registration. This resident group is also commonly known as the *liudong renkou* ('floating population') and it does not belong to the *de jure* resident population. Owing to the different purposes, coverage, and criteria used in defining the geographic boundary and the minimum duration of stay, the numbers representing the non-*hukou* population in each series may be quite different even for the same year.

Finally, the urban population Series H. This *de facto* urban population (based on a six-month residence criterion) is added to show the growth of the urban population, an important metric of China's urbanisation, mainly driven by migration. In other countries, this *de facto* urban population is the common, perhaps only, statistic of 'urban population' known at the national level. In China, however, multiple series of 'urban population' statistics exist that also have often caused confusion (see Chan 2007, 2012a).

Trends since 1982

Based on Table 55.1, one can identify some broad migration trends. The annual number of *hukou* migrants recorded by the Ministry of Public Security remained relatively stable, hovering between 17 and 21 million in the three decades from 1982. In fact, the rate of *hukou* migration, as a percentage of China's total population, declined significantly, from 1.7 per cent in 1982 to only 1.3 per cent in 2010. A portion of *hukou* migration is rural–rural migration, mainly involving marriage, and a small amount of rural–urban migration. Systematic information about the composition is not available, but it is quite certain that *hukou* migration to large cities remains very stringently controlled (Chan 2014; Chan and Buckingham 2008).

On the other hand, the non-*hukou* migrant population, irrespective of the statistics on which it is based, shows a rapid increase in the two decades until about 2012. For example, Series D ('floating population') expanded from about 30 million in 1995 to 121 million in 2000, and increased by another 100 million in the first decade of the twenty-first century. The population of those in the urban areas but with rural-*hukou* (Series G) increased from 66 million in 1990 to 210 million in 2010 – a jump of 144 million in two decades! As a percentage of the urban population, the non-*hukou* population rose from 20–23 per cent in the late 1980s and the early 1990s to 35 per cent in 2014.

Based on Series D, the average annual increase in the size of the floating population was less than 2 million in 1987 and 1995 but surged to about 10 million in 2000–10. Furthermore, the gap, both in absolute and relative terms, between the *de facto* urban population and those without urban-*hukou* widened in the period between 1995 and 2014 (shown in the steady rise in Series G), suggesting a rather disturbing trend that a higher proportion of people in cities and towns fell into the disadvantaged category 'in the city but not of the city' (Chan 2011). The rapid swelling of the non-*hukou* population in the city coincided with China's ascendency to being the 'world's factory'. This widening trend was finally reversed in 2015, following the new *hukou* reform initiatives in 2014. More migrants have been granted local *hukou*, hence depressing the value of G in 2015. This percentage has remained more or less stable at around 28 per cent hereafter, partly as a result of the end of the one-child policy, which helped to boost urban-*hukou* population by natural increase (Chan 2018).

China's internal migration is mainly labour migration in response to disparities in wages between the urban and rural sectors and between regions in China (Cai 1999, 2000; Fan 2008). The lack of sufficient gainful employment in the countryside in many agricultural provinces has pushed many rural-*hukou* workers to leave home. They move to make monetary gains through employment as wage-workers or self-employment. Many go to nearby towns outside the villages and most of them move within provinces, but about a quarter to one-third migrates to big cities on the coast (Chan 2012b).

Drawing on the data from China's last two censuses and three mini-censuses (1 per cent National Population Surveys), Table 55.2 is a summary of the major interprovincial migration statistics covering five 5-year periods between 1990 and 2015 (for the population aged 5 and above), and the aggregate pattern. This type of long-distance migration also increased steadily and significantly from only 10.7 million in 1990–95 to a peak of 55.2 million in 2005–10. This rise, however, has stopped in 2010–15, suggesting a likely turning point. These cross-province flows are largely village-to-city migrations. The total interprovincial migration in those two and a half decades (based on those five 5-year periods) totalled 189.5 million. This number counts more than once those who moved more than once in those five 5-year periods. By 2015, 97.2 million people lived in a place with a *hukou* registered in another province, compared to only 42.4 million in 2000 (SC and NBS 2002, 2016). The more than doubling of the out-of-province *hukou* population mirrors a similar rapid scale of change in the overall non-*hukou* population in the same period, as shown in Table 55.1.

Table 55.2 also ranks of the provinces according to the net migration volumes in different periods. Until recently, major in-migration and out-migration flows between provinces were basically uni-directional (Chan 2012b). For example, in 1995–2000, the ratio of in-migration to out-migration was 26:1 in the largest net in-migration province, Guangdong (see Chan 2013). Conversely, in the largest net out-migration province, Sichuan, in the same period, the ratio of out-migration to in-migration was 1:7.5. Those ratios mean that the major players in interprovincial flows were essentially either export provinces (such as Sichuan and Henan) or import provinces (such as Guangdong). Because of that, the net migration statistics can readily capture the importance of each province in the interprovincial flows until 2010, when the dominance of uni-directional flows has begun to weaken significantly. For instance, in the 2010–15 period, the ratio of in-migration to out-migration in Guangdong dropped to only 4:1.

In terms of the aggregate volume of net migration in the two and a half decades, Guangdong (the largest net importer) tops the list and Henan (the largest net exporter) is at the bottom. The predominant flows are from inland to the coast: the top seven provinces are all from the coastal region, and the bottom eight, from the inland region. This same pattern is also obvious in Figure 55.2, showing the 20 largest interprovincial flows.

Further examination of Table 55.2 shows that net in-migration is dominated by two provinces, Guangdong and Zhejiang. For the entire 1990–2015 era, these two provinces account for 31.5 per cent of all the interprovincial migration. In 1995–2000 when their combined share

Table 55.2 Interprovincial Migration in China, 1990–2015 (in thousands)

	1990–95			1995–2000			2000–05			2005–10					2010–15					1990–2015 Aggregate		
	Net migration	NET percent	Rank	Net migration	NET percent	Rank	Net migration	NET percent	Rank	In-migration	Out-migration	Net migration	NET percent	Rank	In-migration	Out-migration	Net migration	NET percent	Rank	Net	NET percent	Rank
Guangdong	1799	19.6	1	11063	34.3	1	10281	27.0	1	13,890	1613	12,277	22.23	1	10,692	2585	8106	15.22	1	43,526	22.96	1
Zhejiang	−273	−3	24	1745	5.4	3	4021	10.6	2	8407	1339	7067	12.80	2	5654	1775	3879	7.28	2	16,439	8.67	2
Beijing	606	6.6	3	1715	5.3	4	1916	5.0	5	3851	406	3445	6.24	4	3990	744	3247	6.09	3	10,929	5.77	3
Jiangsu	319	3.5	5	667	2.1	7	1963	5.2	4	4895	1894	3002	5.43	5	5100	2129	2971	5.58	4	8,921	4.71	4
Shanghai	610	6.6	2	2005	6.2	2	2650	7.0	3	4934	401	4533	8.21	3	3530	823	2707	5.08	5	12,505	6.60	5
Fujian	104	1.1	10	722	2.2	6	1132	3.0	6	2515	1114	1401	2.54	6	2263	1159	1105	2.07	7	4,464	2.36	6
Tianjin	171	1.9	7	388	1.2	8	802	2.1	7	1499	213	1286	2.33	7	2728	332	2396	4.50	6	5,043	2.66	7
Xinjiang	437	4.8	4	925	2.9	5	395	1.0	8	841	287	554	1.00	8	875	427	448	0.84	8	2,759	1.46	8
Hainan	38	0.4	12	88	0.3	11	33	0.1	10	339	236	103	0.19	11	338	291	47	0.09	9	309	0.16	9
Tibet	27	0.3	13	35	0.1	14	−6	0.0	12	92	62	29	0.05	14	100	63	37	0.07	11	123	0.06	10
Nei Mongol	159	1.7	8	−116	−0.4	18	−23	−0.1	14	829	648	181	0.33	10	677	632	45	0.08	10	246	0.13	11
Liaoning	248	2.7	6	375	1.2	9	257	0.7	9	1181	685	495	0.90	9	781	808	−27	−0.05	14	1,349	0.71	12
Qinghai	17	0.2	14	−46	−0.1	16	−12	0.0	13	183	150	33	0.06	13	205	170	34	0.06	12	26	0.01	13
Ningxia	4	0	15	41	0.1	13	7	0.0	11	239	151	89	0.16	12	189	209	−20	−0.04	13	120	0.06	14
Chongqing	NA	NA	NA	−655	−2.0	23	−1010	−2.7	23	737	1844	−1107	−2.01	22	990	1478	−487	−0.91	16	−3,260	−1.72	15
Shaanxi	−25	−0.3	17	−296	−0.9	20	−572	−1.5	21	735	1347	−613	−1.11	18	1127	1372	−245	−0.46	15	−1,751	−0.92	16
Jilin	−134	−1.5	22	−275	−0.9	19	−315	−0.8	18	345	854	−509	−0.92	17	315	817	−502	−0.94	17	−1,734	−0.92	17
Yunnan	104	1.1	9	335	1.0	10	−132	−0.3	15	632	1089	−457	−0.83	16	793	1462	−669	−1.26	18	−819	−0.43	18
Heilongjiang	−188	−2	23	−639	−2.0	22	−825	−2.2	22	323	1463	−1140	−2.06	23	472	1313	−841	−1.58	19	−3,633	−1.92	19
Gansu	−77	−0.8	20	−357	−1.1	21	−376	−1.0	19	260	1047	−787	−1.42	20	387	1241	−854	−1.60	20	−2,450	−1.29	20
Shanxi	87	0.9	11	49	0.2	12	−135	−0.4	16	499	794	−295	−0.53	15	429	1295	−866	−1.63	21	−1,160	−0.61	21
Shandong	−9	−0.1	16	26	0.1	15	−199	−0.5	17	1341	2015	−674	−1.22	19	1306	2220	−914	−1.72	22	−1,770	−0.93	22
Hebei	−74	−0.8	19	−102	−0.3	17	−378	−1.0	20	925	2017	−1092	−1.98	21	1159	2513	−1354	−2.54	23	−3,000	−1.58	23
Guizhou	−107	−1.2	21	−970	−3.0	24	−1235	−3.2	24	592	2681	−2088	−3.78	24	999	2496	−1497	−2.81	24	−5,897	−3.11	24
Hubei	−44	−0.5	18	−1604	−5.0	26	−2214	−5.8	27	846	3804	−2958	−5.36	27	1544	3041	−1497	−2.81	25	−8,317	−4.39	25

Jiangxi	−347	−3.8	25	−2445	−7.6	28	−1977	−5.2	26	699	3483	−2784	−5.04	26	896	2676	−1780	−3.34	27	−9,333	−4.92	26
Guangxi	−450	−4.9	26	−1551	−4.8	25	−1726	−4.5	25	600	2821	−2221	−4.02	25	860	2622	−1763	−3.31	26	−7,710	−4.07	27
Sichuan*	−1294	−14.1	30	−3806	−11.8	31	−3178	−8.4	31	1055	4988	−3933	−7.12	29	1623	3672	−2049	−3.85	28	−14,259	−7.52	28
Anhui	−662	−7.2	29	−2579	−8.0	29	−3165	−8.3	30	824	5526	−4702	−8.51	30	1121	4243	−3122	−5.86	30	−14,230	−7.51	29
Hunan	−532	−5.8	28	−2899	−9.0	30	−2827	−7.4	28	690	4592	−3902	−7.07	28	1276	3754	−2478	−4.65	29	−12,638	−6.67	30
Henan	−514	−5.6	27	−1839	−5.7	27	−3154	−8.3	29	432	5430	−4999	−9.05	31	856	4915	−4059	−7.62	31	−14,564	−7.68	31
Total interprovincial migration	**10,661**			**32,330**			**38,042**			**55,228**					**53,276**					**189,537**		

Sources and notes: Interprovincial migration refers to those who lived in a different province 5 years prior to the survey time. Total interprovincial migration is the sum of all provincial in-migration. Net per cent = Net migration as a per cent of nation's total interprovincial migration. Data for 1990–2010 are from Chan (2012b); 2010–15 numbers are computed from SC and NBS (2016).

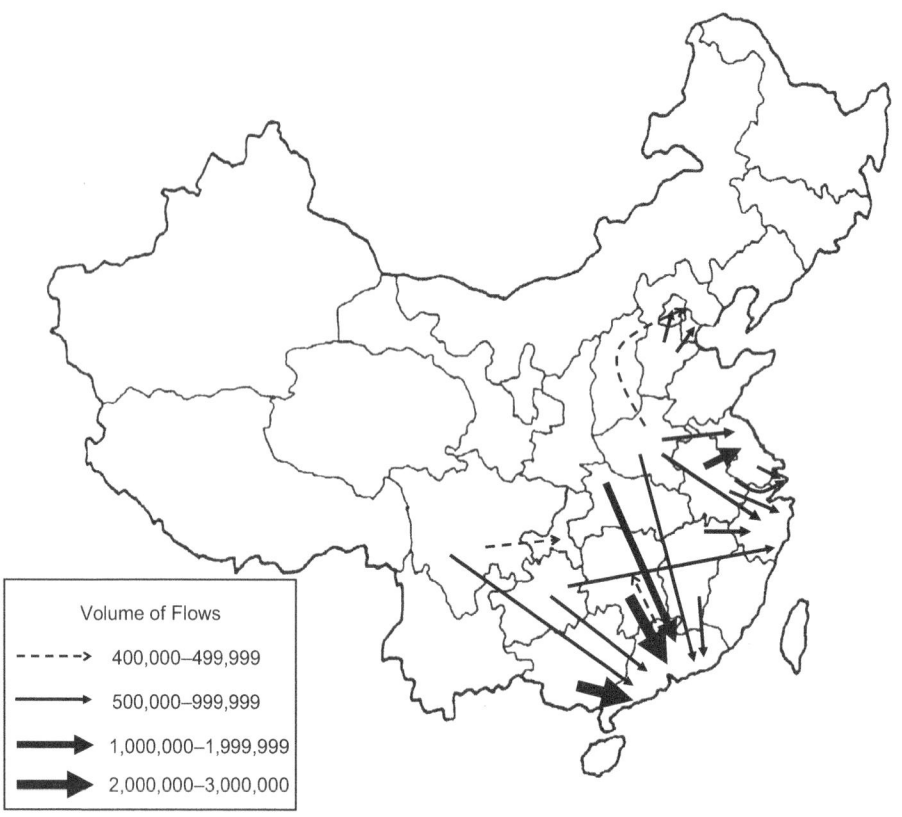

Figure 55.2 The 20 largest interprovincial migration flows, 2010–15
Source: compiled from SC & NBS (2016)

reached the highest, at 40 per cent, with Guangdong alone taking up 34.3 per cent! The province was the most sought-after destination of interprovincial migrants for every period under study though its share has declined steadily since 2000. The second largest migration receiving province is Zhejiang. It was actually a net exporter in 1990–95, yet it flipped to become the third largest net importer in 1995–2000 and climbed to be the second largest thereafter. In the late twentieth century, the Zhejiang migrants were known for their entrepreneurial skills and ubiquity in the country (and even in Europe); the high economic growth of the province since the mid-1990s has turned it into a major and increasingly popular destination of migrants in the twenty-first century. Interestingly, Guangdong and Zhejiang were also the main sources of international migration from China until recently. It could well be that the labour vacuums created in these provinces by the international emigration stimulated the massive internal in-migration. Since 2005, however, the combined share of Guangdong and Zhejiang has dropped, with more people moving out and fewer moving in. This change reflects the change in the national pattern of interprovincial migration identified earlier, as more first-generation migrants return to their home provinces than the younger migrants coming to these two provinces. Such a change is the result of the past family planning policy and the recent relocations of many industrial jobs inland under a state-led development regime.

In terms of sending provinces, several major exporters have emerged in recent years in contrast to the one single dominant player of Sichuan in the pre-2000 era, when it alone, for example, accounted for 12 per cent of the nation's total interprovincial migration in 1995–2000. In the 2000–05 and 2005–10 periods, the share of the total migration of each of the four largest net population exporters (Sichuan, Anhui, Henan, and Hunan) was very close (7 to 9 per cent). Hence, while in general only two major destination provinces existed (Guangdong and Zhejiang), the sources of these flows had become more diverse. This pattern reflected the intensification of regional industrial restructuring beginning in the late 1980s, whereby inland provinces lost proportionally more manufacturing jobs to the coastal provinces in the second half of the 1990s and onwards (Yang 2004), giving rise to the emergence of Guangdong (and to a lesser extent, Zhejiang) as the 'world's factory' in those 10 years. At the same time, many poorer provinces (both their governments and people) actively pursued labour export as an economic strategy, modelled after Sichuan. This greater geographic spread of labour migration over longer distances has parallels to what Skeldon (1990) observed for the 'diffusion' of the origins of migration in Peru.

In general, the relative rankings of the provinces over time in Table 55.2 show remarkable stability from 1995 through to 2015. The rankings in 2005–10 are almost exactly the same as those in the previous period and strongly reflect the economic regional specialisation in that time. The pattern is somewhat different in the earliest period (1990–95), as demonstrated by the phenomenal reversal of Zhejiang from a major net exporter in the early 1990s to a top net importer thereafter. Another point worth noting is that in 2010–15, the smaller net migration to the two largest net import provinces, Guangdong and Zhejiang, corresponds with the decreased net migration out of the four largest export provinces, Sichuan, Anhui, Henan, and Hunan. An important reason is that many factories have been relocated from the coastal region to the inland region, as a response to the rising labour and other costs in Guangdong and Zhejiang. This likely heralds a turning point in migration directions as well as the slowing down of (interprovincial) migration nationwide.

Current migration issues

While China's success in becoming the world's factory relied heavily on the army of low-cost migrant workers, recent years have seen a series of rather dramatic and significant events, which have shown an emerging new reality: the factors that made the 'China model' tick, may be on the verge of a tectonic change. The model of China's development also looks more fragile than outsiders have portrayed, which has serious implications for both China and for the global economy. In the following, we briefly examine two major issues.

a) *The precarity of migrant labour and the Lewis turning point*

Occupying the bottom of the global supply chain, migrant labour was badly hit when the global economy crashed and thousands of factories were closed in Guangdong and Zhejiang as the global economic crisis unfolded during the last quarter of 2008. This led to massive layoffs of factory workers, almost all of whom were migrants without local *hukou*. Many of these factories closed almost overnight without any warning and without paying the workers in full or the required severance. Dongguan in Guangdong province, the hub of China's export industry, was devastated by the slump and angry workers staged numerous mass protests demanding full payment of wages and layoff compensation (Foreman 2008).

Drawing on data from NBS in late March 2009, Chan (2010b) estimated that the total unemployment of the rural migrant labour in early 2009 was about 23 million, or 16.4 per cent. The sharp loss of migrants' jobs of 16 per cent, contrasts with a reduction of only 4.3 per cent for the urban-*hukou* workers in formal employment in March 2009. Indeed, more than 95 per cent of the newly laid-off workers in the non-agricultural sector were rural migrant workers, pointing to the extreme vulnerability of this particular group. Such a situation put China dangerously on the verge of a major crisis, which was only avoided through implementing a gigantic stimulus package and taking a conciliatory approach to labour disputes by local governments (Csanádi 2010). The massive investment in high-speed train projects, for example, created millions of jobs in 2009 and was able to redeploy some of the laid-off workers quickly to reverse the situation.

As China's economy began to recover in the early months of 2010, factories in a few coastal cities were reported as having difficulties finding workers to help fill export orders. It was reported that some factories in Guangdong even resorted to hiring illegal workers from Vietnam and elsewhere (Singtao Daily 2010a). This situation came as a surprise to many observers, because just about a year earlier, the situation had been completely the opposite with some 23 million migrant workers laid off as the global financial crisis spread. It is also hard to conceive that severe labour shortages would occur at a time when China's working-age population, the world's largest, had climbed to a new high, reaching 981 million in 2010, and is projected to continue expanding until 2015 (Hu et al. 2010; Kroeber 2010). The shortages and the abundance appear to be contradictory.

Furthermore, in May 2010, the world was shocked by news of a serial tragedy related to the treatment of labour in one of China's famed export-processing zones. Between 14 and 16 suicide attempts of migrant workers, which resulted in 12 deaths, took place in just the first five months of the year, in a single giant factory complex, Foxconn in Shenzhen, the world's largest assembler of electronic products for major brand names such as Apple, Dell, and Toshiba (Moore 2010). Media reports revealed more about the harsh conditions experienced by young Chinese migrant workers. In the same week, as Foxconn moved into damage-control mode by offering raises of about 25 per cent to workers, multiple serious strikes took place at several Honda assembly plants in the nearby cities of Foshan and Zhongshan in the Pearl River Delta. Those strikes ended after two to three weeks with the workers winning 10–30 per cent wage increases, workers at another Honda subsidiary in Foshan also went on strike in July (Singtao Daily 2010b).

The increasing wages and the militancy of the migrant workers have led both the Chinese and international media in late 2010 to pronounce a labour 'shortage' and 'the end of surplus labour' in China (Demick and Pierson 2010). More critically, some observers have argued that China has reached a Lewis turning point (Hamlin 2010; Zhang et al. 2010) or the point when the dualistic rural–urban labour market in a country begins to break down and merge into one. It is also the point where a labour surplus economy is transformed into a full-employment 'normal' economy (Huang and Jiang 2010). According to Lewis, a developing country's industrial wages will begin to rise quickly at that point when the supply of surplus labour from its rural areas tapers off. In the case of China, reaching this point would signal that its dualistic rural–urban socioeconomic structure, which has existed for the entire six decades of the PRC era, and the root cause of a host of social and economic ills, is beginning to end. Reaching the turning point would bring real hopes of closing the sharp rural–urban economic and social differences in the near future. Obviously, too, the significance of this change would extend far beyond China (Garnaut 2010; Huang and Jiang 2010).

However, it is equally clear that an abundance, not a shortage, of rural labour still existed in the country (Yao 2010). Seemingly a paradox of migrant labour shortages co-exist with rural labour supply abundance in China. According to some authors (Green 2008; Han et al. 2009), rural labour supply remained plentiful in the first decade of the twenty-first century, with the surplus estimated at about 100 million, almost all in the age groups of 35 and above (Cai and Wang 2009, Table 7.2). This paradox can be explained with reference to China's special socioeconomic contexts, which are often overlooked in the literature.

First, the lack of a local *hukou* places migrant workers in a weak bargaining position and employers in the export industries are able to 'cherry-pick' workers with the most 'desirable attributes'. For example, they select young workers as easily trainable with the dexterity to handle fast-paced, sometimes military-style, repetitive assembly work (especially in the electronics industry). They have the endurance for long hours of work, often for 28–29 days per month, and 'work attitudes' such as obedience and capacity for long periods of residence in dormitories or barrack-type shelters (Lee 1998; Pun 2005). These qualities are mainly found in young, mostly unmarried, especially female workers. Indeed, the great majority of Foxconn's employees in China fit very well into the above description. As a result, rural migrant labour hired in the export sector falls overwhelmingly in a highly selective age cohort between ages 16 and 30, with new workers typically hired before they reach 20. With an increasing prevalence of education beyond elementary school in the countryside, these young rural migrants are more educated than their predecessors and better suited for assembling modern electronics, which often involves exacting specifications.

Second, China's one-child policy has depressed fertility leading to a drop in the supply of rural labour of some 40 per cent in the 10 years since 2000, from about 18 million to only 11 million (Chan 2010a). Moreover, the rather deplorable (mis)treatments of migrant labour by employers during the global crisis in the Pearl River Delta and Zhejiang also discouraged some of the rural migrants from coming back to seek work in the coastal region later, even when jobs were available. At the same time, the general improvement in rural economic conditions in the inland region in the last few years owing to the policy taken by the Hu-Wen administration (Chan and Wang 2008), and especially the millions of new jobs created by the fiscal stimulus package in 2009 in projects such as high-speed railways, in the interior, also created the intervening opportunities for many young rural labourers closer to home. Overall, labour shortages have occurred in specific age segments and are mostly confined to the coastal region, and the dwindling supply of young migrant workers in coastal areas contributes to the slowdown in interprovincial flows shown earlier.

b) *The plight of the children of migrants*

A significant social issue which has emerged in the last ten years is the plight of the children of migrants, which is related to the high age-selectivity of the Chinese internal migration discussed above. Associated with China's current 170 million migrant labourers are about 100 million children of migrants, accounting for about one-third of China's child population. These are children whose lives have been profoundly disrupted, mostly negatively, by a fractured family as their parents migrate to work in urban areas and leave the children behind. And it has become increasingly obvious that these children are a major victim of China's *hukou*-based migration and urbanisation (Ye et al. 2013).

Public attention on this issue has greatly intensified in recent years because of several heart-breaking tragedies, including one in 2012 when five boys died of carbon-monoxide poisoning in a dumpster as they sought shelter in winter in a poor village in Guizhou.

These boys, unsupervised, were children of migrant workers away from home. In the last two decades, as rural–urban migration expanded, it increasingly involved married couples and their children (Qu et al. 2015). However, migrant workers moving to cities with their children are considered only temporary residents and do not have the rights to urban services, including public education. As expected, children accompanying migrant parents face tremendous educational obstacles at their destination, and an estimate of 67 million children of migrants were thus left behind without both parents in 2015 (Chan and Ren 2018).

The great majority of children left-behind are disadvantaged, some facing multiple and serious challenges in their life (Duan et al. 2013; Ye and Pan 2008), of which the most notable directly affect their future capacity to function adequately as workers and citizens. These include poor or inadequate education, whether in the cities or in the countryside and parental absence and family separation in growing up, which can lead to all kinds of short-term and long-term problems, ranging from stress, to more serious psychological problems, falling behind in school or/and falling victim to sexual abuse (The Economist 2015). Some of the parallels are found in the discussions in Chapters 16–18 in this Handbook.

Under China's 2014 urbanisation and *hukou* reform initiatives, large cities are asked to limit their population size by stringently restricting in-migration (Chan 2014). Many city governments have seized the opportunity to further curb migrant children's access to education, resulting in more migrant children losing their spots in city schools and forcing many more to return or remain in villages. The continued large numbers of deprived children of migrants point to a serious future challenge for China.

Concluding remarks

The volume of internal migration in China has increased steadily since the early 1980s. As China urbanised rapidly, rural–urban migration also accelerated in the first half of the 1990s, and again in the first decade of the twenty-first century though the momentum has slowed in recent years. While the volume of annual *hukou* migration has remained quite stable since 1982, non-*hukou* migration has expanded significantly and this 'Great Migration' supplied China with a huge army of low-cost human labour to power its economic machine.

The rapid industrial growth since China's accession to the World Trade Organization in December 2001, saw 'shortages' of migrant labour emerging in 2004 in the Pearl River Delta, where double-digit industrial growth was recorded every year until 2008. Global financial events since the summer of 2008, however, drastically altered the economic landscape of the Chinese export industry, at least temporarily, where most migrant labour was employed. About 23 million migrant workers lost their jobs in late 2008/early 2009, but China's massive fiscal stimulus programme was able to re-absorb most of the unemployed. As China's export sector recovered in early 2010, migrant labour 'shortages' resurfaced in the coastal region, leading many major manufacturers to relocate some of their plants inland to be close to the sources of migrant labour. However, the shortage is limited primarily to the cohort of those 16–35 years of age, while simultaneously a large surplus labour pool persists among older age groups in the countryside.

Long-distance, interprovincial migration also increased rapidly from the early 1990s spurred by significant wage differentials between inland provinces and coastal provinces, where major centres of industrial growth are located. Guangdong, which has since the early 1990s, risen to become the core of the 'world's factory', is the major hub of long-distance migrants. Over time, the number of inland provinces from which large numbers of labour migrants originate has also increased. Migrating long-distance for a better job has gained precedence over time in many provinces, including those in the western region of China. The rising internal migration trends in the 1990s were also associated with narrowing economic disparities among provinces in statistical terms, though it may not be the case in real terms (Chan and Wang 2008). Migration has helped alleviate poverty in the countryside in the short term by giving underemployed farmers jobs, but simply *migration* is not enough when institutionalised exclusion and discrimination through the *hukou* system remain effective.

It is essential that migrants are allowed to settle in the cities when they find jobs in order to generate true and 'complete' urbanisation (Chan 2018; Lu 2016). The various *hukou* reforms launched in recent decades have so far only marginally weakened the foundation of an exclusionary system that separates the population into two segments, to the disadvantage of the rural segment. Enormous obstacles remain for migrants to settle in big cities in particular, where most of the jobs are to be found. Breaking up families, creating tens of millions of left-behind children, is also economically and socially counter-productive. As Chinese society ages rapidly, the mistreatment of such a large number of rural-*hukou* children will cost China dearly in the future.

Note

1 This is updated from Kam Wing Chan (2012) "Migration and development in China: Trends, geography and current issues," *Migration and Development*, 1:2, 187–205 with the permission of Taylor & Francis Ltd, www.tandfonline.com.

References

Cai F. (1999) "Spatial patterns of migration under China's reform period" *Asian and Pacific Migration Journal, 8(3)*, 313–27.

Cai F. (2000) *Zhongguo liudong renkou* [*Floating Population in China*], Henan Renmin Chubanshe, Zhengzhou.

Cai F. and Chan K. W. (2009) "The global economic crisis and unemployment in China" *Eurasian Geography and Economics, 50*, 513–31.

Cai F. and Wang M. (2009) "The counterfactuals of unlimited surplus labour in rural China" in Cai F. and Du Y. eds., *The China population and labour yearbook, volume 1: The approaching Lewis turning point and its policy implications*, Brill, Leiden, 121–36.

Chan K. W. (1994) *Cities with invisible walls: Reinterpreting urbanization in post-1949 China*, Oxford University Press, Hong Kong.

Chan K. W. (2007) "Misconceptions and complexities in the study of China's cities: Definitions, statistics, and implications" *Eurasian Geography and Economics, 48(4)*, 382–412.

Chan K. W. (2009) "The Chinese *hukou* system at 50" *Eurasian Geography and Economics, 50(2)*, 197–221.

Chan K. W. (2010a) "A China paradox: Migrant labour shortage amidst rural labour supply abundance" *Eurasian Geography and Economics, 51*, 513–30.

Chan K. W. (2010b) "The global financial crisis and migrant workers in China: There is no future as a labourer; returning to the village has no meaning" *International Journal of Urban and Regional Research, 34(3)*, 659–77.

Chan K. W. (2011) "Urban myth" *South China Morning Post, August 24 A13*.

Chan K. W. (2012a) "Crossing the 50 percent population Rubicon: Can China urbanize to prosperity?" *Eurasian Geography and Economics, 53(1)*, 63–86.

Chan K. W. (2012b) "Migration and development in China: Trends, geography and current issues" *Migration and Development, 1(2)*, 187–205.

Chan K. W. (2013) "China: Internal migration" in Ness I. and Bellwood P. eds., *Encyclopedia of global human migration*, Wiley-Blackwell, Oxford, https://onlinelibrary.wiley.com/doi/pdf/10.1002/9781444351071.wbeghm124.

Chan K. W. (2014) "China's urbanization 2020: A new blueprint and direction" *Eurasian Geography and Economics, 55(1)*, 1–9.

Chan K. W. (2018) *Urbanization with Chinese characteristics: The hukou system and migration*, Taylor & Francis, London.

Chan K. W. and Buckingham W. (2008) "Is China abolishing the *hukou* system?" *China Quarterly*, *195*, 582–606.

Chan K. W., Liu T., and Yang Y. (1999) "Hukou and non-hukou migration: Comparisons and contrast" *International Journal of Population Geography*, *5(6)*, 425–48.

Chan K.W. and Y. Ren (2018) "Children of migrants in China in the twenty-first century: trends, living arrangements, age-gender structure, and geography" *Eurasian Geography and Economics*, *59(2)*, 133–163.

Chan K. W. and Wang M. (2008) "Remapping China's regional inequalities, 1990–2006: A new assessment of *de facto* and *de jure* population data" *Eurasian Geography and Economics*, *49(1)*, 21–56.

Csanádi M. (2010) "Institutional reactions to the impact of global crisis at source and destination cities of migration in China" Institute of Economics, Hungarian Academy of Sciences, Discussion Paper, MT-DP 2010/13, Budapest.

Demick B. and Pierson D. (2010) "People, people everywhere in China, and not enough to work" *Los Angeles Times*, March 28 (http://articles.latimes.com/2010/mar/28/world/la-fgchina- labour28-2010mar28) Accessed 28 May 2010.

Duan C., Lv L., Wang Z., and Guo J. 2013. "Woguo Liudong Ertong Shengcun He Fazhan: Wenti Yu Duice - Jiyu 2010 Nian Diliuci Quanguo Renkou Pucha Shujv De Fenxi" [The Living and Development Status of Migrant Children in China: An Analysis of the Sixth Population Census Data.] *Nanfang Renkou* [South China Population], *28(4)*, 45–55.

Fan C. C. (2008) *China on the move: Migration, the state, and the household*, Routledge, New York.

Foreman W. (2008) "Restless migrants challenge order in difficult economy" *Post-Intelligencer*, 20 December.

Garnaut R. (2010) "Macro-economic implications of the turning point" Paper presented at International Workshop on Debating the Lewis Turning Point in China, Beijing, April 6, 2010.

Green S. (2008) "On the world's factory floor: How China's workers are changing China and the global economy" *Standard Chartered Special Report*, January 14, 2008.

Hamlin K. (2010) "China reaching a Lewis turning point as inflation overtakes low-cost labour" *Bloomberg News* (www.bloomberg.com/apps/news?pid=20601068&sid=aOEXbd09bloM) Accessed 11 June 2010.

Han J., Cui C., and Fan A. (2009) "Rural labour-force allocation report—an investigation of 2,749 villages" in Cai F. and Du Y. eds., *The China population and labour yearbook, volume 1: The approaching Lewis turning point and its policy implications*, Brill, Leiden, 137–52.

Harney A. (2009) *The China price: The true cost of Chinese competitive advantage*, Penguin Books, London.

Hu Y., Cai F., and Du Y. (2010) "Shierwu shiqi renkou bianhua ji weilai renkou fazhan qushi yuce" [Population changes and forecast of population development trend in "the Twelfth Five-Year-Plan" period] in Cai F. eds., *Zhongguo renkou yu laodong wenti baogao No.11—houjinrong weiji shiqi de laodongli shichang tiaozhan* [*Report on Chinese population and labour problem No.11 − Challenge of the labour market in the post-financial crisis period*], Shehui kexue wenxian chubanshe, Beijing, 48–77.

Huang Y. and Jiang T. (2010) "What does the Lewis turning point mean for China?" China Center for Economic Research, Peking University, Working Paper Series, Beijing, 2010-03.

Kroeber A. (2010) "The end of surplus labour" *China Economic Quarterly*, *1*, 35–46.

Lee C. K. (1998) *Gender and the south China miracle*, University of California Press, Berkeley.

Lewis W. A. (1954) "Economic development with unlimited supplies of labour" *Manchester School of Economic and Social Studies*, *22*, 139–91.

Liang Z. (1999) "Foreign investment, economic growth, and temporary migration: The case of Shenzhen Special Economic Zone, China" *Development and Society*, *28(1)*, 115–37.

Liang Z. (2007) "Internal migration: Policy changes, recent trends, and new challenges" in Zhao Z. and Guo F. eds., *Transition and challenge: China's population at the beginning of the 21st century*, Oxford University Press, Oxford, 197–215.

Lu M. (2016) *Daguo dacheng* [Great State Needs Bigger Cities], Shanghai remin chubanshe, Shanghai.

Lu M., Zhao S., and Bai N. (2002) "Woguo nongmingong laodongli liudong di huigu yu yuce" [The past and future of the movement of the rural labor force in China] in H. Ma and M. Wang eds., *Zhongguo fazhan yanjiu* [*China development studies*], Zhongguo chubanshe, Beijing, 555–87.

Ministry of Public Security (MPS). (1988–2012) *Zhonghua renmin gongheguo quanguo fenxianshi renkou tongji ziliao* [*Statistical materials on population of counties and cities of the People's Republic of China*], Qunzhong, Beijing.

Ministry of Public Security (MPS), Household Administration Bureau. (1997–2014) *Quanguo zanzhu renkou tongti ziliao huibian* [*Collection of statistical materials on temporary population in China*], Zhongguo gongan daxue chubanshe, Beijing.

Moore M. (2010) "Inside Foxconn's suicide factory" *Telegraph*, May 27 (www.telegraph. co.uk/finance/china-business/7773011/A-look-inside-the-Foxconn-suicide-factory.html) Accessed 19 July 2010.

National Bureau of Statistics & Ministry of Public Security (NBS & MPS). (1988) *Zhonghua renmin gongheguo renkou tongji ziliao huibian* [*Collections of statistical materials on population of the People's Republic of China*], Zhongguo caizheng jingji chubanshe, Beijing.

National Bureau of Statistics (NBC). (1983-2017c) *Statistical yearbook of China*, Zhongguo tongji chubanshe, Beijing.

National Bureau of Statistics (NBS). (1988) *Zhongguo 1987 nian 1 per cent renkou chouyan diaocha ziliao* [*Tabulations of China's 1987 1 per cent population sample survey*], Zhongguo tongji chubanshe, Beijing.

National Bureau of Statistics (NBS). (2010-2017b) *Nongmingong jiance baogao* [*Monitor report on rural migrant labour*], Zhongguo tongji chubanshe, Beijing.

National Bureau of Statistics (NBS). (2018) *Zhonghua renmin gonghequo 2017nian guomin jingji he shehui fazhan tongji gongbao* [*The statistical report of national economy and social development of People's Republic of China*] (www.stats.gov.cn/tjsj/zxfb/201802/t20180228_1585631.html) Accessed 1 March 2018.

National Health and Family Planning Commission (NHFPC). (2013–2018) *Zhongguo liudong renkou fazhan baogao* [*Report on China's floating population development*], Zhongguo renkou chubanshe, Beijing.

National Population and Family Planning Commission (NPFPC). (2011) *Zhongguo liudong renkou fazhan baogao* [*Report on China's floating population development*], Zhongguo renkou chubanshe, Beijing.

National Population Sample Survey Office (NPSSO). (1997) *1995 Quanguo 1 percent renkou chouyang diaocha ziliao* [*Data on the sample survey of 1 percent of the national population in 1995*], Zhongguo tongji chubanshe, Beijing.

Pun N. (2005) *Made in China: Women factory workers in a global workplace*, Duke University Press and Hong Kong University Press, London and Hong Kong.

Qu X., Yang G., and Cheng J. (2015) "Renkou liudong qushi yu nongmingong jiuye" [Population migration Trends and the employment of rural migrant labour] in Cai F. and Zhang J. eds., *Zhongguo renkou yu laodong wenti baogao No.16* [*Reports on China's population and labour No. 16*], Social Sciences Academic Press, Beijing, 35–84.

Sing Tao Daily. (2010a) "Yuexin shuizhang waiji heigong yongru" [Wage raises in Guangzhou led to influx of foreign illegal labour] July 3, A11.

Sing Tao Daily. (2010b) "Foshan bentian qipeichang caibao gongchao" [Strike broke out again in Honda subsidiary in Foshan] July 16, A10.

Skeldon R. (1990) *Population mobility in developing countries*, Belhaven, London.

Solinger D. (1999) *Contesting citizenship in urban China*, University of California Press, Berkeley.

State Council and National Bureau of Statistics (SC & NBS). (1985) *Zhongguo 1982 nian renkou pucha ziliao* [*Tabulation on the 1982 population census of the People's Republic of China*], Zhongguo tongji chubanshe, Beijing.

State Council and National Bureau of Statistics (SC & NBS). (1993) *Zhongguo 1990 nian renkou pucha ziliao* [*Tabulation on the 1990 population census of the People's Republic of China*], Zhongguo tongji chubanshe, Beijing.

State Council and National Bureau of Statistics (SC & NBS). (2002) *Zhongguo 2000 nian renkou pucha ziliao* [*Tabulation on the 2000 population census of the People's Republic of China*], Zhongguo tongji chubanshe, Beijing.

State Council and National Bureau of Statistics (SC & NBS). (2007) *2005 nian quanguo 1 percent renkou chouyang diaocha ziliao* [*Data on the sample survey of 1 percent of the national population in 2005*], Zhongguo tongji chubanshe, Beijing.

State Council and National Bureau of Statistics (SC & NBS). (2012) *Zhongguo 2010 nian renkou pucha ziliao* [*Tabulation on the 2010 population census of the People's Republic of China*], Zhongguo tongji chubanshe, Beijing.

State Council and National Bureau of Statistics (SC & NBS). (2016) *2015 nian quanguo 1 percent renkou chouyang diaocha ziliao* [*Data on the sample survey of 1 percent of the national population in 2015*], Zhongguo tongji chubanshe, Beijing.

The Economist. 2015. "Little match children." October 17. Accessed November 10. www.economist.com/news/briefing/21674712-children-bear-disproportionate-share-hidden-cost-chinas-growth-little-match-children

United Nations. (2012) "International migration and development: Report of the Secretary-General" August 3.

Wang F.-L. (2005) *Organizing through division and exclusion*, Stanford University Press, Stanford.

Wu J.-M. (2011) "Yongyuan de yixiangke? Gongmin shenfen chaxu yu zhongguo nongmingong jieji" [Strangers forever? Differential citizenship and China's rural migrant workers] *Taiwanese Sociology*, *21*, 51–99.

Yang Y. (2004) "Jiushi niandai yilai woguo renkou qianyi de ruogan xin tedian" [New features of population migration in the 1990s in China] *Nanfang renkou* [*Southern Population*], *75*, 13–20.

Yao Y. (2010) "The Lewisian turning point has not yet arrived" *The Economist*, July 16 (www.economist.com/economics/by-invitation/questions/era_cheap_chinese_labour_over) Accessed 21 July 2010.

Ye J. and Pan L. 2008. *Bieyan Tongnian: Zhongguo Liushuo Ertong* [Another Type of Childhood: Left-behind Children in China], Social Sciences Academic Press, Beijing.

Ye J., Wang C., Wu H., He C., and Liu J. (2013) "Internal migration and left-behind populations in China" *The Journal of Peasant Studies 40(6)*, 1119–46.

Zhang X., Yang J., and Wang S. (2010) *China has reached the Lewis turning point*, International Food and Policy Research Institute, Discussion Paper, 000977, Washington, DC.

IN LIEU OF A CONCLUSION
Tracing the way forward in migration and development

A general conclusion is inappropriate for such an extensive and varied collection of essays, even if it has revolved around a common theme. We have taken the topic of migration and development which, perhaps more implicitly, was an underlying theme of so much research into migration from its earliest days but which, towards the very end of the twentieth century, emerged as a much more explicit and politically sensitive issue.

Despite its length, this Handbook is not exhaustive; some aspects could not be covered because appropriate authors could not be found but, more importantly, this work is certainly not the last word on the topic. All books are children of their time and this Handbook is no exception. One of the editors of this Handbook published a volume on the same topic, *Migration and Development*, some 25 years ago before it had emerged as a major international concern (Skeldon 1997). Thinking has clearly moved on in the interim, which is reflected in the contributions to this Handbook. In another 25 years, we can expect thinking to have changed again. Partly, this will be due to shifts in the nature of both migration and development themselves, partly it will stem from the incorporation of new datasets, but partly, too, it will reflect changing ways to think about migration and development. These concluding words simply make a few observations on where next for migration and development.

Amidst all the uncertainty involved in looking towards the future, perhaps one reliable prediction can be made: a continued emphasis on improving the quality of data on both migration and development. Significant progress was achieved over recent decades, particularly in the form of the United Nations/World Bank Origin and Destination database, imperfect though it may be, and we can surely expect to extend its coverage and reliability. Refinement, too, can be expected with more small-area data, particularly on urban origins and destinations. Data on key development variables at sub-national data levels can also be expected and on specific issues such as the measurement of urban poverty. Greater refinement in comparative measures of migration across countries, following in the footsteps of researchers such as Bell and his team (2015a, 2015b, 2018), can also surely be expected.

While improvements in the evidence base on which to analyse future dimensions of migration and development can virtually be taken as a given, other predictions are less certain, even if some scenarios might appear more likely than others. Perhaps three groups of factors in particular are emerging: socio-economic-demographic; climate-related; and political. First, continued progress towards the reduction in gender inequalities and the improvement in the education of women should see the continued trend towards lower fertility, leading to declining populations across much of the world by 2050. When combined with global shifts in technology and increased use of robotics, the volume of migration, too, is likely to decline as already observed in most of the developed countries today (Champion et al. 2018). Declining migration appears likely to be accompanied by increasing mobility as individuals base themselves in one area but travel further, faster, and for shorter periods in order to engage in work (in cases when they cannot work directly from home) or for recreational travel.

However, this pattern of declining migration and rising mobility may be mitigated by the second scenario: the likely impacts stemming from climate change. Rising sea levels and the increased incidence of severe coastal storms are likely to displace large numbers of people but perhaps locally more than regionally or globally. However, the growing realisation among populations that their actions are combining to damage the environment may discourage long-distance mobility for recreation. Governments may even impose taxes on air travel to dampen such travel further. Of course, technological development and the emergence of electric aircraft could sustain what is the largest and fastest-growing population flow in the world at present: international tourists. The fact that this aspect is missing from the current migration and development debate seems a major lacuna. Tourists are not migrants but they both facilitate migration, by providing a regular channel of entry, and cause migration by generating employment and by forcing local populations to leave particular hot spots. Tourism, predicated upon the largest flows of people, is also one of the world's largest industries and hence deserves to be part of any migration, mobility, and development debate.

The third group of future scenarios will probably revolve around political change. The migration and development debate, and as reflected in most of the contributions to this Handbook, has focused primarily on economic and social issues. Migration and political change has either been largely side-lined, or assumed to be about the forces generating conflict and refugee flows. While increasing interest in the political participation of migrants and on the impact of migrants on the diffusion of political ideas is emerging, systematic attempts to examine changing patterns of migration and political regimes have been lacking, although for a partial exception see Moses (2011). Given the current anti-globalisation turn, this political dimension of the topic seems destined to rise as states re-interpret their roles across the globe. More to the point, the emerging tensions between metropolitan and national governments over migration seem destined to increase as populations become more urban. Different demographics and different attitudes in the largest cities, the drivers of national, regional, and global economies, underlie sharply different political attitudes when compared with their hinterlands. It is in the cities where ethnic mixing is greatest, Vertovec's 'super-diversity' (2007), and a return to the polyethnic norm (McNeill 1986) will emerge to challenge national political systems. Politically this plays out differently in different contexts. Some national governments hold more of an anti-immigration stance, while their respective capital cities are more open and welcoming to migrants, in other contexts this is the other way around.

Other scenarios will emerge and the individual chapters of this Handbook identify pathways for further research. However, in this Handbook, our intention has been to summarise where we are now in many of the sub-fields of migration and development and, where possible, to identify the best way forward. As should have been clear, the theme of migration and development is highly varied and we can expect that variety to increase in coming years as the debate is transformed to meet changing circumstances, which is itself an exciting prospect.

References

Bell, M., Charles-Edwards, E., Bernard, A. and Ueffing, P. (2018) "Global trends in internal migration" in Champion, T., Cooke, T. and Shuttleworth, I. eds., *Internal migration in the developed world: are we becoming less mobile?* Routledge, London, 76–97.

Bell, M., Charles-Edwards, E., Kupiszewska, D., Kupiszewski, M., Stillwell, J. and Zhu, Y. (2015a) "Internal migration and development: comparing migration intensities around the world" *Population and Development Review*, 41, 33–58.

Bell, M., Charles-Edwards, E., Kupiszewska, D., Kupiszewski, M., Stillwell, J. and Zhu, Y. (2015b) "Internal migration data around the world: assessing contemporary practice" *Population, Space and Place*, 21, 1–17.

Champion, T., Cooke, T. and Shuttleworth, I. eds. (2018) *Internal migration in the developed world: are we becoming less mobile?* Routledge, London.

McNeill, W. H. (1986) *Polyethnicity and national unity in world history*. University of Toronto Press, Toronto.

Moses, J. W. (2011) *Emigration and political development*. Cambridge University Press, Cambridge.

Skeldon, R. (1997) *Migration and development: a global perspective*. Longman, London.

Vertovec, S. (2007) "Super-diversity and its implications" *Ethnic and Racial Studies*, 30, 1024–1054.

INDEX

Numbers in **bold** are whole chapters or sections in chapters.